D1573245

EMPLOYMENT LAW
Third Edition

By

Mark A. Rothstein
Herbert F. Boehl Chair of Law and Medicine
University of Louisville
General Editor

Charles B. Craver
Freda H. Alverson Professor of Law
George Washington University

Elinor P. Schroeder
Paul E. Wilson Professor of Law
University of Kansas

Elaine W. Shoben
Edward W. Cleary Professor of Law
University of Illinois

Abridged from Rothstein, Craver, Schroeder & Shoben,
"Employment Law", Vols. 1 & 2,
Practitioner Treatise Series (West, 2004)

HORNBOOK SERIES®

Mat #40185204

Hornbook Series, Westlaw, and West Group are trademarks
registered in the U.S. Patent and Trademark Office.

COPYRIGHT © 1994 WEST PUBLISHING CO.
COPYRIGHT © 1999 WEST GROUP
© 2005 West, a Thomson business
　　　610 Opperman Drive
　　　P.O. Box 64526
　　　St. Paul, MN 55164–0526
　　　1–800–328–9352

Printed in the United States of America

ISBN 0–314–15028–5

TEXT IS PRINTED ON 10% POST
CONSUMER RECYCLED PAPER

Preface

Employment law is a dynamic and, at times, seemingly disconnected field of law. We have written this hornbook to provide law students with a conceptual framework and explanations of the legal doctrines involved in the field. Because employment law is the study of the nonunion employment, the book does not discuss the law of unionization and collective bargaining under the National Labor Relations Act.

The book is organized chronologically. It proceeds through the employment relationship from formation, through terms and conditions of employment, to termination. This approach recognizes that a potential legal controversy at any stage of the employment relationship may simultaneously implicate numerous statutory and common law considerations.

Throughout the book, references have been kept to a minimum. Students interested in more detailed reference material, such as citations to every applicable state statute or more expansive case citations, should consult our two volume work, *Employment Law*, in West's Practitioner Treatise Series.

M.A.R.
C.B.C.
E.P.S.
E.W.S.

October, 2004

*

WESTLAW® Overview

Employment Law, by Mark A. Rothstein, Charles B. Craver, Elinor P. Schroeder, and Elaine W. Shoben offers a detailed and comprehensive treatment of the basic rules, principles, and issues relating to employment law. To supplement the information contained in this book, you can access Westlaw, West's computer-assisted legal research service. Westlaw contains a broad array of legal resources, including case law, statutes, expert commentary, current developments, and various other types of information.

Learning how to use these materials effectively will enhance your legal research abilities. To help you coordinate the information in the book with your Westlaw research, this volume contains an appendix listing Westlaw databases, search techniques, and sample problems.

The instructions and features described in this Westlaw overview are based on accessing Westlaw via westlaw.com® at **www.westlaw.com**.

THE PUBLISHER

*

Summary of Contents

*

Table of Contents

EMPLOYMENT LAW

*

INTRODUCTION

American employment law faithfully followed the English common law of master and servant from the founding of the colonies until the second half of the nineteenth century. Accordingly, early American law was consistent with the English rule that employment contracts without a stated duration were presumed to be for one year. This presumption was based on equitable considerations stemming from a largely agrarian and originally feudal society. It prevented masters from terminating servants after they had planted and harvested the crops, and it also prohibited servants from quitting after receiving room and board from the master but before the planting season.

In 1877, the law took a decidedly American turn. Horace Gray Wood, a lawyer and prolific treatise writer from Albany, New York, published a much-read work on master and servant law in which he confidently proclaimed:

> With us the rule is inflexible, that a general or indefinite hiring is *prima facie* a hiring at will, and if the servant seeks to make it a yearly hiring, the burden is upon him to establish it by proof....
> [I]t is an indefinite hiring and is determinable at the will of either party, and in this respect there is no distinction between domestic and other servants.[1]

There is some controversy over whether Wood misinterpreted the case law on which he relied for his conclusion, thereby "inventing" the at-will rule, or accurately summarized the controlling precedents. In either event, it is clear that Wood established the authority for the at-will rule, which soon swept the United States. Perhaps one reason why Wood's rule was so widely followed is that it fit perfectly with the late-nineteenth century mood among industrialists in favor of laissez-faire capitalism.

At the turn of the century, a series of cases added a constitutional dimension to employment at will, thereby creating the "freedom of contract" theory. First, in *Lochner v. New York*,[2] the Supreme Court struck down a New York law prohibiting bakers from working more than sixty hours a week. Then, in *Adair v. United States*,[3] the Court struck down a federal law making it a crime for an agent of an interstate carrier to fire an employee because of membership in a union. Finally,

1. Horace G. Wood, A Treatise on the Law of Master and Servant § 134, at 272 (1877)(footnotes omitted).

2. 198 U.S. 45, 25 S.Ct. 539, 49 L.Ed. 937 (1905).

3. 208 U.S. 161, 28 S.Ct. 277, 52 L.Ed. 436 (1908).

1

Coppage v. Kansas[4] struck down a Kansas statute making it unlawful for any firm or individual to require nonmembership in a union as a condition of employment. In all of these cases the Court held that legislative or judicial interference with contract formation violated the constitutional freedom of contract. Between 1915 and 1935, freedom of contract also was used to justify injunctions against labor strikes.

The demise of freedom of contract was caused less by a doctrinal shift than it was the result of the dire economic conditions during the Depression. This was especially true with regard to employment relations, where mass unemployment, wage deflation, and other problems were pervasive. Much of the focus of the New Deal was on getting people back to work, and challenges to the newly enacted federal legislation once again put the Supreme Court in the middle of reviewing American labor and employment law.

The Norris–LaGuardia Act[5] of 1932 outlawed "yellow-dog" contacts[6] and prohibited the federal courts from issuing injunctions in labor disputes. The following year, Congress passed the National Industrial Recovery Act (NIRA), section 7(a) of which granted employees the right to organize and bargain collectively. In 1935, the NIRA was declared unconstitutional in *A.L.A. Schechter Poultry Corp. v. United States*.[7] Less than two months later, Congress enacted the National Labor Relations Act (NLRA or Wagner Act).[8] The NLRA declared it to be the policy of the United States to encourage collective bargaining; established the National Labor Relations Board (NLRB) to regulate union organizing, representation elections, and unfair labor practices; gave employees the rights of self-organization and collective bargaining; and prohibited certain employer unfair labor practices.

The NLRA was held to be constitutional by the Supreme Court by a five-to-four vote in *NLRB v. Jones & Laughlin Steel Corp.*[9] In attempting to downplay the NLRA's burden on employers, the Court stated, "The act does not interfere with the normal exercise of the right of the employer to select its employees or to discharge them."[10] In effect, the Court said that the NLRA does not take away an employer's "normal" (in other words, common law) right to select or discharge employees, but the Court never expressed just what those rights were. Nevertheless, this specific quotation from *Jones & Laughlin* has been widely cited for the broad principle that an employer has the common law right to hire and fire employees at will.

In 1938, Congress passed the Fair Labor Standards Act, (FLSA)[11] which set minimum wage rates, required higher pay for overtime, and

---

4. 236 U.S. 1, 35 S.Ct. 240, 59 L.Ed. 441 (1915).

5. 47 Stat. 70 (1932), as amended, 29 U.S.C.A. §§ 101–115.

6. A "yellow dog" contract is a contract in which the employee promises not to join a union.

7. 295 U.S. 495, 55 S.Ct. 837, 79 L.Ed. 1570 (1935).

8. 29 U.S.C.A. §§ 151–169.

9. 301 U.S. 1, 57 S.Ct. 615, 81 L.Ed. 893 (1937).

10. 301 U.S. at 45.

11. 29 U.S.C.A. §§ 201–219.

prohibited the use of child labor in goods or services involved in inter-state commerce. In *United States v. Darby*,[12] the Court considered the constitutionality of the FLSA. Based upon Congress' commerce power, the FLSA prohibited the shipment in interstate commerce of goods manufactured by employees earning less than the prescribed minimum wage. The Court in *Darby* reversed much of its prior commerce clause doctrine, holding that Congress' power to regulate interstate commerce was not limited to formal distinctions between manufacturing and commerce.

In the immediate aftermath of World War II, some unions were quite powerful and largely unchecked by existing labor laws. Asserting a need to return a balance to labor-management relations, Congress passed the Labor Management Relations Act (LMRA or Taft–Hartley Act)[13] in 1947 over President Truman's veto. Taft–Hartley amended the NLRA to give employees the right to refrain from (as well as participate in) union activities, it expanded the NLRB from three to five members, and it added a series of prohibited unfair labor practices by unions.

To control internal union affairs, in 1959 Congress enacted the Labor–Management Reporting and Disclosure Act (LMRDA or Land-rum–Griffin).[14] This "bill of rights" for union members required periodic financial and other reports from unions, regulated union elections and union funds, and prohibited Communists and certain ex-felons from holding union office. The LMRDA also made some minor changes in the NLRA.

Beginning in the 1960s, a new wave of federal and state civil rights laws were enacted to prohibit discrimination in employment on the basis of: race, color, religion, sex, and national origin under Title VII of the Civil Rights Act of 1964;[15] age, under the Age Discrimination in Employment Act;[16] handicap, under the Rehabilitation Act;[17] and disability, under the Americans With Disabilities Act.[18] This legislation made the workplace a key focal point in societal efforts to end discrimination and promote economic and social equality of opportunity.

Beginning in 1970, Congress and state legislatures enacted a variety of laws regulating a wide range of conditions of employment. Among the federal laws are the Occupational Safety and Health Act,[19] Mine Safety and Health Act,[20] Employee Retirement Income Security Act,[21] Employee Polygraph Protection Act,[22] Worker Adjustment and Retraining Notification Act,[23] Family and Medical Leave Act,[24] and Health Insurance Porta-

12. 312 U.S. 100, 61 S.Ct. 451, 85 L.Ed. 609 (1941).

13. 29 U.S.C.A. §§ 141–197.

14. 29 U.S.C.A. §§ 401–531.

15. 42 U.S.C.A. § 2000e.

16. 29 U.S.C.A. §§ 621–634.

17. 29 U.S.C.A. §§ 701–796i.

18. 42 U.S.C.A. §§ 12101–12213.

19. 29 U.S.C.A. §§ 651–678.

20. 30 U.S.C.A. §§ 801–962.

21. 29 U.S.C.A. §§ 1001–1461.

22. 29 U.S.C.A. §§ 2001–2009.

23. 29 U.S.C.A §§ 2101–2109.

24. 29 U.S.C.A. §§ 2601–2654.

bility and Accountability Act.[25] These laws attempted to promote workplace safety and health, safeguard the availability of health and pension benefits, and protect employees from the harsh consequences of economic dislocations and personal obligations. This wave of legislation ushered in an era of federal workplace regulation at the same time that the percentage of employees working under collective bargaining agreements was declining.

Partly in response to these statutes, and in recognition of the rights afforded to both public sector and unionized workers, the previously entrenched employment at will rule came under increasing attack and was successfully challenged under a variety of contract and tort theories. By the end of the 1980s, virtually every state had adopted one or more exceptions to the at-will rule. The new era in employment law had begun. Today, employment law is characterized by a complex system of constitutional, statutory, administrative, and common law rights and duties. It continues to evolve in response to society's changing values regarding the employment relationship.

25. 29 U.S.C.A. §§ 1181–1191c.

Chapter 1

ESTABLISHING THE EMPLOYMENT RELATIONSHIP

Table of Sections

---

§ 1.1   Introduction

As discussed in the Introduction, modern employment law has limited traditional employer prerogatives essentially in a negative way.

5

Especially in the private, nonunion sector, in which employment is regulated by neither civil service laws nor collective bargaining agreements, the law has been more proscriptive than prescriptive—prohibiting employers from behaving in certain ways rather than requiring that they behave in certain ways.

The hiring process is an excellent illustration of this general principle. Employers have fairly wide discretion in adopting hiring practices they deem valuable to the enterprise. For example, they may use want ads, employment agencies, hiring halls, or any other method of developing a pool of applicants; they may use application forms, interviews, references, or other methods of soliciting information from or about the individual; they may check an individual's credit record or criminal record; they may require aptitude tests, physical ability tests, or drug tests. The employer's selection method will run afoul of the law only if it violates a specific legal proscription.

There are four main categories of legal doctrines regulating the hiring process. First, for public sector employees and some governmentally-regulated employees, constitutional protections apply. For example, Fourth Amendment principles apply to the drug testing of both public employees and private sector employees where the drug testing is government mandated. Second, federal statutes regulate various aspects of the hiring process. For example, the Employee Polygraph Protection Act[1] prohibits most polygraph testing in the private sector. Third, state constitutional law and state and local statutes regulate the hiring process. For example, numerous states have laws prohibiting blacklisting and inquiring into an applicant's HIV status. Fourth, there may be common law, primarily tort, remedies available to applicants to redress defamation, invasion of privacy, intentional infliction of emotional distress, and other wrongs, as well as remedies available to third parties, such as for negligent hiring, to redress harms caused by the hiring process.

Although this chapter is concerned with the hiring process, a number of the cases cited in the chapter are actually discharge cases. This is because there are relatively few hiring cases brought by unsuccessful applicants for employment. One reason for this is that the law is less sympathetic to the claims of individuals who have been denied an opportunity to obtain employment as opposed to employees whose employment, perhaps after a long tenure, has been wrongfully ended. For example, there is a large body of case law on common law wrongful discharge actions in tort and contract, but there is little if any case law involving actions for wrongful refusal to hire. Second, unsuccessful job seekers are much less likely than discharged employees to file a lawsuit, because the loss to them is less tangible and other employment options are usually being pursued concurrently. The other reason for including non-hiring cases in this chapter is simply that it is more efficient to discuss, for example, all of drug testing in one place.

§ 1.1
1.   29 U.S.C.A. §§ 2001–2009.

Much of the controversy surrounding legal regulation of the hiring process has to do with the regulation of access to information. While employers still may not be told whom to hire or how to hire, if employers are limited in the types of information available to them to use in deciding employability, then the hiring process can be regulated indirectly and, perhaps, less pervasively. At the same time, this type of regulation also furthers other interests, such as protecting confidentiality and privacy.

The final sections of this chapter deal with the contract and tort issues arising from hiring. They discuss the formation of employment contracts and their express and implied terms. They also focus on the determinants and significance of the employment relationship for tort purposes, including the vicarious liability of employers for torts committed by their employees within the scope of employment.

§ 1.2 Want Ads

Section 704(b) of Title VII of the Civil Rights Act of 1964 provides that it is an unlawful employment practice for an employer, labor union, or employment agency to publish any notice or advertisement indicating any preference, limitation, specification, or discrimination in employment based on race, color, religion, sex, or national origin.[1] Most of the cases involving alleged violations of this provision have centered on gender-based preferences. According to Equal Employment Opportunity Commission (EEOC) guidelines, section 704(b) prohibits placing advertisements in gender-segregated newspaper columns.[2]

Although employers, unions, and employment agencies would violate Title VII by placing gender-segregated want ads, it is not clear from the statute and regulations whether newspapers could be held responsible under Title VII for running the discriminatory ads. Based on the legislative history of Title VII, the courts have been unanimous in holding that newspapers are not liable for these ads under Title VII.

To bring an action under section 704(b), an individual must be aggrieved. In *Hailes v. United Air Lines*,[3] the Fifth Circuit held that for purposes of section 704(b), an aggrieved person is someone who is "able to demonstrate that he has a real, present interest in the type of employment advertised [and is] able to show he was effectively deterred by the improper ad from applying for such employment."[4] In *Hailes*, the court held that the plaintiff had met this test because, even though he did not apply for United's "stewardess" position under a "help wanted-female" column, he had been rejected because of gender when he had answered a similar ad run by another airline.[5]

§ 1.2

1. 42 U.S.C.A. § 2000e–3(b).

2. 29 C.F.R. § 1604.5.

3. 464 F.2d 1006 (5th Cir.1972).

4. Id. at 1008.

5. Id.

Section 4(e) of the Age Discrimination in Employment Act (ADEA) contains a similar prohibition on age-based want ads.[6] Although want ads traditionally have not been segregated by age, they often have contained language indicating a preference for younger applicants. In *Hodgson v. Approved Personnel Service, Inc.*,[7] the Fourth Circuit rejected the Department of Labor's guidelines, which indicated that certain "trigger" words, such as "young," "boy," and "recent college graduate," were per se illegal under the ADEA. Instead, the court held that the context must be considered. If the trigger words are used as part of a general invitation to prospective customers to use the employment agency's services, then they are not illegal; if they refer to qualifications for a specific job, then they are.[8]

Both Title VII and the ADEA provide for coordination with state fair employment acts and nearly every state has enacted legislation restricting the content of want ads similar to section 704(b) of Title VII and section 4(e) of the ADEA. Some of the state laws prohibit discrimination based on other factors, such as marital status or sexual orientation, and want ad restrictions therefore are also broader. In addition, several states have enacted "aiding and abetting" laws, which have been used to charge newspapers with violations for running discriminatory want ads. In *Pittsburgh Press Co. v. Pittsburgh Commission on Human Relations*,[9] the Supreme Court held that the newspaper's First Amendment rights were not violated by finding that its gender-segregated want ad column violated the "aiding and abetting" provision of the city's fair employment ordinance. As commercial speech, the want ads were entitled to a lesser degree of First Amendment protection.

Want ads also may support an action for breach of contract. In *Belknap, Inc. v. Hale*,[10] the employer advertised in the newspaper for "permanent replacements" for striking workers. When the strike was settled and the original employees returned to their jobs, the replacements were laid off. The Supreme Court held that the replacements' suit against the employer in state court for breach of contract was not preempted by federal labor laws.

§ 1.3 Employment Agencies

Most states began licensing and regulating employment agencies during the Great Depression, when high unemployment led to some exploitative and unscrupulous employment agency practices. These laws remain on the books, although many have been amended and updated. Today, about two-thirds of the states have laws that regulate employment agencies in some way. Some state laws also prohibit employers from charging a fee to employees seeking to obtain or continue employment.

6. 29 U.S.C.A. § 623(e).

7. 529 F.2d 760 (4th Cir.1975).

8. Id. at 765.

9. 413 U.S. 376, 93 S.Ct. 2553, 37 L.Ed.2d 669, rehearing denied, 414 U.S. 881, 94 S.Ct. 30, 38 L.Ed.2d 128 (1973).

10. 463 U.S. 491, 103 S.Ct. 3172, 77 L.Ed.2d 798 (1983).

Most state laws require employment agencies to be licensed and bonded, prohibit them from charging in advance, and set maximum fees. Some of the laws have been challenged on constitutional grounds, but without success. In upholding the validity of New York's law, Judge Augustus Hand wrote: "It seems quite incredible that a condition of a business practice, adopted largely in the interest of fair dealing, can be regarded as an unlawful usurpation of legislative power."[1]

In addition to state regulation of the business practices of employment agencies, discrimination in referrals is prohibited by section 703(b) of Title VII of the Civil Rights Act of 1964, which provides:

> It shall be an unlawful employment practice for an employment agency to fail or refuse to refer for employment, or otherwise to discriminate against an individual because of his race, color, religion, sex, or national origin, or to classify or refer for employment on the basis of his race, color, religion, sex, or national origin.[2]

The Equal Employment Opportunity Commission, in its sex discrimination guidelines interpreting Title VII,[3] has determined that an employment agency is engaging in an unlawful employment practice when it deals exclusively with one sex, unless the employment agency is engaged in providing employees for jobs in which sex is a bona fide occupational qualification (BFOQ). The guidelines also provide that an employment agency shares responsibility with an employer that indicates a gender specification in its job order if the agency knows that the preference is not based on a BFOQ.[4]

Section 701(c) of Title VII defines the term "employment agency" as "[a]ny person regularly undertaking with or without compensation to procure employees for an employer or to procure for employees opportunities to work for an employer and includes an agent of such a person."[5] A law school placement office has been held to be an employment agency under this definition. A newspaper that runs want ads, however, has been held not to be an employment agency.[6]

Every state has its own employment service, which attempts to find appropriate jobs for the unemployed. These state agencies, which are mandated by a provision of the Federal Unemployment Tax Act,[7] also are responsible for the distribution of unemployment compensation benefits.

In addition to statutory duties, employment agencies owe a common law duty of reasonable care to both the individuals they attempt to place and the employers to which they refer potential employees. For example, in one case an employment agency received a telephone call from a man

§ 1.3

1. National Employment Exch. v. Geraghty, 60 F.2d 918, 921 (2d Cir.1932).

2. 42 U.S.C.A. § 2000e–2(b).

3. 29 C.F.R. § 1604.6(a).

4. Id.

5. 42 U.S.C.A. § 2000e(c).

6. Brush v. San Francisco Newspaper Printing Co., 315 F.Supp. 577 (N.D.Cal. 1970), affirmed, 469 F.2d 89 (9th Cir.1972), cert. denied, 410 U.S. 943, 93 S.Ct. 1369, 35 L.Ed.2d 609 (1973).

7. 42 U.S.C.A. § 503.

who asked it to send over someone to do routine office work at a motorcycle repair shop. Without making a check on the employer, the employment agency dispatched a woman to the caller's "office," which turned out to be an empty room. The woman was abducted and sexually assaulted. In an action for negligence against the employment agency, the court held that the employment agency owed a duty of care to the woman based on their contractual relationship, its ability to foresee some danger to her, and its ability to exercise some control over the employers it made available.[8]

An employment agency also has a duty of reasonable care to employers in the referral of prospective employees. For example, an employment agency was held liable to an employer because a referred employee stole the employer's property. The court termed "perfunctory" the agency's compliance with the minimum statutory requirements of recording the name and address of the applicant, and contacting former employers. Because the employee was to be placed in a private home, reasonable care demanded a more thorough investigation.[9]

Employment agency cases also have involved the issue of fees. For example, in *Michele Matthews, Inc. v. Kroll & Tract,*[10] the court held that the agency was entitled to its fee from an employer who interviewed a candidate from the agency but did not extend an offer, and later hired the same candidate after she answered the firm's newspaper ad.

§ 1.4 Hiring Halls and Training Programs

In some industries, such as construction and longshoring, unions serve as a job referral service, known as a hiring hall. An employer needing workers merely contacts the union and the union sends out the workers. In theory, this system benefits both employers and workers. For employers, it simplifies recruitment and allows flexibility in hiring a work force only as needed. For workers, it centralizes the job search process.

The problem with hiring halls has centered around the union's role in administering them. Section 8(b)(2) of the National Labor Relations Act (NLRA)[1] makes it an unfair labor practice for a union "to cause or attempt to cause an employer to discriminate against an employee" in violation of section 8(a)(3) of the NLRA.[2] Section 8(a)(3) makes it an unfair labor practice for an employer "by discrimination in regard to hire or tenure of employment or any term or condition of employment to encourage or discourage membership in any labor organization."

In *Local 357 International Brotherhood of Teamsters v. NLRB,*[3] the Supreme Court held that union hiring halls are not illegal per se under

---

8. Keck v. American Employment Agency, Inc., 279 Ark. 294, 652 S.W.2d 2 (1983).

9. Janof v. Newsom, 53 F.2d 149 (D.C.Cir.1931).

10. 275 N.J.Super. 101, 645 A.2d 798 (App.Div.1994).

§ 1.4

1. 29 U.S.C.A. § 158(b)(2).

2. Id. § 158(a)(3).

3. 365 U.S. 667, 81 S.Ct. 835, 6 L.Ed.2d 11 (1961).

the NLRA. According to the Court, section 8(a)(3) only prohibits encouragement or discouragement of union membership accomplished by discrimination. Therefore, even if a hiring hall encourages union membership, it is not illegal if the hiring hall is run in a nondiscriminatory manner. In other words, union members may not be given preference over nonunion members in job referrals. It also has been held to be an unfair labor practice for a hiring hall to discriminate against employment applicants because they are members of a sister union (a different local affiliate of the same international union), participated in intraunion dissent, or filed a grievance.

A union hiring hall may use other reasonable, nondiscriminatory criteria in making referrals. Referrals have been permitted on the basis of seniority in the industry, residence in a particular area, or passing a union-administered examination.

Discrimination by a union in hiring hall referrals also may be actionable under section 301 of the Labor Management Relations Act[4] and the Labor Management Reporting and Disclosure Act,[5] in addition to being a breach of the duty of fair representation and an unfair labor practice under the NLRA. For example, it has been held to be a denial of fair representation for a union to fail to timely and fully inform all users of the hiring hall of the changes in the operating procedures and rules of the hiring hall or to misapply hiring hall procedures.

Another area in which unions control job opportunities is through apprenticeships and training programs. Section 703(d) of Title VII[6] specifically prohibits discrimination on the basis of race, color, religion, sex, or national origin by an employer, union, or joint labor-management committee in the controlling of apprenticeships or training programs. Some of the practices found to be discriminatory include the use of tests and admissions criteria which are not job related, discriminatory recruitment efforts, and discriminatory applications of admissions requirements.

Access to employment opportunities also is controlled by apprenticeship programs. The National Apprenticeship Act (also known as the Fitzgerald Act)[7] was originally enacted in 1937. The purpose of the law is to formulate federal and state standards for apprenticeship programs. It is administered by the Department of Labor.

The Job Training Partnership Act (JTPA)[8] authorizes programs to train youth and unskilled adults for entry into the labor force. It also provides training to the economically disadvantaged and to individuals facing language, education, disability, and other barriers. The JTPA is a cooperative program of the federal and state governments and private employers. It attempts to train workers for occupations where there is demonstrated local need.

---

4. 29 U.S.C.A. § 185.

5. 29 U.S.C.A. §§ 401–531.

6. 42 U.S.C.A. § 2000e–2(d).

7. 29 U.S.C.A. §§ 50–50b.

8. 29 U.S.C.A. §§ 1501–1781.

The Workforce Investment Act of 1998[9] was enacted in an effort to streamline job training programs in the United States. Its cornerstone is the "one-stop" customer service system. Funding is provided through individual training accounts; programs that rely on federal funding must attract participants to retain that funding. Finally, the Act stresses accountability and performance monitoring of all funded programs.

§ 1.5 Application Forms

The first direct contact between an applicant and an employer often involves the completion of an application form. Although forms vary widely, they customarily solicit personal information, such as name, address, telephone number, educational background, and work history. Application forms are lawful unless they have the purpose or effect of discriminating on the basis of one or more statutorily proscribed criteria.

Title VII of the Civil Rights Act of 1964 does not specifically prohibit an employer from asking applicants to indicate their race, color, religion, sex, or national origin. Nevertheless, "inquiries which either directly or indirectly disclose such information, unless otherwise explained, may constitute evidence of discrimination prohibited by Title VII."[1] Moreover, because the *use* of such information in making decisions regarding hiring violates Title VII, virtually all employers exclude such questions from their application forms.

The fair employment laws of some states take the approach of Title VII. Most states, however, actually go beyond Title VII and expressly prohibit various preemployment questions on application forms. These preemployment inquiry guides often go beyond simply prohibiting questions that ask for the applicant's race, color, religion, sex, national origin, age, or disabilities. They prohibit application forms from asking questions that indirectly reveal this information. Thus, questions such as hair color, eye color, height, weight, photograph, arrest record, marital status, birthplace, names and addresses of parents, ages of dependents, and reference of a religious leader are often prohibited as well. These provisions have been upheld.

Falsifications

There are a number of cases involving the falsification of application forms. Falsification of information will justify an employer's refusal to hire as well as the discharge of an employee who already has been hired. If the falsification involves the answer to a question that the employer was not lawfully permitted to ask, then the falsification may not justify the discharge.

In *McKennon v. Nashville Banner Publishing Co.*,[2] the Supreme Court resolved the conflict in the lower courts on the use of "after-

9. 29 U.S.C.A. §§ 2801–2945, 9201–9253.

§ 1.5

1. EEOC, Pre–Employment Inquiries (Office of Pub. Affairs 1981).

2. 513 U.S. 352, 115 S.Ct. 879, 130 L.Ed.2d 852 (1995).

acquired evidence." The plaintiff, a thirty-year employee of the defendant, alleged she was discharged in violation of the Age Discrimination in Employment Act (ADEA). In her deposition, the plaintiff indicated she had copied several financial documents bearing upon the employer's financial condition to which she had access as secretary to the defendant's comptroller. The district court granted the defendant's motion for summary judgment and the Sixth Circuit affirmed on the ground that the plaintiff's misconduct provided grounds for her discharge.

The Supreme Court reversed. According to the Court, the purposes of the ADEA are deterrence and compensation. "It would not accord with this scheme if after-acquired evidence of wrongdoing that would have resulted in termination operates, in every instance, to bar all relief for an earlier violation of the Act."[3]

The employee's wrongdoing, however, cannot be overlooked, and serious misconduct will affect the available remedies. "Where an employer seeks to rely upon after-acquired evidence of wrongdoing, it must first establish that the wrongdoing was of such severity that the employee in fact would have been terminated on those grounds alone if the employer had known of it at the time of the discharge."[4] According to the Court, as a general rule, neither reinstatement nor front pay is an appropriate remedy. Back pay, however, is available from the date of discharge until the date the new information was discovered.

Although *McKennon* involved misconduct many years after the plaintiff was hired, many cases involve alleged misstatements on applications. Therefore, this case is extremely important to the application stage of employment. *McKennon*'s analysis also has been applied by state courts in a range of cases.

The nature of the misstatement is an extremely important factor. If it is a "material" misstatement, or if the misstatement is related directly to the job, the courts are more likely to bar the action by applying the after-acquired evidence rule. For example, in *Camp v. Jeffer, Mangels, Butler & Marmaro*,[5] a couple was discharged from their jobs with a law firm after it was discovered that they had lied on the application form and a federal certification form required of contractors of the Resolution Trust Corp. Specifically, the couple failed to note that they had served time in prison after pleading guilty to the felony of using false information to defraud a federally insured bank. The court upheld the discharge because their felony convictions "relate directly" to the basis of the discharge. Similar results have been reached in cases involving resume fraud.

Disclaimers

In order to minimize the risk of a breach of contract claim following termination of an employee, some employers have begun to place dis-

---

3. 513 U.S. at 358, 115 S.Ct. at 884.
4. Id. at 362–63, 115 S.Ct. at 879.

5. 35 Cal.App.4th 620, 41 Cal.Rptr.2d 329, opinion modified (June 29, 1995).

claimers of any job security in their application forms. Most courts will consider the existence of such a disclaimer as a factor, although not necessarily dispositive, of whether there is an implied contract, such as may be created by language in a company handbook or personnel manual. To be effective, the disclaimer must be conspicuous, such as where it was in its own paragraph, highlighted in bold, and printed in large letters. Even without an express "disclaimer," language in an employment application may be used to show that employment was at will. Similarly, it has been held that a statement on an application that the employee had "job security rights" was no bar to termination at will.

§ 1.6 Interviews

The job interview is a well-established practice in American employment. Although some civil service laws specify the particulars of job interviews, in the private sector the specifics of job interviews are left to the employer. Because the interview is often a crucial step in the process of deciding which applicant to hire, it is frequently a focus of applicants who believe they were denied employment unfairly. The courts have held, however, that it is lawful for an employer to refuse to hire an applicant who had a poor interview, which was caused by the applicant's "abrasive personality" or unresponsive and unassertive demeanor.

The most common lawsuits involving interviews are Title VII actions based on alleged gender discrimination. A variety of interview conduct has been held to violate Title VII, such as discouraging females from seeking the traditionally male job of administrator or highway maintenance worker and asking a female meter patrol applicant whether she could wield a sledge hammer when this was not a part of the job. It also has been held to violate Title VII for employers to ask women about their childbearing plans. On the other hand, it has been held not to be a per se violation of Title VII for an employer to ask only female applicants "family oriented" questions about marital status and child care arrangements.

Similar issues have arisen under state gender discrimination laws. Sexist comments, including asking an applicant how she felt about sleeping with her boss, have not necessarily resulted in the finding of gender discrimination. Asking a woman applicant whether she would be afraid of loud machinery or working at night also did not, without more, establish gender discrimination. Plaintiffs also have asserted that discriminatory job interviews resulted in race, national origin, and age discrimination. A perfunctory interview also may be evidence of discrimination.

Statements made to an applicant at a job interview also have been used in an attempt to establish an oral contract that, for example, precluded termination without just cause. For example, in *Weiner v. McGraw–Hill, Inc.*,[1] the applicant was assured in the initial employment

§ 1.6
1.   57 N.Y.2d 458, 457 N.Y.S.2d 193, 443 N.E.2d 441(1982).

interview that the employer terminated employees only for just cause. The application form also specified that termination would be only for just cause. The New York Court of Appeals held that an action for breach of contract would lie based on a dismissal without just cause. Most courts, however, have held to the contrary and have refused to find that statements made at an interview established an oral contract.

Applicants who make false statements at an interview may be discharged when the misstatement is discovered. In *Lysak v. Seiler Corp.*,[2] the applicant volunteered during a job interview that she planned to have no more children when, in fact, she was expecting her third child. The applicant was hired, but she was later fired when her employer learned that she had lied at her interview. In affirming a jury verdict for the employer in a pregnancy discrimination action, the Massachusetts Supreme Judicial Court held that the employer could base a termination decision on a misrepresentation at the interview, even if the subject matter of the misrepresentation was one that would be improper for the employer to have raised.

§ 1.7   References

Along with application forms and interviews, the use of references is a standard element of the hiring process. Despite a lack of empirical data about the efficacy of reference checks in employee selection and a growing reluctance of former employers to provide negative references for fear of liability, the use of references remains pervasive.

There is little direct regulation of references, except for state statutes conferring a good faith immunity from liability for defamation on employers that write letters of reference in good faith. Also common are the "service letter" statutes, which provide that, upon the request of a former employee, the employer must provide a letter indicating the former employee's job title, dates of employment, and, in some cases, the reason for leaving employment. The failure to provide a service letter or the provision of a deficient letter may lead to a range of statutory remedies, including punitive damages.

References also may implicate Title VII of the Civil Rights Act of 1964. For example, former employees may bring Title VII discrimination claims against their former employers alleging retaliatory employment references regardless of whether they cause tangible harm to employment opportunities. The argument also has been made that reliance on a negative reference as a basis for rejecting an applicant constitutes disparate impact discrimination. The use of references, however, has been upheld as job-related, even if there is evidence of a disparate impact.

If an employer provides a reference, is there a duty to provide an accurate reference and, if so, to whom is the duty owed? In *Moore v. St.*

2. 415 Mass. 625, 614 N.E.2d 991 (1993).

Joseph Nursing Home,[1] an employee of the defendant was discharged after twenty-four disciplinary warnings for violence and use of alcohol and drugs. The employee was later hired by another employer, in whose employ he savagely beat and murdered a co-worker. The estate of the deceased worker contended that the original employer had a duty to disclose the violent propensities of the employee to the second employer. The Michigan Court of Appeals, while conceding that this type of information *should* be made known, nevertheless held that, in the absence of a special relationship between the employer and the victim, there was no *duty* to disclose the information. "[W]e conclude that a former employer has no duty to disclose malefic information about a former employee to the former employee's prospective employer."[2]

Other courts have reached contrary results. For example, when an individual applied for the position of vice principal of a school, his former employers wrote letters of recommendation for him in which they described him as dependable and reliable, as having a pleasant personality, and as an "administrator who relates well to his students." They failed to disclose that he had resigned under pressure due to charges of sexual misconduct involving several incidents of touching or molesting female students. After he was hired and engaged in additional acts of sexual misconduct, the victim sued the man's former employer. The California Supreme Court held that the former employers owed a duty to the plaintiff and they could be liable for misrepresentation.[3]

§ 1.8 Defamation

Various types of written and oral statements in the employment setting have given rise to actions for defamation. These include statements made about current or former employees by employers, former employers, co-employees, and other parties. Although these actions may arise at any stage of the employment relationship, from preemployment to post-termination, all of the various actions are discussed in this section.

Defamation, the act of harming another person's reputation through the publication of an injurious falsehood, may be based on a written (libel) or verbal (slander) statement. It consists of a false, unprivileged, and defamatory statement published to another with fault on the part of the publisher, which is either actionable per se or upon a showing of special harm. The four categories of statements considered defamatory per se are: (1) imputation of a crime; (2) imputation of a loathsome communicable disease; (3) imputation of an inability to perform or lack of integrity in office or employment; and (4) imputation of lack of ability in trade, profession, or office.

§ 1.7

1. 184 Mich.App. 766, 459 N.W.2d 100 (1990).

2. 459 N.W.2d at 103.

3. Randi W. v. Muroc Joint Unified Sch. Dist., 14 Cal.4th 1066, 60 Cal.Rptr.2d 263, 929 P.2d 582 (1997).

The first element of an action for defamation is a showing that the statement is defamatory. "A communication is defamatory if it so tends to harm the reputation of another as to lower him in the estimation of the community or to deter third persons from associating or dealing with him."[1] It is not necessary that the communication actually harm another person's reputation so long as it has a "general tendency to have such an effect."[2] In addition, the statement need only prejudice the individual in the eyes of a "substantial and respectable minority" of members of the community.[3]

Although defamation actions generally require a written or verbal statement, defamation by action may exist where the defendant's conduct clearly conveys a defamatory message about the plaintiff. The defamatory conduct, however, may need to be severe. For example, in one case a treatment center director accompanied a discharged social worker to his office, watched him pack his belongings, and escorted him out of the building in the middle of a business day in the full view of coworkers. According to the court, the defendant's actions were insufficient to establish a cause of action for defamation.[4]

It is important to distinguish defamatory statements from statements of opinion. Although this is an extremely important concept, it is often difficult to make this distinction. Derogatory assertions of fact are clearly defamatory. Thus, saying that an employee was fired for stealing, that a former employee was "unethical," that an employee was fired for falsifying time cards, and that an employee attempted to bribe a coworker into engaging in unauthorized conduct have been held to be defamatory. Even less assertive or more equivocal statements have been held to be defamatory. For example, saying that fellow physicians "lacked confidence" in a physician, declining to tell a customer why an employee had been dismissed in an effort not to "embarrass" the former employee, and saying that "after what he did it is no wonder" a reference would not be given also have been held to be defamatory.

The mere statement of opinion, however, is not defamation. A former employer's referring to an employee as an "emotional problem," characterizing an employee as "unprofessional," "insubordinate," and "abusive," asserting that an employee was "disorganized and ill-prepared," and even saying that he "would not trust the plaintiff as far as he could throw him" have been held to be mere opinion and thus not defamatory. If an opinion also implies underlying factual assertions capable of a defamatory meaning, then it will be actionable. This has been referred to as "informational opinion." Statements that an individual did not properly perform job obligations and had poor rapport with other administrators, that an individual was too detail-oriented, and that an airline pilot was "paranoid" have been held to be defamatory.

---

§ 1.8

1. Restatement (Second) of Torts § 559.

2. Id. § 559 at comment d.

3. Id. at comment e.

4. Bolton v. Department of Human Servs., 540 N.W.2d 523 (Minn.1995).

In *Saucedo v. Rheem Manufacturing Co.*,[5] the court held that a former employer's refusal to provide a reference about the plaintiff-former employee did not constitute defamation. The court also held that the plaintiff's failure to obtain job offers from other potential employers after they made reference checks is insufficient to show the publication of a defamatory statement.

Based on the doctrine of *New York Times Co. v. Sullivan*,[6] actions for defamation also must satisfy First Amendment considerations. The publisher of a false and defamatory statement concerning a private person, or concerning a public figure in relation to a purely private matter, is subject to liability only if the publisher knows that the statement is false, acts in reckless disregard for the falsity of the statement, or acts at least negligently in failing to ascertain the truth or falsity of the statement.

Because written statements have a greater degree of permanence, libel is actionable without a showing of special harm to the plaintiff. The harm is presumed. In an action for slander, however, there must be evidence of special harm unless the statement involves particular subjects that constitute slander per se. The imputation of criminal activity, loathsome disease, serious sexual misconduct, or misconduct involving the individual's business, trade, profession, or office have been held to be slander per se. It is this last category that is important to employment law. Thus, a statement that an employee had been fired for drunkenness, an accusation of theft, and allegations about excessive absenteeism and misrepresentation of salary have been held to be slander per se.

Publication

An important element of the tort of defamation is publication, defined as the intentional or negligent communication of the defamatory matter to someone other than the person defamed. In the employment context there have been several issues. First, most courts hold that dictation of defamatory matter to a secretary or stenographer constitutes publication, even though the publication is often held to be privileged. Some courts, however, hold that this does not constitute publication. Second, some courts hold that communication among supervisory and managerial personnel is not publication, although others hold that there is publication, but there is a qualified privilege to do so. Third, most courts hold that simply placing material in an individual's personnel file does not constitute publication. Fourth, communicating with the plaintiff's agent is the same thing as communicating with the plaintiff and therefore does not constitute publication.

Traditionally, courts held that, to be published, the defamatory statement must be communicated directly to a third person. There was no publication if the statement was communicated only to the person defamed, even if the person defamed subsequently communicated what was said to another person. There is a trend in employment cases,

5. 974 S.W.2d 117 (Tex.App.—San Antonio 1998).

6. 376 U.S. 967, 84 S.Ct. 1130, 12 L.Ed.2d 83 (1964).

however, to permit actions for defamation to be based on self-publication by the defamed party to a third person. Typically, these cases involve employees who were discharged by a prior employer, allegedly for some misconduct. When a subsequent, potential employer asks why the individual left the prior employer, if the applicant is truthful, he or she will repeat the defamatory reason that was given to the individual by the former employer. Some courts hold that this self-publication of defamatory material is tantamount to a defamatory communication by the former employer to the potential employer and therefore should be actionable.

The jurisdictions are divided on the viability of defamation actions based on self-publication. The modern cases rejecting the theory generally adopt the position that self-publication fails to satisfy the traditional definition of publication. Other courts reject the theory on other grounds, such as the floodgates argument, privilege, or the existence of a state statute precluding such actions. The cases adopting the theory of self-publication generally require either that the originator of the statement knew or had reason to know that the defamed party would repeat the statement to a third party or that it was foreseeable to the originator of the defamatory matter that the person defamed would be *compelled* to communicate the matter to a third person.

At least two states have enacted statutes to limit defamation actions based on compelled self-publication. In Minnesota, an employee who is discharged may, within five working days of the discharge, request in writing the reason for the discharge. The employer then has five working days to provide, in writing, the "truthful reason." No defamation action may be based on this written reason.[7] Colorado simply prohibits all defamation actions based on self-publication.[8]

Because truth is an absolute defense in a defamation action, defendants in self-publication cases sometimes have asserted that the statement made to the former employee was not defamatory because it was truthful. For example, an employer could assert that the employee *was* discharged for stealing; that was the true reason for the discharge, regardless of whether the employee actually stole anything. Nevertheless, courts have not necessarily focused on the literal meaning of the words used, but their implication. According to one court: "Requiring that truth as a defense go to the underlying implication of the statement, at least where the statement involves more than a simple allegation, appears to be the better view."[9]

Privileges

Statements made in the employment context may be absolutely or conditionally privileged. If a communication is absolutely privileged, the privilege is a bar to a defamation action, irrespective of whether the statement was known to be false, and thus made maliciously or in bad

---

7. Minn. Stat. Ann. § 181.933.

8. Colo. Rev. Stat. Ann. § 13–25–125.5.

9. Lewis v. Equitable Life Assurance Soc'y, 389 N.W.2d 876, 889 (Minn.1986).

faith. There is an absolute privilege for statements made in judicial or administrative proceedings so long as they are pertinent to the subject of controversy. This includes statements to the EEOC, labor grievance hearings, and National Labor Relations Board hearings. Statements made during investigations prior to or in conjunction with judicial or administrative proceedings also are absolutely privileged. Statements made in unemployment compensation proceedings may be absolutely or conditionally privileged, depending on the jurisdiction. Communications made to police for the purpose of reporting criminal activity, however, are generally subject to a conditional privilege unless a statute makes the privilege absolute. Consent to the publication of defamatory matter by the person defamed is also a complete defense.

A publication may be subject to a conditional or qualified privilege if there is a reasonable belief that the recipient or a third party has an important interest in the information and there is either a legal duty to disclose it or it is within the bounds of decent conduct. For example, a defamatory statement may be conditionally privileged if there is a common interest between the publisher and the recipient and the publisher reasonably believes that the recipient has an interest and is entitled to know. For example, it has been held that an employer has a qualified privilege to send out an internal memo stating that a former employee was fired without giving the reason for the discharge. The privilege arises from the social necessity of permitting and encouraging full and unrestricted disclosure. Unlike absolute privileges, however, conditional privileges will be lost if abused.

Generally, if an employer communicates the reason for firing an employee to fellow employees, the communication is qualifiedly privileged based on common interest. Thus, employers have been privileged to tell other employees, including groups of employees, that an employee was discharged for being drunk and misbehaving, stealing, altering a time card, falsifying a document, selling drugs, and vandalism. Reports by and to supervisory and managerial personnel concerning an employee's work performance are generally held to be conditionally privileged based on interest and duty, as well as public policy. A qualified privilege also has been extended to reports made to a small-town newspaper that certain employees had been discharged for possession, sale, or use of controlled substances. Also, a laboratory has been held to have a qualified privilege to report to an employer the results of employee drug tests.

As mentioned earlier, a conditional privilege may be lost if it is abused, such as where: the publisher has knowledge of the falsity of a statement or a reckless disregard for whether the statement is true or false; a statement is published for a purpose other than the one for which the privilege applies; the statement is published to a person not reasonably necessary to accomplish the purpose for which the material is privileged; the publisher is motivated primarily by ill will; or if there is excessive publication.

Courts often use the term "actual malice" in relation to losing a conditional privilege, and that term can mean one of two things. First, it may refer to constitutional malice, which is making a statement with knowledge that it is false or with reckless disregard of the truth. Second, it may refer to common law malice, or simple malice, which is conduct of the publisher evidencing personal ill will, insult or oppression, or reckless and wanton disregard of another's rights. Although either constitutional or common law malice will defeat a conditional privilege, there is a significance to the distinction in the area of damages, but that is beyond the scope of this work.

§ 1.9 Criminal Records

The National Child Protection Act of 1993[1] established the National Criminal History Background Check System. A criminal justice agency in each state must report child abuse crime information to the national system according to guidelines established by the Attorney General. Qualified entities are then required to perform a national background check to determine whether an individual has been convicted of a crime that bears upon his or her fitness to have responsibility for the safety and well-being of children.

Many employers attempt to discover whether applicants for employment have a criminal record, including both arrests and convictions. The legality of such inquiries varies widely, depending on the nature of the job, the method of inquiry, and the existence of a relevant state law. The three different types of criminal records laws are those that require, permit, or prohibit the use of criminal records.

A variety of state laws mandate a preemployment criminal record review for all applicants seeking employment in certain particularly sensitive jobs, including the following: child care employees, child welfare employees, youth detention employees, employees who supervise or discipline children, youth correction employees, school employees, home health employees, nursing home aides, pawnbrokers, police officers, security guards, corrections employees, commercial vehicle locators, nuclear workers, and lottery employees. Some state laws also set the fees (if any) that school districts and private schools may require job applicants to pay for a criminal background check if the applicant passed an initial review.

If the employer investigates the applicant's criminal record, the employer must then determine the extent to which the information will be used in the hiring process. The employer may decide or may be required to enforce a rule that anyone convicted of a felony will be rejected from certain jobs. The employer also may establish or may be required to establish a time period after convictions that will result in disqualification from certain jobs. Another approach is for the employer to consider each hiring decision on an individual basis.

§ 1.9

1. 42 U.S.C.A. § 5119.

If an employer fails to perform a state-mandated criminal record review, this fact may be introduced as evidence of negligence in a negligent hiring case, although the states differ over whether the non-compliance constitutes negligence per se, prima facie negligence, or some evidence of negligence. In deciding which standard to use, the courts consider the legislative intent and state evidentiary principles.

The second category is comprised of state laws authorizing employers to gain access to criminal records, even though employers are not required to use them. Some of the laws grant a more general right of access to the records of certain types of crimes, such as sex crimes. More frequently, however, for both public and private sector employers, criminal records access is available only for specific jobs. In the public sector, the job categories include the following: school teachers, child care employees, private security employees, employees of facilities for the mentally ill, employees of juvenile detention facilities, public housing employees, employees of certain counties, employees of the state militia, and employees of the state auditor general. In the private sector, the job categories include the following: private school employees, employees with disciplinary power over minors, public utilities employees, bank employees, credit union employees, nuclear employees, gaming employees, and higher education security employees.

The third category of state laws includes laws that restrict the access to or use of criminal records. Some states limit the availability of criminal records information to employers or allow individuals to apply for jobs without revealing their criminal records. Other states limit employer access to arrest records or prohibit employers from asking about arrests not leading to conviction.

The purpose of the laws restricting access to and disclosure of criminal records is to prevent discrimination in employment against individuals with criminal records. Some specific statutes attempt to accomplish this end directly, by prohibiting unreasonable discrimination against individuals with prior criminal offenses. More frequently, however, challenges to employment discrimination on the basis of prior conviction or arrest are based on constitutional grounds or are alleged to violate Title VII.

In *Butts v. Nichols*,[2] a challenge was brought against an Iowa law that barred all convicted felons from civil service positions. The court held that the absolute prohibition on hiring for all positions constituted a violation of equal protection. State constitutional law also has been used to challenge the refusal to hire individuals with arrest records.

Private sector challenges to refusal to hire based on criminal records have been brought under Title VII. The leading case is *Green v. Missouri Pacific Railroad*,[3] in which the Eighth Circuit held that criminal convictions may be considered on an individual basis, but that blanket rejections of all convicted criminals may constitute disparate impact race

2.   381 F.Supp. 573 (S.D.Iowa 1974).   **3.**   523 F.2d 1290 (8th Cir.1975).

discrimination. The Ninth Circuit has applied this principle with even greater force to the use of arrest records.[4]

Besides the individual determinations, the courts also have looked to the relationship between the criminal record and the position sought and the length of time of being barred from consideration. Again, restrictions on employment based on convictions are more likely to be upheld than restrictions based simply upon arrests.

§ 1.10 Fingerprinting

Fingerprinting is used by employers to verify the identity of applicants and employees, often as part of a review of criminal records. As might be expected, fingerprinting is most often used in jobs where there is concern about possible criminal activity or public safety.

A variety of federal statutes and regulations require the fingerprinting of applicants and employees. Numerous state laws also require the fingerprinting of school employees, child care employees, juvenile services employees, gambling industry employees, alcohol licensing commission employees, police and security officers, and certain health care providers. Other laws permit the fingerprinting of: gambling industry employees, lottery employees, museum and hospital employees, bar and restaurant employees, and employees of the liquor licensing and enforcement board.

Mandatory fingerprinting laws have been challenged under several federal and state constitutional theories. In *Iacobucci v. City of Newport*,[1] the plaintiff asserted that a municipal ordinance requiring the fingerprinting of employees serving alcoholic beverages violated the First, Ninth, and Fourteenth Amendments to the U.S. Constitution. The Sixth Circuit upheld the ordinance and termed the fingerprinting requirement "only minimally intrusive."[2] Fourth and Fifth Amendment arguments against fingerprinting also have been rejected.

In constitutional challenges the governmental entities have asserted the need for criminal deterrence as the primary reason for the fingerprinting requirement. This claim has been well received by the courts. For example, in *Iacobucci* the court stated that "[b]ecause the ordinance bears a rational relationship to a legitimate governmental interest, we view it as a proper exercise of the City's police power."[3] The courts also have relied on the minimal intrusion of fingerprinting.

Fingerprinting requirements generally are imposed on public employees or private sector employees in regulated industries. For other private sector employees, although fingerprinting is not required by the government, it may be required by the employer. The only exception

4. Gregory v. Litton Sys., Inc., 472 F.2d 631 (9th Cir.1972).

§ 1.10

1. 785 F.2d 1354 (6th Cir.1986), reversed and remanded on other grounds, 479 U.S. 92, 107 S.Ct. 383, 93 L.Ed.2d 334 (1986).

2. 785 F.2d at 1357.

3. Id. at 1355–56.

seems to be if there is a specific state statute that prohibits private sector employers from requiring fingerprints as a condition of employment.

§ 1.11 Credit Records

Some employers use credit information about applicants and employees as an indication of whether the individual is responsible, trustworthy, and stable. Use of this information for an employment purpose, however, may implicate the federal Fair Credit Reporting Act, state credit reporting laws, common law, and the federal Bankruptcy Act.

The Fair Credit Reporting Act (FCRA)[1] is the principal federal law regulating the use of consumer credit information. The FCRA was designed to protect consumers from inaccurate or arbitrary information in a consumer report being used as a factor in determining an individual's eligibility for credit, insurance, or employment. The FCRA attempts to achieve this goal by limiting the types of information contained in consumer reports, restricting access to consumer files, requiring notice to the consumer when an adverse action is based on a consumer report, mandating consumer access to review credit files, and permitting the inclusion of consumer statements in disputed files.

The FCRA governs the use of both "consumer reports" and "investigative consumer reports." A "consumer report" is any communication bearing on a consumer's creditworthiness, credit standing, reputation, or character used in whole or in part to establish a consumer's eligibility for credit, insurance, or employment. An "investigative consumer report" is a more detailed consumer report which contains subjective, personal information on a consumer obtained from interviews and other communications with a consumer's friends, neighbors, and acquaintances. Because these reports may contain subjective views about an individual's marital status, drinking habits, and other personal information, there is concern that inaccurate or irrelevant information could be entered into the reports.

The FCRA regulates "consumer reporting agencies," but employers that check an applicant's references or interview an applicant's neighbors, friends, and associates are not considered consumer reporting agencies. This permits employers, for example, to investigate employees being considered for a promotion without requiring the employer to divulge the consideration.

Under the FCRA, "employment purposes" means the use of a report "for the purpose of evaluating a consumer for employment, promotion, reassignment or retention as an employee." It has been held to be unlawful for an employer to obtain reports: on the relatives or business interests of a job applicant, on the spouse of an employee being considered for promotion, for litigation related to employment, and about former employees.

§ 1.11
1. 15 U.S.C.A. §§ 1681–1681t.

Under the FCRA, credit reporting agencies must maintain procedures to ensure the accuracy of their consumer reports and that users of the reports are using them only for lawful purposes. The FCRA also provides for the exclusion of obsolete information. Consumer reports may not include bankruptcies more than ten years old, nor any lawsuits, judgments, paid tax liens, accounts placed on collection or charged to profit or loss, information regarding the consumer's arrest, indictment or conviction of a crime or other adverse information more than seven years old. These restrictions, however, do not apply to reports used for employment, in which the annual salary reasonably may be expected to exceed $20,000. The FCRA also requires that credit reporting agencies furnishing reports for employment purposes notify the consumer whenever any public record information is reported which could have an adverse effect on the consumer's ability to obtain employment.

If an employer takes adverse action based on a credit report, the employer is required to inform the applicant or employee of the reason for the decision and supply the individual with the name and address of the reporting agency from which the report was obtained. To obtain a more detailed "investigative consumer report" on an applicant or employee, the employer must disclose to the individual, within three days of the request, that it has ordered such a report. The notice must disclose that the report will include information about the applicant's character and reputation, and that the applicant has the right to request full disclosure of the report's contents. If the individual requests a full disclosure of the report, this information must be provided within five days of the request. These notice requirements do not apply if the individual is being considered for a position for which the individual has not applied.

The Fair and Accurate Credit Transactions Act (FACT Act) of 2003,[2] substantially amends the FCRA. Although the main purposes of the amendments were to address identity theft and fraud, there are several provisions with applicability to employment. As amended, for an employer to obtain a consumer report, it must make a "clear and conspicuous" disclosure in writing to the consumer before the report is procured that a report will be obtained for employment purposes and the consumer has authorized the report in writing. Special rules apply when there is an employment application by mail, telephone, computer, or similar means. Before taking an adverse action based on a consumer report, the employer must provide to the consumer a copy of the report and a written description of the rights of consumers under the FCRA. An exception exists for national security investigations.

The FACT Act adds special protections for medical information. A consumer reporting agency may not disclose medical information about a consumer in connection with employment unless: (1) the information is "relevant to process or effect the employment"—in other words, it is job-related; (2) "the consumer provides specific written consent for the

---

2. Pub. L. 108–159 (2003).

furnishing of the report that describes in clear and conspicuous language the use for which the information will be furnished''; and (3) the information furnished relates solely to debts arising from the receipt of medical services and does not provide sufficient information to allow an inference of the specific medical services provided. Any medical information obtained by an employer from a consumer report may not be redisclosed.

Private causes of action under the FCRA may be brought against consumer reporting agencies, employees of reporting agencies, and users of consumer reports (including employers). In actions for both negligent and willful noncompliance with the Act, actual damages, costs, and attorney fees may be recovered. Punitive damages may be awarded in the court's discretion for willful noncompliance, even without proof of malice. Cases arising under the FCRA may be brought in any United States district court, regardless of the amount in controversy. There is a two-year statute of limitations.

The FCRA also provides for civil and criminal sanctions against individuals who obtain information about a consumer from a consumer reporting agency under false pretenses. A violator may be fined up to $5,000 and imprisoned for up to two years. The same penalties apply to any officer or employee of a credit reporting agency who provides any information to an unauthorized person. About one-third of the states have laws regulating some aspect of the consumer reporting industry. As amended, the FCRA broadly preempts state statutes, even those granting consumers greater rights.

Applicants and employees adversely affected in their employment opportunities by a credit report also may have state common law remedies available in the form of tort actions for defamation, negligence, or invasion of privacy. The FCRA, however, provides a qualified immunity against such lawsuits if there has been compliance with the procedures set forth in the FCRA and the disclosure was not done maliciously.

The federal Bankruptcy Act[3] also provides protection against employment discrimination against applicants and employees. Section 525 of the Bankruptcy Act prohibits public and private employers from denying or terminating employment solely because an individual has declared bankruptcy, discharged a debt, or not paid a discharged debt. Although most cases involving section 525 involve employees being terminated subsequent to their filing for or being discharged in bankruptcy, some courts have held that the law also applies to an employer's preemployment inquiries. On the other hand, section 525 protection has been held not to apply to the discharge of an employee allegedly because of his intent to file for bankruptcy.

A number of section 525 cases have involved the meaning of "solely because" of discrimination. Some courts take the position that the law is not meant to prohibit employer actions based on a "mixed motive."

3. 11 U.S.C.A. §§ 101–1330, 1501, 15101–151326.

Other courts have taken a broader reading of "solely because" to prohibit employer conduct in which the bankruptcy proceeding played a "significant role" in the decision to deny or terminate employment.

Discrimination in employment because of outstanding debt also may be actionable under a state garnishment statute or under Title VII. Most states prohibit the discharge of employees for at least some aspect of garnishment, such as child support or wage assignment. Several of the statutes provide for back pay, reinstatement, or damages.

Employer policies providing for the discharge of employees after multiple wage garnishments has been held to violate Title VII because of the disparate impact on minorities. Employer defenses of inconvenience, annoyance, and expense have been insufficient to establish business necessity. Although garnishment-based discrimination has been applied to reprimands, the discipline for failure to pay "just debts" was held not to violate Title VII in the absence of clear evidence of the racial effects of the policy.

§ 1.12 Negligent Hiring

Negligent hiring is a direct cause of action against an employer for injuries to an employee or third party caused by an employee's intentional or negligent acts. The plaintiff's action against the employer is based upon the negligence of the employer in hiring the employee and not vicarious liability. Because negligent hiring is an independent basis of liability, it has been held that no action for negligent hiring will lie if the employer is liable under respondeat superior. Therefore, the courts have held that the employee's actions do not have to have occurred within the scope of employment in order to find the employer negligent. A virtually identical cause of action is based on negligent retention; the only difference is that in negligent retention the employee's conduct after hiring did or should have put the employer on notice of the incompetence or dangerousness of the employee. Thus, the employer's breach of duty was the failure to discharge the employee. Similar actions also have been recognized for the negligent hiring of an independent contractor, the negligent hiring of a former employee, negligent training, and negligent supervision.

As in any negligence action, the starting point is the existence of a duty, which is a question of law. The duty to a third party or fellow employee is based on the foreseeability of harm. The court needs to determine if the employer owed a duty of care to a particular plaintiff. The court will examine whether the plaintiff was in the "zone of risk" or if there was a "sufficient nexus" between the injured party and the employment to create a duty for the employer. There may be a difference between the foreseeability necessary to create a duty and the foreseeability required to establish that the employer's negligence was the proximate cause of the injury. "The concept of foreseeability as it relates to the imposition of a duty 'is based on common sense perception of the risks created by various conditions and circumstances.' "[1]

The courts have been fairly expansive in the relationships that will satisfy the nexus requirement. For example, a sufficient nexus has been found in the relationship between: a doctor and patient, a housing inspector and the tenants of the apartment complex he inspected, an armed security guard and the customers of a convenience store, and the resident manager and the tenants of an apartment complex. In some cases, however, the courts have been unwilling to find a duty of care from the employer to a party injured by the employee. For example, in one case the court held that an employer was not required to search the criminal record of an applicant for a cashier's position.

There also is generally no duty to a party whose relationship with the employee arose through casual contact unrelated to the employment. "[T]he mere existence of the employer-employee relationship does not entitle a third person to seek recovery for injuries inflicted by the employee on the theory of negligence in hiring."[2] For example, in one case the defendant's employee met the plaintiff at a cocktail lounge where she was a waitress. He then drove her to his employer's premises, where he raped her. In an action for negligent hiring, the court affirmed a directed verdict for the employer, observing that the plaintiff was not a customer, patron, or invitee of the defendant-employer and therefore she was beyond the scope of the duty owed by the defendant to the public.[3]

Where an employee is hired pursuant to a work release program, the courts have refused to recognize the existence of a special duty to supervise the employee outside the scope of employment. It also has been asserted, however, that imposing any liability would frustrate the public policy of fostering innovative release and rehabilitation programs. The courts have rejected this argument. According to one court, "[a]n employer's duty to select competent employees is not abrogated because employees are hired in connection with a job program operated by a private rehabilitation center."[4] Nevertheless, some state statutes limit the availability of criminal records because of the public policy of seeking the gainful employment of individuals following their release from incarceration.

Another interesting question of duty was raised in the case of *Moore v. St. Joseph Nursing Home, Inc.*,[5] in which a security guard was savagely beaten and murdered by a coworker. The decedent's estate brought an action against the coworker's former employer, which failed to disclose to the subsequent employer that the employee had been discharged after twenty-four warnings about violence, alcohol use, and

§ 1.12

1. Connes v. Molalla Transp. Sys., Inc., 817 P.2d 567, 570 (Colo.App.1991), affirmed, 831 P.2d 1316 (Colo.1992).

2. Lange v. B. & P. Motor Express, Inc., 257 F.Supp. 319, 323 (N.D.Ind.1966).

3. Baugher v. A. Hattersley & Sons, 436 N.E.2d 126, 128 (Ind.App.1982).

4. Nigg v. Patterson, 233 Cal.App.3d 171, 276 Cal.Rptr. 587, 588 (1990).

5. 184 Mich.App. 766, 459 N.W.2d 100 (1990).

and drug use. The court held that "a former employer has no duty to disclose malefic information about a former employee to the former employee's prospective employer."[6]

Although there should be no general duty on the part of a former employer to seek out prospective employers and inform them about a former employee, the courts ought to recognize a duty to disclose such information when the former employer is specifically asked by a prospective employer. This is especially true when the former employee has displayed violent tendencies in the past and is being considered for a position involving public contact.

After a duty has been established, the next step is to determine whether the employer has breached the duty by hiring or retaining the employee. This is a question of fact for the jury. The jury will consider whether the employer acted in a reasonable manner considering the type of position for which the individual was applying, the information available to the employer, the cost and availability of obtaining additional information, and the foreseeability of harm. Not surprisingly, liability is more likely to be found when the employee is responsible for transporting children or carrying a firearm, the employee has access to a master key or to customers' homes, the employee is working in a "highly volatile" atmosphere, or the employee had engaged in a prior incident of similar misconduct.

A common issue is the appropriate amount of weight to be given to the employer's failure to review an individual's criminal record. The majority rule seems to be that, absent special circumstances, the employer has no duty to investigate whether an individual has a criminal record. Even with the existence of a special circumstance, however, "liability of an employer is not to be predicated solely on failure to investigate criminal history of an applicant, but rather, in the totality of the circumstances surrounding the hiring, whether the employer exercised reasonable care."[7]

In *Board of County Commissioners of Bryan County v. Brown,*[8] the Supreme Court held that a municipality is not liable under 42 U.S.C.A. § 1983 where one of its police officers allegedly used excessive force in making an arrest. "Deliberate action" rather than mere negligent hiring is required to establish a constitutional violation. "A failure to apply stringent culpability and causation requirements raises serious federalism concerns, in that it risks constitutionalizing particular hiring requirements that States have themselves not elected to impose."[9]

Another issue is what type of knowledge on the part of the employer will support a finding of liability. The general rule is that an employer's knowledge of an individual's criminal record may support, but does not require, the finding of negligence. The criminal record or other informa-

---

6.   459 N.W.2d at 100.

7.   Ponticas v. K.M.S. Investments, 331 N.W.2d 907 (Minn.1983).

8.   520 U.S. 397, 117 S.Ct. 1382, 137 L.Ed.2d 626 (1997).

9.   520 U.S. at 415.

tion related to incompetence or dangerousness also must be relevant to the job. For example, an employer's knowledge that the individual had past traffic violations was not enough to put the employer on notice that the employee would commit a sexual assault, and a foreman's knowledge that an employee was "hot-headed" was not enough to establish liability for a subsequent assault. Also, if the conviction was several years before the individual was hired or there was inadequate time after an employee's recent hiring to learn of his dangerous propensities, then no liability has been found.

The next step is to determine whether there is proximate cause between the alleged negligence of the defendant and the harm suffered by the plaintiff. This involves a consideration of two factors: whether the negligent employment practices of the employer led to the individual being hired or retained and whether the employment of the individual set in motion or contributed to the chain of events that led to the injury of the plaintiff. Some courts take a strict view of proximate cause and require that the specific harm must be foreseeable; other courts take a broader view and merely require that some kind of harm must be foreseeable.

If the individual who suffered the injury is an employee of the defendant-employer, then workers' compensation may bar any recovery in tort. Negligent hiring is not an exception to the exclusive remedy principle of workers' compensation. The injured employee must be covered under workers' compensation, however, for the common law action to be barred. If there has been a prior determination of the threshold coverage issues of "in the course of" employment, "arising out of" employment, and other issues by a workers' compensation commission, the courts will often afford deference to the prior determination.

The most important exception to workers' compensation exclusivity in negligent hiring cases is the intentional tort exception. Because workers' compensation bars only actions for negligence, it has been held that a cause of action for negligent hiring based on an intentional tort is not barred. This exception has even been extended to actions based on sexual harassment.

§ 1.13 Blacklisting

At the end of the nineteenth century, in an effort to quash labor organizing, some employers created and circulated lists of pro-union workers to prevent them from gaining employment. In reaction, about half the states enacted blacklisting laws, which prohibited employers from attempting to prevent the employment of former employees. These laws were enacted between 1887 and 1930. Most of the state laws made blacklisting punishable by a fine, but a few states also specifically provided for blacklisted individuals to recover damages from the blacklisting employer.

The existence of a state blacklisting law, criminal or civil, is often invaluable to the success of a civil action for damages. Nevertheless, there is some precedent permitting recovery in a common law blacklisting action even in the absence of a statute. The defendant in an action for blacklisting is invariably the plaintiff's former employer, with the allegation that the former employer acted to prevent the employment of the individual with another employer. There is little redress available against the employer that refuses to hire the individual.

Blacklisting laws fell into disuse with the passage, in 1935, of the National Labor Relations Act,[1] which prohibits employers from discriminating in employment to discourage unionization and coercing employees in the exercise of their right to join a labor organization or to engage in other concerted activity for their mutual aid or protection. Because of the NLRA, most state blacklisting laws are preempted with regard to activity within the purview of the NLRA.

Although the primary reason for state blacklisting laws was to protect against anti-union animus, blacklisting laws may still have relevance to other forms of employer activity. For example, during the McCarthy era, blacklisting laws provided some redress for entertainers who were blacklisted because of their ideological beliefs and associations. More recently, blacklisting laws have been used to challenge blacklisting for the filing of workers' compensation claims or a prior lawsuit.

The essence of a civil action for blacklisting is that a former employer attempted to prevent a former employee from gaining subsequent employment. It has been held that only *unsolicited* statements by a former employer are actionable; responses to inquiries from a prospective employer are privileged.

Contemporary blacklisting cases may require the courts to determine the legislative intent of statutes enacted a century ago. For example, in one case, a former employee sued his former employer under an 1897 Kansas blacklisting law. One part of the statute provides for criminal penalties. Another part of the statute provides that "[a]ny person, firm, or corporation found guilty of the violation of this act" is liable to the injured party for treble damages and attorney fees. The Tenth Circuit held that "found guilty" means that "a criminal blacklisting conviction is an element of a civil blacklisting claim under Kansas law."[2]

§ 1.14 Undocumented Aliens

Under the Immigration Reform and Control Act of 1986 (IRCA)[1], it is unlawful for an employer to knowingly recruit, hire, or continue to employ illegal immigrants. IRCA requires that employers verify employment eligibility upon filling a position. Employers must gather proof of an employee's identity and employability and retain records of that

§ 1.13

1. 29 U.S.C.A. §§ 151–169.
2. Anderson v. United Tel. Co., 933 F.2d 1500, 1503 (10th Cir.) cert. denied, 502 U.S. 940, 112 S.Ct. 375, 116 L.Ed.2d 327 (1991).

§ 1.14

1. 8 U.S.C.A. § 1324a.

verification for three years. Thus, employers have an affirmative duty to determine that a person is authorized to work in the United States. Employers must also complete an INS Form I–9 (Employment Eligibility Verification Form) for each new employee and retain those forms for three years. The Immigration and Naturalization Service (INS) is responsible for enforcing IRCA.

IRCA contains sanction provisions that penalize employers for two different types of conduct. The first type is knowingly hiring an alien who is unauthorized to work at the time of hiring or continuing to employ an alien who becomes unauthorized because of a change in immigration status. The employer may have either actual or constructive knowledge. Constructive knowledge involves a "deliberate failure to investigate suspicious circumstances."[2] If an employer receives a citation from the INS or is informed by the INS that one or more employees are unauthorized to work in the United States, then the employer will be considered to have constructive notice that it is employing an unauthorized alien. An employer will not have constructive knowledge if it offers a job to an alien over the phone without first requesting to see the alien's documentation or fails to compare an alien's Social Security card to the example in the INS handbook.

For a violation of the employment provisions, an employer may be assessed three levels of increasingly severe civil penalties. A first offense carries a penalty of at least $250 and no more than $2,000 for each undocumented alien hired. The second level is a penalty of no less than $2,000 and no more than $5,000. The third level is a penalty of no less than $3,000 and no more than $10,000. An employer is also subject to criminal sanctions for pattern or practice violations.

The second type of violation is failing to verify new employees' work authorization. This type of violation occurs when the employer fails to properly fill out the INS Form I–9, or fails to keep the forms for the proper period of time, or fails to allow the INS or the Labor Department to inspect the forms. If an employer has notice that an employee's documentation is incorrect, the employer is in the same position as if the employee had failed to produce the documentation. The employer may be assessed civil penalties for this type of violation, ranging from $100 to $1,000.

Employers have a defense if they comply in good faith with the employment provisions. Complying with paperwork requirements establishes a good faith defense to an allegation of unlawful hiring. Nevertheless, following proper paperwork procedures will not protect an employer from sanctions for unlawfully continuing employment if the employer has the requisite knowledge. An employer fulfills its obligation to verify an employee's authorization by "examining a document which 'reason-

2. New El Rey Sausage Co. v. United States Immigration & Naturalization Serv., 925 F.2d 1153 (9th Cir.1991).

ably appears on its face to be genuine.' "[3] Thus, an employer that examines an employee's false Social Security card and valid driver's license, but fails to detect that the Social Security card is false is not liable for failing to verify the employee's authorization.

An "employer" is a person or entity, including an agent or anyone acting in the interest of the person or entity, who engages the services or labor of an employee. Liability under IRCA stems from the act of hiring, not merely the state of being an employer. Thus, either an employer or its agent may be liable under the Act. A parent corporation also may be liable for a subsidiary's unlawful hiring practices. Nonetheless, a parent corporation and its subsidiary may obtain separate entity status if they can prove that they are "physically distinct subdivisions which do their own hiring" so long as the two entities do not refer to the practices of the other and are not under common control.[4]

If an employer discovers that its employees do not have the proper documentation, the employer does not have to suspend or fire the employees immediately so long as the employer takes immediate steps to investigate. Employers are exempted from IRCA violations for current employees hired before November 6, 1986. If the employee quits or is terminated by the employer, then the employee loses this "grandfather" status.

The Immigration and Nationality Act[5] was amended by the Immigration Act of 1990[6] and the Miscellaneous and Technical Immigration and Naturalization Amendments of 1991.[7] The Amendments and the regulations promulgated by the Department of Labor limit the annual number of temporary visas for skilled workers to 65,000 and require employers to take certain steps to ensure that hiring workers with these visas will not result in the displacement of U.S. workers. The H–1B visas apply to aliens coming to work temporarily in "specialty occupations," which require at least a bachelor's degree.

§ 1.15 Residency Requirements

Many municipal governments and a few state governments have established residency requirements for eligibility for public employment. These requirements are of two main types: durational and continuing. Both types of requirements have been challenged on constitutional and other grounds.

Durational residency requirements, less commonly used, condition eligibility for employment on the individual having resided in the jurisdiction for a minimum period of time. In the leading case of *Shapiro v.*

3. Collins Foods Int'l, Inc. v. United States Immigration & Naturalization Serv., 948 F.2d 549 (9th Cir.1991).

4. Furr's/Bishop's Cafeterias, L.P. v. Immigration & Naturalization Serv., 976 F.2d 1366 (10th Cir.1992).

5. 8 U.S.C.A. § 1101 et seq.

6. Id.

7. 8 U.S.C.A. § 1201 et seq.

Thompson,[1] the Supreme Court held that a one-year durational residency requirement for eligibility for welfare benefits was unconstitutional because it denied equal protection and infringed upon the fundamental right to travel. The Court stated that the right to travel encompassed the right to "migrate, resettle, find a job, and start a new life." This rationale has been used by the lower courts in invalidating durational residency requirements for state and local employment.

Continuing residency requirements are more common. They require residency within or near a specified government unit as a condition of obtaining or continuing employment. Unlike durational residency requirements, continuing residency requirements have been held not to implicate the fundamental right to travel. Therefore, applying the more deferential rational basis test, courts have upheld continuing residency requirements.

Continuing residency requirements have been challenged on a variety of legal theories. Although right to travel, equal protection, and due process are the most frequent constitutional claims, challenges also have been brought under theories of ultra vires, vagueness, ex post facto law, and impairment of contract.

In *McCarthy v. Philadelphia Civil Service Commission,*[2] a firefighter was discharged because he moved his permanent residence from Philadelphia to New Jersey, in violation of Philadelphia's continuing residency ordinance. The plaintiff challenged the ordinance as unconstitutionally abridging the right to travel. The Supreme Court rejected the claim, distinguishing *Shapiro* and similar cases on the ground that they involved durational residency requirements. According to the Court, continuing residency requirements do not implicate the fundamental right to travel and therefore must be evaluated under the rational basis standard. So long as the ordinance was "appropriately defined and uniformly applied," it was constitutional.

Lower court decisions after *McCarthy* have found numerous rational bases to uphold residency requirements. For example, residency requirements for public school teachers and counselors have been upheld because residents: have greater understanding of the urban problems faced by their students; have greater commitment to an urban education system; are more likely to vote for district taxes, less likely to engage in illegal strikes, and more likely to be involved in school and community activities; have a greater personal stake in the district; have reduced tardiness due to traffic delays; and have greater opportunity to become personally acquainted with students.

Lower court decisions upholding continuing residency requirements for police and firefighters have used similar reasoning: enhanced performance due to greater personal knowledge of the city, greater personal

§ 1.15

1. 394 U.S. 618, 89 S.Ct. 1322, 22 L.Ed.2d 600 (1969), overruled in part on other grounds in Edelman v. Jordan, 415 U.S. 651, 94 S.Ct. 1347, 39 L.Ed.2d 662 (1974).

2. 424 U.S. 645, 96 S.Ct. 1154, 47 L.Ed.2d 366 (1976).

stake in the city's progress, reduced tardiness and absenteeism, and economic benefits to the city from local expenditure of salaries; availability in emergencies; crime deterrence due to the presence of off-duty police; and concern for ethnic balance and reduction of unemployment in the inner city.

Many of the reasons given weight by the courts have been questioned by legal commentators. Nevertheless, the courts have rejected various employee claims, such as that the employee could not find suitable housing, the residency requirement was not a written policy, and the benefits of the policy were marginal and the hardship extensive. These decisions upholding residency requirements have been met with some public disfavor. In California, after the Supreme Court of California upheld continuing residency requirements for municipal employment,[3] California amended its constitution to prohibit any city or county from requiring its employees to be residents, except that employees may be required to live a "reasonable and specific" distance from their place of employment.[4]

Equal protection arguments have been raised most frequently when a continuing residency requirement has been applied to only a certain group of municipal employees. The singling out of police and firefighters for residency requirements has been upheld because of the unique, public safety aspects of the two jobs. Even ordinances permitting discretionary waivers of the rule, seemingly problematic under equal protection analysis, have been upheld. These ordinances include the power to grant general waivers, the "grandfathering" of people living outside the municipality at the time of the passage of the ordinance, and the provision of a cash allowance only to administrators for moving into the city.

Continuing residency requirements also have been unsuccessfully challenged on due process grounds. Specifically, employees have alleged that the rules constitute a taking of the employee's property right to continued employment without due process. The courts have rejected this argument, for example, by noting that the residency requirements were only modifications of the employment contract and that holding a teaching certificate does not entitle the holder to a teaching position.

In a related line of cases, the Supreme Court has held that it is constitutional for a municipality to require that on all construction projects funded in whole or in part by the city, at least half of the employees had to be residents.[5] The Court rejected arguments that such requirements violate either the Commerce Clause or the Privileges and Immunities Clause of Article IV.

3. Ector v. City of Torrance, 10 Cal.3d 129, 109 Cal.Rptr. 849, 514 P.2d 433 (1973), cert. denied, 415 U.S. 935, 94 S.Ct. 1451, 39 L.Ed.2d 493 (1974).

4. Cal. Const. art. XI, ch. 10, subd. (b).

5. White v. Massachusetts Council of Constr. Employers, Inc., 460 U.S. 204, 103 S.Ct. 1042, 75 L.Ed.2d 1 (1983).

A final theory used to challenge residency requirements is that they have a disparate impact on minorities. In two cases the courts have held that the plaintiffs established a prima facie case that a residency requirement had a disparate impact on minorities. According to the courts, the defendants failed to prove a business necessity defense simply by asserting, among other things, that a quick response time was needed for police and fire fighters.[6]

§ 1.16 Civil Service

In 1881, President James A. Garfield was assassinated by Charles J. Guiteau, an insane man who was disappointed because he was unable to get a job with the federal government. As a direct consequence, Congress enacted the Pendleton Act[1] to eliminate patronage in federal employment and to institute efficient and objective federal personnel practices. The Pendleton Act established the Civil Service Commission to implement merit selection, management, and adjudication of complaints by applicants and employees. Although the Pendleton Act was subject to a number of minor amendments over the years, a sweeping revision was made in 1978. In enacting the Civil Service Reform Act (CSRA),[2] Congress made major changes in the federal civil service. As described below, the current federal civil service system is extremely complicated and there may be adverse consequences from failing to comply with specific procedures. Accordingly, great care and expert assistance is recommended in handling federal civil service matters.

The CSRA abolished the Civil Service Commission, dividing its functions between two newly created agencies, the Office of Personnel Management (OPM) and the Merit Systems Protection Board (MSPB). The OPM was given responsibility for the administration and enforcement of the civil service, including maintaining the system of competitive examinations and position appointments. The MSPB was assigned the quasi-judicial role of protecting employees against unjust actions.

The CSRA brought a number of important changes to the federal civil service, including the following: merit system principles and sanctions for committing prohibited personnel practices were codified; whistleblower protections were added; the Senior Executive Service was created to cover top level federal employees; and the substance and procedures of employee discipline were revised. The CSRA reaffirmed the federal government's commitment to "merit principles" of fair and open competition, equal opportunity based solely on ability, equal pay for equal work, and freedom from prohibited personnel practices.

6. Newark Branch, NAACP v. Harrison, 940 F.2d 792 (3d Cir.1991); Newark Branch, NAACP v. Township of West Orange, 786 F.Supp. 408 (D.N.J.1992).

§ 1.16
1. The Civil Service Act of 1883, Ch. 27, 22 Stat. 403 (codified as amended at 5 U.S.C.A. §§ 1101–1105 (1966)).

2. Civil Service Reform Act of 1978, Pub. L. No. 95–454, 92 Stat. 1111 (codified in scattered sections of 5, 10, 15, 28, 31, 38, 39 and 42 U.S.C.A.).

The prohibited personnel practices under the CSRA include discrimination on the basis of race, color, religion, national origin, age, sex, disability, marital status, or political affiliation; influencing political activity through coercion or reprisal; interfering with or obstructing any competitor's application; using unauthorized influence to increase or decrease an applicant's prospects; engaging in nepotism; retaliating for whistleblowing or exercising the right to appeal; discriminating on the basis of conduct unrelated to performance; or violating any regulation dealing with merit system principles.

The merit principles and prohibited personnel practices have incorporated by reference into the civil service system the protections of Title VII, the Equal Pay Act, the Americans with Disabilities Act, and the Age Discrimination in Employment Act. In the 1972 amendments to Title VII, Congress extended the protections of Title VII to the federal government and created an avenue for redress separate from those available through the civil service system. The Government Employee Rights Act of 1991[3] established the Office of Senate Fair Employment to protect Senate employees, presidential appointees, and the personal/advisory staff of elected state officials against discrimination on the basis of race, color, religion, sex, national origin, age, or disability.

To be recognized as a federal employee, and therefore subject to protection under the CSRA, an individual must be appointed by a federal officer or employee, engage in the performance of a federal function, and be subject to the supervision of federal officers or employees. Court decisions have held that being hired as a subcontractor, being housed in a government building, or working at an Army commissary are not enough to establish civil service status.

Merit system principles apply only to executive agencies and the Government Printing Office. The executive agencies specifically listed in the statute are the departments of State, Treasury, Defense, Justice, Interior, Agriculture, Commerce, Labor, Health and Human Services, Housing and Urban Development, Transportation, Energy, Education, and Veterans Affairs.

Federal employees are classified by the type of job held. Over ninety percent are "competitive service" employees—civilians in the lower and mid-level ranks of government who have taken and passed a competitive examination. A relatively small number of these civil servants work in the legislative and judicial branches, but most of them work for the executive agencies listed above. A few employees are classified in "excepted" positions because they are not hired on the basis of a competitive examination. The remaining employees are classified in the Senior Executive Service because they work in highly paid (GS–15 and above) and highly responsible positions that involve supervisory authority or policy-making functions. This categorization is significant because the rights of federal employees vary depending on their classification. Each

3. Civil Rights Act of 1991, Pub. L. No. 102–166, §§ 301–325, 105 Stat. 1071.

employee's official classification appears on the employee's appointment form (OPM SF–50), which is kept in the employee's personnel file.

Applicants and probationary employees have fewer rights than non-probationary employees. For example, applicants may be disqualified because of illicit drug use or past criminal conduct. It does not violate due process to refuse to hire an applicant based on a negative investigation report and simply being listed on a selection register does not confer any liberty or property interest. Decisions regarding eligibility or classification are not overturned unless they are arbitrary and capricious and not supported by evidence.

In addition to the federal civil service laws, virtually every state has some version of a merit system applicable to all or most of its civil service and most states use some form of competitive testing. Many states afford their public employees statutory protections exceeding those applicable to federal employees and, for example, prohibit discrimination based on an expunged juvenile record, marital status, parenthood, sexual orientation, or weight.

§ 1.17   Polygraphs

Employers long have been eager to assess whether applicants and employees are honest, trustworthy, and law-abiding. Although no device is capable of measuring whether someone is telling the truth, the polygraph is based on the theory that lying leads to conscious conflict, which induces fear or anxiety, which in turn produces clearly measurable physiological changes. Polygraphs usually measure three different types of physiological responses. The rate and depth of respiration is measured by pneumographs strapped around the chest and abdomen. Cardiovascular activity is measured by a blood pressure cuff (sphygmomanometer) placed around the bicep. Electrodermal response (galvanic skin response) is measured by electrodes attached to the fingertips.

A number of states have regulated polygraphs for many years, but congressional interest in the subject is much more recent. In 1983 the Office of Technology Assessment of the United States Congress (OTA) undertook a detailed review of the scientific literature on the accuracy of polygraphs. OTA concluded that there are serious questions about the accuracy of polygraphs. "[T]here is very little research or scientific evidence to establish polygraph test validity in screening situations, whether they be preemployment, preclearance, periodic or aperiodic, random, or 'dragnet.' "[1] Overall, accuracy rates were estimated at fifty to ninety percent. When used as a preemployment screen, polygraphs may disqualify as many as thirty percent of applicants.

Despite scientific evidence casting doubt on the accuracy of polygraphs, numerous employers have asserted that polygraphs are highly

§ 1.17

1. Office of Technology Assessment, United States Congress, Scientific Validity of Polygraph Testing 8 (1983).

effective in screening out workers who steal or engage in other forms of misconduct. One reason may be that, because people taking the polygraphs believe the test will detect any lies they tell, while taking the polygraph they admit to various kinds of wrongdoing and they are not hired or are fired as a result. The polygraphs are then credited with ferreting out these people. By the mid–1980s, as many as two million polygraphs were performed in the private sector each year, most frequently by banks, jewelers, retail stores, and fast food outlets.

Based in part on the OTA study, Congress enacted the Employee Polygraph Protection Act of 1988 (EPPA).[2] The law prohibits about eighty-five percent of the former polygraph use in the private sector. An employer may not "require, request, suggest or cause an employee or prospective employee to take or submit to any lie detector test"[3] or "discharge, discipline, or discriminate" against an applicant or employee on the basis of or refusal to take a polygraph.[4] The proscription applies not only to polygraphs, but also to the deceptograph, voice stress analyzer, psychological stress evaluator, or any other similar mechanical or electrical device used to determine honesty. The EPPA does not apply to paper and pencil honesty or integrity tests.

There are three exceptions to the ban on the private sector use of polygraphs. First, a polygraph may be given in connection with an ongoing investigation involving economic loss or injury to the employer's business. Second, polygraphs may be performed on prospective employees of an employer whose business consists of providing security services for the protection of nuclear power, electrical power, public water supply, radioactive or toxic waste, public transportation, currency, negotiable securities, precious commodities or instruments, or proprietary information. Third, an employer that manufactures, distributes, or dispenses controlled substances may test prospective employees who will have access to such activities or current employees in connection with an investigation of misconduct involving controlled substances.

These private sector exceptions are qualified. An individual tested pursuant to the "investigation" exception must have had access to the property in question, the employer must have a reasonable suspicion that the employee was involved in the incident, and the employer must set forth in writing the specific incident involved and the basis for testing the particular employee. The employee may not be discharged on the basis of the polygraph without additional supporting evidence. An employer testing employees under the "security" or "controlled substance" exceptions also may not use the polygraph as the sole basis for discharge.

All polygraph testing in the private sector is subject to various procedural limitations. These include written notice of the test date, time, and place; written notice of the test characteristics; opportunity to review the questions to be asked; and the right to legal counsel. The

2. 29 U.S.C.A. §§ 2001–2009.

3. Id. § 2002(1).

4. Id. §§ 2002(3)(A), 2002(3)(B).

polygraph examiner may not ask questions regarding religious, racial, or political beliefs, or about any matter relating to sexual behavior, nor may the examiner ask questions in a manner designed to "degrade or needlessly intrude on" the examinee.

Polygraph examiners are not permitted to make recommendations concerning employment decisions and they must have a current license if required by the state. Disclosure of the results of testing is limited to the examinee, the requesting employer, and a court ordering disclosure. An employer may disclose an admission of criminal conduct to an appropriate governmental agency.

The EPPA is enforced by the Secretary of Labor and provides for the assessment of civil penalties of up to $10,000. The Secretary of Labor also is authorized to bring an action in federal court to enjoin violations of the EPPA. In addition, the EPPA provides for private civil actions by an affected applicant or employee. The available remedies include employment, reinstatement, promotion, and the payment of lost wages and benefits. Civil actions may be brought in state or federal court and have a three year statute of limitations. In its discretion, the court may award attorney fees and costs to the prevailing party (plaintiff or defendant) other than the United States.

While the EPPA applies to virtually all private sector employers, it does not apply to federal, state, or local government employers. There are also exemptions for national defense and security organizations and their consultants, and for contractors of the Federal Bureau of Investigation. Judicial decisions have held that a polygraph examiner may not be held liable as an "employer" under the EPPA. In addition, the EPPA does not prohibit the arbitration of a polygraph grievance pursuant to a contract provision.

The EPPA does not preempt any state or local law or negotiated collective bargaining agreement that is more restrictive with respect to lie detector tests than any provision of the EPPA. About half the states have anti-polygraph statutes and eleven of these states include state governments. The statutes often prohibit requesting as well as requiring the taking of a polygraph.

In *Calbillo v. Cavender Oldsmobile, Inc.,*[5] a former employee who had been terminated based on a polygraph examination sued his former employer and the polygraph examiner alleging common law negligence and violation of the EPPA. The Fifth Circuit held that under Texas law the polygraph examiner owed no duty of care in conducting the examination. To be liable under the EPPA the individual must be an "employer" and, as to a polygraph examiner, this determination is based on whether the examiner (1) decided that the examination should be administered; (2) decided which employees to examine; (3) provided advice to the employer on compliance with the EPPA; or (4) decided whether the examined employee should be subject to disciplinary action.

5. 288 F.3d 721 (5th Cir. 2002).

The most significant of the tort cases are wrongful discharge actions based on the public policy exception to the at-will rule. In states with an anti-polygraph law, the statute may establish a public policy, breach of which is actionable. For example, in one case, a private security guard was discharged after he refused to undergo a polygraph test. In a subsequent wrongful discharge action, the Nebraska Supreme Court held that the Nebraska anti-polygraph statute created a public policy which supported the action for wrongful discharge.[6]

In states without an anti-polygraph statute, the courts generally hold that an employee has no cause of action based on the public policy exception. For example, in one case, following inventory shortages the employer ordered all of its employees to take polygraph tests and discharged the plaintiff when he refused. The Supreme Court of Oklahoma held that in the absence of state anti-polygraph legislation, discharging an employee for refusing to take a polygraph did not violate public policy.[7]

Public sector challenges to polygraphs have been brought under a variety of constitutional theories, including due process and equal protection, self-incrimination, and right to privacy. The actions have been brought in both state and federal courts. For example, in one case a police officer refused to take a polygraph examination and was found guilty of insubordination. The plaintiff brought an action in which he asserted that the state law, under which only employees of law enforcement agencies could be compelled to take a polygraph, violated equal protection. The Supreme Court of Montana held that there was no rational basis for differentiating among law enforcement employees and all other public and private sector employees and therefore the statute violated the state constitution.[8]

A contrary result was reached by the Supreme Court of Washington in a virtually identical case. The court held that the statute's singling out of law enforcement applicants for polygraphs did not deny equal protection because it was rationally related to the state's legitimate interest in ensuring a high level of trustworthiness and personal integrity of law enforcement personnel.[9]

Although arguments based on self-incrimination have not been successful, the right of privacy theory has met with some success. In one case, the Texas Supreme Court held that the right to privacy in the Texas Constitution was violated by a mandatory polygraph testing requirement. The court held that under a heightened scrutiny standard, the defendant's interest in minimizing employee misconduct was "inade-

---

6. Ambroz v. Cornhusker Square Ltd., 226 Neb. 899, 416 N.W.2d 510 (1987).

7. Pearson v. Hope Lumber & Supply Co., 820 P.2d 443 (Okl.1991).

8. Oberg v. City of Billings, 207 Mont. 277, 674 P.2d 494 (1983).

9. O'Hartigan v. Washington Dep't of Personnel, 118 Wash.2d 111, 821 P.2d 44 (1991).

quate to overcome the privacy interests impinged upon by the polygraph testing."[10]

§ 1.18 Honesty Testing

One of the consequences of enactment of the federal Employee Polygraph Protection Act of 1988[1] has been an increase in the use of other tests purporting to measure "honesty" or "integrity." Paper and pencil honesty tests are widely used by various companies, most frequently in retail, fast food, banking, and other service businesses. The tests attempt to screen out individuals who are likely to be dishonest on the job and thereby seek to reduce employee crimes such as theft and bribery.

Although there are several different honesty tests in common use, two main types of questions are used. First, overt questions ask whether the individual has been dishonest in the past, what the individual's attitude is toward theft by others, and similar direct questions. There also may be less direct overt questions, such as "Do you like to take chances?" The second type of honesty test is more personality based. It attempts to measure personality traits such as dependability, cooperation, drug avoidance, organizational delinquency, and "wayward impulse."

The accuracy of honesty tests remains a subject of great controversy. Critics argue, among other things, that individuals who honestly admit to prior indiscretions are often eliminated as dishonest while those who untruthfully assert that they have always been honest pass. Defenders of the tests claim that the tests are less intrusive than polygraphs, cheaper and easier to use than psychological tests, and highly effective in reducing employee theft. Congress has not not yet seen fit to legislate in this area, but it is continuing to study the issue of paper and pencil honesty tests.

The Employee Polygraph Protection Act[2] does not apply to paper and pencil honesty tests. Similarly, state polygraph laws do not prevent the use of these tests. For example, in one case, the Supreme Court of Minnesota construed language in the state's polygraph law prohibiting the use of "any test purporting to test honesty." The court held that the prohibition is limited to tests which "purport to measure physiological changes in the subject tested * * *." Therefore, the statute did not apply to honesty questionnaires. The court was concerned that without such a construction the statute would be unconstitutionally vague.

Only two states so far have enacted legislation specifically directed at paper and pencil honesty tests. The use of the tests is completely prohibited in Massachusetts.[3] In Rhode Island, honesty tests may be

10. Texas State Employees Union v. Texas Dep't of Mental Health & Mental Retardation, 746 S.W.2d 203, 206 (Tex. 1987).

§ 1.18

1. 29 U.S.C.A. §§ 2001–2009.

2. 29 U.S.C.A. §§ 2001(3) and (4).

3. Mass. Gen. Laws Ann. ch. 149, § 19(B)(1).

used so long as they are not the "primary basis for an employment decision."[4]

Because the actual questions asked in honesty tests often deal with personal information, it is possible that challenges could be brought to their use on a variety of legal theories. For public employees, possible sources of protection include constitutional arguments based on due process, self-incrimination, and the right to privacy. Analogous cases challenging the use of personal and security questionnaires often have balanced the governmental employer's need for the information against the individual's right to nondisclosure. For private sector employees, common law actions for wrongful refusal to hire, wrongful discharge, and invasion of privacy remain a theoretical possibility, but there are as yet no reported cases.

§ 1.19   Psychological and Personality Testing

Psychological testing has become an increasingly popular method of screening applicants and employees. Many employers use psychological testing to: facilitate proper job placement to increase productivity; prevent violence, drug and alcohol abuse, and the legal liability that they can cause; reduce the number of workers' compensation claims for mental health disorders; and reduce health insurance claims for mental illness.

A wide variety of scientific (and pseudo-scientific) measures come under the heading of psychological testing. Intelligence testing and integrity or honesty testing are discussed separately. Other measures in common usage are personality tests (both objective and projective), individual psychological assessments, vocational preference tests, and graphoanalysis (handwriting tests).

For the most part, psychological tests are unregulated. The only exceptions are the occasional cases in which the use of a test had the effect of discriminating on the basis of race, color, religion, sex, or national origin. In *Soroka v. Dayton Hudson Corp.*,[1] an applicant for the position of store security officer was required to take a "Psychscreen," a combination of the Minnesota Multiphasic Personality Inventory (MMPI) and the California Psychological Inventory. The test, consisting of 704 true-false questions, asked questions about, among other things, religious attitudes and sexual orientation. Despite being hired for the job, the plaintiff brought an action in which he claimed that the Psychscreen violated the California Constitution's right to privacy, as well as various state statutes. The trial court denied the plaintiff's motion for a preliminary injunction and the California Court of Appeals reversed. The court held that, under California law, applicants have the

---

4. R.I. Gen. Laws §§ 28–6.1–1 to 28–6.1–4.

§ 1.19

1. 18 Cal.App.4th 1200, 1 Cal.Rptr.2d 77 (1991), superseded by grant of review, 4 Cal.Rptr.2d 180, 822 P.2d 1327 (1992), review dismissed after settlement, 862 P.2d 148, 24 Cal.Rptr.2d 587 (Cal.1993).

same rights as employees and that the employer failed to prove that the test was job related. The case was eventually settled while pending on appeal before the Supreme Court of California.

Psychological testing also may be challenged as violating state and federal disability discrimination laws. Under the Americans with Disabilities Act (ADA), psychological testing may be considered a medical examination. Therefore, these examinations may not be given until after a conditional offer of employment. In addition, in California and Minnesota, all medical examinations must be job related. In such a state, the employer may have a difficult time in using any psychological tests for some jobs.

Cases challenging the use of psychological tests under disabilities laws have reached varying results. For example, in one case, the employer, a nuclear power plant operator, administered an MMPI, which revealed that a conditional offeree had a risk of substance abuse. After a personal evaluation by a psychologist revealed "alcoholic tendencies," the individual was terminated. The Michigan Court of Appeals reversed the grant of summary judgment for the defendant, and held that the trial court should have addressed the issue of whether one who has been designated by a psychological test as having "alcoholic tendencies" is covered under the Michigan Handicappers' Civil Rights Act.[2]

A somewhat different result was reached by the Second Circuit. A police officer candidate who was rejected because a psychologist found that he had shown "poor judgment, irresponsible behavior and poor impulse control," was held not to be a "handicapped person" under the Rehabilitation Act.[3] The character traits cited by the psychologist did not amount to a mental condition that substantially limited a major life activity.

Unsuccessful applicants for public employment also have attempted to challenge the use of psychological testing on constitutional grounds. For example, in one case, applicants who were rejected for police officer positions with the Chicago Police Department because they were "psychologically unfit," brought an action under 42 U.S.C.A. § 1983, in which they claimed that they were stigmatized by the rejection, therefore violating their liberty interests under the Fourteenth Amendment. The Seventh Circuit affirmed the district court's dismissal of the claim on the ground that because there had been no publication of the applicant's rejection there was no stigma attached to the use of the test.[4]

One of the most unusual psychological testing cases is *Harrington v. Almy*.[5] A police officer was suspended pending an investigation into allegations that he molested several children. Although no criminal charges were ever brought, he was not permitted to resume his full police duties unless he submitted to a "penile plethysmograph." This is a

2. Adkerson v. MK–Ferguson Co., 191 Mich.App. 129, 477 N.W.2d 465 (1991).

3. Daley v. Koch, 892 F.2d 212 (2d Cir. 1989).

4. Koch v. Stanard, 962 F.2d 605 (7th Cir.1992).

5. 977 F.2d 37 (1st Cir.1992).

procedure that seeks to determine a male's sexual inclinations by placing a gauge on his genitals and flashing sexually explicit pictures at him. The First Circuit held that because the test was of unproven validity, was degrading, and involved bodily manipulation of the most intimate sort, the test violated substantive due process.

Psychological testing also may be required of current employees. In *Redmond v. City of Overland Park,*[6] the court held that there was no invasion of privacy for a police department to require the psychological evaluation of an employee who displayed bizarre and paranoid behavior on the job. Similarly, in *Davis-Durnil v. Carpentersville, Illinois,*[7] a female police officer suffered from post-traumatic stress disorder and atypical depression with panic attacks after shooting a suspect. The court held that it did not violate the ADA or Title VII to place her on administrative duty and require her to undergo a psychological examination.

Employers performing psychological testing on applicants and employees may be required to give the individuals access to their test results pursuant to a state law mandating the disclosure of medical records made by any health care provider. In *Cleghorn v. Hess,*[8] the Nevada Supreme Court, in holding that the individuals had to be provided with test results, rejected the argument that the statute did not apply to the employment setting, where the individuals who took the tests were not the "patients" of the psychologist. According to the court, the fact that treatment was not contemplated was not dispositive.

§ 1.20 Intelligence and Aptitude Testing

Among the commonly used devices for evaluating applicants for initial hire or for promotion are professionally developed ability tests and intelligence tests, similar to ones used by schools for admission of students. In the employment context, the use of such tests can violate federal discrimination law if they operate unfairly to reduce opportunities for groups on the basis of race, national origin, gender, age, or disability.

The Supreme Court has explained when the use of exclusionary tests violates Title VII and when they violate the Constitution. The Court held in *Griggs v. Duke Power Co.*[1] that a test with a disparate impact on the basis of race, gender, or national origin is discriminatory within the meaning of Title VII if the employer cannot prove its validity. There is no requirement under Title VII that a plaintiff establish any particular motive on the part of the employer with respect to the adoption or use of a testing device. In contrast, motive is a requirement for a claim that a testing device is racially exclusive in violation of the

6. 672 F.Supp. 473 (D.Kan.1987).
7. 128 F.Supp.2d 575 (N.D.Ill. 2001).
8. 109 Nev. 544, 853 P.2d 1260 (1993).

§ 1.20
1. 401 U.S. 424, 91 S.Ct. 849, 28 L.Ed.2d 158 (1971).

Constitution. The Supreme Court held in *Washington v. Davis*[2] that the statutory standard of employment discrimination does not apply to constitutional challenges. Such challenges require proof of the employer's intent to discriminate.

A test that disproportionately excludes on a basis covered by the federal employment discrimination statutes violates those acts unless the employer can satisfy the requirements of job validation. An employer can establish validity only by satisfying the court that there is a close connection between one's level of performance on the test and one's level of performance on the job. There are three types of validity: predictive validity, content validity, and construct validity. An employer can establish predictive validity by demonstrating the statistical relationship between scores on the test and objective measures of job performance. This type of validity, also called criterion-related validity, is necessary to show that an aptitude test predicts the level of job performance. Content validity is achieved when the test replicates essential portions of the job, such as a typing test for a typist. Construct validity requires the identification of a psychological trait or characteristic that is predictive of successful job performance, such as aggressiveness for a sales representative. Like predictive validity, construct validity requires a statistical demonstration of the correlation between the strength of the identified trait and the level of job performance.

A test that is demonstrably job-related, and for which there is no alternative selection device with lesser impact, does not violate any federal employment discrimination act unless the employer adopted the test for the express purpose of exclusion. With respect to invidious motive, the Civil Rights Act of 1991 amended Title VII specifically to provide that a "demonstration that an employment practice is required by business necessity may not be used as a defense against a claim of intentional discrimination" under the Act.[3] In the absence of invidious motive, job-related tests are permissible, provided the employer administers the tests and uses the results consistently. The problem, however, is that an employer cannot be assured in advance of litigation whether a test is job-related. That characterization is a matter of legal determination after trial.

> Title VII contains a specific testing proviso saying that it is not unlawful for an employer to give and to act upon the results of any professionally developed ability test provided that such test, its administration or action upon the results is not designed, intended, or used to discriminate because of race, color, religion, sex, or national origin.[4]

2. 426 U.S. 229, 96 S.Ct. 2040, 48 L.Ed.2d 597 (1976).

3. P.L. 102–166, 105 Stat. 1071 (1991), amending § 703(k)(1)(C)(2) of the Civil Rights Act of 1964, 42 U.S.C.A. § 2000e.

4. 42 U.S.C.A. § 2000e–2(h).

Adopting a test for the purpose of exclusion is only one way that a test may be "used" to discriminate within the meaning of this proviso. The Supreme Court has explained that an employer also may have unlawfully "used" a test to discriminate if that test is not demonstrably related to the job and if that test disproportionately excludes on the basis of race or other bases protected by the Act. In *Griggs v. Duke Power Co.,*[5] the Court held that this proviso does not insulate an employer from liability if exclusionary tests are not job-related, even when the employer used a professionally developed test in good faith. "What Congress has commanded," the Court explained, "is that any tests used must measure the person for the job and not the person in the abstract."[6]

In *Griggs* the defendant power company used standardized aptitude tests for assignment to jobs other than ones in the labor department. Labor department jobs, which were the lowest paying and least desirable jobs, were historically the only jobs available to black workers. When segregation was open and legal, only the labor department was available to African–Americans in this North Carolina company. The aptitude test requirement was adopted when Title VII became effective in 1965. The effect of this testing requirement, as well as a high school diploma requirement also imposed, was to perpetuate the racial segregation of job categories. The company made no effort to establish any connection between the testing requirement and job performance. Instead, it defended on the grounds that there was no racial animus in the adoption of the tests, that the tests were a good faith effort to improve the quality of the work force, and that the Act approved the use of professionally developed tests in the Title VII testing proviso.

The trial judge made a finding of fact that the company was not using the tests for intentional racial exclusion. This finding was not against the manifest weight of the evidence and thus was not disturbed on appeal. Therefore, the specific question before the Supreme Court was whether the use of tests that are not job-related violates the Act, even if the employer adopts the tests in good faith. The Court answered in the affirmative; employers cannot use tests that disproportionately disadvantage groups covered by the Act unless the tests are demonstrably related to the job. *Griggs* was thus the first case to use a disparate impact theory of discrimination and to introduce the concepts of business necessity and job validation as defenses.

Even if an employer successfully establishes the job-relatedness of an exclusionary testing device, the plaintiff may still prevail. At this stage of the litigation—after the plaintiff establishes the disproportionate exclusion of a test and the employer defends with proof of its validity—it remains open to the plaintiff to show that there is an alternative selection device with a lesser disparate impact that would serve the employer's needs as well. This concept of alternative selection

5. 401 U.S. 424, 91 S.Ct. 849, 28   **6.** 401 U.S. at 436.
L.Ed.2d 158 (1971).

devices was introduced by the Supreme Court in *Albemarle Paper Co. v. Moody*[7] in 1975. The Court there held:

> If an employer does then meet the burden of proving that its tests are "job related," it remains open to the complaining party to show that other tests or selection devices, without a similarly undesirable racial effect, would also serve the employer's legitimate interest in "efficient and trustworthy workmanship." * * * Such a showing would be evidence that the employer was using its tests merely as a "pretext" for discrimination.[8]

In a subsequent Supreme Court opinion, *Watson v. Fort Worth Bank & Trust*,[9] the Court made further observations on the subject of alternative selection devices:

> Factors such as the cost or other burdens of proposed alternative selection devices are relevant in determining whether they would be equally as effective as the challenged practice in serving the employer's legitimate business goals. The same factors would also be relevant in determining whether the challenged practice has operated as the functional equivalent of a pretext for discriminatory treatment.[10]

The Civil Rights Act of 1991 codified the *Albemarle* and *Watson* holdings with respect to alternative selection devices. Section 105 of that Act amends section 703 of Title VII to provide that a violation of the Act is established if the complaining party demonstrates that there is an alternative employment practice and the respondent refuses to adopt it.

This provision of the 1991 Act concerning alternative selection devices is further explained in the interpretative memorandum authored by Senator Dole which was specifically endorsed by President Bush when he signed the Act. That memorandum says that the standards outlined in *Albemarle* and *Watson* should apply.

Section 105 of the Civil Rights Act of 1991 specifically rejects the most recent holding of the Supreme Court on the subject of alternative selection devices. The Court had held in *Wards Cove Packing Co. v. Atonio*[11] that in order to require an alternative with a less disparate impact the complainant must prove that the proposed alternative is "equally effective" as the employer's procedure.[12] In response, the Civil Rights Act of 1991 provides that the complainant's demonstration of an alternative selection device "shall be in accordance with the law as it existed on June 4, 1989,"[13] the day before the Supreme Court decided *Wards Cove*.

---

7. 422 U.S. 405, 95 S.Ct. 2362, 45 L.Ed.2d 280 (1975).

8. 422 U.S. at 425.

9. 487 U.S. 977, 108 S.Ct. 2777, 101 L.Ed.2d 827 (1988).

10. 487 U.S. at 998.

11. 490 U.S. 642, 109 S.Ct. 2115, 104 L.Ed.2d 733 (1989).

12. 490 U.S. at 661.

13. Civil Rights Act of 1991, § 105(a), amending Title VII, § 703 (k)(1)(C).

Employers seeking to use tests for the selection or promotion of employees should follow the procedures outlined in the Uniform Guidelines on Employee Selection Procedures.[14] Various provisions of these guidelines detail recordkeeping requirements and procedures for test validation. In the context of test validation, the Supreme Court has said that the guidelines are to be accorded great deference.[15] Although the Court has not always followed the guidelines in all regards, the deference to the guidelines' validation requirements has been a significant influence in Title VII litigation. The Supreme Court has further noted, however, that there are no absolutely fixed rules for how an employer must defend requirements, even standardized tests. The Court said in dicta in *Watson* that Title VII does not necessarily require employers "to introduce formal 'validation studies' showing that particular criteria predict actual on-the-job performance."[16]

In contrast, the guidelines require that all aspects of a test be validated, including any cutoff score. A common source of invalidity for tests has been the employer's failure to validate the use of tests to rank applicants, or the use of a cutoff score. The guidelines state that a cutoff score should be set "so as to be reasonable and consistent with normal expectations of acceptable proficiency within the work force." An otherwise valid exam, such as a content valid physical agility exam for firefighters, must also have a valid cutoff score. The cutoff score cannot simply serve to eliminate a fixed percentage of the applicants, for example. In one case the validity of a firefighter's physical agility exam was called into question because the cutoff score for the maximum number of seconds the firefighter candidates must complete the content valid tasks varied on a yearly basis.[17]

The statutory requirement that exclusionary exams be job-related is not diminished by the presence of an affirmative action plan that produces a balanced work force. The Supreme Court held in *Connecticut v. Teal*[18] that an employer cannot defend the use of an unvalidated promotion exam by showing a "bottom line" of promotees that racially matches the pool of applicants. Title VII is process-oriented rather than outcome-oriented; a racially exclusionary test that is not job-related violates the Act regardless of the employer's good faith efforts to offer employment opportunities to all members of the community. "It is clear," the Court explained, "that Congress never intended to give an employer license to discriminate against some employees on the basis of race or sex merely because he favorably treats other members of the employees group."[19] Therefore, an employer must defend the use of every selection device that disproportionately excludes on a basis covered by federal employment discrimination law.

14. 29 C.F.R. Part 1607 [Guidelines].

15. Albemarle Paper Co. v. Moody, 422 U.S. 405, 95 S.Ct. 2362, 45 L.Ed.2d 280 (1975).

16. 487 U.S. 977, 998, 108 S.Ct. 2777, 101 L.Ed.2d 827 (1988).

17. Evans v. City of Evanston, 881 F.2d 382 (7th Cir.1989).

18. 457 U.S. 440, 102 S.Ct. 2525, 73 L.Ed.2d 130 (1982).

19. 457 U.S. at 455.

§ 1.21   Physical Ability Testing

Many employers require applicants to demonstrate that they have the physical ability to perform the job. The actual tests used vary widely and range from typing tests to agility tests for public safety positions. The three main legal issues raised by these tests relate to the Americans with Disabilities Act (ADA), Title VII of the Civil Rights Act of 1964, and common law negligence.

Under the ADA, employers "may make preemployment inquiries into the ability of an applicant to perform job-related functions, and/or may ask an applicant to describe or to demonstrate how, with or without reasonable accommodation, the applicant will be able to perform job-related functions."[1] In addition, physical agility tests (a subset of physical ability tests) are not "medical examinations" and therefore may be given at any time, including at the pre-offer stage.[2] Nevertheless, if the test screens out or tends to screen out individuals with disabilities, the employer has the burden of proving that the test is job-related and consistent with business necessity.

Physical ability tests, if they adversely affect employment opportunities based on race, color, religion, sex, national origin, or age, also may be challenged under Title VII or the Age Discrimination in Employment Act (ADEA). The most common allegation is gender discrimination. For example, in *Harless v. Duck*,[3] a class action was brought challenging the physical ability test used by the Toledo, Ohio, Police Department. Applicants were required to complete three of the following four tests: fifteen push-ups; twenty-five sit-ups; six-foot standing broad jump; and a twenty-five-second obstacle course. The Sixth Circuit, while conceding that physical abilities were essential to safe and effective police work, nevertheless concluded that "there is no justification in the record for the types of exercises chosen or the passing marks for each exercise."[4] A contrary result was reached in *Lanning v. Southeastern Pennsylvania Transportation Authority*.[5] All applicants for the transit authority police force were required to run 1.5 miles in twelve minutes. In rejecting a disparate impact sex discrimination claim, the Third Circuit held that the transit authority had established that the requirement measured the minimum qualifications necessary to perform the job. Other cases considering the disparate impact of physical standards have reached varying results.

Employees injured during ability tests are limited to their remedies under workers' compensation. Applicants, however, are not barred from bringing an action for negligence. In one case,[6] an applicant for a police

---

§ 1.21

1. 29 C.F.R. § 1630.14A.

2. 29 C.F.R. Part 1630, App. to § 1630.14(a), 56 Fed. Reg. 35,750 (1991).

3. 619 F.2d 611 (6th Cir.), cert. denied, 449 U.S. 872, 101 S.Ct. 212, 66 L.Ed.2d 92 (1980).

4. 619 F.2d at 616.

5. 308 F.3d 286 (3d Cir. 2002).

6. Younger v. City & County of Denver, 810 P.2d 647 (Colo.1991).

officer's position was injured during a preemployment physical agility test. The Supreme Court of Colorado held that because he had not begun employment, the applicant was not subject to workers' compensation. In *Dodson v. Workers' Compensation Division,*[7] however, the West Virginia Supreme Court of Appeals held that a claimant was entitled to compensation where the employer made an offer of employment conditioned on the completion of a strength and agility test administered by the employer, and the claimant was injured in the course of performing the test.

§ 1.22   Medical Testing

Medical screening is the process by which a work force is selected by the application of medical criteria. It has been in wide use in the United States since the beginning of the twentieth century when large companies began employing "factory surgeons" to determine whether applicants and employees were free of disease and had the necessary strength, stamina, vision, hearing, and other physical attributes to perform the job.

The use of medical screening has increased greatly in the last quarter century as many companies realized that it was in their economic interests to employ workers who not only were in good health at the time they begin work, but who were also likely to remain in good health in the future. Thus, medical screening became both diagnostic and predictive. It also was concerned with both occupationally-related disorders and nonoccupationally-related disorders.

The traditional time for medical screening was before the individual was hired—at the preemployment stage. By the early 1980s, ninety percent of applicants for jobs at large plants (more than 500 workers) and over fifty percent of applicants for jobs at smaller plants (fewer than 500 workers) were subject to preemployment medical examinations. Over time, preemployment medical examinations became increasingly detailed and sophisticated. One consequence of this trend was that individuals with disabilities became identified early on and, in many instances, experienced limitations on their employment opportunities.

When the Americans with Disabilities Act (ADA)[1] was enacted in 1990, section 102(d) was included, which mandates major changes in the way many companies have traditionally evaluated the fitness for duty of job applicants. Under this section, all preemployment medical examinations and medical inquiries are illegal. "[A] covered entity shall not conduct a medical examination or make inquiries of a job applicant as to whether such applicant is an individual with a disability or as to the nature and severity of such disability."[2]

---

7. 210 W.Va. 636, 558 S.E.2d 635 (2001).

2. Id. § 12112(d)(2)(A).

§ 1.22

1. 42 U.S.C.A. §§ 12101–12213.

The ADA's prohibition on preemployment inquiries includes medical questionnaires, oral inquiries into disabilities, and medical examinations, whether conducted by human resources or medical personnel. The only exception is that "[a] covered entity may make preemployment inquiries into the ability of an applicant to perform job-related functions."[3] These inquiries, however, must be narrowly tailored. The employer may describe or demonstrate a particular job function and inquire whether the applicant can perform the function with or without accommodation. The employer also may ask about the applicant's ability to perform specific job functions, such as lifting boxes or manipulating small parts.

Despite these limitations on preemployment examinations, employers are permitted to make the successful completion of a medical examination a valid condition of employment. The examination, however, may not take place until after the employer has made a conditional offer of employment. Section 102(d)(3) provides that "[a] covered entity may require a medical examination after an offer of employment has been made to a job applicant and prior to the commencement of the employment duties of such applicant, and may condition an offer of employment on the results of such examination * * *."[4]

These "employment entrance examinations" must satisfy three requirements. First, all entering employees in the same job category must be subject to an examination regardless of disability. Second, information obtained at an employment entrance examination must be collected and maintained on separate forms and in separate medical files. The information must be treated as confidential, except that supervisors and managers may be informed regarding necessary restrictions on the work or duties of the employee and necessary accommodations; first aid and safety personnel may be informed, when appropriate, if the disability might require emergency treatment; and government officials investigating compliance with the ADA must be provided with relevant information on request. Third, employers may not use medical criteria to screen out individuals with disabilities unless the medical criteria are job-related.

The employment entrance examination is less clearly regulated by the actual language of the ADA than other types of medical examinations. Under the ADA, preemployment medical inquiries are prohibited entirely and medical examinations of current employees must be job-related or voluntary. For employment entrance examinations, which are given to conditional offerees, the medical exclusionary criteria must be job-related. The key issue left unclear in the ADA is whether the examinations given to conditional offerees must be job-related. According to the Equal Employment Opportunity Commission (EEOC), the agency charged with promulgating regulations under the ADA: "Medical examinations conducted in accordance with this Section do not have to be job-related and consistent with business necessity."[5]

3. Id. § 12112(d)(2)(B).

4. Id. § 12112(d)(3).

5. 29 C.F.R. § 1630.14(b)(3).

The preceding interpretive regulation permits employers to require, as a condition of employment, that individuals accede to broad medical examinations whose results may not be used in deciding employability. The regulation facilitates discrimination and stigmatization; and it sanctions the compelled disclosure of confidential medical information of little or no relevance to job-related abilities. For example, this interpretation permits HIV testing, genetic testing, and other non-job-related medical inquiries, to the extent that they are not prohibited by state law. It is hard to imagine that Congress intended such a result.

Because medical examinations and inquiries at the post-offer stage need not be job-related, employers are permitted to condition an offer of employment on an individual's signing a general medical release for the disclosure of all of the individual's medical records to the employer. Although employers are not covered entities under the Health Insurance Portability and Accountability Act (HIPAA),[6] the health care providers from whom they obtain the medical records are covered entities. Therefore, the employer must obtain a HIPAA-compliant authorization. According to the HIPAA Privacy Rule, a valid authorization must be written in plain language and contain the following elements: (1) a specific description of the information to be used or disclosed; (2) the identity of the person or entity authorized to make the disclosure; (3) the identity of the individual or entity to whom the disclosure may be made; (4) a description of the purpose of the requested disclosure; (5) an expiration date; (6) the signature of the individual and date; (7) a statement indicating that the authorization may be revoked and an indication of how to do so; (8) a statement that the information may be redisclosed and that it will no longer be protected by the Privacy Rule; and (9) a copy of the authorization must be provided to the individual.[7]

Although the ADA is the most important law regulating medical screening by employers, it is not the only one. For example, other disabilities laws may extend protections to individuals not covered by the ADA, such as federal government employees who are covered by section 501 of the Rehabilitation Act and employees of small employers in the private sector who may be covered under a state disabilities law.

Applicants for jobs with public sector employers also may challenge medical screening practices on constitutional grounds. An illustrative case is *Gargiul v. Tompkins*,[8] in which a tenured kindergarten teacher took an extended sick leave because of a back ailment. When she sought to return to work, she was told that she would have to be examined by the school district's physician, who was male. She refused to be examined by a male physician, citing her personal "creed," but offered to go at her own expense to any woman physician selected by the school board or recommended by the local medical society. The school board rejected this offer and denied her reinstatement.

---

6. 42 U.S.C.A. §§ 300gg to 300gg–2.

7. 45 C.F.R. § 164.508(c).

8. 704 F.2d 661 (2d Cir.1983), vacated and remanded on other grounds 465 U.S.

1016, 104 S.Ct. 1263, 79 L.Ed.2d 670 (1984).

The Second Circuit held that, as a tenured teacher, the woman had a property interest in her job that, under the Fourteenth Amendment, could not be denied her without due process. According to the court, the school board's action was so arbitrary that it violated substantive due process. Although applicants lack the property interest in employment to make out a claim under the due process clause of the Fourteenth Amendment, other constitutional theories, such as search and seizure, right to privacy, and equal protection could, theoretically at least, be asserted by applicants.

If medical screening has the purpose or effect of discriminating against applicants on the basis of race, color, religion, sex, national origin, or age then an employment discrimination action may lie. The most common allegation is gender discrimination. At least one age discrimination claim also has been brought. In *EEOC v. Massachusetts*,[9] a statute requiring certain state employees over the age of seventy to take at their own expense, and pass, an annual physical examination to continue employment was challenged as violating the Age Discrimination in Employment Act (ADEA). The court struck down the statute.

> Here, the Commonwealth of Massachusetts allows age to be the determinant as to when an employee's deterioration will be so significant that it requires special treatment. Such a conception of and use of age as a criteria for decline and unfitness for employment strikes at the heart of the ADEA.[10]

A variety of other laws require, prohibit, or regulate specific forms or aspects of medical screening of applicants and employees. The Occupational Safety and Health Act [11] requires various medical examinations before individuals may be assigned to work in certain hazardous environments. HIV testing, genetic testing, and drug testing, regulated by various state and federal laws, are discussed separately. Some other state laws prohibit employers from charging applicants or employees for employer-mandated medical examinations or requiring preemployment pelvic examinations.

Another important set of legal issues related to medical screening involves an employer's or physician's potential liability for negligent medical screening. This may take one of at least five forms. First, a rejected applicant may allege that a physician's negligent assessment of the applicant resulted in the denial of employment. For example, in *Armstrong v. Morgan*,[12] an employee, upon being promoted, was required to have a physical examination performed by a company-retained physician. The physician's report indicated that the employee was in very poor health and, as a result, the employee lost his job. According to the Texas Court of Civil Appeals, a negligence action against the physician stated a valid claim. "Dr. Morgan owed Appellant Armstrong a duty not to injure him physically or otherwise. If Dr. Morgan negligently performed the

---

9.   987 F.2d 64 (1st Cir.1993).

10.   Id. at 71 (footnote omitted).

11.   29 U.S.C.A. §§ 651–678.

12.   545 S.W.2d 45 (Tex.Civ.App.1976).

examination and as a result gave an inaccurate report of the state of appellant's health, and appellant was injured as a proximate result thereof, actionable negligence would be shown."[13]

An independent consulting physician would not be liable under the ADA for a negligent assessment because, even though the physician may have recommended withdrawing a conditional offer of employment, it was the employer that undertook the action. Nevertheless, it is possible that an indemnity action would lie against the physician for ADA-based liability of an employer proximately caused by the negligence of the physician.

Another potential source of liability involves injuries caused during the course of examination or treatment. Not surprisingly, there are few cases in which injuries are alleged to have been caused during an examination. Negligent treatment cases, however, are more common. For example, in *Nolan v. Jefferson Downs, Inc.*,[14] a racetrack physician was found partially at fault in the negligent treatment of a jockey's eye injury. The physician seldom went to the track himself and delegated his duties to a gynecologist who was a convicted felon. The gynecologist's negligent treatment and failure to refer the jockey to an ophthalmologist caused permanent injury. An important fact in *Nolan* was that the racetrack physician was an independent contractor. Most negligent treatment cases brought against company-salaried health care providers have been held to be barred by workers' compensation.

A third theory on which plaintiffs have sued is that a negligent medical assessment resulted in an improper job placement, which caused the individual to be injured on the job. Actions against employer-salaried physicians and employers for improper job placement will normally be found to be barred by workers' compensation, but actions against independent contractor physicians are more likely to be successful.

A fourth source of liability involves actions in which the plaintiff alleges that in conducting a medical examination the physician failed to diagnose a serious injury or illness. The resulting delay in treatment thus is alleged to have aggravated the individual's condition or reduced the likelihood of successful treatment. Even though an employer may be under no duty to conduct an examination, once the duty is assumed, any negligence in performing the examination may be actionable.

In *Green v. Walker*,[15] a physician contracted with an employer to perform an annual physical examination of an offshore cook. The physician then allegedly negligently failed to diagnose the early stages of lung cancer and the employee subsequently died. In a medical malpractice action brought by the man's widow, the district court granted summary judgment for the physician on the ground that there was no physician-patient relationship and thus no duty. The Fifth Circuit reversed. According to the court, even in the absence of a traditional physician-

---

13. Id. at 47.

14. 592 So.2d 831 (La.App.1991), writ denied 596 So.2d 558 (La. 1992).

15. 910 F.2d 291 (5th Cir.1990).

patient relationship, a physician owes a duty to an employee undergoing an employer-mandated medical examination.

> [W]hen an individual is required, as a condition of future or continued employment, to submit to a medical examination, that examination creates a relationship between the examining physician and the examinee, at least to the extent of the tests conducted. This relationship imposes upon the examining physician a duty to conduct the requested tests and diagnose the results thereof, exercising the level of care consistent with the doctor's professional training and expertise, and to take reasonable steps to make information available timely to the examinee of any findings that pose an imminent danger to the examinee's physical or mental well-being.[16]

The holding in *Green* was based, in part, on the court's view that the individual being examined has a reasonable expectation that the physician will issue a warning about any incidental dangers observed. It is not clear whether liability would be found where the physician disclosed at the examination that no such warnings would be issued.

Although some recent cases continue to adhere to the traditional rule that there is no duty and therefore no liability in the absence of a physician-patient relationship, there is a trend toward finding at least some duty. Cases have alleged a negligent failure to diagnose cancer, a brain tumor, a herniated disc, and a heart attack. The cases have arisen from preemployment, annual, post-injury, and disability evaluation examinations.

Finally, a physician may be liable if a negligent medical assessment causes injuries to a third party. For example, in *Wharton Transport Corp. v. Bridges*,[17] a truck driven by a Wharton employee struck the rear of an occupied car parked on the side of a road. The collision resulted in one death and three severe injuries to the occupants. Wharton paid $426,000 to settle the case brought by the occupants and then brought an indemnity action against the third-party physician it had retained to perform the Department of Transportation (DOT) mandated examination to determine whether the driver was physically fit to drive a truck in interstate commerce. Wharton alleged that the physician was negligent in certifying the driver as physically fit when subsequent examination indicated that he had a variety of severe impairments. The Tennessee Supreme Court held that the physician owed a duty to Wharton and that an action for indemnity would lie. It further held that a jury could find that the injuries sustained by the occupants were reasonably foreseeable as a result of the physician's negligence.

§ 1.23 HIV Testing

In 1985, the Food and Drug Administration approved the first commercial tests to detect antibodies to the human immunodeficiency virus (HIV). Almost immediately, concerns were raised that these tests,

16. Id. at 296.   **17.** 606 S.W.2d 521 (Tenn.1980).

designed to screen donated blood, might be used by employers and insurers to screen people. Although there have been some reports of screening being performed on applicants and employees, these incidents have been relatively isolated. Nevertheless, HIV testing by employers, particularly in settings such as the health care industry, continues to be an important topic that raises a variety of legal issues.

There are five main reasons why an employer would possibly consider the HIV testing of job applicants. They are to protect coworkers and customers from exposure to the virus, to protect the HIV-positive individual from exposure to an unhealthy work environment, to mollify customers and coworkers that the work force is "AIDS or HIV free," to reduce health insurance costs by excluding individuals who are likely to require expensive medical care in the near future, and to promote public health by identification of infected individuals.

It is important to understand that HIV tests do not diagnose AIDS, do not indicate when a seropositive individual will develop AIDS, and do not even detect the HIV virus itself. The tests detect the non-neutralizing antibodies produced by the body after exposure to HIV. Development of antibodies usually occurs six to eight weeks after infection and thus an HIV test administered in this time period will be negative, even though the individual has been exposed to HIV and is presumably capable of transmitting the infection to others. It is also important to note that the Centers for Disease Control and Prevention (CDC) has indicated that HIV cannot be transmitted through casual contact in the workplace. Similarly, the Presidential Commission on HIV has stated that "there is no justification for fear of transmission of the virus in the vast majority of workplace and public settings."[1]

In 1991, the CDC issued updated guidelines on HIV-infected health care workers.[2] Its prior directives had emphasized the use of universal precautions against infection and experts agreed that the risk of transmission from a patient to a health care worker was greater than from a health care worker to a patient. Nevertheless, because of the much-publicized case of an AIDS-infected dentist transmitting the infection to some of his patients, the CDC seemed to modify its position. While continuing to support universal precautions as the primary technique for prevention of transmission of HIV, the CDC also suggested that health care workers performing certain "exposure prone" procedures determine their own HIV status and refrain from performing those procedures if they are HIV infected. These guidelines are quite controversial and could result in both state legislative proposals to implement them and legal challenges to prevent adoption by hospitals.

§ 1.23

1. Report of the Presidential Commission on the Human Immunodeficiency Virus Epidemic 113 (1988).

2. *Recommendations for Preventing Transmission of Human Immunodeficiency* *Virus and Hepatitis B Virus to Patients During Exposure–Prone Invasive Procedures*, 40 Morbidity & Mortality Weekly Rep. 1 (1991).

A variety of local, state, federal, and common law issues have been raised by HIV in the workplace. It is important to distinguish between the laws that deal with HIV testing and the laws that deal with HIV-based and AIDS-based discrimination. Another way of analyzing the issues is to separate the HIV-specific laws from the laws of general applicability relevant to HIV testing.

There are several different types of state laws that attempt to prevent the use of HIV testing by employers. For example, some states prohibit employers from performing HIV tests or requiring the disclosure of the results of an HIV test. Other states ban HIV testing of employees but not applicants, ban only the HIV testing of current health care employees, or ban only the HIV testing of state applicants and employees. Another group of states permits HIV testing only if being HIV negative is a bona fide occupational qualification, which is certified by the state epidemiologist or proven by the employer.

The next category consists of HIV legislation which does not prohibit the testing of individuals, but prohibits the use of HIV test results or HIV-based discrimination. A number of cities also have enacted ordinances that prohibit discrimination in employment on the basis of AIDS or HIV status.

Besides these HIV-specific laws, virtually every state and the federal government have enacted laws prohibiting discrimination in employment on the basis of disability. In several states, employers are prohibited from inquiring into non-job-related disabilities, which would include HIV. In other states and under the federal Americans with Disabilities Act, the use of HIV test results or other HIV status information is prohibited.

AIDS and HIV infection have been held to be handicapping conditions under the Rehabilitation Act. Cases decided under the Rehabilitation Act, however, have not always prohibited HIV testing in the workplace. For example, in *Leckelt v. Board of Commissioners*,[3] an employee was fired from his position as a licensed practical nurse when he refused to disclose the result of his HIV test. The nurse claimed that this action amounted to discrimination on the basis of a perceived handicap; the hospital argued that he was not fired because of an actual or perceived handicap, but because his refusal to provide the information prevented the hospital from taking any necessary steps to prevent the spread of infection. The Fifth Circuit agreed with the hospital, in a decision that has been widely criticized.

HIV testing in the workplace also has been challenged on constitutional grounds. In *Glover v. Eastern Nebraska Community Office of Retardation*,[4] the Eighth Circuit held that a policy requiring the mandatory HIV testing of employees of a center for the mentally retarded violated the Fourth Amendment. Because there was no risk of transmis-

---

3.   909 F.2d 820 (5th Cir.1990).

4.   867 F.2d 461 (8th Cir.), cert. denied, 493 U.S. 932, 110 S.Ct. 321, 107 L.Ed.2d 311 (1989).

sion of HIV from the kind of contact between the employees and their clients, the court held that the testing was an unreasonable search and seizure. On the other hand, mandatory HIV testing of all full-time firefighters and paramedics as a part of their annual physical examinations was upheld on the ground that they are at risk of contracting and transmitting HIV because of their exposure to blood and bodily fluids.

Another issue related to HIV testing is the problem of confidentiality. Indeed, legitimate concern about protecting employee confidentiality is one of the main reasons why most employers would be reluctant to perform HIV testing even if it were legal. Some states have statutes specifically providing for criminal or civil liability for wrongfully disclosing an individual's HIV status. Even without such a law, however, common law actions for defamation, invasion of privacy, or other torts are possible. For example, in one case, the defendant was found liable for slander per se for merely passing on a rumor that the plaintiff had AIDS. Similarly, actions have been based on company officials telling a large group of the plaintiff's co-workers that the plaintiff had AIDS and an insurance company physician's disclosure to parties in a workers' compensation case that the plaintiff was HIV positive.

§ 1.24   Cigarette Smoking

Many employers restrict cigarette smoking in the workplace. Many of the restrictions are mandated by state and local laws, but the increased activism of non-smokers, the attempt to please non-smoking customers, and a desire to reduce health insurance and workers' compensation costs also have contributed to the proliferation of restrictions on workplace smoking.

Laws restricting workplace smoking may be viewed as a subset of laws restricting smoking in public places. Virtually every state has a law of some kind restricting smoking in public places. Most of these states have laws that apply to smoking in the workplace. Twenty states restrict smoking in public sector and private sector workplaces; eighteen states restrict smoking only in public sector workplaces. Public sector restrictions apply either to government workplaces or to any building owned or leased by the government. Private sector restrictions include allowing an employer to restrict smoking by posting a sign prohibiting smoking, requiring employers to establish or negotiate a smoking policy through collective bargaining, and banning smoking except in designated areas in any enclosed workplace.

Besides these state laws, at least 500 local smoking ordinances have been enacted, affecting over 57 million people. Thus, numerous employers are required to have policies on smoking, including separating smokers from nonsmokers. Many other employers have voluntarily adopted strict smoking rules and policies. These policies are expressly permitted under the Americans with Disabilities Act, which provides: "Nothing in this chapter shall be construed to preclude the prohibition of, or the imposition of restrictions on, smoking in places of employment * * *."[1]

An increasing number of employers also have attempted to regulate off-the-job smoking in order to facilitate on-the-job restrictions, reduce health insurance costs, and because of synergistic effects of cigarette smoking and occupational exposures. In addition, some jurisdictions have "heart and lung" statutes, which presume that any cardiovascular or respiratory impairment in a firefighter, police officer, or other designated public employee is work-related. Because the effect of these laws is to presume that smoking-induced impairments are "work-related" for purposes of workers' compensation, some of these jurisdictions, either by statute or other mandate, prohibit certain public employees from smoking on or off the job.

Employers attempting to regulate off-the-job smoking have run up against a variety of challenges. In *Grusendorf v. City of Oklahoma City*,[2] a firefighter trainee was fired for violating an agreement that he would not smoke on or off duty for one year after being hired. He brought suit under 42 U.S.C.A. § 1983, claiming his constitutional rights of liberty, privacy, property, and due process had been violated. The Tenth Circuit, applying a rational basis test, held that the plaintiff failed to prove that the ban on smoking was irrational. "Good health and physical conditioning are essential requirements for firefighters."[3]

In *Best Lock Corp. v. Review Board*,[4] however, the plaintiff's employer, a private company, had a rule prohibiting the use of tobacco, alcohol, and drugs—both on and off the job. When the plaintiff was fired for drinking off the job, he filed for unemployment compensation, claiming that there was no "just cause" for his termination. The court agreed, finding that "just cause" was violating a reasonable rule, and in order for an employer rule regulating off-duty activities to be reasonable, the activity sought to be regulated must bear some reasonable relationship to the employer's business interest. Unlike a constitutional claim, under the unemployment compensation laws, there is no presumption of a rule's validity and the burden is on the employer to show the reasonable relationship to its business interest.

About half the states have recently enacted laws prohibiting discrimination in employment against an applicant or employee based on smoking off the job. The specifics of the laws vary. They may prohibit an employer from discriminating against an employee on the basis of the employee's: participating in lawful activity or use of lawful products off the employer's premises during non-working hours, smoking or using tobacco products, using an "agricultural product" off the job, using consumable products off the employer's premises during nonworking hours, or because the employee is a smoker. Seven of the states link the antidiscrimination protection to the employee's following the employer's

§ 1.24
1. 42 U.S.C.A. § 12201(b).
2. 816 F.2d 539 (10th Cir.1987).
3. Id. at 543.
4. 572 N.E.2d 520 (Ind.App.1991).

smoking policy at work and eight states allow off-the-job restrictions if
they have a rational relationship to the employment or nonsmoking is a
bona fide occupational qualification. Oregon has an exception for collective bargaining agreements. Eighteen of the twenty-two state laws
specifically protect an applicant or prospective employee.

An employer discriminating in employment on the basis of smoking
also could run afoul of the Americans with Disabilities Act, the Rehabilitation Act, or state disabilities laws if a smoker claimed that addiction to
cigarettes constituted a handicap or disability. Such a claim was rejected,
however, in *Ranger Fuel Corp. v. West Virginia Human Rights Commission.*[5] The court held that the use or abuse of tobacco in the absence of
medically verifiable addiction does not constitute a physical or mental
impairment. On the other hand, the courts generally have held that
nonsmokers with hypersensitivity to tobacco smoke are covered by
handicap and disability discrimination laws.

§ 1.25 Genetic Testing

The issue of genetic testing in employment first received public
attention in the early 1980s when there was concern that genetic testing
would be used to screen out individuals who were genetically predisposed
to occupational illness. At that time, a few employers used biochemical
genetic tests to measure the biological effects of genes, including proteins
and enzymes. Because many of the genetic conditions suspected of
predisposing workers to occupational diseases, such as sickle cell trait,
were associated with particular racial or ethnic groups, there was a
significant amount of adverse publicity and congressional attention. This
fact, plus the failure to develop an adequate scientific justification for the
testing, led most observers to believe that biochemical genetic testing in
employment had virtually stopped by the mid–1980s.

At the end of the decade a new concern about possible genetic
testing in employment came to the fore. New developments in molecular
genetics associated with the Human Genome Project (an international
scientific undertaking to map and sequence all of the genes in humans)
promised to be able to predict the genetic factors in each individual that
could lead to illness years in the future. Although these new DNA-based
screening techniques might be used to predict future occupational diseases, the new concern was that these tests could be used to screen out
individuals who were thought to be at an increased risk of developing
nonoccupationally related illnesses. The motivation for this genetic
screening would be the desire to reduce the rapidly increasing cost of
employer-provided employee health insurance.

Laws directed at genetic testing and discrimination in employment
were first enacted in the 1970s to combat irrational sickle cell trait
discrimination that arose out of government-sponsored sickle cell screening programs. Florida, Louisiana, and North Carolina (expanded in 1997)

5. 180 W.Va. 260, 376 S.E.2d 154
(1988).

enacted laws prohibiting discrimination in employment on the basis of sickle cell trait. These laws remain in effect today.

As the prospects increased for more broadly-based genetic discrimination in employment, other states enacted genetic discrimination laws. In 1981, New Jersey enacted a law prohibiting employment discrimination based on an individual's "atypical hereditary cellular or blood trait," defined to include sickle cell trait, hemoglobin C trait, thalassemia trait, Tay–Sachs trait, or cystic fibrosis trait.[1] In 1989, Oregon amended its unlawful employment practices act (amended in 1992 and 1995) to prohibit employers from requiring applicants or employees to undergo "genetic screening," although the term is not further defined.[2] In 1990, New York enacted a law (broadened in 1996) prohibiting discrimination based on sickle cell trait, Tay–Sachs trait, or Cooley's anemia (beta-thalassemia) trait.[3] In 1992, Wisconsin enacted a law prohibiting employers from requiring applicants or employees to undergo genetic testing or from using the information from genetic tests in employment decisions.[4]

Based in large part on public fears that new genetic discoveries would permit employers to discriminate (unfairly) in hiring or benefits, the states responded with a flurry of legislative activity. By the 2003 completion date of the Human Genome Project, thirty-one states had enacted laws prohibiting employers from discriminating in employment on the basis of genetic information (variously defined) as well as requesting or requiring genetic testing as a condition of employment. Unfortunately, the laws are more cosmetic than substantive.

There are only a handful of well-publicized incidents of genetic testing or genetic discrimination by employers. The legitimate social concern is that individuals will decline beneficial genetic testing in the clinical setting because of concerns about employers and other third parties gaining access to the results. The state "anti-discrimination" laws, however well intended, do not change the prevailing law, as evidenced in the ADA, that after a conditional offer of employment an employer may require that individuals sign an authorization for disclosure of all of their medical records to the employer. Only laws, such as those enacted in California[5] and Minnesota,[6] that limit employer access to job-related health information will be effective in preventing the perception and reality of genetic discrimination in the workplace.

Besides specific laws, genetic discrimination may constitute a violation of Title VII of the Civil Rights Act of 1964 because it may have a disparate impact along the lines of race, color, religion, sex, or national origin. For example, discrimination based on sickle cell anemia has been alleged to be disparate impact race discrimination.

§ 1.25
1. N.J. Stat. Ann. § 10:5–12.
2. Or. Rev. Stat. § 659.227.
3. N.Y. Civ. Rights Law art. 4C, §§ 48, 48a.
4. Wis. Stat. § 111.372.
5. Cal. Gov't Code § 12940.
6. Minn. Stat. Ann. §§ 363.01 to .20.

By far, the most likely source of protection for individuals claiming genetic discrimination in employment will be the federal and state laws prohibiting discrimination on the basis of disability. The federal Rehabilitation Act prohibits discrimination against otherwise qualified individuals with disabilities, but it applies only to the federal government (section 501), federal government contractors (section 503), and federal grantees (section 504). Almost every state also has its own law prohibiting discrimination in employment on the basis of handicap or disability, but the coverage, rights, and remedies vary.

The newest and most important law prohibiting discrimination in employment on the basis of disability is the Americans with Disabilities Act (ADA).[7] It is a complex and far-reaching law, but one that was not specifically drafted with the problems of genetic discrimination in mind. Although the ADA clearly prohibits discrimination against individuals who are currently affected with a genetic disease, it is not settled whether the ADA covers other individuals, such as currently unaffected individuals who have the allele for a late-onset genetic disease, unaffected carriers of recessive and x-linked conditions, and individuals at an increased risk of a multi-factorial disorder.

In 1995, the EEOC issued its first official interpretation on the issue genetic discrimination. It indicated that individuals who are discriminated against on the basis of "genetic information relating to illness, disease, or other disorders" are being regarded as having a disability and therefore are covered under the third part of the definition of "disability" under the ADA.[8]

The issue of surreptitious genetic testing was raised squarely in the 1998 case of *Norman-Bloodsaw v. Lawrence Berkeley Laboratory*.[9] Without their express knowledge or consent, blood and urine samples of certain employees obtained during their preplacement medical examinations were tested for pregnancy, syphilis, and sickle cell trait. Seven current and former employees of the research facility sued under the United States and California Constitutions, Title VII of the Civil Rights Act of 1964, and the Americans with Disabilities Act. In dismissing all of the claims, the district court said that because the tests were part of a general medical examination and highly personal questions were asked on the medical questionnaire, the plaintiffs had sufficient notice that these types of tests might be performed. Therefore, any "additional incremental intrusion" caused by performing the testing was minimal.

The Ninth Circuit reversed and remanded the case for trial on the merits. Because performing such tests was inconsistent with sound medical practice, the employees had no reason to think that the tests would be performed without their consent. In holding that the facts alleged raised a valid constitutional claim, the court stated that "[o]ne

---

7. 42 U.S.C.A. §§ 12101–12213.

8. EEOC Compliance Manual, vol. 2, EEOC Order 915.002, Definition of the Term "Disability," at 902–45, reprinted in

Daily Lab. Rep., Mar. 16, 1995, at E–1, E–23.

9. 135 F.3d 1260 (9th Cir.1998).

can think of few subject areas more personal and more likely to implicate privacy interests than that of one's health or genetic make-up."[10] A cognizable Title VII claim for sex discrimination was alleged because of the pregnancy testing of female employees, and a sufficient case of race discrimination under Title VII was alleged because the sickle cell trait testing was limited to black employees. The dismissal of the ADA claims, however, was affirmed because, under the ADA, preplacement medical examinations can be of unlimited scope and need not be job-related.

§ 1.26 Drug Testing

During the 1970s, as a way of monitoring heroin use among people at drug treatment centers, automated and increasingly sophisticated tests were developed to measure the metabolites of drugs in urine. It was not long before these techniques were applied in other settings, such as the military, which began drug testing in 1981. By the mid–1980s drug testing was widely adopted in both public and private sector employment.

Although blood, hair, and other specimens have been used on occasion, urine testing is, by far, the most common. Hair testing, especially when confirmed by other analytic methods, has received increased legislative and judicial approval. There is also a small but growing use of "impairment tests," largely computer programs and eye tests, which attempt to detect impairment from any source. These tests have not yet been widely adopted and have not been challenged in court. More drug testing is performed at the preemployment stage than at any other time, but some employers use preplacement, periodic, random, for cause, post-accident, or return-to-work testing instead of, or in addition to, preemployment testing. Aside from the legal issues, discussed below, there are a number of technical concerns about urine drug testing. These include the following: (1) to ensure that the sample is not adulterated, indirect or direct observation of urination may be necessary; (2) elaborate measures often are required to maintain the chain of custody of the specimen; (3) laboratory quality often varies widely; (4) to be accurate, more expensive confirmatory tests are necessary to augment the initial screening test; (5) a medical review officer may be necessary to evaluate the result in light of possible cross-reacting prescription medications or other substances; (6) drug tests, by revealing prescription medications taken, may reveal an underlying medical condition; (7) the delay between testing and receipt of the results precludes their use to prevent impaired workers from starting on the job; (8) the tests measure the inert metabolites of substances as they are being excreted and do not measure the tested-for substances themselves; (9) the tests do not measure impairment (past or present), the amount of the substance originally ingested, or the length of time between ingestion and the test; and (10) many testing programs are often limited to five or so illicit

10. Id. at 1269.

substances and do not attempt to measure alcohol or other lawful substances of abuse.

Most drug testing is performed by professional laboratories, although "on-site" tests have become an increasingly popular alternative. While on-site tests are less accurate (especially when not confirmed), they are faster, less expensive, and do not require trained personnel. In 1992, however, the Health Care Financing Administration promulgated final regulations implementing the Clinical Laboratory Improvements Act of 1988,[1] which subjects on-site drug testing by employers to the regulation of the Act.[2] The failure to follow approved testing protocols may result in the employer's action being overturned. Among other things, all regulated laboratories must use confirmatory tests, be supervised by a physician, have strict requirements for technicians, and use detailed proficiency testing and quality assurance measures. This regulation may have the effect of making on-site testing infeasible for many employers.

Federal Employees

In 1986, acting on a recommendation by his Commission on Organized Crime, President Reagan issued Executive Order 12,564. The Order requires the head of each executive agency to establish a program to test for illegal drug use by employees in sensitive positions. "Sensitive positions" is defined to include individuals: handling classified information; serving as Presidential appointees; serving in positions related to national security; serving as law enforcement officers; serving in positions charged with protecting life, property, and public health and safety; and serving in jobs requiring a high degree of trust and confidence. In all, about half of the nation's two million federal employees are covered.

The Executive Order authorizes drug testing under four circumstances: (1) where there is reasonable suspicion of illegal drug use; (2) in conjunction with the investigation of an accident; (3) as a part of an employee's counseling or rehabilitation for drug use through an employee assistance program (EAP); and (4) to screen any job applicant for illegal drug use. The Order mandates the use of confirmatory testing and allows the employee to provide a urine specimen in private unless there is reason to believe adulteration will occur.

The Executive Order also prescribes the action agencies must take when an employee's test is positive. Employees will be referred to an EAP and refusal to participate in the EAP will result in dismissal. Employees in sensitive positions are removed from duty pending successful completion of rehabilitation through the EAP. Agencies must initiate disciplinary action against any employee found to use illegal drugs unless the employee satisfies three criteria: (1) the employee must voluntarily identify himself or herself as a drug user before being identified through other means; (2) the employee must seek EAP rehabilitation: and (3) the

§ 1.26
1. 42 U.S.C.A. § 263a.

2. 57 Fed. Reg. 7188 (1992), 42 C.F.R. Pt. 493.

employee must refrain from illegal drug use in the future. The employee must be dismissed if he or she is found continuing to use illegal drugs after initial identification.

The Department of Health and Human Services is charged with promulgating scientific and technical guidelines for the federal drug testing program. The guidelines, originally issued in 1987,[3] specify in great detail the procedures to be used for collection of specimens, chain of custody, laboratory analysis methodology, and transmittal and interpretation of test results. Although the guidelines require testing for marijuana, cocaine, opiates, amphetamines, and PCP, they do not require testing for alcohol or other legal drugs of abuse.

Federal drug testing initiatives led directly and indirectly to increased use of drug testing by private sector employers. The direct effects center on two federal laws. First, the Drug–Free Workplace Act of 1988[4] is directed at federal government contractors and grant recipients. It requires all such entities to certify that they will provide a drug-free workplace. In addition, all holders of grants or contracts in excess of $25,000 must: (1) notify employees that the unlawful manufacture, distribution, dispensation, possession, or use of a controlled substance is prohibited and indicating the sanctions for violations; (2) establish a drug-free awareness program; (3) sanction or require the participation in a drug rehabilitation program for any employee convicted under a criminal drug statute; and (4) make a good faith effort to maintain a drug-free workplace. Significantly, the Drug–Free Workplace Act does not require drug testing.

The second federal law directly affecting private sector drug testing is the Omnibus Transportation Employee Testing Act of 1991.[5] This law codifies earlier Department of Transportation regulations requiring the drug testing of employees in the transportation industry. It also adds the requirement of random alcohol testing for the six million covered employees. Besides these specific enactments, the federal government's lead role in encouraging drug testing has led to the voluntary adoption of drug testing by an increasing number of private sector employers as well as the enactment of drug testing laws and policies by numerous state and local government employers.

Government-mandated drug testing has been challenged on a variety of constitutional grounds, including the right of privacy, procedural due process, substantive due process, self-incrimination, and equal protection. Without question, however, the most substantial claim is that drug testing constitutes a violation of the Fourth Amendment's prohibition against unreasonable searches and seizures. In the companion cases

3. Mandatory Guidelines for Federal Workplace Drug Testing Programs, 52 Fed. Reg. 30,638 (1987); 53 Fed. Reg. 11,970 (1988). Revised drug testing guidelines were promulgated in 1994. 59 Fed. Reg. 29,908 (1994).

4. 41 U.S.C.A. §§ 701–707.

5. Pub. L. 102–143, 105 Stat. 917, 49 App. U.S.C.A. §§ 1618a, 2717.

of *National Treasury Employees Union v. Von Raab*[6] and *Skinner v. Railway Labor Executives' Association*,[7] the Supreme Court addressed the constitutionality of government-ordered drug testing.

In *Von Raab*, a federal employees' union sought to enjoin the United States Customs Service from mandating drug tests of three groups of employees seeking promotions. The positions involved: (1) drug interdiction; (2) carrying firearms; or (3) handling classified materials. Although it held that a drug test is a search subject to the Fourth Amendment, the Court, five-to-four, held that the tests on the first two groups of employees could be conducted without a warrant, probable cause, or any individualized suspicion. Using a balancing test, Justice Kennedy's majority opinion noted that the government has a compelling interest in ensuring that front-line drug enforcement personnel are physically fit and have unimpeachable integrity and judgment. Because of the nature of the job, the Court concluded that the employees have a diminished expectation of privacy. The Court discounted the fact that only five of the first 3,600 people tested positive, by asserting that the testing program may well have a deterrent effect on the use of drugs by employees. With regard to the employees seeking to handle classified material, the Court held that the category was too vague because it could result in the testing of mail clerks, attorneys, and other employees not on the front line in the fight against drugs.

In a pointed dissent, Justice Scalia asserted that the drug testing of Customs Service employees is entirely "symbolic" and that whatever value this symbolism may have, it is not enough to override important constitutional protections. He complained that the government failed to cite any instances in which the "speculated horribles" of employing people who had not been subject to drug testing actually had occurred. He also argued that the safety rationale was so broad that it could be used to justify the testing of automobile drivers, construction workers, and school crossing guards.

In the companion case of *Skinner*, the Court considered a challenge to the Federal Railroad Administration's drug and alcohol testing regulations requiring blood and urine tests for railroad employees involved in train accidents or who violate certain rules. The tests are administered automatically, without a warrant, probable cause, or individualized suspicion. With analysis similar to *Von Raab*, Justice Kennedy's majority opinion held that the drug tests were searches under the Fourth Amendment, but that the government had demonstrated a compelling interest due to the safety-sensitive nature of the positions involved.

Von Raab and *Skinner* established the validity of some drug tests of federal government employees and federally-mandated tests of some private sector employees. To a large extent, the decisions are fact-sensitive and the Court was concerned in both cases with what it deemed to be persuasive evidence of the need to test to ensure public safety. The

6. 489 U.S. 656, 109 S.Ct. 1384, 103 L.Ed.2d 685 (1989).

7. 489 U.S. 602, 109 S.Ct. 1402, 103 L.Ed.2d 639 (1989).

cases did not resolve the constitutionality of the drug testing of numerous other categories of public and private employees.

Numerous lower court cases have considered the validity of federal drug testing programs as applied to various federal employees. In general, the validity of the testing depends on the degree to which the testing is essential to ensure public safety. For example, the Navy's random drug testing of civilian employees required to hold top secret security clearances[8] and the Defense Logistics Agency's random testing of employees with top secret security clearances, police officers, fire fighters, nurses, first line environmental protection specialists, motor vehicle operators, heavy equipment operators, and locomotive operators[9] both have been upheld. On the other hand, the testing of all federal prison employees regardless of their position was struck down.[10]

Perhaps the most instructive cases are the ones in which part of the testing program was upheld and part of the program was struck down. For example, the D.C. Circuit upheld the random drug testing of Department of Agriculture motor vehicle operators, but struck down the suspicionless testing of employees who did not hold safety-sensitive or security-sensitive jobs.[11] The court also prohibited the direct observation of specimen collection. Similarly, the D.C. Circuit upheld the random testing of Army civilian employees working as air traffic controllers, aviation mechanics, armed civilian police and guards, and drug counselors, but struck down the testing of civilian laboratory workers and those in the chain of custody of drug specimens.[12]

Most of the federal sector cases challenging drug testing have been brought by current employees. In *Willner v. Thornburgh,*[13] however, applicants for the position of attorney with the Antitrust Division of the Department of Justice argued that the preemployment drug testing requirement was unconstitutional. Despite the absence of a safety rationale, the D.C. Circuit upheld the drug testing requirement. The court, unreceptive to the privacy assertions of the applicants, stated: "If individuals view drug testing as an indignity to be avoided, they need only refrain from applying."[14]

State and Local Government Employees

Challenges to the drug testing of state and local government employees often have paralleled the challenges brought by federal employees. If the employees are in safety-sensitive positions, drug testing is usually

---

8. American Fed'n of Gov't Employees Local 1533 v. Cheney, 944 F.2d 503 (9th Cir.1991).

9. Plane v. United States, 796 F.Supp. 1070 (W.D.Mich.1992).

10. American Fed'n of Gov't Employees v. Thornburgh, 720 F.Supp. 154 (N.D.Cal. 1989).

11. National Treasury Employees Union v. Yeutter, 918 F.2d 968 (D.C.Cir.1990).

12. National Fed'n of Fed. Employees v. Cheney, 884 F.2d 603 (D.C.Cir.1989), cert. denied, 493 U.S. 1056, 110 S.Ct. 864, 107 L.Ed.2d 948 (1990).

13. 928 F.2d 1185 (D.C.Cir.1991), cert. denied 502 U.S. 1020, 112 S.Ct. 669, 116 L.Ed.2d 760 (1991).

14. Id. at 1190.

upheld. For example, in *Penny v. Kennedy*,[15] Chattanooga, Tennessee police officers and firefighters challenged the city's mandatory, suspicionless urine drug testing program. The Sixth Circuit upheld the program, noting the city's compelling interest in ensuring that there is no risk of impairment of these public safety officials. The court, however, remanded the case for consideration of whether the manner and means of the testing were reasonable. Similar results have been reached in other cases. In *Jackson v. Gates*,[16] however, the Ninth Circuit held that the Los Angeles Police Department unconstitutionally ordered a police officer to take a drug test because he associated with an officer under investigation by the department. According to the court, the department had no "articulable, individualized bases" for singling out the particular officer for for-cause testing.

Drug testing of corrections officers and personnel has been upheld because of the government's compelling interests in avoiding the dangers of a drug-impaired prison work force and in preventing drug smuggling to prisoners. These justifications resulted in the Seventh Circuit's upholding of the testing program in *Taylor v. O'Grady*,[17] but it also caused the court to limit testing to those officers with prisoner contact or the opportunity to smuggle drugs to prisoners.

A number of cases have involved the drug testing of municipal transit employees. The courts generally have permitted the testing because of the dire results of a drug-induced accident, although there have been some distinctions drawn between the timing of the tests (e.g. preemployment, periodic) and the basis of the tests (e.g. random, reasonable suspicion, post-accident). For example, the Third Circuit upheld the random drug testing of transportation workers in safety-sensitive positions, but it required a particularized suspicion to validate return-to-work testing.[18] Post-accident drug testing has been upheld, but the courts have struck down random drug testing of workers not in safety-sensitive positions.

For a variety of other state and municipal employees, the constitutionality of drug testing depends on whether the job is considered to be safety-sensitive. For positions such as school bus driver, the courts have had an easy time finding that the jobs are safety-sensitive. Other positions are not as clear-cut. In making these determinations, courts often have been quite deferential to employer safety claims and they have not required a showing of an imminent threat to *public* safety. For example, the drug testing of an emergency room resident, a surgery scrub technician, and a licensed waste water operator have been upheld on the ground of safety. On the other hand, a probationary city sanitation employee's occasional need to drive a car while on duty was held to

15. 915 F.2d 1065 (6th Cir.1990).

16. 975 F.2d 648 (9th Cir.1992), cert. denied, 509 U.S. 905, 113 S.Ct. 2996, 125 L.Ed.2d 690 (1993).

17. 888 F.2d 1189 (7th Cir.1989).

18. Transport Workers' Union v. Southeastern Pa. Transp. Auth., 884 F.2d 709 (3d Cir.1989).

be insufficient justification for suspicionless drug testing. Overbroad statutes also may invite challenge under the Fourth Amendment.

Some courts apply different standards to the drug testing of applicants versus current employees. Thus, the Supreme Court of California has upheld the suspicionless testing of all applicants, but struck down as violative of the Fourth Amendment the suspicionless testing of all current employees who were offered a promotion.[19]

While safety-sensitive employees may be tested without reasonable suspicion, few cases have discussed what constitutes reasonable suspicion for the testing of nonsafety-sensitive employees. According to the Tenth Circuit, direct observation or physical evidence of on-duty impairment is not required; "information which would lead a reasonable person to suspect ... on-the-job drug use, possession or impairment is sufficient under the Fourth Amendment."[20] Nevertheless, predictable and infrequent testing was held to be insufficiently efficacious to justify the testing of mechanics who repaired city trash trucks.

In *Knox County Education Association v. Knox County Board of Education*,[21] the Sixth Circuit adopted the broadest interpretation of "safety sensitive" to date. It upheld the suspicionless drug testing of school personnel including principals, assistant principals, teachers, aides, substitute teachers, secretaries, and bus drivers. Because of the unique roles of the individuals in the lives of children the positions were deemed "safety sensitive."

The method of testing also has been challenged. The direct observation of urination during a correction officer's drug testing was held to violate the right to privacy provision of the California Constitution. The court said that there were less intrusive means for accomplishing the drug testing objectives.[22] On the other hand, a similar challenge brought by firefighters under the Fourth Amendment and common law invasion of privacy was unsuccessful.[23]

Government–Regulated Private Sector Employees

With regard to the drug testing of private sector employees, the most important factor affecting legality is whether the testing is government mandated. If so, then this "state action" or "governmental action" will permit the employees to assert constitutional arguments similar to those raised by public sector employees. Again, the degree to which the job involves public safety is often controlling. For example, the testing of applicants and employees in nuclear power plants has been upheld.

19. Loder v. City of Glendale, 14 Cal.4th 846, 59 Cal.Rptr.2d 696, 927 P.2d 1200 (1997), cert. denied, 522 U.S. 807, 118 S.Ct. 44, 139 L.Ed.2d 11 (1997).

20. Benavidez v. City of Albuquerque, 101 F.3d 620, 624 (10th Cir.1996).

21. 158 F.3d 361 (6th Cir.1998), cert. denied, 528 U.S. 812, 120 S.Ct. 46, 145 L.Ed.2d 41 (1999).

22. Hansen v. California Dep't of Corrections, 920 F.Supp. 1480 (N.D.Cal.1996).

23. Wilcher v. City of Wilmington, 139 F.3d 366 (3d Cir.1998), on remand, 60 F.Supp.2d 298 (D.Del.1999).

The largest group of private sector employees subject to federal drug testing mandates is transportation workers. The Department of Transportation's regulations have been challenged by various groups and with little success. Thus, the drug testing of railroad crews, airline pilots, airline ground employees in safety-sensitive positions, crews of private vessels, and pipeline workers all have been upheld on the basis of safety.

Pursuant to the Omnibus Transportation Employee Testing Act of 1991, in 1994 the Department of Transportation issued its final rule on drug testing for 7.4 million workers who perform "safety-sensitive functions" involving airlines, railroads, trucking and commercial vehicles, mass transit, pipeline operations, and maritime vessels.[24] For the first time, alcohol testing is also required. The regulation was vacated as to alcohol testing of all "would-be motor carrier operators" prior to their first performance of a safety-sensitive function.[25]

Challenges to state drug testing requirements brought by private sector employees have varied more widely, with the results depending on the nature of the position, the method of testing, and other factors. For example, New Jersey and Illinois laws mandating the drug testing of horse racing personnel were upheld by the Third and Seventh Circuits, but a similar Massachusetts law was struck down by the Supreme Judicial Court of Massachusetts.

State Constitutions and Statutes

Because unregulated private sector employees cannot use federal constitutional grounds to challenge drug testing, they sometimes have asserted that the testing violates state law, either constitutional or statutory. The two principal claims have been unlawful search and seizure and invasion of privacy. Most of the state search and seizure cases involve state and local government employees. State courts have viewed state constitutional search and seizure arguments similar to search and seizure arguments based on the Fourth Amendment. The more unique, and in some respects, more promising argument is that drug testing is an unconstitutional invasion of privacy.

In most states, government action is required before an individual may claim a violation of the state constitution. Under certain state constitutions, however, there is no governmental action requirement. At least seven state constitutions expressly recognize a constitutional right of privacy that might be violated by at least some types of drug testing in the private sector workplace. For example, in California the suspicionless preemployment drug testing of applicants is permissible, but the suspicionless drug testing of employees is not.[26]

A variety of state drug testing laws also have been enacted. Many of the laws mandate or authorize drug testing for certain state and local

24. 49 CFR Part 40.

25. American Trucking Ass'ns, Inc. v. Federal Highway Admin., 51 F.3d 405 (4th Cir.1995).

26. Loder v. City of Glendale, 14 Cal.4th 846, 59 Cal.Rptr.2d 696, 927 P.2d 1200 (1997), cert. denied, 522 U.S. 806, 118 S.Ct. 44, 139 L.Ed.2d 11 (1997).

employees. Some of them track the language of the federal Drug–Free Workplace Act and apply to state contractors and grantees. Challenges to these types of laws have been discussed earlier. In addition, many states have enacted laws related to drug testing in the private sector. These laws either limit drug testing, regulate the procedures for drug testing, or encourage or mandate the drug testing of certain employees in the private sector.

Seven states, Connecticut, Iowa, Maine, Minnesota, Montana, Rhode Island, and Vermont have enacted laws that seek to limit, but not prohibit, drug testing in the private sector. All of the laws permit the preemployment testing of applicants and some permit the periodic testing of employees if advance notice is given. Exceptions are often made for public safety officers and employees in safety-sensitive jobs. "For cause" testing is generally permitted if there is "probable cause," "reasonable cause," or "reasonable suspicion" that an employee is impaired. Most of the laws require that the sample collection be performed in private and that drug testing records are kept confidential. Most of the laws require confirmatory testing. State drug testing laws, however, have been held to be preempted by federal law when they seek to restrict federally-mandated testing.

Nine states, Florida, Hawaii, Illinois, Louisiana, Mississippi, Nebraska, Nevada, North Carolina, and Oregon, regulate various procedures used in private or public sector drug testing. For example, they specify that notices must be posted to advise employees of the testing, require the use of certified laboratories, or grant employees the right to have the sample retested.

Other state laws permit or require drug testing. The Utah Drug and Alcohol Testing Act[27] permits drug testing as a condition of hiring or continued employment so long as employers and managers also submit to testing periodically. Employers performing drug testing must have a written policy and confirmatory tests must be used. Employers that satisfy these requirements are immune from liability for defamation or other torts based on the drug testing. The law also prohibits any action based on the failure to conduct a drug test. Arizona law encourages private sector employees to test for drugs and alcohol, and Alaska law limits the liability of employers that test in good faith and reasonably rely on the results of the test.

In *Chandler v. Miller,*[28] the Supreme Court struck down a Georgia statute that required candidates for designated state offices to present a certificate from a state-approved laboratory that they have taken and have had a negative result on a urinalysis drug test within 30 days prior to qualifying for nomination or election. The Court held that the purely "symbolic" function of the law was insufficient to pass scrutiny under the Fourth Amendment.

27. Utah Code Ann. §§ 34–38–1 to 34–38–15.

28. 520 U.S. 305, 117 S.Ct. 1295, 137 L.Ed.2d 513 (1997).

More general state statutes also may be used as the basis for challenging workplace drug testing. For example, in *Webster v. Motorola, Inc.*,[29] an account executive and a technical editor of an electronic equipment manufacturer sued under the Massachusetts Civil Rights Act and the Massachusetts Privacy Act. The Supreme Judicial Court of Massachusetts upheld the random drug testing of the account executive, who drove 20,000 to 25,000 miles per year in a company-owned vehicle. It struck down the testing of the technical editor because "the nexus between his job duties and the harms feared is attenuated."[30]

A few local laws also have been enacted that attempt to regulate drug testing in the private sector. For example, an ordinance enacted in San Francisco in 1985[31] applies to any person working in San Francisco except uniformed police, fire fighters, police dispatchers, and emergency vehicle operators. It prohibits employee drug testing unless "the employer has reasonable grounds to believe that an employee's faculties are impaired on the job; and * * * the employee is in a position where such impairment presents a clear and present danger to the physical safety of the employee, another employee or to a member of the public."

Disabilities Laws

The Americans with Disabilities Act (ADA) has several provisions dealing with illegal drugs and alcohol. Section 104(a) excludes from the definition of "qualified individual with a disability" "any employee or applicant who is currently engaging in the illegal use of drugs, when the covered entity acts on the basis of such use." Nevertheless, three categories of individuals are still considered "individuals with disabilities." These are an individual who: (1) has successfully completed drug rehabilitation and is no longer engaging in the illegal use of drugs; (2) is participating in a rehabilitation program and is no longer using drugs; or (3) is erroneously regarded as engaging in such use but is not engaging in such use. The term "currently engaging" is not limited to a period of days or weeks, but applies to any recent use that indicates that the individual is actively engaged in such conduct.

The ADA gives employers wide discretion to combat the use of illegal drugs and alcohol in the workplace. Covered employers may prohibit the use of illegal drugs and alcohol in the workplace; require that employees not be under the influence of alcohol or illegal drugs at the workplace; require that employees behave in conformance with the federal Drug–Free Workplace Act; hold an employee who engages in the illegal use of drugs or who is an alcoholic to the same qualification and job performance standards as other employees; and require that employees comply with applicable Department of Defense, Nuclear Regulatory Commission, and Department of Transportation regulations.

The ADA is neutral on the issue of drug testing; the tests are not encouraged, prohibited, or authorized. In addition, the ADA provides

29. 418 Mass. 425, 637 N.E.2d 203 (1994).

30. 637 N.E.2d at 208.

31. San Francisco Police Code art. 33A, §§ 3300A.1 to 3300A.11.

that "a test to determine the illegal use of drugs shall not be considered a medical examination." This means that drug tests, unlike "medical examinations," may be performed at the preemployment stage. Nevertheless, employers that perform drug tests prior to a conditional offer of employment may have a problem. Employers subject to federal testing standards (as well as other employers using a good testing protocol or subject to the Clinical Laboratory Improvements Act) must use a medical review officer to interview the subject of any initial positive result. The medical review officer is required to ask the individual about prescription medications that could have produced a false positive result. Under the ADA, however, it is illegal for an employer or any agent of the employer to inquire into the medications taken by an individual at the preemployment stage. In 1994, EEOC issued an interpretation in which it indicated that under the ADA, drug tests may be given at the preemployment stage. After an initial positive screening test an employer may inquire as to what prescription medications the individual is taking. This problem is avoided, however, by simply performing the drug testing after a conditional offer of employment.

Courts interpreting the ADA will undoubtedly rely on the drug cases decided under the Rehabilitation Act. Cases brought under section 504 of the Rehabilitation Act have held that it was unlawful for the city of Philadelphia to deny jobs to former drug abusers; it was not unlawful to dismiss a New York City police officer because of his addiction to heroin; it was not unlawful to discharge a civilian computer specialist for the Navy who concealed a cocaine addiction and alcoholism when he filled out forms needed to renew his security clearance; and it was not unlawful to reject fire fighter applicants in Detroit who tested positive for marijuana, because they were not covered "handicapped individuals" under the Rehabilitation Act. Courts also will need to evaluate employees' claims that they have been "regarded" as a substance abuser.

Virtually every state has its own disabilities law and these laws differ in their coverage. Some states have included alcoholics, drug abusers, and rehabilitees by statute, regulation, or case law; in other states they are excluded; some other states have not yet decided the issue. It is quite possible that a substance abuser would have more protection under state law than federal law.

Other Statutes

Drug testing may affect a wide range of other federal and state laws. For example, an employer's ability to implement a drug testing program may be limited if the employees are represented by a labor union. Thus, drug testing has raised important issues under the National Labor Relations Act, Railway Labor Act, and labor arbitration. These issues, however, are beyond the scope of this book. There are also important questions of eligibility for workers' compensation and unemployment compensation for individuals who refuse to take drug tests or who test positive. These issues are discussed elsewhere. The Public Health Service Act, is another law that may affect the records generated by drug testing. Regulations issued under that act contain severe sanctions for the unauthorized disclosure of alcohol and drug abuse patient records and information by covered facilities.

Common Law

Workplace drug testing has given rise to a variety of common law actions, the most common of which are invasion of privacy, negligence, defamation, and wrongful discharge. The actions have been based on the conduct of the employer and other third parties at all stages of the employment relationship, from preemployment to post-employment.

A wide range of employer conduct has been alleged to constitute an invasion of privacy, and there has been a wide range of results. For example, one court rejected the argument that an employer's requirement that an employee divulge the medications she was taking established common law invasion of privacy. Similarly, the drug testing of all at-will employees did not amount to an invasion of privacy, even though the failure to consent was grounds for dismissal. The method of testing often is the key factor in establishing liability. In one case, damages for invasion of privacy and negligent infliction of emotional distress were affirmed where a drilling rig employee was "disgusted" by a drug testing procedure in which he was forced to submit a urine sample under direct observation.[32]

Actions for negligence may be brought against an independent laboratory for failing to perform a drug test in a reasonable manner. Although some courts have recognized a duty running from the laboratory to an employee and from the laboratory to an applicant, some courts have refused to recognize an action by an employee against an employer for negligence due to the laboratory's error or an action against the laboratory for negligent interference with contract. Actions also may be brought by the employer for negligence against the laboratory, especially where laboratory errors led to liability by the employer to employees.

Drug test results sometimes are shared with co-workers, supervisors, prospective employers, or other individuals or entities. The publication of drug test results to supervisory personnel and co-workers has been held to be privileged. Nevertheless, the privilege may be lost if there is excessive publication or malice.

Common law actions for wrongful discharge also have been brought on several theories, mostly allegations that discharging an individual for refusing to take a drug test or because of the results of a drug test violates public policy. Although originally these arguments were uniformly rejected, and still often are, an increasing number of jurisdictions have been willing to entertain common law challenges to drug testing. For example, in West Virginia drug testing of current employees will violate public policy unless it is based on a "reasonable good faith objective suspicion" or it is to protect public safety or the safety of

32. Kelley v. Schlumberger Technology
Corp., 849 F.2d 41 (1st Cir.1988).

others,[33] but drug testing of all applicants is lawful.[34] In Pennsylvania[35] and New Jersey,[36] the public policy exception also may be violated by drug testing, although the testing of employees in safety-sensitive jobs is still likely to be upheld. In Alaska, drug testing that focuses on a single employee without prior notice has been held to violate the implied covenant of good faith and fair dealing.[37] In California, the discharge of an employee for refusing to submit to a drug test also is actionable.[38]

Finally, employees working under a collective bargaining agreement may find that their ability to bring a common law action to challenge employer drug testing is preempted by federal labor law. In such event, their exclusive remedy is to pursue their claims under the collective bargaining agreement.

§ 1.27   Formation of the Employment Relationship

The previous sections of this chapter focused on several of the numerous ways (e.g. interviews, drug tests) in which employers select their employees. The other side of the selection process involves the potential employee selecting the employer, and this may involve consideration of wages, hours, fringe benefits, location, opportunity for advancement, and other factors.

Regardless of the selection criteria or method used to create it, the employer-employee relationship is a contractual relationship. The actual contract may be oral or written; express or implied by the conduct of the parties; bilateral or unilateral. Generally, however, employment contracts are unilateral contracts requiring the traditional contract elements of offer, acceptance, and consideration.

The American rule is that oral contracts of indefinite duration (the most common form of employment contract) are presumed to be "at will" contracts. Essentially, this means that the employment relationship may be terminated by either the employer or the employee without notice and for any reason. This rule, of course, has spawned great controversy and numerous exceptions. The courts have generally refused to recognize a common law action for wrongful refusal to hire.

The terminability provisions which characterize at-will contracts may be altered in both written and oral contracts by an agreement of the parties that employment will not be terminated except for "cause," "good cause," or similar language. Such written provisions or assertions of oral representations to that effect often raise interesting factual and

33. Twigg v. Hercules Corp., 185 W.Va. 155, 406 S.E.2d 52 (1990).

34. Baughman v. Wal–Mart Stores, Inc., 215 W.Va. 45, 592 S.E.2d 824 (2003).

35. Borse v. Piece Goods Shop, Inc., 963 F.2d 611 (3d Cir.1992).

36. Hennessey v. Coastal Eagle Pt. Oil Co., 129 N.J. 81, 609 A.2d 11 (1992).

37. Luedtke v. Nabors Alaska Drilling, Inc., 834 P.2d 1220 (Alaska 1992).

38. Luck v. Southern Pac. Transp. Co., 218 Cal.App.3d 1, 267 Cal.Rptr. 618, cert. denied, 498 U.S. 939, 111 S.Ct. 344, 112 L.Ed.2d 309 (1990).

doctrinal issues, but do not alter the basic contractual nature of the relationship between the parties.

Offer

An offer for employment need not be exceedingly formal. The offer may be oral or written. It may be made by telephone, by letter, by an employee manual or handbook, or by an advertisement. An offer also may be implied through the conduct of the employer. Most states do not have strict requirements and will uphold an offer unless the intent of the offering party cannot reasonably be inferred from the outward manifestations of the parties.

At a minimum, an offer of employment must be clear, definite, and explicit. An offer must be sufficiently certain to allow a court to determine the duties of each party. The mere possibility of future employment, expression of good will or good intentions, or a general expression of policy are not sufficient to constitute an offer. Thus, not every utterance by an employer is an offer. A statement indicating specific pay, hours, location, and responsibilities is generally required.

Acceptance

Acceptance of an offer need not be made in the same form as the offer. For example, an employee may accept a written offer orally or through action. An oral offer and an oral acceptance are subject to statute of frauds limitations because of the parol nature of the agreement. Some courts hold that if the employment contract is a unilateral contract, then the employee may only accept by performance (i.e., beginning work).

If an employer and employee fail to reduce their agreement to a final written version, but the parties act affirmatively upon their negotiations, the courts are free to find that an enforceable agreement exists because of the manifestation of the parties' intent to be bound. If the parties do not agree on material terms, however, then the employee cannot be deemed to have accepted any offer. Also, if an employee attempts to change terms of the offer in an acceptance, the employee's actions constitute a counter-offer, not an acceptance.

Consideration

To be enforceable, an employment contract must be supported by consideration. The importance of the type of consideration provided arises mostly in the context of determining whether employment is at will or terminable only for cause. As noted earlier, at-will employment contracts usually are unilateral contracts. The employer makes an offer or a promise which the employee accepts through performance. The employee's action in reliance upon the employer's promise is sufficient consideration to make the employer's promise binding.

Additional consideration may be necessary if a contract is not at will, but terminable only for cause. Even a contract that lacks a specific duration may be regarded as a termination for cause contract if the employee furnishes "independent and additional consideration." If an employee provides consideration beyond performing duties under the employment contract, then the presumption of employment at will may be rebutted. Merely continuing to work in the same employment relationship is not sufficient. But, if the relationship changes through the addition of a new agreement, such as an agreement to pay severance wages or a new noncompetition clause, then continuing to work under the revised agreement is sufficient consideration to make the new provisions binding.

As a general rule, services and obligations associated with beginning new employment will not be considered sufficient additional consideration to override the presumption of at-will employment. Thus, moving to another city, resigning from a former position or job, or foregoing other employment or ceasing to search for other employment are not sufficient consideration to alter at-will status.

Statutory Disclosures

Some states have begun requiring disclosures of wages, hours, conditions, and other terms of employment to be made in English and Spanish, or in other languages that are spoken by more than ten percent of the work force. The main purpose of these laws is to protect migrant farmworkers.

Employee Handbooks, Manuals, and Policy Statements

Employee handbooks, manuals, and policy statements may modify an existing employment relationship or become part of a new employment relationship. The issue usually arises in the context of wrongful discharge litigation, in which the former employee asserts that the employer breached promises made in an employee handbook.

In order for a handbook or manual to become part of the employment contract, the language must be definite and it must be communicated to the employee. If an employment handbook contains detailed procedures for discipline and discharge and expressly contains an obligation to discharge only for good cause, then the courts will recognize that the at-will rule has been modified. An employer, however, may include a disclaimer preventing the handbook from becoming part of a binding contract. If a disclaimer is prominently displayed within a handbook or manual, courts will generally uphold the disclaimer. A minority of courts go further and indicate that the disclaimer need not be in the manual or may be placed within the employment manual years after the date that a particular employee was hired.

It has been held that an employer may unilaterally modify an employee handbook only if it contains a reservation of the right to do so. Without such a reservation of right, additional consideration is required, and the employee's continuing to work for the employer will not suffice as the consideration.

Probationary Periods

Many private and public sector employees must successfully complete a probationary period before becoming a permanent employee.

Whether a special probationary period exists depends on the agreement of the parties, and this agreement may be found in a variety of sources. For example, provisions for probationary periods have been based on personnel manuals, written employment contracts, city council resolutions, and government policy manuals.

The effect of having a probationary period varies and depends, in the first instance, on the agreement specifying a probationary period. Frequently, the agreement will specify that probationary employees may be discharged at will, whereas permanent employees may be discharged only for cause. For public employees, they may have no property interest in their jobs until after the end of the probationary period.

Statute of Frauds

As a general rule, if any promise in a contract cannot be performed fully within a year from the time that a contract is made, the contract falls within the statute of frauds and must be in writing to be enforced. If any contingent event would make it possible for the contract to be performed within a year, the contract would not fall under the statute. For example, if an employer orally promises to employ an employee for life or permanently, and the employee promises to work for the employer for life, the contract does not fall within the statute of frauds. The employee could die or retire within a year and thus the terms of the contract would be fulfilled. If an employer and an employee agree on a contract for a definite term of years greater than one year, however, then the contract must be in writing to be enforceable. If the employee died under a contract for a specific term, the employee's death would not complete the terms of the contract, but the contract would be discharged or excused.

A writing cannot satisfy the statute unless it contains the material terms of the agreement between the parties. The material terms include the nature of the services to be performed, the compensation to be paid, and the length of employment. If the parties to an employment contract have prepared a draft agreement, but have failed to agree and reduce to writing material terms, the draft agreement will not be sufficient to satisfy the statute.

Estoppel

When an employment relationship lacks the formal requirements of an employment contract, the doctrine of promissory estoppel may create an employer-employee relationship. Generally, the elements of estoppel are the following: (1) an unambiguous promise; (2) reliance on that promise; (3) that the reliance was expected and foreseeable; and (4) detriment resulted from that reliance. The effect of promissory estoppel is often to require employment termination to be based on just cause or to take an agreement outside of the statute of frauds.

To be unambiguous, a promise must be more than a statement of good will. It must be an actual promise. Thus, if an employer states that an employee's prospects are good and that the employee might receive a pay increase in the future, that statement is not unambiguous enough to support a claim for estoppel. On the other hand, where an employer stated that an employee has "nothing to worry about" and that he would be employed "until he retired or decided he did not want the job anymore," those statements and the context in which they were made, were sufficient to preclude summary judgment for the employer.

The most important element of estoppel is reliance. The employer's promise must induce some action or forbearance on the part of the employee that would not have occurred but for the employer's promise. That reliance also must be reasonable. Generally, reliance on a promise of at-will employment will be held to be unreasonable because at-will employment does not create enforceable rights in the employee other than the right to be paid. The mere prospect of employment is not sufficient to support a claim of estoppel, but reliance on a promise of permanent employment is sufficient. Thus, an employee's intent to remain with an employer until retirement is not sufficient reliance to support a claim of promissory estoppel.

Allegations that an employer promised lifetime employment and lured an employee from prior employment are insufficient to establish a cause of action based upon promissory estoppel. Merely abandoning a job search also does not demonstrate sufficient reliance to sustain an estoppel claim. If an employer merely promises an employee a certain salary and certain benefits which induce that employee to leave a former position and forego looking for other employment, no action for promissory estoppel will lie. On the other hand, reliance on formal promises by an employer that an employee will be discharged only for cause may be sufficient reliance under a theory of promissory estoppel to support a finding of an employment relationship.

The employee's reliance must be foreseeable and expected. If an employer knows that an employee must resign another position in order to accept a new position, then that reliance would be foreseeable and expected by the new employer.

False representations as to length, stability, and compensation of new employment have been held to establish a claim for promissory fraud in the cases of terminated employees who alleged they were induced to give up secure jobs and relocate. On the other hand, promissory estoppel has been rejected where allegations that misrepresentations as to income potential caused a salaried accountant to leave his position to become a commission-paid financial planner failed to state a claim for fraudulent inducement because the plaintiff understood the uncertain nature of his earnings, where the employee handbook contained a specific disclaimer, where the employee changed residence based on indefinite assurances of continued employment, and where the employee quit in reliance on an interview to be held on the following day.

§ 1.28 Arbitration

Contract provisions requiring the arbitration of all disputes arising under the contract have long been common in collective bargaining agreements. Often the *quid pro quo* for an agreement not to strike, arbitration is considered valuable to both labor and management. For unionized employees, arbitration establishes a fast, inexpensive method of challenging a discharge or other alleged unfair treatment, and it places the burden of proof on the employer. For management, arbitration confines employment disputes to a single forum with limits on the available remedies.

During the 1990s, in an attempt to limit their exposure to various statutory and common law causes of action, an increasing number of employers attempted to impose arbitration on nonunion, at-will employees as the sole remedy for a range of common law and statutory claims. The validity of these provisions has been raised in a series of Supreme Court and lower court cases, and the contours of arbitration outside of collective bargaining are still being developed.

In *Circuit City Stores, Inc. v. Adams,*[1] the employee signed an employment application that established arbitration as the exclusive remedy for all disputes arising out of his employment. When the employee subsequently filed state law claims, the employer removed the case to federal court and sought to compel arbitration under the Federal Arbitration Act (FAA) of 1925.[2] The Supreme Court held that an exemption in the FAA for contracts of employment of "seamen, railroad employees, or any other class of workers engaged in foreign or interstate commerce" applies only to contracts of transportation workers.

The following year, in *EEOC v. Waffle House, Inc.,*[3] the Supreme Court held that the FAA did not prevent the EEOC from bringing an action alleging a violation of the ADA, even though the employee on whose behalf the action was brought had signed an agreement to arbitrate all disputes. "The FAA does not mention enforcement by public agencies; it ensures the enforceability of private agreements to arbitrate, but otherwise does not purport to place any restriction on a nonparty's choice of judicial forum."[4]

A number of issues are still unresolved. In general, although mandatory arbitration provisions contained in employment applications have been upheld, it is not clear whether similar provisions in personnel handbooks would be upheld. In addition, compulsory arbitration may violate state law. For example, in *Armendariz v. Foundation Health Psychcare Services, Inc.,*[5] the Supreme Court of California held that a contract requiring employees to waive their rights to bring actions for sexual harassment under state law was contrary to public policy, and that limitations of remedies under the arbitration provision constituted a contract of adhesion. A Texas court held that an employer could not compel a worker injured on the job to submit his personal injury claim to

§ 1.28

1. 532 U.S. 105, 121 S.Ct. 1302, 149 L.Ed.2d 234 (2001).

2. 9 U.S.C.A. §§ 1–16.

3. 534 U.S. 279, 122 S.Ct. 754, 151 L.Ed.2d 755 (2002).

4. 534 U.S. at 289.

5. 24 Cal.4th 83, 99 Cal.Rptr.2d 745, 6 P.3d 669 (2000).

arbitration because the employer retained the right to terminate or alter its obligations under arbitration at any time.[6]

§ 1.29   Tort Liability and the Employment Relationship

Although many aspects of modern employment law differ greatly from earlier common law rules, the tort consequences of the employment relationship still follow closely traditional common law doctrines. In particular, liability principles of employment law today are substantially based on the common law of master and servant. These rules remain extremely important and govern a wide range of tort actions, including the liability of an employer for the torts committed by an employee within the scope of employment.

Masters

Generally, a master is a person who controls or has the right to control the details of the work of another person engaged in providing services for the master. Whether a particular person is the master of another becomes important when the other person commits a tort. A master may be liable to third parties for a servant's torts under the doctrine of respondeat superior. This liability is not based upon fault or agency, but rather on the public policy that a business enterprise should not be able to disclaim responsibility for actions which may fairly be said to be characteristic of its own activities.

As a general rule, a master is subject to liability for the torts of a servant when the servant commits the tort while acting within the scope of employment. A master may be liable for the torts of a servant even if the servant's action is outside the scope of employment if the master intended the conduct, the master was negligent or reckless, the servant's conduct violated a nondelegable duty, or the agent committed the tort with the aid of the agency relationship with the master. The term "employer" has displaced the term "master" in statutes and case law, and the terms are now used interchangeably.

In order to hold a master or employer liable for injury to a third party caused by a servant or an employee, the third party must first show that a master-servant or employer-employee relationship exists. Under one formulation, four factors are used to make this determination: (1) the method of selection and engagement of the servant; (2) the basis of payment of compensation; (3) the power of dismissal; and (4) the power of control.[1] The Restatement (Second) of Agency uses a ten-factor test to evaluate a putative "master-servant" relationship,[2] which has been adopted by a number of courts. The most important element is the employer's right to control the physical details of the employee's work.

---

6. In re Jobe Concrete Prods., Inc., 101 S.W.3d 122 (Tex. App. 2003).

§ 1.29

1. Dickinson v. City of Huntsville, 822 So.2d 411 (Ala. 2001).

2. See Restatement (Second) of Agency § 220(2) (1958).

Servants

A servant is a person who performs services for another and whose physical conduct while performing those services is subject to the control of the other. The term "servant" is not limited to persons who perform manual labor. Servants also need not even be paid for their services; they may be employed without compensation. The term "servant" has been displaced by the term "employee" in statutes and cases; thus, the terms are often used interchangeably. If a person performs the work of another, a presumption exists that the person is employed by the person whose work is being done.

Scope of Employment

Generally, an employer is liable for its employee's torts committed only within the employee's scope of employment. The conduct of an employee is not within the scope of employment if the employee's actions are different in kind from those authorized, exceed the employee's authorized time or space limitation, or are not performed with a purpose to serve the employer. The Restatement (Second) of Agency uses a ten-factor test to determine whether conduct is within the scope of employment.[3] Neither the Restatement nor the courts limit an employer's liability to the negligent torts of an employee; thus, an employer may also be liable for the intentional torts of an employee.

An employer will not be liable for the acts of an employee engaged in a "frolic." In other words, if the employee's action is wholly motivated by his or her own interests with no underlying purpose to further the employer's business, then the employer will not be liable for the employee's negligent or intentional torts. An employee may temporarily depart from the scope of employment in time or space and reenter the scope of employment by resuming activity within the scope of employment. If an employee's deviation from the employer's business is slight and not unusual, a court may find that the employee continued to act within the scope of employment. If the employee's deviation is "marked and unusual," however, a court may find that the employee acted beyond the scope of employment.

Problems arise in determining scope when an employee is motivated both by a personal motive and a motive to serve the employer. Various courts have applied different tests under this circumstance. Some courts require that the employee's act be primarily for the benefit of the employer before liability attaches. Thus, if an employee's action is wholly motivated by personal reasons, the employer will not be liable for the employee's negligence. Other courts focus upon whether the employee's action is in furtherance of the employer's interests or business. Consequently, if an employee acts while engaged in an activity falling within the scope of employment, even though the act is not authorized or directed by the employer, the employer will be held liable. Under this analysis, whether the employee's act is "fairly and naturally incident to

---

3. Restatement (Second) of Agency § 229(2) (1958).

the employer's business" is important. Nevertheless, if the employee is engaged in a purely social act, the employer will not be liable. Some courts focus upon whether the employee's action is foreseeable. Thus, even if an employee disregards the employer's instructions or violates the employee's duties, the employer will be liable if the employee's actions are foreseeable.

The courts are divided on whether an employer may be held liable for injuries arising from an employee's intoxication. Some courts hold that there is no duty owed by the employer to the third party or that the employee and not the employer was the proximate cause of the injury. Other courts find liability by focusing on whether the employee was acting within the scope of employment at the time of the injury or whether attendance at the function at which the employee became intoxicated was mandatory.

If an employee commits an intentional tort, some courts require not only that the employee's acts be within the scope of employment, but also that the acts facilitate or promote the employer's business. Other courts use a foreseeability standard. Thus, no single test exists to determine what constitutes "scope of employment."

Generally, employees are not within the scope of employment while travelling to and from work. If the employer pays for employment related travel, however, the employee is considered to be acting within the scope of employment. Also, if travel is part of employment, an employer will be liable for the employee's actions if the employment created the necessity for the travel. Accordingly, if an employee is on a purely personal errand while operating an automobile, the employer will not be liable for the employee's negligence. But, if an employee is engaged in a work-related errand, the employer will be liable for the employee's negligence.

An employer does not automatically escape liability when an employee uses physical force. On the other hand, if an employee who uses excessive violence was not expected to use force in the normal course of work, then the employer will not be liable for the acts of the employee. Therefore, if an employee, such as a police officer or a night club bouncer, is authorized to use force, the employer may be held liable for the employee's excessive use of force.

Employees have not been held liable under vicarious liability for intentional acts committed for personal reasons unrelated to the employee's duties and unforeseeable to the employer. This principle has been applied to cases of sexual assault and sexual harassment.

Independent Contractors

Generally, an employer or master is not liable for torts committed by an independent contractor. The commonly accepted theory behind nonliability for the acts of an independent contractor is the fact that the employer has no right of control over the manner in which the contractor's work is done, and thus the work is regarded as the contractor's own enterprise.

An independent contractor is a person who, while pursuing an independent business, undertakes a specific job for another using his or her own means and methods without submitting to the control of the other except for the results of the work. An independent contractor may or may not be the agent of an employer. To determine whether an individual is a servant or an independent contractor, several factors are important: (1) the extent of the master's control over the details of the work; (2) whether the person employed is engaged in a distinct occupation or business; (3) the kind of occupation; (4) the skill required; (5) who supplies the tools; (6) the length of employment; (7) the method of payment; (8) whether the work is part of the regular business of the employer; (9) how the parties view their relationship; and (10) whether the employer is in business.[4] No single factor is determinative; the relationship must be determined from all of the factors as a whole. Nevertheless, the extent of the master's control is the most important factor. The extent of the master's control does not mean the extent of actual control; it means the extent of the right to control.

Courts look at the hiring party's right to control the means or manner in which a worker performs a specific task. If the hiring party merely retains the right to require certain results, then the parties will be considered to have an independent contractor relationship. Thus, merely retaining the right to supervise or inspect the work of an independent contractor for compliance with the terms of a contract does not create a master-servant relationship.

In some states, an important exception to the rule of nonliability of independent contractors exists in the hospital setting, where a hospital may be liable for the torts of independent contractor physicians unless written notice is given to the patient that the hospital is not the employer of the physicians.

A contract between parties establishing an independent contractor relationship is generally determinative of the parties' relationship unless proof exists that the contract was a sham, the hiring party exercised control inconsistent with an independent contractor relationship, or sufficient indicia of a master-servant relationship exist.

A common exception to the rule of nonliability for the acts of independent contractors involves inherently dangerous activities. If an independent contractor is engaged in an inherently dangerous activity, the employer may be liable for the contractor's tortious conduct. "Inherently dangerous" means that an instrumentality has a type of danger which requires special precautions and is part of the instrument at all times and does not arise from the collateral negligence of others. This means that the instrumentality is dangerous in its nondefective or normal state. The work involved need not be the type of work which

4. Restatement (Second) of Agency § 220(2) (1958).

cannot be done without risk or that the work involve a high degree of risk of harm. The key is that the work must be inherently risky and the risk must be recognizable in advance.

No bright line test exists for what work constitutes inherently dangerous activity. An activity may be inherently dangerous in some circumstances, but not in others. Examples of inherently dangerous activities include blasting, installing electrical wires, and clearing land by fire.

Under a related exception, an employer also may be liable for the acts of independent contractors if the employer has a nondelegable duty arising out of a special relationship with the public or a particular person or if the independent contractor's work is peculiarly or inherently dangerous. It is often difficult to predict which activities the courts will consider to be inherently dangerous. Working on an electrical utility project, grain inspection on top of railroad cars, and performing maintenance work at a power generating plant have been held to be *not* inherently dangerous. On the other hand, trenching and excavating has been held to be inherently dangerous.

A nondelegable duty is a duty that the employer is not free to delegate because the work is so specialized or hazardous that the work cannot be delegated. The duty may be imposed by statute, contract, or common law. For example, under the common law, a building owner has a nondelegable duty to safely maintain the areas over which the owner retains control. Thus, a city has been held to have a nondelegable duty to maintain the city convention center in a reasonably safe condition. On the other hand, concert hall owners have been held not to have a nondelegable duty to ensure that independent contractors acting as security guards for a concert perform their services correctly. The effect of the nondelegable duty rule is that both the independent contractor and the property owner are liable for the failure to maintain the property.

A person who employs an independent contractor may be held vicariously liable for the torts of that independent contractor if the contractor is employed to do work that involves "a special danger to others which the employer knows or has reason to know to be inherent in or normal to the work."[5] The employer has a nondelegable duty to ensure that precautions are taken. The application of this exception is not limited to "intrinsically hazardous work." An employer may be liable if the employer could have anticipated the injury as a probable consequence of the contractor's work and if the employer took no precautions to prevent the injury.

Borrowed Servants

A borrowed servant is a servant directed or permitted by the master to perform services for another. A general employer may assert the borrowed servant doctrine as a defense to a third party action involving

---

5. Restatement (Second) of Torts § 427 (1984).

the negligence of an employee while rendering services for a special employer. The general employer may assert this defense under the following conditions: (1) the employee consented to work for the special employer; (2) the employee entered the work of the special employer under an express or implied contract; and (3) the special employer had the power to control the details of the employee's work, how the work was to be performed, and when the work was to stop or continue. The most important factor is the degree of control that a general employer has over the employee. Most courts hold that to escape liability the general employer must completely relinquish control over the employee's conduct during the particular work.

The test is to determine whether the employee performs the particular service in question subject to the direction and control of the general employer or the special employer. If the special employer has complete control and direction over the employee while the employee is rendering services to the special employer, the special employer has the exclusive right to discharge the employee, and the general employer has no control or direction over the employee while the employee renders services to the special employer, then the employee will be considered to be a borrowed servant. A general presumption exists that the employee remains in the employment of the general employer so long as the employee is performing the services entrusted to the employee by the general employer. Thus, the mere fact that an employee obeys the special master's signals or directions does not make an employee a borrowed servant.

§ 1.30   Regulation of Employee Leasing Companies

Licensing Statutes

Laws enacted in ten states require that employee leasing companies register with the state before operating. These statutes typically define employee leasing companies as entities that agree with client companies to place all or substantially all of the client's employees on the leasing company's payroll and then lease them back to the client, for a fee. Some states require that the leasing agreement provide that the leasing company retains traditional employer duties such as hiring, firing, and assignment decisions. One state, South Carolina, requires that the agreement between the employee leasing company and client contain terms ensuring that the leasing company retains the right to hire, fire, and assign leased employees, set safety rules for the workplace, and pays the leased employees from its own accounts.[1]

The laws also draw distinctions between employee leasing companies and temporary employment services. In general, these statutes expressly exclude temporary employment companies from coverage under the state's regulatory structure. Oregon excludes temporary employment by defining "employee leasing companies" as not including the provision of employees to clients on a temporary basis to cover shortages, seasonal

§ 1.30
1. S.C. Code Ann. § 40–68–70(A).

fluctuations, and special assignments.[2] Other states are less clear, but exclude temporary employment agencies from their regulatory scheme. For example, Utah's statute provides that the definition of "employee leasing company" excludes companies that provide leased employees to clients for anything less than an unrestricted duration.[3]

Workers' Compensation Insurance Payments

While only ten states have extensively regulated the operation of employee leasing companies, many more have enacted statutes that define who the leased employee's employer is for the purposes of workers' compensation. A large majority of these laws provide that the employee leasing company is the employer of the leased employees for the purposes of workers' compensation insurance payments. Some states, however, have elected to allow the client and employee leasing company to decide who should provide workers' compensation coverage for the leased employees.

In addition to defining who is liable for workers' composition premiums, several states prohibit employee leasing companies from being self-insured. Most states, however, allow employee leasing companies to provide workers' compensation insurance to leased employees just as any other employer in the state would. Indeed, it would seem that the net worth and surety bond requirements found in many states are designed to ensure that employee leasing companies are able to fulfill their obligations for workers' compensation coverage.

Unemployment Insurance Payments

Employee leasing arrangements present problems of which employer entity, the employee leasing company or the client, is responsible for unemployment insurance payments. To remedy this situation, many states have provided by statute that either the client or the employee leasing company is liable for these payments. The clear majority of these states hold the employee leasing company responsible for unemployment insurance payments. In an attempt to ensure that the leased employees are not denied unemployment coverage, some states provide that if the leased employee is not provided by a properly licensed employee leasing company, the client is responsible for unemployment insurance payments.

2. Or. Rev. Stat. § 656.850(1).   **3.** Utah Code Ann. § 58–59–102(3).

Chapter 2

DISCRIMINATION: RACE, NATION-AL ORIGIN, GENDER, RELI-GION AND AGE

Table of Sections

---

§ 2.1   Introduction

This chapter explores the federal statutory constraints on employment practices that disadvantage applicants and employees because of race, national origin or ethnicity, gender, religion, or age. It also examines state statutory protections against discrimination and constitutionally based claims.

The first major federal legislation providing sweeping protection against employment discrimination was Title VII of the Civil Rights Act of 1964.[1] Title VII prohibits employment discrimination on the basis of "race, color, religion, sex, or national origin" by employers, labor organizations, and employment agencies. The Age Discrimination in Employment Act (ADEA)[2] was enacted three years later to extend similar coverage on the basis of age discrimination. Both Acts have been amended and expanded several times.

Title VII's coverage is broad. The term "race" refers to all racial groups. "National origin" "refers to the country where a person was born, or, more broadly, the country from which his or her ancestors came." Discrimination on the basis of religion refers not only to disadvantage to a worker because of religious affiliation, but also to the employer's duty to make reasonable accommodation to the religious beliefs of employees.

Although these two Acts provide broad protection against discrimination in employment, their coverage is not all-inclusive. First, in Title VII, the term "sex" does not include sexual orientation and there is no other federal protection against employment discrimination on the basis of sexual orientation. The term "sex" in Title VII refers to "gender" rather than anything else. Next, the ADEA does not protect against all age discrimination in employment. The Act limits its protection to individuals who are aged forty and over and thus permits discrimination against younger people on the basis of their age. Although some state and local laws protect individuals from employment discrimination on the basis of sexual orientation and on the basis of any age, the federal law does not extend that far.

Other sources of federally guaranteed rights against employment discrimination are examined at the end of this chapter. Section 2.39 examines constitutional claims of employment discrimination. Claims

---

§ 2.1

1.   42 U.S.C.A § 2000e et seq.

2.   29 U.S.C.A. § 623 et seq.

derived from the Reconstruction Era Civil Rights Act, including in particular under 42 U.S.C.A. § 1981, are addressed in § 2.40.

This chapter does not include discrimination on the basis of disability. Claims of discrimination based on disability under the Rehabilitation Act and the Americans with Disabilities Act are covered in Chapter 3.

§ 2.2　Coverage and Exemptions

When Congress enacted Title VII of the Civil Rights Act of 1964 it used the outer limit of its constitutional power to regulate activities that "affect commerce," but included within the Act numerous limitations and exceptions in the Act's coverage. Three years later Congress enacted the Age Discrimination in Employment Act (ADEA), and that Act similarly requires employers to "affect commerce" and similarly provides numerous limitations and exceptions from coverage. This section covers these basic topics of coverage and exemptions shared by these Acts, including the requirement that employers affect commerce, the preemption of conflicting state law, and the coverage and exemption of certain employers, and the question of individual liability.

Employers Must "Affect Commerce"

The requirement that employers "affect commerce" for coverage under Title VII and the ADEA is not an arduous one. The Supreme Court has interpreted broadly when activities "affect commerce" so that even local activities may have an effect on interstate commerce. Congress tempered the reach of these acts by defining "employer" to exclude very small enterprises. Under Title VII, an employer must have a minimum of fifteen employees for coverage and under the ADEA the minimum is twenty.

The statutory minimum number of employees under the acts functions virtually to guarantee that a covered employer will affect interstate commerce. In a Title VII case, the Ninth Circuit observed that it would be rare for an employer with the statutory minimum number of fifteen employees not to affect commerce. For example, in one case a law firm that practiced only in state law nonetheless reached the threshold for affecting interstate commerce with minimal contacts because: (1) the partners occasionally traveled interstate; (2) the firm purchased out-of-state office equipment; and (3) the firm owned a few thousand dollars worth of reference books bought from an out-of-state publisher.

As this case illustrates, it is only the employer whose operations are almost completely confined within one state that will avoid coverage of the Act for failure to affect commerce. An example of such a rarity is one employer whose interstate phone calls and purchases totaled only a few hundred dollars; these slight contacts were not sufficiently substantial to "affect commerce" for coverage under the Act.

Preemption of State Law Inconsistent with Federal Antidiscrimination Statutes

Title VII preempts inconsistent state law, including laws with which employers cannot comply without violating Title VII. Such laws include "protective" statutes that reflected the desire of state legislatures in an earlier era to protect women from the hazards of the workplace by limiting their hours and working conditions. The Supreme Court explained in a 1908 case that the justification for such laws was the state's interest in protecting women from strenuous work that might produce "injurious effects upon the body" because "healthy mothers are essential to vigorous offspring" and thus "the physical well-being of women because an object of public interest and care." The effect of such legislation was not only to protect but also to disadvantage women from jobs where the employer needed flexibility in assigning workers, such that women tended to hold jobs with regular hours but lower wages. Title VII thus preempts these laws.

The Supreme Court in *California Federal Savings & Loan Association v. Guerra*[1] declined to apply the Supremacy Clause to preempt state legislation that required employers to provide leave and reinstatement to employees disabled by pregnancy. The Court noted that this statute does not actually conflict with Title VII because it covers only the period of actual disability and was not based on stereotyped assumptions based on gender and was not otherwise inconsistent with the purposes of the Act. Further, because Congress did not intend to "leave no room" for supplementary state legislation, there was no preemption. Employers can comply with both laws, the Court noted, by providing equal benefits to all disabled employees of either gender.

The West Virginia Supreme Court of Appeals had occasion to consider Title VII's preemption of state law in a different context. At issue in *Cutright v. Metropolitan Life Insurance Co.*[2] was a state statute prohibiting discharge of an insurance agent except for "good cause" as specifically enumerated in the act. An agent who was discharged for creating a sexually hostile atmosphere sued his employer under the statute and recovered a million dollar jury verdict. The court overturned the award on the grounds that Title VII preempts the state law. Although the state statute did not enumerate this ground as a permissible "good cause," the federal law was inconsistent and Congress intended to preempt inconsistent state law.

Employers Covered

Title VII and the ADEA each apply to a "person" in an industry affecting commerce, including an employer, a labor organization, or an employment agency. A private "employer" is defined primarily by the number of employees. Coverage of a union can be either as an employer if it meets the minimum number of employees, or as a "labor organization" if it represents or seeks to represent employees of a covered employer, without regard to meeting the definition of employer. Similarly, an employment agency can be sued as an employer if it meets the numerical definition, or as an "employment agency" without regard to

§ 2.2
1. 479 U.S. 272, 107 S.Ct. 683, 93 L.Ed.2d 613 (1987).

2. 201 W.Va. 50, 491 S.E.2d 308 (1997).

the number of employees if it acts to secure employees for a covered employer.

The federal government is not an "employer" within the meaning of either Title VII or the ADEA, but separate provisions of the Acts prohibit discrimination by the federal government. Enforcement procedures and remedies are also different for federal employees because the ones provided for actions against "employers" do not apply.

State and local governments are not exempt from Title VII. Congress amended the Act in 1972 to include these employers, and the amendment withstood constitutional challenge. The basis of Congressional power to extend coverage to state and local governments in its 1972 amendments to Title VII was section 5 of the Fourteenth Amendment.

Congress attempted to apply the ADEA to state and local governments as well when it amended that Act in 1974 to include such entities in the definition of "employer." The Supreme Court since held in *Kimel v. Florida Board of Regents*[3] that Congress exceeded its power under Section 5 of the Fourteenth Amendment when it applied the ADEA to the states. Therefore, claimants of age discrimination may no longer sue state employers under federal law, although state statutory law is still available.

Employers Exempted

The congressional exercise of power under the Commerce Clause does not exclude many employers from the coverage of Title VII and the ADEA, but Congress voluntarily imposed more significant limitations and courts have found other sources of law that add further exemptions. These limitations, discussed below, include bona fide membership clubs, Indian tribes, foreign employers, and some employee relationships of religious organizations.

Employers Exempted—Bona Fide Membership Clubs

There is no exemption in Title VII for charitable institutions, provided that they "affect commerce." In contrast, there is an exemption for bona fide private membership clubs, other than labor organizations. Such clubs must (1) be exempt from taxation under the Internal Revenue Code; and (2) have a defined social or recreational purpose or promote a common literary, scientific, or political objective, and demand meaningful conditions of membership. For example, a credit union does not have a sufficient purpose for exemption, nor does a retirement home restricted to members of a fraternal order. One case has found that the Girl Scouts of America has such purpose, however, and found it exempt from Title VII despite its large membership because it selects members on the basis of age, gender, and agreement to uphold the Scout pledge.

Unlike Title VII, the ADEA does not exempt private clubs. A private membership club that qualifies for the Title VII exemption can discrimi-

---

3. 528 U.S. 62, 120 S.Ct. 631, 145 L.Ed.2d 522 (2000).

nate on the basis of race, color, religion, sex, and national origin, but not age. Thus, a club could have enough employees to be an employer covered by the ADEA, but also be exempt from Title VII as a bona fide private membership club. Such a club may require its lifeguards to be blond males, for example, but may not require that they be young. Title VII would not apply to prohibit any race/national origin restriction implicit in "blond" nor the gender requirement explicit in "males," but the ADEA would apply to make the age restriction unlawful unless the club could prove that age is a bona fide occupational qualification.

The restriction of the ADEA on private membership clubs applies only to a club's employment practices and does not include its membership practices. This distinction can be difficult when the club hires some of its own members to perform work at a salary. The issue arose in *EEOC v. First Catholic Slovak Ladies Association*,[4] where a club hired some of the members of its board of directors but had an age restriction on membership to the board. The club's by-laws required members of the board to be sixty-six or fewer years old. This club, whose membership was limited to individuals who were Slovak and Catholic, could lawfully restrict its employees to members with the requisite religious and national origin credentials, but could not impose the age limitation indirectly by requiring its employees to belong to the age-restricted board.

The statutory restriction on private membership clubs is arguably a violation of the members' First Amendment freedom of association. This argument is weak, however, after the Supreme Court's holding in *New York State Club Association v. City of New York*,[5] where the Court upheld state regulation of a club's membership restrictions. Given this broad authorization, the statutory regulation of a club's employment practices is probably constitutional.

Employers Exempted—Indian Tribes

Title VII expressly exempts "Indian tribes" from the definition of "employer." The Supreme Court has characterized this exemption as consistent with the longstanding Congressional policy of providing a unique legal status to Indian tribes in matters of tribal employment.

The Act does not define "Indian tribe." It has been held to include corporations of a tribe designated to administer tribal assets. Tribal law concerning employment policies governs tribal employers as well as providing additional constraints on non-tribal lessees operating on trust land. For the latter group, however, constraints may be waived in the lease if the lease is binding on the tribal nation.

The Fifth Circuit has held that the exemption for "Indian tribes" includes an unincorporated business wholly owned by the Choctaw Nation regardless of whether it was a legal entity separate from the

---

4. 694 F.2d 1068 (6th Cir.1982), cert. denied, 464 U.S. 819, 104 S.Ct. 80, 78 L.Ed.2d 90 (1983).

5. 487 U.S. 1, 108 S.Ct. 2225, 101 L.Ed.2d 1 (1988).

tribe. In so holding that circuit expressly endorsed the position of other circuits that the exemption of Indian tribes by Congress removes the subject matter jurisdiction of federal courts to hear complaints brought against unincorporated commercial enterprises entirely owned and operated by recognized Indian tribes.

The spirit of the Title VII exception for Indian tribes governed the Tenth Circuit's reasoning in *Duke v. Absentee Shawnee Tribe of Oklahoma Housing Authority*.[6] The court held that the employer could not be sued for race and sex discrimination under Title VII because it was an "Indian tribe" despite the fact that the employing housing authority had been created under state law. The employer, which provided low-income housing for members of the Absentee Shawnee Tribe, was implemented under the Housing Act of 1937. Under this Act, such housing authorities could be created either by tribal ordinance or under state law. Despite the fact that this employer had been created under state law, the court reasoned that it was nonetheless covered by the Title VII exemption because the employer's members were selected by the tribe, its function was to serve the needs of the tribe, and its activities were supervised by the tribe. Finding that the purpose of the exemption was to promote the ability of sovereign Indian tribes to control their own economic enterprises, the court held that all ambiguities must be construed in favor of Indian sovereignty. Moreover, the court noted that the exemption would apply even if the employer had expressly declared its intention to subject itself to federal law, because the exemption relates to the subject matter jurisdiction of the federal court. As such, a party could not confer that jurisdiction on the court by agreement.

In contrast to the express exemption of Indian tribes in Title VII, the ADEA has no such provision. The Tenth Circuit in *EEOC v. Cherokee Nation*[7] implied an exemption from federal jurisdiction for employment discrimination claims of all types based on the tribe's right of self-government. The Eighth Circuit in *EEOC v. Fond du Lac Heavy Equipment & Construction Co.*[8] reached the same result but under narrower reasoning. The case involved a dispute between an Indian applicant and an Indian tribal employer located on the reservation. The court characterized it as a "strictly internal matter" and held: "Subjecting such an employment relationship between the tribal member and his tribe to federal control and supervision dilutes the sovereignty of the tribe. The consideration of a tribe member's age by a tribal employer should be allowed to be restricted (or not restricted) by the tribe in accordance with its culture and traditions."[9]

The Ninth Circuit also came to the conclusion that the ADEA does not apply to Indian tribes, but employed a slightly different analysis than the other circuits. It held in *EEOC v. Karuk Tribe Housing Authority*[10]

6. 199 F.3d 1123 (10th Cir.1999), cert. denied, 529 U.S. 1134, 120 S.Ct. 2014, 146 L.Ed.2d 963 (2000).

7. 871 F.2d 937 (10th Cir. 1989).

8. 986 F.2d 246 (8th Cir. 1993).

9. Id. at 249.

10. 260 F.3d 1071 (9th Cir. 2001).

that the Act does not apply to a relationship between an Indian tribe housing authority and an Indian employee because it is a "purely internal matter" related to the tribe's self-governance. The court noted that the housing authority functions as an arm of the tribal government and is not simply a business entity that happens to be run by the tribe or its members.

Employers Exempted—Foreign Corporations

Foreign corporations are exempt from both Title VII and the ADEA. Title VII excludes "foreign operations of an employer that is a foreign person not controlled by an American employer" and the ADEA provides that it does not apply "where the employer is a foreign person not controlled by an American employer." This language exempts at least the foreign operations of foreign employers in the absence of an American employer altogether. Any other configuration is open to question. A leading opinion from the Second Circuit, *Morelli v. Cedel*,[11] interpreted the ADEA language not to exempt a United States branch of a foreign employer. Thus, the Act covered the domestic employees of the New York branch of a Luxembourg bank. The same reasoning has been applied to Title VII.

The applicability of American antidiscrimination law to foreign corporations may also be affected by the presence of a treaty between the United States and the country of the foreign corporation. One question is whether a wholly owned United States subsidiary of a foreign corporation can assert its parent company's rights to discriminate under a treaty. This question was left open in the Supreme Court's opinion in *Sumitomo Shoji America, Inc. v. Avagliano*.[12] The Seventh Circuit answered this question affirmatively in *Fortino v. Quasar Co.*[13] At issue in that case was an American–Japanese treaty that permits Japanese employers to engage managers of its own choosing. When Quasar, a formerly American corporation, became an American subsidiary of a Japanese company, the new owners fired American managers and replaced them with Japanese nationals. The Seventh Circuit concluded that a wholly owned United States subsidiary of a Japanese company could assert the treaty rights of the parent company to the extent that the parent dictated the conduct challenged as discriminatory.

The Fifth Circuit came to the same conclusion in a case interpreting a commercial treaty that pre-dated the Civil Rights Act of 1964, the Convention of Establishment between the United States and France following World War II. In *Bennett v. Total Minatome Corp.*,[14] a wholly owned American subsidiary of a French corporation replaced an American manager with a French expatriate. The replaced manager sued on several grounds, including national origin discrimination. The company successfully defended under a provision of the treaty that permits "accountants and other technical experts, lawyers, and personnel who by

11. 141 F.3d 39 (2d Cir. 1998).

12. 457 U.S. 176, 189–90 n.19, 102 S.Ct. 2374, 72 L.Ed.2d 765 (1982).

13. 950 F.2d 389 (7th Cir. 1991).

14. 138 F.3d 1053 (5th Cir. 1998).

reason of their special capacities are essential to the functioning of the enterprise." The court interpreted this provision as exempting the company from American antidiscrimination law, even though Congress could not have intended this exemption from statutes not yet conceived at the time of the treaty. The court agreed further with the Seventh Circuit's reasoning in *Fortino* that such discrimination must be at the direction of the foreign parent corporation.

Foreign-employment exemption issues have arisen not only with respect to Americans working for foreign companies in the United States but also for Americans working for American companies in other countries. Congress amended Title VII to cover the latter category of workers, overturning a contrary Supreme Court ruling. The Court had held in *EEOC v. Arabian American Oil Co.*[15] that Title VII does not have extraterritorial effect and therefore does not apply to American citizens employed abroad by American companies. Congress responded by amending Title VII to cover such employees with the proviso that Title VII does not require American companies to engage in practices that would violate the laws of the host country.

Employers Exempted—Special Issues with Religious Organizations

Religious employers are not exempt from Title VII or the ADEA, but the First Amendment imposes limitations on their coverage. Because they do not have a blanket exemption, religious employers may not discriminate on the basis of race, color, national origin, gender or age. Title VII, which otherwise prohibits discrimination in employment on the basis of religion, does make a specific exception to allow religious employers to hire on the basis of religious belief and practice. The Supreme Court has held that this provision of the Act does not violate the Establishment Clause of the First Amendment, even though the exemption applies to the nonprofit secular activities of religious organizations.

Courts have interpreted the Acts to exempt religious organizations from all interference with the employment relationship between a church and its minister. Therefore, the Act's prohibition against discrimination on the basis of race, gender, and national origin does not apply to this relationship to avoid state encroachment into religious freedom in violation of the First Amendment.

The ministerial exception includes all matters involving a minister's salary, place of assignment, and duties to perform even though the application of laws such as Title VII could be considered "general laws" with which a church must comply. The Eleventh Circuit so held in its opinion in *Gellington v. Christian Methodist Episcopal Church,*[16] on the reasoning that investigation into a church's employment of clergy would almost always entail excessive entanglement.

---

15. 499 U.S. 244, 111 S.Ct. 1227, 113 L.Ed.2d 274 (1991).

16. 203 F.3d 1299 (11th Cir., 2000) (applying the reasoning of the Supreme Court's First Amendment cases).

Title VII and the ADEA do protect employees of religious institutions if their duties do not go to the "heart" of the church's function. There is no encroachment into religious freedom to regulate the employment of sectarian employees, and Congress chose to prohibit religious institutions from discriminating on the basis of race, gender, and national origin—but not religion—of its nonministerial employees. For example, an editorial secretary of a church-affiliated publishing house could sue under Title VII for gender discrimination and retaliation even though her duties were administrative and discretionary. The court further held that her retaliation claim was not barred even though it was a violation of church doctrine for her to file a complaint about gender discrimination in the first place.

The important issue with religious organizations is whether the employee's function goes to the "heart" of the church's function. If so, then the First Amendment prohibits government interference with the freedom of the religious institution to discriminate on any basis whatsoever. The nature of the claim does not matter. As the Fourth Circuit explained in *EEOC v. Roman Catholic Diocese*,[17] the ministerial exception is a "robust" one and the "exception precludes any inquiry whatsoever into the reasons behind a church's ministerial employment decision. The church need not, for example, proffer any religious justification for its decision[.]"[18]

In contrast, religious institutions that hire nonministerial employees are free to discriminate only on the basis of religion because of their specific exemption on this dimension under the Act. They are not free to discriminate against this second group of employees on the basis of race, gender, or national origin, however.

Employer Liability versus Individual Liability

One noteworthy limitation is that the Act does not expressly provide for individual liability, such as personal liability for a supervisor who discriminates. The Act addresses the conduct of "a person" in an industry affecting commerce and the "agents" of such a person. Therefore, there is no co-worker liability under federal law, even for harassing acts, although state law may provide relief against such individuals. The difficult issue under federal law has been individual liability of supervisors under the "persons in industries" language of the statute.

The strong trend among the federal circuits has been not to allow individual liability under the federal employment discrimination acts. The Seventh Circuit has leading opinions rejecting such liability, first under the ADA[19] and then under Title VII.[20] That circuit has made clear its position that although all the federal employment discrimination statutes are ambiguous on the subject of individual liability, the struc-

17. 213 F.3d 795 (4th Cir. 2000).
18. Id. at 802.
19. EEOC v. AIC Sec. Investigations, Ltd., 55 F.3d 1276 (7th Cir. 1995).

20. Williams v. Banning, 72 F.3d 552 (7th Cir. 1995).

ture of each dictates that only employers should be liable. Other circuits that have considered the issue since then have generally agreed.

The issue of individual liability was not litigated significantly during the first quarter century of Title VII jurisprudence. In the usual case of discriminatory hiring or discharge, an action against the individual supervisor is duplicative and unnecessary; the deeper pocket of the employer was sufficient in the usual case. The issue of supervisor liability has surfaced in harassment cases, especially following the provision of more effective damage remedies under the Civil Rights Act of 1991. Plaintiffs have sued individual harassers under state tort law and have sought a federal remedy against them as well. The liability of the individual harasser under Title VII becomes particularly important to plaintiffs when the employer itself is not liable. When an employer makes a sufficiently prompt and reasonable response to hostile environment harassment complaints, there is no employer liability even though the plaintiff was already injured before the response, and even though the response might not have been effective in stopping the conduct.

The Seventh Circuit's opinion in *Williams v. Banning*[21] is the leading opinion denying personal liability under Title VII against an individual in a harassment case even when the employer was not liable because it had taken prompt action to stop the conduct. Earlier opinions denying individual liability had involved situations where the plaintiffs had claims against the employers for the harassment by the individually named defendants, but the Seventh Circuit applied the principle in *Williams* even when the employer was not liable. The court reasoned that the plaintiff's Title VII relief was limited to the relief provided voluntarily by the employer when it fired the harasser and retained the complainant. The court noted that this relief is "considerable recompense, albeit not in monetary form,"[22] and that the plaintiff can sue the individual supervisor under state tort law if she has suffered mental and emotional distress, embarrassment and humiliation from the harassment.

Although federal law is generally foreclosing individual liability, state law remains an avenue for plaintiffs to sue individual supervisors, either under common law tort or state employment discrimination statutes. In one New Jersey case, for example, the court noted that the rationale for excluding individual liability under the federal statutes does not apply to the state statute. Unlike Title VII, the New Jersey statute does not restrict coverage to employers with fifteen or more employees, and there is no calibration of maximum allowable damage awards to the size of the employer. Therefore, the structure of the state statute did not demonstrate an intention to exclude individuals from liability. Such liability requires affirmative discriminatory acts, however, and not mere passivity.

21. 72 F.3d 552 (7th Cir. 1995).   **22.** Id. at 555.

West Virginia has gone further in interpreting its Human Rights Act to permit suit against both other employees and employers. The supreme court of that state held in *Holstein v. Norandex, Inc.*[23] that the act's provision for liability by "persons" included both principal and agent. A claim in that state may be brought on the theory that another employee aided and abetted an employer in engaging in an unlawful employment practice. A New York district court reached the same conclusion in interpreting the New York Human Rights Law to reach supervisors who aid, abet, incite, compel, or coerce any conduct forbidden by that Act.

In federal law, the trend against individual liability appears to apply also to individuals who have the power to hire and fire and thus may be considered "agents" of the employer within the meaning of the Act. Title VII, as well as the ADEA, defines "employer" as "a person engaged in an industry affecting commerce who has fifteen or more employees" and any "agent" of such person. The leading case discussing and rejecting individual liability of corporate supervisors as "agents" is *Tomka v. Seiler Corp.*[24] That opinion notes that a literal reading of the language of the Act suggests that corporate supervisors might be liable as employers, but that this situation presents the "rare case" in which the literal application of the statute will produce a result "demonstrably at odds with the intentions of its drafters" to protect small employers. Moreover, the court noted that if individuals may be liable as "agents" of the employer, courts would be burdened with the difficult factual determinations to distinguish among supervisors with actual power to hire and fire and those without such power.

For purposes of injunctive relief rather than monetary relief, individual employees with supervisory capacity may be named individually under appropriate circumstances. For monetary relief in the form of back pay, the reasoning of cases following *Tomka* finds that only the employer is liable. Less clear is the potential liability of individuals who participated in the discrimination for compensatory and punitive damages under the Civil Rights Act of 1991. The Ninth Circuit was the first circuit to address this issue and answered in the negative in *Miller v. Maxwell's Int'l, Inc.*[25] Applying familiar reasoning that because Congress protected small employers with limited resources, the court found it was "inconceivable" that Congress intended to allow civil liability against individual employees under either Title VII or the ADEA. The court added in dicta, with a strong dissent, that it was also clear that Congress did not intend such individual liability under the Civil Rights Act of 1991. Other courts have since agreed that the Civil Rights Act of 1991 does not provide an independent basis for the liability of corporate supervisors as "agents." The Sixth Circuit has explained that the calibrated damages scheme in that Act begins with employers with fifteen employees and thus precludes liability of individual "agents" who are not otherwise mentioned within the limitation scheme.

23. 194 W.Va. 727, 461 S.E.2d 473 (W.Va. 1995).

24. 66 F.3d 1295 (2d Cir. 1995).

25. 991 F.2d 583 (9th Cir. 1993).

Defining the Employment Relationship

The relationship between the complainant and the respondent must be one of "employment" even if the respondent is otherwise an employer within the meaning of the Act and even if the complainant performs useful services. Thus, students are not employees, even if they assist in research or teaching at the direction of a professor, as long as the purpose of these compensated activities is "educational." The distinction between educational activities and work for the benefit of the university can be difficult to ascertain.

An unpaid volunteer is also not an employee and is therefore not protected by the Act. The label "volunteer" is not controlling; economic reality can transform a volunteer into an employee covered by the Act. Someone called a "paid volunteer" may qualify as an employee under the Act, but incidental remuneration is not sufficient to change the status of a volunteer to an employee. Payment to a trainee by someone other than the defendant also does not change the volunteer status of a worker with respect to the person who does not pay, even if work is received. The person who pays may nonetheless qualify as an "employer" if other conditions are met. Thus, in one case, a state training program placed a trainee in a company where harassment allegedly occurred; the company was not an employer, but the state could be an employer because trainees were paid while in the program.

The compensation to a worker does not need to be monetary and does not need to be direct to cross the line from volunteer to employee. In *United States v. City of New York*,[26] the United States sued on behalf of participants in New York City's work experience program, a mandatory welfare work program, and alleged racial and sexual harassment. The Second Circuit held that there were sufficient allegations that these workers were "employees" under Title VII because they were required to perform meaningful work for the city, and in exchange received substantial benefits in remuneration for their work, including cash and food stamps, transportation and child care expenses, and eligibility for workers' compensation.

Although the remuneration of a worker need not be monetary, it must be for the benefit of the employer and not the worker. In *York v. Association of the Bar of the City of New York*,[27] an attorney who volunteered at the New York City Bar Association was a volunteer even though she did the work for the purpose of advancing her career. The attorney was involved in several projects involving international environmental law for the association and expected in return the opportunity to network with other attorneys. Her claim was that when she rejected the sexual advances of two men who were powerful in the association, she suffered adversely in her advancement in the association's committee structure and in support for her projects. Although her claim might have

---

26. 359 F.3d 83 (2d Cir. 2004).

27. 286 F.3d 122 (2d Cir.), cert. denied, 537 U.S. 1089, 123 S.Ct. 702, 154 L.Ed.2d 633 (2002).

been cognizable as sexual harassment if she had been an employee, her volunteer status did not change simply because she expected professional advancement from her efforts. Such benefits were incidental to the activity and not compensation sufficient to transform her status.

Prisoners are not ordinarily employees even when they perform compensated work while incarcerated, unless the position particularly passes the economic realities test. Factors relevant to the economic reality test include the extent of the employer's right to control the means and manner of the worker's performance, the availability of leave time, retirement benefits, and the payment of Social Security taxes.

Independent contractors are not "employees" and thus are not covered by the Act. The requirement of an employment relationship also excludes military personnel from coverage under the Act, as distinguished from civilian personnel.

Defining Protected Classes

Title VII proscribes "race" discrimination, which includes members of groups who trace their ancestry to Africa or Asia. The prohibition against "race" discrimination also encompasses indigenous Americans, including Native American Indians, Eskimos, Samoans, and Native Hawaiians.

The Supreme Court held in *McDonald v. Santa Fe Trail Transportation Co.*,[28] that the proscription applies not only to historically excluded "minorities" but to all racial groups. In that case the employer had discharged three Caucasian employees guilty of theft, but retained an African–American employee guilty of the same offense. The Court held that when such unequal treatment of similarly situated employees is premised upon race, it violates the Act.

The prohibition against race discrimination further includes discrimination because of the applicant's or employee's spouse. The most prominent case for this principle is *Parr v. Woodmen of the World Life Insurance Co.*,[29] where the employer unlawfully discriminated against an applicant because of his interracial marriage. The court held that the discrimination was "because of" race within the meaning of the Act and rejected the employer's contention that the discrimination was caused by interracial marriage rather than race. The court reasoned that the adverse employment action was caused by the plaintiff's race because the employer would not have been bothered by the plaintiff's marriage to a black woman if the plaintiff himself had been black rather than white. Therefore, the discrimination was "because of" the plaintiff's race.

Another problem that has arisen under defining protected classes under Title VII concerns the meaning of discrimination on the basis of "sex." Congress did not provide much guidance on its intention with respect to this prohibition; there is virtually no legislative history on the subject. This proscription became part of the Act only because a south-

28. 427 U.S. 273, 96 S.Ct. 2574, 49   **29.** 791 F.2d 888 (11th Cir. 1986).
L.Ed.2d 493 (1976).

ern congressman who opposed the entirety of Title VII added "sex" as an amendment at the last minute in an effort to defeat the entire bill. Congress subsequently provided some additional clarification of the meaning of discrimination on the basis of "sex" when it amended Title VII with the Pregnancy Discrimination Act in 1978. This Act defined discrimination on the basis of "sex" to include pregnancy, childbirth, and related medical conditions.

The concept of national origin is broadly construed under Title VII. In the legislative history to Title VII Congress explained the term to mean the country from which one's forebearers came. The term appears to be synonymous with "ancestry," but a number of state statutes prohibiting discrimination in employment include "ancestry" as a term separate from "national origin."

The Title VII meaning of "national origin" includes the physical, cultural, or linguistic characteristics of a national origin group. An allegation of discrimination on the basis of the plaintiff's Ukrainian roots, therefore, was sufficient to establish a Title VII claim. The concept encompasses claims of discrimination against "hyphenated-American" groups such as Asian–Americans, Polish–Americans, and Italian–Americans. Discrimination on the basis of Spanish surname is discrimination on the basis of national origin. Further, it is not necessary for plaintiffs to allege a "nation" from which "national origin" discrimination can arise; groups such as Gypsies and Cajuns are covered by the concept.

National origin discrimination does not encompass discrimination on the basis of something simply correlated with national origin unless the statistical analysis comports with the requirements for showing the disparate impact of a practice on a group. In *El Deeb v. University of Minnesota*,[30] the Eighth Circuit held that the plaintiff doctor could not withstand summary judgment in a claim for salary discrimination on the basis of national origin by showing a statistical relationship between salary and training in the developing world. Whereas the district court had noted that anyone could be trained in the developing world without regard to national origin, the court of appeals faulted the failure of the analysis to account generally for other variables.

Discrimination on the basis of national origin may sometimes be confounded by race discrimination. The fact that both dimensions are covered by the Act makes the distinction unimportant, such as in a case involving prejudicial behavior by Caucasians against black Africans. In some instances the distinction may be important to establish coverage, such as in a case involving prejudicial behavior by African–Americans against black Africans. *Etefia v. East Baltimore Community Corp.*[31] involved a claim by an African-born male employee who alleged a hostile work environment caused by his African–American female supervisors. They taunted him with the epithet "witch doctor" and made comments

30. 60 F.3d 423 (8th Cir. 1995).   **31.** 2 F.Supp.2d 751 (D.Md. 1998).

referring to Africans as having "sold us into slavery." The court found no difficulty with coverage, but the claim failed on other grounds.

Limitations in Class Definitions

Federal employment discrimination law is deceptively comprehensive. Everyone is potentially covered under a protected dimension, because both genders and all majority and minority racial and ethnic groups, as well as religious groups, are covered by Title VII. This breadth is deceptive, however, because the basis of discrimination must be specifically related to the protected dimension. No one is guaranteed fair treatment on grounds unrelated to the protected dimensions.

One of the notable limitations in coverage is that Title VII's prohibition against discrimination on the basis of "sex" does not include sexual orientation. The legislative history of Title VII does not support the extension of sex discrimination to include homosexuality or sexual disorders. Subsequently, Congress expressly declined to include sexual orientation among protected categories in the Americans with Disabilities Act. The Seventh Circuit has observed that "courts have widely agreed that discrimination based on sexual orientation (actual or perceived), as opposed to sex, is beyond the purview of Title VII." Although there may be a claim of discrimination on the basis of sexual stereotyping, the basis of such a claim must be on the gender-related discrimination rather than on actual or perceived sexual orientation.

A few suits have opened the possibility that discrimination on the basis of sexual orientation may support a claim under 42 U.S.C.A. § 1983 as a violation of equal protection. The Ninth Circuit[32] reversed summary judgment in a suit not involving employment where a plaintiff sought to show a denial of equal protection on the basis that he is a gay man. He claimed that after he openly declared his sexual orientation and thus triggered his separation from the service, the service discriminated against him on the basis of his status when it sought to recoup his medical school costs paid pursuant to the Armed Forces Health Professional Scholarship Program. Recoupment is not automatic when there is separation from service, so the question was the basis on which this discretion was exercised. The case was remanded to determine if the Air Force was directing its policies against a service member based on his status as a homosexual.

The Seventh Circuit held in *Nabozny v. Podlesny*[33] that employment discrimination on the basis of sexual orientation could violate section 1983 if the plaintiff can show intentional differential treatment on the basis of class membership. The court explained that the required discriminatory purpose "implies that a decisionmaker singled out a particular group for disparate treatment and selected his course of action at least in part for the purpose of causing its adverse effects on the identifiable group."

32. Hensala v. Department of Air Force, 343 F.3d 951 (9th Cir. 2003).

33. 92 F.3d 446 (7th Cir. 1996).

Following *Nabozny*, a Washington state court case[34] found that a plaintiff alleged facts that could support a section 1983 employment discrimination claim. A hospital sonographer sued her state employer on the basis that she was fired on the basis of her sexual orientation. She claimed that the decisionmaking doctor had refused to work with her on the grounds that she should not be doing vaginal exams because she is a "[expletive deleted] faggot" and a "queer." The court held that her claim under section 1983 should not have been dismissed. Similarly, in *Lovell v. Comsewogue School District*,[35] a district court upheld the equal protection claim of a school teacher who said that her complaints to the district about harassment by students on the basis of sexual orientation were taken less serious than complaints based on other types of harassment.

In federal employment, bias against individuals on the basis of sexual orientation is now prohibited after former President Clinton amended an executive order to include sexual orientation as a prohibited basis of discrimination in federal employment. There is no judicial enforcement of executive orders, however.

Prohibitions against sexual orientation discrimination in employment with judicial remedies is found in state and local laws in some jurisdictions. One litigated example is the San Francisco ordinance prohibiting discrimination in requiring contractors doing business with city to provide the same benefits to employees with domestic partners as to employees with spouses. The Ninth Circuit found that this local legislation was not a violation of either the federal or state constitutions.[36]

It is also significant that the Title VII protection against discrimination on the basis of national origin does not include the basis of citizenship. The Act thus affords no protection against an employer's decision to exclude lawful aliens because of their citizenship status. Citizenship discrimination is prohibited to a limited extent by the Immigration Reform and Control Act of 1986.

Complainants cannot "bootstrap" coverage of an otherwise unprotected class on the basis that a protected class is adversely affected. For example, discrimination on the basis of sexual orientation is not covered by Title VII, even though the effect of this exclusion disproportionately disadvantages men. The fact that gender discrimination is covered by the Act, coupled with the adverse effect on men, does not overcome the fact that Congress did not intend to cover sexual orientation.

Similarly, discrimination on the basis of citizenship is not covered by the Act, even when the effect is to disadvantage on the basis of national origin. This attempt to bootstrap coverage failed in *Fortino v. Quasar Co.*[37] Judge Posner considered the effect of an American–Japanese treaty

---

34. Miguel v. Guess, 112 Wash.App. 536, 51 P.3d 89 (2002).

35. 214 F.Supp.2d 319 (E.D.N.Y. 2002).

36. S.D. Myers, Inc. v. City & County of San Francisco, 253 F.3d 461 (9th Cir. 2001).

37. 950 F.2d 389 (7th Cir. 1991).

that permits foreign employers to engage managers of its own choosing. Quasar, now an American subsidiary of a Japanese company, fired American managers and replaced them with Japanese nationals. Although the effect of this process was to exclude on the basis of national origin, the plaintiffs could not use this effect to show a violation of Title VII. Judge Posner noted that "in the case of a homogeneous country like Japan, citizenship and national origin are highly correlated," but that "to use this correlation to infer national-origin discrimination from a treaty-sanctioned preference for Japanese citizens who happen also to be of Japanese national origin would nullify the treaty."

§ 2.3 Coverage and Exemptions—Private Employers

Title VII prohibits employers from discriminating on the basis of race, color, religion, sex, or national origin. Section 701(b) of the Act defines "employer" as—"a person engaged in an industry affecting commerce who has fifteen or more employees for each working day in each of twenty or more calendar weeks in the current or preceding calendar year * * *."[1] Similarly, the ADEA prohibits discrimination on the basis of age forty and over and defines an "employer" as—"a person engaged in an industry affecting commerce who has twenty or more employees for each working day in each of twenty or more calendar weeks in the current or preceding calendar year."[2]

The legislative history of the Civil Rights Act of 1964 reflects that the reason for numerical restriction was that Congress did not want to burden small businesses with federal requirements. Title VII was amended in 1972 to reduce the threshold for coverage from twenty-five to fifteen employees. The number fifteen was a compromise; the bills that created the 1972 amendments originally called for a reduction to only eight employees. Opponents of the reduction were concerned about the burden on small businesses, which are often family-run and which usually hire friends and relatives of the same ethnicity as the owner. In contrast, state legislatures have not always been so solicitous of small business, and many of the state fair employment statutes have smaller or no minimum number of employees for coverage.

Numerous issues surround the counting schemes for defining an "employer" under Title VII and the ADEA. This section covers: (1) whether the determination of coverage is a jurisdictional issue or a matter of substantive merits; (2) counting employees for the purpose of satisfying the numerical definition of employer; (3) distinguishing between counting employees for coverage and the standing of an individual to sue under the acts; (4) distinguishing employees from independent contractors; (6) partnership issues; (7) liability of third party employers; and (8) distinguishing exempt non-employment corporate conduct from covered employment-related conduct.

§ 2.3

1. 42 U.S.C.A. § 2000e(b).

2. 29 U.S.C.A.§ 630(b).

The "Employer" Determination: Jurisdictional Question or Merits Inquiry?

A threshold question concerning the definition of employer under the federal antidiscrimination statutes is whether the determination is a matter of subject matter jurisdiction or a question of the substantive merits of the case. The Supreme Court left the issue open on two occasions and the circuits are now split on the issue. The first time that the Supreme Court left the issue unresolved was in *Hishon v. King & Spalding*,[3] where the Court expressly noted that its substantive decision made it unnecessary to consider the district court's conclusion that it lacked subject matter jurisdiction. The issue was a claim of partnership denial in a law firm, which the district court believed not covered by the Act and therefore dismissed as lacking jurisdiction rather than as failing to state a claim. The Supreme Court found the Act did apply to this situation because fair consideration to partnership was a term of the pre-partnership employment.

The second time the Court avoided the question was in *Walters v. Metropolitan Educational Enterprises, Inc.*[4] In this case the Court actually had granted certiorari on the question. The Seventh Circuit had dismissed a Title VII suit for lack of subject matter jurisdiction on the grounds that the defendant company lacked fifteen employees during the relevant period. The Court ultimately concluded that the Seventh Circuit had erred in determining the number of employees, and therefore did not address whether the fifteen-employee requirement is jurisdictional or an element of the merits.

The Third Circuit in *Nesbit v. Gears Unlimited, Inc.*,[5] outlined the significance of the distinction and outlined why it is important as a practical matter whether coverage is characterized as subject matter jurisdiction or a question of substantive merits. In that case the court noted first that subject matter jurisdiction is not waivable, such that courts have an independent obligation to satisfy themselves of jurisdiction and can raise the issue *sua sponte*. Second, supplemental jurisdiction over state claims is possible if the fifteen-employee requirement is not jurisdictional. Third, when a court considers a jurisdictional issue, it is not necessary to view the evidence on the question in a light most favorable to either party. This approach stands in contrast to a motion to dismiss for failure to state a claim which must accept the complaint's allegations as true, or a motion for summary judgment in which the judge must view the evidence in the light most favorable to the non-moving party.

Counting Employees for Purposes of Defining "Employer"

The numerical and temporal requirements for "employer" status under Title VII and the ADEA are often not a simple matter. Each Act

3. 467 U.S. 69, 104 S.Ct. 2229, 81 L.Ed.2d 59 (1984).

4. 519 U.S. 202, 117 S.Ct. 660, 136 L.Ed.2d 644 (1997).

5. 347 F.3d 72 (3d Cir. 2003), cert. denied, ___ U.S. ___, 124 S.Ct. 1714, 158 L.Ed.2d 400 (2004).

requires a certain number of persons be employed "each working day in each of twenty or more calendar weeks in the current or preceding calendar year." For Title VII, the certain number is fifteen and for the ADEA that number is twenty. It is noteworthy that the weeks need not be consecutive, but a week does not count unless the minimum is met each day of the week. The weeks with the minimum number of employees may be cumulated throughout the calendar year. The Acts also provide that an employer that meets this standard in the preceding calendar year is covered even if the standard is not met in the current calendar year.

A dispute arose among the circuit courts concerning the proper way to count "in each working day." Some held that the term meant that the employer had to have the minimum number of workers actually paid on each day, and others held that the employer had to have the minimum number workers on the payroll on each day even if they each did not work. In *Walters v. Metropolitan Educational Enterprises, Inc.*,[6] the Supreme Court held that the "payroll method" is the appropriate way of counting employees for purposes of Title VII coverage. Under the payroll method, the court will look to whether an employee is on the payroll on any particular day and not whether the employee worked and was compensated on that day.

Title VII defines "employee" as "an individual employed by an employer" and the ADEA uses the identical language. As noted above, an "employer" is defined simply as having the requisite number of "employees" in the provided time period, and neither term is clarified further in the Acts. One court has aptly characterized the definition of employee as "magnificently circular"[7] and another has complained that it is a "turn of phrase which chases its own tail."[8]

Because of the inadequacy of the definition of "employee" in the Acts, the decisional law has established some principles. First, everyone who receives compensation from an employer is not necessarily an employee. Corporate directors and managing partners of a partnership, for example, are not employees solely on the basis of these functions, even though the corporate legal entity pays them for their services. Shareholder directors who participate in management decisions also are not employees. High-level managers who were employees, however, do not cease to be employees simply because they also become corporate directors.

A Second Circuit opinion, *Drescher v. Shatkin*,[9] emphasized the importance of looking beyond form to decide who is an employee. The court focused instead on corporate control in order to distinguish true employees from others. The plaintiff in that case worked in a dentist's office which was incorporated and had a sole shareholder, the senior

---

6. 519 U.S. 202, 117 S.Ct. 660, 136 L.Ed.2d 644 (1997).

7. Broussard v. L.H. Bossier, Inc., 789 F.2d 1158, 1160 (5th Cir. 1986).

8. Serapion v. Martinez, 119 F.3d 982, 985 (1st Cir.1997).

9. 280 F.3d 201 (2d Cir. 2002).

dentist. The worker sued under Title VII for sexual harassment perpetrated by one of the other dentists, who was a son of the sole shareholder. She had complained to the father about the son's persistent sexual behavior and he allegedly ignored her. Her claim for harassment against the employer depended upon a finding that the father was also an employee in order to meet the statutory minimum of fifteen employees. The Second Circuit held that this sole shareholder of the professional corporation was not an "employee" despite his performance of traditional employee duties and despite the possible characterization of him as an agent of the corporation. His dominant position in managing the firm was the most significant factor in removing him from the count. He was president, sole director, and sole shareholder of the corporation. Unlike someone who is only one director among many, the court noted, he had absolute power to change corporate policy because he was the sole director. He was thus not an "employee" for purposes of determining whether the corporation was subject to Title VII.

The cases have developed several other principles in defining and counting employees. First, all employees of the employer's legal entity will be counted toward the minimum number, not just those in the particular department or branch where the discrimination took place. Furthermore, the plaintiff can amalgamate the number of employees of two or more distinct legal entities if they qualify as joint employers. The requirements are common ownership, unified control over both entities, an integrated economic relationship, and a common or centralized labor relations policy.

In order for an individual to count as an employee for purposes of defining employer, the relationship between that individual and the employer must be one of actual employment. For example, a circuit court declined to find an employment relationship between the Women's Professional Rodeo Association (WPRA) and its members. A male aspirant for membership thus could not use Title VII to challenge the WPRA's exclusivity on the basis of gender.[10] The court found that the relationship was not one of employment because the association does not pay its members nor do the members perform services for the association; the nonprofit organization simply sanctions rodeo barrel races and facilitates participation by its members. Without counting the WPRA members as employees, the defendant did not employ the requisite fifteen individuals for coverage under the Act for any purpose.

The limitation to "employment" relationships is not necessarily required by Title VII or the ADEA, but courts have found such a limitation consistent with the overall structure and purpose of the Acts. The literal language prohibits discrimination against "any individual" but limits the prohibited conduct to employment related matters. Because of the context, courts have been unanimous in the conclusion that

---

10.   Graves v. Women's Professional Rodeo Ass'n, 907 F.2d 71 (8th Cir.1990).

Title VII "is directed at, and only protects, employees and potential employees."[11]

Counting Employees for Coverage versus Standing to Sue

Counting employees for the purpose of establishing the statutory minimum under Title VII and the ADEA is distinguishable from the issue of whether a worker has standing as an employee to sue for discrimination. Some employees who do not count for coverage nonetheless have standing to sue, and some employees who are not covered by the act because of an exemption may nonetheless count toward the minimum for coverage.

First, part-time workers do not count toward the minimum fifteen employees necessary for coverage, but once the employer reaches the minimum for coverage, all employees are protected by the substantive provisions of the Act. It is not necessary to be a "counted" employee in order to have standing to complain of unlawful discrimination. Moreover, because the statute says that twenty weeks of fifteen employees in the *previous* calendar year suffices for coverage, the employer is covered by Title VII for a year after meeting the minimum, even if the employer reduces the work force.

Courts have had more difficulty with the second issue of whether employees who cannot sue under the acts because of some exemption may nonetheless count for purposes of coverage. For example, consider an employer that has both exempt and nonexempt employees, such as a foreign corporation in the United States employing both foreign nationals covered by a treaty as well as domestic workers. The employer's relationship with the foreign nationals in this situation is exempt from federal antidiscrimination law, but not the relationship with the domestic workers if the acts otherwise apply. The question is who counts as an "employee" for purposes of federal antidiscrimination law.

Do foreign employees count toward the minimum for statutory coverage? This issue first surfaced in the 1990s and some early opinions assumed that foreign employees overseas could not be counted even if they might count if they worked in the United States. The leading case holding that foreign employees working overseas could count toward the minimum is *Morelli v. Cedel*.[12] Although *Morelli* has developed a following, it has also attracted criticism. The Ninth Circuit followed the reasoning of *Morelli* in a Title VII case, *Kang v. U. Lim America, Inc.*[13] The foreign employer in *Kang* had only six employees in the United States, but numerous ones in Mexico. The majority agreed with *Morelli* but a strong dissent by Judge Fernandez questions the very premise of the Second Circuit opinion. He argued that because Title VII expressly provides coverage for an individual who is a citizen of the United States working abroad, it must mean that "it does not include 'an individual who is [not] a citizen of the United States,' working abroad. Each

---

11. Serapion v. Martinez, 119 F.3d 982   **13.** 296 F.3d 810 (9th Cir.2002).
(1st Cir. 1997).

12. 141 F.3d 39 (2d Cir.1998).

instance is encompassed by the hypostasis of that old rule of construction (rather than of logic): inclusio unius est exclusio alterias.''

Employees versus Independent Contractors

Independent contractors are not covered by Title VII and the ADEA. The Acts specifically refer to "employment" opportunities which would seemingly apply to everyone providing services for pay to employers. The problem is that the relationship between such workers and the employer is a contractual one to provide services rather than to provide employment. The distinction is often elusive.

Courts have adopted three tests for determining whether an individual is an employee: (1) the common law agency test; (2) the economic realities test; and (3) the hybrid test, a combination of the common law agency and economic realities tests. Although the matter is not free from doubt, it appears that the common law agency test is the current trend. Those circuits that still adhere to the other tests have made a point to indicate that their alternative tests are consistent with the agency test, indicating the preeminency of that test in federal antidiscrimination law.

The agency test relies upon common law principles of agency to determine the status of a worker. The Supreme Court approved this test in a case involving the interpretation of a similarly circular definition of employer and employee in ERISA.[14] In *Nationwide Mutual Insurance Co. v. Darden*,[15] the Court held that Congress was presumed to intend the conventional master-servant relationship as understood at common law. The Court explained that the common law test involves the hiring party's right to control the manner and means by which the product is accomplished. The relevant factors are the skill required, the source of the instrumentalities and tools, the location of the work, the duration of the relationship between the parties, whether the hiring party has the right to assign additional projects to the hired party, the extent of the hired party's discretion over when and how long to work, the method of payment, the hired party's role in hiring and paying assistants, whether the work is part of the regular business of the hiring party, whether the hiring party is in business, the provision of employee benefits, and the tax treatment of the hired party. The Court stressed that the common law test requires assessment of all aspects of the relationship; no one factor is decisive.

The economic realities test was originally designed to be more expansive than the common law agency test. The Supreme Court first adopted this test in the context of the Fair Labor Standards Act in order to further the purpose of the Act. The Court's retreat from this test in *Darden* was occasioned in part by congressional disapproval of a similarly expansive reading under the National Labor Relations Act. *Darden*, an

---

14. 29 U.S.C.A. § 1002(6).

15. 503 U.S. 318, 112 S.Ct. 1344, 117 L.Ed.2d 581 (1992).

ERISA case, does not control the antidiscrimination statutes, but it has been persuasive in the circuits.

Under current interpretation, the economic realities test focuses upon factors such as who furnishes the equipment, the duration of employment, the availability of leave, the accumulation of retirement benefits, the payment of Social Security taxes, and the intention of the parties. The key factor is the extent of the employer's right to control the means and manner of the worker's performance. The difference between this test as it is currently formulated and the agency test in *Darden* is slight, and at least one court has found no substantive conflict between the two.

The Seventh Circuit also has attempted to reconcile *Darden* with its longstanding use of the economic realities test. In *Alexander v. Rush North Shore Medical Center*,[16] that circuit concluded that the *Darden* factors were all subsumed within the five-factor economic realities analysis previously adopted. Those five factors are: (1) the extent of the employer's control and supervision over the worker, including directions on scheduling and performance of work; (2) the kind of occupation and nature of skill required, including whether skills are obtained in the workplace; (3) the responsibility for the costs of operation, such as equipment, supplies, fees, licenses, workplace, and maintenance operations; (4) the method and form of payment and benefits; and (5) the length of job commitment and/or expectations. The Seventh Circuit now calls this test the "functional" economic realities test.

The hybrid test is a combination of the agency test and the economic realities test. It takes into consideration traditional common law agency principles and combines them with economic tests like employee benefits and tax treatments. Because the Supreme Court mentioned some economic realities in its list of factors purporting to be common law agency principles, it is arguable that the Supreme Court's test is in reality a hybrid test more than a traditional common law agency test. The Eighth Circuit, which had expressly repudiated the economic realities test before *Darden*, made the observation that there is no significant difference between the test articulated in *Darden* and the hybrid test. That circuit observed in *Wilde v. County of Kandiyohi*[17] that "by adding employee benefit and tax treatment factors to the Restatement factors in its explanation of the common-law test, the Supreme Court recognized the common-law test encompasses economic factors." In subsequent application, that circuit court applied the *Darden* factors and focused on length of service and regular course of business. Finding the factual question a close one, the court permitted the issue to go to the jury rather than deciding the issue as a matter of law.[18]

16. 101 F.3d 487 (7th Cir.1996).

17. 15 F.3d 103 (8th Cir.1994).

18. Jenkins v. Southern Farm Bureau Casualty, 307 F.3d 741 (8th Cir.2002).

The Supreme Court has indicated in dicta that *Darden* applies to the antidiscrimination acts.[19] The Court has also clarified in an earlier opinion that reference to common law principles is not a license to apply the differing common law among the states, but rather "general common law principles" independent of any particular state.

Employees versus Partners

Title VII and the ADEA are limited to employer-employee relations and exclude entrepreneurial decisions such as the initial formation of a partnership or professional corporation. Although initial formation is clearly not covered by antidiscrimination law, more difficult has been the question whether the Acts cover related partnership issues.

One partnership question is whether Title VII and the ADEA cover the alteration of established entities. When they break up and reorganize, can a discriminatory exclusion of some partners be actionable? The First Circuit has taken a bold lead on this subject in *Serapion v. Martinez*.[20] The plaintiff in this case claimed gender discrimination motivated the break-up of a law partnership in which she was a partner with a much smaller equity interest than the name partners. She alleged that the firm broke up and reformed without her in order to avoid honoring an agreement that she would eventually achieve parity. The First Circuit concluded that courts must make a case-by-case determination of whether the circumstances of the plaintiff's position bears a close enough resemblance to that of an employee to enjoy the protections of Title VII. Drawing upon the cases that consider whether an individual is an employee or independent contractor, the panel found that the plaintiff's degree of ownership, method of compensation, and participation in governance indicated that she did not have employee status and therefore no claim under Title VII.

A second question concerns an individual's change in status from an employee to a partner presents related issues. The issue is whether the Act applies to the promotion of associates to partnership. The Supreme Court resolved that question only in part in its 1984 decision in *Hishon v. King & Spalding*.[21] In that case the firm had included as a term of employment for associates the promise of consideration for partnership. The Court reasoned that because the evaluation for partnership was a term of employment for the associate, it was therefore a term of employment within the meaning of Title VII. The evaluation therefore must be free of gender bias to comply with the proscription of the Act. The case left unresolved whether Title VII covers partnership decisions in other contexts, but in a subsequent partnership case the Court cited *Hishon* for the proposition that "decisions pertaining to advancement to a partnership are, of course, subject to challenge under Title VII." This dictum strongly suggests that promotion to partnership is always covered by the Act and that *Hishon* was an example of the rule of coverage

---

19. Walters v. Metropolitan Educ. Enter., Inc., 519 U.S. 202, 117 S.Ct. 660, 136 L.Ed.2d 644 (1997).

20. 119 F.3d 982 (1st Cir.1997).

21. 467 U.S. 69, 104 S.Ct. 2229, 81 L.Ed.2d 59 (1984).

rather than an exception to a rule of noncoverage. The issue nonetheless remains unresolved.

Liability of Third Party Employers

The requirement that the discriminatory conduct relate to "employment" for coverage under federal antidiscrimination acts has presented a question with respect to third party employers. The issue is whether a plaintiff who is employed by Employer X can sue Employer Y for interfering with employment conditions. The language of the Act would suggest that it is not necessary for the employee to be working for the defendant employer, and most of the circuits to consider the issue have permitted an action.

The leading case is *Sibley Memorial Hospital v. Wilson*,[22] which held that the employment relationship does not necessarily have to be a direct one as long as there is an employment relationship with someone. The exception is independent contractors, who are not "employed" by anyone except themselves. In *Sibley*, the defendant was a hospital that ran a nursing office to assist placement of private nurses for patients who requested them. These private nurses were employees of the patient, not the hospital. The plaintiff was a male private nurse who alleged that upon arrival at the hospital, he was sent away more than once by supervisory nurses who worked for the hospital on the grounds that he was male and the patients were female. The hospital objected to the lack of an employer-employee relationship but the court held that Title VII does not explicitly require a direct employment relationship as long as there is some employment relationship involved. The court noted that the Act covers labor unions and employment agencies, which are "institutions which have not a remote but a highly visible nexus with the creation and continuance of direct employment relationships between third parties." The relationship of the hospital was similar and "its daily operations are of such a character as to have such a nexus to the third parties in this case."[23]

Most courts that have considered the issue have followed the *Sibley* approach, but the issue is an open one. In *King v. Chrysler Corp.*,[24] for example, the plaintiff was a cafeteria worker employed by an independent contractor in the Chrysler plant. She sued for the sexual harassment by one of Chrysler's employees and Chrysler moved for summary judgment on the grounds that it had no employment relationship with the plaintiff. The court rejected this argument and held that although the Act protects only interference with employment, the parties need not have an employment relationship themselves.

Non-Employment versus Employment–Related Conduct

Corporate decisions that do not involve employment are not within the scope of Title VII and the ADEA. Such decisions include the selection

22. 488 F.2d 1338 (D.C. Cir.1973).

23. 488 F.2d at 1344.

24. 812 F.Supp. 151 (E.D.Mo.1993).

of corporate directors and the determination of eligibility to purchase stock.

Federal antidiscrimination law is applicable, however, if such decisions relate to employment. For example, stock allocation can be related to employment if it is allocated as part of compensation to employees. In such a situation, a discriminatory allocation may violate Title VII or the ADEA. Similarly, an employer may not grant preferences to stockholder employees in terms of hiring, salary, job assignments, and promotion.[25] It is not the naked corporate act of governance that is itself exempt. The question is always whether the act relates to hiring and firing employees or other "terms, conditions, or privileges of employment" on the basis of race, color, national origin, gender, religion, or age.

§ 2.4 Coverage and Exemptions—Unions and Employment Agencies

Unions

Title VII[1] and the ADEA[2] impose obligations on labor organizations even if the organization itself does not employ enough employees to be an "employer" within the meaning of the Acts. A "labor organization" is defined by the aggregate number of its members and by its purpose of dealing in whole or in part with employers concerning grievances, labor disputes, wages, rates of pay, hours, or other terms or conditions of employment. Under Title VII the minimum aggregate number of members is twenty-five. The ADEA uses the same number for unions after the effective date of the Act in 1968 and fifty is the number before that date. Small labor organizations with fewer than the required number of members are not covered unless they are covered separately as "employers" under the Acts.

Section 703(c) of Title VII specifically addresses the obligations of labor organizations. The Act makes unlawful the following actions on the basis of an individual's race, color, religion, sex, or national origin: (1) excluding or expelling from membership; (2) limiting, segregating, or classifying its members or applicants for membership, and failing or refusing to refer for employment any member; and (3) causing or attempting to cause an employer to discriminate. The ADEA prohibits the same actions by a union on the basis of age for individuals who are forty and over. Section 703(d) of Title VII prohibits discrimination on the same grounds in training programs, including apprenticeship and on-the-job training programs. There is no equivalent provision in the ADEA.

These provisions convey the two-fold obligations of labor organizations, both internal and external. Internally, the union cannot discriminate in admissions, dues, facilities, allocation of union offices, and so

25. Bonilla v. Oakland Scavenger Co., 697 F.2d 1297 (9th Cir. 1982).

2. 29 U.S.C.A. § 630(d).

§ 2.4

1. 42 U.S.C.A. 2000e(d).

forth. A union's internal obligation is violated when it segregates its membership according to race, color, religion, national origin, or gender, even if there is no direct economic consequence resulting from the segregation. Externally the union cannot discriminate in its referrals and other relations with employers. The Supreme Court held in *Goodman v. Lukens Steel Co.*[3] that a union's external obligation included the obligation to process employees' grievances against the employer in a nondiscriminatory manner. The union, which failed to process grievances of race discrimination against the employer, could not defend on the ground that its actions were intended for strategic advantage on other issues that would benefit all employees.

It is also noteworthy that a plaintiff has standing under these provisions even in the absence of union membership. A union certified or lawfully recognized to represent exclusively all employees in a bargaining unit must meet its obligations to all employees represented by the union. A union further has a duty of fair representation imposed upon it by the labor relations statutes. That duty obligates the union to represent all workers in the bargaining unit over which it exercises exclusive bargaining rights "without hostile discrimination, fairly, impartially, and in good faith."[4]

Goodman left open the question of whether a union is required to take affirmative steps to oppose an employer's discriminatory practices. The Court of Appeals had held that Title VII imposed an affirmative duty to combat discrimination by an employer with which the union had an exclusive bargaining relationship. The Supreme Court declined to address this broader obligation and affirmed on the narrower ground of the union's obligation to process grievances in a nondiscriminatory manner.

The affirmative obligation of the union is clearer when an employer and union are engaged in a joint operation such as a training program. Section 703(d) of Title VII prohibits discrimination in training programs, including joint labor-management apprenticeship training programs. The failure of a union to monitor a joint apprenticeship committee or to police discrimination practiced by employers that employ journeymen referred to them as part of the apprenticeship training program, is a violation of the Act.

When the union and the employer jointly violate the Act, they can be jointly and severally liable. Neither is an indispensable party, and both can be held liable for the full amount of the plaintiff's recovery. There is no right of contribution between the employer and the union because none is provided for in the Act, and the Supreme Court has declined to find such an implied right in the statutory scheme.[5]

---

3. 482 U.S. 656, 107 S.Ct. 2617, 96 L.Ed.2d 572 (1987).

4. Steele v. Louisville & N.R.R., 323 U.S. 192, 65 S.Ct. 226, 89 L.Ed. 173 (1944).

5. Northwest Airlines v. Transport Workers Union, 451 U.S. 77, 101 S.Ct. 1571, 67 L.Ed.2d 750 (1981).

An international union may be liable for the acts of a local union either on a theory of agency or on the basis that the international union has an affirmative duty to oppose discrimination when it knew or should have known of the activities of a local. Liability can be premised on the theory that the international should have known about the hiring practices of the local and its "overall picture."

Under Title VII a union may be liable for discriminatory referrals by its agents and for harassment that creates a hostile environment in the union. In *Daniels v. Pipefitters' Ass'n Local 597,*[6] for example, the union was liable under both theories of intentional racial discrimination and for the disparate impact of its referral practices. The Seventh Circuit held that its refusal to provide referrals for the plaintiff was racially motivated and that the plaintiff's expulsion for fighting following a sham hearing was racially motivated retaliation for protesting the union's racial practices. The union was also liable under Title VII for the racially hostile environment in the union. The hostile environment was created by racial epithets that pervaded the hiring hall and by comments such as those of one union official who complained about union activism by black members because "this has been a white man's union."[7]

In addition to these claims of intentional discrimination, the plaintiff in *Daniels* also established Title VII liability under a disparate impact theory. The statistical expert established that the referral practices adversely affected the plaintiff's group. In one year black members received only fourteen percent of the referrals even though thirty to fifty percent of the union members were black. The probability of such a low number of referrals to black members by chance alone was less than one in a trillion.

Unions may also be liable under Title VII for a failure to make reasonable accommodation of a member's religion. In *EEOC v. Union Independiente de la Autoridad de Acueductos y Alcantarillados de Puerto Rico,*[8] the plaintiff was a Seventh–Day Adventist who objected to union membership because of his personal interpretation of religious commands. The court observed that the obligation to accommodate religion under Title VII reads literally to cover only "employers" but noted further that courts have uniformly imposed the same duty upon labor organizations the same duty to be consistent with the purposes of the Act.

Employment Agencies

Title VII[9] expressly covers discrimination on the basis of race, color, religion, sex, or national origin by employment agencies, and the ADEA[10] similarly protects individuals age forty and over from discrimination by employment agencies. Agencies may not discriminate in job referrals in the same way that employers are prohibited from discrimination in

---

6. 945 F.2d 906 (7th Cir.1991).

7. 945 F.2d at 910.

8. 279 F.3d 49 (1st Cir. 2002).

9. 42 U.S.C.A. § 2000e(b). For a further discussion of employment agencies see § 2.3.

10. 29 U.S.C.A. § 623(b).

hiring. Employers may not request discriminatory referrals, and agencies may not honor such requests.

Both Title VII and the ADEA define the term employment agency: "The term 'employment agency' means any person regularly undertaking with or without compensation to procure employees for an employer * * * and includes an agent of such a person." The number of employees at the agency and the volume of business of the agency are not material in the definition. Coverage is based upon "regularly undertaking" the procurement of "employees" for "employers." Each of these terms has presented difficulties in interpretation. For example, an agency that operates a service to place nurses with out-patients who need private nursing in their homes is not covered by the Act as an "employment agency" because the employer to whom the employees are sent is not an "employer" covered by the Act. The size of the agency's business does not control; it is the size of the employer's work force that controls. Once an agency is covered by procuring employees for any employer of sufficient size, however, then the agency is covered for all purposes. It cannot then make discriminatory referrals to anyone, even employers that are too small to be themselves in violation of the Act by requesting a discriminatory referral.

A newspaper is not an "employment agency" if it simply prints advertisements from employers in a "Help Wanted" section. An employment agency or employer covered by the Act cannot publish discriminatory advertisements, however. Section 704(b) provides that it is an unlawful employment practice for "an employer, labor organization, or employment agency to print or publish, or cause to be printed or published, any notice or advertisement relating to employment * * * or relating to any classification or referral for employment by such an employment agency, indicating any preference, limitation, specification, or discrimination" on the basis of race, color, religion, sex, or national origin.

An educational institution, such as a college or a technical school, is an "employment agency" if it has a placement office. Its obligation under the Act is to refrain from discriminatory referrals. There is no affirmative obligation to monitor the practices of employers that recruit on campus, although many such institutions do so voluntarily.

It is clear that an agency has a duty to refrain from discriminatory referrals, but one problem is how the agency should distinguish between a legitimate request for limited referrals as opposed to an unlawful one. For example, an employer that wishes to interview only women for an acting role for a woman is legally permitted to do so under the defense of "bona fide occupational qualification."[11] How can an agency distinguish between a lawful request for an employee defined by national origin or gender and an unlawful request that is facially discriminatory? The EEOC Guidelines say that the agency should receive such requests in

---

11. See § 2.18.

written form for evaluation, and if they appear reasonable, the agency itself is protected.

§ 2.5 Coverage and Exemptions—Public Employers

State and Local Government Employers—Sovereign Immunity Issues

The employment decisions of state and local governments are covered by section 701(a) of Title VII[1] if these employers otherwise meet the statutory minimum of fifteen employees. These employers were excluded from coverage when the Act was originally passed in 1964, but Congress extended Title VII to state and local governments in the Equal Employment Opportunity Act of 1972. Before that time employment discrimination claims under federal statutory law against such employers could be brought only under the Reconstruction Era Civil Rights Acts.[2] The Supreme Court has found constitutional the extension of the Act to state and local governments and the authorization of suits against state agencies. It held in *Fitzpatrick v. Bitzer*,[3] that the extension was a proper exercise of congressional power under the Fourteenth Amendment and that the Eleventh Amendment does not prohibit the award of back pay and attorneys' fees against state employers.

Since its holding in *Bitzer*, the Supreme Court has refined its analysis of congressional powers under Section 5 of the Fourteenth Amendment. Most notably, the Supreme Court held in *Kimel v. Florida Board of Regents*[4] that Congress exceeded its power under Section 5 when it applied the Age Discrimination in Employment Act to the states. Therefore, claimants of age discrimination may no longer sue state employers under federal law. Although congressional power to apply the ADEA to the states had previously been acceptably premised on its Commerce Clause power, the Supreme Court's opinion in *Seminole Tribe v. Florida*[5] held that Congress lacks power under Article I to abrogate state sovereign immunity granted by the Eleventh Amendment.

Kimel explained that Congress cannot enact legislation under Section 5 that permits suits against states unless, first, Congress makes it unmistakably clear that it intends to do so. Although the ADEA satisfied this test, it failed the next prong of the analysis as "appropriate legislation" under Section 5.[6] The Court held that in order for legislation to be appropriate it must pass the "congruence and proportionality" test between "the injury to be prevented or remedied and the means adopted to that end." The Court in *Kimel* concluded that the ADEA fails this test because the legislative record suggested that extension of the Act to the states was an unwarranted response. It was unwarranted because Con-

§ 2.5

1. 42 U.S.C.A. § 2000e(a).

2. See § 2.40.

3. 427 U.S. 445, 96 S.Ct. 2666, 49 L.Ed.2d 614 (1976).

4. 528 U.S. 62, 120 S.Ct. 631, 145 L.Ed.2d 522 (2000).

5. 517 U.S. 44, 116 S.Ct. 1114, 134 L.Ed.2d 252 (1996).

6. Section 5 of the Fourteenth Amendment provides Congress with the power to enforce the Amendment with appropriate legislation. U.S. Const. Amend. 14.

gress did not identify a pattern of age discrimination by the states that amounted to a constitutional violation.

Lower courts have struggled since *Kimel* to understand its application to other federal statutes that permit suits against states. It appears not to affect the ability of claimants to sue states under Title VII, at least with respect to claims for discrimination on the basis of race and gender, because the Supreme Court in *Kimel* distinguished age classifications as "unlike governmental conduct based on race or gender." The opinion notes that these groups enjoy greater status under the Fourteenth Amendment, and therefore when states discriminate on these grounds there is "a tighter fit between the discriminatory means and the legitimate ends they serve." The Court's activism in this area leaves it ripe for further developments.

State and Local Government Employers—Statutory Exemptions

Before the Civil Rights Act of 1991, there was a Title VII exemption for employment decisions affecting three groups of officials appointed to assist elected officials: personal staff, immediate legal advisers, and policy-making assistants. Their exemption in section 701(f) meant that they could be appointed or fired without the protection of the Act. Moreover, these employees did not count toward the statutory minimum number of fifteen necessary for the Act's coverage. The Government Employees Rights Act of 1991, enacted as a part of the Civil Rights Act of 1991,[7] extended the coverage of the Act to all except elected officials. Therefore, personal staff, legal advisers, and all assistants are now protected under Title VII. Under section 321 of the Act they can file complaints with the EEOC for agency review.

The Act provides for special procedures and limited remedies for complainants under section 321. The procedures are unlike those for other complainants under Title VII. Under section 321 the EEOC has the power to provide for relief when it determines a violation has occurred.

Review is to a federal court of appeals which can set aside the award if it is: (1) arbitrary, capricious, an abuse of discretion or not consistent with law; (2) not made according to the required procedures; or (3) unsupported by substantial evidence. This provision is a dramatic departure from Title VII procedure, which provides for de novo review in federal district court.

Section 321 of the Government Employees Rights Act further provides that where state or local law prohibits the practice alleged to be discriminatory, and where an enforcing authority exists, the EEOC must not act until it has notified the authority and given it sixty days to remedy the complaint. Finally, section 321 provides for remedies like those accorded to other Title VII plaintiffs except that punitive damages are not allowed.

7. P.L. 102–166, 105 Stat. 1071.

Federal Government—Generally

Title VII[8] and the ADEA[9] cover federal employees. When Title VII was originally enacted it did not provide coverage for any public employers, including the federal government. The 1972 amendments to the Act extended the definition of employer to include state and local employers, but these amendments provided different coverage for federal employees. Title VII provides that its coverage of employers does not include the federal government or corporations wholly owned by the United States government. Although the federal government is not covered in the main body of Title VII, section 717 of the Act, as amended in 1972, provides substantive protection.

Employees bringing Title VII and ADEA suits against the federal government as employer must meet the requirement that there be an adverse employment action, like their counterparts in the private sector, although the statutory basis of the requirement is different. One court[10] has held that the language of section 717 creates the basis for the requirement because the federal claimant must be "aggrieved" in order to bring an action. It therefore applied the same standards applied in actions under section 703 and concluded that a lateral transfer was not an actionable injury unless the employee could show that it affected the terms, conditions, or privileges of her employment. The court noted that mere idiosyncrasies of personal preference are insufficient to demonstrate an adverse employment action, even when the employer is aware of the preference.

Federal Government—Procedures

The primary difference between complaints against a federal employer and other employers covered by Title VII and the ADA is in the enforcement procedures. The employing federal agency has the primary responsibility for hearing complaints of discrimination against it because the procedural philosophy is to encourage resolution of the dispute within the agency itself. Therefore, prior to filing a formal complaint, an aggrieved person must file an informal complaint with the EEO counselor of the employer agency within forty-five days of the alleged act of discrimination or of the effective date of the challenged personnel action. If the counselor fails to resolve the complaint, the employee may file a more formal charge. After an investigation, an investigator makes a recommendation. If the complainant demands a hearing, one is then held before an administrative hearing officer. Those findings are reviewed by the head of the agency to make a final determination. If the charging party is dissatisfied with the final determination, further appeals to the EEOC and to court are available.

Prior to the inclusion of federal employees in Title VII and the ADEA, the Civil Service Commission had jurisdiction over the complaints filed against agencies. This jurisdiction was transferred to the

8. 42 U.S.C.A. § 717.
9. 29 U.S.C.A. § 633a(a).
10. Brown v. Brody, 199 F.3d 446 (D.C.Cir.1999).

EEOC, whose regulations for federal employees are substantially identical to the former Civil Service Commission procedural regulations, with increasing emphasis on alternative dispute resolution.

Federal Government—Congressional Accountability Act

In 1995, Congress enacted the Congressional Accountability Act,[11] also known as the Shays Act, to apply eleven employment laws to Congress. Those laws include: Title VII of the Civil Rights Act of 1964, the Age Discrimination in Employment Act, the Americans with Disabilities Act, the Fair Labor Standards Act of 1938, and the Family and Medical Leave Act of 1993. Covered employers include the House of Representatives, the Senate, the Capitol Police, the Congressional Budget Office, and the Office of the Architect of the Capitol.

The Act requires counseling and mediation of claims before more formal resolution. It also creates a new Office of Compliance for enforcement. Appeals from hearings may go to a new Board of Directors for this Office. Judicial review goes to the Federal Circuit. Alternatively, a complainant may sue in federal district court after completing the counseling and mediation requirements.

The Act also directed the Judicial Conference to study and report to Congress on the application to the judicial branch of a variety of labor and employment laws, including Title VII. The result was the Model Employment Dispute Resolution Plan ("Model EDR Plan") adopted by the Judicial Conference of the United States. The Model EDR Plan approved by the Judicial Conference recommends rights and protections for employees of the United States courts which are comparable to those provided to legislative branch employees under the Congressional Accountability Act of 1995.

Federal Government—Military

Title VII does not cover the relationship of the military to its uniformed military personnel because that relationship is not one of "employment." Issues involving the recruitment, enlistment, pay, discipline, discharge, or harassment of uniformed military personnel are thus beyond the scope of the Act. Civilian employees of the military are distinguishable and the military is not exempt from Title VII with respect to these employees.

Title VII's coverage of civilian personnel employed by the military includes an individual in a hybrid military-civilian position unless the challenged employment action is integrally related to the military's unique structure. In one case,[12] an Hispanic technician in the National Guard could not invoke Title VII's prohibition against retaliation because the allegedly retaliatory act was the denial of a military promotion. In order to hold his civilian position the technician was required to hold the commensurate military position. The decision not to promote him as

---

11. 2 U.S.C.A. §§ 1301 et seq.   **12.** Mier v. Owens, 57 F.3d 747 (9th Cir.1995).

an officer was an inherently military decision, even though the officer would not be on active duty.

§ 2.6 Intentional Discrimination

Title VII and the ADEA together provide that it is an unlawful employment practice for an "employer" "to discriminate against any individual" on the basis of race, color, religion, sex, national origin, or age forty and over.[1] The Act does not define the word "discriminate," so that task has been left to the courts.[2] Although violations of the Acts need not be intentional, an employment action premised upon an individual's race, color, religion, sex, national origin, or age is unlawful in the absence of a defense.

An individual claim of intentional discrimination requires proof that an employer-defendant failed to treat the individual plaintiff the same as other applicants or employees *because of* race, color, religion, sex, national origin, or age.[3] These claims of motivated discrimination are known as "disparate treatment" claims under Title VII. The controlling question of fact is the motivation of the employer.

The same analysis of intentional discrimination governs claims of race or ethnicity discrimination under 42 U.S.C.A. § 1981.[4] Unlike Title VII, however, proof of intentional conduct is always necessary to prevail in a claim under section 1981. In contrast, under Title VII a plaintiff who fails to establish intentional discrimination still may attempt to establish disparate impact discrimination.[5] Under the ADEA the circuits are split as to whether it is always necessary to establish intentional conduct or whether disparate impact claims are also permitted.

Discriminatory Animus in General

The meaning of intentional discrimination in employment is not defined in the federal acts, but the caselaw has established that the ordinary meaning of words like "discrimination" and "prejudice" is broader than the statutory coverage. For example, the Tenth Circuit has held that a jury's reliance on the dictionary definitions of these words was prejudicial to the defendant and supported a new trial.[6] The plaintiff in that case alleged intentional discrimination and retaliation as a result of her complaints of racial discrimination. The claims were brought under both Title VII and section 1981 and the case was tried before a jury. A handwritten note in the jury room revealed that the jury had improperly relied upon dictionary definitions, rather than legal definitions, of prejudice and discrimination.

§ 2.6

1. 42 U.S.C.A. § 2000e–2(a); 29 U.S.C.A. § 623(a).

2. See Owen M. Fiss, *A Theory of Fair Employment Laws*, 38 U. Chi. L. Rev. 235 (1971).

3. Furnco Constr. Corp. v. Waters, 438 U.S. 567, 577, 98 S.Ct. 2943, 2949, 57 L.Ed.2d 957 (1978).

4. See § 2.40.

5. See § 2.21.

6. Mayhue v. St. Francis Hosp., 969 F.2d 919 (10th Cir.1992).

The dictionary definition of prejudice used by the jury was "an opinion formed without taking time and care to judge fairly * * *." The definition of discrimination was "to make or see a difference." Both of these definitions were improper because they focused upon a mental process rather than action. Further, the dictionary definition of "discriminate" was overly broad and did not accurately reflect the law because it focused upon difference in treatment rather than the *basis* of differential treatment. A claim of intentional employment discrimination under federal law requires that the plaintiff suffer from an adverse employment decision on the basis of a prohibited consideration.

The Supreme Court had occasion to consider one aspect of the meaning of intentional conduct in *Personnel Administrator v. Feeney*.[7] In *Feeney*, the issue was a state statutory scheme that created a preference for veterans in employment. The foreseeable effect of the preference was to disadvantage women because veterans are disproportionately male. Applying constitutional analysis, the lower court said that the effect was so obvious that the legislature must have intended the result, but the Supreme Court disagreed. Intent means doing something because of, not in spite of, a particular consequence.

Similarly, a challenge to a teacher competency test failed to establish that the cutoff score was set intentionally to discriminate against African–Americans because the commissioner already knew the impact of the cutoff on the group.[8] The court noted that over ninety-five percent of the African–American teachers passed the test even with the challenged cutoff point and thus it was not credible that the purpose of the commissioner's action was to exclude teachers on the basis of race.

Adverse Employment Actions

In addition to demonstrating that the challenged conduct was intentionally discriminatory, plaintiffs must also establish that the conduct affected them with respect to some aspect of employment. Discriminatory animus that does not manifest itself in any way related to employment opportunity is not covered by Title VII or the ADEA.

The evidence of animus must bear upon the adverse employment decision that is the subject of the plaintiff's complaint. It is not sufficient to show unrelated animus. For example, in an age discrimination claim the plaintiff sought unsuccessfully to prove her case through management conversations expressing the philosophy that older workers should be replaced with younger ones. Her case failed because she did not establish any connection between these discussions and the adverse employment decision in her case.[9]

Plaintiffs have also failed to establish a causal connection between animus and action when the animus is reflected by someone who is not

---

7. 442 U.S. 256, 99 S.Ct. 2282, 60 L.Ed.2d 870 (1979).

8. Frazier v. Garrison I.S.D., 980 F.2d 1514 (5th Cir.1993).

9. Henson v. Liggett Group, Inc., 61 F.3d 270 (4th Cir.1995).

the decision maker. For example, a plaintiff alleging religious discrimination failed to satisfy the causation requirement because he could not establish any connection between his religion and his discharge two months after he had missed some important meetings in order to celebrate the Jewish holidays of Rosh Hashanah and Yom Kippur.[10] The only evidence of religious animus was that someone without supervisory authority had jokingly criticized him for missing the meetings on the holidays. He had said that the only excuse for missing such meetings "is if you're dead, and even that is not a good excuse." This evidence was insufficient to support the inference that the employer was motivated by animus.

Similarly, a plaintiff failed to demonstrate age discrimination when he was fired after the director of operations had commented that "maybe we need to get some 20–year-olds down here in the pressroom."[11] Plaintiff's discharge was decided by his supervisor, who was subordinate to the director of operations and present when the comment about "needs" was made. The director of operations was not directly involved in the decision to fire the plaintiff and there was no other evidence to suggest that age was a determining factor in the discharge. The age-biased statement by the superior was not attributable to the decision-making supervisor and thus there was no proof of animus in the decision, even though that supervisor might well have been implementing his superior's expressed preferences.

Special Causation Problems Linking Animus to Adverse Employment Actions

The causal element also has been problematic in cases where the employer was motivated by animus that is related to race but is not hostile to the plaintiff's racial identity. Cases where the plaintiff has social relations with members of the disfavored group present such a problem. The law firm in *Rosenblatt v. Bivona & Cohen*,[12] for example, was alleged to be prejudiced against interracial marriages and for that reason fired a newly-wed attorney who had been with the firm for twelve years. The court considered this case of first impression in the circuit and rejected a line of older cases that focused upon the wording of the statute to exclude such actions. The key wording in Title VII is "because of such individual's race" which the earlier opinions had interpreted to mean that the race of the plaintiff must be the subject of the employer's prejudice. The court in *Rosenblatt* nonetheless found the claim sufficient under Title VII. Relying on authority from the Eleventh Circuit in *Parr v. Woodmen of the World Life Insurance Co.*,[13] the court found that the employer excluded the plaintiff because he and his spouse were of different races and that this reason was a form of racial animus covered

---

10. Lawrence v. Mars, Inc., 955 F.2d 902 (4th Cir.1992), cert. denied, 506 U.S. 823, 113 S.Ct. 76, 121 L.Ed.2d 40 (1992).

11. Smith v. New York Times, 955 F.Supp. 558 (D.S.C. 1996), affirmed, 107 F.3d 867 (4th Cir.1997).

12. 946 F.Supp. 298 (S.D.N.Y.1996).

13. 791 F.2d 888 (11th Cir.1986).

by the Act. The court reasoned that if the plaintiff lawyer had been black, his marriage would not have been biracial and therefore "such individual's race" affected the decision to terminate him.

The Fifth Circuit had occasion to consider this question as a matter of first impression in that circuit in *Deffenbaugh-Williams v. Wal–Mart*.[14] Following *Parr*, the circuit rejected the store's defense that discharging a white woman because she was dating a black co-worker could not be discriminating against her "because of" her race.

The Sixth Circuit reached a similar result with language that reaches further. At issue in *Tetro v. Elliott Popham Pontiac, Oldsmobile, Buick, & GMC Trucks, Inc.*[15] was the employer's discharge of a Caucasian employee because his child was biracial. The discharge of the father was not related to his race nor to the opposition of his race to his child's; rather the racial animus was directed at the biracial daughter. In broad language, the court reasoned that Title VII was meant to reach "victims of discriminatory animus towards third persons with whom the individuals associate."

Protection also extends to individuals who protest discrimination directed toward others. An employer may not retaliate against a white male, for example, who protests the discriminatory treatment of others on a protected basis. In *Wehr v. Ryan's Family Steak Houses, Inc.*,[16] a male manager in a restaurant protested to his supervisor the harassment of female waitresses by other managers. He claimed that waitresses who acquiesced to "dating" the managers were given more favorable assignments. Despite the lack of objection by any of the women affected, the plaintiff's discharge upon his complaint to the supervisor was a violation of Title VII even though he was not complaining on his own behalf. That circuit came to the same result in another case involving an affirmative action officer in a university who sued on the grounds he was discharged for his ardent advocacy for women and minority groups.[17]

A similar problem with the sufficiency of the causal connection between the adverse action and the plaintiff's race arose in a case in which a supervisor promoted his "drinking buddy" whom he knew from social occasions.[18] The supervisor and his drinking buddy were both Caucasian; the plaintiff was a more qualified African–American who had not had the same opportunities to participate in these social occasions. The trier of fact did not find that the supervisor was motivated by racial animus; the supervisor testified credibly that the more qualified plaintiff simply never entered his mind as a possible promotee. The court found that although the promotion was literally based upon preference for the social relationship rather than racial preference, there was a sufficient

14. 156 F.3d 581 (5th Cir.1998) (collecting cases), vacated and reinstated in relevant part en banc, 182 F.3d 333 (5th Cir. 1999).

15. 173 F.3d 988 (6th Cir.1999).

16. 49 F.3d 1150 (6th Cir.1995).

17. Johnson v. University of Cincinnati, 215 F.3d 561 (6th Cir.), cert. denied, 531 U.S. 1052, 121 S.Ct. 657, 148 L.Ed.2d 560 (2000).

18. Roberts v. Gadsden Mem. Hosp., 835 F.2d 793 (11th Cir.1988).

connection between race and the social relationship itself for satisfaction of the causal requirement in the Act. The court described the promotion as "nothing more than a typical 'good ole boy' appointment that the Act intended to reach."

In contrast, the First Circuit came to an opposite conclusion about cronyism as a basis for hiring. In *Foster v. Dalton*,[19] a naval hospital failed to promote the most qualified candidate, who was a black woman, in favor of the "fishing buddy" of the decision-maker. The court held that the superior candidate could not prevail in the absence of discriminatory animus. Whereas the Eleventh Circuit found in *Roberts* that the Act intended to reach "old boy" practices that had the effect of causing discrimination based on proscribed criteria, the *Foster* court required proof that the motivation of the decision-maker was discriminatory animus rather than social networking. Although the court found the cronyism distasteful, it found no connection between favoritism for same-race friends and the purpose of Title VII in eliminating racial barriers to employment. Although not citing *Roberts*, the *Foster* court was apparently unpersuaded by the *Roberts'* approach of addressing cronyism with a racially disparate result as a practice that is inherently covered by the Act without further proof of a racial connection.

More consistent with *Foster* than with *Roberts* is the opinion of the Eighth Circuit in *Brandt v. Shop 'n Save Warehouse Foods, Inc.*[20] The plaintiff in this case alleged that she lost the opportunity to become a meat cutter because the hiring supervisor tailored the description of the job with unnecessary qualifications in order to hire a friend who was looking for a job. The Eighth Circuit said that a jury verdict in the plaintiff's favor should be overturned because there was no evidence that pointed to gender discrimination. The dissenting opinion noted that there was bolstering evidence of job segregation that should have been sufficient to present the issue to the jury. That evidence was that the job categories of meat cutter and meat wrapper were traditionally segregated as male and female jobs respectively in this employer's work force, such that the plaintiff's rejection despite her qualifications for the traditionally male job should be sufficient to present a triable issue of motivation.

In a related line of cases, one court has found that a preference for a relative of a current employee is not sufficiently connected to racial animus to be a violation of Title VII.[21] The case challenged several such preferences on a theory of intentional discrimination rather than for the impact of the nepotism practice, and the court found the preference for relatives not to be sufficiently connected to racially premised exclusion.

Favoritism Cases: *Animus Issues*

Similar analytic difficulties have arisen in the cases where plaintiffs have alleged sexual favoritism. These cases involve claims of employment

19.　71 F.3d 52 (1st Cir.1995).
20.　108 F.3d 935 (8th Cir.1997).

21.　Holder v. Raleigh, 867 F.2d 823 (4th Cir.1989).

disadvantage caused by a preference for an employee or applicant with whom the decisionmaker is romantically involved. In one case, the court found that such a preference is sufficiently related to gender bias to meet the causal requirement of Title VII,[22] whereas another found that the preference is based upon sexual attractiveness, not upon gender discrimination.[23]

The current weight of authority holds that it is not gender discrimination to favor a paramour. A California case, *Proksel v. Gattis*,[24] relied upon an EEOC interpretation to conclude that such conduct, without more, does not violate California law. The court reasoned that isolated instances of preferential treatment based upon consensual romantic relationships do not discriminate against either men or women because both are disadvantaged for reasons other than gender.

The Tenth Circuit came to the same conclusion under Title VII that favoritism to a paramour is not gender discrimination. In *Taken v. Oklahoma Corporation Commission*,[25] the court concluded that female employees' do not have a claim of gender discrimination when a male supervisor granted a promotion to a less qualified woman with whom he had a voluntary romantic relationship. The opinion explains that male candidates for promotion would have been as disadvantaged as the female plaintiffs and therefore the disadvantage was not based upon gender. The Fifth Circuit took a slightly different approach in *Ackel v. National Communications*.[26] Under similar facts, the court found no gender discrimination against the woman who was replaced by the male supervisor's lover. It noted that although such favoritism is unfair, it disadvantages both men and women for reasons other than gender. The woman who was transferred so that the paramour could take her job was not moved because of gender discrimination but because she "happened to occupy" the position wanted for the lover.

Different problems arise when employees terminate consensual relationships. When a relationship is not consensual, it can be actionable as sexual harassment. The problem in the context of intentional discrimination is when the relationship was originally consensual, but then terminates. A number of cases have claimed gender discrimination when a former lover takes an adverse employment action following the end of a consensually romantic relationship. A New York case[27] rejected such a claim as "fatally flawed" because the plaintiff's only theory was she would not have lost her job if she had not engaged in a sexual relationship with her employer. The employer broke off the relationship and fired the plaintiff because he wanted to attempt a reconciliation with his wife. The court did not find credible the theory that the employer's

22. King v. Palmer, 778 F.2d 878 (D.C.Cir.1985).

23. DeCintio v. Westchester County Med. Ctr., 807 F.2d 304 (2d Cir.1986), cert. denied, 484 U.S. 825, 108 S.Ct. 89, 98 L.Ed.2d 50 (1987).

24. 41 Cal.App.4th 1626, 49 Cal.Rptr.2d 322 (1996).

25. 125 F.3d 1366 (10th Cir.1997).

26. 339 F.3d 376 (5th Cir.2003).

27. Mauro v. Orville, 259 A.D.2d 89, 697 N.Y.S.2d 704 (App.Div.1999).

desire not to continue an intimate relationship with an employee was discrimination "because of" the employee's gender. Termination on the basis of a failed sexual relationship did not support a claim even if it was "antithetical to good business practice" because it was not premised on gender.

The Fifth Circuit came to the opposite conclusion and found that a former lover could recover for gender discrimination in *Green v. Administrators of Tulane Educational Fund*.[28] In that case a crucial fact was that after the termination of the consensual relationship, the male supervisor pressured the plaintiff to resume their intimacy. Although the initial relationship had been consensual, the conduct in retaliation for rejecting continued advances was sexually harassing and thus discrimination on the basis of gender. Other cases have found no gender discrimination when there is no pressure to resume a terminated relationship because then there is no harassment. The key in these cases is whether the adverse employment action was based upon a repudiation of the prior relationship or upon a desire to resume it. In the first instance, there is no gender discrimination because the basis of the adverse action is on the past consensual conduct, and in the second instance it is sexually harassing because it is premised on pressuring the employee for future sexual conduct.

A twist on this problem arose in a case involving adverse action because of the perception of a romantic relationship with a third party. In *Bush v. Raymond Corp., Inc.*,[29] an employee alleged that she was discharged because her new supervisor believed that she had received special treatment because of her romantic relationship with the previous supervisor. This allegation alone was insufficient to support a claim of gender discrimination.

Causation Issues

The favoritism cases present problems with connecting animus to adverse employment actions, as seen in the last subsection. Causation problems also appear in cases where there is a temporal lapse between an expression of animus and an adverse employment action. This causation issue often appears in retaliation cases when there is a significant amount of time between the allegedly triggering event and the perceived retaliation. Conversely, plaintiffs often want the fact of temporal proximity between an event and an adverse action to be sufficient to show causation. The Third Circuit has noted that temporal proximity alone is insufficient to establish the necessary causal link unless the timing is "unusually suggestive."[30] The plaintiff must show the causal link for retaliation, including in claims for quid pro quo harassment, from other evidence. That link, however, need not be proof of actual antagonistic conduct, but the entire record will be viewed with a "wide lens."

28. 284 F.3d 642 (5th Cir.2002).
29. 954 F.Supp. 490 (N.D.N.Y.1997).
30. Farrell v. Planters Lifesavers Co., 206 F.3d 271 (3d Cir.2000).

Discerning causation from temporal proximity is particularly challenging when the asserted retaliation is not an immediately identifiable adverse action but a process that begins shortly after the complaint. Uncertain how to interpret conflicting signals from the Eighth Circuit on this issue, for example, a district court in Iowa considered the very close temporal connection when the plaintiff was given a warning for failure to use the right procedure for sick call in the same meeting called to discuss her complaint about a co-worker's harassment. That fact, coupled with the retaliatory behavior of other co-workers (not the decision-makers) immediately after the meeting, was sufficient to withstand summary judgment for her claim of retaliation when she was ultimately discharged.[31]

Causation issues appear in many different contexts in federal anti-discrimination law. They all have in common the need to connect the employer's animus to the adverse employment action to establish that it was "because of" the plaintiff's race, national origin, gender, religion, or age forty and over.

§ 2.7 Intentional Discrimination—Direct Evidence of Discriminatory Animus

Title VII and the ADEA make unlawful employment decisions adverse to an individual on the basis of race color, religion, sex, national origin or age forty and over.[1] An employer may not, for example, refuse to consider an applicant for a job because of that individual's race.

The Supreme Court has explained that a Title VII or ADEA plaintiff in a case alleging intentional discrimination has the burden of production and persuasion on the ultimate question of the employer's motivation.[2] There are two methods of doing so. First, the intent may be established with direct evidence and may be proven through direct evidence of the employer's discriminatory motive. Alternatively, a claimant may use the indirect, burden-shifting approach first articulated by the Supreme Court in *McDonnell Douglas Corp. v. Green*[3] as refined by subsequent cases. This section covers the first method.

Definition and Nature of "Direct Evidence"

Plaintiffs may establish the employer's intent to discriminate with "direct evidence" of such animus. Although this term is a misnomer because a state of mind must always be inferred, it has been adopted to refer to statements that reflect the mental bias of the decision-maker. Courts have defined such evidence in a variety of ways that appear to differ only in form rather than substance. For example, one circuit

---

31. Hanna v. Boys & Girls Home & Family Services, Inc., 212 F.Supp.2d 1049 (N.D. Iowa 2002).

§ 2.7

1. 42 U.S.C.A. § 2000e–2(a); 29 U.S.C.A. § 623(a).

2. Reeves v. Sanderson Plumbing Prods., 530 U.S. 133, 120 S.Ct. 2097, 147 L.Ed.2d 105 (2000); Hazen Paper Co. v. Biggins, 507 U.S. 604, 113 S.Ct. 1701, 123 L.Ed.2d 338 (1993).

3. 411 U.S. 792, 93 S.Ct. 1817, 36 L.Ed.2d 668 (1973).

defines it as "evidence of remarks or comments which indicate discriminatory animus on the part of those with decision making authority."[4] Another defines it as "evidence of conduct or statements that both reflect directly the alleged discriminatory attitude and bear directly on the contested employment decision."[5]

Although the definitions have been relatively consistent, courts have struggled to understand the meaning of "direct evidence" in the employment discrimination context. Some courts have approached the term in the classic meaning of the term: Direct evidence is that which, if believed, is sufficient to prove the fact in question without inference or presumption. In the context of intentional employment discrimination, that fact would be the discriminatory animus of the decision-maker when making the adverse decision. Without this connection, it is reasoned, the evidence bears directly only on the bias of the decision-maker and not directly on the challenged action. Other courts have treated the term more generally in intentional employment discrimination cases and include as "direct" any evidence of a discriminatory attitude that more probably than not affected the adverse employment decision.

The statement that is offered as direct evidence of discrimination cannot be too ambiguous or it loses its probative value as evidence of improper motive. In one case, a decision-maker's comment that the plaintiff was "not a selling person" was insufficient to show race discrimination.[6] An earlier case had also found excessive ambiguity in an age discrimination case when a supervisor noted that the plaintiff's approaching birthday was "a cause for concern."[7] In another case,[8] the plaintiff wanted to use a supervisor's silence in the face of an accusation to be direct evidence, but the attempt was unsuccessful because of the ambiguity of silence.

Remarks that have been accepted as direct evidence of discriminatory animus, particularly when coupled with additional evidence, include the following: calling an employee a "damn woman" for gender discrimination;[9] telling an employee that she "needed a good Christian boyfriend to teach her to be submissive" for religious discrimination;[10] saying that age is a criterion in which employees would retain jobs as evidence of age discrimination;[11] and calling an employee a "black radical" who would stir up racial discontent as evidence of racial discrimination.[12]

---

4. Campos v. City of Blue Springs, 289 F.3d 546, 552 (8th Cir.2002).

5. Taylor v. Virginia Union Univ.,193 F.3d 219, 232 (4th Cir.1999) (en banc), cert. denied, 528 U.S. 1189, 120 S.Ct. 1243, 146 L.Ed.2d 101 (2000).

6. Betkerur v. Aultman Hosp. Ass'n, 78 F.3d 1079 (6th Cir.1996).

7. Phelps v. Yale Sec., Inc. 986 F.2d 1020 (6th Cir.) cert. denied, 510 U.S. 861, 114 S.Ct. 175, 126 L.Ed.2d 135 (1993).

8. Weston–Smith v. Cooley Dickinson Hosp., Inc., 282 F.3d 60 (1st Cir.2002)

9. Hill v. Lockheed Martin Logistics Mgmt. Inc., 354 F.3d 277 (4th Cir. 2004).

10. Campos v. Blue Springs, 289 F.3d 546 (8th Cir. 2002).

11. Febres v. Challenger Carribean Corp., 214 F.3d 57 (1st Cir. 2000)

12. Ross v. Douglas County, Neb., 234 F.3d 391 (8th Cir. 2000).

Direct evidence of discrimination has usually involved statements or other facts that bear upon the separate fact of an adverse employment action. In one case,[13] the plaintiff attempted unsuccessfully to use the fact of her termination itself as direct evidence of discrimination. She argued that the timing of her discharge a few weeks after announcing her pregnancy was evidence of discrimination, but the court said that this evidence would not support such an inference.

In some rare cases plaintiffs have attempted to present direct evidence that the setting of the actual qualifications for a job was a process tainted by discrimination. In *Burns v. Gadsden State Community College*,[14] the plaintiff alleged that the defendant college discriminated against her application as an administrator on the basis of gender. The direct evidence included a conversation among college officials about the need to hire more minority and women administrators, but not for the higher positions. The plaintiff further alleged that her application for one of those higher administrative positions was rejected because the employer deliberately defined the job to require experience that women were unlikely to have. Specifically, the job description said that the position required a background of five years industrial experience. The plaintiff alleged that the decision-maker for the position sought by the plaintiff decided that the five years experience would have to be in "heavy industry" because few women would meet that narrowly defined qualification. The court held that such direct evidence would be sufficient to establish the plaintiff's case of intentional discrimination. In an older case, the plaintiff presented direct evidence that a police commissioner set the minimum height standard by asking an assistant how many women on the applicant list were at each height. This evidence was bolstered by the commissioner's reference to women as "balls of fluff" in his deposition.[15]

Stray Remarks Distinguished

Because statements that are direct evidence of discrimination reflect upon the employer's animus when making an adverse employment decision, courts must distinguish between "direct evidence" and "stray remarks" in the workplace. Whereas direct evidence of animus relates to the actor's state of mind at the time of making an adverse decision, a stray remark is simply a prejudicial comment that does not bear upon the challenged employment decision. Even remarks directed at plaintiffs personally may not suffice to show direct evidence of discrimination when they are not contemporaneous with an adverse employment decision. In *Heim v. Utah*,[16] for example, the supervisor said that he hated having "f* * *ing women in the office" and noted that the female plaintiff occasionally swore "during her mood period of time." The Tenth Circuit held that these comments were boorish and reflected a stereotypical view of women, but that no evidence connected them with

---

13. Marshall v. American Hosp. Ass'n, 157 F.3d 520 (7th Cir. 1998).

14. 908 F.2d 1512 (11th Cir. 1990).

15. Vanguard Justice Soc'y v. Hughes, 471 F.Supp. 670, 711 n.77 (D.Md. 1979).

16. 8 F.3d 1541 (10th Cir.1993).

any employment decision. The plaintiff, who was the only woman on the crew, had claimed that the supervisor had denied her an opportunity to train in another department. In the court's opinion, the remarks were insufficient in themselves to show that the supervisor's actions were improperly motivated.

A "stray remark" is in general an expression of personal opinion that does not reflect a discriminatory intent to limit employment opportunities. Its remoteness in person from the individual plaintiff and in time from the adverse decision makes it insufficiently probative of the ultimate question of intent. For example, in *Taken v. Oklahoma Corp. Commission*,[17] white plaintiffs alleged that a black male supervisor disadvantaged them in favor of a black woman because of racial favoritism. The direct evidence was a statement he had once made that "someone has to look after these black girls." The court held that this evidence was insufficient to establish a nexus between the statement and the adverse action. Similarly, a comment by an employer's general counsel at an industry dinner party that gender salary inequity is justified because "women don't work as hard as men" was a stray remark unrelated to the salary of a female vice president which the general counsel played no role in setting.[18]

The Causal Link of the Direct Evidence of Animus to the Adverse Action

Animus alone is insufficient for a claim of intentional discrimination under Title VII or the ADEA. The plaintiff must also establish that the adverse employment action was caused by the discriminatory animus. A statement of bigotry with reference to the plaintiff at the exact time of the adverse action is strong evidence of discriminatory intent. For example, in a case challenging the denial of a promotion to a qualified candidate, the manager had said, "As long as I'm the warehouse manager, no Jew will run the warehouse for me."[19] The statement was contemporaneous with the challenged employment decision and it was made with direct reference to the plaintiff.

Even when there is not a statement specifically referring to the plaintiff, direct evidence of discriminatory animus toward the plaintiff's group at the time of making an adverse decision toward the plaintiff also helps probe the ultimate question: Was the employment decision adverse to the plaintiff based upon a prohibited factor? The plaintiff must establish the causal link between the animus and the challenged employment decision. When prejudiced expressions are contemporaneous with the decision, or closely related to it, the trier of fact can draw the inference of the causal connection. For example, the trier of fact could draw the inference of intentional gender discrimination when an employer asserted that "women are not good sailors" and subsequently denied

17. 125 F.3d 1366 (10th Cir.1997).

18. Stopka v. Alliance of Am. Insurers, 141 F.3d 681 (7th Cir.1998).

19. Weiss v. Parker Hannifan Corp., 747 F.Supp. 1118 (D.N.J. 1990).

a woman a job that included such work.[20] Similarly, the Eleventh Circuit remanded a case in which the comment was that women were not "tough enough" for a job. Such a remark could be direct evidence of discriminatory animus.[21]

Evidentiary Value of Stray Remarks versus a Pattern of Hostile Remarks

A pattern of comments that reflect a general prejudice toward plaintiff or plaintiff's group may be sufficient as direct evidence of discriminatory animus if they are sufficiently pervasive and have probative force even in the absence of a clear connection to an adverse employment decision. A supervisor's use of racial slurs in *Brown v. East Mississippi Electric Power Association*,[22] for example, was direct evidence of discrimination because they reflected a discriminatory attitude that affected his behavior toward the African–American plaintiff. The frequency of the slurs and the duration of the pattern gave them cumulative significance in bearing on animus in decision-making even though each remark in itself was a stray one.

In contrast, a single reference to the black male plaintiff as "boy" is insufficient. Epithets in general do not tend to be sufficient as direct evidence of animus unless they are tied with other conduct indicating discrimination. In one case, calling an older employee "pops" was direct evidence of age discrimination when coupled with other comments reflecting stereotyped assumptions about older workers. Comments directly reflecting stereotyped assumptions are generally received as more probative of discriminatory animus than epithets alone. Although pervasive epithets such as those used in *Brown* are useful evidence of hostility, occasional slurs are more likely to be considered stray. In contrast, evidence of stereotyped assumptions may be direct evidence of animus even if they are favorable stereotypes rather than hostile ones. In *Kang v. U. Lim America, Inc.*,[23] the Korean–American plaintiff sued for physical and verbal abuse by his Korean supervisor because he failed to live up to supervisor's stereotypical notions that Korean workers were better than "Americans" and his primarily Mexican co-workers. His allegation that the supervisor told him that he had to work harder and longer because Koreans are superior was sufficient for direct evidence of national origin discrimination.

The difficulty of determining the probative value of a pattern of hostile remarks is illustrated by the Seventh Circuit opinion in *Indurante v. Local 705, International Brotherhood of Teamsters*.[24] The plaintiff argued that his discharge was caused by animus toward Italian Americans and he offered evidence of slurs such as "all the Italians were going to be fired," "all the Italians were nothing but mobsters and

20. Grant v. Hazelett Strip–Casting Corp., 880 F.2d 1564 (2d Cir.1989).

21. Haynes v. W.C. Caye & Co., 52 F.3d 928 (11th Cir.1995).

22. 989 F.2d 858 (5th Cir.), rehearing denied, 995 F.2d 225 (5th Cir.1993).

23. 296 F.3d 810 (9th Cir. 2002).

24. 160 F.3d 364 (7th Cir.1998).

gangsters," and "the days of the goombahs are over." The court considered these remarks to be "stray" ones that did not support any theory of discrimination even given their cumulative nature. Important factors were that the remarks did not refer to any question of employment, that they did not refer to the plaintiff personally, that they were not made to him personally, and that they were not contemporaneous with his discharge. The dissenting opinion found that the remarks readily support the inference that bias against Italian Americans could have played a role, thus creating a fact question under either theory of evidence.

As *Brown* and *Indurante* indicate, there is a fine line between (1) direct evidence, (2) stray remarks, and (3) a pattern of hostile remarks that have some probative value even though they are not direct evidence. The second category of the purely "stray" remark does not reflect animus and therefore is not probative of intentional discrimination under any theory. The third category can be further divided into three types: First are cumulative remarks that rise to the level of direct evidence even though they do not bear directly on the adverse action, as in *Brown*. Second is the use of cumulative remarks as evidence of pretext in a case seeking to prove indirectly the discriminatory animus under the scheme originally set forth by the Supreme Court in *McDonnell Douglas Corp. v. Green*.[25] This latter category is not direct evidence because of the lack of causal nexus, but it is admissible to support a claim supported with circumstantial evidence under the *McDonnell Douglas* scheme of proof. Such "bolstering" evidence is relevant even though not direct. Third is the use of a pattern of hostile remarks to support a claim that the employer is responsible for creating an abusive working condition under the theory of hostile environment harassment. There are additional and separate criteria for these claims and their use of prejudiced remarks in the workplace.

Yet another use of prejudiced remarks is to impeach contradictory testimony of a decision-maker. The Seventh Circuit upheld the admission of some remarks because they were part of a pattern of falsehoods and contradictions that were relevant to the credibility of the decision-maker with respect to the requirements and standards for the job. In that case, *Hasham v. California State Board of Equalization*,[26] the decision-maker had commented that he did not want to hire any more foreigners. That comment was more than a year prior to his failure to promote the plaintiff, a Pakistani-born auditor. In another remark related to the claimant, the decision-maker complained about the claimant's accent and commented that he could not expect to be promoted if he cannot communicate with people. The plaintiff's case did not proceed under the theory that these comments sufficed as direct evidence, but they were admissible because of the decision-maker's contradictory testimony about other matters relating to the promotion.

25. 411 U.S. 792, 93 S.Ct. 1817, 36 L.Ed.2d 668 (1973).

26. 200 F.3d 1035 (7th Cir.2000).

§ 2.8　Intentional　Discrimination—Indirect　Evidence, Nondiscriminatory Purpose, and Pretext

Direct evidence of discriminatory animus is not always present in claims alleging intentional discrimination in employment. A plaintiff also may establish a case of intentional discrimination with indirect evidence. The Supreme Court has held that a plaintiff in such a case has the burden of "showing actions taken by the employer from which one can infer, if such actions remain unexplained, that it more likely than not that such actions were based on a discriminatory criterion illegal under the Act."[1]

Indirect Evidence: The McDonnell Douglas Paradigm

In the landmark case of *McDonnell Douglas Corp. v. Green,*[2] the Supreme Court first introduced a three-part approach to cases with circumstantial evidence of discrimination. Under that paradigm, a plaintiff must first establish treatment that is differential on a proscribed dimension, such as the claim of race discrimination involved in *Green.* If the plaintiff is successful, the defendant has the evidentiary burden of articulating a legitimate business purpose for the adverse decision. The defendant's articulation of a legitimate reason for the decision has the effect of dispelling the inference of improper motivation created by the plaintiff's proof. The burden remains with the plaintiff at all times, however, to convince the trier of fact that the adverse employment decision was intentionally discriminatory. The third part of this approach permits the plaintiff to introduce evidence to show that the defendant's articulated reason is a pretext to hide the discriminatory animus. This apparently simple scheme for proof has dominated employment discrimination law for over a quarter of a century, during which time it has been explained and expanded into a complex and difficult doctrine.

The *McDonnell Douglas* case, in which the Court introduced this evidentiary scheme, was a hiring case involving alleged race discrimination. The Court detailed how the plaintiff can establish the first prong of the test for a claim of intentional exclusion in hiring in order to create the inference of improper motivation. To carry this initial burden of establishing a prima facie case of intentional discrimination, the Court said, the plaintiff may show

> (i) that he belongs to a racial minority; (ii) that he applied and was qualified for a job for which the employer was seeking applicants; (iii) that, despite his qualifications, he was rejected; and (iv) that, after his rejection, the position remained open and the employer continued to seek applicants from persons of complainant's qualifications.[3]

§ 2.8

1. Furnco Constr. Corp. v. Waters, 438 U.S. 567, 98 S.Ct. 2943, 57 L.Ed.2d 957 (1978).

2. 411 U.S. 792, 93 S.Ct. 1817, 36 L.Ed.2d 668 (1973).

3. 411 U.S. at 802, 93 S.Ct. at 1824.

The Supreme Court emphasized the importance of flexibility in the application of the *McDonnell Douglas* factors in *Swierkiewicz v. Sorema*.[4] Noting that *McDonnell Douglas* requirements were not meant to be a "pleading requirement" but merely an "evidentiary standard," the Court held that Rule 8(a)(2) of the Federal Rules of Civil Procedure simply requires "a short and plain statement of the claim showing that the pleader is entitled to relief" and does not require the allegation of facts to satisfy the evidentiary burden.

Courts have generally been consistent with the spirit of *Swierkiewicz* that the *McDonnell Douglas* requirements were never meant to be rigid, mechanized, or ritualistic. They have modified the original *McDonnell Douglas* formulation to make it suitable for a variety of claims under Title VII and the ADEA. Because *McDonnell Douglas* itself was framed in terms of a race claim for discrimination in hiring, many modifications have been needed. The Supreme Court has embraced and encouraged the flexible application of the prima facie case.

The Supreme Court has never held that the *McDonnell Douglas* approach is also applicable to claims brought under the ADEA. The Court specifically noted this fact in *Reeves v. Sanderson Plumbing Products*,[5] but did not address this issue there because the parties had not disputed it. The circuit courts universally apply the approach to the ADEA.

The Prima Facie Case

First, the initial requirement in *McDonnell Douglas* is that the plaintiff show his membership in a racial minority. Some courts have interpreted this requirement to mean simply that the plaintiff belongs to a "protected class." Under the ADEA it is necessary to plead membership in the age-protected category because federal law does not prohibit discrimination against individuals who are under forty years of age.

Pleading membership in a protected category is more complex under Title VII. With respect to race, the Supreme Court held in *McDonald v. Santa Fe Trail Transportation Co.*[6] that Title VII and section 1981 also protect members of the racial majority. When the plaintiff is a member of the majority racial group, however, some courts have modified the first prong of *McDonnell Douglas*. The Sixth Circuit has explained that the rationale of the first prong was to reflect congressional efforts "to address this nation's history of discrimination against racial minorities, a legacy of racism so entrenched that we presume acts, otherwise unexplained, embody its effect."[7] Courts have thus held in reverse discrimination suits that the plaintiff must make a special showing in order to enjoy the *McDonnell Douglas* presumption that discrimination is the most likely explanation for the adverse action unless the employer otherwise explains it. The Tenth Circuit explained that a Title VII

---

4. 534 U.S. 506, 122 S.Ct. 992, 152 L.Ed.2d 1 (2002).

5. 530 U.S. 133, 120 S.Ct. 2097, 147 L.Ed.2d 105 (2000).

6. 427 U.S. 273, 96 S.Ct. 2574, 49 L.Ed.2d 493 (1976).

7. Murray v. Thistledown Racing Club, Inc., 770 F.2d 63, 67 (6th Cir.1985).

disparate treatment plaintiff who pursues a reverse discrimination claim under *McDonnell Douglas* "must, in lieu of showing that he belongs to a protected group, establish background circumstances that support an inference that the defendant is one of those unusual employers who discriminates against the majority."[8]

The Tenth Circuit had an opportunity to explore this principle further in an usual case, *Taken v. Oklahoma Corporation Commission.*[9] The plaintiffs in this case were white men and women who were complaining that they were more qualified for a promotion than the black woman who was chosen. They alleged that the promotion had been premised upon the recommendation of their black male supervisor, who had preferred the successful candidate because of their romantic relationship. On the race aspect of the claim, the plaintiffs contended that they should be entitled to the *McDonnell Douglas* presumption because the decision-maker and beneficiary were both of the same race, different from theirs. They lost on this point because the final decision to promote had been made by a committee of three persons, only one of whom was their black supervisor; the remaining members were two white males. The court left open the possibility that if the promotion had been decided "solely by non-whites" that the plaintiffs would have been entitled to the presumption.

For gender discrimination, the first step of the prima facie case requires only a statement of complaint on the basis of gender, because both men and women are protected classes. Remarkably, there have been few cases involving a man claiming gender discrimination under the *McDonnell Douglas* approach. One such claim of disparate treatment involved a man claiming gender discrimination on the basis of sexual favoritism. It was unsuccessful for reasons other than an inability to plead his status as a protected category under Title VII. In other contexts, Supreme Court cases have established that men are protected from discrimination "because of sex" under Title VII. First, the Supreme Court held that Title VII protected male employees from a facially discriminatory benefits policy in *Newport News Shipbuilding & Dry Dock Co. v. EEOC.*[10] The employer in that case provided pregnancy benefits for employees but not for their spouses, which was facially discriminatory against men because only male employees could have spouses capable of becoming pregnant. Next, the Supreme Court in *Oncale v. Sundowner Offshore Services., Inc.,*[11] expressly held in the context of same-sex harassment that Title VII protects both genders from discrimination.

The next requirement under the *McDonnell Douglas* approach is that the plaintiff "apply" for a position with the defendant. This requirement is meaningful only in cases complaining of discrimination in

8. Notari v. Denver Water Dep't, 971 F.2d 585 (10th Cir.1992).

9. 125 F.3d 1366 (10th Cir. 1997).

10. 462 U.S. 669, 103 S.Ct. 2622, 77 L.Ed.2d 89 (1983).

11. 523 U.S. 75, 118 S.Ct. 998, 140 L.Ed.2d 201 (1998).

initial hire or promotion. This requirement has been modified in the context of discharge.

The failure to make a formal application is not always fatal for a plaintiff, particularly in cases involving promotion or job assignment. The Supreme Court explained in *International Brotherhood of Teamsters v. United States*,[12] that application for promotion to a racially exclusive division is not necessary when the plaintiff can demonstrate the futility of such application. An employer can create an atmosphere where it is understood that there is no prospect of some individuals holding certain jobs because of race, gender, or national origin. Similarly, in a gender discrimination case,[13] a plaintiff did not apply for the job after she was discouraged from doing so by the statement that it was a "man's job."

The third step of the *McDonnell Douglas* approach is to show qualification for the job. There has been some confusion in the case law concerning whether this requirement means qualification for the job in the abstract or qualification in the sense of meeting the employer's stated criteria. This distinction is explored further is the discussion below concerning the defendant's burden of articulating a legitimate business purpose.

The confusion between the plaintiff's burden to show "qualification" and the defendant's burden to articulate a legitimate business purpose is well-illustrated by the Sixth Circuit case of *Cline v. Catholic Diocese*.[14] In that case a teacher was discharged for violating the rule against pre-marital sex when she was noticeably pregnant shortly after her marriage. The question was whether "non-pregnant if single" was part of the "qualification" for being a teacher and thus part of the plaintiff's prima facie case, or whether it was the employer's burden to establish pre-marital sex as the reason for the discharge. The circuit court held that the trial court erroneously found that she could not show qualification for the prima facie case because her violation of the morality rule was disqualifying. The opinion explains that the consideration of her pregnancy was the employer's burden under legitimate business purpose. It explained that the inclusion of the justification into the prima facie case would have the effect of precluding the plaintiff from challenging the policy as pretext, as she properly can do when the defendant articulates it as a legitimate business purpose.

The fourth requirement of the prima facie case under the *McDonnell Douglas* approach is that the employer continued to seek applicants for the position. This requirement has been adapted generally to require only that the plaintiff show that there was a job opening. Some courts have required further that the plaintiff demonstrate that the job was filled by someone outside of the plaintiff's group, but this requirement now appears inconsistent with the Supreme Court's decision in *O'Con-*

---

12. 431 U.S. 324, 97 S.Ct. 1843, 52 L.Ed.2d 396 (1977).

13. EEOC v. F & D Distrib., Inc., 728 F.2d 1281 (10th Cir.1984).

14. 206 F.3d 651 (6th Cir.2000).

nor v. Consolidated Coin Caterers Corp.[15] In *O'Connor,* the Court held that in an age discrimination case the plaintiff is not required to show that the favored applicant or employee is outside the protected age group. The Court noted that the ADEA prohibits discrimination on the basis of age, not class membership, and thus it is irrelevant whether one person in the protected class has lost out to another person in that class.

The same reasoning has been applied to Title VII by the Seventh Circuit in *Carson v. Bethlehem Steel Corp.*[16] The court interpreted *O'Connor* to mean that a plaintiff complaining of discrimination on the basis of race, sex, national origin, or religion need not show that the employment advantage was lost to someone outside the protected group. That court thus applied the *O'Connor* reasoning to a race discrimination claim and held that the central question is whether the employer would have taken the same action had the plaintiff been in a different class. This reasoning has also been applied to the Americans with Disabilities Act.

The reasoning has been applied to gender discrimination as well. The District of Columbia Circuit Court held that the key to a woman's case of gender discrimination is not a showing that a benefit went to a man, but showing that she was treated less favorably than similarly situated men. In that case,[17] a woman alleged gender discrimination in a promotion process even though some of the promotions went to women. The court reasoned that a woman claiming gender discrimination can establish a claim by showing that she received "unfavorable treatment" in the promotion process because she is a woman and that the district court erred by concluding that the claim was baseless because of the presence of women among those promoted.

Defendant's Burden—Nondiscriminatory Purpose

After the plaintiff creates the inference of discrimination from the four-part test, the burden then shifts to the employer to articulate some nondiscriminatory reason for the employee's rejection. In *McDonnell Douglas* the Court referred to this stage as the articulation of a "legitimate business purpose." Subsequent caselaw has made clear that the court should not be judging whether the reason is a rational business practice. Even irrational practices may be lawful. The sole reason for inquiring into the business purpose is to dispel the inference of intent. If the defendant fails in this burden of production, the plaintiff prevails. If the defendant satisfies this slight burden, however, the plaintiff retains the burden of persuasion on the ultimate issue of whether the adverse action was discriminatorily motivated. The purpose need not be a "legitimate" business purpose, for example, as long as the employer's purpose was not discriminatory.

The word "articulate" is also a misnomer in the description of the defendant's burden at this stage of the litigation. The defendant must do

15. 517 U.S. 308, 116 S.Ct. 1307, 134 L.Ed.2d 433 (1996).

16. 82 F.3d 157 (7th Cir.1996).

17. Stella v. Mineta, 284 F.3d 135 (D.C.Cir.2002).

more than offer a reason at oral argument; there must be some evidence put before the court. The onus on the employer is not great, however. Articulated reasons sufficient to dispel the inference of discrimination have included the greater "communication skills" of the individual selected instead of the plaintiff[18] and the probability that the selected individual "would stay on the job longer" than the plaintiff.[19]

The defendant's evidence of a nondiscriminatory reason for the adverse action dispels the inference of unlawful discrimination created by the plaintiff's prima facie case. The inference is dispelled as soon as the evidence is produced; the court does not need to be persuaded by the evidence that the defendant was actually motivated by that reason. It remains for the plaintiff to prove that the articulated reason is pretextual and that the employer's motivation was unlawfully discriminatory.

Furthermore, the court need not be persuaded that the employer's articulated reason for the adverse action even reflected good business judgment. The Court caused confusion on this point when it originally characterized the defendant's burden as the production of a "legitimate business reason."[20] This phrase creates the impression that the employer's reason for the adverse action affecting the plaintiff must be rational, but the Supreme Court clarified the limited nature of the burden in *Furnco Construction Corp. v. Waters*.[21] The Court noted:

> A prima facie case under *McDonnell Douglas* raises an inference of discrimination only because we presume these acts, if otherwise unexplained, are more likely than not based on the consideration of impermissible factors. And we are willing to presume this largely because we know from our experience that more often than not people do not act in a totally arbitrary manner, without any underlying reasons, especially in a business setting. Thus, when all legitimate reasons for rejecting an applicant have been eliminated as possible reasons for the employer's actions, it is more likely than not the employer, whom we generally assume acts only with *some* reason, based his decision on an impermissible consideration such as race.[22]

In *Furnco* the court of appeals had held that the employer violated Title VII by refusing to accept applications of bricklayers. The employer specialized in relining blast furnaces with firebrick and had no permanent workforce of bricklayers. The job supervisor for each relining contract had authority to hire bricklayers known to be experienced and competent or recommended as highly skilled. The district court found that Furnco's practice of hiring only persons of known quality was a legitimate nondiscriminatory reason for the plaintiffs' rejections. The

18. Lucas v. Burnley, 879 F.2d 1240 (4th Cir.1989).

19. Woody v. St. Clair County Comm'n, 885 F.2d 1557 (11th Cir.1989).

20. McDonnell Douglas Corp. v. Green, 411 U.S. 792, 93 S.Ct. 1817, 36 L.Ed.2d 668 (1973).

21. 438 U.S. 567, 98 S.Ct. 2943, 57 L.Ed.2d 957 (1978).

22. 438 U.S. at 578, 98 S.Ct. at 2950.

court of appeals disagreed and noted that Furnco could take written applications and then compare those qualifications with those of other bricklayers already known to the superintendent.

The Supreme Court held that the appellate court had gone too far in substituting its own judgment as to proper hiring practices. The Court noted: "We think the Court of Appeals went awry, however, in apparently equating a prima facie showing under *McDonnell Douglas* with an ultimate finding of fact as to discriminatory refusal to hire under Title VII[.]"[23] When the defendant dispelled the inference of discrimination by explaining its procedures, the court could not complain that it did not particularly like the procedures, or that the defendant did not maximize the opportunities for minority bricklayers. Moreover, "Courts are generally less competent than employers to restructure business practices, and unless mandated to do so by Congress they should not attempt it."[24]

The inquiry does not end with the defendant's proof of justification, as the Court further observed in *Furnco*. Once the plaintiff has created the inference of discrimination and the defendant has dispelled it, the burden returns to the plaintiff to prove that the defendant's nondiscriminatory explanation is pretextual. At this stage the plaintiff can offer proof that the defendant's proffered nondiscriminatory reason for the adverse employment action was simply a pretext to cover the employer's discriminatory motive. The plaintiff retains the burden of persuasion. During the pretext stage of disparate treatment litigation, the plaintiff must focus on the defendant's specific reasons for taking the challenged actions. When the plaintiff offers such proof, it is an abuse of the trial judge's discretion not to receive it. It does not matter that the evidence could have been offered during the first stage of the litigation as long as it relates to the defendant's proffered nondiscriminatory reason.

Plaintiff's Proof of Pretext

The third stage of a case alleging disparate treatment through indirect evidence is the pretext stage. Under the *McDonnell Douglas* burden shifting scheme, the plaintiff can show that the defendant's proffered explanation for the adverse employment action was pretextual and that the real reason was discrimination.

The Supreme Court expressly discussed in *McDonnell Douglas* the type of evidence that the plaintiff might produce during this "pretext" stage of the litigation. That case involved a claim of individual disparate treatment discrimination when the employer failed to rehire a laid off worker solely because of his involvement in an illegal civil rights demonstration directed against the company. The Court found that the employer's concern about the illegal demonstration against it was a reason that dispelled the inference of discrimination. The burden then shifted back to the plaintiff to prove pretext. The Court suggested types of evidence that would be relevant to such an inquiry, including: the employer's treatment of the plaintiff during his prior term of employment; the

---

23. 98 S.Ct. at 2949.   **24.** Id. at 2950.

employer's reaction to the plaintiff's legitimate civil rights activities; and the employer's general policy and practice with respect to minority employment. With respect to the last example, the Court said that statistics may be helpful to a determination of whether the treatment of the plaintiff conformed to a general pattern of discrimination against African–American workers. The Court cautioned, however, that it would not be sufficient to find that the racial composition of the employer's workforce reflected exclusionary practices. "We caution that such general determinations, while helpful, may not be in and of themselves controlling as to an individualized hiring decision, particularly in the presence of an otherwise justifiable reason for refusing to rehire."[25]

When a plaintiff introduces statistics during the pretext phase of a disparate treatment claim, it is necessary to connect those statistics to the plaintiff's case. Statistical proof of a pattern of exclusion of a plaintiff class may be a separate cause of action for group disparate treatment. Such a claim may be tied to the individual claim of disparate treatment, but it is a separate theory under which the individual plaintiff may or may not be able to recover. For the individual claim, however, the statistics must in some way bear upon the treatment of the particular plaintiff. In one case,[26] for example, the plaintiff attempted to establish pretext with a racial analysis of the employer's workforce, but the court found the evidence did not relate to his individual claim. The employer's articulated reason for not hiring the plaintiff was his bad reference from a previous job. The court explained that such evidence does not reflect motive absent a connection between the statistics, the employer's practices, and the applicant's case.

The Supreme Court further detailed the type of evidence relevant to the plaintiff's proof of pretext in *McDonald v. Santa Fe Trail Transportation Co.*[27] In that case the employer fired Caucasian workers who claimed individual disparate treatment on the basis of race. The company articulated a legitimate business purpose; the employees were guilty of theft from the employer. The plaintiff had evidence of pretext; an African–American employee equally guilty of theft was not discharged.

The mere fact of unequal discipline of employees belonging to different groups is not dispositive. The question before the court is whether the employer's articulated reason is pretextual. The essence of a claim of disparate treatment is that an employer has treated some individuals "less favorably than others because of their race, color, religion, sex or national origin."[28] An inequality of discipline did not violate the Act, for example, in *Jones v. Gerwens.*[29] The black plaintiff alleged that he was discharged for violating rules that white employees had violated without penalty. The court explained that the Act does not

25. 93 S.Ct. at 1826 n. 19.

26. Gadson v. Concord Hosp., 966 F.2d 32 (1st Cir.1992).

27. 427 U.S. 273, 96 S.Ct. 2574, 49 L.Ed.2d 493 (1976).

28. International Bhd. of Teamsters v. United States, 431 U.S. 324, 97 S.Ct. 1843, 52 L.Ed.2d 396 (1977).

29. 874 F.2d 1534 (11th Cir.1989).

require identity of treatment, but differences in treatment must not be grounded in discriminatory animus. In *Jones,* the plaintiff police officer received discipline for violating rules about the personal use of city vehicles. Although the prior supervisor had allowed such violations, the new supervisor had announced that he would not tolerate deviations from "the book." The black plaintiff's infractions occurred after this warning whereas the white employees occurred before the warning. The inequality of the discipline alone was insufficient to establish disparate treatment.

The key is the employer's underlying motivation. In *Jones,* the plaintiff alleged that he did not commit all the rule violations for which he received discipline. The employer received a summary judgment, however, because at the internal disciplinary hearing the employee had admitted to all the rule violations. This circumstance created a legitimate, nondiscriminatory reason for the discharge. The court explained that it was "no consequence" that the plaintiff later disputed the charges. "The law is clear that, even if a Title VII claimant did not in fact commit the violation with which he is charged, an employer successfully rebuts any prima facie case of disparate treatment by showing that it honestly believed the employee committed the violation."[30]

The principle applies broadly; it does not matter if a court finds that similarly situated employees received unequal discipline if the court also finds that the employer honestly believed in differences between them. Similarly, a nondiscriminating employer may be completely wrong about whether an employee has acted improperly at all. An employer may be wrong about which employee started a fight,[31] or who had caused client dissatisfaction,[32] as long as the adverse action is not motivated by a proscribed dimension.

The plaintiff might not prevail in a disparate treatment claim even when the court finds that the articulated reason is indeed pretextual. The plaintiff must still persuade the court that the adverse action was motivated by unlawful animus rather than some other factor, such as personal animosity toward the plaintiff. The Supreme Court, in *St. Mary's Honor Center v. Hicks,*[33] held that the employer had met its burden of production by producing reasons for the adverse action, even if the court did not find them credible. The plaintiff retains the ultimate burden of persuasion that the motivation was unlawful.

The district court in *Hicks* had found that the plaintiff established a prima facie case of discriminatory demotion and discharge. The employer articulated two legitimate reasons for the adverse actions: the severity and the accumulation of violations. The plaintiff proved by a preponderance of the evidence that both of these reasons were pretextual because similarly situated employees were not demoted and discharged. The trial

---

30. Id. at 1537.

31. Morgan v. Massachusetts Gen. Hosp., 901 F.2d 186 (1st Cir.1990).

32. Menard v. First Sec. Serv. Corp., 848 F.2d 281 (1st Cir.1988).

33. 509 U.S. 502, 113 S.Ct. 2742, 125 L.Ed.2d 407 (1993).

court found that the plaintiff had failed to convince the court that the reason for the adverse action was unlawful discrimination, however. There remained the possibility that personal animosity motivated the employer, although the employee never suggested such a reason.

The Eighth Circuit reversed and held that once the plaintiff has established that the employer's articulated reasons are pretextual, the plaintiff has satisfied the ultimate burden of persuasion. "Because all of the defendant's proffered reasons were discredited," the court explained, "defendants were in a position of having offered no legitimate reason for their actions. In other words, defendants were in no better position than if they had remained silent, offering no rebuttal to an established inference that they had unlawfully discriminated against plaintiff on the basis of his race."

The Supreme Court disagreed and held that the employer had met its burden by articulating reasons even though the factfinder did not credit them. The falsity of the employer's explanation alone was not sufficient to establish that it was a pretext for racial discrimination against the African–American plaintiff.

The plaintiff, Melvin Hicks, had had a good employment record as a correctional officer with a halfway house operated by the Missouri Department of Corrections and Human Resources until there were changes in the administrative personnel. He was disciplined, demoted, and ultimately dismissed for violations that the trial judge found were not treated as serious for some other employees. Nonetheless, the judge did not find the " 'crusade' " to terminate him was " 'racially rather than personally motivated.' "[34] The plaintiff could not prevail without meeting the ultimate burden of persuasion on this issue as long as the defendant proffers some reason to meet its burden of production. "We have no authority," the Court explained, "to impose liability upon an employer for alleged discriminatory employment practices unless an appropriate factfinder determines, according to proper procedures, *that the employer has unlawfully discriminated.*"[35]

Although there was significant confusion about the application of *Hicks* in the years immediately following the decision, the Supreme Court resolved the matter in an age discrimination case, *Reeves v. Sanderson Plumbing Products.*[36] The Court in *Reeves* sought to resolve the conflict among the circuits that came to be known as the presence or absence of "pretext plus" requirements. The dispute following *Hicks* was whether it was adequate for a plaintiff to combine a prima facie case with evidence sufficient to reject the employer's articulation of a legitimate business purpose. Some circuits found this combination sufficient, but others required additional evidence of pretext in order for a plaintiff to prevail.

34. 113 S.Ct. at 2748.
35. Id. at 2751 (emphasis in original).
36. 530 U.S. 133, 120 S.Ct. 2097, 147 L.Ed.2d 105 (2000).

Reeves involved an age discrimination claim by a manager who was fired for inadequate record-keeping. After establishing the prima facie case and rebutting the employer's record-keeping rationale, the plaintiff offered evidence of additional remarks made by a management employee that suggested animus on the basis of age. The jury found for the plaintiff, but the Court of Appeals directed a verdict for the employer on the grounds that the additional evidence was insufficient to establish pretext. The Supreme Court granted certiorari in order to resolve the question "as to whether a plaintiff's prima facie case of discrimination * * *, combined with sufficient evidence for a reasonable factfinder to reject the employer's nondiscriminatory explanation for its decision, is adequate to sustain liability for intentional discrimination."[37] Although the context of the case is the ADEA, it would appear that the holding is a general clarification of the Court's opinion in *Hicks* and thus is applicable to Title VII cases as well.

First, the opinion begins by reiterating that in employment discrimination cases "liability depends on whether the protected trait (under the ADEA, age) actually motivated the employer's decision."[38] Specifically, "age must have actually played a role" in the decision-making process and "had a determinative influence on the outcome." To establish a claim, "a plaintiff's prima facie case, combined with sufficient evidence to find that the employer's asserted justification* * * is false, may permit the trier of fact to conclude that the employer unlawfully discriminated."[39]

The facts in *Reeves* clarify the Court's articulation of the plaintiff's burden in an individual disparate treatment claim. Reeves was a 57–year-old employee who had worked for forty years for the defendant manufacturer of toilet seats and covers. He was a supervisor in a department where his duties included recording the hours and attendance of employees under his supervision. Believing that production was down in Reeves' department because of poor supervision, a manager ordered an audit of the time records and found irregularities. Reeves was fired upon the recommendation of that manager and two others. Reeves sued for age discrimination and established a prima facie case. Then he offered evidence that there were not irregularities on the time records. He also had pretext evidence of age-based animus in comments and behavior by only one of the three decision-makers. The comments were that the plaintiff "must have come over on the Mayflower" and that he was "too damn old to do the job." The behavior concerned harsher treatment toward the plaintiff than toward similarly-situated younger employees. The Court of Appeals found this pretext evidence insufficiently connected with the discharge and thus concluded that there was insufficient evidence for a rational jury to conclude that age had motivated the decision.

37. 120 S.Ct. at 2104.   **39.** Id. at 2109.
38. 120 S.Ct. at 2105.

The Supreme Court reversed on the grounds that it was sufficient for the jury to combine the prima facie case with their disbelief of the proffered reason for the termination, specifically the irregularities in the time records. The Court noted that *Hicks* explains that the factfinder is not compelled to find animus upon disbelief of the proffered reason, but *Reeves* clarifies that disbelief of the employer's reason is nonetheless sufficient to support a finding of animus in conjunction with the plaintiff's prima facie case.

The Seventh Circuit has noted[40] that *Reeves* is a "cautionary note not to grant summary judgment too readily when facts are susceptible to two interpretations."[41] Similarly, the Second Circuit has noted from *Reeves* the lesson that "trial courts should not 'treat discrimination differently from other ultimate questions of fact.' "[42]

The Ultimate Question of Fact

The Supreme Court noted in *McDonnell Douglas* that these four steps were not meant to be rigid and that lower courts should apply them flexibly. Since that time the courts have used this flexibility to adapt the steps to cases involving promotion, discharge, and constructive discharge. Courts often note that any test formulated for a prima facie case for any type of employment discrimination must be flexible. The Supreme Court in *Texas Department of Community Affairs v. Burdine*[43] clarified the nature of each party's burden in a disparate treatment case. The plaintiff has the ultimate burden of persuasion on the question whether the defendant intentionally discriminated against the plaintiff. After the plaintiff establishes the four-parts of the prima facie case under *McDonnell Douglas*, it is only the burden of production, not persuasion, that shifts to the defendant.

The ultimate question of fact is whether the defendant intended to treat the plaintiff disparately because of race, color, religion, sex, or national origin. A race-blind rating system, for example, can defeat an inference that a plaintiff received disparate treatment on the basis of race, as long as the trier of fact believes that the raters were truly ignorant of racial information about the candidates.

The causal connection is crucial. It does not suffice to show that the plaintiff was treated unfairly if the grounds are unrelated to a dimension proscribed by the Act. In *Holder v. City of Raleigh*,[44] for example, the employer chose to hire someone who was favored solely because he was the nephew of an interviewer and the son of a crew supervisor. The plaintiff, who belonged to a minority group, was better qualified. The court held that although the decision was distasteful, it did not violate Title VII because the decision-maker was not invidiously motivated.

40. Adams v. Ameritech Servs., 231 F.3d 414 (7th Cir.2000).

41. Id. at 428.

42. Weinstock v. Columbia Univ., 224 F.3d 33, 40 (2d Cir.2000), cert. denied, ___ U.S. ___, 124 S.Ct. 53, 157 L.Ed.2d 24 (2003), quoting Reeves v. Sanderson Plumb-ing Prods., Inc., 530 U.S. 133, 120 S.Ct. 2097, 2109, 147 L.Ed.2d 105 (2000).

43. 450 U.S. 248, 101 S.Ct. 1089, 67 L.Ed.2d 207 (1981).

44. 867 F.2d 823 (4th Cir.1989).

Once a case has been tried on the merits, it is no longer relevant whether the plaintiff correctly established a prima facie case in the first instance.[45] The Supreme Court has identified the reason for the *McDonnell Douglas* rules as simply "to govern the basic allocation of burdens and order of presentation of proof."[46] The prima facie case is no longer relevant once the case has been tried on the merits because the defendant already has been required to present evidence as if the plaintiff had made a prima facie case.

After-Acquired Evidence

Another group of individual disparate treatment cases are known as "after acquired evidence" cases. The question they pose is whether an employer can justify a discriminatory action against an employee by the later discovery of wrongful conduct on the job, such as stealing, that would have justified dismissal. Do the legitimate grounds, unknown at the time of the dismissal, preclude the discrimination claim?

The Supreme Court resolved this issue in *McKennon v. Nashville Banner Publishing Co.*[47] In this case the plaintiff alleged that her discharge from her position as a confidential secretary was a violation of the ADEA. She admitted in deposition that she had copied several confidential documents during her final year of employment because she feared an unlawful discharge and wanted to gather proof for her case. The district court granted summary judgment for the employer because her misconduct was grounds for termination and therefore no remedy was available even if the employer had also violated the ADEA in the initial discharge. The Supreme Court reversed and held that she was not barred from all relief.

The Court held that when an employer discovers evidence of wrongdoing that, in any event, would have led to termination on lawful and legitimate grounds had the employer known of it, an employee may recover back pay only until the point of this discovery. Reinstatement and front pay are inappropriate remedies. The Court thus adopted a remedial compromise similar to that chosen by Congress with respect to the related, but distinct, type of cases known as "mixed motive cases." Whereas an after acquired evidence case involves a discriminatory discharge later justified by evidence found after the wrongful act, a mixed motive case involves both legitimate and illegitimate motives simultaneously motivating an adverse employment decision.

One significance of the *McKennon* decision is that it reflects the Court's unspoken willingness to accept the priorities of Congress as reflected by the Civil Rights Act of 1991, even when interpreting provisions not affected by the 1991 Act. Congressional intent is reflected in the 1991 Act's approach to Title VII mixed motive cases, overturning the

---

45. United States Postal Serv. Bd. of Governors v. Aikens, 460 U.S. 711, 714–715, 103 S.Ct. 1478, 1481–1482, 75 L.Ed.2d 403 (1983).

46. 103 S.Ct. at 1482.

47. 513 U.S. 352, 115 S.Ct. 879, 130 L.Ed.2d 852 (1995).

Supreme Court's approach in *Price Waterhouse v. Hopkins*.[48] The Court originally resolved the mixed motive question in that case by holding that there was no unlawful employment practice if the legitimate ground was a motivating factor in the adverse decision. Congress disagreed in the Civil Rights Act of 1991 and provided for limited relief in Title VII mixed motive cases. In *McKennon* the Court reached the same resolution as Congress for this ADEA after acquired evidence case.

An open question is whether the rationale of *McKennon* applies to cases where the after acquired evidence involves resume fraud. Whereas *McKennon* involved wrongful conduct on the job, a resume fraud case is one where the employer argues that the plaintiff never would have been hired but for fraud in the application. In *Mardell v. Harleysville Life Insurance Co.*,[49] for example, the plaintiff claimed discriminatory discharge, but the employer defended by showing that she exaggerated her resume when she was initially hired. Her resume had failed to note that some of her work experience was unpaid student experience. She also claimed she received a B.A. degree, but the registrar's office did not have notification that she had completed all her course work, and her earned degree had never been conferred. This pre-*McKennon* case resolved the issue in the same manner as *McKennon* later did in the employee misconduct case. The court rejected the approach of some other cases that reasoned the plaintiff cannot complain about discriminatory conduct occurring on a job obtained by fraud. *McKennon*'s reasoning will probably control this line of resume fraud cases, but the matter is not free from doubt.

The practical effect of *McKennon* and related cases is to provide plaintiffs' attorneys with an incentive to pursue a legitimate claim of discrimination even if additional, nondiscriminatory reasons legitimate the action. Although the individual plaintiffs do not recover further accumulated back pay nor any equitable relief, they can recover attorney's fees for the prevailing part of the claim.

The other practical effect of the "after acquired evidence" rule is to provide employers with an incentive to search for wrongdoing. After discharging an employee who alleges discrimination, an employer's hunt for evidence of wrongdoing on the job or of a material misrepresentation in the plaintiff's initial application for employment may be rewarded with reduced liability. The Supreme Court noted this potential effect and cautioned that sanctions would be appropriate for abusive conduct.

The application of *McKennon* to Title VII is gaining rapid acceptance in the circuit courts. The basis for this application is the common substantive features and common purposes of the two acts. A few courts have considered "after after-acquired" evidence cases in which the employer seeks to introduce evidence of wrongdoing by the plaintiff after

48. 490 U.S. 228, 109 S.Ct. 1775, 104 L.Ed.2d 268 (1989).

49. 31 F.3d 1221 (3d Cir.1994), affirmed in part, vacated in part, 65 F.3d 1072 (3d Cir.1995).

the employment relationship has ended. In one case,[50] the employer sought to introduce evidence that a youth worker smoked marijuana. In another,[51] a law firm wanted to introduce evidence of misconduct by the plaintiff, one of its former lawyers, with respect to documents that she had copied after her employment had ended. Both courts held that *McKennon* is premised on conduct that occurs during employment rather than afterwards.

§ 2.9 Intentional Discrimination—Mixed Motives

A mixed motive case is one in which the adverse employment action was caused by both unlawful discrimination and legitimate factors interacting together on the outcome. They occur when the plaintiff establishes improper motivation and the defendant establishes that there were additional legitimate factors that affected the adverse decision. It is because of these two causes that the case becomes one called "mixed motive" because of the simultaneous presence of legitimate and illegitimate factors motivating the decision process.

Mixed motive cases have had a turbulent history in the Supreme Court and Congress. Although the definition of such cases has not changed, everything else has: procedures, remedies, and the nature of the evidence that plaintiffs may present.

"Mixed Motive" History—Hopkins and the Civil Rights Act of 1991

The Supreme Court addressed the relative burdens in a mixed motive case, but Congress overturned the decision in the Civil Rights Act of 1991. The Court had held in *Price Waterhouse v. Hopkins*[1] that when a plaintiff proves that illegal factors played a motivating part in the employment decision, the defendant may prevail by proving that it would have made the same decision regardless of the illegal factors.

In *Hopkins* the plaintiff proved that the defendant had engaged in gender stereotyping when denying the plaintiff partnership status. The plaintiff was advised that in order to improve her chances for partnership the next time, she should "walk more femininely, talk more femininely, dress more femininely, wear make-up, have her hair styled, and wear jewelry." In addition to this illegal stereotyping, the employer also was motivated by a legitimate factor. The trier of fact had found that Hopkins was not promoted because of her difficulty in relating to her coworkers. Because the employer established it would have reached the same adverse employment decision regardless of the gender stereotyping, the plaintiff lost in her initial trial.

Congress specifically addressed the *Hopkins* issues in the Civil Rights Act of 1991. It amended Title VII to provide for the burdens of proof and the remedial consequences in a mixed motive case. Liability

---

50. Carr v. Woodbury County Juvenile Detention Ctr., 905 F.Supp. 619 (N.D.Iowa 1995).

51. Sigmon v. Parker Chapin Flattau & Klimpl, 901 F.Supp. 667 (S.D.N.Y.1995).

§ 2.9

1. 490 U.S. 228, 109 S.Ct. 1775, 104 L.Ed.2d 268 (1989).

attaches when the plaintiff establishes that a decision was caused in part by illegal animus. Section 703(m) of the Act now provides that liability is established whenever "the complaining party demonstrates that race, color, religion, sex, or national origin was a motivating factor for any employment decision, even though other factors also motivated the practice."

Mixed Motive Cases—Remedies

The 1991 Act further amended Title VII to provide for limited remedies in mixed motive cases. Section 706(g) now provides that when a plaintiff has established that illegal animus motivated a decision, the defendant can limit the available remedies by proving that it would have taken the same adverse decision in the absence of the impermissible motivating factor. Remedies are then limited to declaratory relief, affirmative relief that cannot include hiring or reinstatement, and attorney's fees.

In the context of mixed motive cases, the practical effect of the 1991 amendments to Title VII is to remove the litigation disincentive that *Hopkins* created. Plaintiffs with evidence of discrimination will more easily find attorneys to pursue their claims, because attorneys will be assured of recovering statutory fees from defendants once improper animus is established as a motivating factor. In choosing to take a case with direct evidence of discrimination, attorneys need not fear that the entire case will be lost if the employer can prove that the motivation was mixed.

Nature of Plaintiff's Evidence

Following *Hopkins*, lower courts assumed for many years that mixed motive cases were triggered only when the plaintiff presented direct evidence of discrimination. There was nothing in the opinion to require only direct evidence, but the facts of that case had contained such evidence. The plaintiff had been told that her chances of partnership would be improved if she behaved in a more feminine manner. In opposition to the plaintiff's direct evidence of discrimination, the employer established that her abrasiveness with staff was a legitimate reason for not promoting her. The concurring opinion by Justice O'Connor characterized the case as one of "mixed motive" combining *direct* evidence with legitimate factors, and afterwards the lower courts proceeded in mixed motive cases only when there was direct evidence of discrimination.

During the years after *Hopkins* and before the Supreme Court decided *Desert Palace Inc. v. Costa*,[2] courts struggled with the difference between cases proceeding with direct evidence under the mixed motive line of cases and indirect evidence under the scheme of *McDonnell Douglas* to establish pretext. For example, the First Circuit in *Fernandes v. Costa Brothers Masonry*[3] offered a framework for mixed motive cases

---

2. 539 U.S. 90, 123 S.Ct. 2148, 156 L.Ed.2d 84 (2003).

3. 199 F.3d 572 (1st Cir.1999).

that began with the difficulty of identifying "direct" evidence of discrimination.

The Supreme Court considered in *Desert Palace* whether direct evidence is required for a plaintiff to obtain a mixed-motive instruction under section 2000e–2(m). The Court held that no such "heightened showing" through direct evidence is required. Further, the Court held that a Title VII plaintiff need only demonstrate that an employer used a forbidden consideration with respect to any employment practice, and that "to obtain an instruction under section 2000e–2(m), a plaintiff need only present sufficient evidence," direct or circumstantial, "for a reasonable jury to conclude, by a preponderance of the evidence, that race, color, religion, sex, or national origin was a motivating factor for any employment practice."[4]

The significance of *Desert Palace* is that plaintiffs no longer need to establish direct evidence of discriminatory motive in order to receive a mixed motive instruction. The full impact of this difference in litigation has yet to be seen.

Causation in Mixed Motive Cases

It is essential to the plaintiff's mixed motive claim that the evidence of animus be connected to the adverse decision. It is not sufficient to demonstrate unrelated animus, such as a harassing environment, unless there is a connection between that unlawful animus and the employment decision. This principle applies even when the harassing environment itself may be actionable.

In one case,[5] for example, a woman brought a claim of discriminatory discharge against her employer as well as a claim of hostile environment. She had been the first woman assigned to the installation and repair department and the evidence revealed that the employer was responsible for a sexually harassing atmosphere in the warehouse out of which she worked. The trier of fact found that there were sexually suggestive gestures and comments and lewd cartoons posted and distributed. Moreover, women in the warehouse were assigned to undesirable work when similarly situated men were not so assigned. The finding of a hostile work environment supported the award of nominal damages. The court did not sustain the plaintiff's claim of discriminatory discharge, however. The employer offered proof that she was discharged for poor performance, and the plaintiff did not show this reason to be pretextual. Her evidence of the hostile work environment was relevant to the claim, and separately actionable, but the trier of fact was not persuaded that the employer's reasons for her discharge were pretextual. She failed to establish a mixed motive claim because the trier of fact found the employer's motivation in her discharge to be only legitimate—not mixed.

Once the causal connection is established, however, the plaintiff in a mixed motive case is in a better position to establish the presence of

---

4. 123 S.Ct. at 2155.

5. Parton v. GTE N., 971 F.2d 150 (8th Cir.1992).

discrimination than a plaintiff in a purely pretext case under the *McDonnell Douglas* burden-shifting scheme. In pretext cases plaintiffs retain the burden of showing that discrimination played a role and had a determinative influence on the outcome. In contrast, in a mixed motive case, the plaintiff need only show that discrimination was a motivating factor. The reason for the difference is caused by the Civil Rights Act of 1991. As noted earlier in this section, a portion of that Act that was responding to the Supreme Court's *Hopkins* decision. The legislative solution was to make the burden shift to the defendant to show that the same result would have been reached in the absence of discrimination. Under the mixed motive scheme as modified by the 1991 Act, however, the effect of the defendant's successful proof is to limit the plaintiff's remedies. Although the mixed motive plaintiff thus has a greater chance of establishing the presence of discrimination than the purely pretext plaintiff, the chance of recovering compensatory and punitive damages is greater for the purely pretext plaintiff.

§ 2.10　Discharge and Constructive Discharge

The disparate treatment theory of individual discrimination applies to discharge and constructive discharge cases as well as to hiring cases. Although the original burden shifting scheme of *McDonnell Douglas Corp. v. Green*[1] was premised on hiring, the Supreme Court has now provided a model of its application in a discharge case, *Reeves v. Sanderson Plumbing Products*.[2] To prove a prima facie case of discrimination in a discharge case following *Reeves*, the plaintiff generally needs to prove: (i) at the time he was fired, he was a member of a protected class; (ii) he was otherwise qualified for the position held; (iii) he was discharged by the employer; and (iv) the employer subsequent held the position open.

The Supreme Court's opinion in *Swierkiewicz v. Sorema*,[3] subsequent to both *McDonnell Douglas* and *Reeves*, emphasized that the prima facie case is a "flexible evidentiary standard" and that it should not be applied rigidly. Some circuits have reduced the standard to its bear bones. The District of Columbia Circuit has observed: "This court, like our sister circuits, requires a plaintiff to state a prima facie claim of discrimination by establishing that: (1) she is a member of a protected class; (2) she suffered an adverse employment action; and (3) the unfavorable action gives rise to an inference of discrimination."[4]

Special Issues with the Prima Facie Case in Discharge Cases

The *Reeves* formulation for the prima facie case of discriminatory discharge closely parallels the original *McDonnell Douglas* recitation with simple adaptation from "hiring" to "firing" language. Circuits had

§ 2.10

1. 411 U.S. 792, 93 S.Ct. 1817, 36 L.Ed.2d 668 (1973).

2. 530 U.S. 133, 120 S.Ct. 2097, 147 L.Ed.2d 105 (2000).

3. 534 U.S. 506, 122 S.Ct. 992, 152 L.Ed.2d 1 (2002).

4. Stella v. Mineta, 284 F.3d 135 (D.C. Cir. 2002).

made such a parallel before the Supreme Court decided *Reeves*, creating a body of law that would appear not to be altered by the *Reeves* formulation of the prima facie case.

The "qualification" step of the prima facie case in a discharge case has created difficulty for some plaintiffs. Some courts have required plaintiffs to prove that they were performing at a level of the employer's legitimate expectations at the time of discharge. Others have reasoned that the reason for the discharge should not be considered part of the qualification requirement for a prima facie case because it is the employer's burden to show legitimate business purpose.

Some cases have found a failure of the prima facie case if a discharged plaintiff was not replaced by members outside their racial, ethnic, or gender group. The theory is that the employer could not have been acting out of animus against the plaintiff's group if someone from the same group is favored.

The Supreme Court has answered this question for the ADEA, and the District of Columbia Circuit rejected this requirement for Title VII as well. The Supreme Court case addressing the question under the ADEA is *O'Connor v. Consolidated Coin Caterers Corp.*[5] The fifty-six year old plaintiff in *O'Connor* pleaded that he was discharged despite his satisfactory job performance and replaced by a younger person. The Fourth Circuit found a problem with the fourth element of the plaintiff's prima facie case, which it characterized as "following his discharge or demotion, he was replaced by someone of comparable qualifications outside the protected class,"[6] because the plaintiff's replacement was forty and thus inside the ADEA protected class. The Supreme Court held that in an age discrimination case the plaintiff is not required to show that the favored applicant or employee is outside the protected age group. Noting that the ADEA prohibits discrimination on the basis of age rather than class membership, the Court found it irrelevant whether one person in the protected class has been favored over another person in that class.

Burden Shifting Scheme in Discharge Cases

Once the plaintiff establishes the prima facie case, the burden shifts to the employer to articulate a legitimate nondiscriminatory reason for the discharge. This burden is one of production, not persuasion. The employer does not necessarily need to prove that the discharged employee's performance was inadequate; the employer need only dispel the inference of unlawful discrimination. It was sufficient in one case, for example, for the employer to dispel the inference of intent in a discharge case by citing the employee's refusal to commit to the job. The plaintiff had expressed doubts about his future in Kansas City, where the employer was located, because his wife had remained in Indiana and the plaintiff was uncertain whether she would move. The discharge was not

5. 517 U.S. 308, 116 S.Ct. 1307, 134   **6.** 116 S.Ct. at 1313.
L.Ed.2d 433 (1996).

related to the plaintiff's performance, but it was not unlawfully motivated under Title VII.[7]

The ultimate question of fact remains whether the employer was motivated to terminate the employee because of race, color, religion, sex, or national origin. In a typical case, the employee can establish a prima facie case and the employer rebuts with evidence of poor job performance. The plaintiff then must establish by a preponderance of the evidence that the proffered reason is pretextual. Even direct evidence of animus or general evidence of disparate working conditions is not sufficient to establish that the termination itself was discriminatory.

For example,[8] an Hispanic female plaintiff failed to show unlawful motivation in her discharge. She presented evidence that she was required to perform menial duties, such as preparing coffee, and that the president told her that she needed to work twice as hard as equivalent employees because she was young, Hispanic, and female. The district court judge believed that the employer discharged her because of her poor job performance, however, and not for unlawfully discriminatory reasons. Any claim for disparate working conditions would have to proceed as a separate theory of recovery under Title VII and not as a claim for discriminatory discharge.

Constructive Discharge

Cases involving constructive discharge are slightly different from those involving express discharge. A constructive discharge occurs if working conditions are such that a reasonable person in the plaintiff's circumstances would feel compelled to resign. The employer has committed a constructive discharge "[w]hen an employee involuntarily resigns in order to escape intolerable and illegal employment requirements."[9]

A few decisions have focused upon the intent of the employer in constructive discharge cases and required the plaintiff to show that the employer intended to force the resignation. The Eighth Circuit led the minority of circuits adopting this stricter view, but the most recent opinion from that jurisdiction has abandoned the position. *Hukkanen v. International Union of Operating Engineers Local No. 101*[10] held that the employer's state of mind is not controlling in a claim of constructive discharge. If the employer has created intolerable conditions that a reasonable person could not endure, then it does not matter that the employer only intended to have "fun" with the employee rather than to compel resignation. The conditions that support a claim of constructive discharge must be ones that have occurred and not simply feared. Otherwise there is no adverse action to support the claim.

The prima facie case based upon *McDonnell Douglas* is modified for constructive discharge to require: (i) membership in a protected class, (ii)

---

7. Harris v. Board of Pub. Util., 757 F.Supp. 1185 (D.Kan.1991).

8. Valdez v. San Antonio Chamber of Commerce, 974 F.2d 592 (5th Cir.1992).

9. Henson v. Dundee, 682 F.2d 897 (11th Cir.1982).

10. 3 F.3d 281 (8th Cir.1993).

satisfactory performance, (iii) constructive discharge despite qualification, and (iv) circumstances giving rise to an inference of discrimination. Constructive discharge claims often arise in the context of racial or sexual harassment. The employee's resignation must be related to the employer's actions or inactions, rather than to personal reasons. The plaintiff need not prove that the employer intended to force the resignation, but the constructive discharge must be the reasonable and foreseeable result of the employer's conduct.

Constructive Discharge versus Hostile Environment Harassment Claims

The Fourth Circuit in *Amirmokri v. Baltimore Gas & Electric Co.*[11] compared and distinguished the requirements of constructive discharge with those of harassment. The court noted that claims for workplace harassment and constructive discharge are both governed by two-part tests. The first part of each test is the severity of the conditions. Whereas the conduct must be "severe and pervasive" for an harassment claim, the work environment for a claim of constructive discharge must be "intolerable." Second, the employer's response is critical in both types of claims. To defeat liability in a hostile environment harassment claim, the employer must have taken prompt and adequate action. To defeat a constructive discharge claim, the employer must have taken action reasonably calculated to end the intolerable working environment.

Focusing upon this last test, the court explained by means of example that a superficial response by the employer should not be sufficient to defeat a constructive discharge:

> To hold that any response by an employer, however superficial, negates any inference of intent in a constructive discharge claim might paradoxically deny relief to employees who suffer from the "intolerable" conditions necessary for constructive discharge rather than less severe conditions that might give rise to an ordinary workplace harassment claim. Suppose, for example, that an employee suffers workplace harassment on account of his national origin and his employer responds with token action that does not sincerely address the problem. If the harassment is severe and pervasive, the employee can bring a workplace harassment claim and obtain relief. If, however, the environment became intolerable and the employee were forced to resign, he would be unable (in the face of a token response) to bring a constructive discharge claim and would therefore be without a remedy. Requiring a response reasonably calculated to end the intolerable environment avoids this inequitable result.[12]

Constructive discharge claims in harassment cases play a particular role with respect to the statute of limitations. If the last act of harassment occurs more than 180 days before the complaint is filed the harassment claim may be time-barred. If the working conditions from

11. 60 F.3d 1126 (4th Cir.1995).   **12.** 60 F.3d at 1133.

the harassment make an intolerable condition for employment, however, such that the plaintiff quits and can establish constructive discharge, then the constructive discharge itself is a discriminatory act for purposes of the statute of limitations.

Constructive discharge in the context of harassment may become more important to establish following a decision of the Seventh Circuit that restricts damages in the absence of actual or constructive discharge. *Hertzberg v. SRAM Corp.*[13] held that recovery for back pay as well as front pay requires proof of actual discharge or constructive discharge. The unwillingness of a harassment victim to remain on the job is insufficient to support these elements of recovery. This restriction, if widely adopted, is particularly significant in light of the Supreme Court's opinion in *Pollard v. E.I. du Pont de Nemours & Co.*,[14] which held that front pay is a form of equitable relief rather than compensatory damages and therefore not included in the damages cap. The Seventh Circuit has provided a different form of restriction on front pay awards, as well as back pay awards.

§ 2.11 Retaliation for Opposing Discrimination

Title VII provides that it is an unlawful employment practice for a person covered by the Act to discriminate against an individual "because he has opposed any practice made an unlawful employment practice by this title, or because he has made a charge, testified, assisted, or participated in any manner in an investigation, proceeding, or hearing under this title."[1] This provision creates the cause of action for retaliation caused by "opposition" or "participation."

The elements of a cause of action for retaliation are: (1) the plaintiff engaged in a protected activity; (2) the plaintiff suffered an adverse employment decision; and (3) the adverse decision was motivated by the protected activity such that there was a causal connection between the two. The last element may be established by direct evidence of retaliatory animus or by indirect evidence of disparate treatment. When a plaintiff uses the indirect method of proof, the *McDonnell Douglas*[2] allocation of burdens apply.

Retaliation for Opposition to Discrimination

This protection against retaliation applies when the plaintiff is opposing discrimination directed against the plaintiff or third parties. For example, an employer may not retaliate against a supervisor for hiring diverse employees.[3] Moreover, an employer may not retaliate

13. 261 F.3d 651 (7th Cir.2001), cert. denied, 534 U.S. 1130, 122 S.Ct. 1070, 151 L.Ed.2d 973 (2002).
14. 532 U.S. 843, 121 S.Ct. 1946, 150 L.Ed.2d 62 (2001).

§ 2.11
1. 42 U.S.C.A. § 2000e–3(a).
2. McDonald v. Santa Fe Trail Transp. Co., 427 U.S. 273, 96 S.Ct. 2574, 49 L.Ed.2d

493 (1976), citing McDonnell Douglas Corp. v. Green, 411 U.S. 792, 93 S.Ct. 1817, 36 L.Ed.2d 668 (1973). See also Reeves v. Sanderson Plumbing Prods., 530 U.S. 133, 120 S.Ct. 2097, 147 L.Ed.2d 105 (2000).

3. EEOC v. St. Anne's Hosp., 664 F.2d 128 (7th Cir.1981).

against an employee or applicant because of the protected activities of a spouse, relative, or close friend.[4]

Plaintiffs have increasingly brought claims of retaliation on the basis that the opposition to discrimination was directed against them. The typical case involves a plaintiff who is discharged following a complaint of sexual harassment or other gender discrimination directed against her. The plaintiff may have a claim for harassment but the retaliation claim provides advantages if the plaintiff is not barred by the same defenses that apply to harassment claims. The Third Circuit considered the relationship of the two types of claims in *Farrell v. Planters Lifesavers*.[5] In that case a female employee rejected a supervisor's sexual advance and was discharged several weeks later. The employee "opposed" discrimination for her retaliation claim only by rejecting the sexual advance. The district court rejected the claim on the basis that she did not allege that the supervisor had threatened retaliation. The circuit court reversed and held that she did not need to show a threat of retaliation, either implicitly or explicitly, in order to demonstrate that she was terminated in retaliation for rejecting the sexual advance.

An open question is whether a claim for retaliation under section 704 can be based upon opposition to a practice that is not unlawful under Title VII but which the employee reasonably believes in good faith to be unlawful. Although the Supreme Court has never addressed the issue, the courts of appeal have followed this rule.[6] For example, in *Jurado v. Eleven–Fifty Corp.*,[7] the Hispanic plaintiff was a radio announcer in Los Angeles who protested a new rule restricting his broadcast to all English words. He had been accustomed to sprinkling street Spanish phrases into the program. Although the language restriction was not discriminatory, the court observed that opposition to the practice would be protected.

The Supreme Court has noted that it has never resolved the question whether a good faith, reasonable belief that discrimination has occurred is sufficient for a claim under section 704. In *Clark County School District v. Breeden*,[8] the Court reversed a decision from the Ninth Circuit in which it applied the standard of "reasonable belief." The Supreme Court found it unnecessary to address whether that standard is the correct one because the Court disagreed with the lower court that, under the circumstances of the case, the belief could be reasonable. The Justices therefore remanded the case without resolving the issue whether a reasonable belief that discrimination has occurred suffices for a section 704 opposition claim.

4. Aquino v Sommer Maid Creamery, Inc. 657 F.Supp. 208 (E.D.Pa.1987).

5. 206 F.3d 271 (3d Cir.2000).

6. Leading cases adopting this rule are Jennings v. Tinley Park Community Consolidated Sch. Dist., 796 F.2d 962 (7th Cir. 1986) and EEOC v. Crown Zellerbach, 720 F.2d 1008 (9th Cir.1983).

7. 813 F.2d 1406 (9th Cir.1987).

8. 532 U.S. 268, 121 S.Ct. 1508, 149 L.Ed.2d 509 (2001).

The facts in *Breeden* involved a woman's offense at a laugh shared between two male employees over a sexual innuendo that surfaced as part of a required meeting. The plaintiff and the two male employees were going over a job applicant's file and they were discussing a notation in the file of a remark made by the applicant in the past. The remark, made to a woman not involved in the lawsuit, was: "I hear that making love to you is like making love to the Grand Canyon." The male supervisor at the meeting said that he "didn't get it" and the other male employee laughed and said that he would "explain it later." The plaintiff later consulted the employer's regulations on harassing behavior, which specifically mentioned sexually explicit jokes. She then complained that she found the laugh between the two men to be offensive and contrary to the employer's policy. She also filed a complaint with the Nevada Equal Rights Commission and the EEOC. When she was subsequently transferred to a position she found less desirable, she sued for retaliation. The district court granted summary judgment, but the court of appeals remanded for consideration whether the transfer was retaliatory. The Ninth Circuit said that the plaintiff was protected from retaliation from complaining about a sexually explicit remark because, although the remark did not rise to the level of unlawful harassment, the plaintiff had a good faith, reasonable belief that it did.[9]

Retaliation for "Participation" in Proceedings Concerning Discrimination

A retaliation claim based upon "participation in proceedings" is different from one based upon "opposition to discrimination" in one respect. In contrast to the requirements of good faith and reasonableness for an opposition claim, a claim based on retaliation for participation in proceedings may stand even if the plaintiff's conduct was malicious. This principle was established in *Pettway v. American Cast Iron Pipe Co.*,[10] where an employee made knowingly false statements in a request for reconsideration of his race discrimination case before the EEOC. The court treated the request as the equivalent of a petition for reconsideration and thus part of the "proceeding" of the Commission. Noting that the employer's interest in being free from libelous attacks could be vindicated through defamation law, the court feared the chilling effect of a rule that protected only some statements from retaliation against the speaker. Therefore, the court held that even malicious materials contained in a charge or communication with the EEOC entitled the employee to protection from retaliation. His discharge violated Title VII and the court awarded reinstatement, back pay, and protective orders as needed for his protection.

Participants in proceedings who are answering questions under oath may reveal their own inappropriate behavior at work as a by-product of the proceedings. The question then becomes whether discipline or dis-

9. Breeden v. Clark County Sch. Dist., 232 F.3d 893 (9th Cir. 2000) (unpublished opinion), rev'd, 532 U.S. 268, 121 S.Ct. 1508, 149 L.Ed.2d 509 (2001).

10. 411 F.2d 998 (5th Cir.1969).

charge based upon information acquired in this fashion is retaliation for participation in the proceedings. The difficulty of distinguishing the participation from the conduct can be a troubling factual question. In *Merritt v. Dillard Paper Co.,*[11] an employer discharged an employee after he revealed in a deposition that he had personally engaged in acts of sexual harassment against a co-worker who was claiming harassment against a third party. The company president was furious that the deposition was so damaging to their case. He fired the employee with the comments that his deposition had been "the most damning" to the company's case. The court held that the discharge could be illegal retaliation if the employee was fired for the deposition rather than for the sexual harassment to which he confessed. Relevant to this inquiry was the fact that the president made no independent investigation of the harassment but simply fired the employee upon reading his deposition.

Breeden may signal the Supreme Court's hostility to retaliation cases in general with this holding, but it may simply be a case of unsympathetic plaintiffs making "bad law." The dissenting opinion by Judge Fernandez in the Court of Appeals decision may have best identified the problem with this case. His full dissent said:

> I respectfully dissent because, as I see it, Breeden has unreasonably built a whole edifice of alleged harassment and retaliation upon the shaky foundation of a single comment at a single meeting. No doubt workplaces are not Panglossian retreats. But this is not the best of all possible worlds, and I doubt that we improve it when we encourage litigation of this ilk.[12]

Whatever the underlying reason the Supreme Court rejected this claim, the language of the holding leaves open questions for section 704 suits. First, it opens the question that the circuits had resolved: Is it sufficient for a plaintiff to have a good faith, reasonable belief that the employer has engaged in conduct unlawful under Title VII, or must the conduct in fact be a violation of the Act? Second, what kind of causal proof must the plaintiff produce to link an adverse employment action to the protected conduct? The Court did not reject the cases relying on temporal proximity, but it did hold temporal proximity may be inadequate proof in situations where it may previously have been found sufficient.

Who is Protected from Retaliation?

Retaliation against federal employees is not expressly prohibited by the Act. The federal government is not a defined "employer" under section 701(b) and thus the provisions relating to retaliation do not directly apply. There are no parallel provisions under section 717(a) which prohibits discrimination by the federal government. Courts have implied such protection against retaliation, however.

---

11. 120 F.3d 1181 (11th Cir. 1997).

12. Breeden v. Clark County School District, 232 F.3d 893 (9th Cir.2000) (Fernandez, J., dissenting) (unpublished opinion), rev'd, 532 U.S. 268, 121 S.Ct. 1508, 149 L.Ed.2d 509 (2001).

The Act also does not literally prohibit retaliation against former employees. Claims of retaliation with respect to employment records or references have presented this issue. The question is whether an employer violates Title VII by informing other prospective employers of the fact that a former employee filed charges of discrimination or by giving an unjustifiably negative reference in retaliation. The Supreme Court resolved a split among the circuits on this issue in *Robinson v. Shell Oil Co.*,[13] where the Court held that the word "employee" included former as well as current employees in the context of the antiretaliation provision. The opinion explains that it would be destructive of the purpose of the antiretaliation provision for an employer to be able to retaliate against complaints of discriminatory termination and that the Act must be read in its broader context.

Basis for Employer Liability

An open question under Title VII's antiretaliation provision is the standard to which employers should be held with respect to knowledge of the retaliating conduct of a supervisor. The Eighth Circuit had occasion to address this issue for the first time in *Cross v. Cleaver*.[14] A female police officer filed a complaint of sexual harassment, after which the police chief allegedly used his authority to retaliate against her with reassignments and a suspension. The employer was the city police board of commissioners, so any retaliation by the police chief was in his capacity as supervisor. The employer argued that the appropriate standard was whether it "knew or should have known" of the conduct. The court held that a strict vicarious liability standard was appropriate where the police chief was acting under his authority from the employer. The court cautioned that the standard of employer liability applicable to a retaliation claim may depend on the status of the retaliator and the nature of retaliation. It thus leaves open the possibility that an employer may not be strictly liable for retaliatory conduct by someone who is not so high in the hierarchy that the conduct is necessarily imputed to the employer.

§ 2.12   Racial Harassment

Among the prohibitions of Title VII is discrimination against any individual with respect to "compensations, terms, conditions, or privileges" of employment.[1] The Supreme Court held in *Meritor Savings Bank, FSB v. Vinson*[2] that the harassment of an employee on a basis covered by the Act can be actionable as affecting a condition of employment. The principle of that case, which was a sexual harassment case, has been extended to racial and other forms of harassment. Such claims are known as "hostile environment" or "abusive working environment" cases.

---

13. 519 U.S. 337, 117 S.Ct. 843, 136 L.Ed.2d 808 (1997).

14. 142 F.3d 1059 (8th Cir. 1998).

2. 477 U.S. 57, 106 S.Ct. 2399, 91 L.Ed.2d 49 (1986).

§ 2.12

1. 42 U.S.C.A. § 20003–2(a).

The topic of this chapter section is when harassment on the basis of race is a violation of Title VII as a discriminatory condition of employment. Plaintiffs may also bring racial harassment claims under state statutory law. In addition, common law actions for intentional infliction of emotional distress may be brought for intentional racial disparagement conducted in a rude, insolent, or violent manner for the purpose of causing emotional and physical distress.

Employer Policies Creating a Hostile Environment

The plaintiff in a Title VII racial harassment case must show the existence of a "hostile environment" on the basis of race. The essence of the action is that the employer created or permitted an intimidating, offensive work environment. The Supreme Court explained in the context of a sexual harassment case, *Harris v. Forklift Systems*,[3] that a hostile environment claim must show harassment "sufficiently severe or pervasive to alter the conditions of the victim's employment and create an abusive working environment." Such an environment may be created by policies or practices of the employer or by failure to take action to correct the harassing atmosphere created by other employees or customers.

There have not been many recent cases involving policies, as opposed to practices, that create a hostile environment. *Rogers v. EEOC*[4] was a 1971 landmark case where the Fifth Circuit recognized that an employer's policy may affect a condition of employment under Title VII. The defendant optometrist in Texas had a policy of segregating patients on the basis of national origin. The plaintiff was the only Spanish-surnamed employee and she alleged that the segregation of patients created a hostile work environment for her. The district court found that any offense to her "sensibilities" caused by the segregation was not an employment practice within the meaning of Title VII. The Fifth Circuit disagreed and held that the "practice of creating a working environment heavily charged with ethnic or racial discrimination" is prohibited by Title VII.

Environments Made Racially Abusive by Co–Workers

The most common type of claim of hostile environment discrimination involves conduct of co-workers and supervisors rather than policies of the employer. Claims of this type may be defended with proof that the employer did not and should not have known about the harassment or that the employer took all reasonable steps to prevent the harassment. This defense will be examined later in the section, after examining the elements of the claim.

The elements of a claim of hostile environment harassment vary somewhat among circuits and even within circuits. The general formulation is that the plaintiff must show that he or she was subjected, on the

3. 510 U.S. 17, 114 S.Ct. 367, 126 L.Ed.2d 295 (1993).

4. 454 F.2d 234 (5th Cir.1971), cert. denied, 406 U.S. 957, 92 S.Ct. 2058, 32 L.Ed.2d 343 (1972).

basis of race, to unwelcome harassment which was severe and pervasive enough to create an objectively and subjectively hostile or abusive work environment.

The severity and pervasiveness of the harassment is a question of fact that turns on the totality of the circumstances. The plaintiff must establish that the harassing environment was severe and pervasive. The Supreme Court explained in *Harris v. Forklift Systems*[5] that conduct that will rise to the level of severe and pervasive harassment must be more than rude, abrasive, unkind, or insensitive. It is generally said that federal antidiscrimination laws do not create a general "civility code."

First, the gravity of the offensive conduct is relevant to assessing its severity. In *Daniels v. Essex Group, Inc.*,[6] for example, the African–American plaintiff was subjected to racial harassment which included race-oriented graffiti, racial slurs, and a doll hung in effigy. In upholding a finding of unlawful discrimination, the Seventh Circuit considered the threatening nature of the conduct and its direction toward the plaintiff as the only African–American on the site. In general, gravity is greater if the conduct is personally directed at the plaintiff and if there are explicit or implicit threats of physical violence.

Next, the frequency and duration of the acts of racial harassment are important to establishing the severity and pervasiveness of the conduct. Sporadic and brief episodes are given less weight than ones that occur often and regularly. Although severity is normally established by demonstrating a series of incidents, it is not a requirement to show a series or pattern of conduct. Even isolated acts, if sufficiently serious, can create a racially hostile environment. In one case, a black employee produced sufficient evidence to create a jury question when she twice found a noose hanging from the light fixture above her work station and also found that some of her work had been sabotaged.

The character of non-threatening harassment is relevant. Conduct that is humiliating is more severe than conduct that is a "mere offensive utterance" or "simple teasing." Some racial harassment cases have relied on conduct that is belittling in a way that is historically racial in character. One early case involved the discharge of an employee after she filed a complaint with the NAACP regarding the employer's practice of deference to white employees but not to African–Americans. The employer referred to white employees as "Miss" or "Mrs." but referred to black employees by their first name.[7] The court in that early case found a Title VII violation. The facts, which sound insufficient for severe and pervasive harassment in current times, can be understood only in the context of the historical setting. The totality of the circumstances includes the surrounding societal norms.

Many cases of harassment involve the use of racial epithets in the work place and an open question is whether "mere epithets" in the

---

5. 510 U.S. 17, 114 S.Ct. 367, 126 L.Ed.2d 295 (1993).

6. 937 F.2d 1264 (7th Cir.1991).

7. Johnson v. Lillie Rubin Affiliates, 5 FEP Cases 547 (M.D.Tenn.1972).

absence of more directly threatening behavior can ever be sufficient to establish a hostile working environment. In *Johnson v. Bunny Bread Co.*,[8] African–American employees complained that their supervisors and coworkers often referred to them in racially derogatory terms. The Eighth Circuit held that there was no Title VII violation because the remarks were merely a part of casual conversation, accidental, or sporadic. Another case observed that Title VII was not intended to be a "clean language" act, but that an employer may not hide racist comments behind a "thicket of race-neutral insults and profanities."[9] Other cases have found that the use of repeated, racially abusive language can violate the Act.

The Second Circuit reversed the trial court's finding of no racial harassment in *Whidbee v. Garzarelli Food Specialties, Inc.*[10] on the grounds that the lower court failed to consider the totality of the circumstances in judging the severity and pervasiveness of the conduct. Although the duration of the incidents was shorter than in many cases, the African–American employees were subjected to a stream of derogatory comments for two or three months and at least one comment was physically threatening. The trial court also erred in according less weight to incidents that occurred after the plaintiffs submitted their notice of intended resignation. The Second Circuit noted that employees are not worthy of less protection simply because they have declared their intention to leave. The subsequent remarks were also relevant for assessing the severity of the harassment prior to the declaration of intent to resign.

When a single employee does not have a claim for racial harassment, a group of employees subjected to individualized incidents may have a claim sufficient to support injunctive relief to force an employer to respond. The Sixth Circuit held that a series of individualized acts could support such a claim brought by the EEOC.[11] Nooses in the workplace, KKK symbols, and other conduct need not be directed at individuals to support the claim for injunctive relief.

Objective and Subjective Standard

The harassment must be both objectively and subjectively offensive. The Supreme Court held in *Harris v. Forklift Systems*,[12] that it is not necessary for a plaintiff to show tangible psychological injury in a harassment case, but that it is necessary to demonstrate that a reasonable person would have found the environment to be hostile. Moreover, in addition to the objective standard, the plaintiff must show that he or she found the environment hostile; an unusually resilient victim cannot recover.

---

8. 646 F.2d 1250 (8th Cir.1981).

9. Rodgers v. Western–Southern Life Ins. Co., 792 F.Supp. 628, 635 (E.D.Wis. 1992), aff'd 12 F.3d 668 (7th Cir. 1993).

10. 223 F.3d 62 (2d Cir.2000).

11. EEOC v. Northwest Airlines, Inc., 188 F.3d 695 (6th Cir.1999).

12. 510 U.S. 17, 114 S.Ct. 367, 126 L.Ed.2d 295 (1993) (sexual harassment).

In *Daniels v. Essex Group, Inc.,*[13] the Seventh Circuit applied both an objective standard of abusiveness and a subjective standard of injury to the plaintiff, in upholding a verdict in the plaintiff's favor. In that case a black plaintiff was subjected to race-oriented graffiti, racial slurs, and a doll hung in effigy which the court found would be abusive to a reasonable person and was in fact abusive to the plaintiff.

The objective standard used in harassment cases is whether a reasonable person would find the environment to be hostile or abusive. Thus, a plaintiff who experienced an abusive work environment because of the supervisor's "sharp looks" could not state a claim if a reasonable person would not be affected in the same way by the conduct.[14]

The "reasonable person" standard has been controversial in the context of sexual harassment, but little has been written on the subject in the context of other types of harassment. Commentators have considered whether the standard for sexual harassment should be that of a "reasonable woman" as distinct from a "reasonable person" because women may find offensive conduct that men do not. The parallel question for racial harassment is whether to use a "reasonable black person" standard. A district court in Maine adopted this standard to assess the severity of racial harassment under Title VII and the Maine Human Rights Act (MHRA) in *Harris v. International Paper Co.*[15] The court reasoned that employing a "reasonable person" standard would permit discriminatory conduct and speech based on racial beliefs and stereotypes to remain unremedied.

The incident in question in *Harris* concerned the placement of a post card next to the time clock within a week of the African–American plaintiff's arrival at the paper mill. The post card depicted "Our Gang" and the handwritten caption said: "The new generation of papermakers." It depicted the "Little Rascals" attempting to wash a dog and the black character "Buckwheat" was set apart from the other children, who were white. The term "Buckwheat" was also used routinely in the mill as a racial epithet. The court found that these circumstances could reasonably be perceived by an African–American to be abusive. "Since the concern of Title VII and the MHRA is to redress the effects of conduct and speech on their victims," the court said, "the fact finder must 'walk a mile in the victim's shoes' to understand those effects and how they should be remedied." The court then explicitly adopted the "reasonable black person" standard by which to measure the hostility of the environment. Other courts have continued to use the "reasonable person" test in racial harassment as in sexual harassment cases.

The subjective standard asks whether this plaintiff personally experienced an abusive working environment because of the harassment. The Act protects individuals from interference with employment, so in the absence of such interference there is no violation. Thus, the "thick-

13. 937 F.2d 1264 (7th Cir.1991).

14. Ramsey v. Henderson, 286 F.3d 264 (5th Cir.2002).

15. 765 F.Supp. 1509 (D.Me.1991), vacated in part for other reasons, 765 F.Supp. 1529 (D.Me.1991).

skinned" plaintiff does not recover even when a "reasonable person" who would be offended and affected by the harassment could recover. This principle is illustrated by *Newman v. Federal Express Corp.*[16] where the plaintiff was subjected to racially harassing conduct that he subjectively did not find abusive. One incident involved a racially-charged hate letter received by a number of African–American employees. Another was a personal voice mail to him that contained the sounds of gun fire. The plaintiff admitted in deposition that at the time of receiving the letter he was not "surprised, shocked or disturbed" by it. He did not consider it a "big deal" and said that he would not lose sleep over it. He referred to the voice mail message with gun shots as "silly." In the absence of evidence that he was subjectively harassed by the incidents, there was no claim.

Causation

The harassment claim must establish a causal link between the abusive conduct and the plaintiff's race for Title VII coverage. Pranks and other forms of hazing, for example, will be unlawful only upon a showing that they were motivated by race. For example, in *Vaughn v. Pool Offshore Co.*,[17] the Fifth Circuit held that the hazing of a black oil rig worker was not racial harassment, even when the pranks were accompanied by racial epithets. The court noted that nearly all of the employees were subject to similar pranks, regardless of race, and that the environment was "coarse, rowdy, and generally abusive, but not polluted with discrimination."[18]

Similarly, federal law does not cover mere personality conflicts, even when the employees in conflict are racially different. In *Vore v. Indiana Bell*,[19] white employees complained about the conduct of a co-worker who was the only African–American employee in the office. He allegedly engaged in physical threats, angry tirades, and vulgarities toward them, but none was racial in nature. The court noted that federal law does not cover personality conflicts and upheld the grant of summary judgment for the defendant employer. The court observed that "Title VII is not implicated by the nebulous claim that Indiana Bell discriminated against white employees by permitting an unpleasant black employee to work with them."[20] There is no Title VII claim without racial animus.

The white co-workers further argued disparate treatment, claiming that the employer would have responded to their complains if the races of the co-workers had been reversed. There was evidence of a statement by a supervisor that the African–American employee was not disciplined for fear that he would file an EEOC complaint. The court affirmed summary judgment for the employer on this claim as well because there was no evidence of a policy of such disparate treatment nor any instances of such disparate discipline. Even if the supervisor made the alleged statement, the court reasoned, it could not "vilify every employer that

---

16. 266 F.3d 401 (6th Cir.2001).

17. 683 F.2d 922 (5th Cir.1982).

18. Id. at 925.

19. 32 F.3d 1161 (7th Cir.1994).

20. Id. at 1164.

exercises caution in the handling of delicate employment situations where race might factor."[21]

The animus that connects the harassment to the plaintiff must be racial in nature for a claim based on race. It is insufficient to prove harassment by persons of a different race unless the harassment is based on racial animus. In *Ramsey v. Henderson*,[22] the plaintiff was a postal worker of multiple ethnicities: Spanish, Chinese, American Indian, and Irish origin. She alleged harassment by her African–American female co-workers, and that the harassment became more severe when she dated an African–American man and had a baby with him. Her claim failed because of her failure to provide specific incidents of harassment and to connect her co-workers' general disapproval of her relationship to the race of the persons involved.

Basis for Employer Liability

The Supreme Court clarified the standard for employer liability in harassment cases in two important cases, *Burlington Industries, Inc. v. Ellerth*[23] and *Faragher v. City of Boca Raton*.[24] Both of these cases are sexual harassment cases whose holdings have been applied to all types of harassment claims under Title VII and the ADEA. The Court held in *Ellerth* that an employer in hostile environments harassment cases has an affirmative defense. The employer is liable unless it can show that (1) it exercised reasonable care to prevent and promptly correct the harassment and (2) that the employee unreasonably failed to use the employer's remedial procedures. Liability for workplace harassment by other co-workers or third-parties is determined according to a negligence standard. That standard is met if the employer knew or should have known of the harassment and failed to take corrective action.

This liability principle was further clarified by the Supreme Court in *Faragher*. The plaintiff was a female lifeguard living in close quarters with male lifeguards and supervisors who harassed her. Applying the affirmative defense, the Court noted that the city could not be found to have exercised reasonable care to prevent the harassment because the district court found that the city had entirely failed to disseminate its policy against sexual harassment among its beach employees and that it had made no attempt to keep track of conduct of supervisors. Moreover, the city's policy did not include any assurance that harassing supervisors could be bypassed when complainants reported their conduct.

The plaintiff's failure to invoke an employer's complaint procedure is a defense to the employer's liability when that procedure meets the standard of availability. In *Mems v. City of St. Paul, Department of Fire & Safety Services*,[25] the city had an appropriate complaint procedure in

21. Id.

22. 286 F.3d 264 (5th Cir.2002).

23. 524 U.S. 742, 118 S.Ct. 2257, 141 L.Ed.2d 633 (1998) (sexual harassment).

24. 524 U.S. 775, 118 S.Ct. 2275, 141 L.Ed.2d 662 (1998) (sexual harassment).

25. 327 F.3d 771 (8th Cir.2003), cert. denied, ___ U.S. ___, 124 S.Ct. 1052, 157 L.Ed.2d 891 (2004).

place and evidence that the four plaintiff firefighters had not availed themselves of it to complain about the racial harassment that was subject of their later suit. The court thus approved a jury instruction saying: "Plaintiffs claim that they were subjected to a racially hostile or abusive working environment. Defendant City of St. Paul denies this charge and claims that Plaintiffs unreasonably failed to take advantage of corrective opportunities." The jury found in favor of the defendant for three of the four plaintiffs and the verdict was upheld.

Employers are not liable for harassment under Title VII if they respond reasonably and promptly to known conditions. Although it is not necessary for the steps to stop the harassment as long as the measures are reasonably calculated to do so, the cessation of the harassment after action by management is almost always fatal to a claim of hostile environment. For example, in *Woodland v. Ryerson & Son, Inc.*[26] the plaintiff first complained to management about a racist poem strewn about the plant, whereupon management promptly collected and destroyed it. Later the plaintiff complained about graffiti in the bathroom, including KKK and a swastika and a hooded figure drawn on the walls. Management covered it immediately and held a meeting with employees to say that such graffiti would not be tolerated. Later management further told employees that such conduct would be disciplined severely. The behavior stopped, and the plaintiff had no claim for racial harassment as a result.

In *Newman v. Federal Express Corp.*[27] the plaintiff did not complain about every harassing episode that was later named in his suit for racial harassment. The failure to complain was found relevant to whether the plaintiff found the conduct subjectively harassing as well as to the basis for employer liability.

The Limitations Problem

A recurring problem in harassment cases is the short limitations period for Title VII claims. When conduct continues into the past, beyond the limitations period, it is called a continuing violation. The character of harassment claims is that they are usually established over a period of time, so the question becomes whether conduct lying outside the time period may be used to establish the severity and pervasiveness of the harassment.

The Supreme Court clarified this issue in *National Railroad Passenger Corp. v. Morgan.*[28] The claim was one of racial harassment and involved the application of the continuing violation theory. *Morgan* held that although a plaintiff may not recover damages for conduct that occurs outside the limitations period, such conduct is nonetheless admissible for the purpose of establishing the severity and pervasiveness of the harassment necessary for recovery for violations within the limitations period. The Court explained that a "hostile work environment claim is

26. 302 F.3d 839 (8th Cir. 2002).
27. 266 F.3d 401 (6th Cir.2001).
28. 536 U.S. 101, 122 S.Ct. 2061, 153 L.Ed.2d 106 (2002).

comprised of a series of separate acts that collectively constitute one 'unlawful employment practice.' "[29]

§ 2.13 Harassment on the Basis of National Origin, Religion and Age

The last section of this chapter covered cases involving hostile environment claims based on race. This section extends the topic of harassment to explore special issues when the abusive environment is discriminatory on the basis of national origin, religion and age. For national origin and religion, the claim is based on the Title VII prohibition of discrimination against any individual with respect to "compensations, terms, conditions, or privileges" of employment.[1] For age, the ADEA similarly prohibits discrimination with respect to "terms, conditions, or privileges of employment" for individuals forty and over.[2] The Supreme Court has held[3] that harassment of an employee on a protected basis can be actionable as affecting a condition of employment.

The topic of this chapter section is the federal statutory basis for hostile environment claims on the basis of national origin, religion, and age. Plaintiffs may also bring related claims for harassment under state statutory and common law.

National Origin

A claim of hostile environment harassment based on national origin must show that the employer created or permitted an intimidating, offensive work environment. Such an abusive environment must be "sufficiently severe or pervasive to alter the working conditions" of the plaintiff individual or class.[4] A hostile environment may be created by policies or practices of the employer or by failure to take action to correct the harassing atmosphere created by other employees or customers.

An employer may have a explicit or implicit policy that creates a hostile environment on the basis of national origin because if it makes an atmosphere of isolation, inferiority, and intimidation. A number of cases have challenged English-only rules in a work place on this grounds. The EEOC Guidelines have taken the position that an English-only rule in the workplace is harassing for these reasons unless the employer can provide a business justification.[5]

The Ninth Circuit rejected that Guideline in *Garcia v. Spun Steak Co.*[6] The court there held that the enactment of an English-only policy does not "inexorably" lead to an abusive environment for those whose primary language is not English. Therefore, the court reasoned, the

---

29. 122 S.Ct. at 2074.

§ 2.13

1. 42 U.S.C.A. § 20003–2(a).

2. 29 U.S.C.A. § 623.

3. Meritor Savings Bank, FSB v.Vinson, 477 U.S. 57, 106 S.Ct. 2399, 91 L.Ed.2d 49 (1986)(sexual harassment).

4. Harris v. Forklift Systems, 510 U.S. 17, 114 S.Ct. 367, 126 L.Ed.2d 295 (1993).

5. EEOC National Origin Guidelines, 29 C.F.R. § 1606.7 (1993).

6. 998 F.2d 1480 (9th Cir.1993), cert. denied, 512 U.S. 1228, 114 S.Ct. 2726, 129 L.Ed.2d 849 (1994).

adoption of an unjustified English-only rule is not per se a harassing condition. To prevail on such a claim the plaintiffs must demonstrate that the rule contributes to ethnic tension and that such tension alters a condition of employment under the standard of hostile environment claims. The majority opinion further notes that nothing in Title VII "requires an employer to allow employees to express their cultural identity."[7]

Judge Boochever's dissenting opinion questions how plaintiffs can produce such evidence and speculated that the EEOC Guideline may be premised on the difficulty of such proof. He reasoned that it is far easier for employers to justify a language restriction, such as proving its reasonable necessity for safety, than it is for plaintiffs to show its harassing effect. Judge Reinhardt filed an opinion dissenting to the denial of a rehearing en banc in which he observed that the majority displayed insensitivity to the history of ethnic discrimination because language is intimately tied to national origin and cultural identity.

Subsequent cases involving language rules have tended to rely on *Garcia* to deny relief. Courts have been particularly likely to reach this result in situations where the employees are bilingual and thus can comply with the English-only rule.

A district court case from Illinois distinguished the *Garcia* line of cases in a fact situation that involved employees who were not bilingual. In *EEOC v. Synchro–Start Products, Inc.*[8] the court held that the EEOC's claim of national origin discrimination could survive a motion to dismiss at least with respect to the effect of the employer's English-only rule on employees who spoke little or no English. The employer in that case had many employees or Polish and Hispanic national origin who had little proficiency in English. The court further said that because the issue was one of first impression in the circuit, it held open the possibility that the EEOC's guideline might properly be applied to some bilingual employees as well.

An employer's practice does not need to be an explicit one, such as English-only rules, to be challenged as harassing. *Rogers v. EEOC*[9] involved the *de facto* practice of an optometrist in Texas of segregating patients on the basis of national origin. The plaintiff, who was the only Spanish-surnamed employee, successfully claimed that this segregation of patients created a hostile environment because even though the offensive conduct was not directed toward her, it was a working environment heavily charged with ethnic discrimination.

In addition to claims for harassment on the basis of an employer policy such as an English-only rule, claims may also be premised on the employer's failure to take action to correct the harassing atmosphere created by other employees or customers. Such claims proceed along the same lines as racial harassment cases. The plaintiff must establish that

7. 998 F.2d at 1487.

8. 29 F.Supp.2d 911 (N.D. Ill.1999).

9. 454 F.2d 234 (5th Cir.1971), cert. denied, 406 U.S. 957, 92 S.Ct. 2058, 32 L.Ed.2d 343 (1972).

there was severe or pervasion harassment that caused an abusive working condition on the basis of national origin and the employer may defend by showing that it exercised reasonable care to prevent and promptly correct the harassment.

In a national origin harassment case the plaintiff needs to show more than a lack of civility or the occasional presence of ethnic slurs. As with the racial harassment cases, the courts have been reluctant to find national origin harassment based solely on brief, isolated name calling. For example, in one case,[10] a supervisor of Mexican ancestry was verbally abused by subordinates for disciplining a union employee. The court held that the harassment, including calling her a "wetback" and asking to see her green card, was not sufficient to violate 42 U.S.C.A. § 1981 because the harassment continued for only fifteen minutes on one occasion.

Courts will look at the entire workplace atmosphere to determine whether the complained of conduct created a hostile environment. For example, in *Valdez v. Mercy Hospital*,[11] a supervisor who was known for telling ethnic jokes, circulated among the employees a handwritten "Mexican Sex Manual" and a "Polish Sex Manual." The Eighth Circuit held the action was not sufficiently severe or pervasive to be actionable under Title VII, especially in light of the ongoing personality conflict between the plaintiff and his supervisor.

The court in *Amirmokri v. Baltimore Gas & Electric Co.*,[12] held that there was sufficient evidence of pervasive national origin discrimination in a claim brought by an Iranian immigrant who worked as an engineer for the employer utility. The evidence showed that for six months the plaintiff was subjected to daily epithets and name-calling, such as "the ayatollah" and "camel jockey." His supervisor also harassed him by the assignment of objectively impossible tasks and saying in front of co-workers that he did not know what he was doing.

Religion

Title VII also supports claims of hostile working environment based on religion. The Third Circuit has identified the elements of a claim for religious harassment in *Abramson v. William Paterson College of New Jersey*.[13] First, a claim for religious harassment required proof of intentional discrimination because of religion. Next, that harassment must be pervasive and regular. Third, the harassment must have detrimentally affected the plaintiff, and fourth, it must be of such a nature that it would have detrimentally affected a reasonable person of the same religion in that position.

What is particularly interesting about this formulation is that, unlike sexual harassment, there is no requirement that the harassment be "severe" as well as pervasive. It is also noteworthy that the court adopted, without discussion, a "reasonable person of the same religion"

10. Nieto v. United Auto Workers Local 598, 672 F.Supp. 987 (E.D.Mich.1987).

11. 961 F.2d 1401 (8th Cir.1992).

12. 60 F.3d 1126 (4th Cir.1995).

13. 260 F.3d 265 (3d Cir.2001).

test rather than a "reasonable person" test. The parallel in sexual harassment would be the difference between a "reasonable person" and a "reasonable woman."

Conduct that is not religious in nature cannot be religious harassment unless it directed at the employee for the purpose of harassment, however. Thus, swearing by co-workers would not rise to the level of religious harassment of an objecting co-worker unless the behavior was motivated by that purpose.

In one case[14] an employee complained that the employer played "Satanic death metal music" in the store where he worked. The plaintiff claimed that his supervisor also offended his Lutheran religion by using characters from the game Dungeons and Dragons on memos used to congratulate employees and posted on the bulletin board. One such fictional character was identified as a skeleton from hell who had returned to wreak havoc on the world. The plaintiff was disturbed by the evil eyes in the depiction and concerned that it was posted near his desk. The court clarified that a claim for religious harassment must be based on conduct that is based on the plaintiff's protected status and is sufficiently severe or pervasive as to alter the conditions of employment. In the absence of religious character or purpose, there is no action because the conduct would not be based on the plaintiff's protected status. Here the court found no evidence that the music or characters were directed at the plaintiff because of his religion. The offensive conduct was not causally connected to his religion and therefore not protected.

As with racial and national origin harassment, a frequent type of religious harassment is the use of demeaning and offensive slurs. The conduct must be highly offensive or on a continual basis. Conduct considered simply unpleasant and isolated is insufficient, such as occasional references to the plaintiff as a "Jewish–American princess."[15]

Harassment based on religious ancestry is also unlawful. For example, a Title VII violation was found where an employee was subjected to a course of harassment because his paternal grandmother was Jewish, even though the plaintiff was never a member of the Jewish faith.[16]

In an unusual case, the Maine Supreme Judicial Court held that a fundamentalist Christian subject to sexually explicit taunts in the workplace may sue his employer for religious harassment under state law.[17] Because his co-workers knew that his objection to the language was religious, their continued use of vulgarities was harassing him on the basis of religion.

14. Cook v. Cub Foods, Inc., 99 F.Supp.2d 945 (N.D.Ill.2000).

15. Meek v. Michigan Bell Tel. Co., 193 Mich.App. 340, 483 N.W.2d 407 (1991), appeal denied, 440 Mich. 872, 486 N.W.2d 743 (1992) (action based on state law).

16. Compston v. Borden, Inc., 424 F.Supp. 157 (S.D.Ohio 1976).

17. Finnemore v. Bangor Hydro–Electric Co., 645 A.2d 15 (Me.1994).

One case clarified the level of personal commitment to work that a company can expect from employees without creating religious harassment.[18] The employee in that case failed to establish a claim of religious harassment when the employer told supervisory employees at a weekend training program that they should put their job as their "first priority" in life. The employee said that God was her first priority, so that this requirement was religious harassment. The court found that she failed to produce evidence of how the employer's expectation created an actual conflict with her religion. In the absence of such evidence, the company was permitted to attempt to motivate its employees to make their jobs the top priority in their lives.

Age

Claims of harassment on the basis of age forty and over are covered by the ADEA. but the Title VII framework for analysis is used in this area as well as others. The plaintiff must establish that there was severe or pervasive harassment that caused an abusive working condition on the basis of age and the employer may defend by showing that it exercised reasonable care to prevent and promptly correct the harassment.

A wide range of conduct may give rise to an action for age-based harassment. For example, it has been held to be unlawful age harassment to taunt an employee by calling him "old man" and "grandpa,"[19] to repeatedly urge that an employee retire,[20] and, among other things, to tell a senior employee that he need not make a contribution to the office "flower fund" because he would not be around to work that much longer, as well as sending him out in the rain to do another employee's work.[21] On the other hand, where the harassment was not directly based on the employee's age, it was not continuous, pervasive, and concerted, and where the employee failed to complain about the conduct to supervisors, no age-based harassment was found.

§ 2.14   Sexual Harassment and Gender Stereotyping

Since the publication in 1979 of Catherine MacKinnon's book[1] about the nature and types of sexual mistreatment of women in the workplace, there has been extensive litigation of sexual harassment claims and various theories of legal liability. The first circuit to recognize sexual harassment as a violation of Title VII of the Civil Rights Act of 1964 was the Eleventh Circuit in *Henson v. Dundee*[2] in 1982. That case presented the then-novel question of whether it violates Title VII to retaliate against a woman who declines the sexual advances of her male superior.

18. Beasley v. Health Care Serv. Corp., 940 F.2d 1085 (7th Cir.1991).

19. City of Billings v. State Human Rights Comm'n, 209 Mont. 251, 681 P.2d 33 (1984).

20. Kelewae v. Jim Meagher Chevrolet, Inc., 952 F.2d 1052 (8th Cir.1992).

21. Lewis v. Federal Prison Indus., Inc., 786 F.2d 1537 (11th Cir.1986).

§ 2.14

1. Catherine MacKinnon, Sexual Harassment of Working Women (1979).

2. 682 F.2d 897 (11th Cir.1982).

In 1986, the Supreme Court found that sexual harassment could violate Title VII as a condition of employment in *Meritor Savings Bank, FSB v. Vinson.*[3] Following the EEOC Guidelines,[4] the Court held that Title VII covers mandatory sexual conduct as well as severe and pervasive hostile environments. The Court later clarified that both men and women are covered because the statutory basis for harassment claims is as a "term" or "condition" of employment "because of" the individual man's or woman's "sex" within the meaning of the Act.[5]

Although racial, ethnic, age, religious, and disability harassment cases are always based on hostile environment claims, there are two types of sexual harassment claims: ones involving tangible employment actions, including "quid pro quo" harassment, and ones involving the creation of a hostile environment. Mandatory sexual conduct is known generally as quid pro quo ("this for that") harassment. The essence of a claim of this type is that an employer conditions employment benefits upon unwelcome sexual conduct, as in *Henson v. Dundee.* The second type, hostile environment harassment, means a work environment that is hostile or abusive because of severe and pervasive harassment based upon gender.

This section discusses both of these types of claims, including their elements, special causation issues, and employer defenses. It also covers harassment more generally based on gender stereotyping. The origin of this claim was *Price Waterhouse v. Hopkins,*[6] where the woman plaintiff was not promoted because she was considered too masculine. In most recent years there have been numerous claims by men about harassment by other men and/or women for failure to conform to conventional notions of masculinity.

Tangible Employment Actions, including Quid Pro Quo Harassment

The uncertain scope of "tangible employment actions" is addressed later in this subsection, but it includes the category of cases traditionally known as "quid pro quo." The essence this claim is the employer conditions a benefit on some form of sexual favor. The "director's couch" is a classic example, which posits that a discriminatory director does not hire an actress who refuses to make herself available to him on his couch. The conditional benefit may be initial employment, continued employment, promotion, or other tangible employment action. The key is the connection between the sexual conduct and the benefit, such that the sexual favor need not even be for the gratification of the person making the demand. Requiring that an employee submit to the unwanted sexual advances of a customer as a condition of continued employment is also quid pro quo harassment.

3. 477 U.S. 57, 106 S.Ct. 2399, 91 L.Ed.2d 49 (1986).

4. 29 C.F.R. § 1604.11(a)

5. Oncale v. Sundowner Offshore Servs., Inc., 523 U.S. 75, 118 S.Ct. 998, 140 L.Ed.2d 201 (1998).

6. 490 U.S. 228, 109 S.Ct. 1775, 104 L.Ed.2d 268 (1989).

When the Supreme Court first recognized in *Meritor Savings Bank, FSB v. Vinson*[7] that harassment could violate Title VII, the Court drew upon the Sexual Harassment Guidelines promulgated by the EEOC in 1980. Those Guidelines provide that under Title VII "unwelcome sexual advances, requests for sexual favors, and other verbal or physical conduct of a sexual nature constitutes sexual harassment when: (1) submission to such conduct is made either explicitly or implicitly a term or condition of an individual's employment; (2) submission or rejection of such conduct is used as the basis for employment decisions affecting such an individual; or (3) such conduct has the purpose or effect of unreasonably interfering with an individual's work performance or creating an intimidating, hostile or offensive working environment."[8] The first category is classic "quid pro quo" harassment. The second is a broader formulation known as "tangible employment action" following the Supreme Court's decision in *Burlington Industries, Inc. v. Ellerth*.[9] The third is the "hostile environment" claim for sexual harassment discussed later in this section.

As the Guidelines reflect, the sexual conduct involved in quid pro quo harassment does not need to amount to sexual intercourse; other kinds of unwelcome sexual conduct suffice. In *Priest v. Rotary*,[10] for example, a waitress was subjected to unwanted touching on her breasts and leg by the owner of the restaurant. Numerous other incidents of unwanted suggestive contact included kissing her, putting his arms around her, rubbing his body against hers, and fondling various parts of her body. The plaintiff rejected these advances and received less favorable work assignments than waitresses who acquiesced to them. Eventually the plaintiff was fired for reasons which the trial court found were pretextual. These facts were sufficient for quid pro quo harassment because tangible job benefits were conditioned upon acquiescence in unwanted sexual conduct and the plaintiff was fired in retaliation when she refused to comply.

A "tangible employment action" encompasses quid pro quo, but it is a broader category. The term comes from the Supreme Court 's opinion in *Ellerth* where the Court explained that an employee who rejects the sexual demands of a superior but does not suffer any consequence does not have a claim under the first two categories in the EEOC Guidelines. Because of the absence of a tangible employment action, the claim must fall into the third category, hostile environment.

The Supreme Court also explained in *Ellerth* the significance of the difference. The plaintiff is in a better position to establish employer liability when the harassment involves a tangible employment action because the employer is strictly liable for it. In contrast, as the Supreme Court further explained in *Faragher v. City of Boca Raton*,[11] the employ-

7. 477 U.S. 57, 106 S.Ct. 2399, 91 L.Ed.2d 49 (1986).

8. 29 C.F.R. § 1604.11(a).

9. 524 U.S. 742, 118 S.Ct. 2257, 141 L.Ed.2d 633 (1998).

10. 634 F.Supp. 571 (N.D.Cal.1986).

11. 524 U.S. 775, 118 S.Ct. 2275, 141 L.Ed.2d 662 (1998).

er is not liable for a hostile environment claim if it has reacted reasonably to known harassment. This defense is discussed later in this section.

Although the distinction between tangible employment actions and hostile environment harassment has been central to the development and litigation of harassment law, the line between them is often difficult to draw. Sexual conduct such as the fondling in *Priest v. Rotary* can also create a hostile environment. It becomes quid pro quo harassment at the point at which tangible job benefits turn on acquiescence, such as when the manager assigned the plaintiff waitress to less desirable work because she rejected his advances and when he ultimately discharged her for the same reason.

The Supreme Court has explained that a "tangible employment action" is one that constitutes a significant change in employment status: hiring, firing, failing to promote, reassignment with significantly different responsibilities, or a decision causing a significant change in benefits.[12] Lower courts have identified actions that are not sufficiently tangible under this standard: A "bruised ego" is not enough, and demotion without change in pay, benefits, duties, or prestige is also insufficient. Reassignment to a more inconvenient job or prank phone calls also do not suffice.

It is less certain what claims, other than classic quid pro quo ones, fall within the category of tangible employment actions. The question is whether there is a requirement that a tangible employment action needs to be an adverse action. The recurring fact pattern involves female employees who succumb to sexual demands to retain job security rather than risk retaliation by rejecting their supervisors. Because the submission keeps their employment status unchanged, there is no adverse action.

The question remains an open one, but the first circuit courts to consider the issue have rejected the requirement that the tangible employment action be an adverse one. The leading opinion is *Jin v. Metropolitan Life Insurance Co.,*[13] which involved an insurance agent who submitted to the unwanted sexual demands of her supervisor who explicitly required weekly sexual acts to retain her job. The Second Circuit held her acquiescence under threat of a tangible employment action was itself a tangible employment action. The trial court erred by instructing the jury that the plaintiff must show a "tangible adverse action."

The Ninth Circuit agreed and went a step further in *dicta* in *Holly D. v. California Institute of Technology.*[14] In that case the plaintiff was an assistant to a professor in his university laboratory who submitted to unwanted sexual demands which she believed the professor implicitly demanded. The Ninth Circuit agreed in principle that a tangible employment action occurs when a supervisor explicitly or implicitly conditions a

12. Burlington Indus., Inc. v. Ellerth, 524 U.S. 742, 118 S.Ct. 2257, 141 L.Ed.2d 633 (1998).

13. 310 F.3d 84 (2d Cir.2002).

14. 339 F.3d 1158 (9th Cir.2003).

job, a job benefit, or the absence of a job detriment, upon an employee's acceptance of sexual conduct. Further, that circuit held that it is not necessary to show the subjective intent of the supervisor but only that a reasonable person would have believed that job security depended on fulfilling the demands. Under the facts of that case, however, there was insufficient evidence that the professor had abused his authority in that manner. In the absence of evidence that the professor had explicitly or implicitly demanded sex for her job security, her claim became a hostile environment one with the defense that she had not notified the employer or availed herself of available complaint procedures.

Hostile Environment Claims of Sexual Harassment

In addition to quid pro quo harassment, Title VII provides a cause of action for hostile environment harassment. This type of sexual harassment involves a work atmosphere that is infused with conduct that is sexual in nature even though not involving the demand for favors. Such a working condition is actionable under Title VII if it is "severe and pervasive." The Supreme Court in *Meritor Savings Bank, FSB v. Vinson*[15] first held that both types of harassment were actionable under Title VII. The Court thus rejected any requirement of economic loss or tangible disadvantage in order to be a "condition" of employment under the Act.

Meritor Savings Bank, FSB v. Vinson involved a claim by a former bank employee who alleged that her supervisor fondled her, exposed himself, and had sexual relations with her on numerous occasions. She did not allege that any tangible job benefit was conditioned on acceptance of this behavior, but that she endured it only because he was her supervisor. The defendant bank denied the conduct and further defended on the ground that any such conduct was based on a voluntary social relationship. In *Vinson*, the Court determined that the key inquiry is not whether the victim's conduct is voluntary, but whether the sexual advances were unwelcome.

The Court in *Vinson* drew further upon the EEOC's Sexual Harassment Guidelines for the hostile environment theory. The Guidelines provide that under Title VII "unwelcome sexual advances, requests for sexual favors, and other verbal or physical conduct of a sexual nature constitutes sexual harassment when * * * such conduct has the purpose or effect of unreasonably interfering with an individual's work performance or creating an intimidating, hostile or offensive working environment."[16] Relying upon the last basis, the Court held that the existence of sexual harassment must be assessed "in light of the record as a whole and the totality of the circumstances."[17]

It is the totality of the circumstances that determines whether harassing incidents collectively amount to an harassing environment. Isolated incidents may not rise to the level of severe and pervasive

---

15. 477 U.S. 57, 106 S.Ct. 2399, 91 L.Ed.2d 49 (1986).

16. 29 C.F.R. § 1604.11(a).

17. 106 S.Ct. at 2406.

harassment necessary for a claim. In *Weiss v. Coca–Cola Bottling Co.,*[18] for example, the plaintiff alleged that her supervisor asked her for dates, called her a "dumb blond," put his hand on her shoulder several times, placed "I love you" signs in her work area, and attempted to kiss her in a bar. The Seventh Circuit held that these "relatively isolated" incidents were insufficient to establish sexual harassment.

After *Vinson* established that acquiescence in unwelcome sexual conduct can create a hostile environment in violation of Title VII, the Supreme Court in *Harris v. Forklift Systems*[19] further clarified the nature of the plaintiff's claim. *Harris* explained that a plaintiff need not suffer psychological harm to establish a hostile environment claim. The Court noted that although "the effect on the employee's psychological well-being is, of course, relevant to determining whether the plaintiff actually found the environment abusive, no single factor is required."[20]

The Eighth Circuit in *Hathaway v. Runyon*[21] noted that *Harris* provides no clear standard and leaves "virtually unguided juries" to determine whether conduct is sufficiently egregious to be actionable. In *Hathaway* the court held that a woman who worked as a postal employee presented sufficient evidence for a jury to find that male co-workers interfered with her work. One of the co-workers flirted with her and, when she made it clear she was not interested, he and a friend made noises at her every time she walked by. The noises consisted of leering, snickering, laughing, and other insinuating sounds for eight months. The defendant maintained that this conduct was merely unpleasant, but the court concluded that "a work environment is shaped by the accumulation of abusive conduct, and the resulting harm cannot be measured by carving it 'into a series of discrete incidents.' "[22]

Despite complaints about the vagueness of the standard for a hostile environment claim, the Supreme Court in its 1998 opinion *Faragher v. City of Boca Raton*[23] reaffirmed that it is a factual inquiry and not subject to a bright line standard. The plaintiff in that case was one of a few female lifeguards living in close quarters with male lifeguards and supervisors who assaulted her, made remarks about her body, and pantomimed sexual actions. These acts were sufficient to create an objectively abusive working environment.

One circuit court has found that a hostile environment can exist when the victim does not even witness the offensive behavior directly. The case involved offensive behavior behind the woman plaintiff's back. Her awareness of the conduct was sufficient for the claim even though she did not witness it herself.[24]

---

18. 990 F.2d 333 (7th Cir.1993).

19. 510 U.S. 17, 114 S.Ct. 367, 126 L.Ed.2d 295 (1993).

20. 114 S.Ct. at 371.

21. 132 F.3d 1214 (8th Cir.1997).

22. Id. at 1222.

23. 524 U.S. 775, 118 S.Ct. 2275, 141 L.Ed.2d 662 (1998).

24. Torres v. Pisano, 116 F.3d 625 (2d Cir.1997), cert. denied, 522 U.S. 997, 118 S.Ct. 563, 139 L.Ed.2d 404 (1997).

Courts have generally used the "reasonable person" standard to assess whether the harassment was sufficiently severe and pervasive to create a hostile environment. Some commentators have urged the acceptance of a "reasonable woman" standard and some courts have used the standard. The Supreme has continued to phrase the test in terms of the "reasonable person" standard.

Harris explained that although the plaintiff need not suffer from psychological harm, the plaintiff must nonetheless perceive her working conditions as hostile. The standard of offense is an objective one of reasonableness, but it is also subjectively required that the particular plaintiff be adversely affected. Thus, the plaintiff must show both that the offending conduct created an objectively hostile environment and that she subjectively perceived her working conditions as abusive.

The standard for an objectively abusive hostile environment was clarified somewhat in a case where the plaintiff alleged retaliation for complaining about a sexually explicit joke in a meeting she attended with her male supervisor and another male co-worker. In *Clark County School District v. Breeden*,[25] the three employees were going over a job applicant's file and they were discussing a notation in the file of a remark made by the applicant in the past. The remark, made to a woman not involved in the lawsuit, was: "I hear that making love to you is like making love to the Grand Canyon." The male supervisor at the meeting said that he "didn't get it" and the other male employee laughed and said that he would "explain it later." The plaintiff complained that she found the laugh between the two men to be offensive. When she was subsequently transferred to a position she found less desirable, she sued for retaliation. The Supreme Court held in a per curiam opinion that no one could have reasonably believed that the incident violated Title VII. It was merely an isolated incident that "cannot remotely be considered 'extremely serious' as required for a Title VII violation. The Court concluded: 'No reasonable person could have believed that the single incident recounted above violated Title VII's standard.' "

Another element of a claim for sexual harassment is unwelcomeness. The plaintiff's proof that conduct is "unwelcome" can be the employee's own testimony, but the employer is free to rebut with evidence that the employee encouraged the conduct. In *Vinson*, the Supreme Court noted that testimony about the plaintiff's provocative dress and sexual fantasies is relevant in determining if sexual harassment occurred. A woman plaintiff need not be a "perfect lady" to bring suit, however. Evidence that a woman plaintiff frequently used vulgar language,[26] or even posed nude for a magazine during non-work hours[27] does not mean that harassment on the job is welcome.

25. 532 U.S. 268, 121 S.Ct. 1508, 149 L.Ed.2d 509 (2001).

26. Carr v. Allison Gas Turbine Div., 32 F.3d 1007 (7th Cir. 1994).

27. Burns v. McGregor Electronic Indus., Inc., 989 F.2d 959 (8th Cir.1993).

In general, the plaintiff's personal lifestyle is not relevant unless it bears directly on the question whether the workplace harassment is unwelcome. In *Stacks v. Southwestern Bell Yellow Pages, Inc.*,[28] the district court erred by focusing on the plaintiff's private life to reject her hostile environment claim. The plaintiff sales representative complained about behavior that included parties in hotels after sales canvasses. The male sales representatives invited women whom they called "road whores" and whom they "berated, talked down to, made fun of, and passed around." The plaintiff said that these parties made her feel "less than human" and that the behavior conveyed that there was something wrong with being a woman. The district court discounted her reaction, however, because the plaintiff admitted to having an affair with a married co-worker. This finding was reversed as a matter of law because the plaintiff's private and consensual sexual activities do not constitute a waiver of harassment claims.

The Causation Problem

In both quid pro quo cases and hostile environment claims, plaintiffs must establish the causal link between the conduct and gender for coverage under Title VII. Moreover, the plaintiff must also establish the link between the gender-motivated conduct and the adverse action or abusive environment. If the conduct is not linked to gender discrimination, or if it is not linked to an adverse employment action or condition, then it is merely a personal matter between the parties that does not invoke federal antidiscrimination law.

First, quid pro quo or other tangible employment action cases require proof that the adverse employment action was causally connected to the rejection of sexual conduct. The unpleasant situation for an employee who has rejected a supervisor's sexual advance is not actionable unless there is a causally related adverse action or unless the situation becomes a hostile environment. Otherwise, an advance is not actionable in itself even when it makes the employee uncomfortable. It is also not actionable even when the employee is later terminated unless the employee can connect the termination with the rejection. The trial court in one case said that the passage of three or four weeks between the rejection and the discharge was not sufficiently proximate to suggest causation. The Third Circuit reversed[29] and held that temporal proximity is simply one factor and that other evidence may be probative of the causal link. The court also noted that it is not necessary to demonstrate antagonism after the rejection in a quid pro quo case.

Issues of temporal proximity in the quid pro quo context may be affected by the Supreme Court's comments on temporal proximity in the context of a retaliation claim. In *Clark County School District v. Breeden*,[30] the Supreme Court noted that temporal proximity may be causal

---

28. 27 F.3d 1316 (8th Cir.1994).

29. Farrell v. Planters Lifesavers, 206 F.3d 271 (3d Cir. 2000).

30. 532 U.S. 268, 121 S.Ct. 1508, 149 L.Ed.2d 509 (2001).

only when the connection in time is "very close." When there is any delay or uncertainty, the plaintiff must have other proof of causation.

For hostile environment claims, it is also necessary for the plaintiff to connect the hostility of the environment to the plaintiff's gender. The employer in *Cross v. Alabama*[31] created a hostile work environment through a supervisor's abrasive management style, but it was not related to gender. The court held that conduct that was equally offensive to men and women would not be a hostile environment on the basis of gender. In *Ocheltree v. Scollon Productions, Inc.*,[32] a woman worked in an all-male department and was subjected to sexually-laden and explicit language and pantomiming. She sued for hostile environment harassment and a jury found in her favor. The Fourth Circuit reversed but then vacated the opinion and reheard it en banc to affirm the jury verdict. The Fourth Circuit at first reversed on the grounds that there was insufficient evidence of causation. The initial Fourth Circuit opinion noted that all the employees were exposed to the same conduct regardless of gender and that Title VII does not require "gentlemanly conduct" to replace a rough workplace simply because a woman is present. The rehearing en banc affirmed the jury verdict because there was sufficient evidence for the jury to find that the conduct has been directed at the plaintiff as a woman. Specifically, there was evidence that the offensive conduct was for the purpose of making her self-conscious and uncomfortable and to provoke her reaction as a woman, such as by showing her a picture of pierced male genitalia and asking her opinion. Although it was true that other men in the room were also offended by the conduct of the perpetrators, no other person besides the plaintiff was asked to react to sexually-laden material while the whole room watched. The jury could infer that the conduct was directed toward the plaintiff because of her gender.

Other harassment causation problems have occurred when a supervisor has favored a consensual lover to the disadvantage of all other men and women in the workplace. A hostile environment may be created by a sexually charged atmosphere at the workplace, but it is not sufficient to allege only that an employer gives preferential treatment to an individual with whom there is a consensual romantic relationship. Such cases, generally known as paramour cases, are not consistent, but the majority view is that it is not gender discrimination against other employees when an employer favors a paramour. A 1996 California case, *Proksel v. Gattis*,[33] addressed the split among courts on this issue and concluded that under California law there is no claim of sexual harassment, even when the conduct of the office lovers is indiscreet, if there is no conduct other than favoritism that creates the adverse environment.

---

31. 49 F.3d 1490 (11th Cir.1995).

32. 308 F.3d 351 (4th Cir.2002), vacated en banc, 335 F.3d 325, cert. denied, ___ U.S. ___, 124 S.Ct. 1406, 158 L.Ed.2d 77 (2004).

33. 41 Cal.App.4th 1626, 49 Cal.Rptr.2d 322 (1996).

Causation also fails if the motivation for harassment is personal animosity rather than gender discrimination. Thus, a male teacher had no claim for harassment in *Succar v. Dade County School Board*[34] even though he alleged that the school took inadequate steps to stop the verbal and physical abuse directed at him by a female teacher. The reason for the abuse was a personal feud occasioned by the termination of their consensual romantic relationship. The Eleventh Circuit observed that Title VII prohibits discrimination rather than "personal animosity" and that the Act "is not a shield against harsh treatment at the work place."[35]

In a related development concerning causation, a court has held that a hostile environment cannot be suffered indirectly unless the direct victims of the harassment are in the plaintiff's same gender group. Thus, a man does not have standing to claim a hostile work environment that was not directed at him or at members of his group. In *Lyman v. Nabil's Inc.*,[36] a male restaurant manager claimed that the owner created a hostile working environment through his harassment of female employees. The court rejected this theory on the grounds that a sexual harassment claim requires that the plaintiff personally suffer unwelcome harassment. A section 704 claim of retaliation for opposing discrimination is distinguishable and available if the plaintiff meets the elements required under that section of the Act.

When the pattern of harassment has occurred over a long period of time, the limitations period creates a problem with respect to conduct that happened more than 300 days before the complaint. The Supreme Court held in *National Railroad Passenger Corp. v. Morgan*[37] that as long as an act contributing to the claim occurs within the limitations period, the entire series of acts constituting the hostile environment may be considered for liability. Once a court determines that the acts are part of a pattern, they are admissible to support the hostile environment claim.

Basis of Employer Liability for Harassment

Title VII covers "employers" so the plaintiff must establish a basis of employer liability in any claim under the Act. Plaintiffs often name supervisors individually in a suit as well, especially in harassment cases, as "agents" of employers, but the trend holds against individual liability. Recovery against the individual perpetrator usually requires a common law tort claim. The plaintiff in *Priest v. Rotary*, for example, established additional claims for battery, false imprisonment, and intentional infliction of emotional distress on the basis of the manager fondling her, pinning her body against the wall, and causing her severe distress by requests for sexual favors when he knew she was already distressed by a health problem and the burden of single parenthood. The advantage of the tort claims in addition to Title VII from the plaintiff's perspective is

34. 229 F.3d 1343 (11th Cir.2000).

35. Id. at 1345.

36. 903 F.Supp. 1443 (D.Kan.1995).

37. 536 U.S. 101, 122 S.Ct. 2061, 153 L.Ed.2d 106 (2002).

damages. Whereas Title VII did not provide for compensatory and punitive damages before it was amended by the Civil Rights Act of 1991, the tort claims were essential for such damages. They are less essential now that Title VII supports such damages, but the Act has caps. The tort claims remain necessary for a plaintiff to recover beyond the statutory caps on compensatory and punitive damages.

Because a Title VII claim is against an "employer," the plaintiff must establish a basis for holding the employer liable for the conduct of harassers. When harassment is committed by an employer-owner, there is no difficulty with finding liability under Title VII because the person perpetrating the harassment is the employer. The owner-manager of a restaurant, for example, creates liability as an "employer" when engaging in harassment of the staff. Once the employer and the perpetrator are distinct, however, the issue becomes the connection between the two for purposes of employer liability under Title VII.

The Supreme Court has clarified the standard for employer liability in two cases, *Burlington Industries, Inc. v. Ellerth*[38] and *Faragher v. City of Boca Raton.*[39] These cases establish that employers are strictly liable for the conduct of supervisors. Nonetheless, in hostile environment claims, the employer has an affirmative defense. *Ellerth* involved a claim by a woman whose supervisor made sexual suggestions and explicit threats but then did not follow through on the threats when she did not acquiesce. Her boss allegedly told her that he could make things "hard" on her if she didn't "loosen up" sexually, but nothing happened to her when she rebuffed him. Moreover, even though she ignored his suggestive comments relating to how she could receive a desired promotion, she received the promotion anyway. These allegations were sufficient to meet the severe and pervasive requirement for hostile environment harassment, but the plaintiff attempted to fit within the quid pro quo definition. The strategic reason that the plaintiff wished to bring the case as a quid pro quo claim rather than a hostile environment one was to find a basis of employer liability. She had never complained about her supervisor's conduct before she left the company and thus would have difficulty showing that the employer failed to take reasonable steps to stop the harassment. Prior case law had required such notification for any hostile environment claim, but not a quid pro quo claim, so the plaintiff sought to characterize her claim as quid pro quo in order to hold the employer liable.

The Supreme Court disagreed with the characterization of these facts as quid pro quo, but modified the degree of the advantage of a quid pro quo claim compared with a hostile environment claim. The Court concluded that an employer is strictly liable for any sexual harassment caused by a supervisor. When that harassment is quid pro quo, there is no defense once the plaintiff establishes that the sexual conduct was an unwelcome condition of employment. When that harassment is a hostile

38. 524 U.S. 742, 118 S.Ct. 2257, 141 L.Ed.2d 633 (1998).

39. 524 U.S. 775, 118 S.Ct. 2275, 141 L.Ed.2d 662 (1998).

environment created by the supervisor, the employer is liable unless it can show as an affirmative defense that (1) it exercised reasonable care to prevent and promptly correct the harassment and (2) that the employee unreasonably failed to use the employer's remedial procedures. Liability for workplace harassment by other co-workers or third-parties is determined according to a negligence standard. That standard is met if the employer knew or should have known of the harassment and failed to take corrective action.

This liability principle was further clarified by the Supreme Court in *Faragher v. City of Boca Raton.*[40] The plaintiff was a female lifeguard living in close quarters with male lifeguards and supervisors who harassed her. Applying the affirmative defense, the Court noted that the city could not be found to have exercised reasonable care to prevent the harassment because the district court found that the city had entirely failed to disseminate its policy against sexual harassment among its beach employees and that it had made no attempt to keep track of conduct of supervisors. Moreover, the city's policy did not include any assurance that harassing supervisors could be bypassed when complainants reported their conduct.

The circuit courts have attempted to provide further guidance first on when an employer may be strictly liable even for a hostile environment claim. The Fifth Circuit[41] has endorsed the Seventh Circuit's interpretation of the Supreme Court's holdings in *Faragher* and *Ellerth*. In *Johnson v. West,*[42] the Seventh Circuit held that the employer is vicariously liable for its employees' activities in two types of situations: (1) there is a tangible employment action or (2) the harassing employee is a proxy for the employer. Applying the "proxy" concept, the Seventh Circuit found the Chief of Police at a hospital was not a proxy for the hospital because he had at least two superiors at the location and more within the employer's overall structure. He was therefore not a high-level manager whose actions "spoke" for the employer. Further, this harasser had no authority to change the terms and conditions of the plaintiff's employment because the plaintiff worked for several supervisors.

The Fifth Circuit further clarified in *Ackel v. National Communications*[43] that acting as a proxy for the employer does not require stock ownership. It is simply a question of fact whether an individual holds a sufficiently high position in the management hierarchy to be considered an alter-ego of the employer.

The second method by which employers may be liable for harassment occurs when they fail to take reasonable steps to stop known harassing conduct. The first step of this analysis is whether the employer has adequate procedures in place for employees to make complaints. As

40. 524 U.S. 775, 118 S.Ct. 2275, 141 L.Ed.2d 662 (1998).
41. Ackel v. National Communications, 339 F.3d 376 (5th Cir. 2003).
42. 218 F.3d 725 (7th Cir. 2000).
43. 339 F.3d 376 (5th Cir. 2003).

illustrated by *Faragher*, the inability of employees to notify the employer may be caused by inadequate communication and the remote location of the assignment. Another example of inadequate procedures is *Ocheltree v. Scollon Productions, Inc.*[44] The fairly small company had general handbook policies requiring employees to avoid verbally abusing each other and had an "open door" policy about complaints, but it lacked any specific mention of harassment. Moreover, there was no training of personnel about handling harassment complaints and no duty of supervisors to report incidents. The plaintiff's attempts to approach the president through the "open door" policy were discouraged. The employer was thus charged with constructive knowledge of the harassment, which it then failed to take reasonable steps to control.

For employers that do have adequate complaint machinery in place, the issue is the reasonableness of the employer's response once it is on notice of the harassing conduct. Courts focus on this issue by examining the steps taken to stop the harassment. *Spicer v. Virginia Department of Corrections*[45] is particularly instructive in this regard. In that case a female employee of a correctional institution complained about harassment that she received after the distribution of a memorandum concerning proper employee dress. The thrust of the memorandum was that employees should adhere to the same standards of dress required of the inmates' visitors. The plaintiff was singled out in the memorandum as someone who wore revealing attire. It cited her in particular as an example of inappropriate dress because she had worn a blouse so revealing that it showed her nipples. Immediately afterward, the plaintiff was subjected to ridicule and crude jokes by male co-workers.

The Fourth Circuit held in *Spicer* that the employer's response was adequate because it took swift and reasonable action. That action included (1) steps to prevent the public posting of the memorandum, (2) counseling the employees who wrote and distributed the memorandum about the sensitivity of the matter, and (3) admonishing the employees who made sexual remarks that such conduct would not be tolerated. After the plaintiff's complaint she was no longer harassed about the memorandum. The court thus held that the district court erroneously faulted the employer for not taking additional steps. Specifically, the district court criticized the effectiveness of two training sessions designed to educate employees and to prevent the recurrence of such remarks. Attendance at these sessions was voluntary and there was no evidence that the harassers had attended. Moreover, the district court found that the EEO manager who conducted the training was insensitive to sexual harassment. Accordingly, the district court granted as the sole relief an order that the defendant formulate a training program and "take positive steps to assure the effectiveness of its existing policy against sexual harassment." The Fourth Circuit reversed this order and

44. 308 F.3d 351 (4th Cir.2002), vacated en banc, 335 F.3d 325, cert. denied, ___ U.S. ___, 124 S.Ct. 1406, 158 L.Ed.2d 77 (2004).

45. 66 F.3d 705 (4th Cir.1995).

observed: "While we have never suggested that an employer must make the most effective response possible and we have consistently held that an employer is only liable for sexual harassment committed by its employees if no adequate remedial action is taken, the record in this case does not even colorably support a conclusion that the Virginia Department of Corrections' response was inadequate."[46] In dissent, Judge Motz complained that the trial judge's conclusion that the employer failed to take effective remedial action was a finding of fact that the en banc majority improperly reversed.[47]

An interesting aspect of *Spicer* is that the district court found that the harassing co-workers were not convinced by counseling that they had done anything wrong. This fact was not relevant, however, because the harassment stopped. The key to appropriate employer response is to take steps to stop the harassment; it is not necessary to change the beliefs of the harassers.

Since *Ellerth* and *Faragher* the lower courts have considered the adequacy of a variety of employer responses to sexual harassment complaints. The Fourth Circuit has held that an employer's policy was inadequate when it considered only sexual advances as a basis for complaint and not other forms of harassment on the basis of gender.[48] The Ninth Circuit held that an employer's remote location was distinguishable from *Faragher* because the policy was adequately disseminated, a manager flew to the location immediately upon hearing the complaint, and disciplinary actions were taken swiftly.[49]

The Seventh Circuit accepted a different line if argument from an employer in *EEOC v. Indiana Bell*.[50] In that case the hostile environment claim concerned conduct by a male co-worker about which the employer had received complaints from many women over the course of twenty years. The trial court refused to admit evidence that the employer's delay in addressing the problem was motived in part by a concern over arbitration that may result from any discipline on the matter. The collective bargaining agreement covered the employee who was the subject of the complaint and the employer wanted to offer evidence that it was fearful of the possible outcome of that arbitration. The majority accepted this argument and remanded for admission of this evidence on the grounds that the employer could be legitimately concerned about possible grievance and reinstatement of the disciplined employee. The court found inapplicable the principle that Title VII obligations trump collective bargaining agreements because the two are not in conflict in this circumstance. A dissenting opinion complains that the "door should not be open to this defense" because Title VII imposes an unequivocal duty on employers to take reasonable steps to stop harassment.[51]

46. Id. at 710.

47. Id. at 716 (Motz, J. dissenting).

48. Smith v. First Union Nat'l Bank, 202 F.3d 234 (4th Cir.2000).

49. Montero v. Agco, 192 F.3d 856 (9th Cir.1999).

50. 214 F.3d 813 (7th Cir.2000).

51. Borneman v. United States, 213 F.3d 819, 826 (4th Cir.2000) (Ilana, J., dis-

Employers may also defend under *Ellerth* and *Faragher* with a showing that the plaintiff failed to use available complaint procedures. The Supreme Court in those cases emphasized the publication of the procedures and availability of the process. In *Reed v. MBNA Marketing System*,[52] the First Circuit further considered the age of the employee in evaluating the reasonableness of her response to a sexual assault in the work place. It was appropriate to take into consideration that the employee was only seventeen with respect to the defense that she unreasonably failed to take advantage of any preventive or corrective opportunities provided by the employer or to avoid harm.

Harassment by Nonemployees

The EEOC Guidelines on Sexual Harassment provide that an employer may be liable for the conduct of nonemployees if the employer knew or should have known of the harassment and failed to take immediate and appropriate remedial action.[53] The case law has been limited. One case involved harassment by the defendant's employees of a worker at a shared workplace. The plaintiff in that case, *King v. Chrysler Corp.*,[54] was a cafeteria worker employed by an independent contractor in the Chrysler plant. She sued for the sexual harassment by one of Chrysler's employees and Chrysler moved for summary judgment on the grounds that it had no employment relationship with the plaintiff. The court rejected this argument and held that although the Act protects only interference with employment, the parties need not have an employment relationship themselves.

When the employer takes affirmative steps that are reasonably foreseen to encourage harassment by third parties, it can be liable for the resulting conduct by them. In *EEOC v. Sage Realty Corp.*,[55] an employer became liable for the harassing behavior of the public when it changed the attire required of lobby attendants. The plaintiff, who began working for the employer when the required dress was professional, suddenly found herself harassed by the public when she was required to wear an outfit which revealed her buttocks and the side of her body above the waist when she raised her arms. The outfit prompted lewd comments from the public she served.

There are few reported cases involving the harassment of an employee by non-employees when the employer's conduct did not contribute to the harassment or otherwise made it foreseeable. One case from the Third Circuit held that a restaurant could be liable for the harassment of a waitress by a customer.[56] The facts of that case did not support liability, however, because the conduct of the customer was isolated and did not create a hostile work environment.

senting), cert. denied, 531 U.S. 1070, 121 S.Ct. 759, 148 L.Ed.2d 661 (2001).

52. 333 F.3d 27 (1st Cir. 2003).

53. 29 C.F.R. § 1604.11(e).

54. 812 F.Supp. 151 (E.D.Mo.1993).

55. 507 F.Supp. 599 (S.D.N.Y.1981).

56. Hallberg v. Eat'n Park, 70 Fair Empl. Prac. Cases 361 (W.D.Pa.1996).

"Conditions" Claims and "Retaliation" Claims

Although *Vinson* established that a hostile environment claim is actionable as "sex discrimination" within the meaning of section 703 of Title VII, the loss of a tangible job benefit may still be necessary for a retaliation claim under section 704. The Fifth Circuit in *Mattern v. Eastman Kodak*[57] found no violation of section 704 when co-workers retaliated against a woman who reported incidents of sexual harassment. The plaintiff, a woman who was in a mechanic's apprenticeship program, alleged that after she reported some harassing conduct to management, her co-workers treated her with hostility and attempted to sabotage her work. The jury found in her favor on the section 704 claim but in the employer's favor on the section 703 claim.

The court of appeals in *Mattern* noted the necessity of distinguishing between harassment under sections 703 and 704. Noting that the prohibition in section 704 is limited to "discrimination," the court concluded that it relates only to ultimate employment decisions and not to "conditions" of employment such as harassment under section 703. The majority reasoned that whereas section 703 prohibits a wider range of employment situations and conditions, section 704 has a more narrow proscription. The dissenting opinion criticized the majority for its failure to adhere to the spirit of the Supreme Courts's decision in *Vinson* that discrimination under Title VII is not limited to the loss of tangible benefits.

The availability of hostile environment harassment claims under section 704 is important to plaintiffs in some situations. First, a section 704 hostile environment claim is important if the section 703 harassment claim fails to stand on its own, as in *Mattern*. Second, the section 704 hostile environment claim is important in the circumstances where a plaintiff fails to make a timely administrative complaint about the initial harassing conduct and must rely upon the subsequent retaliatory conduct that falls within the statute of limitations. Other courts of appeal have not yet considered the availability of a retaliatory harassment claim using a hostile environment theory.

Sexual Orientation Harassment versus Sexual Stereotyping Harassment

Claims of harassment based on sexual orientation have become increasingly common, but federal law provides no relief. State statutory law can provide a cause of action in those jurisdictions that prohibit discrimination on the basis of sexual orientation, but a statutory prohibition on "sex" discrimination is insufficient. For example, neither Title VII nor state discrimination law afforded relief to an employee who was subject to continuous derogatory comments, such as "faggot," as well as physical assaults.[58]

---

57. 104 F.3d 702 (5th Cir.), cert. denied, 522 U.S. 932, 118 S.Ct. 336, 139 L.Ed.2d 260 (1997).

58. Carreno v. Local Union No. 226, IBEW, 1990 WL 159199 (D.Kan.1990).

The Supreme Court's decision in *Oncale v. Sundowner Offshore Services, Inc.*[59] addressed same-sex harassment in a fact situation that involved men harassing men, but not on the basis of homosexuality. The Court found that Title VII's prohibition against discrimination on the basis of "sex" applied to both men and women. Thus, a Title VII claim is available if a plaintiff can establish that the harassment was directed toward him or her "because of" gender. This holding did not address discrimination on the basis of sexual orientation.

The Third Circuit outlines the ways in which a plaintiff may bring a claim for same-sex harassment in *Bibby v. Philadelphia Coca Cola Bottling Co.*[60] A plaintiff may (1) demonstrate that the harassment is motivated by the aggressors sexual desire, or (2) show that a harasser displays hostility towards the participation of plaintiff's gender in the workplace, either in general or with reference to a particular function, or (3) illustrate that the "harasser's conduct was motivated by a belief that the victim did not conform to the stereotypes of his or her gender."[61]

Other circuits have agreed that, following the reasoning of the Supreme Court in *Oncale*, it is fatal to a plaintiff's case if the harassment is on the basis of a belief that the plaintiff is homosexual, regardless of whether the belief is true. In *Centola v. Potter*[62] the plaintiff had not revealed his sexual orientation to his co-workers but they correctly guessed that he was homosexual. The court emphasized that his claim must be premised upon the gender stereotyping by the co-workers and not on their bigotry toward homosexuals. Finding that the evidence supported a claims that the harassment was based on both the covered ground of stereotyping and the uncovered ground of sexual orientation discrimination, the court applied "mixed motive" analysis and permitted the plaintiff's claim. In contract, in *Bianchi v. City of Philadelphia*[63] a firefighter lost his claim because of his insistence that the harassment directed against him was premised on the mistaken assumption that he was homosexual and not based on a failure to conform to societal male norms.

Tort law can provide a cause of action in some situations. In *Zaks v. American Broadcasting Cos.*,[64] an action for intentional infliction of emotional distress was permitted where an employer and co-workers allegedly harassed, vandalized, assaulted, stabbed, and stuffed an unconscious employee into a closet because of his homosexual orientation. State common law governs these claims.

§ 2.15   Intentional Exclusion of Groups

Title VII makes it an unlawful employment practice for employers to "fail or refuse to hire or to discharge any individual, or otherwise to

59. 523 U.S. 75, 118 S.Ct. 998, 140 L.Ed.2d 201 (1998).

60. 260 F.3d 257 (3d Cir.2001), cert. denied, 534 U.S. 1155, 122 S.Ct. 1126, 151 L.Ed.2d 1018 (2002).

61. Id. at 262–63.

62. 183 F.Supp.2d 403 (D.Mass.2002).

63. 183 F.Supp.2d 726 (E.D.Pa.2002).

64. 626 F.Supp. 695 (C.D.Cal.1985).

discriminate" on the basis of race, color, religion, sex, or national origin[1] as well as to "limit, segregate, or classify" individuals in any way which would "deprive or tend to deprive" them of employment opportunities "or otherwise adversely affect" them on those grounds.[2] The ADEA has identical prohibitions to protect individuals who are age 40 and over.[3] These two Acts thus prohibit employers from intentionally disadvantaging groups defined by race, color, religion, sex, national origin, and age. It is unlawful, for example, for persons covered by the Acts to post a Help Wanted sign in a store window with the specification that "No Irish need apply," such as was common in Boston at one time, or to advertise in a newspaper with descriptions such as "man's job" or "woman's job," or "young executive position," as was common nationwide at the time the statutes were enacted.

Because employers may not lawfully "segregate or classify" employees on the protected dimensions, they may not assign all African–American or Mexican–American employees to the least desirable job categories, another practice that was open and overt before Title VII. The Acts specifically provide that facial classification is permissible in the few circumstances where a limitation on the basis of religion, sex, national origin, or age is a "bona fide occupational qualification." This defense, known as BFOQ, is a limited concept. First, it never applies to race, because Title VII does not list race as a permissible basis for the BFOQ defense. Second, courts apply the defense narrowly on the basis of religion, sex, national origin, and age because the defense arises in circumstances in which the employer refuses to consider any individual applicant except in the favored category. Because the thrust of the Acts is to provide equal opportunity, there are not many circumstances in which employers may rely upon the BFOQ defense in order to deny opportunity altogether to a group otherwise protected by the Acts. The classic example of a legitimate BFOQ is gender restrictions on applications for casting acting roles in the entertainment industry.

Apart from the narrow BFOQ defense, employers may not operate on stereotyped assumptions in offering employment opportunities. The Supreme Court observed in *Hazen Paper Co. v. Biggins* that the ADEA was prompted by congressional concern that older workers were being deprived of employment on the basis of "inaccurate and stigmatizing stereotypes." An age stereotype, for example, is that older employees are less able to handle stressful jobs or less able to adjust to technological change. It is similarly unlawful to make work assignments on the basis of racial stereotypes, or sexual stereotypes unless they meet the BFOQ standard. As one court explained: "In forbidding employers to discriminate against individuals because of their sex, Congress intended to strike at the entire spectrum of disparate treatment of men and women resulting from sex stereotypes."[4]

§ 2.15

1. 42 U.S.C.A. § 2000e–2(1).

2. 42 U.S.C.A. § 2000e–2(2).

3. 29 U.S.C.A. § 623(a)(1)(2).

4. Sprogis v. United Air Lines, Inc., 444 F.2d 1194, 1198 (7th Cir.), cert. denied, 404

One early case that litigated gender stereotyping was *Diaz v. Pan American Airways, Inc.*[5] The defendant airline employed only women as flight attendants on the belief that men were not suited for the job. In an effort to establish stereotyped assumptions as a BFOQ, the airline introduced at trial expert testimony by a psychiatrist concerning the unique ability of women to calm passengers in the air. The expert explained that the cabin of a modern airplane is a "special and unique psychological environment"—a "sealed enclave"—in which typical passengers have three emotions: primarily apprehension, but also boredom and excitement. In this enclave females are psychologically better suited to act as flight attendants because both men and women passengers would respond better to them. The psychiatrist explained that "many male passengers would subconsciously resent a male flight attendant perceived as more masculine than they, but respond negatively to a male flight attendant perceived as less masculine, whereas male passengers would generally feel themselves more masculine and thus more at ease in the presence of a young female attendant."[6] For women passengers, he further explained, a male flight attendant might seem intrusive and inappropriate.

The Fifth Circuit opinion rejected this basis for a BFOQ. The trial judge's finding that the expert's testimony was persuasive was not sufficient to support the defense. Noting that the primary function of the airline is to transport passengers safely, the court said: "No one has suggested that having male stewards will so seriously affect the operation of an airline as to jeopardize or even minimize its ability to provide safe transportation from one place to another."[7]

The truth or falsity of a stereotype is not the central issue. Even a stereotype that is factually true cannot be the basis of an employment decision in the absence of a BFOQ. In *City of Los Angeles, Department of Water & Power v. Manhart*,[8] the Supreme Court found unlawful the use of a gender-based rule for contributions to a pension plan. In *Manhart*, the Court noted that unsubstantiated beliefs cannot support employment decisions. "Myths and purely habitual assumptions about a woman's inability to perform certain kinds of work are no longer acceptable reasons for refusing to employ qualified individuals, or for paying them less."[9] In this case the employment decision was based upon the "unquestionably true" fact that women as a group live longer than men as a group. In order to provide equal monthly pension benefits upon retirement, therefore, the employer withheld more from the paychecks of women than of men to fund these later benefits.

The Court said that the central issue is whether it is unlawfully discriminatory to operate on class characteristics rather than on individ-

U.S. 991, 92 S.Ct. 536, 30 L.Ed.2d 543 (1971).

5. 442 F.2d 385 (5th Cir.), cert. denied, 404 U.S. 950, 92 S.Ct. 275, 30 L.Ed.2d 267 (1971).

6. Diaz v. Pan American World Airways, Inc., 311 F.Supp. 559, 566 (S.D. Fla. 1970).

7. Diaz v. Pan American World Airways, 442 F.2d 385, 388 (5th Cir.1971).

8. 435 U.S. 702, 98 S.Ct. 1370, 55 L.Ed.2d 657 (1978).

9. 98 S.Ct. at 1374.

ual characteristics. Even when the characteristics attributable to the class are true for the group as a whole, there are individual differences within the class. Although women as a group outlive men as a group, not every woman will outlive every man born at the same time. Because the Act refers to discrimination "because of such individual's race, color, religion, sex, or national origin," the Court found "unambiguous" the focus of the statute: "Even a true generalization about the class is an insufficient reason for disqualifying an individual to whom the generalization does not apply."[10]

Discrimination on the basis of pregnancy has been a facial classification since 1978, when Congress amended Title VII with the Pregnancy Discrimination Act. With this amendment, discrimination on the basis of "sex" includes "pregnancy, childbirth, or related medical conditions." Further, the Act provides that women affected with these conditions "shall be treated the same for all employment-related purposes" as other persons "not so affected but similar in their ability or inability to work." Therefore it is facial discrimination for an employer to require all pregnant women to quit or take leave at a certain point during pregnancy, unless such a rule is justified as a BFOQ. It is also a violation of Title VII for an employer to create a hostile or abusive work environment for an employee on the basis of her pregnancy. The plaintiff must establish the connection of the adverse treatment to her pregnancy, however, and not to behavior that resulted in the pregnancy.

Congress enacted the Pregnancy Discrimination Act as a response to a Supreme Court decision that failed to find discrimination on the basis of pregnancy to be facial discrimination. In *General Electric Co. v. Gilbert*,[11] the Court upheld an employer's disability plan that provided employees with compensation during periods of disability resulting from nonoccupational causes and excluded only one condition—pregnancy. The Court reasoned that the exclusion of pregnancy is not gender-based discrimination because the plan divided potential recipients into two groups: pregnant women and nonpregnant persons. It was this reasoning that Congress explicitly rejected when it enacted the Pregnancy Discrimination Act.

The prohibition against unjustified facial classification on the basis of pregnancy now includes "receipt of benefits under fringe benefit programs,"[12] such as the one involved in *Gilbert*. Employers need not provide such benefits at all, but any benefits provided cannot treat pregnancy, childbirth, and related conditions differently from other conditions.

The Pregnancy Discrimination Act further provides that employers are not required to pay for health insurance benefits for an abortion "except where the life of the mother would be endangered if the fetus were carried to term, or except where medical complications have arisen

---

10. Id. at 1375.

11. 429 U.S. 125, 97 S.Ct. 401, 50 L.Ed.2d 343 (1976).

12. 42 U.S.C.A. § 2000e(k).

from an abortion." A proviso in the Act clarifies that although an employer need not provide abortion benefits, it is nonetheless permissible for an employer to provide such benefits. The EEOC interprets the Act to require an employer to grant sick leave for an abortion under the same terms that the employer grants sick leave for other medical conditions.[13] The EEOC interpretation of the Act also includes a prohibition on discharging an employee for having an abortion.

Prohibited facial classification of employees with respect to benefits is not limited to benefits for the employees themselves. The Supreme Court clarified this point in *Newport News Shipbuilding & Dry Dock Co. v. EEOC*.[14] The Supreme Court held that the prohibition against discrimination on the basis of pregnancy affects the ability of employers to fashion health benefits for dependents. The employer provided pregnancy benefits for employees but not for their spouses. This rule was facially discriminatory against men because only male employees could have spouses capable of becoming pregnant.

The exclusion of contraceptive devices such as birth control pills from an employer's health plan was found violative of the Pregnancy Discrimination Act by one district court. The court noted that nearly all other prescription drugs were covered by the employer's health plan and, after consideration of the legislative intent behind the Pregnancy Discrimination Act, concluded that this plan was equivalent to the one excluding pregnancy in *Gilbert*, which Congress expressly repudiated. The district court found irrelevant the lack of intent by the employer to discriminate because the classification was facial.

In *Saks v. Franklin Covey Co.*,[15] the employer denied coverage for surgical infertility procedures under its health benefits plan. A female employee sued on the theory that the health plan violated the PDA because it provided fewer benefits for infertility procedures than for treatment of other conditions. Applying the *Newport News* standard of the relative comprehensiveness of coverage, the court considered first whether sex-specific conditions exist, and if so, whether exclusion of benefits for those conditions results in inferior coverage on the basis of gender. The court noted that infertility is a medical condition that affects men and women with the same frequency, such that the exclusion of surgical infertility procedures equally disadvantages men and women. Therefore, although the PDA covers conditions "related" to pregnancy, it did not violate the Act by providing inferior coverage for infertility procedures.

Discrimination against a woman employee because of the disability of her baby, rather than her own disability, is not discrimination on the basis of gender or pregnancy. Several cases have held that Title VII and the Pregnancy Discrimination Act protect only the mother and do not prohibit discrimination on the basis of the medical condition of a child.

13. Questions & Answers on the Pregnancy Discrimination Act, 29 C.F.R. Part 1604 (44 Fed. Reg. 23804).

14. 462 U.S. 669, 103 S.Ct. 2622, 77 L.Ed.2d 89 (1983).

15. 316 F.3d 337 (2d Cir. 2003).

In *McNill v. New York City Department of Correction*,[16] for example, the employee missed several months of work after childbirth in order to breast feed as a matter of medical necessity because of the baby's cleft palate and lip. The PDA did not cover this situation because it was the child's medical needs rather than the mother's that caused the absence. Any claim would need to come under the Family and Medical Leave Act. Similarly, in another case[17] a self-insuring employer discharged the mother because of the condition of the dependent child. Because the condition of the dependent did not depend upon the gender of the parent, Title VII did not apply. The employee's proper claim was under ERISA.

Pregnancy discrimination is also not the proper claim for employment disadvantage related to medical conditions other than pregnancy or child birth. In a California state case[18] interpreting a California statute similar to the PDA, the court found that refusing to rehire an employee after leave for a diagnostic hysterectomy was not covered by the statute. The court refused to accept the argument that any surgery relating to a woman's reproductive organs falls within the act without some connection to pregnancy, termination of a pregnancy, or childbirth.

Discrimination on the basis of rearing children is another example of discrimination that is not gender specific and therefore is not facially discriminatory in violation of Title VII. In *Fisher v. Vassar College*,[19] the college denied tenure to a biology professor who had taken eight years away from her field in order to rear children. Whatever bias there may have been against her, it was not on the basis of gender. The plaintiff was unable to establish that the college had a practice that treated fathers different than mothers, or married men different from married women.

An employment practice need not affect all members of a group in order to be prohibited as an unjustified facial classification. Any rule that applies only to one group is a facial classification even if the entire group is not subject to the rule. For example, a rule that prohibits the employment of women with pre-school-age children is facial discrimination when the rule does not apply equally to men. The Supreme Court held that such a rule violated Title VII, in *Phillips v. Martin Marietta Corp.*[20] It did not matter that not all women have pre-school-age children, nor did it matter that the rule did not have the effect of reducing employment opportunities for women in general because the job category in question was seventy to seventy-five percent women. Nonetheless, the facially discriminatory rule affected employment opportunities for some individuals solely on the basis of gender. Because men were not subject

---

16. 950 F.Supp. 564 (S.D.N.Y. 1996).

17. Fleming v. Ayers & Assoc., 948 F.2d 993 (6th Cir.1991).

18. Williams v. MacFrugal's Bargains 67 Cal.App.4th 479, 79 Cal.Rptr.2d 98 (1998).

19. 66 F.3d 379 (2d Cir. 1995), aff'd, 114 F.3d 1332 (2d Cir. 1997), cert. denied, 522 U.S. 1075, 118 S.Ct. 851, 139 L.Ed.2d 752 (1998).

20. 400 U.S. 542, 91 S.Ct. 496, 27 L.Ed.2d 613 (1971).

to the same rule, the employer could only defend such facial discrimination as a BFOQ.

Rules that apply only to some members of one gender group are known as "sex-plus" rules. In *International Union, United Auto., Aerospace and Agr. Implement Workers of America, U.A.W. v. Johnson Controls, Inc.*,[21] the Supreme Court found illegal a sex-plus rule that excluded women of childbearing capacity from jobs with potential exposure to lead. Another sex-plus case found unlawful a no-marriage rule that applied only to female flight attendants.[22] Similarly, rules regulating the weight of employees can violate the Act if they apply only to women.[23]

Sex-plus rules can violate Title VII if they result in any form of employment disadvantage. The Supreme Court held in *Nashville Gas Co. v. Satty*[24] that an employer could not place a special burden, such as loss of seniority, on women who take a pregnancy leave. The Court distinguished its earlier decision in *Gilbert*, where it had found no gender discrimination in a benefit plan that excluded only pregnancy. The important difference to the Court in *Satty* was that the employer was imposing a burden on women who took pregnancy leave as opposed to excluding them from a benefit. It can become a question of fact whether the employer has placed a burden on pregnancy, such as whether the employer was impermissibly influenced by an employee's pregnancy when her position was eliminated through downsizing while she was on maternity leave.

The key question is whether there is a burden placed on women, or some subset of women, that is not placed on others. For example, in *Urbano v. Continental Airlines, Inc.*,[25] the Fifth Circuit held that employer did not violate the PDA in failing to give light duty assignments to a pregnant worker because the employee was treated the same as other employees. The employer's policy was to give priority for light-duty assignments to employees who were injured on the job, and then to assign remaining jobs to employees injured off the job. The pregnant plaintiff in *Urbano* requested a light-duty assignment after her doctor restricted her from lifting over twenty pounds, but there were no light-duty assignments available at the time of her request. The court explained that there was no disparate treatment because the PDA requires employers to treat pregnant employees as it treats non-pregnant employees. The court concluded that the PDA does not require special treatment of women whose conditions fall under its protection from adverse treatment.

21. 499 U.S. 187, 111 S.Ct. 1196, 113 L.Ed.2d 158 (1991).

22. Sprogis v. United Air Lines, 444 F.2d 1194 (7th Cir.1971). See also Romasanta v. United Air Lines, Inc., 717 F.2d 1140 (7th Cir.1983).

23. See Laffey v. Northwest Airlines, Inc., 567 F.2d 429 (D.C.Cir.1976), cert. denied, 434 U.S. 1086, 98 S.Ct. 1281, 55 L.Ed.2d 792 (1978).

24. 434 U.S. 136, 98 S.Ct. 347, 54 L.Ed.2d 356 (1977).

25. 138 F.3d 204 (5th Cir.1998).

The fact that federal law does not require special treatment on the basis of pregnancy or related conditions does not mean that states cannot require such special treatment, however, as long as the state requirement does not adversely affect the rights of men in violation of federal law. The Supreme Court explained in *California Federal Savings & Loan Association v. Guerra*[26] that Title VII does not preempt a California statute requiring that employers provide female employees unpaid pregnancy leave of up to four months with guaranteed reinstatement or placement in a substantially similar job. The Court majority reasoned that the PDA does not prohibit preferential treatment of pregnancy because Congress intended the PDA to be a "floor" beneath which benefits may not fall rather than a "ceiling" above which they cannot rise. Employers in that state may avoid violation of either the federal or state statute under the Court's explanation by providing equivalent benefits to other disabled employees.

It is important to note that in the sex-plus cases there is no violation of the Act unless there is a difference in treatment on the basis of gender. A rule applied equally to men and women, such as a rule against extra-marital sexual relationships, is not a facial classification. *Boyd v. Harding Academy*[27] exemplifies this principle. The employer was a Christian school that required its teachers to adhere to Christian moral standards, including a ban on sex outside of marriage while employed by the school. The plaintiff, who was not married, was fired when she admitted that she was pregnant. Her claim of pregnancy discrimination failed because the school had consistently adhered to the practice of firing both male and female employees for cohabitation outside marriage, without regard to pregnancy. The plaintiff's pregnancy had simply confirmed the fact that she had had an extra-marital affair.

Because there was no issue in *Boyd* whether the plaintiff's pregnancy had resulted from sex outside of marriage, the court had no occasion to consider whether an employer could fire an employee for an unwed pregnancy by artificial insemination. Such a category of employees—those with a pregnancy by artificial means—would necessarily be all female and therefore the employer could not demonstrate that men were held to the same standard. It was critical in *Boyd* that the category of adversely affected employees was defined as those who engaged in extramarital sex and that the category included both men and women.

A rule that applies equally to all groups can become unlawful when the employer applies it differentially, however, such as discharging females for transgressions while tolerating similar behavior from males. A rule also can violate the Act when there is greater chance that transgression of the rule will be observed for one group. For example, an employee's violation of a rule against unwed parenthood is more easily

26. 479 U.S. 272, 107 S.Ct. 683, 93 L.Ed.2d 613 (1987).

27. 88 F.3d 410 (6th Cir.1996).

ascertained for women who conceive a child out of wedlock than for men who commit the same act.[28]

Sex-plus rules are distinguishable from rules directed toward a category of workers who are all the same gender. It is not unlawful to apply rules to such workers unless the rules are directed at this job category precisely because of the gender of the workers. For example, a restriction on the weight of employees is permissible if applied in a similar fashion to men and women, even if gender-specific height and weight tables are used. It can be gender discrimination, however, to apply a stringent weight-maintenance requirement to a job category of all women solely because the employer values a svelte appearance more in women than in men.[29]

Similarly, an employer violates Title VII by disadvantaging a single-sex category of workers because of their gender. The Supreme Court held in *County of Washington v. Gunther*[30] that an employer cannot pay less to female guards in county jails than the employer's own study indicated that they were worth, if the basis of that differential is gender-based. The Court emphasized that it was not addressing the issue of comparable worth. Instead, "respondents seek to prove, by direct evidence, that their wages were depressed because of intentional sex discrimination, consisting of setting the wage scale for female guards, but not for male guards, at a level lower than its own survey of outside markets and the worth of the jobs warranted."[31]

An employer may use race-conscious or gender-conscious criteria for the selection and promotion of employees pursuant to a bona fide affirmative action plan. Voluntary affirmative action plans must meet criteria specified by the Supreme Court for such plans to be bona fide. It is important to distinguish voluntary affirmative action plans from remedial hiring orders that are race or gender specific. Voluntary affirmative action plans are not court-ordered remedies following a finding of liability. Rather, employers adopt such plans in order to achieve a more diverse work force in job categories where groups have been historically underrepresented. The adoption of such a plan is not an admission of historical exclusion by the employer; it reflects only societal exclusion, for whatever reasons. Federal contractors adopt voluntary affirmative action plans in order to comply with Executive Order 11246.

Claims of intentional discrimination against a group may take several forms. A claim of facial discrimination against a group, such as those described in this section, is distinguishable from a claim of group disparate treatment in which there is no express exclusion by the employer. A plaintiff class claiming unlawful disparate treatment must establish the intentional exclusion or underrepresentation of the group

---

28. See Chambers v. Omaha Girls Club, Inc., 834 F.2d 697 (8th Cir.1987).

29. Gerdom v. Continental Airlines, Inc., 692 F.2d 602 (9th Cir.1982), cert. denied, 460 U.S. 1074, 103 S.Ct. 1534, 75 L.Ed.2d 954 (1983).

30. 452 U.S. 161, 101 S.Ct. 2242, 68 L.Ed.2d 751 (1981).

31. 452 U.S. at 167, 101 S.Ct. at 2246.

by the employer. The plaintiff's proof in a group disparate treatment case can include statistical patterns and anecdotal evidence of individual disparate treatment. Such claims should be further distinguished from disparate impact claims, in which it is not necessary to prove intent.

§ 2.16 Intentional Exclusion of Groups—Restrictive Advertising and Race Coding

Newspaper "Help Wanted" pages historically differentiated on the basis of gender and age. Before the Civil Rights Act of 1964 (Title VII) and the Age Discrimination in Employment Act (ADEA) in 1967, virtually all newspapers had columns labeled "Help Wanted—Male" and "Help Wanted—Female," and it was routine to find advertisements requesting "young" applicants. Indeed, these advertising practices were so deeply ingrained in the culture that they persisted for many years after the federal guarantees of equal opportunity were enacted.

It is now well established that advertisements may not expressly describe desired applicants by gender or age. Nor may an advertisement use terms that suggest such preferences, such as "Gal Friday" or "recent graduate." The only defenses to such restrictions in advertising are the same that apply to hiring. Specifically, the employer must be able to establish a bona fide occupational qualification (BFOQ) or the employer must be acting pursuant to a bona fide affirmative action plan.

Section 704(b) of Title VII provides:

It shall be unlawful for an employer, labor organization, or employment agency to print or publish, or cause to be printed or published, any notice or advertisement relating to employment by such an employer * * * indicating any preference limitation, specification or discrimination based on race, color, religion, sex, or national origin.[1]

Who Can Sue and Be Sued for Restrictive Advertising

Because the Acts apply only to employers, labor organizations, and employment agencies, a newspaper is not liable simply for printing discriminatory advertisements for other employers. As an employer itself, of course, the newspaper cannot advertise discriminatorily for its own employees. For other employers, however, a newspaper does not become an "employment agency" subject to the Acts by printing advertisements for other employers.

One issue that has caused difficulty in challenging discriminatory advertisements is standing. The EEOC has standing to challenge such practices, but a private individual has standing only when such a plaintiff has a genuine interest in the position.

Explicit and Implicit Preferences

As with gender and age discrimination in advertising and job assignment, racial restrictions on job categories were commonplace before the

---

§ 2.16
1. 42 U.S.C.A. § 2000e–3(b).

Section 4(e) of the ADEA contains a similar provision. 29 U.S.C.A. § 623(e).

passage of the Civil Rights Act of 1964. The fact that such segregation was open and legal motivated Congress to pass the Act. The Act made illegal the practice of relegating minority workers to the least desirable jobs. In the modern context, such overt segregation is rarely seen. Explicit references to race, religion, national origin, gender, or age are rare in modern advertising and recruitment, except in instances where an employer is acting pursuant to a bona fide affirmative action plan, or where the employer limits the job on the basis of gender or national origin as a bona fide occupational qualification.

Efforts to restrict jobs with explicit but secretive preferences are as unlawful as the overt segregation of the past. An interesting example of secretive job coding is alleged in *EEOC v. Recruit U.S.A.*[2] This case involved an appeal from an injunctive order requiring two employment agencies not to destroy records. The agencies operated referral agencies primarily for Japanese companies. The EEOC sought the preliminary injunction after receiving information from former employees that suggested invidious discrimination. The basis of the EEOC complaint was the alleged practice of these agencies to accommodate the racial, ethnic, gender, and age preferences of their clients. A former employee provided information that one agency had a secret coding system to keep track of the requests: "See Maria" meant that the client would prefer or accept Hispanics; "See Mary" meant Caucasians; "See Mariko" meant Japanese; "See Adam" restricted the job to males; "See Eve" restricted the job to females; "Suite 20–35" limited the job to ages 20–35; and "Floor 40" meant a person in the forties.

The advent of computerized resume reviews presents new opportunities for coding that may create Title VII problems. Key word searches on resumes performed by some commercial software has the potential for segregating and classifying applicants on a grand scale. A zip code search, for example, can be a form of race coding where housing patterns are racially distinctive.

Lawful versus Unlawful Race Coding

Racial, ethnic, gender and age coding can occur lawfully in several situations. First, employers have recordkeeping requirements under the EEOC's Uniform Guidelines on Employee Selection Procedures.[3] Title VII provides that employers and employment agencies and labor organizations "shall (1) make and keep such records relevant to the determinations of whether unlawful employment practices have been or are being committed, (2) preserve such records for such periods, and (3) make such reports therefrom, as the Commission shall prescribe."

Lawful coding can be for the purpose of employment opportunity assessment or in preparation for litigation. The most common method of determining an individual's race, national origin, gender, or age is self-identification. Courts have sometimes accepted statistics based upon a visual survey and name review even when self-identification records

---

2. 939 F.2d 746 (9th Cir.1991).   **3.** 29 C.F.R. § 1607.4.

were available. In *Clady v. County of Los Angeles*,[4] for example, the plaintiff class of black and Hispanic applicants used self-identification figures for their statistical analysis, whereas the employer used figures based upon visual inspection and surname review. The court adopted the employer's method because it was the only way to compare the tests over time.

Because notations of race or other protected dimensions can be lawful in some circumstances, but evidence of intentional discrimination in others, the trier of fact must determine the purpose of the notations. In one case,[5] for example, the trial judge found as a matter of fact that applications for certain positions were racially coded by a circle in the lower lefthand corner of the first page. A supervisor testified that the purpose of this coding was to keep records for purposes of assessing equal employment opportunity. The judge found this assertion discredited by the fact that when a black applicant filed a charge of discrimination against the company, someone in the company had whited out the racial coding on her application. If the notation had a lawful purpose, then it would be unnecessary to hide the notation in the face of litigation.

When employers surreptitiously make racial codes on applications, the secretive character can be evidence that the coding was invidious rather than lawful. An employer that relies heavily upon subjective evaluations by interviewers who make racial notations is especially vulnerable to a claim of intentional exclusion.

Although the use of such notations is evidence of discriminatory intent, it is not dispositive. An example of this principle is *EEOC v. Chicago Miniature Lamp Works*.[6] In that case the trial judge found that the employer had numerous applications with the letter "B" written by hand on them, apparently as a racial code. On appeal, the circuit court reversed the judgment of liability because of flaws in the plaintiff-EEOC's statistical analysis. The evidence did not support a finding of disproportionate exclusion in the employer's method of recruitment, and the applicant flow showed that African–American applicants were hired at a favorable rate. With respect to the evidence of racial coding, the appellate court noted that "ordinarily the probative value of any race-coding would relate to its effect on Miniature's hiring rate vis-a-vis its applicant pool."[7] Because there was no adverse effect, the racial coding was not invidious.

The court further explained in *Chicago Miniature* that the good applicant flow data would not compel a finding for the employer if there were evidence that the employer had a reputation for discrimination. "Of course," the opinion explains, "if an employer gets a reputation that

4. 770 F.2d 1421 (9th Cir.1985), cert. denied, 475 U.S. 1109, 106 S.Ct. 1516, 89 L.Ed.2d 915 (1986).

5. Calloway v. Westinghouse Elec. Corp., 642 F.Supp. 663 (M.D.Ga.1986).

6. 947 F.2d 292 (7th Cir.1991).

7. Id. at 304.

it will not hire black workers, because of actions such as race-coding, then black applicants will be deterred from applying."[8]

This principle was explained more fully in *Mister v. Illinois Central Gulf Railroad*.[9] If the employer has a reputation for discrimination, or if employment agencies know of the employer's discrimination, then very few of the disfavored group will apply. If, for example, an employer has a reputation for discrimination against African–Americans, then "[t]he firm could hire as large a percentage of the (few) black applicants as of white applicants while still discriminating."[10] Further, the court explained that known discrimination not only deters many potential applicants, but results in application from only highly qualified black applicants who would find the costs of applying worthwhile. "The observation that the firm hires black and white applicants in such a pool with equal probability would show only that it is happy to hire high-quality blacks while it is satisfied to use medium quality whites—people who could not get in the door if they were black." The court concluded that "discrimination affects the applicant pool in a way that makes the discrimination harder to detect."[11]

§ 2.17   Intentional Exclusion of Groups—Segregation or Classification of Employees

Title VII and the ADEA prohibit employers, labor organizations, and employment agencies covered by the Act from limiting, segregating, or classifying employees or applicants on the basis of race, color, religion, sex, national origin and age.[1] The case law since Title VII's effective date in 1965 has identified many areas of such impermissible limitation, segregation, or classification.

Job segregation on the basis of race and gender was open and legal before 1965. In the landmark case of *Griggs v. Duke Power Co.*,[2] for example, the employer had segregated overtly before 1965 by relegating all African–Americans to the labor department and reserving the "operating" departments with better pay for the preferred racial group. The openly racial assignments ended on July 2, 1965, which was the date that the Act became effective.

It was generally understood by employers like the Duke Power Company that Congress had targeted racial job segregation with the Civil Rights Act. The assignment of jobs or duties on the basis of race is a prohibited segregation or classification under section 703(a)(2), which provides that it is an unlawful employment practice for an employer

> to limit, segregate, or classify his employees or applicants for employment in any way which would deprive or tend to deprive any

---

8. Id. at 304 n.11.

9. 832 F.2d 1427 (7th Cir.1987), cert. denied, 485 U.S. 1035, 108 S.Ct. 1597, 99 L.Ed.2d 911 (1988).

10. 832 F.2d at 1436.

11. Id.

§ 2.17

1. 42 U.S.C.A. § 2000e–2; 29 U.S.C.A. § 623(a)(2).

2. 401 U.S. 424, 91 S.Ct. 849, 28 L.Ed.2d 158 (1971).

individual of employment opportunities or otherwise adversely affect his status as an employee, because of such individual's race, color, religion, sex, or national origin.[3]

Identical statutory language is present in the ADEA.[4]

Overt and covert classification

Overt classification of employees is well illustrated by *Slack v. Havens*,[5] an early Title VII case. In that case there were four women who worked in the same job category in the defendant employer's manufacturing plant. Although heavy cleaning was not part of their job description, the supervisor decided that production would stop for one day because he wanted to do some heavy cleaning. Three of the four women, all of whom were African–American, were told they had to do the cleaning and were fired when they refused to do so. The fourth woman, a Caucasian, was excused from the department for that day so that she wouldn't have to do the undesirable work. The supervisor made express the racial classification when he said that black people should stay "in their place" and are suited to cleaning. The district court found in favor of the three discharged women because regardless of the employer's motivation, they had been disadvantaged by the overtly racial classification.

Covert classification is more common and becomes overt when a practice is expressed in racial terms. A covert classification is one where the real reason for the different treatment of employees is racial but that basis is not immediately apparent. One case, *Hurde v. Jobs Plus–Med*,[6] involved facts similar to *Slack* without express articulation of the basis for the classification. The plaintiff alleged that he was assigned work to move sand more often and for longer periods than other employees and he was the only employee who had to drain the parking lot by digging ruts. His claim was that the basis of the assignments was race and that similarly situated employees did not have to do such work. The case survived summary judgment because the essence of his claim was that he had been categorized for work assignment on the basis of race. Another case, *Lams v. General Waterworks Corp.*,[7] involved a similar claim and adds evidence of overt classification to bolster the evidence of covert classification. The African–Americans in the defendant company were concentrated in the construction department and rarely promoted out to better departments. When asked at trial for the reason, a key manager responded: "I would presume that's the type of work that they like."[8] He discouraged inquiries from black workers about promotions and transfers, but facilitated the advancement of white workers about whom he did not have the same stereotyped attitude concerning their work preferences.

---

3. 42 U.S.C.A. § 2000e–2(a)(2).

4. 29 U.S.C.A. § 623(a)(2).

5. 1973 WL 339 (S.D.Cal. 1973).

6. 299 F.Supp.2d 1196 (D.Kan. 2004).

7. 766 F.2d 386 (8th Cir.1985).

8. Id. at 392.

A supervisor's mental classification of employees can be expressed by actions as well as words. In one case,[9] a supervisor rarely asked the Hispanic section chief attorney to lunch even though he regularly asked other section chief attorneys. The same supervisor also assigned all three of the Hispanic attorneys to the same division as the Hispanic section chief. These patterns were evidence of his mental categorization of these workers and this evidence was admissible to show intent when the Hispanic section chief was not promoted.

A classification of minority workers as the group most suspected of criminal conduct may also support a theory that the employer engaged in racial stereotyping. For example, in *EEOC v. Riss International Corp.*,[10] a discharged black employee established that the suspicion of him for dishonesty was the product of "a common prejudicial stereotype of 'typical' black dishonesty * * * apparently drawn and acted upon with hardly a scintilla of evidence."[11] The court said that it appeared the company was hiring African–Americans on something of an experimental basis and that a nervous all-white management held the plaintiff to a higher standard than would be imposed on other employees. Also relevant was the racial stereotyping of job assignments, such that the few black employees were assigned to be maintenance men and elevator operators.

Discriminatory versus Non–Discriminatory Classifications

All classifications of employees are not necessarily unlawful employment practices. An employer's general awareness of employee classifications is not in itself unlawful even when the classifications are based on race or other protected categories. In one case,[12] a hospital president kept aware in a general way of the percentage of medical staff who were foreign-trained because he wanted to know how his hospital compared with peer hospitals on that dimension. This concession in itself was not sufficient to draw an inference of improper motivation with respect to employment opportunities nor an "inappropriate awareness of the race or ethnicity of the members of the hospital staff."[13]

The focus of the classification inquiry is on the deprivation of employment opportunity. For example, the same conduct of classification by an employer could be discriminatory toward one group but not another. Consider the classification of employees for changing facilities or rest rooms. A racial or ethnic classification of such work-related areas would be impermissible classification. The effect of such segregation is inherently demeaning and adversely affects the status of minority employees.

Contrast the segregation of employees on the basis of gender for purposes of privacy in dressing and toilet. Such classification of employees is on a protected dimension, but it does not have the same demean-

---

9. Perdomo v. Browner, 67 F.3d 140 (7th Cir. 1995).

10. 525 F.Supp. 1094 (W.D.Mo.1981).

11. Id. at 1100.

12. Betkerur v. Aultman Hosp. Ass'n, 78 F.3d 1079 (6th Cir.1996).

13. 78 F.3d at 1097.

ing effect. This distinction is further discussed at the end of this section which distinguishes an employer's obligation to prevent harassment from the obligation not to segregation and classify employees in a demeaning or oppressive manner.

Problems of Proof with Covert Classifications

An employer's assignment of desirable jobs on the basis of a protected dimension is actionable whether it is overt or covert, but the manner of proof between the two is very different. Overt classification takes direct evidence, as illustrated by the cases earlier in this section. Covert classification requires proof of a pattern that uncovers the true nature of the regular practice.

Such pattern and practice cases are also called group disparate treatment cases. The plaintiff class alleging disparate treatment in work conditions or assignments must show a deliberate pattern of disadvantage on the basis of membership in a protected group. Statistics can help to establish such as pattern, as in *International Brotherhood of Teamsters v. United States*.[14] In that case the employer had two truck driving classifications: city drivers and over-the-road drivers. The second category was considered more desirable and the drivers were virtually all white. All the minority drivers were in the less desirable category. Impressed by the "inexorable zero" of minorities in the over-the-road job, the Court found that this fact, bolstered by anecdotal evidence, was sufficient to establish a pattern of intentional exclusion.

The inexorable zero reflecting historical exclusion was relevant in a case involving the gender preference of a restaurant in hiring male waiters, *EEOC v. Joe's Stone Crabs, Inc.*[15] In the five-year period prior to the EEOC's charge, the restaurant hired 108 waiters and all of them had been men. The restaurant had a practice of hiring food servers during an annual "roll call" to which aspiring workers came. Because the job was considered a very desirable one among experienced food servers, roll call was generally well-attended. The court concluded that the relative absence of women from the event reflected the continued effect of the historical exclusion of women from its work force and the perceived futility of application.

Self-segregation versus Employer Segregation

It is necessary to distinguish between an invidious classification that is the employer's responsibility and self-imposed segregation of employees that is beyond the scope of the employer's responsibility. Notably, an employer has no affirmative duty to eliminate self-segregation of employees at social events or eating places during non-working hours.

In contrast, the employer cannot condone unofficial but invidious segregation of work-related areas even if the segregation is not required or encouraged by the employer. This issue appeared in *Firefighters*

---

14. 431 U.S. 324, 97 S.Ct. 1843, 52 L.Ed.2d 396 (1977).

15. 296 F.3d 1265 (11th Cir.2002), cert. denied, 539 U.S. 941, 123 S.Ct. 2606, 156 L.Ed.2d 627 (2003).

Institute for Racial Equality v. St. Louis,[16] where the employees were firefighters who worked on long shifts that required them to eat and sleep on the job. The employees grouped themselves by race for these activities, with the minority employees suffering from social exclusion by the Caucasian firefighters. The Eighth Circuit found that the employer had an affirmative duty in that situation to control the work environment to prevent demeaning exclusions on the basis of race and national origin.

Even when the self-segregation of employees is not demeaning, employers should monitor such conduct to assure that there is no indirect loss of employment opportunity as a result. In *Carmichael v. Birmingham Saw Works*,[17] for example, the employees tended to self-segregate by race in the lunchroom but the circumstances were not in violation of Title VII because of the nature of the practice. Nonetheless, this self-segregation was relevant to a different type of claim against the employer. In that case, an African–American employee was not an applicant for a promotion that went to a less qualified white worker because word of the promotion opportunity was spread informally. The problem was that the white supervisor revealed the promotion opportunity at a lunch table, such that all the recipients of the information were white. The court observed that the plaintiff "never reaped the benefits of the white grapevine" because of the informality of the procedure and the social segregation of the lunch room.

"Segregation" of Employees versus Harassing "Conditions" of Employment

The affirmative duty to prevent demeaning segregation such as that in *Firefighters Institute for Racial Equality v. St. Louis*[18] is distinguishable from the duty of employers to control behavior that creates a hostile working environment on a basis protected by the Acts. This difference is between "classification," which is the topic of this section, and harassment. Harassment claims, which are far more commonly litigated, concern the creation of an adverse "condition" of employment, without the need to show a more general "classification" of employees.

Another distinction between a claim for "classification" or "segregation" versus a claim for harassment is that off-site conduct may support a claim for harassment even though off-site self-segregation does not support a claim for classification.[19] The difference is that a claim for a hostile condition of employment can involve conduct outside the workplace that adversely affects conditions on the job. It does not matter where harassing conduct occurs if the effect is to create a hostile working environment. In contrast, employers are responsible for demeaning classifications and segregation only on the job.

16. 549 F.2d 506 (8th Cir.), cert. denied, 434 U.S. 819, 98 S.Ct. 60, 54 L.Ed.2d 76 (1977).

17. 738 F.2d 1126 (11th Cir. 1984).

18. 549 F.2d 506 (8th Cir.), cert. denied, 434 U.S. 819, 98 S.Ct. 60, 54 L.Ed.2d 76 (1977).

19. Domingo v. New Eng. Fish Co., 727 F.2d 1429 (9th Cir.1984).

Another difference between a segregation claim and an harassment claim is the group nature of the former and the individual nature of the latter. It is not possible to classify or segregate only one member of a class; by definition, the conduct is group based in its intent. In contrast, harassment of one employee on a protected dimension need not affect any other employee.

The essence of the employer's obligation with respect to segregation of employees is to avoid classification or segregation that disadvantages or oppresses a protected group. On the other hand, the obligation to avoid harassing working conditions for protected groups may dictate *segregation* for the purpose of protecting *conditions* of employment as also required by the Acts. Thus, the *failure* to segregate on the basis of gender for toilet facilities or changing areas may have the effect of creating a harassing work environment, and concomitantly, such segregation of groups on the basis of gender will not be unlawful segregation because it is not oppressive. It is important for employers to focus on whether the segregation is demeaning or oppressive such that it adversely affects employment opportunities.

§ 2.18 Bona Fide Occupational Qualification

The defense of "bona fide occupational qualification" (BFOQ) allows for intentional classification of applicants or employees in the narrow circumstances where such classification is "reasonably necessary to the normal operation of that particular business or enterprise." This defense appears in both Title VII[1] and the ADEA.[2] Title VII limits this defense to exclusion on the basis of gender, national origin, and religion. Notably, race is specifically excluded, such that an employer can never say that classification by race is necessary to the operation of the business.

This section will explore the various tests developed to establish a BFOQ defense. The Supreme Court has clarified the nature of this defense in three opinions. Two of these opinions concerned BFOQ for gender,[3] and one involved the BFOQ defense under the ADEA. The Court has not indicated that the defense operates any differently under these two Acts.

BFOQ Basis–Generally

The effect of the defense is that an employer can lawfully refuse to consider or hire certain individuals solely on the basis of their religion, gender, or national origin. The EEOC Guidelines interpret the defense narrowly, with a focus on its permissibility for authenticity.[4] For example, a movie producer may restrict the screening for acting parts on the basis of gender; it is not necessary to consider men for the role of a

§ 2.18

1. 42 U.S.C.A. § 2000e–2(e).

2. 29 U.S.C.A. § 623(f)(1).

3. International Union, UAW v. Johnson Controls, Inc., 499 U.S. 187, 111 S.Ct.

1196, 113 L.Ed.2d 158 (1991); Dothard v. Rawlinson, 433 U.S. 321, 97 S.Ct. 2720, 53 L.Ed.2d 786 (1977).

4. 29 C.F.R. § 1604.2(a).

woman or women for the role of a man even if individual actors and actresses can credibly play opposite gender roles. According to EEOC, ethnic restaurants may refuse to consider as chefs any individual who does not match the ethnic character of the restaurant for purposes of authenticity, even when other individuals can cook the native cuisine as well. This interpretation, however, is more questionable, and it has never been challenged in court.

It is never permissible under the BFOQ defense to refuse to consider an individual on the basis of race. If a producer is casting a movie about historical characters, it is not permissible to refuse to consider individuals who are racially different from the historical people. Although it would be permissible to refuse to hire anyone whose appearance is too dissimilar to the historical figure, there can be no blanket refusal to consider all individuals on the basis of their racial identification. Thus, the producer of a movie about the life of Christopher Columbus cannot permissibly announce that the title role will be limited to individuals whose racial identification is Caucasian, although the producer can require that the person ultimately cast in the role bear a credible resemblance to the historical figure. The producer can refuse to consider any women for the title role, however, because of the BFOQ defense.

BFOQ Basis–Rejection of Romantic Pateralism

The Supreme Court has explained that the BFOQ defense is narrow. In *Dothard v. Rawlinson*,[5] the Court held that romantic paternalism is not sufficient to establish gender as a BFOQ for prison guards in a male penitentiary. Legitimate concerns for the safety of third parties is a legally sufficient basis for BFOQ, however. In the unique situation in that case, the male prisoners in the defendant-employer's penitentiary system were not segregated by type of offense. As a consequence, sex offenders were interspersed throughout the system and created a special threat to female guards. The Court said it was not permissible to deny women guard positions on the grounds that the employer was worried about their individual safety in any such possible attack, but it was permissible to deny such placement because of the threat such an attack would pose to third parties when the guard lost control.

Although a BFOQ does not need to be grounded in factual studies, it may not be based on unjustified stereotypes or romantic paternalism. As *Dothard* rejected romantic paternalism as a basis for its decision about women as prison guards, other cases have rejected the motivation to protect women from jobs that are dirty, dangerous, or strenuous.[6] State protective statutes that limited the times and conditions of work for women reflected similar concerns. Employers could not use these statutes as a BFOQ defense to Title VII if the state requirement conflicted with the federal standard. Citing the Supremacy Clause in Article I of the Constitution, courts held that the state or local requirement could not restrict the federal legislation.

5. 433 U.S. 321, 97 S.Ct. 2720, 53 L.Ed.2d 786 (1977).

6. Weeks v. Southern Bell Tel. & Tel. Co., 408 F.2d 228 (5th Cir.1969).

BFOQ Basis–Privacy

In prison systems where the inmates are properly segregated on the basis of offense, the safety justification in *Dothard* does not apply to most of the guard positions. The question then becomes whether the employment of guards of the opposite gender threatens the privacy interest of the inmates. The Seventh Circuit held in *Torres v. Wisconsin Department of Health & Social Services*[7] that the privacy interests of the female inmates was insufficient for creating a BFOQ. Instead, prison officials need to adopt measures to afford privacy to inmates whenever it is possible to do so. In *Torres*, the female inmates could cover windows in the doors of their rooms with "privacy cards" for up to ten minutes during certain hours to allow privacy when they dress or use the toilet. Similarly, the Ninth Circuit also has held that prisoners as a group have a limited right of privacy and that a BFOQ for corrections officers cannot be supported on the privacy right alone.[8]

Privacy has not been the only concern of prison officials in assigning correctional officers on the basis of gender, however, and courts have found other grounds to uphold a BFOQ for such jobs. In *Robino v. Iranon*,[9] the Ninth Circuit found that gender was a BFOQ for a correctional facility's female-only posts where the officers would be required to observe inmates in the showers and toilet areas. The court accepted that the rationale was not primarily privacy but security, rehabilitation, and morale. The security interest was reducing the risk of sexual conduct between officers and the inmates. The state's assertion of these penological interests sufficed despite the fact that they were not supported by any empirical data to show an improvement in security or an increase in rehabilitation and morale when only female officers are assigned to the unit, although there had been an internal study of allegations from the unit of sexual abuse and morale problems. In *Torres* the Seventh Circuit also upheld the BFOQ for certain posts because the warden had made a study and found that "a high percentage of female inmates has been physically and sexually abused by males." Although in *Torres* the abuse by males had occurred outside the prison setting, the court nonetheless found that the employer had demonstrated a sufficient ground to exclude male guards in order to foster the rehabilitation of the prisoners.

The privacy interest of male prisoners has also failed to prevent the assignment of female officers to guard them. In *Timm v. Gunter*,[10] for example, the court found reasonable the prison's practice of allowing female guards in a male penitentiary to conduct surveillance of all areas and to pat-search male prisoners on the same basis as male guards. The prison provided reasonable privacy protection by allowing the inmates to

---

7. 859 F.2d 1523 (7th Cir.1988), cert. denied, 489 U.S. 1017, 109 S.Ct. 1133, 103 L.Ed.2d 194 (1989).

8. Somers v. Thurman, 109 F.3d 614 (9th Cir.), cert. denied, 522 U.S. 852, 118 S.Ct. 143, 139 L.Ed.2d 90 (1997).

9. 145 F.3d 1109 (9th Cir.1998).

10. 917 F.2d 1093 (8th Cir.1990), cert. denied, 501 U.S. 1209, 111 S.Ct. 2807, 115 L.Ed.2d 979 (1991).

use a covering towel while dressing and body positioning while using the urinal or shower.

BFOQ Basis—Rejection of Customer Preference

Customer preference is not a sufficient reason for a BFOQ, except when privacy interests are involved. Even documented proof of customer preference, rather than mere assumptions, is not sufficient to create a BFOQ. In one early case, for example, an airline demonstrated through customer surveys that there was a preference for young female flight attendants among its passengers, who were primarily businessmen. Such evidence was not sufficient for a BFOQ.[11]

In another case,[12] customer preference was insufficient for the defense, even though the strength of the preference threatened the ability of the employee to perform the job. A woman was wrongfully denied a job as a sales representative who would need to conduct some overseas business out of her hotel room. The defendant argued that in Latin America she could not be effective as a sales representative because the cultural condition was such that men would be reluctant to do business with her. The court rejected the argument as a basis of a BFOQ. Similarly, an employer may not use a racial criterion when hiring a minority recruiter on the assumption that such an individual would be more credible with the target group. Such an assumption was a stereotype about the preferences of the target group. Similarly, an employer may not use racial or gender restrictions when hiring a social worker who would serve in part as a positive role model for young urban black males.[13]

Other litigation on the BFOQ defense has concerned positions that require heavy lifting, arduous work, or providing physical security. In some cases, employers have argued that because men as a group are stronger, have more endurance, and are more physically threatening than women as a group, gender is a BFOQ for jobs requiring these traits. The Supreme Court established in *Los Angeles Department of Water & Power v. Manhart*,[14] however, that even true stereotypes cannot be the basis of restricting employment opportunities under Title VII.

BFOQ Basis—"All or Substantially All" Cannot Perform Job Safely and Efficiently

Physical stereotypes on the basis of gender–even true ones–are not alone a sufficient basis for a BFOQ. If a job requires upper body strength to lift weight that more men than women can achieve, the employer may not refuse to consider women on that basis. Those women who are strong enough to do the job would be unfairly excluded if the defense applied so easily. Thus, an employer cannot reject a woman applicant

---

11. Diaz v. Pan Am. World Airways, 442 F.2d 385 (5th Cir.), cert. denied, 404 U.S. 950, 92 S.Ct. 275, 30 L.Ed.2d 267 (1971).

12. Fernandez v. Wynn Oil Co., 653 F.2d 1273 (9th Cir.1981).

13. Jatczak v. Ochburg, 540 F.Supp. 698 (E.D.Mich.1982).

14. 435 U.S. 702, 98 S.Ct. 1370, 55 L.Ed.2d 657 (1978).

who is capable of performing the job requirements solely because many other members of her gender group cannot do so.

In *Weeks v. Southern Bell Telephone & Telegraph Co.,*[15] the employer refused to hire women for the position of "switchman" because the job required strenuous lifting. The Fifth Circuit held that a BFOQ can be supported only if "all or substantially all" members of the excluded class would be unable to perform the essential job duties safely and efficiently. Otherwise it is necessary to test individual applicants to see if they can perform the tasks required for the job. This opinion has been influential and the test of "all or substantially all" has sometimes been called the *Weeks* test. Although the Supreme Court has not spoken directly to this issue, in *Dothard v. Rowlinson*[16] the Court cited *Weeks* with approval.

The exception to the "all or substantially all" test for a BFOQ is when there is a risk to third parties and it is not practicable to test all individuals for this risk. *Dothard* illustrates this principle; the Court upheld the BFOQ for the prison guard when the unusual prison setting meant that there was increased risk of prison unrest posed by the possibility that unsegregated sex offenders might attack a woman guard.

The Supreme Court examined the safety principle in an age discrimination case concerning the BFOQ. In *Western Air Lines, Inc. v. Criswell,*[17] the Court provided a two-part approach. First, the employer must show that there are unacceptable risks to third parties if members of the protected class are employed. Second, the employer must show that it is impracticable to identify through individual evaluations those persons who cannot safely and efficiently perform those tasks. Although this case was brought under the ADEA, the principles are relevant to BFOQ litigation under Title VII.

In *International Union, United Auto Workers v. Johnson Controls, Inc.,*[18] the Supreme Court clarified the "safety" exception and held that the defense applies only to qualifications that affect an employee's ability to do the job. The employer in that case had adopted a gender-based fetal protection policy that excluded all fertile female employees from certain jobs because of a concern for the health of the fetus that a fertile woman might conceive. The employer manufactured batteries and workers were exposed to lead during the manufacturing process. The Court held that the total exclusion of all women of child-bearing capacity from jobs involving exposure to certain levels of lead violates the Act. The BFOQ defense did not apply because the rule did not relate to the ability of the employees to perform the job.[19]

---

15. 408 F.2d 228 (5th Cir.1969).

16. 433 U.S. 321, 97 S.Ct. 2720, 53 L.Ed.2d 786 (1977).

17. 472 U.S. 400, 105 S.Ct. 2743, 86 L.Ed.2d 321 (1985).

18. 499 U.S. 187, 111 S.Ct. 1196, 113 L.Ed.2d 158 (1991).

19. See also Elinor P. Schroeder, *The Other Question in Johnson Controls*, 1 Kan. J.L. & Pub.Pol'y 145 (1991).

The majority opinion in *Johnson Controls* also relied upon the Pregnancy Discrimination Act (PDA). Congress enacted the PDA in 1978 to amend Title VII to include discrimination on the basis of pregnancy as a type of discrimination on the basis of gender. The Act provides that women affected by pregnancy, childbirth, or related medical conditions shall be treated the same for all employment-related purposes "as other persons not so affected but similar in their ability or inability to work."[20] The Court noted that the legislative history of the PDA made clear that "this statutory standard was chosen to protect female workers from being treated differently from other employees simply because of their capacity to bear children."[21]

The three Supreme Court cases concerning BFOQ make clear that the defense is most likely to be upheld when the issue is the safety of third parties for whom the employer has responsibility. In *Dothard*, the issue was the safety of those threatened by a prison riot. In *Criswell*, the safety of airline passengers was at issue. The employer in *Johnson Controls* presented the safety argument with respect to the possible health hazard to the potential fetuses that the women employees might carry. The safety argument in *Dothard* and *Criswell* related to the ability of the employees to do a job that has a safety component. In contrast, in *Johnson Controls* the safety argument was unrelated to any direct aspect of the job. The Supreme Court thus made clear the essential focus of the defense; it applies only to "qualifications that affect an employee's ability to do the job."

§ 2.19   Voluntary Affirmative Action

Voluntary affirmative action refers to a choice by employers to take steps to ensure employment opportunities for members of groups historically excluded from various job categories. Such steps may include special efforts at recruiting, special training, and express consideration of race, national origin, and gender in decision-making. These voluntary actions are distinguishable from court-ordered remedies against employers for violations of Title VII. They are voluntary in the sense that employers need not adopt such a plan, although as a practical matter such plans are adopted because of the obligations of any employer who does business with the federal government, as described below. They remain controversial in our society as courts and commentators[1] struggle with defining discrimination and equality.

---

20. 42 U.S.C.A. § 2000e(k).

21. 499 U.S. at 203, 111 S.Ct. at 1206.

§ 2.19

1. See generally Deborah C. Malamud, *Class-Based Affirmative Action: Lessons and Caveats,* 74 Tex. L. Rev. 1847 (1996); Deborah Jones Merritt, *Sex, Race, and Credentials: The Truth About Affirmative Action in Law Faculty Hiring,* 97 Colum. L. Rev. 199 (1997); David Benjamin Oppen-

heimer, *Understanding Affirmative Action,* 23 Hastings Const. L. Q. 921 (1996); Laura F. Rothstein, *The Affirmative Action Debate in Legal Education and the Legal Profession: Lessons from Disability Discrimination Law,* 2 J. Gender, Race & Justice 1 (1998). See also David Schwartz, *The Case of the Vanishing Protected Class: Reflections on Reverse Discrimination, Affirmative Action, and Racial Balancing,* 2000 Wis. L. Rev. 657.

Sources of Obligations and Restrictions

Title VII makes no mention of preferential treatment except in two contexts. One is a provision to clarify that the Act does not require preferential treatment even if the employer has a workforce that is not representative of the surrounding community. The other is a provision that preferential treatment is permissible in the context of businesses near Indian reservations. Such businesses or enterprises may grant preferential treatment to any individual "because he is an Indian living on or near a reservation."[2]

Federal contractors have affirmative action obligations under Executive Order 11246,[3] which is implemented by Department of Labor regulations. This Executive Order applies to all employers with construction contracts financed by the federal government and to employers with significant federal service or supply contracts. Their obligation is to remedy any underutilization of minorities and women, even though the individual employer may bear no responsibility for the relative underrepresentation of these groups in various job categories. The employer must adopt an affirmative action plan, which may include specific numerical goals and timetables.

The EEOC has promulgated guidelines with respect to the adoption of affirmative action plans for compliance with Executive Order 11246 or other purposes. The guidelines permit plans if the employer's self-analysis indicates that one of the following three conditions exists: (1) the employer's practices have a potentially adverse effect on opportunities for women and minorities; (2) the effect of past discrimination has a continuing effect in the workforce; or (3) the employer has a limited labor pool from which to select diverse candidates because of historical circumstances.[4]

An employer that is not covered by Executive Order 11246 has no affirmative obligation to address any underutilization of groups in the workforce except to the extent that the employer's own post-Act conduct is causing discriminatory exclusion. The Act specifically provides that employers are not under any affirmative obligation to achieve a workforce representative of the population. Section 703(j) provides:

> Nothing contained in this title shall be interpreted to require any employer, employment agency, labor organization, or joint labor-management committee subject to this title to grant preferential treatment to any individual or to any group because of the race, color, religion, sex, or national origin of such individual or group on account of an imbalance which may exist with respect to the total number or percentage of persons * * * in comparison with the total number of percentages of persons of such race, color, religion, sex, or national origin in any community, State, section, or other area, or in

2. 42 U.S.C.A. § 2000e–2(i).   **4.** 29 C.F.R. § 1608.3.
3. 3 C.F.R. § 1964.

the available work force in any community, State, section, or other area.[5]

Voluntary Affirmative Action–Private Sector

The Supreme Court considered the relationship of section 703(j) to the obligation of employers under Executive Order 11246 in *United Steelworkers of America v. Weber*.[6] This case concerned the legality of the admissions procedures for a special skills training program at a Kaiser aluminum plant. The plant was located in Gramercy, Louisiana, where the area population was approximately two-fifths African–American. The plant had a skills trade workforce that was less than two percent African–American. As a federal contractor, Kaiser had affirmative action obligations that the Department of Labor enforced. Under federal pressure, the company and the steelworkers union agreed to a skills training program with a racial quota of equal numbers of black and white trainees. The plaintiff was a rejected white applicant who had more seniority than and qualifications at least equal to some of the accepted black trainees. He sued for reverse discrimination.

The Court in *Weber* first reconfirmed its prior holding that Title VII protects all groups from discrimination, not just the historically excluded groups that were the focus of the Act. The Court had held in *McDonald v. Santa Fe Trail Transportation Co.*[7] that an employer violated the Act by discharging white employees who had committed the same offense as a retained black employee. Unless the employer can explain the disparate treatment of the white employees with a nondiscriminatory reason, the employer's reverse discrimination was unlawful.

The *Weber* opinion explained that the *McDonald* principle did not compel a decision in favor of the plaintiff because the spirit of the Act is to provide opportunities for the historically excluded groups to advance in employment. The Act therefore permits voluntary efforts to remedy past patterns of exclusion. Although section 703(j) says that nothing in the Act "requires" affirmative action, the Court found that the section "permits" voluntary action. The plan in this case was voluntary despite the fact that the employer enacted it in response to the pressure of the Executive Order for federal contractors. The economic threat to the employer of losing federal contracts is not the kind of coercion that keeps the action from being "voluntary" under the Act.

Weber further clarified that voluntary affirmative action is lawful under Title VII only if it is pursuant to a valid plan. In order for a plan to be valid it must remedy conspicuous racial imbalances in traditionally segregated job categories. Moreover, it must be temporary; its purpose must be to eliminate a manifest racial imbalance rather than to maintain a racial balance. Further, it must not unduly trammel the rights of the majority. The Court found significant in the Kaiser plan that no white employees were discharged for replacement with black workers, and

5. 42 U.S.C.A. § 2000e–2(j).

6. 443 U.S. 193, 99 S.Ct. 2721, 61 L.Ed.2d 480 (1979).

7. 427 U.S. 273, 96 S.Ct. 2574, 49 L.Ed.2d 493 (1976).

there was not an absolute bar to the advancement of all white employees. When these criteria are met, as in *Weber,* the plan does not violate Title VII because the Act "does not condemn all private, voluntary, race-conscious affirmative action plans."[8]

The Supreme Court further explained the permissible reaches of voluntary affirmative action under Title VII in a subsequent opinion, *Johnson v. Transportation Agency.*[9] This case involved the use of an affirmative action plan to promote a woman named Diane Joyce to a position as a road dispatcher. No women had held this position in the defendant county previously. One of the components of the selection process was a highly subjective rating by a panel that interviewed the applicants. Joyce protested the objectivity of some of the members of her panel who had had poor interactions with her in the past. She complained that one panel member once had refused—until she filed a grievance—to issue her the same protective clothing that the men had, and that another had described her as a "rebel-rousing, skirt-wearing person." Her overall ratings from this panel were adequate for the promotion, but not as high as those of a man named Paul Johnson, who became the plaintiff in the suit. Rather than address the complaint by Joyce about the objectivity of her panel, the employer promoted Joyce instead of Johnson pursuant to its affirmative action plan.

The Supreme Court upheld the validity of this type of affirmative action. It was lawful for the employer to use gender as a factor in the selection among qualified candidates. It was important in this case that the employer was acting under a valid affirmative action plan that met the criteria outlined in *Weber*.

There are two noteworthy differences between *McDonald* and *Johnson* that make the distinction between actionable reverse discrimination and lawful affirmative action. First, an employer cannot make an ad hoc decision preferring a member of an historically underrepresented group over another person similarly situated. A generalized desire to improve the opportunities for minorities or women is not sufficient. The employer in *McDonald* was not acting pursuant to a plan. Second, even if there were an affirmative action plan in the company, its existence would not justify different disciplinary standards on the basis of race. The fact that there was good cause to fire the plaintiffs in that reverse discrimination case would not justify preferential treatment to the black employee if the cause to discharge was equally strong. The Court explained: "The Act prohibits *all* racial discrimination in employment, without exception for any groups of particular employees[.]"

Johnson further clarified the *Weber* standards for a valid affirmative action plan. First, the plan must be a temporary one. Its purpose must be to remedy underrepresentation, not to maintain racial or gender balance indefinitely. The Court explained in *Johnson* that the plan must be "intended to *attain* a balanced work force, not to maintain one." The

---

8. 99 S.Ct. at 2729.

9. 480 U.S. 616, 107 S.Ct. 1442, 94 L.Ed.2d 615 (1987).

fact that a plan does not have a stated termination date may be fatal to a plan that imposes quotas, as in *Weber*, but it is not fatal to a plan like the flexible one in *Johnson* which did not set aside positions according to specific numbers, but simply took minority or gender status into account. There is an assumption that once the employer reaches the expressed goal in a flexible plan, the plan will cease. A plan that uses quotas carries no implication that it will become inoperative when the quota is met, and therefore it needs an express assurance that achievement of the goals will terminate the plan.

A valid plan must not only be temporary, but it must also be limited to the purpose of redressing a "manifest imbalance" in "traditionally segregated job categories." It is not sufficient to compare the representation of the group in question to the general population to assess whether there is a manifest imbalance unless the job is one that requires no special expertise. Otherwise, the comparison should be with "those in the labor force who possess the relevant qualification."[10] The Court further noted that the imbalance need not be so great that it would rise to the level of establishing a prima facie case if the employer were a defendant in a Title VII claim.

Finally, the *Weber* standards require that a valid affirmative action plan must not "unnecessarily trammel" the interests of the white male applicants or employees. In *Weber*, the special training program had half the positions reserved for white applicants. There was no absolute bar to white males, nor positions reserved for targeted groups. *Weber* noted that the Kaiser plan did not require the discharge of any employee. A subsequent court of appeals decision found that this condition was not met when an employer made racially-premised layoffs during an economic downturn and attempted to justify the practice as necessary to preserve gains under its affirmative action plan.[11]

In *Johnson,* the promotion of the qualified woman was at the expense of a qualified man whose subjective ratings were higher, but that fact alone was not sufficient to invoke the "unduly trammel" standard. The Court noted the promotion did not upset any "legitimate firmly rooted expectation." The woman who was promoted in *Johnson* was qualified for the job, but the plaintiff male was "more qualified" because of the higher rating on the subjective interview. Without regard to whether that rating was a fair one, the employer was free to prefer the lower rated woman even if the man was more qualified. The flexibility of this affirmative action plan compared with *Weber* did not invalidate it. The Court did not need to decide in *Johnson* whether an employer would be free to favor a candidate who was unqualified, but the implication of the *Johnson* holding is that the candidate must meet a threshold level of qualification in order for a preference to be valid under a flexible affirmative action plan.

10. Id. at 1452.

11. Britton v. South Bend Community Sch. Corp., 819 F.2d 766 (7th Cir.1987).

Voluntary Affirmative Action–Public Employers

The Supreme Court has not squarely addressed the question of *Weber*-type voluntary affirmative action by a public employer. A plurality opinion by the Court the year prior to *Johnson* had established that affirmative action plans by public employers are subject to exacting judicial scrutiny whenever racial or ethnic distinctions are involved. In *Wygant v. Jackson Board of Education*,[12] a plurality of the justices held unconstitutional a school board plan that required laying off white teachers who were more senior than minority teachers hired recently under this affirmative action plan. The divided Court found several infirmities. The plurality and concurring opinions noted several problems with the plan, including its generalized desire to make the composition of the teachers represent the community rather than to redress underutilization of qualified teachers, its permanent nature, and its layoff policy that unduly trammeled the interests of the senior white teachers. Although the *Johnson* case a year later involved a public employer, the Court did not use that opportunity to expand upon *Wygant* and focused on the Title VII question clarifying *Weber*. The *Johnson* opinion did note, however, that it was leaving open the question of whether there were identical constraints on voluntary affirmative action plans under Title VII and the Constitution. Thus, the question is whether a public employer with an affirmative action plan that meets the *Weber/Johnson* standards may nonetheless violate the equal protection clause of the Fourteenth Amendment.

The Supreme Court has considered extensively the constitutionality of affirmative action in the contexts of allocating public contracts and judicial remedies and has sustained the use of hiring and promotion ratios. The Court has found a compelling state interest to permit "narrowly tailored" race conscious affirmative action to remedy past and present discrimination by the state actor.[13]

The Supreme Court further considered the constitutionality of governmental affirmative action project awards in *Adarand Constructors, Inc. v. Pena*.[14] In this case a subcontractor who produced guardrails was not awarded a portion of a federal highway project and challenged the constitutionality of the federal program designed to provide highway contracts to disadvantaged business enterprises. Under this program contractors for highway projects were given an additional one percent of the bid price if the contractor met relevant "goals" for the hiring of minority subcontractors. The Court held that all racial classifications imposed by a federal, state, or local government must be analyzed by strict scrutiny review. Such classifications are constitutional only if they are "narrowly tailored measures that further compelling governmental interest." After setting the standard, the Court remanded the case for

12. 476 U.S. 267, 106 S.Ct. 1842, 90 L.Ed.2d 260 (1986).

13. United States v. Paradise, 480 U.S. 149, 107 S.Ct. 1053, 94 L.Ed.2d 203 (1987).

14. 515 U.S. 200, 115 S.Ct. 2097, 132 L.Ed.2d 158 (1995).

application of the principle to the challenged program. The Court thus left open many questions, including the possible application of this standard to employment discrimination cases.

The Court clarified the application of the strict scrutiny standard in the educational context, where affirmative action was used in the selection of students for admission to the University of Michigan Law School. In *Grutter v. Bollinger,*[15] the Court endorsed the view that "student body diversity is a compelling state interest that can justify the use of race in university admissions."[16] The Court found that the benefits of diversity were substantial, and that the effective participation "by members of all racial and ethnic groups in the civic life of our Nation is essential if the dream of one Nation, indivisible, is to be realized."[17] The Court therefore concluded that the law school had a compelling interest in attaining a diverse student body and could engage in race-conscious affirmative action for a limited time.

The lower courts have struggled to apply these standards. The remedial aspect of affirmative action has been particularly difficult as defendants have sought to show underrepresentation of minority groups without admitting to past discrimination themselves. While defendants have been reluctant to attribute exclusion to their own practices, courts have also been reluctant to permit claims of general societal discrimination to suffice. Several noteworthy cases from the Fifth Circuit illustrate the point. In *Police Association of New Orleans v. City of New Orleans,*[18] the city attempted to defend its race-conscious promotion and transfer program from an equal protection challenge without any specific evidence of past discrimination. The justification was that the program would allow a better reflection of the racial composition of the city so that "more African–American supervisors could better supervise African–American officers who in turn were needed to relate to the larger African–American population."[19] The court rejected this basis for a racial classification. In a similar case involving an equal protection challenge to the promotion of firefighters,[20] the Fifth Circuit found that even mild advantages on the basis of race in the promotion program were not justified in the absence of egregious or pervasive past discrimination by the department. Moreover, out of rank promotion of female firefighters also did not survive an equal protection challenge despite the less exacting nature of intermediate scrutiny, because there was no showing whatsoever that the underrepresentation of women among the city firefighters was attributable to past discrimination by the department or even by the industry in general.

In contrast, the Seventh Circuit had the benefit of the Supreme Court's reasoning in *Grutter* when it considered the value of diversity for

15. 539 U.S. 306, 123 S.Ct. 2325, 156 L.Ed.2d 304 (2003).

16. 123 S.Ct. at 2337.

17. Id. at 2340–41.

18. 100 F.3d 1159 (5th Cir. 1996).

19. Id. at 1168.

20. Dallas Firefighters v. Dallas, 150 F.3d 438 (5th Cir. 1998).

a police force in *Petit v. City of Chicago*.[21] That case found that the Chicago police department established a compelling operational need for diversity at the rank of sergeant. Relying on *Grutter*, the court agreed that diversity in this setting was compelling to set the proper tone in the department and earn the trust of the community. Because Chicago operates a large metropolitan police force in a racially and ethnically divided city, affirmative action was warranted to enhance the department's effectiveness. That enhancement would be both external with respect to the perception of the force in the city, and internal with respect to changing attitudes of officers.

The Supreme Court's endorsement of diversity in the *Grutter* case now calls into question the failure of this argument in the defense of an affirmative action case involving teacher layoffs. This Title VII case, *Taxman v. Board of Education of Township of Piscataway*,[22] from the Third Circuit, concerned the layoff of a teacher from the business department of a public high school. The district needed to lay off one of two teachers, one Caucasian and one African–American, who were identical in seniority and otherwise indistinguishable in credentials. The school chose to keep the African–American teacher because she was the only black teacher in the business department, although there were many black teachers in other departments. There was no showing of underrepresentation of African–American teachers in the district as a whole—only in this one small department. The employer thus could not defend with a remedial purpose, only a diversity goal, which the court rejected. Finding that the non-remedial plan unduly trammeled the interests of the majority, the Third Circuit rejected the affirmative action plan under the *Weber* standard.

An array of dissenting opinions in this en banc decision would have upheld the district for a variety of reasons. Some would have permitted the consideration of diversity in the teachers for the benefit of the students; some would have found that this plan did not unduly trammel the rights of the majority; and some would have permitted race as one among many permissible factors in the lay off decision. The Supreme Court granted certiorari in the case, but it was settled out of court before argument. Although *Grutter* emphasized the individuality of the inquiry about compelling state interests, it is possible that racial diversity within high school departments would meet its standard. The question then becomes whether the plan would nonetheless violate Title VII under the *Weber* standard, as the Third Circuit held in *Taxman*.

The existence of an affirmative action plan is relevant in a case alleging reverse discrimination, but affirmative action is not technically an affirmative defense. The employer can respond to a claim of disparate treatment by a disappointed white plaintiff by presenting the affirmative action plan and by demonstrating that the challenged decision was made

21. 352 F.3d 1111 (7th Cir. 2003), cert. denied, ___ U.S. ___, 124 S.Ct. 2426, 158 L.Ed.2d 984 (2004).

22. 91 F.3d 1547 (3d Cir. 1996)(en banc), cert. dismissed, 522 U.S. 1010, 118 S.Ct. 595, 139 L.Ed.2d 431 (1997).

pursuant to that plan. The Court made clear in *Johnson v. Transportation Agency* that the burden then shifts to the plaintiff to attack the validity of the plan.

§ 2.20 Proof of Patterns of Invidious Exclusions

Claims that an employer engaged in a pattern of intentional exclusion under Title VII or the ADEA, may be brought by a plaintiff class or by the EEOC. The EEOC has authority to bring suit when it "has reasonable cause to believe that any person or group of persons is engaged in a pattern or practice of resistance to the full enjoyment of any of the rights" secured by the Act.[1] A plaintiff class that is properly certified may challenge the disparate treatment of the group. In either action, the plaintiff must prove by a preponderance of the evidence that discrimination was the employer's "standard operating procedure—the regular rather than the unusual practice."[2]

Manner and Order of Proof

In a case alleging pattern or practice, or group disparate treatment, the *McDonnell Douglas/Reeves*[3] prima facie case is not applicable because that model is based upon proof of discrimination against only one individual. Such individual proof is relevant to the class claim as anecdotal evidence of intentional discrimination, and individual claims are also relevant to the relief stage of the litigation. In a class claim, however, "[s]tatistics are equally competent in proving employment discrimination."[4]

Although the prima facie case for a class claim is different from an individual claim, it is unclear whether the *McDonnell Douglas/Burdine* burden-shifting scheme nonetheless applies in a pattern or practice or group disparate treatment case. As Judge Easterbrook explained in the Seventh Circuit opinion in *Mister v. Illinois Central Gulf Railroad*:[5]

> The pattern-or-practice case starts with a stronger showing than the individual disparate treatment case; the "prima facie case" under *McDonnell Douglas Corp. v. Green* supports only a weak inference of discrimination, while the statistical showing in a pattern-or-practice case leaves a smaller possibility of race-neutral conduct. This suggests that *Burdine's* allocation of burdens may be inappropriate in pattern-or-practice litigation. Even if that allocation applies—as we assume today—what the employer must "articulate" is an *explanation* of its activity.[6]

§ 2.20

1. 42 U.S.C.A. § 2000e–6(a).

2. International Bhd. of Teamsters v. United States, 431 U.S. 324, 336, 97 S.Ct. 1843, 1854, 52 L.Ed.2d 396 (1977).

3. McDonnell Douglas Corp. v. Green, 411 U.S. 792, 93 S.Ct. 1817, 36 L.Ed.2d 668 (1973); Reeves v. Sanderson Plumbing

Prods., 530 U.S. 133, 120 S.Ct. 2097, 147 L.Ed.2d 105 (2000).

4. International Bhd. of Teamsters v. United States, 431 U.S. 324, 339, 97 S.Ct. 1843, 52 L.Ed.2d 396 (1977).

5. 832 F.2d 1427 (7th Cir.1987).

6. Id. at 1434 (internal citation omitted).

The assumption that the *McDonnell Douglas/Burdine* burdens apply to class claims is not universally shared. The Eleventh Circuit, for example, has held that this allocation of burdens does not hold for class actions, and that the usual procedure is to consider the evidence as a whole to determine whether the plaintiffs have established a pattern or practice of discrimination.[7]

Role of Statistical Proof to Establish Intent

There are two Supreme Court opinions involving pattern or practice cases, *International Brotherhood of Teamsters v. United States*[8] and *Hazelwood School District v. United States*.[9] Both were brought by the Department of Justice, which had the authority to bring pattern or practice suits before Congress transferred that authority to the EEOC. Although it was unclear at the time whether the term "pattern or practice" required a showing of intentional discrimination, the Department of Justice avoided the legal issue by pleading that these employers had intentionally discriminated on the basis of race.

Teamsters involved a challenge to the assignment of employees to job categories. One group of truck drivers, line drivers, received higher pay than another group, city drivers. Nationwide the employer had 1,802 line drivers, all of whom were white except for thirteen minority drivers. In the less desirable city driving jobs, there were 1,117 white employees and 167 minority employees. The government based its claim of intentional discrimination on these figures, plus anecdotal evidence of specific instances when African–American or Latino city drivers were discouraged from attempting to transfer to the better position.

Hazelwood involved a challenge to a school district's pattern of hiring school teachers. Less than two percent of the teachers in the entire school system were minority group members. The school district was in a suburb of St. Louis, whose school system employed many minority teachers. The Hazelwood School District had a practice of allowing the principals in the individual schools to hire the certified teachers of their choice. The plaintiff's claim was that the subjective hiring practices of the employer resulted in a virtually all white work force.

The Supreme Court explained the value of statistics in these cases. "Statistics showing the racial or ethnic imbalance are probative in a case such as this one," the Court noted, "only because such imbalance is often a telltale sign of purposeful discrimination."[10] The purpose of statistical analysis is simply to probe such motivation and not to require employers to maintain a balanced work force.

Types of Group Comparisons to Show Underrepresentation

The Supreme Court has recognized three methods by which the plaintiff can attack the exclusionary effect of an employer's hiring

---

7. See Perryman v. Johnson Prods. Co., 698 F.2d 1138, 1143 (11th Cir.1983).

8. 431 U.S. 324, 97 S.Ct. 1843, 52 L.Ed.2d 396 (1977).

9. 433 U.S. 299, 97 S.Ct. 2736, 53 L.Ed.2d 768 (1977).

10. Id. at 1856 n.20.

practices. The three methods of assessing disproportionate exclusion in employment discrimination cases are: applicant flow analysis, population comparison analysis, and requirement effect analysis. An individual case may involve one or all of these methods, as appropriate to the nature of the claim and the facts. The Court has refused to endorse any particular method.

In *Watson v. Fort Worth Bank & Trust*,[11] the Court acknowledged the difficulty that the lack of specific guidance causes lower courts and litigators. There is no clear rule for when to use which method of analysis nor for when the extent of exclusion is legally significant. "At least at this stage of the law's development," the Court explained, "we believe that such a case-by-case approach properly reflects our recognition that statistics 'come in infinite variety and * * * their usefulness depends on all of the surrounding facts and circumstances.' "[12]

A further uncertainty is whether each of these three methods of demonstrating exclusion is probative of intentional exclusion. Equally uncertain is whether each of these methods may probe disparate impact, where statistical analysis examines exclusionary effects without regard to intent. Courts and litigators glean guidance from the Court only by examining the theory of the case in which particular methods of analysis were endorsed. The Court's pattern or practice cases utilized the population comparison approach.

The Supreme Court provided the framework for population comparison analysis in the pattern or practice cases of *International Brotherhood of Teamsters v. United States*[13] and *Hazelwood School District v. United States*.[14] The premise of population comparison is that "absent explanation, it is ordinarily to be expected that nondiscriminatory hiring practices will in time result in a work force more or less representative of the racial and ethnic composition of the population in the community from which employees are hired." The Court further explained: "Evidence of longlasting and gross disparity between the composition of a work force and that of the general population thus may be significant[.]"[15]

For this population comparison analysis the Court first distinguished between skilled and unskilled jobs. The facts of *Hazelwood* and *Teamsters* differ in that one case involved school teachers and the other concerned truck drivers. The Court observed that in *Teamsters* the comparison between the representation of minority group members among the over-the-road truck drivers and the percentage in the general population was "highly probative, because the job skill there involved— the ability to drive a truck—is one that many persons possess or can fairly readily acquire."[16] By contrast, when jobs require special qualifica-

11. 487 U.S. 977, 108 S.Ct. 2777, 101 L.Ed.2d 827 (1988).

12. 108 S.Ct. at 2789 n.3 (quoting *Teamsters*).

13. 431 U.S. 324, 97 S.Ct. 1843, 52 L.Ed.2d 396 (1977).

14. 433 U.S. 299, 97 S.Ct. 2736, 53 L.Ed.2d 768 (1977).

15. 97 S.Ct. at 1856 n. 20.

16. Hazelwood School Dist. v. United States, 433 U.S. 299, 308 n.13, 97 S.Ct. 2736, 2741 n. 13, 53 L.Ed.2d 768 (1977).

tions, "comparisons to the general population (rather than to the smaller group of individuals who possess the necessary qualifications) may have little probative value."[17] In *Hazelwood*, the district court properly limited the comparison to the special skills group of school teachers.

In *Hazelwood*, the Supreme Court further clarified the population comparison approach and its relationship to the applicant flow analysis. The defendant employer argued that applicant flow data would be better evidence of intentional exclusion than the comparative skilled population statistics, which have less probative value. Applicant flow statistics would show the actual percentage of white and minority applicants for teaching positions. The Court noted that there was no evidence of applicant flow statistics in the record, but agreed that such evidence "would, of course, be very relevant."

Significance Levels and Standard Deviations

The Supreme Court's opinion in *Hazelwood* further considered the degree of disparity between the population and the employer's workforce necessary to show disproportionate exclusion. When the representation of the plaintiff class in the relevant population is a certain percentage, the employer's expected number of employees from the class is easily calculated. The issue then becomes how to assess the degree of the disparity between the expected and the actual number of employees from the class. The Court explained how to interpret the result of the statistical calculation:

> A precise method of measuring the significance of such statistical disparities was explained in *Castaneda v. Partida* * * *. It involves calculation of the "standard deviation" as a measure of predicted fluctuations from the expected value of a sample. Using the 5.7% as the basis for calculating the expected value, the expected number of Negroes on the Hazelwood teaching staff would be roughly 63 in 1972–1973 and 70 in 1973–1974. The observed number in those years was 16 and 22, respectively. The difference between the observed and expected values was more than six standard deviations in 1972–1973 and more than five standard deviations in 1973–1974. The Court in *Castaneda* noted that "[a]s a general rule for such large samples, if the difference between the expected value and the observed number is greater than two or three standard deviations," then the hypothesis that teachers were hired without regard to race would be suspect.[18]

The Court's observations were not intended to suggest that "precise calculations of statistical significance are necessary in employing statistical proof, but merely to highlight the importance of the choice of the relevant labor market area."

The Court has since declined to provide further clarification. Justice O'Connor's plurality opinion in *Watson v. Fort Worth Bank & Trust*

---

17. 97 S.Ct. at 2741 n.13.   **18.** 97 S.Ct. at 2742 n. 14.

noted that although the Court has "emphasized the useful role that statistical methods can have in Title VII cases," it has "not suggested that any particular number of 'standard deviations' can determine whether a plaintiff has made out a prima facie case in the complex area of employment discrimination."[19]

The Circuit Courts have tried to provide as much guidance as possible in light of the "case by case" nature of the inquiry. The Seventh Circuit has had occasion to consider the matter frequently and has noted that ordinarily a result of two standard deviations is sufficient to conclude that a disparity is not the result of chance alone.[20] On the other hand, that circuit has rejected any bright-line rule and held that a significance level of two standard deviations is not a necessary minimum and that a lesser showing may still suffice.[21]

The sufficiency of a disparity between two groups of employees on the basis of race was the issue in *Frazier v. Garrison Independent School District*,[22] where the plaintiffs challenged a teacher competency test administered by the state. Plaintiffs alleged that the commissioner was aware of the exclusionary effect of the test on African–American teachers at the time that he recommended raising the cutoff score. The court rejected the claim that raising the cutoff score was intentional race discrimination, however, because the evidence revealed that the overall pass rate for all racial groups was over ninety-five percent.

The Sufficiency of "Statistics Alone"

Yet another area of uncertainty in the litigation of group disparate treatment or pattern or practice claims is whether a class claim can rest on statistics alone. In the usual case, plaintiffs present evidence of specific instances of discrimination, because anecdotal evidence can bring "the cold numbers convincingly to life."[23] The class representatives typically have personal claims of individual disparate treatment, and there are usually other witnesses testifying to incidents of discriminatory treatment. The uncertainty in the law is whether such evidence is necessary for the prima facie case or whether specific incidents of discrimination simply bolster the statistics. Some cases have indicated that statistics alone can create a prima facie case of intentional group exclusion, but the issue remains an open one.

§ 2.21 Disparate Impact

The disparate impact theory of discrimination is fundamentally different from the disparate treatment theory. The disparate treatment theory is premised upon motive; the plaintiff must establish that the defendant acted intentionally to treat the plaintiff class or the individual plaintiff differently. In contrast, motive is irrelevant in the disparate

19. 108 S.Ct. at 2790 n. 3.

20. Adams v. Ameritech Servs. Inc., 231 F.3d 414 (7th Cir.2000).

21. See Kadas v. MCI Systemhouse Corp., 255 F.3d 359 (7th Cir. 2001).

22. 980 F.2d 1514 (5th Cir.1993).

23. International Bhd. of Teamsters v. United States, 431 U.S. 324, 339, 97 S.Ct. 1843, 52 L.Ed.2d 396 (1977).

impact theory of discrimination. This latter theory is premised upon unjustified exclusion caused by some hiring device that disproportionately disadvantages a group defined by race, color, religion, sex, or national origin.

This section explores the origin and application of the disparate impact theory of discrimination and introduces future sections that explore more specialized topics of application. This section examines the general use of disparate impact theory under Title VII and the effect of the codification of the concept in the Civil Rights Act of 1991. Finally, it explores the limitations on its use. Not included in this section is the current split among the circuit courts as to the availability of the theory under the ADEA, which is instead covered in the section on special issues with respect to the ADEA.

Disparate Impact Theory: Origin and Title VII Application

The Supreme Court first accepted the concept of disparate impact discrimination in its 1971 landmark decision in *Griggs v. Duke Power Co.*[1] The employer in that case required a high school diploma and a passing score on general aptitude tests for placement in any department except the lowest one. Historically, the employer had relegated all of its black workers to that department, but after the passage of the Act these new requirements replaced the former racially premised rules. The district court had ruled that Title VII requires proof of invidious motive; the court of appeals had held that liability could attach either to conduct that was invidiously motivated, or to unequal treatment of similarly situated individuals on the basis of race, color, religion, sex, or national origin.

The Supreme Court reversed and held that the Act covers more than the conduct identified by the lower courts in this case. The unanimous opinion written by Chief Justice Burger said that Title VII proscribes conduct that is "fair in form but discriminatory in operation."[2] When an employer uses procedures or testing mechanisms unrelated to measuring job capability, the Court said, the absence of discriminatory intent does not redeem the conduct. The high school diploma requirement disproportionately excluded black applicants from the desirable jobs, and the aptitude tests were found also to impact applicants on the basis of race. When such disparate impact occurs, it is incumbent upon the employer to demonstrate that its requirements are job-related and governed by principles of business necessity.

In 1977, the Court held in *Dothard v. Rawlinson*[3] that the disparate impact theory applies to gender discrimination. The plaintiff had been excluded from a position as a prison guard in Alabama penitentiaries because of a minimum height requirement for the job. The plaintiff's national statistics on the difference in height on the basis of gender were

2. 91 S.Ct. at 853.

1. 401 U.S. 424, 91 S.Ct. 849, 28 L.Ed.2d 158 (1971).

3. 433 U.S. 321, 97 S.Ct. 2720, 53 L.Ed.2d 786 (1977).

sufficient to establish a prima facie case of disparate impact and thus shifted the burden to the defendant to establish the business necessity of the requirement.

The disparate impact theory of discrimination has been controversial since its application to Title VII in *Griggs*. Whereas some scholars and commentators advocated this approach and applauded its acceptance, others have reviled it as contrary to the intent of Congress in enacting the statute in 1964. The debate about *Griggs* continues to rage even though Congress formally included the concept in its amendments to Title VII in the Civil Rights Act of 1991.[4]

The criticism that the disparate impact theory is contrary to congressional intent in 1964 is largely moot now that Congress has codified the theory in the Civil Rights Act of 1991. In that Act Congress sought to change the result of a number of Supreme Court decisions in the late eighties that were perceived to erect barriers for employment discrimination plaintiffs. Among the decisions that Congress targeted was *Wards Cove Packing Co. v. Atonio*,[5] which reconsidered the nature of the burden shifting in *Griggs*. Congress specifically declared as one of the purposes of the Act to reinstate the *Griggs* scheme and, in so doing, codified disparate impact theory for the first time.

Limitations on the Use of Disparate Impact Theory

The disparate impact concept of discrimination has been limited to statutory foundations, and may even be limited to Title VII and the Americans with Disabilities Act. Notably, disparate impact discrimination is not sufficient for a constitutionally-based claim in the United States, although the concept has been accepted in Canada as a basis for a constitutional claim. The Supreme Court held in *Washington v. Davis*[6] that a plaintiff class could not prevail with a Fifth Amendment claim against the Washington, D.C., police department upon a showing of the disparate impact of an aptitude test used to screen applicants for training. The employer in a constitutionally-based claim cannot be liable in the absence of motive.

Similarly, the disparate impact theory cannot be used in a claim brought under 42 U.S.C.A. § 1981. The Supreme Court held in *General Building Contractors Association v. Pennsylvania*[7] that discriminatory intent must be shown in a section 1981 claim. Although the *Griggs/Dothard* disparate impact model cannot be used in a claim brought under section 1981, the requirement that the plaintiff must show intent does

4. See Richard A. Epstein, Forbidden Grounds: The Case Against Employment Discrimination Laws (1992); Kingsley R. Browne, *Discrimination, Affirmative Action, and Freedom: Sorting Out the Issues*, 43 Case W. Res. L. Rev. 287 (1993); Roger Pilon, *The Civil Rights Act of 1991: A "Quota Bill," a Codification of Griggs, a Partial Return to Wards Cove, or All of the Above?*, 45 Am. U. L. Rev. 775 (1996).

5. 490 U.S. 642, 109 S.Ct. 2115, 104 L.Ed.2d 733 (1989).

6. 426 U.S. 229, 96 S.Ct. 2040, 48 L.Ed.2d 597 (1976).

7. 458 U.S. 375, 102 S.Ct. 3141, 73 L.Ed.2d 835 (1982).

not mean that the plaintiff must show invidious discrimination; it is sufficient to show that race was a significant factor in the decision.

The Court noted that classifications based on race and gender are distinguishable because they are "so seldom relevant to the achievement of any legitimate state interest that laws grounded in such considerations are deemed to reflect prejudice and antipathy."[8] The question is whether the Court's emphasis on the intentional nature of state discrimination in this context indicates that the federal regulation of disparate impact discrimination by the states is beyond its section 5 power.

The validity of the application of Title VII disparate impact analysis against a state employer is open to question after the Supreme Court's decision in *Kimel v. Florida Board of Regents*.[9] The Court there held that the ADEA was not a proper exercise of congressional power under section 5 of the Fourteenth Amendment, but distinguished the categories of race and gender discrimination. A decision by the Eleventh Circuit considered this issue before the Court's opinion in *Kimel*, but in light of the Court's earlier opinion in *Seminole Tribe v. Florida*.[10] At issue in *Crum v. State of Alabama*[11] was the use of a high school diploma requirement by the state as an employer. The Eleventh Circuit concluded that disparate impact analysis was a valid exercise of section 5 power, but only because it found that the method was a means of penetrating intentional discrimination. Noting that the Constitution prohibits only intentionally discriminatory action by state actors, and not state action that leads to a merely exclusionary result, the court reasoned that disparate impact analysis as used in this case was simply a means of probing such use. The use, however, is restricted to probing the state employer's motive through the telltale sign of imbalance. *Kimel* would not appear to alter either the *Crum* analysis or conclusion, although *Crum* itself raises the issue whether the use of disparate impact analysis against a state employer is limited to its probative value for intentional discrimination.

Disparate Impact of "Employment Practices"

In a disparate impact case under Title VII the plaintiff bears the initial burden of establishing the exclusionary effect of a specific selection device. The Seventh Circuit has held that disparate impact analysis can be used for any "employment practice," including single decisions. In *AFSCME v. Ward*,[12] the plaintiff union challenged a decision by the Illinois Department of Employment Security to concentrate layoffs in the offices that served the Chicago area. This decision, the plaintiffs contended, had a disparate impact on the basis of race. The district court had held that a single decision cannot be the basis of a disparate impact

---

8. 120 S.Ct. at 659, quoting Cleburne v. Cleburne Living Ctr., Inc., 473 U.S. 432, 105 S.Ct. 3249, 87 L.Ed.2d 313 (1985).

9. 528 U.S. 62, 120 S.Ct. 631, 145 L.Ed.2d 522 (2000).

10. 517 U.S. 44, 116 S.Ct. 1114, 134 L.Ed.2d 252 (1996).

11. 198 F.3d 1305 (11th Cir.1999), rehearing and suggestion for rehearing en banc denied, 212 F.3d 602 (11th Cir.2000).

12. 978 F.2d 373 (7th Cir.1992).

claim because there is no repeated customary method of operation. The Seventh Circuit disagreed and reasoned that "employment practice" should be interpreted the same for disparate impact cases as for disparate treatment cases. Single decisions, such as a layoff, can violate the Act when the plaintiff alleges intentional exclusion; therefore, a single decision is sufficient for a disparate impact claim.

Although it is not necessary to demonstrate the employer's motive in selecting any challenged selection device, the plaintiff's proof must be specific to establish the disproportionate impact of the device. It is not sufficient simply to assert that a selection criterion has an impact, nor is it sufficient to show that the employer's workforce does not mirror the racial, ethnic, and gender composition of the surrounding population. The Supreme Court so held in *Wards Cove Packing Co. v. Atonio*,[13] and this aspect of the case remains good law even after the Civil Rights Act of 1991 reversed other portions of this case.

No "Bottom Line" Defense

Just as plaintiffs may not establish a prima facie case with a mere showing that the employer's work force does not mirror the surrounding population, it is conversely not sufficient for an employer to defend a disparate impact case with similar kind of evidence. Specifically, the employer cannot defend with evidence of a favorable "bottom line" of individuals hired whose composition matches the racial, gender, and ethnic characteristics of the applicants. In *Connecticut v. Teal*,[14] the Supreme Court held that an employer could not avoid the need to defend with business necessity the use of a test that has a disparate impact. The employer had a large pool of employees who were eligible for promotion to supervisor. The employees were given a test which disproportionately excluded black applicants. The employer then attempted to eliminate this effect by a second part of the selection process, which the Court characterized as an affirmative action program. The result was that the employer hired supervisors whose racial composition was very close to the composition of the applicants. The Court held that a favorable "bottom line" is not a defense when there is an identifiable selection device that disproportionately excludes on the basis of race. Unless the employer can demonstrate the business necessity of this device, individuals who would be otherwise qualified for the promotion are unfairly excluded. It is not sufficient that other members of the same racial group as the excluded individuals were advantaged by a subsequent selection device.

Although the holding in *Teal* is phrased broadly, the lower courts have limited its application to situations involving a series of separate pass/fail selection devices. If a test or other discrete pass/fail barrier has a disparate impact, it must be individually validated even if there is no bottom line impact for the entire multicomponent selection process. Although the Uniform Guidelines take the opposite view, that bottom

13. 490 U.S. 642, 109 S.Ct. 2115, 104 L.Ed.2d 733 (1989).

14. 457 U.S. 440, 102 S.Ct. 2525, 73 L.Ed.2d 130 (1982).

line effect is all that matters,[15] the Guidelines are not binding and the Supreme Court refused to follow them in *Teal*.

Methods for Establishing Disparate Impact–Effect on Population

One method by which the plaintiff may prove the impact of a challenged selection device is to demonstrate the effect of the requirement on the relevant population. When a device has a demonstrable impact on the group from which the employer draws employees, the impact on that population establishes the prima facie case. For example, in *Griggs v. Duke Power Co.*,[16] it was sufficient for the plaintiff to produce the state census figures for educational attainment by race to demonstrate that the employer's high school diploma requirement adversely affected African–Americans. Similarly, in *Dothard v. Rawlinson*, the plaintiff established a prima facie case of disparate impact against women with national statistics concerning the relative height of men and women.

Methods for Establishing Disparate Impact–Applicant Flow

The second method by which the plaintiff may demonstrate the disparate impact of a challenged selection device is applicant flow. This method is preferred by the EEOC in the Uniform Guidelines on Employee Selection Procedures,[17] which the agency uses to guide its prosecutorial discretion. Applicant flow analysis is the examination of the relative pass rates, or acceptance rates, of applicants on the basis of race, gender, and national origin. This method can be used to examine the effect of each separate requirement or to examine the effect of all the requirements taken together.

The Civil Rights Act of 1991 provides that the plaintiff must identify the particular practice that causes the impact, unless it is not possible to separate the employer's practices for individual analysis. Section 703(k)(1)(B)(i) provides that with respect to showing that particular requirements have a disparate impact, the complaining party shall demonstrate that each particular challenged employment practice causes a disparate impact, except that if the complaining party can demonstrate to the court that the elements of a respondent's decisionmaking process are not capable of separation for analysis, the decisionmaking process may be analyzed as one employment practice.[18]

If the plaintiff satisfies the court that the requirements are "not capable of separation," then presumably the plaintiff may demonstrate impact with the applicant flow throughout the entire process or perhaps by a general population comparison that would not otherwise be permitted.

One problem with applicant flow analysis is that potential applicants may be deterred from making a formal application because of the employer's reputation for discrimination or because the challenged re-

15. 29 C.F.R. § 1607.4(c).

16. 401 U.S. 424, 91 S.Ct. 849, 28 L.Ed.2d 158 (1971).

17. 29 C.F.R. § 1607.4.

18. 42 U.S.C.A. § 2000e–2.

quirement is known in advance such that potential applicants who do not satisfy the requirement do not pursue the position further. In *Dothard*, for example, the Supreme Court observed that plaintiffs need not always establish the prima facie case with comparative statistics concerning actual applicants. The Court reasoned:

> The application process might itself not adequately reflect the actual potential applicant pool, since otherwise qualified people might be discouraged from applying because of a self-recognized inability to meet the very standards challenged as being discriminatory. A potential applicant could easily measure her height and weight and conclude that to make an application would be futile. Moreover, reliance on general population demographic data was not misplaced where there was no reason to suppose that physical height and weight characteristics of Alabama men and women differ markedly from those of the national population.[19]

One court has noted that a finding of taint in an applicant pool is not the equivalent of finding a violation of the Act. When historical exclusion adversely affects the applicant pool, the exclusion of applicant flow data is not the equivalent of finding discrimination. It merely reflects the inaccuracy of such data to show whether the employer is currently excluding. The court in *EEOC v. Joe's Stone Crab, Inc.*[20] found that a restaurant chain's reputation for hiring only men as waiters prevented some women from attending the "roll call" where waiters were hired.

It is unclear whether the exception to the "particular requirement" provision of the Civil Rights Act of 1991, as previously quoted, applies in situations where the applicant flow is tainted for some reason. In such cases the requirements may be capable of separation, yet there may be no meaningful data because the employer's reputation for discrimination or announcement of exclusionary requirements. In the absence of clarifying case law, it remains unclear whether in such situations the plaintiff has failed to make out a prima facie case or whether the plaintiff may use a comparison of the individuals hired with the relevant population to establish a prima facie case of disparate impact. *Dothard*, which was decided before the 1991 amendments to the Act, makes a passing reference to such a comparison, but the availability of statistics of the effect of a height requirement on the general population was alone sufficient in that case.

Plaintiffs must establish not only the fact of the impact but its causal relation to the denial of an employment opportunity. In cases involving hiring requirements, this burden is easily met. In other types of challenges, however, the causality issue can be more problematic. In one interesting case,[21] for example, female plaintiffs attempted to estab-

---

19. 97 S.Ct. at 2727.

20. 296 F.3d 1265 (11th Cir.2002), cert. denied, 539 U.S. 941, 123 S.Ct. 2606, 156 L.Ed.2d 627 (2003).

21. Donnelly v. Rhode I. Bd. of Governors, 110 F.3d 2 (1st Cir. 1997).

lish the disparate impact of a three-tier salary system used by the defendant university to pay its professors. The court held that the plaintiffs not only failed to establish the causal requirement of disparate impact analysis, but also that their argument seemed "to be introducing a comparable worth argument" into Title VII. The opinion further noted that a Title VII wage claim requires proof that similarly situated males were better paid, even when plaintiffs claim that some wage-related practice has a disparate impact on women.

Establishing Disparate Impact–The Four–Fifths Rule

The degree of disparity necessary to establish disparate impact is also unclear. When the Supreme Court cited the racial disparity in high school graduation rates in *Griggs* and the gender disparity in height in *Dothard*, it did not comment on the magnitude of disparity that was necessary for a prima facie case. The Uniform Guidelines on Employee Selection Procedures, used to guide the prosecutorial discretion of the EEOC and other federal enforcers of employment law, have chosen a rule of thumb to assess the sufficiency of the disparity in the applicant flow data. The rule of thumb is called the "four-fifths rule" or "eighty percent rule."

The "four-fifths rule" considers a selection device to have an adverse impact when it produces a pass rate for one group protected under the Act that is less than four-fifths, or eighty percent, of the pass rate of the group with the highest pass rate. For example, assume that there are 100 male applicants and 100 female applicants. The employer uses a timed test that requires applicants to sort cards alphabetically into bins. An applicant fails the test by taking longer than a prescribed cutoff time to sort the cards.

Assume first with this hypothetical employer that sixty of the 100 men pass the test and only thirty of the 100 women pass the test. The pass rate of the men is sixty percent and the rate for the women is thirty percent. The pass rate for the women is thus only half of the rate of the men. Under the "four-fifths rule" this difference is sufficient to show adverse impact because the comparative pass rate is only one-half and not at least four-fifths. If fifty of the women had passed, however, the female pass rate would have been fifty percent. To compare this pass rate with that of the men, divide the .50 rate by the .60 rate. The result is .83, which is greater than eighty percent (four-fifths).

To continue the example, assume now that the sorting test of this hypothetical employer results in fifty of the 100 women passing and fewer of the men passing. The pass rate for the women is one-half. Four-fifths of this rate is .40. Therefore, there will be adverse impact unless at least forty of the men pass.

Establishing Disparate Impact–Alternatives to the Four–Fifths Rule

Some cases have followed the four-fifths rule of thumb to assess the sufficiency of the disparity for the prima facie case in disparate impact, but others have not.[22] In *Clady v. County of Los Angeles*,[23] for example, the court observed that the Uniform Guidelines are not binding and do not have the force of law. The four-fifths rule has been criticized by courts and commentators, the court noted, as an ill-conceived rule capable of producing anomalous results and trial courts need not adhere to it.

The Supreme Court subsequently confirmed that observation about the four-fifths rule and expressly refused to identify any single method by which the prima facie case for disparate impact can be established. In *Watson v. Fort Worth Bank & Trust*,[24] the plurality opinion noted: "At least at this stage of the law's development, we believe that a case-by-case approach properly reflects our recognition that statistics come in a variety and their usefulness depends on all the surrounding facts and circumstances."[25] In the same case, the Court similarly refused to identify any single measure for assessing the sufficiency of the disparity in the success rate of the two groups being compared. The Court observed that although statistics can be very useful, it has never specified any guiding rule of thumb to determine whether a plaintiff has made out a prima facie case. Neither the four-fifths rule of the Uniform Guidelines nor any particular number of standard deviations provides a clear threshold.

One case that illustrates the difficulty of applying the doctrine is *Frazier v. Garrison Independent School District*,[26] where the court considered the facts under both group disparate treatment and disparate impact theories. The court found that a difference in pass rates of African–American and white teachers on a state competency exam was insufficient to establish a prima facie case of disparate impact. The cumulative pass rate for the black teachers was 95.58 percent, for Hispanic teachers was 99.16 percent, and for white teachers was 99.75 percent. The plaintiffs did not offer a statistical analysis and the court noted that it is not always necessary for plaintiffs to do so.

Although the court did not discuss the point, the data arguably represented the performance of the entire relevant pool rather than just a sample of it. Like the statewide high school graduation rates in *Griggs*, these numbers arguably reflected the performance of all teachers in the state over a period of years. The issue is not free from doubt, however, because these data were not reflective of all future teachers and therefore were not truly representative of the entire relevant population, like the height and weight data used in *Dothard*. The court apparently found it unnecessary to decide whether these data represented the entire pool

22. For criticism of the rule, see Elaine W. Shoben, *Differential Pass–Fail Rates in Employment Testing: Statistical Proof Under Title VII*, 91 Harv. L. Rev. 793 (1978).

23. 770 F.2d 1421 (9th Cir.1985), cert. denied, 475 U.S. 1109, 106 S.Ct. 1516, 89 L.Ed.2d 915 (1986).

24. 487 U.S. 977, 108 S.Ct. 2777, 101 L.Ed.2d 827 (1988).

25. 108 S.Ct. at 2789 n.3.

26. 980 F.2d 1514 (5th Cir.1993).

or only a sample of it, however, because the court found the magnitude of the difference to be legally insufficient under any analysis.

Although there are many uncertainties about the current status of the law concerning disparate impact, it remains clear that this theory of discrimination is still valid under Title VII in the sense that it does not require any proof of motivation. Disparate impact discrimination is a separate theory of discrimination, distinct from disparate treatment discrimination. The confusing similarity in the names of these two theories of discrimination is the unfortunate result of the Supreme Court's footnote in *International Brotherhood of Teamsters v. United States*,[27] in which the Court drew the distinction between *Griggs*-based impact claims and individual claims of intentional exclusion. The Court used the terms disparate impact and disparate treatment to make the distinction, and those terms have prevailed. The EEOC Guidelines refer to "adverse impact," and *Griggs* itself referred to "disproportionate exclusion." These latter terms are thus used as synonymous with "disparate impact."

§ 2.22   Disparate Impact—Discretionary Evaluations for Promotion and Hire

The use of the disparate impact theory of discrimination under Title VII originated with cases concerning identifiable selection practices that adversely affected one group's opportunities for employment. In the landmark case establishing the principle, *Griggs v. Duke Power Co.*,[1] there were aptitude tests that disproportionately excluded on the basis of race, and there was a high school diploma requirement with a racial impact. Similarly, in *Dothard v. Rawlinson*,[2] a height requirement adversely affected employment opportunities on the basis of gender. The question that arose was whether disparate impact analysis could apply to discretionary evaluations for promotion and hire. This chapter section details how the Supreme Court answered "yes" to that question and the issues that still remain open with this application.

Discretionary Reviews–Adverse Impact Generally

The Supreme Court held in 1988 that disparate impact theory can be applied to selection procedures that are not objective standards. Justice O'Connor's plurality opinion in *Watson v. Fort Worth Bank & Trust*[3] observed that disparate treatment rather than disparate impact has conventionally been used to review employment decisions based on the exercise of personal judgment or the application of inherently subjective criteria. Nonetheless, *Watson* approved the examination of subjective practices with disparate impact analysis. The Court reasoned:

27. 431 U.S. 324, 97 S.Ct. 1843, 1854 n.15, 52 L.Ed.2d 396.

§ 2.22

1. 401 U.S. 424, 91 S.Ct. 849, 28 L.Ed.2d 158 (1971).

2. 433 U.S. 321, 97 S.Ct. 2720, 53 L.Ed.2d 786 (1977).

3. 487 U.S. 977, 108 S.Ct. 2777, 101 L.Ed.2d 827 (1988).

We are persuaded that our decisions in *Griggs* and succeeding cases could largely be nullified if disparate impact analysis were applied only to standardized selection practices. * * * We are also persuaded that disparate impact analysis is in principle no less applicable to subjective employment criteria than to objective or standardized tests. In either case, a facially neutral practice, adopted without discriminatory intent, may have effects that are indistinguishable from intentionally discriminatory practice.[4]

In *Watson,* the plaintiff was a black woman employee who had repeatedly failed in her quest for promotion. The employer defended each of the adverse decisions through subjective comparisons of the plaintiff to other candidates. The Court held that the plaintiff could establish a prima facie case if she could demonstrate that this subjective system had a disparate impact on black applicants. The burden would then shift to the defendant to justify the "legitimacy" of its subjective practices.

Discretionary Reviews–Proof of Impact

Subsequent to *Watson,* two events have left uncertainties concerning the nature of the plaintiff's proof in disparate impact claims involving subjective selection procedures. Those events were another Supreme Court case on a related issue, and the Civil Rights Act of 1991. Neither bears directly on *Watson,* but each touches upon issues closely related to the *Watson* principle.

First, a year after *Watson* the Supreme Court held in *Wards Cove Packing Co. v. Atonio*[5] that a plaintiff could not establish a prima facie case simply with evidence of a racial imbalance in a workforce. That case was largely overturned by the Civil Rights Act of 1991,[6] but this evidentiary aspect of the case is still the law. The implication for subjective evaluation cases like *Watson* is that the plaintiffs must produce applicant flow evidence or some type of evidence other than the racial, ethnic, or gender makeup of the workforce. Because *Watson* involved a claim of discrimination in promotion, it is less clear what kind of evidence would be acceptable to prove the disparate impact of initial hiring decisions when the sole basis of the hiring decision is subjective evaluation. If a reputation for discrimination taints the applicant pool, then applicant flow is not probative of the practices.

The Ninth Circuit approached a promotion case in a manner consistent with *Watson* without ever citing the case. It permitted a jury to find disparate impact in promotions when the plaintiff presented evidence of disparity between the men and women through the percentages of each group that moved to higher levels of management. The jury found disparate impact in the subjective process used by the employer in promotions, salaries, and benefits.[7]

4. 108 S.Ct. at 2786.

5. 490 U.S. 642, 109 S.Ct. 2115, 104 L.Ed.2d 733 (1989).

6. P.L. 102–166, 105 Stat. 1071 (1991).

7. Hemmings v. Tidyman's Inc., 285 F.3d 1174 (9th Cir. 2002), cert. denied, 537 U.S. 1110, 123 S.Ct. 854, 154 L.Ed.2d 781 (2003).

Particularity Requirement

A second area of remaining uncertainty about the disparate impact provisions of the Civil Rights Act of 1991 is the particularity requirement. The 1991 Act amended Title VII to provide that the plaintiff in a disparate impact case must identify a particular employment practice that is causing the impact. *Watson* itself talked about a particularity requirement and by implication the Court found that the subjective process in that promotion case was a "particular requirement." It is unclear how the particularity requirement applies to nonpromotion cases where the decision maker uses subjective procedures.

The 1991 Civil Rights Act revisions to Title VII include a further provision with respect to the particularity requirement. Section 703(k)(1)(B)(i) says with respect to the particularity requirement for disparate impact cases:

> the complaining party shall demonstrate that each particular challenged employment practice causes a disparate impact, except that if the complaining party can demonstrate to the court that the elements of a respondent's decisionmaking process are not capable of separation for analysis, the decisionmaking process may be analyzed as one employment practice.[8]

These provisions taken together in the context of subjective hiring decisions open possibilities for plaintiffs. If applicant flow is tainted because of the employer's reputation for discrimination, then perhaps the plaintiff can use a comparison of the individuals hired to the relevant labor market. One district court used this approach, but was overturned on appeal. The Eleventh Circuit held in that case, *EEOC v. Joe's Stone Crab, Inc.,*[9] that the plaintiff had to prove that at least one facially neutral employment practice proximately caused the disparity between the labor pool and the employer's work force. The job in that case was waiting tables at a restaurant that prided itself on its ambiance. The very subjective method of recruiting servers who would satisfy the requirements of ambiance resulted in the hiring of no women in the chain of restaurants during the relevant time period. Although the EEOC was able to establish on remand that the reputation of the employer for gender discrimination was relevant to a claim of intentional discrimination, it was insufficient for the particularity requirement for disparate impact.

Watson has left open many issues with respect to subjective processes that only future litigation can resolve. It is unclear which subjective processes besides promotion from within are sufficiently particular to permit disparate impact analysis, and it is unclear what type of proof of impact is appropriate. The *Watson* plurality opinion acknowledged the difficulty posed by the lack of specific guidance for lower courts and litigators on these issues and others relating to disparate impact. The

---

8. 42 U.S.C.A. § 2000e–2(k)(1)(B)(I).

9. 220 F.3d 1263 (11th Cir. 2002), cert. denied, 539 U.S. 941, 123 S.Ct. 2606, 156 L.Ed.2d 627 (2003).

Court saw no alternative to the case-by-case determination of these issues because of the importance of surrounding facts and circumstances.[10]

§ 2.23　Disparate Impact—Scored Tests

The Supreme Court in *Griggs v. Duke Power Co.*[1] established the principle that employers must prove the job relatedness of any challenged testing device that operates to exclude a group covered by Title VII. Once the plaintiff establishes a prima facie case showing the disparate impact, the burden shifts to the defendant to demonstrate the validity of the device. The tests involved in *Griggs* were the Bennett and Wonderlic aptitude tests, which had a disproportionate impact on the basis of race.

In *Griggs* the Court relied upon crude data that demonstrated the racial effect of the employer's tests. The sole evidence presented on the question was detailed only in a footnote. The Court noted that "with respect to standardized tests, the EEOC in one case found that use of a battery of tests, including the Wonderlic and Bennett tests used by the Company in the instant case, resulted in fifty-eight percent of whites passing the tests, as compared with only six percent of the blacks."[2] The crudeness of this evidence reflects the fact that the issues being litigated in this landmark case were the basic definitions of discrimination rather than the exact nature of the evidence to fit such definitions. Subsequent decisions and the agency Guidelines[3] have provided additional guidance.

Once the employer becomes aware of the adverse effect of a selection procedure, it is incumbent upon the employer to study the validity of the requirement. Moreover, if the employer can use another device that is equally valid but with lesser disparate impact, the Guidelines require the employer to do so. This obligation arises when "two or more selection procedures are available which serve the user's legitimate interest in efficient and trustworthy workmanship, and which are substantially equally valid for a given purpose," then "the user should use the procedure which has been demonstrated to have the lesser adverse impact."

Proving the Causal Link Between the Test and the Loss of Employment Opportunity

The plaintiff's essential proof in a disparate impact claim is that employment opportunities were lost by the employer's use of the challenged selection criterion. It is not sufficient to identify an irrational component of the procedure if its use has not affected opportunities. For

---

10. Watson v. Fort Worth Bank & Trust, 487 U.S. 977, 995–96 n.3, 108 S.Ct. 2777, 2789–90 n.3, 101 L.Ed.2d 827 (1988).

§ 2.23

1. 401 U.S. 424, 91 S.Ct. 849, 28 L.Ed.2d 158 (1971).

2. 91 S.Ct. at 853 n.6.

3. Uniform Guidelines on Employee Selection Procedures, 29 C.F.R. Pt. 1607.

example, in *EEOC v. Sears, Roebuck*,[4] the employer used a test designed to measure "vigor" for hiring commissioned sales representatives. The plaintiff's claim of gender discrimination failed because there was no proof that the test had ever prevented a woman from being hired. Although *Griggs* talked about measuring the person for the job and not measuring the person in the abstract, it is essential for the plaintiff first to prove that the abstract measurement has prevented employment opportunities.

The Uniform Guidelines on Employee Selection Procedures require employers covered by the Act to document the effect of each selection procedure for each job. When the passing rate for each group defined by race, national origin, and gender is at least four-fifths of the passing rate for the group with the highest rate, the Uniform Guidelines say that there is no adverse impact of a selection device.

Devices to Avoid Impact: Unlawful Manipulations

The general difficulty and uncertainty of defending the validity of a selection procedure, has led some employers to try to eliminate the disparate effect of a testing device. One method for eliminating the adverse effects of an exam is to create a cutoff score above which the relative performance of candidates on the exam is irrelevant. Any such cutoff score itself needs validation, however. The selection of candidates among those above the cutoff score must also pass the requirements of the Act.

In one case, the employer attempted to minimize the adverse effects of an exam on the basis of race and gender by changing the relative weight given to the exam compared with other component parts of the selection process.[5] The court of appeals rejected such a result-oriented approach because it was overtly race and gender conscious in a manner that did not satisfy the requirements of affirmative action.

Another technique that employers developed to eliminate the adverse effects of tests—and thus to avoid the necessity of demonstrating predictive validity—was to take the top scorers in each racial and gender group. Using this procedure, an employer would hire the top scoring man and top scoring woman, or the top scorers in groups defined by race or national origin, without regard to the possibly higher scores of other candidates in other groups. This practice, known as "race norming," is now prohibited by the Civil Rights Act of 1991. The Act amends Title VII to provide that it is unlawful "to adjust the scores of, use different cutoff scores for, or otherwise alter the results of, employment related tests on the basis of race, color, religion, sex, or national origin."[6] Employers thus may not impose an indirect quota system on test takers by taking the top scorers from each group without regard to the scores of other test takers.

4. 839 F.2d 302 (7th Cir.1988).

5. San Francisco Police Officers' Ass'n v. City & County of San Francisco, 869 F.2d 1182 (9th Cir.1988), cert. denied, 493 U.S. 816, 110 S.Ct. 68, 107 L.Ed.2d 35 (1989).

6. 42 U.S.C.A. § 2000e–2(*l*).

The case of *Officers for Justice v. Civil Service Commission*[7] concerned yet another method for reducing the adverse effect of an examination. The employer "banded" scores on a test so that applicants who fell within a range of scores were treated as scoring identically. This public employer then used race as the sole basis for hiring within the band. The court disapproved the second part of this practice as a violation of equal protection. It was permissible under the employer's valid affirmative action plan, however, to use a variety of other criteria in addition to race to choose among individuals within the band.

The court in *Officers for Justice* left open the question whether the practice of banding scores is generally permissible under Title VII. The plaintiff union argued that this practice of grouping scores together and then treating them as identical is a violation of the new provision in the Civil Rights Act of 1991 that prohibits altering scores. This provision against race norming, the union maintained, also applies to banding scores. The court left the matter unresolved, however, because of a procedural irregularity. Aside from this ambiguity, the court endorsed the use of banding in this case as "a facially neutral way to interpret actual scores and reduce adverse impacts on minority candidates while preserving merit as the primary criterion for selection."[8]

When employers use aptitude tests or similar selection devices, any adverse effect on the basis of race, gender, or national origin is irrelevant as long as the employer can establish the validity of the exam. The problem is that the employer cannot be reassured as to the validity of the exam in advance of litigation. This fact, combined with the difficulty of complying with the requirements of the Uniform Guidelines for predictive validity, has led some employers to seek ways to avoid any adverse impact caused by the exam. One of those methods, race norming, is now clearly unlawful under the Civil Rights Act of 1991. The legality of other methods, such as banding scores, remains unclear.

§ 2.24 Test Validation—Predictive Validity

Once a plaintiff class has established that a test has a disparate impact on a dimension covered by Title VII, the employer must then show that the exclusionary device is job-related. The Supreme Court held in *Griggs v. Duke Power Co.*[1] that Title VII forbids the use of employment tests that are exclusionary in effect unless the employer demonstrates that any given requirement has a "manifest relationship" to the job.

Predictive Validity–Generally

Predictive validity is one important method by which an employer can establish that a test is job-related and thus permissible to use under

---

7. 979 F.2d 721 (9th Cir.1992), cert. denied, 507 U.S. 1004, 113 S.Ct. 1645, 123 L.Ed.2d 267 (1993).

8. 979 F.2d at 728.

§ 2.24

1. 401 U.S. 424, 91 S.Ct. 849, 28 L.Ed.2d 158 (1971).

Title VII despite any unintended impact on the basis of race, color, religion, sex, or national origin. Predictive validity, also called criterion-related validity, means that a selection device is valid because empirical evidence establishes a close connection between the procedure and the job. Specifically, the evidence must show that there is a strong relationship between the results of the selection procedure and important elements of work behavior. In such a situation the selection device is predictive of performance because one's level of performance on the device predicts one's level of performance on the job.

The exact requirements for any method of validation are not fixed and inflexible. The key is whether the employer can establish a sufficiently strong relationship between the test and the job to convince the judge that the test predicts good job performance. The lack of specific requirements is best reflected in the observation made by the Supreme Court in *Watson v. Fort Worth Bank & Trust*,[2] a plurality opinion containing frequently cited dicta on the nature of disparate impact analysis and business necessity. The Court there said that employers are "not required, even when defending standardized or objective tests, to introduce formal 'validation studies' showing that particular criteria predict actual on-the-job performance."[3]

The Uniform Guidelines on Employee Selection Procedures provide the greatest source of guidance for assessing the sufficiency of a predictive validity study. These Guidelines require formal validation according to the standards of the American Psychological Association. In 1975, the Supreme Court held in *Albemarle Paper Co. v. Moody*,[4] that the Guidelines were entitled to great judicial deference. The Guidelines, endorsed strongly in *Albemarle*, are very specific about validation requirements. The requirements of predictive validity (called criterion-related validity in the Guidelines) have minimum technical standards with respect to: (1) feasibility; (2) analysis of the job; (3) criterion measures; (4) representativeness of the sample; (5) statistical relationships; (6) operational use of selection procedures; (7) overstatement of validity findings; and (8) fairness.[5]

In *Albemarle* the Court found inadequate a professional study that attempted to demonstrate the validity of the employer's aptitude tests. One problem was that the expert conducted the study only on current employees. This method of validation, called concurrent validation, is permissible but less persuasive than a more extensive study. A second problem was that the expert did not engage in a job skills analysis, but simply grouped together jobs on the basis of their proximity in the lines of progression rather than on the basis of the similarity of tasks performed.

2. 487 U.S. 977, 108 S.Ct. 2777, 101 L.Ed.2d 827 (1988).

3. 108 S.Ct. at 2790.

4. 422 U.S. 405, 95 S.Ct. 2362, 45 L.Ed.2d 280 (1975).

5. 29 C.F.R. § 1607.14.

The Court further found that the study was "materially defective" in several respects. First, the expert did not find statistically significant results for all the lines of progression; there was a significant correlation for only three of the eight lines. The aptitude tests that were used for all the lines of progression were therefore not demonstrably related to most of the jobs for which they were used.

Second, the study compared the employees' test results with very subjective supervisor ratings. The EEOC Guidelines in force at the time of *Albemarle*, now the Uniform Guidelines, specifically require that supervisor ratings must be based upon criteria that are fully described with as much specificity as possible. The work behavior under review must represent "major or critical work behaviors as revealed by careful job analyses."[6] Because of the danger of bias in subjective evaluations, a study must take every care to avoid subtle effects caused by prejudice or relative unfamiliarity with some employees. Moreover, a study undertaken in anticipation of litigation needs special sensitivity to the danger of finding the desired results.

Predictive Validity–Differential Validity and Related Issues

Another defect of the *Albemarle* study was the failure of the expert to attempt "differential validity." This concept refers to a demonstration that a selection device is equally valid for minority group members as it is for majority group members. The cultural bias of a test, for example, could make it a valid predictor for one group but not for another. The original EEOC Guidelines required that employers study whether a test is predictive for all groups, and the employer in *Albemarle* failed to do so. Subsequently, the successor to these Guidelines, the Uniform Guidelines on Employee Selection Procedures,[7] relaxed this requirement and eliminated the term "differential validity." The new Guidelines refer to "fairness" and urge examination of the fairness of the testing device to all groups.

One area of uncertainty about differential validity is whether adjustment of scores following a differential validity study is lawful under the new provisions added to Title VII in the Civil Rights Act of 1991. A section designed to end the practice of "race norming" uses broad language that an employer may not "adjust the scores of, use different cutoff scores for, or otherwise alter the results of, employment related tests on the basis of race, color, religion, sex, or national origin."[8] Although adjustments based upon differential validity are completely distinguishable from a quota system like race norming that is not based upon empirical findings, the broad language of this new amendment may disallow both practices.

The inquiry into the fairness of an exam, as endorsed by the Uniform Guidelines, may be in conflict with the new provision that prohibits any adjustment. A professional study may find that an exam is

---

6. 422 U.S. at 432 n.30, 95 S.Ct. at 2379 n.30.

7. 29 C.F.R. Pt. 1607.

8. 42 U.S.C.A. § 2000e–2(*l*).

differentially valid but only when the scores are adjusted. For example, a test in English may predict job performance equally well for native speakers of the language as well as non-native speakers, but the latter group may have an overall lower scale of test results. The test is differentially valid if the individuals with the best scores among the lower scoring group are able to perform the job as well as the best scorers from the native-speakers group. Under the Uniform Guidelines an employer is required as a matter of fairness to make such an adjustment when different scores predict the same job performance. The key is the prediction of the job performance. It remains unclear under the new amendments, however, whether acting on such information is an unlawful adjustment of scores. Congress aimed the provision at race norming, which is totally unrelated to differential validity, but the literal language of the provision would make unlawful any adjustment in scores, even if scientifically supportable.

In general, the Supreme Court's strong endorsement of the Guidelines in *Albemarle* has been highly influential on the lower courts, but the difficulty of defending selection devices with predictive validity under the Guidelines has led lower courts to greater flexibility. The stringent validation requirements of the Uniform Guidelines are not binding on a court in its assessment of whether an employer has met its burden of demonstrating differential validity. One court explained that noncompliance is "not necessarily fatal" but that it "diminishes the probative value of the defendant's study."[9]

The difficulty of compliance with the requirements of predictive validity has prompted some employers to attempt to eliminate the adverse effect of testing requirements. The elimination of testing requirements has accomplished that goal for some employers, but large public employers have been unable to avoid testing for jobs such as police officers and fire fighters. Much of the recent litigation about predictive validity has centered on these jobs. As the next section explores, many of these employers have abandoned predictive tests in favor of ones that attempt content validity because the Guidelines pose more generalized requirements for content validity.

§ 2.25 Test Validation—Content and Construct Validity

There are three types of test validation that may be used to demonstrate that any given requirement has a "manifest relationship" to the job as required by *Griggs v. Duke Power Co.*[1] once the plaintiff has demonstrated the disparate impact of the requirement on the basis of a dimension protected by Title VII. The first type is predictive validity, also known as criterion-related validity, which was the subject of the

9. Craig v. County of Los Angeles, 626 F.2d 659, 665 (9th Cir.1980), cert. denied, 450 U.S. 919, 101 S.Ct. 1364, 67 L.Ed.2d 345 (1981).

§ 2.25

1. 401 U.S. 424, 91 S.Ct. 849, 28 L.Ed.2d 158 (1971).

previous section. The second is content validity, and the third is construct validity, which are covered in this section.

These three types of validation are recognized by the American Psychological Association and therefore endorsed by the Uniform Guidelines on Employee Selection Procedures. The significance of establishing the validation of a requirement is that the it demonstrates its job-relatedness and thus justifies under *Griggs* the business use of such a test despite any disparate impact it may have on groups defined by race, gender and national origin.

Content Validity

Content validity is the simplest form of test validation. It refers to a demonstration that the test replicates major portions of the job, such as a typing test for a typist. The test must be representative of major portions of the job and the actual content of the job must require the tested abilities. The Uniform Guidelines require for content validity that the employer, union, or labor organization "show that the behavior(s) demonstrated in the selection procedure are a representative sample of the behavior(s) of the job in question."[2]

The test need not measure all aspects of job performance in exact proportion to the job in order to be content valid, but the matters tested must be important aspects of the job. A firefighter exam, for example, may include the performance of specific tasks that a firefighter must undertake during the job itself: climbing ladders, removing ladders, carrying ladders, placing ladders, connecting and disconnecting hoses, turning on hydrants, dragging hoses, dragging and carrying tarpaulin. It does not matter that a firefighter does not perform these tasks constantly on the job; what is crucial is that they are essential tasks.

The measurement of the content valid exam is important to its validity. A typing test for a typist may not measure speed, for example, if the job itself requires typing information on the lines of forms, such that accuracy rather than speed constitutes good job performance.

Because a firefighter's speed in performing physical tasks during a fire is crucial, an exam that measures abilities to perform essential tasks may measure the speed with which the tasks are successfully performed. The cutoff score must be logically and consistently applied, however. An employer cannot require a different minimum level of speed for the same job with each group of applicants.

A content valid test may be a paper and pencil test that asks questions about the tasks closely related to the job. In *Guardians Association v. Civil Service Commission*,[3] the employer used a written test for police officers. The test included an explanation of laws or circumstances under which arrests could be made. Then the test asked the applicant to apply the law to a certain fact situation. For example, it asked if a man making obscene gestures on the subway is committing (1)

2.   29 C.F.R. § 1607.14C(4).   **3.**   630 F.2d 79 (2d Cir.1980).

harassment, (2) jostling, (3) menacing, or (4) sexual misconduct. Because the ability to apply rules to factual situations was a skill that was a significant part of the job duties of a police officer, the test was content valid.

As with other content related tests, a written test must also bear close relation to the skills actually needed for the job. In one case, for example, a written test measured certain knowledge and skills required of a fire captain.[4] The test did not measure "supervisory skill," however, despite the fact that almost half of the fire captain's job was spent in supervision. Therefore, the test was insufficiently related to the job to be content valid.

Construct Validity

Construct validity refers to a showing that a test measures identifiable traits or characteristics important for successful job performance, such as leadership or aggressiveness. Such "constructs" may be measured by a testing device. Whereas content validity is appropriate for the measurement of a "skill" which comprises a significant portion of a job, construct validity is appropriate for the measurement of some personal trait or quality, called a "construct," desirable for the job. To defend any disparate impact on the basis of race, gender, or ethnicity that such tests may cause, the employer must show that the test accurately measures the construct and that the construct is necessary for successful job performance.

Validation of a test that measures a construct requires proof that the construct itself is correlated statistically to the quality of job performance. In effect, employers need to validate such tests according to the standards demanded for criterion related studies.

The greater difficulty in establishing construct validity compared with content validity makes the line between the two quite significant, but identification of the distinction can be difficult. "Intelligence" or "knowledge" are constructs because they are traits or characteristics, whereas the ability to read and effectively express oneself, and the knowledge of the subject matter that is the part of the job, could be considered a "skill" that is a part of the content of the job. The court in *Guardians Association v. Civil Service Commission*[5] indicated that "memory," ability to fill out forms, and the ability to apply rules to factual situations were skills that are a significant part of the job duties of a police officer. Thus, a police employer could defend with content validity a test that accurately measured those skills.

In a case involving testing teachers,[6] the plaintiffs argued that the written test for obtaining a teaching credential should be defended with construct validity rather than content validity since the test measured

---

4. Firefighters Inst. v. City of St. Louis, 549 F.2d 506 (8th Cir.1977).

5. 630 F.2d 79 (2d Cir.1980).

6. Association of Mexican–American Educators v. California, 937 F.Supp. 1397 (N.D.Cal. 1996), affirmed, 231 F.3d 572 (9th Cir.2000).

general rather than specific skills. The court rejected the argument because the "specific, well-defined skills" involved in the test were "reading, mathematics, and writing" rather than abstract skills like mental aptitude or intelligence.

Another case, *Firefighters Institute for Racial Equality v. St. Louis,*[7] noted:

> Paper-and-pencil tests which are intended to replicate a work behavior are most likely to be appropriate where work behaviors are performed in paper and pencil form (e.g., editing and bookkeeping). Paper-and-pencil tests of effectiveness in interpersonal relations (e.g., sales or supervision), or of physical activities (e.g., automobile repair) or ability to function properly under danger (e.g., firefighters) generally are not close enough approximations of work behaviors to show content validity.[8]

This passage was quoted with approval in a release by the EEOC.[9] A clear distinction between tests appropriate for content validity and those that require the more difficult proof of predictive validity or construct validity nonetheless remains elusive.

Test validation by any method is a defense and the burden of proof remains on the defendant to establish validation by a preponderance of the evidence. If the court finds that the employer has demonstrated the validity of a testing device, it remains open to the plaintiff to show that the employer failed to use a selection device with a less disparate impact. In the absence of such further evidence, proof of validity is a complete defense to any disparate impact caused by a testing device.

§ 2.26 Other Criteria for Hiring or Promotion

The hiring and promotion of workers may involve the use other kinds of selection criteria besides tests and discretionary review. Disparate impact analysis is equally available for Title VII plaintiffs to attack the effect of other criteria that employers may use. The impact of such requirements on the basis of race, gender, or national origin can be measured by their effect on actual applicants. This section explores ways in which plaintiffs may establish the existence of disparate impact with data other than the effect of the requirement on applicants.

Effect of Requirement on Population

The landmark disparate impact case, *Griggs v. Duke Power Co.,*[1] involved not only aptitude tests with a disparate impact, but also a high school diploma requirement. The Court noted that this requirement had a disparate impact on African–Americans in the state where the employer was located. The census data revealed a racial difference in the attainment of a high school diploma.

7. 616 F.2d 350 (8th Cir.1980).

8. Id. at 361.

9. 44 Fed. Reg. 12,007 (1979).

§ 2.26

1. 401 U.S. 424, 91 S.Ct. 849, 28 L.Ed.2d 158 (1971).

The rudimentary nature of the evidence in *Griggs* did not give courts much guidance on how to determine the existence of a prima facie case. The fact that Duke Power Company did not draw employees from the entire state did not dilute the probative value of the statewide evidence. One can assume that the educational statistics in the area from which the employer draws employees are consistent with the statewide data in the absence of contrary evidence.

Similar logic was the underpinning of another major Supreme Court case concerning disparate impact, *Dothard v. Rawlinson*.[2] This case concerned height and weight requirements that had a disparate impact on the basis of gender. The evidence to support this effect was national population statistics. The Court found acceptable such evidence in the absence of information suggesting that the group of people who would desire the job position in question would have physical characteristics different from the population at large.

When the employer's requirement has a demonstrable effect on the plaintiff's group in the general population, that evidence may be sufficient to establish a prima facie case. Data showing the effect of a requirement on the plaintiff's group in general, such as an education requirement or height requirement, establish a prima facie case because of the inference that the relevant population from which the employer could hire has the same characteristics. It remains open to the defendant to introduce evidence to rebut this inference. The Court observed in *Dothard* that if the employer discerns fallacies in the plaintiff's statistics, "he is free to adduce countervailing evidence of his own."[3]

Subsequent to these cases, the Supreme Court clarified that the plaintiff's proof nonetheless needs to be specific when the plaintiff seeks to establish that a requirement has a disparate impact on the basis of population data. In *New York City Transit Authority v. Beazer*,[4] the Supreme Court considered a challenge to the employer's rule that excluded all drug users, including individuals on methadone maintenance treatment. The plaintiff introduced evidence that approximately two-thirds of all persons in the city's methadone treatment programs were minorities, compared with a city population that is only one-third minority. The district court inferred from these numbers that the rule excluded a higher percentage of otherwise qualified minorities than nonminority applicants. The Second Circuit affirmed, but the Supreme Court reversed.

The Supreme Court found numerous faults with several aspects of the plaintiff's proof in *Beazer*, including this evidence comparing the city's minority population to the representation of minority groups in the public methadone treatment programs. A crucial flaw in this evidence was that it related only to public methadone programs; there was no evidence concerning the private treatment programs. One could

---

2. 433 U.S. 321, 97 S.Ct. 2720, 53 L.Ed.2d 786 (1977).

3. 97 S.Ct. at 2727.

4. 440 U.S. 568, 99 S.Ct. 1355, 59 L.Ed.2d 587 (1979).

speculate that if all of the persons receiving treatment in private facilities were nonminority, then there may be no impact caused by the no-methadone rule. An equivalent flaw in data concerning education, for example, would be if the plaintiff provided data for high school graduation rates from only public or only private schools. The *Beazer* opinion reflected an unwillingness to take judicial notice of disparate impact; the plaintiff must produce competent evidence.

Effect of Requirement on Applicants

Another method for establishing the disparate impact of any requirement is to examine its effect on the pool of applicants. If the requirement disproportionately excludes a group defined by race, gender, or national origin, the next question is whether that exclusion is sufficiently large. Because applicants represent only a sample of the relevant population, it is necessary for the different rates of exclusion to be statistically significant and/or to satisfy the four-fifths rule of the Uniform Guidelines on Employee Selection Procedures. If there are not enough applicants or workers to examine for the impact of a requirement, plaintiffs may seek to establish the impact through other means.

Nontesting requirements have been particularly challenging for plaintiffs to establish their adverse impact. Rules against nepotism, for example, are difficult to challenge under disparate impact analysis. If there are an insufficient number of instances to show the impact of the rule on actual applicants or employees, then it is difficult to find proof that anti-nepotism rules affect employment opportunities on a dimension protected by the Act. In *Thomas v. Metroflight, Inc.,*[5] the plaintiff challenged the adverse effect of a no-spouse rule on the basis of gender. The plaintiff, who resigned after her marriage to a fellow employee with more seniority, alleged that the rule more frequently worked to the disadvantage of females. There were very few examples of the effect of the rule on actual employees within the company, so that evidence failed for the sample size. The plaintiff then attempted to argue that the generally larger salaries of the male employees, and their generally greater seniority, would inevitably lead to greater employment disadvantage for women who marry coworkers than for men.

The district court found this evidence insufficient, and the Tenth Circuit affirmed. The appellate opinion observed that it was reluctant to affirm on the issue of impact because "we suspect, as others have claimed, that 'no-spouse' rules in practice often result in discrimination against women, and are generally unjustified." Despite this sense of regret, the court noted that "we cannot accept our own speculations or others' conclusions as a substitute for plaintiff's required proof, nor may we take judicial notice of evidence that might have been but was not presented."[6]

5. 814 F.2d 1506 (10th Cir.1987).   6. Id. at 1509 (footnote omitted).

In contrast to these difficulties with producing evidence of disparate impact, however, is *Chambers v. Omaha Girls Club, Inc.*[7] The plaintiff challenged the employer's rule against unwed pregnancy on several grounds, including its disparate impact on the basis of race. The evidence to support the disparate impact claim was the greater fertility rate among black females. The court found this evidence sufficient to support the claim that a rule against unwed pregnancies would impact more harshly on black women. This evidence failed to relate directly to birth rates among unwed women rather than among women in general and thus failed to address squarely the issue presented about the effect of the unwed pregnancy rule. Any defects in the prima facie case were overcome, however, by the finding of business necessity for the rule.

Cases such as *Beazer, Thomas,* and *Chambers* all involved more creative forms of evidence presented by the plaintiffs because the cases demanded less conventional evidence. In the absence of straightforward population figures, such as for a height requirement, or large numbers of applicants for significant applicant flow data, it is not possible to establish the disparate impact of the requirement without some evidence that probes the fundamental question: Does the requirement adversely affect the employment opportunities of plaintiff's group defined by race, gender or ethnicity?

§ 2.27 Business Necessity and Justification

Griggs v. Duke Power Co.,[1] the Supreme Court's landmark case in 1971 that embraced the disparate impact theory of discrimination, held that Title VII proscribes conduct that is "fair in form but discriminatory in operation."[2] When an employer uses procedures or testing mechanisms unrelated to measuring job capability, the Court said, it is incumbent upon the employer to demonstrate that its requirements are job-related and governed by principles of business necessity.

As a general rule, the concept of "job-relatedness" has applied to testing procedures capable of being validated under the Uniform Guidelines for Employee Selection Procedures. When nontesting devices, such as education requirements and physical standards, have a disparate impact, the employer may defend with "business necessity." This chapter section explores this defense for nontesting selection procedures.

Codification of Business Necessity in the Civil Rights Act of 1991

There were a number of Supreme Court decisions in the late eighties that Congress perceived as a retrenchment of employment discrimination rights. Among the decisions that Congress targeted was *Wards Cove Packing Co. v. Atonio,*[3] which had reconsidered the nature of

7. 834 F.2d 697 (8th Cir.1987).

§ 2.27
1. 401 U.S. 424, 91 S.Ct. 849, 28 L.Ed.2d 158 (1971).

2. 91 S.Ct. at 853.

3. 490 U.S. 642, 109 S.Ct. 2115, 104 L.Ed.2d 733 (1989).

the burden shifting in *Griggs*. Congress specifically declared as one of the purposes of the Act to reinstate the *Griggs* scheme with respect to the business necessity defense. Section 703(k)(1)(A) of Title VII, as amended by the Civil Rights Act of 1991, provides:

> An unlawful employment practice based on disparate impact is established under this title only if (i) a complaining party demonstrates that a respondent uses a particular employment practice that causes a disparate impact on the basis of race, color, religion, sex, or national origin and the respondent fails to demonstrate that the challenged practice is job related for the position and consistent with business necessity * * *.[4]

This amendment expresses the congressional intent that business necessity is a defense in Title VII litigation and that the employer has the burden of establishing it. The Supreme Court's 1989 opinion in *Wards Cove Packing Co. v. Atonio*[5] had placed the burden on the plaintiff to show the lack of business necessity. The Civil Rights Act of 1991 returned employment discrimination law to the earlier understanding of the meaning of *Griggs v. Duke Power Co.* and overturned that part of *Wards Cove* by defining "demonstrate" to mean "meets the burdens of production and persuasion."[6]

The Supreme Court explained in *Griggs* that "Congress has placed on the employer the burden of showing that any given requirement must have a manifest relationship to the employment in question." It also stated: "The touchstone is business necessity. If an employment practice which operates to exclude Negroes cannot be shown to be related to job performance, the practice is prohibited."[7]

Non-Empirical Proofs

A requirement such as an educational attainment need not be strictly validated in order to meet business necessity. A court will not assume the required relationship, however, between a certain level of education and jobs that require general skills, as in *Griggs*. Employers have generally not been successful in establishing the business necessity of an education requirement for semi-skilled jobs in production, transportation, maintenance, sales, and clerical positions. Courts have been more receptive to education requirements for professional jobs.

Employers must validate or defend with business necessity other kinds of nontesting requirements if they have a disparate impact. A disqualification of applicants with a criminal record, for example, may have a disparate impact. If the job does not specifically require trust and integrity more than most jobs, it is difficult for an employer to demonstrate the business necessity of such a requirement.

Courts have generally been deferential to public safety as an element of business necessity when the job clearly involves entrusting the

4. 42 U.S.C.A. § 2000e–2(k)(1)(A).

5. 490 U.S. 642, 109 S.Ct. 2115, 104 L.Ed.2d 733 (1989).

6. 42 U.S.C.A. § 2000e(m).

7. 401 U.S. at 432, 91 S.Ct. at 854.

public safety, such as airline pilots. In one case involving airline flight engineers, *Spurlock v. United Airlines*,[8] the court articulated a sliding scale, with a lesser showing of necessity required for jobs that require a high risk of harm to the public. Because piloting a commercial airliner clearly implicates public safety, the employer can require a college education—notwithstanding the absence of an empirical study correlating education and performance in the cockpit.

For some requirements, courts have permitted employers to meet the requirement of "demonstrating" business necessity without any effort to make an empirical demonstration of the fact. In *Chambers v. Omaha Girls Club, Inc.*,[9] for example, the employer operated a club for teenage girls in an inner city. One of the stated missions of the club was to provide positive role models for the girls through the club's employees. Only women staffed the club, and the issue before the court was the discharge of one unmarried female staffer who became pregnant.

The court in *Chambers* found that the rule against single mothers had a disparate impact on the basis of both race and gender, but that the employer successfully defended the rule with business necessity. The employer's evidence was not extensive; expert testimony confirmed the employer's assumption that an employee who is an unwed mother would defeat the employer's legitimate goal of providing positive role models. The lack of a validation study was not disqualifying. The court observed that although a validation study can be helpful in evaluating a business necessity defense, it is not required to maintain a successful business necessity defense.

It was unclear in the *Chambers* case whether the trial court believed that it was possible to validate the effect unwed pregnancy had on the club's patrons. If empirical proof is not possible, the question becomes whether defendants can nonetheless prevail with a business necessity defense. The court here observed that the role model rule by its nature may not be suited to validation in an empirical study. "Although validation studies can be helpful in evaluating such questions," the court held, "they are not required to maintain a successful business necessity defense."[10]

Testing versus Non–Testing Requirements

Business necessity has been more easily established as a defense, generally speaking, than job-relatedness because of the difficulty of showing test validation. For that reason it is important to distinguish testing requirements that require job validation from other requirements that require business necessity. Sometimes employers use vague, subjective evaluations that are simply unscientific types of tests, such as looking for "leadership" or "presence." Other times employers have used a proxy for such characteristics, such as height and weight. The Supreme Court considered a height requirement for prison guards in

8. 475 F.2d 216 (10th Cir.1972).   **10.** Id. at 702.

9. 834 F.2d 697 (8th Cir.1987).

Dothard v. Rawlinson[11] and concluded that the impact of such requirements shifts the burden to the employer to demonstrate job-relatedness.

Following *Dothard*, courts will not assume that general physical requirements are a business necessity without empirical evidence or validation. In *Lanning v. SEPTA*,[12] for example, the employer transit authority had requirements that security officer applicants have a certain level of pre-training aerobic capacity and a post-training ability to run one and a half miles within twelve minutes. The requirements had a disparate impact on women but the employer was able to demonstrate the job-relatedness of the requirements with a statistically significant validation study showing that aerobic and running ability is related to arrests. Further, the employer successfully connected the relationship of arrests to public safety and thus the ability to perform the job.

A common requirement for police officers or firefighters is physical strength. The necessity for such strength cannot be assumed without studies of the job itself, and hiring cannot be based on gender or appearance. The concept of "test" is not limited to paper and pencil tests, and tests of physical strength need to be validated like other tests. Typically tests of physical strength withstand scrutiny if they are content valid, such as requiring firefighter or police applicants to demonstrate an ability to do tasks specifically required for the job.

Business Necessity versus Business Justification

Many questions remain about the nature of the business necessity defense, despite the attempt by Congress to clarify the law in the Civil Rights Act of 1991. The amendments to Title VII contained in this Act do not provide clear guidance, however. First, the Act now specifies that business necessity is a defense to disparate impact analysis, and not to cases of overt discrimination or disparate treatment.[13] It also clarifies that business necessity is a defense and that the burden of production and persuasion rests with the defendant to establish the presence of business necessity. Beyond these provisions, the Act is silent as to the nature of the defense. The legislative history on the subject indicates the following: "The terms 'business necessity' and 'job related' are intended to reflect the concepts enunciated by the Supreme Court in *Griggs v. Duke Power Co.* and in other Supreme Court decisions prior to *Wards Cove Packing Co. v. Atonio.*"[14]

This cryptic history refers to a rejection of the *Wards Cove* holding with respect to business necessity. The Court had said in that case:

> Though we have phrased the query differently in different cases, it is generally well-established that at the justification stage of such a disparate impact case, the dispositive issue is whether a challenged practice serves, in a significant way, the legitimate employment goals of the employer. The touchstone of this inquiry is a reasoned

11. 433 U.S. 321, 97 S.Ct. 2720, 53 L.Ed.2d 786 (1977).

12. 181 F.3d 478 (3d Cir. 1999).

13. 42 U.S.C.A. § 2000e–2(k).

14. 137 Cong. Rec. 515276 (Oct. 25, 1991)(citations omitted).

review of the employer's justification for his use of the challenged practice. A mere insubstantial justification in this regard will not suffice, because such a low standard of review would permit discrimination to be practiced through the use of spurious, seemingly neutral employment practices. At the same time, though there is no requirement that the challenged practice be "essential" or "indispensable" to the employer's business for it to pass muster, this degree of scrutiny would be almost impossible for most employers to meet, and would result in a host of evils * * *.[15]

This *Wards Cove* concept of "business justification" as equivalent to "business necessity" signaled a weakening of the standard, and Congress sought to reject the Court's approach. A troubling aspect of the congressional intent to reject *Wards Cove* and to return the law of business necessity to *Griggs* is that the Court itself did not purport to find the two standards incompatible. Indeed, at the opening of the passage from *Wards Cove* quoted above the Court described this phase of the litigation as "well-established." Unless the Court did not truly believe that it was describing existing law in this *Wards Cove* passage, then there is a conflict between congressional understanding of the business necessity requirement in *Griggs* and the Court's understanding of it. The failure of Congress to provide more guidance beyond the cryptic reference to returning to *Griggs* may necessitate further judicial clarification.

The relationship of the business necessity defense to the defense of legitimate nondiscriminatory reason in a class action claim of disparate treatment was addressed by the Fifth Circuit in *Allison v. Citgo Petroleum Corp.*[16] The court reasoned:

It is the rare case indeed in which a challenged practice is job-related and a business necessity, yet not a legitimate nondiscriminatory reason for an adverse employment action taken pursuant to that practice. Thus, a finding that a challenged practice is job related and a business necessity in response to a disparate impact claim strongly, if not wholly, implicates a finding that the same practice is a legitimate nondiscriminatory reason for the employer's actions in a pattern or practice claim.[17]

The significance of this observation was that it prevented the severance of the disparate impact claim from the other claims that were tried to the jury. The Civil Rights Act of 1991 permits jury trials for claims of intentional discrimination where the plaintiff is seeking compensatory damages, but claims for disparate impact are still tried to the judge without a jury. The effect of this ruling, therefore, was to prevent the plaintiff from presenting similar evidence to multiple factfinders.

§ 2.28 Less Discriminatory Alternatives

Title VII litigation brought under the disparate impact theory proceeds with the same three-part burden shifting that characterizes indi-

15. Wards Cove Packing Co. v. Atonio, 490 U.S. 642, 659, 109 S.Ct. 2115, 2125, 104 L.Ed.2d 733 (1989) (citations omitted).

16. 151 F.3d 402 (5th Cir. 1998).

17. Id. at 424.

vidual claims of disparate treatment under *McDonnell Douglas* scheme.[1] First, the plaintiff must establish the disproportionate exclusion based upon a statistical showing that a specific selection procedure has a disparate impact on a protected group. If the plaintiff succeeds in establishing this prima facie case, the burden of production and persuasion shifts to the defendant to justify the exclusionary effect with job-relatedness or business necessity. If the defendant succeeds with this proof, the burden shifts back to the plaintiff to demonstrate that the employer failed to use a selection device that is equally effective but has a lesser disparate impact. This section explores this final phase of disparate impact litigation.

Less Discriminatory Alternative–Origin

The Supreme Court introduced this third phase, proof of less discriminatory alternative, in its 1975 opinion in *Albemarle Paper Co. v. Moody*.[2] The Court explained:

> If an employer does then meet the burden of proving that its tests are "job related," it remains open to the complaining party to show that other tests or selection devices, without a similarly undesirable racial effect, would also serve the employer's legitimate interest in "efficient and trustworthy workmanship." Such a showing would be evidence that the employer was using its tests merely as a "pretext" for discrimination.[3]

The Court further clarified this concept in *Watson v. Fort Worth Bank & Trust*.[4] The plurality opinion reviewed much of Title VII law in dicta, including many facets of disparate impact claims. On the subject of alternative selection devices with lesser disparate impact, Justice O'Connor's opinion for the plurality noted that relevant to the inquiry are factors such as the cost or other burdens of proposed alternative selection devices. The fundamental inquiry is determining whether they would be equally as effective as the challenged practice in serving the employer's legitimate business goals. The opinion then added: "The same factors would *also* be relevant in determining whether the challenged practice has operated as the functional equivalent of a pretext for discriminatory treatment."[5] Comparing the references to pretext in *Albemarle* and *Watson* leads to the conclusion that the underlying inquiry is not one of pretext—an intentional discrimination concept—at this phase of disparate impact litigation, although the matter is not free from doubt.

§ 2.28

1. McDonnell Douglas Corp. v. Green, 411 U.S. 792, 93 S.Ct. 1817, 36 L.Ed.2d 668 (1973); Reeves v. Sanderson Plumbing Prods., 530 U.S. 133, 120 S.Ct. 2097, 147 L.Ed.2d 105 (2000). See § 2.8.

2. 422 U.S. 405, 95 S.Ct. 2362, 45 L.Ed.2d 280 (1975).

3. 95 S.Ct. at 2375.

4. 487 U.S. 977, 108 S.Ct. 2777, 101 L.Ed.2d 827 (1988).

5. 108 S.Ct. at 2790–91 (emphasis added).

Subsequent to these opinions, the Supreme Court held in *Wards Cove Packing Co. v. Atonio*[6] that if plaintiffs demonstrate that there are alternatives to the employer's hiring practices that reduce the disparate impact of practices currently being used, and employers "refuse to adopt these alternatives, such a refusal would belie a claim" that "their incumbent practices are being employed for nondiscriminatory reasons."[7] This approach creates a greater burden on the plaintiff than a mere demonstration of the availability of an alternative practice. As discussed in the next section, Congress has explicitly rejected the *Wards Cove* characterization of this phase of disparate impact litigation and reinstated the pre-*Ward Cove* understanding of the concept.

Lesser Discriminatory Alternatives–The Civil Rights Act of 1991

In the Civil Rights Act of 1991, Congress amended Title VII to specify that the concept of "alternative employment practice" shall be "in accordance with the law as it existed on June 4, 1989."[8] That date is the day before the Supreme Court decided *Wards Cove*. Moreover, the Act provides that the exclusive legislative history on the subject of alternative business practices is a brief paragraph in the *Congressional Record* that refers to a rejection of *Wards Cove* in favor of *Griggs*.

The Act codifies the alternative business practice concept with a provision that an unlawful employment practice exists if the plaintiff makes a "demonstration" of such a practice "in accordance with the law as it existed on June 4, 1989" and the employer "refuses to adopt such alternative employment practice."[9] The language about a "refusal to adopt" comes from the passage of *Wards Cove* quoted above, despite the Act's overt rejection of that case. The apparent contradiction of the stated congressional intent with these provisions has left the courts with little guidance.

The case law has focused on the stated congressional intent to reinstate the prior law more than on the literal wording of the statutory amendment. The Seventh Circuit in *Price v. City of Chicago*[10] rejected the plaintiff's argument that the language of the amendment altered the fundamental burden of plaintiffs in disparate impact litigation. In that case the employer used the neutral device of birth date for breaking ties for promotions when applicants had identical scores on tests and requirements. The plaintiff said that the rule preferring older employees had a disparate impact on minorities because of the historical pattern of hiring, but failed to establish a disparate impact. The plaintiff's next argument was that the employer should be liable in the absence of an impact because there were alternative selection procedures that would result in greater minority representation. The Seventh Circuit opinion analyzed the language of statutory purpose and the amendment and concluded that Congress did not intend to alter the burden-shifting

---

6. 490 U.S. 642, 109 S.Ct. 2115, 104 L.Ed.2d 733 (1989).

7. 109 S.Ct. at 2127.

8. 42 U.S.C.A. § 2000e–2(k)(1)(C).

9. 42 U.S.C.A. § 2000e–2(k)(1)(A)(ii), (k)(1)(C).

10. 251 F.3d 656 (7th Cir. 2001).

approach of *Griggs*. In the absence of disparate impact, the plaintiff did not have a prima facie case.

A similar result has been reached by other circuits although those cases have not needed to focus on the conflicting language because of the nature of the facts. The Fifth Circuit in *Brunet v. City of Columbus*[11] considered the concept in the context of a cutoff score on a firefighters exam. The court rejected the plaintiff's contention that the city should have used a different cutoff score that would have had a lesser disparate impact on female applicants. The trial court had made a finding of fact that there was no equally valid cutoff score with a lesser adverse impact, and it was not required to consider all possible alternative hiring procedures in this portion of the analysis. In another firefighter case, the Eighth Circuit in *Smith v. City of Des Moines*[12] considered an age discrimination challenge to a physical agility test. The court rejected the argument that the city should use alternative means of assessing fitness with a lesser disparate impact on older workers because the plaintiff failed to demonstrate that the proposed alternative would actually have a lesser impact nor that it would serve the city's legitimate interests equally well.

The paucity of cases interpreting the conflicting language of the amendments in the 1991 Act leave open the question of its interpretation. If the Act did make a radical change in the nature and burden of proof in disparate impact cases, as some plaintiffs have argued, the revolution has not yet occurred.

§ 2.29   Procedural Requirements

Procedural Guiding Principles in Federal Antidiscrimination Law

The procedural requirements under Title VII and the ADEA reflect congressional intent that employment discrimination disputes should not be handled like common law civil disputes. Plaintiffs must exhaust complicated state and federal administrative procedures before filing suit. During this time of administrative deferral, the state and federal agencies charged with investigating claims may attempt to conciliate or otherwise to resolve the dispute before litigation. If this process is not successful, the federal agency may sue in its own name or issue the complainant a "right-to-sue" letter. Congress put these procedural impediments to litigation in Title VII in order to promote the conciliation of employment discrimination claims before litigation.

A second guiding principle in Title VII procedures is deference to state administrative agencies in states where there is a statutory scheme substantially similar to Title VII. Plaintiffs must first exhaust state administrative remedies and then exhaust federal administrative remedies. Under Title VII a charge of discrimination against a non-federal employer must be filed with the Equal Employment Opportunity Commission (EEOC) within a certain number of days after the discriminato-

---

11.   58 F.3d 251 (6th Cir.1995).   **12.**   99 F.3d 1466 (8th Cir.1996).

ry act. The Supreme Court has held that timely filing with the EEOC is a prerequisite to suit.[1]

Limitations Period

The complainant has a limited number of days after the discriminatory act during which to file. The number of days is either 180 or 300, depending upon whether the complainant lives in a state with a state agency charged with enforcing state law prohibiting race, sex, national origin, and religious discrimination.[2] Such state agencies, known as "deferral agencies" or "706 agencies," must have an opportunity to resolve employment discrimination charges before the federal agency. Because of this policy of deference to an available state agency, the time limitation depends upon the presence of such an agency. A complainant in a state without such an agency has 180 days in which to file with the EEOC, whereas a complainant in a state with a deferral agency has 300 days.

The 300–day limitation is deceiving, however, because the complainant must file with the state agency before filing with the EEOC. Although the state filing does not have to be timely under state law, the state charge must precede the federal charge. The EEOC must grant exclusive jurisdiction to the state agency for sixty days unless the state agency terminates its jurisdiction earlier. If the state agency terminates its jurisdiction before the sixty days have run, the complainant must file the federal EEOC charge within thirty days of the state's termination. If the state agency has not terminated its jurisdiction within sixty days, the complainant may proceed to file with the EEOC within the 300–day period. If the complainant has not filed a charge with the state agency, the EEOC will refer the charge to the state agency for the sixty-day period and then reactivate the charge for its own jurisdiction after that time. For purposes of counting the 300 days, however, the charge is not "filed" with the EEOC until after the 60–day referral period.[3] Therefore, as a practical matter, a complainant filing with the EEOC needs to do so within 240 days of the discriminatory act.

The initial limitations period runs from the time of the discriminatory act. In hiring and promotion cases the discriminatory act is normally the date that the vacancy was filled on a discriminatory basis. It can also be the date on which the employer made the decision adverse to the plaintiff if the facts give notice that the decision was discriminatory.

In discharge cases the discriminatory act occurs on the day that notice is given. The Supreme Court had occasion to consider that issue in *Delaware State College v. Ricks*.[4] In this case an assistant professor

§ 2.29

1. Zipes v. Trans World Airlines, Inc., 455 U.S. 385, 102 S.Ct. 1127, 71 L.Ed.2d 234 (1982); United Air Lines, Inc. v. Evans, 431 U.S. 553, 97 S.Ct. 1885, 52 L.Ed.2d 571 (1977).

2. 42 U.S.C.A. § 2000e–5(e).

3. Mohasco Corp. v. Silver, 447 U.S. 807, 100 S.Ct. 2486, 65 L.Ed.2d 532 (1980).

4. 449 U.S. 250, 101 S.Ct. 498, 66 L.Ed.2d 431 (1980).

sued his employer for discriminatory refusal to grant him tenure. Under the terms of his agreement with the college he continued to be employed under a terminal contract for another academic year after the tenure denial. During this time he pursued internal appeals and then brought his claim to the EEOC. His complaint was untimely, despite the fact that it was filed while he was still employed under the terminal contract. The Court reasoned that the discriminatory act occurred on the date he received the unequivocal notice of termination, not the last day on the job or the day on which he received notice that his final appeal was denied. The unequivocal notice of the college's decision not to grant him tenure and to give him the terminal contract was the date of the allegedly discriminatory act. The limitations period ran from that date.

A subsequent Supreme Court opinion applied the *Ricks* principle to a change in a seniority system. In *Lorance v. A T & T Technologies*,[5] the Court considered a challenge to a change in a seniority system which the plaintiffs alleged was intentionally discriminatory on the basis of gender. The Court never addressed the substantive issue because the claim was untimely. The limitations period began to run, the Court held, when the change in the seniority system became effective and not when the plaintiffs were injured by it. The dissenting justices complained that the decision is "glaringly at odds with the purposes of Title VII," and Congress subsequently agreed. The Civil Rights Act of 1991 amended Title VII to provide that in a challenge to a seniority system as intentionally discriminatory, the unlawful practice occurs at any one of three times: (1) when the system is adopted; (2) when the complainant becomes subject to it; or (3) when a person aggrieved is injured by its application.[6] An open question is whether the *Lorance* rationale is still applicable to challenges under the ADEA. The Seventh Circuit held in *EEOC v. City Colleges of Chicago*[7] that because the Civil Rights Act of 1991 overruled *Lorance* only with respect to Title VII, *Lorance* remains controlling for cases brought under the ADEA.

The Court's rationale in *Lorance* would not necessarily be restricted to seniority system challenges, so that the continued vitality of the rationale in other areas remains open to question.

Continuing Violations

Some violations are called "continuing" violations in the sense that the discriminatory act does not stop in a way that begins the limitations period. Discrimination in pay or in other forms of compensation is a continuing violation that may be challenged within 180 or 300 days of any receipt of such discriminatory pay or other compensation. The recovery period for such discrimination is limited by the Act, however, to a period of two years prior to the filing of the charge.

5. 490 U.S. 900, 109 S.Ct. 2261, 104 L.Ed.2d 961 (1989).

6. 42 U.S.C.A. § 2000e–5(e)(2).

7. 944 F.2d 339 (7th Cir. 1991).

The Supreme Court clarified the continuing violation theory in *National Railroad Passenger Corp. v. Morgan.*[8] The trial judge in this hostile environment racial harassment case had permitted the jury to consider conduct prior to the 300–day limitations period only for background, but not as the basis for any liability. The plaintiff appealed the unfavorable jury verdict. The Supreme Court held that as long as an act contributing to the claim occurs within the limitations period, the entire series of acts constituting the hostile environment may be considered for liability. Once a court determines that the acts are part of a pattern, they are admissible to support the hostile environment claim. In that case, the plaintiff presented evidence that managers made racial jokes, performed racially derogatory acts, and used racial epithets that could have been found to be part of a pattern.

Res Judicata

Once the federal court has tried a Title VII claim and appeals have been exhausted, the principle of res judicata prevents relitigation of the claim. By the same principle, the resolution of issues under parallel statutes, such as 42 U.S.C.A. § 1981, has preclusive effect and prevents relitigation under Title VII or vice versa.

The same principle applies to the resolution of issues by state courts to the same extent that such determinations would be preclusive in subsequent state proceedings. The Supreme Court explained this principle in *Kremer v. Chemical Construction Corp.*[9] In *Kremer*, an employee filed a complaint with the EEOC, which referred it to the state agency charged with administering the state's employment laws. The state agency investigated and dismissed the claim, and the complainant appealed within the state court system. The state courts reviewed and affirmed the administrative judgment under the arbitrary and capricious standard. Therefore, judicially reviewed determinations from a state agency have preclusive effect, even if the judicial review at the state level was not de novo.

The Court premised its decision in *Kremer* on the statutory requirement that federal courts must give the same preclusive effect to state judicial determinations that those determinations would have been given in the courts of the state from which the determination came. The Court subsequently held that only judicial determinations or judicial review of agency determinations have res judicata effect to preclude subsequent litigation; unreviewed agency determinations do not. In *University of Tennessee v. Elliott,*[10] the Court explained that if such preclusive effect were given to state agency determinations in Title VII cases, there would be virtually no federal jurisdiction in employment discrimination claims because deferral to state agencies is mandatory under the Act.

8. 536 U.S. 101, 122 S.Ct. 2061, 153 L.Ed.2d 106 (2002).

9. 456 U.S. 461, 102 S.Ct. 1883, 72 L.Ed.2d 262 (1982).

10. 478 U.S. 788, 106 S.Ct. 3220, 92 L.Ed.2d 635 (1986).

In general, the procedural philosophy with respect to administrative agencies in the field of employment discrimination is to maximize chances for early resolution without diminishing the variety of fora available to the complainant. On the one hand, the statute requires administrative exhaustion. On the other, the Court has noted that the legislative history of Title VII "manifests a congressional intent to allow an individual to pursue independently his rights under both Title VII and other applicable state and federal statutes."

Arbitration

The same philosophy of encouraging early resolution without diminishing choices for the complainant governs the Court's current attitude toward the arbitration of employment discrimination claims. The Court held in *Gilmer v. Interstate/Johnson Lane Corp.*[11] that an employee could not avoid a contractual obligation to arbitrate simply by asserting that the dispute is a violation of federal discrimination law. Although there is a statutory scheme and administrative structure to process discrimination claims, the obligation to arbitrate remained. This employee's arbitration agreement was in his registration with the New York Stock Exchange rather than directly with his employer, thus avoiding the exemption for "contracts of employment" in section 1 of the Federal Arbitration Act.

Long before *Gilmer*, the Court held in Alexander v. Gardner-Denver Co., *Alexander v. Gardner–Denver Co.*,[12] that an arbitrator's determination does not have a preclusive effect on subsequent Title VII litigation. As with administrative determinations, the proceedings are de novo. The Court extended this principle in *McDonald v. West Branch*[13] to hold that the findings of arbitrators also do not have a binding effect in a subsequent suit under 42 U.S.C.A. § 1983.

In *Circuit City Stores, Inc. v. Adams*,[14] the Supreme Court considered whether a preemployment arbitration agreement could be enforced pursuant to the Federal Arbitration Act (FAA). In this case, a provision in the employer's application for work, signed by all applicants, required all employment disputes to be settled by arbitration. After being employed for two years, the employee filed a state-law employment discrimination claim as well as related tort claims. The employer then sued in federal court to enjoin the state lawsuit and to compel arbitration pursuant to the FAA. A provision in the FAA exempts from its coverage "contracts of employment of seamen, railroad employees, or any other class of workers engaged in foreign or interstate commerce."[15] The Ninth Circuit held that this provision exempts all employment contracts of individuals engaged in interstate commerce. The Supreme Court, five-to-

11. 500 U.S. 20, 111 S.Ct. 1647, 114 L.Ed.2d 26 (1991).

12. 415 U.S. 36, 48, 94 S.Ct. 1011, 1019, 39 L.Ed.2d 147 (1974).

13. 466 U.S. 284, 765 n.11, 104 S.Ct. 1799, 80 L.Ed.2d 302 (1984).

14. 532 U.S. 105, 121 S.Ct. 1302, 149 L.Ed.2d 234 (2001). See also Charles B. Craver, *The Use of Non–Judicial Procedures to Resolve Employment Discrimination Claims,* 11 Kan.J.L. & Pub. Pol'y 141 (2001).

15. 9 U.S.C.A. § 1 (2000).

four, reversed. According to the majority, if all employees engaged in interstate commerce were exempt, there would be no point in Congress specifically mentioning seamen and railroad employees. Therefore, the "residual phrase" of all other workers engaged in foreign or interstate commerce must be interpreted as applying only to the subjects of the specifically enumerated categories. Thus, the exemption applies only to transportation employees.

These cases have produced a dramatic shift in the resolution of employment discrimination claims beginning in the 1990s. In a 2000 case,[16] the Supreme Court cited the estimate by the American Arbitration Association that by 1997 more than 3.5 million employees were covered by private arbitration agreements that precluded the resolution of their claims in court. Commentary on the effect of this change has been large and most scholars have disapproved of the trend as undermining the goals of federal antidiscrimination law.[17]

§ 2.30 Judicial Remedies

The remedial provisions of Title VII and the ADEA reflect congressional intent that employment discrimination disputes should not be handled like other civil disputes. On the one hand, the statutes encourage a victim of employment discrimination to pursue claims like a "private attorney general" to vindicate the public interest in eradicating discrimination. On the other hand, the statutes provide limited judicial remedies. The limitations were particularly narrow for Title VII when it was first enacted, but have since been expanded under the Civil Rights Act of 1991.

Remedial Evolution of Title VII

When Title VII was enacted as part of the Civil Rights Act of 1964, Congress severely limited its remedies compared with state tort claims. The difference is that the Act also provided for attorney's fees for prevailing parties, to encourage individual vindication of rights. In addition to these fees, however, plaintiffs could not get monetary relief because the Act provided only equitable remedies like reinstatement and back pay. The Civil Rights Act of 1991 later included compensatory and punitive damages for intentional discrimination under Title VII, but with statutory caps. Thus, a prevailing Title VII plaintiff still receives less potential recovery than a prevailing plaintiff with a state tort claim

16. EEOC v. Waffle House, Inc., 534 U.S. 279, 122 S.Ct. 754, 151 L.Ed.2d 755 (2002).

17. See Geraldine Szott Moohr, *Arbitration and the Goals of Employment Discrimination Law*, 56 Wash. & Lee L.Rev. 395 (1999); Lewis L. Maltby, *Private Justice: Employment Arbitration and Civil Rights*, 30 Colum. Hum.Rts.L.Rev. 29 (1998); Jean R. Sternlight, *Panacea or Corporate Tool? Debunking the Supreme Court's Preference* *for Binding Arbitration*, 74 Wash.U.L.Q. 637 (1996); Katherine Van Wezel Stone, *Mandatory Arbitration of Individual Employment Rights: The Yellow Dog Contract of the 1990s*, 73 Denv. U.L.Rev. 1017 (1996). But see David Sherwyn et al., *In Defense of Mandatory Arbitration of Employment Disputes: Saving the Baby, Tossing Out the Bath Water, and Constructing a New Sink in the Process*, 2 U.Pa.J.Lab. & Empl.L. 73 (1999).

arising from the same conduct or a prevailing plaintiff under 42 U.S.C.A. § 1981 or 42 U.S.C.A. § 1983.

Jury Trials

Although the ADEA has had jury trials since its enactment, there were no jury trials under Title VII until the Civil Rights Act of 1991. Although jury trials are relatively new to Title VII, there is controlling precedent. Federal courts are governed by the Seventh Amendment right to trial by jury in civil actions. Under that jurisprudence there is no right to a jury trial when a plaintiff seeks only equitable relief, such as reinstatement and back pay.[1] Conversely, when a plaintiff seeks only legal remedies, such as compensatory and punitive damages, either party may demand a jury trial.[2] When a plaintiff's claim is a mixed one seeking both legal and equitable remedies, either party may demand a jury trial for resolution of the legal issues. The factual issues common to both claims are tried to a jury first. The judge may then resolve the equitable claims in a manner not inconsistent with the jury determination. Thus, for example, in a sexual harassment claim, the plaintiff may seek compensatory damages and reinstatement. The jury hears the evidence, resolves any factual disputes, decides whether to award damages and, if so, determines the amount. The judge then determines whether reinstatement is an appropriate remedy, but only in a manner consistent with the jury verdict.

§ 2.31 Judicial Remedies—Compensatory and Punitive Damages

The 1991 Act makes a limited provision for both compensatory and punitive damages for violations of Title VII. Congress did not make this new provision as an amendment to Title VII, but as an amendment to 42 U.S.C.A. § 1981 with specific reference to Title VII. It provides that compensatory damages are available in actions brought under Title VII where the respondent has engaged in intentional discrimination. It further provides for punitive damages against non-governmental defendants under Title VII "if the complaining party demonstrates that the respondent engaged in a discriminatory practice or discriminatory practices with malice or with reckless indifference to the federally protected rights of an aggrieved individual."[1] These remedies are considered respectively below.

Compensatory Damages for "Intentional" Discrimination

The Civil Rights Act of 1991 provides that compensatory damages are available in actions brought under Title VII where the respondent has engaged in intentional discrimination. The meaning of "intentional discrimination" is not defined, except that the term is followed by a

§ 2.30

1. See Beacon Theatres, Inc. v. Westover, 359 U.S. 500, 79 S.Ct. 948, 3 L.Ed.2d 988 (1959).

2. Curtis v. Loether, 415 U.S. 189, 94 S.Ct. 1005, 39 L.Ed.2d 260 (1974).

§ 2.31

1. 42 U.S.C.A. § 1981A.

parenthetical explanation: "(not an employment practice that is unlawful because of its disparate impact)."

The 1991 Act enumerates types of compensatory damages that may be awarded: future pecuniary losses, emotional pain, suffering, inconvenience, mental anguish, loss of enjoyment of life, and other nonpecuniary loss. Courts have found guidance on entitlement and measurement of compensatory damages of these types from general damage law because compensatory damages have historically been permissible to compensate civil rights victims for humiliation, mental suffering, and other physical and mental injuries resulting from the stress of the experience. Courts have also found guidance through the case law involving compensatory damages in those employment discrimination cases that have been brought under 42 U.S.C.A. § 1981 for three decades.

Punitive Damages

The 1991 Act provides for punitive damages under Title VII "if the complaining party demonstrates that the respondent engaged in a discriminatory practice or discriminatory practices with malice or with reckless indifference to the federally protected rights of an aggrieved individual." This provision is limited to respondents "other than a government, government agency or political subdivision."[2]

The substantive requirement for punitive damages under Title VII reflects the standard that has been used for the recovery of punitive damages in employment discrimination cases brought under 42 U.S.C.A. § 1981. The terms "malice" and "reckless indifference" to the plaintiff's rights have governed entitlement. Plaintiffs never recover punitive damages as a matter of right; they are always discretionary with the trier of fact.

The Supreme Court clarified the requirements for punitive damages under the Civil Rights Act of 1991 in *Kolstad v. American Dental Association*.[3] The issue in that case was whether a plaintiff could get an instruction for the jury on punitive damages in the absence of evidence beyond that necessary to establish intentional discrimination. The D.C. Circuit had held that for punitive damages a plaintiff must have evidence of egregious behavior beyond the level of intentional conduct necessary to establish the disparate treatment claim. The dissenting opinion focused upon the statutory language permitting punitive damages when the defendant acted with reckless indifference to federally protected rights and concluded that it is sufficient for a plaintiff to show that the employer was aware that the conduct violated antidiscrimination law. The majority claimed that the position of the dissenting judges failed to create a distinction between the basis for liability and the basis for punitive damages and that such a two-tier system is an established part of punitive damages jurisprudence.

2. 42 U.S.C.A. § 1981A.

3. 527 U.S. 526, 119 S.Ct. 2118, 144 L.Ed.2d 494 (1999).

The Supreme Court agreed with parts of each side of this issue as it was framed by the circuit court. The Court first agreed with the majority opinion in the circuit court case and said that punitive damages are authorized in only a subset of intentional discrimination cases. It explained that they are permissible in those cases in which the employer acts with malice or reckless indifference to the plaintiff's federally protected rights. This inquiry is centered around the subjective knowledge or intent of the employer. The Court then said that this means that an employer must at least discriminate in the face of a "perceived risk" that its actions will violate federal law.

Damage Caps

The 1991 Act specifies some express limitations on the recovery of compensatory damages and punitive damages under Title VII. For compensatory damages, in addition to the substantive requirement that the conduct be intentional, the Act provides that the complaining party must not be able to recover under section 1977 of the Revised Statutes, known as 42 U.S.C.A. § 1981.[4] Congress added this limitation to avoid the potential for double recovery for those individuals who could use both statutes in a claim of employment discrimination. Second, the recovery for compensatory damages cannot include any recovery for back pay or other relief already available under Title VII. The final limitation for both compensatory and punitive damages is the monetary ceiling that the Act imposes. There is a cap of $50,000 for respondents (employers, unions, and employment agencies) with more than fourteen and fewer than 101 employees in each of twenty or more calendar weeks in the current or preceding calendar year. These latter terms mirror the definitional language used for the coverage of the Act, and their interpretation should be consistent with prior case law. The ceiling on recovery for defendants with more than 100 but fewer than 201 similarly defined employees is $100,000. The next bracket is 200 to 501, with a top of $200,000. Finally, a defendant with more than 500 employees may be liable for $300,000.

Pecuniary losses in the form of back pay are not subject to the cap. The Act specifically excludes from compensatory damages "backpay, interest on backpay, or any other type of relief authorized under section 706(g) of the Civil Rights Act of 1964." The effect of this exclusion is twofold: (1) it keeps backpay and interest on it independent of the dollar ceiling; and (2) it keeps back pay separate from the other forms of equitable relief and thus prevents the future characterization of back pay as damages subject to jury trial.

§ 2.32 Judicial Remedies—Reinstatement and Back Pay

Reinstatement and back pay were among the original remedies provided for violations of Title VII as it was enacted in the Civil Rights Act of 1964. Section 706(g) provided that a court may enjoin unlawful employment practices and may order "such affirmative action as may be

4. 42 U.S.C.A. § 1981A.

appropriate, which may include, but is not limited to, reinstatement or hiring of employees, with or without back pay * * *.''[1]

Remedies under the ADEA include "such legal or equitable relief as may be appropriate to effectuate the purposes" of the Act.[2] Like Title VII, such injunctions may include reinstatement and other affirmative orders. Back pay and front pay may also be granted, on the same principles as under Title VII. Additional discussion of the unique history of remedies under the ADEA appears later in this chapter.

Reinstatement

The statutory provision for reinstatement orders was contrary to the common law rule that equity would not force the acceptance of unwanted services. The basis for the common law avoidance of such orders was a fear that a court-ordered working relationship would require constant court supervision and would not result in a productive endeavor. In the employment discrimination context, the statutory authority for reinstatement orders has prevailed over the common law concerns. Because the Act does not apply to very small employers, there is less concern that a reinstatement order will produce an intolerable situation for the parties.

A court nonetheless may deny a reinstatement order on the grounds that the antagonism of the parties would preclude an effective working relationship. The antagonism must be more than the feelings of hostility that are normally generated in a lawsuit, however. A court may deny the order if the position requires an unusually close working relationship, or confidential relationship, between the antagonistic parties.

Back Pay

Back pay is an appropriate equitable remedy, with or without hiring or reinstatement, for violations of Title VII. The Supreme Court held in *Albemarle Paper Co. v. Moody*[3] that back pay should be awarded as a matter of course upon a finding of employment discrimination. The trial court had denied back pay because the employer had not acted in bad faith. This approach is inconsistent with the goal of the Act to make whole the victims of discrimination, the Court held. Instead, a court should deny back pay awards only upon a showing of why an award would be inconsistent with equitable principles.

When a district court declines to award back pay, it is incumbent upon the court to "carefully articulate its reasons." The Court suggested, but did not hold, that one such reason for denial of back pay might be inconsistency in pleading that prejudiced the defendant. In general, courts should fashion "the most complete relief possible" under the Act.[4]

The Supreme Court found sufficient reason to deny back pay relief in a case concerning contributions to a pension plan. The employer

§ 2.32

1. 42 U.S.C.A. § 2000e–5(g).

2. 29 U.S.C.A. § 633(a), (c).

3. 422 U.S. 405, 95 S.Ct. 2362, 45 L.Ed.2d 280 (1975).

4. 422 U.S. at 422, 95 S.Ct. at 2373.

discriminated on the basis of gender by requiring women employees to pay more into the retirement plan than men because, the employer had reasoned, the plan offered equal payout benefits and women as a group live longer than men as a group. In this case, *Los Angeles Department of Water & Power v. Manhart*,[5] the Court found unlawful the employment practice, but reversed the district court's back pay order. Reaffirming the *Albemarle* test that back pay should ordinarily be granted, the Court found that this case met the exception. "The *Albemarle* presumption in favor of retroactive liability can seldom be overcome," the Court observed, "but it does not make meaningless the district court's duty to determine that such relief is appropriate."[6]

§ 2.33 Judicial Remedies—Seniority and Bona Fide Seniority Systems

Discrimination in seniority systems and retroactive seniority relief are two related but distinctly different topics involving the role of seniority in federal antidiscrimination law. Congress accorded seniority rights special treatment in both Title VII[1] and the ADEA.[2] These two topics are included together in this section for the purpose of comparing and contrasting the related issues.

Retroactive Seniority Relief

Retroactive seniority is an appropriate remedy for unlawful employment practices under federal antidiscrimination law. For an employee whose employment was delayed or interrupted for unlawful reasons, reinstatement alone provides incomplete relief. Only the addition of back pay and lost seniority can put the individual in as good a position as he or she would have occupied in the absence of discrimination. For example, if an employer unlawfully lays off employees when they become pregnant in the erroneous belief that there was a bona fide occupational qualification, then after the plaintiffs prevail on the claim their relief would be incomplete without back pay for the time they were wrongfully laid off and retroactive seniority for the time they could not work.

As with back pay, victims of discrimination ought ordinarily to receive retroactive seniority with a hiring or reinstatement order. The Supreme Court explained this principle in *Franks v. Bowman Transportation, Inc.*[3]

> No less than with the denial of the remedy of back pay, the denial of seniority relief to victims of racial illegal discrimination in hiring is permissible "only for reasons which, if applied generally, would not frustrate the central statutory purposes of eradicating discrimina-

5. 435 U.S. 702, 98 S.Ct. 1370, 55 L.Ed.2d 657 (1978).

6. 98 S.Ct. at 1381.

§ 2.33

1. 42 U.S.C.A. § 2000e–2(h).

2. 29 U.S.C.A. § 623(f)(2).

3. 424 U.S. 747, 96 S.Ct. 1251, 47 L.Ed.2d 444 (1976).

tion throughout the economy and making persons whole for injuries suffered through past discrimination."[4]

Remedial seniority under *Franks* allows the victim of discrimination to receive seniority credit from the date of the discriminatory act. Although this approach affects the rights of innocent incumbent employees, the Court found more significant the interests of the victims of discrimination to receive complete relief.

Perpetuating Past Discrimination Through Seniority Systems

One way in which a seniority system may be discriminatory is when the system perpetuates the effects of past discrimination. Consider an employer that previously had a discriminatory leave policy that unlawfully disadvantaged women on disability for childbirth. Employees who were wronged by this policy in the past argue that even though the limitations period has passed for the previous wrong, its effects are still felt through the perpetuation of the disadvantage in the seniority system. As this section explores, the employer will be protected if the plan was adopted at a time before it violated federal law and if it is part of a bona fide seniority plan. It will not be protected if the genesis of the plan was discriminatory or if it resurrects the discriminatory effects in the present through a new plan that builds on the old one, such as a retirement incentive plan built on the prior service credit.

First, a seniority system that perpetuates the effects of past discrimination is not subject to challenge under a disparate impact theory because Title VII contains a special proviso in section 703(h): "Notwithstanding any other provision of this title, it shall not be an unlawful employment practice for an employer to apply different standards of compensation, or different terms, conditions, or privileges of employment pursuant to a bona fide seniority or merit system * * *."[5] This provision insulates bona fide seniority systems from attack on the grounds that pre-Act discrimination is perpetuated by the system after the Act.

The Court subsequently expanded the protection of the proviso for post-Act discrimination. In *United Air Lines v. Evans*,[6] the Court held that the perpetuation of discrimination through the effect of the seniority system is not itself grounds for an unlawful employment practice. If the statute of limitations has otherwise expired, the perpetuation of the effects of the discrimination through the seniority system does not make a continuing violation that the victim can still challenge.

Limitations on the Exemption of Discriminatory Seniority Systems

The question that remains open is what factors would remove a system from the protection of the proviso. Title VII refers to "a bona fide seniority system." The burden is on the plaintiff to challenge whether a system falls within the protection of this provision, because it does not define a true defense. Rather, the Supreme Court has explained, it

---

4. 96 S.Ct. at 1267 (citation omitted).

5. 42 U.S.C.A. § 2000e–2(h).

6. 431 U.S. 553, 97 S.Ct. 1885, 52 L.Ed.2d 571 (1977).

simply delineates which employment practices are illegal and which are not.[7] Therefore, the defendant need only demonstrate that a challenged practice was done pursuant to a seniority system, and the burden remains with the plaintiff to prove the defendant's improper motivation in the adoption or use of the system. The determination of the motivation behind the adoption or use of a system is one of fact which will not be disturbed on appeal unless it is clearly erroneous.

Definition of "Seniority System"

In order to qualify as a "bona fide seniority system" under section 703(h) it is necessary for the system to be one of "seniority." The Supreme Court had occasion to consider the features of a seniority system in *California Brewers Association v. Bryant*.[8] The employer had a system for layoffs and recall which gave preference to employees who had worked over forty-five weeks in one classification in one calendar year. These employees were considered "permanent" and they were given preference over all "temporary" employees, regardless of the total amount of time individuals in this second group had worked for the employer.

The plaintiff class in *California Brewers* challenged these rules on the grounds that minorities disproportionately failed to satisfy the forty-five week minimum to become permanent employees. The Supreme Court held that the forty-five week requirement was part of a bona fide seniority system. The principal feature of every seniority system is that preferential treatment is awarded on the basis of some measure of time in employment, the Court reasoned. The definition of a seniority system, however, is not limited to rewarding the length of employment with the defendant. The system can include ancillary rules such as the forty-five week rule. Seniority systems need rules to "delineate how and when the seniority time clock begins ticking," as well as rules that "define which passages of time will 'count' toward the accrual of seniority and which will not." The Court further noted that seniority systems must contain rules that specify which working conditions will be governed or influenced by seniority. Therefore, "[r]ules that serve these necessary purposes do not fall outside § 703(h) simply because they do not, in and of themselves, operate on the basis of some factor involving the passage of time."[9]

§ 2.34   Judicial Remedies—Affirmative Action and Other Affirmative Orders

Among the remedies specifically provided in section 706(g) of Title VII is "such affirmative action as may be appropriate."[1] The court sitting in equity has the discretion to require the employer to undertake

---

7. Lorance v. A T & T Technologies, Inc., 490 U.S. 900, 109 S.Ct. 2261, 104 L.Ed.2d 961 (1989).

8. 444 U.S. 598, 100 S.Ct. 814, 63 L.Ed.2d 55 (1980).

9. 100 S.Ct. at 820–21.

§ 2.34

1. 42 U.S.C.A. § 2000e–5(g).

affirmative action in hiring and promotion to remedy past discrimination. This provision gives the court further power to order other appropriate relief, such as requiring an employer to educate its personnel about the requirements of the Act.

Judicially-ordered affirmative action is distinguishable from voluntary affirmative action. When an employer undertakes voluntary affirmative action, there is no admission of past discrimination. Such action is simply a response to the underutilization of minorities or women in a job category without regard to why the underrepresentation exists. In contrast, court-ordered affirmative action is a judicial remedy that occurs after the plaintiff has prevailed in a claim of employment discrimination. The purpose of the court-ordered affirmative action is to correct the continuing effects of past discrimination by this particular defendant rather than the effects of generalized societal discrimination.

Whereas voluntary affirmative action by private employers must comply with the standards set by the Supreme Court in *United Steelworkers of America v. Weber*,[2] court-ordered affirmative action is subject to the constraints of the Constitution. As with public employers that wish to pursue a voluntary affirmative action plan, court-ordered affirmative action involves governmental classifications on the basis of race and ethnicity that are "inherently suspect and thus call for the most exacting judicial examination."[3]

The Supreme Court confirmed in a 1986 plurality opinion that section 706(g) allows courts under appropriate circumstances to adopt numerical hiring ratios in order to reach racial, ethnic, or gender goals. *Local 28, Sheet Metal Workers v. EEOC*[4] held that courts may order affirmative action programs to remedy "persistent or egregious discrimination" when it is necessary "to dissipate the lingering effects of pervasive discrimination."[5] It is not necessary that the beneficiaries of such orders be themselves identifiable victims of prior discrimination.

The Supreme Court affirmed this principle in its 1995 affirmative action case, *Adarand Constructors, Inc. v. Pena*.[6] This case concerned affirmative action for federal contractors and applied the principle of strict scrutiny for federal programs, which the Court had previously done for state and local programs.[7] *Adarand Contractors* confirmed, however, that federal courts may order affirmative action to remedy an employer's "pervasive, systematic, and obstinate discriminatory conduct."[8]

2. 443 U.S. 193, 99 S.Ct. 2721, 61 L.Ed.2d 480 (1979).

3. Wygant v. Jackson Bd. of Educ., 476 U.S. 267, 273, 106 S.Ct. 1842, 1846, 90 L.Ed.2d 260 (1986).

4. 478 U.S. 421, 106 S.Ct. 3019, 92 L.Ed.2d 344 (1986).

5. 478 U.S. at 446, 106 S.Ct. at 3034.

6. 515 U.S. 200, 115 S.Ct. 2097, 132 L.Ed.2d 158 (1995).

7. City of Richmond v. J.A. Croson Co., 488 U.S. 469, 109 S.Ct. 706, 102 L.Ed.2d 854 (1989).

8. 515 U.S. at 2117.

§ 2.35 Judicial Remedies—Attorneys' Fees and Costs

An important feature of the remedial provisions of Title VII and the ADEA is the availability of attorney's fees. Section 706(k) of Title VII provides:

> In any action or proceeding under this title the court, in its discretion, may allow the prevailing party, other than the Commission or the United States, a reasonable attorney's fee (including expert fees) as part of costs and the Commission and the United States shall be liable for costs the same as a private person.[1]

The availability of such fees encourages attorneys to take employment discrimination cases even in the absence of a large monetary recovery by the plaintiff. Unlike most civil litigation where the costs are funded through private contingency contracts between the plaintiffs and their attorneys, employment discrimination litigation can proceed without concern about the source of funds for fees if the plaintiff prevails. This difference enables individuals to act as "private attorneys general" to vindicate the national interest is eradicating discrimination in the workplace.

Fees to "Prevailing Party"

Title VII and the ADEA provide for attorneys' fees to "prevailing parties." When it is the plaintiff who is the prevailing party, the award of fees is supported by the statutory embodiment of the private attorney general theory. When it is the defendant who is the prevailing party, the same rationale does not support the recovery of fees. The question before the Supreme Court in *Christiansburg Garment Co. v. EEOC*[2] was how to interpret the statutory provision for fees to "prevailing parties" when the rationale for such recovery was much stronger for prevailing plaintiffs than for prevailing defendants.

In *Christiansburg Garment* the Court rejected the defendant's argument that prevailing defendants should recover attorneys' fees on the same basis as prevailing plaintiffs. The Court held that although the statute simply uses the word "parties," Congress intended plaintiffs to vindicate the public interest as private attorneys general, and the same rationale does not apply to defendants. Nonetheless, there are equitable considerations on the side of prevailing defendants. The Court observed that "many defendants in Title VII claims are small-and moderate-size employers for whom the expense of defending even a frivolous claim may become a strong disincentive to the exercise of their legal rights."[3]

The Court equally rejected the plaintiff's claim that defendants should recover attorneys' fees only when the plaintiff has litigated in bad faith. The Court held that defendants can recover attorneys' fees in a

§ 2.35

1. 42 U.S.C.A. § 2000e–5(k). Under the ADEA, section 7(b), 29 U.S.C.A. § 626(b), incorporates by reference 29 U.S.C. § 216(b) in the Fair Labor Standards Act providing for attorney's fees.

2. 434 U.S. 412, 98 S.Ct. 694, 54 L.Ed.2d 648 (1978).

3. 434 U.S. at 422 n. 20, 98 S.Ct. at 701 n. 20.

Title VII case "upon a finding that the plaintiff's action was frivolous, unreasonable, or without foundation, even though not brought in subjective bad faith."[4]

The Eleventh Circuit has listed factors for assessing whether a claim is frivolous for purposes of awarding attorneys' fees to a prevailing employer. They are: (1) whether the plaintiff established a prima facie case; (2) whether the defendant offered to settle; and (3) whether the trial court dismissed the case prior to trial or held a full-blown trial on the merits.[5] An Alabama court applied these factors with approval in a case where fees were awarded against a frivolous claim despite the fact that two Justices on the Alabama Supreme Court had voted to grant certiorari to the dismissal of the claim. The court rejected the contention that these votes reflected upon the merits of the claim because the vote on a petition to the Supreme Court has no precedential value.[6]

In contrast, an award of attorneys' fees to a prevailing defendant was reversed in a case where the plaintiff's evidence was sufficiently credible to withstand a motion to dismiss after the presentation of the plaintiff's case.[7] The trial court had found it necessary to hear evidence from both sides and took the matter under consideration for several weeks. These facts suggested that the plaintiff's claim was not frivolous.

Calculation of Attorney's Fees

The ordinary procedure for the computation of attorneys' fees is the calculation of the lodestar. The lodestar is the amount representing the multiplication of the number of hours spent on the case times the hourly rate. In order to determine this amount, the trial court judge must first determine how many of the billable hours were reasonably spent on the portion or portions of the case on which the attorney prevailed. Next the trial judge must determine a reasonable hourly rate for someone of the attorney's experience. Once calculated, the lodestar is the presumptively reasonable fee, although the trial judge may adjust it upward or downward in circumstances where the lodestar may not actually represent a reasonable fee. Such adjustment should be rare because the lodestar already accounts for many factors, such as the difficulty of establishing the claim.

Relevant to the calculation of the lodestar is any contingency fee arrangement that the parties may have made. The Supreme Court held in *Blanchard v. Bergeron*[8] that the court may consider the terms of a contingency arrangement in setting the statutory fee, but that the amount recoverable under the private agreement does not serve as a ceiling for the court-awarded fee. The Court was interpreting the Civil Rights Attorney's Fee Awards Act[9] in that case, but the rationale would

---

4. 434 U.S. at 421, 98 S.Ct. at 700.

5. Sullivan v. School Bd. of Pinellas County, 773 F.2d 1182 (11th Cir.1985).

6. Shepherd v. Summit Mgmt., 794 So.2d 1110 (Ala.Civ.App.2000).

7. Glymph v. Spartanburg Gen. Hosp., 783 F.2d 476 (4th Cir.1986).

8. 489 U.S. 87, 109 S.Ct. 939, 103 L.Ed.2d 67 (1989).

9. 42 U.S.C.A. § 1988.

apply equally to other civil rights statutes. The Court reasoned that the statute contemplates reasonable compensation in order to ensure the availability of competent counsel for civil rights plaintiffs. If the plaintiff obtained counsel for less than a reasonable fee, the defendant should not be the beneficiary.

The calculation of the reasonable number of hours spent must focus not only on the extent to which the attorney prevailed in the case, but also on which hours were "duplicative, unproductive, excessive, or otherwise unnecessary."[10] When setting the reasonable hourly rate, a trial judge may appropriately consider the prevailing rate for comparably qualified attorneys in the community. Relevant to the inquiry is the exceptional quality of the performance and the results.

§ 2.36 Judicial Remedies—Court Enforcement of Consent Decrees

When the parties voluntarily settle a class-based employment discrimination claim, the settlement is reviewed and adopted by the trial court as a consent decree. Typically, the settlement includes an express statement that the defendant has not violated the law, but agrees voluntarily to take measures for the benefit of the class. The parties to a consent decree are bound by the agreement once it has been approved by the court, although it may be modified by changes in the law or other conditions.[1]

Consent decrees often include an affirmative action component. Because affirmative action plans are subject to different requirements if they are voluntary than if they are a judicial remedy, the question is the status of a court-approved plan as a component of a consent decree. The Constitution governs orders imposed judicially, so the standard for affirmative action plans as part of a judicial remedy is more demanding than the one imposed by Title VII on private plans. The Supreme Court addressed that question in *International Association of Firefighters Local 93 v. City of Cleveland*[2] and held that an affirmative action plan adopted pursuant to a settlement was a "voluntary" plan, despite the judicial oversight.

Although consent decrees need not meet the standard of judicial remedies, they must meet the standards of *United Steelworkers of America v. Weber*[3] in order not to violate Title VII. Consistent with the *Weber* standards, a police department does not need to admit past

---

10. Grendel's Den, Inc. v. Larkin, 749 F.2d 945, 950 (1st Cir.1984), citing Hensley v. Eckerhart, 461 U.S. 424, 103 S.Ct. 1933, 76 L.Ed.2d 40 (1983).

§ 2.36

1. Rufo v. Inmates of Suffolk County Jail, 502 U.S. 367, 112 S.Ct. 748, 116 L.Ed.2d 867 (1992).

2. 478 U.S. 501, 106 S.Ct. 3063, 92 L.Ed.2d 405 (1986).

3. 443 U.S. 193, 99 S.Ct. 2721, 61 L.Ed.2d 480 (1979). See § 2.19.

discrimination in order to have a valid consent decree that requires an increase in the number of black officers promoted to sergeant.[4]

§ 2.37 Religious Discrimination and Accommodation of Religion

Title VII prohibits discrimination on the basis of religion, but it provides an exemption for religious institutions that discriminate on the basis of religious affiliation. Religious discrimination can take two forms. One form is discrimination based on religious faith or affiliation; the Act prohibits discrimination for or against persons because they belong to a certain religious group. The other form of religious discrimination is a failure to make a reasonable accommodation to an employee's religious observances and practices.

The subsections below also examine the exemption for religious employers, the exemption for religious schools, religion as a bona fide occupational qualification, and the definition of religion and religious practices. Title VII also prohibits harassment on the basis of religion, with the same legal standards as other claims of harassment based on a protected dimension.

Discrimination on the Basis of Religious Beliefs

Discrimination for or against a person because of religious beliefs is a prohibited basis for providing employment opportunities. The plaintiff may establish a case with direct evidence of discriminatory animus or by the indirect evidence method of disparate treatment based on *McDonnell Douglas Corp. v. Green* approach.[1] The only difference is that a case of religious discrimination requires proof that the employer was on notice of the plaintiff's religious beliefs.

This aspect of religious beliefs claims is different from claims based on race, gender, and national origin because the employer's awareness of the protected dimension is assumed in those cases. If it happens that the employer was unaware of the plaintiff's racial, ethnic, or gender identity, that fact can rebut the inference of intent established by the plaintiff's prima facie case. Notably, the plaintiff does not have the burden of pleading awareness of the protected dimension in order to establish intent in race, national origin, and gender cases.

In contrast, plaintiffs must prove awareness of their religious beliefs in order to establish the intent of the employer to discriminate against them. Judge Posner explained this aspect of the claim in *Reed v. Great Lakes Cos.*[2] In that case the plaintiff was a hotel employee had embarrassed his supervisor when he walked out of a meeting with the Gideons. The purpose of the meeting had been to receive free bibles from the Gideons for distribution in the hotel rooms. The plaintiff had been

4. Association of Afro–American Police v. Boston Police Dep't , 780 F.2d 5 (1st Cir. 1985); cert. denied, 478 U.S. 1020, 106 S.Ct. 3334, 92 L.Ed.2d 740 (1986).

§ 2.37

1. 411 U.S. 792, 93 S.Ct. 1817, 36 L.Ed.2d 668 (1973). See §§ 2.8–2.10.

2. 330 F.3d 931 (7th Cir.2003).

offended when the Gideons unexpectedly started to pray during the meeting. He was later fired for insubordination when he argued with his supervisor about his right to walk out of a religious meeting. The Seventh Circuit noted that his claim of religious discrimination must begin with proof that the employer was aware of his religion. In this case, the plaintiff refused to reveal his beliefs about divinity, even in his deposition. Noting that even atheism is a protected "religious" belief because it takes a position about divinity, the opinion concludes that the plaintiff could not have been a victim of discrimination about his beliefs when the employer (and even the court) does not know what they are. Indeed, the plaintiff had refused even to deny that he was a Gideon.

After the element of notice is satisfied, the other evidentiary requirements are the same. The plaintiff may establish discrimination through direct evidence or circumstantial evidence under the *McDonnell Douglas* approach. An example of direct evidence is *Campos v. City of Blue Springs*.[3] In that case the plaintiff alleged that she was forced to resign because she was not Christian. The plaintiff was hired as a crisis counselor for the city's Youth Outreach Unit. She alleged that she got along well with her co-workers until the day that she revealed that she practiced aspects of Native American spirituality rather than Christianity. She introduced evidence that she was taken off counseling assignments because she refused to use Christian scripture in them. There was also evidence that her supervisor attempted to interfere with the plaintiff's continued employment by impeding her certification because the supervisor wanted a Christian in the position. Relevant statements included that she "needed to find a good Christian boyfriend to teach her to be submissive."

An example of a case claiming religious discrimination under the *McDonnell Douglas* model is *Peterson v. Hewlett–Packard Co.*[4] In that case the plaintiff alleged discrimination against his religious beliefs when his employer insisted that he remove anti-homosexuality scriptures hung on the walls of his cubicle. The plaintiff had written the scriptures in response to company posters that were designed to foster tolerance of diversity. The scriptures were in large typeface that could be read by individuals passing in the hallway outside his cubicle. The plaintiff described himself as a "devout Christian" who believed that homosexuality violates biblical commandments. He further explained that he intended his scriptures to be hurtful to homosexual co-workers because they needed to repent and be saved. After attempts to have the plaintiff comply with company policy, he was fired for continuing to violate the policy against harassment.

The company's policy favoring diversity and prohibiting harassment was broader than required by federal law because it encompassed homosexuality. The court did not accept the plaintiff's theory that the policy was discriminatory against his religious beliefs. He was not required to

3. 289 F.3d 546 (8th Cir.2002).   **4.** 358 F.3d 599 (9th Cir.2004).

change his beliefs but only to avoid offensive behavior directed toward co-workers. The plaintiff had no evidence that the company had acted inconsistently in this regard and thus the company policy and its application were not pretextual.

Discrimination on the Basis of Religious Practices: Reasonable Accommodation

Congress clarified the meaning of discrimination on the basis of religion in its 1972 amendments to Title VII. Section 701(j) now provides that the term religion includes all aspects of religious observance, practice, and belief "unless an employer demonstrates that he is unable to reasonably accommodate to an employee's or prospective employee's religious observance or practice without undue hardship on the conduct of the employer's business."[5] Although this amendment refers only to an "employer's" obligations, the First Circuit in *EEOC v. Union Independente de la Autoridad de Acueductos y Alcantarillados de Puerto Rico*[6] interpreted the obligation to apply also to unions through the general statutory prohibition on unions not to "discriminate." Summary judgment was thus precluded in that case where a Seventh Day Adventist objected to membership in a labor organization on the grounds that his religion prohibited it.

The Supreme Court has taken two occasions to consider the nature and extent of the employer's obligation to accommodate religious practices. The Court considered the relationship between "reasonable accommodation" and "undue hardship" in *Ansonia Board of Education v. Philbrook.*[7] The plaintiff was a high school teacher who converted to the Worldwide Church of God. The tenets of his new church required him to refrain from secular activities on numerous holy days. The union contract with the defendant school district provided teachers with three days off for religious purposes and other days off for personal convenience, not including religious observance. The plaintiff needed more than three days for holy days. The school board allowed him to take unauthorized days leave without pay, but he was dissatisfied with this arrangement. He unsuccessfully sought permission either to use the personal convenience days for religious observance or to pay for the cost of the substitute (approximately $30 at the time) himself rather than lose the full amount of his own day's pay (approximately $130). After the rejection of these alternatives, he sued.

The Supreme Court reversed the holding of the court of appeals in the plaintiff's favor. The court of appeals had held that Title VII requires the employer to accept the alternatives for religious accommodation proposed by the employee unless that accommodation causes undue hardship. That court had therefore remanded the case for a finding whether the teacher's proposed alternatives would produce a hardship for the employer. The Supreme Court found that this approach demand-

5. 42 U.S.C.A. § 2000e(j).

6. 279 F.3d 49 (1st Cir. 2002).

7. 479 U.S. 60, 107 S.Ct. 367, 93 L.Ed.2d 305 (1986).

ed too much of the employer. The statute only demands that the employer make a reasonable accommodation, the Court explained. It is not necessary for the employer to prove that each of the alternatives suggested by the employee would produce an undue hardship. The Court held that "an employer has met its obligation under § 701(j) when it demonstrates that it has offered a reasonable accommodation to the employee."[8] This holding has the effect of collapsing the two statutory elements of "reasonable accommodation" and "undue hardship" into one element, which is a fairly relaxed standard of reasonableness.

The remaining issue in *Ansonia* was whether the school board's policy was a reasonable one. The Court noted that generally permitting an employee to take an unpaid leave for holy days beyond the number permitted in the collective bargaining agreement would be a reasonable accommodation. The Court explained that Congress was motivated by a desire to assure individuals an opportunity to observe religious practices, "but it did not impose a duty on the employer to accommodate at all costs."[9] Nonetheless, if an employer has a policy that permits employees to take a paid leave for all purposes except religious ones, then permission to take unpaid leave for religious observance would not be reasonable. The Court concluded: "Such an arrangement would display a discrimination against religious practices that is the antithesis of reasonableness."[10] Because the policy in *Ansonia* was between these hypothesized extremes, the Court remanded the case for further factual inquiry.

The Court had earlier clarified the limited scope of the requirement of reasonableness in *Trans World Airlines, Inc. v. Hardison*.[11] This case involved a clerk in the supply department of the airline's twenty-four hour maintenance operation. The clerk gained sufficient seniority in one line of progression to be able to select shifts that avoided conflicts with religious observances. When the clerk successfully bid to change building assignment in this operation, he fell to the bottom of the seniority list in accordance with the collective bargaining agreement. With less seniority, he lost the ability to avoid conflict with his Sabbath. The employer expressed willingness to permit the union to alter the seniority rules, but the union was unwilling to do so. The employer eventually fired the clerk for insubordination when he refused to report for work during his assigned shift.

Before the conflict that led to the discharge, the employee had suggested several methods of accommodation that were rejected. Unlike the teacher in *Ansonia*, this employee was willing to take a cut in pay to have time off on the weekend for his religious observances, but the employer established that the work was essential on the weekend. To make this accommodation, the company would have to pay premium wages to someone not ordinarily assigned to that shift. The employee sued both the union and the employer.

8. 107 S.Ct. at 372.
9. Id.
10. Id.

11. 432 U.S. 63, 97 S.Ct. 2264, 53 L.Ed.2d 113 (1977).

The Court found that neither the union nor the employer violated the duty to make a reasonable accommodation of the employee's religious observances. The employer took reasonable steps by holding several meetings with the employee to attempt to find a solution to the problem. Further, the company allowed the plaintiff to observe special religious holidays and authorized the union steward to search for someone who would voluntarily swap shifts for regular Sabbath observances. The company also attempted to find the employee another position that did not pose the weekend conflict. These steps were sufficient. It was not necessary to pay premium wages to another employee to cover for the plaintiff, nor was it necessary to override the collective bargaining agreement and force an unwilling employee with no religious objection to work on the plaintiff's Sabbath.

The Court's minimal interpretation of the statutory obligation to accommodate religious practices avoided the potential constitutional conflict that lower courts had discussed in cases pre-dating *Hardison*. An employee who is forced to work on the Sabbath of another employee is disadvantaged because of the lack of religion. Because the prohibition of discrimination on the basis of religion includes the lack of religion, such an employee also would have a claim of religious discrimination. If the Act required the employer to make the accommodation in this fashion, the constitutionality of the Act under the First Amendment would be very questionable.

The "hardship" exception also applies to general disruption. Seniority rights may completely bar a claim of religious accommodation if disruption of the assignments on the basis of seniority would impose too great a hardship. For example, a truck driver who had religious objections to assignment of "sleeper runs" with female co-workers could not be accommodated without excessive disruption to the seniority assignment system.[12]

Hardship may also be found when the safety of other employees is at issue. In *Bhatia v. Chevron U.S.A., Inc.*,[13] the employee sought accommodation of the requirement of the Sikh religion that males not shave any body hair because his beard interfered with the use of a safety respirator. The respirator was not used often by workers in his job, but it was necessary at times to comply with federal safety requirements. The court found that the employer had taken reasonable steps for accommodation by offering the employee another position that would not require wearing a respirator. The employee objected to the lower-paying alternative and argued that the employer should allow him to keep his old job and simply to exempt him from the occasional assignments that require a respirator. The court held that because the assignments requiring a respirator were more dangerous than other assignments, it was not reasonable to expect coworkers to take the greater risk. The company

12. Virts v. Consolidated Freightways Corp., 285 F.3d 508 (6th Cir. 2002).

13. 734 F.2d 1382 (9th Cir.1984).

had made a good faith effort to accommodate the employee's religious beliefs, but further efforts would be an undue burden.

Exemption for Religious Employers

The exemption of religious institutions is a narrow one. Section 702 provides that the Act does not apply to a "religious corporation" with respect to "employment of individuals of a particular religion to perform work connected with carrying on by such corporation of its activities."[14] It is not a general exemption of religious corporations from the definition of "employers" covered by the Act. Rather, it is an exemption from the prohibition against religious discrimination by religious institutions. Thus, such employers may discriminate for or against individuals on the basis of religion, but they are still subject to the general proscriptions of the Act and may not discriminate on the basis of race, gender, or national origin.

The Supreme Court considered in part the constitutionality of section 702 in *Corporation of the Presiding Bishop of the Church of Jesus Christ of Latter–Day Saints v. Amos.*[15] The plaintiff in *Amos* was a discharged employee of a gymnasium run by the Latter–Day Saints Church. The section 702 exemption applied because the employer was a religious institution, which premised the discharge upon the failure of the employee to remain a member in good standing in the church. The plaintiff argued that the exemption of a church's secular economic enterprises has the effect of "establishing" religion in violation of the First Amendment. The plaintiff's First Amendment argument was that when a religious corporation engages in a secular enterprise, it should be treated as a secular employer subject to the basic prohibitions of the Act and thus prohibited from discriminating on the basis of religion. The plaintiff argued that if section 702 is applied to secular activities of religious organizations so as to permit them to discriminate on the basis of religion, they would then enjoy freedom from a limitation imposed on similarly situated secular enterprises. Such favoritism toward religious corporations thereby "establishes" religion in violation of the First Amendment, the plaintiff concluded. Under the facts of this case, the Supreme Court disagreed and upheld the constitutionality of section 702 as applied in this case.

The Court explained in *Amos* that section 702 is a valid attempt by Congress to avoid the entanglement of courts in the fine distinction between religious and nonprofit secular activities. The Court further reasoned that any other rule would create potential liability for religious organizations because they would have to anticipate how courts later would draw the religious-secular distinction. Such concerns about potential legal liability could interfere with the ability of religious organizations to carry out their religious missions. The Court left open, however, whether section 702 can constitutionally exempt profit-making secular enterprises. When such enterprises are unrelated to religious activity,

---

14. 42 U.S.C.A. § 2000e–1(a).   **15.** 483 U.S. 327, 107 S.Ct. 2862, 97 L.Ed.2d 273 (1987).

their exemption from religious discrimination under section 702 may violate the establishment clause of the First Amendment.

Few cases have had occasion to consider the scope of section 702 with respect to which organizations qualify for its exemption. The provision refers to "a religious corporation, association, educational institution, or society."[16] Because most cases have concerned churches, synagogues, and other organizations closely associated with a religion, there has been little occasion to consider the coverage of this section.

One case that considered the coverage of section 702 was *EEOC v. Townley Engineering & Manufacturing Co.*[17] In this case a manufacturer of mining equipment held mandatory devotional services for its employees. The company was a closely held corporation whose founders and principal owners made a covenant with God to operate the business as a Christian, faith-operated business. They manifested this covenant in ways additional to the devotional meetings, such as printing gospel verses on all commercial documents of the company. The company was not affiliated with any church, however. The court held that the beliefs of the company's owners were not enough to qualify for the section 702 exemption.

Religious Schools Exemption

Section 703(e)(2) of Title VII specifically exempts certain educational institutions from the prohibition on religious discrimination in hiring and employing individuals. The Act provides that it is not unlawful for a school, college, university, or other institution of learning to "hire and employ employees of a particular religion" if such institution is

> in whole or in part, owned, supported, controlled, or managed by a particular religious corporation, association, or society, or if the curriculum of such school, college, university, or other educational institution or institution of learning is directed toward the propagation of a particular religion.[18]

The EEOC has interpreted this section as providing two alternative exemptions. One is for a school "owned, supported, controlled, or managed" by a particular religion. The other is for a school whose curriculum is "directed toward the propagation of a particular religion."[19] There is little case law on the meaning of this provision, probably because few religious schools are run by groups not already exempted as religions under section 702.

One case interpreting solely the application of section 703(e)(2) concerned the Kamehameha School in Hawaii, founded by the estate of Bernice Pauahi Bishop.[20] Her will provided that teachers in the school "shall forever be persons of the Protestant religion." The complainant

16. 42 U.S.C.A. § 2000e–1(a).

17. 859 F.2d 610 (9th Cir.1988), cert. denied, 489 U.S. 1077, 109 S.Ct. 1527, 103 L.Ed.2d 832 (1989).

18. 42 U.S.C.A. § 2000e–2(e)(2).

19. EEOC Dec. No. 75–186 (1975).

20. EEOC v. Kamehameha Schs./Bishop Estate, 990 F.2d 458 (9th Cir.), cert. denied 510 U.S. 963, 114 S.Ct. 439, 126 L.Ed.2d 372 (1993).

applied for a job and the school rejected her because she was not Protestant. Among several grounds for decision, the district court held that the religious and moral curriculum of the school alone would be sufficient to exempt it under section 703(e)(2). The Ninth Circuit reversed and held that the school did not qualify for the religious exemption.

Religion as a Bona Fide Occupational Qualification

Section 703(e) of Title VII provides a bona fide occupational qualification (BFOQ) defense for religion as for gender and national origin. The provision allows employers, labor organizations, and employment agencies otherwise covered by the Act to hire, employ, or classify individuals on the basis of religion in "those certain instances" where religion is a "bona fide occupational qualification reasonably necessary to the normal operation of that particular business or enterprise."[21]

The BFOQ defense is a narrow defense for religion, as it is for gender and national origin. The Supreme Court explained in a gender discrimination case that to qualify as a BFOQ "a job qualification must relate to the 'essence' or to the 'central mission of the employer's business.' "[22]

There are only a few cases involving religion as a BFOQ, because it is a rare situation where an employer claiming a religion BFOQ would not already be a religious employer exempt under section 702 from the prohibition against religious discrimination. One case in which the BFOQ defense did appear was *Pime v. Loyola University of Chicago.*[23] In *Pime* the defendant was a former Jesuit university seeking to maintain its religious identity even after it had evolved into a secular institution. It required that three vacancies in the department of religion and philosophy be filled by Jesuits in order to maintain some "Jesuit presence" on campus. The plaintiff, who was Jewish, was a part-time professor in the philosophy department who wanted one of the full-time positions reserved for Jesuits. In the university at large, ninety-four percent of the teaching staff was non-Jesuit, and the great majority of the faculty in the philosophy department was not Jesuit.

The plaintiff applied for the position and was rejected because he was not a Jesuit. He sued, but the court held that religion was a BFOQ in this case. The court found that "Jesuit presence" was important to the successful operation of the university. The educational tradition and character of the university made it important for students to have occasional contact with Jesuits. Although Jesuit training was not a superior qualification for any other reason, the court found that "having a Jesuit presence in the Philosophy faculty is 'reasonably necessary to

21. 42 U.S.C.A. § 2000e–2(e).

22. International Union, UAW v. Johnson Controls, Inc., 499 U.S. 187, 203, 111 S.Ct. 1196, 1205, 113 L.Ed.2d 158 (1991).

23. 803 F.2d 351 (7th Cir.1986).

the normal operation' of the enterprise, and that fixing the number at seven out of thirty-one is a reasonable determination."[24]

The BFOQ for religion also applied to a job of transporting Moslem pilgrims into Mecca by helicopter. The employer limited the job to persons of that faith because only Moslems may enter the holy areas; others are subject to execution. The court upheld this religious BFOQ because of the threat of harm to third parties, not just to the non-Moslem pilot.[25]

Defining Religion and Religious Practices

Section 701(j) of Title VII defines the term "religion" as including "all aspects of religious observance and practice, as well as belief."[26] This definition encompasses more than membership in traditional religious groups. The EEOC Guidelines on religious discrimination follow the Supreme Court's guidance under the First Amendment and define religious practices to include "moral or ethical beliefs as to what is right and wrong which are sincerely held with the strength of traditional religious views."[27] Under this interpretation, it is not necessary for a religious group to espouse the individual's beliefs, nor is it necessary for the religious group to which the individual professes to belong to accept all the particular beliefs held by the individual.

Courts have relied generally on definitions of religion that have evolved in First Amendment litigation.[28] A "religion" does not require a God or deity or even a written theology, but to be a "religion" the ideology must be more than a political, economic or social philosophy. The Supreme Court has explained with respect to the free exercise clause:

> There is no doubt that "only beliefs rooted in religion are protected by the Free Exercise Clause". Purely secular views do not suffice. Nor do we underestimate the difficulty of distinguishing between religious and secular convictions and in determining whether a professed belief is sincerely held.[29]

§ 2.38 Age Discrimination in Employment Act—Special Issues

Congress enacted the Age Discrimination in Employment Act (ADEA) in 1967 to prohibit discrimination against older workers. The basic substantive provisions of the Act are identical to Title VII, with the substitution of the word "age" as the prohibited basis for discrimination in place of "race, color, religion, sex, or national origin." The purpose of the ADEA, the Supreme Court has explained, is to eradicate the arbitrary exclusions of older workers and the consequent individual and

---

24. Id. at 354.

25. Kern v. Dynalectron Corp., 577 F.Supp. 1196 (N.D.Tex.1983), affirmed, 746 F.2d 810 (5th Cir.1984).

26. 42 U.S.C.A. § 2000e.

27. 29 C.F.R. § 1605.1.

28. See Frazee v. Illinois Dep't of Employment Sec., 489 U.S. 829, 109 S.Ct. 1514, 103 L.Ed.2d 914 (1989).

29. 109 S.Ct. at 1517.

social costs of such discrimination.[1] Therefore, the Act "broadly prohibits arbitrary discrimination in the workplace based on age."[2]

In contrast to the substantive provisions, the procedural and remedial provisions of the ADEA originally paralleled those of the Fair Labor Standards Act because Congress originally designated the Secretary of Labor to enforce the Act. Congress subsequently transferred the enforcement power to the EEOC, but left unchanged until recently the different procedural requirements. General confusion about the differences resulted in traps for unwary litigants, and many age discrimination claims met unexpected procedural barriers. Consequently, Congress cured the situation with the Civil Rights Act of 1991. The filing procedures and time limitations of the ADEA now are virtually the same as those of Title VII.

The original impetus for the ADEA was a report from the Secretary of Labor which documented the problem of discrimination against older workers. Congress had directed the Secretary to prepare such a report when it decided not to include "age" as one of the prohibited bases of discrimination in the Civil Rights Act of 1964. When Congress enacted the ADEA in 1967, it was not acting to redress the omission of "age" in the 1964 Act. The ADEA is more narrow in its scope because the ADEA does not protect persons under forty. Its protection extends only to individuals at least forty years old. Originally the Act prohibited discrimination against individuals between the ages of forty and sixty-five. Congress amended the Act in 1978 to extend the upper age limit to seventy. Then in the 1986 amendments Congress removed the upper cap altogether. In its current form, section 12(a) of the Act provides: "The prohibitions in this chapter shall be limited to individuals who are at least 40 years of age."[3]

Although Congress attempted to extend coverage of the ADEA to state employers, the Supreme Court held in *Kimel v. Florida Board of Regents*[4] that such an extension violated the states' Eleventh Amendment immunity because it exceeded congressional power under Section 5 of the Fourteenth Amendment. This holding followed the Court's earlier decision in *Seminole Tribe v. Florida*[5] that Congress lacks power under Article I to abrogate state sovereign immunity granted by the Eleventh Amendment. *Kimel* explained that Congress cannot enact legislation under Section 5 that permits suits against states unless it meets two tests: first, there must be a clear intent by Congress to exercise the power, and second, there must be congruence and proportionality between the wrong addressed and the remedy against the state. The Court in *Kimel* concluded that the ADEA satisfies the first prong but fails the second. The congruence and proportionality test was not met because

§ 2.38

1. EEOC v. Wyoming, 460 U.S. 226, 103 S.Ct. 1054, 75 L.Ed.2d 18 (1983). See also Johnson v. Mayor & City Council, 472 U.S. 353, 105 S.Ct. 2717, 86 L.Ed.2d 286 (1985).

2. Lorillard v. Pons, 434 U.S. 575, 577, 98 S.Ct. 866, 868, 55 L.Ed.2d 40 (1978).

3. 29 U.S.C.A. § 631(a).

4. 528 U.S. 62, 120 S.Ct. 631, 145 L.Ed.2d 522 (2000).

5. 517 U.S. 44, 116 S.Ct. 1114, 134 L.Ed.2d 252 (1996).

Congress did not identify a pattern of age discrimination by the states that amounted to a constitutional violation, nor even any pattern at all. Therefore, states retain Eleventh Amendment immunity in ADEA cases.

Eleventh Amendment immunity is not absolute immunity, however. It provides immunity from suit by private individuals but not from cases brought by the federal government, The Supreme Court explained in *Alden v. Maine*[6] that states consented to suit by the federal government when they ratified the Constitution. Therefore, the EEOC may still bring claims based on the ADEA against state and local governments. The question that remains open is whether EEOC suits can provide remedies for individuals. The Seventh Circuit answered that question in the affirmative by analogizing to the Supreme Court's 2001 opinion in *EEOC v. Waffle House, Inc.*[7] In that case the Court found that the EEOC could pursue a claim on behalf of an individual even when an arbitration agreement precluded the individual from pursuing an claim personally. The Seventh Circuit reasoned in *EEOC v. Board of Regents of the University of Wisconsin System*[8] that *Waffle House* sent a clear signal that the EEOC may pursue victim-specific relief and that in the face of that clear signal, any distinction between arbitration agreements and sovereign immunity should be drawn by the Supreme Court rather than the circuit courts. The issue has not been widely addressed and is ripe for further litigation.

Special Issues in Coverage

Although some state statutes protect all adults from discrimination on the basis of age, the ADEA limits its protection to those forty and over and does not recognize a cause of action for "reverse" age discrimination against the young. The Supreme Court established this principle in *General Dynamics Land Systems, Inc. v. Cline.*[9] In that case the employer implemented a collective bargaining agreement that eliminated the employer's retiree health insurance benefits program for workers then under fifty but retained the program for workers then over fifty. Those employees who were between forty and fifty sued on the basis that they were entitled to protection under the ADEA and were being discriminated against on the basis of "age." The EEOC agreed in an interpretative regulation that the plain meaning of the Act prohibited discrimination on the basis of age against anyone entitled to the Act's protection.

The great majority of the circuit courts had agreed that there was no claim for reverse discrimination under the Act. The Sixth Circuit in *Cline* disagreed and, following the lead of the EEOC's interpretative regulation, held that the Act prohibited reverse age discrimination. The Supreme Court reversed. Rejecting the argument that a word like "age" has to have the same meaning in all parts of the Act, the majority held

6. 527 U.S. 706, 119 S.Ct. 2240, 144 L.Ed.2d 636 (1999).

7. 534 U.S. 279, 122 S.Ct. 754, 151 L.Ed.2d 755 (2002).

8. 288 F.3d 296 (7th Cir. 2002).

9. 540 U.S. 581, 124 S.Ct. 1236, 157 L.Ed.2d 1094 (2004).

that the reference to "age" in the context of discrimination means "old age" even though its reference in the provision for the affirmative defense of bona fide occupational qualification can mean "age" as a qualification means comparative youth. The Court concluded that "social history emphatically reveals an understanding of age discrimination as aimed against the old, and the statutory reference to age discrimination in this idiomatic sense is confirmed by legislative history."[10]

The coverage of the ADEA is similar to Title VII in that the ADEA regulates only the actions of "employers," "labor organizations," and "employment agencies." The definitions of these terms for ADEA coverage closely parallel those for Title VII. One difference is that the ADEA requires that the "person affecting commerce" have twenty or more employees rather than the requirement of fifteen or more under Title VII.

Congress chose to treat the federal government differently, as it also had done under Title VII. Rather than include the federal government as an employer, Congress made separate provisions to protect federal employees from age discrimination. The Act provides that all personnel actions involving employees or applicants at least forty years of age in executive agencies "shall be made free from any discrimination based on age."[11] Federal employees with an ADEA complaint are not burdened with the complicated requirements of agency exhaustion as they are under Title VII. The enforcement of their rights rests with the Equal Employment Opportunity Commission, but they have different waiting periods than other ADEA claimants.

One source of confusion about the coverage of the ADEA has been its application to bona fide employee benefit plans. The Supreme Court held in *Public Employees Retirement System v. Betts*[12] that such plans were exempt from the ADEA. Congress responded a year after that decision with the Older Workers Benefit Protection Act of 1990.[13] This Act provides that the ADEA prohibits discrimination against older workers in all employee benefits except when significant cost considerations justify an age-based reduction in employee benefits. Employers may observe the terms of a bona fide employee benefit plan provided that the payments made, or costs incurred, for older employees are not less than those for younger employees.

Proving and Defending Age Discrimination

The substantive prohibition of section 4(a) of the ADEA is the same as section 703(a) of Title VII. It prohibits discrimination against an individual "because of such person's age." As previously noted, this protection extends only to individuals at least forty years old. Because of the similar wording of these two provisions the substantive requirements for ADEA claims closely parallel those of Title VII. An individual may

10. 124 S.Ct. at 1246.
11. 29 U.S.C.A. § 633a(a).
12. 492 U.S. 158, 109 S.Ct. 2854, 106 L.Ed.2d 134 (1989).
13. P.L. 101–433, 104 Stat. 978, codified in portions of 29 U.S.C.A. §§ 623–630. See § 10.9.

bring an individual claim of disparate treatment, or a plaintiff class can bring a claim of group disparate treatment. Because the underlying purposes of Title VII and the ADEA differ, however, some courts have concluded that it is not appropriate to permit claims of disparate impact under the ADEA.

Direct Evidence

For an individual claim of age discrimination, a plaintiff may introduce direct evidence of discrimination in the same manner as under Title VII. In one case, for example,[14] the jury found that the employer violated the ADEA when it demoted an employee on the basis of age. When the plaintiff complained about his small annual bonus after his division produced outstanding profits that year, he was told, "At your age, you shouldn't be rocking the boat." Shortly afterwards he was demoted. In another case, an employee in a cabaret survived summary judgment by alleging she was told that she could not be promoted from waitress to entertainer because she was "too old."[15]

In *Lowe v. J.B. Hunt Transport,*[16] an older employee was fired only two years after he was hired. In upholding the employer, the Eighth Circuit focused upon the fact that it was the same decision-makers in the company who made both the hiring and the firing decision. The court found improbable that the same individuals had developed an aversion to older workers in so short a period of time.

Disparate Treatment under ADEA

Under the disparate treatment model of establishing discrimination the plaintiff in an ADEA claim also proceeds under the *McDonnell Douglas Corp. v. Green*[17] framework. Although the Supreme Court noted in *Reeves v. Sanderson Plumbing Products,*[18] that it has never so held, the circuits have uniformly applied the Title VII case law on disparate treatment to the ADEA. A plaintiff thus creates an inference of unlawful disparate treatment in a hiring case by showing membership in the protected age category, qualification for a job, rejection despite that qualification, and the job remained open or was filled by a younger person. In a discharge case the plaintiff must show membership in the protected category, satisfactory job performance, discharge, and replacement by a younger person. A plaintiff may also pursue a claim of retaliation under section 4(d) of the ADEA, which is identical to the provision in Title VII.

In *O'Connor v. Consolidated Coin Caterers Corp.,*[19] the Supreme Court considered whether replacement by someone under forty is a proper element of the prima facie case for disparate treatment under the ADEA. The Court held that it is not a proper requirement because the

14. Reyher v. Champion Int'l Corp., 975 F.2d 483 (8th Cir.1992).

15. Lindsey v. Prive Corp., 987 F.2d 324 (5th Cir.1993).

16. 963 F.2d 173 (8th Cir.1992).

17. 411 U.S. 792, 93 S.Ct. 1817, 36 L.Ed.2d 668 (1973).

18. 530 U.S. 133, 120 S.Ct. 2097, 147 L.Ed.2d 105 (2000).

19. 517 U.S. 308, 116 S.Ct. 1307, 134 L.Ed.2d 433 (1996).

Act prohibits discrimination on the basis of age, not class membership. The Court reasoned that it is irrelevant whether one person in the protected class has lost out to another person in that class because of their age. The Act simply limits the protected class to individuals forty or older, but expressly forbids age-based decisions. The Court further noted that replacement of a plaintiff by someone substantially younger is a far more reliable indicator of age discrimination than is the fact that the plaintiff was replaced by someone outside the protected class.

Reeves v. Sanderson Plumbing Products[20] involved an age discrimination claim by a fifty-seven year-old employee who had worked for forty years for the defendant manufacturer of toilet seats and covers. He was a supervisor in a department where his duties included recording the hours and attendance of employees under his supervision. Believing that production was down in Reeves' department because of poor supervision, a manager ordered an audit of the time records and found irregularities. Reeves countered with evidence that there were no irregularities in his records and with proof of some comments with age-based animus by one of three decision-makers. The comments were that the plaintiff "must have come over on the Mayflower" and that he was "too damn old to do the job." There was also evidence concerning harsher treatment toward the plaintiff than toward similarly-situated younger employees. The Supreme Court held that it was sufficient for the jury to combine the prima facie case with their disbelief of the proffered reason for the termination, specifically the irregularities in the time records.

In the plaintiff's case for age discrimination in discharge, difficulty also can arise with the requirement that the plaintiff demonstrate performance that meets the employer's reasonable expectation. Courts have phrased this requirement in various ways and applied it in a general way. As one court noted, the *McDonnell Douglas* scheme was never meant to be "fetishized."[21] If the plaintiff is challenging the legitimacy of the expectation as a pretext for age discrimination, for example, the defendant cannot be insulated from liability by creating an unreasonable expectation and thus preventing a prima facie case. The plaintiff may attack the legitimacy of the expectation. The mere fact that the employer holds more experienced workers to a higher standard than less experienced workers, however, is not in itself age discrimination.

The defendant may dispel the inference of intentional discrimination by articulating a legitimate business reason for the adverse action. In an ADEA discharge case, the employer typically dispels the inference with evidence of the older employee's poor work performance. The burden then shifts back to the plaintiff to convince the trier of fact that the employer's proffered reason is pretextual. In one case,[22] for example, an employer discharged a waitress for violating a rule against leaving work

20. 530 U.S. 133, 120 S.Ct. 2097, 147 L.Ed.2d 105 (2000).

21. Palucki v. Sears, Roebuck & Co., 879 F.2d 1568, 1570 (7th Cir.1989). See also the Supreme Court's general observations in Swierkiewicz v. Sorema, 534 U.S. 506, 122 S.Ct. 992, 152 L.Ed.2d 1 (2002).

22. Lindsey v. Prive Corp., 987 F.2d 324 (5th Cir.1993).

in the company of a customer. The court noted that the plaintiff could establish pretext if she convinced the trier of fact that younger waitresses were not punished for violating the same rule.

A case of constructive discharge under the ADEA is governed by standards like those under Title VII. In *Wilson v. Monarch Paper Co.*,[23] for example, the employer reassigned a vice president with thirty years of experience to janitorial duties, sweeping the floors and cleaning up the employees' cafeteria. These demeaning conditions and additional age harassment caused a deep depression that eventually required hospitalization and lasted several years. The court held that the jury was justified in finding that the employer intentionally and systematically humiliated the plaintiff for the purpose of forcing his resignation.

The plaintiff in a disparate treatment case retains at all times the burden of persuasion. In *Colosi v. Electri–Flex Co.*,[24] an ADEA plaintiff failed to show that the employer's articulated reasons for firing him were pretextual, even though no corporate record mentioned any of his alleged shortcomings and one affidavit was allegedly perjurious. The court noted that small, family-owned companies often conduct operations with less formality. Even disregarding the perjurious affidavit, there were still eight uncontradicted affidavits enumerating grounds for firing him.

It does not matter if the reasons for firing an older employee are related to age in some way if the motivation for the adverse action was not actually age discrimination. There is often a thin line between an employer's action based upon discriminatory stereotypes about age and action relating to the particular qualities of an older worker. In the *Colosi* case, for example, the articulated reasons for the employee's discharge included his failure to adapt to the company's new computer system. The company instituted the system in order to keep better track of inventory, but the plaintiff refused to change from the old method and would not accept the computer's output. This behavior by the plaintiff established a legitimate, non-age based ground for the employer's action, whereas a stereotyped assumption that older employees cannot adapt to new methods would be age discrimination.

Similarly, the plaintiffs in a group disparate treatment claim under the ADEA failed to establish that age was the employer's motive for replacing older striking employees with younger employees who had been temporary help during the strike.[25] Although the seniority of the fired workers may have been a factor in the decision, that fact was not sufficient to support an inference of intentional discrimination. The question was whether the employer was motivated by the age of the striking workers who were not recalled. A few stray remarks about the age of the workers were not enough to demonstrate animus toward the group on the basis of age, nor to suggest that the legitimate reasons the employer had for preferring the replacement workers were pretextual.

23. 939 F.2d 1138 (5th Cir.1991).

24. 965 F.2d 500 (7th Cir.1992).

25. Britt v. Grocers Supply Co., 978 F.2d 1441 (5th Cir.1992).

Defenses to Intentional Age Discrimination

Employers may defend against a claim of intentional age discrimination not only by rebutting the plaintiff's evidence, but also by proving a specific defense. The Act provides for several defenses to intentional discrimination on the basis of age. First, the Act protects actions that are based on the use of a bona fide seniority system. Although seniority is related to age in the sense that it is time-based, an employer nonetheless is permitted "to observe the terms of a bona fide seniority system that is not intended to evade the purposes of this chapter."[26] The defense includes a proviso, however, that "no such seniority system shall require or permit the involuntary retirement" of individuals because of age.[27]

The definition of a "bona fide seniority system" under the ADEA is the same as under Title VII in most respects. A seniority system is one that improves employment rights as the length of an individual's employment increases. In one interesting case,[28] the plaintiffs alleged a violation of the ADEA because senior employees were disadvantaged in job assignment because of their greater seniority. The postal service had difficulty with staffing fourteen chronically understaffed offices and therefore had a policy of transferring the most senior postal inspector to such vacancies unless that inspector had already served five years in one of these positions. The employer successfully defended this practice on grounds other than the exception for bona fide seniority systems; a system that reduces benefits with tenure rather than increases them cannot meet the definition of seniority.

The proviso for retirement plans in the seniority defense simply notes that the system must not "require or permit" involuntary retirement.[29] Voluntary early retirement incentive plans are permissible when they are consistent with the purposes of the statute to eradicate discrimination against older workers. It is not permissible to coerce employees to choose between early retirement with benefits and discharge without benefits. Following the guiding principle of the Act to prevent arbitrary age bias, courts have considered various retirement incentives to assess whether they are meaningful choices for employees or unlawful discrimination. The ADEA does specifically permit certain pension plan practices, such as Social Security "bridge payments," which might not otherwise meet the standard of consistency with the Act.

Another statutory defense under the ADEA is bona fide occupational qualification (BFOQ). The Act provides that it is not unlawful to take any action otherwise prohibited under the Act "where age is a bona fide occupational qualification reasonably necessary to the normal operation of the particular business."[30] Like this defense under Title VII, the defendant must prove a factual basis for the BFOQ and cannot rely upon stereotyped assumptions. Thus, it is not sufficient to say that a job is

---

26. 29 U.S.C.A. § 623(f)(2).

27. Id.

28. Arnold v. United States Postal Serv., 863 F.2d 994 (D.C.Cir.1988), cert.

denied, 493 U.S. 846, 110 S.Ct. 140, 107 L.Ed.2d 99 (1989).

29. 29 U.S.C.A. § 623(f)(2).

30. 29 U.S.C.A. § 623(f)(1).

restricted to younger workers because it requires heavy work or long hours.

Although stereotyped assumptions are not sufficient for a BFOQ, the defense nonetheless does represent a congressional recognition that age may sometimes serve as a necessary basis for some employment decisions when it is not possible to use neutral qualifications instead. Like Title VII, the employer must show that all or substantially all individuals in the protected group would be unable to perform the job. In one case,[31] the court allowed a BFOQ for an upper age limit of forty-five for rookie campus officers on a university campus. Part of the rationale was that younger officers relate better to college students.

The Supreme Court considered the BFOQ defense under the ADEA in *Western Air Lines, Inc. v. Criswell*[32] and confirmed that the defense is governed by the same principles as Title VII. *Criswell* held that an employer can establish age as a BFOQ by proving that some members of the age-defined group cannot perform the job safely and efficiently, and that they cannot be identified by means other than age. The case concerned a challenge to an airline's rule that flight engineers could not be over sixty because of the employer's concern for the safety of its passengers. The Court rejected a "rational basis" test, even where safety is concerned, and made clear that the standard for a BFOQ is a stringent one. *Criswell* developed a two-part approach for cases involving safety as a BFOQ. First, the employer must establish that there is a potential for unacceptable risk to the employer or third parties that older employees are more likely to pose. Second, the employer must prove that it is impractical to perform individual evaluations that could identify which of those older workers pose that risk.

Rejecting the airline's argument that deference should be given to its rule, the Court held that mere convenience of the employer is not enough. There must be an objective justification. Applying this test in another case,[33] the Eleventh Circuit refused to allow an age BFOQ for a school bus driver because the private school failed to show any factual basis for believing that all or substantially all persons over sixty-five would be unable to perform the job safely and efficiently and that it was impractical to deal with older employees on an individual basis.

In a second case involving flight engineers, the Supreme Court struck down an employer's rule that differentiated only on the basis of age. The rule in *Trans World Airlines v. Thurston*[34] allowed former captains to "bump" into flight engineer positions for any reason except mandatory retirement at age sixty. The Court found no justification for this overt classification on the basis of age.

The ADEA also specifically provides that it is not an unlawful employment practice to take action "where the differentiation is based

31. EEOC v. University of Texas Health Science Ctr., 710 F.2d 1091 (5th Cir.1983).

32. 472 U.S. 400, 105 S.Ct. 2743, 86 L.Ed.2d 321 (1985).

33. Tullis v. Lear Sch., Inc., 874 F.2d 1489 (11th Cir.1989).

34. 469 U.S. 111, 105 S.Ct. 613, 83 L.Ed.2d 523 (1985).

on reasonable factors other than age."[35] Cost-cutting can be a legitimate, non-discriminatory reason for discharging an older worker, but not if the employer's motivation is to replace the more highly paid older employee with a cheaper, younger person in the same position.

This *Metz* type of cost-cutting is distinguishable from reductions that result from general company reorganization to trim the overall expense of the operation. When there is a general reduction in force (RIF), an individual plaintiff or class may claim intentional group discrimination on the basis of age if a disproportionate number of older employees are affected. As with other claims of group disparate treatment, statistics are relevant to probe the employer's motivation.

RIFs often result in the offer of retirement packages to older workers that are accompanied with waivers of ADEA claims. Such waivers were specifically addressed by Congress in the Older Workers Benefit Protection Act.[36] A waiver is not effective as a knowing and voluntary waiver of rights unless it gives the employee time to consider options and specifically makes reference to ADEA claims. The Supreme Court has held that the mere retention of the monies paid under a release that is not in compliance with the Act is insufficient to ratify an otherwise invalid release.[37]

Disparate Impact Under the ADEA

An open question, on which the Supreme Court has granted certiorari in 2004,[38] is the applicability of disparate impact analysis to the ADEA. When the Act was new, the courts generally held that disparate impact analysis was applicable to ADEA claims in the same manner as to Title VII. After the Supreme Court expressly noted that it has never held that disparate impact analysis is appropriately applied to an ADEA case,[39] several circuits called into question the established doctrine.

An early, and frequently cited, case permitting disparate impact analysis under the ADEA was *Geller v. Markham*.[40] In *Geller*, the defendant school board established a policy that in order to save money no newly hired teacher should have enough experience to be in the "sixth step" of the pay scale. The plaintiff was an experienced fifty-five year old teacher who lost an employment opportunity to a less experienced twenty-five year old because of this policy. The Second Circuit upheld the use of disparate impact analysis and permitted the plaintiff to establish a prima facie case with evidence that 92.6 percent of the teachers in the protected age group have enough experience to be in the

35. 29 U.S.C.A. § 623(f)(1).

36. 29 U.S.C.A. §§ 626(f)(1).

37. Oubre v. Entergy Operations, Inc., 522 U.S. 422, 118 S.Ct. 838, 139 L.Ed.2d 849 (1998).

38. Smith v. City of Jackson, 351 F.3d 183 (5th Cir. 2003), cert. granted, ___ U.S. ___, 124 S.Ct. 1724, 158 L.Ed.2d 398 (2004).

39. Hazen Paper Co. v. Biggins, 507 U.S. 604, 113 S.Ct. 1701, 123 L.Ed.2d 338 (1993).

40. 635 F.2d 1027 (2d Cir.1980), cert. denied, 451 U.S. 945, 101 S.Ct. 2028, 68 L.Ed.2d 332 (1981).

sixth step. The school district attempted to show business necessity with its budgetary problems, but the court rejected this justification. Chief Justice Rehnquist (then Justice) dissented from the Supreme Court's denial of certiorari because he questioned whether the plaintiff had established a prima facie case and whether the cost-cutting defense should be allowed.

This issue is unique to age discrimination in federal antidiscrimination law because there is express statutory authorization for disparate impact under Title VII and the ADA. The Supreme Court had occasion to consider a fact pattern that might have raised the issue but the plaintiff was a single individual with a disparate treatment claim. In *Hazen Paper Co. v. Biggins*,[41] the employer fired the plaintiff when he was within a few weeks of the vesting of his pension benefits upon ten years of service. The Court observed that although years of service is correlated with age, it is an independent factor. Noting that a young employee may have worked for the same employer long enough for the pension to vest and that an older employee may be newly hired, the Court found age and years of service to be "analytically distinct." Therefore, it was incorrect to say that a decision based upon years of service is age-based and intentionally discriminatory under the disparate treatment theory. The proper claim in such a case is under ERISA. An ADEA disparate treatment claim, the Court said, requires proof that the employer acted on the basis of the employee's age and not just the employee's pension status.

The concurring opinion by Justice Kennedy, joined by Chief Justice Rehnquist and Justice Thomas, noted that this opinion does not involve a disparate impact theory and that the Court has never approved the use of disparate impact analysis under the ADEA. Because this case involved a claim by a single individual as a disparate treatment discharge, it left open the question whether the Act permits a regular practice of discharging employees after a certain number of years of service solely because of those years of service. It is unclear whether a plaintiff class could prevail on a disparate impact theory that such a practice disproportionately disadvantaged the protected class of workers over forty. If so, then the burden would shift to the defendant to establish the business necessity of the practice.

Procedure and Remedies

Although the substantive provisions of the ADEA were patterned after Title VII, Congress originally modelled the procedural and remedial provisions generally after the Fair Labor Standards Act. Congress changed these requirements in the Civil Rights Act of 1991 such that ADEA claims now have procedural requirements based on Title VII.

Remedies under the ADEA include "such legal or equitable relief as may be appropriate to effectuate the purposes" of the Act.[42] Like Title

41. 507 U.S. 604, 113 S.Ct. 1701, 123   **42.** 29 U.S.C.A. § 633(a), (c).
L.Ed.2d 338 (1993).

VII, such injunctions may include reinstatement and other affirmative orders. Back pay and front pay may also be granted, on the same principles as under Title VII. The ADEA does not permit damages for pain and suffering. Attorneys' fees are available as a remedy under the ADEA, but only for prevailing plaintiffs.

Unlike Title VII, the ADEA provides for double damages as liquidated damages in cases where the defendant commits a willful violation of the Act. In *Trans World Airlines v. Thurston*,[43] the Supreme Court defined willful conduct as occurring when the defendant "knew or showed reckless disregard" for whether the conduct was prohibited by the statute. This standard is greater than negligence, in the sense that the plaintiff must prove more than simply that the defendant "should have known" that its conduct violated the Act. Nonetheless, the willfulness standard does not require a specific intent to violate the Act nor conduct that is "outrageous."

The Supreme Court provided further clarification of the willfulness standard in a Fair Labor Standards Act case, *McLaughlin v. Richland Shoe Co.*[44] The issue in that case was whether the three-year limitations period for "willful" violations of that Act should be governed by the same standards as *Thurston* established for liquidated damages under the ADEA. The Court held that the standard should be the same. Acknowledging that the term willfulness is not used consistently in the law, the Court observed that the term "is generally understood to refer to conduct that is not merely negligent."[45] The Court reaffirmed the *Thurston* standard of knowledge or reckless disregard and rejected the expansive definition of willfulness as knowing that the Act was "in the picture." Such an expansive standard, the Court noted, would "virtually obliterate any distinction between willful and nonwillful violations."[46]

In *Hazen Paper Co. v. Biggins*,[47] the Court reaffirmed these holdings and clarified the application of the standard for purposes of assessing liquidated damages under the ADEA. Following *Thurston*, some lower courts had held that the standard applied only to formal policies and not to individual cases where age had entered into the employment decision. *Thurston* itself involved a challenge to a rule by the airline that captains facing mandatory retirement cannot become flight engineers but that captains leaving their positions for any other reason could do so. *Biggins* involved an individual claiming that his discharge was caused by age discrimination. This difference between a formal policy and an "informal" disparate treatment claim does not affect the willfulness standard, the Court held. The Act permits liquidated damages in any case where the employer acted with knowledge or reckless disregard of the employee's ADEA rights. Liquidated damages are not permissible if the employ-

---

43. 469 U.S. 111, 126, 105 S.Ct. 613, 83 L.Ed.2d 523 (1985).

44. 486 U.S. 128, 108 S.Ct. 1677, 100 L.Ed.2d 115 (1988).

45. 486 U.S. at 133, 108 S.Ct. at 1681.

46. 486 U.S. at 132–33, 108 S.Ct. at 1680–81.

47. 507 U.S. 604, 113 S.Ct. 1701, 123 L.Ed.2d 338 (1993).

er acted with an incorrect but good faith belief that the statute permitted the age-based distinction.

§ 2.39 Constitutional Claims

Some claims alleging discrimination in employment on the basis of race, national origin, or gender are constitutional claims. The Fifth Amendment broadly limits the power of the federal government to deprive a person of "life, liberty or property, without due process of law."[1] The Fourteenth Amendment limits state governments with the same language, as well as prohibiting states from denying to any person "the equal protection of the laws."[2] Despite the absence of the words "equal protection" in the Fifth Amendment, the Supreme Court has interpreted the constraint on the federal power to include the equal protection guarantee.[3] The Supreme Court has permitted the use of a constitutional basis for a claim only in the limited circumstances where there is no adequate statutory basis to enforce an important right. In the employment discrimination area, this category is now very limited.

Claims under the Fifth Amendment

A few employment discrimination claims brought against federal employers have been supported solely by the Fifth Amendment. The Supreme Court first held in a constitutional tort case that the Constitution itself could be the basis of a claim.[4] The Court recognized the inherent power of the federal courts as a matter of general jurisdiction to hear claims of constitutional violations against the federal government.[5]

The constitutional remedy does not supplant the statutory scheme for resolving employment discrimination suits, however. A plaintiff with a claim against the federal employer cannot avoid the short limitations period specified in Title VII by bringing a constitutional claim. The Supreme Court held in *Brown v. General Services Administration*[6] that the time limitation for bringing Title VII employment discrimination suits against the federal government could not be avoided by the simple expedient of bringing the action directly under the Constitution. The remedies provided under Title VII are exclusive for federal employees.

The Fifth Amendment was also the basis of the constitutional claim of race discrimination in *Washington v. Davis*.[7] This employment discrimination case is noteworthy in constitutional law for establishing the principle that plaintiffs must prove intentional discrimination to establish a constitutional claim of race discrimination; proof of disparate impact on the basis of race is not sufficient. In this case the plaintiff

§ 2.39

1. U.S. Const. Amend. V.

2. U.S. Const. Amend. XIV.

3. Bolling v. Sharpe, 347 U.S. 497, 74 S.Ct. 693, 98 L.Ed. 884 (1954).

4. Bivens v. Six Unknown Named Agents, 403 U.S. 388, 91 S.Ct. 1999, 29 L.Ed.2d 619 (1971).

5. See also Butz v. Economou, 438 U.S. 478, 98 S.Ct. 2894, 57 L.Ed.2d 895 (1978).

6. 425 U.S. 820, 96 S.Ct. 1961, 48 L.Ed.2d 402 (1976).

7. 426 U.S. 229, 96 S.Ct. 2040, 48 L.Ed.2d 597 (1976).

class challenged the use of an aptitude test for the selection of police officer trainees in Washington, D.C. A few years prior to *Washington v. Davis*, the Court had established the disparate impact theory for Title VII claims in *Griggs v. Duke Power Co.*[8] and the validation requirements in *Albemarle Paper Co. v. Moody*.[9] The test in *Washington v. Davis* had a disparate impact on the basis of race and the department had not validated the test under the Title VII standards for test validation. Because the federal government was not an employer covered by Title VII until the 1972 amendments to the Act, the plaintiff class could not rely upon the statute at the time the suit arose.

The opinion of the court of appeals in *Washington v. Davis* had held that the *Griggs* standard should apply in this constitutional claim and that plaintiffs need only prove the disproportionate pass rate in order to establish a prima facie case. The Supreme Court reversed on the grounds that the constitutional standard is not identical to the statutory standard. The Court reasoned that a neutral element does not become a "suspect" racial classification merely because there is an adverse impact on one race. A suspect classification triggers strict scrutiny that the government can defend only by demonstrating a compelling state interest. In *Washington v. Davis* the Court said that disparate impact alone cannot create such a classification; it is necessary for the plaintiff to prove purposeful discrimination. Because there was no such evidence in this case, the employment practice that was adverse to black applicants was measured simply by its rationality. The Court found that the use of a standardized aptitude test to screen potential police officers easily met the rationality test.

§ 2.40 Reconstruction Era Civil Rights Acts

The Reconstruction Era Civil Rights Acts provide additional bases for employment discrimination claims. After the Civil War, Congress addressed issues of race discrimination and deprivation of federally guaranteed rights in numerous acts that are independent of the Civil Rights Acts enacted in the second half of the twentieth century, despite their significant overlap. Congress did not by implication repeal the overlapping provisions when it enacted the Civil Rights Act of 1964. Plaintiffs may sue under both Title VII and a Reconstruction Era Act if both apply. In some cases the older laws provide additional relief, and in other cases they reach conduct that the modern acts do not reach for reasons of coverage or procedure.

Section 1981–Generally

The purpose of the Reconstruction Era Acts was to grant civil rights to the newly freed slaves. One of these acts of particular relevance to employment discrimination law is 42 U.S.C.A. § 1981. Congress originally passed this act in 1866, following the abolition of involuntary servitude in the Thirteenth Amendment. This brief act provides to "all

8. 401 U.S. 424, 91 S.Ct. 849, 28 L.Ed.2d 158 (1971). See also § 2.18.

9. 422 U.S. 405, 95 S.Ct. 2362, 45 L.Ed.2d 280 (1975). See also § 2.21.

persons" the same right "to make and enforce contracts * * * as enjoyed by white citizens."[1] Section 1981 was recodified in 1871, following the ratification of the Fourteenth Amendment, which provided citizenship for all persons born in the United States and prohibited states from making or enforcing any law that abridges privileges or immunities of citizens or denying them equal protection of the laws.

Because of the recodification of section 1981 following the ratification of the Fourteenth Amendment, courts assumed for decades that state action was a prerequisite to a claim. It was not until the modern civil rights era that the Supreme Court considered section 1981 in a new light. Section 1981 now reaches conduct besides state action, such as the refusal of a private party to make a contract on the basis of race. The Court reasoned that Congress enacted such legislation pursuant to its power under the Thirteenth Amendment to remove the "badges and incidents of slavery."[2]

Section 1981 reaches the relationship between an individual and an employer because it is a contractual one. In modern law it applies to both public and private employers and to unions. Section 101 of the Civil Rights Act of 1991 now codifies that interpretation by amending section 1977 of the Revised Statutes to add section (2)(c): "The rights protected by this section are protected against impairment by nongovernmental discrimination and impairment under color of State law."

Unlike Title VII, a plaintiff bringing a claim under section 1981 must prove intentional discrimination; it is not sufficient to demonstrate discrimination on the basis of disparate impact. The Supreme Court held in *General Building Contractors Association v. Pennsylvania*[3] that recovery under section 1981 requires proof of motivation. Therefore, a plaintiff with only a claim of disparate impact discrimination must use Title VII and cannot rely upon either section 1981 or the Constitution.

Section 1981–Who May Sue

Not all employment discrimination victims have the advantage of claims under section 1981. Section 1981 covers employment discrimination on the basis of race and ethnicity, but not religion or gender. The literal wording of the statute refers to the right of all persons to make contracts the same as "white citizens." The Supreme Court has interpreted this term to mean that the Act prohibits race discrimination as well as discrimination on the basis of ethnicity.

In *McDonald v. Santa Fe Trail Transportation Co.,*[4] the Court held that section 1981 prohibits discrimination on the basis of race whether it is invidious discrimination against African–Americans or reverse discrimination against the majority Anglo–American racial group. Later,

§ 2.40

1. 42 U.S.C.A. § 1981.

2. Runyon v. McCrary, 427 U.S. 160, 96 S.Ct. 2586, 49 L.Ed.2d 415 (1976); Jones v. Alfred H. Mayer Co., 392 U.S. 409, 88 S.Ct. 2186, 20 L.Ed.2d 1189 (1968).

3. 458 U.S. 375, 102 S.Ct. 3141, 73 L.Ed.2d 835 (1982).

4. 427 U.S. 273, 96 S.Ct. 2574, 49 L.Ed.2d 493 (1976).

the Court explained that the term "race" is not limited to our modern usage of that term. The Court held in *St. Francis College v. Al–Khazraji*[5] that the Act covered discrimination against an Iraqi-born U.S. citizen who claimed that his employer discriminated against him because he was an Arab. The Court noted that there was a very broad understanding of the term "race" at the time that section 1981 was enacted in the middle of the nineteenth century. At that time "race" included groups that are considered ethnic groups in current usage. Various groups fell into this "racial" category, including Finns, Gypsies, Basques, Hebrews, Arabs, Swedes, and so forth. Therefore, the Court concluded that section 1981 covers those identifiable classes of persons who are subjected to discrimination "solely because of their ancestry or ethnic characteristics."[6] In a companion case, the Court held that the Reconstruction Era act applies to discrimination against Jews and reiterated that it is not necessary for a plaintiff to prove that the group in question is a separate "race" by modern standards.

The expansive interpretation of racial discrimination for purposes of section 1981 coverage nonetheless does not include other grounds that are covered by Title VII. Specifically, section 1981 does not address discrimination on the basis of gender, alienage, or religion.

Section 1981–Who May Be Sued

Unlike Title VII, there is no minimum number of employees necessary for an employer to be covered by section 1981. It covers private employers, but there is uncertainty about its coverage of state employers. The Supreme Court held that section 1981 may not be the basis of suit against a state employer, although there is a division among the circuit courts whether this decision was overturned by the Civil Rights Act of 1991. In *Jett v. Dallas Independent School District*,[7] the Supreme Court held that a plaintiff may not rely upon section 1981 to bring a claim against a state employer and thus may not have the benefit of the theory of respondeat superior, which is otherwise available in a claim against private employers under section 1981. The dissent complained bitterly that the majority in *Jett* ignored the history of section 1981 before *Runyon v. McCrary*,[8] in which the Court for the first time interpreted section 1981 to reach private action as well as state action. Indeed, it is with considerable irony that the Court in 1989 interpreted this Act not to reach state action when originally it was thought that section 1981 was restricted to state action. The majority nonetheless held in *Jett* that plaintiffs may not use section 1981 for violations by state governmental units and that the exclusive federal remedy is under another of the Reconstruction Era statutes, section 1983, which is explored in the following portion of this section. The significance of this limitation for the plaintiff in *Jett* was that section 1983 will not support

5. 481 U.S. 604, 107 S.Ct. 2022, 95 L.Ed.2d 582 (1987).

6. 481 U.S. at 612, 107 S.Ct. at 2027.

7. 491 U.S. 701, 109 S.Ct. 2702, 105 L.Ed.2d 598 (1989).

8. 427 U.S. 160, 96 S.Ct. 2586, 49 L.Ed.2d 415 (1976).

the doctrine of respondeat superior; plaintiffs must establish an official policy or custom in order to prevail.

Section 1983

Congress enacted what is now 42 U.S.C.A. § 1983 in 1871 pursuant to its powers under the Fourteenth Amendment. It prohibits any person acting under color of state law from depriving any person of "any rights, privileges, or immunities secured by the Constitution and laws." The statute itself creates no rights; it merely provides a remedy for the violation of established rights. Among those rights is the right to equal protection of the laws, as guaranteed by the Fourteenth Amendment. Section 1983 thus prohibits invidious discrimination by governmental employers on the basis of race, national origin, religion, and gender because these are established rights.

Because there is no established federal right to be free from employment discrimination on the basis of sexual orientation, section 1983 does not afford the basis of protection. The lesbian plaintiff in *Able v. United States*[9] tried unsuccessfully to challenge her discharge on the basis of her sexual orientation by casting it in terms of the established right of intimate association.

Section 1983 does not govern private employers, only public ones. Before Congress amended Title VII in 1972 to cover state and local governments, this section was the only statutory basis to challenge discrimination by such employers. Noteworthy employment discrimination cases brought under section 1983 have included claims against police departments, fire departments, and public schools.

Section 1983 remains the exclusive tool in many employment claims, such as the discharge of public employees for exercising their freedom of expression. In the context of employment discrimination on the basis of race, gender, or national origin, the enforcement of constitutional rights through section 1983 has diminished in importance because Congress amended Title VII in 1972 to include state employers and in 1991 to include damages as well as equitable relief. Nonetheless, it remains a useful tool in employment cases against public employers for the recovery of damages without the statutory caps in the Civil Rights Act of 1991.

§ 2.41   State Fair Employment Practice Statutes

State Deferral Agencies

Most states, and many municipalities, have laws to promote fair employment, often as part of larger human rights legislation. These statutes play an important role in providing additional grounds for employment discrimination claims, especially in light of the Supreme Court's decisions limiting the reach of federal law. *Alden v. Maine*[1] and

---

9.   155 F.3d 628 (2d Cir. 1998).

§ 2.41

1.   527 U.S. 706, 119 S.Ct. 2240, 144 L.Ed.2d 636 (1999) (Congress cannot make

Kimel v. Florida Board of Regents[2] have restricted the availability of federal antidiscrimination law against state actors and thus increased the significance of the state law remedy against state employers. Because the states typically prohibit discrimination in employment much the same as the federal statutes, the state statutes fill the gap left by the inability of Congress to make a valid abrogation of the states' immunity. Crucial to recovery against state employers is an abrogation of immunity, however, even under the state scheme.

State agencies to enforce these laws are present in most states as well. When these agencies qualify as deferral agencies for the federal Equal Employment Opportunity Commission (EEOC), all complaints from those jurisdictions are deferred to the state agency for resolution before there is any federal involvement. Complainants also may file directly with a state or municipal agency. These agencies are known variously as equal opportunity agencies, civil rights commissions, or human rights bureaus.

Unlike the federal law, state and local laws that prohibit employment discrimination are not restricted in their coverage to those persons who affect interstate commerce. Typically, state laws follow the federal law in their coverage of employers, labor organizations, and employment agencies, but there are many differences between state and federal coverage and among the various states.

First, there are major differences among the statutes in the grounds on which employment discrimination is prohibited. The federal proscriptions include race, color, religion, sex, and national origin, as well as age and disability. Some states have fewer proscriptions. Alabama and Mississippi have no comprehensive fair employment practice statute for private employers and no fair employment practice agencies. Several states do not prohibit discrimination on the basis of age, or limit that protection to public employees. Many of the states that do prohibit age discrimination provide for an upper age limit, typically seventy. The federal Age Discrimination in Employment Act previously had this limitation, and the state statutes were generally modelled after the earlier version of the federal act. Some states subsequently amended their statutes to remove the upper age limit after the federal amendment, but others did not.

Many state statutes provide coverage that is virtually identical to the federal coverage. The significance of the overlap is that the state statute provides a state forum. Typically, there is an enforcing agency and state remedies that supplement the federal scheme.

Beyond the identity of coverage between the federal law and most states, many of the state statutes are more expansive in their coverage than the federal law. These states thus permit grounds of complaint not

states subject to suit under federal law in state courts without state consent).

2. 528 U.S. 62, 120 S.Ct. 631, 145 L.Ed.2d 522 (2000) (ADEA not constitutionally applied to private claims against states).

otherwise covered by law, such as sexual orientation. Notably, the federal law does not include sexual orientation as a basis of proscribed employment discrimination, but several states have included this basis.

Local laws have been more expansive than either federal or state law in some instances, notably with respect to employment bias on the basis of sexual orientation. The Colorado electorate disapproved of the more expansive local legislation in this regard in the cities of Aspen, Boulder, and Denver and voted to amend the state constitution to prohibit such enactments. The United States Supreme Court found this state amendment unconstitutional in *Romer v. Evans*[3] as a violation of equal protection, but crafted the opinion in very narrow language.

In addition to differences between state and federal law on which categories are protected from employment bias, state statutes can also vary from federal ones in the scope of the protection for an otherwise overlapping category. Greater state protection for discrimination on the basis of age is the most prominent example. Several states extend the prohibition against age discrimination to protect younger applicants and employees. Unlike the federal law, which only protects individuals over forty, several states prohibit discrimination on the basis of age for anyone over the age of eighteen. Some have no minimum age requirement for protection against age discrimination.

In addition to differences in the substantive coverage of the state statutes and federal law, there are differences in who is subject to the acts. First, the state fair employment practice statutes sometimes list exemptions or partial exclusions from coverage that differ from the federal law.

Next, there are differences between some states and the federal approach to the coverage of small employers. Some states follow the federal rule requiring fifteen or more employees for coverage of private employers. The federal minimum of fifteen employees reflects the concern of Congress that small businesses should not be burdened with this federal requirement, and those states agreed that small businesses also should not be burdened by the state requirement.

Most state legislatures were less solicitous of the small businesses within their states. Several statutes require a minimum of only one employee. Other state legislatures chose a number between one and the federal number of fifteen.

Remedial differences between Title VII and some state statutes have been important, especially before the expansion of federal remedies in the Civil Rights Act of 1991. It still remains true that many states provide criminal penalties or civil fines, unlike Title VII, for the violation of their employment discrimination laws. These sanctions are in addition to or in lieu of private remedies. Like Title VII, most states provide for attorneys' fees.

3. 517 U.S. 620, 116 S.Ct. 1620, 134 L.Ed.2d 855 (1996).

Most of the state statutes provide for equitable remedies, similar to the original provision in Title VII. Many provide for some form of damages, expanding upon the original federal limitation to equitable relief. Particularly before the enactment of the Civil Rights Act of 1991, the states that allowed such damages under their statutes provided a significant alternative forum for claimants. Although federal law now permits limited compensatory and punitive damages under Title VII, the availability of such damages under state law remains important because of the ceiling on the recovery of non-economic damages under Title VII and because of the caps on compensatory and punitive damages under Title VII.

Chapter 3

DISABILITY DISCRIMINATION

Table of Sections

§ 3.1 Introduction

Disability discrimination law has become an important part of employment law, and the significance of the field is likely to increase in the future. An aging population, medical and other technologies that permit people with disabilities to enter and remain in the work force, and changing societal notions about the value of individuals with disabilities all point toward more litigation related to claims of discrimination based on disability.

Although laws prohibiting employment discrimination against individuals with disabilities have been enacted in nearly every state, the federal Americans with Disabilities Act of 1990 (ADA) is the primary statutory basis of the field. Because of the broad wording of the ADA, legal challenges have considered a range of definitional and interpretive issues, many of which have reached the Supreme Court.

§ 3.2 Rehabilitation Act

The Rehabilitation Act of 1973[1] was, in many ways, the groundbreaking piece of federal legislation prohibiting discrimination against individuals with disabilities. Its language has been adopted in many state laws, and it served as the conceptual framework for the Americans with Disabilities Act. The main problems with the Rehabilitation Act are its limited coverage and remedies.

Section 501, applicable to all federal departments, agencies, and other "executive instrumentalities," requires nondiscrimination, reasonable accommodation, and affirmative action for the "hiring, placement, and advancement" of individuals with disabilities.

Section 503 provides that any contract in excess of $10,000 entered into with any federal department or agency shall contain a provision requiring that the contracting party take affirmative action to employ and promote qualified individuals with disabilities. The term "individual with disabilities" is defined as "any person who (A) has a physical or mental impairment which substantially limits one or more of such person's major life activities, (B) has a record of such an impairment, or (C) is regarded as having such an impairment." "Major life activities" means functions such as caring for one's self, performing manual tasks, walking, seeing, hearing, speaking, breathing, learning, and working.[2]

Responsibility for enforcing section 503 is vested in the Office of Federal Contract Compliance Programs (OFCCP) in the Department of Labor. By regulation, the director of the OFCCP may seek to (1) withhold progress payments on the contract; (2) terminate the contract; or (3) bar the contractor from future contracts. The Labor Department also has awarded back pay to individuals who have been denied employment or advances in employment because of disability. Individuals who believe they have been discriminated against may only pursue their administrative remedies through the OFCCP; most courts have held that there is no express or implied private right of action.

Section 504 provides that no otherwise qualified individual with disabilities shall, solely by reason of disability, be (1) excluded from the participation in, (2) denied the benefits of, or (3) subjected to discrimination under, any program or activity receiving federal financial assistance. Unlike section 503, there is no monetary minimum amount of financial assistance required for coverage under section 504. There is also no minimum number of employees required and therefore an employer could be covered under section 504, but not under the ADA. The procedures for enforcement of section 504 by each federal agency are the same as those used to implement Title VI of the Civil Rights Act of 1964. Also, unlike section 503, the courts have recognized a private right of action under section 504.

§ 3.2

1. 29 U.S.C.A. §§ 701–796.

2. 45 C.F.R. § 84.3(j)(2)(ii) (§ 504 regulation).

The Rehabilitation Act and the ADA differ in some respects. For example, the Rehabilitation Act may apply to employers with fewer than 15 employees. Also, it has been held that the ADA's quantum of proof, in which the individual must prove that discrimination was a motivating factor, does not apply to the Rehabilitation Act, which requires that discrimination was "solely by reason" of the individual's disability.

§ 3.3 Americans With Disabilities Act—Coverage

The Americans with Disabilities Act of 1990 (ADA)[1] was the first comprehensive federal law to prohibit discrimination in employment against the estimated 43 million Americans with physical or mental disabilities. The ADA's five titles deal with employment (Title I),[2] public services (Title II),[3] public accommodations operated by private entities (Title III),[4] telecommunications (Title IV),[5] and miscellaneous issues (Title V).[6] The ADA draws heavily upon Titles II and VII of the Civil Rights Act of 1964 and the Rehabilitation Act of 1973.

Title I of the ADA, dealing with employment discrimination, took effect in 1992 for employers with twenty-five or more employees; it was extended to employers with fifteen or more employees in 1994. Since that time, the coverage of Title I of the ADA is identical to Title VII of the Civil Rights Act of 1964. Besides most private sector employers, the ADA applies to state and local government employers and the United States Congress. Federal employees are not covered by the ADA, but they remain covered by comparable provisions of section 501 of the Rehabilitation Act. Because Congress enacted the ADA and Rehabilitation Act pursuant to a valid exercise of its powers under section 5 of the Fourteenth Amendment, as well as the commerce clause, the Eleventh Amendment is not a bar to the federal government in enforcing the ADA against the states, although the Eleventh Amendment bars ADA suits against states by private individuals.

In *University of Alabama v. Garrett,*[7] the Supreme Court held, that ADA actions in federal court by state employees to recover money damages are barred by the Eleventh Amendment. Following reasoning used in recent decisions on federalism, the Court stated that there was an inadequate history of irrational employment discrimination by the states and that discrimination based on disability is examined under only a "rational basis" standard. Therefore, Congress did not have constitutional authority under Section 5 of the Fourteenth Amendment to impose on the states a money damages remedy for violations of the ADA.

Several cases have considered whether certain individuals are "employees" for purposes of determining whether the employer has met the ADA's statutory threshold for coverage. In *Clackamas Gastroenterology*

---

§ 3.3

1. 42 U.S.C.A. §§ 12101–12213.

2. 42 U.S.C.A. §§ 12111–12117.

3. Id. §§ 12131–12165.

4. Id. §§ 12181–12189.

5. 47 U.S.C.A. §§ 152, 221b, 225, 610.

6. 42 U.S.C.A. §§ 12201–12213.

7. 531 U.S. 356, 121 S.Ct. 955, 148 L.Ed.2d 866 (2001).

Associates v. Wells,[8] the Supreme Court held that in determining who is a business partner, and therefore not counted as an employee for ADA purposes, the court should examine whether the partner operates independently and manages the business or if the partner is subject to the firm's control. If the latter, the partner will be counted as an employee. Similar considerations have been applied to determine whether a shareholder and director in a closely-held corporation should be considered an employee: (1) whether the director has undertaken traditional employee duties; (2) whether the director was regularly employed by a separate entity; and (3) whether the director reported to someone higher in the organization.[9] The courts are in agreement that independent contractors are not employees.

It is important to determine who is a "covered entity" or employer under the ADA. The courts have adopted a broad definition. In one case, the court remanded for a determination of whether an association of employers that sponsored group health benefits could be considered a "covered entity" amenable to suit, even though the association was not an employer of the plaintiff.[10] In other cases, related firms with fewer than the statutory minimum number of employees may be treated as one employer for purposes of coverage under the ADA if satisfying the agency test. Most courts have held that neither owners, supervisors, nor public officials may be sued individually under the ADA.

It is important for the plaintiff to prove that the named defendant is the actual employer. There is no liability where the alleged discrimination was committed by an independent contractor. Successor employers, however, may be liable for their predecessor's violations. According to the EEOC, temporary employees are covered by the ADA. Although unions may be liable for violations, bona fide private clubs are exempt from coverage.

A few cases have concerned the issue of who has standing to bring an action under the ADA. An employee's former wife, who was a beneficiary under a health benefits plan, and an employee's wife, whose disabilities prevented her from attending social events related to employment, were held not to be within the zone of interest protected by the ADA. In other cases, the estates of ADA plaintiffs have sought to continue the action following the plaintiffs' deaths. Because the ADA does not address the issue, the courts have looked to state law.

§ 3.4 Americans With Disabilities Act—Definition of Disability

Section 102(a) of the ADA contains the general prohibition on employment discrimination. "No covered entity shall discriminate against a qualified individual with a disability because of the disability of

8. 538 U.S. 440, 123 S.Ct. 1673, 155 L.Ed.2d 615 (2003).

9. Trainor v. Appollo Metal Specialties, Inc., 318 F.3d 976 (10th Cir. 2002).

10. Carparts Distrib. Ctr., Inc. v. Automotive Wholesaler's Ass'n, 37 F.3d 12 (1st Cir.1994).

such individual in regard to job application procedures, the hiring, advancement, or discharge of employees, employee compensation, job training, and other terms, conditions, and privileges of employment." This broad language is intended to be construed in a manner consistent with section 504 of the Rehabilitation Act. The ADA makes it unlawful for an employer to discriminate "because of the disability of such individual." Therefore, there can be no liability if the employer did not know that the individual had a disability at the time it took the adverse action.

The definition of "disability" in section 3(2) of the ADA also relies on the Rehabilitation Act and its three-part definition of "disability" as a physical or mental impairment that substantially limits one or more of the major life activities of the individual, has a record of such an impairment, or is regarded as having such an impairment. Section 101(8) of the ADA specifies that the term " 'qualified individual with a disability' means an individual with a disability who, with or without reasonable accommodation, can perform the essential functions of the employment position that the individual holds or desires." The ADA expressly provides that homosexuality and bisexuality are not impairments and the following sexual and behavioral disorders are excluded from coverage under the Act: transvestism, transsexualism, pedophilia, exhibitionism, voyeurism, gender identity disorders not resulting from physical impairments, other sexual behavior disorders, compulsive gambling, kleptomania, and pyromania.

The first prong of the three-prong definition of "disability" is a physical or mental impairment that substantially limits one or more of the major life activities of such individual. Although these terms are not further defined in the ADA, the legislative history clearly indicates that in adopting the same language as used in section 504 of the Rehabilitation Act, Congress intended that the regulations and case law under section 504 should be applied to the same terms when used in the ADA.

The EEOC used the section 504 regulations to define "physical or mental impairment" under the ADA. It includes any physiological disorder of various body systems, such as neurological, musculoskeletal, and sense organs, and therefore encompasses a wide range of medical conditions. Only physical or mental impairments that *substantially* limit a major life activity are covered as disabilities under the ADA. The definition of impairment does not include physical characteristics such as eye color, hair color, handedness, or height, weight, or muscle tone that are within the "normal" range and are not the result of a physiological disorder. Personality traits and environmental, cultural, or economic factors also are not impairments.

To be a disability, the impairment must substantially limit a "major life activity," defined in the EEOC regulations as including, but not limited to, "caring for oneself, performing manual tasks, walking, seeing, hearing, speaking, breathing, learning, and working." These are "basic activities that the average person in the general population can perform with little or no difficulty." In proving a substantial limitation of a major life activity, several courts have required that the individual present "comparator evidence" demonstrating the difference between the plaintiff's limitations and the average person's.

What does it mean to "substantially limit" a major life activity? According to the regulations, whether an individual is "substantially limited" depends on the nature and severity of the impairment, the duration or expected duration of the impairment, and the permanent or long-term impact of the impairment. In *Sutton v. United Air Lines, Inc.,*[1] twin sisters with correctable vision problems were denied an opportunity to become airline pilots because their uncorrected vision did not meet the airline's medical standards. Yet, in their ADA action the airline argued that they were not covered by the ADA because in their "mitigated" state they did not have a substantially limiting impairment. The Supreme Court, rejecting the EEOC's interpretation that impairments should be considered in their unmitigated state, held that the court was required to consider the effect of eyeglasses on their condition. In a companion case, the Court said that in evaluating the severity of the plaintiff's hypertension, the effect of his medication should be considered. The burden of documenting an impairment rests with the employee. An employee who fails to control a controllable disability may lose the protection of the ADA.

Sutton and its companion cases are undoubtedly the most controversial decisions under the ADA because they severely restrict the coverage of the statute, especially for medical impairments, such as epilepsy, diabetes, and cardiovascular disease. If the condition can be "mitigated" by medications or other measures, then the individual is not covered; if the condition cannot be mitigated, then the individual is unlikely to be qualified for the position. Thus, it has been asserted that the only individuals now clearly covered by the ADA are those who are blind, deaf, or use wheelchairs. Although there have been a variety of proposals to amend the ADA to address the definition of disability, Congress has yet to consider the issue.

Courts in ADA cases have determined that a variety of minor impairments are not covered. These include "hammer toes," shift work sleep disorder, irregular heartbeat, colitis, "seasonal affective disorder," strabismus, mild degenerative joint disease, and epicondylitis (tennis elbow). Other minor conditions deemed not covered by the ADA include depression, anxiety, hypertension, hypercholesterolemia, mitral valve prolapse, asbestosis, shortness of breath and chest pains, tendinitis, nearsightedness, allergies, chronic diarrhea, and fear of snakes.

The courts are divided on the issue of whether an employee who exhibits the minor symptoms of a serious illness is covered under the ADA. For example, the Ninth Circuit has held that an employee who

§ 3.4

1. 527 U.S. 471, 119 S.Ct. 2139, 144 L.Ed.2d 450 (1999).

took a four-month leave of absence to recover from a psychological impairment caused by colon cancer surgery did not have a covered disability because the psychological impairment was only temporary.[2] Similarly, the Eleventh Circuit held that the side effects of chemotherapy for lymphoma, weakness, dizziness, swelling of the ankles and hands, numbness of the hands, the loss of body hair, and vomiting, were not disabling conditions.[3] Other courts have held that occasional "flare-ups" of chronic diseases are not disabilities. In a much better reasoned opinion, however, the Seventh Circuit held that the intermittent pressure ulcers of a paraplegic employee, which caused her to stay at home for several weeks, were part of her overall disability, and therefore subject to ADA protection.[4]

The courts also have had a difficult time in deciding whether an individual who has recovered from a serious health condition to the point of being able to resume work without restrictions is nonetheless covered under the statute as having a disability. The First Circuit held that a scrap metal salesperson, who suffered a heart attack and spent seven days in the hospital undergoing angioplasty, was covered under the ADA despite his subsequent full recovery.[5] In reversing the district court, the First Circuit cited with approval to the EEOC's compliance manual, which provides that an impairment does not have to be permanent to be a disability under the ADA. According to the court, severe conditions that last more than a few months and are potentially long term may constitute disabilities. In a questionable, contrary decision, the Fifth Circuit held that a woman with breast cancer who underwent a lumpectomy and radiation treatment was not disabled because she was able to return to work.[6]

Temporary impairments, such as broken limbs, sprained joints, concussions, appendicitis, and influenza are not disabilities. Temporary coughs, broken legs, knee injuries, ankle injuries, and minor back injuries also are not disabilities. It has even been held that an employee who requested two months of unpaid leave following abdominal surgery was not an individual with a disability because her inability to work was "of limited duration."[7] Similar reasoning produced a questionable result in a case where an employee who took a four-month leave of absence to recover from a psychological impairment caused by colon cancer surgery was held not to have a covered disability.[8]

In *Bragdon v. Abbott*,[9] the Supreme Court held that an asymptomatic, HIV-positive woman who was denied dental services in a dentist's

---

2. Sanders v. Arneson Prods., Inc., 91 F.3d 1351 (9th Cir.1996), cert. denied, 520 U.S. 1116, 117 S.Ct. 1247, 137 L.Ed.2d 329 (1997).

3. Gordon v. E.L. Hamm & Assoc., Inc., 100 F.3d 907 (11th Cir.1996), cert. denied, 522 U.S. 1030, 118 S.Ct. 630, 139 L.Ed.2d 610 (1997).

4. Vande Zande v. State of Wis. Dep't of Admin., 44 F.3d 538 (7th Cir.1995).

5. Katz v. City Metal Co., 87 F.3d 26 (1st Cir.1996).

6. Ellison v. Software Spectrum, Inc., 85 F.3d 187 (5th Cir.1996).

7. McDonald v. Commonwealth of Pennsylvania, 62 F.3d 92 (3d Cir.1995).

8. Sanders v. Arneson Prods., Inc., 91 F.3d 1351 (9th Cir.1996), cert. denied, 520 U.S. 1116, 117 S.Ct. 1247, 137 L.Ed.2d 329 (1997).

9. 524 U.S. 624, 118 S.Ct. 2196, 141 L.Ed.2d 540 (1998).

office was covered under Title III of the ADA. This same reasoning undoubtedly applies to employment cases under Title I. The Court held that being HIV positive was a substantial limitation on the major life activity of reproduction of the plaintiff, although some lower courts have held that HIV infection did not interfere with a substantial life activity. Pregnancy and related medical conditions, however, are not, absent unusual circumstances, considered to be physical impairments under the ADA.

An increasingly important issue is whether currently asymptomatic individuals who are at increased risk of developing a disorder or who have a chronic infection are covered by the ADA. In *Furnish v. SVI Systems, Inc.*,[10] the plaintiff, an electrical engineer responsible for technical work in installing video systems in hotels, was diagnosed with chronic hepatitis B and severe septal fibrosis suggestive of liver disease, as well as hepatitis-caused cirrhosis. The plaintiff was being treated with Interferon, which caused fatigue, nausea, and achiness. The plaintiff was discharged for unsatisfactory work performance caused by his need to take time off when the side effects of his treatment made him unable to work. The Seventh Circuit held that liver function is not a major life activity and, even if it is, the plaintiff failed to prove that his liver function was substantially limited.

It is important to note that many impairments differ widely in their severity. Thus, conditions such as migraine headaches, asthma, arthritis, diabetes, epilepsy, high blood pressure, and vision impairment must be evaluated on a case-by-case basis. The coverage of other conditions, such as infertility, obesity, and allergies to tobacco smoke, have yet to be resolved, but the more recent cases tend to find these conditions are not covered.

Because working is considered a major life activity, there has been some question whether the denial of a single job is a limitation of a major life activity. The regulations address this specifically: "The inability to perform a single, particular job does not constitute a substantial limitation in the major life activity of working." Whether an individual is substantially limited in the major life activity of working depends on the geographical area to which the individual has reasonable access, the number and types of similar jobs from which the individual is disqualified because of the impairment, and the number and types of other jobs from which the individual is disqualified because of the impairment. Weight lifting restrictions and the inability to work more than forty hours a week are not disabilities. The courts also have held that carpal tunnel syndrome does not substantially limit the major life activity of working. An employee's inability to perform his or her former job or all of the duties of the former job does not necessarily mean that the employee is substantially limited in the major life activity of working. The inability to work for a particular supervisor because of stress also is not a disability.

10. 270 F.3d 445 (7th Cir. 2001).

The courts have held that an individual assessment is needed to determine whether an individual is substantially limited in the major life activity of working. The court must compare the plaintiff's ability to work to the average person having comparable training, skills, and abilities.

In *Toyota Motor Manufacturing, Kentucky, Inc. v. Williams,*[11] the Supreme Court addressed the issue of when working is considered a major life activity. The Court unanimously held that an individual's inability to perform manual tasks associated with her job, due to work-induced carpal tunnel syndrome, did not constitute a substantial limitation of the major life activity of working. The Court said that "major life activities" must be strictly construed to effectuate the congressional intent that the ADA have limited coverage. It is not enough that the impairment prevents the employee from performing her job. "When addressing the major life activity of performing manual tasks, the central inquiry must be whether the claimant is unable to perform the variety of tasks central to most people's daily lives, not whether the claimant is unable to perform the tasks associated only with her specific job."[12] As a result of this case, it will be more difficult for individuals to establish a covered disability under the ADA by asserting that they are substantially limited in the major life activity of working.

The second prong of the definition of "disability" protects individuals with "a record of such impairment." Congress was aware that individuals with a history of cancer, heart disease, and other illnesses often face discrimination long after recovery from their illness. According to the EEOC's interpretive regulations, "[h]as a record of such impairment means has a history of, or has been misclassified as having, a mental or physical impairment that substantially limits one or more major life activities." The mere presence of a report in the employee's personnel file, which listed his prior workers' compensation claims, was held to be inadequate evidence that the employee's discharge was based on his "record of impairment." Also, the condition must substantially limit a major life activity to establish a "record" of impairment.

The third prong of the definition of "disability," "being regarded as having such an impairment," is conceptually the most difficult. The EEOC has limited "being regarded as having a disability" to three situations: (1) individuals who have impairments that are not substantially limiting but are erroneously regarded as substantially limiting; (2) individuals who have impairments that are only substantially limiting because of the attitude of others; and (3) individuals who have no impairment at all but who are erroneously regarded as having a substantially limiting impairment.

In general, the courts have held that a perceived impairment must be substantially limiting. In other words, the condition the plaintiff is "regarded" as having must be a covered disability. An employer's expression of concern about an individual's health, or its attempts to accommodate an individual's impairment, however, does not establish

---

11.   534 U.S. 184, 122 S.Ct. 681, 151   **12.**   122 S.Ct. at 693.
L.Ed.2d 615 (2002).

that the individual is being regarded as having a disability under the ADA. Also, the individual must prove that the employer was aware of the health condition.

Section 102(b)(4) of the ADA provides that it is unlawful to discriminate against a qualified individual "because of the known disability of an individual with whom the qualified individual is known to have a relationship or association." The purpose of this provision is to prevent employment discrimination against the family and friends of individuals with disabilities. The basis of the discrimination may be stigma associated with the disability or, in the case of dependents of employees, it may be concerns about higher health insurance costs. The plaintiff must prove that the employer knew about the disability of the "associate." Brief contact is not enough to establish an association. Other association cases have involved a faculty member at a boarding school whose son with bipolar disorder caused disruptions and breaches of the peace, and a discount store employee whose husband had a mental breakdown, which allegedly caused too much stress for the employee. The plaintiff must prove a causal connection between an adverse employment action and the disability of the plaintiff's "associate."

The ADA has a special provision for infectious and communicable diseases. Section 103(d) directs the Secretary of Health and Human Services to publish a list of infectious and communicable diseases transmitted through handling food. An employer may refuse to assign an individual with one of the listed diseases to a job involving food handling. In 1991, the Public Health Service published a notice containing a list of six pathogens, such as hepatitis A, often transmitted by food contaminated by infected persons who handle food. HIV was not on the list.

§ 3.5 Americans With Disabilities Act—Illegal Drugs and Alcohol

The ADA also has special provisions for illegal drugs and alcohol. Section 104 excludes from the definition of "qualified individual with a disability," "any employee or applicant who is currently engaging in the illegal use of drugs, when the covered entity acts on the basis of such use." "The illegal use of drugs" includes both the use of illegal drugs and the abuse of legal controlled substances. In addition, employees who engage in the illegal use of drugs or who are alcoholics may be held to the same qualification standards as other employees and they may be subject to discipline for poor performance or drug-related activity, such as possession or distribution of drugs.

The Fifth Circuit has held that an alcoholic is not covered under the ADA unless there is evidence that the effects of "alcoholism-induced inebriation are qualitatively different than those achieved by an overindulging social drinker * * *."[1] In other words, the physical and mental impairments caused by the alcoholism must be substantially limiting. Such an approach makes it extremely difficult for an alcoholic to obtain

§ 3.5
1. Burch v. Coca–Cola Co., 119 F.3d 305, 316 (5th Cir.1997), cert. denied, 522 U.S. 1084, 118 S.Ct. 871, 139 L.Ed.2d 768 (1998).

coverage under the ADA, and those who are so severely impaired by alcohol are unlikely to be able to perform essential job functions.

Individuals who are no longer using illegal drugs and who are in or who have completed a rehabilitation program and individuals who are erroneously regarded as engaging in illegal drug use are covered. Merely entering a rehabilitation program, however, "does not immediately convert a 'current' user into an individual with a disability protected under the ADA." There is, as yet, no shorthand test for when drug use is "current." According to one court, " 'no longer engaging in such use' can be read to mean that the person has been in recovery long enough to have become stable."[2] Enrolling in a treatment program while the ADA charge is pending before the EEOC is too late.

Employees who use drugs and those who are alcoholics are not protected by the ADA if their substance abuse renders them unfit to perform the job. For example, in one case, a police officer was diagnosed with manic-depression, alcoholism, and post-traumatic stress syndrome.[3] His firing was held not to violate the ADA where the record indicated that he had been suspended for thirty days for striking a prisoner; on two other occasions he drove away from a gas station with the pump nozzle still in his gas tank, and after one incident he suffered blackouts after which his hands were shaking so violently that he was unable to write a report. It has been held not to be a violation of the ADA to discharge an employee with some driving duties when his driver's license was revoked for driving under the influence, or to refuse to provide treatment for an employee whose security clearance was revoked after hospitalization for mental illness and alcoholism. In other cases, the discharges of employees have been upheld where they were driving while intoxicated, engaged in sexually inappropriate behavior on the job, made disparaging remarks about the employer's product in public, and failed a test after signing a "last chance agreement."

As with drug abuse rehabilitation, an important issue is the length of time an individual must be in successful alcohol rehabilitation in order to be protected under the ADA. In one case, the court upheld a hospital's refusal to reinstate the chief of internal medicine after he completed a month-long in-patient alcoholism treatment program.[4] The court observed that the individual had a history of relapses, and it was concerned about the risks to public safety in the event of another relapse. In other cases, a nurse who used drugs "in the weeks and months before her discharge," and a firefighter with a recent history of cocaine use were held not be protected under the ADA.

Once it is established that the individual with a substance-related disability is covered under the ADA, the same analysis regarding rights,

2. McDaniel v. Mississippi Baptist Med. Ctr., 877 F.Supp. 321, 328 (S.D.Miss.1994), affirmed without opinion, 74 F.3d 1238 (5th Cir.1995).

3. Graehling v. Village of Lombard, 58 F.3d 295 (7th Cir.1995).

4. Altman v. New York City Health & Hosp. Corp., 903 F.Supp. 503 (S.D.N.Y. 1995), affirmed, 100 F.3d 1054 (2d Cir. 1996).

duties, and procedures is applied. Employers, however, also may assert any relevant defenses, including that the individual's employment would constitute a direct threat to the individual, coworkers, or the public.

In *Raytheon Co. v. Hernandez*,[5] a twenty-five year employee of the company was required to take a drug test when he was suspected of being under the influence of drugs or alcohol. When the test was positive, he was forced to resign. Two years later, after completing a rehabilitation program, he applied for his former position and was denied employment because of an unwritten company rule prohibiting the rehire of individuals who left the company for violating personal conduct rules. The Ninth Circuit held that, as applied to the plaintiff, the rule had a disparate impact on substance abusers who were later rehabilitated. The Supreme Court held that the Ninth Circuit erred in deciding the case on a disparate impact theory that was not pled timely and in failing to resolve the case on the disparate treatment claim. It reversed and remanded.

The unresolved issue in *Raytheon,* the validity of the employer's no-rehire policy, is important to consider. Although there is a facial justification for the rule, if Raytheon can refuse to rehire its former employees who were terminated for violations, then it would seem that other employers could adopt an even broader policy of not hiring any individual who was discharged for cause (including violating a substance abuse policy) by itself or *any other* employer. Such a result, however, would undermine the intent of section 510(b)(1) of the ADA, which provides that the protections of the ADA apply to an individual who "has successfully completed a supervised drug rehabilitation program and is no longer engaging in the illegal use of drugs, or has otherwise been rehabilitated successfully and is no longer engaging in such use * * *."

It is not clear whether an individual who has a false positive drug test is covered under the ADA as someone erroneously regarded as engaging in illegal drug use. The ADA gives employers wide discretion to combat the use of illegal drugs and alcohol in the workplace and neither requires nor prohibits drug testing. Because drug tests are expressly excluded from the definition of medical tests, they may be given at any time.

An important issue regarding drug testing under the ADA concerns the timing of the tests. For employers subject to federal testing standards (as well as other employers using a good testing protocol), after a positive test result, a medical review officer will interview the subject to inquire whether the individual is taking any medications that could have caused a false positive result. Under the ADA, however, as described below, it is illegal for an employer or any agent of the employer at the preemployment stage to inquire into the medications taken by an individual. The EEOC has taken the position that after a positive test an employer may validate the test results by inquiring as to medications taken "or other biomedical explanations for the positive result." Merely

5. 540 U.S. 44, 124 S.Ct. 513, 157 L.Ed.2d 357 (2003).

deferring drug testing to the preplacement stage, however, eliminates this problem.

§ 3.6 Americans With Disabilities Act—Qualification Standards

The ADA prohibits discrimination against a *"qualified* individual with a disability." Thus, it is essential to determine what it means to be "qualified." According to section 101(8), the term means "an individual with a disability who, with or without reasonable accommodation, can perform the essential functions of the employment position that such individual holds or desires."

In practice, determining whether an individual is medically qualified for a particular job is a two-step process. First, there must be an evaluation of the physical and mental demands of the job. Second, the applicant must undergo a job-related medical assessment. Under the ADA, there must be an individualized determination of fitness. In matching job demands with individual abilities, the individual need only be able to perform the "essential functions" of the job. Congress specifically intended that individuals with disabilities not be excluded because of their inability to perform functions that are "marginal" to the job. Whether a function is "essential" or "marginal" depends upon, among other things, the amount of time the employee spends on the activity and the effect on the business if the employee did not perform the function. Absent evidence that the employer has used qualification standards as a subterfuge for discrimination, the courts often give deference to an employer's judgment in determining essential functions.

An individual who is not qualified for the position need not be hired or retained. Determining whether an individual is "qualified" for the job must be done on a case-by-case basis, considering the nature of the disability and the nature of the job. Some of the reasons why individuals were found not to be qualified include: having frequent seizures in a store resulting in a disruption of the business; frequent absenteeism; panic attacks, outbursts, and mood swings; depression and anxiety that prevented performance of the job; a police officer who drove erratically after collapsing into a diabetic coma; an airline fleet service clerk applicant with serious breathing and movement impairments; a city bus driver who had difficulty distinguishing traffic light colors; a "door greeter" at a wholesale store whose bad back prevented her from standing; truck drivers whose disabilities prevented them from obtaining DOT certification; a teacher whose learning disabilities prevented her from passing even an accommodated teacher certification test; a nuclear power employee who was denied a security clearance based on a psychological examination; a nurse whose fatigue-induced seizures prevented her from working evening and night shifts; and employees whose back injuries prevented them from bending and doing heavy lifting. Individuals also may not be qualified because they are unable to perform the job for reasons unrelated to their disability.

One of the many reasons an individual with disabilities may be considered medically unqualified for a particular job is the employer's concern that the individual may pose a safety or health threat to the individual, coworkers, customers, or the public. Section 103(b) provides that "[t]he term 'qualification standards' may include a requirement that an individual shall not pose a direct threat to the health or safety of other individuals in the workplace." Although this language is narrow and does not include harm to the individual employee with a disability, the interpretive regulation of the EEOC is broader. It defines "direct threat" to include the affected individual, requires these determinations to be made on the basis of reasonable medical judgment, and lists four factors to consider. These factors are the duration of the risk, the nature and severity of the potential harm, the likelihood that the potential harm will occur, and the imminence of the potential harm. The legislative history and the EEOC regulations make it clear that a "direct threat" claim of an employer is difficult to prove. Patronizing assumptions, generalized fears, and speculative or remote risks are insufficient.

In *Chevron U.S.A. Inc. v. Echazabal*,[1] an employee who had worked for independent contractors at a Chevron Oil refinery applied for a job with Chevron. On two occasions the employer withdrew conditional offers of employment following medical examinations which indicated that Echazabal had hepatitis C. Although he had worked at the Chevron facility for over 20 years without experiencing any health problems, Echazabal was denied employment by Chevron on the ground that exposure to toxic chemicals at the refinery would damage his liver. He was laid off by his contractor-employer when Chevron requested that he be removed from further exposures. Echazabal then sued under the ADA.

The Supreme Court unanimously upheld the validity of the EEOC interpretation of the direct threat provision, which provides a defense to employers if employment of an individual would constitute a threat to "self" as well as "others." The Ninth Circuit, in striking down EEOC's regulation, had relied on the interpretive maxim of *expressio unius exclusio alterius* (express mention and implied exclusion). According to the lower court, because the ADA mentions only threat to others as a defense under section 103(b) of the ADA, threat to self is excluded. The Supreme Court, however, said the *expressio unius* principle is inapplicable because section 103(b) uses threat to others as a nonexclusive example of a lawful qualification standard. Having dispensed with the textual argument, the Court had no trouble in finding that the interpretation was reasonable. On remand, the Ninth Circuit reversed the district court's granting of summary judgment for the employer, and remanded for a factual determination of whether the employer had proven a significant risk of substantial harm.

§ 3.6

1. 536 U.S. 73, 122 S.Ct. 2045, 153 L.Ed.2d 82 (2002).

Although Congress intended that the "direct threat" defense be construed narrowly, it has been applied in a variety of circumstances. A direct threat has been found where a city bus driver had insulin-dependent diabetes, where an employee with epilepsy worked near fast-moving press rollers and conveyor belts, where a United States marshal with a paranoid personality disorder would create a risk if he carried a firearm, where a neurologist with attention deficit hyperactivity disorder had short-term memory loss that led to mistakes in patient care, where a "line cook" with uncontrolled epilepsy was a direct threat to himself and others, where a firefighter with asthma was susceptible to breathing difficulties at work, and where HIV-infected health care workers performed invasive procedures. The safety defense, however, must be substantiated by an individualized determination of fitness and objective, reliable evidence about the nature of the risk.

§ 3.7 Americans With Disabilities Act—Medical Examinations and Inquiries

The ADA mandated major changes in the way some companies and physicians traditionally assessed the health status of applicants and employees. Section 102(d)(2) prohibits preemployment medical examinations and questionnaires. An employer may not "conduct a medical examination or make inquiries of a job applicant as to whether such applicant is an individual with a disability or as to the nature or severity of such disability." The only permissible inquiries are about the ability of the applicant to perform job-related functions. For example, an employer may ask if the individual is able to climb telephone poles, drive a truck, or manipulate small parts, if these are essential job functions. The employer also could ask, more generally, if the individual had any physical or mental impairment that would prevent the individual from performing essential job functions.

Because of the prohibition on preemployment medical inquiries, it is important to determine what is a "medical" examination or inquiry. According to the EEOC: "Medical examinations are procedures or tests that seek information about the existence, nature, or severity of an individual's physical or mental impairment, or that seek information regarding an individual's physical or psychological health." The following factors are used to determine whether any particular test is medical: (1) whether the test is administered by a health care professional or trainee; (2) whether the results of the test are interpreted by a health care professional or trainee; (3) whether the test is designed to reveal an impairment or the state of an individual's physical or psychological health; (4) whether the test is given for the purpose of revealing an impairment or the state of an individual's physical or psychological health; (5) whether the test is invasive (e.g., requires drawing blood, urine, breath, etc.); (6) whether the test measures physiological/psychological responses (as opposed to performance of a task); (7) whether the test is normally done in a medical setting; and (8) whether medical equipment/devices are used for the test.

In particular, skill or physical agility tests are not medical examinations. If these, or any, tests tend to screen out individuals on the basis of disability, however, the employer has the burden of proving that the tests are job-related and consistent with business necessity. Psychological tests are considered medical examinations if they provide evidence concerning whether an applicant has a mental disorder or impairment listed in the American Psychiatric Association's *Diagnostic and Statistical Manual of Mental Disorders (DSM)*. If, however, the test is designed to measure such factors as honesty, tastes, and habits, it is not a medical examination.

The ADA prohibits preemployment medical inquiries, but it may be difficult for the adversely affected individual to prevail on such a claim. It is not clearly established whether a nondisabled individual subjected to illegal medical questions is protected under the ADA, although the better reasoned opinions so hold. Furthermore, even if the individual has a covered disability, the employer may still avoid liability by proving that the employment decision was not affected by the unlawful inquiry. On the other hand, the ADA prohibits the unauthorized disclosure of medical information by employers regardless of whether the individual has a disability.

After a conditional offer of employment, an employer may require an "employment entrance examination" (preplacement examination) pursuant to section 102(d)(3). To be lawful under the ADA: (1) all entering employees in the same job category must be subject to an examination, regardless of disability; and (2) all medical information must be collected and maintained on separate forms and in separate medical files and treated as confidential. The only exceptions to the confidentiality rules are that supervisors and managers may be informed about necessary work restrictions and accommodations, safety and first aid personnel may be informed if the disability might require emergency treatment, and government officials investigating compliance with the ADA may be provided with relevant information on request.

Because medical examinations at the post-offer stage need not be job-related, it is lawful for an employer to condition employment on the individual's signing an authorization for the employer to obtain the individual's medical records obtained in the clinical setting. Medical information concerning employability may be disclosed to decision makers within the company. As a result, the issue has arisen regarding whether an employer may require individuals to sign a broad authorization for the disclosure of medical information to supervisors and managers. According to the EEOC, although individuals may *voluntarily* disclose medical information to nonmedical personnel, the employer may not "request, persuade, coerce, or otherwise pressure the individual to disclose such information." Consequently, the mandatory signing of an unlimited authorization probably would be held to be unlawful.

Even though post-offer medical examinations need not be job-related, an employer may not withdraw a conditional offer of employment based on a medical examination unless the withdrawal is based on the individual's inability to perform the essential functions of the job. Thus, it was held to be unlawful for a city to perform nonconsensual HIV testing at the post-offer stage and then withdraw conditional offers from those who tested positive.

Pursuant to section 102(d)(4), all medical examinations and inquiries of current employees must be "job-related and consistent with business necessity." Employers may require medical assessments, including those by independent medical examiners, to determine whether an employee remains capable of performing job-related functions safely and efficiently or is entitled to a medical leave of absence. On the other hand, an employer may not require an employee to submit to medical examinations that are not job-related, and the employer has the burden of proving that a medical examination of a current employee is job-related.

Employers also may offer medical examinations of a non-job-related nature, such as comprehensive medical examinations and wellness programs, but employee participation must be voluntary. As with examinations at the post-offer stage, employers may not engage in unauthorized activity to obtain medical information about a current employee. In one case,[1] the plaintiff, a law firm associate, alleged that after he began looking ill a partner of the defendant-law firm searched the plaintiff's office, discovered a letter from the Johns Hopkins University AIDS Services, and placed it in the plaintiff's personnel file. The court held that these allegations stated a claim under section 102(d)(4) of the ADA. Similarly, requiring employees to disclose to their supervisors all prescription medications they were taking has been held to violate the ADA.

Employers frequently require employees to undergo a medical examination before returning to work from a disability leave of absence. The courts have upheld medical examinations, psychological evaluations and specialized second opinions before permitting employees to resume work. Employees may not be subject to examinations merely because they are returning from a leave under the Family Medical Leave Act without a showing of "business necessity." Similarly, it has been held that an employer's policy requiring employees to provide medical diagnoses whenever they took unauthorized absences for any length of time violated the ADA's prohibition against medical inquiries likely to reveal employee disabilities.

§ 3.8 Americans With Disabilities Act—Reasonable Accommodation and Undue Hardship

If an individual is unable to perform the essential functions of the job because of a disability, then the employer must determine whether reasonable accommodation would enable the individual to perform the essential functions. Under section 102(b)(5)(A), employers have a duty to

§ 3.7

1. Doe v. Kohn Nast & Graf, P.C., 866 F.Supp. 190 (E.D.Pa.1994).

make reasonable accommodations to the known physical or mental limitations of an otherwise qualified applicant or employee. Section 101(9) provides that reasonable accommodation may include making facilities accessible, job restructuring, part-time or modified work schedules, reassignment to a vacant position, acquisition or modification of equipment or devices, appropriate adjustment or modification of examinations, training materials or policies, and the provision of qualified readers or interpreters. Reasonable accommodation is not required, however, if it results in "undue hardship" to the employer, defined in section 101(10) as "an action requiring significant difficulty or expense" in light of factors such as the nature and cost of the accommodation and the size and financial resources of the company.

Although employers have a duty of reasonable accommodation, the initial burden is on the individual to request accommodation and to make a facial showing that accommodation is possible. The burden of production then shifts to the employer to present evidence of its inability to accommodate. An accommodation is not reasonable if it strips the job of its principal duties. It also need not be the best possible accommodation so long as it will permit the employee to perform the job. An employer has no duty to create a new job category or to transfer the employee's essential job duties to co-workers.

Devising a reasonable accommodation is an interactive process in which both parties bear a responsibility for good faith and prompt action. An employee who fails to engage in the process, terminates the process, or unreasonably rejects alternatives proposed by the employer will not succeed in a claim under the ADA. The employer's duty, which begins when it has information that the employee might have a disability, is to find a reasonable accommodation that will permit the individual to perform the essential functions of the job without undue hardship on the enterprise.

A common accommodation is the use of leave. The courts generally have held that the use of leave, especially accrued leave or unpaid leave, is a reasonable accommodation, and the failure to permit an employee to use leave violates the ADA. A leave of absence to obtain psychological treatment and alcoholism treatment also have been held to be reasonable. There are no specific time limits on what length of leave is reasonable, and courts consider such factors as the nature of the employee's duties and the effect of the leave on the employer. Requiring an employer to provide an indefinite leave until the employee's considerable health problems were resolved, and allowing the employee to continue with unpredictable absences, however, have been held to be unreasonable.

Although providing accommodations to permit an employee to remain in his or her current position is preferred, reassignment of the employee to another position also is a reasonable accommodation, including reassignment from one shift to another. Most courts have held that there is no duty to reassign an employee to a permanent light duty position. There is also no duty to reassign an employee to a position for which the employee is unqualified, where there is no vacant position, where the reassignment would be a promotion, and where the reassignment would advance the employee with a disability over a more qualified nondisabled candidate.

The employee has the burden of proving that a vacancy exists. Nevertheless, it was not reasonable to transfer an employee to a position that did not have the same opportunity for advancement or to reassign an employee to a lesser position when a comparable position was vacant. In other cases involving reassignment the courts have held there is no requirement to train en employee to take a new position where such training was not provided to employees without disabilities, no duty to pay the employee more than the regular rate of the reassigned position, and no duty to offer a former employee a position that became available six months after his termination.

In *US Airways, Inc. v. Barnett*,[1] the plaintiff injured his back while working as a cargo handler and was transferred to a less physically demanding position in the mailroom. Over his request to continue in the position as a reasonable accommodation, the mailroom position was given to another employee pursuant to the employer's unilaterally imposed seniority system. The Supreme Court was faced with the issue of whether the ADA or the seniority system took precedence. Justice Breyer's plurality opinion rejected both absolute positions—that the seniority system always or never takes precedence over the ADA. Instead, he wrote that ordinarily, if a proposed accommodation conflicts with a seniority system, the seniority system will prevail. The employee, however, may show special circumstances to override the seniority system, such as where the employer changes the seniority system so frequently that it reduces employee expectations and where the seniority system already contains exceptions.

Reasonable accommodation cases often have unique facts. In some of the more generally applicable cases, the courts have held that employers have no duty under the ADA to provide a completely smoke-free environment, no duty to change an employee's supervisor when doing so would be unduly burdensome, no duty to create a flexible schedule for an employee when doing so would create a hardship, no duty to create a new position or a part-time position, no duty to allow an employee to work at home, no duty to create a special job rotation, no general duty to hire an assistant to help perform essential job functions, no duty to hire a "job coach" for a mentally retarded employee, and no duty to ensure that an employee would be guarded against stress and criticism. On the other hand, a disabled legal aid attorney's claim that providing her with a paid parking space near work was a reasonable accommodation was held to be actionable. It is not a violation of the ADA for an employer to

§ 3.8

1.   535 U.S. 391, 122 S.Ct. 1516, 152 L.Ed.2d 589 (2002).

discontinue accommodations it had been making that exceeded its legal obligations. The failure to provide reasonable accommodation, however, may establish constructive discharge.

Although the issue is far from settled, most courts have held that there is no duty to provide reasonable accommodation for individuals with disabilities who are covered under the "third prong" of the three-part definition of disability because they are regarded as having an impairment.

§ 3.9 Americans With Disabilities Act—Defenses

Employers have asserted a variety of defenses in ADA cases, and many of these defenses have proved successful. For example, there is no violation where the employer had no knowledge that the individual had a disability at the time that the alleged discriminatory act took place. In general, the defenses involve either business justifications or misconduct on the part of the employee. With regard to business justifications, it does not violate the ADA for an employer to hire a more qualified and experienced nondisabled, incumbent employee rather than a disabled applicant. In addition, "downsizing" has been held to be a lawful justification for discharging or laying off employees.

A variety of employee actions have been held to constitute serious misconduct that justified the employer's adverse treatment of an employee. These include deliberate falsifications on an application or reports, theft, fighting, sleeping on the job, excessive absenteeism, submitting false workers' compensation claims, shoplifting, insubordination, being under the influence, failing to comply with a supervisor's orders, repeated tardiness, making threats, relapsing into substance abuse, disruptive behavior, rude behavior, repeatedly entering private homes without invitation, refusing to conceal an "HIV positive" tattoo that disturbed hospital patients, and inappropriate conduct toward female employees and members of the public. Unacceptable performance and lack of essential skills also have been held to be defenses to ADA claims. The employer need not be correct in its assessment of cause for the adverse action; a reasonable and honest mistake is a defense to intentional discrimination.

§ 3.10 Americans With Disabilities Act—Health Care and Other Benefits

Section 501(c) of the ADA, provides that the ADA does not prohibit insurers, HMOs, or similar providers of medical services from underwriting medical risks so long as permitted by state law. It also permits employers who sponsor commercially written health insurance coverage as well as self-insured employers to classify and underwrite medical risks. Thus, although employers may not deny all health insurance coverage to employees with disabilities, under the ADA they need not offer identical coverage at identical rates, but failure to do so will violate HIPAA. In addition, the EEOC has said that employers may provide "relevant information" to insurance companies where the company requires a medical examination as a precondition to health or life insurance coverage.

In 2000, the EEOC issued enforcement guidance on the application of the ADA to employer-provided health benefits. Employers are free to make any distinctions in health benefits that are not disability based. Some examples of benefit plan distinctions that are not disability based are preexisting condition clauses, lifetime or other universal limitations, experimental drugs and treatment, elective surgery, and other limitations on particular medical procedures, such as blood transfusions or x-rays, so long as they are not exclusively used for the treatment of a particular disability.

When limitations are found to be disability based, then the employer has the burden of proving that the limitation comes within the saving provision of section 501(c) and that it is not a subterfuge for discrimination. The first step, proving the applicability of section 501(c) is easier to prove, and would seem to be satisfied by merely showing the existence of a lawful, bona fide benefit plan. Proving that it is not a subterfuge, however, is more difficult. The employer has the burden of demonstrating that the benefit plan is based on valid actuarial principles for underwriting, classifying, or administering risks. According to the EEOC, some potential justifications include that the plan covers all similarly catastrophic conditions the same way, the limitation is necessary to preserve the fiscal soundness of the plan, the limitation is necessary to preserve meaningful and affordable health benefit coverage for employees, and the limitation excludes coverage for treatments that would not provide any meaningful benefit.

A few ADA cases already have been decided on the issue of health benefits. Group health insurance plans were held to have violated the ADA by reducing the maximum AIDS-related benefits per eligible plan member from $1 million to $25,000 and by failing to pay for high dose chemotherapy with autologous bone marrow transplant to treat breast cancer. Also, an employee with inoperable cancer who was on disability leave was held to remain an active employee and therefore could not be disqualified from life insurance benefits. Most courts to consider the issue have held that health benefits plans do not have to provide the same benefits for mental and physical disabilities. The exclusion of fertility treatments has been held not to violate the ADA.

Medical examinations and employer inquiries of current employees must either be job-related and consistent with business necessity or voluntarily. At least one court has held, however, that it did not violate the ADA for an employer to discharge an employee who refused to provide health history information needed for submission with the employer's application to enroll all of the employees in a new health insurance plan.

Former employees who retired with disability pensions have been held to be "qualified individuals with a disability" under the ADA and therefore could challenge alleged discrimination in the payment of their benefits. Specifically, the Second Circuit held that the city's alleged policy of requiring individuals to retire with a disability pension before allowing them to receive the more generous regular retirement pension violated the ADA.

§ 3.11 Americans With Disabilities Act—Discriminatory Treatment

Section 102(a) of the ADA prohibits a wide range of discriminatory conduct, including application and hiring procedures, compensation, job training, discharge, and other terms and conditions of employment. This provision has been broadly construed. "Discharge" includes constructive discharge, in which the employee's working conditions are made so intolerable that the employee has no other choice than to quit. "Other terms and conditions of employment" includes demotion, transfer, reassignment, and job assignments.

A variety of alleged conduct has been held to be actionable under the ADA, including restricting jobs for employees with disabilities to the least desirable ones and refusing to train employees with disabilities on additional machinery. However, an employer's making minor and temporary changes in work hours, assigning mandatory overtime work, and not ensuring that an individual employed on an as-needed basis received job assignments have been held not to be actionable.

It is well established that a claim for disability-based hostile environment harassment is actionable under the ADA. As with other forms of harassment, to violate the ADA the harassment must be severe. For example, an employee with asthma stated a claim for harassment where coworkers and supervisors intentionally smoked in his presence because they knew this bothered his asthma. On the other hand, a single negative comment did not constitute harassment, and calling an employee "crip" was not enough to demonstrate that the employer "regarded" the individual as having a disability under the third prong of the definition.

§ 3.12 Americans With Disabilities Act—Retaliation

As with other antidiscrimination laws, section 503 of the ADA prohibits retaliation against any individual for asserting any right under the ADA or participating in any proceeding under the ADA. The most common basis for retaliation claims has been requesting an accommodation and filing a charge with the EEOC. A range of employer actions also have been held to be covered under section 503, including discharge and delay in approving an assignment. In a case where a father and son worked for the same employer, retaliating against the son due to the father's ADA action also was held to be actionable. Individual defendants may be sued in their personal capacities for violating the ADA's anti-retaliation provision.

Individuals alleging retaliation must exhaust their administrative remedies by alleging retaliation in the charge they file with the EEOC. The plaintiff must establish (1) that he or she had engaged in protected activity; (2) that the employer took adverse action; and (3) there was a causal relationship between the protected activity and the adverse action. The first two elements are relatively straightforward, but direct proof of a connection between the protected activity and the adverse action is usually lacking. Consequently, the courts have approved relying on circumstantial evidence of motive. The courts have uniformly applied the burden-shifting approach of *McDonnell Douglas Corp. v. Green*[1] to retaliation claims under the ADA.

> [O]nce the plaintiff has established a prima facie case of retaliation, the employer has the burden of coming forth with a legitimate, nondiscriminatory reason for its adverse action. If the employer does so, the plaintiff may then present evidence that the reason given by the employer is a mere pretext for the real, discriminatory reason for the adverse action.[2]

The timing of the events is often an extremely important factor. A long delay between the protected activity and the adverse action gives rise to an inference that there was no retaliation. For example, no retaliation was found where there was a four-month interval between the employee's request for accommodation and discharge, and where there was a one-year delay between filing a charge with the EEOC and the employee's reassignment. Even where there is a short time between the protected activity and the adverse action, the employer may be able to rebut the inference of retaliation. For example, an employee was discharged two days after a dispute with her supervisor, but the employer rebutted the inference of retaliation by proving that the discharge was based on budgetary considerations and the supervisor played no part in the decision. A variety of other reasons have been held to justify the adverse action, including the employee's failing to pay group health premiums, insubordination, and falsifying reports.

If the "protected activity" underlying an action for retaliation is the filing of a claim alleging discrimination in violation of the ADA, what happens to the retaliation claim if the original discrimination claim fails, such as because the individual is held not to be covered under the definition of "individual with a disability"? The courts to consider the issue have held that the retaliation claim may still succeed if the employee can a demonstrate a good faith belief that there was a violation of the ADA, acted on the basis of the belief, the employer knew of the employee's conduct, and the employer took adverse action against the employee because of the protected activity.

§ 3.12

1. 411 U.S. 792, 93 S.Ct. 1817, 36 L.Ed.2d 668 (1973).

2. Doebele v. Sprint/United Mgmt. Co., 342 F.3d 1117 (10th Cir. 2003), quoting

Butler v. City of Prairie Village, 172 F.3d 736 (10th Cir. 1999).

§ 3.13 Americans With Disabilities Act—Procedure, Burden of Proof, and Remedies

The procedures and burden of proof under the ADA are quite similar to that used in Title VII cases. The plaintiff must first exhaust administrative remedies before the EEOC before filing suit. The statute of limitations and the bases for extending it under the ADA are the same as under Title VII. State statutes of limitation do not apply. The continuing violation doctrine, which may result in extending the time for filing a complaint, has been held to apply to ADA cases. The plaintiff's prima facie case includes showing: (1) that he or she is an individual with a disability under the ADA; (2) that he or she is qualified with or without reasonable accommodation to perform the essential functions of the job; and (3) that the employer discharged or otherwise discriminated against the plaintiff because of the plaintiff's disability. The plaintiff has the burden of proving that the employer knew that the individual has a disability. The length of time between the employer's learning of the disability and the adverse action is also relevant.

The courts have applied the burden-shifting approach of *McDonnell Douglas Corp. v. Green*[1] to ADA cases. To prove that an adverse action was taken "because of" an individual's disability, it is not necessary to prove that the action was taken "solely because of" the disability. According to the Eleventh Circuit: "In everyday usage, 'because of' conveys the idea of a factor that made a difference in the outcome."[2]

Under *McDonnell Douglas*, after the plaintiff establishes a prima facie case, the burden shifts to the employer to state a lawful reason for the employment decision. The plaintiff may then attempt to discredit the employer's proffered reason as pretextual. The courts in ADA cases have not agreed on whether the plaintiff must merely establish that the employer's stated reason is false ("pretext only"), that the stated reason is false and the real reason is discriminatory ("pretext plus"), or some middle ground. At least one court has held that an employer's "honest belief" in the facts used to base its employment decision cannot be a pretext for discrimination, even if the facts are not true.

Two other important allocations of the burden of proof in ADA cases have been recognized in addition to disparate treatment analysis applying the *McDonnel Douglas* burden-shifting approach. First, in *Raytheon Co. v. Hernandez*,[3] the Supreme Court explicitly approved the use of disparate impact claims under the ADA, based on the statutory language of section 102(b), which defines "discriminate" to include "utilizing standards, criteria, or methods of administration * * * that have the effect of discrimination on the basis of disability" and "using qualification standards, employment tests or other selection criteria that screen

§ 3.13

1. 411 U.S. 792, 93 S.Ct. 1817, 36 L.Ed.2d 668 (1973).

2. McNely v. Ocala Star–Banner Corp., 99 F.3d 1068, 1077 (11th Cir.1996), cert. denied, 520 U.S. 1228, 117 S.Ct. 1819, 137 L.Ed.2d 1028 (1997).

3. 540 U.S. 44, 124 S.Ct. 513, 157 L.Ed.2d 357 (2003).

out or tend to screen out an individual with a disability." Second, some courts have applied the Supreme Court's mixed-motive analysis of *Desert Palace, Inc. v. Costa*[4] to ADA cases, but other courts have decline to apply this approach.

As amended by the Civil Rights Act of 1991, remedies available under Title I of the ADA include reinstatement, back pay, equitable relief, compensatory damages, and punitive damages. Damages are only available for intentional violations and the total amount of damages available is limited by the size of the company: $50,000 for employers with 15–100 employees; $100,000 for employers with 101–200 employees; $200,0000 for employers with 201–500 employees; and $300,000 for employers with more than 500 employees. The responsibility for promulgating implementing regulations and enforcement of Title I of the ADA rests with the Equal Employment Opportunity Commission (EEOC). State and federal courts have concurrent jurisdiction over ADA cases.

Class action certification may be granted to ADA cases under appropriate circumstances. Available remedies include equitable relief, back pay, front pay, and interest and punitive damages. The employer has the burden of proving that the plaintiff failed to mitigate damages. Attorney fees also may be awarded to prevailing parties, by applying standards used in Title VII cases. There is no right to a jury trial.

§ 3.14 Americans With Disabilities Act—Relationship to Other Laws

There are several laws that have been affected directly or indirectly by the ADA. One group of laws is workers' compensation. In general, actions brought under the ADA are not barred by the "exclusive remedy" provisions of workers' compensation laws. Thus, receipt of workers' compensation will not be a bar to an action for discrimination under the ADA. Similarly, receipt of damages for discrimination cannot be used as an offset to receipt of workers' compensation benefits. The failure to pay workers' compensation and distinctions among individuals with disabilities for purposes of benefits under workers' compensation do not violate the ADA.

An extremely contentious issue is whether employees who assert that they are totally disabled in applying for Social Security disability benefits and other compensation are barred from bringing an action for disability discrimination under the ADA. If individuals were "totally disabled" and unable to work, this would prevent their being "qualified" under the ADA. In *Cleveland v. Policy Management Systems Corp.*,[1] the Supreme Court held that filing for or receiving Social Security benefits does *not* estop a claim under the ADA nor does it establish a presumption against the plaintiff. To the extent that the plaintiff has made

4. 539 U.S. 90, 123 S.Ct. 2148, 156 L.Ed.2d 84 (2003).

§ 3.14

1. 526 U.S. 795, 119 S.Ct. 1597, 143 L.Ed.2d 966 (1999).

contradictory assertions, however, the plaintiff has the burden of explaining the discrepancy.

Another source of overlapping laws is federal labor law. Although it should be clear that federal and state disability discrimination claims are not preempted by the National Labor Relations Act or section 301 of the Labor Management Relations Act, there is currently some support to the contrary. The Supreme Court has held that an employee's failure to arbitrate a claim did not bar an action under the ADA where the collective bargaining agreement did not contain a "clear and unmistakable waiver" of the employee's statutory rights.

In *Circuit City Stores, Inc. v. Adams*,[2] the Supreme Court held that provisions in individual employment contracts providing that arbitration is the sole remedy for all employment disputes are enforceable. The Court held that only employment contracts of transportation workers are exempt from the Federal Arbitration Act. In *EEOC v. Waffle House, Inc.*,[3] however, the Court held that arbitration agreements do not bar the EEOC from bringing actions, as the EEOC is not a party to the agreement to arbitrate all disputes.

The other law with potential overlap with the ADA is the Family and Medical Leave Act (FMLA). For example, a reasonable accommodation under the ADA may be to grant leave time in addition to that required by the FMLA, although leave under the ADA does not require maintaining health insurance coverage. In addition, if an employee is entitled to leave under the FMLA, an employer may not require the employee to take another job as a reasonable accommodation under the ADA.

§ 3.15　State Disabilities Laws

Nearly every state has its own civil rights law prohibiting discrimination in employment on the basis of disability or handicap. Section 501(b) of the ADA provides that the ADA does not preempt any state or local law "that provides greater or equal protection for the rights of individuals with disabilities than are afforded by this Act."

There are three main ways in which state laws are important to complement the protections of the ADA. First, the state law may apply to a wider class of employers. Twenty-five states and the District of Columbia have laws that apply to employers with fewer than fifteen employees. Second, the state law may apply to a wider range of impairments than the ADA, such as individuals who are obese, who have substance abuse problems, or whose disabilities are not severe enough to meet the ADA definition. Third, the state law may more closely regulate certain medical or hiring procedures in employment. For example, in

2. 532 U.S. 105, 121 S.Ct. 1302, 149 L.Ed.2d 234 (2001).　　**3.** 534 U.S. 279, 122 S.Ct. 754, 151 L.Ed.2d 755 (2002).

Minnesota preplacement medical examinations must be limited to assessing job-related health conditions.[1]

An amendment to California's Fair Employment and Housing Act[2] extends protections beyond the ADA in several ways, including the following: an impairment need not substantially limit a major life activity but need only make it more difficult; the degree of limitation is considered without regard to mitigating measures; some conditions, such as HIV, epilepsy, and diabetes are per se disabilities; and working is considered a major life activity regardless of whether the impairment affects entry into a broad range of jobs.

§ 3.15
1. Minn. Stat. Ann. § 363A.20.
2. Cal. Gov't Code § 12926.1

Chapter 4

WAGES, HOURS, AND BENEFITS

Table of Sections

§ 4.1   Introduction

Although laws regulating wages and hours can be traced to colonial times, early regulation took the form of caps on the wages of skilled workers, who were in short supply. Organized concern about protecting the conditions under which workers toiled did not arise until the mid–1800s. In 1840, an Executive Order issued by President Van Buren established a ten-hour day for workers at government shipyards. State legislatures began to enact maximum hours legislation and restrictions on child labor. In *Lochner v. New York*,[1] however, the Supreme Court struck down a New York law limiting work in bakeries to ten hours a day on the ground that it interfered with the freedom of contract between employers and employees. *Lochner* suggested that states might be able to regulate working conditions if they could show a specific health threat, and the Court did uphold some statutes governing the work of women and children,[2] but as a general matter, *Lochner* ushered in a thirty-year period during which courts routinely invalidated most state and federal protective labor legislation.

The *Lochner* era did not end until March 29, 1937, when the Supreme Court sustained the constitutionality of a state minimum wage law in *West Coast Hotel Co. v. Parrish*.[3] President Roosevelt had made wage-hour legislation a major issue in the 1936 campaign, and the Fair Labor Standards Act (FLSA) was passed and signed into law on June 25, 1938. The FLSA established a minimum wage of twenty-five cents per hour for the first year it was in effect, with an increase to thirty cents in the second year, and forty cents in the seventh year. The FLSA did not limit hours of work, but dealt with the maximum hours issue by requiring the payment of an overtime rate of one-and-one-half times the regular rate of pay for all hours over forty-four per week for the first year it was in effect, forty-two per week for the second year, and forty per week in the third year. The child labor provisions prohibited the interstate shipment of goods produced by an establishment employing children under the age of sixteen, or eighteen in the case of hazardous industries. In *United States v. Darby*,[4] the Supreme Court upheld the FLSA against commerce clause and due process attacks.

The FLSA has been amended a number of times since 1938, although its basic scheme has remained essentially unchanged. The first major amendments were made by the Portal–to–Portal Act of 1947, which was a congressional reaction to various court decisions over the first decade of FLSA enforcement. The Fair Labor Standards Amendments of 1949 strengthened the child labor restrictions, elaborated on the overtime standard, revised some exemptions, and raised the mini-

§ 4.1

1. 198 U.S. 45, 25 S.Ct. 539, 49 L.Ed. 937 (1905).

2. See, e.g., Muller v. Oregon, 208 U.S. 412, 28 S.Ct. 324, 52 L.Ed. 551 (1908) (upholding limit on hours of work for women).

3. 300 U.S. 379, 57 S.Ct. 578, 81 L.Ed. 703 (1937).

4. 312 U.S. 100, 61 S.Ct. 451, 85 L.Ed. 609 (1941).

mum wage to seventy-five cents. Other significant amendments came in 1961, when the concept of enterprise coverage was introduced, in 1966, when the equal pay standard was added, and in 1985, when special provisions governing public sector workers were enacted. The most recent increase in the minimum wage was in 1996, when it was raised in stages from $4.25 to $5.15 per hour.

Although the FLSA is the cornerstone of federal wage policy, several other federal statutes establish minimum wage requirements. These include the Davis–Bacon Act of 1931, the Walsh–Healey Public Contracts Act of 1936, and the Service Contract Act of 1965. Davis–Bacon and Walsh–Healey were both enacted at a time when courts were routinely striking down protective labor laws. To avoid the constitutionality problem, these statutes adopted the concept of a prevailing wage, rather than a statutorily fixed minimum wage. The FLSA does not preempt state laws, and most states have wage-hour laws, although many are less protective than the FLSA. Most states also have laws protecting workers' rights to receive payment of their wages.

Since World War II employee benefits other than cash wages, such as pensions, health insurance, paid vacations, and leaves of absence, have become increasingly important aspects of compensation. Some benefits, such as unemployment compensation insurance coverage and Social Security taxes, are required by federal law, and many states require certain benefits, most commonly time off for jury duty, voting, or childcare. Until recently, however, Congress has resisted universal government-mandated benefits, and employers provide most benefits either unilaterally or as a result of collective bargaining with unions representing their workers. The Family and Medical Leave Act of 1993, which requires covered employers to grant leaves of absence for the birth or adoption of a child, or for the serious health conditions of the employee or close family members, thus represents a significant departure from past practice.

Historically, a more common statutory approach to employee benefits has been not to require employers to provide a benefit, but rather to impose certain obligations once an employer chooses to offer one. Take, for instance, health care coverage. Except in Hawaii, no law currently requires employers to offer health care coverage to their workers. Once an employer provides this benefit, however, the Employee Retirement Income Security Act (ERISA) requires the provision of continuation coverage rights and limits the operation of pre-existing condition exclusion provisions. If an employer provides health care benefits through the purchase of insurance, every state requires some minimum level of coverage through its insurance laws, although the specific coverage requirements differ greatly from state to state. In addition, Title VII of the Civil Rights Act of 1964, as amended by the Pregnancy Discrimination Act of 1978, requires employers that offer health coverage to include coverage for pregnancy and childbirth.

ERISA has been one of the most significant developments in the law regulating employee benefits. Although primarily concerned with pensions, it also covers a vast array of nonpension benefits. It imposes certain procedural obligations on employers that provide covered benefits, including reporting and disclosure requirements and the requirement of internal claims and appeal mechanisms, and it creates a federal cause of action for challenges to benefits denials. Its most important and controversial aspect, however, is its broad preemption provision, which has displaced large bodies of state law dealing with the enforcement of benefit promises.

§ 4.2 Fair Labor Standards Act—Coverage

The Fair Labor Standards Act (FLSA) contains four major requirements: a minimum wage, an overtime standard, restrictions on child labor, and equal pay. These requirements apply to all covered employees unless the Act specifically exempts them from one or more of its provisions. There are three types of coverage: individual employee (traditional) coverage, enterprise coverage, and coverage of public employees.

Individual Employee Coverage

As originally enacted in 1938, the FLSA defined coverage only on the basis of an employee's job duties, not on the nature of the employer's business. Under this traditional coverage, employees are covered only if they are "engaged in commerce" or in the "production of goods for commerce."[1] Congress intended the term "engaged in commerce" to extend to the limits of the commerce clause. Employees are "engaged in commerce" if their work involves the movement of goods, people, or communications across state lines or is closely related to that activity. The term includes, for example, employees in communications industries, those who load, unload, or otherwise handle goods received directly from outside the state, those who regularly use channels of commerce such as telephones and the mail, and those who maintain, repair, or improve instruments of commerce.

Employees are engaged in the "production of goods for commerce" if they manufacture, mine, produce, handle, or otherwise work on goods that cross state lines. The term also includes tasks closely related or essential to production, such as supervising, packing, warehousing, and shipping. Coverage is present if the employer hopes or has reason to believe that the goods will cross state lines, even if the goods are in fact sold locally.

Enterprise Coverage

Under individual employee coverage, with its focus on each worker's duties, some employees of a company can be covered by the FLSA, while others are not. In 1961, Congress broadened the scope of the Act by

§ 4.2

1. FLSA §§ 6(a), 7(a), 29 U.S.C.A. §§ 206(a), 207(a).

adding enterprise coverage, which focuses instead on the nature of the employer's business. Although enterprise coverage is grounded on a commerce test similar to that used for traditional coverage, all employees of a covered enterprise are automatically covered without regard to the duties of each individual worker. To qualify for enterprise coverage a business must satisfy three requirements: the statutory definition of "enterprise," a commerce standard, and a dollar volume test.

The Act defines "enterprise" as "related activities performed (either through unified operations or common control) by any person or persons for a common business purpose, and includes all such activities whether performed in one or more establishments * * *."[2] This broad definition can include activities performed at physically separate locations by legally distinct entities, and it can result in coverage of a group of establishments that do not meet the dollar volume requirement on an individual basis.

Although the definition of enterprise has three components, related activities, unified operations or common control, and common business purpose, the same facts can help satisfy more than one part of the definition. Activities are related if they are the same or similar, part of a vertical structure, auxiliary or service operations, or otherwise reasonably related to the main function of the enterprise. For example, a bank owned an office building, occupied part of it for its banking operations, and rented the remaining floors to other tenants. The bank employed some workers whose only duties were to clean and maintain the leased portions of the building. Maintenance of the real estate was found related to the operation of the bank itself, because the bank depended on the rental income and the tax advantages of ownership to enable it to occupy the building, and it used the building as its symbol in advertising and promotion. Therefore, the real estate activities and the banking activities constituted a single enterprise, and the maintenance employees were covered by the FLSA.[3]

Unified operation or common control will be found if there is common ownership, substantially overlapping or integrated operations, or a common entity with the power to control operations. The third part of the definition is a common business purpose. A profit motive or commercial activity, even if conducted by a nonprofit organization, establishes a business purpose. In addition, the statute specifies that the operations of a hospital, nursing home, or other similar residential institution, school, college, or university, various types of urban and interurban mass transit, and public agencies are all for a business purpose.[4] A common business purpose depends on many of the same factors that establish the requirement of related activities. For instance, the activities of renting and maintaining houses and apartments were

---

2. FLSA § 3(r)(1), 29 U.S.C.A. § 203(r)(1).

3. Wirtz v. Savannah Bank & Trust Co., 362 F.2d 857 (5th Cir.1966).

4. FLSA § 3(r)(2), 29 U.S.C.A. § 203(r)(2).

held to have a common business purpose because the services were substantially similar from project to project and had the common purpose of maintenance and operation.[5]

Besides satisfying the statutory definition of enterprise, a business must also meet a commerce test and a dollar volume test to qualify for enterprise coverage. The commerce test requires that an enterprise have two or more employees "engaged in commerce or in the production of goods for commerce, or * * * handling, selling, or otherwise working on goods or materials that have been moved in or produced for commerce."[6] The third prong of this commerce test is not part of the commerce definition for traditional coverage. It applies to tasks performed on goods after the end of their interstate journey, when employees might not be "engaged in commerce." Thus, an enterprise with no employees covered by traditional coverage can nevertheless be a covered enterprise, if it has employees who handle goods that have been moved in commerce.

The third component of enterprise coverage is a dollar volume test, the amount of which has varied over the years. In 1989, Congress simplified this part of the statutory scheme, which had contained several different industry-specific amounts and grandfather provisions, by setting an across-the-board standard of a minimum of $500,000 in annual gross volume of sales made or business done.[7] Hospitals, nursing homes, and other similar residential institutions, schools, colleges, universities, and public agencies qualify for enterprise coverage without regard to either the commerce test or the dollar volume test.[8]

An establishment whose only regular employees are its owner or a member of the owner's immediate family is not to be considered an enterprise engaged in commerce or the production of goods for commerce, and its sales may not be included in determining whether an enterprise meets the dollar volume test.[9]

Employee Status

Protection of individual workers under any form of coverage depends on the existence of an employer-employee relationship. The most common dispute over employee status involves the distinction between employee and independent contractor. If an individual hired to perform work for a firm is a true independent contractor, no employment relationship and therefore no FLSA coverage exist. The FLSA, however, contains expansive definitions of the relevant terms. An "employer" includes "any person acting directly or indirectly in the interest of an employer in relation to an employee,"[10] an "employee" is "any individual employed by an employer,"[11] and "employ" is "to suffer or permit to work."[12]

5. Brock v. Hamad, 867 F.2d 804 (4th Cir.1989).

6. FLSA § 3(s)(1)(A)(i), 29 U.S.C.A. § 203(s)(1)(A)(i).

7. FLSA § 3(s)(1)(A)(ii), 29 U.S.C.A. § 203(s)(1)(A)(ii).

8. FLSA § 3(s)(1)(B), (C), 29 U.S.C.A. § 203(s)(1)(B), (C).

9. FLSA § 3(s)(2), 29 U.S.C.A. § 203(s)(2).

10. FLSA § 3(d), 29 U.S.C.A. § 203(d).

11. FLSA § 3(e)(1), 29 U.S.C.A. § 203(e)(1).

12. FLSA § 3(g), 29 U.S.C.A. § 203(g).

Common law definitions of employee and independent contractor are not controlling, nor is any agreement between the parties about the nature of their relationship. Rather, the overarching consideration is economic reality; are individuals economically dependent on the business for which they labor? The economic realities test does not require that workers be completely dependent on a business for their basic source of income. Otherwise, workers in seasonal businesses that operate for only a few weeks a year, part-time workers, and workers with more than one job might never be covered. Rather, the question in such situations is whether workers depend on the business for their continued employment during the period the business operates.

In interpreting the economic realities test, courts have applied a number of factors, many of which are drawn from common law principles. They include: (1) the degree of control exercised by the alleged employer; (2) the extent of the relative investments in equipment and material; (3) the worker's opportunity for profit and loss through managerial skill; (4) the skill and initiative required by the work; (5) the permanence of the relationship; and (6) the extent to which the service rendered is an integral part of the alleged employer's business. Of necessity, the inquiry into employee status is highly fact-dependent and requires examination of all the circumstances. For instance, lack of actual day-to-day control over an individual's work does not preclude a finding of employee status if the nature of the job prevents direct supervision. Similarly, lack of permanence in the relationship will not negate a finding of employee status if the other factors point in that direction.

Application of these factors can sometimes result in a finding that two or more entities or individuals are statutory employers of the same workers and jointly responsible for compliance with the FLSA. Often the workers' status as employees is clear, but the identity of the joint employer may come as a surprise. For instance, *Donovan v. DialAmerica Marketing, Inc.*[13] involved a telephone marketing company and its relationship to two groups of workers, those who researched telephone numbers in their homes and those who recruited some of the home researchers and distributed research work to them. The court found that the home researchers were statutory employees, but the distributors were independent contractors, primarily because their opportunity for profit or loss was based on their skill in recruiting and retaining their own home researchers and in controlling their expenses. It went on to hold, however, that DialAmerica was the statutory employer of all the home researchers, including the employees of the distributors. The distributors' status as independent contractors and statutory employers of the researchers did not prevent application of the economic realities

13.   757 F.2d 1376 (3d Cir.), cert. denied, 474 U.S. 919, 106 S.Ct. 246, 88 L.Ed.2d 255 (1985).

test to DialAmerica as well. Even though the company had given control over the researchers' rate of pay to the distributors, it was a joint employer and jointly liable for failure to pay the minimum wage to the researchers.

Similarly, agents of employers can also be statutory employers if they exercise enough control over employees. In *Falk v. Brennan*,[14] a real estate management company that performed services for a number of separately owned apartment complexes was found to be the statutory employer of the maintenance workers at each of the complexes. Although these workers were employees of the building owners, they were also statutory employees of the management company, which supervised them and exercised substantial control over the terms and conditions of their work.

Courts disregard sham arrangements set up to provide the appearance of an independent contractor relationship. For example, an employer might arrange to have an admitted employee perform after-hours work, either on the employer's premises or at home. Except under highly unusual circumstances, the worker remains a statutory employee, even if the after-hours work is different from the work he or she performs during normal business hours. Similarly, alleged independent contractors who do the same kind of work as individuals on the employer's payroll are likely to be classified as employees as well. The economic realities, rather than contractual provisions, determine whether an individual is an independent contractor or an employee.

Another question of employee status concerns students and trainees. Although on-the-job training of employees is compensable activity, there are situations in which individuals who are being trained but do not hold any formal job are not statutory employees. In *Walling v. Portland Terminal Co.*,[15] the Supreme Court held that individuals being trained as railroad brakemen in a week-long course were not statutory employees of the railroad because the railroad received no immediate benefit from the work done by the trainees and the trainees did not expect any remuneration for their work. The Act was "obviously not intended to stamp all persons as employees, who, without any express or implied compensation agreement, might work for their own advantage on the premises of another."[16]

Accordingly, the Department of Labor has developed six criteria indicative of a training rather than an employment relationship: (1) the training is similar to that provided by a vocational school; (2) the training is for the benefit of the trainees; (3) the trainees do not displace regular employees, but work under close observation; (4) the employer gets no immediate advantage from the training, and in fact may have its operations impeded by the training; (5) the trainees are not necessarily

---

14. 414 U.S. 190, 94 S.Ct. 427, 38 L.Ed.2d 406 (1973).

15. 330 U.S. 148, 67 S.Ct. 639, 91 L.Ed. 809 (1947).

16. 330 U.S. at 152, 67 S.Ct. at 641.

entitled to a job at the end of the training period; and (6) the employer and the trainees understand that the trainees are not entitled to wages for the time spent in training.[17]

Closely related to the trainee question is the status of volunteers. A true volunteer, one who performs services for humanitarian, charitable, or civic purposes, does not expect compensation for those services and is not a statutory employee. Most examples of true volunteerism occur, of course, in the public sector or with nonprofit, noncommercial organizations. Commercial operations have a very difficult time arguing that individuals performing work on their behalf do not expect compensation in some form. In *Tony & Susan Alamo Foundation v. Secretary of Labor*,[18] a religious foundation operated many commercial businesses staffed by the Foundation's "associates," most of whom were former drug addicts and criminals. These associates received no cash wages, but the Foundation did provide them with food, clothing, and shelter. Although they vehemently disavowed any desire for compensation, their complete dependence on the Foundation proved that they did expect to receive in-kind benefits for their labors. Therefore, they qualified as statutory employees.

§ 4.3   Fair Labor Standards Act—Wages

Section 6 of the Fair Labor Standards Act (FLSA) requires the payment of a minimum hourly wage, currently $5.15, to all covered employees who are not specifically exempt.[1] The unit of measurement for determining compliance with the minimum wage requirement is the workweek, defined as 168 hours, or seven consecutive days. Each workweek is considered separately; a workweek in which an employee receives less than the minimum wage can not be averaged with one in which he or she receives more than the statutory minimum.

Although the minimum wage is expressed as an hourly rate, the statute does not require that employees be paid by the hour. Other compensation systems, such as piece rates and weekly, monthly, or yearly salaries, are perfectly legal, as long as the employee's total straight-time compensation for a workweek divided by the number of hours worked equals at least the minimum wage. The result of this computation will also be the "regular rate of pay," which determines the amount of any overtime compensation required under section 7. Items excluded in determining the regular rate also may not be included in determining compliance with the statutory minimum.

With two exceptions, employees must receive the minimum wage in cash or negotiable instrument, free and clear. Section 3(m) allows employers to credit against the minimum wage the reasonable value of board, lodging, or other facilities customarily furnished to their employ-

---

17. See Wage & Hour Manual (BNA) 91:416 (1975).

18. 471 U.S. 290, 105 S.Ct. 1953, 85 L.Ed.2d 278 (1985).

§ 4.3

1. 29 U.S.C.A. § 206(a)(1).

ees.[2] Reasonable cost may not exceed the employer's actual cost, and the employer is responsible for maintaining and preserving records documenting its costs. Under Department of Labor regulations the facilities must be of a kind normally furnished by the employer, such as meals provided by a restaurant, and they must be furnished primarily for the benefit of the employees; the employees must be told that the value of the facilities is being deducted from their wages; and acceptance of the facilities must be voluntary.[3] At least two Courts of Appeals have rejected the regulation's voluntariness requirement, which was first promulgated in 1940, as inconsistent with the statutory language.[4] Under the courts' view, a restaurant may take a credit for meals provided to employees even though the employees do not have the choice of receiving the cash instead.

Items that do not meet the requirements of section 3(m) may not be credited against payment of the minimum wage. They include tools of the trade, set-offs for breakage, and uniforms. The FLSA does not prohibit employers from requiring employees to wear uniforms. Employees may not, however, be required to pay for the uniforms or even for the cost of cleaning them, if those payments reduce their hourly rate below the minimum wage in the week in which the uniforms are bought or cleaned. Similarly, employers may not deduct from an employee's pay losses for events like breakage, cash register shortages, or suspected pilferage if the deduction will have the effect of reducing the employee's hourly wage for that week below the statutory minimum. Deductions for theft that would result in less than the statutory minimum may be made only following an adjudication of guilt against the employee in a criminal proceeding.

Deductions may be made for the employee's share of Social Security and any other federal, state, and local taxes, but not for any tax the employer is required to bear. Deductions for amounts ordered paid to a third party under garnishment, wage attachment, or bankruptcy proceedings are lawful, as long as the employer does not derive any benefit from the transaction. In addition, amounts deducted pursuant to a voluntary assignment by the employee to a third party will be treated as if they had been paid directly to the employee for purposes of determining compliance with the minimum wage requirement. Once again, the employer may not derive any benefit or profit from these assignments. Typical assignments include union dues, charitable contributions, and insurance premiums.

These restrictions on deductions from an employee's pay apply only when the effect of the deduction is to reduce the employee's hourly rate of pay below the required minimum wage for the workweek in which the deduction is made. Otherwise, the FLSA does not limit the items or

2. 29 U.S.C.A. § 203(m).

3. 29 C.F.R. §§ 531.30–531.32.

4. Herman v. Collis Foods, Inc., 176 F.3d 912 (6th Cir. 1999); Davis Bros. v. Donovan, 700 F.2d 1368 (11th Cir.1983); Morrison, Inc. v. Donovan, 700 F.2d 1374 (11th Cir.1983).

amounts of deductions. State law, however, often does regulate deductions for all employees, including those who are exempt from the federal minimum wage requirement or so highly paid that compliance with the federal requirement is not in jeopardy.

The second statutory exception to the requirement that the minimum wage be paid free and clear is for tipped employees. Section 3(m) allows the employer to take a tip credit for employees who customarily receive over $30 a month in tips, as long as the employer has informed the employees of the tip credit and the employees retain the tips they receive.[5] In 1996, Congress froze the amount of the minimum cash wage for tipped employees at $2.125 per hour, as long as the employees receive at least the difference between that amount and the minimum wage in tips.

§ 4.4　Fair Labor Standards Act—Hours—Overtime

The Fair Labor Standards Act (FLSA) does not restrict the number of hours adult employees may be compelled to work. It simply requires that employees not specifically exempt from the minimum wage and overtime provisions be paid at least the minimum wage for the first forty hours they work in a workweek and at least one-and-one-half times their regular rate of pay for all additional hours worked. As with the minimum wage requirement, the basic unit of measurement for computation of overtime is the workweek. For instance, if an employee works thirty hours in one week and fifty the next, the employer may not average the two weeks to avoid payment of overtime; the employee is entitled to ten hours of overtime for the second week.

Although employees may be paid on an hourly, salary, piece rate, commission, or some other basis, each employee has a "regular rate of pay," which must be computed in order to determine the amount of overtime pay required. The regular rate is an hourly rate. For employees paid by the hour it is their hourly rate. For other workers, the regular rate is calculated by dividing the employee's total compensation for a workweek, less statutory exclusions, by the number of hours the employee actually worked during that week. An employer's regular rate may be more than the minimum wage, but it can never be less.

Section 7(e) defines "regular rate" as "all remuneration for employment paid to, or on behalf of, the employee,"[1] with eight specific employer payments excluded from the determination of the regular rate. These exclusions include gifts on special occasions, vacation and holiday pay or payment for occasional absences, reimbursement for travel expenses, discretionary bonuses, talent fees, irrevocable contributions to benefit plans, premium payments for daily or weekly overtime or for weekend and holiday work, so-called "clock pattern" overtime pay, and stock options. Under section 7(h), overtime premiums excluded from the

---

5. 29 U.S.C.A. § 203(m), (t).

§ 4.4
1. 29 U.S.C.A. § 207(e).

regular rate are "creditable toward overtime compensation payable pursuant to" section 7(a).[2] Included in determining the regular rate are such items as noncash wages in the form of board, lodging, and other similar facilities, commissions, non-overtime premium payments, and nondiscretionary bonuses. Permissible deductions from wages, such as voluntary assignments, garnishments, union dues, and withholding taxes, are included in the determination of the regular rate.

Calculation of the amount of overtime due to a worker paid on an hourly basis is simple. In addition to the straight-time hourly earnings for all hours worked, the employee must receive one-half the hourly rate for every hour over forty. An employee with an hourly rate of $8.00 who works forty-four hours in a workweek is entitled to $368 (forty-four hours at $8.00, plus four hours at $4.00).

Computing overtime due salaried employees can be more complex. A salaried employee's regular rate of pay is the amount of the salary divided by the number of hours of work for which the salary is intended to compensate. Therefore, a worker whose weekly salary of $500 is intended to compensate for a workweek of forty hours has a regular rate of $12.50 and must be paid, in addition to the salary of $500, one-and-one-half times that rate, or $18.75, for each hour over forty. If the salary is intended to cover only a thirty-five hour workweek, the employee's regular rate is $14.29. The Department of Labor's position is that this employee would be entitled to receive the salary plus $14.29 per hour for hours thirty-six to forty, and $21.44 ($14.29 x 1 1/2) for all hours in excess of forty.

The calculation becomes more complicated if the salary is intended to compensate for fluctuating workweeks. The courts and the Department of Labor permit employers to use the fluctuating workweek method to compute overtime pay under certain circumstances. Under this method, the regular rate must be computed anew every week, with resulting lower earnings per hour as the number of overtime hours increases. Therefore, the employer and the employee must have a "clear mutual understanding" about the use of the fluctuating workweek method at the time of hire.[3] The Fourth Circuit has held this clear mutual understanding does not require that employees understand the manner in which their overtime pay is calculated or that they have acknowledged in writing that the pay plan has been explained to them.[4] Further, the fluctuating workweek method requires only that employees' schedules fluctuate, not that that they be unpredictable. This method of payment may, of course, be used only when an employee's salary is large enough so that the regular rate every week is always at least the minimum wage.

For example, assume that an employee is hired at a weekly salary of $500, which is intended to compensate for all hours worked. Under the

2. 29 U.S.C.A. § 207(h); 29 C.F.R. § 778.201.

3. 29 C.F.R. § 778.114.

4. Griffin v. Wake County, 142 F.3d 712 (4th Cir.1998).

fluctuating workweek method, the salary is intended as straight-time compensation for all hours worked, and the regular rate for any week is the salary divided by the number of hours worked in that week. The required overtime payment is the number of overtime hours multiplied by one-half the regular rate. If the employee works fifty hours one week, the regular rate is $10.00 ($500/50), and the employee's total compensation for the week is $550 ($500 salary plus ten hours of overtime at $5.00 per hour). If the employee works forty-eight hours the next week, the regular rate is $10.42 ($500/48), and the total compensation must be $541.68 ($500 salary plus eight hours of overtime at $5.21 per hour).

Another method of reducing overtime costs available in some situations is the so-called Belo contract, a form of guaranteed compensation that includes a certain amount of overtime. This method, named after *Walling v. A.H. Belo Corp.*,[5] was codified in the 1949 amendments and is now found in section 7(f).[6] Belo contracts may be used only pursuant to a specific agreement between the employer and the employees.[7] The employee's duties must "necessitate irregular hours of work," and the fluctuation must not be entirely in the overtime range. If employees regularly work forty hours a week, and only the overtime hours vary, a Belo contract may not be used. The contract must guarantee a weekly overtime payment, and the employee must receive that payment regardless of the number of hours actually worked. The weekly guaranty cannot exceed sixty hours per week.

§ 4.5 Fair Labor Standards Act—Hours—Compensable Time

The FLSA requires that employees be paid at least the minimum wage for the first forty hours they work in a workweek and one-and-one-half times their regular rate of pay for all additional hours worked. Therefore, a key to compliance with the Act's minimum wage and overtime requirements is determining the number of "hours worked." The FLSA defines "employ" as "to suffer or permit to work,"[1] but it does not contain any general definition of "work" or of compensable time. In an early trilogy of cases, the Supreme Court mandated liberal tests for determining compensable time. Employees must be paid not only for all time spent in "physical or mental exertion (whether burdensome or not) controlled or required by the employer and pursued necessarily and primarily for the benefit of the employer or his business,"[2] but also for idle time or time spent in incidental activities.[3]

5. 316 U.S. 624, 62 S.Ct. 1223, 86 L.Ed. 1716 (1942).

6. 29 U.S.C.A. § 207(f).

7. 29 C.F.R. § 778.407.

§ 4.5

1. FLSA § 3(g), 29 U.S.C.A. § 203(g).

2. Tennessee Coal, Iron & R. Co. v. Muscoda Local 123, 321 U.S. 590, 598, 64 S.Ct. 698, 703, 88 L.Ed. 949 (1944).

3. Armour & Co. v. Wantock, 323 U.S. 126, 65 S.Ct. 165, 89 L.Ed. 118 (1944); Skidmore v. Swift & Co., 323 U.S. 134, 65 S.Ct. 161, 89 L.Ed. 124 (1944).

Under this test, time actually spent in production and related activities is clearly compensable. This includes not only the normal work day, but also any other time employees are required or permitted to perform work. Work not required or requested by the employer counts as hours worked if the employer has actual or constructive knowledge of it. For instance, if an employee arrives early and performs tasks incidental to the normal working day, like starting machines or answering the phone, the time so spent is compensable if the employer knew or should have known of the employee's actions. The same is true if an employee stays late to finish a project or takes work home and completes it there. Employers who wish to avoid liability for these hours should forbid unauthorized work beyond the normal working day and establish a system to police compliance with the rule.

Whether time not spent in physical or mental exertion is compensable depends on a variety of factors, including the relationship of the activity to the employee's principal duties, the nature and extent of the restrictions the employer imposes on the employee during that time, the primary beneficiary of the activity, and any agreement between the employer and the employee. Resolution of the question depends on the specific facts of a case, although general guidelines have developed over the years for particular types of nonproductive activities.

Cases involving waiting time always invoke the catchy, but conclusory, distinction between periods when employees are "engaged to wait" and when they are "waiting to be engaged." The critical issue in most waiting time cases is whether employees can make effective use of the time for their own purposes. If they can not, the time is considered primarily for the employer's benefit, the employees are "engaged to wait," and the time is compensable. Time spent waiting for work during the work day because of machinery breakdowns, delivery delays, a shortage of customers, or other similar reasons is normally compensable. Even if employees are permitted to leave the employer's premises, courts generally find the waiting time compensable if it is too short for employees to use the time for their own benefit. Waiting time can be compensable even during periods when employees are technically not on duty, if they are required to wait or remain at or near the employer's premises. On the other hand, if employees are completely relieved of duty during the waiting time and the periods are long enough to permit them to pursue their own activities, they are "waiting to be engaged," and the time is not compensable. This can be true even in atypical employment settings in which employees have agreed to remain on the employer's premises, if they are in fact relieved of duty.

A similar analysis applies to employees who are "on call" and must be available to return to work on short notice. Obviously, these employees are not completely free to do whatever they want when they are off duty but on call. Depending on the employer's requirements, they may not be able to leave their homes, travel out of town, or even be alone with their children without having a babysitter on call too. Constraints on an employee's freedom are, however, inherent in the concept of being on call and do not by themselves render on-call time compensable. If employees must remain on the employer's premises or so near it they can not engage in personal activities, the on-call time is compensable. If employees are permitted to go home while on call, the on-call time is rarely found compensable, regardless of the relative restrictions on their movements.

In *Bright v. Houston Northwest Medical Center Survivor, Inc.*,[4] for instance, a biomedical equipment repair technician had to wear a beeper, arrive at the hospital within twenty minutes after being called, and not be intoxicated or so impaired that he could not work on the equipment. The court held that the on-call time was not compensable, even though the employee was on call during all of his off-duty hours and had had no relief from this status for almost an entire year. Only where callbacks are so frequent that employees can not effectively use their time or where the employer's on-call system is so distracting or burdensome that personal activities are inhibited will on-call hours be compensable.

In *Renfro v. City of Emporia*,[5] firefighters were subject to constraints almost identical to those in *Bright* and a number of other cases, but with one critical difference. The firefighters were called back to work for at least an hour on an average of three to five times during a twenty-four-hour on-call period. The court found frequency of the callbacks so burdensome that the entire on-call time became compensable. Similarly, in *Cross v. Arkansas Forestry Commission*,[6] employees had to monitor hand-held radios twenty-four hours a day while on call and had to respond immediately to emergencies. This requirement restricted their travel, forced them to pay attention to the radio constantly, and prevented them from going places where radio noise was unwelcome. The on-call time was held compensable under these circumstances.

Sleep time is compensable under certain circumstances. Employees who are on duty for less than twenty-four hours are considered to be working even if they are allowed to sleep during part of that time. Employees who are on duty for twenty-four hours or more may agree with their employer to exclude from compensable time bona fide meal periods and bona fide sleeping periods of no more than eight hours. The employer must furnish adequate sleeping facilities, and employees must normally have an uninterrupted sleep period. Any actual interruptions for calls to duty are compensable, and if employees do not get at least five hours' sleep during a sleep period, the entire time is compensable. Employees who reside on their employers' premises permanently or for extended periods of time are probably not working the entire time they are on the premises. The Department of Labor will recognize any "reasonable agreement" between the parties concerning exclusion of sleep time and time spent in other personal pursuits.

4. 934 F.2d 671 (5th Cir.1991) (en banc), cert. denied, 502 U.S. 1036, 112 S.Ct. 882, 116 L.Ed.2d 786 (1992).

5. 948 F.2d 1529 (10th Cir.1991), cert. dismissed, 503 U.S. 915, 112 S.Ct. 1310, 117 L.Ed.2d 510 (1992).

6. 938 F.2d 912 (8th Cir.1991).

Travel from home to work and back is normally not compensable time.[7] If, however, employees are required to report to one location, such as the employer's dispatching office, to receive assignments or instructions, and then travel to a job site, the time spent traveling from the office to the job site is compensable. The Department of Labor makes an interesting distinction as to the status of travel time for employees who are called back after the end of their workday. The regulations provide that if the off-duty employee must travel to the premises of one of the employer's customers to perform the emergency work, the travel time is compensable, but the Department takes no position on the compensability of travel time if the employee must simply report to the employer's premises.[8] Presumably this distinction is based on the notion that normal commuting is personal, not working time. If, however, travel is part of an employee's principal job activities, travel time is compensable. Overnight travel is compensable if it occurs during regular working hours, but not otherwise, unless the employee is required to perform work while traveling. Under a 1996 amendment to section 4(a) of the Portal-to-Portal Act, the use of an employer's vehicle for commuting and incidental activities is not part of the employee's principal activities and therefore not compensable if the use of the vehicle is within the employee's normal commuting area and subject to an agreement between employer and employee.

Rest and meal periods are governed by straightforward rules established by the Department of Labor. Break periods of twenty minutes or less are compensable. Meal periods are not compensable if employees are completely relieved of duty during that time. If employees are required to remain at their work station while eating, they are not completely relieved of duty and must be paid for the time. Several courts of appeals have held that employees who remain on call during their meal period need not be compensated if they are not "primarily engaged in work-related duties" during that time. This test is also referred to as the "predominately-for-the-benefit-of-the-employer" standard; if the meal time is not predominately for the employer's benefit, it is not compensable. Although most of these decisions involved public sector law enforcement officers, the courts purported to rely on standards applicable to the private sector as well.

Although the FLSA has no definition of compensable time, there are three express statutory exceptions from the determination of hours worked. In 1947, Congress enacted the Portal–to–Portal Act, partially in response to court decisions defining as compensable such activities as washing-up and changing clothes. Section 4 of the Portal–to–Portal Act excludes from hours worked "activities which are preliminary to or postliminary to * * * principal * * * activities," unless the time is made compensable by contract, custom, or practice.[9] Thus, time spent in activities characterized as "preliminary" or "postliminary" is not com-

---

7. Portal–to–Portal Act § 4(a), 29 U.S.C.A. § 254(a); 29 C.F.R. § 785.35.

8. 29 C.F.R. § 785.36.

9. 29 U.S.C.A. § 254.

pensable. If, however, the activities are considered an integral part of the principal activities, they will be characterized as "preparatory" or "concluding" and compensable. The second statutory exemption is the 1996 amendment to section 4 concerning use of employer vehicles, discussed above. The third, section 3(o) of the FLSA,[10] excludes from "hours worked" time spent changing clothes or washing at the beginning or end of the workday, if the express terms of, or custom or practice under a collective bargaining agreement excludes that time from working time. In all other situations, changing or washing time will be compensable if it is part of the principal activities of the job or is found to be preparatory or concluding in nature.

As with many of the other distinctions in the area of working time, the difference between preliminary and postliminary, on the one hand, and preparatory and concluding, on the other, can be elusive and is heavily dependent on the facts of a particular case. One important factor is whether the employer or the employee is the primary beneficiary of the activity. For instance, sharpening knives before or after a shift at a meatcutting plant was held to be preparatory and therefore compensable,[11] as were changing clothes and showering in a battery plant where the manufacturing process involved use of toxic materials.[12]

Many other miscellaneous activities may be compensable if they are required by the employer or primarily benefit the employer. These include attendance at lectures, meetings, and training programs, unless attendance is voluntary, outside of normal working hours, and not related to the employee's job. Time spent adjusting grievances during the regular workday is compensable, unless otherwise agreed in a collective bargaining agreement. Time spent waiting for and receiving medical attention on the employer's premises or at the employer's direction during normal working hours is compensable.

Finally, the Supreme Court has articulated the de minimis doctrine, which renders noncompensable otherwise compensable time because of the small amount of time involved. Insubstantial and insignificant activity does not have to be counted as compensable time. "[A] few seconds or minutes of work beyond the scheduled working hours * * * may be disregarded. Split-second absurdities are not justified * * *. It is only when an employee is required to give up a substantial measure of his time and effort that compensable working time is involved."[13] An often-cited test for whether activity falls under the de minimis rule looks at three factors: the administrative difficulty of recording the time, the size of the aggregate claim, and whether the employees performed the work on a regular basis.

10. Id. § 203(o).

11. Mitchell v. King Packing Co., 350 U.S. 260, 76 S.Ct. 337, 100 L.Ed. 282 (1956).

12. Steiner v. Mitchell, 350 U.S. 247, 76 S.Ct. 330, 100 L.Ed. 267 (1956).

13. Anderson v. Mt. Clemens Pottery Co., 328 U.S. 680, 692, 66 S.Ct. 1187, 1194, 90 L.Ed. 1515 (1946).

§ 4.6   Fair Labor Standards Act—Exemptions

The FLSA contains a complex scheme of exemptions, under which covered employees may be fully or partially exempt from the Act's minimum wage or overtime requirements, or its restrictions on child labor. The majority of the FLSA exemptions apply to specific industries, but the most significant, the "white-collar exemptions," are based on job duties and cut across all sectors of the economy.

Most exemptions are measured on a workweek basis. If an employee performs both exempt and nonexempt work during a workweek, the exemption is lost for the entire week. Some exemptions do, however, permit the performance of some nonexempt work, as long as all the other requirements of the exemption are met. Exemptions are narrowly construed, and the employer bears the burden of persuasion on the issue.

White–Collar Exemptions—August 2004 Regulations

The white-collar exemptions, contained in section 13(a)(1), for those employed "in a bona fide executive, administrative, or professional capacity,"[1] relieve the employer from both the minimum wage and the overtime requirements. Of all the exemptions, these contain the greatest potential for error, with possibly devastating results. White-collar employees are often highly paid and therefore have high regular rates of pay, and they may routinely work more than forty hours a week. A mistake in classifying them as exempt can result in large awards for unpaid overtime.

In April 2004, the Bush administration promulgated sweeping revisions to the regulations defining the section 13(a)(1) white-collar exemptions.[2] These revisions took effect on August 23, 2004. The new regulations maintain both the duties test and the salary basis test from the previous regulations, but with major modifications, including a significant increase in the minimum salary, from $155 to $455 per week.

Common to all three classifications is the requirement that employees be paid on a salary basis. Hourly rates of pay, no matter how high, are antithetical to the concept of a salary, and, with one exception, employees found to be paid on an hourly basis do not qualify for the white collar exemptions. The exception is for computer employees, who can qualify for exemption under either section 13(a)(1) or section 13(a)(17), which is discussed below.

Being paid on a salary basis means that for each week during which employees perform any work, they must receive a predetermined amount of money that constitutes all or part of their compensation. The salary may not be "subject to reduction" because of the quality or quantity of work performed.[3] Under the pre-August 2004 regulations, exceptions to this no-reduction rule existed for deductions for absences of one day or

§ 4.6

1. 29 U.S.C.A. § 213(a)(1).

2. 69 Fed. Reg. 22122 (April 23, 2004), revising 29 C.F.R. Part 541.

3. 29 C.F.R. § 541.602(a) (effective August 23, 2004); 29 C.F.R. § 541.118(a) (effective until August 23, 2004).

more for personal reasons, deductions for absences of one day or more because of sickness or disability if the employer has a sickness or disability compensation policy, and penalties for infractions of safety rules of major significance.[4] The new regulations retain these exceptions and they also permit deductions from pay for disciplinary suspensions of a full day or more imposed in good faith for infractions of workplace conduct rules, such as rules prohibiting sexual harassment or workplace violence.[5] They also make clear that an employer is not required to pay the full salary for weeks in which an exempt employee takes unpaid leave under the Family and Medical Leave Act.[6]

The new regulations go into great detail about the effect of improper deductions on an employee's exempt status. An employer's actual practice of making improper deductions demonstrates that it did not intend to pay employees on a salary basis, although the regulations go on after this statement to enumerate factors to consider in determining whether an actual practice exists. If the facts show that the employer has an actual practice of making improper deductions, the exemption is lost during the time when the deductions were made only for employees in the same job classification working for the same managers responsible for the actual improper deductions.

Under the new regulations, improper deductions that are "either isolated or inadvertent" will not cause a loss of the exemption if the employer reimburses the employees for the deductions.[7] In addition, the new regulations provide a safe harbor for employers. If the employer has a clearly communicated policy prohibiting improper deductions and containing a complaint mechanism, reimburses employees for any improper deductions and makes a good faith commitment to comply in the future, the exemption will not be lost for any employees unless the employer willfully violates the policy by continuing to make the improper deductions after receiving employee complaints.[8] The best evidence of a clearly communicated policy is a written policy distributed to employees before the improper deductions by, for instance, giving a copy to new employees at the time of hire, or publishing it in an employee handbook or on the employer's Intranet.

For each of the categories of exemptions, executive, administrative, and professional, there is now one minimum salary–$455 per week.[9] The regulations also define a new set of workers, the "highly compensated employees," who are exempt under section 13(a)(1) if they have a total

4. 29 C.F.R. §§ 541.118(a)(2), (3), (5) (effective until August 23, 2004).

5. 29 C.F.R. § 541.602(b)(5) (effective August 23, 2004).

6. 29 C.F.R. § 541.602(b)(7) (effective August 23, 2004).

7. 29 C.F.R. § 541.603(c) (effective August 23, 2004).

8. 29 C.F.R. § 541.603(d) (effective August 23, 2004).

9. 29 C.F.R. §§ 541.100(a)(1) (executive employee), 541.200(a)(1) (administrative employee), 541.300(a)(1) (professional employee). See also 29 C.F.R. § 541.400(b) (for computer employees, either $455 per week on a salary basis or $27.63 an hour on an hourly basis.) (All effective August 23, 2004).

annual compensation of at least $100,000 and they customarily and regularly perform any one or more of the exempt duties or responsibilities of an executive, administrative, or professional employee, which are about to be discussed.[10] The total annual compensation of these highly compensated employees must include at least $455 per week paid on a salary basis.

For each of the categories of exemptions, the existing difference between the long and the short tests has been eliminated, and there is only one duties test for each category. Employees will be exempt executives if their primary duty is management of the enterprise in which they are employed or a customarily recognized department or subdivision of that enterprise; they customarily and regularly direct the work of two or more employees; and they have the authority to hire or fire other employees or their suggestions and recommendations as to hiring, firing, advancement, promotion, or any other change of status of other employees are given particular weight.[11] Employees who own at least a bona fide twenty percent equity interest in an enterprise are exempt as executives only if they are actively engaged in its management.[12]

The new regulations also address the issue of the "working supervisor." They take the position that as a general matter exempt executives decide when they will perform nonexempt work and still remain responsible for the success or failure of the business while they are doing the nonexempt work. Thus, an assistant manager in a retail store may serve customers or stock shelves, but he or she can still supervise employees at the same time. On the other hand, a working supervisor whose primary duty is performing nonexempt work on the production line in a manufacturing plant does not qualify for the exemption merely because he or she occasionally is responsible for directing the work of other nonexempt production line employees.

To qualify as exempt administrative employees, employees must have a primary duty of performing office or non-manual work directly related to the management or general business operations of the employer or the employer's customers, and their primary duty must include the exercise of discretion and independent judgment as to "matters of significance."[13] The term "matters of significance" refers to the level of importance or consequence of the work performed. The regulations give examples of employees whose work qualifies them under the duties requirement for the administrative exemption. These include insurance claims adjusters, certain employees in the financial services industry, human resources managers, and purchasing agents.

To qualify as an exempt professional employee, employees must have a primary duty of the performance of work requiring knowledge of an advanced type in a field of science or learning customarily acquired by

10. 29 C.F.R. § 541.601(a) (effective August 23, 2004).

11. 29 C.F.R. § 541.100(a)(2)-(4) (effective August 23, 2004).

12. 29 C.F.R. § 541.101 (effective August 23, 2004).

13. 29 C.F.R. § 541.200(a)(2), (3) (effective August 23, 2004).

a prolonged course of specialized intellectual instruction or requiring invention, imagination, originality, or talent in a recognized field or artistic endeavor.[14] Again, the regulations set forth examples of workers who would normally satisfy this duty requirement, including registered or certified medical technologists, nurses, dental hygienists, physician assistants, accountants, chefs, athletic trainers, and funeral directors or embalmers.

White-Collar Exemptions—Pre–August 2004 Regulations

A major issue with respect to the salary test under the previous white-collar regulations was the meaning of the requirement that an exempt employee's salary not be "subject to reduction," except for certain specified reasons. In *Auer v. Robbins,*[15] the Supreme Court upheld as reasonable the Secretary of Labor's interpretation that the salary basis test is not met when an employee's compensation may "as a practical matter" be adjusted in ways inconsistent with the test. That standard is met if there is an actual practice of making such deductions or a policy that creates a "significant likelihood" of such deductions. Thus, if there have been no actual deductions, there must be "a clear and particularized policy—one which 'effectively communicates' that deductions will be made in specified circumstances." In *Auer,* a group of police sergeants relied on a policy contained in a section of the Police Manual that listed fifty-eight possible rule violations and the range of penalties accompanying them. The manual nominally covered all department employees, and some of the specified penalties involved disciplinary pay deductions. The Court agreed with the Secretary that the manual did not "effectively communicate" that pay deductions were an expected form of punishment for the plaintiff sergeants; it was possible to give complete effect to the entire manual without drawing that inference.

Auer also contained an issue involving the Secretary's "window of correction" regulation. The department made a one-time pay reduction in the case of a sergeant who violated its residency requirement. The regulations at issue provided "where a deduction not permitted [by the salary-basis test] is inadvertent, or is made for reasons other than lack of work, the exemption will not be considered to have been lost if the employer reimburses the employee for such deductions and promises to comply in the future."[16] The grounds for taking advantage of the window were in the alternative, said the Court, and therefore the department did not lose it even though the deduction was not inadvertent. The deduction was for a reason other than lack of work and so satisfied the second ground under the regulation. The Court also agreed with the Secretary's view that the reimbursement does not have to occur immediately upon discovery of the nonpermitted deduction.

14. 29 C.F.R. § 541.300(a)(2) (effective August 23, 2004).

15. 519 U.S. 452, 117 S.Ct. 905, 137 L.Ed.2d 79 (1997).

16. 29 C.F.R. § 541.118(a)(6) (effective until August 23, 2004).

Each exempt executive, administrative, or professional employee must also satisfy a duties test, either the "short test," or the "long test," depending on the amount of the employee's salary. To claim any exemption at all for its executive and administrative employees, an employer must pay them a salary of at least $155 per week; the minimum salary for professional employees (except attorneys, physicians, and teachers, for whom there is no minimum) is $170 per week.

Executive Employees

Under the long test, workers are exempt as executive employees if they receive a salary of at least $155 per week and meet five other requirements: (1) their primary duty must be management of an enterprise or one of its subdivisions or departments; (2) they must customarily and regularly direct the work of two or more employees; (3) they must have the authority to hire or fire or to make recommendations about employment decisions that are accorded weight; (4) they must customarily and regularly exercise discretionary powers; and (5) they must not spend more than twenty percent of their time (forty percent for retail or service establishments) performing nonexempt work.[17] The percentage limitations on nonexempt work do not apply to an employee who is in sole charge of an independent establishment or a physically separate branch, or who owns at least a twenty percent interest in the enterprise. The short test for "high-salaried" executives applies to employees who receive a salary of at least $250 per week and who meet the first two criteria discussed above.

Under all of the white-collar exemptions, the primary duty criterion is often measured by the amount of time the employee spends performing the specified duties. An employee who spends over half of his or her time in management duties clearly satisfies that part of the test for an executive employee. Time is not the only measurement, however, especially under the short test, which contains no limits on the percentage of nonexempt work, or for store managers and other similar employees who are in charge of a separate establishment and who also have no percentage restriction. The primary duty of these employees will generally be the work they do that is of principal value to their employer. For example, in *Murray v. Stuckey's, Inc.*,[18] store managers spent sixty-five to ninety percent of their time performing nonmanagerial duties, but neither that fact nor the fact that they were actively supervised by regional managers eliminated their exempt status. They were clearly in charge of their individual stores, and therefore management was their primary duty.

Administrative Employees

Employees who qualify for the administrative exemption generally perform office work. They include executive and administrative assis-

---

17. 29 C.F.R. § 541.1 (effective until August 23, 2004).

18. 939 F.2d 614 (8th Cir.1991), cert. denied, 502 U.S. 1073, 112 S.Ct. 970, 117 L.Ed.2d 135 (1992).

tants; specialists in technical areas, such as credit managers, purchasing agents, and labor relations directors; and individuals who work on special assignments with only general supervision and who are often away from the employer's place of business, such as field representatives and account executives. The long test for administrative employees requires a weekly salary of at least $155 and satisfaction of the following tests: (1) the employee's primary duty must be either (a) office or nonmanual work directly related to management policies or the general operations of the company, or (b) administration of a school system or educational institution in work directly related to academic instruction or training; (2) the employee must customarily and regularly exercise discretion and independent judgment; (3) the employee must either (a) regularly and directly assist a proprietor or bona fide executive or administrative employee, or (b) work under only general supervision along specialized or technical lines, or (c) execute special assignments and tasks under only general supervision; (4) the employee must not spend more than twenty percent of his or her time (forty percent for retail or service establishments) performing nonexempt work.[19] Under the short test, employees who receive salaries of at least $250 per week qualify for the exemption if they satisfy the primary duty test doing work that requires the exercise of discretion and independent judgment.

Professional Employees

The exemption for professional employees includes the traditional professions of law, medicine, and theology, as well as work requiring advanced instruction in a field of science or learning and work that is original and creative in character. Exempt professional status requires knowledge that is normally acquired only through a prolonged course of specialized intellectual instruction, rather than through experience on the job. Under the long test, employees are exempt if their salary is at least $170 per week and (1) their primary duty consists of either (a) work requiring advanced knowledge acquired by a prolonged course of scientific or specialized study, (b) original and creative work depending on imagination, talent, or invention, (c) teaching, or (d) computer programming or other highly-skilled computer work; (2) they consistently exercise discretion and judgment; (3) their work is predominately intellectual, varied, and incapable of being standardized by time; and (4) they must not spend more than twenty percent of their time in work not essential and necessarily incident to the work described above.[20] The short test is satisfied if employees receive a salary of at least $250 per week, they satisfy either (a) or (c) of the primary duty criteria, and their work requires the consistent exercise of discretion and judgment, or of invention, imagination, or talent in a recognized field of artistic endeavor. The salary requirement does not apply to attorneys, physicians, and teachers, or to highly skilled computer workers who are paid on an hourly basis at a rate exceeding six-and-one-half times the minimum

19. 29 C.F.R. § 541.2 (effective until August 23, 2004).

20. 29 C.F.R. § 541.3 (effective until August 23, 2004).

wage. Congress also has enacted a separate exemption for highly skilled computer workers, which is discussed below.

"Outside Salesmen"

The fourth exemption contained in section 13(a)(1) is for any "employee employed * * * in the capacity of outside salesman." There is no salary test for this category. Employees qualify for this exemption if (1) they are employed for the purpose of and are customarily and regularly engaged away from their employer's place of business in either (a) making sales or (b) obtaining orders or contracts for services or for the use of facilities for which the customer will pay, and (2) their hours of work in activities other than those described in number one, above, "do not exceed 20 percent of the hours worked in the workweek by nonexempt employees of the employer."[21]

Outside salespeople must perform their work away from the employer's place of business; inside salespeople do not come within the exemption. Selling services as well as goods qualifies for the exemption, but performing services does not. Therefore, a serviceperson who both sells the services and then performs them is not an "outside salesman." Similarly, route drivers whose primary responsibility is delivery of their employer's products to retail outlets, with little or no direct sales activity, do not come within the exemption.

The new white-collar regulations covering "outside sales employees" are virtually identical to the previous regulations for outside salesmen, except that the twenty percent limit on nonexempt work has been eliminated.[22]

Other Exemptions from Minimum Wage and Overtime Requirements

Aside from the white-collar exemptions in section 13(a)(1), the FLSA contains other exemptions from both the minimum wage and overtime requirements. These include employees employed by seasonal amusement and recreational businesses, certain employees in fishing and other fishing-related and aquatic businesses, and agricultural workers under certain circumstances. Employees exempted by special orders, regulations, or certificates issued by the Department of Labor are exempt from the minimum wage and overtime requirements. These include certificates for the employment of apprentices, learners, messengers, workers with disabilities, and students at special rates below the minimum wage. "Seamen" on foreign vessels are exempted from both the minimum wage and overtime. Domestic employees employed on a casual basis to provide babysitting services and those employed to provide companionship services to aged and infirm individuals are exempt. Other exemptions include employees of small newspapers and certain switchboard operators.

Under a 1996 amendment, a worker is exempt from both the minimum wage and overtime requirements if he or she is "a computer

21. 29 C.F.R. § 541.5 (effective until August 23, 2004).

22. 29 C.F.R. § 541.500 (effective August 23, 2004).

systems analyst, computer programmer, software engineer, or other similarly skilled worker," and his or her primary duty is "(A) the application of systems analysis techniques and procedures, including consulting with users, to determine hardware, software, or system functional specifications; (B) the design, development, documentation, analysis, creation, testing, or modification of computer systems or programs, including prototypes, based on and related to user of system design specifications; (C) the design, documentation, testing, creation, or modification of computer programs related to machine operating systems; or (D) a combination of duties described in ... (A), (B), and (C) the performance of which requires the same level of skills."[23] If the employee is compensated on an hourly basis, he or she must be paid at a rate of not less than $27.63 an hour.

Exemptions from Minimum Wage Only

In 1996, Congress created a subminimum "Opportunity Wage" of $4.25 per hour for the first ninety consecutive calendar days of employment for workers under the age of twenty.[24] Displacement of incumbent employees, including partial displacements like reductions in hours, wages, or benefits, for the purpose of hiring teenagers at the subminimum wage, is prohibited.

Exemptions from Overtime Only

Section 13(b)[25] establishes a number of exemptions from the Act's overtime requirements only. The major provisions affect the transportation industry. Employees with respect to whom the Secretary of Transportation has the power to establish qualifications and maximum hours of service under the Motor Carriers Act, employees of employers engaged in the operation of a common carrier by rail and subject to part I of the Interstate Commerce Act, and employees of an air carrier subject to the Railway Labor Act are all exempt from FLSA overtime requirements. "Seamen" on American vessels are exempt from overtime. In addition, a number of employees in agriculture and related industries are exempted from the overtime requirements, as are other specialized workers, including certain television and radio broadcasters, live-in domestic workers, and houseparents for institutionalized orphans. Special overtime rules for fire fighters and law enforcement officers are discussed below.

In addition to the section 13 exemptions, section 7 contains some special rules on overtime. Under section 7(i), employees of retail or service establishments are not entitled to overtime if their regular rate of pay exceeds one-and-one-half times the minimum wage and more than half of their compensation for a representative period is commissions on goods and services.[26]

---

23. FLSA § 13(a)(17), 29 U.S.C.A. § 213(a)(17).

24. FLSA § 6(g), 29 U.S.C.A. § 206(g).

25. 29 U.S.C.A. § 213(b).

26. 29 U.S.C.A. § 207(i).

§ 4.7 Fair Labor Standards Act—Child Labor

The FLSA restricts the employment of minors by means of an elaborate statutory definition of "oppressive child labor," complemented by Department of Labor regulations.[1] In nonagricultural employment, the minimum age for most jobs is sixteen. For occupations declared hazardous by the Secretary, the minimum age is eighteen. Seventeen hazardous occupation orders are currently in effect. They include such occupations as coal mining, logging, driving motor vehicles, and operating power woodworking machines.

The Secretary of Labor has authorized the employment of fourteen- and fifteen-year olds in certain specified jobs in office and sales work, retail, food service, and gasoline service establishments, under conditions that do not interfere with their education, health, or well-being. The regulations also limit the number of hours these minors may work, both per day and per week. Their employment must be outside of school hours and between the hours of 7:00 a.m. and 7:00 p.m., except from June 1 to Labor Day, when the evening limit is 9:00 p.m. Additionally, during the school year, fourteen-and fifteen-year-olds may work no more than three hours per day and eighteen hours per week. During vacation periods, they may work no more than eight hours per day and forty hours per week.[2]

As with its other requirements, the FLSA provides certain exemptions from the child labor prohibitions. The child labor exemptions are not, however, identical to the exemptions from the Act's minimum wage and overtime requirements. Therefore, the child labor restrictions can apply to employers whose employees are not subject to the minimum wage and overtime provisions. The child labor exemptions cover agriculture, actors and performers, newspaper delivery, evergreen wreath making, and employment by a parent or guardian in nonhazardous occupations.[3] A 2004 amendment added an exemption permitting Amish teenagers between ages 14 and 17 to work in sawmills under certain conditions.[4]

The most significant and controversial exemption is that for agriculture. Minors fourteen and older may work in any agricultural occupation outside of school hours unless that occupation has been declared hazardous by the Secretary.[5] Twelve-and thirteen-year olds may work in agriculture outside of school hours on the same farm where their parent is employed or on another farm with parental consent. Children under twelve may be employed by their parent on the parent's farm.

The child labor ban has two different enforcement mechanisms, a direct prohibition on unlawful employment of minors and an indirect

§ 4.7

1. FLSA § 3(*l*), 29 U.S.C.A. § 203(*l*).

2. 29 C.F.R. § 570.119.

3. FLSA §§ 3(*l*), 13(c), (d), 29 U.S.C.A. §§ 203(*l*), 213(c), (d).

4. FLSA § 13(c)(7), 29 U.S.C.A. § 213(c)(7).

5. FLSA § 13(c)(1), (2), 29 U.S.C.A. § 213(c)(1), (2).

prohibition by means of an injunction against the interstate shipment of goods. Section 12(c), the direct prohibition, simply bans the employment of oppressive child labor. It applies on the same bases as the Act's minimum wage and overtime requirements, individual employee coverage and enterprise coverage.[6] The indirect prohibition contained in section 12(a), however, goes beyond these traditional forms of coverage. Section 12(a), the "hot goods" provision, prohibits the shipment or delivery for shipment in commerce of goods produced in an establishment "in or about which" oppressive child labor has been employed within the preceding thirty days.[7] Unlike the direct prohibition, the hot goods ban applies without regard to the nature of the work performed by the minor or the enterprise in which the minor worked. Thus, employers not subject to the Act's minimum wage and overtime requirements or to the direct prohibition on oppressive child labor can be subject to the hot goods ban.

The Secretary of Labor has the authority to prosecute violations of each of these provisions. The Act provides for civil penalties of up to $10,000 per violation, injunctive relief, "hot goods" injunctions, and criminal prosecution for willful violations.

Although a major goal of the child labor restrictions is to protect children from workplace hazards, there is no private cause of action under the FLSA for wrongful death or injuries to minors employed in violation of the Act.[8]

§ 4.8 Fair Labor Standards Act—Public Employees

The history of FLSA coverage of public employees is tortuous, to say the least. The FLSA initially applied only to private sector employees. In 1966, Congress extended coverage to schools, hospitals, nursing homes, and local transit agencies. Two years later the Supreme Court upheld the constitutionality of these amendments.[1] The Court later held, however, that the Eleventh Amendment prohibited suits by public employees to enforce the FLSA.[2] In 1974, Congress amended the Act again to abrogate the states' Eleventh Amendment immunity and to extend coverage to virtually all government employees. Then, in *National League of Cities v. Usery*, the Court held application of the FLSA to states and their subdivisions violated the Tenth Amendment by intruding on state sovereignty in "areas of traditional governmental functions."[3] Nontraditional or proprietary governmental functions remained covered, however, and for the next nine years courts attempted to find

---

6. 29 U.S.C.A. § 212(c).

7. 29 U.S.C.A. § 212(a).

8. See, e.g., Breitwieser v. KMS Indus., Inc., 467 F.2d 1391 (5th Cir.1972), cert. denied, 410 U.S. 969, 93 S.Ct. 1445, 35 L.Ed.2d 705 (1973).

§ 4.8

1. Maryland v. Wirtz, 392 U.S. 183, 88 S.Ct. 2017, 20 L.Ed.2d 1020 (1968).

2. Employees of Dep't of Pub. Health & Welfare v. Department of Pub. Welfare, 411 U.S. 279, 93 S.Ct. 1614, 36 L.Ed.2d 251 (1973).

3. 426 U.S. 833, 852, 96 S.Ct. 2465, 2474, 49 L.Ed.2d 245 (1976).

the line between traditional and nontraditional functions. Finally, in *Garcia v. San Antonio Metropolitan Transit Authority*,[4] the Court overruled *National League of Cities* and held that the Tenth Amendment posed no barrier to application of the FLSA to state and local governments.

Over a decade later, in *Seminole Tribe of Florida v. Florida*,[5] the Supreme Court held that Congress lacks the power under Article I to abrogate a state's sovereign immunity, preserved by the Eleventh Amendment, from suit in federal court by private parties.

Three years later, in *Alden v. Maine*[6] the Court held that Congress did not have the authority under Article I to abrogate a state's sovereign immunity from actions brought against it in its own courts. The Court noted three limitations on state sovereign immunity: First, states can waive their immunity; second, sovereign immunity bars suits against states, but not against lesser entities such as cities or against state offices for injunctive or declaratory relief or for money damages if sued in their individual capacity; and third, appropriate federal agencies, such as the Department of Labor, retain the power to enforce Commerce Clause statutes against states and state agencies.

The substantive requirements of the FLSA apply generally to public sector employers, but there are a number of provisions unique to the public sector. In the wake of *Garcia v. San Antonio Metropolitan Transit Authority*, Congress enacted the Fair Labor Standards Amendments of 1985, which dealt with the fiscal problems and historical practices of public employers. These include the use of compensatory time off instead of cash payments for overtime, the status of volunteers, and additional overtime rules for public safety employees.

The 1985 amendments modified the overtime provisions of the FLSA by adding section 7(*o*), which permits public employers to continue a common practice of making compensatory time off, or "comp time," available instead of paying for overtime in cash.[7] Comp time must be awarded at a rate of at least one-and-one-half hours off for each hour of overtime worked. There are limits on the amount of comp time employees may accumulate before they must either receive time off or be paid in cash for any additional overtime. For employees engaged in public safety, emergency response, and seasonal activities, the limit is 480 hours of comp time, which is the equivalent of 320 hours of overtime. For all other employees, the cap is 240 hours of comp time, or 160 hours of overtime. An employee's request to use comp time must be honored within a reasonable period unless the time off would unduly disrupt the agency's operations. When employees leave a job, they must be paid for any unused comp time at their final regular rate, or at their average regular rate for the last three years, whichever is greater. In *Christensen*

4. 469 U.S. 528, 105 S.Ct. 1005, 83 L.Ed.2d 1016 (1985).

5. 517 U.S. 44, 116 S.Ct. 1114, 134 L.Ed.2d 252 (1996).

6. 527 U.S. 706, 119 S.Ct. 2240, 144 L.Ed.2d 636 (1999).

7. 29 U.S.C.A. § 207(*o*).

v. Harris County,[8] the Court held that nothing in section 7(o) prohibits public employers from requiring employees to use their accrued compensatory time.

Section 7(o) allows the use of comp time only pursuant to an agreement between the employer and the employee. The statute describes three kinds of agreements. First, under section 7(o)(2)(A)(i) the public agency may address the issue in a collective bargaining agreement or other similar agreement with the employees' representative. Second, for employees not covered by section 7(o)(2)(A)(i) and hired after April 15, 1986, the employer must reach an agreement with each individual employee before the performance of any work. Third, for employees not covered by section 7(o)(2)(A)(i) but hired before April 15, 1986, the regular practice in effect on that date constitutes an agreement that satisfies the statute. The last two categories include both unrepresented employees and employees in a state that prohibits public sector bargaining but who have nevertheless designated a representative.[9]

The 1985 amendments also modified the definition of "employee" to make clear that individuals performing volunteer services for state and local governments would not be covered, even if they receive expenses or a nominal payment for their work.[10] For instance, a volunteer school crossing guard is not an employee merely because he or she receives a uniform allowance or travel expenses. To prevent abuse and undue pressure, however, public employees may not volunteer to perform the same kind of services for which they are employed for the same public agency that employs them.

Another recognition of the situation of public sector employers appears in a Department of Labor regulation governing the exemption under section 13(a)(1) for white-collar workers. Under the regulation,[11] an otherwise exempt public sector executive, administrative, or professional employee does not lose his or her exempt status under a regulated public sector pay and leave system that requires partial-day or hourly deductions from pay for employee absences not covered by accrued leave, or for budget-driven furloughs. The Department's revisions to the white-collar exemptions, discussed above preserve this rule.[12]

The FLSA contains three different kinds of overtime exemptions for firefighters and law enforcement personnel. First, section 13(b)(20) provides a complete exemption from the overtime requirements of section 7 for public employees engaged in fire protection or law enforcement activities for workweeks in which the agency has fewer than five employees employed in such activities.[13]

8. 529 U.S. 576, 120 S.Ct. 1655, 146 L.Ed.2d 621 (2000).

9. Moreau v. Klevenhagen, 508 U.S. 22, 113 S.Ct. 1905, 123 L.Ed.2d 584 (1993).

10. FLSA § 3(e)(4), 29 U.S.C.A. § 203(e)(4).

11. 29 C.F.R. § 541.5d (effective until August 23, 2004).

12. 29 C.F.R. § 541.710 (effective August 23, 2004).

13. 29 U.S.C.A. § 213(b)(20).

Second, public employers too large for the complete exemption in section 13(b)(20) may structure their employment practices to come within the partial exemption contained in section 7(k).[14] This exemption recognizes that firefighters and law enforcement personnel often are on duty twenty-four hours a day, and therefore the normal standard of a forty-hour workweek is not appropriate. For fire protection employees with work periods of twenty-eight consecutive days, overtime must be paid for all hours over 212 in a work period; if their work period is less than twenty-eight consecutive days but more than six, no overtime compensation is required until the ratio of the number of hours worked to the number of days in the work period exceeds that of 212 hours to twenty-eight days. For instance, if a city established a work period of fourteen consecutive days for fire fighters, overtime would be required for all hours in excess of 106 (106/14 = 212/28). For employees engaged in law enforcement activities, the rules are the same, but the number of hours that triggers overtime is 171 for a work period of twenty-eight consecutive days. Thus, a city with a work period of fourteen consecutive days would owe overtime to its police officers after eighty-six hours (86/14 = 171/28). Employees with a work period less than seven consecutive days do not qualify for the section 7(k) exemption, and must receive overtime for all hours over forty in a workweek.

The third exemption is contained in section 7(p)(1), enacted in 1985. It allows public employers to exclude from the computation of hours worked special detail work performed for a separate and independent employer by the public employer's fire protection or law enforcement employees, as long as this work is at the employee's option.[15] Section 7(p) also permits public employees, at their option, to engage in occasional or sporadic part-time employment for the same employer but in a different capacity, without having the hours worked on the occasional job count toward calculation of overtime in the regular job. Employees may also trade shifts with other employees, and those hours will be excluded from calculation of overtime.

A 1999 amendment added section 3(y),[16] which defines "employee in fire protection activities" as including "a firefighter, paramedic, emergency medical technician, rescue worker, ambulance personnel, or hazardous materials worker" who is trained in fire suppression and is engaged in the prevention, control, or extinguishment of fires or response to emergency situations where life, property, or the environment is at risk. This amendment helped eliminate much of the litigation over whether ambulance and rescue service employees could be treated as fire protection personnel for purposes of the section 7(k) exemption. Under Department of Labor regulations that predate the 1999 amendment, the term also includes employees of public agencies charged with fighting forest fires who perform fire spotting or lookout activities, fight fires on the fireline or from aircraft, or operate equipment to clear fire breaks,

14.   29 U.S.C.A. § 207(k).   **16.**   29 U.S.C.A. § 203(y).
15.   29 U.S.C.A. § 207(p)(1).

regardless of whether they are full-time, part-time, or temporary or casual employees.[17] Civilian employees of fire departments, fire districts, or forestry services who perform various support services like dispatching, equipment repair, and maintenance are not included in this definition.

The term "law enforcement activities" refers to employees who (1) are uniformed or plainclothed members of a body of officers empowered by local law to enforce laws to maintain public peace and order, protect life and property, and prevent and detect crimes; (2) have the power to arrest; and (3) are undergoing, will undergo, or have undergone on-the-job training or a course of instruction that typically includes such matters as physical training, self-defense, firearm proficiency, and investigative and law enforcement techniques.[18] Also included by express reference in the statute are security personnel in correctional institutions.

Performance of nonexempt work by fire protection or law enforcement personnel will not defeat the exemptions as long as the nonexempt work does not exceed twenty percent of the total hours worked by an employee during the applicable work period. These overtime exemptions may be used only by public employers. Private companies are not exempt from the Act's normal overtime requirements, even if they are under contract with a state or local government to provide police or fire protection services.

§ 4.9   Fair Labor Standards Act—Retaliation

Like most other remedial labor legislation, the FLSA contains protection for employees who assert rights under the statute. Section 15(a)(3) prohibits discrimination against employees because they have filed complaints or instituted or testified in proceedings under the Act.[1]

The victim of the retaliation must be an "employee." Section 15(a)(3) applies to employers that attempt to blacklist or otherwise retaliate against former employees, although it may not prohibit employers from discriminating against job applicants who were never hired by the allegedly retaliating employer.

On the other hand, the prohibition against retaliation applies to "any person." This choice of wording led the Seventh Circuit to hold that section 15(a)(3) protected an employee who alleged he was fired for reporting violations of the FLSA, even if there could be no violation because his employer was not covered by the minimum wage and overtime provisions of the Act.[2]

Most of the courts to consider the issue have held, contrary to the express language of the statute, that an employee may gain the protec-

---

17. 29 C.F.R. § 553.210(a).
18. Id. § 553.211(a).

2. Sapperstein v. Hager, 188 F.3d 852 (7th Cir. 1999).

§ 4.9
1. 29 U.S.C.A. § 215(a)(3).

tion of section 15(a)(3) even if he or she has not filed a complaint with the Department of Labor. Discussing a problem with a Department investigator, refusing to release back pay claims or return back pay awards, and even protesting violations to the employer all have been found protected. At least two courts of appeals have, however, limited the cause of action under section 15(a)(3) to employees who have filed formal complaints, instituted a proceeding, or testified.[3]

In *McKenzie v. Renberg's Inc.,*[4] the Tenth Circuit held that a personnel director who discussed with the company's attorney her concerns that certain employees of the company were not being properly paid had not engaged in activities protected under section 15(a)(3). The court reasoned that the "hallmark" of protected activity is "the assertion of statutory rights (i.e., the advocacy of rights) by taking some action adverse to the company." In this case, the plaintiff never crossed the line from performing her duties as personnel director to making a personal complaint about her employer's wage-hour practices or asserting a right against her employer. The court also remarked in a footnote that it had never addressed whether section 15(a)(3) protects actions taken by an employee on behalf of other employees, noting that section 15(a)(3) does not contain an "opposition" clause similar to that found in Title VII and the ADEA.

The FLSA protects an employee from retaliation even where the employer erroneously believed the employee had filed a complaint. The employee does not have to be correct in asserting a FLSA violation; a good faith belief that the employer is violating the Act is enough.

Section 15(a)(3) can be enforced by the government through an injunction action under section 17. In addition, employees may sue under section 16(b). Remedies under section 16(b) for unlawful retaliation include "legal or equitable relief * * *, including without limitation employment, reinstatement, promotion, and the payment of wages lost and an additional equal amount as liquidated damages." This language has been held to authorize awards of compensatory damages for emotional distress and punitive damages.

§ 4.10 Fair Labor Standards Act—Administration and Enforcement

The FLSA is administered and enforced by the Secretary of Labor and the Administrator of the Wage–Hour Division of the Department of Labor, to whom the Secretary has delegated most statutory responsibilities. The FLSA authorizes five enforcement actions, three by the Secretary of Labor, one by private plaintiffs, and one by the Department of Justice.

3. Ball v. Memphis Bar–B–Q Co., 228 F.3d 360 (4th Cir.2000); Lambert v. Genesee Hosp., 10 F.3d 46 (2d Cir.1993), cert. denied, 511 U.S. 1052, 114 S.Ct. 1612, 128 L.Ed.2d 339 (1994).

4. 94 F.3d 1478 (10th Cir.1996), cert. denied, 520 U.S. 1186, 117 S.Ct. 1468, 137 L.Ed.2d 682 (1997).

First, the Secretary may sue under section 16(c) on behalf of affected employees to recover unpaid minimum wages and overtime compensation and an equal amount in liquidated damages.[1]

Second, the Secretary may seek injunctive relief under section 17 to restrain any violation of the Act, including minimum wage, overtime, retaliation, and child labor violations.[2] The Secretary may recover unpaid minimum wages and overtime compensation on behalf of affected employees in either a section 16(c) or a section 17 action, but liquidated damages are not available in a section 17 action. A section 17 injunction may also prohibit the interstate shipment of goods produced in violation of the FLSA. This "hot goods" ban, contained in section 15(a)(1), applies to "any person" who ships goods produced in violation of the Act's minimum wage and overtime requirements.[3] It contains exemptions for common carriers and some good faith purchasers, but not for creditors. In *Citicorp Industrial Credit, Inc. v. Brock*,[4] the Supreme Court upheld an injunction issued against the shipment of inventory seized by an employer's secured creditor.

In addition, section 17 is the only provision under which recordkeeping violations may be prosecuted. Section 11(c) requires employers subject to the Act to make, keep, and preserve records of the individuals they employ and their wages, hours, and other conditions of employment.[5]

Although failure to comply with the recordkeeping requirements is a violation of the FLSA independent of any other violations, the most significant impact of an employer's failure to keep required records is its effect on the proof in a suit seeking unpaid minimum wages or overtime. If the employer has not maintained records from which an employee's hours of work and wages can be determined, the employee will be permitted to produce evidence to show the "amount and extent of that work as a matter of just and reasonable inference."[6] If the employee does so, the burden shifts to the employer to rebut the inference, a difficult task if it has not kept adequate records.

Injunctions under section 17 are generally retrospective in nature. If, however, the employer's behavior makes future compliance questionable, a prospective injunction should issue. Because section 17 relief is equitable in nature, there is no right to a jury trial.

Third, section 16(e) authorizes civil penalties of up to $10,000 for each violation of the child labor provisions and up to $1,000 per violation for repeated or willful violations of the minimum wage and overtime provisions.[7] The amount of the proposed civil penalty is determined

§ 4.10

1. 29 U.S.C.A. § 216(c).

2. 29 U.S.C.A. § 217.

3. Id. § 215(a)(1).

4. 483 U.S. 27, 107 S.Ct. 2694, 97 L.Ed.2d 23 (1987).

5. 29 U.S.C.A. § 211(c). Depending on their type, records must be preserved for either two or three years.

6. Anderson v. Mt. Clemens Pottery Co., 328 U.S. 680, 66 S.Ct. 1187, 90 L.Ed. 1515 (1946).

7. 29 U.S.C.A. § 216(e).

administratively by the Secretary of Labor. Employers objecting to the penalty may request a hearing before an Administrative Law Judge, with an appeal to the Secretary of Labor. Ultimately, the Secretary may sue to collect the penalty.

Fourth, employees may bring an action under section 16(b) for unpaid minimum wages and overtime compensation and an equal amount as liquidated damages.[8] The Act's antiretaliation provision, section 15(a)(3), may also be enforced through a suit under section 16(b). In addition to any judgment for the plaintiffs, the court "shall * * * allow a reasonable attorney's fee to be paid by the defendant, and costs of the action." This language limits attorney's fees awards under the statute to prevailing plaintiffs. Employees lose their right to sue under this section if the Secretary of Labor files an action under section 16(c) or section 17 on their behalf.

The FLSA authorizes a unique form of representative action in employee suits under section 16(b). Unlike the normal "opt-out" scheme of Federal Rule of Civil Procedure 23(b)(3), under which members of a plaintiff class remain members unless they affirmatively exclude themselves, no employee may be a party to an FLSA suit under section 16(b) unless he or she has consented in writing and filed that consent with the court. Although courts may assist efforts to join potential plaintiffs by allowing discovery of the names and addresses of similarly situated individuals and authorizing notice to them, the normal reluctance of many people to disturb the status quo, plus the difficulty in understanding legal notices, mean that few FLSA representative actions are brought by private plaintiffs.

The fifth action authorized by the FLSA is a criminal prosecution for willful violations, under section 16(a).[9] The Department of Justice prosecutes these actions, and maximum sanctions are a fine of not more than $10,000 or imprisonment for not more than six months, or both. Prison sentences may not be imposed for a first conviction.

The Portal–to–Portal Act of 1947 established two good faith defenses for employers found in violation of the Act. The first, in section 10 of the Portal–to–Portal Act,[10] provides a complete defense to liability if the employer proves that it acted in good faith in conformity with and reliance on a written opinion of the Wage–Hour Administrator, even if the opinion is later rescinded or invalidated. The opinion must be in writing, and it must come from the Wage–Hour Administrator. Oral statements from any official or written opinions from low-level officials within the Wage–Hour Division do not satisfy the statute. To be "in conformity with" a written opinion, the employer's situation must be identical to the facts described in the opinion. If some elements are missing or different, or if the opinion does not take a clear position on the issue, the employer may not take advantage of the section 10 defense. "Good faith" is an objective test and requires that the employer

8. 29 U.S.C.A. § 216(b).

9. 29 U.S.C.A. § 216(a).

10. Id. § 259.

have "no knowledge of circumstances which ought to put [it] on inquiry."[11] If the section 10 defense applies, the employer may not be subject to "any liability or punishment" for failure to pay the minimum wage and overtime. This language bars issuance of a prospective injunction as well as back pay liability.

The second defense, created by section 11 of the Portal–to–Portal Act, authorizes the court, in its discretion, to reduce or eliminate an award of liquidated damages if the employer proves that it acted in good faith and had reasonable grounds for believing that it was not violating the FLSA.[12] Unlike the absolute defense in section 10, this defense applies only to the liquidated damages portion of the plaintiff's recovery. There can be no reduction of liability for unpaid minimum wages and overtime compensation. Because a written opinion from the Wage–Hour Administrator is not required under section 11, courts can consider such factors as reliance on advice of counsel or personnel experts. The employer must satisfy both the subjective and objective prongs of the defense, however. If the law in an area is clear, the employer will not be able to prove it reasonably believed it acted lawfully.

Another defense raising similar questions of good faith and reasonableness is the statute of limitations. The statute of limitations for FLSA actions is two years, or three years in cases of "willful" violations. Because FLSA violations are classic examples of continuing violations, the statute of limitations often serves to determine the amount of liability rather than the timeliness of the plaintiff's claim. Use of the three-year statute will significantly increase the total amount of back pay liability. In *McLaughlin v. Richland Shoe Co.*,[13] the Supreme Court resolved a three-way split in the circuits and adopted a "reckless disregard" standard; an employer commits a willful violation if "the employer either knew or showed reckless disregard for the matter of whether its conduct was prohibited by the statute." The Court held that Congress intended to create a two-tiered statute of limitations and to draw a real distinction between willful and ordinary violations. In fact, there now appear to be three tiers of violations: those to which the three-year statute of limitations applies; those to which the two-year statute of limitations applies, and in which plaintiffs receive an award of liquidated damages; and those to which the two-year statute of limitations applies, but in which there is no award, or a reduced award, of liquidated damages. If a violation is willful, liquidated damages should always be awarded, because the employer's actions could never satisfy the good faith and reasonableness test of section 11. By rejecting an unreasonableness test for willful violations, however, *Richland Shoe* contemplates situations in which an employer's actions are not willful, but not reasonable enough to justify a reduction of liquidated damages under section 11.

11.   29 C.F.R. § 790.15.

12.   29 U.S.C.A. § 260.

13.   486 U.S. 128, 133, 108 S.Ct. 1677, 1681, 100 L.Ed.2d 115 (1988).

The FLSA severely restricts the ability of employees to waive, release, or settle their claims. The original act contained no reference to settlement, but early cases held that public policy prohibited employees from waiving bona fide disputes about coverage or liquidated damages without government supervision. In reaction to these decisions and a decline in voluntary payments by employers, Congress amended the Act in 1949 to add a sentence to section 16(c) authorizing the Secretary of Labor to supervise the payment of unpaid wages and providing that employees' agreements to accept these payments constitute a waiver of their right to sue under section 16(b). Government-supervised settlements under section 16(c) or settlement of a section 16(b) lawsuit are now the only ways in which individual employees' FLSA claims may be compromised.

§ 4.11   Prevailing Wage Laws

In addition to the Fair Labor Standards Act, three federal prevailing wage statutes govern wages paid to certain workers in certain industries. They are the Davis–Bacon Act, which applies to the construction industry, the Walsh–Healey Act, which applies to the manufacturing and supply industries, and the Service Contract Act, which applies to companies that supply services. Instead of mandating a fixed minimum wage as the FLSA does, the prevailing wage statutes require covered employers to pay their workers the wages that prevail for workers in their area doing similar work on similar projects. These prevailing wage rates are determined by the Secretary of Labor. Although all three statutes use the same concept, the prevailing wage is determined by a different method under each one.

Davis–Bacon Act

The Davis–Bacon Act,[1] the first federal law that set a floor on wages for nonfederal workers, was originally enacted in 1931, substantially amended in 1935, and then repealed and reenacted in 2002. It requires that the advertised specifications for every federal construction project in excess of $2000 contain minimum wage provisions for each class of laborer and mechanic based on the prevailing wage for those workers in the locality where the work is to be performed. The Davis–Bacon Act applies by its terms only to contracts to which the federal government or the District of Columbia is a party, but many statutory schemes providing federal financial assistance to construction projects adopt the Davis–Bacon standards. The prevailing wage includes the amount of certain fringe benefits, such as contributions to retirement plans, disability and accident insurance, health care benefits, and vacation and holiday pay.

The Secretary of Labor is responsible for determining the prevailing wages in a locality. The statute does not define the term "prevailing" or give any guidance on how the Secretary is to arrive at a determination. The method developed by the Secretary was used from 1935 until 1985, when it was modified by the Reagan Administration. Under this method,

§ 4.11
1.   40 U.S.C.A. §§ 3141–3148.

known as the thirty percent rule, the prevailing wage could be set at the rate paid to a thirty percent plurality of local workers. In heavily unionized areas this rate was often the union rate. In 1982, the Department of Labor promulgated regulations eliminating the thirty percent rule and substituting a process by which the prevailing rate would be the rate paid to a majority of workers in the area, or, if no majority rate existed, the weighted average of all area rates.

The Davis–Bacon Act is enforced by the Department of Labor and the federal contracting agency. If the contractor fails to comply with the Act, the government may cancel the contract and complete the work itself. The Comptroller General may withhold the amounts of any unpaid wages from payments otherwise due the contractor and pay them directly to the covered workers. If these payments do not satisfy all claims for unpaid wages, covered workers may sue the contractor on the payment bond required by the Miller Act. The government may also debar a noncomplying contractor for three years. In *Universities Research Association, Inc. v. Coutu*,[2] the Supreme Court held that the Davis–Bacon Act does not confer a private cause of action for unpaid wages. Although the Court noted that in *Coutu* the Department of Labor had determined that the contract did not call for work covered by Davis–Bacon, and accordingly the contract did not contain a prevailing wage determination, the courts appear to be ignoring this distinction.

Walsh–Healey Public Contracts Act

The Walsh–Healey Public Contracts Act of 1936[3] applies to all contracts entered into by the federal government for the manufacture or furnishing of materials, supplies, articles, or equipment in excess of $10,000. It requires that all covered contracts contain stipulations about minimum wages, maximum hours, child and convict labor, and health and safety. Contractors must pay their workers not less than the "prevailing minimum wages" for similar work in the same locality, as determined by the Secretary of Labor.

In *Wirtz v. Baldor Electric Co.*,[4] the D.C. Circuit struck down the Secretary of Labor's determination of the prevailing minimum wage in the electrical motors and generators industry. After *Baldor Electric*, the Department of Labor stopped issuing Walsh–Healey determinations. Although existing determinations remained in effect, their rates were gradually overtaken by increases in the federal minimum wage.

This and other developments have rendered the Walsh–Healey Act virtually meaningless today. Originally the Act required that covered

---

2. 450 U.S. 754, 101 S.Ct. 1451, 67 L.Ed.2d 662 (1981).

3. 41 U.S.C.A. § 35–45.

4. 337 F.2d 518 (D.C.Cir.1963).

employees receive overtime on a daily basis; that provision was repealed in 1985. The prohibitions on the use of child labor have been replaced by those in the FLSA, the use of convict labor has never been a major problem, and the Occupational Safety and Health Act has superseded its safety provisions.

Service Contract Act

The O'Hara–McNamara Services Act of 1965,[5] generally called the Service Contract Act, covers federal contracts and subcontracts in excess of $2500 that furnish services to the United States through the use of service employees. It requires that covered employees be paid at least the "prevailing rates for such employees in the locality," including fringe benefits, as determined by the Secretary of Labor. The Service Contract Act also requires all contractors with service contracts, regardless of amount, to pay their workers the minimum wage set forth in the FLSA. In 1965, many service employees were not covered directly by the FLSA, so the Service Contract Act was a way to provide some of them with a federal minimum wage protection.

In 1976, Congress reacted to a district court decision that the Service Contract Act applied only to blue-collar workers doing jobs similar to the "wage-board" classifications of the federal civil service by amending the Act to define a service employee as any person working on a government service contract except a bona fide executive, administrative, or professional employee within the meaning of the FLSA. Because the Act applies to contracts "the principal purpose of which is to furnish services," the 1976 amendments meant that employees of many computer and other high technology firms contracting with the government became covered. Lobbying by various employer groups led to the promulgation of regulations that exempted contracts that, taken as a whole, do not have the provision of services as their principal purpose, and certain contracts for the maintenance and repair of computers, scientific and medical apparatus, and office and business machines.

As with the other federal prevailing wage statutes, the Service Contract Act is administered and enforced by the Secretary of Labor. There is no private cause of action for aggrieved employees. Penalties for violations include withholding of amounts owed to employees, cancellation of the contract, and debarment.

Other Statutes

The Contract Work Hours and Safety Standards Act[6] complements the Davis–Bacon Act by imposing overtime and health and safety standards for laborers and mechanics on most federal and federally-financed projects. Unlike Davis–Bacon, the Contract Work Hours Act does not require that the federal government be a direct party to the contract.

---

5. 41 U.S.C.A. §§ 351–358.   **6.** 40 U.S.C.A. §§ 327–332.

The Copeland Anti–Kickback Act[7] makes it a crime for a federal contractor to require or coerce workers to return part of their pay to their employer. It also mandates that the Secretary of Labor issue regulations requiring federal construction contractors to furnish weekly statements of the wages paid their workers.

Over thirty states and the District of Columbia have prevailing wage laws. Although they vary greatly, they generally cover only public works construction and for that reason are often referred to as "little Davis–Bacon Acts."

§ 4.12   Restrictions on Garnishment

Title III of the Consumer Credit Protection Act of 1968[1] restricts creditors' abilities to garnish workers' earnings and employers' rights to fire workers whose wages have been garnished. The legislative history shows that Congress was concerned about rising amounts of consumer credit and what it saw as "a causal connection between harsh garnishment laws and high levels of personal bankruptcies," especially in states with no restrictions on garnishments.

The Act generally prohibits garnishments of more than twenty-five percent of a worker's disposable earnings in any week. "Earnings" is defined as compensation for services, including periodic payments from a pension plan, and "disposable earnings" is the earnings left after deduction of any amounts withheld by law. Exceptions to the general twenty-five percent limit exist for (1) support orders issued by a court of competent jurisdiction or in accordance with a state administrative procedure that affords "substantial due process" and is subject to judicial review; (2) orders of bankruptcy courts; and (3) debts due for federal or state taxes. Support orders may garnish as much as fifty percent of a worker's disposable income, and as much as sixty percent if the individual subject to the support order is not also supporting a spouse or dependent child apart from the spouse or child involved in the support order. These percentage limitations increase to fifty-five and sixty-five, respectively, if the worker is more than twelve weeks behind in support payments.

The second prong of the Act is its restriction on discharges. Employers are prohibited from firing any employee because his or her earnings "have been subject to garnishment for any one indebtedness." The phrase "subject to garnishment" means that the earnings must actually be withheld from the employee's pay. Therefore, mere service on the employer of a second garnishment order does not constitute garnishment for a second debt. This is the case even if the only reason the employer does not withhold for the second garnishment is that the maximum amount allowed by law is already being withheld for the first garnishment. Willful violation of the restriction on discharge is punishable by a fine of $1,000 or imprisonment for one year, or both. The statute

---

7. 18 U.S.C.A. § 874; 40 U.S.C.A. § 276c.

§ 4.12
1. 15 U.S.C.A. §§ 1671–1677.

provides for enforcement by the Secretary of Labor, and there is no private cause of action for employees who claim they were fired in violation of this restriction.

The Act specifically does not preempt state laws prohibiting garnishments or imposing greater restrictions on garnishments than federal law, or laws providing greater rights against discharge because of garnishments.

§ 4.13   State Wage and Hour Regulation

Almost every state has a wage-hour law setting at least a minimum wage. Most also contain an overtime requirement and restrictions on child labor. While some states have no statutory minimum wage or overtime requirement, others provide more protection for workers than does the Fair Labor Standards Act (FLSA). The FLSA expressly does not preempt state laws that impose higher standards than federal law. Therefore, if the state minimum wage is higher than the federal minimum, if state law imposes a daily overtime requirement, or if it covers workers who are exempt under the FLSA, state law controls. Similarly, state law may limit tip credits or other set-offs against the minimum wage that federal law allows, and the state may impose more severe restrictions on child labor than does the FLSA.

A more significant source of wage-related rights is found in state wage payment or wage collection statutes. These laws regulate the specifics of wage payment in ways not touched by federal law. Although statutes vary from state to state, they share some common elements. They contain a definition of "wages" and require that employers pay wages in legal tender. They generally require payment of wages on a regular periodic basis, either monthly, semi-monthly, or weekly. Many states require employers to notify workers of the dates on which they will be paid and the place where they will receive their paychecks. In several states, unclaimed, unpaid wages, which remain unclaimed for periods between one and five years, become property of the state.

State wage payment laws commonly limit deductions and withholding from employees' pay. Most states prohibit deductions unless required or permitted by law or with the written consent of the employee. Some states prohibit deductions for damage to the employer's property, shortages, robberies, or debts, while others permit deductions for such items if the losses result from the worker's gross negligence, willful misconduct, or dishonesty.

Most state wage payment laws also regulate the payment of wages upon termination of employment. In some states, the employer must pay all accrued wages on the last day of employment, while in others the payment may be made on the next regularly scheduled payday. Some states draw a distinction between voluntary and involuntary separation from employment and require immediate payment only in cases of involuntary separation. If there is a dispute about the amount of wages owed to an employee, some states require the employer to pay the amount it concedes to be due. On the death of an employee, some states permit the employer to pay a specified portion of the wages due the deceased worker to his or her surviving family members before transferring the rest to the estate.

Enforcement of wage payment laws is generally entrusted to an administrative agency, with an appeal of the agency's decision to the state trial courts. Aside from unpaid wages, penalties often include liquidated damages, and criminal sanctions may be available, especially for willful violations. Generally, employees may not waive their rights under state wage payment statutes, and at least one state statute specifically provides that undocumented workers come within its protections.

A dispute under a state wage payment law may involve the question whether the employer actually owes certain amounts to the employee. Resolution of the issue may require looking to the same kind of evidence, some form of agreement or practice, written or oral, that is often used to support claims of discharge in breach of an implied contract. Thus, for instance, whether a worker who quit or was fired before his or her employment anniversary date is entitled to vacation pay for the year depends, in most states, on the terms of the employer's vacation policy, which might normally be found in an employee handbook or other similar document.

A caveat to this discussion of rights under state wage payment or collection laws is that under some circumstances they may be preempted by federal law. For instance, because severance pay plans are covered by ERISA, state wage payment laws may not regulate the circumstances under which employees receive severance pay. The employee's recourse is under section 502(a)(1)(B) of ERISA. Claims to vacation pay, however, are normally not preempted by ERISA, because ERISA does not cover unfunded, single-employer vacation pay plans.[1] Similarly, state law claims for wages due under a collective bargaining agreement may be preempted by section 301 of the Labor Management Relations Act.[2]

§ 4.14　Equal Pay Act—Overview

The Equal Pay Act of 1963 (EPA), the first modern employment discrimination statute, was enacted as an amendment to the Fair Labor Standards Act (FLSA).[1] Coverage under the EPA is identical to that of the FLSA, based on individual employee coverage, enterprise coverage, or federal, state, and local government coverage. Although the Supreme Court's decisions on state sovereign immunity in *Seminole Tribe of*

§ 4.13

1. Massachusetts v. Morash, 490 U.S. 107, 109 S.Ct. 1668, 104 L.Ed.2d 98 (1989). See also §§ 4.19, 4.30.

2. 29 U.S.C.A. § 185. See, e.g., Wheeler v. Graco Trucking Corp., 985 F.2d 108 (3d Cir.1993).

§ 4.14

1. 29 U.S.C.A. § 206(d).

Florida v. Florida[2] and *Alden v. Maine*[3] preclude private party suits against states and their agencies for violations of the FLSA, several courts of appeals have continued to hold that the extension of the EPA to the states could have been authorized by section five of the Fourteenth Amendment and therefore validly abrogated state immunity.

With one major exception, employees exempt from the FLSA's minimum wage requirement are also exempt from the EPA. A 1972 amendment eliminated the EPA exemption for executive, administrative, and professional employees, and outside salespeople, all of whom remain exempt from the FLSA's minimum wage and overtime requirements.

As an amendment to the FLSA, the EPA shares the enforcement procedures and remedies of that statute. The Department of Labor initially administered the EPA; in 1979, administration and enforcement were shifted to the Equal Employment Opportunity Commission (EEOC).

The EPA's substantive proscription is brief and narrow. It requires that men and women doing "equal work" in the same "establishment" receive equal pay, unless the employer can justify a pay differential by a seniority, merit, or piecework system, or by "any other factor other than sex." Equal work is described as work that requires equal skill, effort, and responsibility, and is performed under similar working conditions. Although enacted to correct wage discrimination against women, the EPA also protects men who receive lower pay than women who perform the same work. The EPA does not directly address gender discrimination in any other aspect of employment, but job segregation and discrimination in assignments, common elements in many EPA cases, often invalidate employer defenses to pay differentials. The EPA prohibits only one form of gender-based wage discrimination—unequal pay for equal work. Unequal pay for unequal work is not illegal under the EPA, even where intentional discrimination caused the inequality in work assignments. Remedies, if any, for this problem lie under Title VII.

In *Corning Glass Works v. Brennan,*[4] to date the only Supreme Court case arising under the EPA, the Court articulated the allocation of the burdens of proof in EPA litigation. Reading the statutory language literally, the Court held that the plaintiff has the burden of persuasion on the issues of unequal pay, equal work, and on the basis of sex. The case did not raise the question whether the work at issue was performed in the same establishment, but clearly the Court would have placed the burden of persuasion on that issue on the plaintiff as well. Unlike Title VII individual disparate treatment litigation, in which proof of the employer's intent is all-important, motive is not an element of a prima facie case under the EPA. If motive or intent enters the case at all, it will

---

2. 517 U.S. 44, 116 S.Ct. 1114, 134 L.Ed.2d 252 (1996).

3. 527 U.S. 706, 119 S.Ct. 2240, 144 L.Ed.2d 636 (1999).

4. 417 U.S. 188, 94 S.Ct. 2223, 41 L.Ed.2d 1 (1974).

be through the assertion of one of the statutory affirmative defenses, as to which the Court held the employer bears the burden of persuasion.

Corning illustrates the application of these rules and the importance of the allocation of the burdens of persuasion perfectly. The case involved the job category of inspector. The pay differential at issue originated at a time when the company operated segregated shifts, with male inspectors on the night shift and female inspectors on the day shift. Before institution of the night shift, women did all of the inspection work. When the night shift began in the 1920s, applicable state law prohibited the employment of women at night, so the company transferred men from the day shift. These men, however, refused to take the inspection jobs for the wages paid to the day shift women; the evidence showed "that additional compensation was necessary because the men viewed inspection jobs as 'demeaning' and as 'women's work.'" Thus, Corning paid the night shift inspectors, all male, higher wages to perform the same work done by the day shift inspectors, all female. By the time of the litigation, the day and night shifts had long since been integrated, but the pay differential between day shift and night shift workers continued.

Corning contended that a difference in shifts was not "similar working conditions" within the meaning of the EPA. The Court rejected that argument. Congress chose the terms defining equal work—skill, effort, responsibility, and working conditions—because they were widely used in industry job evaluation systems. In those systems, "working conditions" refers to hazards and surroundings, not time of day. A shift differential, therefore, can be justified only under the affirmative defense of "any other factor other than sex." Because the pay difference in the case had its origins in sex segregation, Corning could not satisfy its burden of proving the factor was "other than sex." The allocation of the burdens of persuasion was crucial to the outcome in *Corning*. If the difference between day work and night work had made the working conditions dissimilar, the Secretary of Labor would not have established an element of his prima facie case. The company would have won, regardless of the discriminatory origins of the shift differential.

Corning is also important for its rejection of the market defense. The company's defense "reflected a job market in which Corning could pay women less than men for the same work." This reason, that women's wages were depressed because the market did not value their work as highly as men's, was precisely why Congress passed the EPA, and Corning could not rely on it.

§ 4.15 Equal Pay Act—Prima Facie Case

The Equal Pay Act (EPA) requires, within any establishment, the payment of equal pay to men and women, for "equal work on jobs the performance of which requires equal skill, effort, and responsibility and which are performed under similar working conditions." The plaintiff bears the burden of persuasion on the elements of: (1) same establishment, (2) unequal pay, (3) on the basis of sex, and (4) equal work.

The establishment requirement is often overlooked in discussions of the EPA. The term "establishment" appears in other contexts in the Fair Labor Standards Act (FLSA) as well,[1] but neither the FLSA nor the EPA defines it. The EEOC interprets establishment to mean a "physically separate place of business."[2] Thus, wages paid to employees who work in separate facilities operated by the same employer may generally not be compared for EPA purposes. The EEOC says, however, that "unusual circumstances," such as centralized hiring, frequent interchange of employees, and identical duties among locations, may result in the treatment of two or more distinct physical parts of a business as a single establishment. To the extent that any trend can be perceived in the relatively small number of cases involving this issue, it is toward a broad, nongeographic construction of the term, especially for public-sector employers. The leading case, *Brennan v. Goose Creek Consolidated School District*,[3] concluded that while a narrow construction of the concept of establishment may be appropriate under the FLSA, it is not under the EPA. In the FLSA, "establishment" appears in an exemption, which should be construed strictly against the employer. In the EPA, on the other hand, it is one of the elements of the plaintiff's case, and therefore should be read broadly to facilitate proof of discrimination. Thus, the court found that where a centralized administration controlled all personnel decisions and each building had essentially the same working conditions, all of the schools in a school district constituted a single establishment under the EPA.

The second element of the plaintiff's prima facie case is unequal pay. The EPA prohibits an employer from paying "wages to employees * * * at a rate less than the rate at which he pays wages to employees of the opposite sex * * *." The statute commands equal *rates of pay*, not necessarily an equal bottom line. In *Bence v. Detroit Health Corp.*,[4] the managers of the men's division of a chain of health spas received a higher percentage commission on their membership sales than did the managers of the women's division. Although the total remuneration for both groups was equal because more women than men bought memberships, the court found the employer in violation of the equal pay requirement. The rate of pay was the unequal commission rate, not the equal bottom line.

To prove pay discrimination on the basis of gender, a female plaintiff need only find one man doing equal work at a higher rate of pay. Although she must find that male comparator, once he has been identified, the plaintiff may also use statistical evidence of a gender-based disparity to bolster her case.

§ 4.15

1. See, e.g., 29 U.S.C.A. §§ 203(r), 213(a)(3).

2. 29 C.F.R. § 1620.9(a).

3. 519 F.2d 53 (5th Cir.1975).

4. 712 F.2d 1024 (6th Cir.1983), denied, 465 U.S. 1025, 104 S.Ct. 1282, 79 L.Ed.2d 685 (1984).

That some men also receive the same pay as the plaintiff does not defeat her prima facie case, although that fact may help the employer establish an affirmative defense by attributing the pay differential to some factor other than gender. Plaintiffs may also compare their pay to that of a predecessor or successor in the same position, if no intervening changes in job content or other circumstances destroy the equality of the job held by different employees. In one case, the female plaintiff received the same pay as her immediate male predecessor, but less than several men who preceded him. The court allowed her to use the nonimmediate predecessors for comparison in her EPA suit.[5]

The equal work standard is the battleground in many EPA cases. In performing an equal work analysis, actual job content, not job title or description, controls. Similarly, courts look to the requirements of the job itself, not the skills and qualifications of the individual holding the job. Factors such as experience and training may justify a pay differential between two employees performing equal work, but they enter the case as affirmative defenses, not as part of the plaintiff's prima facie case.

In an influential early decision, the Third Circuit held that "equal" means "substantially equal," not "identical,"[6] and all the circuits to consider the issue have adopted this standard. The substantially equal test prevents employers from avoiding EPA liability by assigning one inconsequential task to male workers only, but otherwise it does not significantly advance resolution of the equal work determination. It is clear that for work to be equal, the jobs at issue must look alike. Although Congress specifically chose the concepts of skill, effort, responsibility, and working conditions because of their common use in industry job evaluation plans that establish wage structures among a wide range of very different jobs, the courts have construed the EPA's equal work requirement as applying only to jobs within the same job family.

To satisfy the substantial equality test, jobs must share a common core of tasks; "a significant portion" of the two jobs must be identical. No more precise test or percentage requirement has emerged to help determine when jobs share this crucial common core. Individual decisions, which often involve a "calorie-counting" treatment describing in great detail the various tasks employees perform, remain fact-bound, and the case law has provided few guidelines for a broad analysis of the statute's requirements.

Rarely are two sets of jobs identical; one or both jobs may have additional duties that the other does not. Once a court determines the existence of a common core of tasks, it must then evaluate the differences between the jobs and decide whether those differences render the jobs unequal. The statute's three criteria, skill, effort, and responsibility,

5. Broadus v. O.K. Indus., Inc., 226 F.3d 937 (8th Cir.2000).

6. Shultz v. Wheaton Glass Co., 421 F.2d 259 (3d Cir.), cert. denied, 398 U.S. 905, 90 S.Ct. 1696, 26 L.Ed.2d 64 (1970).

generally come into play at this point, although the decisions often do not treat them separately or with much meaningful analysis.

According to the EEOC, skill includes "consideration of such factors as experience, training, education and ability."[7] Very few cases have dealt specifically with the skill criterion. *Forsberg v. Pacific Northwest Bell Telephone Co.*[8] contains one of the more thorough discussions of the skill factor. The court found that jobs involving seemingly similar tasks, identifying the cause of malfunctions on telephone lines, actually required qualitatively different skills, where one job required independent problem-solving abilities and the other did not.

Effort is "the physical or mental exertion needed for the performance of the job."[9] Most of the cases dealing with the significance of additional duties involve the equal effort requirement.

Responsibility is "the degree of accountability required in the performance of the job, with emphasis on the importance of the job obligation."[10] For instance, supervisory responsibilities, if they actually exist, can render jobs unequal.

A test developed in *Hodgson v. Brookhaven General Hospital,*[11] an extra effort case, states principles courts often use in assessing the significance of extra duties to the equal work determination. Generally, extra duties assigned to the higher paid workers will not destroy the substantial equality of two jobs unless the extra duties (1) actually require extra effort (or skill or responsibility), (2) take a significant amount of the time of all of the higher paid workers, and (3) have an economic value to the employer commensurate with the pay difference. Extra duties that do not require extra effort, skill, or responsibility are treated as inconsequential, and the jobs retain their substantial equality. If not all members of the higher-paid group perform the extra duties, the obvious conclusion is that the basis for the pay differential is something else, like the gender of those holding the higher-paid jobs. Moreover, if a lower-paid woman can point to just one higher-paid man whose work is substantially equal to hers and who does not perform the extra duties, she has established her prima facie case. That other men receive the same higher pay but actually do the extra tasks is irrelevant.

The third factor in assessing the importance of extra duties is the economic value of the extra duties. Although the EPA does not address the relative, or "comparable" worth of jobs across job families, courts consider the value of specific duties in determining the equality of jobs with a common core of tasks. They do this, however, not through some abstract measure of worth, but through evidence of the value the employer itself assigns to the duties. In *Shultz v. Wheaton Glass Co.,*[12] the company paid male "selector-packers" $2.355 per hour, while it paid

---

7. 29 C.F.R. § 1620.15(a).

8. 840 F.2d 1409 (9th Cir.1988).

9. 29 C.F.R. § 1620.16(a).

10. Id. § 1620.17(a).

11. 436 F.2d 719 (5th Cir.1970).

12. 421 F.2d 259 (3d Cir.), cert. denied, 398 U.S. 905, 90 S.Ct. 1696, 26 L.Ed.2d 64 (1970).

female selector-packers only $2.14. The men and women performed all of the same tasks, but in addition some of the men did work that was normally performed by a third group of workers, "snap-up boys," who were paid $2.16 per hour. Because the company placed approximately the same value on the jobs done by the female selector-packers and by the snap-up boys, the court refused to believe that the snap-up boys' tasks, when performed by the male selector-packers, were really worth an additional twenty-one cents an hour. Without some sort of independent evidence of the value the employer places on the performance of a particular task, the economic value inquiry may become more problematic, although if there is a large pay disparity between very similar jobs, courts may simply find the employer's justification not worthy of belief.

The statute's fourth requirement, similar working conditions, is the only one the Supreme Court has specifically addressed. In *Corning Glass Works v. Brennan*,[13] the Court held that Congress chose the phrase "similar working conditions" as a term of art, to be defined according to commonly used principles of job evaluation. Under those principles, "working conditions" means "surroundings" and "hazards," not, as Corning argued, time of day. Thus, a finding of dissimilar working conditions requires jobs with exposure to a greater level of risk or a more unpleasant environment than those to which they are compared.

§ 4.16 Equal Pay Act—Defenses

Once the plaintiff in an Equal Pay Act (EPA) case has made out a prima facie case of unequal pay for equal work, the defendant can prevail only by justifying the pay differential under one of the EPA's four exceptions: "(i) a seniority system; (ii) a merit system; (iii) a system which measures earnings by quantity or quality of production; or (iv) a differential based on any other factor other than sex." In *Corning Glass Works v. Brennan*,[1] the Supreme Court held that these exceptions are affirmative defenses as to which the defendant bears the burden of persuasion.

The first three defenses share the requirement that the employer have a "system." A formal written document may not be necessary, but an employer must regularly use an organized and structured procedure with identified criteria to determine wage differences. Employees should be aware of the system, and, of course, the system must not be based on sex.

The seniority system and incentive system defenses have generated little litigation. Perhaps this is because formalized seniority or incentive systems are unlikely to contain explicit gender-based distinctions that would open them to attack under the EPA, and employers using longevity or production in an unstructured manner may be relying on other factors as well and for that reason they assert one of the other defenses.

---

13. 417 U.S. 188, 94 S.Ct. 2223, 41 L.Ed.2d 1 (1974).

§ 4.16

1. 417 U.S. 188, 94 S.Ct. 2223, 41 L.Ed.2d 1 (1974).

An employer satisfies the seniority system or incentive system defenses as long as it uses the same basis for measuring the seniority or production of all workers and applies the rules of its system equally to workers of both sexes.

The merit system defense, on the other hand, raises more problems. "Merit" is a vague term, and a scheme of merit evaluations can disguise the very kinds of gender discrimination the EPA was intended to eliminate. Ratings under a merit system must be based on predetermined criteria applied systematically, not on highly subjective, standardless factors applied haphazardly. Post hoc testimony about an employee's merit does not constitute a merit system. An employer should be able to explain how it used its merit system to arrive at each worker's rating and how that rating caused any pay discrepancies among employees doing equal work. A system that merely classifies jobs without providing a basis of evaluation, advancement, or reward does not qualify as a merit system.

Most of the case law on the EPA affirmative defenses involves the fourth, catch-all defense, "any other factor other than sex." Although the courts and the EEOC have developed rules, some fairly detailed, for evaluating a few employer practices, the exact contours of the defense remain fuzzy. Overt gender considerations of any sort obviously preclude its use, as does blatant reliance on gender-biased market forces. Beyond that bright line, however, courts are split on whether the defense should be read literally, to allow an employer to rely on *any* factor other than sex, or whether the employer's reason should bear some relationship to traditional wage-setting criteria, to the particular job, or to the employer's business.

The statutory language might seem to support a broad reading of the defense. Assuming a factor is not simply a pretext for discriminatory intent, a facially neutral reason for a pay disparity is, logically, "any other factor other than sex." On the other hand, the purpose of the EPA is to eradicate gender bias in wages, and many facially neutral policies can perpetuate the undervaluation of women's work. Factors like experience and training may adversely affect women who have not had the same opportunities as men, but employers who are not acting with discriminatory motives will undoubtedly be able to demonstrate a job-related reason for their use of these criteria. Other factors, such as use of prior salaries in setting wages or payment of a head-of-household supplement, can also affect women adversely, but they are not as obviously job-related. Requiring that a "factor other than sex" bear some relationship to the job would prohibit the use of such factors in many cases.

The Supreme Court has not decided any cases involving the application of the EPA's fourth affirmative defense to a facially neutral reason that is not part of a traditional job evaluation system. Language in its decisions construing the EPA can be read to support both broad and narrow views of the defense. *Corning Glass*, the landmark EPA case, involved a pay practice grounded in historical gender segregation, so the

Court did not have to clarify the role of job-relatedness in the factor other than sex defense. The case also stands for the proposition, however, that an employer may not rely on market forces to take advantage of the inferior bargaining power of women workers, even when that reliance is economically rational from the employer's point of view.

County of Washington v. Gunther,[2] involving the relationship of Title VII and the EPA, contains dicta suggesting that the factor other than sex defense precludes the use of disparate impact analysis, which challenges facially neutral practices, in Title VII wage discrimination cases. Thus, any truly neutral factor not adopted or used with discriminatory intent would fall within the fourth affirmative defense. In its cryptic discussion of this point, however, the Court stated that Congress included the EPA's fourth affirmative defense "because of a concern that bona fide job-evaluation systems used by American business would otherwise be disrupted." This example, the only one given in the Court's brief treatment of the issue, could be read as limiting the factor other than sex defense to those criteria typically used in job evaluation systems.

Not surprisingly, this lack of Supreme Court guidance has resulted in a variety of formulations of the factor other than sex defense in the lower courts. These range from the Seventh's Circuit's blanket statement that the factor does not have to be "related to the requirements of the particular position in question, or * * * a business-related reason,"[3] to the Ninth Circuit's "acceptable business reason" test,[4] to the Second Circuit's requirement that the employer prove "a bona fide business-related reason."[5] If employers may advance any facially neutral reason for a pay disparity, as the Seventh Circuit apparently allows, plaintiffs can win only by showing that the employer's reason is in fact a pretext for discriminatory intent. Because the EPA does not require plaintiffs to prove intent, EPA plaintiffs ought to be able to cast doubt on the defendant's reason with less evidence of pretext than a Title VII case would require. Therefore, arguably the more abnormal and non-business-related the reason offered by the employer, the more likely a court should be to find the employer's reason not credible. Unfortunately, little analysis of this sort has taken place, and courts tend to use Title VII precedent in dealing with pretext issues under the EPA.

On the other hand, if employers must prove that their factor other than sex is job-related, EPA cases start to resemble Title VII disparate impact cases. In *Aldrich v. Randolph Central School District*,[6] the employer justified a pay differential between the job of custodian and that of cleaner on the basis of a civil service examination and classification system. The court remanded so that the school district could

2. 452 U.S. 161, 101 S.Ct. 2242, 68 L.Ed.2d 751 (1981).

3. Fallon v. Illinois, 882 F.2d 1206, 1211 (7th Cir.1989) (internal quotation marks omitted).

4. Kouba v. Allstate Ins. Co., 691 F.2d 873, 876 (9th Cir.1982).

5. Brinkley v. Harbour Recreation Club, 180 F.3d 598 (4th Cir.1999).

6. 963 F.2d 520 (2d Cir.) cert. denied, 506 U.S. 965, 113 S.Ct. 440, 121 L.Ed.2d 359 (1992).

attempt to prove that both the custodian's exam and the district's practice of filling custodian positions only from among the top three scorers were related to performance of the job. The court's language was similar to the description of the burden the school district might have borne if the civil service examination had been challenged in a Title VII disparate impact case. Under the EPA, however, the plaintiff did not have to show that the test disproportionately excluded women; it was enough for her to prove that men who had passed the test and therefore received higher pay performed work substantially equal to hers.

In theory, any justification could be advanced under the fourth affirmative defense, but in practice, most of the case law centers on a handful of reasons. These include various factors related to the labor market, the economic value of the work performed, head-of-household classifications, training programs, red-circling, temporary or part-time work, and shift differentials. The following paragraphs should be read with the transcending question of the scope of the defense, discussed above, in mind. A court's conclusion about an employer's reason may be determined by its choice of test, or it may simply follow a previous court's decision involving the same employer practice without analyzing the issue of the scope of the defense.

One of the most difficult questions is the role of market forces in setting wages. Employers may not pay men more than women simply because men have greater bargaining power in the market, but that rule is not always easy to apply in individual cases. For instance, in settings where salary bargaining takes place on an individual basis and the employer has a random pay structure, one man may receive a higher salary because he in fact has more experience or greater skills, and not because of any gender bias in the market. In *Horner v. Mary Institute*,[7] a school hired a male teacher at a higher salary than a female teacher after the man refused to accept the amount offered to (and accepted by) the woman. The Eighth Circuit upheld a finding of unequal work but went on to remark that, in any event, the pay difference was based on a factor other than sex. In distinguishing *Corning*, the court said that the school had merely "consider[ed] the market place value of the skills of a particular individual."

In *Winkes v. Brown University*,[8] on the other hand, a female professor received an offer from another school with a sixty-four percent salary increase, and Brown matched it in order to retain her. The district court found that Brown would not have made the same counter-offer to a man, and therefore the University had violated the EPA. In other words, Brown was acting on the basis of gender bias in the market, albeit one of the rare markets in which females may be valued more highly than males in some situations. The First Circuit reversed the factual finding as clearly erroneous, although its result was also affected by the exis-

7. 613 F.2d 706 (8th Cir.1980).   8. 747 F.2d 792 (1st Cir.1984).

tence of a consent decree requiring Brown to recruit and retain female faculty.

A related issue is an employer's use of an employee's prior salary in setting initial wages. This practice allows the current employer to take advantage of gender biases in the market and thus perpetuates the undervaluation of women's work. In *Kouba v. Allstate Insurance Co.*,[9] a Title VII case dealing with the factor other than sex defense, Allstate based an employee's initial salary on several elements, including his or her prior salary. The court recognized that this practice could result in the incorporation of prior discriminatory practices into Allstate's wage structure. It remanded to allow Allstate to show that its use of prior salaries served as a sales incentive or as a predictor of ability. Similarly, *Price v. Lockheed Space Operations Co.*[10] held that basing an employee's pay on prior salary is not a factor other than sex unless the employer can prove business reasons for the practice.

Employers sometimes contend that a pay differential is justified by the economic benefit provided by the more highly paid workers. If the economic benefit results from extra duties performed by male workers, the issue is often resolved as part of the equal work analysis, but if plaintiff proves equal work, the issue can appear again as an asserted factor other than sex. In *Hodgson v. Robert Hall Clothes, Inc.*,[11] sales personnel in the men's clothing department were paid more than sales personnel in the women's department, on the ground that the men's department as a whole was more profitable than the women's department. The two departments were also segregated by sex, and the plaintiff did not challenge on appeal the district court's finding of the validity of the same-sex rule. *Robert Hall* has been harshly criticized and may well be limited to its facts, because discriminatory job assignments generally negate any claim that a factor is "other than sex."

In *Bence v. Detroit Health Corp.*,[12] the employer paid male health club managers more than female health club managers and argued that the difference was justified by the size of the markets for men's and women's memberships. The court rejected the employer's reliance on *Robert Hall,* because the female managers produced more, not less, profit on their sales. It went on to state that the segregation of male and female employees into separate departments, combined with a lower commission rate to the women, could not qualify as a factor other than sex.

Another category of "factor other than sex" cases that tends to disadvantage women is the payment of benefits only to a "head-of-household." If the employer defines the head of household as the man, the factor is explicitly gender-based and unlawful. If the head of house-

---

9. 691 F.2d 873 (9th Cir.1982).

10. 856 F.2d 1503 (11th Cir.1988).

11. 473 F.2d 589 (3d Cir.), cert. denied, 414 U.S. 866, 94 S.Ct. 50, 38 L.Ed.2d 85 (1973).

12. 712 F.2d 1024 (6th Cir.1983), cert. denied, 465 U.S. 1025, 104 S.Ct. 1282, 79 L.Ed.2d 685 (1984).

hold is defined in neutral terms as an employee who earns more than his or her spouse, men continue to be the primary beneficiaries because of the market forces that undervalue work done by women. Moreover, unlike prior salary, a head-of-household rule is not even arguably job related. Nevertheless, all of the courts of appeals to consider this practice have upheld it as a factor other than sex.

One of the first factors other than sex discussed by the courts was the training program. Typically, men and women performed the same tasks, but the employer claimed the more highly paid men were participating in a training program leading to their eventual placement in unequal jobs. Such programs can easily be used as subterfuges for wage discrimination, and the courts developed elaborate requirements to determine their bona fides. A training program must be open to both men and women; the program's existence must be communicated to all employees; the program must have an ascertainable ending point, with advancement to a higher job dependent solely on completion of the program, not on personnel needs; and it must actually amount to training, with a structured course of education.

Another factor other than sex upheld by the courts is so-called red circle rates, which maintain the higher wages of workers temporarily working outside their regular job assignment in a lower-paying position. Both the legislative history of the EPA and the Supreme Court in *Corning Glass* specifically mention red circle rates, and such maintenance of salary upon reassignment has generally been upheld by the lower courts. Courts have also allowed employers to pay different wages to workers employed on a temporary or part-time basis, even though they are doing the same work as permanent workers being paid more. As the Supreme Court recognized in *Corning Glass*, shift differentials can be factors other than sex. Although experience and skills not actually used in performing a job cannot be considered in determining whether work is equal, the employer can raise them as factors other than sex.

§ 4.17   Equal Pay Act—Curing Violations

The Equal Pay Act (EPA) contains a "no wage reduction" proviso, which states: "An employer who is paying a wage rate differential in violation of this subsection shall not, in order to comply with this subsection, reduce the wage rate of any employee." Employers can come into compliance with the EPA only by raising the wages of the lower-paid employees immediately, not merely by opening opportunities in the higher-paid jobs that may previously have been unavailable to those workers.

The Supreme Court's landmark EPA case, *Corning Glass Works v. Brennan*,[1] illustrates the operation of this requirement. For forty years Corning had operated segregated shifts, with men working at night paid

§ 4.17
1.   417 U.S. 188, 94 S.Ct. 2223, 41 L.Ed.2d 1 (1974).

more than women working during the day. In 1966, the company allowed women to bid for night shift jobs, and within two years half of the night shift jobs were filled by women. In 1969, Corning signed a collective bargaining agreement establishing a uniform wage rate for all new workers on both shifts. The collective bargaining agreement, however, provided for a higher "red circle" rate for incumbent night shift workers that effectively preserved the forty-year differential between day and night shift workers. By this time both shifts were fully integrated, so that the incumbent red circled night shift consisted of both men and women, as did the lower-paid incumbent day shift. The Court held that the 1966 integration of the night shift was not enough; Corning could cure its violation only by equalizing the wages of the female day shift workers. The red circle provision in the 1969 collective bargaining agreement suffered from the same flaw, for the rates it preserved violated the EPA. To cure the violation, the incumbent day shift workers had to receive the same higher red circle rate as the night shift workers.

Corning also illustrates the importance of historical inquiry into a company's wage structure. An observer of the status quo under the 1969 collective bargaining agreement would have seen that all of the day shift and some of the night shift received one wage, and some of the night shift received a higher wage, but both groups consisted of both men and women. That some men receive the same wage as a woman plaintiff does not defeat her prima facie case, but it was necessary to unravel the background of the pay differential in order to defeat Corning's affirmative defenses. Similarly, where a unique job is held by only one person, or where all of the incumbents are female, investigation may reveal that previous male holders of the positions were more highly paid. If the work has remained equal, so that there is an EPA violation, the cure is to raise the pay of the female incumbents to that of the male predecessors.

Another problem for employers, particularly those with random salary structures, is curing one violation without creating another. In *Board of Regents of the University of Nebraska v. Dawes,*[2] the university, concerned about possible loss of federal funds because of wage discrimination against women, reviewed its salary structure and devised a formula comparing the salaries of individual female faculty members with the salary of the average male faculty member, reached by taking into account education, specialization, experience, and merit. Thirty-three women identified as receiving less than the male average received a salary supplement increasing their pay to that average. The result was that the average male salary became the minimum female salary. Obviously, some men, ninety-two in all, received less than the female minimum. The Eighth Circuit found an EPA violation in the university's failure to pay the minimum salary it established for women to the ninety-two men. That some faculty members of both sexes were paid more than the female minimum did not matter, because EPA plaintiffs

2. 522 F.2d 380 (8th Cir.1975), cert. denied, 424 U.S. 914, 96 S.Ct. 1112, 47 L.Ed.2d 318 (1976).

do not have to show that all members of their gender receive lower wages.

Dawes was distinguished, however, in *Ende v. Board of Regents*,[3] a very similar case in which Northern Illinois University (NIU) established a formula based on a variety of factors and raised the salaries of female faculty members the formula identified as underpaid. The Seventh Circuit held that NIU did not have to equalize the pay of men who received less than the formula amount. One difference between *Dawes* and *Ende* was that in response to a complaint filed by a female faculty member, the Office of Civil Rights of the then-Department of Health, Education, and Welfare had found reasonable cause to believe NIU discriminated against women in salary matters, whereas there was no such determination in *Dawes*. As with affirmative action generally, that distinction frustrates the goal of voluntary compliance by requiring a finding of discrimination before the university could act. The *Ende* court specifically did not base its decision on affirmative action concepts, however. Instead, it held that the increase paid to individual female faculty members was a factor other than sex within the meaning of the EPA's fourth affirmative defense. "We think that an increase which restores a victim of past discrimination to the salary level he/she would have enjoyed in the absence of discrimination qualifies as defense (iv) even where the discrimination itself was based on sex." Perhaps the third distinction is that *Ende* involved a much more sophisticated attempt to eliminate wage discrimination against women, with no set amount as the minimum salary for all female faculty members. The university could argue that it was merely applying the same standards to women that it had always applied to men.

§ 4.18 Equal Pay and Comparable Worth Under Title VII

The Equal Pay Act (EPA) applies to gender-based wage discrimination only where men and women perform substantially equal work. Title VII of the Civil Rights Act of 1964 (Title VII), enacted the year after the EPA, prohibits gender discrimination in all aspects of employment, including compensation, without an equal work requirement. Concern that the broader language of Title VII would nullify the carefully-crafted restrictions of the EPA led Congress to add to Title VII a coordinating provision offered by Senator Bennett. It provides:

> It shall not be an unlawful employment practice under [Title VII] for any employer to differentiate upon the basis of sex in determining the amount of the wages or compensation paid or to be paid to employees of such employer if such differentiation is authorized by the provisions of [the Equal Pay Act].[1]

During the mid to late 1970s, the interpretation of the Bennett Amendment became an important issue in the development of the theory

---

3. 757 F.2d 176 (7th Cir.1985).   **§ 4.18**
                                        1. 42 U.S.C.A. § 2000e–2(h).

of comparable worth. The premise of this theory is that widespread occupational segregation has caused some jobs to be filled predominately by women, while other, entirely different jobs are held predominately by men. The theory asserts that, precisely because women hold them, predominately female jobs receive lower wages than male-dominated jobs of equal value, or comparable worth, to the employer. Comparable worth claims have involved such disparate jobs as nurse and tree trimmer, and secretary and carpet layer. The EPA does not reach this kind of discrimination, because admittedly the two sets of jobs do not satisfy that Act's equal work requirement. The vehicle for asserting claims of comparable worth had to be Title VII, and therefore the ambiguous language of the Bennett Amendment became crucial.

Under one view, the Bennett Amendment incorporated the EPA's equal work requirement into Title VII and thus prevented a finding of a Title VII violation in gender-based wage discrimination cases unless the employer's practice also violated the EPA. Under this reading, an employer who told a female employee that her wages would be fifty percent higher if she were male would not violate Title VII as long as it did not also employ a man doing substantially equal work. The competing view held that the Bennett Amendment merely incorporated the EPA's four affirmative defenses into Title VII. Pay differences "authorized" by the EPA are those that come within one of its four affirmative defenses. Thus, a female plaintiff claiming gender-based wage discrimination does not have to prove the existence of a male doing equal work in order to state a claim.

In *County of Washington v. Gunther*,[2] the Supreme Court adopted the latter interpretation by a five-to-four vote. *Gunther* presented appealing facts for a broad reading of the Bennett Amendment. The county paid female "matrons," who worked in the female section of the county jail, less than it paid male "correction officers" in the male section of the jail. Male prisoners significantly outnumbered female prisoners, so not only did each correction officer supervise more prisoners than each matron, but the matrons devoted much of their time to less valuable clerical work. This difference in duties was enough to make the work unequal, even though the positions were obviously similar. The plaintiffs alleged, however, that the county had intentionally underpaid them because they were women. They claimed that the county had determined through both an internal job evaluation and an external wage survey that the matrons should be paid ninety-five percent of the rate paid the correction officers, but "because of intentional discrimination," the county had set their wages at seventy percent of the male rate.

Gunther is as notable for what the Court did not say as for what it did. The Court specifically remarked that it was not deciding "the precise contours of lawsuits challenging sex discrimination in compensation under Title VII." Indeed, beyond the Court's narrow holding that the Bennett Amendment does not import the EPA equal work require-

2. 452 U.S. 161, 101 S.Ct. 2242, 68 L.Ed.2d 751 (1981).

ment into Title VII, the majority opinion in *Gunther* left virtually every other question about the scope of comparable worth claims unanswered. It declined to decide whether the *Gunther* plaintiffs themselves had stated a prima facie case. At several points the majority pointed out that plaintiffs were not basing their claims on a comparable worth theory that would require a comparison of the intrinsic worth of jobs or consideration of statistical evidence quantifying the role of sex discrimination in wage rates. Rather, the *Gunther* plaintiffs were trying to prove, "by direct evidence," that the county intentionally depressed their wages because they were women.

The best argument for the employer in *Gunther* was that the Court's reading of the Bennett Amendment created a redundancy. The section of Title VII to which the Bennett Amendment was added already contained defenses for seniority, merit, and piecework systems, the subjects of the first three EPA defenses, and the fourth EPA defense, "any other factor other than sex," is implicit in Title VII's prohibition on sex discrimination. The Court responded that the Bennett Amendment guaranteed a consistent interpretation of the first three defenses under both the EPA and Title VII. "More importantly," incorporation of the fourth affirmative defense through the Bennett Amendment "could have significant consequences for Title VII litigation." Title VII encompasses the disparate impact theory, which prohibits the use of a facially neutral practice with a discriminatory effect on members of protected groups unless the employer proves the practice is job related and consistent with business necessity. The EPA's fourth defense, said the Court, "was designed differently, to confine the application of the Act to wage differentials attributable to sex discrimination * * *. Equal Pay Act litigation, therefore, has been structured to permit employers to defend against charges of discrimination where their pay differentials are based on a bona fide use of other factors 'other than sex.'"

Although courts have not given much attention to this enigmatic remark, some commentators have concluded that it may preclude the use of disparate impact theory in Title VII gender-based wage discrimination litigation. Under this view, an employer's reliance on prevailing market rates in setting wages, without more, could not be challenged under a disparate impact argument, despite any negative effect the practice has on women's compensation rates. In the years immediately following *Gunther* the lower courts did not have to interpret the Supreme Court's language because there was another reason barring application of disparate impact theory to comparable worth claims, the line of cases restricting disparate impact theory in all Title VII claims to challenges to single, objective employer practices.[3] By the time the Supreme Court rejected that restriction in *Watson v. Fort Worth Bank & Trust*,[4] a number of influential lower court decisions had refused to recognize comparable worth arguments on either disparate treatment or disparate impact

3. See, e.g., American Fed'n of State, County, & Mun. Employees v. State of Wash., 770 F.2d 1401 (9th Cir.1985).

4. 487 U.S. 977, 108 S.Ct. 2777, 101 L.Ed.2d 827 (1988).

grounds, and this precedent was well-established. The decision the next year in *Wards Cove Packing Co. v. Atonio*[5] and then the Civil Rights Act of 1991 both now require a plaintiff alleging disparate impact to identify the particular practice or practices causing the impact, unless the employer's practices are incapable of separation.[6] This requirement imposes almost insurmountable barriers to proof of an adverse impact comparable worth claim.

Although a few recent cases have turned to the *Gunther* dicta to support rejection of disparate impact theory, there has been no exploration of the meaning of the EPA's fourth affirmative defense in Title VII litigation similar to the current debate under the EPA itself. The irony is that while the courts reject the use of disparate impact theory in Title VII wage discrimination claims, some of the EPA cases construing the fourth affirmative defense have described the nature of the employer's burden in language very similar to the Title VII business necessity defense. Moreover, using the EPA's fourth affirmative defense to disallow disparate impact claims in Title VII wage discrimination litigation lets employers rely on a defense, prevailing market rates, which is not available under the EPA itself.

Cases litigated under a disparate treatment theory have not fared much better. While *Gunther* removed the statutory barrier to assertion of comparable worth claims, the lower courts have shown great reluctance to find that a wage scheme violates Title VII absent strong "smoking gun" evidence of intentional sex discrimination. *Taylor v. Charley Brothers*[7] illustrates the kinds of proof that may be necessary in the post-*Gunther* era. The employer created two segregated divisions at its warehouse and paid workers in the female division thirty percent less than workers in the male division. There was no attempt to maintain a rational wage structure; men performing difficult work were paid the same as men doing easier unskilled work. Some women were in fact performing work equal to that done by some men; those disparities violated the EPA. While other female jobs required less effort than the male jobs, the plaintiffs' job evaluation expert testified that the relatively minor differences in the work did not begin to justify the large differences in pay. The court relied on the employer's intentional discrimination in job assignment and the EPA violations as strong circumstantial evidence for its finding that the wage disparities among the unequal jobs were the result of gender discrimination.

Charley Brothers was an easy case. The more difficult problem arises when virtually the only evidence of discriminatory intent is a job evaluation or wage survey revealing an undervaluation of predominately female jobs. In *American Federation of State, County & Municipal Employees (AFSCME) v. Washington*,[8] the state commissioned a job evaluation study that disclosed serious disparities between wages paid in

5. 490 U.S. 642, 109 S.Ct. 2115, 104 L.Ed.2d 733 (1989).

6. 42 U.S.C.A. § 2000e–2(k)(1)(B)(i).

7. 1981 WL 27045 (W.D.Pa.1981).

8. 770 F.2d 1401 (9th Cir.1985).

predominately female jobs and those paid in predominately male jobs with similar rankings in the study. When the state did not rectify the situation immediately, plaintiffs sued, claiming, among other things, that a failure to correct the known undervaluation of women's jobs supplied the necessary discriminatory intent. The Ninth Circuit disagreed. The state's practice of setting wages for various jobs based on market rates, rather than on their rating in the job evaluation study, was not enough to prove intentional discrimination. Any other result, concluded the court, would discourage employers from conducting job evaluations and engaging in voluntary efforts to correct pay inequities.

In addition, the court cited *Personnel Administrator v. Feeney*[9] for the proposition that mere knowledge of a wage disparity is not enough; plaintiffs must prove that the employer chose the policy because of its discriminatory effect. This unfortunate language was picked up and elaborated on by Judge Posner in a similar case, *American Nurses' Association v. Illinois*,[10] another influential decision rejecting a comparable worth claim. *Feeney* was not a Title VII disparate treatment case, and under Title VII discriminatory intent does not require a finding of invidious, evil motives. Rather, intent can be inferred from the fact of the disparate treatment, without any finding that the employer intended to hurt the plaintiff. With this "because of" standard, *AFSCME* created a burden of proof that will be almost impossible for Title VII wage discrimination plaintiffs to meet.

AFSCME was a major blow to the comparable worth movement. Although technically it held that plaintiffs failed to establish a prima facie case, it is also cited for the proposition that an employer's mere reliance on prevailing wages in the labor market is a defense to a Title VII wage discrimination claim. Pre–*Gunther* courts were inhospitable to claims challenging an employer's reliance on the market, and post-*Gunther* courts have been no different. Even where plaintiffs produce some additional background evidence of discriminatory intent, it is generally insufficient to defeat the market defense. In *Briggs v. City of Madison*,[11] involving two positions within the same job family, the court held that plaintiffs had established a prima facie case with their proof that public health nurses, who were predominately female, were paid less than sanitarians, who were predominately male, and that the two jobs involved work that, while not equal, was similar in skill, effort, and responsibility. The employer, however, prevailed with its defense that it had to pay more to its sanitarians in order to recruit and retain them.

§ 4.19 ERISA—Overview and Coverage

Aside from basic wages or salaries, employers often provide part of an employee's compensation in the form of fringe benefits, such as paid vacations, severance pay, medical coverage, or disability payments. In 1974, Congress transformed the law governing most fringe benefits by

---

9. 442 U.S. 256, 99 S.Ct. 2282, 60 L.Ed.2d 870 (1979).

10. 783 F.2d 716 (7th Cir.1986).

11. 536 F.Supp. 435 (W.D.Wis.1982).

enacting the Employee Retirement Income Security Act (ERISA).[1] Although much of the legislative history dealt with abuses in the administration and investment of private pension plans, ERISA also covers a wide variety of other common employment fringe benefits. ERISA does not require employers to provide pensions or any other benefit, nor, with certain exemptions, does it mandate any specific level of benefits if employers choose to offer plans. Rather, it protects the interests of participants in employee benefit plans and their beneficiaries in enforcing any benefit promise the employer does make by establishing certain minimum standards for all covered plans.

ERISA contains four titles. Title I deals with the protection of employee rights. It consists of seven parts: Reporting and Disclosure; Participation and Vesting; Funding; Fiduciary Responsibility; Administration and Enforcement; Continuation Health Coverage; and other Group Health Plan Requirements. Title II amended the Internal Revenue Code and deals with the tax consequences of coverage. Title III divides responsibility for administration and enforcement among the Department of Labor, the Internal Revenue Service, and the Pension Benefit Guaranty Corporation. Title IV creates the Pension Benefit Guaranty Corporation and establishes a system of insurance for pension plan termination.

ERISA covers any employee benefit plan established or maintained by an employer, a union, or both.[2] Exempted are governmental plans; tax-exempt church plans; plans maintained solely to comply with workers' compensation, unemployment compensation, or disability insurance laws; plans maintained outside the United States primarily for nonresident aliens; and excess benefit plans. Under ERISA the universe of benefit plans is divided into two types, pension benefit plans (or just "pension plans") and welfare benefit plans (or "welfare plans"). Both are subject to statutory structural requirements, reporting and disclosure obligations, fiduciary standards of care, broad preemption of state law, federal court enforcement by the government and private plaintiffs, and civil and criminal remedies for violations. While pension plans are subject to participation, vesting, and funding requirements, ERISA contains almost no substantive requirements for welfare plans. ERISA displaces much of the preexisting state law governing welfare benefits, but it does not impose any significant content regulation of its own.

A welfare benefit plan under ERISA is (1) "any plan, fund or program" (2) established by (3) an employer, an employee organization, or both, (4) for the purpose of providing certain enumerated benefits, through the purchase of insurance or otherwise, (5) to participants and their beneficiaries.[3] A plan must cover participants because of their status as employees. In *Nationwide Mutual Insurance Co. v. Darden*,[4] the Supreme Court held that ERISA's definition of the term "employee"

§ 4.19
1. 29 U.S.C.A. §§ 1001–1461.
2. ERISA § 4(a), 29 U.S.C.A. § 1003(a).
3. ERISA § 3(1), 29 U.S.C.A. § 1002(1).
4. 503 U.S. 318, 112 S.Ct. 1344, 117 L.Ed.2d 581 (1992).

incorporates traditional principles of agency law for identifying master-servant relationships. A plan, fund, or program in which none of the participants are employees, former employees, or union members is not a welfare benefit plan under ERISA.

ERISA's statutory definition of welfare plans enumerates many common employment fringe benefits: medical, surgical, or hospital care or benefits; benefits in the event of sickness, accident, disability, death, or unemployment; vacation benefits; apprenticeship or training programs; day care centers; scholarship funds; prepaid legal services; and any benefit allowed by section 302(c) of the Labor Management Relations Act (LMRA) other than pensions. Section 302(c) of the LMRA authorizes collectively bargained trust funds, jointly administered by employers and unions, that provide certain fringe benefits to employees. It largely duplicates the benefits enumerated in the ERISA definition, except for the addition of holiday and severance benefits and financial assistance for employee housing.[5]

The Department of Labor has exempted from ERISA coverage certain payroll practices and one-time payments by employers to employees. They include overtime, shift, holiday, or weekend premiums; wage payments out of an employer's general assets, rather than from a trust fund, for absences because of illness, vacations, holidays, active military duty, jury duty, training periods, or sabbatical or other educational leave; and holiday gifts such as turkeys or hams. In *Massachusetts v. Morash*,[6] a preemption case, the Supreme Court held that an employer's practice of paying discharged employees a lump sum for unused vacation time out of its general assets is not a welfare plan under ERISA. In specifically approving the Department of Labor regulation, the Court noted that an unfunded vacation plan maintained by a single employer does not pose the risks ERISA was intended to address, the mismanagement of accumulated benefit plan funds and the resulting failure to pay benefits from those funds when the contingency for which they were promised occurs. Because the risk that employees will not receive their vacation pay from the employer's general assets is no different from the risk they will not receive their wages, the Department of Labor acted reasonably in excluding this kind of vacation pay plan from coverage under ERISA.

The terms "plan, fund, or program" are not defined by the statute. In the leading case of *Donovan v. Dillingham*,[7] the Eleventh Circuit said that an ERISA plan exists "if from the surrounding circumstances a reasonable person can ascertain the intended benefits, a class of beneficiaries, the source of financing, and procedures for receiving benefits." In *Fort Halifax Packing Co. v. Coyne*,[8] another preemption case, the Supreme Court observed that a plan requires an ongoing administrative

5. 29 U.S.C.A. § 302(c)(6), (7)(C).

6. 490 U.S. 107, 109 S.Ct. 1668, 104 L.Ed.2d 98 (1989).

7. 688 F.2d 1367 (11th Cir.1982) (en banc).

8. 482 U.S. 1, 107 S.Ct. 2211, 96 L.Ed.2d 1 (1987).

program, the hallmarks of which include the obligations to determine claimant eligibility, calculate benefit levels, make payments, monitor the availability of funds, and keep records.

Although the statute imposes various structural requirements on ERISA plans, compliance with these requirements is not necessary for coverage. Courts have found that very casual practices, including oral promises, are covered plans, even when the employer was not aware it was maintaining an ERISA plan. For instance, in *Firestone Tire & Rubber Co. v. Bruch*,[9] the Supreme Court's seminal decision on the scope of judicial review of plan administrators' decisions, the severance pay plan in question consisted of two sentences in an employee handbook. The company had not set up a claims procedure or complied with the statute's reporting and disclosure requirements, but the severance pay promise was clearly a "plan" under ERISA.

§ 4.20   ERISA—Structure

ERISA requires all benefit plans to be in writing.[1] Failure to comply with this requirement does not, however, affect coverage. If a plan meets the statutory definition, which does not contain a written document requirement, ERISA applies. Lack of a written instrument undoubtedly means that other statutory obligations, such as the reporting and disclosure requirements, have been ignored as well, but these are independent violations with their own penalties, and they do not affect the question of coverage.

Plan documents must address certain topics. They must provide for one or more named fiduciaries, "who jointly or severally shall have authority to control and manage the operation and administration of the plan." The plan documents must describe any procedures for allocation of responsibilities for administration of the plan. If the plan does not designate an administrator, the plan sponsor becomes the administrator by default; for single employer plans, the employer is the plan sponsor. The plan documents must also provide a funding procedure and specify the basis for payments to and from the plan. Every plan must also provide "a procedure for amending such plan, and for identifying the persons who have authority to amend the plan."[2] In *Curtiss-Wright Corp. v. Schoonejongen*,[3] the Supreme Court held that a plan provision stating that "[t]he Company reserves the right at any time and from time to time to modify or amend, in whole or in part, any or all of the provisions of the Plan" sets forth an amendment procedure that satisfies section 402(b)(3). The Court reasoned that the term "person" is defined in ERISA to include a corporation, and corporate law principles should be consulted to determine who has the authority to make decisions on

9. 489 U.S. 101, 109 S.Ct. 948, 103 L.Ed.2d 80 (1989).

§ 4.20

1. ERISA §§ 102, 402, 29 U.S.C.A. §§ 1022, 1102.

2. ERISA § 402(b)(3), 29 U.S.C.A. § 1102(b)(3).

3. 514 U.S. 73, 115 S.Ct. 1223, 131 L.Ed.2d 94 (1995).

behalf of the company. The Curtiss–Wright plan also properly provided a procedure for amendment, a unilateral company decision.

An interesting ramification of the written instrument requirement is its effect on the application of the doctrine of estoppel. Employees routinely ask questions about the terms of their coverage under their employer's benefit plans, and the plan administrator or fiduciary responds, often orally. Sometimes the employee is told coverage exists and acts on the basis of that advice, only to have the claim for benefits ultimately denied because the terms of the plan documents do not in fact provide coverage. Claims of estoppel under state law are preempted by ERISA, and suit under section 502(a)(1)(B)[4] to enforce the terms of the plan will fail, unless the employee can successfully argue that the plan is estopped by its misrepresentations from denying coverage.

The federal courts have the power to develop a body of federal common law of rights and obligations under ERISA plans. That power does not, however, allow the courts to contradict the express requirements of the statute. At least seven courts of appeals have held that ERISA's writing requirement, coupled with the requirement that plans specify a formal means of amendment, prevent oral or informal written modifications of written ERISA plans. Oral representations conflict with "ERISA's emphatic preference for written agreements." The courts reason that ERISA's written document and reporting and disclosure requirements give participants and beneficiaries ready access to plan documents and ensure that by examining those documents they may determine their rights under the plan. Even when the plan has failed to comply with the Act's requirements, the policy favoring written documentation prevails. For instance, a plan might consist of only a few sentences in an employee handbook, but as long as it is in writing, it may not be modified orally. One court has even questioned whether the benefit provisions in a written plan that does not contain an amendment procedure, as ERISA requires, can be amended at all until an amendment procedure is added and complied with.[5]

Courts also point out that emphasizing the written documents protects the actuarial soundness of benefit plans and the legitimate expectations of other participants and beneficiaries; if an administrator's promises to some participants or beneficiaries to pay benefits not expressly allowed by the plan could be enforced, the funds available to pay the benefits the plan does allow would be diminished. Seizing on this point, the Seventh Circuit has permitted the use of estoppel in cases involving single-employer unfunded welfare benefit plans, arguing that no particular fund will be depleted by enforcing the plan administrator's promises.[6] The problem with this approach, attractive as it may be in many cases, is that ERISA's writing requirement applies to all benefit

4. 29 U.S.C.A. § 1132(a)(1)(B).

5. Frank v. Colt Indus., Inc., 910 F.2d 90 (3d Cir.1990).

6. Black v. TIC Investment Corp., 900 F.2d 112 (7th Cir.1990).

plans, both pension and welfare, whether established with a separate fund or unfunded.

This refusal to permit participants to enforce oral representations about their eligibility for benefits can certainly lead to harsh results where the participant has reasonably relied on information provided by the plan administrator or its agents. Many eligibility questions, particularly those involving health care plans, are complex, and the plan administrator is in a better position than the average participant or beneficiary to determine the answers. That so many courts prohibit the use of estoppel to provide benefits in the face of a contrary plan provision illustrates the significance of ERISA's written document requirement. In *Kane v. Aetna Life Insurance*,[7] the Eleventh Circuit attempted to alleviate some of the harshness of the rule by distinguishing between interpretations of an ambiguous plan term, which can be enforced against the plan, and modifications of the plan, which can not. Later cases in the Eleventh Circuit have emphasized that the plan provision in question must be ambiguous and capable of differing reasonable interpretations and that the representations to the participant or beneficiary must have been an interpretation of that provision.[8]

Some of the unfairness of the no-oral-modification rule is reduced by the statutory requirement that the plan administrator issue a summary plan description (SPD), providing a "plain English" version of the plan to participants and beneficiaries. As an integral part of ERISA's structure, the terms of a summary plan description (SPD) can often be enforced when they are at odds with the plan documents themselves.

§ 4.21   ERISA—Reporting and Disclosure

ERISA imposes extensive reporting and disclosure requirements on all covered plans, both pension and welfare.[1] The plan administrator must file an annual report and other information with the Department of Labor. In addition, the plan administrator must furnish certain documents and information directly to participants and beneficiaries on a periodic basis. These include summary annual reports, summary plan descriptions, summaries of material modifications, and for pension plans, statements of total accrued benefits and vested pension benefits. Information must also be provided upon the written request of participants and beneficiaries, or upon the occurrence of a COBRA qualifying event.

One of the most important documents mandated by ERISA is the summary plan description (SPD), the statute's "plain language" requirement. The SPD must be in writing, written in a manner calculated to be understood by the average plan participant, and sufficiently accurate and

---

7. 893 F.2d 1283 (11th Cir.) (en banc), cert. denied, 498 U.S. 890, 111 S.Ct. 232, 112 L.Ed.2d 192 (1990).

8. See, e.g., Simmons v. Southern Bell Tel. & Tel. Co., 940 F.2d 614 (11th Cir. 1991); Alday v. Container Corp. of Am., 906 F.2d 660 (11th Cir.1990), cert. denied, 498 U.S. 1026, 111 S.Ct. 675, 112 L.Ed.2d 668 (1991).

§ 4.21

1. ERISA §§ 101–111, 29 U.S.C.A. §§ 1021–1031.

comprehensive to apprise participants and beneficiaries of their rights and obligations under the plan.[2] The statute and accompanying regulations set forth a detailed list of the information the SPD must contain, including the name and address of the plan administrator and any trustees, requirements for participation and eligibility, circumstances that may result in disqualification, ineligibility, or denial or loss of benefits, and the plan's claims procedures. The plan administrator must furnish an SPD to each participant or beneficiary within ninety days after that person becomes a participant or starts receiving benefits. Updated SPDs must be provided periodically. In addition, the administrator must furnish a copy of the latest updated SPD upon written request of a participant or beneficiary.

Although the formal plan document can sometimes serve as the SPD as well, normally the SPD is a separate document, printed in booklet or brochure form, like an employee handbook. The SPD may be the only written explanation employees receive about their benefits. Although the SPD must be an "accurate" summary of the plan, subtleties in eligibility and coverage may become lost in the transition from the formal plan document to the SPD. When the SPD entitles an employee to benefits, but the formal plan document does not, courts generally enforce the SPD if the participant or beneficiary reasonably relied on it, even if the SPD contains a statement that the plan document will control in case of conflict. On the other hand, if there is no direct conflict between the plan and the SPD, if the SPD is silent on an issue that is described in the plan documents, or if the plan is more favorable to the participant than even unambiguous language in the SPD, the language of the plan controls.

Participants and beneficiaries may seek redress for a plan administrator's failure to provide information through suit under section 502(a)(1)(A),[3] which authorizes the court to award a civil penalty of up to $100 per day under section 502(c).[4] With three exceptions for which no prior request is necessary,[5] section 502(c) penalties are not triggered unless the participant or beneficiary has made a request for information covered by a statutory disclosure duty and the administrator has failed to comply within thirty days. Reasoning that penalty provisions should be construed strictly, the courts have refused to impose section 502(c) penalties unless all statutory conditions have been met. The request must be for information covered by section 502(c), and the statute must specifically impose the duty to supply the information on the plan administrator, not on the plan or some other entity. Further, the decisions whether to impose the penalty and, if so, in what amount are within the discretion of the trial court.

2. ERISA § 102(a)(1), 29 U.S.C.A. § 1022(a)(1).

3. 29 U.S.C.A. § 1132(a)(1)(A).

4. 29 U.S.C.A. § 1132(c).

5. ERISA § 502(c)(1), 29 U.S.C.A. § 1132(c)(1) (notice of right to elect health care continuation coverage); ERISA § 502(c)(1), (3), 29 U.S.C.A. § 1132(c)(1), (3) (certain notices concerning pension plans).

§ 4.22   ERISA—Claims Procedures

Section 503 requires every ERISA plan to establish and maintain a claims and appeals procedure. The plan must give participants or beneficiaries whose claims for benefits have been denied written notice of the specific reasons for the denial and provide them a reasonable opportunity for a full and fair review of that decision.[1] Congress apparently thought that internal claims procedures would promote the consistent treatment of claims for benefits, enhance efficient and expert plan management, provide a nonadversarial method of claims settlement, minimize the costs to the parties, and reduce frivolous suits.

Every plan is thus required to establish a "reasonable claims procedure," as defined in Department of Labor regulations,[2] and the summary plan description must describe the procedures for presenting claims for benefits and the remedies available under the plan if a claim is denied. Claimants must follow the requirements of a reasonable claims procedure.

Under the regulations, a description of all claims procedures and applicable time limits must be included in the summary plan description. Plans may not set up procedures that "unduly inhibit[ ] or hamper[ ] the initiation or processing of claims for benefits." The plan may not charge a fee or impose costs as a condition of pursuing an appeal, it may not require the filing of more than two appeals of an adverse determination before the claimant may bring suit in court, and in most situations, mandatory arbitration is prohibited. A plan's claims and appeals procedures must contain administrative safeguards to ensure that determinations are made in accordance with governing plan documents and that the plan provisions have been consistently applied with respect to similarly situated claimants.

The regulations mandate time limits for resolutions of initial claims and appeals; the limits differ, depending on the nature of the benefit that has been denied. The claim determination must be in writing and must state the specific reason for the determination, refer to the specific plan provision on which the determination was based, describe any additional information or material necessary to perfect the claim, explain why this information or material is necessary, and describe the plan's appeal procedures. If the claim involves health or disability benefits, the written determination must also include an internal rule, guideline, protocol, or similar criterion upon which the determination was based. If the determination was based on the fact that the claim was for services that were either not medically necessary or experimental, the determination must include an explanation of the scientific or clinical judgment upon which the determination was based.

Plans must establish procedures for appeals of adverse benefit determinations. The plan must permit the claimant to submit written

§ 4.22   **2.**   29 C.F.R. § 2560.503–1.

1.   ERISA § 503, 29 U.S.C.A. § 1133.

comments, documents, and other information; it must provide, upon request and without charge, all documents, records, and other information relevant to the claim for benefits; and the review process must take into account all information submitted by the claimant. For appeals involving group health plan claims, the plan must not give any deference to the initial determination, and the appeal must be decided by a named fiduciary of the plan who did not make the initial determination and is not a subordinate of the person who made the initial determination. If the appeal involves consideration of medical necessity or the experimental nature of the treatment, the named fiduciary must consult with a health care professional, and the plan must disclose to the claimant the identity of all experts consulted. The notice of denial of an appeal must be written in a manner calculated to be understood; it must include the specific reasons for the denial and refer to the specific plan provisions upon which the denial was based; it must state that the claimant is entitled to receive, upon request and without charge, all documents, records, and other information relevant to the claim; and it must explain that the claimant has a right to challenge the denial in court.

Generally, a participant or beneficiary may not bring a suit under section 502(a)(1)(B) challenging a denial of benefits unless he or she has exhausted the plan's claims procedures. ERISA does not explicitly require initial resort to these internal procedures, but the courts have unanimously imposed the exhaustion requirement, at least when the claim is based on an interpretation or application of the terms of the plan. Courts justify exhaustion with the same policy reasons that support section 503's claims procedure requirement and with analogies in ERISA's legislative history to section 301 of the Labor Management Relations Act, for which the courts also have created an exhaustion requirement. Issue or theory exhaustion is not required; claimants need only pursue their claims through the internal review procedure. Failure to exhaust the plan's claims procedure before filing suit can lead to a stay pending exhaustion or a dismissal without prejudice, although some courts have dismissed with prejudice when the plan's time period for seeking review of a benefit denial has expired.

As with exhaustion requirements generally, courts may decline to require exhaustion of plan remedies on the grounds of futility, denial of meaningful access to the appeals procedure, or the likelihood of irreparable injury during appeal. Exhaustion is not futile, however, merely because the same person or group of people who denied the claim for benefits initially will decide the appeal from that denial. Although the regulations impose some requirements on the identity of the decision-maker on appeal, they do not require independent decisionmakers for the internal appeal. As a practical matter, the person who makes the initial decision and any appeals body will share common interests or affiliations in almost every case.

There is no substantive remedy for violations of the claims procedures requirements of section 503. The appropriate remedy is normally a remand to the plan fiduciary for a new determination of the claim, including, if necessary, consideration of new evidence.

§ 4.23   ERISA—COBRA

While ERISA contains detailed substantive regulation of pension benefit plans, as originally enacted it did not regulate any of the terms of welfare benefit plans. The departure from this norm began with the Consolidated Omnibus Budget Reconciliation Act of 1985 (COBRA),[1] which amended ERISA, the Internal Revenue Code, and the Public Health Service Act to require sponsors of group health plans to offer participants and beneficiaries the chance to elect continuation coverage under the plan when a "qualifying event" that would otherwise cause a loss of coverage occurs. COBRA applies to group health plans maintained by all employers except churches, federal government entities (including the District of Columbia and United States territories and possessions), state and local government entities that do not receive funds under the Public Health Service Act, and employers that "normally employed fewer than 20 employees on a typical business day during the preceding calendar year."

Qualified Beneficiary

ERISA requires the plan to offer continuation coverage to "each qualified beneficiary" who suffers a "qualifying event." A qualified beneficiary is an employee who was covered by the plan on the day before the qualifying event, as well as the covered employee's spouse or dependent children who were covered on the day before the qualifying event. The term "qualified beneficiary" also includes a child born to or placed for adoption with the covered employee during the period of COBRA coverage. Retired employees, their spouses (or surviving spouses), and their dependent children can also be qualified beneficiaries in certain circumstances.

Qualifying Event

An event is a qualifying event only if it would result in loss of coverage under the plan but for the right to elect continuation coverage. For employees, there are two qualifying events, a termination of employment for any reason other than discharge for "gross misconduct," or a reduction of hours. The statute does not define the kind of termination for "gross misconduct" that will cause the loss of COBRA rights. A few courts have adopted the gross misconduct standard used under state unemployment insurance laws, which requires proof of willful, wanton, intentional, or substantial disregard of the employer's interests.[2] The Seventh Circuit has held the gross misconduct standard requires the employer to prove that the employee actually engaged in the bad

---

§ 4.23

1. The amendments to ERISA are found at ERISA §§ 601–608, 29 U.S.C.A. §§ 1161–1168.

2. See, e.g., Burke v. American Stores Employee Benefit Plan, 818 F.Supp. 1131 (N.D.Ill.1993).

behavior; a good faith belief that the employee engaged in gross misconduct will not permit it to deny COBRA benefits.[3]

For spouses and dependents, the qualifying events are the same as
for employees, plus the death of the covered employee, divorce or legal
separation from the employee, the employee's becoming entitled to
Medicare benefits, and a dependent child's ceasing to be a dependent
under the terms of the plan. Additionally, for retired employees, a
bankruptcy reorganization proceeding that results in a "substantial
elimination of coverage" within one year of its commencement is a
qualifying event.

Commencement and Length of Continuation Coverage

As a general matter, the period of continuation coverage begins on
the date of the event leading, under the terms of the plan, to loss of
coverage, not on the date on which coverage would otherwise have been
lost, if these do not occur at the same time. The date of notice that a
qualifying event will take place has, however, been found not to be a
qualifying event itself. Thus, a tender of resignation with notice is not
the qualifying event; rather the qualifying event occurs when the employee actually stops working for the employer. A plan may choose to
follow this general rule, or it may choose to defer the beginning of the
COBRA period until the loss of coverage actually occurs.

The length of required continuation coverage depends on the qualifying event. If the qualifying event is termination of employment or
reduction in hours, the COBRA period is normally eighteen months. If,
however, the qualified beneficiary is determined, under Title II or XVI of
the Social Security Act, to have been disabled at any time during the
first 60 days of COBRA coverage resulting from the loss of employment
or reduction of hours, the COBRA period for all qualified beneficiaries is
extended to twenty-nine months. If another qualifying event, like a
divorce or separation, occurs during the original eighteen-or twenty-
nine-month period, that period is extended to thirty-six months, but only
for individuals who were qualified beneficiaries when the first qualifying
event took place and who remained covered at the time of the second
event.

If the qualifying event is the death of the employee, divorce or
separation, loss of dependent child status, or eligibility for Medicare, the
COBRA period is thirty-six months. Any time an employee becomes
eligible for Medicare, regardless of whether there is a qualifying event,
COBRA coverage must be provided for the spouse and dependent children for at least thirty-six months following the date of eligibility. For
retirees whose qualifying event is the employer's bankruptcy, COBRA
coverage must be offered for the life of the retiree. If the retiree dies and
leaves a surviving spouse or dependent children, COBRA coverage for
them extends an additional thirty-six months beyond the date of the
retiree's death.

3. Kariotis v. Navistar Int'l Transp.
Corp., 131 F.3d 672 (7th Cir.1997).

COBRA coverage can end before the expiration of any of these periods if the employer ceases to provide any group health plan to any employee, if the beneficiary fails to pay the premium, or if the beneficiary becomes entitled to Medicare benefits. In addition, COBRA coverage can end on the date when the qualified beneficiary "first becomes," after the date of the COBRA election, covered under another group health plan that does not contain any exclusion or limitation as to any preexisting condition the beneficiary has, unless that exclusion or limitation does not apply to, or is satisfied by, the beneficiary under the Health Insurance Portability and Accountability Act of 1996 (HIPAA). In *Geissal v. Moore Medical Corp.,*[4] the Supreme Court held that an employer may not deny COBRA coverage to a qualified beneficiary on the ground that he or she was covered under another group health plan at the time of the COBRA election.

Type of Coverage and Premium

Coverage offered under COBRA must be identical to the coverage available to the beneficiary immediately before the qualifying event. If coverage provided similarly situated active employees is changed, the COBRA beneficiary must be given the same rights with respect to the new coverage as active employees who have not had a qualifying event. The plan may charge a COBRA beneficiary a premium for continuation coverage of no more than 102 percent of the plan's cost for a similarly situated beneficiary; a disabled beneficiary who is entitled to twenty-nine months of coverage may be charged 150 percent of the applicable premium after the first eighteen months of COBRA coverage. The plan may not require payment of any premium until forty-five days after the date on which the beneficiary makes the initial election.

Notice Requirements and Election Rights

COBRA contains two separate notice requirements. Upon the commencement of coverage under a health care plan to which COBRA applies, plan administrators must provide each participant and his or her spouse a notice of continuation coverage rights. Coverage can commence because an employee is hired by the plan sponsor, or because the plan becomes subject to COBRA by, for instance, meeting the twenty-employee requirement. The second notice requirement is triggered by a qualifying event. The employer must notify the plan administrator within thirty days after a covered employee's death, termination of employment, reduction of hours, or Medicare eligibility, or the commencement of bankruptcy proceedings. If the employer continues to pay for coverage after the qualifying event, it may delay this notice until the date coverage is lost, but then the COBRA period does not begin to run until the loss of coverage. The qualified beneficiary has the duty to notify the plan administrator within sixty days after a divorce, legal separation, or a child's loss of dependency status. Following any notice of a qualifying event, the plan administrator then has fourteen days to notify each qualified beneficiary of the right to elect continuation coverage. Should a

4. 524 U.S. 74, 118 S.Ct. 1869, 141 L.Ed.2d 64 (1998).

dispute arise, the plan administrator has the burden of proving that proper notice was given following a qualifying event.

A qualified beneficiary must elect coverage within sixty days after the date coverage terminates under the plan because of the qualifying event or the date he or she receives notice of COBRA election rights from the plan administrator, whichever is later. An election made any time during the sixty-day period relates back to the date coverage was lost because of the qualifying event. The Eleventh Circuit has held that if the plan administrator is aware that the qualified beneficiary is incompetent at the time of the qualifying event, the COBRA notification is effective only if it is mailed to a person capable of making, and willing to make, an informed decision about the election of continuation coverage on behalf of the beneficiary.[5] Similarly, the time limits for making a COBRA election can be subject to equitable tolling if, for instance, the qualified beneficiary becomes incapacitated during the election period.

Remedies

Failure to comply with COBRA requirements can be remedied through suit under section 502(a) of ERISA, and relief can include all the benefits that would have been paid if no violation had occurred.[6] In addition, failure to provide the required notices can subject plan administrators to the $100 per day penalty under section 502(c).[7] Unlike most of the other kinds of disclosure obligations subject to section 502(c) penalties, there is no requirement that participants or beneficiaries have made a prior request for information; the notice obligation is triggered when the administrator learns of the qualifying event.

§ 4.24 ERISA—HIPAA

The Health Insurance Portability and Accountability Act of 1996 ("HIPAA") continued the substantive regulation of both insured and self-insured health care plans that began with COBRA. In a new Part 7 to Title I of ERISA,[1] HIPAA severely limits the ability of insurance companies offering group health insurance coverage and self-insured plans to apply pre-existing condition exclusions, most particularly with respect to individuals who move from one job that provides health care benefits to another.

Limits on Pre-existing Condition Exclusions

With some exceptions, HIPAA establishes a general rule that ERISA health plans, whether insured or self-insured, may impose a pre-existing condition restriction only under certain carefully defined circumstances.

---

5. Meadows v. Cagle's, Inc., 954 F.2d 686 (11th Cir.1992).

6. 29 U.S.C.A. § 1132(a).

7. 29 U.S.C.A. § 1132(c).

§ 4.24

1. ERISA §§ 701–734, 29 U.S.C.A. §§ 1181–1191c.

First, the restriction must relate to a physical or mental condition for which medical advice, diagnosis, care, or treatment was recommended or received within the six-month period preceding the participant's or beneficiary's "enrollment date." Genetic information may not be treated as a condition unless it has led to an actual diagnosis of the condition related to the information. "Enrollment date" is defined as the date of enrollment or, if earlier, the first day of the waiting period for enroll-ment. For example, if a group health care plan requires a two-month waiting period for all new employees, the six-month "look-back" period for purposes of determining whether the plan's pre-existing condition exclusion may be applied is the date of hire. In this situation, the plan could not apply a pre-existing condition exclusion to an employee who had not received medical treatment or had treatment recommended to him or her during the six-month period immediately preceding hire by the new employer, but who became ill and received treatment during the two-month waiting period after the date of hire.

Assuming the participant or beneficiary has a pre-existing condition as defined by HIPAA, the period of coverage denial with respect to that condition can not last longer than twelve months, or eighteen months if the individual is a "late enrollee." A late enrollee is a participant or beneficiary who enrolls under the plan other than during the first period he or she is eligible to enroll, or during a "special enrollment period," discussed below. This period of coverage denial must be reduced by the aggregate periods of "creditable coverage" applicable to the participant or beneficiary. "Creditable coverage" includes coverage under a group health plan, health insurance, Medicare Part A or B or Medicaid, health coverage provided by the military, health coverage offered by the federal government to federal employees, a medical care program of the Indian Health Service or of a tribal organization, a "public health plan," a state health benefits risk pool, or a health benefit plan under the Peace Corps Act. Creditable coverage does not include coverage of "excepted bene-fits." HIPAA thus eliminates one of the most widely discussed "failures" of the health care benefit system, the loss of coverage solely because of a change in jobs. An employee who works twelve months or longer for one employer that provides health care coverage (thereby accumulating twelve months of creditable coverage) and then switches jobs may not have any pre-existing condition exclusion applied to him or her by the new employer's plan.

A plan may refuse to count creditable coverage if there is a sixty-three day break between the end of the creditable coverage and the date of enrollment under the new plan. In calculating the sixty-three day period, however, the new plan may not count a waiting period for coverage under a group health plan or an affiliation period for coverage under an HMO. For example, assume that (1) an employee has at least twelve months of creditable coverage under a former employer's plan, (2) that coverage expires on July 1, (3) the employee is hired by a new employer on September 1, and (4) the new employer's health care plan has a thirty-day waiting period for enrollment. The thirty-day waiting period can not be included in determining whether a break in coverage sufficient to cause the loss of the employee's creditable coverage has occurred. In fact, under this example, it has not; the employee suffered a sixty-two day break in creditable coverage (from July 1 to September 1), and his or her earlier creditable coverage must be taken into account by the new employer's plan.

Individuals prove their periods of creditable coverage by presenting certifications of coverage to the new plan. This document is a written certification of the individual's period of coverage under the prior plan and the coverage, if any, under the prior plan's COBRA provisions, and the waiting period, if any (or affiliation period, if any, in the case of an HMO), imposed on the individual before his or her coverage under the prior plan. The prior plan or insurer must provide an individual with a certificate (1) when he or she ceases to be covered under the plan or becomes covered under COBRA, (2) when the individual's COBRA coverage ends, and (3) upon the individual's request within twenty-four months after the first two dates.

In addition, a group health plan or insurer may not apply any pre-existing condition exclusion to a newborn child if that child is covered under creditable coverage as of the thirtieth day after his or her birth, unless there was a sixty-three day period during which the child was not covered under any creditable coverage. Similarly, if a child is adopted or placed for adoption before attaining age eighteen and is covered under creditable coverage as of the thirtieth day following the adoption or placement for adoption, the plan or insurer may not impose any pre-existing condition exclusion as to that child, unless he or she has a sixty-three day break in creditable coverage. A group health plan or insurer may not impose any pre-existing condition exclusion relating to pregnancy.

Special Enrollment Periods

HIPAA also changes, under certain circumstances, the common practice of health plans and insurers of limiting the periods when employees may enroll themselves or their dependents if they could have enrolled earlier but did not. If one of the special enrollment periods applies to an employee or his or her dependents, the plan must use the twelve-month exclusion period for pre-existing conditions (subject to the creditable coverage rules), rather than the eighteen-month period otherwise permitted for late enrollees.

If an employee or his or her dependent is eligible for coverage but not enrolled, the plan or insurer must permit the employee or dependent to enroll if (1) the employee or dependent was covered under another group health plan or had health insurance coverage at the time coverage was previously offered under the employee's new group health plan; (2) the employee stated in writing at that time that he or she was declining coverage because of the other coverage, although this requirement applies only if the plan sponsor or insurer requires such a statement and gives the employee notice of the requirement and its consequences; (3)

the employee's or dependent's other coverage was either COBRA coverage that was later exhausted, or non-COBRA coverage that was lost because of loss of eligibility or termination of employer contributions toward the other coverage; and (4) the employee requested the enrollment not later than thirty days after the exhaustion of COBRA coverage or the termination of eligibility for non-COBRA coverage or employer contributions toward the non-COBRA coverage.

In addition, group health plans that provide dependent coverage must provide a "dependent special enrollment period" if an employee who is a participant or could have enrolled during a previous enrollment period acquires a dependent through marriage, birth, adoption, or placement for adoption. During that period, the plan must permit the employee, if he or she is not already enrolled, and the new dependent to enroll. Further, in the case of the birth or adoption of a child, the employee's spouse, if not already enrolled but otherwise eligible for coverage, must be permitted to enroll during the dependent special enrollment period. The dependent special enrollment period must be at least thirty days long and must begin on the later of the date dependent coverage is made available under the plan, or the date of the marriage, birth, adoption, or placement for adoption. Coverage of the dependent must become effective, in the case of marriage, not later than the first day of the first month beginning after the date the request for enrollment is made, or in the case of birth, adoption, or placement for adoption, the date of the event.

Prohibition on Discrimination Based on Health Status

HIPAA prohibits a group health plan or an insurer from establishing rules for eligibility or continued eligibility, including waiting periods, of an individual based on the individual's or the individual's dependent's health status; medical condition, including both physical and mental illnesses; claims experience; receipt of health care; medical history; genetic information; evidence of insurability, including conditions arising out of acts of domestic violence; or disability. These prohibitions do not, however, require a group health plan or insurer to provide particular benefits, nor do they prevent a plan or insurer from establishing limits or restrictions on the amount, level, extent, or nature of the benefits or coverage for similarly situated individuals enrolled under the plan. A group health plan or an insurer may not require an individual to pay a larger premium than that charged to similarly situated individuals, because of the health status factors listed above. A plan or insurer is not prohibited from establishing premium discounts or rebates, or modifying copayments or deductibles in connection with a wellness program.

§ 4.25   ERISA—Other Health Care Mandates

In addition to COBRA and HIPAA, Congress has acted in a piecemeal fashion by mandating specific benefits relating to health care, primarily for the benefit of children. This section will discuss those provisions.

Qualified Medical Child Support Orders

The 1993 budget law added two mandates for group health care plans. The first requires plans to recognize qualified medical child support orders (QMCSOs) that require a divorced spouse to provide health care coverage for his or her children.[1] The QMCSO is facially similar to the qualified domestic relations orders pension plans are required to honor. To be a QMCSO, a judgment, decree, or order (including approval of a settlement agreement) must be made pursuant to a state domestic relations law and must provide for child support or health benefit coverage for the child of a participant under a group health plan. (The child is called an "alternate recipient.") The order must clearly specify the name and last known mailing address of the participant and of each alternate recipient, a reasonable description of the type of coverage to be provided by the plan, the period to which the order applies, and each plan to which the order applies. A QMCSO may not require a plan to provide any type or form of benefit, or any option, the plan does not otherwise provide.

Orders that meet the QMCSO standards are exempted from preemption by ERISA. Plan administrators must establish procedures for determining whether a state court medical support order qualifies as a QMCSO. The plan is protected from liability to the participant or the alternate recipient if it makes these determinations in accordance with ERISA's fiduciary standards. Alternate recipients under a QMCSO are considered beneficiaries under the plan for purposes of ERISA and participants under the plan for purposes of ERISA's reporting and disclosure requirements. Reimbursement for expenses for the alternate recipient must be made to the parent who actually paid them, not necessarily the participant.

Health Coverage of Adopted Children

The second mandate added by the 1993 budget law is a requirement that a group health care plan provide coverage for children placed for adoption with a participant or beneficiary under the same terms and conditions that apply for biological children.[2] Coverage must begin when the child is placed in the adoptive home, even if the adoption is not yet final, and plans may not exclude preexisting conditions of adopted children if they do not apply a similar exclusion to biological newborns.

There is one major exception to the rule that adopted children must be treated in the same manner as biological children. A group health plan may not restrict coverage of a child adopted by a participant or beneficiary, or placed for adoption with a participant or beneficiary, solely on the basis of a preexisting condition that the child has at the time he or she would otherwise become eligible for coverage under the plan.

§ 4.25

1. ERISA § 609, 29 U.S.C.A. § 1169.

2. ERISA § 609(c), 29 U.S.C.A. § 1169(c).

Pediatric Vaccine Coverage

Group health plans are required to continue to provide the same level of coverage for pediatric vaccines as they provided on May 1, 1993.[3]

Minimum Maternity Lengths of Hospital Stay

The Mothers' and Newborns' Health Protection Act of 1996 amended ERISA to add section 711,[4] prohibiting health plans that provide hospitalization benefits and health insurance issuers offering group health coverage from limiting covered maternity stays to less than forty-eight hours after a vaginal delivery and ninety-six hours after a cesarean section, unless the attending health care provider, in consultation with the mother, decides an earlier discharge is appropriate.

Mental Health Benefit Parity

The Mental Health Parity Act of 1996 amended ERISA to provide that a group health care plan providing medical and surgical benefits and mental health benefits may not impose aggregate lifetime limits or annual limits on mental health benefits, unless it imposes the same limits on "substantially all" medical and surgical benefits.[5] The rule applies to "mental health benefits," as defined in the plan, provided that it does not include treatment of substance abuse or chemical dependency. The rule, however, does not require plans to offer mental health benefits, nor does it prohibit plans from limiting the amount, duration, or scope of mental health benefits, except as required by the provisions on aggregate annual and lifetime limits. There is also a provision that the parity requirement will not apply if it would cause an increase of at least one percent in plan costs.

§ 4.26   ERISA—Retiree Health Benefits

Unlike pension benefit plans, welfare benefit plans are not covered by ERISA's mandatory vesting rules. The statute does not require that the right to welfare benefits become nonforfeitable after a specified period of time, and employers are normally free to modify levels of benefits offered under their welfare plans or to eliminate benefits entirely. In *Inter-Modal Rail Employees Association v. Atchison, Topeka and Santa Fe Railway Company,*[1] the Court confirmed that "unless an employer contractually cedes its freedom, it is generally free under ERISA, for any reason at any time, to adopt, modify, or terminate its welfare plan." Thus, although the statute does not require it, employers may voluntarily create a vested welfare benefit through the use of appropriate language in the plan documents, so that a provision for the payment of retirement welfare benefits could obligate the employer to

---

3. ERISA   § 609(e),   29   U.S.C.A. § 1169(e).

4. 29 U.S.C.A. § 1185.

5. ERISA § 712, 29 U.S.C.A. § 1185a.

§ 4.26

1. 520 U.S. 510, 515, 117 S.Ct. 1513, 1516, 137 L.Ed.2d 763, 769 (1997) (internal quotation marks and citations omitted).

continue benefits for the retirees' lifetimes. During the past twenty years, the issue of an employer's obligation to continue to provide retiree welfare benefits, especially health care benefits, has been hotly litigated. The escalating costs of health care, the increasing number of retirees, the troubled economy, and waves of corporate mergers and acquisitions led many companies to reduce or eliminate health care benefits for their retirees.

Suits by retirees challenging an employer's termination or modification of their welfare benefits fall into two groups: suits under Labor Management Relations Act section 301 when the employer terminates benefits after the expiration of a collective bargaining agreement, and suits under ERISA section 502(a)(1)(B) when the employer changes benefits for its former nonunion workers. In each case, however, the dispositive issue is the same—did the employer (or the employer and the union) intend to create an irrevocable right to retiree welfare benefits?

Collectively Bargained Benefits

Unionized workers will trace their claim to retiree welfare benefits to the collective bargaining agreement between their employer and their union. In interpreting collective agreements under section 301, courts follow a straightforward contract analysis. If the contract unambiguously provides either that retiree benefits survive its expiration or that they are limited to its duration, the inquiry is at an end. Few cases have found such unambiguous language, although examples do exist.[2]

Courts also look to other provisions in the collective bargaining agreement as an aid to interpreting the provision concerning retiree benefits. In *International Union, UAW v. Yard–Man, Inc.*[3] the court viewed a contract provision limiting the duration of coverage for a retiree's spouse and dependent children as an indication that the parties did not intend to limit benefits for retirees themselves. Conversely, specific durational language concerning retiree benefits, or reaffirmation and continuation clauses in each successive collective agreement are evidence of an intent to limit benefits to the life of the contract.[4] Contract language explicitly preserving the right to amend, modify, or terminate benefits or referring to summary plan descriptions containing that language have resulted in a finding for the employer.

If the contract is ambiguous, courts look to extrinsic evidence for indications of the parties' intent. This can include summary plan descriptions and other company documents, bargaining history, and past practice. Past practice can also be evidence of intent, especially if the employer has continued to pay retiree welfare benefits during strikes and other periods when no collective bargaining agreement was in effect.

2. See, e.g., United Steelworkers of America v. Connors Steel Co., 855 F.2d 1499 (11th Cir.1988), cert. denied sub nom. H.K. Porter Co. v. United Steelworkers of Am., 489 U.S. 1096, 109 S.Ct. 1568, 103 L.Ed.2d 935 (1989).

3. 716 F.2d 1476 (6th Cir.1983), cert. denied, 465 U.S. 1007, 104 S.Ct. 1002, 79 L.Ed.2d 234 (1984).

4. See, e.g., Murphy v. Keystone Steel & Wire Co., 61 F.3d 560 (7th Cir.1995).

Finally, courts may look to representations by management, especially those made to union officers, as evidence of an intent to vest benefits.

Casting an influential shadow over every analysis of the right to receive retiree welfare benefits after the expiration of a collective bargaining agreement is the Sixth Circuit's decision in *International Union, UAW v. Yard–Man, Inc.*[5] The employer stopped providing life and health insurance benefits for retirees after the expiration of the collective bargaining agreement and two years after the closing of the plant covered by the agreement. After a typical section 301 contract analysis, the court went on to remark that "retiree benefits are in a sense 'status' benefits which, as such, carry with them an inference that they continue so long as the prerequisite status is maintained." In other words, "normally retirement benefits vest." The court reasoned that retirement benefits of any kind are really a form of deferred compensation for work performed during the employee's active years. After retirement, employees no longer have any bargaining power and the union is not obligated to bargain on their behalf; therefore, a presumption of vesting best fulfills the parties' expectations.

The discussion of status benefits in *Yard–Man* was dicta, and immediately after the statement quoted above the court noted that no federal labor policy presumptively favors the finding of irrevocable rights to retiree welfare benefits. Some courts have criticized *Yard–Man* and refused to infer an intent to vest retirement welfare benefits because of the status of retirement. In later cases the Sixth Circuit itself stated that *Yard–Man* does not stand for the proposition that retiree status creates a legal presumption in favor of vesting.[6] Nevertheless, the concept continues to influence the courts and allows them to disregard clear contract language of intent or to find an intent to vest retiree welfare benefits on very uncertain objective evidence.

Nonunion Plans

Nonunion retirees claiming a right to continued welfare benefits may sue only under ERISA. As with collectively bargained plans, the first step is to determine whether the ERISA plan unambiguously reserves the right to modify or terminate benefits. If it does, the benefits are not vested, and the employer may make any change it wishes. That employees have retired in reliance on receiving welfare benefits and have in fact received them for some time does not render the benefits irrevocable in the face of clear language allowing termination or modification. Undoubtedly, because nonunion plans are drafted by the employer and are not the subject of negotiation with a union, clear reservations of the right to modify or terminate are much more common than in section 301 cases.

5. 716 F.2d 1476 (6th Cir.1983), cert. denied, 465 U.S. 1007, 104 S.Ct. 1002, 79 L.Ed.2d 234 (1984).

6. See, e.g., International Union, United Auto. Workers v. BVR Liquidating, Inc., 190 F.3d 768 (6th Cir.1999), cert. denied, 529 U.S. 1067, 120 S.Ct. 1674, 146 L.Ed.2d 483 (2000) (in construing a benefit plan negotiated by a company and a union, *Yard-Man* creates "an inference that the parties intended for benefits to vest ... ").

If the plan documents and the SPD are ambiguous, courts may examine extrinsic evidence of the employer's intent. This can include whether the employer has reduced benefits in the past, thus acting consistently with its argument that it reserved the authority to do so. Although oral representations cannot modify the clear terms of a plan, they can help interpret ambiguities. For instance, evidence that company officials told employees that retirement welfare benefits were a reward for spending their careers with the company could illuminate the employer's intent.

Retiree Benefits Bankruptcy Protection Act

In July 1986, LTV Corporation, the nation's second largest steel manufacturer, filed for reorganization under Chapter 11 of the Bankruptcy Code and at the same time notified approximately 78,000 retirees that it was discontinuing their medical and life insurance benefits. The congressional response to this move was the passage of the Retiree Benefits Bankruptcy Protection Act of 1988, adding section 1114 to the Bankruptcy Code.[7]

Section 1114 classifies many retiree welfare benefits, including those for health care, as administrative expenses that must be paid before confirmation of a reorganization plan under Chapter 11. These benefits must continue to be paid during reorganization until the parties agree to a modification or the court orders one upon finding that it "is necessary to permit the reorganization of the debtor and assures that all creditors, the debtor, and all of the affected parties are treated fairly and equitably, and is clearly favored by the balance of the equities." The difference between benefits paid under the original agreement and those paid under any modification are treated as an unsecured claim.

§ 4.27 ERISA—Interference With Benefit Accrual

Like most other remedial labor legislation, ERISA contains an antiretaliation provision that safeguards workers' statutory rights by protecting the underlying employment relationship on which those rights are based. Section 510 makes it unlawful

> for any person to discharge, fine, suspend, expel, discipline, or discriminate against a participant or beneficiary for exercising any right to which he is entitled under the provisions of an employee benefit plan, [or] this title, * * * or for the purpose of interfering with the attainment of any right to which such participant may become entitled under the plan, [or] this title * * *. It shall also be unlawful for any person to discharge, fine, suspend, expel, or discriminate against any person because he has given information or has testified or is about to testify in any inquiry or proceeding relating to this Act * * *.[1]

7.   11 U.S.C.A. § 1114.

    § 4.27
1.   ERISA § 510, 29 U.S.C.A. § 1140.

Section 510 contains three separate protections. The first, patterned on the antiretaliation provisions of other labor laws, is straightforward; it prohibits any adverse employment action in retaliation for the exercise of a right to seek benefits. For instance, an employer violates section 510 if it fires an employee because the employee filed a claim for benefits under an ERISA plan or sued under ERISA to recover denied benefits.

The third protection listed in section 510, for individuals who have given information or testified in any proceeding under the Act, has not generated much litigation. There is a difference of opinion as to the scope of the term "proceeding," with the Fourth Circuit holding that it refers only to administrative or legal proceedings, not to a complaint made within the company,[2] and the Ninth Circuit holding that the statute protects intra-office complaints.[3]

The second form of protection listed in section 510 is unique to ERISA. The legislative history contains stories of employees who were fired after many years of faithful service, just before they were to become eligible for a pension or other employment benefit. Congress sought to deter this kind of employer misconduct both by imposing relatively short vesting requirements for pension plans, and, in section 510, by prohibiting employers from discriminating against employees in order to prevent them from attaining rights under ERISA plans. An employer that fires an employee in order to block that employee's vesting in the employer's pension plan violates section 510. Although Congress was concerned with protecting employees' ability to obtain vested pension rights, the courts have given section 510 a much broader reading. Section 510 prohibits discrimination intended to interfere with the attainment of *any* rights under an ERISA plan. Employees who are already fully vested in the employer's pension plan are protected from discharge or other adverse actions aimed at preventing them from accruing additional pension rights.

Section 510 also protects participation in ERISA welfare plans, even though welfare plans rarely provide for vested rights. In *Inter–Modal Rail Employees Association v. Atchison, Topeka & Santa Fe Railway Co.*,[4] the employer contracted out work previously done by its employees to another company, which provided fewer pension and welfare benefits. Workers who continued their employment with the new company thus had a large reduction in their benefits. They sued under section 510, claiming they had been fired "for the purpose of interfering with the attainment of * * * right[s] to which" they would have "become entitled" under their former employer's ERISA plans. The Ninth Circuit permitted the plaintiffs to proceed on their claim for interference with their pension benefits, but not on their claim as to welfare benefits. The court's reasoning was that welfare benefits do not vest, and a section 510

---

2. King v. Marriott International, Inc., 337 F.3d 421 (4th Cir. 2003).

3. Hashimoto v. Bank of Hawaii, 999 F.2d 408 (9th Cir. 1993).

4. 520 U.S. 510, 117 S.Ct. 1513, 137 L.Ed.2d 763 (1997).

claim depends on the existence of a present "right." The Supreme Court reversed, holding that the Ninth Circuit's reading of section 510 is contradicted by the plain language of the statute, which uses the word "plan," and thus is not limited to pension plans. The Court agreed that employers do have the power to amend or abolish welfare benefit plans, but that power does not include the power to "discharge, fine, suspend, expel, discipline, or discriminate against" participants or beneficiaries "for the purpose of interfering with [their] attainment of * * * rights * * * under the plan."

Section 510 protects "participants" from interference with their rights under an ERISA plan. Participants are employees or former employees who are or may become eligible for benefits under an ERISA plan.[5] Thus, section 510 has been held to protect a part-time employee who was not eligible for benefits, where the employer had intended to move her into a full-time position with benefits. Section 510 also protects participants from retaliation because their spouses or children have made or may make claims. Applicants for employment would not, however, seem to be protected by section 510 because they do not satisfy the statutory definition of participant, which is pegged to employee status. Therefore, applicants who are refused employment because they or their dependents may make large claims against the employer's health care plan may not have a claim under section 510. Those applicants may, however, have rights under the Americans with Disabilities Act.

A threshold question in section 510 cases is whether the plaintiff must exhaust the internal appeal procedures established by the ERISA plan before bringing suit. Exhaustion is required in actions under section 502(a)(1)(B) seeking benefits from a plan, but the courts have not agreed whether exhaustion is required in suits for violation of section 510, which are brought under section 502(a)(3). The rationale for requiring exhaustion is certainly not as clear in section 510 suits as in challenges to benefit denials. Those courts that require exhaustion reason that it will further private dispute resolution, reduce the number of frivolous ERISA suits, minimize the costs of dispute resolution, prevent premature judicial interference with decisionmaking by plan fiduciaries, and allow the development of a complete record for eventual judicial review, if necessary. On the other hand, section 510 claims involve statutory rights, rather than interpretation of a plan document. They involve interference with a participant's ability to meet the requirements for receipt of benefits under the plan, not with whether the participant has in fact qualified for benefits. The key question is the employer's intent, not the reasonableness of a benefit denial. Moreover, while the plan as such can grant claims for benefits, it cannot give the relief typically sought in a section 510 case, reinstatement of the employment relationship.

A major problem under section 510, as with other discrimination statutes, is proof of the necessary employer intent. In one sense, every

---

5.   ERISA § 3(7), 29 U.S.C.A. § 1002(7).

discharge interferes with the employee's ability to accrue and receive benefits offered by the employer, because fired employees normally lose all nonvested benefits. The courts have not allowed section 510 to become a general wrongful discharge statute, however. Section 510 plaintiffs must prove more than the fact that their discharge prevented them from receiving future benefits; they must prove that the employer acted with specific intent to interfere with their ERISA rights. The loss of benefits must have been a motivating factor for the employer's actions, not merely a consequence of them. The mere fact that the employer's actions resulted in a savings is not enough, standing alone, to prove the necessary intent. Absent evidence that the employer was concerned only with benefit costs, as opposed to general payroll costs, plaintiffs have to find other strong circumstantial evidence, such as proximity to vesting, to avoid summary judgment.

Instead of firing an employee to avoid paying benefit claims, an employer might decide simply to eliminate the particular benefit. ERISA does not require employers to provide benefits, nor does it regulate the level of benefits that employers do offer. While ERISA regulates some kinds of pension plan terminations, employers can freely terminate or modify welfare plan benefits unless they have promised not to do so. This is the issue in the retiree health benefits controversy. Additionally, some courts have held that termination of a benefit plan, without more, does not affect the employment relationship and therefore does not violate section 510.

The troubling case of *McGann v. H & H Music Co.*,[6] involved not a plan termination, but a modification affecting only the plaintiff. After learning that McGann had been diagnosed as having AIDS, his employer modified its health care plan by becoming self-insured and placing a $5,000 cap on lifetime benefits for AIDS. It retained the preexisting $1 million lifetime cap for all other medical conditions. The company conceded that its action was prompted by knowledge of McGann's illness and a desire to avoid the high medical costs associated with AIDS. McGann's claim that this change violated section 510 was rejected by the Fifth Circuit. The court reasoned that the employer had never promised not to change the terms of its health care plan, and therefore it had an absolute right to do so. Because McGann did not have a right to the continued availability of the $1 million cap, he was not deprived of any right to which he was entitled under the employer's plan. The court noted that although McGann was the company's first employee with AIDS, the $5,000 limit on AIDS coverage applied to all employees. To get past summary judgment on the issue of specific intent, McGann apparently would have had to produce evidence that the employer disliked him personally and that the change was made as part of that dislike.

McGann illustrates a major advantage to employers of having a self-funded health care plan. Commercial health insurance is subject to

6. 946 F.2d 401 (5th Cir.1991), cert. denied sub nom. Greenberg v. H & H Music Co., 506 U.S. 981, 113 S.Ct. 482, 121 L.Ed.2d 387 (1992).

regulation by each state. In many states, changes without notice to policyholders and the exclusion, differentiation, or elimination of coverage for particular medical conditions are unlawful. Indeed, following *McGann*, Texas amended its insurance laws to prohibit the cancellation of an accident or sickness policy during its term because the insured has been diagnosed with HIV infection or AIDS. Even if the amendment had predated his illness, however, it would not have benefited Mr. McGann. ERISA permits the operation of state insurance laws, but it neither allows states to regulate the content of self-funded ERISA plans nor imposes its own substantive requirements for those plans.

§ 4.28   ERISA—Civil Enforcement of Benefit Rights

ERISA Causes of Action

The civil enforcement provision of section 502 of ERISA[1] authorizes a number of causes of action, four of which are relevant for benefit claims litigation. In terms of day-to-day enforcement of ERISA rights, the most important provision is section 502(a)(1)(B), which authorizes participants or beneficiaries to bring an action to recover benefits due them under the plan, to enforce their rights under the plan, or to clarify their rights to future benefits under the plan. This is the only purely personal cause of action authorized by ERISA. It does not depend on statutory violations; it enforces individual rights under the terms of the ERISA plan.

The second major civil enforcement provision is section 502(a)(3), which permits participants, beneficiaries, or fiduciaries to sue to enjoin any act that violates ERISA or the terms of the plan, or to obtain "other appropriate equitable relief" to redress statutory or plan violations or to enforce provisions of the statute or the plan. This cause of action is broader than that authorized by section 502(a)(1)(B). It includes claims to enforce statutory rights, as well as personal rights under the plan, it permits plan fiduciaries, as well as participants and beneficiaries, to sue, and it reaches a broader group of defendants. A section 502(a)(3) claim may be brought, for instance, by a plan participant against an employer for violation of section 510, ERISA's antidiscrimination provision, by a fiduciary to recover money paid to a physician in violation of the terms of a health care plan, or by a fiduciary to enforce an employer's statutory obligation to make contributions.

Third, section 502(a)(2) permits a participant, beneficiary, fiduciary, or the Secretary of Labor to seek relief under section 409[2] for breach of ERISA's fiduciary obligations. This cause of action is essentially the reverse of a section 502(a)(1)(B) claim. It vindicates statutory rights, not individual rights under a plan. Whereas any monetary relief under section 502(a)(1)(B) is paid to the individual claimant from plan assets, relief under section 502(a)(2) is paid by the individual fiduciaries to the plan.

§ 4.28   **2.** Id. § 1109.
1. 29 U.S.C.A. § 1132.

Fourth, section 502(a)(1)(A) authorizes a plan participant or beneficiary to sue the plan administrator for failure to comply with a request for information that ERISA requires the administrator to furnish. The remedy for this violation is a civil penalty of up to $100 per day, as authorized by section 502(c).

Other ERISA causes of action include section 502(a)(4), which permits the Secretary of Labor, participants, or beneficiaries to seek relief for failure to provide statements of benefits as required by section 105(c). The Secretary of Labor may seek injunctive relief to enforce the statute under section 502(a)(5) and civil penalties under section 502(a)(6). Plan administrators, fiduciaries, participants, and beneficiaries may seek review of final orders of the Secretary of Labor under section 502(k).

Standing

Section 502 describes three classes of private parties who may bring actions: participants, beneficiaries, and fiduciaries. Most courts limit standing in ERISA suits to members of those groups, for causes of action they are specifically authorized to bring. Although section 502(d)(1) provides that plans "may sue or be sued * * * as an entity," there are no enumerated section 502 causes of action in which a plan is authorized to act as a plaintiff. Therefore, most courts refuse to permit a plan to bring a section 502 claim, although in many situations a plan could avoid the standing problem by suing in the name of its fiduciary.

A "participant" is defined as "any employee or former employee of an employer * * * who is or may become eligible to receive a benefit of any type from an employee benefit plan which covers employees of such employer * * *."[3] In *Firestone Tire & Rubber Co. v. Bruch*,[4] the Supreme Court interpreted the definition of participant to cover "employees in, or reasonably expected to be in, currently covered employment" and "former employees who have * * * a reasonable expectation of returning to covered employment or * * * a colorable claim to vested benefits." Seizing on this explanation, several courts have held that former employees who have received all their vested benefits and have no reasonable expectation of returning to work are not participants.[5]

ERISA defines "beneficiary" as "a person designated by a participant, or by the terms of an employee benefit plan, who is or may become entitled to a benefit thereafter."[6] Courts have sometimes construed this term broadly to include individuals claiming they should have been designated by the participant. For instance, in *Brown v. Connecticut General Life Insurance Co.*,[7] the plaintiff's divorce decree ordered her ex-husband to maintain her as the beneficiary of his life insurance, but after his remarriage he designated his second wife as the beneficiary

---

3. ERISA § 3(7), 29 U.S.C.A. § 1002(7).

4. 489 U.S. 101, 109 S.Ct. 948, 103 L.Ed.2d 80 (1989).

5. See, e.g., Shawley v. Bethlehem Steel Corp., 989 F.2d 652 (3d Cir.1993).

6. ERISA § 3(8), 29 U.S.C.A. § 1002(8).

7. 934 F.2d 1193 (11th Cir.1991).

under an ERISA group life insurance plan. Upon his death, the first wife sued to collect the proceeds from the ERISA plan, and the court permitted her to maintain an action as a beneficiary.

Jurisdiction and Venue

The federal courts have exclusive jurisdiction over all ERISA causes of action except claims under section 502(a)(1)(B), which may be brought in either state or federal court. Venue is proper where the plan is administered, where the breach took place, or where a defendant resides or may be found, and nationwide service of process is authorized.

Statute of Limitations

The only express statute of limitations in Title I of ERISA is the six- or three-year period for actions alleging a breach of fiduciary obligations.[8] For other actions the courts borrow the most analogous state limitations period. Thus, actions for denial of benefits under section 502(a)(1)(B) are generally governed by the state statute of limitations for breach of written contracts. Suits under section 502(a)(3) for retaliation in violation of section 510 are generally analogized to employment discrimination or wrongful discharge claims.

Jury Trial

ERISA does not expressly provide a right to jury trial for any of the section 502 causes of action. The courts of appeals are virtually unanimous in characterizing relief under ERISA as equitable in nature, so that there is no right to jury trial under the Seventh Amendment. Some of the ERISA causes of action, like section 502(a)(3), explicitly provide for "appropriate equitable relief," but even suits for benefits denials under section 502(a)(1)(B), which does not contain similar language, are held to be equitable in nature.

Remedies

In *Massachusetts Mutual Life Insurance Co. v. Russell*,[9] a beneficiary whose benefits under a disability plan had been terminated and later reinstated sued for damages. The plan had paid her full retroactive benefits; she sought instead "extra-contractual compensatory or punitive damages caused by improper or untimely processing" of her claim. She relied solely on section 409(a), which allows "such other equitable or remedial relief as the court may deem appropriate,"[10] and not on section 502(a)(3). The Court noted that section 409 focuses on the relationship between the fiduciary and the plan and that its remedies serve to make the plan whole against wayward fiduciaries. It also explained that section 502's "six carefully integrated civil enforcement provisions," none of which expressly authorizes monetary awards other than benefits due under the plan, are strong evidence that Congress did not intend to permit other remedies. Therefore, the Court held that extracontractual

---

8. ERISA § 413, 29 U.S.C.A. § 1113.

9. 473 U.S. 134, 105 S.Ct. 3085, 87 L.Ed.2d 96 (1985).

10. 29 U.S.C.A. § 1109.

damages caused by improper or untimely processing of benefit claims cannot be recovered under section 409(a).

The Court in *Russell* carefully remarked that it had "no occasion to consider whether any other provision of ERISA authorizes recovery of extracontractual damages." That occasion arose in *Varity Corp. v. Howe*,[11] where a group of beneficiaries of a welfare plan sued the plan administrator for breach of fiduciary duty, claiming that the administrator had, "through trickery," caused them to withdraw from the plan and lose their benefits. They sought an order reinstating them as participants in the plan. The Supreme Court held that the authorization in section 502(a)(3) of "appropriate equitable relief" permitted individual participants or beneficiaries of ERISA plans to sue plan administrators seeking relief for themselves, not for the plan, for breaches of fiduciary obligations. The Court distinguished *Russell* as involving section 502(a)(2), which limits remedies by virtue of its cross-reference to section 409, not section 502(a)(3), upon which the *Russell* plaintiff specifically refused to rely. Further, the Court said that in *Russell* another part of section 502, section 502(a)(1), already provided specific relief for the harm plaintiff had suffered, whereas no other action authorized by section 502 applied to the *Varity* plaintiffs' claims. The Court saw the language in section 502(a)(3), authorizing "appropriate equitable relief" to "redress" any "act or practice which violates any provision of this title," as broad enough to cover individual relief for a breach of fiduciary duty. The Court characterized section 409, which authorizes relief running to the plan, as "reflecting a special congressional concern about plan asset management," not an intent to provide the only remedies for every kind of fiduciary breach.

Attorney's Fees

Section 502(g)(1) allows the court, in its discretion, to award reasonable attorney's fees to *either* party. An early Tenth Circuit case, *Eaves v. Penn*,[12] set forth five factors to consider in determining whether to award fees, and this list has been widely cited. The factors are

(1) the degree of the offending parties' culpability or bad faith; (2) the degree of the ability of the offending parties to personally satisfy an award of attorneys fees; (3) whether or not an award of attorneys fees against the offending parties would deter other persons acting under similar circumstances; (4) the amount of benefit conferred on members of the * * * plan as a whole; and (5) the relative merits of the parties' position.

Unlike the fee-shifting provisions of the civil rights statutes, section 502(g)(1) does not by its terms create a presumption in favor of a prevailing plaintiff's request for fees and against that of a prevailing defendant. Nevertheless, application of the *Eaves v. Penn* factors tends to result in fee awards to most prevailing participants with very few

11. 516 U.S. 489, 116 S.Ct. 1065, 134   **12.** 587 F.2d 453 (10th Cir.1978).
L.Ed.2d 130 (1996).

awards to plans that prevail against individual participants. For awards to prevailing defendants the Seventh Circuit has borrowed the standard of the Equal Access to Justice Act[13] that an award should be made unless the plaintiff's position was "substantially justified" or "special circumstances make an award unjust."[14] The Ninth Circuit has held that section 502(g)(1) does not authorize the award of fees for work performed during the plan's internal claims review process.[15]

§ 4.29 ERISA—Judicial Review of Fiduciary Decisions

Questions of coverage under welfare benefit plans, especially health care plans, arise constantly. Some involve interpreting the terms of the benefit plan and applying them to undisputed facts, while others may require decisions about the underlying facts. For example, is a particular medical procedure an "experimental" treatment excluded from coverage under a health care plan? Are services rendered to a patient at an extended care facility medical treatment or merely "rehabilitative" or "custodial" in nature? When a company sells a plant or a division, are employees who continue in the buyer's employment without missing a day of work entitled to benefits under the seller's severance pay plan? Because ERISA preempts state law governing benefit claims, all of these questions, plus many more, find their way to federal court as suits under section 502(a)(1)(B). Those courts must then determine the standard of review to apply to the plan fiduciary's decision.

Before the enactment of ERISA, courts had developed federal common law doctrines governing collectively bargained labor-management trust funds authorized by section 302(c) of the Labor Management Relations Act of 1947.[1] One of these doctrines was that a denial of benefits by fund trustees would not be reversed unless the decision was arbitrary or capricious. This standard was derived from the requirement in section 302(c)(5) that trust funds be established for "the sole and exclusive benefit of the employees" and their families. If the trustees' denial of a benefit claim was "arbitrary, capricious, or made in bad faith, not supported by substantial evidence, or erroneous on a question of law," the decision violated the exclusive benefit rule.

Although ERISA authorizes suits against fiduciaries and plan administrators, it does not specify the standard for judicial review of a fiduciary's denial of a benefit claim. In *NLRB v. Amax Coal Co.*,[2] the Supreme Court remarked that ERISA "was designed to reinforce, not to alter, the long-established duties of a trustee." Taking their cue from that language, all of the courts of appeals adopted the so-called arbitrary and capricious standard as the appropriate test for judicial review of a plan administrator's decisions under ERISA. This standard, "the least

13. 28 U.S.C.A. § 2412(d)(1)(A).

14. Bittner v. Sadoff & Rudoy Indus., 728 F.2d 820 (7th Cir.1984).

15. Cann v. Carpenters' Pension Trust Fund, 989 F.2d 313 (9th Cir.1993).

§ 4.29

1. 29 U.S.C.A. § 186(c).

2. 453 U.S. 322, 101 S.Ct. 2789, 69 L.Ed.2d 672 (1981).

demanding form of judicial review of administrative action," accorded great deference to the decisions of plan administrators and fiduciaries. While some of the lower courts applied a less deferential standard where a conflict of interest existed between plan participants and employer-controlled fiduciaries, the arbitrary and capricious standard was used in most cases.

In *Firestone Tire & Rubber Co. v. Bruch*,[3] the Supreme Court rejected the blanket use of a deferential standard of review, at least at first glance. In 1980, Firestone sold five plants to Occidental Petroleum Company. Occidental took over the facilities as going concerns, and most of the former Firestone employees continued in their jobs without interruption. Nevertheless, some of them sought severance pay under the provisions of a Firestone employee handbook. Firestone denied their request on the ground that the sale to Occidental did not constitute a "reduction in work force" within the meaning of the handbook. Applying the arbitrary and capricious standard of review to this decision, the district court granted summary judgment for Firestone. The Third Circuit reversed, noting that Firestone totally controlled its unfunded severance pay plan, and that any benefits paid by the plan would come out of the general assets of Firestone, not, as under LMRA section 302(c), from a separate trust fund. Because Firestone had a conflict of interest between its role as plan fiduciary and its role as profit-making enterprise, its decision to deny severance benefits was not entitled to judicial deference. Rather, principles of contract law and de novo review should be used.

The Supreme Court affirmed the Third Circuit, but on different grounds. It rejected the analogy to the LMRA and held that because "ERISA abounds with the language and terminology of trust law," those principles dictate the appropriate standard of review under section 502(a)(1)(B). "Trust principles make a deferential standard of review appropriate when a trustee exercises discretionary powers." That meant, said the Court, that benefits decisions should be reviewed under a de novo standard, "unless the benefit plan gives the administrator or fiduciary discretionary authority to determine eligibility for benefits or to construe the terms of the plan." Thus, the Court rejected the lower courts' use of the arbitrary and capricious standard in all cases, because that standard afforded "less protection to employees and their beneficiaries than they enjoyed before ERISA was enacted," when state law governed the enforceability of an employer's benefit promises. At the same time, however, it allowed plans to trump this rule merely by amending the plan documents (if necessary) to grant the appropriate discretionary authority to the fiduciary.

Obviously, the threshold question in the period immediately after *Firestone* is whether the plan language gives the administrator or fiduciary the kind of discretionary authority sufficient to invoke a deferential, rather than a de novo, standard of review. Clauses granting

3. 489 U.S. 101, 109 S.Ct. 948, 103 L.Ed.2d 80 (1989).

administrators the power "to interpret," "to construe," "to determine eligibility," "to determine coverage," and "to determine all questions arising in connection with the administration, interpretation, and application of the Plan" have been held to confer *Firestone*'s discretionary authority.[4] These clauses are often found in combination with statements that decisions of the administrator or fiduciary will be "final and conclusive" or "binding." On the other hand, language that fails clearly and expressly to delegate some form of discretion in decisionmaking does not invoke deferential review. While the Seventh Circuit has commented that "magic words (such as 'the committee has discretion to * * *') are unnecessary,"[5] presumably a body of judicially approved clauses is fast developing, and plan sponsors and administrators who want to be certain of obtaining deferential review of their benefits decisions will amend their plans to include that language. After that happens, plan participants will be back in the position the Court decried, with less protection of their benefit rights than before the enactment of ERISA.

Firestone also rejected the specific holding of the Third Circuit and refused to create different standards of review for funded and unfunded plans. The Court noted that if a plan gives discretion to an administrator or fiduciary operating under a conflict of interest, reviewing courts must weigh the conflict as a "factor in determining whether there is an abuse of discretion." In *Brown v. Blue Cross & Blue Shield of Alabama, Inc.*,[6] the Eleventh Circuit discussed at length the inherent problem of self-interest when an insurance company serves as the decisionmaking fiduciary for a benefit plan and pays those benefits out of its own assets. The health benefit plan at issue in *Brown* clearly gave the insurance company discretionary authority in its role as fiduciary, but the court held that the concept of arbitrary and capricious review must be tailored to reflect the conflict between the fiduciary's obligations to plan participants and beneficiaries and its business interests in making a profit. When the fiduciary has a "substantial conflict of interest," the burden shifts to the fiduciary to prove that its decision was not affected by its own self-interest.

The court in *Brown* distinguished insurance policy plans from other types of ERISA plans, but the self-interest problem occurs in any single employer unfunded welfare plan. Sometimes the plan's structure separates the decisionmaking and payment functions, as when a self-funded health care plan contracts with an insurance company to act as the plan administrator. The insurance company processes the claims and makes the benefits decisions, but payment ultimately comes from the plan sponsor (the employer). In that situation, one might argue that no immediate conflict of interest exists as to any particular claim. On the

---

4. See, e.g., Halpin v. W.W. Grainger, Inc., 962 F.2d 685 (7th Cir. 1992); Pratt v. Petroleum Prod. Mgmt. Inc. Employee Sav. Plan & Trust, 920 F.2d 651 (10th Cir. 1990).

5. Sisters of the Third Order of St. Francis v. SwedishAmerican Group Health Benefit Trust, 901 F.2d 1369, 1371 (7th Cir.1990).

6. 898 F.2d 1556 (11th Cir.1990), cert. denied, 498 U.S. 1040, 111 S.Ct. 712, 112 L.Ed.2d 701 (1991).

other hand, if the employer's management personnel make decisions on claims for benefits from a self-funded plan, as ERISA permits,[7] the same conflict identified in *Brown,* and present in *Firestone,* arises. Moreover, no matter how the plan is funded, or who makes the benefits decisions, ultimately the employer pays for those claims. Either the employer pays the claims directly in the case of a self-funded plan, or the insurance company raises its premiums on the next year's policy to reflect the group's experience. In both cases, the employer has an economic interest in the amount of claims paid by the plan.

In the wake of *Firestone* and *Brown,* the other courts of appeals appear to be settling on one of three standards of review when the fiduciary has a conflict of interest. Under the "sliding scale" approach, the court continues to use the arbitrary and capricious standard, but decreases the level of deference given to the fiduciary's decision based on the seriousness of the conflict.[8] The second approach treats decisions by a fiduciary who has failed to rebut the plaintiff's showing of self-interest as "presumptively void" and applies the de novo standard.[9] The First Circuit has adopted what appears to be a third position on review of a benefits denial by a conflicted administrator.[10] It held that "the requirement that [the administrator's] decision be 'reasonable' is the basic touchstone ... and that fine gradations in phrasing are as likely to complicate as to refine the standard. The essential requirement of reasonableness has substantial bite itself * * *."

Firestone involved review of a denial of benefits based on interpretation of the terms of the plan. A few courts have held that when an administrator's eligibility decision turns on a question of law, review is de novo regardless of the terms of the plan. Additionally, *Firestone* also raised the issue whether, in the absence of an express grant of discretion in the plan, de novo or deferential review applies to an administrator's factual determinations.

Under a discretionary standard of review, a decision denying benefits will be upheld if it is based on a reasonable interpretation of the plan's terms and the evidence before the fiduciary at the time of the decision. Procedural violations, such as failure to file required documents with the Department of Labor, failure to provide summary plan descriptions to participants and beneficiaries, or failure to comply with requests for information, normally do not affect the application of the deferential standard of review. De novo review, on the other hand, means that the reviewing court is free to make its own decision, without regard to the decision of the administrator. Courts are split on whether *Firestone* contemplated a de novo hearing, at which the claimant is permitted to present additional evidence, or a de novo review of the record before the administrator.

---

7. ERISA § 408(c)(3), 29 U.S.C.A. § 1108(c)(3).

8. See, e.g., Pinto v. Reliance Standard Life Insurance Co., 214 F.3d 377 (3d Cir. 2000).

9. See, e.g., Armstrong v. Aetna Life Ins. Co., 128 F.3d 1263 (8th Cir.1997).

10. Doe v. Travelers Ins. Co., 167 F.3d 53 (1st Cir.1999).

In *Black & Decker Disability Plan v. Nord*[11] the Supreme Court held that the courts may not require ERISA plans to adopt the "treating physician rule," which was originally developed under the Social Security Act. Under this rule, the opinion of the plaintiff's treating physician as to the plaintiff's medical condition is entitled to deference unless there is substantial evidence in the record to support a contrary conclusion. The Court said that the Secretary of Labor has not promulgated regulations requiring such a rule in ERISA benefit determinations. Moreover, whether the opinion of a treating physician warrants greater credit than that of plan consultants requires an empirical investigation that "courts are ill equipped to conduct." The Court did go on to say that administrators "may not arbitrarily refuse to credit a claimant's reliable evidence, including the opinions of a treating physician."

§ 4.30 ERISA—Preemption

ERISA contains a preemption provision of "unparalleled breadth."[1] It bars state regulation of benefit plans even as to matters on which ERISA is silent. For that reason, ERISA preemption has had its most dramatic effect on welfare plans. Although state laws relating to pensions are also preempted, ERISA contains substantive federal standards for pension plans. ERISA does not, however, regulate the content of welfare plans. Federal preemption thus displaced a vast body of state law dealing with fringe benefits and left a void in its place. ERISA preemption often comes as a surprise to state court plaintiffs, who start out relying on state law causes of action and may end up with no remedy at all under federal law.

Section 514(a)[2] of ERISA preempts "any and all State laws insofar as they may now or hereafter relate to any employee benefit plan" covered by the Act. Exceptions to this provision include state laws that regulate insurance, banking, or securities; generally applicable criminal laws; parts of Hawaii's Prepaid Health Care Act; qualified domestic relations orders that are exempted from ERISA's anti-alienation provision; and state laws prohibiting health care plans from requiring beneficiaries to use Medicaid before they may receive plan benefits.

For purposes of section 514, "State law" is broadly defined to include "all laws, decisions, rules, regulations, or other State action having the effect of law, of any State," and "State" is defined as "a State, any political subdivision thereof, or any agency or instrumentality of either, which purports to regulate, directly or indirectly, the terms and conditions" of ERISA-covered plans. Thus, ERISA preempts state

---

11. 538 U.S. 822, 123 S.Ct. 1965, 155 L.Ed.2d 1034 (2003).

§ 4.30

1. Holland v. Burlington Indus., Inc., 772 F.2d 1140, 1147 (4th Cir.1985), cert. denied sub nom. Slack v. Burlington Indus.,

Inc., 477 U.S. 903, 106 S.Ct. 3271, 91 L.Ed.2d 562 (1986), and aff'd mem. sub nom. Brooks v. Burlington Indus., Inc., 477 U.S. 901, 106 S.Ct. 3267, 91 L.Ed.2d 559 (1986).

2. 29 U.S.C.A. § 1144(a).

common law that relates to covered plans, as well as state statutes and regulations.

Covered Plan

ERISA's preemption provision applies only to employee benefit plans covered by the statute. States may apply their own laws to plans that are exempt from ERISA coverage, such as government plans and church plans.

In *Fort Halifax Packing Co. v. Coyne*,[3] the Supreme Court held that ERISA did not preempt a Maine statute requiring employers to make a one-time severance payment to employees who lose their jobs as a result of a plant closing and are not covered by an express contract providing for severance pay. While recognizing that ERISA covers severance pay plans, the Court held that Maine's law did not "relate to an employee benefit plan," because it did not establish, or require employers to establish, a plan. The Court explained that a plan involves an "ongoing administrative program" to perform such functions as determining claimant eligibility, calculating benefit levels, making payments, monitoring the availability of funds, and keeping records. The one-time lump-sum payment, triggered by a single event, required by the Maine law did not involve any of these functions, and therefore the law did not undermine the purpose of section 514, protecting benefit plans from the administrative burdens of conflicting state regulation.

In *Massachusetts v. Morash*,[4] the Court approved Department of Labor regulations exempting from ERISA coverage certain "payroll practices," including the payment of vacation pay out of an employer's general assets. Under the regulations the employer's practice of paying terminated employees for their unused vacation time was not a covered plan, and therefore Massachusetts could apply its wage payment law to require payment in full on the date of the discharge.

"Relate to"

Section 514 preempts state laws that "relate to" an ERISA-covered plan. The Supreme Court has said that these words should be construed expansively, and that a law "relates to" an employee benefit plan "if it has a connection with or reference to such a plan."[5] Both direct and indirect state actions that relate to covered plans are preempted. In *Alessi v. Raybestos–Manhattan, Inc.*,[6] the Court held that ERISA preempted a portion of New Jersey's workers' compensation law that prohibited a setoff of workers' compensation benefits against pension benefits. It was irrelevant that the state action took the form of a workers' compensation law, rather than a pension law. The Court noted that the New Jersey law conflicted with ERISA because it eliminated one method for calculating pension benefits, integration, that federal law

3. 482 U.S. 1, 107 S.Ct. 2211, 96 L.Ed.2d 1 (1987).

4. 490 U.S. 107, 109 S.Ct. 1668, 104 L.Ed.2d 98 (1989).

5. Shaw v. Delta Air Lines, Inc., 463 U.S. 85, 103 S.Ct. 2890, 77 L.Ed.2d 490 (1983).

6. 451 U.S. 504, 101 S.Ct. 1895, 68 L.Ed.2d 402 (1981).

permits. In *UNUM Life Insurance Co. v. Ward*,[7] the Court held that a state common law agency rule that an employer may be deemed the agent of an insurance company was preempted by ERISA on the ground that it would have a "marked effect" on plan administration, as it would require the employer to have a role in plan administration. Therefore, the rule "related to" employee benefit plans.

In *Egelhoff v. Egelhoff*,[8] the Court found that a Washington state statute providing that designation of a spouse as beneficiary of a nonprobate asset is automatically revoked upon divorce was preempted by ERISA because it implicated an area of core ERISA concern, adherence to plan documents. Specifically, the Washington statute conflicted with ERISA's requirements that the plan specify the basis on which payments are made and that the fiduciary administer the plan in accordance with the plan documents, making payments to a beneficiary who is designated by a participant or by the terms of the plan. It also interfered with the goal of nationally uniform plan administration.

State laws that relate to ERISA plans are preempted even if they do not conflict with ERISA's requirements, even if they are aimed at effectuating ERISA's underlying purposes, and even if they deal with matters that ERISA does not address. For example, ERISA does not mandate that plans provide any particular level of welfare benefits, yet in *Shaw v. Delta Air Lines, Inc.*,[9] the Court held that ERISA preempted a New York law requiring disability benefit plans to provide coverage for pregnancy-related disabilities. In addition, ERISA preemption is not restricted to state laws specifically designed to affect employee benefit plans. *Pilot Life Insurance v. Dedeaux*[10] prohibited the application of state common law contract and tort doctrines to an ERISA plan's failure to pay benefits.

Not every state law that has a relationship to an ERISA plan is preempted, however. In a footnote in *Shaw*, the Court remarked that "[s]ome state actions may affect employee benefit plans in too tenuous, remote, or peripheral a manner to warrant a finding that the law 'relates to' the plan." Unfortunately, the Court has failed to give a coherent test to aid the lower courts in determining which laws that relate to benefit plans are not preempted. In the same footnote in *Shaw* the Court cited with apparent approval *American Telephone & Telegraph Co. v. Merry*,[11] in which the Second Circuit held that a state garnishment of a spouse's pension income to enforce alimony and child support orders was not preempted by ERISA because it touched on pension plans "in the most remote and peripheral manner." In 1984, Congress ratified this result by amending both the antialienation[12] and the preemption provisions[13] of

---

7. 526 U.S. 358, 119 S.Ct. 1380, 143 L.Ed.2d 462 (1999).

8. 532 U.S. 141, 121 S.Ct. 1322, 149 L.Ed.2d 264 (2001).

9. 463 U.S. 85, 103 S.Ct. 2890, 77 L.Ed.2d 490 (1983).

10. 481 U.S. 41, 107 S.Ct. 1549, 95 L.Ed.2d 39 (1987).

11. 592 F.2d 118 (2d Cir.1979).

12. ERISA § 206(d)(3)(A), 29 U.S.C.A. § 1056(d)(3)(A).

13. ERISA § 514(b)(7); 29 U.S.C.A. § 1144(b)(7).

ERISA to permit the enforcement of qualified domestic relations orders against ERISA plans.

Mackey v. Lanier Collection Agency & Service, Inc.[14] was the first post-*Shaw* case in which the Court found no ERISA preemption of a state law that related to a benefit plan. First, however, the Court held that a Georgia statute specifically prohibiting the garnishment of benefits of an ERISA-covered plan was preempted because it clearly related to ERISA plans through its express reference to them. The Court then went on to find that Georgia's general garnishment statute was not preempted and could be applied to garnish benefits from an ERISA welfare plan, even though garnishment would subject ERISA plans to administrative burdens and costs. The Court noted that Congress permitted plans to sue and be sued without restriction, and therefore it must have intended that state law methods for collecting money judgments against plans would not be disturbed. In addition, ERISA's antialienation provision covers only pension benefits, and by negative implication Congress must have intended to permit the alienation and assignment, including garnishment, of welfare benefits.

In *New York State Conference of Blue Cross & Blue Shield Plans v. Travelers Insurance Co.*,[15] the Court may have signaled the beginning of a restriction on the scope of ERISA preemption, at least as to state laws that do not refer to ERISA plans. The Court held that a New York law imposing surcharges on the bills of patients whose hospital bills are paid by commercial insurance and on HMOs is not preempted by ERISA because it does not "relate to" employee benefit plans within the meaning of section 514(a). The state law did not single out insurance purchased by ERISA plans or HMOs funded by ERISA plans, so it did not make "reference to" ERISA plans. The question for the Court was whether the surcharge laws have a "connection with" ERISA plans. The Court surveyed its prior preemption cases and concluded that in each case where preemption was found, the state law mandated employee benefit structures or their administration, or it provided alternate enforcement mechanisms for rights arising under ERISA. The purpose of the New York law was clearly to encourage health plans to purchase coverage from Blue Cross/Blue Shield, but the Court said that this indirect economic effect was not sufficient to trigger preemption. The Court remarked that while there might be a point at which an exorbitant state tax could have the effect of forcing ERISA plans to adopt a certain scheme of substantive coverage or restrict their choice of insurers, no showing had been made that the New York surcharges operated in that manner. Rather, the state law's indirect effect on the relative prices of insurance policies was no different from that of many state laws in areas traditionally subject to local regulation.

14. 486 U.S. 825, 108 S.Ct. 2182, 100 L.Ed.2d 836 (1988).

15. 514 U.S. 645, 115 S.Ct. 1671, 131 L.Ed.2d 695 (1995).

In *California Division of Labor Standards Enforcement v. Dilling-ham Construction, N.A., Inc.,*[16] the Court relied on *Travelers* to hold that a California law requiring payment of prevailing wages to employees in apprenticeship programs that have not received state approval but allowing the payment of lower apprentice wages to employees participating in state-approved programs is not preempted by ERISA. As with the New York surcharge, the prevailing wage statute, said the Court, does not bind ERISA plans to anything. Nothing requires apprenticeship programs to meet the California standards; the effect of the statute is "merely to provide some measure of economic incentive to comport with the State's requirements.... " Similarly, in *De Buono v. NYSA–ILA Medical & Clinical Services Fund,*[17] the Court held that a New York tax on gross receipts for patient services at hospitals, residential health care facilities, and diagnostic and treatment centers was not preempted by ERISA but was rather "one of 'myriad state laws' of general applicability that impose some burdens on the administration of ERISA plans but nevertheless do not 'relate to' them within the meaning of the ... statute."

In pre-*Travelers* decisions, the lower courts developed a number of questions to determine which state laws are "too tenuous, remote, or peripheral" to fall within ERISA's preemption provision. Does the state law address areas of exclusive federal concern, such as the right to receive benefits under an ERISA plan? Does the law represent a traditional exercise of state authority? Does the law directly affect relationships among the traditional ERISA entities—the plan, its fiduciaries, the participants, and the beneficiaries? Does it interfere with the calculation of benefits under ERISA plans? For instance, in *Memorial Hospital System v. Northbrook Life Insurance Co.,*[18] a hospital asserted state law claims against an ERISA plan that had authorized treatment of a participant and later, after the hospital provided the treatment, denied coverage. The court held that the claims the hospital asserted as an assignee of the participant's benefits were preempted, because they involved the right to receive benefits under the plan. On the other hand, the claims asserted in the hospital's independent status as a third-party health care provider were not preempted. They were independent of the plan's actual obligations and did not seek to modify the plan or its obligations to its participants in any manner. Similarly, in *Perkins v. Time Insurance Co.,*[19] there was no preemption of a health care plan participant's claim that an independent insurance agent fraudulently induced him to surrender coverage under an existing policy in order to participate in an ERISA plan that did not provide the coverage the agent promised.

Laws of general application that affect ERISA plans only indirectly are most likely to be found outside the scope of section 514. For instance,

16. 519 U.S. 316, 117 S.Ct. 832, 136 L.Ed.2d 791 (1997).

17. 520 U.S. 806, 117 S.Ct. 1747, 138 L.Ed.2d 21 (1997).

18. 904 F.2d 236 (5th Cir.1990).

19. 898 F.2d 470 (5th Cir.1990).

a state may apply its discrimination laws to a pension plan employee's claim that the plan fired him because of his race and age. State laws defining the fiduciary duties of a corporate officer to the corporation's shareholders are not preempted merely because an ERISA plan is a shareholder. A municipal income tax that affects employee contributions to benefit plans is not preempted, nor is a state law setting rates hospitals must charge private payors, including benefit plans. In *Aetna Life Insurance Co. v. Borges,*[20] the Second Circuit held that ERISA does not preempt the application of Connecticut's escheat law to benefit checks issued by ERISA plans but not presented for payment by the beneficiaries within three years.

The Insurance Saving Clause and the Deemer Clause

Although the scope of section 514(a) is very broad, ERISA's "saving clause," section 514(b)(2)(A), returns significant power to the states by exempting from the scope of the preemption provision "any state law that regulates insurance * * * "[21] and permitting states to continue their traditional role as primary regulators of the insurance industry. At the same time, Congress apparently wanted to prevent the states from subjecting ERISA plans to their general insurance laws by claiming the plans were insurers under state law. The "deemer clause," section 514(b)(2)(B), qualifies the saving clause by providing that no employee benefit plan shall be deemed to be an insurance company "for purposes of any law of any state purporting to regulate insurance companies, [or] insurance contracts * * *."[22] The combination of these clauses means that any entity engaged in the business of insurance, except an ERISA plan, is subject to state insurance regulation.

In a series of ERISA preemption cases involving the insurance saving clause, *Metropolitan Life Insurance Co. v. Massachusetts,*[23] *Pilot Life Insurance Co. v. Dedeaux,*[24] *UNUM Life Insurance Co. v. Ward,*[25] and *Rush Prudential HMO, Inc. v. Moran,*[26] the Supreme Court looked to the criteria developed under the McCarran–Ferguson Act[27] interpreting the term "business of insurance." Then, in *Kentucky Association of Health Plans, Inc. v. Miller,*[28] the Court abruptly changed course. Stating that the use of McCarran–Ferguson precedent "has misdirected attention, failed to provide clear guidance to lower federal courts, and * * * added little to the relevant analysis," the Court set out a new two-part test for deciding whether a state law regulates the insurance industry and therefore falls within the insurance saving clause. "First, the state law must be specifically directed toward entities engaged in insurance. Sec-

20. 869 F.2d 142 (2d Cir.), cert. denied, 493 U.S. 811, 110 S.Ct. 57, 107 L.Ed.2d 25 (1989).

21. 29 U.S.C.A. § 1144(b)(2)(A). The saving clause also exempts state laws that regulate banking or securities.

22. 29 U.S.C.A. § 1144(b)(2)(B).

23. 471 U.S. 724, 105 S.Ct. 2380, 85 L.Ed.2d 728 (1985).

24. 481 U.S. 41, 107 S.Ct. 1549, 95 L.Ed.2d 39 (1987).

25. 526 U.S. 358, 119 S.Ct. 1380, 143 L.Ed.2d 462 (1999).

26. 536 U.S. 355, 122 S.Ct. 2151, 153 L.Ed.2d 375 (2002).

27. 15 U.S.C.A. §§ 1011–1015.

28. 538 U.S. 329, 123 S.Ct. 1471, 155 L.Ed.2d 468 (2003).

ond, * * * the state law must substantially affect the risk pooling arrangement between the insurer and the insured." Applying the new rule to Kentucky's any-willing-provider laws, the Court held they were saved from preemption. As to the first part of the test, the Court rejected the petitioner's argument that the laws were not specifically directed toward insurers, but also at doctors who wanted to form limited provider networks. That a law might have significant effects on noninsurers is not inconsistent with its being directed specifically toward the insurance industry. As to the second factor, the laws expanded the number of health care providers from whom an insured could receive services and therefore "alter[ed] the scope of permissible bargains between insurers and insureds."

In *Metropolitan Life Insurance Co. v. Massachusetts*,[29] the Supreme Court held that a Massachusetts statute requiring general health insurance policies covering state residents to include certain minimum mental health care benefits was not preempted by ERISA. Although the law bore "indirectly but substantially on all insured benefit plans" by requiring the inclusion of the mental health benefits in any insurance policy they bought, it fell within the saving clause as a law regulating insurance. The insurers argued that the saving clause applies only to traditional insurance laws, such as those that regulate the manner in which insurance may be sold, and not to laws that mandate the substantive terms of insurance contracts. The Court rejected that contention on the ground that it would render the saving clause meaningless, because laws that regulate only the insurer do not "relate to" benefit plans in the first place. Moreover, if laws mandating the substantive content of insurance policies do not come within the saving clause, the deemer clause's exemption for laws regulating insurance contracts that apply directly to benefit plans would not have been necessary.

The Court returned to the relationship between the saving clause and the deemer clause in *FMC Corp. v. Holliday*,[30] and held that Pennsylvania could not apply its statute prohibiting welfare benefit plans from exercising subrogation rights against a claimant's tort recovery to a self-funded ERISA health care plan. As it suggested in *Metropolitan Life*, the Court read the deemer clause to create a distinction between insured and uninsured plans. To come within the saving clause and thus avoid ERISA preemption, state laws must directly regulate only insurance companies. This direct regulation of insurance companies will result in indirect regulation of insured ERISA plans by controlling the content of the policies the plans buy. Direct state insurance regulation cannot reach self-funded ERISA plans, however, because self-funded plans do not purchase insurance policies, and the deemer clause prohibits states from deeming ERISA plans to be insurance companies under state laws purporting to regulate insurance. Any attempt by a state directly to regulate self-funded plans "relates to" those plans and is not saved by the saving clause because it does not regulate insurance. An

---

29. 471 U.S. 724, 105 S.Ct. 2380, 85 L.Ed.2d 728 (1985).

30. 498 U.S. 52, 111 S.Ct. 403, 112 L.Ed.2d 356 (1990).

interesting question on which the courts are split is whether a self-insured plan that buys an excess or "stop-loss" insurance policy to protect it from catastrophic claims can be regulated by the states.

The reasoning of *FMC* and *Metropolitan Life* results in different treatment of insured and uninsured plans. Employers that are able to self-insure can avoid the increasing number of state laws mandating minimum health care benefits. This distinction has enormous significance for health policy. Our current system of health care relies heavily on benefits provided through employment. Any state attempts at improving the delivery of health care services or controlling health care costs through regulation of employer-provided health care plans will never be fully effective because of ERISA preemption. States can regulate insured plans through their insurance laws, but they can not reach self-insured plans. *Standard Oil Co. v. Agsalud*[31] struck down the Hawaii Prepaid Health Care Act, which required all workers in the state to be covered by a comprehensive health care plan, on exactly these grounds. After years of effort, Hawaii's congressional delegation obtained passage of an amendment to section 514 exempting portions of the Hawaii law.[32] Hawaii remains the only state whose health care law is exempted, albeit partially, from ERISA preemption. Any further state efforts at reform in this area would require a waiver from ERISA.

Examples of ERISA Preemption—Failure to Pay Benefits

The lesson of *Pilot Life Insurance Co. v. Dedeaux*[33] is that state law claims for denial of benefits are preempted by ERISA, whether the claim is characterized as a breach of contract, as a tort, or as some sort of statutory violation. The sole vehicle for assertion of these claims is suit under section 502(a) of ERISA. Similarly, ERISA preempts state law actions for improper handling or processing of benefit claims, for damages resulting from the failure to pay benefits, and for improper administration of benefit plans even when the state law cause of action could give remedies not available under ERISA.

A disturbing example of the application of these rules is *Corcoran v. United HealthCare, Inc.*[34] Mrs. Corcoran, a participant in her employer's health care plan, was pregnant with her second child. Her physician classified her as high-risk for complications and recommended hospitalization late in her pregnancy, but United, which administered a utilization review program for the plan, decided that limited home nursing care would suffice and refused to authorize any hospitalization. The fetus went into distress and died while Mrs. Corcoran was at home during a period when no nurse was on duty. She and her husband sued United under state law for malpractice and the wrongful death of their child. The court agreed that United made medical decisions and gave medical

31. 442 F.Supp. 695 (N.D.Cal.1977), affirmed, 633 F.2d 760 (9th Cir.1980), affirmed, 454 U.S. 801, 102 S.Ct. 79, 70 L.Ed.2d 75 (1981).

32. ERISA § 514(b)(5), 29 U.S.C.A. § 1144(b)(5).

33. 481 U.S. 41, 107 S.Ct. 1549, 95 L.Ed.2d 39 (1987).

34. 965 F.2d 1321 (5th Cir.), cert. denied, 506 U.S. 1033, 113 S.Ct. 812, 121 L.Ed.2d 684 (1992).

advice, but found that it did so in the context of determining the availability of benefits under an ERISA plan. Accordingly, the Corcorans' action had to be characterized as an attempt to recover for a tort involving benefit determinations, and under *Pilot Life* it was preempted. The court remarked that ERISA preemption in cases like this eliminates an important check on the burgeoning utilization review system by removing the financial incentive to comply with an appropriate standard of care. Any changes in the scope of section 514, however, must come from Congress.

Examples of ERISA Preemption—Wrongful Discharge

In *Ingersoll–Rand Co. v. McClendon*,[35] the Supreme Court held that ERISA preempted an employee's wrongful discharge claim under Texas common law alleging he was fired to prevent him from becoming vested in his employer's ERISA pension plan. The existence of the pension plan was

> a critical factor in establishing liability under [Texas'] wrongful discharge law. As a result, this cause of action relates not merely to pension benefits, but to the essence of the pension *plan* itself.

The Court also remarked that even if section 514 did not exist, the Texas cause of action would nevertheless be preempted because it conflicts directly with an ERISA cause of action, section 510.

There are very few cases dealing with the question of ERISA preemption in suits in which the plaintiff challenges a discharge on some basis totally unrelated to benefit plans, but seeks recovery of benefits under an ERISA plan as part of the remedy. In *Martori Bros. Distributors v. James–Massengale*,[36] an employer tried to prevent enforcement of a make-whole order issued by the California Agricultural Labor Relations Authority to remedy unfair labor practices, to the extent it ordered the payment of fringe benefits under ERISA plans. The court held that the remedy did not relate to the ERISA plans, because it did not require any changes in the plans, but merely ordered the payment of benefits the workers would have received but for the unlawful behavior.

Examples of ERISA Preemption—State Fair Employment Practice Laws

Shaw v. Delta Air Lines, Inc.[37] held that ERISA preempts state fair employment practice laws to the extent that they require ERISA plans to provide benefits not required by federal law. *Shaw* involved mandated benefits for pregnancy-related disabilities at a time when federal law permitted employers to discriminate on the basis of pregnancy. ERISA, of course, preempts state discrimination laws only as they relate to benefit plans; claims involving matters such as hiring, promotion, or

35. 498 U.S. 133, 111 S.Ct. 478, 112 L.Ed.2d 474 (1990).

36. 781 F.2d 1349 (9th Cir.), cert. denied, 479 U.S. 1018, 107 S.Ct. 670, 93 L.Ed.2d 722 (1986).

37. 463 U.S. 85, 103 S.Ct. 2890, 77 L.Ed.2d 490 (1983).

wages are not affected. Although ERISA does not preempt most state claims alleging discriminatory discharges, some claims may implicate ERISA plans, especially pension plans.

Examples of ERISA Preemption—Mandated Benefit Laws

As with state fair employment practice laws, ERISA will preempt state laws mandating the provision of specified benefits under ERISA covered plans that are not required by federal law. *District of Columbia v. Greater Washington Board of Trade*[38] invalidated a District of Columbia law requiring employers to provide the same level of health insurance for employees receiving worker's compensation benefits as they provided for active employees. Under this reasoning, a state family leave law requiring the maintenance of health insurance coverage during the period of leave will be preempted by ERISA as it applies to employers not covered by the federal Family and Medical Leave Act. Similarly, the Ninth Circuit held that a state law requiring employers to pay for employees' medical examinations is preempted by ERISA.[39]

§ 4.31 Leaves of Absence—Federal Law—Family and Medical Leave

The Family and Medical Leave Act of 1993 (FMLA) requires that employers provide leaves of absence for childbirth or adoption, for the care of children or other family members, or for an employee's own illness.[1] The FMLA covers employers with fifty or more employees and state and local government agencies. In *Nevada Department of Human Resources v. Hibbs*,[2] the Supreme Court held that Congress properly used its authority under section 5 of the Fourteenth Amendment to abrogate the states' sovereign immunity and thus subjected the states to suit by their employees for money damages for violations of the family-care provisions of the Family and Medical Leave Act.

Covered employers must permit eligible workers to take up to twelve weeks of unpaid leave in any twelve-month period for the birth, adoption, or placement for foster care of a child, to care for a child, spouse, or parent with a serious health condition, or for the worker's own serious health condition that makes him or her unable to perform the job. To be eligible for FMLA leave, a worker must have been employed by the employer for at least twelve months and have at least 1,250 hours of service in the twelve-month period preceding the leave. In addition, the employer must have at least fifty employees within a seventy-five mile radius of the employee's worksite. Thus, an employee who works at a

38. 506 U.S. 125, 113 S.Ct. 580, 121 L.Ed.2d 513 (1992).

39. Aloha Airlines v. Ahue, 12 F.3d 1498 (9th Cir.1993).

§ 4.31

1. 29 U.S.C.A. §§ 2601–2654. Department of Labor regulations implementing the Act are at 29 C.F.R. Part 825.

2. 538 U.S. 721, 123 S.Ct. 1972, 155 L.Ed.2d 953 (2003).

small, relatively isolated branch of a major employer might not be eligible for FMLA leave, even though the employer itself is covered by the Act.

A "serious health condition" is an illness, injury, impairment, or physical or mental condition that involves inpatient care or continuing treatment by a health care provider. The legislative history indicates that Congress did not intend to include short-term conditions from which people recover quickly. The Department of Labor's regulations therefore restrict the scope of the continuing treatment prong of the definition to periods of incapacity that require absence from work, school, or other regular daily activities for more than three consecutive calendar days, and that involve either (A) treatment two or more times by a health care provider, or (B) treatment by a health care provider at least once with a resulting regimen of continuing treatment under the provider's supervision. The Eleventh Circuit has construed the three consecutive day requirement as meaning a period of continuous incapacity extending more than seventy-two hours.[3] Obviously, determining whether a individual has a serious health condition under this part of the regulations depends on the facts of each case. By permitting intermittent leave, however, the FMLA does envision the use of leave for therapy or doctor's visits, even though the employee or the employee's family member is not totally incapacitated. Therefore, the regulations also include within "continuing treatment" chronic or long-term health conditions that are incurable or so serious that they would result in a period of incapacity of more than three days if not treated. If an employee needs FMLA leave because of his or her own serious health condition, the employee must either be unable to work at all or be unable to perform any of the essential functions of the job, within the meaning of the Americans with Disabilities Act.

Leave for birth, adoption, or placement for foster care must be completed within one year of the event. If a husband and wife work for the same employer, the employer may limit their aggregate number of weeks of leave for birth, adoption, placement for foster care, or care for a sick parent to twelve in a twelve-month period. Employees taking leave to care for a sick family member or because of their own serious health condition may take their leave intermittently or on a reduced leave schedule when medically necessary. When an employee requests intermittent or reduced schedule leave, the employer may temporarily transfer him or her to a different job that can better accommodate the recurring periods of leave, as long as the employee is qualified for the job and the new job has equivalent pay and benefits.

When leave for childbirth, adoption, or placement for foster care is foreseeable, the employee must give at least thirty days' notice of his or her intention to take a leave. When the need for medical leave is foreseeable because of a planned treatment, the employee must make a reasonable effort to schedule the treatment in a manner that will not

3. Russell v. North Broward Hospital, 346 F.3d 1335 (11th Cir. 2003).

unduly disrupt the employer's operations, and give thirty days' notice. If the employee cannot give thirty days' notice, he or she must give notice as soon as practicable. The regulations provide that if an employee fails to give thirty days' notice for foreseeable leave with no reasonable excuse for the delay, the employer may deny the taking of leave until at least thirty days after the date the employee does give notice. The Act itself does not deal with the kind of notice an employee must give when the need for leave is unforeseeable, but the regulations state the employee should give notice as soon as practicable, normally within one or two working days of learning of the need for the leave. The circuits are split on whether an employer may enforce a policy requiring notice of unforeseen leave within a certain period of time against employees taking FMLA leave. The employer may not delay the leave, however, if the employee did not have actual notice of the requirement to notify the employer. Moreover, it is not necessary that the employee expressly invoke his or her rights under the FMLA; the requirements of the Act can be triggered by, for instance, a statement that the employee will need leave for the birth of a child. At that point, the employer may have to obtain further information from the employee in order to determine whether he or she is seeking FMLA leave.

An employer may require medical certification, including a second or third opinion at its expense, of the need for a leave to care for a sick relative or for the employee's own illness. An employee who fails to cooperate with the second opinion process loses the right to take or continue a leave. The employer may request recertification at reasonable intervals, but not more than once every thirty days. The Americans with Disabilities Act generally prohibits employers from asking about employees' or applicants' medical conditions or from requiring physical examinations of employees unless the examinations are job-related and consistent with business necessity. The medical certification provisions of the FMLA create one situation in which employers may acquire information about an employee's health condition. In *Rhoads v. Federal Deposit Insurance Corp.*,[4] however, the Fourth Circuit rejected an employee's argument that an employer that wants to contest the validity of a medical certification must follow the Act's second opinion procedures. The court noted that the second opinion procedures are permissive, and that nothing in the statute indicates that failure to follow those procedures forever forecloses the employer from challenging whether the employee had a serious health condition.

In *Ragsdale v. Wolverine World Wide, Inc.*,[5] the Supreme Court struck down as contrary to the Act and beyond the Secretary of Labor's authority a regulation requiring the employer to notify an employee that his or her leave would be treated as FMLA leave and providing that any leave taken before the designation may not be counted toward the

---

4. 257 F.3d 373 (4th Cir.2001), cert. denied, 535 U.S. 933, 122 S.Ct. 1309, 152 L.Ed.2d 219 (2002).

5. 535 U.S. 81, 122 S.Ct. 1155, 152 L.Ed.2d 167 (2002).

employee's FMLA entitlement.[6] In *Ragsdale*, the employer had granted the employee thirty weeks of leave for cancer treatments. When she sought a further extension of the leave, the employer refused and fired her. Under the Department of Labor regulations, the employee was entitled to an additional twelve weeks of FMLA leave, because the employer had never told her that the thirty-week absence would count against her FMLA entitlement. The Court found that the regulation imposed a penalty on the employer that is "unconnected to any prejudice the employee might have suffered from the employer's lapse" and "incompatible with the FMLA's comprehensive remedial mechanism."

The FMLA does not require paid leave, although an employee may elect, or the employer may require, the substitution of accrued paid leave for any part of the twelve-week leave provided by the Act. An employer that intends to designate paid leave as FMLA leave must "promptly (within two business days absent extenuating circumstances)" notify the employee of this fact, or it will be considered to have waived that option. The Act specifically states that providing unpaid FMLA leave to a salaried employee who would otherwise come within one of the FLSA's white-collar exemptions will not cause the loss of the FLSA exemption.

During the leave the employer must continue to provide health care benefits at the same level and under the same conditions as if the employee were actively at work. Thus, an FMLA leave is not a "qualifying event" under COBRA, because it does not result in a loss of health care coverage. An employee's COBRA rights will be triggered, if at all, when or if the employee tells the employer that he or she will not be returning to work. The regulations state that an employee may choose not to retain health coverage during the leave, but the employer must restore coverage at the end of the leave, without any qualifying period, physical examination, or exclusion for preexisting conditions. Thus, as a practical matter, under health care plans that require the employee to pay a portion of the premium, the employer may have to pay that portion on behalf of an employee on FMLA leave who fails to maintain coverage. Otherwise, the employer risks becoming a self-insurer for complete coverage following the leave. The regulations do provide that after the employee returns to work the employer may recover the employee's share of any missed premium payments if it chose to maintain the employee's coverage by making the payments itself.

If the employee fails to return from unpaid leave for a reason other than the continuation, recurrence, or onset of a serious health condition that would entitle the employee to FMLA leave, or for some other reason beyond the employee's control, the employer may "recover" any premium it paid to maintain the employee's coverage during the leave. The employer may not recover its share of the premium for any part of the FMLA leave taken as paid leave, however. The FMLA does not specify how this "recovery" is to be made. If the employer deducts the premiums from any amounts due to the employee, it may violate the restric-

---

6.   29 C.F.R. § 825.700(a).

tions on deductions contained in most state wage payment laws. Unless the courts find that the recovery of premiums provision of the FMLA preempts state law, an employer may be limited to suing an employee who does not voluntarily repay the premiums.

When the employee returns from leave, the employer must restore him or her to the same or an equivalent position, with no loss of employment benefits accrued before the date the leave began. Employees on FMLA leave are not entitled to any employment right to which they would not have been entitled had they not taken leave. Therefore, if the employer can show that the employee would have been fired or laid off if he or she had not been on FMLA leave, the employer is relieved of its obligation of restoration. In addition, an employee who is unable to perform the essential functions of his or her job at the end of FMLA leave is not entitled to restoration to his or her former position.

The statute creates an exception to the restoration requirement for "key employees." The employer may deny restoration (but not the taking of leave in the first place) to a salaried employee who is among the highest paid ten percent of its workforce, if the denial is "necessary to prevent substantial and grievous economic injury" to its operations, if the employer notifies the employee of its determination, and if the employee does not return to work after receiving this notice.

The enforcement mechanisms of the FMLA are similar to those under the Fair Labor Standards Act. The FMLA may be enforced through suit in either federal or state court by employees individually or on behalf of themselves and other similarly situated employees, or by the Secretary of Labor. An employee's right to bring suit terminates if the Secretary brings an action on his or her behalf. The statute of limitations is two years from the last event constituting a violation or three years for willful violations. The Department of Labor may receive and investigate employee complaints, but, as under the FLSA, there is no administrative prerequisite to suit.

The Act creates three separate causes of action for violations. The first, the "entitlement" or "interference" claim, prohibits employers from interfering with "the exercise of or the attempt to exercise, any right" provided by the FMLA. To prevail under this section, the plaintiff must show only that he or she was denied a substantive benefit under the FMLA, such as leave or restoration from leave, for a reason connected with the FMLA leave. Interference can include not only the denial of leave entirely, but actions such as discouraging employees from taking leave, or requiring them to perform work-related tasks while on leave. The second cause of action is the "retaliation" or "discrimination" claim. It is unlawful for an employer to fire or otherwise discriminate against an employee "for opposing any practice made unlawful" by the FMLA. This claim requires proof that the employer's actions were motivated by retaliatory or discriminatory animus, and the courts use the burdens of proof developed under Title VII of the Civil Rights Act of 1964 to analyze such actions. Finally, the FMLA prohibits discrimination against individuals because they have filed charges, given information, or testified in any proceeding under the Act.

Remedies for violations of the Act include lost wages and benefits plus interest, or, if the employee has not lost any wages or benefits, any actual monetary losses the employee sustained as a direct result of the violation, up to the equivalent of twelve weeks' pay, plus interest. The statute mentions the cost of providing care as an example of these non-wage losses. Plaintiffs may recover an amount equal to the monetary recovery as liquidated damages, subject to reduction by the court if the employer proves it acted in good faith and with reasonable grounds for believing it was not in violation of the Act. In addition, the statute authorizes "such equitable relief as may be appropriate, including employment, reinstatement, and promotion." Several courts have held that this provision includes the award of front pay.[7] The court must award a victorious plaintiff reasonable attorney's fees, reasonable witness fees, and costs. Because the statute speaks only of fee awards from defendants to plaintiffs, fee awards under the FMLA are not available to prevailing defendants. There is a right to jury trial under the FMLA.

Employers with fewer than fifty employees are not covered by the Family and Medical Leave Act and therefore are not required by that Act to grant any leaves, and even employers covered by the FMLA are not required to grant FMLA leaves to employees who do not meet the statute's eligibility standards. The provision of leaves of absence is also regulated, albeit less directly, by Title VII. If an employer not covered by the Family and Medical Leave Act does choose to offer leaves, or if covered employers offer leaves under more generous conditions than required by the Act, they must do so on a nondiscriminatory basis.

The Pregnancy Discrimination Act (PDA) requires that employers treat workers disabled by pregnancy, childbirth, or related medical conditions the same for all employment-related purposes as employees disabled by other conditions.[8] Therefore, if an employer provides leaves of absence for employees who cannot work because of illness or injury, it must provide leaves on the same basis and with the same conditions for the period of a female employee's pregnancy-related disability. An employer may not, for instance, limit the length of a leave for pregnancy-related disabilities if it does not place the same limit on other kinds of medical leaves. In addition, a failure to provide any leave at all for pregnancy-related disabilities, or the provision of seriously inadequate leave, may, upon a proper statistical showing, constitute unlawful pregnancy discrimination under Title VII's disparate impact theory.

Employers may, if they wish, treat workers with pregnancy-related disabilities more favorably than they treat workers with other condi-

7. See, e.g., Arban v. West Publishing Co., 345 F.3d 390 (6th Cir. 2003); Smith v. Diffee Ford–Lincoln–Mercury, Inc., 298 F.3d 955 (10th Cir. 2002).

8. Title VII, § 701(k), 42 U.S.C.A. § 2000e(k).

tions. In *California Federal Savings & Loan Association v. Guerra*,[9] the Supreme Court held that the PDA did not preempt a California statute requiring employers to provide up to four months' unpaid leave to workers disabled by pregnancy and childbirth. One of the Court's rationales was that "Congress intended the PDA to be a floor beneath which pregnancy disability benefits may not drop—not a ceiling above which they may not rise." The Court carefully noted that the California statute was limited to the period of actual disability and therefore did not reflect stereotypes about the general abilities of pregnant workers. Under *Cal Fed*, then, employers may provide a leave of absence for the period of disability caused by pregnancy and childbirth, even if the Family and Medical Leave Act does not require them to offer any other form of disability leave.

It is important to distinguish between a leave granted because of the disability caused by pregnancy and childbirth and a leave granted for other reasons. If a "maternity leave" extends beyond the time when the female worker is actually disabled by pregnancy and childbirth, it becomes to that extent a childcare, or personal, leave. *Cal Fed* does not apply to nondisability personal leaves of absence for reasons such as childcare, and such leaves must be equally available to men and women. An employer would violate Title VII if, for example, it allowed female employees, but not male employees, to take a one-year leave of absence to care for a newborn child, without regard to the length of time the woman was actually disabled.

Employers may not require pregnant workers to take a leave of absence at any particular point in their pregnancy or to delay their return to work until a specified period after they have given birth, unless the employer can prove that the employee is unable to perform her job duties because of her pregnancy. In *International Union, UAW v. Johnson Controls, Inc.*,[10] the Supreme Court held that to establish a bona fide occupational qualification on safety grounds, an employer must prove that pregnancy actually interferes with ability to perform. Concern about possible harm to an employee's unborn child that might be caused by exposure to toxic substances in the workplace does not satisfy the strict requirements of the BFOQ defense and may not be used to justify a mandatory transfer or leave requirement.

§ 4.32   Leaves of Absence—Federal Law—Leaves for Military Service

The Uniformed Services Employment and Reemployment Rights Act of 1994 (USERRA)[1] replaced the Veterans' Reemployment Rights Act (VRRA),[2] also known as the Vietnam Era Veterans' Readjustment Assis-

9. 479 U.S. 272, 107 S.Ct. 683, 93 L.Ed.2d 613 (1987).

10. 499 U.S. 187, 111 S.Ct. 1196, 113 L.Ed.2d 158 (1991). For a further discussion, see § 2.15 and § 5.36.

2. 38 U.S.C.A. §§ 4301–4307. The VRRA was essentially a reenactment of legislation in effect since the Selective Training and Service Act of 1940.

§ 4.32

1. 38 U.S.C.A. §§ 4301–4331.

tance Act. While it codified some of the case law that had developed under the 1940 Act, it also significantly expanded job protections for members of the military services.

The USERRA applies to all employers, regardless of size, including the federal and state governments and their political subdivisions. The Act applies to individuals who have been absent from work because of "service in the uniformed services" and who have been separated from service under honorable conditions. "Uniformed services" means the Armed Forces, the Army and Air National Guard, the commissioned corps of the Public Health Service, and any other category of individuals designated by the President in time of war or emergency. "Service" means duty on a voluntary or involuntary basis, including active duty, active duty for training, initial active duty for training, inactive duty training, full-time National Guard duty, and absence from work for an examination to determine an individual's fitness to perform these duties. The USERRA eliminates the distinctions that existed under prior law among different types of military service.

Employers are prohibited from discriminating against individuals who are members of, apply to be members of, perform, apply to perform, or have obligations to perform service in a uniformed service. The USERRA prohibits discrimination in initial employment, reemployment, retention in employment, promotion, or any benefit of employment. The Act codifies the "motivating factor-same decision" burden of proof: the employer will be found to have discriminated against the service member if his or her service, application for service, or obligation for service was a "motivating factor" in the adverse employment decision, unless the employer can prove that it would have taken the same action in the absence of the service, application for service, or obligation for service. In addition, it prohibits retaliation against individuals because they have taken actions to exercise their rights or enforce their protections under the Act, have testified or made a statement in connection with any proceeding under the Act, or have otherwise participated in an investigation under the Act. The antiretaliation provision applies to individuals even if they have not actually served in the uniformed services. The motivating factor-same decision test also applies to retaliation claims, and both causes of action apply to any employment position, including brief, nonrecurrent jobs for which there is no reasonable expectation of continued employment.

To be entitled to reemployment rights and benefits, employees must give their employers advance written or oral notice of their military obligation, unless military necessity prevents the giving of notice or the giving of notice is otherwise impossible or unreasonable. With certain exceptions, the cumulative length of the absence and of all previous absences from the employer's employment because of the service may not exceed five years. One of these exceptions is service in which the employee is "ordered to or retained on active duty (other than for training) under any provision of law because of a war or national emergency declared by the President or the Congress, as determined by the Secretary concerned." After the terrorist attacks of September 11, 2001, President Bush declared a national emergency;[3] this would seem to bring service of any person ordered to, or retained on, active duty in response to this declaration within the tolling provision

The time within which a service member must notify the employer of his or her intention to return to work varies with the length of the military service. If the service was less than thirty-one days, or if the reason for the absence was a fitness-for-service examination, the individual must report to his or her employer by the beginning of the first full regularly scheduled work period on the first full calendar day that begins at least eight hours after the individual returns home. If reporting within that period is impossible or unreasonable through no fault of the individual, he or she must report as soon as possible. If the length of service was between thirty-one and 180 days, the service member must submit an application for reemployment no later than fourteen days after the completion of the service. If submission of an application within fourteen days is impossible or unreasonable through no fault of the employee, he or she must submit it on the next calendar day when submission is possible. If the service was for more than 180 days, the individual must submit an application for reemployment no later than ninety days after the completion of service. All of these periods can be extended for up to two years if the individual is hospitalized for, or convalescing from, a service-related illness or injury. If the employee fails to report or apply within the applicable time period, he or she does not automatically lose reinstatement rights, but rather becomes subject to the employer's regular rules and policies concerning absence from work. An employer may request that a service member who has been absent from work for a period of service of more than thirty days provide documentation showing that the application for reemployment is timely, that the service member has not exceeded the five-year service limitation, and that his or her separation was honorable.

Under the USERRA, the conditions governing reinstatement to employment are determined by the length of the military service. An individual whose service was for no more than ninety days must be "promptly reemployed" in the position he or she would have occupied if continuously employed with no uniformed service, unless he or she is not qualified for the job and cannot become qualified after reasonable efforts by the employer to qualify him or her. If the individual cannot become qualified for that job, he or she must be reinstated to the preservice position he or she held. If the individual cannot become qualified for either of these positions, the employer must place him or her in any other position that is the "nearest approximation" to these positions, with full seniority. The same rules apply to service members whose

---

3. Proclamation No. 7463, 66 Fed. Reg. 48199 (September 14, 2001).

period of service was for more than ninety days, except that for each contingency, the employer also has the option of placing the individual in a position of equivalent seniority, status, and pay. The Act defines "qualified" to mean having the ability to perform the essential tasks of the position. "Reasonable efforts" means actions, including training, that do not place an undue hardship on the employer.

Employers must make reasonable efforts to accommodate a disability incurred in or aggravated during uniformed service. If these efforts fail to qualify the employee for the position he or she would have held if continuously employed, the employer must place that person in any other position that is equivalent in seniority, status, and pay that the person is qualified to perform or in a position that approximates that position.

The USERRA provides only three exceptions to the duty to reemploy a returning service member. They are: (1) if the employer's circumstances have so changed as to make reemployment impossible or unreasonable; (2) in the case of an individual who is not entitled to reemployment because he or she is no longer qualified despite the employer's efforts at requalification, if reemployment would impose an undue hardship; and (3) if the employment the individual left was for a brief, nonrecurrent period with no reasonable expectation of continued employment.

After the individual has been reinstated, the employer can fire that person only for cause for a period that depends on the length of service. If the period of service before the reemployment was more than 180 days, the cause protection lasts one year; if the period of service was more than thirty-one and less than 180 days, the cause protection lasts only 180 days.

Upon reemployment, the employee is entitled to all seniority and seniority-based rights and benefits he or she had at the time the service began plus any additional seniority and rights that he or she would have attained if continuously employed. As to non-seniority-based rights and benefits, the employer must treat the returning service member in the same manner it would treat an employee on furlough or leave of absence, including requiring the payment of the employee cost of non-seniority benefits. An employee who is absent because of uniformed service may waive the right to receive non-seniority-based benefits by knowingly providing written notice of his or her intent not to return to employment after service. The employer has the burden of proving this issue. The Act does not contain a similar waiver provision for seniority-based benefits.

Employers must provide COBRA-like coverage in their health plans for both the employee who is absent for service and for his or her eligible dependents. Coverage must be continued for the lesser of the eighteen-month period beginning on the date on which the employee's absence begins, or the day after the date on which the employee fails to apply for or return to employment as required by the Act. As with COBRA, the employer may charge no more than 102 percent of the total health care premium (both the employer's and the employee's share), unless the period of service is for less than thirty-one days. In that case, the service member may not be required to pay more than the employee's share. Unlike COBRA, however, the continuation requirements of USERRA do not contain COBRA's restriction to "group health plans" as defined by COBRA or its twenty-employee size threshold; all employers covered by USERRA that provide health plans are required to offer this continuation coverage. Moreover, the USERRA does not spell out the many details associated with continuation coverage, such as whether and how notice of continuation rights must be given, the length of time within which the employee must elect continuation coverage, or whether coverage may be terminated for failure to pay the premium. It also does not provide how its continuation coverage rights interact with rights under COBRA, for those employers who are covered by both acts. In addition, USERRA requires that no exclusion or waiting period, except for illness or injury determined by the Secretary of Veterans Affairs to be service-related, may be applied upon reemployment to employees or their dependents who did not continue their health coverage during the service-related absence. This restriction parallels that found in the Family and Medical Leave Act and, as with that Act, may have the effect of causing employers with insured plans to continue to pay health care premiums on behalf of employees on military leave, rather than face the prospect of becoming a self-insurer for health conditions occurring during the period of noncoverage. Individuals on active duty on the date of the Act's enactment have the right to elect continuation coverage for the remaining part of the eighteen-month period that began on the date of separation from civilian employment or the period of service, whichever is lesser.

USERRA also contains protections for rights under ERISA-covered pension benefit plans, church plans, and state or federal laws governing pension benefits for government employees. Individuals reemployed under USERRA may not be treated as having incurred a break in service because of their period of military service. Military leave must be deemed to be service with the employer or employers maintaining the plan for the purpose of determining vesting and accrual of benefits under the plan. The employer must fund any obligation of the plan to provide benefits during the break period. If accrued benefits are contingent on employee contributions or elective deferrals, the returning service member is entitled to those benefits only if he or she pays the plan the appropriate amounts.

Complaints alleging violations or impending violations of the USERRA may be filed with the Secretary of Labor, who is then required to investigate. If the Secretary determines a violation has occurred, he or she must make reasonable efforts to effect compliance. If these efforts are unsuccessful, the Secretary must notify the complainant of the results and advise him or her of the enforcement rights under the Act.

At this point, if the respondent is a state or a private employer, the complainant may request that the Secretary of Labor refer the case to the Attorney General, and if the Attorney General is reasonably satisfied that a violation has occurred, the Attorney General may commence an action on behalf of the complainant. If the suit is against a state, the action must be brought in the name of the United States. Alternatively, an individual who has chosen not to file a complaint with the Secretary of Labor, who has chosen not to request referral to the Attorney General, or who has been refused representation by the Attorney General may file an action to enforce his or her rights under the Act. Although 1998 amendments dealt with the issue of the authority of federal courts to entertain suits by private parties against the states under the Eleventh Amendment by providing for state court jurisdiction over suits against a state brought by an individual, it seems unlikely that these suits may be maintained absent the state's consent. In all other suits (actions brought by the United States and those brought against private employers by an individual), jurisdiction lies in the federal district courts.

Remedies for violations may include an order requiring compliance with the Act, compensation for lost wages or benefits suffered because of the failure to comply, and, in the case of willful violations, an equal amount as liquidated damages. In addition, the court may award reasonable attorney's fees, expert witness fees, and other litigation expenses to the prevailing plaintiff; the Act specifically provides, however, that no fees or court costs shall be taxed against the plaintiff. Actions under the USERRA may be initiated only by the United States or a person claiming rights or benefits, and not by an employer, prospective employer, or other entity with obligations under the Act. Only an employer or potential employer shall be a necessary defendant. No state statute of limitations may apply to USERRA actions.

In 1998, Congress amended the USERRA to include provisions on employment and reemployment rights in foreign countries. The term "employee" now includes individuals who are citizens, nationals, or permanent resident aliens of the United States employed in a foreign country by an employer that is incorporated or otherwise organized in the United States or is controlled by an entity organized in the United States. If an employer controls an entity that is incorporated or otherwise organized in a foreign country, any denial of employment, reemployment, or benefit by the foreign entity is presumed to be by the controlling U.S. employer. The determination whether an employer controls an entity is to be based on interrelations of operations, common management, centralized control of labor relations, and common ownership or financial control. The amendments contain an exemption from compliance as to an employee in a foreign country if compliance would cause the employer or the entity it controls to violate the law of the foreign country.

§ 4.33 Leaves of Absence—State Law

Family and Medical Leave

The federal Family and Medical Leave Act of 1993,[1] which covers employers with fifty or more employees, does not preempt state and local laws providing more generous leave rights. Over half the states have legislation requiring covered employers to provide family or medical leaves in certain circumstances. Most of these laws apply only to state employees. These are often part of general personnel or civil service statutes governing the state and its subdivisions, and they will not be discussed in this section.

The most comprehensive of the state laws applicable to the private as well as the public sector require covered employers to grant employees of either sex unpaid leave for the birth or adoption of a child or for the serious illness of an immediate family member. Nine states, California, Connecticut, Hawaii, Maine, New Jersey, Oregon, Rhode Island, Vermont, Wisconsin, plus the District of Columbia currently have such family leave laws; of these, six, Connecticut, the District of Columbia, Maine, Rhode Island, Vermont and Wisconsin also require leaves for the employee's own medical condition.

The length of the required leave varies from four weeks in one calendar year to four months in a twenty-four month period. A few states impose restrictions similar to those in the FMLA on the aggregate amount of leave a husband and wife may take.

All of these family leave statutes require that employees have worked for the employer for a specified period of time before being eligible for family leave. Employees are generally required to give advance notice of the need for a leave whenever possible, and many statutes permit the employer to require medical certification of the illness. In some states, employers may deny family leave to certain highly compensated employees, generally on the conditions that the employer demonstrate its need to deny the leave and give the employee notice of the decision.

Two states that do not have family leave laws have parental leave legislation, which requires employers to provide leave for the birth or adoption of a child. Minnesota's law permits leave only for birth or adoption, but it also requires employers to permit workers to use their sick leave to care for an ill or injured child. Washington permits leave for birth, adoption, or to care for a terminally ill child. Colorado and New York simply require that employers give adoptive parents the same leave privileges they provide to biological parents. Maryland and Nebraska have joined the states with laws requiring employers to give adoptive parents the same leave privileges they provide to biological parents.

Finally, the statutes of six states, California, Iowa, Louisiana, Massachusetts, Montana, and Tennessee, require employers to provide disability leaves to pregnant workers. At least one additional state, Kansas, imposes that requirement by regulation. In *California Federal Savings*

§ 4.33

1. 29 U.S.C.A. §§ 2601–2654.

& *Loan Association v. Guerra,*[2] the Supreme Court upheld California's statute against a challenge that it was preempted by the Pregnancy Discrimination Act (PDA). The Court reasoned that the PDA merely required employers to treat pregnancy-related disabilities no worse than other disabilities, and that it did not prohibit more favorable treatment of pregnancy-related disabilities, at least where the leave of absence was for the period of the woman's actual physical disability. In addition, the Court remarked that California's law did not prohibit employers from voluntarily granting paternity leave to male workers. This reasoning protects other state maternity leave statutes from challenges that they unlawfully discriminate against non-pregnant workers, but the Massachusetts law, which also requires employers to give female employees adoption leaves, should be vulnerable to attack.

At the conclusion of any of the leaves described in this section, the employer must normally reinstate the worker to his or her former job or a substantially equivalent position, with no loss of accumulated seniority or benefits. The Family and Medical Leave Act requires employers to continue health insurance coverage while workers are on leave. State laws imposing the same requirement, however, are preempted by ERISA to the extent they apply to employers covered by the federal law.

The Family and Medical Leave Act does not preempt state and local laws providing more generous leave rights. For instance, a state's leave law may apply to smaller employers that are not covered by the FMLA. The FMLA permits those laws to continue to operate, and eligible employees may take leave under state law, even though they have no rights under the FMLA. A more difficult problem occurs when an employer is covered by both the FMLA and a state leave law. The Department of Labor has taken the position that if leave qualifies under both the FMLA and state law, the leave used counts against the employee's entitlement under both laws. For instance, if the state law provides for sixteen weeks of leave in a two-year period, the employee would be entitled to take sixteen weeks one year under the state law and twelve weeks the next under the FMLA.

Leave for Bone Marrow or Organ Donation

Four states, Louisiana, Minnesota, New York, and Utah, require covered private sector employers to give time off so that an employee can donate organs or bone marrow. At least nine states, Arkansas, California, Delaware, Illinois, Indiana, New York, Oklahoma, Virginia, and Wisconsin, have similar statutes, some as part of their civil service laws, covering state workers only. Nebraska's statute is hortatory only; it merely "encourages" employers to give employees time off for bone marrow donation. South Carolina has a very detailed statute on the matter, but the language in the leave provision is permissive, not mandatory.

2. 479 U.S. 272, 107 S.Ct. 683, 93 L.Ed.2d 613 (1987).

Short-Term Leave for School–Related and Other ParentalActivities

Illinois, Louisiana, North Carolina, and Rhode Island require employers to provide employees time off to attend school conferences concerning their children. Massachusetts has a family obligation leave law that requires that employees be allowed up to twenty-four hours off in any twelve-month period to attend school conferences, to take children to medical appointments, or accompany elderly relatives to medical appointments or for other professional services, such as interviewing at nursing homes. Nevada, Oregon, and Utah require employers to give workers time off to attend juvenile proceedings involving their children.

Leave for Victims of Domestic Violence and Other Crimes

Several states including Arizona, California, Colorado, Maine, Ohio, and Wyoming, mandate leave for employees who have been victims of domestic violence or other crimes, for activities such as attending court proceedings, obtaining restraining orders, ensuring personal safety or the safety of children, or to obtain medical treatment or counseling.

Leaves to Vote

Most states permit an employee statutorily protected time off from work to vote. Generally, voters are permitted time off to vote in any election held within a state. Some states, however, limit time off to general, primary, and special elections. Generally, an employee is allowed time off to vote varying from one to four hours unless the employee has the same amount of time to vote outside of working hours while the polls are open. Minnesota allows an unspecified amount of time off during the morning of election day. Ohio allows a "reasonable time" off to vote.

As a general rule, an employer may not deny an employee compensation for the time that an employee is away from work to vote. Nevertheless, some states have struck down pay-while-voting regulations as unconstitutional.[3] Furthermore, if an employee does not vote, a number of states allow the employer to deduct wages for the time off or discipline the employee. Many states allow an employer to designate what hours may be taken off for voting and to request notice before an employee takes time off to vote.

Although most states do not indicate what penalty exists for violation of the voting time off laws, a number of statutes indicate that an employer will be guilty of a misdemeanor for violations.

§ 4.34   Jury Service Laws

Federal Law

Under the Jury System Improvements Act,[1] an employee is protected from discharge, intimidation, and coercion by an employer because of

3. See, e.g., Heimgaertner v. Benjamin Elec. Mfg. Co., 6 Ill.2d 152, 128 N.E.2d 691 (1955); Illinois Central R.R. v. Commonwealth, 305 Ky. 632, 204 S.W.2d 973 (1947), cert. denied, 334 U.S. 843, 68 S.Ct. 1511, 92 L.Ed. 1767 (1948).

§ 4.34

1. 28 U.S.C.A. § 1875.

the employee's service on a jury in federal court. If an employer commits a violation of the Act, the employee may recover lost wages and benefits. The term "benefits" means "employment-related benefits-other than wages-that an employee lost as a result of his employer's hostility to jury service," including "commissions, insurance benefits, sick leave, vacation pay, use of a company car, or any other economic or fringe benefits." The employee also may receive injunctive or other appropriate relief, including reinstatement, and reasonable attorney's fees, but compensatory damages are not available. Additionally, an employer is subject to a civil penalty up to $1000 for violating the Act.

Often, an employee will bring an action under the Act after being discharged, but a judge may hear an action sua sponte if a juror in his or her court is being harassed or coerced while serving on a jury in his or her court. One court found no violation of the Jury System Improvements Act for an employer to require employees to give advance notice of absences for jury duty and then to fire an employee when he failed to do so.[2] An employee also may bring an action against an employer if the employer intimidates, but does not discharge the employee. The courts consider an employer's hostile comments regarding an employee's jury service as evidence of coercion.[3] Hostile comments also may indicate the employer's true reasons for discharging an employee.

Under the Act, an employer may not change the conditions under which an employee works while the employee serves as a juror. Thus, a company may not reassign an employee to a new position or change an employee's work schedule during jury service without an explanation unrelated to jury service. Furthermore, an employer may not suggest that an employee will be discharged in the future if the employee serves as a federal juror, nor may an employer withhold wages while an employee serves on a federal jury.

The Jury System Improvement Act does not expressly provide for the right to a jury trial, but because it provides for legal remedies, the Seventh Amendment right to trial by jury applies.

State Laws

Every state except Montana has a statutory provision protecting an employee from discharge because of serving on a jury panel in state or federal court. Protection under state law, however, is usually not as broad as protection under the Jury System Improvements Act. A number of states prohibit an employer from threatening or coercing an employee because of jury service, but many states focus merely on protection against wrongful discharge. Some states specifically protect an employee's benefits, such as seniority, vacation time, or sick-leave, but many statutes do not address benefits. In some states, an employee must give reasonable notice to the employer of impending jury service in order to receive statutory protection.

---

2. In re Scott, 155 F.R.D. 10 (D.Mass. . 1994).

3. See Hill v. Winn–Dixie Stores, Inc., 934 F.2d 1518 (11th Cir.1991).

Many states allow an employee to pursue a civil action for violation of the state statute. Statutes of limitation range from thirty days to one year after the violation. At least one state, however, allows employees who do not file within their prescribed time limit to bring a nonstatutory action for retaliatory discharge under the public policy exception to the employment at will rule.[4] Such actions often are used in states without a statutory civil cause of action.[5]

Generally, employees may recover lost wages and reasonable attorney fees as well as gain reinstatement for discharge. Some states allow an employee to recover punitive damages. A number of states also allow a court to impose civil contempt against an employer. Many states provide for criminal sanctions in addition to or instead of providing for a civil cause of action. These statutes classify violations as crimes ranging from criminal contempt to misdemeanors. The criminal sanctions range from fines to imprisonment.

Most state statutes do not address whether an employer must pay an employee while the employee serves on a jury. Some statutes provide that the employer is not required to compensate the employee for time on jury duty; a few states require the employer to compensate the employee; other states have determined that an employer is simply not legally bound to pay an employee during an absence for jury duty.

Some state statutes protect both potential and actual jurors, while others do not address the issue. At least one state recognizes statutory protection for a potential juror appearing for the limited reason of claiming an exemption from jury duty.[6]

---

4. See Call v. Scott Brass, Inc., 553 N.E.2d 1225 (Ind.App.1990); Hodges v. S.C. Toof & Co., 833 S.W.2d 896 (Tenn.1992) (permitting recovery of compensatory damages, even though not authorized by statute).

5. See Shaffer v. Frontrunner, Inc., 57 Ohio App.3d 18, 566 N.E.2d 193 (1990).

6. See Wright v. Faggan, 773 S.W.2d 352 (Tex.App.1989).

Chapter 5

CONDITIONS OF EMPLOYMENT

Table of Sections

---

§ 5.1 Introduction

Traditionally, employers have had wide discretion to establish all of the conditions of employment. It was the employer's property and the employer's business and therefore the employer decided the means of operation and employee conduct in the workplace. It is precisely this point which differentiates an employee from an independent contractor. Simply stated, the employer retains the right of control over employees.

The common law principle of the master (later the employer) having plenary control of the servants' (later employees') activities in the workplace and beyond increasingly has conflicted with emerging societal values. Specifically, contemporary American society increasingly values individual autonomy, privacy, freedom of expression, and freedom of association. Thus, although employers still have unchallenged authority to determine the essential aspects of the business operation, unreasonable intrusions or other practices by employers are less likely to be countenanced by either employees or the courts and legislatures.

As in some other areas of employment law, many of the first successful actions challenging employer prerogatives have involved public sector employees. Using the governmental action of public employment, employees have invoked constitutional protections, such as free-

440

dom of expression and association, search and seizure, and liberty. In the private sector, employees have relied on civil rights statutes and common law principles, with varying degrees of success. The expectations of individual employees also have been influenced by collective bargaining agreements, which have set industry standards regarding conditions of employment.

For private sector employees, where the law is least developed, it is important to distinguish between at-will employees and employees who may be discharged only for just cause. As to the former, in the absence of egregious employer conduct or infringement upon statutory rights, employees are still likely to have relatively few legal rights. As to the latter, for conditions of employment related to both on-the-job (e.g., grooming, dress) and off-work (e.g., associations, political activities) activities, employers are likely to have a difficult time establishing just cause for discharge.

This chapter considers a range of conditions subject to regulation by employers. It is an area of employment law that is likely to see tremendous growth for the following reasons. First, as the nature of what people do on the job continues to change, it will raise new questions regarding the legitimate rights of employers and employees. For example, computer monitoring and other surveillance measures raise a conflict between privacy and productivity. Second, the range of employee interests deemed worth protecting, through legislative action or litigation, is likely to continue to expand. The privacy of employment records, the right to dress or be groomed as one wants, and the right to be free from employer interference with off-work activities are examples of employee interests seriously asserted only recently.

§ 5.2 Grooming and Appearance

Employers sometimes establish grooming standards for their employees which regulate hair length, hair style, facial hair, or hair coverings. The policies are most often imposed in two contexts: health and sanitation, and public contact situations. Grooming policies have been challenged on constitutional grounds, under Title VII,[1] and under various state statutes similar to Title VII. Other policies dealing with appearance have been challenged under the Americans with Disabilities Act[2] and other disabilities laws.

Constitutional Arguments

Constitutional challenges to grooming policies are usually based on: (1) the First Amendment right to personal expression; or (2) the Fourteenth Amendment right to equal protection and due process, based on either gender or religious discrimination. In the leading case of *Kelley v. Johnson*,[3] a police officer challenged a county regulation limiting the

§ 5.2
1. 42 U.S.C.A. § 2000e.
2. 42 U.S.C.A. §§ 12101–12213.

3. 425 U.S. 238, 96 S.Ct. 1440, 47 L.Ed.2d 708 (1976).

length of male police officers' hair. The Supreme Court, applying the test of whether the regulation was rationally related to the promotion of safety of persons and property, held that the regulation did not violate any right guaranteed by the Fourteenth Amendment. Justice Rehnquist's majority opinion noted that law enforcement officers are subject to many regulations not applicable to the public at large, such as those requiring them to wear a police uniform, prohibiting them from smoking in public, and requiring them to salute the flag while in uniform. Viewed in this context, the Court considered the hair-length regulation a reasonable restriction. Furthermore, according to the Court, the Fourteenth Amendment liberty interest in personal grooming is subject to abridgment by the state police power for reasons of health and safety. In this case, the county's interest in a disciplined and easily recognizable police force outweighed the plaintiff's right to wear his hair as long as he wished.

Based on *Kelley,* the First Circuit also upheld a ban on mustaches and goatees as well as beards for police officers.[4] The court, applying the rational basis test, held that ease of recognition and promotion of esprit de corps were sufficient reasons to uphold the rule. According to the court, *"Kelley's* grip on the instant case is unrelenting."[5]

Kelley's grip on cases involving other types of public safety officers is also significant. For example, the Supreme Court has held that hair-length regulations for firefighters were rationally related to safety because the rules ensure proper functioning of gas masks and promote discipline within the department.[6] The Eighth Circuit also has held that a county policy prohibiting emergency medical technicians from wearing mustaches or beards did not violate due process.[7] The policy was justified by the need for esprit de corps, a professional image, and possible interference with the performance of their job. In a somewhat unique case, a hirsute firefighter was suspended without pay for refusing to either put on a t-shirt or shave the chest hair showing from under his uniform shirt.[8] The court upheld the suspension, rejecting the firefighter's First Amendment claim.

Grooming policies also have been challenged as unconstitutional religious discrimination. There is no clear trend in the cases. For example, the Third Circuit held that a police department rule prohibiting the wearing of beards, but allowing an exemption for medical reasons, violated the free exercise rights of Muslim police officers who desired to wear a beard for religious reasons.[9] On the other hand, the Fourth Circuit upheld the discipline of a Rastafarian correctional officer who

4. Weaver v. Henderson, 984 F.2d 11 (1st Cir.1993).

5. Id. at 13.

6. Quinn v. Muscare, 425 U.S. 560, 96 S.Ct. 1752, 48 L.Ed.2d 165 (1976).

7. Hottinger v. Pope County, 971 F.2d 127 (8th Cir.1992).

8. Stalter v. City of Montgomery, 796 F.Supp. 489 (M.D.Ala.1992), affirmed, 993 F.2d 232 (11th Cir. 1993).

9. Fraternal Order of Police Newark Lodge No. 12 v. City of Newark, 170 F.3d 359 (3d Cir. 1999), cert. denied, 528 U.S. 817, 120 S.Ct. 56, 145 L.Ed.2d 49 (1999).

wore his hair in "modified" dreadlocks, as required by his religion, in violation of the grooming policy.[10]

Several rationales have been applied in the dismissal of constitutional gender discrimination claims by lower courts. The cases often have involved regulations requiring only men to have short hair. One court stated that the right to wear one's hair in a certain way is not a right found within the periphery of any specific constitutional right. Another said that the right to personal expression is subject to abridgment in the interest of health and safety. Courts have shown deference to police grooming policies because they believe that law enforcement officials have greater expertise than the courts in determining reasonably necessary regulations. Some courts have cited a strong need to regulate in order to maintain discipline in a "quasi-military" organization.

In another constitutional case, the plaintiff alleged that her employer's refusal to allow her to wear a "corn-row" hairstyle imposed on her the "badges or incidents of slavery" forbidden by the Thirteenth Amendment. The court dismissed the claim because hairstyles are not immutable and enjoy no constitutional protection.

Title VII Actions

While Title VII does not specifically address grooming policies, courts have regularly accepted that the policies fall within "terms and conditions of employment," about which discrimination is forbidden by Title VII. The grooming policies most often attacked under Title VII are those setting different hair-length standards for males and females. In general, the courts hold that the application of different grooming standards to the sexes is not gender discrimination under Title VII where the standards reflect cultural norms and do not single out one of the sexes for harsher treatment. A few early cases had held that different-sex grooming policies violate Title VII.

Title VII also has been used to challenge regulations related to hair coverings worn in the workplace. A regulation allowing long-haired women who work with exposed food to wear hair nets, but required men in the same position to wear hats, was found to be discrimination on the basis of gender. The court held that grooming regulations must be rationally related to a legitimate goal and may not be based on stereotypes.

The vast majority of courts, however, have found that enforcing different grooming policies for males and females does not necessarily constitute gender discrimination under Title VII. For example, in one case, different hair length standards applied to the male and female employees of a food store chain were found to have no significant effect upon the employment opportunities afforded one sex in favor of the other. Grooming standards also have been held to be nondiscriminatory when applied to diverse employees, including employees who service and repair bank equipment, bus drivers, copy layout artists, artist-craftper-

---

10. Booth v. Maryland, 327 F.3d 377 (4th Cir. 2003).

sons for an amusement park operator, and railroad procedures analysts. These decisions have been explained in different ways. One rationale is that it is an employer's right to impose standards necessary to the success of its business. The D.C. Circuit took judicial notice that "reasonable regulations prescribing good grooming standards are not at all uncommon in the business world."[11] Another court reasoned that discrimination is illegal only when based on immutable or protected characteristics, such as unchangeable gender characteristics, being married, or having children. Because hair length is easily changeable, it does not qualify as an immutable characteristic.

Most race discrimination claims related to grooming policies involve no-beard rules. Pseudofolliculitis barbae is a skin disorder resulting from hairs in the beard area of the face and neck when the individual is clean-shaven. Because the condition is found in twenty-five percent of black males but far less than one percent of white males, black men have asserted that no-beard rules constitute disparate impact race discrimination. Some cases have upheld no-beard rules on the rationale that the health and sanitation, cleanliness, hygiene, and public image involved in certain businesses outweighed the disparate impact resulting from the grooming policy. Other cases, however, have found that no-beard rules constitute disparate impact race discrimination for which employers have the burden of proving job-relatedness or business necessity.

No-beard rules also have been alleged to constitute religious discrimination under Title VII. Whether the plaintiff wins or loses generally turns on the overall conduct of the employer and the type of business in which the employer is engaged. Employer grooming rules are more likely to be upheld if they are applied consistently and based on substantial concerns, such as safety. For instance, a company was required to accommodate a Jewish computer programmer's religious beliefs requiring him to have a beard when it was shown that the company accommodated members of other religions. On the other hand, accommodation may not be possible because of the nature of the business. This rationale was applied to a plaintiff who was the manager of a family restaurant and to an employee who had potential exposure to toxic gases and who was unable to wear a respirator because of a beard.

Americans with Disabilities Act

A variety of disability cases have involved alleged discrimination based on appearance. These include individuals who had missing teeth or a disfigured eye socket. The greatest number of such cases have alleged discrimination based on obesity. Generally, the courts have held that obesity is not a disability under the Americans with Disabilities Act (ADA). Therefore, the ADA has not reached employer conduct such as denial of a promotion to senior management because the individual's obesity was inconsistent with the image the company was trying to project.

11. Fagan v. National Cash Register Co., 481 F.2d 1115, 1117 n.3 (D.C.Cir.1973).

State Fair Employment Laws

Plaintiffs also have brought race, sex, religion, and national origin discrimination claims under state law. For example, a prospective busboy sued successfully under New York state law when a restaurant hired females with long hair, but refused to hire him.[12] On the other hand, some courts have been extremely deferential to employers by stating that a "hiring policy that distinguishes on some other ground [than a fundamental right], such as grooming codes or length of hair, is related more closely to the employer's choice of how to run his business than to equality of opportunity."[13]

In Illinois, a prospective mailroom employee claimed discrimination on the basis of race, religion, and national origin.[14] The plaintiff, a Jamaican-born black man, was a member of the Ethiopian Orthodox Church, one of two fundamental branches of the Rastafarian religion. He was rejected because he wore his hair in dreadlocks. His employment discrimination action was dismissed because there was no evidence that the employer knew or should have known the plaintiff's hairstyle was mandated by religion or national origin, and because no pretext was shown for hiring another employee. The result may be questioned, however, as sanctioning disparate impact discrimination without requiring an employer defense so long as the employer is ignorant of the disparate impact.

The District of Columbia is the only jurisdiction with a statute specifically prohibiting discrimination based on personal appearance, including grooming practices. Personal appearance is defined in the statute as "the outward appearance of any person, irrespective of sex, with regard to bodily condition or characteristics, manner or style of dress, and manner or style of personal grooming, including, but not limited to, hair style and beards." In a case brought under this law, the employer was held to have violated the statute for discharging a receptionist for, among other things, having disheveled hair and wearing low-cut and tight blouses.[15] This case demonstrates the difficulty in regulating such a variable subject as personal appearance.

§ 5.3 Dress

Employers often regulate the appearance of their employees by establishing dress codes, including regulation of uniforms, eyeglasses, headcoverings, earrings, and certain types of religious garb. As with grooming rules, discussed in the preceding section, dress codes have been

---

12. Doyle v. Buffalo Sidewalk Cafe, Inc., 70 Misc.2d 212, 333 N.Y.S.2d 534 (1972).

13. Pik–Kwik Stores, Inc. v. Commission on Human Rights & Opportunities, 170 Conn. 327, 365 A.2d 1210, 1212 (1976), quoting Willingham v. Macon Tel. Pub'g Co., 507 F.2d 1084, 1091 (5th Cir. 1975).

14. Gayle v. Human Rights Comm'n, 218 Ill.App.3d 109, 161 Ill.Dec. 17, 578 N.E.2d 144, appeal denied, 142 Ill.2d 653, 164 Ill.Dec. 917, 584 N.E.2d 129 (1991).

15. Atlantic Richfield Co. v. District of Columbia Comm'n on Human Rights, 515 A.2d 1095 (D.C.1986).

challenged under the Constitution, as discrimination based on gender, race, and religion under Title VII, and under state law.

Constitutional Law

The leading constitutional dress code case involved the military, but is nevertheless instructive. In *Goldman v. Weinberger*,[1] the plaintiff, an Orthodox Jew and an ordained rabbi, was a captain at a military hospital. The Air Force refused to grant him an exemption to its dress code to allow him to wear a yarmulke while on duty. In holding that the Air Force did not violate the plaintiff's First Amendment right of free exercise of religion, the Court stated that because the military is a specialized society separate from that of civilians, the review of constitutional challenges to military regulations is "far more deferential" than that for regulations applied to civilians. The Air Force argued that the wearing of a yarmulke would open the door to dress code challenges by members of all religions, compelling them to allow all exceptions, including the turbans and dreadlocks worn by those of the Sikh and Rastafarian faiths. It claimed that this would result in numerous health and safety related problems, although it could not establish any in the case at issue. Alternatively, the Air Force argued that refusing exemptions for the religious garb of other faiths would create the appearance of religious favoritism. The Court found that the dress code served a legitimate purpose by encouraging "the subordination of personal preferences and identities in favor of the overall group mission."[2] The Court also found that the regulation was valid because it was based on a "neutral, completely objective standard—visibility."

The Second Circuit applied the rational basis test in upholding a county's requirement that all van drivers wear pants, thereby rejecting the plaintiff's argument that her deeply held beliefs required her to wear a skirt.[3] The Third Circuit upheld a rule requiring guards at Pennsylvania prisons to wear an American flag patch on their uniforms.[4] The court rejected the plaintiff's claim that the regulation was a "compelled expression" in violation of the First Amendment.

Title VII

Title VII also has been used in religion and gender discrimination dress code cases. Dress codes challenged as discriminatory on the basis of gender have involved requiring uniforms for women only, uniforms which subject the wearer to sexual harassment, and the wearing of contact lenses. Personal appearance standards sometimes have been used to deny or terminate employment, as well as to deny promotions.

---

§ 5.3

1. 475 U.S. 503, 106 S.Ct. 1310, 89 L.Ed.2d 478 (1986).

2. 475 U.S. at 508, 106 S.Ct. at 1313.

3. Zalewska v. County of Sullivan, 316 F.3d 314 (2d Cir. 2003).

4. Troster v. Pennsylvania State Dep't of Corrections, 65 F.3d 1086 (3d Cir.1995), cert. denied 516 U.S. 1047, 116 S.Ct. 708, 133 L.Ed.2d 663 (1996).

Where uniforms are prescribed, employers may not discriminate between male and female employees in the nature of the uniform. In *Carroll v. Talman Federal Savings & Loan Association,*[5] a bank required all female tellers to wear uniforms, while male tellers could wear business suits. The women were expected to pay for the cleaning and maintenance of their uniforms and income tax on the value of the uniforms was deducted from their earnings. In ruling that the uniform rule discriminated on the basis of gender, the Seventh Circuit said that it was irrelevant that some female employees liked the uniforms. The uniform rule constituted disparate treatment and was demeaning to women because customers generally assume that uniformed employees have less authority than those in normal business attire. In another case, female sales clerks were required to wear smocks, while male sales clerks could wear customary business attire consisting of slacks, a shirt, and a necktie. The court held that this was disparate treatment discrimination and also ruled that proof of discriminatory intent is not necessary for explicit gender discrimination based on uniforms.

Uniforms which subject women to sexual harassment also constitute discrimination on the basis of gender. In *EEOC v. Sage Realty Corp.,*[6] the plaintiff was a lobby attendant in a building managed by the defendant. The plaintiff was issued a "bicentennial uniform," designed to resemble the American flag and worn as a poncho, with only dancer pants and sheer stockings underneath. Because the plaintiff was tall, the standard-size uniform was very short and revealing. After repeated attempts to have the uniform altered or replaced with a less revealing uniform, the plaintiff wore the uniform at work for two days. While wearing the uniform, she was subjected to repeated sexual harassment, including sexual propositions and lewd comments and gestures from visitors to the building. She was unable to perform her duties properly because of the humiliation. When she resorted to wearing her old uniform, she was given a "lay-off" letter stating that she had lost her job because of a lack of work. The court held that the employer violated Title VII by requiring the plaintiff to wear a uniform which the employer knew was revealing and sexually provocative and could reasonably have been expected to subject her to sexual harassment when worn on the job. The court stated that wearing the uniform was not a bona fide occupational qualification (BFOQ) for her position as lobby attendant.

Cocktail and restaurant waitresses also have alleged gender discrimination when they were required to wear uniforms which subjected them to verbal and physical sexual harassment from customers, as well as to physical discomfort and colds. In one case, cocktail waitresses were instructed to "project an air of sexual availability through the use of provocative outfits."[7] The court held that the plaintiff had established a

5. 604 F.2d 1028 (7th Cir.1979), cert. denied, 445 U.S. 929, 100 S.Ct. 1316, 63 L.Ed.2d 762 (1980).

6. 507 F.Supp. 599 (S.D.N.Y.1981).
7. EEOC v. Newtown Inn Assoc., 647 F.Supp. 957, 958 (E.D.Va.1986).

prima facie case of gender discrimination, but that the defendant would be allowed to assert a BFOQ defense. In another case, the plaintiff survived a motion for summary judgment where the employer required female employees to wear skirts or dresses on certain occasions because a visiting supervisor liked to look at their legs. On the other hand, it has been held not to be actionable sexual harassment for a supervisor to criticize a receptionist for repeatedly wearing inappropriately provocative dress at work.

In some instances, dress codes may be closely related to single-sex employment policies. For example, in *Wilson v. Southwest Airlines Co.,*[8] the airline employed only attractive young women for the positions of ticket agent and flight attendant and required them to wear high boots and hot pants. In defending an action alleging gender discrimination against men, the airline asserted that the dress code and hiring restrictions were BFOQs because the airline was attempting to project an image of "feminine spirit, fun and sex appeal." The court rejected the claim and concluded that female sexual allure was not essential to the airline's primary function of transporting passengers.

A regulation requiring only female employees to wear contact lenses and not eyeglasses also was found to be discrimination on the basis of gender. The court based its decision on the fact that the contact lens requirement imposed a substantially greater cost on female employees and was not reasonably related to performance of the job.

Dress code regulations requiring different attire of male and female employees, but which are not demeaning or costly to the female employees, are sometimes upheld. In one such case, the defendant's dress code prohibited women from wearing pants in the executive office portion of the defendant's offices. The court applied the same analysis as in the "haircut cases," which limit the application of Title VII to those employment policies which discriminate on the basis of: immutable characteristics, characteristics which are changeable but involve fundamental rights, and characteristics which are changeable but which significantly affect employment opportunities afforded to one sex. The court held that the plaintiff's desire to wear pantsuits did not fall into one of the above categories.

General personal appearance standards are often upheld. In *Craft v. Metromedia, Inc.,*[9] a television news station relied partially on market surveys in terminating the employment of a female news anchor. When told that she was fired because she was not feminine enough in her clothing and makeup, the plaintiff sued on the basis of gender discrimination, alleging that the station did not apply similar standards to male news anchors. The court held that while there was some emphasis on the feminine stereotype of "softness" and bows and ruffles, and on the fashionableness of female news anchors, the real reason for termination

---

8.   517 F.Supp. 292 (N.D.Tex.1981).

9.   766 F.2d 1205 (8th Cir.1985), cert. denied, 475 U.S. 1058, 106 S.Ct. 1285, 89 L.Ed.2d 592 (1986).

was a nondiscriminatory concern for appearance, colors, textures, lighting, and conservatism. The court said that the appearance standard was applied equally to males and females and was reasonably necessary within the Kansas City market.

General personal appearance standards have been used to deny promotions to women. In one instance, an employer's requirement that public contact employees maintain appropriate standards of grooming was found to be reasonable and not unfair to any class of employees. Subsequently, in *Price Waterhouse v. Hopkins*,[10] however, the Supreme Court held that the comments of partners in an accounting firm concerning a female candidate's manner and grooming were sufficient to show that her rejection for partnership was based on gender discrimination. The decision was based on evidence that the male partner who explained to the plaintiff the decision to place her partnership candidacy on hold advised her to "walk more femininely, talk more femininely, dress more femininely, wear make-up, have her hair styled, and wear jewelry."[11]

It is not clear to what extent *Price Waterhouse* will be applied in cases involving grooming and dress codes. If viewed more broadly as a case of gender stereotyping, *Price Waterhouse* will have little direct impact. If viewed in a more fact-specific manner, however, *Price Waterhouse* could result in closer judicial scrutiny of employment decisions based on considerations of grooming and dress. Under this latter interpretation, a case such as *Craft* would have to be considered as an exception to the rule of close scrutiny, perhaps because of the image-conscious job of a television newscaster.

Men who challenge dress code restrictions tend to lose when the regulations are based on traditional cultural norms. For example, a male grocery store employee unsuccessfully challenged a tie requirement on the basis that the female dress code had been modified to allow women to wear pants. In another case, a male loan counselor claimed gender discrimination when the dress code prohibited men from wearing earrings, while permitting women to wear them. In ruling for the defendant, the court stated that the "imposition of grooming standards designed to project, in the employer's view, a conservative banking image is within the employer's discretion."

Religious discrimination claims also have been based on employer dress codes. Whether the policy is found to be discriminatory usually turns on the nature of the job in question. In one of these cases, the defendant was a private corporation providing auxiliary services to nonpublic school students under a contract with the school district. The plaintiff, a Muslim woman, alleged religious discrimination when she applied but was not hired for a position as a third-grade counselor for Catholic elementary schools because she wore a head covering. In ruling for the defendant, the court said that although the plaintiff's head covering was worn for a religious purpose, it did not clearly indicate to

10. 490 U.S. 228, 109 S.Ct. 1775, 104 L.Ed.2d 268 (1989).

11. 490 U.S. at 235, 109 S.Ct. at 1782.

others that she belonged to any certain religion, and therefore the refusal to hire her could not have been religious discrimination.

Race and religion discrimination claims also may fail if the employer falls into one of the exceptions to Title VII or would suffer "undue hardship" by allowing the plaintiff to wear religious garb in the workplace. For example, in one case the plaintiff, a receptionist at a Christian retirement home, was hired without discussion of her religious beliefs, then was asked not to wear her Muslim headcovering while at work. The court ruled in favor of the retirement home operators because of Title VII's exemption for religious entities. The court reasoned that to allow the plaintiff to wear her religious garb at work would be to favor her religion over the defendant's.

In *United States v. Board of Education*,[12] the plaintiff, a Muslim school teacher, was not permitted to wear religious headcoverings and other attire. The school district took the action because a Pennsylvania "garb statute" expressly prohibits public school teachers from teaching in any religious garb. In an action brought by the federal government, representing the teacher, the plaintiff argued that the Pennsylvania law was unconstitutional and preempted by Title VII. The Third Circuit upheld the validity of the garb statute. The court said that the law served the compelling state interest of preserving religious neutrality and it barred all religious attire and therefore was religion-neutral. The court further held that accommodating the plaintiff would have imposed an undue hardship.

State Fair Employment Laws

State law gender discrimination claims have paralleled those under Title VII. Thus, for example, they are likely to be successful if the dress codes are based on stereotypes or encourage sexual harassment. In a Michigan case, a hospital's dress code required female technologists to wear a white or pastel-colored uniform and males in the same position to wear a white laboratory coat over regular street clothing. This was found to constitute gender discrimination because the hospital conceded that the regulation was adopted because the administration believed patients expect females to look like nurses and males to look like doctors. The court said that this type of dress code reinforces negative stereotypes; gives women a sense of inferiority, causing them to function less effectively; implies that women are of a lower status than men in the same position; and is more costly and less convenient.

California was the first jurisdiction to enact legislation making it illegal for an employer to prohibit female employees from wearing pants at work, unless special clothing is required as a uniform or costume.

In summary, there is little direct regulation of employer policies prescribing dress codes for employees. An employer may require an employee to wear a uniform or similar attire, but policies which have the purpose or effect of unreasonably discriminating against employees on

---

12. 911 F.2d 882 (3d Cir.1990).

the basis of gender, religion, or other proscribed factors will violate Title VII.

§ 5.4 Searches

Employers sometimes believe it is necessary to search employees, the personal property of employees, and employer property under the control of employees to locate money, merchandise, contraband, or other things. The lawfulness of these searches depends, primarily, on whether constitutional principles apply and the reasonableness of the search.

Public Employers

Workplace searches by government employers are restricted by the Fourth Amendment. Hallways, offices, desks, closets, and file cabinets are considered to be part of the workplace. Fourth Amendment rights do not turn on property interests in either the place searched or its contents. "[The] capacity to claim the protection of the [Fourth] Amendment depends not upon a property right in the invaded place but upon whether the area was one in which there was a reasonable expectation of freedom from governmental intrusion."[1] Whether a reasonable expectation of privacy exists is a question of law. For a search to violate the Fourth Amendment, the employee whose work space is searched must have a subjective expectation of privacy which would be considered reasonable by society.

In the leading case of *O'Connor v. Ortega*,[2] the Supreme Court found a reasonable expectation of privacy in the desk and file cabinets of a physician whose hospital-employer accused him of work-related improprieties. The physician had exclusive use of the office, desk, and file cabinets, he had occupied his office for seventeen years, he kept personal materials there, and he did not store work-related files in his office. In addition, the hospital had no regulation or policy discouraging employees from storing personal papers and effects in their desks or file cabinets.

Lower court cases before *O'Connor* also applied the reasonable expectation test to various factual situations. For example, a reasonable expectation of privacy was found to be held by: a guidance counselor who worked in an office secured by a locked door and whose school district-owned desk contained psychological profiles and other confidential student records; a government employee who discarded papers in the wastepaper basket located next to his desk in his government office; and a police officer who stored personal belongings in his department-issued locker with his personal lock on it.

While employees do not waive their Fourth Amendment rights merely because they work for the government, "the operational realities of the workplace * * * may make some employees' expectations of privacy unreasonable when an intrusion is by a supervisor rather than a

§ 5.4

1. Mancusi v. DeForte, 392 U.S. 364, 368, 88 S.Ct. 2120, 20 L.Ed.2d 1154 (1968).

2. 480 U.S. 709, 107 S.Ct. 1492, 94 L.Ed.2d 714 (1987).

law enforcement official."[3] Thus, employee awareness of the practice of regularly conducted searches, possession of locker keys or combinations by the employer, and workplace regulations that authorize searches have been found sufficient to negate an employee's reasonable expectation of privacy. Abandonment of the property which is the object of the search or a waiver signed by the employee also may negate any privacy right in the subject of the search.

The *O'Connor* case also introduced a second factor into Fourth Amendment search analysis—whether the government employer's search of the area in which the employee has a reasonable expectation of privacy was reasonable under the circumstances. This requires a balancing of the governmental interest in the efficient and proper operation of the workplace with the employee's privacy interests. Thus, for example, the government would have a more compelling interest in searching the lockers of employees of the United States Mint than it would in a search involving clerical workers at another agency. *O'Connor* held that the same standard should be applied for investigations of employee misconduct as for noninvestigatory, routine, work-related searches. Furthermore, the Court held that searches by government employers must be justified at the time they are begun and must be reasonable in scope; reasonableness is determined by the facts leading to the inception of the search.

The purpose of a search may determine the standard of reasonableness applied. In one case a police department was investigating an officer suspected of wiretapping within the department. Because the purpose of the search was in dispute (criminal versus administrative), and because this would determine the reasonableness standard, the purpose of the search was a material fact which the jury should decide.

A heightened standard has been applied in Fourth Amendment challenges to strip searches. Correctional facility officers and other government employees with public safety duties have been found to have a diminished reasonable expectation of privacy. In *McDonell v. Hunter*,[4] the Eighth Circuit held that to determine if an individual's expectation of privacy is reasonable for Fourth Amendment purposes, there must be both an objective and a subjective expectation, and the expectation must be one which society will accept as reasonable. The court adopted a reasonable suspicion standard for strip searches of correctional officers working in correctional facilities based on the legitimate government interest in maintaining security. A "reasonable suspicion" must be based on specific objective facts and rational inferences that the employee is in possession of contraband hidden on his or her person. A government employer cannot require that its employees consent to an unreasonable search as a condition of employment.

Other searches of employee vehicles may be unconstitutional. For example, employees of a commuter railroad parked their cars in a

3. O'Connor v. Ortega, 480 U.S. 709, 717, 107 S.Ct. 1492, 94 L.Ed.2d 714 (1987).

4. 809 F.2d 1302 (8th Cir.1987).

company lot that was posted with the following sign: "Vehicles Entering or Exiting Metra Property are Subject to Search by Metra Police." One day, police officers stopped and searched employee cars as they were leaving work. Although the employees consented, they said they felt they were not free to refuse the request to search. The Seventh Circuit held that the search violated the Fourth Amendment because the employer presented no facts to justify the search. In addition, neither the sign nor the assent at the beginning of the search established valid consent.[5]

Another type of search addressed in *McDonell*, vehicle searches, was found to be much less intrusive than the search of one's person. An individual's expectation of privacy in his or her vehicle is less than in other property and the expectation of privacy as to packages or containers within a vehicle is less than that which would exist if the packages were in the employer's offices. Therefore, privately owned vehicles of correctional facility employees may be searched without cause if parked where they are accessible to inmates and if the search is done uniformly or by systematic random selection of employees whose vehicles are to be searched. Vehicles outside the confines of the institutions may be searched if inmates have unsupervised access to them or if there is a reasonable suspicion that the vehicle contains contraband.

Private Employers

Searches by private employers pose different legal issues than challenges brought under the Fourth Amendment, although privacy standards for public employees may provide a reasonable basis for the privacy expectations of private sector employees. Searches by private employers are usually challenged under state tort law, such as invasion of privacy or intentional or negligent infliction of emotional distress. For example, in one case an invasion of privacy claim was brought where the former employer of a division claims supervisor searched his locked file cabinet, desk, and personal papers. The court found for the defendants because the plaintiff failed to allege a lack of authority for the search. Similarly, the search of an employee's briefcase and random vehicle searches with prior notice of the policy were found not to meet the level of outrageousness necessary for a claim of intentional infliction of emotional distress.

In other cases, however, courts have held that employer searches constituted invasion of privacy. For example, in one case the court held that mere suspicion that another employee had stolen watches or that unidentified employees may have stolen price-marking guns was found insufficient to justify the employer's search of the employee's locked locker and her personal possessions without her consent. In another case, the search of an employee's motel room was held to be an invasion of privacy.

Searches of one's person may raise other issues. For example, in one case a liquor distiller began having security guards conduct pat-down

---

5. McGann v. Northeast Ill. Reg. Commuter R.R., 8 F.3d 1174 (7th Cir.1993).

searches of employees as they left the plant to prevent the theft of tools and small bottles of liquor ("miniatures"). When some of the 500 male workers and their wives objected to a woman guard conducting the pat-down searches, she was transferred and replaced with a male guard. According to the court, her transfer did not violate Title VII.[6]

Strip searches are one of the most intrusive types of searches. In *Bodewig v. K–Mart, Inc.*,[7] an Oregon court found outrageous conduct where a store manager, after concluding that the plaintiff, a part-time checker, did not take a customer's money, nevertheless forced her to submit to a strip search to appease the customer, who was permitted to witness the search. The court found that the manager's conduct was unacceptable by society's standards and showed complete disregard for any subsequent effect on the plaintiff. Because a special relationship was found to exist in the employer-employee context, the conduct need not be deliberate, but only socially intolerable and reckless.

§ 5.5 Surveillance—Visual, Audio, and Video

An emerging issue in employment law involves the surveillance of employees in the workplace by their employers. Workplace surveillance takes various forms, such as using one-way mirrors, surveillance cameras, listening devices, and monitoring of phone conversations.

Federal Law

Most of the current litigation has focused on the monitoring of employee telephone conversations by private or public employees. This is an area specifically covered by federal statute. Title III of the Omnibus Crime Control and Safe Streets Act of 1968[1] protects both wire and oral communication from interception by employers. The statute has two exceptions, which allow monitoring: (1) if it is performed in the ordinary course of business, either in any business or by a telephone service provider, or by a law enforcement officer; and (2) if one party consents or is the interceptor. The law requires that the plaintiff have a reasonable expectation of privacy, defined by the courts as a subjectively held expectation which society would be prepared to regard as reasonable under the circumstances.

Under the statute, "any person whose wire, oral, or electronic communication is intercepted, disclosed, or intentionally used in violation of" the law may recover in an action for civil damages. Appropriate relief includes equitable or declaratory relief; actual, statutory, and punitive damages; and attorney fees and litigation costs. If the conduct is for a tortious or illegal purpose or for purposes of direct or indirect

---

6. Sutton v. National Distillers Prods. Co., 445 F.Supp. 1319 (S.D.Ohio 1978), affirmed, 628 F.2d 936 (6th Cir.1980).

7. 54 Or.App. 480, 635 P.2d 657 (1981).

§ 5.5

1. 18 U.S.C.A. §§ 2510–2521. Title III of the Omnibus Crime Control and Safe

Streets Act of 1968 was amended and retitled by Title I of the Electronic Communications Privacy Act of 1996, P.L. 104–104, 104th Cong., 2d Sess. (1996).

commercial advantage, damages are the greater of the sum of the actual damages suffered by the plaintiff and any profits made by the violator or the statutory damages of between $100 a day for each violation or $10,000. If the conduct is not for one of the purposes described above, the first violation damages are the greater of the plaintiff's actual damages and the statutory damages of between $50 and $500. For the second violation, damages are the greater of the plaintiff's actual damages and the statutory damages of between $100 and $1,000. The statute of limitations is two years.

In *Simmons v. Southwestern Bell Telephone Co.*,[2] the plaintiff operated a phone company "testdesk" from which personal phone calls were not permitted. The company provided an unmonitored phone line for personal use and warned the employee repeatedly about use of the testdesk for personal calls. The employee also knew that the testdesk lines were monitored. These facts led the court to conclude that the plaintiff had no reasonable expectation of privacy with regard to the testdesk lines and therefore there was no violation of the statute.

Under the Omnibus Act, a telephone extension used without authorization or consent to surreptitiously record a private conversation is not used in the "ordinary course of business." Both "sporadic illegal eavesdropping" and indiscriminate wiretapping of private telephone conversations have been held to violate the statute. On the other hand, monitoring of employee phone calls dealing with the general public has been held to fall within the "extension telephone exception" where the employees had advance knowledge of the monitoring and because there was a legitimate business purpose for the practice.

In *Deal v. Spears*,[3] the owners of a small liquor store, in attempting to discover whether an employee played a role in a recent burglary, secretly recorded and listened to more than twenty-two hours of employee phone calls. Many of the calls were sexually provocative and involved an extramarital affair. When the recording was finally used to justify the discharge of an employee for selling a keg of beer to a friend at cost, the two employees whose calls were taped sued the store owners. The Eighth Circuit affirmed an award for the plaintiffs and rejected the owner's claim that the recordings were made in the "ordinary course of business."

In *Briggs v. American Air Filter Co.*,[4] the court addressed the issue of consent to monitoring by one of the parties to the call. The court noted that nonconsensual interception within the "ordinary course of business" is lawful. There was no statutory violation because the call was business-related and not personal, the act of listening-in was limited in purpose and time (just long enough to determine if business matters

2.   452 F.Supp. 392 (W.D.Okl.1978), affirmed, 611 F.2d 342 (10th Cir.1979).

3.   980 F.2d 1153 (8th Cir.1992).

4.   630 F.2d 414 (5th Cir.1980).

were being discussed), and because the act of listening-in was not part of a general practice of surreptitious monitoring.

Briggs also raises the related issue of what determines whether a telephone conversation is business or personal. The Eleventh Circuit has held that a personal call may not be intercepted in the ordinary course of business, except to the extent necessary to guard against unauthorized use of the telephone or to determine whether a call is of a business or personal nature.[5] Thus, interception of an employee's personal phone conversation with a friend regarding the employee's job interview with another company was not in the ordinary course of business. The conversation was personal because although the company was interested in whether its employee would be leaving, she was an at-will employee free to resign and interview with any company at any time. A contrary result was reached where a business call was between two employees, occurred during office hours, was over a specialized phone extension, and concerned unflattering remarks about supervisory employees in their capacities as supervisors.[6] The court concluded that the call was business-related and therefore could be monitored.

Prior consent is another exception that may make employer monitoring of personal phone calls permissible. The knowledge of monitoring capability alone, however, does not constitute implied consent. Also, the consent must extend to the specific nature of the call. For example, where an employee did not consent to general monitoring but only to the monitoring of sales calls, the asserted consent was ineffective. The court concluded that consent can be limited and that the presence of a general monitoring policy does not submit the employee to unlimited surveillance.

The Omnibus Act contains a very specific exception for an investigative or law enforcement officer in the ordinary course of duties. Thus, there was no violation of the Act for a police department to monitor the calls of a police officer who was using a regularly recorded police telephone line to place a personal call to his lover. The court stated that Congress did not intend the Act to apply to routine recording of emergency and investigative calls as an integral part of a police telephone system. On the other hand, the Sixth Circuit held that the police department was not acting in the ordinary course of duty when it "tapped" a pager provided by the department to the officer. The department did not routinely monitor pagers and did not provide notice of possible monitoring.

In a case involving the monitoring of a two-way radio system for communication between school bus drivers and their dispatchers, the court said that a person broadcasting by radio did not have a reasonable expectation of privacy under the Act because anyone with a radio could monitor the communications. In a case involving the surreptitious cassette recording of an argument between the plaintiff and his foreman,

---

5. Watkins v. L.M. Berry & Co., 704 F.2d 577 (11th Cir.1983).

6. Epps v. St. Mary's Hosp. of Athens, Inc., 802 F.2d 412 (11th Cir.1986).

the court held that there was no reasonable expectation of privacy under the Act because the argument took place in a small shop with no walls and other workers could enter and leave the area freely. Industry practice, the employee's true expectations, and the nature of the communications will be considered in determining whether the expectation of privacy was reasonable.

State Law

Nearly forty states protect privacy rights in personal communications by statute, many of which are based on the federal statute. Some states protect privacy rights in the state constitution, usually by creating a general right to privacy. A few states specifically protect the privacy of communications. For example, Connecticut law prohibits "an electronic surveillance device or system, including but not limited to the recording of sound or voice or a closed circuit television system, or any combination thereof, for the purpose of recording or monitoring the activities of [his] employees, video in areas designed for the health or personal comfort of employees or for safeguarding of their possessions, such as rest rooms, locker rooms or lounges."[7]

Some states require the consent of all parties to a conversation before it may be recorded; others require consent by only one of the parties. California prohibits monitoring without a beeptone or verbal announcement.

Electronic surveillance in the workplace also may constitute common law invasion of privacy. For example, an employer was liable for invasion of privacy where a supervisor concealed an electronic listening device in the ceiling of an employee's office and monitored her private conversations for four years.

The First Circuit has held that there was no violation of the Fourth Amendment for a quasi-public telephone company to monitor employee work stations continuously by using unconcealed video cameras not equipped with microphones. According to the court, "[t]he mere fact that the observation is accomplished by a video camera rather than the naked eye, and recorded on film rather than in a supervisor's memory, does not transmogrify a constitutionally innocent act into a constitutionally forbidden one."[8]

5.6   Surveillance—Computer

A variety of new computer technologies have enabled employers to monitor the activities of employees. In general, there have been few legislative or case law restrictions, although computer monitoring is certain to be an area of increasing activity in the future.

Employers use computers to monitor employee productivity in numerous ways. For example, computers can monitor the number of

---

7. Conn. Gen. Stat. § 31–48B.

8. Vega–Rodriguez v. Puerto Rico Tel. Co., 110 F.3d 174, 181 (1st Cir.1997) (footnote omitted).

keystrokes of clerical employees and the total number of reservations booked by travel industry personnel. Computers can monitor the pace of sales of cashiers. Using global positioning systems, they can even track the location and speed of delivery drivers and note all the unscheduled and personal stops being made. Despite occasional calls to limit employer prerogatives in this area, at least in the nonunion workplace, employers have wide discretion.

Thus far, most of the litigation has involved employer access to employee computers and e-mail, and monitoring of employee use of the Internet. Overwhelmingly, the courts have held that employees have no reasonable expectation of privacy in computers provided by employers for exclusive use at work. Thus, for example, there was no liability where a state employer obtained a list from the employee's computer and learned that the employee had unauthorized programs that he was using for personal business on state time, and where the employer accessed an employee's e-mail messages transmitted over the Internet.

An employer's case is even stronger where policies are disclosed to employees and acknowledged by the employee on logging in, where the employer policy reserved ownership of computer data, and where the policy of monitoring Internet activity was clearly shared with employees. A former state employee, however, had a reasonable expectation of privacy in private files stored on his work computer where employees were permitted to place private information secured by a password.

On the other hand, employees who use the Internet to criticize their employers may be subject to employer sanctions. In *Konop v. Hawaiian Airlines, Inc.*,[1] an airline pilot maintained a secure website where he posted bulletins critical of his employer, employer's officers, and union. He was suspended after his employer's vice president gained unauthorized access to the site under false pretenses and disclosed its contents. The Ninth Circuit held that the employer's action did not violate the Wiretap Act because there was no "interception" during transmission.

§ 5.7   Interrogation

An employee suspected of stealing or other serious misconduct frequently will be brought in for questioning by a manager, supervisor, or security guard as part of an internal investigation. Employers have a privilege to conduct investigations and there is no common law right to refuse to participate in an interrogation or to insist upon having one's attorney present. Although union employees have the right to have a representative present at a disciplinary interview, the right has not been extended to nonunion employees.

If an interrogation is conducted in an unreasonable manner, the employee may have an action in tort. The most frequently alleged torts

---

§ 5.6

1. 302 F.3d 868 (9th Cir. 2002), cert. denied, 537 U.S. 1193, 123 S.Ct. 1292, 154 L.Ed.2d 1028 (2003).

are false imprisonment, intentional infliction of emotional distress, invasion of privacy, and defamation.

False Imprisonment

False imprisonment is usually the most serious tort arising from an interrogation. It occurs when the employer or its representative intentionally confines the employee within a fixed area. For example, in one case, while accusing the plaintiff of stealing, the defendant repeatedly put his hands on the plaintiff's shoulders to restrain her when she rose in an attempt to leave the room. Threats made during the course of the interrogation and excessively long interrogations are also factors accounting for liability.

If the interrogation is conducted in a generally reasonable manner, then there will be no liability. For example, the defendants have prevailed in false imprisonment cases where the questioning was done in a reasonable manner, where the plaintiff showed no apprehension or fear, where the employee was questioned during business hours in familiar surroundings, and where the defendant was acting in good faith.

Frequently, the employer's representative will tell the employee being interrogated that discharge will result if he or she leaves the room. If the employee remains to keep his or her job or to "clear" his or her name, has the employee been "confined" by the employer sufficiently to establish false imprisonment? The courts are in agreement that this "compulsion" is inadequate to establish false imprisonment. Even a threat to call the police if the employee does not remain has been insufficient to establish false imprisonment.

Another issue is whether a "shopkeeper's privilege" statute, which shields merchants from liability for detaining and interrogating individuals suspected of shoplifting, applies to the detention of employees. At least one court held that it did not apply, and even if it did, it did not protect the defendant's conduct consisting of shouting at the employee in a four-hour interrogation and forcing her to admit to a crime she did not commit.

Because false imprisonment is an intentional tort, most courts will not bar a claim for false imprisonment by applying the exclusive remedy provisions of workers' compensation.

Intentional Infliction of Emotional Distress

Unreasonable employer interrogation also has been alleged to constitute intentional infliction of emotional distress. The employee must prove that the employer intentionally or recklessly engaged in conduct "so outrageous in character and extreme in degree as to go beyond all bounds of decency."[1] The employer-employee relationship establishes a clear duty not to engage in such behavior. The more difficult question is

§ 5.7

1. National Loss Control Serv. Corp. v. Dotti, 126 Ill.App.3d 804, 81 Ill.Dec. 815, 467 N.E.2d 937, 942 (1984).

determining what type of employer conduct is sufficiently outrageous to establish liability. For example, liability was found where the defendant intended to frighten the plaintiff by raising his voice, pounding his fist on the table, and threatening to have her arrested, but there was no liability where the interrogation lasted only 30 minutes and was done in a pleasant voice.

Factors considered by the courts in similar cases include the length of the interrogation, whether the employee was paid for the time spent in the interrogation, whether the employer's conduct during the interrogation was reasonable, and whether the employer had a good faith belief in the employee's guilt. Often, the plaintiff must meet a stringent burden of proof to show that the defendant's actions were so "terrifying or insulting as naturally to humiliate, embarrass, or frighten the plaintiff."[2] If the employer acts in good faith, or if the plaintiff failed to request that the interview be terminated, or if the plaintiff was rude to the interviewer as well, then the claim has failed.

Regardless of the severity of the standard, unfortunately, a few employers have exceeded it. Thus, in one case, while interrogating a female manager, one of the employer's representatives left his pants unzipped, the employee was laughed at and accused of lying, she was not permitted to smoke or eat, she was accused of having a lesbian affair with a coworker, and she was not permitted to leave until she signed a statement.[3] In another case, store security officers questioned a female sales representative in a small, windowless room for over three hours, during which time she was led to believe that she was not free to leave.[4]

In deciding whether the defendant's conduct is sufficiently outrageous, the courts consider whether it would be considered extreme and outrageous by the plaintiff of ordinary sensitivities—unless the defendant knew that the plaintiff was a person of special sensitivities. For example, in one case the employer knew that the employee was emotionally frail. Nevertheless, the employee was interrogated most of the day at thirty-minute intervals without a lunch break, and he was cursed at, accused of stealing, threatened with arrest, and denied access to and use of his prescription tranquilizer.[5]

A part of the plaintiff's prima facie case is establishing that the defendant's conduct caused the plaintiff to suffer severe emotional distress. In one case, the plaintiff failed to prove emotional distress where her physical symptoms were associated with a preexisting medical condition and she failed to see her physician immediately after the incident.

Defamation

Defamatory accusations made by a representative of the employer to the employee are generally not actionable because there is no publication

---

2. Sossenko v. Michelin Tire Corp., 172 Ga.App. 771, 324 S.E.2d 593 (1984).

3. Mansfield v. American Tel. & Tel. Corp., 747 F.Supp. 1329 (W.D.Ark.1990).

4. Smithson v. Nordstrom, Inc., 63 Or. App. 423, 664 P.2d 1119 (1983).

5. See Tandy Corp. v. Bone, 283 Ark. 399, 678 S.W.2d 312 (1984).

to a third party and the communication may be privileged. Occasionally, however, the interrogation is conducted in such an unreasonable manner that an action for defamation may lie. For example, in one case, the employer's security guards interrogated the employee in a glass-enclosed guardhouse at the plant gate through which numerous employees passed as they entered or left the large plant. Even though none of the passers-by could hear what was being said, the court held that an action for slander would lie because of the clear nonverbal implication that the employee had engaged in some serious wrongdoing.[6]

Invasion of Privacy

The tort of invasion of privacy has been used infrequently in the context of interrogations, although probing into irrelevant personal matters could certainly be considered "intrusion." In one case, the court held that the distribution of a confession signed after an interrogation was privileged and therefore it was not an invasion of privacy.

§ 5.8 Employment Records

Both personnel files and employee medical records make up employment records. Statutory and case law involving employment records has centered around three factual situations. First, an employee may seek access to his or her own records. This is usually pursuant to a state statute. Second, a third party may seek access to an employee's records. Examples of third parties include journalists, unions, co-employees, attorneys, plaintiffs in personal injury actions against the employer, and citizen groups. Third, the employee may claim that improper information is contained in his or her employment records or that the contents of the records have been wrongfully disseminated. Actions for negligent maintenance of employment records, defamation, and invasion of privacy have been brought based on this third category.

Legislation has been enacted to regulate various aspects of employment records. Fourteen states have laws giving public and private sector employees access to their own personnel files, two states allow access only to private employees, and seven states allow access only to public employees. These laws usually grant an employee "reasonable" access to his or her own records, but employers may be able to limit the frequency of access to the records. Private sector employees in nine states can request that inaccurate information be expunged from their personnel file, and if there is a dispute about the accuracy of the information, employees may write an explanatory letter which is then included in the file and sent out any time the disputed information is requested. A Minnesota law requires an employer to provide a copy of a personnel record to an employee after the employee reviews his or her record and files a written request.

---

6. General Motors Corp. v. Piskor, 281 Md. 627, 381 A.2d 16 (1977).

Access to one's own file is generally limited by the type of information contained in the file. In *Board of Trustees v. Superior Court*,[1] a physician sought access to his own personnel, tenure, and promotion files. The court balanced the physician's right of access to private information about himself with the rights of the individuals whose confidential letters of reference were in the requested files. A California statute allowed an employee access to his own personnel file, excluding letters of reference. The court found no compelling state purpose to maintain the confidentiality of the information contained in the letters, but required that the letters be disclosed with identifying information deleted to maintain the rights of privacy of those who had furnished the information.

The rights of third parties to access the personnel files of federal employees is regulated by the Freedom of Information Act and the Privacy Act. Virtually all of the states have some type of public records statute using language similar to that of the Privacy Act, and regulate access to the files of state or other public employees. Some states regulate access to employee files of specific public or private employees, including police officers and firefighters, employees of licensed hospitals, "peace officers," personnel in hospitals for the mentally disordered, and teachers. Public records statutes usually limit access to personnel files of public employees if that access would constitute an "unwarranted invasion of personal privacy," and require balancing the public's right to government information with the employee's right of privacy.

In *Ollie v. Highland School District No. 203*,[2] a discharged school library aide sought access to information contained in coworkers' personnel files to support her claim that she had been subject to harsher treatment. Under the state's public disclosure act, public records were exempt from disclosure if they were "personal information, maintained for employees, [and] disclosure * * * would violate the employee's right to privacy." The court held that information contained in personnel evaluations and personnel records was privileged, but information about public, on-duty job performances could be disclosed if the employees' names and identifying information were removed to protect their privacy.

This method of deleting information to maintain privacy was discussed in *Department of the Air Force v. Rose*,[3] in which the United States Supreme Court interpreted the section of the Privacy Act dealing with personnel files. The Supreme Court stated that courts would have to examine any records to which access was requested and require disclosure of information to which the exemption would not apply.

The "routine use" exception of the Privacy Act has been held to justify the disclosure of confidential medical information to a union representative, where the employee's mental health was a central issue

§ 5.8

1. 119 Cal.App.3d 516, 174 Cal.Rptr. 160 (1981).

2. 50 Wash.App. 639, 749 P.2d 757, review denied, 110 Wash.2d 1040 (1988).

3. 425 U.S. 352, 96 S.Ct. 1592, 48 L.Ed.2d 11 (1976).

in deciding whether to place the employee on an enforced leave of absence.

The tort of negligent maintenance of employment records has been asserted for the improper inclusion and dissemination of information in personnel files. In *Quinones v. United States*,[4] the Third Circuit recognized such an action where an individual was rejected for employment when his former employer told prospective employers that the individual was unfit for employment, despite his exemplary record. The essence of the claim is that the employer breached a duty to the employee of maintaining the records in a reasonable manner, and it is not based on whether information within the files is inaccurate. Nevertheless, even with negligent methods of recordkeeping, unless the information were inaccurate or wrongly disseminated, the employee would suffer no damages. Thus, the basis of the action is related to defamation. It has not been asserted in many other reported cases. Although it has been followed in a district court case within the Third Circuit, it has been rejected by the other courts in which it has been asserted.

Laws enacted in five states give employees a right of access to some or all of their medical records within the possession of their employer. Certain medical information, however, may be withheld if, in the opinion of the employer's physician, it would be injurious to the health of the employee. In addition, under many workers' compensation laws, employees have a right of access to any physician report prepared for workers' compensation purposes. Perhaps the most sweeping right of access for employees to their medical records is contained in a regulation issued pursuant to the Occupational Safety and Health Act.

§ 5.9 Freedom of Expression

Employers have long been interested in regulating what employees say, where they say it, and to whom they say it. Where there is a legitimate basis for the employers' concerns, such as trade secret disclosures, the law has sanctioned employer regulation of employee expression. Where the employers' interests are less direct, however, the law has sometimes granted a remedy to employees whose freedom of expression has been limited. As with many of the conditions of employment explored in this chapter, the most important consideration in analyzing the rights of employees is whether the employment at issue is public or private.

Public Employment

Public employee freedom of expression is protected by the First Amendment. In *Pickering v. Board of Education*,[1] the Supreme Court established a three-part test to determine whether the discharge of a

---

4. 492 F.2d 1269 (3d Cir.1974).

§ 5.9
1. 391 U.S. 563, 88 S.Ct. 1731, 20 L.Ed.2d 811 (1968).

public employee was made on the basis of protected speech. First, the employee must be speaking on a matter of public concern. Second, the court must balance the interests of the employee, as a citizen, in commenting on matters of public concern against the government employer's interest in running an efficient operation. Third, the employee's protected conduct must be a motivating factor in the government employer's decision to discharge. The third element, causation, is a question for the trier of fact only if the court has resolved the first two elements in favor of the employee.

The first issue, whether the speech addresses a matter of public concern, is evaluated according to the "content, form, and context of the statement." The manner, time, and place of the statement is very important. The burden is on the employee to show that the speech deserves First Amendment protection. Although the Supreme Court has not defined "public concern," statements addressing matters of public concern tend to fall within certain categories. These include speech related to broad social or policy issues or allegations of discrimination, inefficiency, or improprieties by a government office. These types of statements have been held to be matters of public concern.

On the other hand, mundane employment grievances relating primarily to the individual employee have been held not to be matters of public concern. Some examples include individual job evaluations, complaints about individual working conditions, and employer grooming requirements.

Because these general distinctions are not always easy to apply to the wide range of cases, the Supreme Court has said that the context of the statement is important. If a statement is made in the course of an ongoing debate about public issues, such as in testimony before the legislature or in comments to the news media, then the speech is more likely to be considered to involve a matter of public concern. On the other hand, the Eleventh Circuit upheld the dismissal of a police officer's claim that we was retaliated against in violation of the First Amendment when he was subjected to disciplinary action after testifying against a fellow officer in a criminal case.

If employee speech is found to involve a matter of public concern, then the *Pickering* balance test is applied. The test is an attempt to balance the employee's interest in speaking on matters of public concern with the government employer's interest in promoting workplace efficiency. The Court in *Pickering* suggested seven factors to consider: (1) maintenance of discipline by immediate superiors; (2) preservation of harmony among coworkers; (3) maintenance of personal loyalty and confidence when necessary to the proper functioning of a close working relationship; (4) maintenance of the employee's proper performance of daily duties; (5) public impact of the statement; (6) impact of the statement on the operation of the government entity; and (7) the existence or nonexistence of an issue of legitimate public concern.

In *Connick v. Myers*,[2] the Supreme Court added three additional factors to consider: (1) whether the speaker was in a position in which the need for confidentiality was so great as to justify dismissal for even completely accurate public statements; (2) whether narrowly drawn grievance procedures required submission of complaints about the operation of the agency to superiors for action prior to taking complaints to the public; and (3) whether a statement that was knowingly or recklessly false would still be protected by the First Amendment.

Not surprisingly, application of these myriad factors has proven to be difficult. For example, *Rankin v. McPherson*[3] involved a nineteen year-old, probationary, clerical employee with the title of "deputy constable," who worked in a room where there was no public access in the Harris County, Texas constable's office. On March 30, 1981, upon hearing a radio report that there had been an attempt to assassinate President Reagan, the plaintiff told a coworker, who was her boyfriend, "If they go for him again, I hope they get him." After another employee overheard the remark, she was summoned into the constable's office and fired.

The Supreme Court, five-to-four, held that the employee's First Amendment rights outweighed the employer's interests. The majority relied on the fact that the employee served no confidential, policymaking, or public contact role; the employee was not a peace officer, did not wear a uniform, and was not authorized to make arrests or carry a weapon; and the statement was made in a private conversation in an area where the public did not have access. The dissent challenged whether a distinction should be drawn between nonpolicymaking and policymaking employees. It further argued that the need to maintain esprit de corps and public image of a law enforcement agency outweighed the employee's First Amendment freedom of expression. Because of the closeness of the case and the changes in Court composition, it is hard to predict how a comparably close case would be decided today.

In *Waters v. Churchill*,[4] a nurse working at a public hospital was fired because of statements made to coworkers during a dinner break that were critical of the hospital. It was disputed whether the statements were "disruptive." The district court granted summary judgment for the hospital, but the Seventh Circuit reversed. The Supreme Court, seven-to-two, vacated the judgment and remanded the case for trial. Writing for a four-justice plurality, Justice O'Connor, relying on *Connick*, held that the government's interests are greater when it acts as an employer than when it acts as a sovereign. Therefore, it may restrict more of employee speech in the interest of efficiency. In reviewing the facts, the key is what the employer reasonably believed was said, rather than what the trier of fact ultimately determines was said. In dissent, Justices Stevens

2.　461 U.S. 138, 103 S.Ct. 1684, 75 L.Ed.2d 708 (1983).

3.　483 U.S. 378, 107 S.Ct. 2891, 97 L.Ed.2d 315 (1987).

4.　511 U.S. 661, 114 S.Ct. 1878, 128 L.Ed.2d 686 (1994).

and Blackmun argued that nondisruptive speech on a matter of public concern is protected, and whether it is protected should not turn on whether the employer believed the speech was protected.

Although there was little question in *Rankin* that the discharge was based on the speech in question, the third part of the *Pickering* test requires that the court determine that the protected activity was a motivating factor in the action of the public employer. In *Mount Healthy City School District Board of Education v. Doyle*,[5] the Supreme Court enunciated a test which "protects against the invasion of constitutional rights without commanding undesirable consequences not necessary to the assurance of those rights."[6] The test formulated by the Court places the initial burden of proving causation on the employee, who must show that the conduct was a "motivating" or "substantial" factor in the termination of employment. Once the employee has carried that burden, the employer must show by a preponderance of the evidence that the discharge would have occurred even if the protected conduct had not occurred. The policy behind this test is to keep an employee who would not otherwise have been retained from being put in a better position merely because the employee also engaged in constitutionally protected conduct.

The Supreme Court also has addressed the issue of remedies for First Amendment claims by federal employees. In *Bush v. Lucas*,[7] an aerospace engineer was demoted for making a statement to the news media which was highly critical of the space center where he worked. The Court refused to create an individual damage remedy against the federal government for First Amendment violations and held that the remedial system overseen by the Civil Service Commission was adequate. Employees of state and local governments do, however, have a cause of action for damages under 42 U.S.C.A. § 1983. Federal and state laws also prohibit retaliation against government employees who engage in whistleblowing.

Freedom of expression also may involve an employee's writings as well as reading materials permitted on employer property. With regard to the former, an assistant state's attorney withstood a motion to dismiss his claim that he was discharged for writing a novel about the criminal justice system. In another case, a police officer, who was an outspoken critic of gun control laws, was lawfully discharged for publicizing his status as a law enforcement officer to lend credibility to his position.

With regard to reading material, in an attempt to combat hostile environment gender discrimination, Los Angeles County adopted a policy that banned the private reading of *Playboy* by firefighters in county fire stations. A district court enjoined the policy as needlessly intruding on the First Amendment rights of off-duty employees.[8]

---

5. 429 U.S. 274, 97 S.Ct. 568, 50 L.Ed.2d 471 (1977).

6. 429 U.S. at 287, 97 S.Ct. at 576.

7. 462 U.S. 367, 103 S.Ct. 2404, 76 L.Ed.2d 648 (1983).

8. Johnson v. County of Los Angeles Fire Dep't, 865 F.Supp. 1430 (C.D.Cal. 1994).

Most courts to consider the issue have held that in cases involving an employee's petition for the redress of girevances, the First Amendment standard is the same as in cases alleging a "mere" free speech violation. In particular, for protection, the petition must involve a matter of public concern.

Private Employment

Because direct federal constitutional protection is limited to governmental action, private sector employees have fewer rights to express their opinions. Potentially, the most likely basis for a sweeping expansion of the right to freedom of expression for private sector employees would be through an expansion of the public policy exception to the at will rule. In a leading but still singular case, *Novosel v. Nationwide Insurance Co.*,[9] a district claims manager for an insurance company was discharged for refusing to lobby the Pennsylvania legislature in opposition to a "no fault" insurance bill under consideration. The Third Circuit concluded that concern for the rights of political expression and association is sufficient to state a public policy under Pennsylvania law. The case was remanded for application of balancing considerations based on *Pickering* and later cases. A related public policy argument also may be based on state constitutional provisions which protect freedom of expression. In addition, some employee speech may constitute "opposition" activity, which is protected under the antiretaliation provisions of Title VII and other civil rights statutes.

In evaluating freedom of expression claims in the private sector, the courts often differentiate between internal and external speech. Statements by employees, often complaints, made within the workplace are generally afforded less protection by the courts. Thus, for example, discharges have been upheld where employees complained about internal accounting practices, inadequate service to customers, and defective products. By contrast, external speech is much more likely to be protected under either whistleblowing laws or common law. This includes statements to government agencies, to the news media, and in public fora.

The discharge of an employee who refused to remove two confederate flag stickers from his tool box has been held not to violate the First Amendment. Similarly, a Connecticut law, prohibiting the discharge of private sector employees in retaliation for exercising their First Amendment rights, was held not to apply to the discharge of an employee who refused to display at his work station an American flag distributed by his employer.

Otherwise protected employee speech may lose its protection if it is made in an unreasonable time, place, or manner. For example, discharges have been upheld where an employee stood in front of the employer's customer's place of business and expressed his dissatisfaction with the customer's product and service and where a hospital employee discussed

---

9.   721 F.2d 894 (3d Cir.1983).

incidents of abuse and improper conduct by hospital employees with her taxi driver, her neighbor, and the newspaper, but later denied discussing the incidents.

Some employers prohibit employees from speaking any language other than English while at work. Although the issue is far from settled, a divided Ninth Circuit upheld such a policy. It rejected the argument that it constituted national origin discrimination and was not justified by any valid business concerns.

§ 5.10 Freedom of Association

The First Amendment protects public sector employees from interference with their right of association outside the workplace. "A fundamental proposition in our constitutional jurisprudence is that government employment may not be conditioned upon a relinquishment of a constitutional right, including the rights to speech and association guaranteed under the First Amendment."[1] While the freedom of association was once held only to apply to the advancing of political beliefs, the concept now includes the right to meet with others and does not apply merely to an association for the advancing of common beliefs.

Public Employees

In *Shelton v. Tucker,*[2] the Supreme Court declared unconstitutional an Arkansas statute which conditioned the employment of every teacher in a state-supported school or college on the annual filing of an affidavit listing, without limitation, every organization to which the teacher belonged or regularly contributed money over the previous five years. While conceding that fitness for teaching depends on many factors, including conduct outside the classroom, the Court stated that to compel a teacher to list every organization with which he or she associates is a clear violation of the freedom of association.

The use of questionnaires by government employers also has been a source of litigation. In *American Federation of Government Employees v. Schlesinger,*[3] employees of the Department of Energy challenged a mandatory questionnaire which required them to divulge employment and financial interests, creditors, and interests in real property owned by them, their spouses, and dependents. The court found that the form also would require an employee to reveal whether the employee or a family member was "an official or adviser of his church, his fraternity, his school, any charity, or almost any cause, whether it be concerned with some aspect of the environment, alcohol, abortion, or union activity."[4] The court stated that while some intrusion upon an employee's privacy will be tolerated when it is relevant to the purpose or function of the

§ 5.10

1. Wilson v. Taylor, 658 F.2d 1021, 1027 (5th Cir.1981).

2. 364 U.S. 479, 81 S.Ct. 247, 5 L.Ed.2d 231 (1960).

3. 443 F.Supp. 431 (D.D.C.1978).

4. Id. at 433.

governmental agency, this sort of broad-sweeping invasion should not be allowed.

In another questionnaire case, an employee who worked as an administrator in a city alternative sentencing program was terminated for her failure to complete a questionnaire which asked about arrests and convictions of the employee or immediate family members, previous sexual relations with a member of the same sex, the details of previous marriages, divorces, and annulments, and all outstanding debts or adverse judgments.[5] The Fourth Circuit upheld dismissal of the employee's suit on the ground that the information was either public information or not constitutionally protected. The court further held that the employer had a legitimate interest in the information and that it took adequate steps to prevent further disclosure. In effect, the court placed the burden on the employee to show that the intrusion was unreasonable rather placing the burden on the government agency to show that the government's need for the information contained in the questionnaire outweighed the individual's right of association.

The choice of marriage partner also may implicate the freedom of association. For example, the Sixth Circuit held that a school board employee made out a prima facie case of a constitutional violation by alleging that her discharge was the result of her marriage to a person with whom the superintendent had a disagreement.[6] The employee had a liberty interest in not being denied employment for exercising her First Amendment right to freedom of association.

The Fourth Circuit, however, upheld a municipal ordinance barring spouses from working in the same department or having supervisory authority over each other because it is rationally related to the government interest of reducing conflicts of interest and in promoting workplace harmony.[7]

Private Employees

Some types of associations may be protected by civil rights statutes. For example, under Title VII it is unlawful for an employer to discriminate against an applicant or employee because the individual is married to or associates with members of another racial, religious, or ethnic group. To be protected under Title VII, however, a religious association must be bona fide. For example, a district court rejected the argument that discharging an employee because he belonged to the Ku Klux Klan was religious discrimination under Title VII. The court ruled that the Klan is a political and social organization and is not a religion for purposes of Title VII.

In addition to Title VII, section 102(b)(4) of the Americans with Disabilities Act expressly includes within the definition of unlawful

---

5. Walls v. Petersburg, 895 F.2d 188 (4th Cir.1990).

6. Adkins v. Board of Educ., 982 F.2d 952 (6th Cir.1993).

7. Waters v. Gaston County, 57 F.3d 422 (4th Cir.1995).

discrimination "excluding or otherwise denying equal jobs or benefits to a qualified individual because of the known disability of an individual with whom the qualified individual is known to have a relationship or association." The purpose of the provision was to prohibit discrimination against family members and friends of people with AIDS, but it has broader applicability, including prohibiting discrimination against individuals who have a spouse or child with a chronic illness.

The right of association has not yet been afforded much recognition in common law actions by at-will employees.

In *McCloud v. Testa*,[8] the Sixth Circuit held that the First Amendment protects public employees against adverse employment actions taken by members of rival factions of the *same* political party, even if the factional differences are non-ideological. For example, a Maryland criminal statute provides: "A person or group may not engage in an act or conduct solely to coerce or intimidate another person to contribute or donate money, goods, materials, or services to a social, economic, or political association or organization." An employee who was terminated for refusing to make a contribution to the United Way brought a wrongful discharge action in which she alleged that her employer was in violation of the Maryland statute on contributions and therefore that her discharge violated public policy. The Maryland Court of Appeals upheld the discharge on the ground that the United Way was not a social or economic organization and therefore the discharge did not violate the statute or public policy.[9]

In other private sector cases employers have been given discretion in making decisions which affect the association of employees. For example, courts have: upheld the discharge of an employee because of a relationship with a subordinate; held that discharge for fraternizing with a fellow employee did not violate freedom of association; held that an anti-nepotism policy did not breach contractual rights nor infringe upon the right to marry; and held that firing an employee for dating a coworker did not constitute marital status discrimination.

§ 5.11 Political Activity

Public Employees

Employee political activity is subject to constitutional protection and statutory regulation. Most of the leading cases involve public sector employees, especially those who have been dismissed because of political patronage. In *Elrod v. Burns*,[1] the Supreme Court reiterated the constitutional rule that a public employee may not be excluded from employment on the basis of political affiliation unless the affiliation is with a subversive organization. The Court found that the state interest in political patronage (preservation of the two-party political system) did

---

8. 97 F.3d 1536 (6th Cir.1996).   **§ 5.11**

9. Ball v. United Parcel Serv., 325 Md.   **1.** 427 U.S. 347, 96 S.Ct. 2673, 49
652, 602 A.2d 1176 (1992).   L.Ed.2d 547 (1976).

not outweigh the freedoms of belief and association upon which the system infringed.

> Patronage, therefore, to the extent it compels or restrains belief and association, is inimical to the process which undergirds our system of government and is "at war with the deeper traditions of democracy embodied in the First Amendment."[2]

Individuals in policymaking positions, however, may be dismissed based on political affiliation because the use of these positions to sabotage the policies of the opposing party would defeat the purpose of representative government.

Based on *Elrod,* it is important to determine whether an employee occupies a policymaking position. A policymaker is an employee whose responsibilities are "not well defined or are of broad scope," or one who "acts as an adviser or formulates plans for the implementation of broad goals."[3] Confidentiality is an indicator of a policymaking position only when the employee obtains access to information of partisan political importance, not information relating only to the needs of individual clients. The Fifth Circuit, in finding that a school superintendent occupied a policymaker position, listed the following relevant factors to be considered: a general statement of responsibilities; a position demanding more than ministerial competence; discretion in performing duties which is not severely limited by statute, regulation, or policy determinations made by supervisors; and the authority to make decisions that create or implement policy.[4] The broad criteria used in defining "policymaking" means that cases must be decided on an ad hoc basis. For example, in one case the court held that decisions regarding mending potholes could be "policymaking" when made by the City of Chicago Finance Committee.[5] In other cases the courts have held that secretaries to policymakers were themselves policymakers and therefore may be fired for political reasons.

In *Branti v. Finkel,*[6] the Court further held that political affiliation may be the basis of a retention decision if the affiliation is relevant to the effective discharge of the duties of the office. The Court rejected inquiries based on policymaking or confidentiality requirements before holding that the proper question is whether the hiring authority can demonstrate that party affiliation is an appropriate requirement for the effective performance of the public office involved. If an individual's private political beliefs would interfere with the discharge of his or her public duties, the interest in maintaining governmental effectiveness and efficiency will outweigh the interest in protecting those beliefs.

---

2. 427 U.S. at 357 (citation omitted).

3. 427 U.S. at 367–68..

4. Kinsey v. Salado Ind. Sch. Dist., 950 F.2d 988 (5th Cir.), cert. denied, 504 U.S. 941, 112 S.Ct. 2275, 119 L.Ed.2d 201 (1992).

5. Hudson v. Burke, 913 F.2d 427 (7th Cir.1990).

6. 445 U.S. 507, 100 S.Ct. 1287, 63 L.Ed.2d 574 (1980).

In *Rutan v. Republican Party,*[7] the Supreme Court expanded the protection against patronage to forbid promotion, transfer, recall, and hiring decisions based on party affiliation and support, unless the employee occupies a position that meets the criteria set out in *Elrod* and *Branti.* The majority asserted in a five-to-four decision that the burdens on free speech and association imposed by patronage hiring are similar to those involved in patronage promotions, transfers, and recalls. While government employees have no entitlement to promotions, transfers, and recalls, the majority held that the government may not withhold these benefits on a basis which violates their First Amendment rights. The Court applied a strict scrutiny standard of analysis. It is important to note that several members of the majority are no longer on the Court. Their absence makes it important to note the dissent written by Justice Scalia.

Justice Scalia first argued that as a "venerable and accepted tradition," with "open, widespread, and unchallenged use that dates back to the beginning of the Republic," the patronage system deserves judicial deference. Second, Justice Scalia argued that a lower-level balancing test should be applied, rather than the strict scrutiny analysis used by the majority. He based his argument on the idea that public employees enjoy a different level of constitutionally protected rights than that of the general public, and that such a distinction is necessary if government offices are to function smoothly. While acknowledging that the patronage system "influences or redirects" political expression and association, he maintained that the benefits and history of the system outweigh its drawbacks, allowing it to survive a balancing test. Finally, Justice Scalia argued that *Elrod* and *Branti* should be overruled because their vague standard had led to unpredictable results and excess litigation.

An employee need not prove that the employer attempted to change his or her political allegiance through coercion, only that the sole reason for the discharge or other adverse action was affiliation with a certain political party. A plaintiff must make a prima facie showing that the discharge grew out of constitutionally protected activities, at which time the defendant has the burden of proving by a preponderance of the evidence that another reason existed for the adverse action.

Refusal to hire on the basis of the political *beliefs* of a potential employee is unconstitutional, but the employee must prove that the political beliefs were a substantial or motivating factor in the decision not to hire. In a Fourth Circuit case, a Marxist political science professor was unable to prove that his Marxist beliefs were a substantial or motivating factor in the decision to deny his appointment.[8] The Supreme Court, however, has held that a requirement that public employees execute affidavits disclosing or denying membership in the Communist

---

7. 497 U.S. 62, 110 S.Ct. 2729, 111 L.Ed.2d 52 (1990).

8. Ollman v. Toll, 518 F.Supp. 1196 (D.Md.1981), affirmed, 704 F.2d 139 (4th Cir.1983).

party was a reasonable requirement of fitness for employment and not a violation of due process.[9]

Loyalty oaths long have been used to restrict public employees' political activities. In early cases, the Supreme Court held that the denial of public employment on the basis of subversive association could not be justified when the employee was innocent of the group's illegal and subversive goals. In the leading case on loyalty oaths, *Elfbrandt v. Russell*,[10] the Court found that an individual's mere knowledge of illegal aims of the "subversive organization" with which he or she is associated is insufficient to justify termination of that individual's employment. The stricken oath prohibited "knowing, but guiltless" behavior. The Supreme Court also has applied the vagueness and overbreadth doctrines to the analysis of loyalty qualifications. In a series of cases, the Court struck down state statutes requiring teachers to fill out affidavits listing all organizations to which they belonged or contributed during the past five years,[11] statutes requiring one to forego any involvement with the Communist Party,[12] as well as statutes which required respect for the flag and the foreswearing of membership in subversive organizations.[13]

Employment may not be conditioned on an oath that one has not or will not engage in protected speech activities such as the following: criticizing institutions of government; discussing political doctrine that approves the overthrow of certain forms of government; and supporting candidates for political office. On the other hand, loyalty oaths are upheld when they paraphrase constitutional oaths, as long as such oaths are addressed to future action and promise constitutional support in broad terms. In contrast, an oath requiring a state employee to swear that he was not a "subversive person" was held to be unconstitutionally vague and overbroad, in violation of the First and Fourteenth Amendments.

The Hatch Act[14] is the federal statute which serves as a restraint on political activity in the federal sector. It prohibits covered employees from using their official authority to interfere with or affect the outcome of an election and from taking an active part in political management or in political campaigns. The purpose of the Hatch Act is to ensure political neutrality of the federal bureaucracy. The statute was meant to prevent the bureaucracy from becoming a unified political power, to prevent the party in power from using government workers improperly, to prevent competition between the party and the department heads, and to prevent employee demoralization based on politics, not merit. All fifty states have passed statutes modeled on the Hatch Act, which limit the political activities of state employees.

---

9. Garner v. Board of Pub. Works, 341 U.S. 716, 71 S.Ct. 909, 95 L.Ed. 1317 (1951).

10. 384 U.S. 11, 86 S.Ct. 1238, 16 L.Ed.2d 321 (1966).

11. Shelton v. Tucker, 364 U.S. 479, 81 S.Ct. 247, 5 L.Ed.2d 231 (1960).

12. Cramp v. Board of Pub. Instruc., 368 U.S. 278, 82 S.Ct. 275, 7 L.Ed.2d 285 (1961).

13. Baggett v. Bullitt, 377 U.S. 360, 84 S.Ct. 1316, 12 L.Ed.2d 377 (1964).

14. 5 U.S.C.A. §§ 1501–1508.

The Hatch Act prohibitions apply to nearly all employees of the executive branch of the federal government, with the exception of certain employees appointed or paid by the executive department, and persons employed as the head or assistant head of an executive department. Nonpartisan political activities, such as voter registration, are exempted from the scope of the Act. Violators of the Act may receive penalties from thirty days' unpaid suspension to removal from office. The Hatch Act applies to state and local government employees only to the extent that they work for agencies whose activities are funded totally or partially by federal funds. Agencies which fail to remove employees in violation of the Act may lose federal funding equal to the amount of two years' salary of the employee.

The Hatch Act Reform Amendments of 1993[15] conferred greater rights on public employees to engage in partisan political activity. In contrast to prior laws, an employee "may take an active part in political management or in political campaigns." There are exceptions, however, including that an individual may not: (1) solicit campaign contributions from subordinates or persons having business pending before the agency; (2) engage in political activity while on duty; (3) use government facilities or property for a political purpose: and (4) run for a partisan political office.

For public employees, an important distinction is whether the political activity is partisan or nonpartisan. While the First Amendment nearly always protects nonpartisan activity, partisan activity can be regulated more closely. In *United States Civil Service Commission v. National Association of Letter Carriers,*[16] a Hatch Act case, the Supreme Court listed various partisan political activities which may be regulated by public employers, including the following: holding a party office; working at the polls; acting as party paymaster for other party workers; organizing a political party or club; actively participating in fund-raising activities for a partisan candidate or political party; becoming a partisan candidate for, or campaigning for, an elective public office; actively managing the campaign of a partisan candidate for public office; or serving as a delegate, alternate, or proxy to a political party convention. Thus, it was held to violate the Hatch Act for a District of Columbia public school teacher to run for a seat on the D.C. City Council.

The outward expression of political affiliation also is constitutionally protected, subject to restriction only when necessary to protect a legitimate government interest. When a ban on the wearing of political buttons was challenged by Veteran's Administration employees, the court found that a balancing test would be required because the wearing of political buttons is not prohibited by the Hatch Act. Factors to be considered include the type of expression, the nature of the agency seeking the ban, and the context in which the expression is made. The court found that restrictions on this type of activity must be based on

15. 5 U.S.C.A. §§ 7321–7326.

16. 413 U.S. 548, 93 S.Ct. 2880, 37 L.Ed.2d 796 (1973).

efficient performance of duties or prevention of conflicts of interest, and that the ban must be restricted to a particular class of employees. On the other hand, placing political posters on a union bulletin board in a nonpublic area of the post office was held to violate the Hatch Act.

Sanctioning public employees who refuse to engage in political activity also may run afoul of the First Amendment. For example, the director of a government-operated group home for children was fired for refusing to participate in a workplace fundraising campaign for a school voucher system. The First Circuit held that conditioning continued employment on political activity violated the First Amendment.[17]

In a somewhat unusual case,[18] the wives of highway patrol troopers placed political campaign signs in the yards of their residences. The troopers and their wives then challenged a state rule prohibiting troopers from displaying partisan signs at their residences. The Tenth Circuit held that the state had important interests for the rule, including demonstrating that police protection is available to the public free of political overtones, and therefore upheld the rule as to troopers who were the sole owners of their residence. As to one trooper who owned his residence as a joint tenant with his wife, however, the court held that the trooper had no right to order his wife to remove the sign, and thus imposing discipline on the trooper would violate his constitutional rights.

Section 501(b) of the Ethics in Government Act of 1978, as amended, prohibits a member of Congress, federal officer, or other federal government employee from accepting an honorarium for making an appearance or speech or writing an article. In *United States v. National Treasury Employees Union*,[19] federal government employees below the grade of GS–16 who had previously received honoraria for speeches and articles on nongovernmental topics such as history, religion, and dance challenged the law. The Supreme Court held that the statute was overbroad and violated the First Amendment.

As mentioned earlier, many states have enacted their own versions of the federal statute. The First Circuit upheld a city version of the Hatch Act in response to an overbreadth claim by a firefighter who ran for city office.[20] Although the election in which the firefighter participated was nonpartisan under Pawtucket law, the reality that the election context was partisan led the court to conclude that the city law was constitutional. The constitutionality of Oklahoma's "Little Hatch Act" also was upheld as applied to the proscription of participation in partisan political activities.[21]

Some state employees' claims are brought on the theory that a governmental defendant's actions violated the state constitution. Oregon

17. Acevedo–Delgado v. Rivera, 292 F.3d 37 (1st Cir. 2002).

18. Horstkoetter v. Department of Pub. Safety, 159 F.3d 1265 (10th Cir.1998).

19. 513 U.S. 454, 115 S.Ct. 1003, 130 L.Ed.2d 964 (1995).

20. Magill v. Lynch, 560 F.2d 22 (1st Cir.1977), cert. denied, 434 U.S. 1063, 98 S.Ct. 1236, 55 L.Ed.2d 763 (1978).

21. United States Civil Serv. Comm'n v. National Ass'n of Letter Carriers, 413 U.S. 548, 93 S.Ct. 2880, 37 L.Ed.2d 796 (1973).

state police officers successfully claimed that official guidelines which did not allow them to be candidates for a partisan office, participate in the management of a partisan political party, campaign for or against partisan political candidates, or solicit contributions for partisan political candidates violated the Oregon State Constitution.[22] The court held that the statute was overbroad and that no judicial or agency interpretation could render it constitutional.

Private Employees

Private sector employees also have alleged that restrictions on their political activity are unlawful. Many states have laws protecting specific political activities of private sector employees, such as joining political parties and running for office. Broader assertions of political rights in the absence of express statutory language have been less successful.

State laws protecting freedom of political activity sometimes conflict with other important legal interests. Washington's Fair Campaign Practices Act, which prohibits employers from discriminating against employees based on their political activity, was held to be unconstitutional as applied to a newspaper copy editor. The court held that the First Amendment protects the editorial integrity of the press, thereby permitting the newspaper to enforce a rule prohibiting its employees from engaging in political activity.[23]

Claims also have been brought under state tort law. In *Novosel v. Nationwide Insurance Co.*,[24] a former employee alleged that the sole reason for his discharge was his refusal to participate in a company-wide effort to lobby the Pennsylvania House of Representatives in support of the "No–Fault Reform Act." The Third Circuit held that Pennsylvania's public policy prohibited hiring and firing on the basis of an employee's political activities, whether the job is in the public or private sector. In effect, it permitted an at-will, private sector employee to assert a First Amendment claim via the public policy exception to the employment at will rule.

§ 5.12   Other Off–Work Behavior

Some employers have long been interested in the off-duty activities of their employees, such as personal associations or behavior which could disrupt the job performance of the employee or fellow workers, favor business competitors, or reflect negatively on the image of the enterprise. Off-duty sexual relationships and illegal activities are most frequently cited as "unacceptable behavior." An employee's right to challenge employer disciplinary action depends on whether the employer is public or private, the nature of the unacceptable activity, and the respective interests of the employer and employee.

22. Oregon State Police Officers Ass'n v. State, 308 Or. 531, 783 P.2d 7 (1989), cert. denied, 498 U.S. 810, 111 S.Ct. 44, 112 L.Ed.2d 20 (1990).

23. Nelson v. McClatchy Newspapers, 131 Wash.2d 523, 936 P.2d 1123 (1997), cert. denied, 522 U.S. 866, 118 S.Ct. 175, 139 L.Ed.2d 117 (1997).

24. 721 F.2d 894 (3d Cir.1983).

Public Employees

Public employees may invoke constitutional protections unavailable to private sector employees. When discipline or dismissal results from lack of adherence to general standards, variously defined as "immoral acts," "conduct unbecoming" or "lack of good moral character," a public sector employee may challenge the action on equal protection, due process, or "void for vagueness" grounds. The results have varied. For example, dismissals have been upheld where a married employee left his wife and moved in with his pregnant girlfriend; where male police officers consorted with the wife of an alleged mobster and with women of "loose morals," and where the employee practiced "plural marriage." On the other hand, dismissals have been held to violate the right to privacy of employees who: refused to answer questions about her sex life, had a relationship with a coworker, cohabited with his girlfriend, and refused to terminate an affair.

Police officers and teachers appear to be held to a higher standard of conduct (and afforded fewer privacy protections) than are other public employees because of their function as "role models" and their potential influence on the public and students. In addition, the quasi-military structure of most police units, with their need for discipline, has also been used by the courts to justify lessened privacy rights for employees. Generally, the courts have required only a rational relationship between a regulation and the government's intended objective in order to uphold the regulation as constitutional.

Federal employees have greater protection against dismissal based on their off-work activities than do other public sector employees because of the federal statutory requirement that the "efficiency of the service" be impaired. The issue has been framed as whether the misconduct has a sufficient relationship to the agency's operations so that disciplinary action would promote the efficiency of the service. It is the agency's burden to show by a preponderance of the evidence that a nexus exists, and the employee may successfully rebut by showing the absence of any adverse impact.

A sufficient relationship may be shown to exist because the egregious nature of the conduct presumes a nexus, because the conduct is so at odds with the employee's job duties that a nexus is created, or because the notoriety accompanying the misconduct has created a nexus by discrediting the agency or affecting the performance of other employees. When the conduct is unrelated to job duties and there is no notorious publicity, a nexus generally is not found. Being charged with a crime does not automatically establish a nexus, although conviction may. The EEOC guidelines require an agency to show it has reasonably refused or terminated employment based on criminal conviction in light of the nature and gravity of the offense, the time elapsed since the conviction, and the nature of the job sought or held.

Courts reviewing the discharges of state and local government employees have reached decisions similar to the federal employee cases when applying a nexus test between the off-duty activity and the impact on the employer. Thus, the discharges of state and local employees have been upheld where an employee was engaged in egregious sexual misconduct, where an off-duty employee engaged in anti-Semitic verbal abuse in public, where an employee assaulted a fellow off-duty employee, and where an employee engaged in disorderly conduct. The Kentucky Supreme Court even upheld the discharge of an at-will public employee, a secretary with the Louisville Housing Authority, who filed a negligence action after her infant son was injured in an apartment owned and managed by her employer.[1] Similarly, a city's antinepotism policy, which prevented the marriage of two police department supervisors, was held not to infringe upon the fundamental right to marry.[2]

Successful challenges, however, have been brought against the refusal to hire unwed mothers, the discharge of a middle-aged, divorced school teacher who had a male guest stay overnight, the discharge of a state college director of residence halls for women who had a child out of wedlock, and the discharge of a teacher for a single, noncriminal homosexual episode with a fellow teacher.

In *Shahar v. Bowers,*[3] the attorney general of Georgia withdrew an offer of employment to an attorney after he learned that she had "married" another woman in a lesbian religious ceremony. In a sharply divided en banc opinion, the Eleventh Circuit held that the state did not violate the woman's rights of intimate and expressive association, freedom of religion, equal protection, or substantive due process. According to the court, the need to maintain the department's credibility with the public and to avoid disruption outweighed any association interests of the attorney.

Private Employees

Private sector employees have fewer protections against employer discipline for off-duty behavior. Thus, the courts have upheld the discharge of employees for dating or marrying coworkers, including subordinates. The courts also have given deference to the rights of religious organizations to oversee the morals of their employees.

Off-duty conduct occasionally falls into the category of behavior protected by the public policy exception to the at-will rule, and employees may also be protected if they are working pursuant to an express or implied contract. In *Rulon–Miller v. International Business Machines Corp.,*[4] an employee was discharged for dating an employee of a competitor. Because there was a written company policy acknowledging the privacy rights of employees with regard to their off-the-job behavior, the court held that the employee had stated a cognizable claim for wrongful

§ 5.12

1. Boykins v. Housing Auth., 842 S.W.2d 527 (Ky.1992).

2. Parks v. City of Warner Robins, 43 F.3d 609 (11th Cir.), rehearing denied, 52 F.3d 1073 (11th Cir.1995).

3. 114 F.3d 1097 (11th Cir.1997)(en banc), cert. denied, 522 U.S. 1049, 118 S.Ct. 693, 139 L.Ed.2d 638 (1998).

4. 162 Cal.App.3d 241, 208 Cal.Rptr. 524 (1984).

discharge. In the absence of such policies, however, the courts will not require a nexus between off-the-job conduct and on-the-job performance, leaving employers largely free to impose whatever standards of conduct or discipline they choose.

Some employer attempts to regulate off-work behavior or lifestyle may implicate Title VII. In *Chambers v. Omaha Girls Club, Inc.*,[5] a black, single woman was employed by the Club as an arts and crafts instructor. When she later informed her supervisor that she was pregnant, she was discharged pursuant to the Club's written "role model" rule. The plaintiff brought a Title VII action in which she alleged that the "role model" rule was disparate treatment gender discrimination (based on pregnancy) and disparate impact race discrimination (based on higher fertility rates among black females). The court upheld the "role model" rule, finding that it satisfied the requirements for both the bona fide occupational qualification (gender) and the business necessity (race) defenses.

In *Brunner v. Al Attar*,[6] the plaintiff, an employee of an auto body shop who worked as a volunteer at the AIDS Foundation on the weekends, alleged that she was fired because the owner of the company feared that she could somehow become infected with the virus and transmit it to him, his family, or other employees. The Texas Court of Appeals, in affirming the grant of summary judgment for the defendant, held that the defendant's alleged conduct did not violate the limited public policy exception to the at-will rule recognized in Texas, and it did not violate the state disability discrimination law because the plaintiff had no disability. Section 102(b)(4) of the Americans with Disabilities Act, which prohibits discrimination against an individual because the individual associated with individuals with disabilities, would now apply to this situation.

Some states have enacted laws forbidding employers from coercing employees to deal with or refrain from patronizing particular stores. These laws date back to the days of "company stores." Additional state legislation to limit employers from inquiring into off-work activities of employees or from discharging employees because of off-work activities is likely. Several states have enacted laws prohibiting employers from refusing to hire or discharging employees because they smoke cigarettes off work. Some of the laws enacted for this purpose are written more broadly to prohibit discrimination because of the use of a "lawful product," or even because of "lawful activity off the premises of the employer during nonworking hours." It remains to be seen how broadly these laws will be construed.

The New York statute, which bars discrimination against employees because of their participation in "legal recreational activity" was held not to encompass "romantic activity." Therefore, an employer's discharge of employees for violating its policy prohibiting a dating relation-

---

5.   834 F.2d 697 (8th Cir.1987).   **6.**   786 S.W.2d 784 (Tex.App.1990).

ship between a married employee and another employee other than a spouse did not violate the statute. In other cases, an employee fired for owning a business in violation of his employer's conflict of interest rule was held to have no recourse under North Dakota's law prohibiting discharge for lawful off-work activities because of the statute's exception for BFOQs, and an employer did not violate the Colorado "lawful activity" statute when it discharged an employee who wrote a letter to the editor critical of the employer because the duty of loyalty is a BFOQ.

§ 5.13 Invasion of Privacy

Employees have become increasingly sensitive about employer intrusions on their privacy and they have brought a wide range of lawsuits seeking redress. Public employees have raised federal constitutional claims. State constitutions and state statutes have been invoked by private sector employees. The most frequently asserted privacy claims, however, have been for common law invasion of privacy.

Invasion of privacy encompasses a wide range of factual situations of alleged wrongdoing. Many of the cases involving issues such as drug testing, psychological testing, and surveillance are discussed in other parts of the book. This section focuses on the substantive legal framework for asserting any common law invasion of privacy action.

The tort of invasion of privacy actually consists of four separate types of cases: public disclosure of private facts, intrusion upon seclusion, false light, and appropriation of name or likeness. Each of these claims has been asserted in the employment context.

Public Disclosure of Private Facts

Public disclosure of private facts is the tort most often asserted by employees in invasion of privacy actions. The Restatement (Second) of Torts describes the requisite level of privacy necessary for a public disclosure of private facts:

> Every individual has some phases of his life and his activities and some facts about himself that he does not normally expose to the public eye, * * *. Sexual relations, for example, are normally entirely private matters, as are family quarrels, many unpleasant or disgraceful or humiliating illnesses, most intimate personal letters, most details of a man's life in his home, and some of his past history that he would rather forget.[1]

The elements necessary to establish a claim for invasion of privacy based on public disclosure of private facts are: "Publication or publicity absent any waiver or privilege of private matters in which the public has no legitimate concern so as to bring shame or humiliation to a person of ordinary sensibilities."[2] "Publicity" occurs when a matter is made public

---

§ 5.13

1. Restatement (Second) of Torts § 652D (1977).

2. Restatement (second) of Torts § 652D (1977).

by communicating to the public at large, or to so many persons that the matter must be regarded as substantially certain to become one of public knowledge. Oral communications as well as written communications may qualify as "publication." Where no publicity is proven, no cause of action exists.

While at least one court has found that the existence of a special relationship between the plaintiff and the "public" to whom the information is disclosed (such as a coworker relationship) may satisfy the public disclosure requirement, most courts disagree. Thus, the majority rule is that private information must be made widely public, with disclosure made to people outside the workplace who have no need to know the information. A balancing of interests usually occurs in these cases, where the court weighs the degree of exposure, the sensitivity of the private facts disclosed, and the need for legitimate business communication.

For example, the publication requirement was not satisfied where a treating psychologist's letter to the employee's division supervisor was reviewed only by supervisors and others with a legitimate and direct interest in the plaintiff's employment. Similarly, a former employer's mailing a letter to the plaintiff's ex-wife requesting verification that the ex-wife would exercise no claim to plaintiff's retirement benefits was held to be a private, and not a public communication.

Discussion of a plaintiff's private matters with fellow employees does not reach the requisite level of publicity to state a claim for public disclosure of private facts. For instance, the disclosing to a few coworkers the fact that the plaintiff-employee was undergoing psychiatric treatment did not reach the requisite level of "publicity." Also, when an employer responded to customer inquiries regarding the reason for the discharge of a sales representative, the court held that there was no invasion of privacy because the customers asked and only a few were told the information.

In *Doe v. Southeastern Pennsylvania Transportation Authority*,[3] the defendant was alleged to have violated the plaintiff's constitutional right to privacy by disclosing among management employees that the plaintiff was taking AZT. The defendant learned this information through an audit of prescription drug records submitted through the employee health benefits plan. The Third Circuit held that the defendant's need to know justified the "minimal intrusion."

The opposite result was reached in *Levias v. United Airlines*.[4] An airline's medical examiner was supplied with the plaintiff flight attendant's medical information by her gynecologist. The medical supervisor then disclosed most of the information to the plaintiff's male flight supervisor, who had no compelling reason to know it, as well as to the plaintiff's husband. In addition, the supervisor repeatedly contacted the

3. 72 F.3d 1133 (3d Cir.1995), cert. denied, 519 U.S. 808, 117 S.Ct. 51, 136 L.Ed.2d 15 (1996).

4. 27 Ohio App.3d 222, 500 N.E.2d 370 (1985).

plaintiff to reveal the details of her medical condition and also raised the issue with the plaintiff in the presence of her appearance supervisor.

The employer-defendant in an invasion of privacy action may claim that a waiver or privilege precludes the invasion of privacy action. Written or oral releases authorizing a physician to reveal information acquired in the course of the employee's examination or treatment may operate as a waiver of any potential invasion of privacy claims by the employee. Where a psychologist revealed information about a patient's neuroses and psychoses to the patient's employer in the course of recommending that she be transferred to a less stressful position, the court found that the plaintiff had waived her right to keep the information confidential.

The defense of qualified privilege operates as a matter of law in the invasion of privacy context. To fall within the qualified privilege defense, a communication must be "made in good faith and on a subject-matter in which the person making it has an interest, or in reference to which he has a duty."[5] It is privileged if "made to a person or persons having a corresponding interest or duty, even though it contains matter which without this privilege would be slanderous * * *."[6]

Courts have applied this defense to invasion of privacy suits in the employment context where public policy was implicated. For example, where work was disrupted at a nuclear power plant due to rumors that the reason for an employee's illness at work was radiation exposure, the court found that the employer had a qualified privilege to tell employees that the plaintiff was ill due to the effects of a hysterectomy. The employer's interest was found to outweigh the plaintiff's interest in keeping the reason for her illness a secret.

Some communications may be absolutely privileged. A communication of private facts is absolutely privileged if required by the law. For example, a claim for damages may arise from the failure to protect persons from the danger of mentally disturbed persons by one bearing a "special relationship." For example, the employer of an employee who worked with potentially dangerous chemicals and was believed by a mental health professional to be lethally dangerous to himself and those around him was found to have an absolute and a qualified privilege to confer with others in order to determine whether the employee should continue working.[7] The employer was found to have an absolute privilege because of the statutory requirement that employers make the workplace safe. The court also found that the company had a qualified privilege based on the legitimate interest in protecting employees from danger and protecting the employment rights of the employee.

Sometimes the existence of a conditional privilege is found to be a jury question, rather than a matter of law. Communications are privileged if the publisher and the recipient each have a legitimate interest in

---

5. Young v. Jackson, 572 So.2d 378, 383 (Miss.1990).

6. Id.

7. Davis v. Monsanto Co., 627 F.Supp. 418 (S.D.W.Va.1986).

the subject matter. For instance, where employees have a proper interest in being informed of the discharge of a fellow employee, a conditional privilege may exist for the employer to reveal that information to them in a manner that the information will not reach the general public.

Matters which are already public knowledge as the result of a public incident, and which are the subject of disciplinary action by a public body, are not sufficiently private to provide an invasion of privacy cause of action. In one case, three public school teachers who became drunk at an end-of-the-year teachers' retirement party and later crashed their car into a cement abutment failed to prove any actionable publicity by the school district, which publicized the disciplinary action taken in regard to the plaintiffs.

Similarly, where the reason for a plaintiff's termination had become common knowledge at the hospital where she formerly was employed, the court found that the facts of the termination were not private. The lack of privacy provided by hospital policy to an employee undergoing termination proceedings, as well as the fact the plaintiff's employment record would be made available upon request by potential future employers, were factors relevant to the court's decision.

An employee's criminal record may qualify as a private matter if the employee has kept a clean record for a fair amount of time since the conviction. Criminals "are the objects of legitimate public interest during a period of time after their conduct * * * has brought them to the public attention * * *."[8] When they have reverted to the lawful life of good citizens, however, their conduct no longer deserves public attention. Therefore, when the crime is recent and the employee cannot definitively be qualified as "rehabilitated," the employee's criminal record is likely to be considered a matter of public record. For example, an employee on probation for a recent charge of first degree burglary did not disclose that information on his application for employment. The court found no actionable intrusion when the employer sent a letter detailing the reason for the employee's termination (falsification of employment records) to five supervisory or recordkeeping employees, to the state department of employment, and to an official in the plaintiff's union.

Another limitation on the cause of action for invasion of privacy is that the private matter disclosed publicly must be outrageous or highly offensive to a reasonable person. In order to constitute outrageous conduct, the defendant's conduct must inflict actual mental suffering on the plaintiff.

While the employment relationship may work against the employee by creating a waiver or privilege, the relationship may also provide a basis for a claim of invasion of privacy. "Where a special relationship exists between the plaintiff and the 'public' to whom the information has been disclosed, the disclosure may be just as devastating to the person

8. Baker v. Burlington N., Inc., 99 Idaho 688, 587 P.2d 829 (1978), quoting Briscoe v. Reader's Digest Ass'n, 4 Cal.3d 529, 93 Cal.Rptr. 866, 483 P.2d 34, 40 (1971).

even though the disclosure was made to a limited number of people."[9] For example, one court found an employee's physical, mental, and emotional distress resulting from her employer's disclosure of the facts surrounding her mastectomy to co-employees to be a question for the jury.

Intrusion Upon Seclusion

The Restatement (Second) of Torts defines intrusion upon seclusion in the following manner: "One who intentionally intrudes, physically or otherwise, upon the solitude or seclusion of another or his private affairs or concerns, is subject to liability to the other for invasion of his privacy, if the intrusion would be highly offensive to a reasonable person."[10] The legitimacy of the reason for inquiring into the employee's private concerns is an important factor in determining liability. The employer may be liable for damages when an intrusion occurs with no legitimate purpose.

In *Mares v. ConAgra Poultry Co.,*[11] the plaintiff's employment was terminated following her failure to fill out a form dealing with drug usage. The court, while recognizing that the absence of public disclosure does not preclude an action for intrusion upon seclusion, nevertheless held that the legitimate business interests cited by the employer (protecting employees from false positives and maintaining the integrity of its drug testing) were enough to support the employer's request for information. Allegations that, an employer harassed and badgered the office of an employee's physician to obtain confidential information, however, have been held to be sufficient to state a claim for intrusion upon seclusion. Similarly, liability has been found where an employer asked the plaintiff-employee's subordinates about the employee's sexual orientation.

Although the Restatement provides that no physical intrusion is necessary, several jurisdictions require a physical intrusion to maintain an action. For example, one court found that a physical intrusion, like that of a trespass, is necessary for the tort of intrusion upon seclusion. The location of the alleged intrusion is often important, and therefore courts generally hold that it is not an invasion of privacy for investigators situated on public property to videotape an employee suspected of committing workers' compensation fraud. Also, if no intrusion actually takes place because of the employee's refusal to participate in the questioning or activity, or because valid consent was given, no cause of action for invasion of privacy will exist.

Attendance records which are well known to an employer and many coworkers are not considered to be private. Where the plaintiff's husband was shown his wife's attendance records and drew his own conclusions from her absences to form the belief that she was having an

9. Miller v. Motorola, Inc., 202 Ill. App.3d 976, 148 Ill.Dec. 303, 560 N.E.2d 900 (1990).

10. Restatement (Second) of Torts, § 652B (1977).

11. 971 F.2d 492 (10th Cir.1992).

extramarital affair, the court found that the records were not sufficiently private to sustain a cause of action. This decision was based on the fact that neither the employer nor the coworkers knew of the plaintiff's affair and the fact that the husband could have called on the telephone at any time and found that his wife was not at work.

Courts generally agree that an employer has a legitimate business interest in determining the mental and physical condition of an employee to the extent that it relates to employment. That interest, however, must be balanced against the nature and extent of intrusion in determining if an invasion of privacy has occurred. Where an employee was discharged after her supervisors questioned her clinical psychologist, with whom she met at her own expense regarding her mental state, the court found an actionable invasion of her privacy. The plaintiff had not consented to the release of the information by her private psychologist, and the court found that her employer had no legitimate business interest in trying to garner information without the plaintiff's consent.

On the other hand, some courts have refused to find an invasion of privacy even where the employer engaged in or authorized deceptive or highly questionable conduct. In one case, investigators conducting an undercover investigation of the plaintiff's husband's workers' compensation claim represented that they were employed by a marketing company and used that story to gain access to the plaintiff's home. They gathered information about the activities of her husband, as well as later asking the plaintiff to test various consumer products and inviting her to participate in a shopping spree, which was later canceled. The court found no invasion of privacy because the purpose and scope of the investigation was limited to gathering information concerning the workers' compensation claim, the investigators never entered the plaintiff's home without her permission, the investigation took place for a relatively short period of time, and the credibility of the plaintiff's husband was called into question by competent evidence.

Courts have construed an "offensive intrusion" to require either an unreasonable manner of intrusion or intrusion for an unwarranted purpose. Searches of employee homes are a frequent source of liability. In one case, two of the plaintiff's supervisors, allegedly concerned about his health, hired a locksmith to open his trailer home, where they observed the plaintiff sleeping and possibly intoxicated.[12] After this incident, during which the two supervisors took notes on the number of liquor bottles present in the plaintiff's trailer, the plaintiff was told he could not return to his place of work in a supervisory capacity, and as a result, he signed a termination agreement. The court held that there was no error in the jury finding that an unreasonable intrusion occurred. In another case,[13] the employee consented to the search of his home only to show that he did not take any fishing equipment from his employer's

12. Love v. Southern Bell Tel. & Tel. Co., 263 So.2d 460 (La.App.), cert. denied, 262 La. 1117, 266 So.2d 429 (1972).

13. Wal–Mart Stores, Inc. v. Lee, 348 Ark. 707, 74 S.W.3d 634 (2002).

store without permission. When the search took place, however, it involved 10–15 of the employer's employees and five police officers, and it lasted over seven hours. The employer seized over 400 items and inventoried them on the employee's front lawn. In affirming the judgment for the employee, the court held that the search went well beyond the limited consent granted.

An action for intrusion upon seclusion may be based on unwanted and repeated demands for sex, such as where the employer frequently went to the employee's home early in the morning, used his status as her employer to gain entry, and repeatedly demanded sex.[14] A successful action for intrusion, however, also may arise in the workplace. Thus, a manager's intrusive interrogation and coercive behavior were found to be so offensive as to support a jury award of damages for the invasion of the plaintiff's privacy.[15] The manager repeatedly called the plaintiff into his office, closed and locked the door, questioned her about her sex life, propositioned her, and threatened to fire her if she did not have sex with him. The plaintiff refused to answer any of the questions and spurned the advances. Significantly, the court held that there was an intrusion, even though the manager was rebuked. If the behavior is sufficiently offensive, actual receipt of the private information is not necessary.

A claim of highly offensive behavior may be precluded if the employee consents to the release of the information or activity. Where consent does not exist, however, an action for invasion of privacy may arise. For example, a stockholder in a corporation alleged that the defendant, another stockholder in the same corporation, opened and read mail which was delivered to the corporation's office, but which was addressed to the plaintiff and marked personal. The court found that people have a reasonable expectation that their mail will not be opened and read without consent, and that such a lack of consent gave rise to an action for invasion of privacy.

Invasion of privacy actions may be based on intrusions in the workplace itself. For example, the surreptitious videotaping of fashion models in their changing area by security guards was held to be an invasion of privacy. On the other hand, the removal of papers from a general manager's locked credenza by his secretary was held not to be actionable because of agency principles, but liability might well have been found if the papers were removed by another employee.

False Light

The Restatement (Second) of Torts defines false light publicity in the following manner:

> One who gives publicity to a matter concerning another that places the other before the public in a false light is subject to liability to the other for invasion of privacy, if:

---

14. Pearson v. Kancilia, 70 P.3d 594 (Colo. App. 2003).

15. Phillips v. Smalley Maintenance Servs., Inc., 711 F.2d 1524 (11th Cir.1983).

a) the false light in which the other was placed would be highly offensive to a reasonable person, and

b) the actor had knowledge of or acted in reckless disregard as to the falsity of the publicized matter and the false light in which the other would be placed.[16]

The injury in a false light claim is mental distress resulting from the publicity.

False light requires that the published matter must be untrue. Therefore, if the published matter is expressed as an opinion and not as a matter of fact, no cause of action exists. The analysis for determining whether a statement is a factual assertion or an opinion is the same as is used in defamation cases.

When a defendant has attributed certain statements or beliefs to the plaintiff, the applicable question is whether the assertions or beliefs were in fact those of the plaintiff. In one case, the plaintiff, a marketing director for the defendant, brought suit when the defendant published in a trade magazine a letter allegedly written by the plaintiff.[17] The letter was a lengthy criticism of FDA policies which had seriously interfered with the defendant's marketing efforts, and as a result of its publication, the plaintiff alleged that his reputation, business opportunities, and earning capacity were seriously impaired. The court found that there was sufficient evidence for the jury to find that the letter attributed to the plaintiff views which were not his own, that this could reasonably have been found to be "highly offensive to a reasonable person," as required by the Restatement, and that the plaintiff was actually "bothered, annoyed, and offended" by the publication of the letter, as would a reasonable person.

Facts must actually be made public in a false light invasion of privacy claim. One court found sufficient publication to uphold a jury verdict for the plaintiff where a supervisor falsely stated to a subordinate in front of other employees that the subordinate's wife was sexually promiscuous. When an employee's former supervisor made comments following the plaintiff's resignation indicating that he was terminated for embezzlement or similar activities, the court found that a jury question existed as to whether any information placing the plaintiff in a false light was communicated to "so many persons that the matter must be regarded as substantially certain to become one of public knowledge."[18] On the other hand, when a former employee did not describe with any specificity the coworkers to whom the reasons for her termination were publicized, a court found that no actionable false light invasion of privacy claim existed. The court noted that there was no evidence of publication to a large group of people, as well as the fact that the

---

16. Restatement (Second) of Torts, § 652E (1977).

17. Jonap v. Silver, 1 Conn.App. 550, 474 A.2d 800 (1984).

18. Krochalis v. Insurance Co. of N. Am., 629 F.Supp. 1360 (E.D.Pa.1985).

employee actually was discharged for inventory shortages—the reason revealed by the defendants to her former coworkers.

The "publication" at the root of an invasion of privacy claim may consist of acts rather than words. In one case, a trader for a securities firm fell out of favor with management for voicing his objection to firm participation in what he believed were unlawful trading practices. The firm, deciding to terminate his employment, made a surprise visit to his office in front of the other traders, refused to allow him to speak to his staff, remained with him while he packed his personal belongings, interrogated his fellow employees about entries in his travel and entertainment expense reports, and then escorted him out of the building. The trader based his false light cause of action on the claim that the series of acts taken by management had the cumulative impact which created a false impression among his coworkers that he had engaged in serious misconduct or a substantial breach of ethics before his discharge. The court found that the series of acts leading up to the trader's dismissal could convey the false and offensive message to many of the trader's coworkers that his discharge was due to unscrupulous conduct on his part.

Appropriation of Another's Name or Likeness

One form of the tort of invasion of privacy which occasionally arises in the employment context is appropriation of name or likeness. The case law in this area generally involves whether the employer used the employee's name, picture, or other likeness for commercial use without the employee's consent.

A common example is a case in which a Boeing Airplane employee was in a photograph used by the company in magazine advertisements.[19] The employee made no complaint at the time the photograph was taken, nor did he complain when the photograph was posted around the plant on company bulletin boards. The focus of the photograph was on the airplane pictured, with the employee serving mainly as a prop, with no identification of him made by name or otherwise. The court, determining that the employee's real complaint was that he had not been compensated for the use of his photograph, not the fact that the photograph was published, found that there was no invasion of the employee's privacy. The court also noted that the right to privacy may be waived, and that the employee in this case had certainly done so through prior inaction.

Similarly, a former laboratory director claimed that his name continued to appear on various forms and documents by the company after his employment with the company was terminated.[20] The court found that the plaintiff had originally consented to the use of his name, but that a question of fact existed as to whether the company had ceased use of the plaintiff's name within a reasonable time after his dismissal. The court also noted that the measure of damages in an appropriation case is the "value of the benefit derived by the person appropriating the other's

19. Johnson v. Boeing Airplane Co., 175 Kan. 275, 262 P.2d 808 (1953).

20. Alonso v. Parfet, 253 Ga. 749, 325 S.E.2d 152 (1985).

name or likeness.''[21] Also, where a defendant-employer had incurred expenses in reliance upon the use of interviews and pictures of the plaintiff, the court found that the plaintiff had irrevocably consented to the use of the pictures and interviews, and that no cause of action was available to him.

21.   325 S.E.2d at 154.

Chapter 6

OCCUPATIONAL SAFETY
AND HEALTH

Table of Sections

OCCUPATIONAL SAFETY AND HEALTH ACT

OCCUPATIONAL SAFETY AND HEALTH ACT

§ 6.1   Overview

The Occupational Safety and Health Act of 1970[1] is the primary federal law regulating workplace safety and health. It covers employment in every state, the District of Columbia, Puerto Rico, and all American territories, at least six million workplaces and ninety million employees. The Act does not apply to working conditions of employees over whom other state and federal agencies exercise statutory authority to prescribe or enforce standards or regulations affecting occupational safety or health.

Among other requirements, each employer must comply with the following two provisions of the Act. First, section 5(a)(1) requires the employer to keep its place of employment free from recognized hazards that are causing or likely to cause death or serious physical harm to its employees. Second, section 5(a)(2) requires the employer to comply with occupational safety and health standards promulgated under the Act.

The Act provides for the promulgation of standards in three ways. Under section 6(a), the Secretary of Labor was authorized to adopt national consensus standards and established federal standards without lengthy rulemaking procedures. This authority ended in 1973. Section 6(b) sets out the procedures to be followed in modifying, revoking, or issuing new standards. The Secretary may also promulgate an emergency temporary standard pursuant to section 6(c). An emergency temporary standard may be established if the Secretary determines that employees are subject to grave danger from exposure to substances or agents known to be toxic or physically harmful and that an emergency standard is necessary to protect employees from danger. These standards are effective upon publication in the Federal Register.

All enforcement functions of the Act rest with the Occupational Safety and Health Administration (OSHA) of the United States Department of Labor. OSHA compliance officers (COs) are empowered by section 8(a) to inspect any workplace covered by the Act. The CO must present his or her credentials to the owner, operator, or agent in charge before proceeding with the inspection tour. The employer and an employee representative have a right to accompany the inspector. After the inspection a closing conference is held, during which the CO and employer discuss safety and health conditions and possible violations. Most COs

§ 6.1
1.   29 U.S.C.A. §§ 651–678.

cannot issue citations "on the spot," but must confer with the OSHA area director.

After the CO files his or her report, the area director decides whether to issue a citation, computes any penalties to be assessed, and sets the date for abatement of each alleged violation. If a citation is issued, it is mailed to the employer as soon as possible after the inspection, but in no event can it be more than six months after the alleged violation occurred. Citations must be in writing and must describe with particularity the violations alleged, including the relevant standards and regulations.

The Act provides for a wide range of penalties. Based on the 1990 amendment to the Act, violations are categorized and penalties may be assessed as follows:

De Minimis Notice	$0
Nonserious	$0–$7,000
Serious	$1–$7,000
Repeated	$0–$70,000
Willful	$5,000–$70,000
Failure to Abate Notice	$0–$7,000 per day

The good faith of the employer, the gravity of the violation, the employer's past history of compliance, and the size of the employer are all considered in penalty assessment. In addition to the above-mentioned civil penalties, there are criminal sanctions for willful violations that have caused the death of one or more employees.

Under the Act, an employer, an employee, or authorized employee representative (union) have fifteen working days in which to file a notice of contest. If the violation, abatement date, or proposed penalty is not contested, the citation becomes final and not subject to review by any court or agency. If a notice of contest is filed in good faith, however, the abatement requirement is tolled and a hearing is scheduled. An employer may also file a petition for modification of abatement (PMA) if unable to comply with any abatement requirement that has become a final order. If the Secretary or an employee contests the PMA, a hearing is held to determine whether any abatement requirement, even if part of an uncontested citation, should be modified.

The Secretary must immediately forward any notice of contest to the Occupational Safety and Health Review Commission (Commission or OSHRC). The Commission is a quasi-judicial, independent administrative agency comprised of three Presidentially-appointed commissioners who serve staggered six-year terms. In cases before the Commission, the Secretary is usually referred to as the complainant, and has the burden of proving the violation; the employer is usually called the respondent. The hearing is presided over by an administrative law judge (ALJ) of the Commission. After the hearing the ALJ renders a decision, affirming, modifying, or vacating the citation, penalty, or abatement date. The ALJ's decision then automatically goes before the Commission. An aggrieved party may file a petition for discretionary review (PDR) asking that the ALJ's decision be reviewed, but even without a PDR any Commission member may direct review of any part or all of the ALJ's decision. In this event, the Commission reconsiders the evidence and issues a new decision. If, however, no member of the Commission directs review within thirty days, the decision of the ALJ is final.

Any person adversely affected by a final order of the Commission may file a petition for review in the United States court of appeals for the circuit in which the violation is alleged to have occurred or in the United States Court of Appeals for the District of Columbia Circuit. The affected party must file within sixty days of the final order.

§ 6.2 Jurisdiction

Section 3(5) of the Act defines "employer" as "a person engaged in a business affecting commerce who has employees, but does not include the United States or any State or political subdivision of a State."[1] Section 3(4) of the Act defines "person" as "one or more individuals, partnerships, associations, corporations, business trusts, legal representatives, or any organized group of persons."[2] Based on these two broad definitions, the Act applies to at least six million workplaces and ninety million employees. Unlike the National Labor Relations Act and Title VII of the Civil Rights Act of 1964, OSHA coverage is not based on volume of business or number of employees. The duties imposed by section 5(a) of the Act apply to "each employer."

The Secretary of Labor has issued interpretive regulations that indicate whether selected "special" employers will be considered by the Secretary to be within the Act's coverage.[3] These six employer groups are as follows: (1) professionals (covered if employing one or more employees); (2) agricultural employers (covered but immediate family of a farm employer are not considered employees); (3) Indians (covered); (4) charities (covered); (5) churches (covered when they employ one or more persons in secular activities); and (6) domestic household employers (not covered).

According to a directive issued in 2000, OSHA has exempted home offices from OSHA inspections. Employees who request inspections will be notified of OSHA's new policy. Employers must still keep records of work-related injuries and illnesses occurring at employees' homes.

Congressional Exemptions

Beginning with fiscal 1977, Congress has restricted some specific aspects of OSHA enforcement by attaching limitations to OSHA Appropriations Bills and continuing resolutions. In all, there are seven limitations currently in effect.

§ 6.2

1. 29 U.S.C.A. § 652(5).

2. Id. § 652(4).

3. 29 C.F.R. Part 1975.

First, and most importantly, OSHA is prohibited from inspecting employers with ten or fewer employees in industries with three-digit Standard Industrial Classification (SIC) injury and illness rates of less than the national average rate for the private sector. There are several exceptions to the limitation, and inspections are still permitted in the following instances: in response to complaints, for failures to correct, for willful violations, to investigate accidents, for imminent dangers, for health hazards, and to investigate discrimination complaints.

Second, OSHA is prohibited from inspecting workplaces in states with approved plans for six months after a state inspection, except for investigations of employee complaints and fatalities, special studies, and accompanied monitoring visits.

Third, OSHA may not undertake any enforcement activity on the Outer Continental Shelf in excess of the authority granted to OSHA in the Outer Continental Shelf Lands Act or the Outer Continental Shelf Lands Act Amendments of 1978.

Fourth, the Secretary of Labor is prohibited from assessing penalties for first-instance nonserious violations of *any* employer unless the inspection discloses ten or more violations. OSHA is still permitted to issue citations for these violations which prescribe an abatement date. Second-instance violations of any nature can carry a penalty, even if fewer than ten violations are detected. According to OSHA regulations, if ten or more violations are found, penalties will be assessed for *all* violations. In computing the ten violations figure, all types of violations are considered, including notices issued for failure to post pursuant to section 17(i).

Fifth, farms with ten or fewer employees at one time during the past year, except those with migrant labor camps, are exempt. Members of a farm employer's immediate family are not considered employees.

Sixth, OSHA may not promulgate or enforce any regulation restricting work activity in any recreational hunting, fishing, or shooting area.

Seventh, no penalties may be assessed against an employer with ten or fewer employees that had a prior on-site consultation and had made good faith efforts to abate the violative conditions prior to the inspection.

State and Local Governments

Section 3(5) of the Act expressly excludes state and local governments from the definition of employer, but this provision has been narrowly construed. Consequently, employers with a contractual or other relationship with a state or political subdivision have been unsuccessful in their attempts to be excluded. For example, an architecture and construction management firm that was supervising the construction of a building at a state university was held to be an employer because the company dealt with the political subdivision "at arm's length." Similarly, the Occupational Safety and Health Review Commission held that joint supervisory control of the cited employer's workers by a municipal sewer department did not relieve the cited employer from complying with the Act.

The political subdivision exemption cannot be transferred by contract. Thus, a firm that leased equipment and operators to a city, which agreed to provide supervision at the worksite, still retained shared control of the employees and therefore was an employer under the Act. Some of the significant factors in determining whether an entity is exempt under the Act as a state or political subdivision are whether it makes a profit, whether it pays taxes, whether it pays the salary of the employees, and whether it is administered by a public official. In *University of Pittsburgh*,[4] the Commission held that a state-supported private university is not exempt from OSHA jurisdiction as a political subdivision. Although the state has some control of the university's affairs, the university was not created directly by the state nor is it administered by individuals responsible to public officials.

The courts also have narrowly construed the political subdivision exemption. In *Brock v. Chicago Zoological Society*,[5] the Seventh Circuit reversed the Commission and held that the zoo was not a political subdivision of the state of Illinois. The court applied the two-part test found in the Secretary's regulation: (1) whether the entity is created directly by the state so as to constitute a department or administrative arm of the government, or (2) whether the entity is administered by individuals who are controlled by public officials and responsible to such officials or to the general public.

Federal Government Compliance

Section 19(a) of the Act requires the head of each federal agency to establish, develop, and maintain a comprehensive OSHA program consistent with promulgated standards. This express congressional mandate of federal government compliance originally was implemented by the executive orders of Presidents Nixon and Ford.

In 1980 President Carter issued a new executive order to give added protection to federal government employees.[6] Among other provisions, the executive order: (1) requires agency heads to comply with OSHA standards except where the Secretary of Labor approves alternatives; (2) requires agency heads to render workplaces free of recognized hazards that are causing or likely to cause death or serious physical harm; (3) assures employees protection against discrimination for exercising protected rights, such as filing reports about unsafe working conditions; (4) allows for the establishment of occupational safety and health committees composed of representatives of management and an equal number of nonmanagement employees to monitor the agency's job safety and health performance; and (5) authorizes the Secretary of Labor to conduct unannounced inspections under certain circumstances and, if violations are found, to report them to the head of the agency and the occupational safety and health committee. The 1980 executive order supersedes all

4. 7 OSHC 2211, 1980 OSHD ¶ 24,240 (1980).

5. 820 F.2d 909 (7th Cir.1987).

6. Exec. Order 12,196, 45 Fed. Reg. 12,769 (1980). OSHA's regulations implementing the executive order are codified at 29 C.F.R Part 1960.

prior executive orders dealing with safety and health protection for federal government employees.

Interstate Commerce Requirement

The Act is based on the congressional finding that workplace injuries and illnesses place a burden upon interstate commerce. To relieve this burden, Congress passed the Act pursuant to the commerce clause. Thus, section 3(5) of the Act defines an employer as "a person engaged in a business affecting commerce who has employees." The use of the words "affecting commerce" indicates a congressional intent to exercise fully its constitutional authority under the commerce clause. Section 3(3) of the Act defines commerce as "trade, traffic, commerce, transportation, or communication among the several states, or between a state and any place outside thereof * * *."[7]

The requirement of section 3(5) that an employer be *engaged* in a business affecting commerce was the main issue in *Godwin v. OSHRC.*[8] The Commission had held that because the employer was merely clearing land in preparation for grape production, it was not *presently engaged* in a business affecting commerce. The Ninth Circuit reversed, finding it "insignificant" that, at the time of the hearing, grapes had been neither planted nor harvested. "The effect on interstate commerce nevertheless exists."[9]

It has also been held that an employer is engaged in a business *affecting* commerce if it does business with other employers engaged in interstate commerce. Thus, the Second Circuit held that a building maintenance service company was engaged in a business affecting commerce because it supplied services to a group of companies engaged in interstate commerce and because it used supplies produced out of state. Similarly, the Tenth Circuit has held that it is irrelevant whether the employer itself was engaged in commerce so long as its relationship to commerce was more than minimal.

Several Commission and judicial decisions indicate that it is quite easy to prove that an employer is engaged in a business affecting commerce. For example, the Ninth Circuit has held that an employer was engaged in a business affecting commerce because it hired employees from a union hall, used the telephone and mails, and purchased supplies from out of state. Similarly, the Commission has held that an employer's use of goods manufactured out of state, which moved in interstate commerce, was sufficient to establish jurisdiction.

Section 4(b)(1) Preemption

Section 4(b)(1) of the Act provides that OSHA does not apply to "working conditions of employees with respect to which other Federal agencies * * * exercise statutory authority to prescribe or enforce standards or regulations affecting occupational safety or health."[10] Congress

---

7. 29 U.S.C.A. § 652(3).

8. 540 F.2d 1013 (9th Cir.1976).

9. Id. at 1016.

10. 29 U.S.C.A. § 653(b)(1).

intended to avoid the duplication of enforcement by OSHA and other federal agencies that regulate employee safety and health. Many questions have arisen, however, including what employers are entitled to an OSHA exemption, what are the limits of exemptions, and what are the procedural implications of exemptions.

The most recent Commission decisions suggest a three-part test to determine whether OSHA is preempted from exercising jurisdiction by virtue of section 4(b)(1). Preemption requires that:

(1) The employer is covered by another federal act directed exclusively at employee safety and health or directed at public safety and health and employees directly receive the protection the act is intended to provide.

(2) The other federal agency has exercised its statutory grant of authority.

(3) The other federal agency has acted in such a manner as to exempt the cited working conditions from OSHA jurisdiction.

The first requirement for preemption under section 4(b)(1) is that the employer is covered by another federal act directed exclusively at employee safety and health or directed at public safety and health and employees directly receive the protection the act is intended to provide. The Commission's original formulation of this first requirement was more limited. According to the Commission, to be exempt, the employer had to be covered by another federal act, the policy or purpose of which must be to assure safe and healthful working conditions for employees.

The second requirement for preemption under section 4(b)(1) is that the other federal agency has exercised its statutory grant of authority. The exercise of statutory authority involves both the prescribing and the enforcing of standards or regulations. The starting point is a determination of whether there is statutory authority to prescribe the appropriate rules and regulations. In *Northwest Airlines, Inc.*,[11] the Commission reviewed the validity of the somewhat unusual regulatory scheme whereby the Federal Aviation Administration (FAA) enforces company maintenance manuals regulating the working conditions of airline ground maintenance personnel. According to the Commission, the employer's maintenance manuals had the force of law because there was statutory authority for the FAA to regulate employer working conditions.

An important factor is the position that the other agency takes with regard to preemption. For example, in *Tidewater Pacific, Inc.*,[12] the Commission gave considerable weight to the Coast Guard's amicus brief in which it "unequivocally disclaims [general regulatory authority and] describes its safety standards applicable to uninspected vessels as 'minimal.' "

11. 8 OSHC 1982, 1980 OSHD ¶ 24,751 (1980), petition for review dismissed, Nos. 80–4248, 80–4222 (2d Cir.1981).

12. 17 OSHC 1920, 1997 OSHD ¶ 31,-267 (1997).

In *Chao v. Mallard Bay Drilling, Inc.*,[13] the Supreme Court addressed the issue of OSHA authority over uninspected vessels. The Court observed that under the Memorandum of Understanding between OSHA and the Coast Guard, the Coast Guard can preempt OSHA and "exercise" its statutory authority either by promulgating specific regulations covering the working conditions at issue or asserting comprehensive regulatory authority through inspections of the vessels. Therefore, the unregulated working conditions aboard uninspected vessels are not preempted from OSHA jurisdiction. Finding preemption in such a case would create "large gaps" in coverage and thus would be "plainly inconsistent with the purpose of the OSH Act."[14]

Another procedural debate has existed over whether an agency's notice of proposed rulemaking is sufficient to preempt OSHA jurisdiction pursuant to section 4(b)(1). In *Consolidated Rail Corp.*,[15] the Commission held that a notice of proposed rulemaking is enough to divest OSHA's jurisdiction under section 4(b)(1). According to the Commission, because a Federal Railroad Administration (FRA) policy statement was the end result of a long deliberative process, including advance public notice and agency investigation, OSHA was preempted from enforcing standards dealing with hazards over which the FRA, in its policy statement, claimed authority.

The Commission has long held that the other agency's regulations need not be similar or equally stringent in order to preempt OSHA. Moreover, enforcement by the other agency need not be similar or equally stringent. According to the Commission, "[a]ny oversight of another agency's enforcement activities is beyond the scope of permissible inquiry under section 4(b)(1)."[16]

The third requirement for preemption under section 4(b)(1) is that the other federal agency has acted in such a manner as to exempt the cited working conditions from OSHA jurisdiction. The first question to be resolved is whether section 4(b)(1) provides for industry-wide exemptions. In the leading cases of *Southern Railway Co. v. OSHRC*[17] and *Southern Pacific Transportation Co. v. Usery*,[18] the Fourth and Fifth Circuits affirmed the Commission and rejected the contention of the railroads that section 4(b)(1) provides the railroads with an industry-wide exemption. The courts based their decisions on a literal reading of the term "working conditions," used in section 4(b)(1) and an inquiry into the statutory objectives of the Act. According to the Fourth Circuit, an industry-wide exemption would result in unregulated working condi-

13. 534 U.S. 235, 122 S.Ct. 738, 151 L.Ed.2d 659 (2002).

14. 122 S.Ct. at 744 n. 9

15. 10 OSHC 1577, 1982 OSHD ¶ 26,-044 (1982), petition for review dismissed, No. 82–3302 (3d Cir.1982).

16. Pennsuco Cement & Aggregates, Inc., 8 OSHC 1378, 1980 OSHD ¶ 24,478 (1980).

17. 539 F.2d 335 (4th Cir.), cert. denied, 429 U.S. 999, 97 S.Ct. 525, 50 L.Ed.2d 609 (1976).

18. 539 F.2d 386 (5th Cir.1976), cert. denied, 434 U.S. 874, 98 S.Ct. 221, 54 L.Ed.2d 154 (1977).

tions for thousands of workers, which would "utterly frustrate the legislative purpose."[19]

The view that there are no industry-wide exemptions under section 4(b)(1) was followed in numerous Commission and judicial decisions. In *Dillingham Tug & Barge Corp.*,[20] however, the Commission overruled prior decisions and held that section 4(b)(1) "in certain circumstances can create industry-wide exemptions." According to the majority opinion, without industry-wide exemptions employers have an unreasonable burden to determine the requirements of two sets of regulations. In addition, the established rule is that there can be no inquiry into the "stringency of another agency's exercise of authority."

The Commission has long held that preemption under section 4(b)(1) is a defensive matter to be raised by the employer. In addition, as an affirmative defense, it must be raised by the employer before the hearing or it will be deemed waived. The Commission's position, however, has been rejected by the Third and Fourth Circuits. According to the Third Circuit in *Columbia Gas of Pennsylvania, Inc. v. Marshall*[21]: "Section 4(b)(1) preempts OSHA of subject matter jurisdiction once concurrent regulation is determined to cover the same working conditions. As such, a section 4(b)(1) claim can be raised initially on appeal or by the court *sua sponte*."[22]

§ 6.3 State Plans and State Regulation

According to section 2(b)(11),[1] one of the express purposes of the Occupational Safety and Health Act is to encourage state participation in safety and health regulation. Section 18 of the Act[2] permits states to assert jurisdiction over job safety and health matters by submitting a plan for OSHA approval. The states, however, are not required to submit a state plan.

The Act sets the minimum acceptable safety standards in order to maintain some semblance of uniformity. Nevertheless, the standards merely serve as starting points for state programs; the Act does not require that state plans be identical to federal OSHA. There is no requirement that approved state plans contain a general duty clause, but several state plans have provisions at least similar to a general duty clause. The standards prescribed for covered employers may be more stringent under a state plan, but no state may exercise wider jurisdiction than federal OSHA.

The Act preempted, at least temporarily, all state job safety and health legislation. In accordance with the constitutional doctrine of federal supremacy the states are precluded from enacting or enforcing any conflicting law. Under section 18(a) of the Act, if the Secretary

19. 539 F.2d at 338.

20. 10 OSHC 1859, 1982 OSHD ¶ 26,-166 (1982).

21. 636 F.2d 913 (3d Cir.1980).

22. Id. at 918.

§ 6.3

1. 29 U.S.C.A. § 651(b) (11).

2. Id. § 667.

determines that a state has promulgated standards comparable to OSHA's and has an enforcement plan meeting the criteria of section 18(c), jurisdiction may be ceded back to the state.

The Act leaves the choice of submitting a plan to the individual state. If a state does not submit a state plan, it is precluded from enforcing state laws, regulations, or standards relating to issues covered by the Act. This preclusion, however, does not extend to a state's enforcement of a law or standard directed to an issue upon which there is no effective OSHA standard. An "issue" is defined as "an industrial, occupational or hazard grouping which is at least as comprehensive as a corresponding grouping contained in [any of the subparts to the general industry standards]."[3] Boilers and elevators are two issues over which OSHA has not promulgated standards and, therefore, over which state enforcement is not preempted.

States without approved plans also retain jurisdiction in three other areas. First, states may enforce standards, such as state and local fire regulations, which are designed to protect a wider class of persons than employees. For example, state and local governments have begun enacting laws regulating procedures to be used in eliminating asbestos hazards, such as in buildings. New Jersey passed a comprehensive act and issued regulations providing for employee education, training, testing, and licensing in the handling of asbestos. The dual purpose of the law was to protect workers and to protect members of the public who occupied buildings where the employees worked. A district court in New Jersey held that the law was preempted under section 18 of the Act insofar as it pertained to health and safety in the workplace.[4] Because the nonoccupational safety concerns were nearly indistinguishable from the occupational safety concerns, the effect was to preempt totally the New Jersey law.

The second area in which states retain jurisdiction is consultation, training, and safety information activities. Third, states may enforce standards to protect state and local government employees. Connecticut and New York are the only jurisdictions with OSHA-approved public employee plans. Six states have enacted laws protecting public employees, but they are not OSHA-approved state plans eligible for matching funds. A variety of other state laws have been held not to be preempted by OSHA, including local zoning ordinances, drinking water and toilet facilities laws, injury reporting laws, and common law damage and indemnity actions.

Section 18(b) of the Act provides: "Any State which, at any time, desires to assume responsibility for development and enforcement therein of an occupational safety and health issue with respect to which a Federal standard has been promulgated under section 6 shall submit a State plan for development of such standards and their enforcement."

3. 29 C.F.R. § 1902.2(c).

4. New Jersey State Chamber of Commerce v. New Jersey, 653 F.Supp. 1453 (D.N.J.1987).

Section 18(c) of the Act lists eight requirements that all state plans must meet, but generally each plan must provide for standards and enforcement "at least as effective as" the federal legislation.

As of 2004, a total of fourteen jurisdictions received final state plan approval: Alaska, Arizona, Hawaii, Indiana, Iowa, Kentucky, Maryland, Minnesota, South Carolina, Tennessee, Utah, Virginia, Virgin Islands, and Wyoming. There are presently twenty-three jurisdictions with approved state plans for private and public sector employees and two state plans covering only state and local government employees.

States with Approved Plans

Alaska	Michigan	Tennessee
Arizona	Minnesota	Utah
California	Nevada	Vermont
Hawaii	New Mexico	Virgin Islands
Indiana	North Carolina	Virginia
Iowa	Oregon	Washington
Kentucky	Puerto Rico	Wyoming
Maryland	South Carolina	

State Plans Covering Only Public Employees

Connecticut
New York

The District of Columbia, Maine, New Hampshire, New Jersey, Rhode Island, West Virginia, and Wisconsin have laws protecting public employees, but they are not OSHA-approved state plans. Because federal grants of ninety percent for planning and development are no longer available, it is unlikely that many new state plans will be submitted for approval. Thus, state plans either have obtained final approval or are at interim stages leading to OSHA's final approval.

In *Gade v. National Solid Wastes Management Association,*[5] the Supreme Court considered whether two Illinois laws, which required state licensing of hazardous waste workers, were preempted by OSHA. The dual purposes of the state laws were to protect both employees and the general public. A detailed OSHA standard also addressed training requirements for hazardous waste workers.

The Court, five-to-four, held that the Illinois law was preempted. Writing for a four-justice plurality, Justice O'Connor stated that the Act "precludes any state regulation of an occupational safety and health issue with respect to which a federal standard has been established, unless a state plan has been submitted and approved pursuant to section 18(b)."[6]

The plurality rejected the argument that states may either "oust" the federal standard by submitting a state plan or "add to" the federal standard without seeking the Secretary's approval. It reasoned that state

5. 505 U.S. 88, 112 S.Ct. 2374, 120 L.Ed.2d 73 (1992).   **6.** 505 U.S. at 102, 112 S.Ct. at 2385.

activity is permitted only if the state "is willing completely to displace the applicable federal regulations."[7] The plurality also rejected the argument that preemption should not apply to state laws that address public safety as well as occupational safety concerns. The state law will be preempted, regardless of whether it serves any other objective, so long as it "directly, substantially, and specifically regulates occupational safety and health."[8]

Justice Kennedy, in a concurring opinion, wrote that he would consider the case one of express rather implied preemption. Justice Souter, writing for four dissenters, asserted that regardless of the preemption theory used, "the key is congressional intent, and I find the language of the statute insufficient to demonstrate an intent to pre-empt state law in this way."[9]

§ 6.4   State Criminal Laws

Beginning in the mid–1980s there has been a substantial increase in the number of state criminal prosecutions brought as a result of fatalities or injuries in the workplace. The charges have included reckless endangerment, manslaughter, and even murder. One reason for this increased local activity is a perception of lax federal enforcement efforts in occupational safety and health.

In many of these cases the defendants have argued that state criminal laws are preempted where the prosecution is based on working conditions regulated by OSHA. The state courts generally have not been receptive to these arguments. Although a decision in Colorado held that state prosecutions are preempted, decisions in Illinois, Michigan, New York, Texas, and Wisconsin, and an advisory opinion by the United States Department of Justice have concluded that there is no preemption.

§ 6.5   Promulgation of Standards—Existing Standards

OSHA standards may be divided into three classes based on the method of promulgation: existing standards (interim standards) adopted under section 6(a) of the Act; new standards (permanent standards) promulgated pursuant to section 6(b) of the Act; and emergency temporary standards adopted under section 6(c) of the Act.

Section 20 of the Act[1] directs the Secretary of Health and Human Services (HHS) to conduct studies and research to develop recommended safety and health standards. To further this purpose, section 22[2] created the National Institute for Occupational Safety and Health (NIOSH) headed by a director appointed by the Secretary of HHS for a term of six

7. 505 U.S. at 99, 112 S.Ct. at 2384.

8. 505 U.S. at 107, 112 S.Ct. at 2388.

9. 505 U.S. at 107, 112 S.Ct. at 2392 (Souter, J., dissenting).

§ 6.5

1. 29 U.S.C.A. § 669.

2. Id. § 671.

years. Within HHS, NIOSH is a part of the Centers for Disease Control and Prevention.

NIOSH has no authority to promulgate or enforce standards, but it is responsible for conducting research and making recommendations to the Department of Labor. In addition to recommending new standards, NIOSH is also responsible for updating and revising all previously promulgated standards. NIOSH has authority under sections 8 and 20(b) of the Act to conduct inspections and question employers and employees for research purposes. Many of these inspections are "health hazard evaluations" initiated by an employee's filing of an inspection request with NIOSH.

Under section 6(a) of the Act, the Secretary was required to adopt as occupational safety and health standards all national consensus standards, unless the Secretary determined that a particular standard or standards would not result in improved safety and health for employees. National consensus standards are privately adopted standards produced by a body of diverse professionals, such as the American National Standards Institute (ANSI). The purpose of section 6(a) was to permit OSHA enforcement activities without a time lag for promulgation of standards. In adopting national consensus standards the Secretary often incorporated by reference other private regulations not appearing in full in the source standard. This procedure has generally been upheld.

National consensus standards (as well as established federal standards, described below) may be partially or fully adopted. Partial adoption usually results from modifications made by omissions and deletions and by changing advisory language to mandatory language. Both types of modifications have generated considerable controversy.

In *Noblecraft Industries, Inc. v. Secretary of Labor*[3] the Ninth Circuit rejected an employer's contention that the section 6(a) promulgation of an ANSI standard represented an impermissible delegation of legislative and administrative authority to a private organization. The employer also argued that the Secretary's omission of an explanatory headnote invalidated the section 6(a) promulgation of an ANSI standard. In rejecting this argument, the court held that the omitted language was "essentially a direction to the enforcing agency that exemptions should be liberally granted" and this would be superfluous in light of section 6(d)'s variance provision. The court ruled, however, that the challenged standard was intended to apply to woodworking and not to a manufacturer of structured plywood or to sawmill operations.

In attempting to give binding effect to previously-optional private standards, the Secretary in some instances has changed the wording of a standard from "should" to "shall." In *Usery v. Kennecott Copper Corp.*,[4] however, the Tenth Circuit affirmed the Commission's holding that the Secretary was not authorized by section 6(a) of the Act to make such

---

3. 614 F.2d 199 (9th Cir.1980).

4. 577 F.2d 1113 (10th Cir.1977). Accord, Marshall v. Union Oil Co., 616 F.2d 1113 (9th Cir.1980).

changes. Furthermore, the court in *Marshall v. Pittsburgh–Des Moines Steel Co.*[5] held that the Secretary's subsequent "interpretation" of an ANSI standard could not change the effect of an already adopted standard from advisory to mandatory.

Section 4(b)(2) of the Act provides that established federal standards, adopted by OSHA under section 6(a) of the Act, supersede the corresponding standards under other safety laws on the effective date of the OSHA standards. Established federal standards are federal safety and health standards previously promulgated under another federal statute, such as the Walsh–Healey Act, which prescribed the working conditions for employees of federal contractors. As with the national consensus standards, the section 6(a) adoption of established federal standards has raised a number of legal issues. Of particular importance are OSHA's changes in language and changes in scope of the original source standards.

In *Deering Milliken, Inc. v. OSHRC,*[6] the Fifth Circuit rejected the employer's argument that the Secretary's adoption of the Walsh–Healey cotton dust standard under section 6(a) was invalid simply because the sampling method required by the standard was changed from air concentrations to personal dust samplers. The employer's objection was termed "frivolous" because personal samplers collect twenty percent less dust than area samplers do and thus the industry's obligation was, if anything, decreased by the new requirement.

The Commission has followed *Deering Milliken* and has held that the Secretary was not required to promulgate section 6(a) standards verbatim. The proper inquiry is whether the Secretary made a substantive change, and the burden of proof is on the employer to show that a change was substantive.

The Commission has held that employers may challenge the validity of the Secretary's section 6(a) standards adoption procedures in an enforcement proceeding before the Commission. The courts of appeals, however, have disagreed on whether procedural challenges to section 6(a) rulemaking may be asserted on judicial review of enforcement proceedings pursuant to section 11(a) of the Act.

§ 6.6 Promulgation of Standards—New Standards

Section 6(b) of the Act provides that any promulgation, modification, or revocation of OSHA standards must comply with specific rulemaking procedures. The Secretary is required to publish a notice of proposed rulemaking in the Federal Register and must allow thirty days after publication for interested parties to submit written data or comments. OSHA's regulations provide that rulemaking proceedings shall be legislative in nature but that fairness may require cross-examination on

5. 584 F.2d 638 (3d Cir.1978).
6. 630 F.2d 1094 (5th Cir.1980).

"crucial issues." In practice, OSHA has usually permitted cross-examination quite freely.

In *Industrial Union Department, AFL–CIO v. American Petroleum Institute (The Benzene Case),*[1] the Supreme Court addressed several important substantive issues in ruling on the validity of OSHA's benzene standard. The Fifth Circuit had invalidated the standard because OSHA failed to provide a quantitative estimate of the benefits to be achieved by reducing the permissible exposure limit (PEL) for benzene from 10 ppm to 1 ppm. The Fifth Circuit based its decision on section 3(8)'s definition of "occupational safety and health standard" as being "reasonably necessary or appropriate" for safe workplaces. From this language the court held that the Secretary must determine "whether the benefits expected from the standard bear a reasonable relationship to the costs imposed by the standard." The court was, essentially, fashioning a three-part test: (1) whether substantial evidence supports the Secretary's estimate of expected benefits; (2) whether substantial evidence supports the Secretary's estimate of expected costs; (3) whether the benefits bear a reasonable relationship to the costs. Because there was inadequate evidence of expected benefits, the other issues were not reached.

The Supreme Court affirmed the decision of the Fifth Circuit, but the Court was sharply divided and issued five separate opinions. Justice Stevens, writing for a plurality of four justices, rejected the government's argument that section 3(8) of the Act is meaningless and is supplanted by section 6(b)(5) of the Act, which details the requirements for standards dealing with toxic materials or harmful physical agents. According to the plurality opinion, section 3(8) must be satisfied before there can be any consideration of a standard under section 6(b)(5). "[Section 3(8)] requires the Secretary, before issuing any standard, to determine that it is reasonably necessary and appropriate to remedy a significant risk of material health impairment."[2] In other words, "the burden was on the Agency to show, on the basis of substantial evidence, that it is at least more likely than not that long-term exposure to 10 ppm of benzene presents a significant risk of material impairment."[3]

In *American Textile Manufacturers Institute, Inc. v. Donovan (The Cotton Dust Case),*[4] The Supreme Court addressed the issue of whether the Act requires the Secretary, in promulgating a standard under section 6(b)(5), to determine that the costs of the standard bear a reasonable relationship to its benefits. The Fifth Circuit, in *The Benzene Case,* had imposed such a requirement. The D.C. Circuit, however, in *The Cotton Dust*[5] and *The Lead*[6] cases had rejected this view.

§ 6.6

1. 448 U.S. 607, 100 S.Ct. 2844, 65 L.Ed.2d 1010 (1980).

2. 448 U.S. at 639, 100 S.Ct. at 2862 (emphasis added).

3. 448 U.S. at 653, 100 S.Ct. at 2869.

4. 452 U.S. 490, 101 S.Ct. 2478, 69 L.Ed.2d 185 (1981).

5. AFL–CIO v. Marshall, 617 F.2d 636, 664 (D.C.Cir.1979), affirmed sub nomine American Textile Mfrs. Inst., Inc. v. Donovan, 452 U.S. 490, 101 S.Ct. 2478, 69 L.Ed.2d 185 (1981).

6. United Steelworkers of Am. v. Marshall, 647 F.2d 1189 (D.C.Cir.1980), cert. denied sub nomine Lead Indus. Ass'n Inc. v. Donovan, 453 U.S. 913, 101 S.Ct. 3148, 69 L.Ed.2d 997 (1981).

In a five-to-three decision, the Court rejected the argument that the Act requires the use of cost-benefit analysis. Relying on the plain meaning of the word "feasible" as "capable of being done," the Court ruled that imposing a cost-benefit requirement would be inconsistent with the mandate of Congress.

> * * * Congress itself defined the basic relationship between costs and benefits, by placing the "benefit" of worker health above all other considerations save those making attainment of this "benefit" unachievable * * *. Thus, cost-benefit analysis by OSHA is not required by the statute because feasibility analysis is.[7]

The Court observed that when Congress has intended that an agency engage in cost-benefit analysis, it has clearly indicated such an intent on the face of the statute. Neither the language of OSHA nor its legislative history indicate such a congressional intent. Moreover, the general definitional language of section 3(8) cannot be used to impose a cost-benefit requirement and thereby "eviscerate" the "to the extent feasible" language of section 6(b)(5).

According to the majority opinion of Justice Brennan, "feasible" as used in section 6(b)(5), includes economic feasibility. After reviewing the record, the Court concluded that the D.C. Circuit did not err in holding that the Secretary's finding that compliance with the cotton dust standard was economically feasible was supported by substantial evidence. Even though no specific economic studies were performed on the final standard, there were studies that showed that compliance with a stricter and more costly standard was feasible.

Revising and updating existing health standards also have been difficult. *AFL–CIO v. OSHA*[8] involved a challenge to OSHA's revision to its air contaminants standard for 428 toxic substances. The Eleventh Circuit held that the Act does not preclude "generic" rulemaking, but that each PEL must be supported by substantial evidence. The court held that OSHA satisfied the section 6(b)(5) requirement of "material impairment," but it failed to prove the "significant risk" posed by each substance or that the new standards eliminated or substantially lessen the risk.

> OSHA merely provided a conclusory statement that the new PEL will reduce the "significant" risk of material health effects shown to be caused by that substance, * * * without any explanation of how the agency determined that the risk was significant.[9]

The court said that OSHA was free to use "safety factors" as a margin of error for setting PELs, but it required that OSHA explain how the safety factor for each substance was determined.

7. 452 U.S. at 509, 101 S.Ct. at 2490   **9.** Id. at 975.
(footnote omitted).

8. 965 F.2d 962 (11th Cir.1992).

While failing to demonstrate the need for some of the new standards, the court also criticized OSHA because some standards were not protective enough. "OSHA established PELs for * * * [two] carcinogens, at levels where OSHA itself acknowledged that the risk of material health impairment remained significant."[10]

The court further criticized OSHA for failing to establish the technological and economic feasibility for each substance regulated and for each affected industry. The court concluded that "OSHA's overall approach to this rulemaking is so flawed that we must vacate the whole revised Air Contaminants Standard."[11]

The Congressional Review Act of 1996[12] provides a mechanism for Congress to consider, and then approve or disapprove, controversial federal regulations. The first use of the law was in 2001 when President Bush signed a congressional resolution of disapproval of the OSHA ergonomics standard.

§ 6.7 Promulgation of Standards—Emergency Temporary Standards

Section 6(c)(1) of the Act provides that if the Secretary determines that employees are "exposed to grave danger from exposure to substances or agents determined to be toxic or physically harmful or from new hazards," an emergency temporary standard (ETS) may be issued.[1] These standards are effective immediately upon publication in the Federal Register without any detailed rulemaking requirements. Under section 6(c)(3) of the Act an ETS may remain in effect for only six months; thereafter, the Secretary must promulgate a permanent standard under section 6(b) of the Act. In this event, the ETS serves as the proposed rule.

An emergency temporary standard must be based on the existence of a grave danger and the need for a standard to protect workers from that danger. The first element, therefore, is proving that there is a grave danger. According to the Third Circuit in *Dry Color Manufacturers' Association v. Department of Labor*,[2] the Act does not require an absolute certainty of the deleterious effect of a substance, but there must be evidence showing "more than some possibility" of a grave danger.

The second element of an ETS is the need to protect workers from the danger. In *Asbestos Information Association/North America v. OSHA*,[3] the Fifth Circuit held that the ETS was invalid and stayed its enforcement. The court's analysis focused on whether OSHA had proven the need to adopt an ETS for asbestos rather than modifying the existing standard after notice and comment rulemaking. The court pointed out that section 6(b) rulemaking can be completed within one year regard-

10. Id. at 976.
11. Id. at 987.
12. 5 U.S.C.A. § 801.

§ 6.7
1. 29 U.S.C.A. § 655(c)(1).
2. 486 F.2d 98 (3d Cir.1973).
3. 727 F.2d 415 (5th Cir.1984).

less of an ETS and therefore "the practical effects of our decision on the regulations enforced in the workplace will endure only a short time."[4] It further added that "the plain wording of the statute limits us to assessing the harm likely to accrue, or the grave danger that the ETS may alleviate, during the six-month period that is the life of the standard."[5]

§ 6.8 Promulgation of Standards—Judicial Review

The validity of OSHA standards may be reviewed by the courts in two ways. First, any party adversely affected by a standard may obtain preenforcement review by filing a petition for review within sixty days of a standard's promulgation. According to the Second Circuit, a standard is "issued" when it is filed in the Office of the Federal Register and a standard is "promulgated" when it is published in the Federal Register.[1] The date of promulgation begins the sixty-day period to seek review of the standard. Pursuant to section 6(f) of the Act, these petitions may be filed in the United States court of appeals for the circuit in which the party resides or has its principal place of business. A copy of the petition must be forwarded to the Secretary by the clerk of the court.

The second method of review, post-enforcement, is available to any person "adversely affected or aggrieved" by a final order of the Commission, by filing a petition for review pursuant to section 11(a) of the Act. Petitions for review under section 11(a) of the Act must also be filed within sixty days in a United States court of appeals for the circuit in which the violation is alleged to have occurred, for the circuit in which the employer has its principal office, or in the District of Columbia Circuit.

Filing a petition for judicial review under section 6(f) does not stay the effective date of a standard, nor does a section 11(a) petition stay a final order of the Commission. A reviewing court, however, may grant a stay. In judicial review under either section of the Act, the Secretary's determinations in promulgating a standard are conclusive if supported by "substantial evidence" in the record considered as a whole.

§ 6.9 Compliance With Standards

OSHA standards are grouped under four industry categories: General Industry, Construction, Maritime and Longshoring, and Agricultural. An employer must be cited under an applicable standard that is appropriate to the employer's business, and the burden is on the Secretary of Labor to prove by a preponderance of the evidence that the standard applies.

---

4. Id. at 420.

5. Id. at 422.

§ 6.8

1. United Technologies Corp. v. OSHA, 836 F.2d 52 (2d Cir.1987).

General Industry

General industry standards apply to all covered employers, subject to two exceptions. First, the general industry standard may be specifically limited to a certain type of business. For example, subpart R of the general industry standards contains "special" standards for bakery equipment, laundry machinery, sawmills, and the like. Nevertheless, employers covered by these "special industry" general industry standards still must comply with all other general industry standards unless the specific condition is actually covered by a "special industry" standard.

Second, the specific working conditions may be subject to a standard contained in the construction, maritime and longshoring, or agricultural standards. General industry standards will apply, however, if there is no specific construction, maritime and longshoring, or agricultural standard covering the hazardous condition. For example, "even in areas properly citable under specific maritime standards, the Secretary may hold an employer to the general industry standards in those situations where no specific standard is applicable."[1]

Construction

The construction standards apply to employers with employees engaged in "construction work," defined as "work for construction, alteration, and/or repair, including painting and decorating." Several cases have involved whether the employer's operations came within this definition. For example, in *Brock v. Cardinal Industries, Inc.,*[2] the employer was manufacturing modular housing units in a factory. It was cited under the general industry standards for failing to have guardrails on two platforms. The ALJ affirmed the violations, but the Commission reversed. The Commission majority concluded that the general industry standards did not apply because the employer was engaged in construction. "Although Cardinal's employees construct housing units in a factory setting, the carpentry, plumbing, roofing, and electrical work they perform is identical to that performed at a construction site, and identical to the kind of work that OSHA specifically intended Part 1926 to cover."[3] The Sixth Circuit reversed the Commission. According to the court, in determining whether the work performed is "construction," it is not the nature of the work in the abstract, but the nexus of the work to a particular construction site.

In *CH2M Hill, Inc. v. Herman,*[4] the Seventh Circuit reversed the Commission and held that the construction standards did not apply to an engineering firm that consulted on a sewer project because the firm did not exercise substantial supervision or control over construction. The court held that although construction standards may apply to professionals (e.g. engineers and architects) in some situations, there was inade-

§ 6.9

1. Dravo Corp. v. OSHRC, 613 F.2d 1227, 1234 (3d Cir.1980).

2. 828 F.2d 373 (6th Cir.1987).

3. Id. at 378.

4. 192 F.3d 711 (7th Cir.1999).

quate evidence that the cited employer exercised "substantial supervision" of construction activities.

Maritime and Longshoring

The terms "ship repairing," "ship building," "shipbreaking," and "longshoring" are defined in the OSHA standards. Ship repair means "any repair of a vessel, including, but not restricted to, alterations, conversions, installations, cleaning, painting, and maintenance work." Shipbuilding means "the construction of a vessel, including the installation of machinery and equipment." Shipbreaking means "any breaking down of a vessel's structure for the purpose of scrapping the vessel, including the removal of gear, equipment, or any component part of a vessel." Longshoring operation means "the loading, unloading, moving, or handling of, cargo, ship's stores, gear, etc., into, in, on, or out of any vessel."

Agricultural

There are two types of OSHA agricultural standards. First, certain general industry standards have been made applicable to agricultural operations. Second, certain standards have been promulgated that apply only to agricultural operations. OSHA has not defined "agricultural operation," but in implementing congressional appropriations limitations it has defined "farming operation" as "any operation involved in the growing or harvesting of crops or the raising of livestock or poultry, or related activities conducted by a farmer, on sites such as farms, ranches, orchards, dairy farms, or similar establishments."

Besides the four broad industry categories, OSHA standards may also be broken down, unofficially, in other ways. For example, standards are often referred to as being "horizontal" or "vertical." Horizontal standards are broadly worded standards covering many employers in various industries. Vertical standards are detailed, specific standards applied to a smaller number of employers—usually in a particular industry. Standards also may be divided into "specification" standards and "performance" standards. Specification standards detail the precise equipment, materials, and work processes required to eliminate hazards. Performance standards indicate the degree of safety and health protection to be achieved, but are more flexible and leave the method of achieving the protection to the employer. Finally, standards may be "general" or "specific." General standards, such as those dealing with housekeeping or personal protective equipment, apply to a variety of workplace settings. Specific standards, such as a requirement that a precise type of machine be guarded in a precise manner, apply only to prescribed situations.

As a general rule, when two or more standards apply to a particular working condition, a vertical standard will take precedence over a horizontal standard and a specific standard will take precedence over a general standard.

Employee Training and Education

Many OSHA standards require that employers provide specific safety training for employees. The failure to provide adequate safety training may constitute a violation of a specific training standard. For example, the Second Circuit held that a standard requiring an employer to designate a competent person to inspect machinery and equipment meant that the employer was required to select a specific employee and to notify the employee of the existence and nature of his or her safety inspection duties.

Along with the duty to comply with specific safety training standards, employers have an overall duty to train employees adequately for their jobs. Employers must take reasonable precautionary steps to protect employees from hazards. "And precautionary steps, of course, include the employer's providing an adequate safety and training program."[5] The reasonableness of training depends upon the obviousness of the hazard, the experience of the employee, the likelihood that an accident will occur, and the degree of harm likely to result from an accident. Inadequate safety training can also be the basis of a section 5(a)(1) violation.

It is important to remember that the degree of safety training required of a particular employee performing a specific job will vary considerably. Some of the factors considered in determining the amount of safety training required are: (1) the employee's experience, expertise, and other qualifications; (2) the nature of the employee's job function; and (3) the nature of the hazards to which an employee may be exposed in the normal course of work.

Supervision

Employers are required to provide adequate supervision of employees, although the degree of supervision required depends on several factors. In general, less supervision is required where employees are well-trained, competent, experienced, and have good safety records; where the work involved is not overly hazardous; or where constant supervision is impractical. The Fifth Circuit held that the owner of a company with an excellent safety program was not required to remain on the job and direct employees himself. The court stated that this would be unreasonable and infeasible. Similarly, the Commission has held that an employer was not required to supervise constantly its employees who were working at another employer's worksite and were under the direction of the other employer.

In another leading case, the Third Circuit declared that "[w]hile close supervision may be required in some cases to avoid accidents, it is unrealistic to expect an experienced and well-qualified laboratory techni-

---

5. Brennan v. Butler Lime & Cement Co., 520 F.2d 1011, 1017 (7th Cir.1975).

cian to be under constant scrutiny."[6] The court further pointed out that requiring each employee to be watched constantly by a supervisor would be "totally impractical and in all but the most unusual circumstances, an unnecessary burden."

Safety Equipment

Many OSHA standards require compliance by adopting prescribed safety procedures or by modifying machinery to include safety devices. Employers also have a duty to supply their employees with tools and equipment in safe condition. The Commission has held, however, that this duty is not absolute, and that employers will not be liable for latent defects in machinery or tools manufactured or repaired by another company. Nevertheless, employers must exercise reasonable diligence in providing safe tools, including periodically examining and testing equipment. It is not necessary for the Secretary to observe defective tools or machinery in use where other evidence indicates that defective tools or machinery were in use at the time of the alleged violation or were available for use.

Employers may also be required to provide, and to insist on the use of, special safety equipment. This equipment is commonly referred to as "personal protective equipment." Examples of personal protective equipment are safety shoes, safety belts, goggles, and hard hats. OSHA does not certify, approve, or endorse brands of safety equipment and manufacturers may not represent that their products are recommended by OSHA.

The Fifth Circuit construed a standard requiring the use of personal protective equipment "wherever it is necessary by reason of hazards of process or environment." The court applied a "reasonable man" test and held that the standard was not impermissibly vague. Furthermore, the need for using safety shoes was not dependent on any evidence of prior accidents.

Many safety standards simply read that the employer must "provide" safety equipment. Thus, it has been important to determine whether "provide" means simply "make available" to employees or whether it means "require the use of." In *Usery v. Kennecott Copper Corp.*,[7] the Tenth Circuit reversed the Commission and held that "provide" does *not* mean "require the use of." According to the court, this result was mandated by the plain meaning of the word, which must be used in interpretation. The Commission has followed the Tenth Circuit's decision in *Kennecott*. The word "provide" requires only that safety equipment be "made available." The Commission attempted to distinguish cases which had held to the contrary by asserting that the standard in those cases specifically mentioned "use."

6. Brennan v. OSHRC (Hanovia Lamp Div.), 502 F.2d 946, 949 (3d Cir.1974).

7. 577 F.2d 1113 (10th Cir.1977). Accord, Borton, Inc. v. OSHRC, 734 F.2d 508 (10th Cir.1984).

The question also has been raised whether the word "provide" means that the employer must pay for personal protective equipment. The Third Circuit has held that the word "provide" in a personal protective equipment standard did not mean that the employer was required to bear the cost for safety shoes worn by employees. Although the question of cost should be resolved during collective bargaining, the court held that the employer still must require the use of protective footwear. The Commission has also held that employers need not pay for personal protective equipment.

Health Hazards

An area in which employers have a heightened duty is in protecting employees from exposure to health hazards such as asbestos, vinyl chloride, and lead. Because of the dangers associated with these substances, preventive duties are extensive and explicit.

The first responsibility of the employer is to conduct periodic atmospheric tests to determine the presence and concentration of hazardous substances. The standards differ on the frequency of the testing, but even stringent requirements have been upheld. For example, the Second Circuit held that an employer must monitor *every* operation in which vinyl chloride was released, regardless of the employer's prediction that only negligible concentrations of the gas were released. The Commission, however, has held that the asbestos standard does not require environmental monitoring or medical examinations where employees are not regularly exposed during the course of their work, even though their sporadic exposures sometimes exceeded the standard.

In detecting health hazards, an employer is only required to exercise reasonable diligence. A citation was vacated where the employer had retained an independent testing laboratory to conduct atmospheric tests, even though those tests failed to discover excess levels of asbestos fibers.

An employer may also be required to provide periodic medical examinations for each employee. The D.C. Circuit affirmed the Commission's holding that this requirement exists where employees are exposed to *any* concentration of asbestos fibers, even if below the permissible limit. In addition, employers are required to keep detailed records of all medical examinations and atmospheric tests.

OSHA's health standards require that medical examinations be provided "without cost" or "at no cost" to the employee. The Commission has held that a provision in the inorganic arsenic standard providing that medical examinations be provided without cost required the employer to compensate employees for time spent taking the examination (outside normal working hours) and for extra transportation expenses.

Variances

Pursuant to section 6(d) of the Act, an employer may petition the Secretary for a "permanent" variance when its safety practices are not in strict compliance with a standard, but still achieve the same result. A "temporary" variance may be sought under section 6(b)(6)(A) of the Act when an employer cannot meet the requirements of a standard within the time specified for compliance. It is essentially a preinspection extension of abatement. The Act also provides for variances in the interest of national defense under section 16 and variances in the aid of research under section 6(b)(6)(C). The Secretary has published regulations to cover the four types of variances.

§ 6.10 Elements of a Violation

To establish a prima facie violation of section 5(a)(2) of the Act, the Secretary must prove by a preponderance of the evidence that (1) the cited standard applies, (2) there was a failure to comply with the cited standard, (3) an employee had access to the violative condition, and (4) the employer knew or could have known of the condition with the exercise of reasonable diligence. The Secretary also has the burden of proving the reasonableness of the proposed abatement date.

Exposure

To constitute a violation of section 5(a)(2) there must be at least some possibility of employee exposure. Early Commission decisions required the Secretary to prove the "actual exposure" of employees, although this term was never adequately defined. It was clear, however, that there could be no violation unless an employee was imperiled by a hazard, as where an employee was "seen by an inspector teetering on the edge of the floor 150 feet or so up from the ground."[1]

In *Gilles & Cotting, Inc.*,[2] the Commission expressly rejected the actual exposure rule and replaced it with the concept of access. Access was said to be present whenever employees in the course of their work, their personal comfort activities while on the job, or their normal means of ingress and egress to their workplaces have been, are, or will be in a zone of danger. Because actual exposure would exist if employees have been or are in a zone of danger, the only new element is when employees "will be in a zone of danger."

Subsequent Commission decisions have modified *Gilles & Cotting* to permit the Secretary to prove exposure by showing that employees may reasonably be expected to come into danger considering the nature of the work, the work activities required, and the routes of arrival and departure.

Access is a way by which exposure can be proved through the use of circumstantial evidence. This broad principle has been reaffirmed by the Commission in a number of decisions. Therefore, the Secretary need not prove the identity of exposed employees; it is not necessary that machinery be observed in operation where other evidence indicates that it was

§ 6.10

1. Brennan v. OSHRC (Underhill Constr. Corp.), 513 F.2d 1032, 1039 (2d Cir.1975).

2. 3 OSHC 2002, 1975–76 OSHD ¶ 20,-448 (1976).

in use at the time of the alleged violation or was available for use; and it is immaterial that a door is locked where the normal duties of employees requires them to enter the room. On the other hand, access was not established where the only employee exposed to the hazard was the employer's walkaround representative during the OSHA inspection and where the Secretary failed to prove reasonable predictability of access to the point of operation of unguarded machinery.

Knowledge

To prove a violation, the Secretary must not only establish that there has been noncompliance with a standard to which employees had access, but the Secretary must also prove an element of "knowledge" on the part of the employer. In this context, "knowledge" refers to an awareness of the existence of the conditions allegedly in noncompliance with OSHA standards. It is not necessary to prove that the employer knew the requirements of the standard.

The knowledge requirement was first applied to serious violations. Indeed, the definition of a serious violation in section 17(k) of the Act requiring a substantial probability that death or serious physical harm could result is qualified by the words "unless the employer did not, and could not with the exercise of reasonable diligence, know of the presence of the violation." The Commission has long held that the Secretary has the burden of proving knowledge for serious violations.

By its terms, section 17(k) indicates that there can be no serious violation unless the employer did not or could not *with the exercise of reasonable diligence* know of the presence of the violation. This indicates that knowledge may be either actual or constructive. "Reasonable diligence" has been defined as "such *watchfulness*, *caution*, and *foresight* as, under all the circumstances of the particular service, a corporation controlled by careful prudent officers ought to exercise."[3] The test of knowledge is whether the employer knew or, with the exercise of reasonable diligence, could have known of the presence of the violation. Where an employer maintains an adequate inspection program the burden of proof is on the Secretary to prove that the employer's failure to discover the violative condition was due to a lack of reasonable diligence.

Constructive knowledge has been found where the employer failed to inspect its workplace to discover readily apparent hazards, where there were inadequate safety instructions, where safety rules were not enforced, where there were prior instances of employee noncompliance, where an employee had been injured previously by the same hazard, and where the employer had received at least three written complaints from employees before the OSHA inspection. Even under the constructive knowledge standard an employer need only do what is reasonable to

---

3. Ames Crane & Rental Serv., Inc., 3 OSHC 1279, 1974–75 OSHD ¶ 19,724 (1975) (separate opinion of Cleary, Comm'r), affirmed, 532 F.2d 123 (8th Cir.1976), quoting Wabash Ry. v. McDaniels, 107 U.S. 454, 460, 2 S.Ct. 932, 27 L.Ed. 605 (1883) (opinion of Harlan, J.) (emphasis added by Cleary, Comm'r).

discover hazards. Thus, the Secretary failed to prove employer knowledge where the employer had retained a consulting firm to conduct atmospheric tests and the consultant failed to discover that employees were exposed to excess levels of airborne contaminants.

Unlike the term "serious violation," defined in section 17(k) of the Act, the term "nonserious violation" is not defined anywhere in the Act. In *Prestressed Systems, Inc.*,[4] however, the Commission held that the Secretary has the burden of proving employer knowledge in both serious and nonserious violations. The Commission clearly indicated that constructive knowledge can be shown if the employer failed to exercise reasonable diligence in detecting hazardous conditions. All hazards in "plain view" would appear to be detectable.

Feasibility

OSHA standards generally specify the means for compliance but do not contain specific language relating to the feasibility of compliance. Thus, the question has been raised whether the Secretary should have the burden of proving that compliance with a standard is feasible or should feasibility be presumed and the burden of proving the lack of feasibility be on the employer?

Unlike section 5(a)(2) of the Act and the specific standards with which compliance is mandated by that section, the general duty clause, section 5(a)(1) of the Act, is couched in broad terms. Therefore, to prove a violation of section 5(a)(1) the Secretary must indicate the specific steps the employer should have taken to avoid citation and must demonstrate the feasibility and likely utility of those measures. Commission decisions have held that the burden of proving feasibility, required for section 5(a)(1) violations, does not pertain to violations of section 5(a)(2) of the Act. In *Ace Sheeting & Repair Co. v. OSHRC*,[5] the Fifth Circuit affirmed the Commission's holding that the Secretary need not prove the feasibility of compliance with a standard. The Commission and court both pointed out that the feasibility requirement of section 5(a)(1) of the Act was designed to allay the fear that employers would not be adequately informed of the nature of the violation and the means for compliance. This problem, however, does not arise when an employer is cited under a precise standard which provides for specific methods of compliance.

A small number of standards, particularly health standards, actually use the word "feasible" in the standard and condition an employer's obligation to comply on the existence of feasible methods. The Commission has held that, when a violation of one of these standards is alleged, the Secretary has the burden of proving technological feasibility. Although the Secretary need not show the feasibility of a detailed abatement program, the Secretary must prove that *some* controls are feasible and that the compliance measures are feasible at the cited employer's workplace.

4. 9 OSHC 1864, 1981 OSHD ¶ 25,358 (1981).

5. 555 F.2d 439 (5th Cir.1977), affirming 3 OSHC 1868, 1975–76 OSHD ¶ 20,256 (1975).

Because the Secretary is presumed to have considered economic factors before promulgating a standard, the Secretary will not normally have the burden of proving the economic feasibility of compliance in a contest before the Commission. But, where the word "feasible" is used in a standard, economic feasibility is considered. In *Sherwin–Williams Co.*,[6] the Commission adopted the following allocation of the burden of proof. The Secretary must prove that proposed engineering and administrative controls are technologically and economically feasible. After the Secretary proves technological feasibility, the burden of producing evidence shifts to the employer, which may raise the issue of economic feasibility and go forward with evidence of the cost of controls and personal protective equipment (PPE). The burden of production then returns to the Secretary to prove that the benefits of the proposed engineering controls justify their costs in relation to other abatement measures. The ultimate burden of persuasion on the feasibility issue remains with the Secretary.

§ 6.11 Defenses

Although OSHA standards have been adopted and promulgated for literal compliance, section 5(a)(2) does not impose strict liability on employers. Thus, despite the rejection of common law defenses such as assumption of risk and contributory negligence, the Commission and courts have recognized several defenses.

The first group of defenses, "substantive defenses," deals with the validity and applicability of a particular standard to the facts of a case, the nature of the employer's conduct, and its effect on the safety and health of employees. These defenses must be proved by a preponderance of the evidence.

The second group of defenses, "procedural defenses," involves the validity of the enforcement procedures of the Secretary and the Commission's adjudication of contested cases. Examples include challenges to inspection procedures, citation issuance, and the hearing process.

Substantive defenses include different types of defensive matters. For example, the employer may challenge the Secretary's prima facie case, such as by proving that there was no exposure or no knowledge, or that the wrong standard was cited or the standard does not apply to the employer. In addition, affirmative defenses, such as vagueness or improper promulgation of the standard, must be raised in the notice of contest or answer.

Improper Promulgation of Standard

In addition to the preenforcement review of standards pursuant to section 6(f) of the Act, the validity of a standard's promulgation may be challenged in an enforcement action before the Commission under sec-

6. 11 OSHC 2105, 1984–85 OSHD ¶ 26,-986 (1984), petition for review withdrawn, No. 84–2587 (7th Cir.1984).

tion 10(c) of the Act and on judicial review of a Commission decision pursuant to section 11(a) of the Act. Commission and judicial decisions have supported this principle. For example, the Third Circuit, in ruling that the Commission may consider the improper promulgation defense, observed that "it would be an exercise in futility for the Commission to enforce a citation under a standard which it knew, perhaps from prior adjudications, would be held invalid by this court."[1]

The Commission has held that it will not consider challenges to established federal standards based on alleged procedural deficiencies in their initial promulgation under their original statutes. The Commission will, however, permit challenges based on alleged procedural errors committed when the same standards were adopted as OSHA standards pursuant to section 6(a) of the Act.

Vagueness of Standard

Some standards containing general language have been attacked on due process grounds because they are allegedly too vague to give employers an adequate explanation of what conduct is required. Although vagueness challenges have been common, they have not met with much success at either the Commission or court of appeals level.

Ryder Truck Lines, Inc. v. Brennan[2] was the first judicial decision to consider the vagueness issue. The Fifth Circuit, in affirming the validity of a general personal protective equipment standard, held that "[s]o long as the mandate affords a reasonable warning of the proscribed conduct in light of common understanding and practices, it will pass constitutional muster."[3] Of particular importance to the court was that the standard involved remedial civil legislation and no First Amendment rights were at issue. The use of an objective, reasonable person test, first applied in *Ryder,* has been followed by other circuits and by the Commission.

Whether a standard provides fair notice to an employer cannot be determined solely from the face of the standard, but the facts of each case must be considered. Nevertheless, some general principles can be discerned from the cases decided on the basis of vagueness. First, flexibility in wording, or even imprecise or inartful drafting, does not necessarily mean that a standard is impermissibly vague. Second, a standard is not vague simply because its application requires the exercise of judgment. Third, a vague standard "may be cured by authoritative judicial or administrative interpretations which clarify obscurities or resolve ambiguities."[4] Fourth, where the standard's terms are "unequivocal," the Commission will not even apply a reasonable person test in rejecting a vagueness challenge.

§ 6.11

1. See, e.g., Atlantic & Gulf Stevedores, Inc. v. OSHRC, 534 F.2d 541, 551 (3d Cir. 1976).

2. 497 F.2d 230 (5th Cir.1974).

3. Id. at 233.

4. Diebold, Inc. v. Marshall, 585 F.2d 1327, 1338 (6th Cir.1978).

Unpreventable Employee Misconduct

Unpreventable employee misconduct is the most important defense. It also has been referred to as "isolated occurrence," "isolated incident," "isolated misconduct," and "employee misconduct." Regardless of the name, the basic premise of this defense is that it would be unfair and would not promote employee safety and health to penalize an employer for hazardous conditions that were created by employees, unpreventable, and not likely to recur.

In *Standard Glass Co.,*[5] the Commission developed a three-part test to determine whether an employer has proved the unpreventable employee misconduct defense: (1) it required an isolated, brief violation of a standard by an employee; (2) which is unknown to the employer; and (3) is contrary to both the employer's instructions and a company work rule which the employer has uniformly enforced. Although *Standard Glass* has never been overruled, the Commission has replaced it with a four-part test first set forth in *Jensen Construction Co.:*[6] (1) the employer has established work rules designed to prevent the violation; (2) it has adequately communicated these rules to its employees; (3) it has taken steps to discover violations; and (4) it has effectively enforced the rules when violations have been discovered. The *Standard Glass* elements still find their way into the *Jensen* test, but the newer rule focuses more on the employer's overall safety program than on the events surrounding the specific incident of violative conduct. Each of the elements has been the subject of litigation.

A slightly different formulation of the first requirement is that the employer's commitment to safety is reflected by the establishment of work rules effectively implementing the requirements of the standard. However this first element is phrased, it will usually be the easiest of the four requirements for the employer to prove.

The second element focuses on the employer's overall safety training, specific work instructions, and hazard warnings. The defense has been rejected where the employer has failed to provide the necessary overall safety training of employees, where there were inadequate specific work instructions—especially where there were inexperienced employees, and where warnings of workplace hazards were absent, incomplete, or ineffective. By contrast, the defense has been sustained where the employees were well trained, experienced, and knew of the rules, and where the work rule was effectively communicated to the employees.

Under the third element, the employer is presenting evidence that it lacked even constructive knowledge of the noncomplying conditions. The success of the defense will depend on whether the employer exercised reasonable diligence in detecting workplace hazards.

Where there is evidence of widespread noncompliance by employees, both in numbers of employees and duration of exposure, there is a strong

5. 1 OSHC 1045, 1971–73, OSHD ¶ 15,-146 (1972).

6. 7 OSHC 1477, 1979 OSHD ¶ 23,664 (1979).

inference that the employer's efforts in detecting and correcting violations have been lacking. This focus on the degree of noncompliance was the fist step in the *Standard Glass* test and there are a number of cases on this point. The defense has been rejected where there were numerous incidents of prior noncompliance and where several employees were engaged in the proscribed conduct. On the other hand, the defense has been sustained where there was a single incident of noncompliance by only one or a few employees.

Another inference arising in this context is that where there is evidence of inadequate supervision or enforcement of safety rules by supervisors, the employer did not take adequate steps to discover violations. Although the defense has been unsuccessful where there was inadequate supervision of employees, supervisory misconduct will not necessarily result in the finding of a violation.

The final element of the defense involves the degree to which the employer has enforced its safety rules through sanctions and disciplining of noncomplying employees. Thus, where the employer did not discipline employees after prior incidents of violative conduct, subsequent violations have not been considered "unpreventable" and the defense has failed. Where there have been sanctions, such as reprimands and the docking of pay, the defense has been upheld. Evidence of discipline following an inspection will be considered by the Commission.

Impossibility/Infeasibility

To establish the defense of impossibility of compliance, an employer was required to prove that (1) compliance with the standard was functionally impossible or would preclude performance of required work, and (2) alternative means of employee protection were unavailable or were in use. It was a difficult burden to meet. The Commission held that it was not enough for the employer to show that compliance was difficult, expensive, would require changes in production methods, or that one means of compliance was unsuccessful. Thus, the defense was rejected where the employer failed to prove that compliance was impossible, where alternative measures were not used, and where compliance was actually achieved after the issuance of the citation.

In *Dun–Par Engineered Form Co.*,[7] the Commission overruled prior precedent and held that the proper focus should be on infeasibility rather than impossibility. The Commission held that once the employer proves that compliance is infeasible, the burden shifts to the Secretary to prove the existence of a feasible alternative. On judicial review, the Eighth Circuit reversed the Commission and held that the burden of proving the existence of a feasible alternative does not shift to the Secretary. Subsequently, the Commission has followed the Eighth Circuit's approach to the infeasibility defense.

7. 12 OSHC 1949, 1986 OSHD ¶ 27,650 (1986), reversed, 843 F.2d 1135 (8th Cir. 1988).

To establish an infeasibility defense the employer must prove: (1) the means of compliance prescribed by the applicable standard would have been infeasible under the circumstances in that (a) its implementation would have been technologically or economically infeasible, or (b) necessary work operations would be technologically or economically infeasible after its implementation, and (2) either (a) an alternative method of protection was used, or (b) there was no feasible alternative means of protection.

Greater Hazard

In some instances employers have been able to prove that compliance with a standard would actually create a greater hazard than noncompliance. The Commission will vacate a citation under the greater hazard defense if the employer can prove: (1) the hazards of compliance are greater than the hazards of noncompliance; (2) alternative means of protecting employees are unavailable; and (3) a variance application would be inappropriate. This three-part test has received widespread judicial approval.

The essence of the greater hazard defense is that the hazards of compliance with a standard are greater than the hazards of noncompliance. The evidence of a greater hazard, however, must be clear. The "mere verbalized fears" of employees and an employer's unsupported opinion have been held to be inadequate. Similarly, it is not enough that compliance with the standard will cause momentary lapses of protection or inconvenience to employees. An employer's good faith belief that its own safety policies are safer than those required by OSHA does not constitute a defense.

The issue has been raised whether the greater hazard defense applies where compliance with the standard will eliminate the initial hazard but will create new hazards that, overall, pose greater hazards. In *Russ Kaller, Inc.*,[8] the employer asserted that compliance with a standard's guardrail requirement would prevent employees from jumping clear of a collapsing scaffold. The Commission rejected this defense and held that it is not enough for the employer to show that compliance with a standard will create *new* hazards. The greater hazard defense is limited to instances where the specific hazard covered by the standard would be increased by compliance.

§ 6.12 General Duty Clause

The general duty clause, section 5 (a)(1), was enacted to cover serious hazards to which no specific standard applies. Because section 5(a)(1) was designed to augment rather than supplant standards, citation under section 5(a)(1) is improper where a specific standard is appropriate.

To prove a violation of section 5(a)(1) the Secretary must establish that the employer failed to render its workplace free of a hazard, which

8. 4 OSHC 1758, 1976–77 OSHD ¶ 21,152 (1976).

was "recognized" by the employer or its industry, and which was causing or likely to cause death or serious physical harm. In addition, the Secretary must demonstrate the feasibility and likely utility of specific abatement measures. Nevertheless, as with section 5(a)(2) violations, a prima facie case under section 5(a)(1) does not require the actual occurrence of an accident, nor does the occurrence of an accident, by itself, prove the existence of a violation.

The general duty clause was not intended to impose strict liability on employers under respondeat superior or any other theory. Only "feasibly preventable" forms of hazardous conduct can support a section 5(a)(1) violation. Thus, employers may assert a wide range of defenses, many of which are identical to defenses used for alleged violations of standards. The assertion that section 5(a)(1) is unconstitutionally vague, however, has been rejected.

Decisions of the Commission and courts of appeals have held that citation under section 5(a)(1) of the Act is only proper if no specific standard applies. "The standards presumably give the employer superior notice of the alleged violation and should be used instead of the general duty clause whenever possible."[1] The Commission has not yet specifically addressed the issue of whether the Secretary must show that no standard applies or whether the burden is on the employer to prove that there *is* an applicable standard. It would appear, however, that the existence of an applicable standard is a defense to be raised by the employer.

It is often quite difficult to determine whether a standard applies to the cited condition, and the Secretary has used alternative pleadings and amendments of pleadings to avoid a dismissal when one basis of the citation is found to be inapplicable. There are particular problems raised when a citation is issued under section 5(a)(1) of the Act when there are "similar" advisory or revoked standards or standards with partial coverage of the hazard.

In *A. Prokosch & Sons Sheet Metal*,[2] a majority of the Commission held that section 5(a)(1) does not apply where the Secretary adopted an advisory ("should") American National Standards Institute (ANSI) standard pursuant to section 6(a) of the Act. In dissent, Commissioner Cottine argued that the majority created an unjustifiable void in worker protection. In his view, advisory provisions are not OSHA standards under section 3(8) of the Act because they do not *require* employer conduct and because they were expressly not adopted as standards by OSHA.

In *Pratt & Whitney Aircraft*,[3] the Commission held that section 5(a)(1) can be cited when the applicable specific standard has been

§ 6.12

1. Usery v. Marquette Cement Mfg. Co., 568 F.2d 902, 905 n. 5 (2d Cir.1977).

2. 8 OSHC 2077, 1980 OSHD ¶ 24,840 (1980).

3. 8 OSHC 29, 1980 OSHD ¶ 24,447 (1980), remanded, 649 F.2d 96 (2d Cir. 1981).

revoked. The revocation was published in the Federal Register, and one of the expressed reasons was that the overall purpose of the revoked standard was the protection of property rather than employees. Revocation was viewed as necessary to effectuate employee safety and health. This notice was adequate to apprise employers of their continuing duties under the Act.

In some instances a standard will provide only partial protection against a hazard. The Commission has held that citation under section 5(a)(1) is improper where the applicable standard is inadequate because this would amount to a circumvention of the rulemaking process. Similar reasoning has been used to vacate section 5(a)(1) citations where there were partially applicable standards with arguably limited utility in abating the hazard. According to the Commission, it is impermissible for the Commission to inquire into the adequacy of the abatement measures required by standards.

Elements of a Violation

Section 5(a)(1) of the Act specifically requires that "each employer shall furnish to each of *his employees* employment and a place of employment" free from recognized hazards. Thus, unlike section 5(a)(2) of the Act, which mandates compliance with standards, section 5(a)(1) limits the employer's duty to protecting its own employees from recognized hazards.

The most distinctive and significant element of section 5(a)(1) violations is that they are limited to "recognized hazards." The "recognition" requirement serves to ensure that cited employers at least have constructive knowledge of the existence of specific hazardous conditions. In this way, Congress sought to eliminate the unfairness of assessing first-instance civil penalties based on such a sweeping and broadly worded provision.

As with section 5(a)(2) violations, the relevant inquiry for determining the existence of a violation is whether there are hazardous conditions and not whether there has been an accident. Also, "recognition" refers to knowledge of the hazard and not to recognition of the method of abatement.

The leading case of *American Smelting & Refining Co. v. OSHRC*[4] concerned the issue of whether recognized hazards are limited to those detectable through the senses or whether they extend to hazards only detectable through instrumentation. The Eighth Circuit reviewed the legislative history of section 5(a)(1) of the Act and found of considerable importance the fact that Congress changed the wording from "readily apparent hazards," used in an earlier version of the bill, to "recognized hazards." Moreover, the court pointed out that the ameliorative purpose of the Act would be subverted by a narrow construction of "recognized hazards." "[T]o limit the general duty clause to dangers only detectable by the human senses seems to us to be a folly * * *. Where hazards are

---

4. 501 F.2d 504 (8th Cir.1974).

recognized but not detectable by the senses, common sense and prudence demand that instrumentation be utilized."[5]

A hazard is considered recognized if it is common knowledge in the employer's industry *or* if the employer has knowledge of the hazardous condition. Thus, recognition may be established either objectively or subjectively. In *National Realty & Construction Co., Inc. v. OSHRC*,[6] the D.C. Circuit held that whether a hazard is recognized by an industry is determined by the "common knowledge of safety experts who are familiar with the circumstances of the industry or the activity in question."[7] The Commission has followed *National Realty* and also has held that the expert testimony of an OSHA compliance officer about industry practice may be used to show that a hazard was recognized.

The second way in which a hazard may be recognized is if the employer has knowledge of the hazard. In *Brennan v. OSHRC (Vy Lactos Laboratories, Inc.)*,[8] the Eighth Circuit held that an employer's personal knowledge of the existence of a hazard was sufficient to make the hazard "recognized." This view has been followed by the Commission. It should be emphasized, however, that employer knowledge to show hazard recognition under section 5(a)(1) of the Act refers to knowledge that a condition is hazardous. This contrasts with section 5(a)(2) employer knowledge, which refers to knowledge that a condition exists.

Burden of Proof

The Secretary's burden of proving a violation of the general duty clause is greater than the burden of proving a violation of a standard. In *National Realty* the D.C. Circuit held that the Secretary must prove: (1) that the employer failed to render its workplace free of a hazard which was (2) recognized, and (3) causing or likely to cause death or serious physical harm, and (4) the Secretary must specify the particular steps the cited employer should have taken to avoid citation and demonstrate the feasibility and likely utility of those measures. This formulation of the burden of proof has been adopted by the Commission, the other courts of appeals, and the Secretary.

The Secretary must meet this burden by introducing a preponderance of reliable and probative evidence. Speculation and conjecture will not satisfy the Secretary's burden. Similarly, the Commission may not base the finding of a section 5(a)(1) violation on *its own* speculation. In *National Realty* the court reversed the Commission's finding of a violation because the commissioners had served as "expert witnesses" for the Secretary, speculating what additional steps the employer could have taken to prevent employees from riding on the front of bulldozers and other construction equipment. The court held that Commission expertise cannot operate on an empty record and satisfy the Secretary's burden through conjecture.

5. Id. at 511.
6. 489 F.2d 1257 (D.C.Cir.1973).
7. Id. at 1265 n. 32.
8. 494 F.2d 460 (8th Cir.1974).

As with section 5(a)(2) violations, general duty clause violations require employee exposure and employer knowledge. The knowledge requirement of section 5(a)(1) really consists of two parts. First, the employer must have knowledge that a particular work practice is hazardous or constructive knowledge of this fact because the practice is a recognized hazard in the employer's industry. This establishes that the hazard is "recognized." Second, the employer must have actual or constructive knowledge that the allegedly hazardous condition exists at its workplace.

Defenses

Employers have a wide range of defenses available against alleged section 5(a)(1) violations. Jurisdictional and procedural defenses to section 5(a)(1) violations are identical to those raised in section 5(a)(2) cases. The employer also may introduce any evidence that would rebut the Secretary's prima facie case. The employer can show that a specific standard applied, that the hazard was not recognized, that there was insufficient employee exposure, that the employer had no knowledge of the violation, or that the Secretary failed to indicate what method of compliance was feasible.

Although common law defenses like contributory negligence and assumption of risk do not apply, employers may raise many of the same substantive defenses that can be raised in a section 5(a)(2) case. The Secretary's heightened burden of proof under section 5(a)(1) of the Act, however, has the effect of allocating to the Secretary the burden of proving some of these matters. For example, the Ninth Circuit has held that the Secretary must prove that the proposed method of abatement will not result in a greater hazard. This is part of the Secretary's proof relating to "feasibility." Because feasibility also includes "utility" and "practicality," interference with work, inconvenience, and other defenses would appear to be relevant.

§ 6.13 Multi–Employer Responsibility

In many instances employees will have, simultaneously, employment relationships with more than one employer. Each of these employers may be considered a "joint employer." The most common example of joint employers is where one employer leases from another employer both a piece of heavy equipment, such as a crane, and an employee to operate the crane. If the leased employee operating the crane becomes involved in violative conduct, the question arises whether the original employer (lessor), the secondary employer (lessee), or both employers are in violation.

Employer responsibility is generally based on determining which employer controls, supervises, or directs the loaned employee. The Commission and courts have refused to apply the agency concept of "borrowed servant" to transfer liability to the *secondary* employer. Thus, where the lessee of the crane "relies upon the expertise of the crane operator and gives no particular direction as to the operation of the crane, it is the duty of * * * the actual employer of the crane operator to comply with the minimum safety requirements as set forth in the standards."[1]

For an original employer to avoid liability under the Act, it must provide adequate safety training and instruction. In *A & W Drill Rentals, Inc.*,[2] the Commission vacated a section 5(a)(1) citation based on a crane operator's negligent failure to maintain a safe distance between the crane and power lines. The cited employer, a drill rental firm, was held to have taken adequate precautionary measures by employing an experienced drilling rig operator, instructing him to be careful to avoid overhead lines, informing him of the presence of power lines at the jobsite, and posting clearance limits on the rig. The same criteria of supervision, direction, and control are used to analyze the liability of secondary employers.

The most common multi-employer problem involves prime contractors and subcontractors on construction sites. Because of the nature of the work, employees of one employer may be exposed to hazards created by other employers. In these situations the question is which employer or employers have violated the Act: the employer that controls the work area containing the hazard, regardless of whether this employer's own employees are exposed; the employer that has employees exposed to the hazard; both employers; or maybe some third party, such as the owner of the land or the general contractor.

In *Brennan v. OSHRC (Underhill Construction Corp.)*,[3] the cited employer was part of a joint venture employed as a subcontractor in erecting a high-rise housing project. An inspection disclosed violative conditions, such as storing steel braces a foot over the edge of the unguarded fourteenth floor under which workers passed, and failing to erect perimeter guards on open-sided floors as high as the seventeenth floor. Reversing the Commission on one of the violations, the Second Circuit affirmed both citations, rejecting the contention that none of the cited employer's own employees was exposed to the hazards.

According to the court's well-reasoned opinion, where an employer is in control of an area and responsible for its maintenance, the Secretary need only show that "a hazard has been committed and that the area of the hazard was accessible to the employees of the cited employer or those of other employers engaged in a common undertaking."[4] The court specifically rejected the Commission's "narrow" and "unreasonable" interpretation, and relied on the congressional intent to encourage reduction of safety hazards to employees at their place of employment.

Underhill established that an employer may be in violation of section 5(a)(2) of the Act even if none of its own employees are exposed.

§ 6.13

1. Frohlick Crane Serv., Inc. v. OSHRC, 521 F.2d 628, 631 (10th Cir.1975).

2. 2 OSHC 1394, 1974–75 OSHD ¶ 19,076 (1974).

3. 513 F.2d 1032 (2d Cir.1975).

4. Id. at 1038.

In subsequent decisions, the Commission has expressly adopted the reasoning in *Underhill*. Moreover, the Commission has extended *Underhill* beyond construction to all multi-employer situations where the cited employer creates or controls a hazard to which one or more employees of another employer are exposed. Such an extension, however, has been rejected by at least one court.

In *Anning–Johnson Co.*[5] and *Grossman Steel & Aluminum Corp.*,[6] the Commission held that a noncontrolling employer is not in violation if it did not, and could not with the exercise of reasonable diligence, know of the hazard. The Commission's position also allows an employer to escape liability by taking realistic abatement measures, even though these measures may fall short of literal compliance with applicable standards. A prerequisite to the application of the *Anning–Johnson/Grossman* rule is that there is exposure of the employees of the cited employer, but no control. As expressed by the Commission in *Anning–Johnson*, the cited employer must not have created the violation and must have lacked the "means to rectify" it. To determine whether an employer has the means to rectify a violation, the Commission will look to three factors: (1) whether the employer had the physical capacity to comply or to order compliance by others; (2) whether any constraints imposed by craft union agreements and practices restricted the employer's ability to abate; and (3) whether "contractual or monetary restraints" prevented abatement. Once an employer establishes that it lacked the means to rectify a violation, the employer will be excused from literal compliance with applicable standards. But, the employer will still be in violation if it did not undertake realistic, nonliteral abatement measures. The use of such measures by an employer must be raised as a defense.

In *Don Davis,*[7] the Commission held that control over the manner and means of accomplishing work must include control over the workers and not just the results of the work. "One who cannot hire, discipline, or fire a worker, cannot assign him additional projects, and does not set the worker's pay or work cannot be said to control the worker." The Commission relied on common law agency principles and the statutory definition of "employer." This is a questionable holding because employers having control of the workplace, including the authority to direct workers in their manner of work, would not be liable for exposing workers to hazards simply because of a lack of an employment relationship.

§ 6.14   Recordkeeping

Section 8(c) of the Act vests the Secretary of Labor with comprehensive authority to promulgate regulations requiring employers to main-

---

5. 4 OSHC 1193, 1975–76 OSHD ¶ 20,-690 (1976).

6. 4 OSHC 1185, 1975–76 OSHD ¶ 20,-691 (1976).

7. 19 OSHC 1477, 2001 OSHD ¶ 32,402 (2001).

tain all records necessary to the enforcement of the Act. Specifically, section 8(c)(1) requires each employer to make available to the Secretary of Labor and the Secretary of Health and Human Services (HHS) all records that have been deemed necessary to enforce the Act or prevent occupational injuries and illnesses. Section 8(c)(2) of the Act gives the Secretary of Labor, in cooperation with the Secretary of HHS, authority to promulgate regulations requiring employers to maintain accurate records of work related deaths, injuries, and illnesses. Section 8(c)(3) of the Act requires accurate records of employee exposure to potentially toxic materials or harmful physical agents which are required to be monitored or measured under section 6 of the Act.

While the regulations for recordkeeping and reporting are promulgated by the Occupational Safety and Health Administration (OSHA) in cooperation with the Secretary of HHS, the actual compilation of data is done by the Bureau of Labor Statistics (BLS), a part of the Department of Labor. It should be noted that OSHA recordkeeping and reporting requirements do not supersede an employer's recordkeeping obligations under state workers' compensation laws. In addition, some specific OSHA standards contain other recordkeeping and reporting requirements.

All employers covered under the Act are subject to the recordkeeping and reporting requirements unless specifically exempted. Even federal agencies and state and local government employers in state plan states are required to keep records. An important exemption is provided for small employers. According to the Secretary's regulation, an employer with no more than ten employees at any time during the prior calendar year need not comply with any recordkeeping requirement except the obligation to report fatalities or multiple hospitalization accidents and the obligation to participate in BLS statistical surveys. Other exemptions, such as for certain retail firms and services, farmers, and employers of domestic servants, are set out in the regulations.

Pursuant to section 4(b)(1) of the Act, employees covered by another federal act regulating employee safety and health, such as the Mine Safety and Health Act (MSHA), are exempt from OSHA recordkeeping. Nevertheless, the Commission has held that railroads are *not* exempt from OSHA recordkeeping. Employers claiming a recordkeeping exemption under section 4(b)(1) of the Act, however, have the burden of proving that they are covered by another act. The Secretary's regulations also provide that employers may petition for a recordkeeping exception, whereby records may be kept in an alternative manner if the deviation in form will not affect the substance of the data reported.

The recordkeeping system consists of three forms for the recording of occupational injuries and illnesses: a log, a supplementary record, and a summary. Employers must request each of these forms from OSHA. The records must be kept on a calendar-year basis (January 1 to December 31). The completed forms should *not* be sent to OSHA, but must remain at the establishment and be available for inspection and copying by the BLS, Department of Labor, Department of HHS, or states with authority to inspect and compile records under sections 18 and 24 of the Act. The records must be maintained at the establishment for five years following the end of the year to which they refer.

OSHA's new recordkeeping requirements began in 2002. The OSHA 300 form replaces the 200 form, and it must be used by employers to compile information on injuries and illnesses that occur throughout the calendar year. Another new form, the OSHA 301 ("Injury and Illness Incident Report") is used to provide additional information about how each injury or illness occurred, the nature of any treatment received by the employee, and other details. OSHA has issued enforcement guidance on the new recordkeeping requirements, including the timetable for phase-in of all the recordkeeping measures.

OSHA regulations require records to be kept at each "establishment," defined as a single physical location where business is conducted or where services or industrial operations are performed. If separate activities are performed at a location, each activity is considered a separate establishment. Employers without a fixed establishment, such as construction, installation, and repair and service operations, may maintain records in an established central place.

OSHA's regulation requires that employers provide *access* to the logs for inspection and copying. In *Caterpillar, Inc. v. Reich*,[1] the Seventh Circuit held that the employer did not violate the regulation when it redacted the names and badge numbers of employees sustaining injuries in the copy of the log it provided to OSHA, because it provided access to the unredacted version for inspection and copying.

Each employer is also required to display in each establishment an official poster explaining the protections of employees under the Act. In states with approved state plans, only a state poster need be used. All posters are supplied by OSHA or the applicable state agency responsible for administering an approved state plan.

In *Kaspar Wire Works, Inc. v. Secretary of Labor*,[2] the D.C. Circuit rejected the employer's argument that hundreds of recordkeeping violations were not willful. The employer's personnel had been specifically trained by OSHA on recordkeeping, and the numerous unreported injuries included finger amputations, broken bones, eye injuries, and severe burns.

Employee Access to Exposure and Medical Records

The primary purpose of OSHA's access to exposure and medical records regulation is "to enable workers to play a meaningful role in their own health management." The regulation applies to all covered general industry, maritime and construction employers. It is, however, limited to employers having employees exposed to toxic substances or harmful physical agents. Unlike other OSHA recordkeeping require-

§ 6.14   2.   268 F.3d 1123 (D.C.Cir.2001).
   1.   111 F.3d 61 (7th Cir.1997).

ments, the access regulation does *not* require that certain documents be prepared, but only that existing records be maintained and made available to employees and other parties designated in the regulation.

Any current or former employee or an employee being assigned or transferred to work where there will be exposure to toxic substances or harmful physical agents has a right of access to four kinds of exposure records: (1) environmental monitoring records; (2) biological monitoring results; (3) material safety data sheets; and (4) any other record disclosing the identity of a toxic substance or harmful physical agent. Any worker who has a right of access to exposure records may designate a representative to exercise his or her access rights. Recognized or certified collective bargaining agents (i.e. labor unions) are automatically considered "designated representatives" and have a right of access to employee exposure records without individual employee consent. OSHA also has a right of access to exposure records.

Access to employee medical records is more restricted. Employees have a right of access to their entire medical files regardless of how the information was generated or is maintained. Excluded from the definition of "employee medical record" are certain physical specimens, certain records concerning health insurance claims, and certain records concerning voluntary employee medical assistance programs. A limited discretion is also given physicians to deny access where there is a specific diagnosis of a terminal illness or psychiatric condition. Collective bargaining agents must obtain specific written consent before gaining access to employee medical records. OSHA has a right of access to employee medical records, but those records in a personally identifiable form are subject to detailed procedures and protections. The Commission has held that OSHA has a right of access to employee medical records as part of its enforcement process and in discovery before a Commission hearing. The Commission also has held that a release referring only to medical records did not require the disclosure of employee exposure records.

With a few exceptions, employers must preserve exposure records for at least thirty years and must preserve medical records for the duration of employment plus thirty years. With the exception of x-rays, employers may keep the records in any form, such as microfilm, microfiche, or computer. Upon receipt of a request, access must be provided in a reasonable time, place, and manner within fifteen days. In responding to an initial request, an employer may provide a copy without cost, provide copying facilities at no cost, or may loan the record for a reasonable time. Administrative costs may be charged for subsequent copying requests.

Although identities of substances, exposure levels, and health status data may not be withheld, the employer may delete any other trade secret data which discloses manufacturing processes, or discloses the percentage of a chemical substance in a mixture, as long as the employee or designated representative is notified of the deletion. Access to other trade secrets may be conditioned upon a written agreement not to misuse this information.

In 1988 the Secretary amended the regulation concerning procedures for employers to follow in retaining employee medical records. Some of the new provisions include: exemption from record retention requirements for medical and exposure records of short-term employees (the short term employee may be handed the records); permission for employers to store medical records on microfilm; protections for employer trade secrets; and a requirement that unions must have need before they may see an employee's exposure records without the employee's consent, thereby allowing employers to deny blanket requests.

Hazard Communication/"Right to Know"

OSHA's original Hazard Communication Standard covered an estimated 14 million employees in 300,000 manufacturing establishments.[3] Among other things, it required chemical manufacturers and importers to assess the hazards of chemicals they produce or import, and all employers engaged in manufacturing to provide information to their employees concerning hazardous chemicals by means of hazard communication programs including labels, material safety data sheets (MSDSs), training, and access to written records. One of the purposes of the standard was to preempt state "right to know" laws. The standard originally applied only to chemical manufacturers and importers (SIC Codes 20–39) and applied only to 600 substances and excluded hazardous wastes, foods, drugs, and pesticides. In 1987 OSHA published an amendment to the Hazard Communication Standard that expanded coverage beyond the manufacturing sector to cover all workers.

According to a 1998 OSHA instruction, employers may provide MSDSs to employees via computers, microfiche, the Internet, CD–ROM, and fax machines. If electronic means are used, reliable devices must be available in the workplace at all times, employees must be trained to use them, there must be adequate back-up in case of a power outage or emergency, and there must be an overall hazard communication program. In addition, employees must be able to obtain hard copies and in emergencies copies must be immediately available to medical personnel.

In the 1980s about half the states enacted "right to know" laws. Most of these laws were passed before the promulgation of the Hazard Communication Standard. Although the coverage and requirements of the laws vary widely, many of the laws have a wider reach than merely the workplace. Consequently, a recurring and important issue is whether the state laws are preempted by the OSHA standard. In *New Jersey State Chamber of Commerce v. Hughey*,[4] the Third Circuit considered a challenge to the New Jersey law, including the claim that it was preempted by the OSHA Hazard Communication Standard. The court had previously held that the state law was preempted only as to

3. 48 Fed. Reg. 53,280 (1983), codified at 29 C.F.R. § 1910.1200.

4. 774 F.2d 587 (3d Cir.1985).

employees in the manufacturing sector. The *Hughey* court reaffirmed this position. It also held that there was no preemption of the community disclosure provisions.

> Because OSHA standards by definition govern occupational safety and health issues, they do not preempt state laws that regulate other concerns. The Secretary has authority to promulgate standards only as to occupational safety and health and those standards cannot have a preemptive effect beyond that field.[5]

The court further held that the provision requiring the state to develop hazardous substance lists and the provision requiring employers to complete workplace and environmental surveys are not preempted, with the exception of employers in the manufacturing sector.

> Based on *Hughey*, state right to know laws may protect employees not covered by OSHA's Hazard Communication Standard, they may require employers in all business sectors to comply with non-workplace reporting requirements, and they may regulate substances beyond those covered by OSHA. An unresolved issue, however, is the preemptive effect of the OSHA standard in state plan states with right to know laws.

> The Supreme Court's decision in *Gade v. National Solid Wastes Management Association*,[6] however, casts doubt on this holding. In *Gade*, the Supreme Court considered whether two Illinois laws, which required state licensing of hazardous waste workers, were preempted by OSHA. The dual purposes of the state laws were to protect both employees and the general public. A detailed OSHA standard also addressed training requirements for hazardous waste workers. The Court, five-to-four, held that the Illinois law was preempted. Writing for a four-justice plurality, Justice O'Connor stated that OSHA "precludes any state regulation of an occupational safety and health issue with respect to which a federal standard has been established, unless a state plan has been submitted and approved pursuant to section 18(b)."[7] The plurality rejected the argument that preemption should not apply to state laws that address public safety as well as occupational safety concerns. The state law will be preempted, regardless of whether it serves any other objective, so long as it "directly, substantially, and specifically regulates occupational safety and health."[8]

§ 6.15 Employee Rights

Employees have numerous rights conferred upon them by the Occupational Safety and Health Act, the Secretary's regulations, and the Commission's rules of procedure. The most important of these rights is contained in section 11(c)(1) of the Act,[1] which protects employees from employer discrimination.

---

5. Id. at 593.

6. 505 U.S. 88, 112 S.Ct. 2374, 120 L.Ed.2d 73 (1992).

7. 505 U.S. at 102, 112 S.Ct. at 2385.

8. 505. U.S. at 107, 112 S.Ct. at 2388.

§ 6.15

1. 29 U.S.C.A. § 660(c)(1).

No person shall discharge or in any manner discriminate against any employee because such employee has filed any complaints or instituted or caused to be instituted any proceeding under or related to this Act or has testified or is about to testify in any such proceeding or because of the exercise by such employee on behalf of himself or others of any right afforded by this Act.

This language gives employees a wide range of protections. The use of the words "no person" is broad enough to cover the specific employer, an authorized employee representative, or even some third party like another employer that decides to "blacklist" the employee. The section also covers various forms of discrimination. The words "any manner" protects employees against sanctions imposed by altering compensation, terms, conditions, or privileges of employment. Finally, section 11(c)(1) expressly protects employees against retaliation after exercising rights "related" to the Act, which could include complaints made to other federal, state, or local agencies with authority over matters of occupational safety and health. It has also been held that an employee's safety-related complaints to his or her employer are protected under section 11(c)(1), regardless of whether a complaint is filed with OSHA.

The Secretary's regulations contain two important interpretations of section 11(c). First, the term "employee" is considered to include job applicants and former employees who were employed at the time of the alleged discrimination. Second, the employee's engaging in protected activity need not be the *sole* consideration behind the employer's action. Section 11(c) is violated if protected activity was a substantial reason for the employer's action or if the discrimination would not have taken place "but for" engaging in protected activity. In *Reich v. Hoy Shoe Co.*,[2] the Eighth Circuit held that the Secretary of Labor does not have to prove that the employer had actual knowledge of the protected activity; suspicion is enough to establish a prima facie case of retaliation.

An employer's discharging or otherwise sanctioning an employee will be upheld as long as it is not based on the employee's exercise of rights protected under section 11(c). Thus, unsatisfactory work performance, disruption of the business, insubordination and destruction of the employer's property, lack of cooperation with management, and other "good cause" have been held to be valid reasons for discharge. Similarly, to be protected under section 11(c) employee activity must be in good faith.

Under section 11(c)(2) employees must file a complaint with the Secretary within thirty days after the occurrence of the alleged discrimination. The Secretary's regulations provide for the equitable tolling of this period where there are "strongly extenuating circumstances." The courts have generally supported the principle of equitable tolling, such as where the late filing of the employee's complaint was caused by deliberate deception on the part of the employer. A discrimination complaint may be filed by the employee or by any representative of the employee

2. 32 F.3d 361 (8th Cir.1994).

who is authorized to do so. The complaint may be filed with the area director for the region in which the employee resides or was employed. No particular form of complaint is required. After the filing of a complaint, the Secretary customarily will conduct an investigation to determine the validity of the allegation. This procedure, however, is discretionary with the Secretary. An action by the Secretary under section 11(c)(2) will not be dismissed simply because the Secretary did not conduct an investigation before bringing suit. Similarly, the Secretary's failure to investigate the employee's complaint before filing suit will not preclude discovery after the suit has been filed.

Section 11(c)(3) provides that the Secretary "shall" notify the complainant within ninety days of receipt of the complaint of OSHA's determination. The Secretary's regulations have interpreted this language as directory and this view has been supported by the courts.

If attempts at reaching a settlement are unsuccessful, the Secretary may file an action in United States district court on behalf of the complainant. There is no private right of action under section 11(c), and therefore individuals may not bring actions directly, regardless of whether complaints were initially filed with the Secretary. In *Reich v. Cambridgeport Air Systems, Inc.*,[3] the First Circuit upheld the award of double back pay in the case of two employees who were fired for reporting safety and health violations. The court held that section 11(c) authorized the awarding of all appropriate relief, and that includes exemplary damages. According to the court, the employer's conduct both in and out of court was "consistently brash." In jurisdictions with their own state plans, however, employees may have a private right of action for retaliation.

One final, important procedural matter, which may prevent any section 11(c) action on behalf of the employee, is the Secretary's policy of deferring to other proceedings. Essentially, if there are arbitration proceedings in progress or if a complaint or action has been filed with any other agency or body, OSHA will postpone action on the section 11(c) complaint until the termination of the other proceeding. Also, after the other proceeding has been terminated, OSHA will defer to the results if: (1) the other proceeding has dealt adequately with all factual issues; (2) the proceedings were fair, regular, and free of procedural infirmities; and (3) the outcome of the proceedings was not clearly repugnant to the purpose and policy of the Act.

Employee Duties

Section 5(b) provides that "[e]ach employee shall comply with occupational safety and health standards and all rules, regulations and orders issued pursuant to this Act which are applicable to his own actions and conduct." This language, however, is purely precatory. Neither the Secretary nor the Commission or courts have any power to fine or otherwise sanction disobedient employees.

---

3.   26 F.3d 1187 (1st Cir.1994).

Final responsibility for compliance with OSHA's requirements rests with the employer. Employers are not relieved of their obligations under the Act because of employee reluctance to comply. Therefore, employers must take every measure possible to ensure employee compliance, including the sanctioning of recalcitrant employees. According to the Secretary's regulations, disciplinary measures taken by employers solely in response to employee refusals to comply with appropriate safety rules and regulations are not considered discrimination in violation of section 11(c).

§ 6.16 Inspections

OSHA inspections may be divided into four categories, which have been assigned the following priority: (1) imminent dangers; (2) fatality and catastrophe investigations; (3) investigations of complaints and referrals; and (4) programmed inspections.

In 1998, Congress enacted the Occupational Safety and Health Administration Compliance Assistance Authorization Act. The law amends section 21 of the Act to codify OSHA policies with regard to on-site consultation. Specifically, OSHA is directed to establish and support states to provide on-site consultation, education, and training programs. Employers requesting such services that have ongoing safety and health programs and correct all observed hazards may be exempt from an OSHA inspection for one year from the consultative visit. The exemption does not apply to inspections based on employee complaints or those prompted by a fatality or multiple hospitalization.

Imminent dangers

Section 13(a) defines "imminent danger" as a danger "which could reasonably be expected to cause death or serious physical harm immediately or before the imminence of such danger can be eliminated through the enforcement procedures otherwise provided by this Act." For imminent danger purposes, the Secretary has identified two types of "serious physical harm." First is where there is permanent, prolonged, or temporary impairment, in which part of the body is made functionally useless or is substantially reduced in efficiency on or off the job.[1] Second are illnesses that could shorten life or significantly reduce physical or mental efficiency by inhibiting the normal function of a part of the body.[2] For a

---

§ 6.16

1. E.g., amputations, simple and compound fractures, deep cuts involving significant bleeding and requiring extensive suturing, and disabling burns and concussions. FIRM ch. III–C–2–b(2)(c)(1).

2. E.g., cancer, silicosis, asbestosis, hearing impairment, and vision impairment. FIRM ch. III–C–2–b(2)(c)(2).

health hazard to constitute an imminent danger there must be a reasonable expectation that "irreversible harm" will result.

An imminent danger inspection may result from the filing of an employee complaint, as a result of an on-site consultation, or from some other source. Any allegation of imminent danger is given the highest priority, regardless of weekends, holidays, leave, or other considerations. Except in extraordinary circumstances an inspection will be conducted not later than the next working day of the employer.

Fatality and Catastrophe Investigations

Fatality and catastrophe investigations are second in OSHA priority. The purpose of these inspections is to determine if noncompliance with OSHA standards has caused the injuries, and thereby to prevent future accidents. Most fatality and accident investigations result from the employers' reporting requirement. A fatality or catastrophe investigation will be conducted if an accident has: (1) caused one or more deaths or (2) resulted in the hospitalization of three or more employees for more than twenty-four hours; (3) caused significant publicity; or (4) if specific instructions have been issued for an investigation in connection with a national office special program.

Investigations of Complaints and Referrals

According to OSHA procedures, an inspection will be conducted in response to formal (i.e. written) complaints unless the complainant does not establish reasonable grounds to believe that a violation threatening physical harm or an imminent danger exists, a recent inspection or other objective evidence indicates the hazard is not present or has been abated, or the complaint is not within OSHA's jurisdiction. OSHA will respond to formal complaints alleging an imminent danger within twenty-four hours and other conditions within thirty working days.

If a nonformal complaint is received, OSHA will usually respond by sending a letter to the employer describing the alleged hazard and requesting abatement within a certain time. The complainant will also be notified and requested to inform OSHA if no corrective action is taken by the specified time. An inspection will be conducted if the employer fails to respond to OSHA's letter or if the complainant indicates that no abatement measures have been taken. Inspections also will be conducted for all imminent danger situations and where there is employee exposure to toxic substances.

If a complaint is filed against an employer in an industry with a high accident rate, the scope of the inspection generally will be the entire facility. If the complaint involves a low rate industry, only the conditions identified in the complaint will be inspected. Complaints by former employees alleging unsafe conditions and that they were discharged in violation of section 11(c) of the Act are treated as nonformal complaints.

Programmed Inspections

According to OSHA regulations, programmed inspections for general industry will be conducted only in "high hazard" establishments—

those with lost workday injury rates at or above the national lost workday injury rate for manufacturing. Whether an establishment is considered "high hazard" is based on the nature of the enterprise. For example, scheduling for general industry safety inspections is based on statewide industry ranking reports rating four-digit Standard Industrial Classifications (SICs). General industry health inspection scheduling uses statewide four-digit SICs with high potential for employee exposure to dangerous substances. Construction industry inspections are based on worksites rather than employees.

Administrative exemptions from programmed inspections have been increasing and presently there are four exemptions in effect. First, establishments with ten or fewer employees are not inspected. Second, an employer will be deleted from OSHA's schedule for programmed safety inspections if a substantially complete safety inspection has been conducted within the current or previous fiscal year, regardless of whether violations were cited. Third, an employer will be exempt from a programmed health inspection if one was conducted within the current year or the previous three fiscal years and no serious violations were cited. Fourth, inspections must be in accord with the latest congressional funding limitations.

§ 6.17 Inspection Warrants

In the companion cases of *Camara v. Municipal Court*[1] and *See v. Seattle*,[2] the Supreme Court held that administrative inspections of both commercial and noncommercial premises are generally subject to the warrant requirement of the Fourth Amendment. While the Supreme Court extended the protections afforded for criminal searches to administrative inspections, the Court drew several important distinctions. In securing an administrative warrant there is no need for a showing of probable cause in the criminal law sense. It is not necessary that there be any founded suspicion that a violation has occurred as long as the inspection is pursuant to valid statutory authorization.

The Supreme Court in *See* indicated that licensing inspections, long conducted under state and local law, were valid. The Court did not state, however, that these inspections could be made without a warrant. Nevertheless, in *Colonnade Catering Corp. v. United States*,[3] the Court held that Congress has the power to authorize warrantless searches of liquor dealers. The Court relied on the long history of government regulation of the liquor industry. Only two years later, in *United States v. Biswell*,[4] the Supreme Court extended the *Colonnade* reasoning to uphold the validity of a warrantless search of a pawn shop pursuant to the Gun Control Act of 1968. The Court's decision was based on the

§ 6.17

1. 387 U.S. 523, 87 S.Ct. 1727, 18 L.Ed.2d 930 (1967).

2. 387 U.S. 541, 87 S.Ct. 1737, 18 L.Ed.2d 943 (1967).

3. 397 U.S. 72, 90 S.Ct. 774, 25 L.Ed.2d 60 (1970).

4. 406 U.S. 311, 92 S.Ct. 1593, 32 L.Ed.2d 87 (1972).

following: (1) the overriding governmental interest in the close monitoring of the gun industry; (2) the fact that unannounced inspections better promote effective enforcement; and (3) the theory that by engaging in a pervasively regulated business the individual has waived Fourth Amendment rights and impliedly consented to warrantless administrative inspections.

In *Marshall v. Barlow's, Inc.,*[5] the Supreme Court held that nonconsensual OSHA inspections can only be made pursuant to a warrant. The Court rejected the Secretary's contentions that OSHA inspections should come within the *Colonnade–Biswell* exception and that warrantless inspections are essential to the enforcement of the Act. Although it affirmed the district court, the Supreme Court did *not* agree with the lower court that the Act is unconstitutional; it only agreed that warrantless searches are prohibited. The Court concluded, contrary to the district court, that section 8(a) of the Act is adequate statutory authority for the issuance of warrants and that it would be constitutional for the Secretary to obtain warrants ex parte and to conduct unannounced inspections. Moreover, only administrative probable cause is needed for the issuance of a warrant.

Three exceptions to the warrant requirement, first set out in *Camara* and *See*, apply to OSHA. The first exception is for emergencies. According to this traditional approach, exigent circumstances eliminate the warrant requirement because the urgent need for an immediate search outweighs the right to privacy. The emergency exception, however, can only be invoked in the most extreme instances. For OSHA inspections, the emergency exception would appear to be limited to imminent dangers and other exigencies *and* where it is impossible to obtain consent.

Most administrative inspections are conducted on the basis of consent. In fact, the Supreme Court in *Barlow's* suggested that "the great majority of businessmen can be expected in normal course to consent to inspection without warrant * * *."[6] Valid consent operates as a waiver of the Fourth Amendment right against unreasonable search and seizure. For administrative inspections, the courts have adopted a standard of consent that is less stringent than that required for criminal searches. Consent to an administrative inspection need not be express and the failure to object to a known search constitutes consent. Thus, consent has been found where a company foreman accompanied the compliance officer (CO) on a walkaround without protest.

The failure of the inspector to warn the company managers of their right to insist on a warrant does not render the consent unknowing or involuntary. The COs have been instructed, however, that they may not mislead, coerce, or threaten the employer, and if the employer asks questions about the *Barlow's* decision, the CO must answer in a "straightforward" manner. Consent to an OSHA inspection may be

5. 436 U.S. 307, 98 S.Ct. 1816, 56   **6.** 436 U.S. at 316, 98 S.Ct. at 1822.
L.Ed.2d 305 (1978).

given by any competent management official. Inspections have been upheld where the consent was given by a plant manager, a foreman, and a superintendent. In addition, a general contractor may consent to the inspection of a common worksite where a subcontractor is working.

The Supreme Court in *See* restated the well-settled rule that merely observing what is open to public view does not constitute a search. Thus, a warrant is not required where the premises are open to the public. An important factor is whether an individual or business has a reasonable expectation of privacy, even if the inspection is in an area open to the public. In *Marshall v. Western Waterproofing Co.,*[7] COs attempted to inspect scaffolding on the eleventh floor of a building from which an employee had fallen the previous day. Despite being unable to contact a company official, the COs began the inspection after learning that the scaffolding would be dismantled the next day. Accompanied by the building manager, the COs examined the fifth floor mezzanine, onto which the employee fell. They also viewed the scaffolding from a window of the eleventh floor office of an attorney, who had consented to the presence of the COs. The Eighth Circuit rejected the employer's claim that the search was illegal. The court pointed out that the COs were given consent to enter the mezzanine and office by the building manager and attorney. In addition, the scaffolding was exposed to public view while suspended on the building and was also readily observable by the tenants in the building. "Therefore, Western could have had no reasonable expectation of privacy concerning the viewing of the scaffolding * * *."[8]

Similar results have been reached in other cases. In *Accu–Namics, Inc. v. OSHRC,*[9] the Fifth Circuit upheld the warrantless and nonconsensual inspection of a caved-in trench along a public street. In *Ackermann Enterprises, Inc.,*[10] an agent of the employer directed the CO to wait in the parking lot until the company president or supervisor would arrive and give him permission to conduct an inspection. The Commission held that the CO's observations of violative conditions, which he made from the parking lot, were admissible under the plain view doctrine.

Warrant Procedure

United States magistrates have the authority to issue OSHA warrants and the Secretary and the Secretary's designees (including Labor Department attorneys) have authority to obtain warrants. It is also clear that employers have no right to advance notice of a warrant application, no right to be present or to have counsel present at the warrant hearing, and no right to receive copies of the materials submitted to the magistrate.

---

7. 560 F.2d 947 (8th Cir.1977).

8. Id. at 951.

9. 515 F.2d 828 (5th Cir.1975), cert. denied, 425 U.S. 903, 96 S.Ct. 1492, 47 L.Ed.2d 752 (1976).

10. 10 OSHC 1709, 1982 OSHD ¶ 26,-090 (1982).

OSHA has the authority to seek an ex parte warrant before attempting to make an inspection. Nevertheless, except under special circumstances, a warrant will be sought only after an employer refuses to permit an inspection. In *Donovan v. Enterprise Foundry, Inc.,*[11] the First Circuit held that the face of the warrant need not contain a recital of the reasons for a finding of probable cause, especially where the employer had access to the affidavits upon which the warrant was based. "[T]he principal focus in determining whether a showing of probable cause was made is on the *application*, not the warrant."[12]

Probable Cause

The Supreme Court in *Barlow's* addressed the issue of probable cause as follows:

> For purposes of an administrative search such as this, probable cause justifying the issuance of a warrant may be based not only on specific evidence of an existing violation but also on a showing that "reasonable legislative or administrative standards for conducting an * * * inspection are satisfied with respect to a particular [establishment]." *Camara v. Municipal Court* * * *. A warrant showing that a specific business has been chosen for an OSHA search on the basis of a general administrative plan for the enforcement of the Act derived from neutral sources such as, for example, dispersion of employees in various types of industries across a given area, and the desired frequency of searches in any of the lesser divisions of the area, would protect an employer's Fourth Amendment rights.[13]

OSHA's first priority is the inspection of imminent dangers. There would appear to be little problem in establishing probable cause where a valid imminent danger exists. Indeed, for some imminent dangers a warrant may not even be necessary under the emergency exception.

OSHA's second priority is for the investigation of fatalities and catastrophes. In *Donovan v. Federal Clearing Die Casting Co.,*[14] OSHA sought an inspection warrant based on: (1) the fact that the employer had been cited for violations four years earlier; and (2) the submission of two newspaper articles reporting that an employee of Federal had both hands amputated in a recent accident. The Seventh Circuit held that there was no probable cause because there was inadequate "specific evidence" of a violation. In particular, the court stated that "all newspaper reports are not of sufficient reliability to form the basis of Fourth Amendment probable cause determination."[15]

OSHA's third type of unprogrammed inspection is based on the filing of a complaint. Although the filing of an employee or union complaint will usually establish probable cause, the magistrate must be presented with some additional information. The Seventh Circuit has

---

11. 751 F.2d 30 (1st Cir.1984).

12. Id. at 34 (emphasis in original).

13. 436 U.S. at 320–21, 98 S.Ct. at 1824–25 (footnotes omitted).

14. 655 F.2d 793 (7th Cir.1981).

15. Id. at 797 (footnote omitted).

held that the mere allegation that a complaint has been filed is not sufficient to establish probable cause. There must be an indication that inspections based on employee complaints are part of an overall administrative program and that the specific complaint sets forth adequate facts to justify an inspection.

If possible, a signed employee complaint with supporting affidavits should be presented with the warrant application. Nevertheless, probable cause may be based on an anonymous or informal employee complaint, even without the oath of a compliance officer or other corroborating evidence of the complainant's credibility. According to the Commission, section 8(f) of the Act does not limit the Secretary's authority to inspect to complaints filed by employees or employee representatives. It imposes a duty to do so. The Secretary still has discretionary authority to inspect pursuant to complaints filed by others, including anonymous complaints.

To enforce a subpoena for documents in connection with an OSHA inspection, the Secretary need meet only a four-part test: (1) the purpose of the subpoena is a congressionally authorized one; (2) the subpoena is sought for that purpose; (3) the documents sought are relevant to that purpose and described in sufficient detail; and (4) proper procedures were followed. Once these factors are shown, the subpoena is per se reasonable and deemed not to violate the Fourth Amendment. The more stringent *Barlow's* requirements for administrative searches do not apply to subpoena enforcement actions.

Scope of Inspection

The permissible scope of an OSHA inspection warrant is an important but, as yet, unresolved issue. In *In re Inspection of Workplace (Carondelet Coke Corp.)*,[16] the Eighth Circuit identified three lines of decisions in the cases involving the scope of an OSHA inspection. The Third Circuit and an earlier Eighth Circuit case placed a heavy burden on the Secretary to obtain a wall-to-wall warrant based on an employee complaint. The Seventh and Ninth Circuits established a presumption that a search of the entire workplace is reasonable when based on an employee complaint. A middle standard, developed in a later Seventh Circuit case, and followed by the Eleventh Circuit, would require the Secretary to make "some showing" of why a broad warrant is appropriate in the particular case. The Eighth Circuit in *Carondelet* adopted the middle standard. The court held that the Secretary satisfied his burden by showing that the employer was in a high hazard industry, had a lost work day injury rate nearly four times the national average for manufacturers, and was due to have a programmed wall-to-wall inspection when the complaint was filed.

In *In re Cerro Copper Products Co.*,[17] the Seventh Circuit expressed its agreement with the Eighth Circuit's approach in *Carondelet*. The court specifically endorsed the five factors used to determine whether

16. 741 F.2d 172 (8th Cir.1984).   **17.** 752 F.2d 280 (7th Cir.1985).

the decision to respond to a complaint with a wall-to-wall inspection was a neutral one: (1) whether the employee (complainant) was motivated by a desire to harass the employer; (2) whether the nature of the business at the facility and the employer's safety record qualified it for a general inspection; (3) whether a full inspection had been conducted within the preceding year; (4) whether the facility would be due for a programmed inspection in the near future; and (5) whether OSHA's limited resources were being utilized in the public's best interest.

Despite this persuasive authority, the Commission has agreed with the Third Circuit that when probable cause is based on a specific and extant violation, the inspection must be limited to the alleged violative condition. An exception to the rule would arise only when the Secretary cannot determine the location of the alleged violation.

An increasingly contentious issue in OSHA inspections is the Secretary's right of access to safety records and other written materials. To compel the disclosure of such material over the protest of the employer, the Secretary often will seek a district court to order compliance with a subpoena duces tecum. In *Herman v. Galvin,*[18] a sole proprietor claimed a Fifth Amendment testimonial privilege against producing logs of employee injuries and illnesses. The court rejected the argument based on the required records exception to the privilege. In *Herman, Secretary of Labor v. Avondale Shipyard,*[19] the court ordered the employer to produce accident reports, first aid logs, and medical insurance records to verify the employer's injury and illness records. The union had filed a complaint with OSHA alleging that the employer failed to report all of the injuries and illnesses. The court rejected the employer's argument that the OSHA request was overly broad and infringed upon the confidentiality of employee medical records.

§ 6.18 Inspection Tour

Section 8(a)(1) of the Act conditions the Secretary's authority to inspect on the presentation of proper credentials. This provision protects against forcible entry and snooping as well as guarding against unauthorized individuals representing themselves as COs. Section 8(a)(1) provides that credentials must be presented to the "owner, operator, or agent in charge." As with the general consent provisions, discussed earlier, it is likely that this will include all management personnel with actual or apparent authority. For example, the Commission upheld the validity of an inspection where the CO made a reasonable attempt but was unable to locate the owner and then presented his credentials to the employee authorized to handle matters in the owner's absence. Similarly, the Commission held that an inspection was valid where the CO presented his credentials to the "ship's boss," a joint representative of the union and management. An employer's argument that there was a failure to present credentials will probably not succeed unless there has

18. 40 F.Supp.2d 27 (D.Mass.1999).   **19.** 1999 OSHD ¶ 31,756 (E.D.La.1999).

been prejudice to the employer. The Fifth Circuit in *Accu–Namics, Inc. v. OSHRC*,[1] held that technical violations of section 8(a) of the Act "cannot operate to exclude evidence obtained in that inspection when there is no showing that the employer was prejudiced in any way."[2]

After the presentation of credentials, the CO will conduct an opening conference with a representative of the employer and a representative of the employees, at which time the procedures for conducting the inspection will be discussed. If the inspection is a result of an employee complaint, the complaint will be shown to the employer, although the employee's name will be withheld if the employee has so requested.

The opening conference is as brief as possible. During this time the employer is told what safety records the CO wants to inspect, told what the inspection tour will encompass, and given copies of applicable laws, standards, and regulations. At the opening conference the employer should indicate what trade secrets will be encountered during the inspection and may request confidentiality. The employer also should indicate to the CO any special conditions related to the inspection, such as the need for the CO to wear personal protective equipment or the need to have security clearance.

Section 8(e) provides that an employer and employee representative "shall be given" an opportunity to accompany the inspection tour "for the purpose of aiding such inspection." Despite some early confusion, it is now clear that any defense based on the failure to afford "walkaround" rights must focus on whether there was substantial compliance by the Secretary and whether there was prejudice to the employer.

In *Western Waterproofing Co.*,[3] the Commission held that walkaround rights are "substantial" and not purely a procedural requirement. According to the lead opinion, the employer was prejudiced by not being afforded a walkaround because the Secretary alleged violative conditions that could have been easily explained by the employer. Thus, the employer was required to disprove the allegations at the hearing. The lead opinion also stressed that reasonable efforts were not made to inform the employer of the walkaround. The Eighth Circuit reversed the Commission. The court held that "a showing of prejudice must be made before a citation will be vacated because of a failure by the Secretary's representatives to comply with section 8(e)."[4]

In *Able Contractors, Inc.*,[5] the Commission indicated that it will follow the Eighth Circuit's decision in *Western Waterproofing*. A valid section 8(e) defense requires the employer to show actual prejudice to the presentation or preparation of its case. Thus, it appears that an

§ 6.18

1. 515 F.2d 828 (5th Cir.1975), cert. denied, 425 U.S. 903, 96 S.Ct. 1492, 47 L.Ed.2d 752 (1976).

2. 515 F.2d at 833.

3. 4 OSHC 1301, 1976–77 OSHD ¶ 20,-805 (1976), reversed, 560 F.2d 947 (8th Cir.1977).

4. Marshall v. Western Waterproofing Co., 560 F.2d 947, 951 (8th Cir.1977).

5. 5 OSHC 1975, 1977–78 OSHD ¶ 22,-250 (1977).

employer must prove prejudice *and* a lack of substantial compliance. The prejudice requirement has proved to be the most difficult for employers.

During the course of an inspection the CO is authorized to record all pertinent information, including the making of diagrams and the taking of environmental samples and photographs. An important, related issue is whether, during an inspection, the company may refuse to permit the CO to attach sampling devices to employees to measure the level of noise or airborne contaminants. OSHA has promulgated a regulation providing that personal sampling devices attached to workers may be used by COs as an aid to workplace inspections. Decisions of the First and Fifth Circuits have upheld the validity of OSHA's regulation on the use of personal sampling. The employer has the burden of demonstrating the existence of special or exceptional circumstances which would make the use of personal sampling uniquely burdensome at its workplace.

The closing conference takes place after the inspection tour and its purpose is to review the findings of the inspection with the employer and employee representative. It also affords the employer an opportunity to confer with the CO before a citation is issued. At this time the CO will inform the employer of any apparent violations and the employer may indicate what steps will be taken to abate the hazards. During the closing conference the CO also will describe the apparent violations and discuss other pertinent issues.

§ 6.19 Trade Secrets

Trade secrets are any confidential business devices or processes which give an employer an advantage over competitors. Trade secrets are expressly protected under section 15 of the Act. The confidentiality of trade secrets is maintained because the inspections are conducted by federal employees who are prohibited by law from disclosing such information.

In *Owens–Illinois, Inc.,*[1] the Commission held that independent experts could not be precluded from inspecting the employer's plant. The Commission observed that numerous employers had begun to oppose discovery inspections by non-federal experts. In some instances the objections "may have been raised * * * [simply] as a strategy to hinder the Secretary * * *." According to the Commission, a protective order requiring nondisclosure of trade secrets is adequate protection for the employer. The protective order must contain the following four elements.

First, the Secretary must provide the employer with a resume of the non-federal expert "at a reasonable time" before the discovery inspection. The employer then can challenge (but not veto) selection of the expert on the ground that the expert is closely aligned with a competitor. Second, the expert should be ordered to sign and comply with a written

§ 6.19
1. 6 OSHC 2162, 1978 OSHD ¶ 23,218 (1978).

oath promising not to disclose trade secret information except to OSHA representatives and in proceedings before the Commission. Third, the order should require the Secretary to include in the contract with the expert a nondisclosure provision identical to the oath. The contract must explicitly make the employer a third party beneficiary of the contractual nondisclosure provision. Fourth, the protective order should be broad enough to encompass the Secretary and his or her representatives, and should indicate that the sanctions for violating the order apply to anyone acting on the Secretary's behalf.

In *Salem–Gravure Division of World Color Press, Inc.*,[2] the Commission overruled *Owens–Illinois*. The Commission questioned the effectiveness of protective orders. For example, the Commission lacks contempt powers needed to ensure the deterrent effect of the protective order. The Commission stayed its proceedings to permit the Secretary to obtain a warrant or other appropriate order in federal court, with the nondisclosure provisions subjecting the non-federal expert to contempt in the event of disclosure of trade secrets.

The D.C. Circuit, in *Graphic Communications International Union v. Salem–Gravure*,[3] reversed the Commission's holding that the Secretary must obtain federal district court authorization before permitting a non-federal expert to conduct a discovery inspection of an employer's premises when the employer claims the existence of trade secrets. The D.C. Circuit held that the Commission's ruling was arbitrary and capricious because it failed to provide a reasoned explanation for its departure from established precedent. The court noted the Commission's failure to point to a single case where the protective orders provided for under *Owens–Illinois* had proved inadequate. The court stressed that Congress had given comprehensive authority to the Commission to ensure the safety of workplaces and had not envisioned that federal district court intervention would be required as early as the discovery stage of proceedings.

§ 6.20 Citations

Section 9(a) of the Act provides that a citation must "describe with particularity the nature of the violation, including reference to the provision of the Act, standard, rule, regulation, or order alleged to have been violated." In other words, a citation must contain two elements, a description of the alleged violation and a reference to the standard allegedly violated.

The Commission's rules of procedure have adopted a system of "notice pleading" that parallels the federal rules. In *National Realty & Construction Co. v. OSHRC*,[1] the D.C. Circuit delineated a "fair notice" test for citations.

2. 12 OSHC 2143, 1986 OSHD ¶ 27,697 (1986), reversed, 843 F.2d 1490 (D.C.Cir. 1988), cert. denied, 489 U.S. 1011, 109 S.Ct. 1119, 103 L.Ed.2d 182 (1989).

3. 843 F.2d 1490 (D.C.Cir.1988), cert. denied, 489 U.S. 1011, 109 S.Ct. 1119, 103 L.Ed.2d 182 (1989).

§ 6.20
1. 489 F.2d 1257 (D.C.Cir.1973).

So long as fair notice is afforded, an issue litigated at an administrative hearing may be decided by the hearing agency even though the formal pleadings did not squarely raise the issue * * *. Enforcement of the Act would be crippled if the Secretary were inflexibly held to a narrow construction of citations issued by his inspectors.[2]

Thus, the fair notice test will be satisfied if the employer is notified of the nature of the violation, the standard allegedly violated, and the location of the alleged violation.

The requirement that citations be reasonably specific is designed to apprise the employer of the alleged violation so that corrective action may be taken and so that the employer may be able to decide whether and how to proceed with a contest. It must be remembered, however, that section 9(a) does not require that a citation state the elements of a cause of action or that an employer be informed with particularity how to abate a hazardous condition. A citation will be dismissed only where it fails to contain a description of the alleged violation or a reference to the standard allegedly violated.

Time for Issuance

Until the issuance of a citation an employer is under no legal duty to abate a hazardous condition. To promote the expeditious correction of violations, section 9(a) of the Act provides that citations be issued with "reasonable promptness." This requirement also serves to ensure that the employer receives prompt notice of the Secretary's allegation so that it may begin preparing its defense while the evidence is still fresh.

In *Chicago Bridge & Iron Co.*,[3] a majority of the Commission held that to comply with the reasonable promptness language of section 9(a) a citation must be issued within three working days after the area director formed his or her belief that a violation occurred. Citations not issued with reasonable promptness would be dismissed if the employer asserted a timely defense. On judicial review, the Seventh Circuit held that the rule of the Commission majority was unacceptable. Nevertheless, in remanding the case the court declined to define reasonable promptness. Essentially, the Commission was given the task of devising a more reasonable interpretation.

In *Coughlan Construction Co.*,[4] the Commission adopted a new reasonable promptness rule, which shifted the focus from OSHA to the employer. Regardless of the delay in issuance, up to the six-month statute of limitations in section 9(c), a citation will not be vacated unless the employer was prejudiced by the delay. Under this rule, unless the delay impairs an employer's ability to prepare and present a defense, the citation will be deemed to have been issued in accordance with section 9(a). Decisions of the courts of appeals have supported the Commission's

2. Id. at 1264 (footnotes omitted).

3. 1 OSHC 1485, 1973–74 OSHD ¶ 17,-187 (1974), reversed, 514 F.2d 1082 (7th Cir.1975).

4. 3 OSHC 1636, 1975–76 OSHD ¶ 20,-106 (1975).

view that a citation will not be vacated on "reasonable promptness" grounds absent a showing of prejudice to the employer.

Section 9(c) prohibits the issuance of a citation "after the expiration of six months following the occurrence of any violation." Although the issue has not been resolved, it appears that section 9(c) is a statute of limitations giving rise to an employer defense rather than a substantive condition precedent, which would require the Secretary to plead and prove that a violation occurred within six months of the citation.

Amendments and Settlements

The Secretary's regulations provide that OSHA may unilaterally amend a citation before the filing of a notice of contest or before the expiration of the fifteen working day contest period. For amended items only, a new contest period begins to run upon receipt of the amended citation. This procedure corresponds with rule 15(a) of the federal rules, which permits an amendment as of right before the filing of a responsive pleading. The Secretary's regulations also provide that when a citation is amended both the original citation and the amended version should be posted.

OSHA area directors are authorized to enter into settlement agreements with employers before the filing of a notice of contest. In some instances a settlement results after an informal conference with the employer. Settlements finalized after the filing of a notice of contest must be approved by the regional solicitor.

In *Marshall v. Sun Petroleum Products Co.*,[5] the Third Circuit held that if no notice of contest has been filed the Commission has no jurisdiction to review a settlement. Moreover, even if a notice of contest has been filed (by employees) the Commission's jurisdiction is limited to determining whether the time fixed for abatement is reasonable.

Service

The Act does not specifically provide for a method of service for citations. Section 10(a) of the Act, however, authorizes service of notices of proposed penalties by certified mail and, as a practical matter, the two usually have been sent together by certified mail. Section 10(a) provides for service on the "employer," defined in section 3(5) of the Act as a person engaged in a business affecting commerce who has employees. "Person" is defined in section 3(4) of the Act as one or more individuals, partnerships, associations, corporations, business trusts, legal representatives, or any organized group of persons. Neither definition, however, answers the question of which employee may be served on behalf of a company.

In *Buckley & Co. v. Secretary of Labor*,[6] the Third Circuit reversed the Commission and held that service by mail, sent to the superinten-

5. 622 F.2d 1176, 1185 (3d Cir.1980), cert. denied, 449 U.S. 1061, 101 S.Ct. 784, 66 L.Ed.2d 604 (1980).

6. 507 F.2d 78 (3d Cir.1975).

dent of the cited garage and maintenance shop, was not proper to notify the corporate employer. The court specifically adopted the test for service set out in Chairman Moran's dissenting opinion. That is, notice must be provided to corporate officials with authority to spend corporate funds to either pay the penalty, abate the alleged violation, or contest the enforcement proceedings. Thus, the court held that the notice should have been sent to the corporate headquarters and not to the employee in charge of the cited workplace.

In *B.J. Hughes, Inc.*,[7] the Commission specifically declined to follow *Buckley* and held that service upon the district superintendent at a local jobsite was valid. According to the Commission, service is proper if it "is reasonably calculated to provide an employer with knowledge of the citation and notification of proposed penalty and an opportunity to determine whether to contest or abate." Therefore, it is proper to serve an employee who will know to whom in the corporate hierarchy to forward the documents. *Buckley* was criticized as placing too great a burden on the Secretary to investigate an employer's managerial structure when the local company official has this knowledge as well as first-hand information about the conditions at the workplace. Even if an employee without authority signs the certified mailing receipt, the date of the receipt starts the notice of contest period. An employer's internal mail routing policies are not within the Secretary's control. In *Baker Support Services, Inc.*,[8] the Commission rejected the employer's argument that service was improper where the employer had notified OSHA where to send and how to handle a citation.

Where two companies are closely related, service on one company may be considered adequate service on the other company. Similarly, service on one member of a joint venture constitutes service on the entire joint venture.

Section 9(b) of the Act requires that the cited employer post a copy of the citation at or near each place of a violation referred to in the citation. The posting requirement is for the benefit of employees; therefore, the employer must post the citation at a place where it may be readily observed by all affected employees. Where employers are engaged in physically dispersed activities, the citation may be posted at the location to which employees report each day. If the employees do not report to a single location, the citation may be posted at the location from which the employees carry out their activities.

§ 6.21 Employer Contests

Under section 10(a) of the Act an employer has fifteen working days from the date of receipt of the notice of proposed penalty (or no penalty) in which to file a notice of contest. Weekends and federal holidays are excluded, as is the day on which the employer received the notice of proposed penalty. The notice of contest must be in writing and should be

7. 7 OSHC 1471, 1979 OSHD ¶ 23,675   **8.** 18 OSHC 2200, 2000 OSHD ¶ 32,136 (1979).   (2000).

mailed to the area director who issued the citation and proposed penalty. The postmark date on the notice of contest is controlling. Although the date of receipt of the notice of proposed penalty, rather than the citation, is determinative, OSHA now uses a single form for both the citation and notice of proposed penalty. The short notice of contest period, which begins to run upon receipt of the form, is designed to promote the prompt abatement of hazards while preserving employer due process.

An employer may contest any part or all of the citation, the proposed penalty, the abatement dates, or all of these elements. In no event, however, may the employer take more than the fifteen working day period to file its notice of contest. An uncontested citation is "deemed a final order of the Commission and not subject to review by any court or agency."[1]

There is no prescribed form for a notice of contest. Technically, the communication need only be a notice of "intent to contest." To avoid problems, however, a notice of contest should be signed and dated, list what items are being contested, and indicate whether the notice of contest is of the citation, penalty, abatement date, or all three. It is not necessary to indicate the grounds on which the contest is based.

Although section 10(a) merely requires that an employer "notify" the Secretary of an intent to contest, the Secretary's regulations have interpreted this as requiring that the notification be in writing. In *Acrom Construction Services, Inc.*,[2] the Commission held that a notice of contest must be in writing.

Under section 10(a), the failure to file a notice of contest results in the citation and proposed penalty becoming a final order of the Commission, "not subject to review by any court or agency." This provision has been strictly construed by the Commission. In *Branciforte Builders, Inc.*,[3] however, the Commission held that rule 60(b) of the Federal Rules of Civil Procedure can be used as the basis for setting aside a section 10(a) final order. *Branciforte*, which followed a similar decision of the Third Circuit, was merely a procedural decision and did not add new substantive grounds upon which a section 10(a) final order could be attacked.

An uncontested citation is generally unreviewable. The main substantive basis for an exception to this rule is an employer's allegation that the Secretary's process of citation issuance was fraught with irregularities. For example, in *Atlantic Marine, Inc. v. OSHRC*,[4] the Fifth Circuit remanded a case to determine the validity of an employer's claim that the Secretary's "deceptive practices" or "failure to follow proper procedures" caused the notice of contest to be filed late. In other cases, district courts refused to permit the collection of penalties without a hearing where the employer alleged that an OSHA compliance officer had said that because the hazard had been abated it was not necessary to

§ 6.21

1. § 10(a), 29 U.S.C.A. § 659(a).

2. 15 OSHC 1123, 1991 OSHD ¶ 29,393 (1991).

3. 9 OSHC 2113, 1981 OSHD ¶ 25,591 (1981).

4. 524 F.2d 476 (5th Cir.1975).

file a notice of contest and where the area director allegedly granted an informal extension of the abatement date and the notice of proposed penalty was not received until after the abatement date.

Commission decisions interpreting *Atlantic Marine* have emphasized that the "deceptive practices" defense is objective and is not met by an employer's subjective feeling of "intimidation." Nevertheless, the defense has been upheld by the Commission. In *Merritt Electric Co.*,[5] the employer telephoned the area director on the same day it received a citation, at which time the employer expressed dissatisfaction with the citation and requested a reinspection. The area director failed to inform the employer of the fifteen working day contest period, and the employer did not file a written notice of contest until three months later. The Commission refused to dismiss the employer's notice of contest as untimely and emphasized that the area director had misled the employer into believing that it had done all that was necessary to have the citation reconsidered.

It is not entirely clear when the Commission will hold that there is excusable neglect in the employer's failure to file a notice of contest in a timely manner. For example, it was held *not* to be excusable neglect when a citation was erroneously misdirected within a large company. On the other hand, excusable neglect was found where there was a miscommunication between a company's president and legal counsel. In *Chao v. Russell P. Le Frois Builder, Inc.*,[6] the Commission held that there was excusable neglect for the employer's failure to file a notice of contest where the certified letter containing the citation fell beneath the passenger seat of the company secretary's car after she picked up the mail at the post office. The Second Circuit reversed and held that the Commission does not have jurisdiction to extend the time for filing a notice of contest based on asserted good cause or excusable neglect. According to the court, Commission authority attaches only when proceedings before the Commission have commenced and they only commence upon the filing of a notice of contest.

Limited Contests

An employer need not contest all items in a citation or all citations resulting from one inspection. The uncontested items will be deemed final orders of the Commission pursuant to section 10(a) of the Act and not subject to any later review. Thus, abatement is stayed only for contested items.

A more difficult question involves contests of only the penalty, citation, or abatement date. In *Gilbert Manufacturing Co.*,[7] the Commission overruled existing precedent and held that when an employer notifies the Secretary that it seeks an extension of the abatement date prescribed in a citation, the notification will be treated as a petition for modification of abatement (PMA)—even if it is filed within the fifteen

---

5. 9 OSHC 2088, 1981 OSHD ¶ 25,556 (1981).

6. 291 F.3d 219 (2d Cir.2002).

7. 7 OSHC 1611, 1979 OSHD ¶ 23,782 (1979).

working day notice of contest period. Ambiguous notices and objected-to PMA's will be referred to the Commission. In construing ambiguous notices, the intent of the employer at the time of the original filing is controlling.

In *Florida East Coast Properties, Inc.*,[8] the Commission held that, when only the penalties are contested, the Commission does not have jurisdiction to review the violation, except as incidental to assessing an appropriate penalty. The theory behind the decision was that the abatement requirement should not be stayed during the pendency of a case concerned only with the size of the penalty. The *Florida East Coast* rule was significantly modified by the Commission's decision in *Turnbull Millwork Co.*[9] Without overruling *Florida East Coast,* the Commission held that when an employer contests only the proposed penalty, the employer may subsequently amend the notice of contest to include a contest of the citation. The employer, however, must have intended to contest the citation when it filed its notice of contest, regardless of whether the employer had counsel. The scope of a notice of contest may not be enlarged without evidence of the employer's intent and an administrative law judge may not consider the merits of a citation sua sponte. *Turnbull* did not modify the principle that, when the notice of contest is limited to the penalty, the citation, including the abatement date, becomes a final order of the Commission.

§ 6.22 Employee Contests

Under section 10(c) of the Act "any employee or representative of employees" may file a notice of contest to challenge the reasonableness of the abatement date in a citation. Any "affected employee," including supervisors and officers, or the employees' collective bargaining agent, may file a notice of contest. Like employer contests, employee contests must be sent to the area director who issued the citation and must be postmarked within fifteen working days of the employer's posting of the citation. The area director must then forward the notice of contest to the Commission within seven days. Under Commission rule 7, contesting employees must also serve a copy of the notice on the employer. Pursuant to Commission rule 38(a), the Secretary has ten days after receipt of an employee contest to file a "clear and concise" statement of reasons why the abatement period is not unreasonable. Under rule 38(b), the employees have ten days from the date of receipt of the Secretary's statement to file a response. Rule 38(c) provides that employee contests will be handled as expedited proceedings under rule 103.

Employee contests under section 10(c) are limited to challenging "that the period of time fixed in the citation for the abatement of the violation is unreasonable * * *." Commission and judicial decisions have narrowly construed this provision, with the result of greatly decreasing the effectiveness of employee contests. In *United Auto Workers, Local*

8. 1 OSHC 1532, 1973–74 OSHD ¶ 17,- 272 (1974).

9. 3 OSHC 1781, 1975–76 OSHD ¶ 20,- 221 (1975).

588 (Ford Motor Co.) v. OSHRC,[1] the Seventh Circuit affirmed the Commission's holding that employees may only contest the reasonableness of the date for abatement and may not challenge the adequacy of an abatement plan agreed to by the Secretary.

The Commission has held that in employee contests the burden of proof rests with the Secretary to show that the proposed abatement date is *not* unreasonable. Employers also may elect party status after the filing of an employee notice of contest. Thus, employees and employers may present their own evidence at the hearing.

Even without filing their own notice of contest, affected employees may elect party status and participate at the employer's hearing. This election can be made up to ten days before the hearing, and by permission of the Commission, for good cause within ten days of the hearing.

§ 6.23   Petitions for Modification of Abatement

OSHA regulations provide that within 10 calendar days after the abatement date, the employer must verify to OSHA that each cited violation has been abated. The certification must include the date and method of abatement and a statement that affected employees and their representatives have been informed of the abatement. Documentation of abatement is required for each willful or repeat violation and for any serious violation for which OSHA indicates that documentation is required. Documentation may include evidence of the purchase of repair or equipment, photographic or video evidence of abatement, or other written records. For willful, repeat, and serious violations involving movable equipment, the employer must attach a warning tag or a copy of the citation to the operating controls or to the cited component of the equipment that is moved.

An employer that has made a good faith effort to comply with the abatement requirements of a citation, but has not completed abatement because of factors beyond its reasonable control, may file a petition for modification of abatement (PMA) pursuant to section 10(c). According to the Secretary's regulations and the Commission's rules of procedure, a PMA must be in writing and include the following information: (1) all steps taken by the employer during the prescribed abatement period; (2) the additional time needed and the reasons for requiring it; (3) all interim steps being taken to safeguard employees against the cited hazard during the abatement period; and (4) certification that a copy of the PMA has been posted and served on employees, including the date served. All PMAs must be filed with the appropriate OSHA area director.

According to rules of both the Secretary and the Commission, a PMA must be filed no later than the close of the next working day following the date on which abatement was originally required. Generally, the rule has been strictly followed and when a PMA has been filed late the Commission has refused to consider it. Under the Commission's

§ 6.22
1.   557 F.2d 607 (7th Cir.1977).

procedures, however, only PMAs contested by either employees or the Secretary ever reach the Commission. Therefore, it is possible for the Secretary to waive the filing requirement, but in light of the Secretary's own regulations this is unlikely.

§ 6.24   Degrees of Violations

The Act provides for a wide range of violations, from de minimis to criminal violations.

De Minimis Violations

Section 9(a) of the Act provides for "the issuance of a notice in lieu of a citation with respect to de minimis violations which have no direct or immediate relationship to safety and health." When the Secretary issues a de minimis notice, the employer does not have to post the notice, there is no abatement requirement, and there are no penalties. Because it is not a citation there can be no notice of contest filed. De minimis notices are only issued when there is no direct relationship between the noncomplying conditions and employee safety and health. Thus, de minimis notices have been issued for trifling items like a minor breach of a toilet partitioning standard and a failure to provide a receptacle for disposable cups. A de minimis notice is not proper where there is a direct and immediate relationship to employee safety and health.

The Commission has the authority to amend a citation to a de minimis notice. It has used this authority as a way of removing the abatement requirement where noncompliance with a standard creates no real hazard to employees. De minimis violations have been found only when extremely minor injuries are possible from the hazard, when there was only a "technical noncompliance" with a standard, and when the employer complied with an updated version of a consensus standard not adopted by the Secretary.

In *Caterpillar, Inc. v. Herman*,[1] the Seventh Circuit adopted the Secretary's position that "the Commission cannot label a violation *de minimis* and disregard it; that would transfer the Secretary's prosecutorial discretion ... to the Commission."[2] If a citation is issued, the Commission must determine if a violation occurred and, if so, assess an appropriate penalty. Although the court was critical of the Commission's policy regarding *de minimis* violations, it stopped short of saying the Commission lacked the authority to reduce a violation to a *de minimis* notice.

Nonserious Violations

The Act does not specifically define a nonserious violation. But, because there are express definitions for both de minimis and serious violations, a nonserious violation is between the two. "Accordingly, a non-serious violation is one in which there is a direct and immediate relationship between the violative condition and occupational safety and

§ 6.24   **2.** Id. at 668.
1. 131 F.3d 666 (7th Cir.1997).

health but not of such relationship that a resultant injury or illness is death or serious physical harm."[3]

Section 17(c) of the Act provides that "[a]ny employer who has received a citation for a violation * * * and such violation is specifically determined not to be of a serious nature, may be assessed a civil penalty of up to $7,000 for each such violation." The quoted language would seem to require that the Secretary make a specific determination that a violation is nonserious. In practice, however, the opposite is true. Violations are, in effect, "presumed" to be nonserious unless the Secretary proves the elements of a serious violation.

The most important difference between a serious and nonserious violation is that under section 17(k) of the Act a serious violation requires a "substantial probability that death or serious physical harm could result * * *." This language has been interpreted as referring to the severity of an injury if an accident occurs, rather than the likelihood of an accident. The Secretary's regulations define serious physical harm as a "permanent, prolonged, or temporary impairment of the body in which part of the body is made functionally useless or is substantially reduced in efficiency on or off the job." Also included are "[i]llnesses that could shorten life or significantly reduce physical or mental efficiency * * *." The Commission, however, is not bound by this definition and will determine the seriousness of a violation based on the facts of each case.

Unlike serious violations, discussed below, no penalty need be assessed for a nonserious violation. Although the maximum possible penalties for serious and nonserious violations are the same, $7,000 for each violation, as a practical matter, serious violations usually carry much higher penalties.

Serious Violations

The finding of a serious violation under section 17(k) of the Act requires "a substantial probability that death or serious physical harm could result." Decisions of the Commission and courts have consistently held that it is not necessary to prove that there is a substantial probability that an accident will occur. It is only necessary to prove that an accident is possible and that death or serious physical harm could result. The likelihood of an accident is an important factor in determining the gravity of the violation. Thus, it is quite possible for a serious violation to be of low gravity and a nonserious violation to be of high gravity. Even where there has been a fatality in the workplace, the cited OSHA violation is not necessarily serious. The Secretary must prove a connection between the cited violation and the fatality or that the violative condition could lead to death or serious physical harm.

3. Crescent Wharf & Warehouse Co., 1 OSHC 1219, 1971–73 OSHD ¶ 15,687 (1973).

In the past, the Commission has held that the Secretary was required to prove that death or serious physical harm could result from exposure to toxic substances at the levels and duration at the employer's workplace. In *Anaconda Aluminum Co.*,[4] however, the Commission held that, if a standard is intended to protect against a life-threatening disease, then a violation of the standard is serious. The Secretary need not prove that the levels of exposure at the cited employer's workplace would lead to a serious disease. The Secretary's regulations provide that two or more nonserious violations may be grouped to form a serious violation if the combination of the nonserious violations results in a substantial probability that death or serious physical harm could result. The Commission has specifically approved this procedure. Section 17(b) of the Act provides that an employer that receives a citation for a serious violation *shall* be assessed a penalty of up to $7,000. The Commission has construed this section as requiring that a penalty be assessed for each serious violation.

Repeated Violations

Section 17(a) of the Act provides that "any employer who willfully or repeatedly violates the requirements of section 5 of this Act, any standard, rule, or order promulgated pursuant to section 6 of this Act, or regulations prescribed pursuant to this Act, may be assessed a civil penalty of not more than $7,000 for each violation."

In *Potlatch Corp.*,[5] the Commission set forth the elements of a repeated violation. The Commission was unanimous in holding that: "A violation is repeated under section 17(a) of the Act if, at the time of the alleged repeated violation, there was a Commission final order against the same employer for a substantially similar violation." The majority further held that "the Secretary may establish a prima facie case of similarity by showing that the prior and the present violations are for failure to comply with the same standard." Based on *Potlatch*, to establish a repeated violation the Secretary must prove the following: (1) the same employer (2) was cited at least once before (3) and a final order was issued (4) for a substantially similar violation.

The first element of a repeated violation is that the cited employer is the same one that was cited previously. A change in corporate ownership or supervisors may not preclude the issuance of a citation for repeated violations. It also has been held that the "employer" remains the same for section 17(a) purposes even if the violations occurred in different parts of the same workplace. For example, the Commission has held that a repeated violation will lie where the violations occurred on two different ships in the same shipyard.

The most difficult question in this area is when may employers with no fixed establishment be cited for a repeated violation. The Secretary's regulations provide that employers with no fixed establishment, such as

4. 9 OSHC 1460, 1981 OSHD ¶ 25,300 (1981).   **5.** 7 OSHC 1061, 1979 OSHD ¶ 23,294 (1979).

those involved in construction, painting, and excavation, may be cited for a repeated violation if a prior violation occurred anywhere within the same area office jurisdiction.

Section 17(a) does not mention the number of prior violations required before a citation for repeated violation is proper. The Commission's decision in *Potlatch* and the Fourth Circuit's decision in *George Hyman Construction Co. v. OSHRC*[6] hold that one prior violation may support the finding of a repeated violation.

> The contention that for a violation to be repeated there must be two or more prior violations rests on a strained semantical argument that the word repeated in its adverbial form—repeatedly—could only mean an action which takes place "again and again." * * * Under the circumstances we think a more common usage of the term connotes only that a single prior infraction need be proven to invoke the repeated violation sanction authorized by the Act.[7]

Another issue related to the nature of the prior citation is for how long will a prior citation support the finding of a repeated violation. The Commission in *Potlatch* held that the length of time between violations is relevant only to the good faith criterion for penalty assessment. According to the Secretary's regulations, however, to be cited as a repeated violation, the violation must occur "within three years of the date that the original violation became a final order or within three years of the final abatement date, whichever is later."

In *Potlatch* the Commission reiterated the settled principle that to establish a repeated violation the Secretary "must demonstrate that the earlier citation upon which he relies became a final order of the Commission prior to the date of the alleged repeated violation." Although a settlement agreement can be used as the basis of a subsequent repeated violation, as with any antecedent violation it must be a final order before the inspection for repeated violation begins.

In *Potlatch* the Commission held that the finding of a repeated violation must be based on the employer's having committed a substantially similar violation. A prima facie case of similarity is made out by showing that the prior and present violations are of the same standard. Nevertheless, a repeated violation may be based on a different standard or even where the present, prior, or both violations involved the general duty clause. In situations where a violation of the same standard is not alleged, the Secretary must prove the substantial similarity of the hazardous conditions.

In 1994, OSHA implemented a new penalty structure for willful violations. All willful violations are assessed as serious or other-than-serious (nonserious). Serious violations are assessed a gravity rating of high, medium, or low, allowing for adjustment based on size and history

---

6.   582 F.2d 834 (4th Cir.1978).   **7.**   Id. at 839 (footnote omitted).

of violations. There is a $25,000 minimum penalty. Other-than-serious violations and regulatory violations have a minimum penalty of $5,000.

Citations for repeated violation may be issued for serious and nonserious violations—and conceivably even willful violations. While penalties of up to $70,000 for each violation are possible, the penalty assessment factors of section 17(j) of the Act must be considered. Also, because section 17(a) of the Act provides that penalties up to $70,000 *may* be assessed, it is possible that a repeated nonserious violation could carry no penalty.

According to the Commission in *Potlatch*, in assessing penalties for repeated violations, consideration will be given to, among other things, "an employer's attitude (such as his flouting of the Act), commonality of supervisory control over the violative condition, the geographical proximities of the violations, the time lapse between the violations, and the number of prior violations * * *."

Willful Violations

The Act does not define a willful violation. Section 17(a) of the Act simply provides that an employer "who willfully * * * violates [the Act] * * * may be assessed a civil penalty of not more than $70,000 for each violation, with a minimum of $5,000 for each violation." Although there is no requirement that willful violations be serious, many willful citations are issued where there is death, serious injury, or the potential for serious injury. Willful violations may be alleged under both section 5(a)(1) and section 5(a)(2) of the Act.

The Commission has held that to prove a willful violation the Secretary must prove that (1) the employer has committed a violation of the Act and (2) the violation was committed voluntarily with intentional disregard or demonstrated plain indifference to the Act. In *John W. Eshelman & Sons*,[8] the Commission held that the Secretary need not prove that the employer knew it was violating a specific standard or the Act in general.

> The Commission has found a violation to be willful when it is marked by careless disregard of a standard or of employee safety * * *. Therefore, once careless disregard of employee safety has been established, the Secretary need not prove additionally that an employer knew that it was violating the Act.

Although *Eshelman* is an important case, proof of employer knowledge of the Act or a specific standard will probably continue to be one of the most effective ways of proving that the employer's conduct was marked by "careless disregard of" or "plain indifference to" employee safety and health. Employer knowledge of a standard and a subsequent violation of that standard, however, does not necessarily establish a willful violation.

Willful violations require that the employer have a particular state of mind. The Commission has held that " 'willful' means intentional,

8. 9 OSHC 1396, 1981 OSHD ¶ 25,231 (1981).

knowing, or voluntary as distinguished from accidental conduct and may be characterized as conduct marked by careless disregard." In *Intercounty Construction Co. v. OSHRC*,[9] the Fourth Circuit agreed with the Commission and defined "willful" as action being taken knowledgeably by one subject to the statutory provisions in disregard of the action's legality. No showing of malicious intent is necessary. A conscious, intentional, deliberate, voluntary decision is properly described as willful, "regardless of venial motive." The court pointed out that "[t]o require bad intent would place a severe restriction on the statutory authority of OSHA to apply the stronger sanctions in enforcing the law, a result we do not feel was intended by Congress."[10] This interpretation has been widely followed.

As mentioned earlier, penalties of up to $70,000 may be assessed for each willful violation, with a $5,000 minimum for each violation. The Commission, in applying the section 17(j) penalty assessment factors, has held that the consideration of an employer's good faith is not inconsistent with the finding of a willful violation.

Failure to Abate

The most severe civil penalties in the Act are provided for employers failing to correct (abate) violations for which they were previously cited. Section 17(d) of the Act provides that "any employer who fails to correct a violation * * * may be assessed a civil penalty of not more than $7,000 for each day during which such failure or violation continues." Separate citations are not issued to employers that fail to abate violations. Instead, the Secretary will issue a notice of failure to correct and a notice of proposed additional penalties. A notice of failure to correct may be issued at any time after the abatement date, even during the fifteen working day period in which the employer may contest the original citation or during the pendency of a petition for modification of abatement (PMA). An employer has the same fifteen working days to contest additional penalties for failure to abate, but the notification of additional penalties need not be posted.

The Commission has held that the Secretary may issue a citation for failure to abate more than two years after the expiration of the original abatement date. In *Trico Technologies Corp.*,[11] a failure to abate was discovered during a routine inspection more than two years after the employer had notified OSHA that the violation had been abated. The Commission noted that § 10(b) of the OSH Act imposed no time limit on the issuance of notices for failure to abate.

The Secretary must prove three elements to make out a prima facie case of failure to abate. First, the original citation must have become a final order, or, in the case of a notice of failure to abate issued before the end of the original notice of contest period, no prior notice of contest

9. 522 F.2d 777 (4th Cir.1975), cert. denied, 423 U.S. 1072, 96 S.Ct. 854, 47 L.Ed.2d 82 (1976).

10. 522 F.2d at 780.

11. 17 OSHC 1497, 1996 OSHD ¶ 31,-009 (1996).

could have been filed. Because section 17(d) conditions the issuance of a notice of failure to abate on the entry of a final order, there is no dispute over this first element. Second, the condition on reinspection must be identical. As distinguished from a repeated violation, the evidence of a failure to abate must indicate that the violation has continued uncorrected. Third, the Secretary must establish the presence of a hazard at the time of reinspection. In *Kit Manufacturing Co.*,[12] a majority of the Commission held that, where the initial citation was not contested, the Secretary must "prove that the alleged violative condition was in fact violative at the time of the reinspection * * *." This evidence is not necessary where the prior citation was contested.

Employers have several defenses available in an action for failure to abate. The most obvious defense is that there has been abatement. The physical correction of a hazard or the removal of exposed employees constitutes abatement. Although the Commission originally held that "no exposure" was a defense to be raised by the employer, *Kit* requires the Secretary to prove all the elements of a de novo violation, including exposure. Misunderstanding the abatement requirement is no defense. Finally, even if conditions are violative on reinspection, where the employer can prove that the cited violation was abated but recurred, only a repeated violation is appropriate.

The most important defense to a notice of failure to abate is proof that the original condition was nonviolative. In *York Metal Finishing Co.*,[13] the Commission held that neither res judicata nor collateral estoppel will be applied to preclude an employer from challenging an original, uncontested citation. An employer may not file a notice of contest for a variety of reasons and this does not necessarily mean there was a violation. In addition to factual defenses to the validity of earlier uncontested citations, the Commission has permitted employers to raise two main legal defenses. Employers may allege that the original citation lacked specificity or that the employer was originally cited under the wrong standard.

Imminent Danger

Section 13(a) of the Act defines "imminent danger" as a condition "which could be reasonably expected to cause death or serious physical harm immediately or before the imminence of such danger can be eliminated through the enforcement procedures otherwise provided by this Act." If an OSHA compliance officer finds an imminent danger, the CO will ask the employer to remove endangered employees and to abate the hazard voluntarily. Most employers have abated voluntarily, thereby eliminating the need for other action. If, however, the employer refuses to abate voluntarily, the CO notifies the regional director who, through the regional solicitor, seeks a temporary restraining order (TRO) from the nearest United States district court pursuant to section 13(b) of the

---

12. 2 OSHC 1672, 1974–75 OSHD ¶ 19,-415 (1975).

13. 1 OSHC 1655, 1973–74 OSHD ¶ 17,-633 (1974), petition for review dismissed, No. 74–1554 (3d Cir.1974).

Act. Any TRO issued under section 13(b) without notice may not be effective for more than five days.

Under section 13(c) of the Act, the CO is required to inform all affected employees, as well as the employer, of the existence of any imminent danger discovered. Pursuant to section 13(d) of the Act, if the Secretary "arbitrarily" or "capriciously" fails to seek injunctive relief for an imminent danger, the employees have the right to bring an action for a writ of mandamus in the United States district court where the danger is alleged to exist, where the employer has its principal office, or in the District of Columbia.

Criminal Sanctions

Section 17(e) of the Act provides that "any employer who willfully violates [the] Act, and that violation caused death to any employee" may be punished, upon conviction, by a fine up to $10,000 or six months imprisonment, or both, For second offenses, the punishment may be a fine up to $20,000 or one year imprisonment, or both. Criminal cases under the Act are brought by the Justice Department and are prosecuted by the local United States attorney. The cases are tried in United States district court.

In *United States v. Ladish Malting Co.*,[14] the Seventh Circuit held that conviction of a criminal willful violation requires actual knowledge of the conditions that led to the fatality. It was error for the jury instruction to apply a civil negligence version of willfulness that included what one *ought* to have known. The court also held, however, that general evidence of good faith could not negate a finding of willfulness.

The Act contains other criminal sanctions. Section 17(f) prohibits any person from giving advance notice of an inspection. Section 17(g) makes it a crime to make false statements or file false reports. Section 17(h) makes it a crime to interfere with an OSHA compliance officer by using force. These provisions have been used in only a few cases.

§ 6.25 Penalties

The Act provides for a wide range of penalties. As amended in 1990, the penalty ranges for each of the violations are as follows:

De minimis notice	$0
Nonserious	$0–$7,000
Serious	$1–$7,000
Repeated	$0–$70,000
Willful	$5,000–$70,000
Failure to abate notice	$0–$7,000 per day

Section 17(j) of the Act provides that "the Commission shall have authority to assess all civil penalties provided in this section * * *." In *Brennan v. OSHRC (Interstate Glass Co.)*,[1] the Eighth Circuit held that

14. 135 F.3d 484 (7th Cir.1998).

§ 6.25
1. 487 F.2d 438 (8th Cir.1973).

"the Commission shall be the final arbiter of penalties if the Secretary's proposals are contested and that, in such a case, the Secretary's proposals merely become advisory."[2] The Commission has enthusiastically endorsed the principle that in contested cases it assesses a penalty de novo.

The Commission has held that in assessing penalties under the Act it is not bound to follow the Secretary's penalty computation formula.n applying the penalty assessment factors of gravity, size, good faith, and compliance history, the Commission further declared that it need not accord these factors equal weight. Despite a longstanding rejection of the Secretary's formula, the Commission has never formalized a calculation method of its own. Cases are still decided on an ad hoc basis.

The Commission has held that an administrative law judge (ALJ) may not routinely affirm the proposed penalty of the Secretary, but must make an independent determination based on the section 17(j) factors and the particular facts of each case. This same principle applies to all types of violations. For example, the Commission has held that a blanket $100 per day penalty for failure to abate used by the Secretary was invalid. Penalties for failure to abate must bear a reasonable relationship to the penalties assessed for the violations in the first instance.

Although the Commission has staunchly defended its right to be the final arbiter in penalty assessments, in practice, the Secretary's proposals are often given considerable deference. If the ALJ's assessment, often identical to the Secretary's proposal, is not substantially unreasonable, it is usually upheld. The main reason for this unannounced policy is that penalty assessment is subjective and it is difficult and time consuming for the commissioners to agree on an appropriate penalty.

Assessment Factors

The gravity of the violation is the starting point and most important factor in penalty assessment. "Gravity, unlike good faith, compliance history and size is relevant only to the [specific] violation being considered in a case and therefore is usually of greater significance. The other factors are concerned with the employer generally and are considered as modifying factors."[3] Consequently, it is possible for the gravity to be so high that even with full consideration for good faith, size, and compliance history the penalty assessed will be the maximum amount. The Commission has held that gravity is composed of (1) the number of employees exposed to the hazard; (2) the duration of exposure; (3) whether any precautions have been taken against injury; and (4) the degree of probability that an accident would occur.

Penalties are ordinarily assessed on a per-violation basis, meaning that the failure to comply with a particular standard is considered one violation, even if there are ten machines without the same required guard or there are ten employees without required respirators. On

---

2. Id. at 442.

3. Natkin & Co., 1 OSHC 1204, 1971–73 OSHD ¶ 15,679 (1973).

occasion, OSHA has cited each instance or each employee as a separate violation, with the result that the penalties are greatly increased. These penalties have usually been assessed only for substantial violations, and therefore the penalties became known as "egregious penalties."

In *Eric K. Ho*,[4] the Commission clarified its position on per-instance and per-employee penalties. Although the first use of these penalties was in "egregious" cases, and hence the penalties were termed "egregious penalties," the use of per-instance penalties is *not* tied to egregious conduct. Per-instance penalties are only appropriate when the cited regulation or standard clearly prohibits individual acts rather than a single course of action. In *Ho*, the Commission declined to apply per-instance penalties to violations of the asbestos standard dealing with respirators and training because they were viewed as single violations.

§ 6.26 Occupational Safety and Health Review Commission

Pursuant to section 12(a) of the Act, the Occupational Safety and Health Review Commission is comprised of three members appointed by the President "by and with the advice and consent of the Senate." One of the members is designated as Chairman and is responsible for the administrative operations of the Commission. Members serve six year terms, although the first members were appointed for staggered terms of two, four, and six years. Members of the Commission may be removed by the President only for "inefficiency, neglect of duty, or malfeasance in office." The chairmanship, however, may be changed by the President at any time.

Commission proceedings are governed by three sets of rules. First, the Commission has adopted its own rules of procedure pursuant to section 12(g) of the Act.[1] Second, section 12(g) provides that unless a specific Commission rule applies, "the proceedings [are] in accordance with the Federal Rules of Civil Procedure." This principle is recognized by Commission rule 2 and Commission case law. The final set of rules governing Commission proceedings is the Administrative Procedure Act (APA). Although the APA is not mentioned specifically in section 12 of the Act, the APA has been applied to Commission proceedings. Its applicability is recognized in the legislative history, is made specifically applicable by section 10(c) of the Act, and has been relied on in numerous Commission decisions.

§ 6.27 Pleadings

The Commission rules detail the form of pleadings and other procedural rules.

4. 20 OSHC 1361, 2002 OSHD 32,692 (2003).

§ 6.26

1. The rules are codified at 29 C.F.R. Part 2200.

Complaint

Under Commission rule 34, no later than twenty days after forwarding the notice of contest to the Commission, the Secretary of Labor must file a complaint. Rule 34 also specifies what must be alleged in the complaint. According to the Commission, notice pleading is used to prevent undue delay and undue burden on the parties.

Rule 34(a) requires that the Secretary set forth the following: all violations and proposed penalties being contested; the basis for jurisdiction; the time, location, place, and circumstances of each alleged violation; the considerations upon which all abatement periods and proposed penalties are based; and, if the complaint seeks to amend the citation or proposed penalty, the reasons for the amendment and the change sought.

Answer

Commission rule 34(b) provides that an answer must be filed within twenty days after service of the complaint. The answer must contain "a short and plain statement denying those allegations in the complaint which the party intends to contest." Any allegations not denied are deemed admitted. Answers also must include all affirmative defenses, such as infeasibility, unpreventable employee misconduct, and greater hazard. The failure to raise an affirmative defense in the answer may result in the party being prohibited from raising the defense at a later stage of the proceeding.

The answer is the employer's initial pleading. Commission rule 6 requires that every pleading or document filed by any party contain the filing party's name, address, and telephone number. Any change in this information must be communicated promptly in writing to the ALJ or the Commission, and to all other parties and intervenors. Rule 35 requires that all answers filed by a corporation contain a separate declaration listing all parents, subsidiaries, and affiliates of the corporation or stating that there are none. Failure to file a declaration, or failure to amend the declaration if circumstances change, could lead to a default.

When an employer fails to file an answer, the usual Commission practice is to issue an order to show cause why the notice of contest should not be dismissed. This allows employers a "second chance" to cure a pleading omission that may have been caused by inadvertence or ignorance of the Commission's rules. If the employer fails to respond to repeated notices or to an order to show cause, or fails to prove excusable neglect, the notice of contest may be dismissed. This action may be taken pursuant to Commission rule 41, which gives the Commission discretion to preclude a party from further participation in a proceeding upon a failure to file any pleading in a timely manner.

Amendments

The Secretary's regulations provide that the Secretary may unilaterally amend a citation before the filing of a notice of contest if the amendment is made before the expiration of the fifteen working day contest period. This procedure has never been challenged by the Commission and corresponds closely to rule 15(a) of the Federal Rules of Civil Procedure, which permits an amendment as of right before the filing of a responsive pleading.

Commission decisions interpreting rule 15(a) of the Federal Rules of Civil Procedure have properly held that an employer's first "responsive pleading" is the answer. This determination has had two effects. First, because a notice of contest is not considered a "pleading," it may not be amended after the notice of contest period. Second, a complaint may be amended "as a matter of course" before the filing of an answer.

Even in cases where a responsive pleading (answer) has been filed, the Commission has freely granted leave to amend. The failure of an employer to object to the Secretary's motion to amend has been held to constitute a waiver. In *Long Manufacturing Co. v. OSHRC*,[1] the employer objected to the Secretary's motion to amend a citation to allege a violation under a different standard and to increase the amount of the proposed penalty. The ALJ and the Commission granted the amendment and the Eighth Circuit affirmed. The court held that if an employer "chooses to contest the matter before the Commission, he does not have any vested right to go to trial on the specific charge mentioned in the citation or to be free from exposure to a penalty in excess of that originally proposed."[2]

Withdrawals

If the Secretary determines that there is no merit to a citation, a motion to withdraw the citation will be filed. The main issues that have arisen are whether affected employees have a right to receive notice of the withdrawal, whether they have a right to object, and if so, to what elements of a withdrawal may they object and in what manner.

The Commission has held that, regardless of whether they have elected party status, employees and unions have no right to object to the Secretary's withdrawal of a citation. In *American Bakeries Co.*,[3] the Commission held that, because they have no right to object, employees and unions that have not elected party status have no right to be served with motions to withdraw or to have such motions posted. Employees and unions that have elected party status are entitled to notice that the proceeding is terminated, but they have no right to object.

Dismissals

The Secretary's citation and complaint may be dismissed by the Commission sua sponte or upon the motion of any party. Dismissals of citations may result from procedural violations by the Secretary, because there is insufficient evidence of a violation, or because the employer prevailed with a substantive defense. Motions to dismiss for failure to

---

§ 6.27
1. 554 F.2d 903 (8th Cir.1977).
2. Id. at 907.

3. 11 OSHC 2024, 1984–85 OSHD ¶ 26,-951 (1984).

state a claim upon which relief can be granted, filed pursuant to rule 12(b)(6) of the Federal Rules of Civil Procedure, are rarely granted.

An employer's notice of contest may be dismissed by the Commission and the citation affirmed for "failure to plead or otherwise proceed" pursuant to Commission rule 41. The most common reason for dismissal is the failure to file an answer. Where good cause is shown, however, as where the answer was sent but never received, the contest has been reinstated. The Commission has indicated its reluctance to use the sanction of dismissing a notice of contest. "Dismissal for failure to comply with Commission procedural rules is a matter for the judge's sound exercise of discretion, but a decision on the merits rather than a procedural flaw is favored."[4]

Settlements

Commission rule 100 expresses the policy that settlement is "permitted and encouraged" at any stage of the proceedings. Settlements do not need to include any particular language as long as the terms are expressed clearly, unresolved issues are noted, and any employee parties' objections to the reasonableness of abatement time are indicated. Unless the agreement provides otherwise, the withdrawal of a notice of contest, citation, notification of proposed penalty, or petition for modification of abatement is with prejudice.

The ALJ may impose a time limit for filing the settlement agreement and may impose sanctions, including dismissal of the employer's notice of contest, for failure to comply. However, the ALJ may not modify the terms of the settlement.

Rule 100 specifies that a settlement submitted for approval after the ALJ's report has been directed for review must be filed with the Executive Secretary of the Commission. Other settlement agreements reached after assignment of the case to an ALJ are filed with the ALJ. Along with the settlement agreement, the parties must file a consent order for adoption by the ALJ. Affected employees have ten days to object to a proposed settlement, but rule 100 makes it clear that objections are limited to the reasonableness of the abatement time.

§ 6.28 Discovery

Litigation before the Commission is less formal than federal court practice. Nevertheless, discovery is permitted pursuant to statute and the Commission's rules.

Freedom of Information Act

Both the Commission and the Secretary have promulgated detailed rules describing the subjects and procedure for discovery pursuant to the Freedom of Information Act.[1] Under the Commission's rules, all nonpriv-

---

4. Better Baked Foods, Inc., 10 OSHC 1382, 1982 OSHD ¶ 25,873 (1982).

§ 6.28

1. The Commission's rules are published at 29 C.F.R. Part 2201. The Secretary's regulations appear at 29 C.F.R. Part 70.

ileged information is discoverable, except that the rules may not be used by a party to obtain material from an adverse party that would not otherwise be discoverable. If a request for information is denied, and the denial is upheld by the ALJ, an interlocutory appeal may be filed with the Commission within five days of the adverse ruling.

Requests for Admissions

Commission rule 54 provides that twenty-five or fewer requests for admissions may be served upon any other party without an order of the Commission or an ALJ. In complex cases or in cases with a large number of citations, additional requests for admissions may be approved by the ALJ. The party seeking to serve the additional requests has the burden of proving their necessity and must file a written request for permission with the ALJ.

Each item will be deemed admitted unless within thirty days the party served with the request: (1) files a written answer truthfully denying in whole or in part the requested admission; or (2) files an objection to the request, stating in detail the reasons for the objection. Anything admitted is conclusively established unless the ALJ or the Commission grants permission to withdraw or modify the original response.

Interrogatories and Depositions

Commission rule 55 provides that after the filing of a responsive pleading any party may serve upon any other party twenty-five or fewer interrogatories as of right without an order of the ALJ or the Commission. In cases that are complex or involve large numbers of citations, the ALJ may grant a request for additional interrogatories. All interrogatories must be answered separately, in good faith, and under oath. They must be served on the propounding party within thirty days, but the ALJ is authorized to allow a shorter or longer time for answers.

Commission decisions have emphasized that the scope of permissible discovery is governed by rule 26(b)(1) of the Federal Rules of Civil Procedure. The party seeking the information need not show that the material is admissible, it must merely show that the material is relevant to the case. The Commission has required the full disclosure of all nonprivileged information and the cooperation of both parties.

Commission rule 56 allows depositions only by agreement of all parties or upon an order of an ALJ or the Commission following a motion of a party "stating good and just cause." If ordered or agreed to, the deposition must be under oath and in accordance with rule 30 of the

Federal Rules of Civil Procedure. Expenses in taking the deposition are borne by the party "at whose instance the deposition is taken." Depositions taken pursuant to Commission rule 56 may be used for any purpose permitted by the Federal Rules of Evidence and rule 32 of the Federal Rules of Civil Procedure.

Production of Documents

Commission rule 53 provides that at any time after the filing of a responsive pleading any party may serve on any other party a request to produce or permit the inspection of any document. It also allows for the inspection, copying, or testing of any "tangible thing" in the possession of the other party. The request to produce must set forth with reasonable particularity the items to be produced, inspected, or copied. It also must specify a reasonable time, place, and manner for inspecting. The party upon whom the request is served must serve a written response within thirty days of the request, although an ALJ may allow a shorter or longer time. The response must state whether the request will be permitted and, if not, state the grounds for objection.

Confidential Information

The reason given most frequently for objecting to discovery in OSHA cases is the assertion that confidential information will be revealed. In addition to the claim of trade secrets, three other types of confidential information have been at issue: (1) informants; (2) employee medical records; and (3) attorney work product.

The identity of individuals supplying confidential information to the Secretary is not discoverable. In *Stephenson Enterprises, Inc. v. Marshall*,[2] the Fifth Circuit affirmed the Commission's refusal to order disclosure of the name of an employee who supplied information to the Secretary. Using a balancing test, the court held that the name of the interviewed employee should not be disclosed for the following reasons: (1) because employees have extensive knowledge of an employer's working conditions, the public interest is best served by their assisting OSHA compliance officers; (2) the employee, who did not seek out the CO but was chosen at random, had a particularly strong interest against retaliation; and (3) the employer was provided with all of the CO's notes except for the name of the employee and there is no indication that the CO gained any information from the unnamed employee which formed the basis of an alleged violation. Moreover, the employer already had sufficient information about the course of the inspection because the plant manager took part in the walkaround.

In *West Point–Pepperell, Inc.*,[3] the employer was issued a citation alleging serious violations of the respiratory protection and cotton dust

2.   578 F.2d 1021 (5th Cir.1978).

3.   9 OSHC 1784, 1981 OSHD ¶ 25,356 (1981).

standards. The Secretary requested all medical records of the exposed employees related to pulmonary function. The employer objected on the following grounds: (1) the requested information was irrelevant to the case; (2) the requested information was protected by the physician-patient privilege; and (3) release of the requested information would violate the employees' right of privacy. The Commission rejected each of the employer's arguments. It did, however, attempt to minimize the invasion of employee privacy by including the following protective order: (1) examination of and access to the records were limited to Department of Labor employees and expert consultants; (2) the Secretary, his representatives, and consultants were prohibited from disseminating or copying the records and disclosing any of the information to the public or any other federal agency pursuant to the FOIA; (3) the Secretary was required to arrange for the physical security of the records and for their return to the employer; and (4) the parties were to notify the ALJ of any violation of the protective order.

Materials prepared for litigation in the possession of an opponent's attorney are discoverable only if they are relevant, unprivileged, essential to the preparation of the case, and otherwise unobtainable or a substantial equivalent cannot be obtained without undue hardship. In *Wheeling–Pittsburgh Steel Corp.*,[4] the CO and the employer both took photographs of all alleged violations observed during a walkaround. When it was discovered that the CO's camera had malfunctioned, the Secretary subpoenaed the employer's photographs for use as evidence at the hearing. The employer then moved to quash the subpoena on the grounds that the photographs were privileged attorney work product. The ALJ denied the motion to quash and the Commission affirmed. The Commission held that the presence of five other persons during the taking of the photographs destroyed the confidentiality required for the attorney-client privilege. In addition, photographs do not come within the protected categories of an attorney's mental impressions, conclusions, opinions, or legal theories.

Inspections

Commission rule 53(a)(2) provides that at any time after the filing of a responsive pleading any party may serve on any other party a request to permit entry upon land or property for the purpose of "inspection and measuring, surveying, photographing, testing or sampling the property or any designated object or operation thereon." The procedures are the same as for the production of documents. If the discovery inspection will involve trade secrets, a protective order may be issued in accordance with Commission rule 11(f) and Commission rule 52(d).

In *Pabst Brewing Co.*,[5] an ALJ denied the Secretary's motion to reinspect the employer's worksite because the motion was not made until after notice of the final hearing date, the hearing would be unduly postponed, and "the reinspection was sought to remedy a defective

---

4. 4 OSHC 1578, 1976–77 OSHD ¶ 20,-969 (1976).

5. 4 OSHC 2003, 1976–77 OSHD ¶ 21,-472 (1977).

initial investigation * * *." The Commission reversed and held that discovery inspections are normally permissible, extenuating circumstances justified the delay in filing the motion, and the hearing would not be unduly delayed.

Orders and Sanctions

Commission rule 52(c) provides for the issuance of orders compelling discovery when another party refuses or obstructs discovery. An evasive or incomplete answer is treated as a failure to answer. The party seeking to compel discovery must submit an application to the ALJ for an order compelling discovery. If an order is issued and there is a refusal to comply with the order, the ALJ may issue an order to show cause why sanctions should not be entered. Sanctions may include those specified in rule 37 of the Federal Rules of Civil Procedure, including a dismissal or default judgment.

The Commission has attempted to avoid inappropriately harsh sanctions for refusal to comply with a discovery order. Dismissal of a citation or notice of contest will not be ordered unless the conduct of the non-producing party is contumacious or the requesting party is prejudiced. The Commission also has been more willing to vacate citations which have been abated, believing that such action will not frustrate the remedial purpose of the Act while preserving the integrity of the Commission's orders.

§ 6.29   Hearing Procedures

The Commission's policy is to conduct a hearing in or near the community where an alleged violation occurred. In *Bethlehem Steel Corp.*,[1] the Commission reversed an ALJ's notice of hearing, which set the hearing fifty miles from the employer's plant, and ordered that the hearing be held in a smaller city only six miles from the employer's plant. According to the Commission, a hearing should be held as close as possible to the site of an alleged violation.

If the failure of either party to appear at the hearing was caused by extraordinary circumstances or excusable neglect, the case may be reinstated. Nevertheless, it is difficult to prove that the failure to attend was justifiable. An employer's lack of response to the Secretary's motion for a default order and the Secretary's inadvertent failure to prepare for the hearing have been held to be inexcusable.

Representation

Commission rule 22(a) provides that any party or intervenor may appear in person or through a representative. If utilized, the representative controls all matters related to the interest of the party or the intervenor. Affected employees who are represented by an authorized employee representative may appear only through that representative.

§ 6.29

1. 6 OSHC 1912, 1978 OSHD ¶ 22,982 (1978).

The withdrawal of appearance by any representative may be effected by a written notice of withdrawal.

Commission rule 22 makes clear that a representative need not be a lawyer. Where an authorized employee representative elects party status, other employees in the collective bargaining unit may not do so. Where the authorized employee representative declines to elect party status, however, any individual or group of employees may elect party status as if they were unrepresented.

Burden of Proof

In all proceedings commenced by the filing of a notice of contest, the burden of proof rests with the Secretary. This includes all employer contests and employee challenges to the reasonableness of the abatement date. In petition for modification of abatement (PMA) proceedings, however, the burden of proof rests with the petitioner (employer).

The Commission has held that the civil "preponderance of the evidence" test applies in Commission proceedings. A preponderance of the evidence is also needed to support an affirmative defense. The Commission has defined "preponderance of the evidence" as "that quantum of evidence which is sufficient to convince the trier of fact that the facts asserted by a proponent are more probably true than false."[2]

Evidence

Commission rule 71 provides that the Federal Rules of Evidence are applicable to Commission proceedings. Commission rule 69 provides for the oral examination of witnesses under oath with the opposing party having the right to cross-examine. Under rule 615 of the Federal Rules of Evidence, any party has the right to have witnesses sequestered so that they cannot hear the testimony of other witnesses. Under the rule, however, any party, an officer or employee of a party that is not a natural person, or a person whose presence is shown by a party to be essential to the presentation of the case may not be excluded.

Commission rule 67(j) authorizes an ALJ to call and examine witnesses. A similar provision is contained in rule 614(b) of the Federal Rules of Evidence. The Commission has held that it is not improper for ALJs to examine witnesses. Excessive and vitriolic cross-examination by an ALJ, however, may raise questions about the fairness of a hearing. Commission rule 69 provides that all parties have a right to cross-examine any witness called by an ALJ.

Interlocutory Review

Pursuant to Commission rule 73, a petition for interlocutory review will be granted only if the Commission finds that the review involves "an important question of law or policy about which there is substantial ground for difference of opinion and that immediate review of the ruling may materially expedite the final disposition of the proceedings" or the ruling will result in disclosure of information alleged to be privileged.

2. Ultimate Distribution Sys., Inc., 10 OSHC 1568, 1982 OSHD ¶ 26,011 (1982).

Within five days following receipt of an ALJ's ruling from which review is sought, a party may file a petition for interlocutory review with the Commission. Rule 73(b) requires that a corporate party filing a petition for interlocutory review (or responding to such a petition) must file with the Commission a copy of its declaration of corporate parents, subsidiaries, and affiliates. Any responses to the petition must be filed within five days following service of the petition. A copy of both the petition and responses also must be filed with the ALJ.

Conforming Amendments

Rule 15(b) of the Federal Rules of Civil Procedure provides that when issues not raised by the pleadings are tried by the parties, the pleadings may be amended to conform to the evidence. In Commission practice, a motion to amend the pleadings to conform to the evidence may be raised by any party at the close of the hearing, in post-hearing briefs, and on review before the Commission. In addition, the ALJ or the Commission may sua sponte deem the pleadings amended.

The leading explanation of the policy behind conforming pleadings to the evidence appears in the D.C. Circuit's opinion in *National Realty & Construction Co. v. OSHRC*.[3]

> So long as fair notice is afforded, an issue litigated at an administrative hearing may be decided by the hearing agency even though the formal pleadings did not squarely raise the issue * * *. [C]itations under the 1970 Act are drafted by non-legal personnel acting with necessary dispatch. Enforcement of the Act would be crippled if the Secretary were inflexibly held to a narrow construction of citations issued by his inspectors.[4]

The Commission and the courts have approved the use of rule 15(b) amendments for a variety of issues, such as amending a citation from nonserious to serious, changing the date of an alleged violation, amending the citation from the general duty clause to a specific standard, amending the citation to allege the violation of a different standard than the one originally alleged, and amending the citation from a specific standard to the general duty clause. Because the general duty clause, section 5(a)(1) of the Act, requires proof that a hazard is recognized, as well as other elements, the issue of a section 5(a)(1) violation is not likely to be tried by the parties when the citation alleges a violation of a standard under section 5(a)(2) of the Act. Regardless of the subject, the time raised, or the movant, a prerequisite to the granting of a motion for a conforming amendment is the express or implied consent of the parties. Express consent may be found where a party failed to object to or joined in a conforming amendment request. Implied consent, which is much more common, is found when the other party was on notice that the new allegation was in issue. It is often manifested when both parties introduce evidence relevant to the amended charge or allow relevant evidence to be introduced without objection. For example, in *Usery v.*

---

3. 489 F.2d 1257 (D.C.Cir.1973).   **4.** Id. at 1264 (footnotes omitted).

Marquette Cement Manufacturing Co.,[5] the Second Circuit held that the Commission erred in not granting an amendment pursuant to rule 15(b) of the Federal Rules of Civil Procedure because the employer consented to the trial of the amended charge by stipulating to the undisputed facts underlying the amended charge.

Fees

The recovery of attorney fees against the United States by a private party in an OSHA proceeding is governed by the Equal Access to Justice Act.[6] Under this law, a private party prevailing in an adversary agency adjudication may be awarded attorney fees, expert witness fees, and other costs against the United States unless the adjudicator finds that the agency has made a strong showing that its action was substantially justified. In OSHA cases, fees may be awarded only against the Secretary. There can be no recovery against the Commission because its role is limited to adjudication. The test of whether the Secretary's action is substantially justified is essentially one of reasonableness. Where the Secretary can show that a case had a reasonable basis both in law and fact, no attorney fees will be awarded.

In *H.P. Fowler Contracting Corp.*,[7] the Commission addressed the issue of when an employer is a "prevailing party." The Commission held that an employer that entered into a settlement agreement with the Secretary, which resulted in the withdrawal of one citation and the reduction of two willful violations to serious violations, was a prevailing party as to this portion of the action and therefore could recover attorney fees. Similarly, the Commission has held that the employer was a "prevailing party" when the Secretary withdrew a citation before a hearing.

The Commission's regulations implementing the Equal Access to Justice Act[8] provide: (1) net worth ceilings for eligible parties of $2 million for individuals and $7 million for partnerships, corporations, and other entities; (2) units of a local government (erroneously cited) are eligible for fee awards; (3) "substantially justified" is defined to include the underlying governmental action or failure to act that the proceeding is based on, as well as the government's position in litigation; and (4) the Secretary may seek additional proceedings to show that a position was substantially justified, especially where the action was dismissed before any record was developed.

Reopening Hearings

Commission rule 67(h) authorizes an ALJ to reopen hearings sua sponte if necessary to obtain all relevant evidence upon which to adjudicate cases. In *Brennan v. OSHRC (John J. Gordon Co.)*, the Commission reversed an ALJ who had reopened a hearing sua sponte to take additional evidence on whether the employer was engaged in a business

5. 568 F.2d 902 (2d Cir.1977).

6. 5 U.S.C.A. § 504.

7. 11 OSHC 1841, 1983–84 OSHD ¶ 26,-830 (1984).

8. 29 C.F.R. Part 2204.

affecting interstate commerce. The Second Circuit reversed the Commission and held that the ALJ had acted properly. The court held that the Commission's desire to have the case adjudicated promptly should not take precedence over its obligation to see that the facts of each case are fully elicited and the public interest served. Subsequent decisions of the Commission have demonstrated a greater willingness to reopen a hearing record to receive additional relevant evidence. The Commission has held that motions to reopen the record to take additional evidence are within the discretion of the ALJ.

§ 6.30 Post–Hearing Procedure

Commission rule 74 provides for the filing of post-hearing briefs. In lieu of briefs, the ALJ may even permit or direct the parties to file memoranda or statements of authority. Briefs must be filed simultaneously by all parties on a date established by the ALJ. A motion for an extension must be filed at least three days before the due date and other parties must be advised of the request. Reply briefs are not permitted except by order of the ALJ. Untimely briefs will not be accepted unless accompanied by a motion setting forth good cause for the delay. The ALJ may not issue a decision before the parties have an opportunity to file timely briefs.

Under Commission rule 90, a copy of an ALJ's decision is mailed to every party and the parties then have twenty days in which to file exceptions and petitions for discretionary review with the ALJ. During this period the ALJ is free to reconsider the decision and correct "clerical errors and errors arising through oversight or inadvertence." The ALJ must transmit the decision and all other accompanying documents to the Commission no later than the twenty-first day following the date of mailing to the parties. Until the ALJ's report has been docketed by the Executive Secretary, the ALJ may relieve a party of default or grant reinstatement pursuant to Commission rules 41(b), 52(e), or 64(b).

Once an ALJ's decision is docketed by the Commission, the ALJ has no jurisdiction to amend the decision. Pursuant to section 12(j) of the Act, the ALJ's report becomes a final order of the Commission unless it is directed for review within thirty days of docketing. Commission rule 90(b)(2) provides that the Executive Secretary of the Commission shall notify all parties that an ALJ's decision has been docketed by the Commission.

§ 6.31 Commission Review

Section 12(j) of the Act provides that the "report" of an ALJ becomes a final order of the Commission unless within thirty days any Commission member directs that the report be reviewed by the Commission. The thirty-day review period begins to run from the date the ALJ's report is docketed by the Commission. The date of a direction for review is the date on which the document reaches the Executive Secretary of the Commission, rather than the date written on the direction for review or the date of signing.

Commission rule 91(a) provides that review by the Commission is not a matter of right, but rests within the sound discretion of the Commission. There are two distinct, but related, ways in which an ALJ's decision may be directed for review by the Commission. First, the Commission may grant a petition for discretionary review (PDR) filed by any aggrieved party. Second, a Commission member may direct review of the ALJ's decision on his or her own.

Under section 12(j) of the Act, any member of the Commission may direct a case for review even without the filing of a PDR. Commission rule 92(b) provides that cases in which review will be directed "would normally be limited to novel questions of law or policy or questions involving conflict in administrative law judges' decisions." This rule may be viewed as the formalization of an already-established practice of not directing review in the absence of a PDR unless there is a "compelling public interest" or "novel question of law."

Although a direction for review gives the Commission jurisdiction to review the entire case, "ordinarily" the issues will be limited to those stated in the direction for review or in a later order. In its direction for review the Commission may raise new issues to which the parties will be asked to respond.

Commission rule 92(c) provides that the Commission "ordinarily" will not review issues that an ALJ did not have an opportunity to rule on. In exercising discretion to consider issues raised for the first time on review, the Commission "may consider such factors as whether there was good cause for not raising the issue before the Judge, the degree to which the issue is factual, the degree to which proceedings will be disrupted or delayed by raising the issue on review, whether the ability of an adverse party to press a claim or defense would be impaired, and whether considering the new issue would avoid injustice or ensure that judgment will be rendered in accordance with the law and facts."

When the Commission directs review of an ALJ's decision, the entire decision is on review. The failure to direct a particular citation item for review does not make the ALJ's disposition of that item a final order of the Commission. Therefore, there is no abatement requirement for any contested item until the Commission issues a final order.

If no Commission member directs a case for review, the ALJ's decision becomes a final order of the Commission. No notice need be sent to the employer that review has not been ordered, even if a PDR was filed. In *United States v. Fornea Road Boring Co.*,[1] the employer's PDR was not granted, but no notice was sent to the employer. After the appeal time had run, the Secretary began a collection action in district court pursuant to section 17(*l*) of the Act. In affirming the district court, the Fifth Circuit held that due process did not require that the employer

§ 6.31
1. 565 F.2d 1314 (5th Cir.1978).

be given notice that its PDR was not granted. The Act provides that an ALJ's decision is final unless review is directed within thirty days and the employer was informed by the Commission that it would not receive any further communication unless review was directed.

§ 6.32   Judicial Review

Section 11(a) of the Act provides that "any person adversely affected or aggrieved by a final order of the Commission" may seek review by filing a petition for review in any United States court of appeals for the circuit in which the alleged violation occurred or where the employer has its principal office, or in the Court of Appeals for the District of Columbia Circuit. Under section 11(b) of the Act, the Secretary may seek review only in the circuit in which the alleged violation occurred or where the employer has its principal office.

Petitions for review must be filed with the clerk of the court within sixty days following the issuance of the Commission's final order. The sixty-day period is jurisdictional and may not be extended by pleading excusable neglect. Unlike rule 4(a) of the Federal Rules of Civil Procedure, rule 15 of the Federal Rules of Appellate Procedure does *not* contain a provision permitting late filing because of excusable neglect. For an unreviewed administrative law judge's decision, the sixty-day period begins to run on the day the ALJ's decision becomes a final order of the Commission, *not* thirty days after the Commission's notice to the employer that its petition for discretionary review (PDR) was denied. The date of filing with a court is the date the petition arrives at the office of the clerk of the court.

The filing of a petition does not operate as a stay of the Commission's order, but a supersedeas writ may be sought from the court. The courts of appeals are empowered to affirm, modify, or set aside in whole or in part any order of the Commission. Orders of the courts of appeals are final, but a petition for a writ of cert. may be filed with the Supreme Court.

Exhaustion

The doctrine of exhaustion of administrative remedies applies to the Act. Parties may not seek judicial review before the issuance of a final order of the Commission. As expressed by the Third Circuit: "Where Congress has designated a specific forum for the review of administrative action, that forum is exclusive, and a concerned party must exhaust his administrative remedies prior to seeking relief from the courts."[1] The basic purposes of exhaustion of administrative remedies are to prevent the premature disruption of the administrative process, to allow an agency to develop a factual record and apply its expertise, and to permit an agency to correct its own errors so as to moot judicial controversies.

----

§ 6.32

1. In re Restland Memorial Park, 540 F.2d 626, 628 (3d Cir.1976).

Once an ALJ issues a decision, a party must seek administrative review before the Commission or judicial review will be precluded. In *Keystone Roofing Co., Inc. v. OSHRC*,[2] the employer attempted to "appeal" an ALJ's decision to the court of appeals without having first sought review by the Commission. The Third Circuit held that the employer failed to exhaust its administrative remedies. Thus, the employer was unable to secure any relief, because administrative review was precluded when the unreviewed ALJ's decision became a final order of the Commission. Of particular importance, the court held that judicial review was not possible unless the employer filed a petition for discretionary review with the Commission. If the petitioning party can demonstrate "extraordinary circumstances," however, the failure to file a PDR will be excused.

Even if there has been a decision of the Commission, the case may not be ripe for judicial review under the "finality rule." Generally, only "final orders" or "final agency action" are proper subjects for judicial review. Several cases have held that where the Commission has decided a case on interlocutory review, or reserved ruling on a motion, or ordered the case remanded, the Commission's decision was not a final order subject to judicial review.

Section 11(a) of the Act provides that in cases under the Act "no objection that has not been urged before the Commission shall be considered by the court, unless failure or neglect to urge such objection shall be excused because of extraordinary circumstances." All parties must therefore raise all issues initially before the Commission. The failure to raise an issue before the Commission has resulted in an inability to raise on judicial review issues such as constitutional defenses, alleged improper promulgation of a standard, the particularity of the citation, and evidentiary objections. Even when an issue has not been raised before the Commission it may be raised initially on judicial review if good cause is shown. An intervening decision of the Supreme Court and the fact that the issue was part of the Secretary's prima facie case have been held to be good cause.

Parties

Section 11(a) of the Act provides that a petition for review may be filed by "any person adversely affected or aggrieved by an order of the Commission." While most petitions have been filed by employers or the Secretary, unions or individual employees also may seek judicial review.

An important issue is the right of an employee or employee representative to seek judicial review of a Commission decision when the Secretary declines to seek review. In *OCAW v. OSHRC*,[3] the union sought judicial review when the Secretary refused. The employer argued that because of prosecutorial discretion the union could not, in effect, appeal the Secretary's decision not to appeal. The D.C. Circuit, while

---

2. 539 F.2d 960 (3d Cir.1976).

3. 671 F.2d 643 (D.C.Cir.), cert. denied, 459 U.S. 905, 103 S.Ct. 206, 74 L.Ed.2d 165 (1982).

rejecting this argument and holding that the union had an independent right to seek review, severely limited the right by imposing the following two conditions. First, the union must give the Secretary notice of the appeal. Second, the case will be dismissed as moot if the Secretary informs the court that the case will not be prosecuted regardless of the court's decision.

Scope of Review

Section 11(a) of the Act provides that "[t]he findings of the Commission with respect to questions of fact, if supported by substantial evidence on the record considered as a whole, shall be conclusive." " 'Substantial evidence' means 'such relevant evidence as a reasonable mind might accept as adequate to support a conclusion,' taking into account 'whatever in the record fairly detracts from its weight.' "[4] In other words, "it must be enough to warrant denial of a motion for a directed verdict in a civil case tried to a jury."[5]

In applying the substantial evidence rule to Commission findings of fact, the courts will defer to the Commission's determination of whether the burden of proof has been satisfied.

> [T]he quantum of proof which the Commission, as an independent body appointed by the President, may deem necessary to satisfy it of the existence of the "condition" within the meaning of the statute is a matter on which its experience and expertise is entitled to great deference.[6]

Deference to the Commission is especially appropriate where credibility determinations are involved. "[A]gency credibility resolutions are essentially non-reviewable unless contradicted by uncontrovertible documentary evidence or physical facts."[7]

While the substantial evidence test is used for evidentiary findings, the "abuse of discretion" or "arbitrary and capricious" test is applied in the judicial review of penalty assessment. In *Brennan v. OSHRC (Interstate Glass Co.)*,[8] the Eighth Circuit held that:

> [t]he assessment of penalties is not a finding but the exercise of a discretionary grant of power. And while the court has jurisdiction to review and power to modify, the test of a penalty within the statutory range must be whether the Commission abused its discretion.[9]

Judicial review of contested OSHA cases pursuant to section 11(a) of the Act has followed the well-settled principle that the courts will show

4. Astra Pharmaceutical Prods., Inc. v. OSHRC, 681 F.2d 69, 72 (1st Cir.1982), quoting Universal Camera Corp. v. NLRB, 340 U.S. 474, 477, 488, 71 S.Ct. 456, 459, 464, 95 L.Ed. 456 (1951).

5. Dunlop v. Rockwell Int'l, 540 F.2d 1283, 1287 (6th Cir.1976), quoting Jones v. Priebe, 489 F.2d 709, 710 (6th Cir.1973).

6. Usery v. Hermitage Concrete Pipe Co., 584 F.2d 127, 134 (6th Cir.1978).

7. Olin Constr. Co., Inc. v. OSHRC, 525 F.2d 464, 467 (2d Cir.1975) (citations omitted).

8. 487 F.2d 438 (8th Cir.1973).

9. Id. at 442 (footnote omitted).

"great deference to the interpretation given the statute by the officers or agency charged with its administration."[10] This deference is usually justified by the agency's superior expertise in a particular area.

If statutory interpretations by the Commission and the Secretary have been afforded "great weight," their interpretations of standards have been given "some weight." It is not entirely clear whether this fact reflects a different standard of review or is simply the result of more reasonable statutory interpretation. In any event, the Sixth Circuit has explained the concept of judicial deference in the following way: "We are not called upon * * * to decide whether the OSHRC chose the best course or the most reasonable interpretation of the regulation. We are only asked to decide if it chose a reasonable interpretation * * *."[11] On the other hand, as the Seventh Circuit has observed, "a court need not defer to an interpretation it finds unreasonable * * *."[12]

The strongest case for judicial deference exists when the Commission and the Secretary agree on the interpretation of a standard. Even in these situations, however, there is no assurance that the reviewing court will conclude that the interpretation is reasonable. As the Seventh Circuit has pointed out: "Unlike Humpty Dumpty, the Secretary may not give a word whatever meaning he chooses, and while we would defer to any reasonable interpretation on his part, we are convinced that the interpretation he advances here is unreasonable."[13]

In *Martin v. OSHRC (CF & I Steel Corp.)*,[14] the Supreme Court considered the question of to whom should a reviewing court defer when the Secretary and Commission furnish reasonable but conflicting interpretations of an ambiguous standard. The Court inferred from the structure and history of the statute "that the power to render authoritative interpretations of OSH Act regulations is a 'necessary adjunct' of the Secretary's powers to promulgate and to enforce national health and safety standards."[15] By contrast, the Court held that Congress delegated to the Commission "the type of nonpolicymaking adjudicatory powers typically exercised by a *court* in the agency-review context."[16] Thus, in this allocation of responsibilities, the Commission is authorized to review the Secretary's interpretations of standards "only for consistency with the regulatory language and for reasonableness."[17]

OTHER LAWS

§ 6.33   Federal Mine Safety and Health Act

OSHA does not apply to working conditions regulated under another federal statute. The most detailed and important non-OSHA regulatory

---

10. Udall v. Tallman, 380 U.S. 1, 16, 85 S.Ct. 792, 13 L.Ed.2d 616 (1965), quoted in Southern Ry. v. OSHRC, 539 F.2d 335, 337 (4th Cir.), cert. denied, 429 U.S. 999, 97 S.Ct. 525, 50 L.Ed.2d 609 (1976).

11. RMI Co. v. Secretary of Labor, 594 F.2d 566, 571 (6th Cir.1979).

12. Langer Roofing & Sheet Metal, Inc. v. Secretary of Labor, 524 F.2d 1337, 1339 (7th Cir.1975).

13. Langer Roofing & Sheet Metal, Inc. v. Secretary of Labor, 524 F.2d 1337, 1339 (7th Cir.1975) (footnote omitted).

14. 499 U.S. 144, 111 S.Ct. 1171, 113 L.Ed.2d 117 (1991).

15. 499 U.S. at 152, 111 S.Ct. at 1176.

16. Id. at 154, 111 S.Ct. at 1178.

17. Id.

scheme involves mining. Although mine safety legislation dates back to the late nineteenth century, the first post-World War II federal law was the Federal Coal Mine Safety Act of 1952.[1] This was followed by the Federal Metal and Nonmetallic Mine Safety Act of 1966[2] and the Federal Coal Mine Health and Safety Act of 1969.[3] The Federal Mine Safety and Health Act of 1977,[4] consolidated all federal regulation of coal mining and non-coal mining under one statutory scheme. The Act is enforced by the Mine Safety and Health Administration (MSHA), part of the United States Department of Labor. Contested enforcement proceedings are adjudicated by the independent, five-member Federal Mine Safety and Health Review Commission and its administrative law judges, with appeals going to the United States courts of appeals.

The Act covers every "coal or other mine the products of which affect commerce, and each operator of such mine, and every miner in such mine."[5] According to the legislative history and subsequent case law, the definition of "mine" is to be construed broadly. An "operator" is "any owner, lessee, or other person who operates, controls, or supervises a coal or other mine or any independent contractor performing services or construction at such mine."[6] A miner is simply "an individual working in a coal or other mine."[7] Mandatory standards issued under the 1966 Metal and Nonmetallic Act and 1969 Coal Act were continued as effective until new or revised standards were issued by the Secretary of Labor. The Federal Mine Safety and Health Act provides for both civil and criminal penalties for violating these standards. The regulation of toxic materials, use of labels and warnings, and mine surface construction safety are other areas covered by the standards. All standards are focused toward attaining "the highest degree of health and safety protection for the miner."[8]

Section 103 of the Act provides for "frequent" inspections and investigations for the purpose of: (1) obtaining, utilizing, and disseminating information related to health and safety conditions, the causes of accidents, and the causes of diseases and physical impairments originating in such mine; (2) gathering information with respect to mandatory health or safety standards; (3) determining whether an imminent danger exists; and (4) determining whether there is compliance with the mandatory health and safety standards or with any citation, order, or decision. The Secretary is required to inspect each underground mine at least four times a year and each surface mine at least two times a year.

§ 6.33

1. Pub. L. No. 82–552, 66 Stat. 692 (1952).

2. Pub. L. No. 89–577, 80 Stat. 772 (1966), codified at 30 U.S.C.A. §§ 721—740 (1976) (repealed 1977).

3. Pub. L. No. 91–173, 83 Stat. 742 (1969).

4. 30 U.S.C.A. §§ 801—962.

5. Id. § 802.

6. Id. § 802(d).

7. Id. § 802(g).

8. Id. § 811(a)(6)(A).

The Act also provides for the issuance of regulations requiring operators to maintain accurate records of exposures to potentially toxic materials or harmful physical agents requiring monitoring. Operators also are mandated to notify miners if their exposure exceeds levels proscribed by the Act. Miners may obtain an immediate inspection when there is reasonable grounds to believe that a violation or an imminent danger exists.

Search Warrants

The Act provides for warrantless inspections. In *Donovan v. Dewey*,[9] the Supreme Court held that because the statute mandates regular inspections, this provides a constitutionally adequate substitute for a warrant. The Court also emphasized that there is a substantial federal interest in improving the health and safety conditions in mines and that the mining industry is among the most hazardous. Therefore, Congress could reasonably determine that a system of warrantless inspections was necessary for the law to be effective. This analysis, however, differs significantly from *Marshall v. Barlow's, Inc.*,[10] in which the Court held that nonconsensual, warrantless OSHA inspections violate the Fourth Amendment.

In *Thunder Basin Coal Co. v. Reich*,[11] the Supreme Court held that federal district courts do not have jurisdiction to hear preenforcement challenges to inspection and citation procedures. The Secretary's interpretation of the statute, which permits nonelected labor organizations and nonemployee union representatives to serve as miners' representatives during inspections of nonunion mines, also has been upheld.

Citations

The Act provides for the issuance of a citation to an operator if the Secretary believes that there has been a violation of any standard, rule, order, or regulation promulgated pursuant to the Act. The citation must be: (1) in writing; (2) describe with particularity the nature of the violation; and (3) fix a reasonable time for the abatement of the violation.

Penalties are assessed on the basis of, among other things, whether a citation includes a special finding that a violation is "significant and substantial." A minimum penalty of $60 may be assessed if a violation is not characterized as "significant and substantial." In *National Gypsum Co.*,[12] the Federal Mine Safety and Health Review Commission held that a violation will be considered significant and substantial "if, based upon the particular facts surrounding that violation, there exists a reasonable likelihood that the hazard contributed to will result in an injury or illness of a reasonably serious nature." MSHA does not have the authori-

---

9. 452 U.S. 594, 101 S.Ct. 2534, 69 L.Ed.2d 262 (1981).

10. 436 U.S. 307, 98 S.Ct. 1816, 56 L.Ed.2d 305 (1978).

11. 510 U.S. 200, 114 S.Ct. 771, 127 L.Ed.2d 29 (1994).

12. 3 MSHC 822 (1981).

ty to designate as "significant and substantial" a violation of a regulation that is not a mandatory safety or health standard.

Failure–to–Abate Closure Orders

Section 104(b) provides that a failure to abate closure order may be issued upon a finding by the Secretary upon any follow-up inspection: (1) that a violation described in a citation has not been totally abated within the period of time originally prescribed or subsequently extended; and (2) that the period of time for the abatement should not be further extended. The Secretary must determine "the extent of the area affected by the violation" and issue "an order requiring the operator of such mine or his agent to immediately cause all persons * * * to be withdrawn from, and to be prohibited from entering such area until an authorized representative of the Secretary determines that such violation has been abated."[13]

Unwarrantable Failure Citations and Orders

Four conditions must be met in order for the Secretary to include in a citation a special finding of an unwarrantable failure: (1) a violation of any mandatory health or safety standard; (2) the condition would not cause imminent danger; (3) the violation could significantly and substantially contribute to the cause and effect of a mine hazard; and (4) an unwarrantable failure of an operator to comply with a mandatory standard. The Commission has ruled that an "unwarrantable failure" consists of "aggravated conduct constituting more than ordinary negligence" on the part of the mine operator. Ordinary negligence is insufficient to support a finding of unwarrantable failure. A special finding of unwarrantable failure may be included in a citation even if the violation no longer exists.

A closure order may follow an unwarrantable failure citation. An unwarrantable failure closure order will be issued if another violation is found on a subsequent inspection within ninety days of the previous citation. The violation must be caused by an unwarrantable failure to comply. After an unwarrantable failure citation and subsequent closure order have been issued, the mine operator will continue to receive withdrawal orders for subsequent unwarrantable failure violations issued anywhere in the mine until there has been a full mine inspection with no unwarrantable failure violations. Violations that serve to continue the issuance of an unwarrantable failure closure order, however, must be "similar to those that resulted in the issuance of the withdrawal order."

Pattern of Violations

If the Secretary determines that "an operator has a pattern of violations of mandatory health or safety standards," and that these violations are of "such nature as could have significantly and substantially contributed to the cause of a hazard," the Secretary is required to issue a notice of such a pattern to the operator. If a "significant and

13. 30 U.S.C.A. § 814(b).

substantial" violation is found within ninety days of the notice, MSHA issues a withdrawal order prohibiting all persons from entering an area.

Imminent Danger Withdrawal Orders and Other Safety Provisions

Section 802(j) of the Act defines an "imminent danger" as "the existence of any condition or practice in a coal or other mine which could reasonably be expected to cause death or serious physical harm before such condition or practice can be abated." If an imminent danger is found to exist, the Secretary will issue an order that all miners in the area be withdrawn.

Citations also can be issued for more narrowly defined areas of concern. For example, citations may be issued for violations of coal dust standards. If dust levels remain high in subsequent inspections, closure orders may be issued. The adequacy of miner training is also addressed by the Act. A miner determined to be a hazard to self and others may be withdrawn from the mine and prohibited from reentering until proper training has been given.

Injunctions, Restraining Orders, and Penalties

Section 818 of the Act gives the Secretary authority to "institute a civil action for relief, including a permanent or temporary injunction, restraining order, or any other appropriate order." For example, interfering with or delaying the Secretary in carrying out the provisions of the Act or refusing to permit inspection or access to necessary records can result in civil actions.

Civil and criminal penalties are found in section 820 of the Act. Civil penalties of up to $50,000 may be assessed for each violation of a mandatory standard. An operator also may be assessed up to $5,000 a day for failure to correct a violation. Pursuant to section 820(d), any operator who willfully or knowingly violates or fails or refuses to comply with specified orders shall, upon conviction, be punished by a fine of no more than $25,000, or by imprisonment for not more than one year or by both. This fine and imprisonment can both be enhanced if there has been a prior conviction.

The Act provides that in assessing civil monetary penalties, consideration must be given to the following factors: (1) the operator's history of previous violations; (2) the appropriateness of the penalty to the size of the business; (3) whether the operator was negligent; (4) the effect on the operator's ability to continue in business; (5) the gravity of the violation; and (6) the demonstrated good faith of the person charged in attempting to achieve rapid compliance after notification of the violation. The Commission has held that all these factors must be considered regardless of the amount of probable harm. The Commission also has held that the Secretary's proposed penalty is not binding on the Commission. In other words, when a proposed penalty is contested, the Commission exercises independent review and applies the six statutory criteria without considering the Secretary's regulations.

In certain instances in which a corporate operator violates the Act, "any director, officer, or agent of such corporation who knowingly authorized, ordered, or carried out such violation, failure, or refusal shall be subject to the same civil penalties, fines and imprisonment that may be imposed."[14] In *Richardson v. Secretary of Labor*,[15] the Sixth Circuit rejected the argument that this provision constitutes a denial of equal protection because it imposes liability only on corporate agents. According to the court, Congress intended to assure that the decision-makers responsible for illegal acts of corporate operators would also be held personally liable for violations; thus, there was a rational relationship to the purpose of the Act.

Procedural Rules

An operator has thirty days from receipt of an order or citation in which to contest. Under the Act, contested cases are heard and decided by administrative law judges appointed by the Federal Mine Safety and Health Review Commission. After the ALJ issues a decision, any party adversely affected has thirty days to file a petition for review with the Commission. The Commission also may order review of a case sua sponte where an ALJ's decision is contrary to law or Commission policy. If a petition for review is denied or following the decision of the Commission, any person adversely affected may seek review in the United States courts of appeals. An ALJ's denial of attorney fees and expenses under the Equal Access to Justice Act is not a final decision immediately appealable to the court of appeals.

The rules of procedure of the Commission are similar to and are guided by the Federal Rules of Civil Procedure. The Federal Rules of Evidence, however, do not apply. Miners are encouraged to participate in proceedings concerning citations, penalty assessments, and orders issued under the Act. The courts have upheld the application of the Commission's "adequate cause" standard for excusing the failure to comply with its procedural rules.

Anti–Discrimination Provisions

Miners may request an inspection or investigation by MSHA if they believe there is a violation of the Act or mandatory health and safety standard or that an imminent danger exists. The Act protects miners, representatives of miners, and applicants for employment from discrimination for engaging in this or other forms of protected activity. Specifically, miners may not be discriminated against for: (1) exercising statutory rights; (2) filing or making complaints with the Secretary of Labor, a representative of miners, or the mine operator regarding an alleged danger or safety or health violation in the mine; (3) initiating any proceeding under the Act; (4) testifying, or planning to testify, in any

---

14. 30 U.S.C.A. § 820(c).

15. 689 F.2d 632 (6th Cir.1982), cert. denied, 461 U.S. 928, 103 S.Ct. 2088, 77 L.Ed.2d 299 (1983).

proceeding under the Act; (5) or being evaluated or transferred pursuant to medical standards under the Act. Procedurally, there are two important differences between MSHA and OSHA discrimination actions. First, under MSHA, discrimination actions are brought before the Commission rather than in district court. Second, under MSHA, miners may proceed on their own behalf even if the Secretary decides not to pursue the discrimination claim.

The right of miners to refuse to work in unsafe conditions is another important right that has resulted in extensive case law. The Commission and courts have held that miners have a right to refuse to work in unsafe or unhealthy conditions. This interpretation is based on the legislative history of the Act rather than the statutory language. To qualify for protection, however, it has been held that the miner must notify the operator of the work refusal.

The Commission uses a balancing approach to determine whether discrimination has occurred. The complainant must first establish that the miners engaged in protected health or safety activity and that the adverse action by the operator was based in some part on the protected activity. The operator then has the burden of persuasion that the same adverse action against the miner would have been taken because of the miner's unprotected conduct.

A critical question is, what is protected activity? In *Robinette v. United Castle Coal Co.*,[16] the Commission held that the employee's refusal to work must have been based upon a reasonable, good faith belief that a hazard existed. The burden of proving good faith and reasonableness is on the miner. For example, *Bush v. Union Carbide Corp.*, a mechanic who continued to refuse to unload sulfuric acid from a railroad truck after being told the hazardous conditions were corrected, was not protected because the refusal was based on an unreasonable perception and no reason was given for the refusal.

The Commission is authorized to order appropriate relief, including the award of back pay, in cases of discrimination. The Fourth Circuit has held that the Commission was required to defer to the Secretary's rule that unemployment compensation awards should not be deducted from back pay.

§ 6.34 Migrant and Seasonal Agricultural Worker Protection Act

The Migrant and Seasonal Agricultural Worker Protection Act (MSPA) replaced and repealed the Farm Labor Contractor Registration Act of 1963 (FLCRA). Both laws were enacted to protect migrant and seasonal workers from employers that misrepresented the nature and availability of work, provided inaccurate pay information, used uninsured, unsafe vehicles to transport workers, supplied inadequate housing, and forced workers to pay exorbitant prices for goods. The Farm

---

16.   3 MSHC 803 (1981).

Labor Contractor Act was very flawed, however, so Congress enacted the MSPA to cure its problems. The MSPA was intended to protect all workers protected by FLCRA.

MSPA regulates three classes of persons: farm labor contractors, agricultural associations, and agricultural employers. These are persons who recruit, solicit, hire, employ, furnish, or transport migrant or seasonal agricultural workers. Only farm labor contractors are required to register with the Department of Labor. Farm labor contractors are persons, other than agricultural employers or agricultural associations, who perform any farm labor contracting activity for money or other consideration. "Agricultural association" is a nonprofit or cooperative association of farmers, growers, or ranchers, incorporated or qualified under applicable state law, which recruits, solicits, hires, employs, furnishes, or transports migrant or seasonal agricultural worker. "Agricultural employers" are persons who own or operate a farm, ranch, processing establishment, cannery, gin, packing shed or nursery, or who produce or condition seed, and who recruit, solicit, hire, employ, furnish, or transport migrant or seasonal agricultural workers. All three classes must comply with worker protection requirements. MSPA also regulates persons who own or control farmworker housing. The Act exempts immediate family members of an agricultural employer or a farm labor contractor.

The MSPA protects two classes of workers, migrant agricultural workers and seasonal agricultural workers. A migrant agricultural worker is an individual "who is employed in agricultural employment of a seasonal or other temporary nature, and who is required to be absent overnight from his permanent place of residence." "Migrant worker" is a term of art which has no reference to migratory tendencies of workers. A seasonal agricultural worker is an individual "who is employed in agricultural employment of a seasonal or other temporary nature and is not required to be absent overnight from his permanent place of residence."

The MSPA adopts the meaning of "employ" as defined in the Fair Labor Standards Act. Thus, the terms, "employer," "employee," and "independent contractor" do not have their common law meanings; instead, the terms are construed to open the door for joint-employer situations in which more than one person must fulfill the requirements of the worker protection provisions. "Joint employment" means the situation in which "a single individual stands in the relation of an employee to two or more persons at the same time."[1] "[A]n employer 'cannot shield himself from liability by placing a recruiter-contractor between himself and the laborers, by giving the recruiter-contractor responsibility for direct oversight of the laborers.' "[2]

§ 6.34

1. Howard v. Malcolm, 852 F.2d 101 (4th Cir.1988).

2. Saintida v. Tyre, 783 F.Supp. 1368, 1373 (S.D.Fla.1992) (quoting Monville v. Williams, 1987 WL 42404 (D.Md.1987)).

Farm labor contractors are prohibited from knowingly recruiting, hiring, employing, or using undocumented aliens. The contractor has an affirmative duty to inquire into each worker's employment status.

Violations of MSPA or its regulations may result in criminal sanctions, civil penalties, or injunctions. Workers may also obtain damages for violations in private suits against the violators.

MSPA provides a private cause of action to aggrieved workers. Thus, workers injured in an accident while being transported by a recruiter hired by a farm labor contractor can sue the contractor for damages resulting from the accident. Workers do not have to exhaust any available administrative remedies before pursuing judicial action.

The Migrant and Seasonal Agricultural Worker Protection Act (MSAWPA) was amended in 1995. The amendments reverse the Supreme Court's decision in *Adams Fruit Co. v. Barrett*,[3] which allowed migrant workers injured on the job to collect workers' compensation and to sue under the MSAWPA. Under the amendments, workers' compensation is now the exclusive remedy for injuries or death suffered by a farm worker in states where agricultural workers are covered by workers' compensation.

The amendments also raise the damages from $500 to $10,000 if a worker is injured or killed in an accident where alcohol or drugs are involved, if an employer has a history of violations, where the employer willfully alters a vehicle to make it dangerous, or where the employer uses an unregistered farm labor contractor.

§ 6.35 Common Law

The availability of common law remedies to protect employment opportunities and improve working conditions is severely limited by three legal doctrines: the "at will" employment doctrine, the preemption of state law by the Occupational Safety and Health Act, and the "exclusive remedy" provisions of state workers' compensation laws. Nevertheless, there are some ways in which the common law may be used to protect employment opportunities and improve working conditions.

A growing number of cases have been brought alleging that it violated the public policy exception to the "at will" doctrine for an employer to discharge an employee for refusing to work under hazardous conditions or for reporting safety and health hazards to the government. The courts have reached widely varying results in these wrongful discharge cases. Courts upholding the right to bring these actions usually have found the public policy based in a state or federal statute, such as a state pesticide control law, federal or state OSHA law, or Nuclear Regulatory Commission regulations on the handling of radioactive materials. A public policy need not, however, be based on a statute to support an action for wrongful discharge. There does not seem to be much

---

3. 493 U.S. 808, 110 S.Ct. 49, 107 L.Ed.2d 18 (1989).

difference in results based on whether the employee refused to work or reported the hazards to the government.

Some cases have construed quite broadly the public policy against retaliatory discharge of employees who file occupational safety and health complaints. For example, in *Skillsky v. Lucky Stores, Inc.,*[1] an employee alleged that his subsequent employer discharged him because it learned that he had filed a Cal–OSHA complaint against his former employer. The Ninth Circuit held that the plaintiff alleged facts sufficient to establish that the discharge violated California public policy.

Cases refusing to permit wrongful discharge actions have been based on the asserted preemption of these actions by virtue of section 11(c) of the Occupational Safety and Health Act, the lack of a violation of public policy by the discharge, and substantial justification for the discharge. An action for wrongful discharge requires an independent legal basis and may not be based solely on alleged OSHA or state OSHA violations. It also will fail where the employment is not "at will" but pursuant to an employment contract.

Another theory on which a common law action might be brought is where the negligent assessment of an applicant's or employee's health results in the denial or termination of employment. Although this theory has been used where a physician made a wrongful diagnosis, other possible actions include suits against medical laboratories for negligence in performing tests, against the manufacturers of testing equipment, and against prior employers or other entities that negligently supplied inaccurate information abut the health of an individual.

The "exclusive remedy" provisions of state workers' compensation laws generally apply only to actions for damages and do not apply to actions for injunctive and declaratory relief. In *Shimp v. New Jersey Bell Telephone Co.,*[2] an employee who was allergic to cigarette smoke sought an injunction requiring the employer to prohibit smoking in general working areas. The court held that OSHA did not preempt the "concurrent state power to act either legislatively or judicially under the common law with regard to occupational safety."[3] The action also was not barred by the New Jersey Workmen's Compensation Act. On the merits, the court held that the plaintiff had a common law right to a safe working environment. The employer was ordered "to provide safe working conditions for plaintiff by restricting the smoking of employees to the non-work area presently used as a lunchroom."[4]

Shimp has been followed by a Missouri court,[5] but a similar action brought by federal government employees was dismissed.[6] In *Gordon v.*

§ 6.35

1. 893 F.2d 1088 (9th Cir.1990).

2. 145 N.J.Super. 516, 368 A.2d 408 (Ch.Div.1976).

3. 368 A.2d at 411 (footnote omitted).

4. Id. at 416.

5. Smith v. Western Elec. Co., 643 S.W.2d 10 (Mo.App.1982).

6. Federal Employees for Non–Smokers' Rights v. United States, 446 F.Supp. 181 (D.D.C.1978), affirmed, 598 F.2d 310 (D.C.Cir.), cert. denied, 444 U.S. 926, 100 S.Ct. 265, 62 L.Ed.2d 182 (1979).

Raven Systems & Research, Inc.,[7] an employee with hypersensitivity to cigarette smoke was discharged when she refused to work in an area where other employees smoked. While acknowledging that an employer has a common law duty to supply a reasonably safe place to work, the court rejected the argument that this included protection of this particular employee of special sensitivities. *Shimp* was distinguished because the plaintiff in *Shimp* presented evidence of the threat that cigarette smoking poses to *all* workers, not just those of special sensitivity.

§ 6.36 Title VII of the Civil Rights Act of 1964

Title VII of the Civil Rights Act of 1964[1] prohibits discrimination in the hiring, discharge, compensation, or other terms, conditions, or privileges of employment because of an individual's race, color, religion, sex, or national origin. In some cases, discrimination claims have been brought related to safety and health in the workplace.

Employee claims of religious discrimination have not fared well when the employer has offered a safety-related justification for its challenged employment practice. For example, in *Bhatia v. Chevron U.S.A., Inc.,*[2] the employer had a "no-beard" policy for all employees potentially exposed to toxic gases. The basis for this policy was that the facial hair would prevent a tight face seal when wearing a respirator. The plaintiff, a member of the Sikh religion, which proscribes the cutting or shaving of hair, claimed that the employer's policy constituted religious discrimination. The Ninth Circuit held that, even though the plaintiff established a prima facie case of discrimination, the employer proved that it made good faith efforts to accommodate the plaintiff's religious beliefs.

The most complicated and controversial discrimination issue concerns reproductive hazards in the workplace. The 1978 amendments to Title VII prohibit discrimination in employment based on pregnancy, childbirth, or related medical conditions. The issue is whether Title VII prohibits employer policies which exclude women of procreative capacity from working in environments where there is exposure to conditions which may be harmful to fetal health and development.

The Supreme Court, in *International Union, UAW v. Johnson Controls, Inc.,*[3] held that the company's fetal protection policy violated Title VII. By excluding only women with childbearing capacity from lead-exposed jobs, the employer's policy involved explicit, disparate treatment discrimination, which could be upheld only by application of a bona fide occupational qualification (BFOQ) defense. The Court observed that the statutory defense of BFOQ under section 703(e)(1) of Title VII is narrow. It permits discrimination based on gender only in certain instances where discrimination is reasonably necessary to the normal operation of

---

7. 462 A.2d 10 (D.C.App.1983).

§ 6.36

1. 42 U.S.C.A. § 2000e.

2. 734 F.2d 1382 (9th Cir.1984).

3. 499 U.S. 187, 111 S.Ct. 1196, 113 L.Ed.2d 158 (1991).

the particular business. While safety may establish a BFOQ, the safety exception is limited to instances in which gender or pregnancy actually interferes with the employee's ability to perform the job.

The Court concluded that Johnson Controls failed to establish the BFOQ defense. The company did not prove that all or substantially all women were unable to perform the job safely and efficiently. Furthermore, concerns about the welfare of the next generation did not establish a BFOQ of female sterility. "Decisions about the welfare of future children must be left to the parents who conceive, bear, support, and raise them rather than to employers who hire those parents."[4]

In *Armstrong v. Flowers Hospital, Inc.*,[5] a pregnant home health care nurse refused to treat a patient with AIDS and cryptococcal meningitis because of concern for the health of her unborn child. She challenged her subsequent discharge under the Pregnancy Discrimination Act. In holding for the employer, the Eleventh Circuit recognized that the employee has a difficult choice, but said that "[i]t is precisely this choice ... that is reserved to the pregnant employee under the PDA and *Johnson Controls*."[6]

§ 6.37 Americans with Disabilities Act

Title I of the Americans with Disabilities Act of 1990 (ADA)[1] is the primary federal law prohibiting discrimination in employment on the basis of disability. Virtually every state also has a law prohibiting such discrimination and, in some states, the protections extend more broadly.

One provision of the ADA with direct applicability to occupational safety and health law is section 103(b), which provides that "[t]he term 'qualification standards' may include a requirement that an individual shall not pose a direct threat to the health or safety of other individuals in the workplace."[2] Although this language is narrow and does not include harm to the individual employee with a disability, the interpretive regulation of the EEOC is broader. It defines "direct threat" to include the affected individual, requires these determinations to be made on the basis of reasonable medical judgment, and lists four factors to consider. These factors are the duration of the risk, the nature and severity of the potential harm, the likelihood that the potential harm will occur, and the imminence of the potential harm.

In *Chevron U.S.A. Inc. v. Echazabal*,[3] an employee who had worked for independent contractors at a Chevron Oil refinery applied for a job with Chevron. On two occasions the employer withdrew conditional offers of employment following medical examinations which indicated that Echazabal had hepatitis C. Although he had worked at the Chevron

---

4. 499 U.S. at 205, 111 S.Ct. at 1207.

5. 33 F.3d 1308 (11th Cir.1994).

6. Id. at 1316.

§ 6.37

1. 42 U.S.C.A. 12111–12117.

2. 42 U.S.C.A. 12113(b).

3. 536 U.S 73, 122 S.Ct. 2045, 153 L.Ed.2d 82 (2002).

facility for over 20 years without experiencing any health problems, Echazabal was denied employment by Chevron on the ground that exposure to toxic chemicals at the refinery would damage his liver. He was laid off by his contractor-employer when Chevron requested that he be removed from further exposures. Echazabal then sued under the ADA.

The Supreme Court unanimously upheld the validity of the EEOC interpretation of the direct threat provision, which provides a defense to employers if employment of an individual would constitute a threat to "self" as well as "others." The Ninth Circuit, in striking down EEOC's regulation, had relied on the interpretive maxim of *expressio unius exclusio alterius* (express mention and implied exclusion). According to the lower court, because the ADA mentions only threat to others as a defense under section 103(b) of the ADA, threat to self is excluded. The Supreme Court, however, said the *expressio unius* principle is inapplicable because section 103(b) uses threat to others as a nonexclusive example of a lawful qualification standard. Having dispensed with the textual argument, the Court had no trouble in finding that the interpretation was reasonable.

Another area in which occupational safety and health law and disability discrimination law may overlap is when employees are unable to wear personal protective equipment or otherwise comply with safety and health requirements because of a physical or mental impairment. For example, in one case,[4] the plaintiff alleged that his discharge for failing to wear steel-toed safety shoes violated the ADA because an unspecified impairment prevented him from wearing the shoes without pain. The court granted summary judgment to the employer because the plaintiff failed to prove that he had an impairment that substantially limited a major life activity.

§ 6.38 Admissibility of OSHA Violations and Standards

In several cases plaintiffs have asserted that a private cause of action is implied under the Occupational Safety and Health Act or that there is a federal common law right of action. Both theories have been rejected and the law is clear that the Act does not create a private right of action for injured employees or their estates against employers or third parties.

In *Jeter v. St. Regis Paper Co.*,[1] for example, the Fifth Circuit relied on the language of section 4(b)(4) of the Act to conclude that Congress intended that private rights were to be unaffected by OSHA.

> It seems clear that Congress did not intend OSHA to create a new private cause of action, but, on the contrary, intended private rights to be unaffected thereby.

---

4. Cavallaro v. Corning, Inc., 93 F.Supp.2d 334 (W.D.N.Y. 2000).

§ 6.38
1. 507 F.2d 973 (5th Cir.1975).

The provisions for the enforcement of OSHA and the regulations promulgated thereunder are sufficiently comprehensive to make such a private right of action unnecessary to effectuate the congressional policy underpinning the substantive provisions of the statute.[2]

Similar results have been reached by other courts. Nevertheless, in those civil actions with a valid common law or statutory basis, the admissibility of OSHA standards and violations has raised several legal issues. In general, a plaintiff may not admit into evidence testimonial or documentary evidence of OSHA violations by the employer or an OSHA compliance officer's post-inspection report. This evidence has been held to be inadmissible as irrelevant, prejudicial, and hearsay. Only the Supreme Court of Alabama has held to the contrary.

It is much more common for the plaintiff or defendant to seek to introduce applicable OSHA standards to prove the duty owed to the plaintiff by the defendant. In OSHA-related cases, evidence of the requirements of OSHA standards has been admitted even more freely than the general rule might suggest. Thus, evidence of OSHA's requirements has been held to be admissible even where the standards did not specifically apply to the defendant. Other courts even have permitted experts to testify whether, in their opinion, the defendant violated OSHA requirements.

In common law personal injury actions state courts apply their own law on the admissibility of evidence, and the results have varied widely. Some courts hold that noncompliance with an OSHA standard constitutes negligence per se. Most courts consider noncompliance with OSHA requirements to be "some" evidence of negligence. Other courts hold that OSHA standards are inadmissible.

A related issue is whether OSHA compliance information is discoverable in private litigation. Subject to certain limitations, OSHA investigatory reports are discoverable. The testimony of OSHA personnel, however, usually is not permitted in the absence of a subpoena. In *Moore–McCormack Lines, Inc. v. I.T.O. Corp.*,[3] a subpoena was issued for the testimony of an OSHA compliance officer (CO) and the production of the OSHA accident report he had prepared. All the reports were released except one paragraph containing a conclusion of the CO about the cause of the accident. The district court held that this information was properly withheld under the intra-agency communication exemption of the Freedom of Information Act. The Fourth Circuit reversed and held that the exemption only applies to "materials reflecting deliberative or policy-making processes."[4] The court held that "[i]nferences about the cause of an accident drawn from facts revealed by the investigation,

2. Id. at 977.

3. 508 F.2d 945 (4th Cir.1974).

4. Id. at 948 (quoting EPA v. Mink, 410 U.S. 73, 89, 93 S.Ct. 827, 837, 35 L.Ed.2d 119 (1973)).

though labeled as opinion or conclusions, are not exempt under the guise of deliberative or policy-making material."[5]

Not all information, however, is discoverable. This is especially true with regard to confidential information. In *T.V. Tower, Inc. v. Marshall*,[6] an action was brought under the Freedom of Information Act to obtain the identify of witnesses who had given statements to OSHA investigators. Although OSHA provided the plaintiff with copies of the statements, there were substantial deletions, including the names of the witnesses. In granting summary judgment for the Secretary, the court held that interviewees were "confidential sources," and therefore the statements were exempt from disclosure as investigatory records under Freedom of Information Act exemption 7(D).

5. 508 F.2d at 949.   **6.** 444 F.Supp. 1233 (D.D.C.1978).

Chapter 7

WORKERS' COMPENSATION

Table of Sections

---

§ 7.1   Introduction

Every year, millions of workers sustain employment-related injuries or contract work-related diseases. Some result from single accidents, while others, such as carpal tunnel syndrome, are caused by repeated traumas or the performance of repetitive job tasks. Numerous workers contract diseases, such as asbestosis, silicosis, cancer, pneumoconiosis, and lead poisoning, that are related to their work environments. Job stress may contribute to cardiovascular disease or mental illness.

Many employment-related health problems require medical treatment. A considerable number cause short-term job interruptions, while a few generate prolonged periods of unemployment. Some injuries result in partial or total disabilities of a temporary or permanent nature. In extreme cases, the injury or illness results in death. Industrial injuries cause workers to incur medical expenses and to experience lost earnings and these economic losses may be devastating. Under common law tort concepts, servants adversely affected by work-related conditions could rarely obtain redress from their masters. The absence of adequate, predictable, and efficient remedies led legislatures to enact workers' compensation laws. Although separate and distinct laws have been enacted in every jurisdiction, they are all based on the same model used in the early part of this century.

§ 7.2   The Common Law Era

As economically advanced countries were transformed from agrarian to industrial societies, the number of employment-related injuries and diseases increased sharply. Employees who sustained economic losses had to seek redress through common law tort actions. They had to demonstrate that their medical conditions were caused by the negligence of their employer. If they were unable to prove negligence attributable to their employer, the workers were unable to obtain any relief against the party with the financial capacity to pay their medical expenses and replace their lost earnings.

Even when servants could demonstrate that negligence attributable to their masters through common law agency principles contributed to their work-related injuries, they were not guaranteed favorable verdicts. In *Butterfield v. Forrester*,[1] the court held that any contributory negligence by the injured plaintiff constituted a complete bar to recovery against a negligent defendant. In a later English case, *Priestley v. Fowler*,[2] the court further restricted the ability of workers to sue their masters for injuries caused by the negligence of their fellow employees.

---

§ 7.2
1. East 60 (K.B. 1809).

2. 3 M. & W. 1, 150 Reprint 1030 (1837).

Lord Abinger was concerned about the possibility of holding masters liable for harm to domestic servants caused by the carelessness of chambermaids and cooks. He appeared to be oblivious to the impact his decision would have upon persons injured in factory accidents, even though the industrial revolution had already begun in England.

In *Priestley v. Fowler*, Lord Abinger developed two separate, but related, doctrines to limit the liability of masters for injuries sustained by their workers as a result of the negligent acts of other servants. First, under the traditional respondeat superior principle, masters were only responsible for torts committed by their servants within the scope of their master-servant relationships. Lord Abinger created the "fellow servant" exception to the respondeat superior doctrine, which provided that masters were not liable for harm caused by fellow servants, even though acting within the scope of employment, if the fellow servants were negligent. While the negligent workers could be held personally liable for the consequences of their careless acts, most servants lacked the assets to satisfy meaningful judicial awards.

Lord Abinger formulated a second rule to provide masters with additional protection against suits filed by their servants. He noted that individuals are not required to risk their safety in the employ of careless masters and may, if they think prudent, decline positions they fear would involve unreasonable dangers. Because workers are as capable as masters of acquainting themselves with employment hazards, those who accept employment must assume the risk that they may be injured or killed as a result of dangerous occupational conditions they could have discovered and avoided had they been more alert. Application of the assumption of risk rule meant that employees could not hold their employers legally responsible for most industrial accidents.

These three common law defenses, contributory negligence, fellow servant rule, and assumption of the risk, became known as the "three wicked sisters," because of their preclusive effect on the ability of injured workers to recover. The development of these doctrines occurred at a time when employment relationships were being significantly altered by industrial transformations. As manufacturing firms proliferated, fewer people worked for individual masters. More and more persons found themselves employed by business enterprises that carried out their basic functions through corporate agents. By precluding application of the traditional respondeat superior concept for acts of fellow servants and by presuming that workers assumed the risks associated with their employment, courts made it extremely difficult for employees to recover from their employers for the increasing number of work-related injuries.

By the mid–1800s, United States courts began to accept the English rules restricting employer liability in connection with work-related accidents. *Murray v. South Carolina Rail Road*[3] involved a railroad fireman who lost his leg because of the failure of the engineer to stop the train

---

3. 1 McMullan Law (S.Car.) 385, 1841 WL 2313 (1841).

when a horse ran on the tracks. The court refused to permit a judgment against the railroad.

> A company cannot be supposed to warrant that each servant of the company shall always be watchful and that no servant shall be injured by the negligence of another. * * * These accidents have been numerous. They have for ages been a daily occurrence. * * * [I]n every occupation, where a joint effort is required to perform any piece of business, the employer entrusts many to effect it; and every day it happens that some one of them is injured by the negligence of another. Yet no case can be found where it was ever imagined that the employer was liable for such injury.

The *Murray* court carefully distinguished between passengers, who could rely upon the respondeat superior principle to hold a railroad liable for the negligent acts of its agents, and workers who could not. "The passenger pays the company for carrying him. The agent or servant is paid by the company. The passenger has nothing to do in running the train, and if he should interfere, he would not only lose his claim on the company, but might be made liable to it in case an injury should happen."[4] In 1842, the *Murray* approach was adopted by the Massachusetts Supreme Judicial Court,[5] and it was thereafter accepted by courts throughout the United States.

By the late 1800s, courts began to recognize the harsh results generated by rote application of the fellow servant, assumption of risk, and contributory negligence doctrines. Seemingly deserving victims of employment accidents were being denied all judicial relief. Some judges decided to create exceptions that would permit damage awards against employers in egregious industrial injury cases that would otherwise have been covered by one of the traditional common law defenses.

Two separate concepts were developed to limit the application of the fellow servant rule. The vice principal exception was used to restrict the fellow servant concept to rank and file personnel. Courts using the vice principal approach simply excluded from operation of the fellow servant rule supervisory personnel and others who were empowered to effectuate management policies. Although courts that adopted the vice principal exception still refused to use the respondeat superior principle to impose liability on employers for injuries caused by negligent acts committed by rank-and-file workers, they frequently held firms responsible for the negligent acts of supervisory and managerial employees.

The nondelegable duty concept was developed by some courts to similarly restrict the scope of the fellow servant doctrine. These courts decided that employers should be held legally responsible for the performance of certain basic employment functions, even though management had delegated performance of the actual tasks to lower level workers. Companies were most often found to have a nondelegable duty

---

4. Id. at 395.

5. See Farwell v. Boston & W.R.R., 4 Metc. (45 Mass.) 49 (1842).

to provide employees with reasonably safe employment environments. Courts that applied the nondelegable duty exception were generally willing to impose liability on employers that failed to ensure that these functions were carried out without mishap.

Judicial decisions also eroded the assumption of risk doctrine. Courts believing that strict application of this rule unfairly presumed that workers accepted the risk of dangerous employment conditions that they could not have been expected to discover held that employees could assume the risk only for "ordinary risks." If workers were injured by dangerous employment conditions of which they were unaware, many courts would permit them to sue their responsible employers. Nonetheless, if it could be shown that the injured employees had been aware of the unsafe conditions and had elected to continue their work, they were usually said to have assumed the risks involved.

The courts of a small number of states decided to restrict application of the contributory negligence bar. Although they acknowledged that employers should not be held liable for injuries caused by the negligent acts of the injured workers themselves, they found no reason to permit such contributory negligence to absolve firms from liability arising from the careless acts of other company agents. These courts thus decided that contributory negligence should no longer constitute a complete bar to relief, but should merely reduce the damages the contributorily negligent workers could recover from their employers.

§ 7.3   Liability Without Fault

By the latter 1800s, state legislatures began to acknowledge that application of the fellow servant, assumption of risk, and contributory negligence rules to industrial accident cases created unfair hardships for individuals employed in hazardous occupations. Specific state laws were enacted to preclude or limit application of these defenses in enumerated circumstances. For example, several states adopted legislation that prevented use of the fellow servant principle in cases involving railroad workers. By the early part of the twentieth century, other states had statutorily abrogated the fellow servant defense. Some of these laws pertained solely to the railroad industry, while others applied more generally. None, however, abolished the concept of defendant fault. Injured workers could only prevail if they could demonstrate that their condition was caused by negligence attributable to their employer.

In 1908, Congress expanded protection for persons employed by interstate railroads through enactment of the Federal Employers Liability Act (FELA).[1] Even though the FELA still required plaintiff workers to prove that their injuries were caused by carrier negligence, it severely limited application of the fellow servant and assumption of risk doc-

---

§ 7.3

1. 35 Stat. 65 (1908). The FELA, as amended, is now codified at 45 U.S.C.A. §§ 51–60.

trines. Plaintiff contributory negligence no longer constituted a complete bar to judicial relief. It could only mitigate damages. Nonetheless, if injured railroad workers could not demonstrate the presence of negligence attributable to carrier agents, they were unable to obtain legal redress. In 1920, Congress granted similar protection to seamen injured during the course of their employment through the enactment of the Jones Act.[2]

In *Consolidated Rail Corp. v. Gottshall*,[3] the Supreme Court had to decide whether railroad employees could sue their employers under the FELA for negligent infliction of emotional distress. The Court indicated that the appropriate legal standard should be derived from the fundamental goal of the FELA to compensate workers for injuries resulting from railroad negligence and the common law treatment of such cases. It noted that nearly all states recognize a right of individuals to seek redress for harm resulting from the negligent infliction of emotional distress. The Court then considered the three major common law tests applied to these cases: (1) the "physical impact" test, limiting liability to cases involving direct physical traumas—an approach that had been abandoned by most contemporary courts; (2) the "zone of danger" approach, restricting coverage to plaintiffs who have either sustained a physical impact as a result of the defendant's negligence or were placed in the immediate risk of physical impact by the defendant's negligence; and (3) the "relative bystander" test that determines coverage by asking whether the defendant could reasonably have foreseen the emotional injury caused to the plaintiff. The *Gottshall* Court concluded that the "zone of danger" test should be applied under the FELA.

In *Norfolk & Western Railway Company v. Ayers*,[4] the Supreme Court extended the *Gottshall* rationale to allow railroad workers who developed employment-related asbestosis to recover compensatory damages for mental anguish associated with their fear that the asbestosis might someday develop into cancer. The Court noted that the FELA was intended to authorize monetary relief not only for current injuries but also for reasonable apprehension of future harm. Even though it was unlikely that asbestosis sufferers would develop cancer, the possibility of such a progression was found sufficient to support compensatory awards based upon the claimants' very real fear that their asbestosis might ultimately develop into cancer.

The problem of compensating fairly the growing number of workers injured by industrial production was not unique to the United States. Government officials in several European countries were also concerned about the numerous workers who sustained serious workplace injuries that were not caused by negligence attributable to their employers. Many were unable to afford necessary medical treatment and those who

2. 41 Stat. 1007 (1920), codified at 46 U.S.C.A. § 688.

3. 512 U.S. 532, 114 S.Ct. 2396, 129 L.Ed.2d 427 (1994).

4. 538 U.S. 135, 123 S.Ct. 1210, 155 L.Ed.2d 261 (2003).

suffered prolonged lost earnings experienced extreme financial hardships. In 1884, the comprehensive compensation approach was established with the adoption of the German Compensation Act. The Act created a Sickness Fund to provide all covered employees affected by sickness or accidental disability with up to thirteen weeks of benefits. An Accident Fund provided assistance to individuals disabled for more than thirteen weeks, and a Disability Fund assisted persons who sustained disabling conditions not otherwise covered. The Act required contributions from both employers and employees. This was the first major legislation that did not require claimants to demonstrate fault on the part of their employers. Although the 1884 Act only applied to certain hazardous occupations, its coverage was extended to all industries by 1911. England extended similar protection to employees through the Workmen's Compensation Act of 1897 and other European nations quickly adopted similar legislation.

The compensation without fault concept soon spread to the United States. In 1902, Maryland established an accident fund to protect disabled miners, and Montana enacted a miners' compensation law in 1909. Both of these statutes were declared unconstitutional.[5] These judicial setbacks, however, were temporary. Workers' compensation laws were adopted in New York, Iowa, and Washington, and the constitutionality of these enactments was sustained by the United States Supreme Court.[6] Other states expeditiously created comprehensive workers' compensation schemes.

Workers' compensation laws were designed to provide employees with expansive protection against the consequences of employment-related injuries. Injured workers no longer had to establish negligence attributable to their employer in order to obtain legal redress. They merely had to demonstrate that their conditions arose out of and during the course of their employment. Thus, non-negligent occurrences were covered. Furthermore, the traditional common law defenses—contributory negligence, the fellow servant rule, and assumption of risk—were abolished. Even workers who sustained injuries as a result of their own carelessness were entitled to workers' compensation.

The legislative acceptance of the liability without fault concept was of significant benefit to covered workers, but the new statutes also provided employers with several benefits. While injured employees were guaranteed medical coverage and specified amounts for lost earnings, the liability imposed upon employers was limited. Workers' compensation statutes generally precluded the awarding of compensatory or punitive damages. In addition, by creating the exclusive remedy for employee

---

5. See Franklin v. United Rys. & Elec. Co., 2 Baltimore City Rep. 309 (1904); Cunningham v. Northwestern Improvement Co., 44 Mont. 180, 119 P. 554 (1911).

6. See New York Cent. R.R. v. White, 243 U.S. 188, 37 S.Ct. 247, 61 L.Ed. 667 (1917); Hawkins v. Bleakly, 243 U.S. 210, 37 S.Ct. 255, 61 L.Ed. 678 (1917); Mountain Timber Co. v. Washington, 243 U.S. 219, 37 S.Ct. 260, 61 L.Ed. 685 (1917).

injuries, these laws gave employers immunity against most tort actions arising from the employment relationship.

Workers' compensation enactments established statutorily-mandated social insurance coverage financed by private companies. The limited liability concept and the extension of tort immunity to industrial accidents made it possible for employers to estimate their annual exposure and to obtain insurance policies to cover individuals who sustained work-related injuries. Employees were no longer required to assume the unpredictable risk of employment injuries. Moreover, employers were able to share the risk of industrial accidents with their shareholders, through lower dividends; their consumers, through higher prices; and their employees, through reduced wages.

§ 7.4 Coverage

Most workers' compensation laws cover all private and most public employers.[1] Idaho excludes nonprofit enterprises, and Arkansas, Mississippi, and North Dakota exclude both charitable and religious employers. In states that do not expressly exclude charitable and religious enterprises, courts generally find churches, nonprofit hospitals, the Salvation Army, and other similar organizations covered by workers' compensation statutes. These decisions are based upon the view that these social welfare statutes are intended to provide expansive coverage. In the absence of a specific statutory exclusion, courts appropriately assume that the state legislature intended to protect the workers of all employers. Nonetheless, a few judicial decisions have adopted a contrary approach. They have refused to include charitable enterprises without the express indication of a legislative intent to do so. In many states, sole proprietors may opt for workers' compensation coverage, but they must clearly elect such personal coverage to be entitled to benefits.

The vast majority of workers' compensation laws apply to all employers that have one or more full-time employees and to many that have one or more regular part-time workers. Twelve state statutes, however, specifically exclude private employers that do not regularly employ a minimum number of individuals. Three states require at least five employees, two states require a minimum of four workers, and seven states require three or more employees. Employers that do not regularly employ the minimum number of individuals required by these state laws are exempt from coverage. Some small businesses in states that require three, four, or five regular employees for coverage may employ more than the minimum number during most of the year and fewer than that figure during the remainder of the year. To avoid the uncertainty that would result if such employers were only covered during the periods they employ a sufficient number of workers, courts generally extend full-year

§ 7.4

1. See generally Arthur Larson, Larson's Workers' Compensation Law § 74 (2003).

coverage to firms that regularly employ the minimum number of persons during significant portions of the year.

A separate federal scheme provides workers' compensation protection for maritime employees under the Longshore and Harbor Workers' Compensation Act (LHWCA).[2] Coverage is provided to individuals who are injured while working on piers, wharfs, terminals, buildings, or vessels loading, unloading, building, or repairing ships associated with navigable waters. Claims are filed with the deputy commissioner designated by the Secretary of Labor. Prior to 1972, LHWCA protection was only available to maritime personnel whose injuries were not covered by state workers' compensation laws. In 1972, Congress eliminated this prerequisite. As a result, injured maritime employees may simultaneously seek benefits under both the LHWCA and the applicable state workers' compensation enactment, with the administrative entity making the more recent award deducting amounts previously granted by the other.

Christopher Garris sustained fatal injuries while performing sandblasting work aboard a vessel, the USNS *Maj. Stephen W. Pless*, that was berthed in the navigable waters of the United States. He was then in the employ of Tidewater Temps, a subcontractor for Mid–Atlantic Coatings, which was a subcontractor for Norfolk Shipbuilding and Drydock. Following his death, Christopher Garris' mother sued Norfolk Shipbuilding and Drydock claiming that firm's negligence had caused her son's death. The mother sought relief based on a cause of action for wrongful death that allegedly exists under general maritime law. In *Norfolk Shipbuilding & Drydock Corp. v. Garris*,[3] the Supreme Court sustained the mother's cause of action. It noted that it had previously upheld a maritime cause of action based on breach of the general duty of seaworthiness,[4] and it saw no reason not to extend that duty to injuries caused by the negligent breach of general maritime duties. The Longshore and Harbor Workers' Compensation Act provides non-seamen maritime workers such as Christopher Garris with no-fault workers' compensation coverage against their employer and negligence claims against the vessel, with other claims against these parties being expressly preempted by the LHWCA. The *Garris* Court found the LHWCA preemption provision inapplicable, since Ms. Garris' suit was against neither her son's employer nor the owner of the vessel on which he was killed. The defendant could thus be sued for negligence under general maritime principles without causing any conflict with the LHWCA.

Harbor Tug & Barge v. Papai[5] concerned the Jones Act coverage of an employee who was injured while painting a tug boat. His one-day job included no seagoing activity, nor had his prior twelve jobs with the same employer. A divided Supreme Court concluded that he was not a "seaman" under the Jones Act at the time of his accident. The fact that

---

2. See 33 U.S.C.A. §§ 901–950.

3. 532 U.S. 811, 121 S.Ct. 1927, 150 L.Ed.2d 34 (2001).

4. Moragne v. States Marine Lines, Inc., 398 U.S. 375, 90 S.Ct. 1772, 26 L.Ed.2d 339 (1970).

5. 520 U.S. 548, 117 S.Ct. 1535, 137 L.Ed.2d 800 (1997).

he had worked on ships for other companies did not alter the fact that he had no seagoing duties with respect to his current employer.

All workers' compensation statutes cover some or all government employers. Thirty-nine states extend mandatory protection to all public personnel. Six states cover public employees, but exclude public officials. Georgia requires coverage for the employees of state instrumentalities. Texas extends coverage to county workers and to state highway and college personnel, and it authorizes municipalities to elect coverage for their employees. The Delaware and Tennessee statutes permit voluntary coverage of government workers. Federal civilian employees enjoy statutory protection under the Federal Employees Compensation Act.

Statutory Employers

Businesses frequently hire independent contractors to perform tasks that would otherwise be performed by regular company personnel. Although the independent contractor employees are directly employed by their contractor, they may function like employees of the principal party. Such contractor employees often work for small contractors that are not required to provide workers' compensation coverage or that simply fail to do so. The workers' compensation statutes in the vast majority of states have special provisions pertaining to what are called "statutory employers." These provisions apply to principal parties that are not technically the employers of contractor employees but use those individuals as their own workers.

If the work being performed by contractor employees would ordinarily be accomplished by employees of the principal party, considering the past practices of this particular firm and of comparable companies, the principal party will generally be held secondarily liable for the workers' compensation of those contractor personnel. The principal firm is thus held responsible for injured contractor employees when their actual employers lack adequate workers' compensation coverage. In cases where the principal is found financially liable, it may usually seek reimbursement from the primarily responsible contractors. Principals may protect themselves against such liability in most instances by requiring their contractors to provide sufficient insurance to cover the workers' compensation claims of their employees.

Statutory employer cases frequently involve the use of contractor personnel to perform maintenance, construction, and delivery work. When courts decide statutory employer questions, they usually consider various factors: (1) the past and present practices of the principal firm and of other similar companies; (2) whether the activities are customarily conducted by the principal's own employees; (3) whether the activities of the contractor employees relate to the regular operations of the principal employer; (4) whether the job functions are being performed on the principal's premises or at another location; (5) whether the principal possesses the right to exercise meaningful control over the manner in which the contractor employees perform their work; (6) whether the job tasks are regularly or irregularly carried out; and (7) the specialized or non-specialized nature of the work. If the work being performed by contractor employees is not part of the regular trade, business, or occupation of the principal party, but is merely incidental to that firm's operations, and the principal exercises minimal control over their job functions, the principal would most likely not be held responsible for the workers' compensation coverage of those individuals. On the other hand, if the contractor personnel are carrying out regular maintenance, recurring construction work, or normal delivery runs, the principal would probably be considered their statutory employer.

Statutory employer cases do not merely involve injured contractor employees who are seeking workers' compensation from principal parties. They often arise in a reverse manner when contractor personnel sue principals in tort for injuries allegedly caused by the negligence of principal agents. In these cases, it is the principal parties that argue in favor of statutory employer status, in an effort to obtain the benefit of the tort immunity given to employers liable for workers' compensation. These principals clearly prefer the limited workers' compensation liability to the possibility of unrestricted tort damages.

Exempt Employees

The fact that an employer is covered by workers' compensation does not mean that all of its employees are entitled to statutory protection. Different groups of workers are specifically excluded from coverage in many states. Twenty-six states exempt persons who perform domestic services. The twenty-four states that cover domestic workers, however, provide limited coverage. They typically require a minimum number of hours worked per week or a minimum amount of earnings per calendar quarter. Individuals who perform domestic work on a part-time or sporadic basis are unlikely to be entitled to mandatory coverage. Most state laws permit employers to provide excluded domestic employees with voluntary protection.

Most workers' compensation statutes provide coverage for agricultural workers. Some restrict coverage by requiring a minimum amount of annual earnings, while others limit protection to persons who operate power equipment or work in hazardous jobs. A number of statutes that do not mandate coverage for all agricultural workers allow farmers to voluntarily include otherwise excluded personnel. In states that permit farmers to opt for voluntary coverage, the farmers must usually file written elections to provide their workers with coverage.

The laws in thirteen states expressly exempt agricultural employees. When questions of coverage are raised with respect to farm personnel, courts generally focus upon the work regularly performed by the individuals at issue, rather than the nature of the employer's business. Persons directly involved with the cultivation of crops or the raising of livestock clearly constitute "agricultural" employees. Individuals who process crops or livestock often generate conflicting decisions. If workers perform tasks associated with the initial processing of farm products, as when they cut and gather the crops or transport them to canneries, they are likely to be considered "agricultural" workers. When, however, they carry out functions more directly connected with the production process, they are usually regarded as non-agricultural personnel.

A majority of state workers' compensation laws exclude "casual" employees who perform work on an irregular or sporadic basis. Four states exempt all casual workers, even those who engage in job tasks directly associated with the trade or business of their employer. This exclusion is usually limited to people with truly tenuous employment relationships that are irregular in nature. Twenty-seven states exclude "casual" employees only when the they perform job functions that are outside the normal trade or business of their employer. In these states, intermittent employees who engage in work related to the regular trade or business of their employer are entitled to workers' compensation protection. Eight other states do not exempt "casual" employees, but exclude all persons who perform work not within the normal trade or business of their employer.

Courts are frequently asked to determine the scope of the trade or business limitation. Few cases involve people who engage in tasks immediately related to the fundamental operations of their employer, because the work of such persons is clearly related to the normal trade or business of their employer. Most controverted cases concern individuals who perform maintenance, repair, and construction work. Because firms could not effectively operate without the performance of regular maintenance and necessary repair work, individuals employed in those capacities are generally considered part of the firm's normal trade or business. People who engage in construction work on remodeling projects or on additions to existing facilities are also likely to be included within the regular trade or business of their employer. On the other hand, persons who work on the construction of new buildings are generally found outside the normal trade or business of employers that are not construction firms.

§ 7.5   The Employment Relationship

Workers' compensation laws generally protect only those individuals who are injured while they are "employees." Most enactments define the term "employee" to include any person in the service of another under an express or implied contract of hire. Where there is no express or implied contractual arrangement between the claimant and the covered company, no employment relationship is likely to be found. For example, in *Kennedy v. Forest*,[1] an employed truck driver, without authorization from the truck owner, made arrangements to have another person substitute for himself. The substitute driver was injured and sought compensation from the vehicle owner. Since the court found no implied contract existed between the claimant and the covered business entity, compensation was denied. Furthermore, if there is no indication that claimants have been retained to perform services, they are unlikely to be

§ 7.5
1.   129 Idaho 584, 930 P.2d 1026 (1997).

found entitled to statutory protection. This requirement concerns the belief that employers should not be held responsible for work-related injuries in the absence of mutual relationships. The employment contract prerequisite is also pertinent when determining which party or parties constitute the employer of injured workers.

The contract of employment requirement may affect the compensation rights of persons who lack the legal capacity to establish contractual relationships or who have not established employment affiliations voluntarily. For example, a few states have yet to overrule the archaic common law rule denying wives the capacity to enter into contractual arrangements with their husbands, thereby refusing to extend workers' compensation coverage to wives employed by their husbands. Most state courts that have formally considered this question, however, have rejected the common law approach and have sustained the capacity of wives to establish covered employment relationships with their husbands.

A similar capacity issue is often raised with respect to minor children who perform remunerative services for their parents. Nonetheless, courts generally find that the gainful employment of children demonstrates sufficient emancipation to enable them to enter into covered employment contracts. The more determinative question pertaining to the coverage of minor children working for their parents concerns the distinction between covered remunerative employment and non-covered casual work frequently performed by children at home for minimal compensation without the creation of any real contract of employment.

The most frequently litigated cases raising the voluntariness issue involve people incarcerated in state prisons. Even prisoners who receive modest compensation for their services are usually denied workers' compensation protection either by statutory provision or judicial decision. Many of the court rulings rejecting coverage are based upon the premise that convicts are required to work and cannot be considered to have entered into voluntary employment contracts. On the other hand, when prisoners are farmed out to work for other government agencies or private employers, courts are more likely to find the creation of covered employment relationships. While the lack of workers' compensation protection for incarcerated laborers may seem harsh, it must be acknowledged that correctional institutions are legally obliged to provide injured prisoners with necessary medical treatment. Nonetheless, some state legislatures have sought to guarantee incarcerated workers limited workers' compensation rights through the enactment of special statutory provisions covering their performance of prison employment.

It is generally recognized that employment relationships involve some form of remuneration. As a result, judicial decisions have uniformly concluded that individuals who perform gratuitous services without any expectation of compensation are not entitled to workers' compensation protection. People who voluntarily work for charitable organizations are thus unlikely to obtain compensation for injuries resulting from their uncompensated efforts. The fact that such volunteers are given free meals is usually insufficient to create covered employment relationships. Only in rare instances are covered employment arrangements found.

Judges have a more difficult time deciding the statutory rights of individuals who make monetary pledges to churches or charities and satisfy their pledges through the performance of services that are accorded an hourly credit. Some courts treat these situations as if the persons have effectively donated their services and find no covered employment. Others, however, reach the opposite conclusion. They first treat the pledge as the creation of a legally binding financial obligation, and then find that the subsequent work constitutes covered compensable employment.

The fact that parties do not initially specify the actual remuneration to be paid does not preclude the formation of employment relationships. So long as it is clear that the employer and the worker contemplate gainful employment, courts will find coverage. It is not necessary that workers receive cash for their services. If they receive in-kind payments of a meaningful nature, such as room and board or training, they will probably be found engaged in covered employment. Statutory protection will also be accorded to persons who are hired for brief probationary periods that will be used to determine whether they will obtain permanent employment. These people clearly constitute covered employees during their preliminary terms of work.

Courts occasionally encounter problems with respect to individuals who are asked to provide assistance during emergency situations without the establishment of formal employment relationships. When it is apparent that the parties implicitly intended to create remunerative arrangements, workers' compensation coverage will normally be found. If, however, people merely volunteer their services during exigent circumstances without any expectation of compensation, they will usually be denied statutory protection.

On some occasions, employers either enter into unlawful employment contracts or hire persons to perform illegal services. The most common form of unlawful employment contract involves the engagement of minors. Many workers' compensation statutes have express provisions governing the rights of minors. Most extend coverage to such workers, and many impose a penalty through the awarding of increased compensation to injured minors. Several give unlawfully employed minors the option to accept workers' compensation or to sue the responsible employer in tort. Only five states statutorily deny coverage to illegally employed minors, although often it is the employer that attempts to assert coverage to gain immunity from tort liability. For similar reasons, courts generally extend workers' compensation protection to undocumented aliens who are injured during the course of their unlawful employment. Nonetheless, while undocumented aliens who sustain occupational injuries may receive medical benefits, they may be denied future disability payments, on the ground their loss of earning capacity is due to their unlawful status rather than their employment-related conditions.

Individuals who are hired to engage in illegal conduct are normally denied compensation due to public policy considerations. Courts do not wish to reward people who agree to perform unlawful services. For example, workers' compensation was denied to employees hired as bartenders during prohibition, and to workers employed to drive trucks transporting proscribed alcohol.

Employee or Independent Contractor

Even when persons enter into contractual relationships with employers providing for the performance of remunerative services, they do not necessarily constitute covered "employees." Courts must regularly distinguish between "employees" who are entitled to statutory protection and "independent contractors" who are not. Because it is clear that most state legislatures contemplated common law master-servant concepts when they adopted statutes covering "employees" and excluding "independent contractors," courts frequently consider the factors set forth in section 220 of the *Restatement (Second) of Agency* to determine whether covered employment relationships exist.

In many cases, courts emphasize the "right-to-control" test to resolve questions regarding the existence or nonexistence of an employment relationship. When the evidence demonstrates that the principal possesses the authority to exercise meaningful control over the individual's performance, courts usually find a covered employment relationship. In situations where the principal lacks such authority, excluded independent contractor relationships are normally determined. The critical consideration under the "right-to-control" test concerns the capacity of the principal to regulate the manner and means of job performance. If the principal is merely empowered to specify the final product, but not the way in which it is to be achieved, the control factor would favor an "independent contractor" finding.

Questions most frequently arise with respect to persons with attenuated work arrangements, such as truck drivers, taxi drivers, and commission salespeople. When the principal retains the right to exercise any meaningful control over the actual job performance of such persons, courts tend to find covered employment relationships. For example, when truck drivers drive exclusively or primarily for one carrier and are expected to follow the instructions of that firm's dispatchers, employment relationships are normally found. On the other hand, if the drivers own their own tractors, are able to work for different carriers, and are permitted to determine whether they will carry particular loads, courts focusing on the right-to-control standard often find independent contractor arrangements. If taxi drivers work principally for one company, lease their vehicle from that firm, and are subject to any real company control with respect to their daily job performance, employment relationships tend to be found. When, however, the drivers own their own taxis and basically decide when and how they will work, independent contractor status is likely to result.

Commission salespeople often generate conflicting judicial determinations under the right-to-control test, especially if they work primarily away from any company office. So long as firm managers possess the authority to exercise a reasonable degree of control over the way in which such salespersons function, covered "employee" status is generally found. On the other hand, if they are away from the principal's place of business most of the time and are able to set their own hours and the manner in which they will operate, independent contractor arrangements are usually discerned.

When the right-to-control factor does not sufficiently support an employment or an independent contractor relationship, courts usually evaluate the other nine *Restatement* factors. The criteria supporting a covered master-servant relationship include: (1) the worker is not engaged in a distinct occupation or business; (2) the work is usually performed in the geographical area under the direction of an employer; (3) the work does not require the services of a highly skilled individual; (4) the principal supplies the tools and the place of work; (5) the employment is for an extended period of time and involves regular hours; (6) the worker is to be paid by the hour, week, or month, and has not assumed the risk of loss if the work does not generate profits; (7) the work being performed is part of the regular business of the principal; (8) the parties thought they were creating an employer-employee relationship; and (9) the principal party is engaged in a recognized business.

Most courts do not apply the *Restatement* factors on a strictly numerical basis. The results in specific cases are governed by a weighing of the applicable criteria, and involve a substantial degree of judicial discretion. Even when the number of factors supporting an employment relationship is equal to or fewer than the number of factors suggesting the presence of an independent contractor arrangement, an employer-employee relationship is likely to be found if the employment relationship criteria are found to be more significant than the independent contractor factors. This tendency is attributable to the fact that judges recognize that workers' compensation statutes are designed to protect individuals who sustain occupational injuries, and they interpret those enactments liberally in favor of coverage.

When difficult circumstances are presented, enlightened judges increasingly examine the nature of the work being performed by the injured claimants and the relationship between that work and the overall operations of the company using their services. These judges think that legislators adopted workers' compensation laws to require customers to share the risk of industrial accidents associated with the manufacturing of the products they purchase. Individuals who provide services that regularly and meaningfully contribute to the production process should be granted statutory coverage. Courts that apply the "nature of the work" approach review the type of work being performed by claimants and the relationship between that work and company operations. Where claimants can demonstrate a reasonably direct relationship, they are found eligible for compensation.

Courts that apply the "nature of the work" test frequently find covered employment relationships despite the lack of *Restatement* factors supporting "employee" status. In a classic case,[2] the New York Court of Appeals sustained workers' compensation coverage for a commission salesperson who primarily determined when and how she would work, paid her own expenses, was not obliged to report her activities to firm officials or to attend company meetings, had no company office, and was contractually regarded as an "independent contractor." The salesperson performed regular services that were directly related to the basic operations of the firm, and the Court found this fact sufficient to warrant an employer-employee finding. Other courts have evidenced a growing tendency to rely upon the "nature of the work" approach to permit the awarding of benefits to individuals who would most likely be considered "independent contractors" under more traditional legal doctrines. While other courts continue to rely upon the more conventional *Restatement* standards, it is likely that judges will increasingly employ the "nature of the work" analysis in close cases involving workers they believe should be granted workers' compensation protection.

Professionals and Executives

People who work in professional or executive capacities occasionally raise interesting coverage problems because of the substantial discretion they exercise over their own job performance. Professionals who work regularly for a particular company and are subject to a meaningful degree of management control with respect to their job tasks are clearly entitled to statutory protection. Even independent professionals who enjoy expansive work discretion are likely to be considered covered "employees" if they work continuously for the same party. Nonetheless, professionals who enter into service contracts with various parties and retain complete freedom over their work activities are normally not found entitled to statutory protection.

Most corporate executives, including those who formulate and effectuate basic managerial policies, are provided with statutory coverage. Even officers with substantial or total stock ownership continue to enjoy workers' compensation protection when they perform managerial functions. On some occasions, however, executives who exercise pervasive shareholder power may render the corporations their alter egos and will be denied compensation eligibility. This is particularly likely where they control the company and are injured while acting in an entrepreneurial, rather than an executive, capacity.

Similar issues frequently arise when working equity partners in business firms sustain occupational injuries. Most courts have concluded that equity partners constitute noncovered "employers," rather than covered "employees." Only courts in Louisiana and Oklahoma have reached a contrary result. Michigan has a special statutory provision

2. Gordon v. New York Life Ins. Co., 300 N.Y. 652, 90 N.E.2d 898, motion denied, 300 N.Y. 742, 92 N.E.2d 318 (1950).

including working partners, and the California and Nevada laws expressly cover working partners who receive separate compensation beyond their share of firm profits. The workers' compensation laws in Florida, Nebraska, New Mexico, Oregon, Tennessee, Utah, Vermont, and Virginia permit businesses to cover their equity partners on a voluntary basis.

Borrowed Servants

Employees who work for one company are occasionally required to perform services for a second firm. If they are injured while working for the second party, should they be able to obtain compensation from their usual employer, the second company, or both? Numerous judicial decisions have struggled with the so-called "borrowed servant" doctrine to determine when the borrowing company should be considered the employer of the loaned workers. Because courts generally recognize that no employment relationship can exist without evidence of an express or implied contract of hire, if it is apparent that the loaned employee and the borrowing firm have not entered into an explicit or implicit work arrangement, no covered employment relationship between those two parties is likely to be found. On the other hand, if there is any indication of a consensual agreement between the loaned worker and the borrowing company, courts will usually discover the requisite contract of hire. Such an agreement will often be implied from the fact that the loaned individual voluntarily complied with the work directions issued by the borrowing party. Once courts ascertain an express or implied contractual arrangement, they look for other indicia of employment.

If the borrowing firm is empowered to exercise control over the manner and means of the loaned individual's work and the tasks being performed by that person are essentially for the benefit of the borrowing company, that entity is likely to be held responsible for the workers' compensation pertaining to that "employee." When both the lending company and the borrowing company may simultaneously control the worker's performance, a joint employer situation is usually found, causing both parties to be jointly responsible for that person's workers' compensation coverage. A joint employer finding frequently results when the lending firm is in the business of leasing equipment and equipment operators to other companies, because the loaned employee is expected to maintain the lending firm's equipment while operating it for the other concern.

When the loaned employee engages in separate and distinct activities during discrete time periods for the lending party and the borrowing party, a dual employment relationship is normally found. Each firm is held exclusively responsible for the occupational injuries sustained by the borrowed employee during the performance of his or her duties for that particular firm. If the loaned employee is injured while working exclusively for one dual employer due to negligence attributable to the other employer, the adversely affected worker would usually be able to maintain a tort action against the latter concern. Because that company would not be responsible for the plaintiff's workers' compensation, the tort immunity provided by the compensation statute would not be applicable to that entity.

§ 7.6   Arising During the Course of Employment

Workers' compensation statutes do not protect individuals against all accidental injuries. They only cover employment-related occurrences. Claimants who seek workers' compensation must be able to demonstrate that their conditions arose *during the course of* their employment. If their injuries have no connection with their employment, they are not compensable. On the other hand, if their injuries originated in the employment environment while they were performing work tasks, they are covered.

The most frequently litigated of these cases concern occurrences that have a tenuous relationship with the employment of the injured workers. Employees are injured while they are commuting to or from work, or while they are eating, changing their clothes, cleaning up, resting, or performing other acts of a personal nature. Their misfortune may occur while they are participating in employer-related recreation or social activities, or while they are engaged in horseplay or misconduct. Accidents may befall traveling employees while they are on the road. Individuals may be hurt while they are involved in activities beyond their regular duties, while they are reacting to emergency situations, or before they are actually employed or after they have formally terminated their employment. In all of these situations, administrative officials and judges must decide whether there is a sufficient connection with their employment to warrant the extension of workers' compensation protection.

§ 7.7   Arising During the Course of Employment—Traveling to and From Work

People who are employed travel regularly to and from their places of work, to and from particular jobs during their shift, and to and from meal and rest areas. Their trips are not always uneventful. They may sustain injuries while driving or riding in vehicles or while walking. Courts have developed relatively uniform doctrines to distinguish between uncovered personal excursions and compensable employment-related trips.

Because workers' compensation laws are not designed to provide employees with protection against the general perils of life, claimants may only obtain benefits for injuries having a reasonable nexus to their employment. Courts have thus recognized that persons adversely affected by accidents occurring while they are preparing to leave for work or while they are simply commuting to and from the premises of their employer are not normally entitled to compensation. This is true even when employees receive a travel allowance for their commute. It is only when employees actually enter their employer's premises that their workers' compensation protection commences.

The results of the bright-line "going-and-coming" approach occasionally appear harsh. For example, if persons slip and fall on the sidewalk one block from their place of employment, they will normally not be covered. In fact, if they fall outside their employer's building while reaching for the door handle, they would probably be denied benefits, unless they had already crossed their employer's property line prior to their accident. They must be able to demonstrate that the incident actually occurred on company property.

Freeman v. Twin Falls Clinic & Hospital[1] concerned the compensability of injuries sustained by a claimant when he was on a public street across from his workplace. As he was getting out of his car, he was struck by a fellow employee who backed her car into the claimant's vehicle. Since the claimant's car was parked on a public street, instead of in the employer-provided parking lot, coverage was denied.

Once employees leave employer premises on their way home, the course of employment is usually terminated. If they are injured on the way home away from employer premises, their injuries are not normally compensable. What if individuals who have already left firm property decide to return to work premises for personal reasons and are injured while on company property? In *Tate v. GTE Hawaiian Telephone Co.*,[2] the court denied coverage to an employee who was injured after she had returned to employer premises to retrieve a piece of cake for personal consumption, because the incident occurred during a wholly personal errand. On the other hand, in *Hoffman v. Workers' Compensation Appeal Board*,[3] the court upheld coverage for an off-duty claimant who sustained injury while present at her place of work to obtain her paycheck pursuant to an established employer practice, due to the sufficient relationship between the employer and employee paychecks.

State courts have traditionally followed the same going-and-coming rule with respect to employees injured while traveling to and from external eating establishments during meal or rest breaks. Individuals who sustain injuries while walking, driving, or riding on company premises are considered entitled to compensation, because the critical events occurred during the course of their employment. When, however, accidents take place outside the confines of employer premises, benefit eligibility is usually denied.

Because employees are generally entitled to statutory protection only for accidents occurring on company premises, it is often necessary to determine the exact boundaries of firm property. If a facility is surrounded by a fence, the entire, fenced area will normally be considered company premises. If a contractor is working on a large construction project, even one involving several building sites, the whole project will probably be treated as contractor premises. A parking lot maintained by a company will almost always be regarded as firm property,

§ 7.7
1. 135 Idaho 36, 13 P.3d 867 (2000).
2. 77 Hawai'i 100, 881 P.2d 1246 (1994).

3. 559 Pa. 655, 741 A.2d 1286 (1999), reargument denied (Feb. 16, 2000).

even when the firm shares the lot with other employers or the lot is not contiguous to the main facility.

When employers own several, noncontiguous premises, employees often have to travel from one location to another on public thoroughfares. Judges recognize that it would be illogical to regard worker trips on public streets or sidewalks connecting company facilities as beyond the scope of their employment. As a result, employees who are injured on public roadways while engaged in travel between company facilities are generally found eligible for workers' compensation benefits. The employees are traveling between firm premises for the benefit of their employer, thus their conditions are considered to have arisen during the course of their employment. Even when they are merely traveling from a separate company parking lot to the main facility, most courts cover accidents occurring on public passageways, particularly if the workers were instructed to park in the firm lot. A few courts, however, view employee travel between an employer parking lot and the main site as a continuation of commuting and refuse to provide statutory protection until the individuals enter the firm's principal premises. When employees are injured on public sidewalks while traveling between a non-employer-owned parking lot and employer premises, coverage is normally denied.

Employees injured during normal commuting trips on public passageways are not usually entitled to statutory protection. Nonetheless, courts occasionally extend statutory coverage to injuries caused by special hazards located near company premises, because such hazards may reasonably be considered employment-related. For example, if workers walking on public sidewalks are struck by debris expelled from the premises of their employer, they might well be awarded benefits. Even when the hazards causing their injuries do not emanate from company premises, statutory coverage may be found if the circumstances are unique to the geographical area adjacent to their place of employment. For example, if pedestrians are struck by cars while traveling to or from work in extremely congested areas near their work premises, statutory protection might be provided. To obtain workers' compensation for such injuries claimants must demonstrate that their harm was caused by unusually dangerous circumstances associated with the areas adjacent to their employer's premises.

Ruckman v. Cubby Drilling, Inc.[4] involved employees who sustained injuries in traffic accidents while traveling from their homes to remote drilling sites during special job assignments. Although they were injured on public roads while traveling to work locations, the court applied the "special hazards" rule and sustained coverage. It acknowledged the road hazards common to most commutes, but held that the long distances these claimants were required to travel to reach the remote drilling sites enhanced their risks sufficiently to warrant statutory protection.

4. 81 Ohio St.3d 117, 689 N.E.2d 917, 1998 Ohio 455 (1998).

Special Errands and Travel on Company Conveyances

Employees are sometimes required to make special trips to their place of employment to perform specific tasks. For example, a city worker may be obliged to return to a park each evening to turn off the fountain. The time spent driving to and from the park will greatly exceed the time needed to shut off the fountain. If this person is injured during the trip to and from work, a number of courts would provide compensation. They regard the travel of such employees as a fundamental aspect of their service, because these workers are really being employed to make the special trip each day. Coverage is especially likely when the employees are paid for their travel time or reimbursed for their travel expenses.

Bentz v. Liberty Northwest[5] concerned an employee who worked primarily out of his own home. He was injured one day while traveling from home to his firm office to retrieve mail. Since the court found that such travel between his home office and his employer's premises was a condition of his employment, coverage was provided.

Other "special errands" may also be covered. *Stroud Municipal Hospital v. Mooney*[6] involved a laboratory supervisor at a hospital whose lunch break at home was interrupted by a telephone call directing him to return to the hospital because of an emergency medical situation. While he was returning to work, he was injured in an automobile accident. Since his particular travel back to work was found to constitute a "special errand" for his employer, Mooney's resulting injuries were found compensable. *Barnes v. Children's Hospital*[7] concerned a hospital supervisor who was shopping with her family on Saturday, when she was called to work to perform a task usually assigned to another worker who had failed to report to work that day. She stopped for gasoline as she was preparing to take her family home and then continue to the hospital. Her accidental fall on gas station premises was found covered under the "special errand" exception, since she was leaving the shopping mall early to satisfy the needs of her employer and had to drop her family members off at home before she could return to work. In *Estate of Soupene v. Lignitz*,[8] the court similarly extended coverage to a volunteer firefighter who was injured while responding to an emergency fire call.

The so-called "special errand" rule is normally applied to individuals with specified work hours who are required to make trips back to work during their off-duty hours to perform limited tasks. Their unique work frequently occurs on a regular basis after other employees have gone home or before others are scheduled to begin their shift. To be entitled to statutory coverage, however, the special errands do not have to constitute a normal part of their work. For example, if an employee were injured while returning to work for the purpose of unlocking the shop to admit a repair person, benefits would probably be awarded. On

---

5. 311 Mont. 361, 57 P.3d 832 (2002).

6. 933 P.2d 872 (Okla. 1996).

7. 109 Md.App. 543, 675 A.2d 558 (1996).

8. 265 Kan. 217, 960 P.2d 205 (1998).

the other hand, in *Hoffner v. North Dakota Workers Compensation Bureau*,[9] the court denied coverage for an employee who was injured on his way to work while he was riding as a passenger in his roommate's car even though he and his roommate were transporting empty gas cans to a job site for their employer. This factor was found insufficient to convert a normally uncovered commute into a covered special errand, due to the lack of any inconvenience associated with this task and the fact the claimant was not paid for the trip.

The "special errand" doctrine tends to be limited to persons who return to work to perform relatively minimal tasks. If people return to their place of employment to engage in more extensive service, this exception to the usual "going-and-coming" rule is not likely to be applied. It is no longer reasonable to suggest that the commute of such individuals constitutes the primary part of their service. As a result, they would probably not be considered eligible for statutory coverage while they are traveling to and from work on noncompany premises.

Another exception to the traditional going-and-coming rule has been recognized by most courts for travel on company conveyances. When employees sustain injuries while traveling to and from work in employer-supplied vehicles, they are normally found eligible for workers' compensation. Accidents that occur during commutes in company trucks, vans, or cars are regarded as having taken place during the course of the riders' employment. The fact that the workers may be charged for the company-provided transportation does not usually negate statutory coverage for such trips. Individuals who are given statutory coverage during their transportation in employer vehicles may even be accorded protection by some courts while they are approaching and leaving the firm conveyances. When employees are furnished with employer conveyances to commute to and from work, they may even be covered while they are using their own vehicles due to the servicing of the employer-provided conveyances.

When employers are in the transportation business and they permit their employees to ride their buses or trains to and from work, courts are uncertain whether to include such commuting trips within the course of the riders' employment. Some courts provide statutory protection to the employees riding in those vehicles, because the injuries sustained in vehicular accidents occur on company property. Other courts, however, deny coverage, because the transportation firms provide the company conveyances primarily for the benefit of the riding public, not their own employees.

Some businesses require their employees to bring their own cars to work if they will be expected to use their vehicles to travel from job to job during the work day. If these individuals were to have an accident while driving their own cars to or from their place of employment, they would almost certainly be awarded benefits. They are driving their

---

9. 2000 N.D. 123, 612 N.W.2d 263 (2000).

vehicles to and from work for the direct benefit of their employer, thus their commute constitutes a covered part of their employment.

Dual Purpose Doctrine

Employees occasionally take trips that serve both business and personal interests. For example, a manager may ask someone going on vacation to a particular location to conduct some company business on the way. Or an individual asked to travel to a city on business may decide to take several vacation days in conjunction with that trip. If the employee sustains an injury while on such a trip, would workers' compensation coverage be available? Resolution of this issue is generally determined through application of the so-called "dual purpose" doctrine.

In *Marks' Dependents v. Gray*,[10] Judge Cardozo succinctly enunciated the standard that continues to be followed by most courts in cases involving dual purpose travel:

> If the work of the employee creates the necessity for travel, he is in the course of his employment, though he is serving at the same time some purpose of his own. * * * If, however, the work has had no part in creating the necessity for travel, if the journey would have gone forward though the business errand had been dropped, and would have been canceled upon failure of the private purpose, though the business errand was undone, the travel is then personal, and personal the risk.

When a dual purpose trip combines both business and personal aspects, it is generally considered personal and uncovered if the travel would have been carried out despite the presence or absence of the business objective and would have been canceled without the existence of the personal consideration. Conversely, the trip will constitute covered business travel if it would have had to be carried out by some employee even in the absence of the personal motivation. The critical inquiry is not whether the trip would have been made by the injured worker, but whether it would have had to be undertaken by some employee. Furthermore, the fact that the employer asked the individual to carry out the business objective after it learned of the planned personal trip would not preclude a decision in favor of coverage if the business aspect were of sufficient importance. So long as the business objective would have had to be accomplished by someone, the trip will be considered covered.

The dual purpose doctrine also may be applied to travel to and from employee residences. Although commuting trips normally constitute noncovered personal activities under the going-and-coming rule, the addition of a work-related aspect may render the travel covered. For example, an employer may ask a person to carry out a business function on the way to or from work that had to be performed by some employee. If an accident were to occur during the business part of this trip, the dual purpose doctrine would apply and benefits would be available. Statutory protection would also be likely for individuals who are re-

---

10. 251 N.Y. 90, 167 N.E. 181 (1929).

quired to carry employment-related items back and forth to work, if courts conclude that this service was of significant benefit to their employer. On the other hand, if the business-related aspect was considered relatively insignificant, compensation coverage would probably be denied.

Some employees maintain offices in their homes and regularly perform work there. The work areas of their residences are regarded as employer premises for workers' compensation purposes. Their travel to and from company offices may thus be found covered, because they may be treated as if they were traveling between employer locations as part of their usual employment. To be eligible for statutory protection, however, the claimants must be able to demonstrate that they customarily perform employment functions in their homes.

Even when the personal aspect of a dual purpose trip is found to predominate, statutory protection may still be available with respect to part of the employee's travel. If a firm asks a worker to deviate from a personal trip to perform a noncritical business task, the portion of the trip that may be regarded as the employment-related detour will generally be considered covered. For example, an individual may drive to a vacation spot and then make an employer-requested trip to a business location. Although the travel to and from the vacation site would constitute a noncovered personal trip, the special travel between the vacation spot and the business location would be considered covered.

A converse rule is applied to personal deviations made during business trips. For example, someone may travel to a particular location on business and then make a side trip for personal reasons. While the business segments of the trip would be covered, the personal detour would be excluded. It is only when the individual has effectively returned to the business route that statutory protection is again available. Before the person reaches that point, coverage is usually denied. On the other hand, when a worker deviates slightly from a "special errand" he has performed for his employer to take a more scenic route home and has an accident during that somewhat extended trip, his injuries would most likely be found compensable.

Problems frequently arise when it is not possible to divide a dual purpose trip into distinct business and personal segments. For example, an employee who has to take a business trip from New York to Chicago may make a personal stop in Detroit or St. Louis. Because the personal visit to Detroit would not involve a significant departure from the basic route between New York and Chicago, the entire trip would probably be considered covered, except for the wholly personal portion in Detroit. When, however, the trip to the personal destination involves a substantial departure from the business route, most courts regard that portion of the travel as uncovered. If the worker first flew to Chicago on business, that part of the trip would be covered. The trip from Chicago to St. Louis would most likely be viewed as personal, because it would not be related to the person's return to New York. Nonetheless, the trip from St. Louis back to New York would probably be found covered, because it would be regarded as analogous to the return trip the employee would have had to make from Chicago had there been no personal deviation.

If the personal detour had involved a more substantial departure from the business route, such as a visit to San Francisco, courts would certainly treat the travel from Chicago to San Francisco as personal. Most courts would also consider the portion of the return trip from San Francisco to Chicago as personal. They would only permit the reestablishment of statutory protection once the employee had effectively returned to the employment-related portion of the Chicago to New York expedition. A few courts, however, would provide coverage for the entire return trip from San Francisco to New York. They find that once the personal objective has been accomplished, the individual should be considered back on the business trip.

In cases involving personal deviations from business trips, the critical factor concerns the degree of departure from the direct business route caused by the personal detour. So long as the departure is not substantial, the entire trip (e.g., New York–Detroit–Chicago–New York) may be accorded statutory protection. Nonetheless, when the personal deviation is significant (e.g., St. Louis or San Francisco), the clearly personal part will normally be excluded from coverage.

§ 7.8 Arising During the Course of Employment—The Personal Comfort Doctrine

During their normal work day, employees frequently engage in activities of a personal nature. They eat, drink, relieve themselves, wash up, change clothes, and rest. If they sustain injuries while performing any of these functions, would they be entitled to workers' compensation? Residential employees may live in company housing for their own benefit or for the convenience of their employer. They may have fixed hours of work or they may be on-call for extended periods of time. If they were injured while engaging in personal acts in firm housing, would they receive statutory protection? Courts generally resolve such questions through application of the "personal comfort" doctrine.

Even at work, employees must occasionally engage in conduct to satisfy personal needs. If their actions advance employer interests or are an inherent aspect of the employment relationship, workers' compensation coverage is usually provided. When these activities do not involve a significant departure from their customary employment endeavors, the individuals continue to be considered within the course of their employment. It is only when workers depart substantially from their job functions that coverage is likely to be forfeited.

During their shifts, full-time employees are generally provided with rest and meal breaks. Although they usually receive compensation for their rest breaks, many workers are not remunerated for their meal periods. Nonetheless, if they sustain injuries on company premises during such breaks, their injuries are normally considered covered occurrences. While these actions take place during nonwork time, they have a sufficient physical and temporal proximity to their employment to be viewed as an inherent part of it. Courts even extend statutory protection to persons who unintentionally fall asleep during rest breaks. A disqualifying abandonment of employment is likely to be found only with respect to employees who deliberately choose to sleep for extended periods of time.

Employees injured on company property during rest or meal breaks because of employment-related hazards clearly deserve statutory protection, because the risks causing their harm have a direct connection to their jobs. Even when their plight does not result from conditions indigenous to their employment environment, coverage is still likely to result. The fact that they are still on employer premises and are ministering to personal needs that must be satisfied during their work day would lead most courts to conclude that their injuries arose during the course of their employment. Workers are only likely to be denied statutory protection when they are injured in plant locations they are clearly not permitted to enter, or where they are injured when engaged in conduct wholly unrelated to the purpose for the rest break.

A crucial factor supporting statutory protection for individuals injured during rest or meal breaks concerns their presence on company property. Employees who leave employer premises to obtain food are usually considered to have temporarily abandoned their employment to satisfy personal needs. Unless they can demonstrate that the employer required them to visit the external eating establishments, injuries sustained away from firm property are not likely to be covered.

Employees frequently stop briefly during the work day to drink water or other beverages. Such personal acts do not interrupt the course of their employment. Individuals who sustain injuries while engaged in these activities are thus entitled to statutory protection, even if they get their hand caught in an ice machine, mistake acid for water, or are struck by a fellow employee for cutting in line ahead of that person. Injuries sustained by employees during brief smoking breaks are similarly covered by workers' compensation laws, because they also involve a minimal departure from the regular job functions of the people involved.

Workers often attempt to obtain temporary relief from unusually cold or hot environments. They may light a fire on a cold day or open windows on a hot day. If they were injured while engaging in conduct designed to enhance their personal comfort, statutory protection would almost certainly be available. Some decisions have even extended coverage to individuals who sustained injuries during short swims on hot days. Similar considerations lead courts to provide protection for employees who are hurt while relieving themselves at work. They are generally covered while going to and from the lavatory and while using the facility itself.

Many employees change into work clothes at the beginning of their shift and change back to street clothes at the end. They may wash their hands or face or take showers at the conclusion of the day, or they may otherwise take care of their personal appearance. Such pre-and post-shift activities are generally considered incidental aspects of their employment, even though they do not involve necessary functions. Injuries sustained during these personal ministrations are thus regarded as arising during the course of their employment. When special circumstances require employees to report for work well before the commencement of their shift or to remain at work well after they complete their job tasks, statutory coverage is normally available to them. On the other hand, if individuals are hurt while merely hanging around their employer's premises before or after their shift and their injury has no meaningful connection to their employment, compensation is usually denied.

Coverage questions may be encountered when employees minister to their personal needs in an unreasonable manner. For example, cold workers may carelessly pour gasoline on a fire to warm their environment. Tired persons may decide to take a nap under a company vehicle. If their imprudent actions result in injuries, should they be eligible for compensation? If the workers were merely negligent, statutory protection would generally be available. Even extreme indifference is unlikely to cause a loss of coverage. It is only when workers deliberately engage in dangerous behavior that compensation may be denied on the ground that such actions cannot reasonably be considered incidents of their employment.

Unique coverage issues are raised by employees who reside in company housing. While they may have fixed hours of work, they remain on employer premises during many of their off-duty hours. Because statutory coverage is extended to nonresidential personnel who are injured on company premises while eating, resting, changing clothes, cleaning up, and engaging in other personal activities incident to their employment, courts generally provide similar protection for fixed-hour, residential employees when they carry out those tasks on firm property. Under the so-called "bunkhouse" rule, courts also tend to cover injuries that arise in company residences from conditions indigenous to those dwellings. Thus, workers injured by house fires or from falls out of bed are normally found eligible for benefits. When, however, fixed-hour, residential personnel engage in wholly personal tasks in their company homes that have no real connection to their employment, coverage is usually denied. They also lose their right to statutory protection when they conduct personal business off employer premises.

More extensive statutory coverage is provided for residential employees who are continuously on call. Courts generally include eating, drinking, resting, washing, changing, and other similar endeavors that take place on company property. The fact that they are encouraged or required to remain near their work stations during their on-call hours and may be called to duty at any time provides a sufficient employment connection for most personal activities. The infrequent decisions denying compensation to on-call employees injured while performing personal tasks in company housing usually find the acts in question too distinctly personal to warrant statutory coverage. These cases are rare, however, because doubts regarding incidents on firm property tend to be resolved in favor of coverage. When on-call workers leave company premises to perform wholly personal errands, they normally lose their workers' compensation eligibility.

§ 7.9 Arising During the Course of Employment—Recreational and Social Activities

Many companies permit, encourage, or require employee participation in various recreational or social activities. These undertakings may occur during the regular work day or prior to or after work. They make take place on firm premises or in other locations. If workers sustain injuries while participating in such endeavors, they may be eligible for workers' compensation coverage. Claimants normally have to demonstrate that their injuries arose on company property as an incident of their employment, originated during activities expressly or impliedly required by their employer, or came to pass while they were participating in recreational or social programs of substantial benefit to their firm.

Several state legislatures have concluded that workers' compensation laws should not be applied to some or all injuries that occur while employees voluntarily participate in recreational or social activities conducted during their off-duty hours, even when their firm supports those endeavors through financial contributions. They have thus enacted statutory provisions that effectively preclude coverage for voluntary participation in activities that are not directly sponsored by employers and for which employees receive no remuneration. Employees who sustain injuries while participating in such undertakings in these states are not likely to obtain benefits unless they can establish that the exclusionary language does not apply to their particular circumstances. To prevail, they must normally prove that they were actually required or at least strongly encouraged by their employer to partake.

Courts in jurisdictions that do not have specific statutory provisions pertaining to recreational and social activities apply traditional workers' compensation principles to such endeavors. As a result, they frequently cover injuries that occur during these undertakings on employer premises. This is especially likely when the relevant circumstances arise within the employment environment during scheduled break periods in which such activities regularly take place. In these cases, it is easy for courts to conclude that the injuries have originated during the course of employment. When, however, the harm results from spontaneous and unusual recreational activities, statutory protection is less likely. Firms are probably unaware of these sporadic events, and it is more difficult for courts to treat these situations as accepted incidents of participant employment.

The clearest cases warranting statutory protection involve employees injured while participating in recreational or social activities that are a part of their jobs. They may actually be directed to engage in the conduct in question. For example, they may be ordered to attend a company social event or to take part in a certain athletic endeavor. Coverage would normally be available to individuals participating in these employer-mandated functions. The firm may alternatively encourage workers to participate in external activities. This may apply to persons who are expected to entertain company customers. If employees are injured while engaging in social activities on behalf of their employer, statutory protection would generally be available to them.

Even when companies do not require employee attendance at firm functions, statutory protection may still be accorded. The closest cases involve employer-sponsored social events conducted off company premises. If the evidence indicates that workers were encouraged to attend, coverage may well result. This explains why people who sustain injuries at office parties often obtain benefits. On the other hand, if the firm does not sponsor the event and does not require employee participation, statutory protection will normally be provided only where claimants can demonstrate that the company derived a meaningful employment benefit from their attendance. When the activity in question has not been sponsored by the employer and the injured employees cannot demonstrate that their firm derived any benefit from their participation, coverage will usually be denied.

Although application of the going-and-coming rule usually precludes coverage with respect to accidental injuries that occur during employee commutes off company premises, exceptions are occasionally made for accidents occurring during travel home from firm social events. Persons driving home from office parties are normally found outside the course of their employment. Nonetheless, employees traveling home from firm picnics are frequently awarded benefits. This distinction is based upon the fact that office parties tend to be conducted at or near the employee's customary place of work. Their travel home is thus viewed as analogous to their regular, uncovered commutes. On the other hand, company picnics usually occur at external locations. As a result, travel to and from such firm-sponsored events may reasonably be covered under the "special errand" exception to the going-and-coming rule.

Courts frequently reach opposite conclusions with respect to the statutory protection applicable to individuals who participate in firm-sponsored athletic events. The decisions usually consider four separate factors. If the games occur on company premises, statutory coverage is likely, particularly when they take place during the regular work day. Recreational endeavors that are expressly promoted by the firm are also frequently given coverage, while events that result primarily from worker interest are usually excluded. If the firm supplies the athletic equipment, the uniforms, or the prizes, statutory eligibility may well result. The final factor considered by courts in close cases concerns the commercial and employment benefits companies derive from worker participation in sporting events. Corporations that generate beneficial advertising through their sponsorship of team sports are frequently ordered to provide benefits to individuals injured during such activities. Judges may also base benefit awards on the fact that athletic endeavors enhance employee morale and efficiency. Company policies requiring employees who participate in employer-sponsored recreational activities to waive their right to workers' compensation coverage are unlikely to receive judicial acceptance.

§ 7.10　Arising During the Course of Employment—Traveling Employees

The work of some individuals involves regular travel away from their employers' premises. While they are on the road, they perform various tasks that directly concern their occupation, they minister to personal needs that incidentally relate to their employment, and they engage in activities of a wholly personal nature. Injuries sustained by such persons during their performance of actual job functions are clearly compensable and court decisions increasingly permit the awarding of benefits for injuries arising during their performance of personal endeavors.

Personal tasks that have a meaningful relationship to their employment relationship are generally found to constitute covered activities. Because traveling employees must frequently stay at hotels and motels, courts tend to apply the same rules to these individuals as are applied to residential personnel who reside in company housing. As a result, traveling employees who sustain injuries while obtaining meals on the road are generally given the same statutory protection accorded to residential employees who eat on company premises. They are also likely to be accorded coverage when they walk or drive from their hotel to eating establishments, even though their injuries occur on public thoroughfares. The "special errand" exception to the traditional going-and-coming rule is effectively applied in these cases, with the affected persons being treated as if they were traveling from one part of their employer's premises to another.

Traveling employees who are injured by conditions indigenous to their out-of-town residences are normally awarded benefits. For example, persons injured in hotel fires or from physical attacks by intruders often receive statutory protection. When traveling workers are continuously on call, courts tend to regard almost all reasonable personal activities as within the course of their employment. Even when they work discrete hours while on the road, however, many personal endeavors are now covered. Most contemporary courts recognize that bathing and dressing are necessary for employees who must maintain appropriate appearances, and they regularly award benefits to people injured while performing these tasks.

LaTourette v. Workers' Compensation Appeals Board[1] concerned an employee who suffered a non-occupational heart attack caused by a preexisting medical condition while he was on a business trip. He was hospitalized and had several heart surgeries. While he was being treated, the individual contracted a bacterial infection that caused his death. Although the person sustained the heart attack that led to his demise while on a business trip, the court found that his death did not arise during the course of his employment, since it had no meaningful connection to his employment duties.

Numerous cases have even extended protection to traveling employees injured during wholly recreational trips taken while they are away from home on business. These decisions recognize that "when an employee is required to travel to a distant place on the business of his employer and is directed to remain at that place for a specified length of time, his status as an employee continues during the entire trip, and any injury occurring during such period is compensable, so long as the employee at the time of injury was engaged in a reasonable activity." In the increasing number of jurisdictions following this approach, it has become clear that traveling personnel will receive statutory protection with respect to most activities performed during their business trips. This includes personal endeavors that have any remote relationship to their employment. It is only when they engage in separate and distinct personal acts having no connection to their work that compensation is likely to be denied.

§ 7.11 Arising During the Course of Employment—Horseplay and Employee Misconduct

Employees occasionally engage in horseplay at work. If they are injured during such behavior, should they be entitled to workers' compensation? In most cases of this kind, the critical question concerns whether the claimants instigated or merely participated in the horseplay that caused their injuries. Similar issues are raised when workers are injured by deliberate misconduct. Innocent persons hurt by the misconduct of others are generally eligible for benefits. When, however, the adverse consequences befall the actual perpetrators, the right to compensation may not be certain. Numerous enactments have special provisions disqualifying individuals who sustain injuries while engaging in enumerated forms of misconduct, and courts have to determine the exact scope of these limitations.

It is now generally recognized that employees injured by the horseplay of other workers are entitled to workers' compensation. The fact that the other workers are engaged in prohibited conduct does not affect the statutory protection available to nonparticipating bystanders. On the other hand, individuals who either instigate or participate in the horse-

§ 7.10

1. 17 Cal.4th 644, 72 Cal.Rptr.2d 217, 951 P.2d 1184 (1998).

play that causes their injuries may be denied benefits. Most states apply different approaches to determine which horseplay actors should be permitted to receive compensation.

Courts have traditionally applied an "aggressor" defense that permits employers to defeat compensation claims filed by employees injured by horseplay carried out by themselves. These cases find that the perpetrators of deliberate horseplay temporarily abandon their employment during their inappropriate behavior, causing them to become ineligible for coverage during that period. Nonetheless, if courts conclude that it would be unfair to deny such persons benefits, they may use one of three approaches to extend statutory protection.

Some state courts have developed a rule that distinguishes between employees who participate in horseplay that has become a regular aspect of the employment environment and workers who engage in isolated acts of personal mischief. Individuals who are injured while involved in horseplay that constitutes a customary incident of employment are generally found eligible for compensation. On the other hand, employees who engage in atypical acts of mischief are usually denied benefits, because their conduct cannot reasonably be considered related to their employment circumstances. Although a few decisions have suggested that an established employer tolerance of shop mischief may only be shown through evidence indicating that the company was aware of the behavior in question, most courts have appropriately recognized that the critical issue should concern claimant knowledge. If workers have reason to believe that their horseplay is within the bounds of accepted activity, courts applying this exception find constructive employer acceptance and sustain benefit awards in favor of injured participants.

A second approach merely asks whether it would be reasonable to conclude that an injury caused by horseplay arose out of the employment setting. Courts applying this test cover bystanders injured by the pranks of fellow employees, because their injuries undeniably arose out of their employment. More difficult issues are raised with respect to injured horseplay participants. If the whimsical behavior does not involve any substantial departure from the claimant's regular employment, courts applying this framework tend to award compensation. Benefits would thus be available to a worker performing a prank on the way to the drinking fountain, to a person working with an air hose used in a practical joke, to an employee engaged in an arm-wrestling match with a coworker who teased him about his ability to carry paint buckets, or to a railroad employee injured while striking a torpedo on the track he is walking. So long as the frivolous deviation from their usual employment duties is minimal, these courts are inclined to award benefits to injured pranksters.

Darco Transportation v. Dulen[1] concerned a truck driver who was injured when the vehicle he was operating was struck by a train. The employer challenged the driver's entitlement to compensation by alleging

§ 7.11
1. 922 P.2d 591 (Okla.1996).

that he had been engaged in sexual activity with his coworker at the time of the accident. Since the driver was still operating his vehicle on behalf of the employer at the time of the accident, the court found his injuries covered, despite the possibility he had been simultaneously engaged in sexual behavior. There was no evidence to suggest that he had abandoned his employer's transportation mission at that time.

When the evidence suggests a significant departure from the regular employment of employees injured by their own horseplay, these courts usually deny statutory coverage. They do not believe that the resulting harm may reasonably be considered to have arisen out of claimant employment. Examples of disqualifying deviations include a landscape worker who had an accident while riding a fellow employee's motorcycle off firm premises at the end of the work day, an individual injured while getting off a forklift he was riding as a passenger in violation of an employer rule specifically prohibiting workers from riding on forklifts, an elevator operator who left his post to instigate an altercation with another worker, a salesperson who sustained an injury while shooting staples at a coworker during a lull between customers, and a person who injured himself while attempting to electrify the washroom as a practical joke.

A few courts have sought to expand the statutory protection available to the victims of shop pranks by abolishing the historically recognized distinction between bystanders and participants. Judges utilizing this approach view injuries resulting from shop mischief as a natural byproduct of crowded and stressful employment environments. They believe that employment pranks are to be expected, and they see no reason to deny coverage to those who are participants. Because those individuals are considered victims of the job factors that precipitated their misbehavior, they should be entitled to the same protection that is available to mere bystanders.

Coleman v. State ex rel. Wyoming Workers' Compensation Division[2] involved a death benefit claim filed by the widow of an employee who had died in a vehicular accident. Evidence indicated that the deceased worker had been intoxicated at the time of the accident, and the employer claimed that this misconduct rendered the worker's accident noncompensable. The court agreed and held that employee intoxication is an affirmative defense to a workers' compensation claim.

In *Goebel v. Warner Transportation*,[3] the court indicated that a statute disallowing benefits for injuries due to illegal drug use by claimants does not require proof that the unlawful drug use was the only cause or the main cause of the resulting injuries. Disqualification will result if the drug usage was even a concurrent causative factor. On the other hand, if claimants can demonstrate that their drug or alcohol use did not contribute to their injuries, the statutory presumption against compensability can be negated and compensation may be awarded.

---

2. 915 P.2d 595 (Wyo.1996).   **3.** 2000 S.D. 79, 612 N.W.2d 18 (2000).

Although injuries caused by claimant drug or alcohol abuse may result in benefit disqualifications, coverage will not usually be denied when claimants seek compensation for drug or alcohol problems generated by work-related factors.

Other deliberate employee misconduct may similarly result in a loss of statutory protection. Mere negligence by injured employees will not defeat their right to compensation. Employers claiming willful employee misconduct as a defense to compensation claims must demonstrate that the workers acted deliberately or with reckless indifference to the possibility of harm.

§ 7.12 Arising During the Course of Employment—Activities Beyond the Regular Duties

It is not unusual for employees to engage in acts beyond their normal duties. They may perform job tasks designed to assist fellow workers or to benefit supervisors or their employer. Workers often perform acts intended to benefit customers or members of the general public. They may undertake actions they hope will enhance their own employment skills or perform functions for labor organizations or public service entities. If they undertake the actions in a good faith effort to advance the interests of their employer, their injuries would probably be found to have arisen during the course of employment.

Contemporary courts generally acknowledge that actions taken by employees to assist fellow workers with the performance of their job functions fall within the course of their employment. Although some of the early cases required individuals injured while helping other workers to show that they were simultaneously enhancing their own employment, most recent decisions have eliminated this requirement. They provide statutory protection for persons who assist other employees with their jobs, even when they are not advancing their own work. These courts believe that it would be both unfair and unwise to deny benefits to individuals who are injured while attempting in good faith to assist other employees with the performance of their work. A contrary rule would discourage activities that clearly benefit their employers.

Similar coverage issues arise when employees are instructed by their supervisor or their employer to perform private tasks that will directly benefit the supervisor or the employer. Even though the accomplishment of these private tasks may be beyond their regular job duties, the workers will normally be accorded statutory protection because they are acting in good faith to carry out employment-related directives. For example, if they were asked to perform personal functions at the home of their supervisor, to carry out special errands for that person, or to engage in some other conduct for the private benefit of their employer, they would generally be covered while undertaking those activities.

Workers occasionally decide to exchange jobs with fellow employees. They may be bored with their own job and wish to engage in different work. Most employers are not pleased by such behavior, because they want individuals to perform their assigned work. If people trade jobs with the permission of their employer, they would certainly be acting within the course of their employment while carrying out their new functions. When, however, the exchange occurs without the consent or knowledge of their employer, statutory protection is frequently denied. Courts do not believe that employees further the interests of their employer when they change jobs with other workers for personal reasons. Compensation is especially unlikely in cases in which the individuals who traded jobs violated specific company rules prohibiting such conduct.

Employees may sustain injuries while assisting other workers with wholly personal endeavors. For example, they may drive other employees home when they become ill or take the pay checks of absent workers to their homes. Because these actions do not meaningfully relate to their employment, the persons engaged in such conduct are usually found ineligible for workers' compensation. Benefits are only likely to be awarded when the conduct in question not only furthers the personal needs of the other workers but also advances the interests of their employer.

Employees sometimes perform acts for the benefit of firm customers or members of the general public. When actions on behalf of current clients either facilitate the ability of their employer to serve the customers or generate good will likely to benefit their company, courts regularly find them to be acting within the course of their employment. For instance, an employee may sustain injuries while helping to start a customer's car, while assisting a customer retrieve her stolen purse, or while picking up medication needed by a sick customer. Similar considerations induce courts to rule in favor of statutory coverage for employees who sustain injuries while providing gratuitous assistance to members of the general public who are not presently firm customers. Because these endeavors further the good will interests of their employer, the requisite employment connection is frequently found. Some courts, however, consider good Samaritan acts on behalf of customers or members of the public to be of a personal, rather than an employment-related, nature. They thus deny statutory coverage to the workers involved, even when their activities enhance the good will interests of their firm.

It is not unusual for employees to engage in endeavors designed to enhance their employment skills. They may enroll in formal training programs or undertake casual, self-improvement efforts. These activities are likely to inure to the benefit of their employer, because they help the participants become more proficient workers. Training programs operated by employers in the workplace clearly constitute covered activities. If the employer explicitly or implicitly encourages individuals to attend courses or compensates workers to do so, injuries that occur during those endeavors are likely to be found to have arisen within the course of employment. In the absence of such direct employer support, however, statutory protection tends to be denied—even when the company pays for the cost of the courses.

Employees may enhance their occupational skills by practicing on their assigned equipment or by learning to operate other machinery. Individuals who undertake these self-improvement activities are usually found to be acting within the course of their employment, because they carry out the requisite functions on company premises. Statutory protection will frequently be provided when employees perform wholly personal tasks in their work environments, if they can demonstrate that the employer has customarily permitted employees to work on such jobs. These activities improve their skills and advance employer-employee relationships. Coverage will normally be denied, however, when the personal actions do not constitute a tolerated employment practice. When workers undertake improvement efforts on their own time away from their place of employment, they are usually denied statutory coverage, due to the lack of a sufficient connection to their employment relationship.

Individuals may sustain injuries while attending conventions or seminars related to their occupations. If claimants can show that their employer explicitly or implicitly directed or strongly encouraged them to attend, their injuries would certainly be found to have occurred during the course of their employment. On the other hand, if there were no evidence of specific employer encouragement and the individuals merely decided on their own to attend, statutory protection would normally be denied, even though their employer indirectly benefitted from their endeavors.

Employees represented by labor organizations may decide to participate in union affairs. They may become union officials or shop stewards, or they may engage in other organizational ventures. Some courts have traditionally regarded these activities for the primary benefit of the participants and they have treated these endeavors as beyond the course of participant employment. A growing number of courts, however, have appropriately acknowledged that some union efforts may meaningfully benefit the company involved and they extend coverage to employees injured while performing union acts that have a reasonable relationship to their employment. For example, when shop stewards discuss or present worker grievances or union officials participate in collective bargaining, these courts are likely to find a sufficient connection to the employment setting to warrant statutory protection. Nonetheless, when the activities undertaken on behalf of a labor organization have no actual connection with the business, coverage is denied. A similar lack of statutory coverage applies to picket line activities and other strike-related endeavors directly contrary to the interests of the affected company.

Numerous companies permit their employees to engage in community service activities on firm premises. Workers may participate in Red Cross blood drives, charitable fund raising campaigns, or similar endeavors. Even though these efforts take place on employer property, their overwhelmingly personal nature leads most courts to conclude that the participants are acting outside the scope of their employment. The fact that the company's public image may be enhanced by these actions is not considered sufficient to warrant statutory coverage. When charitable efforts are actively encouraged by firms and take place on company premises, courts should seriously consider the extension of statutory protection, due to the substantial employer involvement. Thus far, however, the only significant expansion of coverage has occurred with respect to the public service endeavors of voluntary fire fighters.

Emergencies

During their employment, individuals occasionally encounter emergency situations threatening fellow workers, customers, or members of the general public. Most people feel a moral obligation to provide assistance to others in distress. Some good Samaritans sustain injuries while attempting to extricate others from dangerous circumstances. If courts can find a reasonable connection between employee rescue efforts and their employment, their resulting injuries are generally held compensable. When no employment nexus is discernible, however, statutory protection is normally denied.

When claimants can demonstrate that employer interests are threatened by emergency situations, coverage is usually made available. Employees injured while attempting to protect firm premises from fire, theft, or other dangers are normally granted benefits. It is clear that these persons are acting to protect employer property and courts consider their endeavors a relevant part of their employment.

Statutory protection is similarly accorded to claimants who are injured while attempting to assist fellow workers endangered by employment-related conditions. Because an employer has an obligation to protect its own employees, courts find that other firm personnel have an implied duty to assist coworkers imperiled by firm-related dangers. Courts even extend statutory coverage to individuals injured during efforts to extricate themselves from dangerous employment circumstances.

Employees sometimes provide aid to customers threatened by hazardous conditions. If the danger emanated from their employer, statutory coverage is normally available to employee rescuers. The fact that they are attempting to limit employer liability is sufficient to support benefit awards. Nonetheless, not all employee assistance to customers in emergency situations is considered covered. When workers merely aid customers during crises having no connection to their employer, the lack of any meaningful employment relationship is likely to result in benefit denials. The fact that the efforts of these employees may enhance firm-customer relations is usually found insufficient to provide the requisite employment nexus.

When employees sustain injuries while attempting to assist strangers threatened by exigent circumstances, the availability of statutory protection is usually dependent upon the establishment of some meaningful employment connection. If the claimants were endeavoring to protect employer interests by limiting the harm caused to members of the general public by dangerous circumstances generated by their employer, compensation would normally be available. On the other hand, many decisions have denied coverage to individuals injured while acting as good Samaritans in emergency situations not attributable to their employer, due to the absence of any reasonable nexus to employment.

Courts wishing to accord coverage to employees injured while providing emergency assistance to complete strangers often use the "positional risk" approach. If the individuals encountering emergency situations were at the relevant locations because of their employment duties, these courts are likely to provide coverage for assistance provided to strangers. "[W]hen a conscientious citizen is in the course of his employment and perceives an imminent danger to the public, * * * his endeavor to alleviate the danger should be considered incidental to his employment."[1] Nonetheless, other courts continue to deny benefits to employees who are injured while providing assistance to strangers whose situations have no direct connection to the claimants' employer.

On rare occasions, private employees are pressed into public service by police officers chasing suspected criminals or firefighters confronting conflagrations. These conscripts may sustain injuries while performing these public tasks and file compensation claims against their employer. When impressed persons are hurt while protecting employer interests, as when they help to pursue criminals who have stolen company property or assist firefighters protecting firm premises, benefits are usually awarded. Statutory protection is also likely when individuals who work for common carriers or taxi companies are directed by government agents to provide public assistance in emergency situations. The fact that their employer provides public services is considered sufficient to warrant the extension of coverage to them when they are conscripted by governmental agents to perform special tasks during public emergencies.

§ 7.13 Arising During the Course of Employment—Pre–Hire and Post–Termination Injuries

Individuals seeking employment may sustain injuries while on the premises of prospective employers. People who are formally hired may injure themselves on firm property before their employment actually commences. Persons who voluntarily terminate their employment or who are involuntarily discharged may suffer harm while they are preparing to remove themselves or their belongings from the premises of their employer. Should any or all of these claimants be entitled to statutory coverage?

Courts generally require evidence of actual employment contracts before they extend workers' compensation protection to injured claimants. As a result, people who seek benefits for injuries sustained while they are endeavoring to obtain work and before they have been formally

§ 7.12

1. In re D'Angeli's Case, 369 Mass. 812, 343 N.E.2d 368, 371 (1976).

hired usually have their claims denied. This lack of statutory protection is even likely with respect to applicants who are injured during preemployment physical ability tests, because their injuries arose prior to the formation of any definitive employment relationship. Consequently, individuals injured before commencing employment are not barred by workers' compensation from bringing actions in tort.

Dodson v. Workers' Compensation Division[1] concerned an individual given an offer of employment by Brown & Root that was conditioned upon his completion of a safety course at his own expense and his subsequent submission to a physical agility test administered under the direction and control of Brown & Root. He suffered a back injury during the physical agility test and sought compensation for his condition. Even though he was not remunerated for the time spent during that test, the court found that an employment contract had already been created between the parties prior to that test. It thus ruled that Dodson's injury had arisen during the course of his employment.

Once it is clear that specific persons have actually been employed, if they are injured while walking or riding to their assigned place of work on company premises or while leaving the personnel office on their way home to retrieve the personal items they need when they start work that afternoon, they would probably be found covered. Statutory protection would also be likely with respect to employees hired at one location who are involved in accidents while traveling on public thoroughfares to their appointed places of work, when their new employer either compensates them for their travel time or pays for their travel expenses.

Some companies require new personnel to complete trial periods before they attain "permanent" status. Individuals who sustain injuries during probationary periods associated with their work are clearly entitled to compensation. The fact that these "temporary" personnel have not yet achieved "permanent" status is irrelevant. So long as their injuries arose during the course of their preliminary employment, they are found eligible for benefits.

Workers who voluntarily relinquish their employment or who are involuntarily terminated must be given the opportunity to pick up their personal belongings and to leave firm premises. They also may be expected to retrieve their final pay checks before they depart. Individuals who sustain injuries while engaged in these activities within a reasonable period of time after the conclusion of their employment are usually found eligible for workers' compensation coverage, because these tasks are considered normal incidents of their employment.

Even when workers whose employment has been terminated remain briefly on company premises to consume food, they are likely to be accorded statutory coverage. Nonetheless, people who remain at work for extended periods of time after the conclusion of their employment to

§ 7.13

1. 210 W.Va. 636, 558 S.E.2d 635 (2001).

engage in wholly personal endeavors, usually forfeit their protection. Courts deciding these cases tend to evaluate the lapse of time between the end of claimant employment, the circumstances surrounding their injuries, and the personal nature of their conduct at the time of the critical events.

Many employees who quit or are discharged are unable to pick up their final pay checks on the date their employment is severed. They may return to firm premises several days later to do so. If they return within a reasonable period after their employment was terminated, their act is likely to be viewed as a final incident of their previous employment relationship. As a result, they will be given statutory coverage with respect to injuries they sustain while on company premises. Cases denying benefits to former employees who are injured while retrieving pay checks are usually based upon an inordinate delay between the dissolution of the employment relationship and the date chosen to obtain the checks. Similar rules are applied with respect to terminated workers who sustain injuries while collecting tools or other personal items at their place of employment several days after the severance of their employment. If they return within a reasonable period of time after the conclusion of their employment, statutory protection is normally available. Benefits tend to be denied only when there is a prolonged hiatus between the claimants' final day of work and the date they returned to retrieve their belongings.

§ 7.14 Arising Out of Employment

The overwhelming majority of state workers' compensation laws require claimants seeking benefits to demonstrate not only that they sustained injuries *during the course of* their employment, but also that their conditions *arose out of* their employment. Courts frequently have to determine the exact scope of these statutory concepts. They have generally recognized that the "course of employment" prerequisite concerns the time, location, and circumstances indigenous to the incident in question, while the "arising out of" component pertains to the underlying cause of claimant injuries.

Various risk concepts have been developed by courts attempting to distinguish between compensable and noncompensable injuries. When the operative circumstances are directly related to the employment of injured claimants, it is obvious that statutory coverage is available. For example, if a machine malfunctions and hurts the operator or a production process runs awry and exposes employees to hazardous substances, the resulting adverse consequences would undeniably arise out of the claimant employment. Many other industrial accident cases involve situations that are more equivocal.

Individuals may sustain injuries during the course of their employment that do not clearly arise out of their work. They may experience unexplainable accidents where the underlying cause is not discernible. For example, they may simply trip and fall on a carefully maintained shop floor. Employees may alternatively sustain injuries at work that are directly attributable to acts of nature. They may be struck by lightning or a falling tree during a storm. Workers may even be involved in vehicular accidents while traveling on public thoroughfares during the course of their employment.

People occasionally suffer injuries that are only related to their employment by virtue of the fact that the operative circumstances occurred at their place of work. For example, they may be struck by stray bullets or assaulted by fellow workers or perfect strangers. Employees may sustain injuries that are directly caused by their own personal situations. They may experience inexplicable dizzy spells or encounter idiopathic falls that appear to be related to their respective physiological compositions. Workers may have heart attacks or develop nervous disorders that are more indigenous to their personal circumstances than to their employment environments.

Employees sometimes suffer harm as a result of items they have brought to their place of employment. For example, they may be injured by a weapon they carried to work. They may become ill because of contaminated food or drink they brought from home. They may even be adversely affected by dangerous clothing they chose to wear in hazardous work environments.

Claimants who have suffered injuries that arose during and out of their employment may seek benefits for subsequently developed complications. Wounds may become infected or fractured bones may not heal properly. Compensable injuries may be exacerbated by careless medical treatment or by the fact that claimants have refused to undergo recommended medical procedures.

Administrative agencies and courts must frequently endeavor to differentiate between conditions that may reasonably be attributed to employment relationships and those that must realistically be considered beyond the scope of workers' compensation coverage. Because judges recognize that most individuals have minimal protection against nonoccupational injuries, there has been a marked tendency over the past fifty years to expand statutory coverage. The decisions moving in this direction have appropriately acknowledged the fact that employers are in a better position to spread the risk of marginal conditions than are individual employees.

§ 7.15 Arising Out of Employment—Traditional Risk Concepts

Some of the early court decisions interpreting workers' compensation enactments found it difficult to embrace the no-fault principle that constituted a fundamental aspect of these new statutes. They often required claimants to provide evidence demonstrating that their employment conditions significantly enhanced the likelihood that employees would suffer the type of harm involved. Under the "peculiar risk" approach, claimants could only obtain benefits if they could establish that their specific work subjected them to a quantitatively greater probability of the harm they sustained. If members of the general public were exposed to similar hazards, compensation would be denied.

Courts soon realized that the "peculiar risk" concept placed too great a burden upon injured workers seeking benefits. As a result, they replaced that approach with the less onerous "increased risk" doctrine that continues to be the predominant American standard. Claimants are no longer obliged to prove that their injuries were caused by risks that are peculiar to their employment. They are, however, required to demonstrate that their employment environment actually increased the likelihood of harm similar to that they sustained.

Moore v. City of Norman[1] involved a police officer who accidentally shot himself in the leg one morning while putting on his uniform at home. Police officers were required to take their guns home each evening. Since he had to put his gun on with his uniform each morning as he prepared to go to work, the court found that his injury arose out of his employment.

Courts that apply the "increased risk" doctrine to workers' compensation cases have developed a special rule for workers required by their employer to travel on public thoroughfares. When employees are injured in accidents while walking, driving, or riding on public roads in connection with their job duties, statutory protection is normally provided. This approach acknowledges that for traveling workers, street risks should be considered risks of their employment. These claimants merely have to demonstrate that the adverse consequences arose during the course of their employment. They are not obliged to establish that they were subject to greater risks of harm than ordinary travelers.

A number of courts have further expanded statutory protection through adoption of the "actual risk" doctrine. These decisions no longer insist upon a showing that claimants worked in settings that exposed them to a greater probability of injury. So long as the type of harm suffered may reasonably be considered a risk associated with the employment of benefit-seeking workers, compensation is available, even though members of the general public are exposed to similar danger.

Some courts have extended the "actual risk" approach through acceptance of the "positional risk" doctrine. Under this progressive formulation, injuries are considered to have arisen out of employment if claimants can establish that their adverse consequences would not have occurred *but for* the fact that their employment functions placed them in the positions in which they were injured. This expansive concept enables employees to obtain benefits for occurrences having no direct relationship to their employment beyond the fact they sustained their injuries while they were at work.

Despite their reliance upon the "increased risk," the "actual risk," and the "positional risk" doctrines, courts occasionally employ tradition-

§ **7.15**

1. 1999 OK 39, 983 P.2d 436 (1999).

al "proximate cause" constructs in workers' compensation cases. When judges utilize this approach, they require evidence that the harm in question resulted from foreseeable risks associated with the claimant's employment and was not superseded by independent intervening factors. Because workers' compensation statutes were designed to establish liability without fault, it seems inappropriate for judges to rely upon the proximate cause doctrine which was specifically developed to govern traditional tort actions grounded upon notions of defendant culpability. If courts would acknowledge that "arising out of" is not intended to be synonymous with "caused by," they would realize that application of the different risk constructs is more consistent with the underlying legislative intent than reliance upon proximate cause standards.

Types of Risks

Courts attempting to distinguish between compensable and noncompensable injuries arising during the course of employment have generally recognized three distinct types of risks. The first group covers "employment risks" that are directly associated with the work environment. These include dangerous equipment, malfunctioning machines, production processes that do not develop properly, and other similar situations. They also concern circumstances unique to employment settings that enhance the likelihood that employees will contract occupational diseases. Legislators certainly envisioned these "employment risks" when they enacted workers' compensation statutes. Injuries caused by these factors are uniformly regarded as having arisen out of employment.

The second category includes "neutral risks" that are neither employment related nor personal to the individuals involved. These entail acts of nature that affect employees while they are at work. Persons may be struck by lightning or falling tree limbs. They may alternatively be injured by external human factors. They may be attacked by strangers or hit by stray bullets. "Neutral risks" also concern accidental injuries that have no apparent cause. For example, workers may inexplicably trip and fall or simply expire from indeterminate causes. Various theories have been developed by courts endeavoring to distinguish between covered and noncovered injuries generated by "neutral risks."

The third group concerns "personal risks" that are related to particular individuals. These risks include persons with heart or vascular conditions who suffer heart attacks or strokes while at work. It also covers workers with other medical disorders that coincidentally manifest themselves in the employment environment. This category even entails dangers that are brought into the work setting by employees themselves. For example, individuals may carry weapons to work or bring in contaminated food or drink. Courts frequently deny compensation to claimants injured at their place of employment by risks personal to themselves, due to the absence of any meaningful causal connection to their employment.

§ 7.16 Arising Out of Employment—Acts of Nature

Employees are occasionally injured during the course of their employment by acts of nature. They may be affected by lightning, wind, earthquakes, or extreme temperatures. Courts have traditionally recognized that claimants who can demonstrate that the nature of their particular employment increased the risk of the harm involved are entitled to benefits. Even when claimant employment does not increase the risk of injury, many courts still provide statutory protection for individuals hurt by acts of nature at work if they are affected by contact with part of their employer's premises. A growing number of courts have further expanded protection in this area through adoption of the "actual risk" or the "positional risk" concept. Under these approaches, coverage is often provided to employees injured while in employment settings, regardless of whether their work enhanced the likelihood of harm.

Many court decisions have involved injuries caused by lightning. Courts applying the "increased risk" doctrine require claimants to show that their specific employment enlarged the probability of harm. For example, because lightning tends to strike prominent points, courts usually award benefits to employees injured while working in high places. They may be performing services on hilltops, roofs, or scaffolding. They may be exposed to a greater risk of lightning by virtue of the fact they are working under a tall tree or are located near large metal objects likely to attract lightning.

Some courts have evidenced a willingness to cover even lightning-related injuries that do not arise in circumstances entailing a greater probability of harm. Through application of either the "actual risk" or the "positional risk" concept, they provide protection for injuries that may reasonably be characterized as actual risks of employment or that affect employees because of the location they are working when the critical circumstances arise. The same doctrines are applied to injuries caused by hurricanes, tornadoes, and earthquakes. Because these acts of nature tend to affect everyone in their path regardless of whether they are at work, home, or someplace else, it is difficult for claimants injured by these storms at work to demonstrate that their employment increased the risk of harm. In states applying the conventional "increased risk" concept, statutory protection is only accorded to employees who can establish that their particular employment duties meaningfully enhanced the probability of harm. They may satisfy this burden by showing that they were working in places that exposed them to greater risks or were assigned to work in buildings that lacked the structural integrity to withstand even moderate natural calamities.

When claimants are unable to demonstrate that they were subject to a greater likelihood of storm injury because of their employment, a number of "increased risk" jurisdictions still award benefits if claimants can prove that their conditions were caused by physical contact with parts of their employer's premises. They are thus entitled to compensation for harm caused by glass from broken windows, flying brick or lumber, collapsed roofs, or fallen walls. Courts that apply the "street risk" doctrine to injuries sustained by employees on public thorough-fares while carrying out their job functions often use this approach to cover workers injured by storms while they are traveling on behalf of their employer. A few states have decided to extend statutory coverage in this area through application of the "positional risk" approach. They thus provide protection to individuals injured by hurricanes, tornadoes, and earthquakes that affect them while they are at their place of work.

Employees who work outdoors may suffer injuries such as frostbite, pneumonia, sunstroke, or related conditions caused by their exposure to extreme temperatures. If they can demonstrate that their job functions increased the risk of these maladies, courts would normally find that their injuries arose out of their employment. Judges have occasionally failed to acknowledge that the appropriate comparison is not with other outdoor workers, but with members of the general public. If only one member of an outdoor crew contracts heatstroke or frostbite, these judges refuse to award benefits because the claimant was exposed to the same risk as the other crew members who were not adversely affected by the elements. The proper comparison, however, should be made with members of the general public. So long as the evidence indicates that outdoor workers were exposed to a greater risk of heat or cold than ordinary persons, this "increased risk" should be sufficient to establish that their temperature-related conditions arose out of their employment. The fact that their fellow employees did not sustain injuries from their similar exposure should not preclude awards of benefits to those workers who were affected by the elements.

Some states have expanded statutory protection for outdoor workers through application of the "actual risk" doctrine. Claimants who are able to demonstrate that their medical conditions arose from actual risks associated with their outdoor employment are granted benefits, even though they were not exposed to a significantly greater likelihood of harm than members of the general public. Courts have generally been unwilling to apply the "positional risk" concept to cases involving exposure to the elements, because this approach would provide outdoor workers with virtually unlimited coverage.

Similar issues are raised by claimants who seek compensation for illnesses caused by their exposure to contagious diseases at work. Most courts limit coverage to claimants who are able to demonstrate that their particular employment exposed them to an "increased risk" of contagion than ordinary citizens. Classic cases involve health care employees who have regular contact with infected patients. Other cases consistently sustaining benefit awards concern individuals whose specific job func-tions require them to work in unsanitary environments that entail increased risk of infection. Courts often reach conflicting results, howev-er, with respect to claimants who appear to have contracted contagious diseases from fellow employees. When they can show that their job duties necessitated unusually close contact with infected coworkers, statutory protection is normally provided, due to the increased probability of contagion. Nonetheless, when claimants are unable to prove that their employment increased the risk of illness, they are unlikely to obtain benefits.

§ 7.17 Arising Out of Employment—Street Risks

Some employees regularly travel on public roads and conveyances in connection with their employment. They may be truck drivers, traveling salespeople, solicitors, delivery workers, or taxi drivers. Other personnel are occasionally required to journey from place to place during their employment. They may be directed to go from one facility to another, or to visit a supplier or customer. While workers are engaged in these excursions they may be injured in vehicular accidents or sidewalk falls. Although it would be clear that their injuries arose *during* their employment, it would not be certain, under the traditional "increased risk" doctrine, that their injuries *arose out of* their employment.

Courts quickly recognized that application of the "increased risk" concept to persons injured during work-related travel created harsh results. Only those claimants who could demonstrate that their work-related travel involved a greater likelihood of harm than was encountered by ordinary travel were entitled to statutory protection. Because judges concluded that this approach was unfair to other employees who were required to take journeys on behalf of their employer, they formulated the "street risk" doctrine.

Under the generally followed "street risk" rule, injuries sustained by workers while they are walking, driving, or riding on public thoroughfares during the course of their employment are given statutory protection. The adverse consequences suffered in these accidents are simply regarded as arising out of their employment, even when the claimants are unable to establish that their work-related travel exposed them to a greater probability of harm than other travelers. The risks associated with streets and highways are simply considered compensable risks of employment for such employees. Claimants injured in vehicular accidents while traveling on behalf of their employer are merely obliged to prove that the relevant incidents occurred during the course of their employment.

The "street risk" doctrine has been applied to diverse accident cases. It has been used to sustain benefit awards to a station attendant struck by a car while crossing the street to make a bank deposit, a construction supervisor injured while crossing the road to reach a telephone, an employee who fell on an icy sidewalk during a work-related errand, and a bookkeeper struck by a car while walking back to the office after mailing several business letters.

The early "street risk" cases usually concerned injuries sustained by employees in vehicular accidents or sidewalk falls. Some courts, however, began to acknowledge that employees who travel on public thoroughfares frequently encounter other dangers that are not directly related to their physical movement.

They have thus expanded the "street risk" concept to cover more than travel-related perils have accorded statutory protection to traveling employees struck by stray bullets, hit by falling debris, stabbed by mentally disturbed persons, harmed by thrown objects, and injured during criminal assaults. Under this comprehensive "street risk" approach, courts normally cover all injuries sustained by employees while they are traveling during the course of their employment.

§ 7.18 Arising Out of Employment—Positional Risks

A majority of courts continue to require claimants to establish that their employment exposed them to a greater risk of relevant harm than is normally experienced by members of the general public. The only significant exception concerns "street risk" cases in which courts provide statutory protection for most, if not all, injuries sustained by employees while they are traveling on public thoroughfares during the course of their employment. A growing number of courts have concluded that the "street risk" concept should be extended to other work-related situations. To accomplish this objective, they have developed the "positional risk" doctrine.

The jurisdictions that apply the "positional risk" formulation tend to award benefits to claimants who can establish that their employment required them to occupy locations that contained the hazards that caused their injuries. Courts applying the "positional risk" doctrine achieve results similar to those reached in "street risk" cases, but they cover dangers encountered throughout the employment relationship. These states have effectively subsumed the "arising out of" prerequisite into the "arising during the course of" requirement. So long as claimants can demonstrate that their conditions arose during the course of their employment, statutory protection is made available to them.

An unusual number of early "positional risk" cases concerned employees injured in the work environment by stray bullets. Although the "street risk" concept had been created to cover these occurrences on public thoroughfares, that doctrine was not initially applicable to wounds sustained on firm premises. Nonetheless, courts in several states have expanded statutory protection for individuals hit by stray bullets without expressly modifying the traditional "street risk" doctrine. For example, New York decisions have upheld benefit awards to workers injured in their employment settings by bullets fired by police officers or strangers. Because the claimants involved in these cases had been struck by stray bullets fired by persons on public streets, the courts concluded that their adverse consequences were caused by "street risks." It must be acknowledged that the "street risk" concept has usually been confined to injuries sustained by workers while they—rather than the individuals causing the harm—were on public streets and sidewalks. Furthermore, it would be extremely difficult to utilize the conventional "street risk" approach to protect workers injured by bullets fired within the shop by other people.

Courts wishing to provide statutory protection for workers injured by neutral risks in the employment setting have usually adopted the "positional risk" approach. For example, judges in states like California, Louisiana, Massachusetts, and New Jersey have decided to cover employees struck at work by stray bullets or other objects emanating from persons outside the employment environment. This expanded protection transcends that available to workers under the traditional "increased risk" doctrine. Courts applying the "increased risk" rule continue to limit awards for such injuries to circumstances in which claimant employment actually exposes employees to a greater probability of harm from such external factors than is encountered by members of the general public. To be eligible for compensation, injured workers must be able to demonstrate that their employment facility is located in an unusually dangerous neighborhood. When they are not able to establish the requisite "increased risk," they are usually denied coverage by the majority of courts that have not adopted the "positional risk" concept.

Similar "arising out of" issues are raised with respect to employees injured in unexplained accidents. For example, individuals may inexplicably fall during the course of their employment. Because claimants hurt in unexplained fall cases are generally unable to demonstrate that their job duties exposed them to a greater probability of harm, it is not possible for courts applying the conventional "increased risk" doctrine to award them benefits. This realization has induced a number of courts to deny compensation in these cases.

A majority of contemporary courts have decided that statutory coverage should be extended to employees who suffer unexplained falls during the course of their employment. They generally find the fact that these incidents occur while the claimants are performing employment-related tasks sufficient to support a conclusion that the harm arose out of their employment. These decisions tend to utilize reasoning analogous to that used in "positional risk" jurisdictions. "[W]here the employee, while about his work, suffers an injury in the ordinary course of the employment, the cause of which is unexplained but which is a natural and probable result of a risk thereof, and the Commission finds from all the attendant facts and circumstances that the injury arose out of the employment, an award will be sustained."[1]

Courts often distinguish between unexplained falls and idiopathic falls. In unexplained fall cases, there is no reason to suspect that circumstances unique to the affected workers caused the resulting harm. Idiopathic fall cases, on the other hand, involve incidents attributable to physical or mental conditions personal to the particular employees. Unlike unexplained falls that concern neutral risks indigenous to the work environment, idiopathic falls relate to wholly personal risks independent of the employment setting. When victims of idiopathic falls are

§ 7.18

1. Robbins v. Bossong Hosiery Mills, 220 N.C. 246, 17 S.E.2d 20, 21 (1941).

able to establish that their employment environment contributed to their injuries, as where they suffer dizzy spells and fall off ladders or strike their heads on machines, this employment connection would usually be enough to warrant complete coverage. Nonetheless, when no such employment nexus can be shown and the evidence indicates that personal claimant circumstances—e.g., epilepsy, vertigo, or a similar condition—precipitated the fall, statutory coverage would normally be denied.

The unexplained/idiopathic distinction also arises with respect to deaths at work that have no clear explanation. When employees die during the course of their employment on firm premises, most courts tend to assume that the fatal conditions arose out of their employment. They treat these circumstances as neutral risk cases and effectively apply "positional risk" concepts. Only when it is clear that deaths are caused by personal conditions that are not exacerbated by employment-related factors is compensation likely to be denied.

§ 7.19   Arising Out of Employment—Personal Assaults

Claimants are occasionally injured during the course of their employment by assaults committed on them by fellow employees, other third parties, or strangers. Individuals who can demonstrate that their particular job duties exposed them to a greater likelihood of attack than ordinary citizens may normally obtain benefits under the conventional "increased risk" approach. Statutory protection is thus provided to public safety personnel, plant guards, couriers carrying valuable items, cashiers, supervisors who direct the work of others, bartenders, bus and taxi drivers, and other workers whose job functions are likely to precipitate physical responses from displeased parties.

Rank-and-file employees assaulted by angry supervisors are normally entitled to compensation in "increased risk" jurisdictions. When employees suffer emotional injuries as a result of sexually harassing conduct by supervisory personnel, some courts similarly find the resulting injuries to have arisen out of claimant employment, while others refuse to do so because of the lack of any apparent increased risk of such harassment. Coverage is usually provided to persons struck by fellow employees during arguments over their job responsibilities or altercations generated by labor disputes because of the direct connection between such incidents and employment circumstances. Courts are only likely to deny statutory protection in those cases in which the disputants had adequate time to calm down between their employment-related disputes and their physical confrontations. When sufficient time has elapsed between the critical events, judges often find the subsequent fights personal, rather than job-related. Since coworkers do not possess the managerial authority of supervisory personnel, verbal and physical sexual harassment by one employee against another may not be found compensable due to the lack of any increased risk of such conduct.

When assaults by fellow employees have no meaningful employment connection and are truly personal in nature, they are generally found beyond the scope of compensation coverage. Nonetheless, close cases involving altercations that have been generated by both personal and employment-related considerations may be granted coverage. In *Stivison v. Goodyear Tire & Rubber Co.*,[1] however, the court refused to extend statutory coverage to an individual assaulted by a fellow employee at a restaurant located near company premises shortly after the conclusion of the work day, even though the fight was in retaliation for the claimant's having informed management that the other worker had violated company rules. The court based its decision on the fact the employer exercised no control over the restaurant and derived no benefit from the claimant's presence at that establishment.

The "increased risk" doctrine also protects employees who must work in environments that are more dangerous than typical public locations. As a result, compensation is generally awarded to individuals assaulted while they are working in high crime neighborhoods. Courts frequently find the risk of assault greater with respect to persons who are required to work in isolated settings, during late night hours, or to park in dimly-lit parking lots.

When claimants are unable to establish that their job functions, work environments, or shift schedules exposed them to a greater probability of assault than members of the general public, the majority of courts that continue to apply the "increased risk" concept are unlikely to provide them with statutory coverage. They can only enhance the likelihood of coverage by proving that they were assaulted on a public thoroughfare during the course of their employment. When these factors are present, they can rely upon the "street risk" approach to obtain compensation without having to show that their specific job duties increased the probability of personal assaults.

Some courts have further expanded statutory coverage through application of the "positional risk" formulation to assault cases. These decisions recognize that the possibility of assault by fellow workers or strangers constitutes a compensable risk of one's employment. Courts applying the "positional risk" doctrine to assault cases generally award benefits in all cases involving employment-related altercations. Nonetheless, they still require evidence that the dispute arose during the course of claimant employment. When it is clear that the underlying animosity developed outside the employment environment due to wholly personal considerations, statutory coverage will generally be denied even though the physical assault occurred at work.

Employees are sometimes assaulted during the course of their employment at work by deranged strangers. If their job duties do not expose them to a greater likelihood of these attacks, they are normally denied coverage in traditional "increased risk" states. "Positional risk" jurisdictions, however, usually award compensation to these victims.

§ 7.19

1. 80 Ohio St.3d 498, 687 N.E.2d 458, 1997 Ohio 321 (1997).

They appropriately recognize that claimant employment positions exposed them to the harm they suffered.

During the first half of the twentieth century, courts uniformly refused to permit assault victims to obtain compensation when the evidence indicated that the claimants instigated the altercations. Some jurisdictions continue to apply the "aggressor" doctrine and deny statutory protection to individuals who are hurt in physical confrontations precipitated by their own conduct. Courts following this approach usually find that the culpability of the aggressor either severed the requisite connection to the employment relationship or rendered the claimant undeserving of statutory protection. Most jurisdictions, however, have rejected the "aggressor" approach and no longer refuse to award benefits to all persons who initiate employment conflicts. They find no reason to believe that state legislatures that created no-fault compensation systems intended to disqualify persons based upon such a culpability concept.

Twenty-three state laws and the Federal Employees Compensation Act contain specific provisions disqualifying claimants whose injuries are caused by their intentional efforts to injure other people. Fifteen statutes limit coverage in this area by expressly disqualifying benefit applicants who are hurt because of their own willful misconduct. Nonetheless, courts in these states do not deny compensation to all claimants injured in confrontations initiated by them. They tend to limit these exclusions to individuals who precipitate altercations through deliberate and premeditated aggression of a serious nature. As a result, impulsive behavior, mere profanity, and even minimal shoving are often found insufficient to warrant a loss of protection under "willful misconduct" provisions.

§ 7.20 Arising Out of Employment—Personal Risks

Employees are frequently injured, not by employment risks associated with their work or by neutral risks indigenous to their employment environments, but by personal risks unique to themselves. Classic cases involve idiopathic falls that result from nonoccupational heart attacks, epileptic seizures, vertigo, or other similar conditions. Should the adverse consequences generated by these conditions be subject to workers' compensation coverage? Unless claimants are able to demonstrate that their job duties contributed to their injuries by increasing the risk of a seizure or an attack or through circumstances exacerbating the effects of their ailments, compensation is usually denied.

When it is clear that idiopathic fall injuries have been entirely caused by medical conditions unique to claimants and have not been aggravated by employment-related factors, benefits are not available. The resulting harm in these cases cannot reasonably be considered to have "arisen out of" claimant employment. The work environment merely provided the coincidental setting for events that could just as easily have occurred in other locations.

Victims of idiopathic falls can obtain benefits if they can establish that the work environment meaningfully contributed to the harm sustained. For example, if people are required to work on ladders or scaffolds and they are injured by falls from those heights, statutory coverage would probably be found. Benefit awards are also likely when employees fall onto machines or other employment-related objects that aggravate their resulting conditions. Compensation is provided in these situations because of the obvious connection between the employment setting and the claimant harm.

Some of the most controverted idiopathic fall cases involve employees who collapse on flat surfaces and are injured when they strike the floor. Most jurisdictions refuse to award benefits to persons hurt in such falls. They logically recognize that the degree of harm caused by the floor is not meaningfully different from the type of harm that would have resulted if the falls had occurred in nonwork settings. Some courts, however, provide statutory coverage in these cases. They usually note that protection is available to employees who strike their heads on production equipment or other work-related objects, and they conclude that shop floors should be treated in a similar manner. While this approach is understandable with respect to falls onto unusually hard cement floors found in many work environments, it is not as defensible with respect to falls onto surfaces that are analogous to those found in typical claimant homes.

Victims of other idiopathic conditions that flare up in work settings may obtain statutory protection if they can establish that employment-related stress, excitement, or exertion aggravated or accelerated their preexisting infirmities. For example, individuals whose pulmonary conditions, such as asthma or lung cancer, are aggravated by the inhalation of particles found in work environments are likely to obtain benefits. Statutory coverage is also likely with respect to workers whose preexisting back weaknesses or heart conditions are aggravated or accelerated by job-related stress, excitement, or exertion. Many courts also cover nervous disorders that are exacerbated by job stress. The fact that the employment environment meaningfully contributes to the final result in these situations is considered sufficient to establish the requisite employment connection. Although the pertinent work-related stress or strain might not cause problems for persons without preexisting personal weaknesses, courts emphasize that workers' compensation laws require employers to take their employees as they find them. Firms are thus held responsible for preexisting personal conditions that are aggravated by employment-related circumstances.

Because many personal risk cases concern preexisting weaknesses or predispositions that have allegedly been aggravated by job-related circumstances, medical testimony is often determinative. To obtain benefits, claimants must be able to establish a causal connection between the employment environment and the relevant harm. Some of the most controverted cases involve medical conditions having no universally accepted causes. Classic cases involve forms of cancer workers claim were exacerbated by job-related factors.

Claimants who are able to demonstrate that employment-related stress, excitement, or exertion meaningfully exacerbated preexisting personal conditions are entitled to compensation. Although five state enactments limit benefit eligibility to the proportion of the resulting harm attributable to job-related factors, courts in the other forty-five states make no such apportionment. Employers are normally held responsible for the entire conditions, even though nonwork factors contributed to the ultimate result.

§ 7.21 Arising Out of Employment—Imported Risks

Employees are occasionally injured at work by personal risks they bring into the employment environment. They may become ill after consuming contaminated food or drink brought from home. Some may be burned while lighting a match or a cigarette. A few may even be wounded by weapons they decide to carry to work. Unless these claimants can demonstrate that their job functions or the employment environment contributed to their plight, statutory coverage normally will be denied.

It is generally recognized that eating and drinking on employer premises constitute covered activities under the personal comfort doctrine. Statutory protection is normally granted with respect to employees harmed by food or drink obtained from their employer's cafeteria or vending machines. Benefits also tend to be awarded to individuals who are required by their employment situations to eat their own meals at near-by restaurants and who become ill as a result of contaminated food. In these cases, the contaminated food is either furnished by the employer or is obtained from commercial establishments the employees were obliged to visit because of their job duties. The rationales underlying these decisions would not readily apply to food and drink imported from home or from commercial eateries for wholly personal reasons. It would be difficult for courts to conclude that harm caused by food and drink brought to work by employees for their own convenience "arose out of" their employment. Only an expansive application of the "positional risk" doctrine would be likely to protect these claimants.

Because cigarette smoking continues to be tolerated during work breaks by most employers, accidents caused by matches, lighters, or cigarettes on firm premises are usually found covered. These activities are viewed as personal ministrations that constitute incidental aspects of the employment relationship. The resulting injuries are thus regarded by most courts as "arising out of" the claimant's employment.

A number of cases concern people injured by guns carried to work. Many hunters are accidently shot while handling guns or related items near their vehicles in company parking lots. When the pertinent circumstances have no reasonable connection to employment, the resulting injuries are generally found beyond the scope of statutory protection.

Coverage is often provided, however, with respect to persons injured by weapons possessed for work-related reasons. For example, compensation would probably be granted to persons shot by guns they carried for protection because of their work in dangerous environments.

§ 7.22 Arising Out of Employment—The Direct and Proximate Consequences

When employees sustain injuries that arise out of and during the course of their employment, they are clearly entitled to workers' compensation coverage. Statutory protection will be available not only for their immediate conditions, but also for the direct and natural consequences of their original injuries. This extended coverage includes aggravation of their initial conditions caused by imperfect medical treatment, as well as subsequent complications resulting from their original injuries. It is even likely to include the results of accidents suffered while claimants are traveling to and from treatment centers. Should benefits be provided for aggravation generated by careless self-treatment or by the refusal of claimants to obtain proper medical treatment? If a weakened condition contributes to a subsequent fall or injury, should compensation be provided for the new predicament?

Workers who sustain employment-related injuries must frequently obtain medical treatment. Courts appropriately recognize that imperfect treatment is a reasonably foreseeable consequence of those injuries. As a result, it is universally acknowledged that the results of careless treatment constitute compensable conditions. For example, exacerbation of initial injuries caused by unsanitary instruments, antibiotics, antitoxins, pain killers, or sedatives would normally be covered. If employees undergo surgical procedures to diagnose or treat job-related injuries, complications resulting from the surgery would be considered compensable. Statutory coverage is also available for entirely new conditions, such as impotence, heart and vascular problems, neurosis, or similar maladies, found to be direct and natural consequences of the treatment. The dependents of workers who die during medical procedures necessitated by employment-connected injuries are entitled to statutorily-prescribed death benefits.

Claimants wishing to obtain workers' compensation for injuries aggravated by careless medical treatment are not obliged to establish negligent conduct. So long as they can demonstrate that their aggravated conditions are the direct and natural consequence of their employment-related incidents, they are entitled to statutory protection. Furthermore, the fact that the health care professionals acted negligently or even recklessly does not normally sever the causal link to their original injuries. Although that issue would be relevant if the claimants were to prosecute third-party tort actions against the responsible parties, it would have no relevance with respect to their right to receive statutory benefits.

Claimants who experience severe discomfort from employment-generated conditions may use prescription drugs or alcohol to alleviate their pain. Individuals may become dependent upon the drugs or alcohol. A number of decisions have found that these personal problems constitute compensable disorders. They have merely required claimants to establish that their drug or alcohol addictions were the foreseeable consequence of their employment-related situations. Other courts, however, have refused to extend statutory coverage to these conditions due to the absence of a clear causal connection or the presence of a statutory provision specifically excluding drug and alcohol problems.

Treatment for compensable injuries may occasionally exacerbate preexisting conditions. Courts generally find aggravation of preexisting conditions subject to statutory coverage as foreseeable results of the work-related circumstances. Typical preexisting conditions aggravated by job-connected incidents include heart disease, phlebitis, varicose veins, pyorrhea, back problems, cancer, and mental disorders. Courts reasonably conclude that these preexisting circumstances would not have become serious problems so quickly had it not been for the impact of the job-related events. These results are thus considered direct and natural consequences of the original injuries.

When compensable injuries prevent treatment of preexisting conditions and those independent maladies deteriorate due to a lack of effective therapy, statutory coverage is generally extended to the worsened preexisting conditions. Typical cases have involved an existing cancer that could not be removed due to an employment-generated infection, an aneurysm that could not be repaired because of a job-related respiratory condition, and a hernia that could not be corrected due to a compensable heart condition. The fact that these preexisting disorders deteriorated because of employment-connected events is sufficient to render them direct and natural consequences of the covered incidents.

Employees injured in employment-related incidents often have to travel to medical offices or hospitals for treatment. Some are required to make return visits for additional treatment. It is not unusual for claimants to sustain further injuries in accidents during their trips to and from these treatment locations. Because their travel is a direct and natural result of their compensable injuries, most courts appropriately recognize that the complications or independent medical problems caused in travel-related accidents should be given statutory coverage. Nonetheless, occasional decisions still refuse to provide statutory protection for these trips, viewing them as outside the course of claimant employment.

Compensable injuries are sometimes worsened by the conduct of claimants themselves. They may negligently treat their own wounds or obtain the assistance of charlatans. They may alternatively refuse to submit to treatment recommended by medical experts. Employers responsible for their initial injuries may challenge the right of these claimants to statutory coverage for the problems precipitated by their own careless treatment or that of unqualified persons, or by their unwillingness to permit proposed medical procedures to be performed. So long as claimant conduct in these regards is not found wholly unreasonable, coverage is usually provided for their aggravated conditions.

Courts properly acknowledge that most individuals who endeavor to treat their own maladies are not health care professionals. Negligent self-treatment is thus considered a foreseeable risk associated with work-related injuries. If claimants worsen their conditions through merely negligent self-treatment, statutory protection is normally provided. Coverage for their exacerbated conditions is only likely to be denied where courts conclude that their own behavior was entirely unreasonable.

Benefits are also denied for aggravation caused by reckless claimant conduct that interferes with the healing process. For example, if claimants participate in athletic events that impede their recovery or perform personal tasks that unreasonably worsen their conditions, they will forfeit coverage with respect to the problems created by their irresponsible behavior. Claimants who ignore specific physician warnings and exacerbate existing compensable conditions through improperly strenuous lifting at work may be denied coverage for their additional injuries, with those conditions being considered caused by deliberate employee misconduct. Because judges view resort to unqualified charlatan healers as completely irrational acts, they generally find that such conduct severs the causal connection between the prior employment-related event and the aggravated result. They thus refuse to provide statutory protection for the difficulties precipitated by such treatment.

Some victims of job-related injuries refuse to allow recommended medical procedures to be performed on themselves. If these decisions inhibit recovery or worsen their conditions, should statutory protection be provided? The answer to this question is usually determined by the reasonableness of their conduct. Courts balance the likely success of the proposed course of treatment against the risk of harm involved. When the probability of medical success is high and the risk to the claimant is minimal, that person's wholly unreasonable refusal to submit to treatment will normally preclude compensation for the aggravation of the original condition attributable to the lack of appropriate treatment. The most shocking cases involve claimants who simply decline to obtain any medical treatment for conditions that require professional care. Other cases resulting in a loss of benefits concern individuals who refuse to have safe diagnostic examinations performed. Some of the most controverted circumstances involve claimants with back problems who decline to permit myelograms to be performed. A majority of courts find the risks and discomfort associated with this procedure sufficient to excuse the unwillingness of persons to undergo the test. A few courts, however, reach the opposite conclusion.

Claimants who fail to engage in prescribed exercise, alcohol detoxification, or other rehabilitative regimens are likely to be denied statutory protection for the aggravation attributable to their omissions. Courts are less strict, however, with respect to claimants who are unable to follow prescribed weight-loss programs. Judges apparently empathize with individuals who find it difficult to lose weight. A loss of benefits is less likely when claimants receive conflicting treatment plans from different physicians and they choose to follow the advice of their personal doctor.

What if claimants refuse to take prescribed medication designed to lessen the pain caused by occupational conditions? In *Vaughan v. State ex rel. Wyoming Workers' Compensation Division*,[1] the court held that a claimant's unwillingness to become dependent upon non-narcotic prescription pain medication did not provide a basis for denying him permanent and total disability benefits. The court found that his actions did not constitute an unreasonable refusal to obtain appropriate treatment for his debilitating pain.

Injured workers are frequently hesitant to undergo surgical procedures. If the probability of success is high and the risk of adverse consequences is minimal, a refusal to have recommended surgery performed is likely to result in a loss of benefits. On the other hand, if there is a real possibility of harm and it is not clear that surgery will rectify the existing condition, coverage will not usually be denied to a person who declines a proposed procedure. Typical cases in this group involve claimants suffering from hernias and disc problems. Close cases tend to be resolved in favor of continued statutory coverage.

When courts determine that the benefit to be derived from a proposed surgical procedure clearly outweighs the minimal risk involved, it is usually impossible for claimants to avoid a loss of continued coverage. The mere fact that they are subjectively afraid of surgery or anesthesia is normally insufficient to excuse their otherwise unreasonable failure to acquiesce in the recommended procedure. Many courts even refuse to permit reliance upon religious convictions forbidding medical treatment to justify an unwillingness to have appropriate surgery performed. Other courts, however, recognize the First Amendment free exercise issues raised by these situations and uphold the right of individuals with contrary religious beliefs to reject proposed medical treatment.

Various workers' compensation statutes provide that claimants must obtain treatment from employer or commission approved physicians. Injured workers occasionally ignore this requirement and visit other health care professionals. When the treatment they receive exacerbates their conditions, their employer often challenges their right to coverage with respect to the aggravated aspects. It is generally recognized that the employer is not liable for the cost of the medical treatment obtained from unapproved physicians unless the claimants can establish that relevant circumstances induced them to seek the assistance of the doctors they chose. Nonetheless, while a few courts have also found that complications caused by unapproved physicians are not compensable,

§ 7.22
1. 2002 WY 131, 53 P.3d 559 (2002).

most have decided to provide coverage when it appears that the claimants choice of doctors was not unreasonable.

Employees who have sustained compensable injuries at work occasionally suffer subsequent injuries outside the employment environment that are at least partially attributable to their previously weakened conditions. If the latter events do not arise out of and during the course of their employment, they would not themselves constitute covered situations. Nevertheless, when claimants can demonstrate a reasonable causal relationship between their prior compensable injuries and their subsequent conditions, statutory protection is normally available for their most recent circumstances. For example, if they sustain nonoccupational falls because of previously weakened legs, ankles, knees, or feet, their resulting conditions would usually be covered. Compensation would also be awarded to claimants who fall off ladders or down stairs as a result of poor balance caused by previously sustained, work-related arm or head injuries.

Even when the prior occupational injuries do not directly cause the subsequent nonoccupational accidents, compensation may still be available for the resulting harm. Claimants need only establish a reasonable relationship between the previous, employment-related events and the current incidents to be eligible for benefits. They may accomplish this by showing that the earlier accidents weakened limbs and made them more susceptible to the types of fractures experienced in the present incidents. Similar reasoning is frequently utilized to provide statutory protection for current heart attacks, leg injuries, and back problems that can be attributed to preexisting weaknesses caused by prior job-related events.

Because statutory coverage is only available for nonoccupational injuries attributable in meaningful part to previous, employment-related conditions, the traditional workers' compensation "no-fault" concept is not directly applicable to these cases. As a result, courts are willing to find that claimant negligence pertaining to current accidents severed the causal link to the prior compensable events. For example, when courts conclude that persons negligently disregarded existing weaknesses and precipitated avoidable injuries, they usually refuse to award benefits for these nonoccupational difficulties. Nonetheless, close cases tend to be resolved in favor of continued coverage. So long as the present, nonoccupational situation is not caused by obvious claimant carelessness, benefits are likely to be awarded if there is any real nexus between the current problems and the prior work-connected injuries.

§ 7.23 Causation

The mere fact that physical or mental conditions arise during the course of employment does not necessarily indicate that workers' compensation coverage will be available. The claimants must also be able to demonstrate that their conditions arose out of their employment. The "arising out of" component is generally considered to include a causation element. To establish that particular injuries arose out of their employment, claimants must usually show a causal connection to their job situations.

Workers' compensation laws in all but ten states either expressly or impliedly mandate proof that injuries were caused by "accidental" events. In jurisdictions that have this requirement, it is generally recognized that claimants are obliged to demonstrate that the circumstances generating their conditions were of an unexpected nature. As a result, if their injury was caused by their own intentional conduct, they will normally be found ineligible for benefits.

Many courts employ a second evidentiary test with respect to the "accidental" injury prerequisite. They require proof that the pertinent incident took place within a relatively definite time frame. This concept becomes especially important with respect to conditions that develop gradually, rather than instantaneously, such as repetitive motion maladies or occupational diseases.

The workers' compensation "exertion" cases most likely to result in benefit awards involve job activities causing immediate "breakage"—i.e., sudden structural changes in the body. For example, almost all jurisdictions provide statutory protection for workers who sustain hernias while performing their normal employment functions. Their conditions clearly arise out of and during the course of their employment, and the fact that their hernias developed unexpectedly and instantly would be sufficient to render them "accidental." Only North Carolina continues to deny coverage for hernias that result from usual efforts and requires evidence of uncommon job exertion.

Similar rules are applied to work-related endeavors that precipitate relatively instantaneous herniated discs, ruptured aneurysms, hemorrhages, or strokes. The vast majority of states find these conditions compensable, even when they result from normal job exertion. The fact that these injuries arise in a relatively immediate fashion is sufficient to establish their "accidental" nature. Nonetheless, a few jurisdictions continue to deny coverage for these conditions when they result from ordinary job exertion. They only award benefits when the conditions are caused by abnormal work effort.

When the conditions in dispute arise out of and during the course of employment and occur at identifiable moments, statutory coverage is generally provided. These cases clearly involve "accidental" injuries of the variety state legislatures intended to include within the expansive scope of workers' compensation enactments. The fact that the operative circumstances have merely involved usual work exertion should not preclude benefit awards. The few jurisdictions that continue to require evidence of abnormal exertion in these cases unreasonably limit the statutory protection available to injured workers.

Heart Conditions

Workers regularly seek benefits for heart attacks, heart disease, and related conditions they claim were caused or aggravated by employment exertion. Employers frequently contest these cases, contending that the claimants suffered from preexisting heart conditions that had no relationship to their employment. Courts have to determine the degree of work exertion that must be shown to make these conditions compensable. They also have to decide whether the existence of nonoccupational heart weaknesses should affect the right of claimants to obtain compensation.

The majority of states have adopted the usual exertion approach. Claimants who sustain heart injuries while engaged in normal work exertion are entitled to benefits in these jurisdictions. They are merely obliged to demonstrate that their conditions arose out of and during the course of their employment. Because employers take their employees as they find them, the fact that these persons have preexisting heart conditions does not preclude coverage for work-related exacerbations. Courts applying the usual exertion doctrine even sustain benefit awards for heart problems that do not manifest themselves instantaneously. So long as claimants can establish that job exertion meaningfully contributed to their conditions, statutory protection is provided, even though their injuries did not become apparent until that evening or the next day.

A sizable minority of jurisdictions have decided that statutory protection should not be extended to heart problems that only have an attenuated connection to the employment relationship. These courts recognize that heart conditions are often caused by congenital weaknesses or other circumstances that affect many members of the general public. They thus believe that benefits should only be awarded to claimants who can demonstrate that their injuries were caused by unusual, rather than ordinary, job exertion. Under this approach, employees who suffer heart attacks while performing strenuous work tasks are ineligible for coverage, if those tasks constitute their usual job functions. Persons who wish to obtain benefits in these jurisdictions must be able to show that the critical event involved exertion beyond that normally associated with their employment.

Several of the courts that generally apply the unusual exertion test have acknowledged that this approach can result in unjust benefit denials for persons who regularly perform strenuous tasks. To ameliorate the impact of the strict unusual exertion doctrine, these courts have decided to compare the degree of exertion involved to the exertion associated with ordinary life, instead of to the regular employment of the claimants. Under this interpretation of the unusual exertion rule, individuals employed in occupations that involve strenuous exertion that transcends the exertion associated with ordinary life are provided with statutory protection for their job-related heart problems.

Many of the unusual exertion cases do not clearly articulate the precise demarcation between covered and uncovered exertion. In some cases, one has the clear impression that the courts are effectively requiring exertion that is unusual for people employed in the line of work of the claimant. Other decisions suggest that coverage will be granted to all employees whose job endeavors involve exertion greater than that of ordinary life.

A small number of states distinguish between claimants who have preexisting heart conditions and those who do not. Workers with no record of heart difficulties are given statutory coverage in these jurisdictions for heart injuries that result from usual employment exertion. Employees with preexisting heart conditions, however, are only awarded benefits for injuries caused by unusual work exertion. Courts following this bifurcated approach have clearly departed from the traditional notion that employers take their workers as they find them.

Back Injuries and Other Conditions

Most states extend workers' compensation coverage to all back injuries that arise out of and during the course of claimant employment, even when the relevant conditions were caused by usual job efforts. This is true whether their normal work exertion is greater than or similar to that associated with ordinary life. Statutory protection is even likely to be afforded to persons who exacerbate preexisting back weaknesses while performing normal job tasks. To obtain benefits, these claimants must simply demonstrate that some employment exertion meaningfully contributed to their back problems. Nonetheless, if claimants are unable to show that employment-related events meaningfully aggravated their preexisting back conditions, coverage will usually be denied.

Some jurisdictions refuse to extend coverage to workers who experience back injuries during usual employment exertion. They require evidence of unusual work exertion as a prerequisite to benefit awards. Individuals who develop back conditions because of normal job exertion are normally unable to obtain compensation in these states. Judicial decisions occasionally distinguish between claimants who have preexisting back weaknesses and those who do not. They permit benefit awards for back injuries caused by usual employment exertion when there is no evidence of preexisting back problems. When there is a record of prior back problems, however, these courts only provide coverage for exacerbations that are generated by unusual job exertion.

Employment endeavors often cause or contribute to other medical conditions that do not involve instantaneous occurrences. Many of these difficulties affect individuals with preexisting weaknesses. Most jurisdictions apply the usual exertion rule to these cases and award benefits to claimants who can establish that their problems arose out of and during the course of their employment. Examples of covered injuries include muscle strains, arthritis, bursitis, cancer, and general arm and leg pain. Nonetheless, some states refuse to cover these conditions if they are precipitated or exacerbated by usual employment exertion. They only sustain benefit awards for injuries caused by unusual job efforts. The decisions denying statutory protection for conditions that result from ordinary work exertion effectively ignore the fact that workers' compensation laws are intended to provide coverage for all injuries that arise out of and during the course of claimant employment.

Extreme Heat and Cold

It is uniformly recognized that claimants who sustain employment-related heatstroke or frostbite have experienced compensable injuries. Their conditions are considered sufficiently sudden and unexpected to constitute "accidental" events. The decisions relating to the coverage of conditions resulting from extreme heat and cold do not ask whether exposure to high or low temperatures was a usual or unusual aspect of the pertinent employment. They merely ask whether the adversely affected employees were subject to temperature extremes that were greater than those associated with ordinary life. So long as this question is answered affirmatively, statutory protection is provided.

Exposure to Diseases

Individuals are frequently exposed to diseases during the course of their employment. The diseases may include pneumonia, pleurisy, influenza, tuberculosis, common colds, and other conditions. Worker exposure may be due to their proximity to sick coworkers, customers, or members of the general public. It may also result from unhealthful conditions in their work environments. Should employees who contract these diseases be entitled to workers' compensation coverage? If their conditions are caused by circumstances indigenous to their particular employment, they would probably be protected under occupational disease provisions. In the absence of such coverage, however, they would have to demonstrate that they sustained "accidental" injuries that arose out of and during the course of their employment.

If workers develop diseases or infections from relatively sudden and unexpected exposure to germs at work, they are generally found eligible for benefits. Courts consider such conditions to constitute "accidental" injuries that arose out of and during the course of claimant employment. For example, diseases transmitted at particular times through cuts or abrasions, pimples on the skin, insect bites, or similar events are normally viewed as compensable "accidental" injuries.

When workers develop diseases or infections due to prolonged exposure to germs, it is more difficult for them to obtain benefits. The absence of a relatively sudden triggering event may induce some courts to find the absence of any "accidental" occurrence. Most courts, however, consider the unexpected nature of claimant contraction sufficient to satisfy the "accidental" requirement.

When claimants contract diseases or infections from routine exposure to germs to which members of the general public are exposed, it is not always easy for them to establish the requisite employment connection. A number of courts refuse to award benefits to individuals who contract nonoccupational diseases from routine exposure to others in the work environment. Some decisions find an absence of causation, because the claimants have not been exposed to appreciably greater risks of illness than ordinary citizens. Other decisions find a lack of any "accidental" occurrence, because normal exposure to the diseases of life can hardly be considered sudden or unexpected.

Although some of the cases reaching contrary results involve routine exposure to the conditions in question, many concern exposure to illnesses that transcend the risks associated with ordinary life. These decisions simply conclude that the diseased conditions arose out of and during the course of the claimant's employment, because the claimant's exposure to the requisite circumstances constituted a risk of his or her work. While members of the general public may be exposed to similar conditions as part of ordinary life, they are not obliged to remain in job settings in which the risk of contagious disease exists.

It is often difficult to distinguish cases denying statutory coverage from those sustaining benefit awards. If the health risk within the employment environment is clearly greater than it is elsewhere, compensation is likely to be available. On the other hand, when the exposure is analogous to that associated with ordinary life, coverage is frequently denied. When it is not clear whether the employment exposure is greater than that experienced by members of the general public, it is often difficult to discern the precise line between compensable and noncompensable circumstances.

Physical Conditions that Develop Over Prolonged Periods

Courts determining benefit eligibility in repeated trauma cases have often been concerned about the absence of any immediate triggering event and the impact of that omission under "accidental" injury statutes. Nonetheless, most jurisdictions have decided to provide statutory protection for physical conditions that develop over prolonged periods. They generally utilize one of three approaches to take care of the "accidental" requirement. A few courts simply eliminate the temporal element that is usually associated with "accidental" injury cases. The fact that the difficulty developed unexpectedly is considered sufficient to warrant statutory protection. Some courts find the time factor satisfied if the physical result arises at an identifiable time. Other courts rely upon the repeated trauma doctrine. They effectively treat each job-related impact or inhalation as a separate "accident" and find the resulting injury "accidental."

States that regularly award benefits to workers who develop employment-related physical problems over protracted periods may deny coverage in close cases. Most of the rejected claims involve individuals who are unable to demonstrate clear employment-related causal connections or who sustain conditions that do not develop at identifiable times. When claimants are able to establish causation and can reasonably identify the time their physical difficulties arose, even courts in these jurisdictions usually favor coverage. The fact that a repetitive motion condition may have been caused by both employment-related and personal factors will not result in a loss of statutory coverage, if the employment-related events were a substantial causative factor.

A few states continue to deny "accidental" injury coverage to employees who develop physical conditions over prolonged periods. Courts in these jurisdictions generally find the absence of any definable triggering event sufficient to preclude benefit eligibility. They occasionally note that if statutory protection is to be extended to these injuries, it must be accomplished through legislative, rather than judicial, action. In these jurisdictions, the adversely affected workers must endeavor to fit their conditions within the scope of occupational disease provisions.

Employment Stress Contributing to Physical Conditions

Employees exposed to employment stress may develop physical manifestations. They may suffer heart attacks, strokes, hypertension, thrombosis, or similar conditions. When health problems are caused by sudden and unexpected shocks, they are generally considered compensable "accidental" injuries. For example, workers who experience relatively immediate physical difficulties as a result of the strain associated with potential or actual vehicular accidents, job-related confrontations with supervisors or strangers, electrical flashes, or similar circumstances, are likely to be awarded benefits.

When the physical manifestations of job stress develop over prolonged periods of time, it is more difficult for claimants to establish the requisite causal relationships. Nonetheless, if adversely affected workers can demonstrate meaningful employment connections, statutory coverage will usually be provided. Cases awarding benefits typically involve individuals who are affected by heavy work loads, job-related tension, worries about serious employment problems, and similar concerns. Favorable awards are especially likely when claimants can establish that they were exposed to unusual levels of job tension or anxiety.

Claimants who suffer physical conditions as a result of prolonged exposure to job stress are occasionally denied benefits. A lack of coverage is most likely when the employment-related stress is not significantly different from that associated with ordinary life. Some courts denying benefits in these circumstances find that the claimants were unable to establish sufficient causal connections to their work. Others decide that the adversely affected individuals did not suffer "accidental" injuries.

Employment Traumas Contributing to Emotional Conditions

Numerous employees are exposed to physical or mental traumas at work that contribute primarily to emotional, rather than corporeal, conditions. Courts frequently have to determine whether the resulting depression, neuroses, or other psychological disorders constitute compensable injuries. When the underlying emotional conditions are generated by physical traumas, statutory coverage is generally provided. When, however, the causative factor is entirely psychological, benefit eligibility is less certain.

Workers may suffer physical traumas that culminate in continuing emotional problems. So long as the causative factors occur in a relatively sudden and unexpected manner and arise out of and during employment, statutory coverage is normally available for these "accidental" injuries. For example, individuals who sustain minor back injuries may develop a neurotic belief that their back is degenerating. Persons struck in the head may become emotionally disabled. Employees who are the victims of unwelcome sexual advances may experience nervous conditions as a result of offensive physical touching. Cases that deny statutory coverage to workers who develop such emotional disorders rely upon the lack of any clear causal connection to claimant employment or the absence of any compensable disability.

The fact that claimants who develop emotional problems as a result of job-related physical traumas had preexisting neurotic tendencies does not usually diminish their right to compensation. Courts apply the traditional rule that employers take their employees as they find them and provide the affected individuals with statutory protection. The persons seeking benefits are only obliged to demonstrate that employment-related physical traumas significantly contributed to their disabling conditions.

Some workers develop mental conditions that result from psychological, rather than physical, traumas. Their disorders may be caused by a single event or may be associated with prolonged exposure to stressful environments. Although the early cases generally denied benefits to individuals with mental difficulties generated by job-related psychological traumas, a majority of courts now find such disabilities compensable.

Statutory coverage is most likely to be provided for mental conditions that arise from particular psychological traumas. Several of the early cases involved workers traumatized by explosions. Even though the claimants sustained no physical injuries as a result of the explosions, they did develop nervous disorders. These emotional problems were found compensable. An early Texas Supreme Court decision[1] provided similar statutory coverage to an iron worker who suffered disabling emotional difficulties after he witnessed the death of a coworker who fell from the defective scaffold on which they were working.

Most contemporary courts have extended the coverage developed in the early cases to emotional disorders precipitated by other single-incident psychological traumas. The sudden and unexpected nature of the triggering events is sufficient to satisfy the "accidental" injury requirement imposed by most jurisdictions. The fact that other nonemployment stress may have affected the psychological state of the claimants does not preclude statutory coverage, so long as the job-related incidents meaningfully contributed to the final result. When the triggering events are not related to the claimants' job functions, however, coverage for the resulting psychological conditions is likely to be denied.

Guess v. Sharp Manufacturing Company of America[2] involved an employee who developed post traumatic stress disorder after she was exposed to the blood of a coworker she suspected was HIV positive. The coworker had cut his hand, and some of his blood got on Guess's hand. Although she had no evidence that her colleague was HIV positive, she

§ 7.23   **2.** 114 S.W.3d 480 (Tenn. 2003).

1. Bailey v. American Gen. Ins. Co., 154 Tex. 430, 279 S.W.2d 315 (1955).

thought that he was since several of his friends had died of AIDS, he received mailings from gay rights organizations, and he "looked and acted gay." Although Guess had been tested five times for HIV and each test was negative, she continued to experience stress related depression. Even though Tennessee allows coverage for psychological conditions that result from stress related employment incidents, the court denied coverage. It held that compensability had to be based upon proof of a rational connection between a work related psychological trauma and the resulting psychological condition. To satisfy this standard, the court held that the claimant had to demonstrate actual–not merely imagined–exposure to HIV. Since Guess's condition was the result of mere speculation about her coworker's HIV status based upon her suspicion that he was gay, the Court found that she failed to establish a rational connection between her condition and her employment.

Not all courts have shown a willingness to provide workers' compensation protection to employees who develop emotional conditions as a result of single-incident psychological traumas. Some courts continue to deny benefits to claimants affected by such circumstances. Most of the decisions denying benefits to these claimants are based upon the absence of any physical ramifications that these courts find expressly or impliedly required for statutory coverage. Some courts continue to deny coverage in such cases when only ordinary circumstances are involved.

Many emotional difficulties arising out of and during the course of employment develop slowly as a result of prolonged stress, anxiety, or frustration. Despite the fact that claimants adversely affected by these circumstances are unable to identify specific events precipitating their disabling mental conditions, a majority of modern courts find these individuals eligible for benefits. *Carter v. General Motors Corp.*[3] is one of the classic cases. A worker on an automotive assembly line was unable to keep up with the machine-driven pace. When he worked on one hub assembly at a time, he fell behind. When he worked on two at a time, in a desperate effort to keep up, he often put the assemblies back on line in the incorrect order. The employee was regularly chastised by his supervisor and he eventually suffered an emotional collapse. The court found the employee's resulting condition compensable. "The case at bar involves a series of mental stimuli or events—(the pressure of his job and the pressure of his foreman)—which caused an injury or disability under the act * * *." Other courts have followed this approach and have awarded benefits to claimants who have suffered disabling emotional conditions as a result of repeated exposure to job stress. These courts either ignore the "accidental" injury requirement under their statutes or find the sudden and unexpected manifestations of the disabling conditions sufficient to satisfy this prerequisite. Some of the courts that extend protection to psychological injuries caused by repeated emotional traumas limit such coverage to mental injuries caused by stress that transcends the ordinary incidents of employment.

3.   361   Mich.   577,   106   N.W.2d   105 (1960).

Some courts draw a critical distinction between mental disorders precipitated by single psychological traumas and those that develop from prolonged stress, anxiety, or frustration. They find that single-trauma conditions constitute compensable "accidental" injuries, due to the existence of sudden and unexpected triggering events, but refuse to extend statutory protection to repeated psychological trauma situations. These courts are unwilling to consider the sudden and unexpected development of the mental problems sufficient to satisfy "accidental" injury requirements. Nonetheless, individuals who develop mental disorders due to their prolonged exposure to employment-related stress may be eligible for coverage under occupational disease provisions.

A number of states currently provide statutory coverage for mental disabilities caused by single or repeated psychological traumas. Courts that do not do so base their decisions on the lack of physical injuries or the absence of sudden and unexpected "accidental" events. Implicit in many of the opinions denying benefits in these cases is the perceived lack of a clear causal connection to employment. The causation concern is likely to diminish with the development of more sophisticated psychological evaluation techniques. As a result, the trend in favor of coverage for psychological trauma/psychological disorder cases will probably continue.

On rare occasions, employees who have been severely affected by physical or mental traumas commit suicide. Although states generally exclude conditions that are intentionally self-inflicted, they cover suicides that may reasonably be attributed to employment-related circumstances beyond claimant control. Early judicial decisions required evidence of uncontrollable impulses or unconscious deliriums as a prerequisite to statutory coverage for suicides, but contemporary courts find suicides compensable whenever job-related traumas generate mental derangement that causes a loss of self-control and results in self-inflicted death. "[W]e believe that in cases where the effects of injuries suffered by the deceased result in his becoming dominated by a derangement of the mind which impairs the ability to resist the impulse to take his own life to the extent that the decedent was in fact unable to control it, the suicide cannot be termed as willful * * *."[4]

A psychological condition that generates more controversy than suicide is called "compensation neurosis." It involves injured workers who assert that anxiety over their industrial accidents or the outcomes of their compensation cases has exacerbated their situations by producing a disabling neurosis that may only be cured through the awarding of additional compensation. If it appears that the claimants are mere malingerers who simply do not want to return to work, their requests for further benefits are usually denied. On the other hand, if psychologists or psychiatrists convince compensation administrators that persons who have sustained employment-related injuries continue to be disabled due to compensation neurosis, a majority of states permit a continuation of

4. Saunders v. Texas Employers' Ins. Ass'n, 526 S.W.2d 515, 517–18 (Tex.1975).

disability benefits. A number of jurisdictions, however, remain skeptical of this condition and refuse to allow continued benefit payments.

§ 7.24 Occupational Disease

The original workers' compensation statutes were designed to substitute no-fault coverage for common law fault remedies. They thus provided coverage for "accidental" injuries that had been the basis for conventional tort liability. Because occupational diseases were not conditions subject to tort liability, state legislatures did not address those particular problems. Although a few early court decisions interpreted general "injury" provisions to encompass some job-related diseases, most non-"accidental" illnesses were not eligible for statutory protection.

Legislators quickly recognized that employees could be as devastated by diseases contracted in work environments as by job-related "accidental" injuries. In 1920, New York became the first state to add specific occupational disease coverage to its compensation law. The New York provision followed the English approach and set forth a schedule of covered illnesses. Other states followed the New York example and adopted express occupational disease provisions.

The Federal Employees Compensation Act and the workers' compensation statutes in all fifty states and the District of Columbia now include specific sections covering occupational diseases. Many enactments currently provide general coverage—i.e., they include all employment-related diseases. Some statutes list scheduled conditions that are covered, but most of these provisions now contain catch-all clauses extending protection to other nonspecified occupational diseases. Several states have adopted entirely separate occupational disease laws. Courts in these states occasionally encounter problems when they attempt to determine whether particular conditions are compensable under the "accidental" injury law, the occupational disease enactment, or both.

Occupational disease coverage is quite different from "accidental" injury protection. Occupational disease provisions do not require evidence of sudden and unexpected triggering events as prerequisites to benefit awards. If a diseased condition arises in a wholly unexpected manner from a relatively definite exposure to particular germs, it is normally regarded, not as an occupational disease, but as an "accidental" injury. Most occupational diseases develop slowly over prolonged periods and are not entirely unexpected occurrences. While occupational diseases are usually unanticipated from the perspective of the particular individuals who contract them, they are hardly unexpected phenomena to people familiar with the hazards associated with the occupations or industries involved. It is the fact that certain diseases are an inherent risk of specific occupations or industries that renders the resulting illnesses compensable.

Courts endeavoring to determine whether particular medical conditions are compensable initially review the relevant statutory language. Most workers' compensation laws expressly define the term "occupational disease." Some include elaborate definitions, while others contain more general provisions. When the applicable enactment does not provide specific guidance, judicial decisions fill the void. Laws in states like Virginia, Illinois, and Indiana provide detailed statutory definitions. Other state codes more generally distinguish between covered "occupational diseases" and uncovered medical conditions associated with ordinary life. Judicial decisions in states that do not expressly define the term "occupational disease" normally use similar language to differentiate between covered and uncovered conditions.

> An ailment does not become an occupational disease simply because it is contracted on the employer's premises. It must be one which is commonly regarded as natural to, inhering in, an incident and concomitant of, the work in question. There must be a recognizable link between the disease and some distinctive feature of the claimant's job, common to all jobs.[1]

Whether the pertinent statutory language is specific, general, or nondefinitive, courts considering occupational disease claims tend to evaluate the cases in a similar manner. They review the medical evidence to determine whether there appears to be a causal connection between the claimant medical conditions and their particular jobs. If no causal link can be established, compensation is generally denied. They also endeavor to ascertain whether claimants are suffering from diseases of ordinary life to which members of the general public are equally exposed. If individuals are seeking benefits for such conditions, they are obliged to demonstrate that their employment exposed them to an unusually high risk of those particular diseases.

Meritorious claims often involve medical conditions caused by specific germs, chemicals, dusts, or similar substances found in the work environment in unusual quantities. For example, health care workers frequently work in close proximity to contagious patients. If it appears that they have contracted tuberculosis, hepatitis, or other diseases from those patients, they will probably be found entitled to statutory protection. Their repeated exposure to contagious patients is considered sufficient to distinguish their conditions from diseases associated with ordinary life. Statutory coverage is also likely for individuals who contract asbestosis, asthma, bronchitis, emphysema, pneumoconiosis, pulmonary fibrosis, or other respiratory diseases because of their excessive exposure in their work environments to the substances that cause those conditions.

Some of the more controverted cases involve respiratory conditions associated with ordinary life that may have been contracted in employment settings. These disputes generally concern causation issues. The mere fact that claimants may have been exposed to germs, fumes, chemicals, or similar substances in their work environments does not

§ 7.24
1. Harman v. Republic Aviation Corp., 298 N.Y. 285, 82 N.E.2d 785, 786 (1948), quoting Goldberg v. 954 Marcy Corp., 276 N.Y. 313, 12 N.E.2d 311, 313 (1938).

prove that their respiratory disorders were precipitated by their employment. Health care workers may contract common diseases outside the hospitals where they work, and causation may be difficult to establish if there is no evidence of unusual exposure to the pertinent germs at their place of work. People who work in dusty facilities may develop pulmonary conditions. If they are unable to demonstrate that their job settings meaningfully contributed to their maladies, they will probably be denied coverage. Benefit denials are especially likely for claimants who have previously experienced similar, nonoccupational conditions or have exacerbated their difficulties through heavy smoking. Nonetheless, the fact that claimants are seeking coverage for common diseases does not automatically result in benefit denials.

The critical question regarding diseases caused by airborne particles or fumes is not whether they are conditions associated with ordinary life, but whether the claimant's employment meaningfully increased the risk of those conditions. Even though statutory protection is more likely to be provided for diseases unique to particular occupations or industries, common ailments are frequently found compensable if the germs, fumes, or other substances causing those disorders are present in the workplace at unusually elevated levels. A lack of statutory coverage for these diseases is only likely to result when courts conclude that state legislatures indicated their clear intention to exclude all ordinary diseases no matter how much the workplace may have contributed to their disorders.

Marlin v. Bill Rich Construction, Inc.[2] involved several construction workers who learned they had inhaled asbestos fibers. Although they suffered no direct physical harm as a result of their asbestos exposure, they developed a substantial fear that they would suffer serious future consequences. When their fears resulted in physical manifestations, they sought compensation. The court concluded that such fear-related consequences, even if physical in nature, do not constitute compensable conditions. In *Metro-North Commuter Railroad Co. v. Buckley,*[3] the Supreme Court used similar reasoning to deny FELA coverage to railroad employees who had been exposed to asbestos and had suffered emotional distress as a result of their apprehension of possible cancer. Since they had no disease symptoms, they were ineligible for either general damages or recovery for medical monitoring costs. To obtain such monetary relief, the claimants would have to demonstrate the existence of resulting physical injury.

Analogous rules are applied to other common conditions that may have been significantly affected by the claimant's job functions. Employees whose work tasks involve heavy lifting or repeated twisting are far more likely to develop back problems than members of the general public. As a result, if these workers can demonstrate a reasonable connection between their back difficulties and their job functions, statutory protection will normally be provided.

2. 198 W.Va. 635, 482 S.E.2d 620 (1996).

3. 521 U.S. 424, 117 S.Ct. 2113, 138 L.Ed.2d 560 (1997).

Individuals who repeatedly move their arms or hands during their work are more likely to develop carpal tunnel syndrome, bursitis, or similar disorders than people engaged in ordinary life activities, and are thus often awarded benefits for these occupational diseases. Nonetheless, some courts continue to deny statutory coverage for these problems. The fact that claimant employment may have meaningfully contributed to their particular conditions is not considered sufficient to overcome the statutory exclusion for diseases of ordinary life. Although carpal tunnel syndrome may constitute a covered occupational disease, if an individual with that condition is able to continue to work despite the resulting pain, he or she is likely to be found ineligible for benefits due to the absence of any "disablement."

Claimants who develop medical conditions while engaged in activities similar to those carried out by members of the general public are not necessarily excluded from statutory coverage. The crucial issue in most jurisdictions is whether the particular job increased the risk of the pertinent disorder. For example, individuals whose job duties require extensive walking or standing may develop varicose veins. Employees who are required to sit for prolonged periods on hard chairs may injure their tail bones. Because persons performing these functions are far more likely to develop the conditions in question, most courts would provide them with occupational disease coverage. Only a few courts have refused to provide coverage for these common diseases.

Judges are occasionally presented with medical conditions that are not clearly included or excluded under applicable "occupational disease" provisions. When workers' compensation laws generally define "occupational disease" to cover disorders peculiar to particular occupations or industries, it is relatively easy for sympathetic courts to expand the scope of protection in appropriate situations. Even though back strains, herniated discs, foot problems, bursitis, arthritis, and similar disorders may not technically constitute "diseases," most courts include these medical problems within general "occupational disease" provisions. They assume that legislators must have intended to provide statutory protection for all medical conditions that are reasonably related to claimant employment, and they interpret the term "disease" accordingly.

Although most workers' compensation statutes provide general "occupational disease" coverage, a number also list specific conditions that are associated with particular occupations or industries. The most frequently listed conditions include anthrax, asbestosis, dermatitis, pneumoconiosis, radiation-related illnesses, silicosis, and various types of chemical poisonings. Workers who develop these conditions are presumptively entitled to statutory protection. Employers seeking to defeat compensation claims are usually obliged to demonstrate that the pertinent disorders did not arise out of and during the course of claimant employment.

If employees develop conditions not specifically mentioned in "occupational disease" provisions but similar to maladies that are included, should the unlisted disorders be granted statutory protection? Some courts have refused to expand the list of covered conditions to cover medical problems that legislators might not have considered. They believe that the legislative, rather than the judicial, branch must determine the scope of statutory coverage. Many other courts, however, have decided to treat the list of specified disorders as illustrative, rather than exclusive. So long as claimants can demonstrate that particular medical problems are associated with their jobs and are similar to conditions listed in the pertinent statutory provision, coverage is likely to be granted.

Some recent judicial decisions have further expanded "occupational disease" coverage by including circumstances that would have traditionally been included within "accidental injury" provisions. Even though "occupational disease" protection has been historically limited to conditions that develop gradually, a few judicial tribunals have evidenced a willingness to include diseases precipitated by identifiable triggering events. They have thus covered infectious conditions contracted by health care workers while in contact with particular patients and other diseases contracted by employees from equipment infected by other personnel. This approach effectively permits adversely affected workers to elect either "accidental injury" or "occupational disease" protection for some unexpected disorders that develop in a relatively sudden manner.

An issue that has begun to generate judicial attention concerns the coverage of stress-related nervous conditions under "occupational disease" provisions. *James v. State Accident Insurance Fund*[4] provides a classic example. The claimant, who had previously suffered from anxiety, became an Information Referral Counselor. She experienced significant personality and professional conflicts with her supervisor. He criticized her work and gave her conflicting job assignments that required her to be in two places at the same time. The claimant became increasingly nervous and took numerous tranquilizers. After she concluded that her nervous condition prevented further employment, she filed a compensation claim. The Oregon Supreme Court decided that emotional disorders caused by unusual job-related stress transcending that experienced by ordinary people could constitute compensable "occupational diseases." If the claimant could establish that "the confrontations with her supervisor were something to which claimant was not ordinarily subjected or exposed to other than during her regular employment," she would be entitled to "occupational disease" coverage.

Other courts have refused to extend "occupational disease" protection to emotional disorders precipitated by stressful employment situations. Even though these jurisdictions have been willing to apply "accidental injury" provisions to maladies resulting from repeated physical traumas, they do not consider it appropriate to include nervous disorders affected by repeated, job-related psychological traumas within either

---

4. 290 Or. 343, 624 P.2d 565, on remand, 51 Or.App. 201, 624 P.2d 644 (1981).

"accidental injury" or "occupational disease" provisions. The courts are divided on the issue of whether stress-related disorders caused by termination of employment or changes in working conditions are compensable.

Allergies and Preexisting Conditions

Most courts extend statutory protection to individuals whose preexisting medical conditions are aggravated by workplace conditions. Some courts, however, ignore the usual admonition that employers take their employees as they find them and deny statutory protection to workers whose allergies are worsened by job-related circumstances.

Even claimants who can establish a direct causal link between their employment and their conditions may be found ineligible for benefits because of their personal susceptibility to the maladies involved.

Most jurisdictions recognize that employees with allergies should not be denied statutory protection for allergic reactions precipitated by their exposure to substances in the work environment. They appropriately acknowledge that the susceptibility of claimants to allergic conditions is not disqualifying. So long as claimants can demonstrate that their medical problems were significantly influenced by job-related factors, statutory coverage is available. Moreover, the fact that a particular allergy affects very few individuals does not diminish their right to compensation for employment-related flare-ups.

The vast majority of courts follow the same practice with respect to workers whose preexisting weaknesses are exacerbated by employment circumstances. A few courts deny "occupational disease" protection to these claimants due to their personal susceptibility to the particular maladies, but most find the propensities of individual workers irrelevant to their benefit eligibility.

The critical factor in states following the majority approach is simply causation. Claimants must be able to establish a meaningful connection between their employment and their conditions.

Diseases Caused by Both Occupational and Nonoccupational Factors

Claimants sometimes seek workers' compensation for conditions that have been jointly caused by employment and nonemployment factors. Typical cases involve individuals with pulmonary problems that appear to have been caused by their inhalation of fumes or substances in the work environment and by their own heavy smoking. When the evidence establishes that job factors substantially contributed to the resulting emphysema, bronchitis, lung cancer, or similar condition, compensation is usually awarded. When, however, the causal connection to the employment environment is not so apparent, courts often find no statutory coverage. An unresolved issue is whether nonsmoking employees may recover for respiratory diseases allegedly caused by second-hand tobacco smoke in the workplace.

Even people who smoke are entitled to benefits for pulmonary diseases that have been significantly affected by job-related considerations. As a result, when claimants can demonstrate that they have worked in employment environments that exposed them to unusual levels of carcinogenic substances, their resulting lung cancer will normally be found compensable. Smokers who can establish that excessive shop fumes meaningfully contributed to their emphysema, bronchitis, or other lung diseases are similarly accorded statutory protection. These cases certainly involve employment settings that contain uncommonly high risks of pulmonary disease that transcend the risks associated with ordinary life.

When the causal link between claimant employment and the relevant medical condition is not so obvious, coverage may be denied. These cases typically involve heavy smokers who work in environments containing various airborne substances that could contribute to pulmonary disorders. If claimants are unable to establish significant causal links between their employment environments and their lung cancer, bronchitis, or similar conditions, courts often attribute their lung problems to their own smoking.

The principal difficulty encountered by claimants who develop pulmonary diseases that may have been generated by occupational or nonoccupational factors concerns the lack of medical certainty about the causes of these conditions. While it is generally recognized that smoking increases the likelihood of bronchitis, emphysema, lung cancer, and other respiratory diseases, many people who do not smoke contract these disorders. Conversely, while millions of persons work in environments that contain airborne substances that contribute to various pulmonary conditions, most do not experience these problems.

A second phenomenon further complicates the causation issue. People who smoke for prolonged periods diminish the ability of their respiratory systems to filter out harmful airborne substances. As a result, when smokers inhale asbestos, cotton fibers, coal dust, and similar substances in their employment environments, more of these particles pass through their innate defense system and enter their lungs.

Most courts acknowledge that claimants are not obliged to prove that the employment-related inhalants were the primary cause of their respiratory diseases. They need only establish that the job-related factors meaningfully contributed to their disorders. Courts also recognize that employers take their workers as they find them and many are willing to conclude that the predisposition of smokers to pulmonary problems does not preclude statutory protection for lung diseases exacerbated by employment-related factors.

Another legal impediment that claimants who smoke must frequently overcome when they seek benefits for respiratory disorders concerns the fact that most workers' compensation statutes expressly or impliedly exclude diseases of ordinary life from coverage. As a result, smokers who develop common pulmonary problems may be unable to establish sufficient employment links to qualify for benefits. Employees who can demonstrate that they were exposed to uncommon airborne substances in their employment environments directly associated with their respiratory disorders or to unusually high levels of more common inhalants at work that significantly contributed to their conditions are likely to prevail. On the other hand, claimants who are unable to establish any meaningful connection between their employment and their ailments will probably be denied coverage.

Several states have sought to accommodate the dual-causation cases through specific statutory provisions that apportion coverage between the occupational and nonoccupational causative factors.

When claimants in states with these statutory provisions seek compensation for disorders affected by employment and nonemployment factors, the courts attempt to determine the degree of disability attributable to the occupational and nonoccupational elements. Benefit awards are based entirely on the proportion pertaining to the occupational component.

Most state legislatures have refused to adopt special apportionment provisions, and courts in these jurisdictions have declined to establish such an approach in their decisions. They continue to believe that employers take their employees as they find them. So long as employment-related factors meaningfully contribute to diseases contracted by employees, full compensation is awarded, despite the fact that nonoccupational elements may have affected the final result.

Timing Issues Relating to Causation, Statutes of Limitation, and Benefit Levels

Some state legislatures were initially concerned that occupational disease coverage would be so expansive that it might jeopardize the financial stability of workers' compensation systems. To prevent fiscal problems, several states adopted special provisions designed to restrict occupational disease protection. Some require minimal periods of exposure to employment-related hazardous substances as a prerequisite to benefit eligibility. Others deny statutory coverage to disorders that do not become apparent within specified periods following the most recent exposure of claimants to the alleged work-related causative factors.

Many occupational diseases develop slowly during prolonged exposure to substances such as asbestos, silica dust, and coal particles. The affected employees may have been exposed to the harmful substances while working for various firms. When their disabling conditions manifest themselves, some states require the different employers to share the cost of claimant benefits in proportion to the degree of claimant exposure associated with each company. It is difficult to apportion liability with any degree of certainty, and this approach deprives employers of any definitive knowledge regarding the end of liability relating to former workers. To avoid these problems, most states have adopted the "last injurious exposure" doctrine. Under this rule, the employer that most recently exposed the claimants to the substances that meaningfully contributed to their disabling conditions is held responsible for their entire compensation.

§ 7.25 Occupational Disease—Special Police and Firefighter Provisions

The workers' compensation laws in eighteen states contain special provisions pertaining to police officers and firefighters. These enactments are generally applicable to heart conditions and respiratory diseases, and are often referred to as "heart and lung" statutes. They establish presumptions in favor of statutory coverage for these "occupational" disorders. These provisions generally apply to all covered police officers and firefighters, but the Minnesota and Virginia provisions limit application to claimants who were found free of heart disease or respiratory problems during their previous medical examinations. Courts usually restrict application of these statutory provisions to active police officers and firefighters who are considered especially vulnerable to heart and lung disorders. Ancillary police and fire department personnel are normally denied the benefit of these sections.

The degree to which an employment link is presumed for heart and lung conditions developed by police officers and firefighters varies from state to state. In several states, courts interpret these provisions as merely creating limited presumptions in favor of compensability. Police and firefighter claimants who develop heart and lung diseases are entitled to preliminary presumptions in favor of benefit eligibility. Nonetheless, if their governmental employers raise meaningful issues regarding the occupational nature of their problems, the statutory presumptions are negated and the affected workers are required to demonstrate actual connections between their employment and their conditions.

In some states, judges believe that these provisions create greater presumptions in favor of coverage. Government entities cannot rebut the presumption by simply raising questions regarding the relationship between claimant employment and their medical conditions. They are required to present substantial evidence indicating that the police or fire duties of the affected persons did not meaningfully contribute to their disorders. Close cases tend to be resolved in favor of statutory protection.

In the third group of states, courts interpret these provisions as establishing almost irrebuttable presumptions in favor of police and firefighter benefit eligibility with respect to heart and lung problems. Judges basically assume that personnel covered by these enactments are entitled to awards for all heart and lung disorders. Government employers can only defeat worker claims by unequivocally demonstrating that their conditions were caused entirely by nonoccupational factors. It is extremely difficult for employers in these jurisdictions to prevent benefit awards to police and fire personnel who develop coronary and pulmonary diseases.

§ 7.26 Occupational Disease—Black Lung

Coal miners' repeated inhalation of coal dust frequently causes black lung disease (pneumoconiosis). By the late 1960s, it had become apparent to federal officials that many state workers' compensation laws were not providing adequate protection for miners who developed this disease. In 1969, Congress enacted a comprehensive compensation system for this particular condition through the enactment of the Coal Mine Health and Safety Act. Title IV of that statute established a compensation program providing monthly benefits for coal miners who became "totally disabled" due to pneumoconiosis. The program also gave death benefits to the dependents of miners who died either from pneumoconiosis or from some other cause while they were totally disabled as a result of that disease.

By 1981, it had become apparent that the Black Lung Disability Trust Fund could not accommodate the substantial number of claims being filed. Congress endeavored to rectify the problem through the enactment of the Black Lung Benefits Revenue Act and the Black Lung Benefits Amendments. These amendments terminated the right of surviving dependents to obtain benefits for miners who died from other causes while totally disabled by pneumoconiosis. Survivor benefits were henceforth limited to miners whose deaths were directly attributable to black lung disease. The 1981 amendments also abolished several presumptions favoring coverage for individuals who worked in mines for specified periods, even when they died from pulmonary disorders other than pneumoconiosis.

Federal Black Lung Act coverage is different from traditional workers' compensation protection. The Black Lung Act contains its own unique definitions and presumptions. Claimants seeking benefits must establish two fundamental propositions: (1) they are "miners" within the meaning of the statute and (2) they are "totally disabled" because of pneumoconiosis. Although the burden of persuasion rests with benefit applicants, they may frequently take advantage of statutory presumptions favoring coverage and liberal judicial proof standards.

The original Black Lung Act defined "miner" as "any individual who is or was employed in an underground coal mine." Subsequent amendments expanded this definition to include surface mines and to cover not only persons employed in mines but also individuals who *work* or *have worked* in mines. The latter change granted statutory protection to self-employed people who work in coal mines operated by others. The amendments also extended coverage to individuals who prepare coal or who work in mine construction or transportation. The current definition reflects these changes:

> The term "miner" means any individual who works or has worked in or around a coal mine or coal preparation facility in the extraction or preparation of coal. Such term also includes an individual who works or has worked in coal mine construction or transportation in or around a coal mine, to the extent such individual was exposed to coal dust as a result of such employment.[1]

§ 7.26

1. 30 U.S.C.A. § 902(d).

Once claimants establish that they are "miners," they must demonstrate that they are affected by mine-related pneumoconiosis. They usually present medical and x-ray evidence to confirm their pneumoconiosis. Nonetheless, the mere fact that their conditions cannot be verified by x-rays does not automatically preclude statutory protection. Claimants may alternatively rely upon other "objective medical evidence such as blood-gas studies, electrocardiograms, pulmonary function studies, physical performance tests, physical examination, and medical and work histories."[2] They must then address the causation issue. Many claimants are able to benefit from either of two important statutory presumptions. If they can prove that they are suffering from "complicated" pneumoconiosis—i.e., the lung opacities disclosed in their chest x-rays exceed one centimeter in diameter—they are entitled to an irrebuttable presumption that they are totally disabled as a result of mine-related, black lung disease. If they are unable to demonstrate "complicated" pneumoconiosis but can establish "simple" pneumoconiosis plus a minimum of ten years of work in coal mines, they can take advantage of a rebuttable presumption that their black lung disease arose out of their work as a miner.

If neither statutory presumption applies to their situations, claimants must independently establish that their pneumoconiosis was caused by their work in coal mines. They generally prove the requisite causal link through testimony regarding their years of work in or around coal mines and the conditions under which they worked. Mine operators are most likely to challenge the causal claims of persons whose own heavy smoking may have significantly affected their pulmonary insufficiencies. If it appears that mine-related exposure to coal dust meaningfully contributed to their diseases, causation is normally found despite the exacerbation attributable to their own smoking. On the other hand, if no reasonable mine link is established and the evidence suggests that most of the pulmonary incapacity is due to personal factors, no mine-related causation is likely to result.

When they adjudicated disability claims under the Black Lung Benefits Act (BLBA), Department of Labor administrative law judges used to apply the "true doubt" rule. This rule effectively shifted the burden of proof to the party opposing compensation, because it resulted in the provision of benefits in cases in which the causation evidence was evenly balanced. In *Director, Office of Workers' Compensation Programs v. Greenwich Collieries*,[3] the Supreme Court decided that this burden-shifting rule was inconsistent with the statutory obligation imposed on claimants under the BLBA to establish their entitlement to compensation.

Claimants who establish mine-related pneumoconiosis must finally demonstrate that their black lung disease has rendered them "totally disabled." The Black Lung Act provides that "a miner shall be consid-

2. 20 C.F.R. § 718.202(a)(4).

3. 512 U.S. 267, 114 S.Ct. 2251, 129 L.Ed.2d 221 (1994).

ered totally disabled when pneumoconiosis prevents him or her from engaging in gainful employment requiring the skills and abilities comparable to those of any employment in a mine or mines in which he or she previously engaged with some regularity and over a substantial period of time."[4] The Act further provides that "if there are changed circumstances of employment indicative of reduced ability to perform his or her usual coal mine work, such miner's employment in a mine shall not be used as conclusive evidence that the miner is not totally disabled."[5]

Once claimants establish benefit eligibility, it becomes necessary to identify the operators responsible for: (1) miner pneumoconiosis exposure and (2) the compensation to be paid. The "most recent one-year rule" is utilized to determine the operators responsible for the exposure of the claimants to black lung disease. "[T]he operator or other employer with which the miner had the most recent periods of cumulative employment of not less than 1 year * * * shall be the responsible operator."[6] To satisfy the "one-year" requirement, individuals must have been employed for at least 125 work days.[7] Some statutes require miners to file claims within a certain number of years since their last exposure to coal dust, and a failure to satisfy this statutory prerequisite may result in a denial of coverage.

Miners eligible for Black Lung Act benefits are provided with comprehensive and unlimited medical coverage that includes nursing care, the cost of travel to obtain medical treatment, and palliative measures for pain. They also receive disability benefits based, not upon their previous earnings as is common with respect to conventional workers' compensation programs, but upon a specified federal standard. Black Lung Act claims are processed by the Department of Labor's Office of Workers' Compensation Programs.

§ 7.27 Compensation—Medical Benefits

In all fifty states, individuals who sustain occupational injuries and illnesses are entitled to medical and hospital benefits. Forty-seven state enactments impose no limits with respect to the amount or duration of medical benefits available to claimants. The right of employees to medical benefits is independent of their right to disability benefits. As a result, individuals who sustain job-related injuries that necessitate medical care but do not prevent their continued employment are entitled to medical benefits even though they have suffered no wage losses.

Under most workers' compensation laws, employers are obliged to provide injured employees with initial medical and hospital services. Many statutes permit claimants to thereafter use their own physicians, with the authorization of workers' compensation administrators. In some jurisdictions, injured workers must select from a panel of physicians compiled by either the state administrative agency or their employ-

---

4. 30 U.S.C.A. § 902(f)(1)(A).

5. Id. § 902(f)(1)(B).

6. 20 C.F.R. § 725.493(a)(1).

7. 20 C.F.R. § 725.493(b).

er. In several other states, employers possess the right to designate the doctors who must be used.

Injured workers must normally apprise their employer of job-related medical problems and give the employer an opportunity to authorize necessary medical assistance. Employees who fail to notify their employer of their problems and seek unauthorized medical help through their own physicians are likely to be held personally liable for the expenses they incur. The fact that workers either have more confidence in their own doctors or have no faith in the employer-authorized physicians is usually insufficient to excuse their failure to give their employer the chance to authorize the necessary treatment. The principal exception to this rule concerns emergency situations. When truly exigent circumstances are involved, injured workers may obtain needed medical care without waiting for employer authorization.

Once injured employees notify their employer of their conditions, the employer has an obligation to provide them with the requisite medical care. The employer is normally required to tell injured workers where they can obtain medical treatment and to inform them of the medical and hospital services available to them. If a company fails to satisfy its obligation to authorize prompt care, the affected workers may make their own health care arrangements and hold their employer liable for the expenses they incur.

Employees with occupational injuries are entitled to all reasonably necessary medical treatment, including the services of physicians, nurses, and rehabilitation specialists. When the services of psychiatrists or psychologists are relevant to treatment, the cost is generally covered. The cost of cosmetic surgery is similarly included for individuals who have suffered disfigurements. In *Asti v. Northwest Airlines*,[1] the court held that a health club membership had to be provided to a claimant with a work-related back injury where the membership was needed to allow the injured flight attendant to maintain his back in a sufficiently strong condition to enable him to continue to carry out his regular job duties.

Some of the more controverted cases have involved the right of claimants to seek chiropractic treatment. Where statutory provisions limit coverage to "medical treatment," courts may find chiropractic services beyond the scope of that language. On the other hand, where more expansive statutory language is involved, courts are likely to include chiropractic treatment.

Transportation costs incurred in connection with appropriate medical treatment are also covered. This is true even when claimants have to travel substantial distances to obtain the assistance of particular specialists. Individuals who develop employment-related respiratory conditions may be advised to relocate to areas with more hospitable climates. The transportation costs relating to these trips are likely to be covered, and

§ 7.27
1. 588 N.W.2d 737 (Minn. 1999).

even their living expenses may be included if the claimants are only going to remain in the new locations temporarily.

Claimants with certain injuries may have to purchase hearing aids, glasses, appliances, hospital beds, or similar items necessitated by their conditions. Such purchases will generally be covered by workers' compensation. Some courts have even included the cost of therapeutic hot tubs and swimming pools. In *Stone Container Corp. v. Castle*,[2] the court ordered an employer to cover the cost of a laptop computer the severely injured claimant required to continue his educational pursuits and to communicate with the outside world. The computer was found to constitute an appliance that was reasonably necessary to treat the claimant's condition.

Although necessary nursing services are covered, courts have not always reached the same result with respect to the right of family members who perform nursing services for claimants at home to be compensated for those services. The early decisions tended to deny payment for these activities, due to the belief that family members are morally obliged to provide such assistance. Most of the more recent cases, however, have reached the opposite conclusion. They recognize that employers are statutorily obligated to provide these services, and they do not believe that individuals who provide bona fide nursing care should be denied compensation simply because they are related to the claimants.

Some job-related injuries result in painful conditions that are unlikely to improve. Should medical benefits cover procedures that are primarily designed, not to improve the underlying disorder, but to alleviate the continuing discomfort? Although these endeavors are not designed to render the affected individuals reemployable, most courts now include these expenses. Only a few continue to deny coverage for palliative measures.

§ 7.28 Compensation—Unscheduled Disability Benefits

Disability benefits are designed to offset the earnings lost by people because of work-related injuries. These benefits are not awarded to all employees who suffer job-related injuries, but are generally limited to workers who can demonstrate reduced earning capacity. All state enactments contain brief waiting periods that must elapse before injured workers become eligible for disability benefits. These are designed to exclude minor injuries. Twenty-two states require the passage of three days, one requires four days, five require five days, and the other twenty-two require seven days. If the disability continues for more than a specified period of time, the disability benefits are made retroactive to the date of the injury. This time frame varies from five days to twenty-eight days.

2. 657 N.W.2d 485 (Iowa 2003).

Workers' compensation systems divide disabilities into four basic classifications: (1) temporary partial, (2) temporary total, (3) permanent partial, and (4) permanent total. Most people who sustain occupational injuries experience temporary total or temporary partial disabilities. During the healing process, they are unable to perform their usual job functions, and they are entitled to temporary disability benefits. If their conditions improve and they are able to resume their regular employment, their right to disability payments normally ends.

In some instances, the healing process runs its course but the conditions stabilize at less than preexisting capacity. Once this "maximum medical improvement" point is reached, the affected persons lose their right to continued temporary disability payments. They must request permanent partial or permanent total disability benefits, depending on the degree of incapacitation involved. Parties occasionally disagree regarding the point at which condition stabilization occurs. If the medical evidence suggests that further improvement is possible, temporary disability payments are usually continued. They only end when it becomes clear that additional improvement is unlikely.

Permanent disability awards may be scheduled or unscheduled. They may be partial or total. Scheduled payments are based upon specific medical conditions and are not directly related to lost earning capacity. For example, statutes generally provide scheduled benefits for the loss of one or both eyes, arms, or legs. The more controverted permanent disability cases do not normally involve scheduled injury situations. They tend to concern requests for unscheduled permanent disability payments.

Courts utilize different tests to determine whether claimants have unscheduled permanent disabilities. The traditional "wage loss" and "earning capacity" approaches used by most courts focus primarily on the claimant's earning potential. Several jurisdictions have adopted the "physical impairment" concept, previously denoted the "whole man theory" by some courts, which closely examines the physical condition of benefit applicants. Even "wage loss" and "earning capacity" jurisdictions provide scheduled benefits for some conditions, and, in this area, they are analogous to "physical impairment" states.

Conventional "wage loss" and "earning capacity" states generally determine eligibility for unscheduled disability benefits by estimating the future impairment of earnings associated with the claimant's occupational injuries. Compensation administrators and courts consider such factors as the claimant's age, education, training, and employment history when endeavoring to calculate the loss of earning potential generated by their conditions. They also examine the actual earnings of claimants at the time they are deciding the benefit eligibility question. Since unscheduled disability benefits are designed to compensate claimants for lost earning capacity, if injured employees elect to retire and are no longer part of the active labor force, they generally forfeit their right to continued disability benefits.

It is generally recognized that actual post-injury earnings create a rebuttable presumption of a claimant's earning capacity. If the wages received by workers following their occupational accidents are as great as or greater than their previous wages, courts tentatively assume that they have suffered no lost earning potential. Nonetheless, this presumption may be rebutted by evidence suggesting that the post-injury earnings do not accurately reflect the true future earning capacity of the individuals involved. For example, current claimant earnings may merely reflect general pay increases, overtime work, special post-injury training, employer sympathy, or other similar factors.

If the overall record indicates that the continuing impact of a claimant's injuries is likely to diminish actual future earnings, the claimant would be entitled to disability benefits despite the present earnings. The controlling factor is the amount of money the claimant would have been likely to earn in future years but for the job-related injuries. In close cases, doubts tend to be resolved in favor of benefit awards.

When claimants who are medically able to resume work unreasonably refuse to accept appropriate employment or fail to seek suitable employment with reasonable diligence, their right to continued disability benefits may be suspended. Individuals who forfeit their right to continued benefit payments because of their unreasonable refusal to accept an offer of suitable work may regain their right to benefits when they accept other appropriate employment, and they may retain their right to continued benefit payments if they subsequently lose their new job and continue to suffer from a partial disability. Claimants who voluntarily abandon presently suitable work may similarly lose their right to continued benefit payments. Claimants who are unable to seek gainful employment due to their incarceration may also forfeit their right to benefits.

If claimants decline employment because of scheduling conflicts with their religious convictions, their right to benefits may not be affected. While voluntary retirement may preclude continued benefit payments, injury-induced retirement will not do so. Furthermore, a claimant who becomes permanently and totally disabled because of an occupational injury sustained before his intended retirement date and who has not "retired or voluntarily withdrawn from the labor force" within the meaning of a statutory disqualification provision covering such withdrawals may continue to receive benefits after his previously planned retirement date.

Most courts define disability in terms of the ability of claimants to perform work commensurate with their training and job experience. If claimants have obtained post-injury employment suitable to their particular backgrounds that compensates them as well as their previous jobs, they will be presumed to have sustained no loss of earning capacity even though they are presently engaged in different lines of work. The fact that these individuals have changed occupations does not negate the fact that they continue to have earning capacities as great as those previously possessed. On the other hand, some claimants are forced to accept employment not commensurate with their training and experience because their occupational injuries prevent them from engaging in suitable work. These persons are likely to be awarded permanent disability benefits even though they are currently earning wages equal to their pre-injury salaries.

Several jurisdictions have evaluated future earning capacity in a more restrictive manner. For a number of years, courts in Louisiana and Michigan found accidental injury claimants disabled if they could no longer perform their prior occupations, regardless of their post-injury earnings in other occupations. More recent statutory changes in both states have modified this approach and generated judicial decisions more analogous to those of other states. Rarely do contemporary courts follow the occupation-specific rule when deciding the disability benefit eligibility of injury claimants presently earning more money in other suitable occupations than they earned prior to their injuries.

The courts in several states, however, continue to apply the occupation-specific doctrine to occupational disease cases. Courts in North Carolina, Maryland, Minnesota, New Mexico, and New York interpret their occupational disease provisions as authorizing permanent disability payments to persons suffering from job-related disorders that preclude their employment in the occupations they previously performed. The fact that these individuals are currently earning as much as before in other occupations is not considered controlling.

Claimants seeking total disability payments are not required to demonstrate that their occupational conditions have deprived them of absolutely all earning capacity. Under the generally accepted "odd-lot" doctrine, courts recognize that even persons who may be able to earn occasional wages or to perform limited kinds of gainful employment may be entitled to total disability awards.

> An employee who is so injured that he can perform no services other than those which are so limited in quality, dependability, or quantity that a reasonably stable market for them does not exist, may well be classified as totally disabled. He who has no reasonable prospect of selling his services has no material earning capacity and is substantially helpless as a self-sustaining unit of society. * * * [S]poratic competence, occasional, intermittent, and much limited capacity to earn something somehow, does not reduce what is otherwise total to a partial disability.[1]

The critical inquiry in odd-lot cases is whether the evidence indicates that the claimants, as a result of their occupational conditions, are simply incapable of obtaining and holding steady employment. Many of these cases involve individuals of limited education who traditionally performed physical labor. When work-related injuries render them unfit

§ 7.28

1. Lee v. Minneapolis St. Ry., 230 Minn. 315, 41 N.W.2d 433, 436–37 (1950).

for any meaningful physical work, they are usually found eligible for total disability benefits. A number of odd-lot claims also concern particularly painful conditions. Most jurisdictions recognize that individuals who cannot engage in gainful employment without experiencing debilitating pain should be considered totally disabled.

Once claimants establish their inability to work regularly in any recognized branch of the labor market, they are presumptively entitled to odd-lot treatment. The burden then shifts to their employer to prove that some kind of suitable employment is actually available to individuals with the backgrounds and conditions of the claimants. If the employer is unable to satisfy this burden, total disability status will be found.

Although most total disability benefit cases involve individuals with work-related conditions that prevent them from engaging in suitable employment, some cases concern persons who possess limited capabilities but are unable to locate meaningful work. These claimants may be affected by the general unavailability of jobs for people with their physical or mental problems or the unwillingness of employers to hire such persons. If their occupational conditions make it impossible for them to obtain gainful employment, they will probably be found totally disabled.

When benefit applicants contend that companies will not employ them because of their occupational conditions, courts usually consider their education, training, and age to determine whether their work-related problems and one or more of these factors have combined to render them unemployable. If it appears that their job-related disorders have significantly contributed to their unemployability, total disability benefits are likely to be awarded. The fact a claimant has been found eligible for Social Security Act disability benefits provides persuasive evidence of a permanent and total disability.

Workers who sustain occupational injuries are occasionally awarded substantial disability benefits despite the fact that their employer continued to carry them on the regular payroll following their accidents. Even though post-injury claimant earnings are the same as pre-injury earnings, compensation administrators may find diminished earning capacities and conclude that post-injury wages have been based more on employer sympathy than worker productivity. If the administrators determine that post-injury wage payments have been intended to be in lieu of disability benefits, they usually permit the company to reduce its disability benefit liability by the amounts paid as post-injury wages.

The critical inquiry when employers seek benefit credit for post-injury compensation is whether the remunerated claimants have actually earned their wages. If the individuals have performed no meaningful work, their earnings are generally considered to have been paid in lieu of disability benefits. On rare occasions, however, the wages paid to such claimants are treated as gratuities and are not credited against disability benefit awards.

While claimants are undergoing rehabilitation treatment designed to restore their pre-injury earning capacities, they are generally entitled to continued disability benefits to make up for their lost earnings. On the other hand, once claimants have been rehabilitated sufficiently to restore their pre-injury earnings potential, their right to continued disability benefits is likely to end. This is true even when they continue to participate in rehabilitation programs.

§ 7.29   Compensation—Scheduled Disability Benefits

The workers' compensation laws in every state, except Alaska, Florida, Kentucky, Maine, Minnesota, Montana, and Nevada, contain special scheduled benefit provisions. These statutory programs usually cover specific physical impairments, such as the loss of one or both eyes, ears, arms, legs, hands, or feet, or one or more fingers or toes. They also include combination losses, such as one arm and one leg, several fingers and one hand, or a foot and a leg. They provide disability payments for a certain number of weeks for each particular injury without regard to the actual wage loss associated with the listed condition. Scheduled benefits normally range from five to thirty weeks for the loss of a finger or toe to approximately 300 weeks for the loss of an arm or leg and 600 weeks or more for the loss of both eyes, legs, arms, hands, or feet.

Scheduled disability benefits are based on the conclusive presumption that people who sustain occupational conditions that cause permanent physical impairment suffer diminished earning capacities. As a result, scheduled benefits are paid to eligible claimants regardless of their actual present or likely future earnings. This enables some individuals to receive scheduled benefits during periods of continuous employment. Claimants with scheduled disabilities may similarly continue to receive full payments despite their concurrent receipt of Social Security Act old age insurance benefits.

It is relatively easy to determine claimant eligibility for scheduled benefits where an entire arm or leg has been amputated or vision in one eye has been completely lost. It is more problematic, however, where amputation does not involve the whole arm or leg or minimal vision is retained in the affected eye. Courts have usually held that the loss of a significant portion of a finger, toe, arm, or leg shall be treated as a loss of the entire limb for scheduled benefit purposes.

In many instances, injured workers merely lose the *use* of one of their limbs. Should these claimants be awarded scheduled or unscheduled disability benefits? If the loss of use of particular limbs is substantial, scheduled benefits are likely to be provided. If the loss is not so substantial, courts tend to resolve these claims under unscheduled disability provisions. Where the applicable statute speaks in terms of "actual loss" of scheduled members, nothing less than actual amputation may suffice. Mere loss of usage may be insufficient to warrant scheduled benefits.

Ehteshamfar v. UTA Engineered Systems[1] concerned a claimant who sought scheduled benefits for an occupational hearing loss. His problem was tinnitus (ringing in ears) which effectively diminished his hearing capacity. Since the statutory definition of "hearing loss" only covered a permanent sensorineural loss of hearing and tinnitus did not fit within that explicit definition, scheduled benefits were denied.

Complex medical issues frequently arise regarding individuals who contend that general occupational injuries to other parts of their bodies have caused them to lose the use of scheduled members. For example, back injuries may cause severe leg pain that impairs the use of those extremities. If courts decide that these claimants have effectively lost the use of one or both legs, they may award them compensation for scheduled losses. If scheduled benefits are not available, these claimants will be limited to unscheduled benefit coverage.

The controlling question with respect to lost use cases concerns the degree of impairment involved. Many courts apply a reasonable use test:

> A total loss of the use of a member exists whenever by reason of injury, such member no longer possesses any substantial utility as a member of the body, or the condition of the injured member is such that the workman cannot procure and retain employment requiring the use of the member.[2]

Some courts apply a stricter standard and refuse to award scheduled benefits for lost limbs unless claimants can demonstrate that their "body is no better off with the member than it would be if the member had been severed." Because scheduled benefits are based more on the physical impairment suffered by injured workers than their loss of earning capacity, most courts appropriately ascertain loss of use from the physical, rather than employment, loss perspective. Nonetheless, some courts continue to focus more on the degree of industrial loss involved.

When compensation administrators decide that scheduled benefits should be awarded to injured workers due to their lost use of particular limbs, they must determine the degrees of lost use involved. If they find that the claimants have lost the complete use of certain members, they normally award them benefits covering the entire limbs. If they conclude that the claimants have only lost the use of fifty or seventy-five percent of the affected appendages, they generally award them fifty or seventy-five percent of the scheduled benefits for the statutorily prescribed number of weeks, except where the applicable statutory provision mandates a reduction in the number of weeks, rather than the weekly amount, of benefits.

Courts do not always agree on whether loss-of-use determinations should evaluate the relevant members in the abstract or as they currently function with the assistance of eye glasses, hearing aids, or artificial limbs. A majority of courts believe that scheduled benefits are to be

§ 7.29
1. 555 N.W.2d 450 (Iowa 1996).

2. Travelers Ins. Co. v. Seabolt, 361 S.W.2d 204, 206 (Tex.1962).

based on the physical impairment sustained by claimants, and they assess industrial loss on the basis of uncorrected sight or hearing. Most courts similarly award full scheduled benefits to employees who lose particular appendages, despite their subsequent replacement with prosthetic devices.

The scheduled benefit provisions in some enactments contain catch-all sections that authorize scheduled awards for the loss of members or body parts not specifically listed in the statute. Under these provisions, if administrators determine that claimants have lost the use of unlisted body parts, they can grant them total or partial scheduled benefit awards. Some of these special sections even include body impairments caused by occupational diseases.

Some industrial accidents do not diminish the actual ability of the affected persons to perform employment tasks, but they do result in serious physical disfigurements. State legislators have appropriately recognized that these conditions may limit future employment opportunities as a result of societal biases. To compensate claimants with these problems, the statutes in thirty-nine states and court decisions in three other states now permit scheduled-type benefit awards for occupational disfigurements. They typically provide a certain percentage of weekly earnings for a specified number of weeks.

In a few industrial accidents, injured workers lose a member or the use of a member and they suffer accompanying disfigurement. Should the affected claimants be able to obtain separate scheduled awards for both the lost members and the disfigurement? The resolution of this question is frequently controlled by the specific language contained in the scheduled benefit and disfigurement provisions. In some jurisdictions, disability benefits for both conditions may be awarded, while in other states, separate awards are not permitted. Because the scheduled benefits concern the lost member and the disfigurement benefits pertain to that separate condition, there is no reason not to permit awards for both conditions in the absence of statutory language expressly precluding joint awards.

When certain occupational accidents cause the loss of particular members, they also affect the use of larger appendages. For example, claimants who lose two or three fingers or toes may effectively lose the use of the affected hands or feet. Should these individuals be compensated merely for the loss of their fingers or toes, or for the loss of the use of their hands or feet? The courts in a number of jurisdictions limit benefits to the exact scheduled losses sustained. Courts in other states, however, reasonably recognize that for some people, the loss of two or three fingers or toes may be the equivalent of a lost hand or foot, and they permit scheduled benefit awards covering the whole hand or foot.

Claimants who suffer isolated scheduled losses sometimes exhaust their awarded benefits but continue to be partially or totally disabled. If they request unscheduled benefits based on their current circumstances, the courts in a number of jurisdictions will deny their benefit applications. They consider the scheduled benefits the exclusive workers' compensation remedy for scheduled losses and refuse to permit extra unscheduled benefits for the same conditions. On the other hand, a growing number of courts have indicated a willingness to reassess the operative circumstances once scheduled benefits have been exhausted. If claimants can demonstrate that they continue to suffer from work-related disabilities, these judges will permit unscheduled benefits awards.

§ 7.30 Compensation—Second Injury Problems

Second injury questions most frequently involve scheduled conditions. They result from the fact that the combined impact of successive injuries may be far greater than the mere sum of the parts. For example, people who lost the use of one arm, leg, or eye in previous occupational or nonoccupational incidents will be more devastated by a subsequent industrial accident that results in the loss of their other arm, leg, or eye than would employees with no preexisting disabilities who sustain the identical later injuries. If the most recent losses are caused by occupational events, should the responsible employer be obliged to compensate the claimants for the loss of one arm, leg, or eye, or should it be required to compensate them for their combined losses? If their immediate employer is obligated to compensate them for their combined losses, should that company have to assume sole financial responsibility for the benefits awarded?

Courts generally acknowledge that employers take their employees as they hire them. When companies hire individuals with one arm, leg, or eye, they necessarily accept the increased risk of loss associated with these persons. As a result, in the absence of a contrary statutory provision, these courts tend to hold employers responsible for the total disabilities resulting from the combined impact of successive injuries. If workers with preexisting losses suffer industrial accidents causing the loss of a second arm, leg, or eye, their current firm will thus be obliged to compensate them for the loss of both arms, legs, or eyes, rather than for the narrow loss sustained in their most recent accidents. The same rule is applicable with respect to other preexisting partial disabilities that are converted to total disabilities as a result of the combined impact of recent occupational injuries. Under the "last injurious exposure" rule, it the claimant's current condition is a mere recurrence or independent aggravation of the prior occupational injury, the claimant's previous employer is liable for the present circumstances, but if the current condition is an aggravation of the prior injury caused by a recent job-related event, the claimant's present employer may be held liable for the resulting disability.

The combined responsibility rule fully compensates injured workers for their actual combined disabilities, but it imposes liability on employers that transcends the degree of financial responsibility related to the most recent occupational accidents. It also discourages companies from employing individuals who have preexisting conditions. Following the judicial decision applying the nonapportionment principle to firms in

Oklahoma, it was estimated that between 7,000 and 8,000 one-eyed, one-legged, one-armed, and one-handed workers were terminated by employers in that state.

A number of state legislatures have sought to limit employer liability for successive injury cases through the enactment of apportionment provisions. These generally provide that firms are not liable for the additional consequences generated by preexisting conditions. When the ultimate disability results from successive occupational events, the adversely affected workers are reasonably protected, with each of the respective employers being held responsible for the degree of disability that arose out of and during claimant employment with them. For an apportionment provision to apply, the preexisting condition must generally have been a "disabling" condition. If it was only a latent weakness— rather than a disabling condition—apportionment will not usually be required.

Suppose an individual who is already receiving permanent total disability benefits as a result of injuries suffered while working for a previous employer sustains further injuries while working for another employer. That claimant may be unable to obtain additional disability benefits from the current firm. Courts recognize that an individual may normally not receive more than permanent total disability benefits.

Apportionment statutes have a harsh impact on employees whose industrial accidents exacerbate preexisting, nonoccupational disabilities. Their employer is normally held responsible for only the proportion of their combined disability attributable to the relevant employment incidents. The adversely affected workers are thus denied compensation for their overall disabilities. This negative aspect of apportionment provisions is ameliorated by the fact that they only apply to claimants who had preexisting disabilities. They do not affect preexisting weaknesses considered the responsibility of the firms that hire these people. If preexisting weaknesses are exacerbated by subsequent industrial accidents, the pertinent employers are held liable for the total consequences.

In some cases, apportionment statutes are limited to situations in which claimant disabilities are the result of previous non-employment related disabling conditions and current employment-related injuries. If the prior disabilities arose from compensable occupational events, the apportionment rule is not applied. As a result, when two successive work-related injuries are involved, the most recent employer is generally responsible for the entire disability resulting from the combined impact of the prior disability and the current injuries.

State legislatures have sought to accommodate the competing interests of employees with successive injuries and their employers through the establishment of second injury funds. Second injury provisions only hold employers responsible for the degree of disabilities attributable to the injuries arising out of and during the course of claimant employment with them. They nonetheless guarantee most individuals who suffer successive injuries full compensation for their combined disabilities by having the second injury funds cover the portion of disability benefits that are beyond what is attributable to the most recent occupational injuries. Second injury funds are most often financed through state appropriations, special employer assessments, or charges imposed on employers in cases of compensable deaths involving workers who leave no dependents eligible for death benefits.

Two-thirds of second injury fund programs are limited to successive injury situations that result in permanent total disabilities. The statutes in eighteen states, however, impose no such restrictions. Fund provisions in approximately half of the state enactments specifically cover scheduled injuries but do not apply to unscheduled disabilities. Statutes that do not contain this limitation are usually found applicable to successive injury cases concerning preexisting unscheduled disabilities. The unrestricted provisions also may be applied to successive disability cases involving occupational diseases, as well as mental disabilities. Because second injury funds were primarily created to protect the employment rights of individuals with preexisting conditions, many jurisdictions, by statute or court decision, limit fund application to conditions that were manifest—i.e., obvious and apparent from observation and examination by lay persons—prior to the occupational event for which benefits are being currently sought.

It is generally recognized that the most recent injury need not be directly related to nor directly affect the preexisting condition to fall within second injury fund jurisdiction. If workers who previously lost the use of a hand or arm lose the use of a foot or leg in a subsequent industrial accident, they will be eligible for second injury fund coverage. On the other hand, claimants seeking second injury fund assistance must be able to demonstrate that the most recent incident combined with the preexisting condition to increase their degree of disability. If the preexisting disorder in no way contributed to the disability that resulted from the most recent occupational injury, their employer would only be responsible for the impact of the current accident, and the second injury fund would have no applicability. Conversely, if the most recent occupational injury would not have produced any disability but for the presence of a preexisting condition, the second injury fund would be responsible for the entire current disability, with the claimant's present employer having no liability.

In some states, eligible benefit applicants obtain their full compensation from their most recent employers. Those firms are then reimbursed by the second injury fund for the portion of benefits attributable to the aggravation of preexisting disabilities. For example, if persons who previously lost the use of one arm, leg, or eye were to lose the use of their other arm, leg, or eye in industrial accidents, they would be awarded benefits based on their combined losses. The responsible employers would then be reimbursed by the fund for the difference between the scheduled benefits pertaining to the loss of both appendages and those applicable to the loss of a single member.

In other states, responsible employers are merely obliged to compensate injured workers for their most recent losses. The affected employees must seek compensation for the remaining portions of their combined disabilities from the relevant second injury funds. Individuals who obtain benefits from both of these sources are compensated fully for their total disabilities.

A number of jurisdictions set maximum weekly benefit amounts that may be awarded to disabled persons. These limits are designed to ensure that claimants with multiple partial disabilities cannot obtain compensation that exceeds the maximum available for total disability. Many statutes similarly specify the maximum number of weeks for which disability benefits may be received. Most courts, however, recognize that these weekly limitations apply separately to distinct occupational conditions. As a result, persons who develop successive industrial disabilities may obtain benefits for more than the maximum number of weeks prescribed.

§ 7.31 Compensation—Calculating Wage Basis

Most state workers' compensation laws provide disabled employees with from one-half to two-thirds of their "average weekly wage." The weekly benefit amounts for claimants with partial disabilities are generally the same as the amounts for totally disabled persons, but they receive their benefit payments for proportionately fewer weeks. It is thus critical to determine the "average weekly wage" for people who develop occupational injuries or diseases.

Statutes generally provide that the three, six, or twelve month period preceding claimant disability will be used to calculate the relevant weekly wage rate. If claimants were employed on a relatively full-time basis during substantially all of the statutorily prescribed period, compensation administrators use their actual earnings to compute their average weekly earnings. If claimants were not employed during substantially all of the specified period, their weekly wage rate is determined by reference to employees of the same class who worked throughout substantially all of the relevant time frame. If there are insufficient data available to permit calculation of the weekly wage rate using the actual earnings of the claimants or of similar workers during the specified time period, statutes generally instruct administrators to use the limited information they have to estimate the wage rate. For people injured shortly after they were hired, their daily or hourly earnings may be used to determine their weekly wage rate at the time of their disability. When a claimant's earnings at the time of the most recent occupational injury does not reflect his or her true earning capacity due to the fact those earnings were diminished because of a previous employment-related injury, the court may use that person's average weekly earnings prior to the first injury to calculate the present benefit level.

The relevant weekly wage rate does not merely encompass base earnings. It includes all items of value received as compensation. As a result, tips, regular bonuses, commissions, and room and board provided to employees are generally included. In the absence of contrary statutory provisions, customary overtime earnings are also taken into account. While most jurisdictions do not include employer contributions to employee fringe benefit programs, because those amounts are not actually received by the workers themselves, several state enactments explicitly authorize the consideration of the value of fringe benefits when average weekly wage determinations are being made. The "wage basis" for covered self-employed individuals is generally calculated by subtracting their business expenses from their gross receipts.

When claimants were working on a part-time basis prior to the development of their occupational conditions, administrators have to decide whether to use their actual part-time earnings as the basis for their weekly wage rate or to calculate that figure using the earnings of full-time personnel performing similar work. Some courts think that weekly benefit rates should reflect claimant earning capacity, not current earnings, and they compute those rates using the full-time earnings of other employees, even when the record indicates that the claimants only intended to work part-time. These courts frequently provide claimants with weekly benefit amounts higher than what they would have earned if they had not become disabled. Other courts believe that disability benefits are intended to compensate claimants for their lost earnings and they calculate weekly benefit rates for voluntarily part-time personnel using their actual part-time earnings. Nonetheless, when claimants who wished to work full-time have recently been forced to accept part-time employment due to circumstances beyond their control, courts generally use the earnings of full-time personnel to determine their weekly wage rates.

Many individuals are employed by two different firms. If they are injured while working for one, should their weekly wage rate be based solely upon their earnings with that company or should it include their total earnings with both employers? A number of jurisdictions use the combined earnings to compute the weekly wage rate only when the two employments are "related" or "similar." Many other states use the combined earnings in their calculations even when the separate employments are not related or similar. A few jurisdictions refuse to combine the earnings from different employments even when they are related or similar.

§ 7.32 Compensation—Death Benefits

Certain surviving dependents of individuals who die as a result of work-related injuries or occupational diseases are entitled to statutorily prescribed death benefits. Surviving spouses and dependent children usually receive specified percentages of the deceased employees' weekly earnings—most frequently one-third, one-half, or two-thirds for surviving spouses and two-thirds or three-fourths for surviving spouses with dependent children. These benefits are normally provided for a set number of weeks, ranging from about 300 to 700 weeks for surviving spouses and continuing for dependent children until they reach age eighteen. Many enactments terminate death benefits for surviving spouses when they remarry. Burial expenses are also provided, ranging from $2,000 to $7,000 in most states.

The right of surviving dependents to death benefits is generally considered independent of the right of the adversely affected workers to disability benefits while they were alive. As a result, previous settlements or releases executed by deceased employees with respect to their workers' compensation rights have no impact in most states on the right of their surviving dependents, unless the surviving dependents have knowingly and voluntarily joined in lump sum settlement agreements entered into by injured workers that expressly waive their future dependency claims. Only workers in California, Illinois, Nebraska, and Wisconsin possess the authority to release not only their own claims, but also the rights of their surviving dependents.

The fact that adversely affected workers were found ineligible for disability benefits while they were alive does not normally prevent their surviving dependents from subsequently establishing their independent claims. Only a few states apply res judicata or collateral estoppel concepts to the later claims of surviving dependents. On the other hand, if the disabled workers established their right to benefits while they were alive, most states do not require their surviving dependents to relitigate all of the eligibility issues. They are usually only required to establish the worker's death, the work-related causal connection, and their dependency status.

On some occasions, individuals who have sustained job-related injuries die from non-occupational conditions during the pendency of their workers compensation claims. Their compensation claims survive their death, with the resulting awards being included in their estates and being passed on to survivors pursuant to will provisions or intestacy statutes.

Survivors who were totally dependent on the deceased workers are entitled to the full amount of the prescribed death benefits. Partially dependent survivors, however, are usually given reduced benefits. The most prevalent approach, followed by sixteen states, requires compensation administrators to calculate the percentage of the deceased worker's earnings given to the partial dependent and to award that survivor the same percentage of the weekly benefit amount provided for total dependents. Seven states mandate an evaluation from the survivor's perspective. They compute the proportion of the dependent's overall support previously provided by the deceased worker, and award that percentage of total dependent benefits. Other state enactments use various other techniques to determine the amounts paid to partial dependents.

Individuals who request death benefits based upon their dependency on employees who died from employment-related conditions must establish that they satisfy the statutorily prescribed eligibility criteria. Most enactments list the relatives of deceased workers eligible for death benefits. They all include surviving spouses and minor children. States may not constitutionally distinguish for death benefit purposes between legitimate and illegitimate minor children, because such disparate treatment would contravene the equal protection clause. Most laws also include dependent parents and some cover siblings, grandparents, and other more distant relatives. People who do not fall within the list of covered dependents are not entitled to death benefits, despite their actual dependency on the deceased. For example, unmarried men and women living together are normally not eligible for benefits following the work-related death of their partners.

State common law definitions of family relationships are generally used to determine whether death benefit claimants meet prescribed relationship prerequisites. In close cases many courts apply liberal tests favoring coverage. For example, several courts have found that divorced spouses who had been residing with decedents when they died should be treated as surviving spouses for benefit purposes. When spouses are living apart at the time of an employee's death, dependency may still be presumed if a conjugal nexus existed between the dependent and his or her injured spouse at the time of that worker's death. Some courts have similarly awarded benefits to children workers were attempting to adopt at the time of their deaths. When employees have been married on several occasions, courts presume that spouses involved with the most recent marriages are the survivors entitled to death benefits.

In many states, spouses and minor children who resided with deceased workers at the time of their deaths are conclusively presumed to be eligible for survivor benefits. They need not present evidence of actual dependency. In the absence of such a statutory presumption, surviving spouses and children must prove that they were financially dependent on the decedents. They are not required to prove that they depended on the deceased workers for their basic needs. They must only demonstrate that they used the funds supplied by those people to maintain their accustomed standard of living.

If survivors received most of their regular financial support from decedents, they would generally be considered totally dependent, even though they sporadically obtained income from other sources. On the other hand, if they regularly received support from other sources, they would be regarded as partial dependents. The critical question concerns the degree to which they were effectively dependent upon the income received from the deceased employees.

What should be the benefit eligibility of surviving relatives who were legally entitled to financial support from deceased workers while they were alive but who actually received no monetary assistance? Many courts believe that dependency must be defined in terms of real financial support, and they refuse to find dependent relationships based solely on unsatisfied legal obligations. A number of other courts, however, have taken a contrary position. They generally find a legal obligation to provide support sufficient to establish dependency, even when no funds were in fact supplied.

§ 7.33 Claims Administration

Almost all workers' compensation laws are enforced by administrative agencies. Louisiana is the only state that relies entirely on the courts to resolve all benefit controversies. Although Alabama, New Mexico, Tennessee, and Wyoming provide some direct judicial involvement, they also use administrative agencies to handle many aspects of the enforcement process. The enactments in the other forty-five states provide for enforcement through specialized administrative agencies.

It is generally recognized that workers' compensation systems were established to assist individuals who are not likely to be knowledgeable regarding technical legal procedures. As a result, administrative agencies apply liberal procedural rules designed to enhance worker coverage. For example, informal benefit applications, such as letters sent to compensation administrators generally describing the pertinent circumstances, are usually found sufficient to begin the claim process.

Employer Notification

Injured employees are generally required to notify their employers promptly of their job-related conditions. They are usually obliged to provide employers with notice of occupational injuries when they occur, and not when they suffer economic harm as a result of those injuries. When latent injuries are involved, notice must be provided as soon as reasonable persons would have recognized the true nature of the compensable conditions. When repetitive trauma injuries are involved, claimants must usually notify employers of their conditions shortly after they realize those conditions have become disabling. The notice obligation is designed to enable firms to provide workers with immediate medical treatment. It is also intended to give companies the opportunity to investigate the underlying circumstances to determine whether the employee conditions are compensable. The failure of injured workers to provide expeditious notice is likely to be excused if the record indicates that the employer was not prejudiced by the omission. In some states, however, failure to provide the employer with timely notice may result in a forfeiture of benefits even when no employer prejudice has been shown.

When it is apparent that interested employers have obtained prompt knowledge of an industrial accident from other sources, the failure of the adversely affected employees to provide the requisite notice will normally be excused. Typical cases involve situations in which company supervisors are apprised of the underlying circumstances, physician treatment reports containing the relevant information are sent to company officials, or firm physicians obtain the pertinent information during their treatment of injured employees. On the other hand, statements to mere coworkers are not likely to constitute adequate notice, because fellow employees are generally not considered responsible company agents. The fact that companies have provided injured personnel with covered medical treatment or have given them workers' compensation benefits generally demonstrates that the firms received sufficient knowledge of the relevant events.

In the absence of legislative language to the contrary, the failure of injured employees to provide employers with prompt notice of their work-related conditions generally precludes benefit awards. Surviving dependents of injured workers who die from their conditions must generally notify employers of the employee deaths within certain time limits, and their failure to provide timely notice may cause a forfeiture of death benefits. Many enactments contain provisions indicating that notice omissions may be excused if employers have suffered no prejudice. Most judicial decisions recognize that notice failures should only be excused when the record demonstrates that claimant conditions were not exacerbated as a result of employer inability to provide expeditious treatment and the firms had a fair opportunity to ascertain the relevant facts. In most jurisdictions, claimants have the burden of establishing that their failure to provide the required notice did not prejudice their employer. If it appears that company interests have been adversely affected by the lack of prompt notification, statutory coverage is usually denied.

Filing of Claims

Individuals who develop employment-related conditions must file benefit claims with state administrative agencies within specified time periods—usually one or two years—following their industrial accidents or injuries, or the manifestation of their occupational diseases. When accidental injuries initially seem insignificant, most courts recognize that claim limitation periods do not begin to run until it would be apparent to reasonable persons possessing the knowledge and experience of the claimants that the conditions are actually serious and probably compensable.

This approach is universally followed under statutes that start the running of limitation periods when job-related "injuries" occur. Typical cases involve minor eye injuries that develop into cataracts or similar disorders and seemingly inconsequential traumas that generate cancerous conditions. Even in jurisdictions with statutes providing for the commencement of limitation periods when employment "accidents" occur, many courts hold that claim periods begin for latent conditions when similarly situated individuals would have become aware of the serious nature of the resulting injuries. On the other hand, some judicial decisions in states with these provisions continue to begin claim periods when the "accidents" take place, even when the compensable nature of the injuries does not become manifest for several years.

Most courts similarly postpone the running of statutory periods for conditions that develop slowly and where it is not immediately apparent that the disorders are employment-related. These cases frequently involve occupational diseases caused by prolonged exposure to airborne contaminants. Nevertheless, when injured workers unreasonably fail to comprehend the true nature of their conditions and file claims belatedly, statutory protection is normally denied. Statutory periods are also tolled when employers mislead workers into thinking they can postpone filing their claims until after the statute of limitations has run, or where employers erroneously induce injured employees to believe that their conditions are not statutorily covered.

Most state enactments include separate statute-of-limitation provisions for death benefits. Because the rights of surviving dependents only accrue when workers die, the limitation periods for dependents do not begin to run until the date injured employees die. Even when statutes fail to contain distinct limitation provisions pertaining to death benefit applications, courts usually recognize that limitation periods for surviving dependents commence at the time of the worker's death. A failure of a surviving dependent to file a claim within the statutory period for the filing of death benefit applications following the worker's death may cause the survivor to lose his or her right to benefits. Nonetheless, courts in states without separate death benefit limitation provisions occasionally apply the periods applicable to all accidental injuries and find death benefit claims filed after those periods are time-barred. Such a strict application of limitation periods unfairly denies compensation to surviving dependents who, obviously, could not apply for death benefits prior to the death of the injured workers.

Because the death benefit rights of surviving dependents are considered independent of the disability benefit rights of injured workers, it is generally acknowledged that the failure of deceased employees to file timely benefit claims during their lifetime does not prevent the award of death benefits to their surviving dependents. On the other hand, the failure of injured workers to notify their employer promptly of their industrial accidents may preclude subsequent death benefit awards to their surviving dependents. When enactments specifically require such notification as a prerequisite to disability *and* death benefits, the absence of employer notice is likely to preclude even death benefits. When no employer notification obligation expressly covers death benefits, courts tend to permit awards to surviving dependents despite the failure of the deceased workers to provide such notice.

§ 7.34 Claims Administration—Adjudication

Administrative proceedings are normally conducted in an informal manner. Technical evidentiary doctrines are usually inapplicable due to express statutory provisions or judicial decisions. Although the exclusion of competent evidence is likely to be considered reversible error, awards are rarely reversed because of the admission of incompetent evidence. For reviewing courts, the critical inquiry is not whether incompetent evidence has been considered, but whether the deciding tribunal relied excessively on that evidence.

The courts in a majority of states follow the "residuum" rule. This doctrine authorizes the affirmance of compensation awards that are partially based on incompetent evidence, so long as there is a residuum of competent evidence to support those determinations. In these jurisdictions, awards based entirely on inadmissible hearsay may not be sustained, no matter how probative the hearsay testimony might be. There must be some admissible evidence underlying the compensation determinations. This admissible evidence may, of course, include hearsay statements that fall within recognized hearsay exceptions.

Courts in some states permit awards to be based totally on inadmissible evidence if that evidence is found to be sufficiently credible. Awards based solely on inadmissible hearsay testimony are only reversed when reviewing courts find that evidence inherently unreliable. Courts in some other states apply an intermediate standard. They do not reject compensation determinations simply because they are based in part on inadmissible hearsay testimony. Nonetheless, they refuse to accept awards that are partially based on incompetent evidence, when they conclude that the benefit decisions would not have been made but for consideration of the inadmissible evidence.

Most controverted cases include medical evidence. The fact that the claimant's medical evidence does not establish a definitive connection between employment and injury or illness, however, is not determinative. The record need only be sufficient to enable administrators to reasonably conclude that the relevant maladies are job-related. Courts recognize that compensation administrators are familiar with the conditions that result from typical industrial accidents, and judges usually permit them to rely upon their personal knowledge to decide whether particular disorders have arisen out of and during the course of employment. Courts even affirm awards that are contrary to the uncontroverted medical testimony provided by expert witnesses where there are reasonable factual bases for the challenged determinations. On the other hand, where the medical evidence indicates the lack of any work connection to claimant injuries and the lay testimony does not establish any meaningful job relationship, courts are unlikely to sustain compensation awards.

Courts occasionally refuse to sustain compensation awards not supported by any expert testimony. These cases usually involve complex medical conditions merely described by the claimants themselves. Some courts believe that causation or disability questions pertaining to these claims can only be resolved with the assistance of medical evidence. Classic cases concern employees with heart conditions, back problems, and eye disorders. Other courts, however, permit benefit awards in these cases without supporting medical evidence, so long as the other evidence is sufficient to establish the requisite employment connection.

Judicial Review

Initial compensation determinations are normally made by administrative examiners. Their factual findings and statutory interpretations are usually subject to thorough administrative review by agency directors or compensation review boards. Internal agency reviewers evaluate hearing records and reach their own factual conclusions. They also decide whether legal issues have been properly resolved. If they find records incomplete, they remand cases to examiners for further proceedings.

Almost all state statutes have created administrative agencies and authorized them to resolve factual disputes pertaining to compensation claims. Many expressly indicate that agency fact findings are conclusive, so long as they are supported by "substantial evidence" in the record. As a result, reviewing judges recognize that they are not empowered to evaluate factual controversies on a de novo basis. They are not to determine whether they would have reached the same factual conclusions had they been the deciding officials. They must simply ask whether there is substantial evidence in the record to support the agency findings. If they answer this inquiry affirmatively, they are obliged to accept the administrative conclusions. When agency review boards have reversed preliminary examiner fact findings, courts generally defer to the agency conclusions. Nonetheless, where credibility questions are involved, some courts give more careful consideration to examiner findings with respect to testimony by witnesses they personally observed.

When courts are asked to review administrative interpretation of statutory provisions, they engage in more intensive evaluations. They examine the statutory language and the relevant legislative history to ascertain the intent of the legislators who adopted the pertinent sections. While it is clear that reviewing judges are not bound by agency interpretations of statutory provisions, they generally give substantial deference to the specialized administrative bodies established to interpret and apply workers' compensation enactments.

It is only when reviewing courts conclude that administrative agencies have clearly misinterpreted or misapplied statutory provisions that they are likely to substitute their views for those of agency officials.

Settlements

The vast majority of workers' compensation claims are resolved through negotiated settlement agreements. Employers or their insurance carriers expressly or implicitly acknowledge that claimant conditions arose out of and during the course of their employment and they agree to provide medical coverage and, where appropriate, disability benefits.

The most controverted settlement issue is the capacity of injured workers to enter into settlements that compromise their benefit rights. For example, suppose a particular injury entitles the affected employee to 300 weeks of disability benefits equal to sixty-seven percent of his or her regular weekly earnings. If it were not unequivocally clear that the person's condition arose out of and during the course of his or her employment, could the parties agree to 150 or 200 weeks of benefits? Could they agree to 300 weeks of benefits at a level equal to fifty percent of the employee's regular weekly earnings?

The enactments in some states contain express language prohibiting the execution of settlement agreements that include waivers of claimants' statutory rights. Courts in most of these states refuse to allow individuals to settle workers' compensation claims for less than the statutorily prescribed benefit amounts. Nonetheless, courts in several jurisdictions that have these specific statutory provisions permit compromise agreements.

Even where this issue is not explicitly addressed in the applicable compensation law, a majority of courts refuse to permit settlements that provide claimants with benefits below those prescribed in the statute. In these jurisdictions, if the parties were to resolve our hypothetical case, the injured worker would have to be given 300 weeks of benefits at a level equal to sixty-seven percent of his or her regular weekly earnings. A number of courts in other states that have no express statutory provisions find no basis for such a strict rule, and they allow parties to reach agreements that provide for compromised benefit amounts.

Compensation laws in a number of states authorize lump-sum settlements. In jurisdictions that do not permit the compromise of worker claims, lump-sum settlements must approximate the present value of the prescribed weekly benefit amounts to which claimants would otherwise be entitled. In states that allow compromise settlements, lump-sum agreements may provide for reduced benefit payments. Some jurisdictions only permit lump-sum settlements where claimants can establish that lump-sum payments are in their best interest.

Reopening Awards or Settlement Agreements

Unlike tort cases, in which a single judgment bars any future claims relating to the same cause of action, all workers' compensation laws permit awards to be reopened in appropriate situations. Although several states allow benefit decisions to be reopened at any time, most statutes impose time limits. Some laws require reopening requests to be filed within specified periods following the initial injuries or benefit awards. Some only permit petitions to be filed while claimants are still receiving benefits. Others allow reopening for set periods following the last benefit payment. These different periods run from one to ten years.

Awards may only be reopened where such action is warranted by changed claimant conditions. Even settlement agreements may be reopened when necessitated by sufficiently changed circumstances. Individuals seeking benefit increases are usually required to demonstrate that their conditions have either deteriorated or have been aggravated by other developments. On the other hand, if benefit recipients experience entirely new medical problems that have no direct relationship to their existing conditions, but which they believe have arisen out of their previous employment accidents, they may not reopen the original case. Their proper course is to file new benefit claims covering their new and distinct conditions. When employers believe that claimant conditions have become less debilitating, they may request benefit reductions or terminations. To prevail in such proceedings the employers must demonstrate not only that claimant conditions have improved but also that their disabilities have declined or ended.

Compensation administrators do not allow parties filing reopening petitions to relitigate issues resolved in the original proceedings. Nor do they permit claimants to raise conditions they were aware of when they filed their initial claims. Persons filing reopening requests must be able to show that their conditions have been affected by occurrences that have taken place since the issuance of their original awards. Those seeking modified benefit awards have the burden of establishing the requisite circumstances.

Even when changed circumstances cannot be established, previous awards may be reopened if petitioning parties can demonstrate that they were procured by fraud. This exception is designed to prevent parties from benefiting from fraudulent misrepresentations that induce administrative agencies to issue unwarranted awards or that cause workers, employers, or insurance carriers to enter into inappropriate settlement agreements.

Attorney Fees, Expenses, Interest, and Penalties

When compensation claims are contested, claimants and employers or their insurance carriers are likely to retain the services of attorneys and medical experts. If benefits are not paid to injured employees promptly, they may request interest to compensate them for the delay. Employers and their insurance carriers must normally assume responsibility for the lawyers and experts they use. Statutes in a number of states authorize the awarding of extra benefits to prevailing claimants to cover the cost of their attorneys and a few permit extra benefits to reimburse claimants for their expert witnesses. In the absence of these special provisions, however, injured workers are usually required to bear their own litigation costs.

Under the American rule, parties to litigation are normally responsible for their respective legal expenses. To ameliorate the impact of this approach, most state legislatures have adopted provisions authorizing add-on awards to at least partially cover the attorney fees of prevailing claimants. In almost all of these jurisdictions, the amount to be included for attorney fees is determined by the administrative agency—either on a case-by-case basis or pursuant to statutorily prescribed guidelines. Where guidelines are provided, they generally authorize add-on amounts ranging from ten to thirty percent of disability benefit awards. Several restrict add-on awards to cases in which the agency decides that employers or their insurance carriers unreasonably contested the right of claimants to receive benefits. A few limit add-on awards to lawyer costs associated with the review process. Claimant lawyers who are not awarded attorney fees generally charge their prevailing clients a percentage of their benefits. Most enactments contain provisions that either require agency approval of lawyer charges or limit contingent fees to twenty, twenty-five, or thirty percent of compensation awards.

Claimants must usually provide medical evidence in contested cases. The statutes in a few states authorize extra awards to cover the costs of these experts. In the absence of special provisions, claimants must normally assume responsibility for their own medical experts. The impact of this doctrine is lessened by the fact that claimants frequently present evidence from treating physicians. While prevailing claimants are not reimbursed for the testimony of these doctors, they do receive medical benefits to cover the costs associated with treatment.

When employers or their insurance carriers contest eligibility, months or years may elapse before prevailing claimants obtain their benefits. A number of statutes permit interest to be awarded on unpaid benefit amounts. Some enactments authorize the imposition of special penalties in cases involving unreasonable nonpayment. These penalties may include percentage increases in awards due, add-on amounts to cover claimant legal costs, or both.

§ 7.35 Exclusivity and Exceptions

The creation of workers' compensation systems involved a critical tradeoff. In exchange for the liability-without-fault protection given to employees, their employers were granted expansive tort immunity with respect to statutorily covered injuries and illnesses. As a result, individuals who sustain job-related conditions are usually unable to sue their employers. The dependents of injured workers are also likely to be denied the right to sue the employers of the adversely affected employees. In most states, individuals are not allowed to sue fellow employees whose negligence contributed to their injuries. Actions may only be brought against employers or fellow employees where intentional misconduct is involved.

Employers wishing to avail themselves of statutory tort immunity must raise the issue in a timely manner and must be able to demonstrate that employee-plaintiff injuries arose out of and during the course of their employment—i.e., are subject to workers' compensation act coverage. The fact that the affected workers chose not to file compensation claims is not controlling. Employees who sustain employment-related injuries that are partially compensable and partly noncompensable may not prosecute tort actions pertaining to the noncompensable aspects of their injuries, since their overall conditions fall within workers' compensation coverage. Similarly, the fact that employees did not sustain *compensable* harm is irrelevant. For example, in several jurisdictions workers who sustain job-related injuries that affect their capacity to have children cannot prosecute tort actions against their culpable employers, nor can employees who suffer an employment-related loss of taste or smell. Workers who sustain noncompensable emotional distress as a result of harassment by company agents also may be denied the right to seek tort damages from their employer. On the other hand, employees who sustain personal injuries that are not subject to workers' compensation coverage may still seek traditional tort damages from their responsible employers. When covered employers fail to carry required workers' compensation insurance, adversely affected employees may obtain regular compensation benefits or elect to seek traditional tort damages.

Horodyskyj v. Karanian[1] involved an individual who had been subjected to workplace verbal and physical sexual harassment by a coworker that caused him to quit his job. He thereafter brought a tort action against his former employer for the economic and emotional damages caused by the harassment. The employer claimed that the former employee's tort action was barred by the immunity provision of the applicable workers' compensation statute, but the court rejected this defense. It indicated that the coworker sexual harassment suffered by the plaintiff was "inherently private" despite the fact it had occurred in the work environment, and thus did not "arise out of employment." As a result, the tort action was not covered by the workers' compensation immunity section.

Relatives and Dependents of Injured Employees

When employees are injured or killed in job-related accidents, their relatives or dependents may also be affected. These people may decide to sue the responsible employers. Spouses may sue for loss of consortium or loss of spousal services. Dependent children may seek damages for loss of support, and parents may sue for the loss of minor children. Suits by such dependents are generally found barred by the statutory immunity afforded to employers.

Some compensation laws specifically prohibit legal actions by the spouses, parents, children, and other dependents of injured workers. Other enactments merely state that workers' compensation coverage shall constitute the exclusive redress available to injured employees. Under both types of statutory provisions, it is usually recognized that husbands and wives affected by job-related conditions sustained by their spouses may not sue the culpable employers for the loss of consortium or the loss of spousal services. Nor may parents sue for the loss of services that were provided by minor children prior to their injuries. Dependent children of adversely affected workers also are denied the right to sue the employers of the injured persons.

In *Pizza Hut of America, Inc. v. Keefe*,[2] the court had to decide whether the child of an employee who suffered fatal prenatal injuries as a result of employment-related negligence by her mother's employer was precluded from seeking tort damages. The court permitted the tort action on behalf of the deceased child to proceed. Although the derivative-injury doctrine prevents the children of injured employees from seeking tort damages for the injuries of their respective parents, the court concluded that the exclusivity doctrine does not apply to injuries directly caused to a non-employee child by the negligence of the employer of that child's parent.

§ 7.35

1. 2001 Colo. J.C.A.R. 4718, 32 P.3d 470 (Colo. 2001).

2. 900 P.2d 97 (Colo.1995).

Parties Entitled to Statutory Immunity

The scope of the civil immunity provided by workers' compensation laws varies from state to state. In ten states statutory immunity is limited to the actual employers of injured workers. In these jurisdictions individuals injured by the negligence of fellow employees may prosecute tort actions against those persons. These third-party suits may include supervisors and even corporate officials whose culpable behavior during the course of their employment contributed to plaintiff conditions. On the other hand, corporate stockholders and business partners who did not engage in personal acts of negligence may not be sued by injured workers based solely on their status as shareholders or partners.

The statutes in most other states, either expressly or as judicially interpreted, extend tort immunity to the coworkers of injured employees. This protection covers not only rank-and-file workers, but also managerial and supervisory personnel. When corporate officers injure workers while acting within the scope of their managerial authority, courts are likely to extend coworker immunity to those officials. Even persons employed by other firms may be granted coworker immunity while they are on loan to and are working for the employer of injured personnel. Statutory immunity also includes the employers of "borrowed servants" and the employees of those firms while the loaned personnel are working for those entities. The immunity extended to coworkers is based on the notion that compensation act protection is intended to provide the exclusive remedy for all employment-related accidents. Nonetheless, the immunity granted to fellow employees is limited to events that occur while they are acting within the course of their employment. When coworkers act outside the course of their employment and their negligence causes harm to fellow employees, they are subject to third-party tort liability.

Civil immunity is not only granted to the actual employers of workers injured in industrial accidents, but also to other firms that are legally responsible for the workers' compensation coverage of those persons. For example, forty-four state enactments contain "statutory employer" provisions that impose compensation liability on general contractors with respect to the employees of uninsured subcontractors they employ to perform work that is part of their regular business, trade, or occupation. When individuals employed by such uninsured subcontractors sustain injuries while performing work on behalf of the general contractor, most courts recognize that their exclusive remedy vis-a-vis the general contractor is through workers' compensation procedures. They are thus precluded from suing that party in tort for damages caused by its negligent agents.

If the subcontractors of statutory employers are insured and able to provide the requisite workers' compensation coverage for their own employees, should their injured workers be able to sue the general contractors for job-related injuries caused by negligence attributable to those parties? A majority of courts have historically permitted third-party tort actions against such general contractors based upon the premise that legislative immunity should only be available to statutory employers that are actually liable for the workers' compensation coverage of uninsured subcontractor personnel.

A number of more recent judicial decisions have held that tort immunity should be granted to statutory employers regardless of the capacity of their subcontractors to satisfy the workers' compensation claims of injured subcontractor employees. These courts note that general contractors who employ the services of subcontractors must obtain insurance to protect themselves against the compensation claims of uninsured subcontractor personnel. They do not believe that statutory employers should be held subject to tort liability when they conscientiously induce their subcontractors to provide the required compensation coverage. Because the statutory employers remain secondarily liable for the compensation coverage of the subcontractor employees, it is likely that the judicial trend extending tort immunity to general contractors even when their subcontractors are insured will continue. Statutory employers who fail to secure the requisite workers' compensation protection for injured contractor employees may be subject to tort liability if their negligence contributes to those injuries.

The courts in several states have held that tort immunity is only available to the actual employers of injured workers. Inasmuch as "statutory employers" are not really the employers of subcontractor personnel, these courts refuse to grant general contractors immunity against tort actions brought by injured subcontractor employees, even when the principal parties are legally responsible for the compensation coverage of those persons.

When no statutory employer relationship is created between a general contractor and a subcontractor because the subcontractor is not performing work within the regular business, trade, or occupation of the general contractor, the principal contractor has no responsibility for the workers' compensation coverage of subcontractor personnel. As a result, the general contractor is not entitled to any legislative immunity vis-a-vis injured subcontractor employees. Furthermore, when the employees of statutory employers sustain job-related injuries due to the negligence of subcontractor agents, they may sue the responsible subcontractors. Because subcontractors have no responsibility for the workers' compensation coverage of general contractor employees, they enjoy no tort immunity with respect to those individuals.

Individuals employed by one firm occasionally sustain job-related injuries caused by the negligence of agents of a corporate parent. Should the parent company be able to rely on the tort immunity available to the subsidiary employer of the plaintiff-employees? When the corporate entities maintain wholly separate identities from a tax and business perspective, they are likely to be treated as distinct firms for immunity purposes. The injured plaintiffs would thus be allowed to sue the parent corporation. On the other hand, if the firms in question have common ownership and common managerial control, the parent company might well be considered the employer of the adversely affected individuals and be afforded statutory immunity.

§ 7.36 Exclusivity and Exceptions—Actions Against Employers

Despite the "exclusivity" of workers' compensation, injured workers still have attempted to bring damage actions against their employers under several different theories. Although a few cases in several jurisdictions have succeeded, the exclusive remedy bar, at least as applied to actions for damages, is alive and well.

Dual Capacity

A theory that has enjoyed some success is the dual capacity or dual persona doctrine, which permits an employee to recover from his or her employer if the employer "possesses a second persona so completely independent from and unrelated to his status as employer that by established standards the law recognizes it as a separate legal person." Although the theory has been widely asserted, it remains a minority view. When a plaintiff in a tort action is unable to demonstrate the existence of a responsible persona that is separate and distinct from the defendant persona as the plaintiff's employer, statutory immunity will usually preclude tort liability.

In the leading case of *Duprey v. Shane*,[1] a nurse employed by a chiropractor was injured in the course of her employment and then was negligently treated by her chiropractor-employer. The California Supreme Court held that the employee could maintain a common law action because her employer's negligent treatment occurred when the employer was acting in his second capacity as a chiropractor. In effect, she was no different from any other patient who was negligently treated by the chiropractor.

Reaction to *Duprey* has varied widely, and the case was legislatively overruled in California in 1982.[2] Some jurisdictions have followed *Duprey,* but other courts have rejected it outright or have limited it to the following situations: where the employer's negligence aggravated a compensable injury and illness, where the employer was not required to render medical treatment, or where the injury or illness for which treatment was initially sought was noncompensable under workers' compensation.

Even fewer jurisdictions permit injured employees to maintain actions against their employers based on injuries or illnesses caused by a product manufactured by the employer if the product was manufactured for sale to the general public. Numerous other jurisdictions, however, have rejected the dual capacity products liability theory, as well as other dual capacity theories.

§ 7.36   **2.** Cal. Lab. Code § 3602(a).
1. 39 Cal.2d 781, 249 P.2d 8 (1952).

Willful and Intentional Torts

Resort to workers' compensation is the exclusive remedy for all "accidental" harms suffered by employees. If an employee is the victim of an intentional act, however, such as assault, battery, or intentional infliction of emotional distress by a company official, the harm is not considered "accidental" and therefore workers' compensation is not a bar. A loss of tort immunity may similarly result when injuries are caused to a worker by an employer's willful *failure to act* in a manner that would have prevented those injuries. Suppose the conduct was not done with the intent to injure, but was willful, wanton, or reckless. Should resort to workers' compensation still be the exclusive remedy?

The overwhelming majority of states have held that there is no common law liability for "accidental injuries caused by the gross, wanton, wilful, deliberate, intentional, reckless, culpable, or malicious negligence, breach of statute, or other misconduct of the employee short of genuine intentional injury."[3]

Intentional misconduct may similarly affect the immunity afforded to a claimant's coworkers. Statutory provisions in twenty-two states and court decisions in twelve other jurisdictions deny statutory immunity to workers whose intentional misbehavior causes injury to fellow employees. In these states, employees injured by the willful misconduct of coworkers may prosecute tort actions against the responsible individuals, but they must establish that the coworkers knew or reasonably should have known that some injury was substantially certain to result.

In addition to private litigation, intentional employer misconduct may increase the amount of the workers' compensation award. Some statutes contain special provisions regulating intentional employer misconduct. Some explicitly give adversely affected employees the option to accept workers' compensation benefits or to seek traditional tort remedies. The laws in Arkansas, Connecticut, Kentucky, Missouri, New Mexico, North Carolina, Ohio, South Carolina, Utah, and Wisconsin authorize ten to fifteen percent extra compensation for individuals whose injuries are caused by employer violations of safety regulations. Statutory provisions in Arizona, Kentucky, Oregon, Washington, and West Virginia, also authorize enhanced awards to claimants injured by other acts of serious employer misconduct.

Fraudulent Concealment

Another line of intentional tort cases is based on the alleged fraudulent concealment from employees of work-related illnesses detected by company physicians in the course of a medical examination. Although an action for contracting the disease in the first place would be barred by workers' compensation, fraudulent concealment cases seek to recover for aggravation of the condition caused by a delay in obtaining treatment.

In *Delamotte v. Unitcast Division of Midland Ross Corp.,*[4] an employee was given periodic chest x-rays by his employer beginning in

3. Arthur Larson, Larson's Workers' Compensation Law § 103.03 (2003).

4. 64 Ohio App.2d 159, 411 N.E.2d 814 (1978).

1952. Although the x-rays revealed a progressively worsening case of silicosis, it was not until 1972 that he was informed of his condition and advised to consult his own physician. The Ohio Court of Appeals held that an action based on fraudulent, malicious, and willful concealment was not barred by workers' compensation. Similar results have been reached in cases involving asbestos-related diseases, lead poisoning, arsenic poisoning, silicosis, and other medical conditions. On the other hand, several other jurisdictions have refused to recognize this theory.

§ 7.37 Exclusivity and Exceptions—Actions Against Third Parties

The relatively low benefits awarded under workers' compensation law and the inability to recover in tort from their employers have led workers to attempt to sue other third parties that are responsible for their harms. Although workers' compensation laws are generally not a bar to these third-party actions, traditional tort concepts—such as proving that the defendant's breach of a duty owed to the plaintiff was a proximate cause of the plaintiff's harm—often cannot be established.

There are numerous potential third-party defendants, including affiliated companies; architects, safety engineers, land owners, and other parties responsible for protecting the safety and health of the worker; and the manufacturers of defective products used by the worker. This latter issue is the source of a great deal of traditional products liability litigation and is beyond the scope of this book. This section will focus on four specific kinds of third-party actions: those against occupational health professionals, insurance companies, unions, and government entities.

Occupational Health Professionals

Improper practices by occupational health professionals have been alleged to be the cause of a variety of personal injuries. In tort actions to recover for these injuries, it has been difficult for plaintiffs to overcome the exclusivity bar of workers' compensation. Nevertheless, a growing number of jurisdictions have recognized actions for negligent health assessments, negligent job placement, and negligent medical treatment.

Traditionally, the courts have held that there is no physician-patient relationship between an employer-provided examining physician and an applicant or employee because the purpose of the examination is not for the benefit or treatment of the individual. In the absence of this contractual relationship there is no legal duty running between the physician and the examinee and without a duty there can be no action for negligence. Nevertheless, more courts seem to be recognizing a duty, even in relationships that do not satisfy the strict test for a physician-patient relationship.

Besides providing medical examinations, company physicians and nurses often become involved, to varying degrees, in the actual treatment of employees, from first aid to ongoing care. A number of lawsuits have alleged malpractice in treatment. Even though most cases have found such personal injury actions barred by workers' compensation, in some cases of alleged negligent treatment the courts have held that the plaintiffs have stated legally cognizable claims. For example, plaintiffs have been permitted to proceed with claims that a company physician failed to diagnose torn wrist ligaments and returned him to work prematurely, causing permanent disability; that negligent treatment in the employer's clinic aggravated a back injury; and that a company physician over-prescribed painkilling drugs for an injury, causing the employee to become addicted. The disparate results reached in these cases is caused by wide differences among the states in whether they recognize exceptions to the workers' compensation exclusive remedy principle.

Insurance Companies

Workers' compensation and other insurance carriers often perform safety and health inspections of the employer-insured's premises as a part of loss-prevention programs. Unable to sue their employer because of immunity, injured employees frequently have alleged that a proximate cause of their injuries was the negligent inspection conducted by the insurer or the failure of the insurer to conduct a safety and health inspection.

The workers' compensation laws in twenty-four states expressly extend workers' compensation tort immunity to insurance companies. In the other states, the courts are divided on whether to permit these actions. Those courts holding that the insurer is amenable to suit often emphasize the reliance placed on such inspections by the employers and employees. Courts rejecting this basis of liability usually stress that insurers are not required to make safety inspections and that permitting the actions would be disruptive of the underwriting relationship and would discourage these beneficial inspections. Even where insurers may be held liable, however, it may be difficult for the plaintiff to prove that the insurer's inspection was negligent or that this negligence was a proximate cause of the injury.

Hough v. Pacific Insurance Co.[1] concerned a lawsuit for emotional and physical suffering caused by a workers' compensation insurance carrier's outrageous and intentional denial of medical and disability benefits. The court recognized that employer-retained compensation insurance carriers owe an independent duty to claimants, as third party beneficiaries to insurance contracts between employers and insurance firms, to process worker claims in an appropriate manner. Insurance companies that act in bad faith and breach this duty may thus be held liable in tort to adversely affected claimants and be denied the right to rely on the workers' compensation immunity that would otherwise be available to those insurers.

§ 7.37

1. 83 Hawai'i 457, 927 P.2d 858 (1996).

Workers injured in vehicular accidents occasionally sue insurance carriers retained by their employers. This type of legal action may occur when individuals have been injured as a result of the negligent driving of company vehicles by fellow employees. If those coworkers are entitled to statutory immunity, the firms insuring the company vehicles are likely to be protected against liability by that same immunity. When workers riding in company vehicles are injured in accidents with automobiles being driven by uninsured third parties, they may seek compensation under the uninsured motorist policies covering company vehicles. Although some decisions extend employer immunity to such insurance carriers, others permit uninsured motorist claims against those carriers.

Unions

Personal injury actions against labor unions have been based on two theories. First, injured employees have alleged that the union's failure to ensure a safe and healthful workplace constituted a breach of the union's duty of fair representation. This theory has been unsuccessful, principally because under federal labor law there is no legal duty for a union to insure against workplace injuries. Moreover, mere negligence will not support an action for breach of the duty of fair representation; liability will attach only if the union's action or inaction is "arbitrary, discriminatory, or in bad faith."

The second theory of liability for unions is that the existence of specific contract language giving safety and health responsibilities to the union or other considerations creates a common law duty, breach of which can lead to liability. This theory has only a remote chance of success.

§ 7.38 Subrogation, Third–Party Defenses, and Contribution Rights

Employers and their insurance carriers that provide employees with workers' compensation benefits for job-related injuries caused by the negligence of third parties are generally granted subrogation rights vis-a-vis those third-party tortfeasors. State enactments specify whether injured employees, their employers, or both should have the first opportunity to sue culpable third parties. They define this subrogation priority in one of four ways. The relatively few jurisdictions that continue to apply the election-of-remedies doctrine have an absolute rule. Injured employees may file workers' compensation claims or tort actions. As soon as they elect the compensation route, they forfeit their right to seek tort redress and their tort rights are assigned to their employer. Conversely, if they file third party tort actions, they forfeit their right to file workers' compensation claims.

Some state enactments provide injured workers and their employers with joint priority. Either may initiate tort suits against third-party tortfeasors. Some of these laws give the other party joinder rights. If employers fail to intervene in employee tort actions, they may lose their right to subrogation. Where no right of intervention is statutorily prescribed, courts often refuse to allow such joinder. When injured employees prosecute third party tort actions and employer compensation insurance carriers intervene in those suits, the employee-plaintiffs may be permitted to retain primary control over the actions with the intervening insurance carriers being restricted to more passive involvement.

Statutes in twenty-one states provide injured workers with initial tort priority. These provisions generally give the employees from three months to two years to file their tort actions, with their employers being unable to do so during these periods. If the workers fail to commence actions within the prescribed time frames, their employers may thereafter file their own suits. The Maine and Maryland laws give the preliminary priority to employers. Under the Maryland provision, employers have two months to file third-party actions. If they do not do so within that period, the injured workers may sue. The Maine enactment requires employers to bring their actions within thirty days after demands by injured employees for such action. If employers fail to do so, the workers may initiate their own suits.

Injured workers who receive workers' compensation benefits and who sue third-party tortfeasors may be statutorily required to obtain the consent of their employer before they settle their tort actions. If their employer unreasonably refuses to grant consent, some enactments authorize them to seek court approval. Employees who settle their tort claims without either employer consent or court approval may forfeit their right to future compensation benefits.

Under the subrogation provisions set forth in most state enactments, employers who have paid medical and disability benefits to injured workers have liens, equal to the amounts they have paid, on third-party tort judgments obtained by those individuals. Employer reimbursement may be limited to the portion of the claimant's tort recovery that duplicates areas covered by workers' compensation payments. The employee-plaintiffs are entitled to the excess. A substantial number of state laws require subrogated employers to share proportionately the legal fees and litigation costs incurred by workers in their third-party tort actions. Even courts in jurisdictions without specific statutory provisions governing this issue tend to require subrogated employers to assume responsibility for their share of the attorney fees and litigation expenses incurred by employee-plaintiffs. When employees who have received workers' compensation benefits for employment-related injuries sue third parties in tort for damages that are not compensable under the workers' compensation statute, their employer does not have a lien on the noncompensable tort proceeds obtained by those workers.

Third–Party Defenses and Right to Contribution From Concurrently Negligent Employers

When injured workers sue third-party tortfeasors, the defendants can raise traditional tort defenses. For example, they may rely upon lapsed statutes-of-limitation or on the contributory or comparative negligence of the plaintiff-employees. On the other hand, they are usually unable to raise the concurrent negligence of plaintiff-employers as a defense. Because the statutory immunity provided to employers prevents tort liability vis-a-vis injured workers, most courts are unwilling to reduce the liability of third-party tortfeasors by amounts not recoverable by the plaintiff-employees themselves. Nevertheless, four states have sought to achieve an accommodation in this area by holding that the liability of third-party tortfeasors should be reduced pro tanto, but only up to the amounts of medical and disability benefits paid to plaintiff-employees by their concurrently negligent employers.

Even when the third-party tort actions are prosecuted by subrogated employers on behalf of injured workers, it is recognized that the lawsuits basically concern the rights of the injured employees. As a result, the defenses that the third-party tortfeasor would be able to assert against employee-plaintiffs may be asserted against their subrogated employers. The most frequently raised defenses of this kind involve statute-of-limitation issues and worker contributory or comparative negligence. On the other hand, because subrogated employers stand in the shoes of their injured workers and third-party tortfeasors could not use concurrent employer negligence as a defense against employee-plaintiffs, courts generally refuse to allow them to raise that defense against subrogated employers.

After injured workers obtain judgments against third-party tortfeasors, those defendants may seek contribution from the workers' concurrently negligent employers. In most jurisdictions, contribution will be denied. This is due to the fact that employers who are provided with statutory immunity with respect to injured workers cannot be considered jointly liable to those individuals. As a result, few courts are willing to permit third-party tortfeasors to obtain contribution from concurrently negligent employers. This is true even when the third party tortfeasors seeking contribution from claimant employers allege that the employer actions that caused the injuries in question were intentional.

The only time that most courts are willing to allow third-party tortfeasors to get contribution from the employers of injured employee-plaintiffs is where they can demonstrate that the employers breached an independent duty owed to them. Classic cases involve situations in which employers have contractually promised to indemnify the third parties from liability generated by their negligence toward employer personnel. The workers' compensation laws in several states forbid the enforcement of indemnity agreements, unless they are reduced to writing. A few state enactments prohibit the enforcement of employer indemnity agreements, preferring to limit employer liability for job-related accidents to the medical and disability benefits available through workers' compensation procedures.

On some occasions, indemnification obligations may arise from special relationships between employers and negligent third parties. The most common cases involve bailor-bailee and lessor-lessee arrangements.

If bailees or lessees negligently injure their own employees while acting on behalf of their bailors or lessors, the workers may obtain compensation benefits from their bailee or lessee employers and prosecute third-party tort actions against the vicariously liable bailors or lessors. The bailors and lessors would then be able to seek indemnification from their bailees or lessees, based upon the independent duties owed by those bailees and lessees to their respective bailors and lessors.

A similar issue may be raised by employers that agree to perform contract work for third parties. If the contractors negligently injure their own workers and those persons sue the principal parties for tort damages, may the principals obtain indemnification from the contractor-employers? A few courts permit indemnification by finding that the contractors owe separate duties of care to their employees and to their principals. The breach of the distinct duty owed to the principals is considered sufficient to enable them to obtain indemnification from the contractors. Most courts, however, refuse to allow such an implied indemnification obligation to negate the usual statutory immunity available to the contractor-employers of the injured workers.

§ 7.39 Retaliation

Numerous state legislatures have enacted specific provisions that make it unlawful for employers to discriminate against individuals because of their filing of workers' compensation claims. Persons who are the victims of retaliatory terminations in some of these states may file complaints with the workers' compensation agency and obtain reinstatement and backpay orders; in other states they are permitted to bring actions in court for damages.

Courts in most states that do not have express antiretaliation provisions in their enactments have decided to protect persons who file compensation claims. They have accomplished this objective through the extension of the generally accepted public policy exception. This exception prohibits terminations that contravene important state policies. The courts in these jurisdictions have recognized that access to compensation benefits is a significant public policy that cannot be thwarted by discriminatory employer action. As a result, employees who are fired in retaliation for filing workers' compensations claims may sue their employer in tort for damages. Because these public policy actions do not involve the enforcement of rights set forth in workers' compensation laws, the culpable employers enjoy no statutory immunity.

§ 7.40 Conflict of Laws

Suppose an Indiana resident enters into an employment contract in Ohio with a New York company to perform work in Kentucky. If the person were to sustain an employment-related injury while working in Kentucky, which state's workers' compensation law should be applied? If the individual files a claim with the administrative agency of a state that is unwilling to apply its statute to this incident, the claim will probably be dismissed. An agency in one state will usually not apply the law of another jurisdiction. It is thus imperative that the claimant file in a jurisdiction willing to apply its own statute. Depending on their conflict of laws approach, the worker may be able to file in one of several states.

Early court decisions viewed workers' compensation laws as statutory substitutes for tort liability and they applied the "tort theory" to resolve conflicts questions. Under this approach, the law of the jurisdiction in which the injury occurred would be applied. Many courts felt uncomfortable with the tort theory, particularly when transient personnel were involved. They wanted a test that would place greater emphasis on the employer's situation. They thus developed the "contract theory." Courts that use this test regard the compensation law of the state in which the contract of employment was made as an implied part of that agreement, and they apply that law to the job-related injuries of the contracting employee.

Many judges recognized that contracts of employment are frequently executed in states having a minimal connection to the place of business of the employing firm or the location of the work to be performed. They wanted a more flexible standard that would place greater emphasis on the actual incidents of employment, and they thus formulated the "place of employment" test. Courts applying this approach consider various factors: (1) where the employment contract was made; (2) where the work is being primarily performed; (3) where the injured worker resides; and (4) where the employing firm conducts significant business.

In 1972, the National Commission on State Workmen's Compensation Laws formulated a conflicts standard it hoped would generate more uniform treatment. Recommendation 2.11 provides that injured workers or their survivors may file compensation claims in the state where the injury or death occurred, where the employment was principally localized, or where the employee was hired. Virtually all states have adopted the Commission's uniform standard.

Compensation agencies usually assert jurisdiction over claims pertaining to job-related injuries that occur within their borders. Several state enactments, however, exclude in-state injuries involving transient workers from other jurisdictions if coverage is available in another state. The more difficult question concerns the willingness of state agencies to cover industrial accidents that occur in other states. Most states now assert jurisdiction over out-of-state injuries whenever the claimants were hired within their borders or the employment was principally localized within their boundaries. A few states only cover out-of-state occurrences for claimants whose contracts of employment were made within their jurisdictions, while a couple continue to require localization of the employment within their boundaries before they provide statutory protection.

Employment contracts occasionally provide that the workers' compensation laws of certain states shall or shall not be applicable to job-related injuries. Most courts ignore such contractual undertakings and simply apply their usual jurisdictional criteria. They do not permit contracting parties to defeat jurisdiction that would otherwise be available, nor do they allow parties to create jurisdiction that would not otherwise exist.

In some instances, the compensation laws of several states may apply to the same industrial accident. Most jurisdictions permit the injured employee to file claims in different states and obtain overlapping benefit awards. To avoid unjust enrichment, the agencies issuing subsequent awards deduct the amounts previously awarded the claimants for the same conditions by agencies in other jurisdictions. Some states, however, hold that employees who sustain occupational injuries in other states and who obtain benefits under the laws of those states may not subsequently obtain compensation for those same injuries in their jurisdiction.

Chapter 8

COVENANTS NOT TO COMPETE
AND RELATED ISSUES

Table of Sections

§ 8.1   Covenants Not to Compete—Generally

Introduction

Covenants not to compete, also known as noncompetition agreements, are contractual provisions where the parties agree not to compete with each other for a certain time period in a particular geographic location. They are common in three circumstances: the sale of a business, the end of a partnership interest, and employment relationships, especially those in highly technical industries and in sales. When an employment relationship is involved, it is not necessary to have an express contract for the separate noncompetition agreement to be enforceable. Thus, an "at will" employee can be bound by a separate agreement not to compete after the termination of the employment relationship.

There are circumstances where noncompetition provisions are essential to the underlying contract, such as in the sale of a business when the goodwill of the enterprise can be destroyed by competition from the seller. For example, consider a contract for the sale of a travel agency

710

named C & T where the buyer purchases the goodwill established by founders Chris and Terry. The goodwill attached to a travel agency would be lost, however, if Chris & Terry simply started a rival business in town as T & C. Their promise not to compete is an essential part of the sale.

Similarly, the promise of a partner not to compete with the partnership after the termination of an interest, as by its sale, is essential to the contract. In exchange for valuable consideration, the departing partner promises not to interfere with the business of the partnership by competing against it.

The same rationale applies when a retiring partner agrees not to start a new practice in competition with the partner's former firm. In *Schoonmaker v. Cummings & Lockwood*,[1] for example, retirement benefits received before the age of 70 were conditioned upon an agreement that the lawyer partner not compete for three years in the counties where the partnership had law offices. This agreement withstood challenge on the rationale that compensation to the retiring partner came from future firm income, in competition with the retired partner's new practice. The Connecticut Supreme Court upheld the validity of the noncompetition agreement in the retirement plan because it was not against public policy, nor a significant interference with client choice, nor an unjustifiable interference with the attorney's mobility. Furthermore, the existence of the firm would have been in jeopardy if the former partner practiced law in the same area.

In contrast, there are circumstances when a covenant not to compete creates an unnecessary and unfair advantage for one party, such as where an employer uses economic coercion to force all employees to promise that they will not work for competitors if they ever leave the company. Although restrictions in the employment setting are often justified, especially when they involve customer lists or trade secrets, agreements between employers and employees are inherently more suspect than agreements incident to the sale of a business. The typical inequality of the parties in bargaining power is one important distinction. Another is the differing nature of the restraint on trade. On the one hand, the sale of a business or partnership interest does not ordinarily contemplate competition between the parties because the sale signals the exit of one party from competition. On the other hand, a restraint on a former employee is inherently anti-competitive to the extent that it prevents competing businesses from gaining a personnel resource.

Because these three types of restraints invoke different policy considerations, the law has developed similar but separate approaches to noncompetition agreements in the contexts of employment versus the sale of an interest in a business or partnership. Notably, state legislatures have been active in enacting statutes that affect such covenants in the employment context, but rarely affecting noncompetition terms in contracts for the sale of interests. Similarly, the common law in virtually

§ 8.1
1. 252 Conn. 416, 747 A.2d 1017 (2000).

every jurisdiction has been more willing to uphold noncompetition agreements made in connection with sales of businesses or partnerships than those made in connection with employment.

The Restatement of Contracts[2] takes the position that a restraint that is ancillary to an otherwise valid transaction or relationship is an unreasonable restraint of trade if one of two conditions is present. The first condition is that the restraint is greater than necessary to protect the promisee's legitimate interest. The second is that the promisee's need is outweighed by the hardship to the promisor and the likely injury to the public. If these conditions are not present, then the covenant cannot be ancillary to an otherwise enforceable agreement and it is simply a naked restraint of trade.

Noncompetition Covenants Incident to Business Sales or Partnership Dissolutions

A contract for the sale of a business may involve a covenant not to compete to prevent the seller from destroying the value of the goodwill transferred. Public policy favors such agreements because of a sense of fairness between the parties and because the restraint on trade is not offensive. In such cases, the parties are usually engaged in an armslength transaction and the new entrant into the market simply supplants the exiting member by purchasing the property, including the goodwill.

Another circumstance in which noncompetition agreements appear outside the context of employment is the dissolution of partnerships. Although this circumstance more closely resembles employment than the sale of a business, it is distinguishable because the partners make a reciprocal agreement to separate their property. If the partners agree who will have which specified areas for a period of time, then they each have the benefit of the restriction on the other. Moreover, dissolutions of partnerships are often regarded legally as the sale of the partnership interest from the departing partner to the remaining partners.

Courts have scrutinized the reasonableness of covenants not to compete in these non-employment areas to assure that they are reasonable in time, geography, and scope. Despite the similarity in the analysis between these cases and employment cases, their different circumstances make it inappropriate to treat case authorities the same.

Because of the dissimilarity between employment contracts and sales contracts, an attempt to avoid the policy restraints on the former by creating the latter was rejected as a "sham" in *Bosley Medical Group v. Abramson*.[3] In this case a creative employer sought to avoid California's statute that permits restraints on trade in sales contracts but not employment agreements. The scheme, which had the employee buy and then sell back company stock, failed to alter the underlying character of the employment relationship.

2. Restatement (Second) of Contracts § 188.

3. 161 Cal.App.3d 284, 207 Cal.Rptr. 477 (1984).

Similarly, the North Dakota Supreme Court found that the sale of 1/200 interest in a company was not a sufficient transfer of a business interest to meet the exception in the statutory prohibition on restraints of lawful professions. The statute prohibits contracts that promote a restraint of business unless it is pursuant to the dissolution of a partnership or the sale of a business. The insurance company in the case[4] sought to enforce a nonsolicitation clause against its departing agent by making it a part of goodwill from the sale of a business because the agent sold back his stock that comprised 1/200th interest in the company. The court held that such a transfer does not constitute a sufficient sale to validate the noncompetition clause under the statutory exception. The court reasoned that although the sale of the stock need not be a controlling interest to qualify under the statutory exception, the sale of such a small amount insufficiently connected the noncompetition agreement with the sale. Any restraint on the agent would need to proceed under the theory of misappropriation of trade secrets rather than enforcement of the covenant.

Courts have found it necessary to distinguish between agreements that are essentially employment relationships and those that truly arise from the sale of a business or partnership because the policy considerations in the two situations are very different. The most useful focus has been on whether the circumstances of the agreement involves a transfer of goodwill as the by-product of a sale or dissolution. If not, then a noncompetition agreement merits greater scrutiny. *Valley Medical Specialists v. Farber*[5] involved an internist and pulmonologist whose practice specialized in treating AIDS and HIV-positive patients and lung cancer patients with procedures that required specialized equipment available at only certain hospitals. At first Dr. Farber was an employee at the defendant clinic VMS, but eventually he became a shareholder and subsequently a minority officer and director. He eventually left VMS and began a practice in the area defined by the noncompetition agreement he signed with VMS. The covenant read: "The parties recognize that the duties to be rendered under the terms of this Agreement by the Employee are special, unique and of an extraordinary character. The Employee, in consideration of the compensation to be paid to him pursuant to the terms of this Agreement, expressly agrees" not to work in competition with VMS for three years anywhere in a five mile radius of any VMS office in existence at the time of the agreement or "any time thereafter."[6]

The trial court treated the departure of the partner doctor as analogous to the sale of a business and thus the noncompetition provisions were not strictly construed against it because it was a transfer of goodwill. The Arizona Supreme Court disagreed and held that, even though this agreement is between partners, it is more analogous to an employer-employee agreement than a sale of a business. The language of

4. Warner & Co. v. Solberg, 634 N.W.2d 65 (N.D. 2001).

5. 194 Ariz. 363, 982 P.2d 1277 (1999).

6. 982 P.2d at 1279.

the agreement itself speaks of employment rather than the transfer of goodwill. It therefore strictly construed the covenant and found it overly broad. Even though the doctor was perhaps not in the inferior bargaining position that is common in employment settings, the public interest in access to his medical specialty weighed in favor of strict construction against the employer. In this case the covenant prohibited the practice of any type of medicine by Dr. Farber, even those that did not compete with VMS, and the geographic restriction was large because of the number of VMS offices. Most importantly, the interest in the patients and the public prevented operation of this agreement. Although this agreement might have been enforceable if it had been a genuine transfer of goodwill pursuant to a sale of a business or partnership interest, it was not enforceable as an agreement incident to employment.

As these cases illustrate, there are many reasons why the party who seeks to enforce a noncompetition agreement finds it advantageous for it to be ancillary to a contract other than an employment contract. Most notably, state statutes disfavoring restraints may provide an exception for sales of interests, and even the common law tends to scrutinize such restraints less closely.

Interplay of Contract Law and Public Policy in Enforcing Post–Employment Covenants

The enforceability of a noncompetition agreement in an employment relationship raises questions of contract interpretation, but the cases invoke public policy to alter pure contract doctrine. Courts have been sensitive to the fact that the underlying issue usually involves the ability of an individual to earn a living. Moreover, even where legislatures have not intervened on the side of the worker, courts have been mindful that public policy is offended in general by restraints on trade. The enforcement of a restrictive covenant therefore has never been a matter of the simple application of contract principles.

Nonetheless, contract issues underlie all questions of interpreting restrictive covenants. Courts have needed to face in this context traditional contract issues such as the adequacy of the consideration for the agreement and the applicability of the statute of frauds. Many of the concerns in enforcing a covenant not to compete, however, are not purely contractual in character. These issues include the reasonableness of the geographic and temporal restriction, the overbreadth of the covenant, and the former employer's legitimate interests with respect to matters such as customer lists.

Considerations of public policy are always featured in cases considering the enforcement of noncompetition agreements. All such agreements are fundamentally a form of restraint on trade, so public policy dictates their curtailment. They are permissible only to protect narrowly defined legitimate employer interests such as an investment in special training or the preservation of trade secrets, confidential business information, customer lists, goodwill or reputation. The interest of the public at large–or even a few innocent individuals–may predominate over a legitimate private interest.

Agreements not to hire

A relatively new phenomenon is called "agreements not to hire" in which employers contract with other employers not to hire each other's employees. Such agreements are similar in effect to covenants not to compete because they prevent employees from working for a competitor, but they are fundamentally different in kind because the contracts are not directly with the employees themselves.

There are only a few cases that have addressed this phenomenon. In *Heyde Co. v. Dove Healthcare,*[7] the Wisconsin Supreme Court held that such an agreement was contrary to public policy because it infringed on the individual employee's freedom of contract. Such agreements between employers, the court further held, may not be enforced unless the employee consents to the restriction. In that case a rehabilitation facility named Greenbriar furnished physical therapists to nursing home facilities and a health-care provider that operated nursing homes. The agreement in question involved placement of physical therapists with the defendant Dove Healthcare and contained a provision by which Dove agreed not to hire Greenbriar's own therapists as employees during their employment and for a period of one year thereafter. Dove eventually terminated the agreement and hired current and former Greenbriar therapists. Greenbriar sued to enforce the contract but the Wisconsin Supreme Court found it to be an unreasonable restraint on trade.

The court in *Heyde* focused on the oppression that the no-hire agreement caused the employees. They were unaware of the agreement and had been told that they would not be asked to sign a covenant not to compete. Under Wisconsin law the employer would have had to support a noncompetition agreement with the employee by consideration, yet the employee received no compensation for this indirect restriction. The court also found relevant the state statute governing restrictive covenants because the restriction was achieved indirectly. Once the court viewed the contract as one to restrain trade, the question of its enforceability then turned on its reasonableness; a restraint of trade is void if it is unreasonable between the parties or if it is injurious to the public. Applying this analysis, the court held that the no-hire provision of the contract between the employers is an unreasonable restraint of trade because it restricts the opportunities of the employees without their knowledge and consent.

In contrast, the Virginia Supreme Court found enforceable a no-hire agreement under very similar circumstances in *Therapy Services, Inc. v. Crystal City Nursing Center, Inc.*[8] Once again the issue involved the provision of physical therapists placed by a provider to nursing homes. The provider sought to prevent the nursing homes from hiring its own therapists by a no-hire provision. The Virginia Supreme Court rejected

7. 258 Wis.2d 28, 654 N.W.2d 830 (2002).

8. 239 Va. 385, 389 S.E.2d 710 (1990).

the claim that such a contract is essentially a noncompetition agreement because it was not between an employer and employee. The court then determined that this restraint was reasonable because otherwise the provider would involuntarily become an unpaid employment agency. Moreover, the court found that the agreement was not so broad as to interfere with the interests of the public in general nor with the interests of the individual employees. Although the employees were restricted from working for the employer subject to the no-hire agreement, they were nonetheless free to work for anyone else. Because there was a shortage of physical therapists in the local area, the court reasoned that they could easily secure employment with third parties if they chose to leave their position with the restricting employer.

It remains open whether no-hire agreements will meet with more favorable judicial reception than covenants not to compete. The policy issues surrounding each type of restraint are similar but the history and precedent are different.

§ 8.2 Employer Breach of Contract—Remedies Generally

This section considers the remedies available to an employee against a former employer when it is the employer who breaches the employment contract in the first instance, usually by firing the employee. The next section considers whether employers can nonetheless enforce separate covenants not to compete when they fire employees. Later sections consider the remedies generally available to an employer when it is the employee who violates the contract by quitting and working for a competitor in violation of a covenant not to compete.

Specific Performance to Receive Services

When the employer breaches an employment contract by firing an employee, the discharged individual sometimes seeks specific performance of the contract to require the employer to continue the employment. The damage to the individual's reputation is the usual motivation for seeking such relief.

The common law rule strongly disfavors specific performance of an employment contract for the policy reason that courts should not compel employers to receive unwanted services. This rule is more compelling in the context of small businesses rather than large ones, where the receipt of services is less personal.

As a practical matter, the rule against specific performance for the receipt of services has been eroded by exception in modern law. The major statutory exception to this common law rule is employment discrimination law, such as Title VII of the Civil Rights Act of 1964 and state fair employment practice laws. Under such statutes, courts routinely order employers to accept the services of employees if the reason for the discharge was discrimination. Therefore, the common law rationale for declining to order receipt of employment services is implicitly rejected in these particular statutory actions.

The rule has been eroded in the common law as well, in the area of wrongful discharge. The rationale parallels that of invidious discrimination; employers may not refuse the services of employees on offensive grounds. Reinstatement orders are thus permissible in these contexts, as exceptions to the general common law rule against ordering specific performance to receive services.

Damages to Employee for Breach of Contract

A suit against an employer for breach of an employment contract supports a claim for compensatory damages in the amount that the plaintiff would have earned during the remaining term of the contract and other consequential damages proven with specificity. Future earnings are reduced to present value at the time of trial.

A damage claim for lost wages triggers a plaintiff's duty to mitigate. An employee who has been discharged in violation of an employment contract must attempt to mitigate damages by seeking other employment during the term of the contract. If the worker finds employment at equal or greater pay, then there is no damage. Alternatively, if the plaintiff leaves the work force to return to school or for another reason, there is no damage unless the reason for leaving the work force was the unavailability of alternative work.

Failure to attempt to mitigate damages results in a reduction of the award to the extent that mitigation was possible. It remains open to the plaintiff to demonstrate that equivalent work was not available, however. The plaintiff is not required to accept work that is not equivalent, such as demeaning work or even simply a different type of work.

Employees with term contracts are typically professionals who suffer loss of reputation when employers no longer want their services. Actors and football coaches are prominent examples of such individuals with term contracts. The resulting lawsuit is thus often an effort to vindicate the individual's reputation. Damages for loss to reputation are nonetheless not available at common law for breach of employment contract. In *Redgrave v. Boston Symphony Orchestra*,[1] for example, the actress Vanessa Redgrave sued the Boston Symphony Orchestra for canceling her contract for a series of concerts following her public support of the Palestine Liberation Organization. She claimed that this breach of contract caused her a loss in reputation, but such damages require an independent basis of recovery, such as an accompanying tort or discrimination claim, neither of which was present in that case.

Breach of contract also typically does not support damages for emotional distress, and employment contracts are no exception. All such noneconomic damages require an additional basis for the claim, such as a tort or discrimination claim. Punitive damages are also not available for a breach of employment contract claim alone, but can be awarded for a tort or discrimination claim.

§ 8.2

1.   855 F.2d 888 (1st Cir.1988).

If the termination of the contract involved circumstances that are falsely injurious to the employee's reputation, there may be a cause of action for defamation. A false accusation of theft, for example, or suggestion of other inappropriate conduct may give rise to such a claim. If successful, presumed damages may be available.

A professional who can claim "lost volume" in the provision of services may successfully claim additional damages in the form of lost income. The usual calculation of damages for a terminated term employee is the contract price minus income actually earned or potentially earned in mitigation of damages, as this section has already explored. The "lost volume" approach to damages does not make any subtraction, however, on the theory that the employee could have earned additional income from the employer without losing any other source. The Connecticut Supreme Court endorsed the lost volume approach for appropriate employment cases in *Gianetti v. Norwalk Hospital*.[2] In that case the defendant hospital failed to comply with its contractual requirement to follow certain procedures before failing to approve the annual renewal of the plaintiff surgeon who performed "on call" emergency room surgery. The lower court had awarded nominal damages because the surgeon had earned more gross income the year of discharge than the year before. The Connecticut Supreme Court held that with appropriate proof, the lost volume theory could establish additional lost income without regard to the comparative gross income.

The court in *Gianetti* explained that the lost volume theory can apply to service contracts even though it is ordinarily associated with contracts for the sale of goods. The question is whether the subsequent employment is a "substitute contract" which the service provider could not have completed if the first contract were not breached.[3] The court adopted a three part test for determination of when the lost volume theory applies to the seller of services: (1) the capacity to perform both contracts simultaneously, (2) the profitability of the second contract, and (3) the probability that the service provider would have entered into the second contract without regard to the termination of the first one.

As *Gianetti* illustrates, circumstances may permit plaintiff employees to seek different kinds of damages even in the absence of a tort claim to accompany the contract claim for breach of an employment contract. In the ordinary case, however, the remedies available to an employee are limited. An employer may breach a contract for a term of employment and generally be liable only for the difference between wages actually earned in subsequent employment and the contract price.

---

2.   266 Conn. 544, 833 A.2d 891 (2003).

3.   See 3 Restatement (Second) of Contracts; § 350, comment (d): "A 'substitute' is a contract which a volume seller who has suffered the loss of one contract through the breach of another party has entered into in place of the broken contract and which the volume seller would not have been able, with his existing personnel and overhead costs, to perform had there been no breach."

§ 8.3   Noncompetition   Agreements   When   Employer Breaches—Employee Obligations

When an employer breaches an employment contract by firing a worker, there may be a severable covenant not to compete that the employer may wish to enforce. The theory behind such a claim is that the employer may engage in efficient breach of contract by paying for the privilege of breaking the term contract but may still enforce other terms. The motivation for enforcing a covenant not to compete in such a situation may be to preserve interests in customer lists or trade secrets, although these interests are separately protectable.

An employer's motivation for enforcing a noncompetition covenant may also be to prevent a competitor from gaining advantage from the employee in other ways. Prominent examples have involved actors, comedians, and sportscasters. A television network may no longer wish the services of a sportscaster or comic actor, for instance, but the network may not want that individual's fans to follow them to a competing network either. One example is *Pathfinder Communications Corp. v. Macy*,[1] where a distinctive radio personality had no trade secrets but the station was concerned that audiences would follow him to a competing station. Relevant to the finding of the radio station's protectible interest was the good name recognition established after the station had spent large amounts advertising his personality.

In the case of term employees, the loss is not monetary because of the employer's responsibility to pay damages. In such cases, the damage to the individual is typically the loss in career advancement by removal from the public eye. For other types of professionals with term contracts, the loss may be the disadvantage of becoming out-of-date by removal from practice. For employees without term contracts, the loss is more poignantly economic. For an at will employee who is discharged, the employer does not have an obligation to pay lost future wages because of the terminable nature of at will employment. When an at will employee has made an agreement not to compete post-termination, the involuntary discharge threatens the individual's livelihood.

The situation of the discharged employee restrained by a noncompetition agreement has sometimes been described as a "double bind." Although freedom of contract permits individuals to bargain for such insecurity, courts increasingly have found that public policy demands careful scrutiny of the circumstances under which a discharged employee may be held to a noncompetition agreement.

A Pennsylvania case that involved such a double bind attracted publicity because the employee was fired for acknowledging his homosexuality. The employee in *DeMuth v. Miller*[2] was an accountant who had not been public with his sexual orientation until he was identified on a

---

§ 8.3

1. 795 N.E.2d 1103 (Ind.App.2003).

2. 438 Pa.Super. 437, 652 A.2d 891 (1995), appeal denied, 542 Pa. 634, 665 A.2d 469 (1995).

local news show as a homosexual calling for an end to gay bashing. His employment contract provided that homosexuality would be a cause for termination and further contained a noncompetition agreement. After being fired, the employee started his own business with some clients who followed him and the former employer sued. The court first upheld the contractual penalty against both state and federal equal protection and due process challenges on the grounds that there was no state action where no property right was asserted. The court thus upheld the validity of the discharge and then enforced the covenant not to compete.

Subsequent to *DeMuth,* a divided Pennsylvania Superior Court considered the same legal issue in a less newsworthy factual situation. The issue in *Insulation Corp. of America v. Brobston*[3] was also the enforcement of a noncompetition agreement against a discharged employee. In this case a sales representative was fired for poor performance. The court held that the restrictive covenant was not enforceable against him in part because of the circumstance of the discharge. The court reasoned that "there is a significant factual distinction between the hardship that is imposed by the enforcement of a restrictive covenant on an employee who voluntarily leaves his employer and that imposed upon an employee who has been terminated for failing to do his job."[4] This case thus casts doubt on the earlier holding in *DeMuth*, although the opinion makes no direct reference to it.

As the Pennsylvania experience reflects, courts have been uncertain how to treat the enforcement of a restrictive covenant against a fired employee. The tension in this area, as in others, is between the desirability of consistent application of contract doctrines and the undesirability of a result that is not sympathetic with the plight of the employee. Some courts resolve the conflict by ignoring contract principles and applying a general reasonableness approach, whereas others manipulate contract principles to obtain results more favorable to employees.

Applying the reasonableness approach, for example, South Dakota analyzes the covenant for fairness under the circumstances when an employer terminates the employee for no cause or bad cause. This jurisdiction concluded that although the circumstances of termination do not preclude enforcement of the covenant, they dictate its scrutiny for fairness.[5]

Those jurisdictions that approach the question with traditional contract principles also often achieve a result favorable to the employee. When faced with a noncompetition clause asserted against a discharged employee, some courts have used the contract principle that other portions of a contract may be unenforceable once one portion has been breached. Thus, the covenant not to compete becomes unenforceable when the employer violates any other portion of the agreement. A district court applying Missouri law concluded that a former employee

3. 446 Pa.Super. 520, 667 A.2d 729 (1995).

4. 667 A.2d at 735.

5. Central Monitoring Serv., Inc. v. Zakinski, 553 N.W.2d 513 (S.D.1996).

was not bound by noncompetition provisions of the contract because the employer was the first to breach other portions of the employment contract with respect to compensation.[6] The employer argued that the employee waived the breach by continuing to work afterwards, but the court found against the employer because the contract did not provide that a waiver by either party of a breach shall not operate as a waiver of any subsequent breach. Achieving the same result, a Georgia court found that if the employer improperly terminates the employee, a noncompetition covenant is not enforceable, at least in the absence of a severability clause in the employment contract.[7]

A district court applying Iowa law similarly found that the employee would not be bound by a covenant not to compete because of the employer's breach, but the court was careful to distinguish the differing sources of the employee's obligation.[8] The employee had a common law fiduciary obligation not to reveal trade secrets that was enforceable regardless of the contractual obligation. The employer's breach of other parts of the employment contract by failing to honor vacation pay and moving expense provisions did not excuse the former employee from fiduciary duties, although it did release him from contractual ones.

The trend appears to be that courts will consider the circumstance of the employee's discharge and are less likely to enforce a covenant not to compete if the employer has fired the employee, especially if the discharge was without cause. One can anticipate that if this trend continues, there will be increasing litigation over the characterization of the employment termination. When employers and employees are in conflict, the severance of their relationship is often mutual and the only question is who initiates the steps that lead to the final parting. In *National Interstate Insurance Co. v. Perro*,[9] for example, the employee tendered a notice of resignation giving two weeks notice. The employer tried to persuade him to stay, but the employee was resolute. At that point, the employer promptly fired him and ended his duties immediately. The court resolved the issue by finding that it was unimportant whether this situation amounted to a resignation or termination because the severance was not wrongful under either characterization. Because this court found that the employer had not been wrongful toward the employee, the circumstances of the employee's departure did not affect the enforceability of the noncompetition agreement.

A discharged employee may fear that the existence of a noncompetition agreement will be an impediment in obtaining a new job. Even without threatened enforcement, prospective employers may fear possible future litigation. One fired worker in such a bind sought a preliminary injunction against the former employer to prevent enforcement of the agreement not to compete. The Second Circuit held in *Levinson v.*

6. Alexander & Alexander, Inc. v. Feldman, 913 F.Supp. 1495 (D.Kan.1996).

7. Marcre Sales Corp. v. Jetter, 223 Ga. App. 70, 476 S.E.2d 840 (1996).

8. Uncle B's Bakery, Inc. v. O'Rourke, 920 F.Supp. 1405 (N.D.Iowa 1996).

9. 934 F.Supp. 883 (N.D.Ohio 1996).

Cello Music & Film Systems[10] that the trial court had abused its discretion in granting such an injunction. An injunction may not be granted without a showing of irreparable harm, and the court found that showing inadequate in this case. The discharged employee argued that he had worked in the "high end" stereo industry all his life and that at age 52 he would suffer great hardship if he were unable to work in the only industry he knew. The court did not find this position to be one of irreparable harm, particularly in the absence of any evidence that the noncompetition agreement was causing the harm he feared. He wanted to use the injunction to calm the fears of potential employers, but he had no evidence that the noncompetition agreement was preventing competitors from making him an offer of employment.

A Texas court considered a similar claim[11] and held that an employee who is fearful that a former employer will wrongfully try to enforce a covenant not to compete may seek an injunction against such enforcement, but not if the apprehension is only a general one. The absence of specific interference by the former employer meant that the former employee could not show irreparable harm. It was insufficient to show that clients were fearful of dealing with the former employee because of the existence of the covenant not to compete.

There is likely to be continued change in this area of post-employment law because the older cases date from an era when employment at will was an absolute rule. The employer's conduct and motivations were as irrelevant to the severance as the employee's reasons. As jurisdictions change their law relating to at will employment, courts will continue to reevaluate the older precedents in this area as well. The lesser amount of litigation with respect to covenants not to compete compared with wrongful discharge makes the law lag in its relative development. Continued developments may bring greater uniformity among the jurisdictions, but currently there is considerable disagreement among courts on whether to enforce covenants not to compete against at will employees who were terminated.

§ 8.4   Employee Breach of Contract—Remedies Generally for Former Employer

The employer faced with the disappearance of a key employee has few options to protect itself from business losses without contractual provisions that anticipate such problems. An at will employee is as free to sever the employment relationship as the employer, and has no obligation to the former employer other than fiduciary obligations not to reveal trade secrets or otherwise to engage in tortious interference with business. The disruption to business and the losses associated with replacing the employee are not compensable in the absence of a contract. A sole practitioner professional whose office manager suddenly departs, for example, may experience considerable losses. Large employers who

---

10. 199 F.3d 1322 (2d Cir.1999) (unpublished opinion).

11. Harbor Perfusion v. Floyd, 45 S.W.3d 713 (Tex.App.2001).

anticipate regular turnover among their employees are more likely to have institutional structures to cope with sudden departures, although for any employer the loss of a key employee is by definition the loss of someone important to the operation.

Even when the employer attempts to protect itself with a written contract, there are practical difficulties with traditional contract remedies when they are applied to the employment context. Notably, specific performance is not available because such involuntary servitude would violate the Thirteenth Amendment. Although equity will not compel personal services, it may prohibit giving services to others in contravention of existing contractual obligations through an express or implied "negative covenant." The negative covenant theory is that a personal service provider under contract with one person has by implication promised not to provide such services inconsistently to another person during the period of performance under the contract. It applies only to unique services, such as those of a performer or athlete, because the enforcement through injunction requires a showing of irreparable harm. If the services are not unique, then damages are an adequate remedy.

Employers sometimes seek to recover damages from departed employees for breach of an employment contract. The issue most commonly arises as an employer defense or counterclaim to a former employee's suit for wages due. There is no claim for damages in the absence of an employment contract and proof of its breach. The damages generally recoverable are limited to the costs of replacing the employee, which may include training costs for the replacement.

As with all contract damages, the employer is under a duty to mitigate damages by finding a replacement employee. The employer may not recover at all if it is able to find a substitute employee at the same or lower salary, although former employees can be liable for the costs associated with securing a replacement.

Reimbursement for the costs of training the breaching employee is a separate theory of recovery from damages for the cost of covering for the departed employee. There are few modern cases, but reimbursement provisions in employment contracts may be unenforceable as a matter of public policy. One such case, *Brunner v. Hand Industries, Inc.*,[1] involved an employee's contractual promise to reimburse the employer for training costs in the event similar work is performed for a competing business within three years of training. The agreement was unenforceable as an attempt by the employer to gain an interest in the general knowledge and skills acquired by the employee during employment. Because employers do not have a protectible property interest in such knowledge and skills, the court reasoned that the contractual agreement could not create one as a matter of public policy. Moreover, the court noted that the agreement was a poorly disguised attempt to restrain competition since the reimbursement agreement applied only in the event the employee subsequently worked for a competitor.

§ 8.4

1.   603 N.E.2d 157 (Ind.App.1992).

Liquidated damages are another possible source of recovery for employers when employees breach their contracts. The Restatement (Second) of Contracts states that damages for breach by either party "may be liquidated in the agreement but only at an amount that is reasonable in the light of the anticipated or actual loss caused by the breach and the difficulties of proof of loss."[2] Further, "A term fixing unreasonably large liquidated damages is unenforceable on grounds of public policy as a penalty."[3]

Liquidated damages in general are not favored when imposed against a breaching employee, unless they are not the product of a meaningful attempt to consider the possible consequences of contract breach at the time the parties enter the employment contract. In *Arrowhead School District No. 75 v. Klyap*,[4] a school district had a form contract for hiring teachers that provided for liquidated damages in the amount of 20% of salary in the event of breach. Although the court found the contract to be one of adhesion, the liquidated damages provision was upheld as a reasonable attempt to estimate the costs associated with breach. The court reasoned that although the teacher Klyap "had no meaningful choice regarding the liquidated damages provision, the clause itself is still not unconscionable because the 20% amount was within Klyap's reasonable expectations as a teacher familiar with the employment needs of the School and the damages the School would suffer upon breach of the contract."[5]

A liquidated damages provision must be a reasonable estimate of projected losses from the loss of the employee's services and not merely a penalty that has an "in terrorem" effect to prevent the employee's breach. In one case,[6] for example, a provision for fees in excess of the annual earnings of the hairdresser bound by the agreement was an impermissible penalty rather than a reasonable attempt to estimate losses. The employer was found to have taken advantage of its "vastly superior bargaining power" to set liquidated damages so "unrealistic and unreasonable that it cannot be considered a good faith pre-estimate of probable damages."[7] In contrast, some courts have upheld very large dollar amounts as reasonable liquidated damages when professionals such as doctors and lawyers have entered into contracts in which they had negotiated freely. In *Ashcraft & Gerel v. Coady*,[8] a law firm and attorney had a contract with a provision for $400,000 in liquidated damages. The District of Columbia Circuit refused to strike the provision as a penalty despite its size. It noted in particular that the contract applied this provision only for "material" breaches rather than for all breaches, and that the amount had increased over time as the attorney's position within the firm had grown in responsibility and importance. Finally, the court lamented that it was not possible to articulate any

2. Restatement (Second) of Contracts § 356(1).

3. Id.

4. 318 Mont. 103, 79 P.3d 250 (2003).

5. Id. at 128.

6. John Jay Esthetic Salon, Inc. v. Woods, 435 So.2d 1051 (La.Ct.App.1983).

7. Id. at 1052.

8. 244 F.3d 948 (D.C.Cir.2001).

narrower test than "reasonableness" for the determination of whether liquidated damages are so large as to violate public policy; case by case determination is necessary.

§ 8.5 Noncompetition Agreements When Employee Breaches—Generally

When a former employee breaches a noncompetition agreement, the employer may seek to enforce it with an injunctive order. The court's first inquiry will be whether the restraint is enforceable as a matter of public policy. If the agreement restrains the individual for too much time or in too great a geographic area, it will be deemed unreasonable and subject to whatever approach to overbreadth is used in the jurisdiction.

Overbreadth

When a covenant not to compete is overbroad, the issue before the courts is whether it has any legal force or is a nullity. Courts have generally taken one of three approaches: nullification, striking offending portions, or rewriting the agreement.

(1) Some courts take the strict view that an overbroad restrictive covenant is not enforceable. The theory is that courts are not in the business of rewriting contracts, and that the party in the superior negotiating position should have an incentive to use restraint in writing the provision in the first place. The Arkansas Supreme Court adopted this strict view in *Rector–Phillips–Morse, Inc. v. Vroman*.[1] The three-year noncompetition covenant in that case was unreasonably long, and the plaintiff employer asked the court to enforce it for a shorter time. The court rejected the request and articulated the rule that when a restriction "is too far-reaching to be valid," the court will not "make a new contract for the parties" by reducing the restriction to a shorter time or to a smaller area.[2]

(2) Other jurisdictions find the strict rule against enforcing overbroad agreements too harsh. Their solution is to delete the offending provisions and enforce the rest. This approach is often called "blue penciling." It was adopted by Indiana, for example, in *Licocci v. Cardinal Associates, Inc.*,[3] where the court chose to enforce only some of the divisible parts of the promise. Not many modern cases use this rule.

A district court applying New York law[4] explained the competing policies. On the one hand, blue-penciling is bad because "[t]oo great a readiness on the part of courts to preserve the valid portions of overbroad restrictions would induce employers to draft such restrictions overbroadly, intimidating the sales force by the ostensible terms of the written contract and relying on courts to enforce the valid portion against an employee who is not intimidated." On the other hand,

§ 8.5

1. 253 Ark. 750, 489 S.W.2d 1 (1973).
2. 489 S.W.2d at 4.
3. 432 N.E.2d 446 (Ind.App.1982), vacated on other grounds, 445 N.E.2d 556 (Ind.1983).
4. Webcraft v. McCaw, 674 F.Supp. 1039 (S.D.N.Y.1987).

"absent good reason, courts should generally try to preserve what is valid in a contract."[5]

The Alaska Supreme Court has explained that the blue pencil rule is unacceptably mechanical.[6] The problem, the court explained, is that this approach "values the wording of the contract over its substance." To illustrate, the court hypothesized two covenants: one that promised not to compete "anywhere in England" and another that promised not to compete "in London or elsewhere in England." Under the blue pencil rule, the whole provision of the first covenant would be void because it could not be narrowed by deleting any words. But the second covenant, promising not to compete "in London or elsewhere in England," would be enforceable as to London because "elsewhere in England" could be "blue pencilled." The court found this difference is merely semantic and therefore rejected it.

(3) The third approach is for the court to redraft an invalid covenant in such a way as to make it valid. The rationale is that unless the court finds the covenant was not drafted in good faith, it is appropriate to uphold the presumed intent of the parties. This position, often referred to as the "reasonableness" position, is followed in the majority of jurisdictions, and it is the one adopted by the Restatement (Second) of Contracts.[7] This approach has the advantage of permitting the courts to fashion a reasonable restriction. It has the disadvantage of failing to provide any incentive for the superior party to use restraint in fashioning the provisions of the original contract.

The Alaska Supreme Court in *Data Management, Inc. v. Greene*[8] identified the factors it found relevant to making a covenant "reasonable" under this approach: limitations as to time and space, presence of confidential information or trade secrets, and degree of benefit to the employer compared with detriment to the former employee. The Ohio Supreme Court[9] included these and other factors: other considerations relevant to enforcement include whether the covenant seeks to "stifle the inherent skill and experience" of the former employee; whether the covenant "operates as a bar" to the former employee's sole means of support; and whether the talent that the employer seeks to suppress was developed during the period of employment.

This third approach is the modern trend. In response to the argument that rewriting covenants fails to give the employer an incentive to avoid overreaching, courts adopting the third approach have noted that there is a general requirement of good faith. An oppressive covenant that is "deliberately unreasonable" should not be enforced regardless of its severability or ability to be enforced reasonably.

---

5. Id. at 1047.

6. Data Mgmt., Inc. v. Greene, 757 P.2d 62 (Alaska 1988).

7. Restatement (Second) of Contracts § 184(2) (1981).

8. 757 P.2d 62 (Alaska 1988).

9. Raimonde v. Van Vlerah, 42 Ohio St.2d 21, 325 N.E.2d 544 (1975).

Statute of Frauds

Although the agreement is contractual in nature, the statute of frauds has rarely been a problem in its enforceability. The Restatement (Second) of Contracts[10] has taken the position that the statute of frauds is not a problem even for promises not to compete that are for an indefinite period. The rationale is that the promise not to compete would be fully performed if the former employee were to die within a year. In contrast, an affirmative promise to do something terminates with death, but may be incomplete. The difference is that the noncompetition agreements promise to refrain from acting and thus can theoretically be completed within a year in the event of death.

The Supreme Court of Alaska in *Metcalfe Investments v. Garrison*,[11] considered as a matter of first impression the applicability of the statute of frauds to a covenant not to compete and concluded that it is not a bar to enforcement. In that case, a real estate broker made an oral commitment not to contact the firm's clients after leaving employment. The court concluded that a promise to forebear from competition is distinguishable from other promises to perform affirmative acts and thus joined the majority position in finding that the oral promise suffices.

Preliminary Injunction

As a practical matter, the availability of a preliminary injunction against a competing former employee is the most important remedy because it is time-sensitive. In most jurisdictions, a preliminary injunction is available upon the showing by the plaintiff that it is likely to prevail on the merits and will suffer irreparable harm without it. Its availability after a rudimentary hearing means that the employer can get legitimate interests protected quickly without waiting until the court has time for a full hearing.

The standards for a preliminary injunction vary with the procedure of each state, but the majority of jurisdictions adhere to a four part test: (1) plaintiff must show a probability of success on the substantive claim; (2) the plaintiff must show that irreparable harm will result without the preliminary injunction; (3) the balance of hardships must tip in the plaintiff's favor; and (4) the public interest must favor the issuance of the preliminary injunction. In the federal system, some circuits have altered this four-part test to permit a sliding test. Under the sliding test, if the plaintiff can show that very great harm will result without the preliminary relief, then it is not necessary to show a "probability" of success on the merits but only that a serious question of liability is present. Conversely, if the plaintiff can show a very high probability of success on the merits, then the degree of irreparable harm need not be as great.

With respect to covenants not to compete, the availability of a preliminary injunction permits the employer quickly to enjoin behavior

---

10. Restatement (Second) of Contracts § 130, comment b and illustration 9 (1981).

11. 919 P.2d 1356 (Alaska 1996).

such as the use of a customer list before the full damage is done. In *A.B. Dick Co. v. American Pro–Tech*,[12] a preliminary injunction was granted against a former technical representative who breached his restrictive covenant not to solicit his customers of the employer, a photocopy repair company. The former employee went to work for a competitor and solicited his old customers. The court noted that in such cases irreparable injury is presumed once a protectable interest is established. If a trial court erroneously issues a preliminary injunction against an employee, the worker's losses may be compensable either procedurally by statute under an injunction bond or at the discretion of the court. Similarly, a case from the Eighth Circuit[13] approved a preliminary injunction against a former employee who was taking customers, even though the employer had lost only a few sales to date. The court reasoned that the real threat was the potential that more customers would switch because of the continued efforts of the former employee.

Some jurisdictions have been willing to relax the required showing of irreparable harm in cases involving violations of noncompetition agreements. Florida has created a "rebuttable presumption" of irreparable harm by statute[14] when an employer has demonstrated the violation of an enforceable restrictive covenant. Thus, in a case involving a former employee of an electronics distributor,[15] it was not necessary to show that the breaching employee had solicited any customers before granting the preliminary injunction against doing so in violation of the noncompetition agreement. Other jurisdictions may accomplish this result without a presumption. The Second Circuit has noted the possibility that New York cases in the "covenant-not-to-compete context apparently assume an irreparable injury to plaintiff."[16] New Hampshire law finds that "[w]henever an employee uses his experience gained from an employer in violation of a reasonable covenant not to compete, irreparable injury occurs and injunctive relief is appropriate."[17] Some other jurisdictions have been similarly willing to simplify the requirement of irreparable harm in cases involving noncompetition agreements.

Texas law has developed a conflict on this question of irreparable injury in noncompetition cases. Applying its state statute, none court held in *Cardinal Health Staffing Network v. Bowen*[18] that an employer must make a showing of irreparable harm before the issuance of a temporary injunction prohibiting the violation of a covenant not to compete. In that case a scheduler for an interim pharmacy staffing business left his employer when the company changed owners. The scheduler violated his noncompetition agreement by working for a competitor, but there was no showing that he was using any confidential

12. 159 Ill.App.3d 786, 112 Ill.Dec. 649, 514 N.E.2d 45 (1987).

13. Safety–Kleen Systems v. Hennkens, 301 F.3d 931 (8th Cir. 2002).

14. Fla.Stat.Ann. § 542.335(j).

15. America II Electronics, Inc. v. Smith, 830 So.2d 906, 908 (Fla.App.2002).

16. Ticor Title Ins. Co. v. Cohen, 173 F.3d 63, 69 (2d Cir.1999).

17. Highdata Software Corp. v. Kothandan, 160 F.Supp.2d 167, 168 (D.N.H.2001).

18. 106 S.W.3d 230 (Tex.App. 2003).

information or soliciting customers. Moreover, the former employer had increased its business considerably after the departure of the employee and the competitor for whom the employee now worked had not had a commensurate increase in business. Although another state court of appeals had concluded that the statutory provision for permanent injunctive relief removed the requirement of irreparable harm for all injunctive relief, this court disagreed. It held that the statute did not apply to temporary relief and thus it applied the traditional rules of equity for temporary injunctions, including the requirement that the employer show irreparable harm. The Texas Supreme Court has not yet resolved the conflict.

Delay in seeking the preliminary injunction is sufficient grounds to deny this interlocutory remedy, even if the delay is not sufficient to bar a permanent injunction. The defense of laches, which can bar permanent relief, requires a showing of both unreasonable delay and prejudice to the defendant. A lesser standard can bar a preliminary injunction because any inexcusable delay undercuts the employer's argument that it will suffer irreparable harm in the absence of immediate relief. Acceptable reasons for delay are investigation and attempts to settle the matter without resorting to court. As the Second Circuit has explained: "Preliminary injunctions are generally granted under the theory that there is an urgent need for speedy action to protect the plaintiff's rights. Delay in seeking enforcement of those rights, however, tends to indicate at least a reduced need for such drastic, speedy action."[19]

§ 8.6   State Statutes Governing Noncompetition Agreements

Statutes govern actions to enforce covenants not to compete in several jurisdictions. The thrust of most of the statutes is to recognize the employee's interest in freedom from unreasonable restraints, while providing exceptions to accommodate an employer's legitimate interests. The courts generally have been left to resolve issues of reasonableness in restraint, which they have done in a way much like the common law analysis used in states without statutes.

A few statutes simply void all covenants not to compete in employment contracts, however, without permitting exception. In contrast, some states have a statutory declaration affirming the validity of reasonable covenants not to compete that arise in a variety of contexts, including the employment relationship.

There are three types of statutes relevant to litigation concerning covenants not to compete. The first type includes those with a very general prohibition on restraints of trade, without specific reference to covenants not to compete. The second type specifically addresses covenants not to compete contained in employment contracts. The third is like the second, but targets only specific professions.

---

19. Citibank, N.A. v. Citytrust, 756 F.2d 273, 276 (2d Cir.1985).

The second type of statute relating to covenants not to compete is the most common: those that relate directly to covenants arising out of the employment context. Some of these statutes approach noncompetition agreements from a negative position; they declare covenants not to compete to be void or disfavored, but provide for exceptions. Other statutes approach the topic in the affirmative; noncompetition agreements are permissible except when they are unreasonable restraints.

Michigan, for example, repealed its negative statute that declared void as against public policy all agreements by which any person promises not to engage in any avocation, trade, employment, or business. In its place the legislature enacted a positive statute that explicitly authorizes covenants not to compete if the covenant protects an employer's "reasonable competitive business interests" and if the covenant is "reasonable as to its duration, geographical area, and the type of employment or line of business."[1] The act was prospective from its enactment such that previously existing covenants that were invalid under the older statute did not become valid under the new act.

The Georgia Legislature enacted a statute that affirmed the validity of noncompetition agreements in employment, but the state's highest court found that the act violated the state constitution. The statute provided: "Every court of competent jurisdiction shall enforce through any appropriate remedy every contract in partial restraint of trade that is not against the policy of the law or otherwise unlawful."[2] This provision was inconsistent with a guarantee in the Georgia Constitution that prohibits the legislature from authorizing contracts in general restraint of trade.[3] The Georgia Supreme Court held that the act was "beyond the power of the General Assembly inasmuch as it is one that authorizes contracts and agreements which may have the effect of or which are intended to have the effect of defeating or lessening competition or encouraging monopoly."[4]

The third category of statutes relevant to litigation concerning covenants not to compete relates to individual professions. Delaware has a statute[5] that nullifies covenants not to compete only with respect to physicians. Colorado has a similar provision[6] with respect to physicians that is a separate section from its general provision voiding such covenants except in particular circumstances. Louisiana has a separate provision for employees who had direct access to computer programs during the course of employment,[7] in addition to that state's general provision permitting limited noncompetition agreements with former employees.

§ 8.6

1. Mich.Comp.Laws Ann. § 445.774a.

2. Ga.Code Ann. § 13–8–2.1(g)(1) (unconstitutional).

3. Ga. Const. art. III, § VI, para. V(c).

4. Jackson & Coker, Inc. v. Hart, 261 Ga. 371, 405 S.E.2d 253, 255 (1991).

5. Del.Code Ann. tit. G, § 2707.

6. Colo.Rev.Stat.Ann. § 8–2–113(3).

7. La.Rev.Stat.Ann. § 23:921(F).

Statutes that prohibit general restraints in trade may also apply to contractual provisions between companies when one promises not to recruit the employees of another for some period of time. Such a provision was not valid in *Communication Technical Systems v. Densmore*.[8] In that case a computer sales and service company hired a consulting company and, as part of their contract, the former agreed not to raid the consulting company for employees. The state's general statute prohibiting restraint of trade was applicable rather than the specific statutory provision permitting noncompetition agreements with former employees for a period of two years. Because the contract was between two companies rather than the employer and former employee, the statutory exception for employees did not apply.

§ 8.7   Injunctions Against Competing Ex–Employees— Common Law Factors Generally

The decision to enjoin a former employee from violating the terms of a covenant not to compete is always discretionary. An injunction is an equitable remedy that is never a matter of right. Therefore, even if the plaintiff employer satisfies the court that the restriction is lawful, the court may still decline to order specific enforcement. In such a case, the plaintiff is left with the damages remedy.

Equitable principles govern the claim seeking injunctive relief. Those principles include equitable defenses of waiver, laches, and unclean hands. These equitable defenses relate to the availability of the injunctive remedy; they do not relate to the substantive right.

If the court finds that the plaintiff employer has failed to act consistently and the defendant was prejudiced by the inconsistent action, waiver may apply. If an employer assures an employee upon discharge, for example, that the noncompetition agreement does not apply, then the employer may be estopped from claiming otherwise in a subsequent lawsuit if the former employee has detrimentally relied in good faith on the representation. Waiver can also operate to the employer's advantage, such as when the employee continues to work after the employer has breached some portion of the employment contract. The employee may then be barred from asserting that the employer's breach invalidated other provisions of the contract, such as the noncompetition agreement.

Laches can bar an injunction to enforce a noncompetition agreement when the plaintiff employer has unreasonably delayed in the pursuit of its rights and the former employee has been prejudiced by the delay. Laches is not determined by the mere passage of time; the key is the unreasonableness of the delay. Thus a ten-month delay can be excessive if the employer did not use that time to investigate or attempt settlement. Diligence in pursuing one's rights is the primary consideration, in addition to any prejudice to the former employee caused by the delay.

---

8.   583 N.W.2d 125 (S.D.1998).

Unclean hands is the equitable defense that is potentially the most troubling to an employer because it not only can act as a bar to an injunction but it can also publicize negative information about the employer's business. This equitable defense applies when the plaintiff has acted in some inappropriate way with respect to the rights asserted in the lawsuit. In *North Pacific Lumber Co. v. Oliver*,[1] for example, a wholesale lumber company sought to enjoin Oliver, a former trader in its employ, from working for a competitor in violation of his noncompetition agreement. Oliver successfully defended by establishing the company's unclean hands. The former trader proved the defense by showing that it was company policy to encourage its traders to cheat customers. Because this practice was a part of the trader's employment, the court reasoned that the company had unclean hands with respect to Oliver's employment contract. Therefore, the company could not receive equitable relief for an otherwise valid restraint. Although the former trader's defense demonstrated that the circumstances where customers were actually cheated rarely occurred, one can speculate that the negative publicity from the case was also costly to the company.

Reynolds & Reynolds Co. v. Hardee[2] involved a fact situation with a successor employer where the defendant alleged unclean hands. The original employer, for which the defendant Hardee was a sales representative, sold its business of printing stationery and other business paper to the plaintiff. The sale purported to include the business, goodwill, and contracts, including employment contracts. The new owner then promptly fired Hardee and offered to rehire him under a contract with a more restrictive noncompetition clause. Hardee declined to sign the new agreement and offered to continue to work under the old contract. The new owner declined and, when Hardee went to work for a competitor, the new owner sued to enforce the original noncompetition agreement. The defendant prevailed on the issue that the noncompetition covenant was not assignable, the court noted in dicta that the unclean hands defense was also "persuasive" given the circumstances of the discharge.[3]

Essential to the unclean hands defense is that it applies only with respect to the behavior of the plaintiff. The defendant's relative wrongdoing is irrelevant. The rationale of the defense is that it is for the protection of the court, such that a court will not enforce the extraordinary remedy of affirmative relief for a litigant who is not worthy of it. When both parties are sullied, therefore, it is crucial which one becomes the plaintiff in the subsequent suit. Thus, when the former employee is the one seeking an equitable order to prevent the employer from enforcing a covenant not to compete, it is the employee's conduct that is scrutinized rather than the employer's. For example, in *Bryan v. Hall Chemical Co.*[4] the employer attempted an unclean hands defense against the former employee's declaratory judgment and injunction action by

§ 8.7
1. 286 Or. 639, 596 P.2d 931 (1979).
2. 932 F.Supp. 149 (E.D.Va.1996), affirmed, 133 F.3d 916 (4th Cir.1997).
3. 932 F.Supp. at 155 n.4.
4. 993 F.2d 831 (11th Cir.1993).

showing that the plaintiff had attended a multi-day strategic planning meeting as a "spy" for the company with whom he had already accepted employment. The defense failed because the evidence showed that the employee had been coerced into attendance by the defendant and that he had resigned before the meetings were completed. Similarly, a mere misunderstanding between the parties will not suffice to create the defense.

Another common law principle relevant to noncompetition agreements is that third parties may be bound by the contractual agreement if they are acting in concert with the promissor. For example, in *Norlund v. Faust*[5] an optometrist had a covenant not to compete with an ophthalmologist whereby he promised not to contact other optometrists who had previously referred patients to the ophthalmologist. This covenant also restricted his wife from engaging in the prohibited activity. Even though she was not a party to the agreement, she could be enjoined from engaging in activities that constituted a breach of the covenant if she was acting in concert with the covenantor. Under these facts, the former employee helped establish his wife's business shortly after leaving his employment with the ophthalmologist. He loaned his wife money to start the business, contacted persons to perform services for the wife's business, and wrote the letter to optometrists in the area concerning their interest in making referrals to the business.

§ 8.8   Injunctions Against Competing Ex–Employees—Circumstances of Making the Agreement

One of the factors relevant to the enforceability of covenants not to compete is the circumstance under which the agreement was made. In many jurisdictions, the employee is not bound unless the circumstances of making the agreement are such that it is equitable to enforce it. The circumstances of making the agreement generally fall into three types: (1) covenants that are simply part of the original written employment agreement, (2) covenants that are signed after employment has begun and for which there is no separate consideration, and, (3) covenants that are signed separately and for which separate consideration is given.

Courts are most likely to enforce those covenants made under the third circumstance because such agreements are conceptually separate contracts. If the exchange of the promise not to compete was for fair compensation, then this bargain should be enforced like any other. The fact that the former employee may not have anticipated the contingency ever occurring is less compelling when consideration was exchanged for the risk, especially when the consideration was tangible.

The majority of courts nonetheless enforce covenants signed under any of the three outlined circumstances. The least sympathetic circumstance is the second, where the employee signs the covenant after employment has begun and receives no separate consideration. The

5.   675 N.E.2d 1142 (Ind.App.1997).

theory is that continued employment is itself sufficient consideration, and the majority rule permits enforcement of covenants under this theory. The Nevada Supreme Court is among the courts most recently to review this issue as a matter of first impression, and it agreed with the majority position that continued employment is sufficient consideration, at least in cases of at will employment.[1]

In contrast, another state has recently considered the issue as a matter of first impression and came to the opposite conclusion. In *Poole v. Incentives Unlimited,*[2] the South Carolina Supreme Court held that continued employment at will of a travel agent by her employer was not sufficient consideration for a covenant not to compete. The rule adopted in that case is that when a noncompetition agreement is presented to an employee any time after the initial employment contract, there must be separate consideration. Continued employment at will is not sufficient for such a covenant to be enforceable.

Those jurisdictions that find continued employment sufficient consideration for a covenant not to compete do not restrict when during the employment period the covenant is executed. In an Arizona case,[3] for example, it was immaterial that two years of employment had passed before the employer asked the employee to sign a noncompetition agreement and offered only continued employment as an incentive for signing. The rationale is that employers otherwise would be forced to fire and rehire employees in order to include the restrictive covenant as part of the "initial" hiring agreement. Such an approach, the courts reason, would be disruptive of seniority and pension rights, and would exalt form over substance.

In many jurisdictions, the key question is not when the covenant was signed but whether the employer acted in good faith in choosing the time to present it. In *American Credit Bureau, Inc. v. Carter,*[4] for example, the court refused to enforce a restrictive covenant that the employer did not mention as a condition for the job until after the employee had quit his former job.

Some jurisdictions reject the rule that continued employment is sufficient consideration for signing a covenant not to compete during the period of employment. The Wyoming Supreme Court took this position in *Hopper v. All Pet Animal Clinic.*[5] That court held that public policy requires that a covenant not to compete that is executed after creation of an employment relationship must be supported by separate consideration. Such separate consideration could be a promotion, a pay raise, special training, new employment benefits, or other advantages beyond continued employment in general. In that case an agreement executed with a veterinarian was not binding when it was first offered as an oral

---

§ 8.8

1. Camco, Inc. v. Baker, 113 Nev. 512, 936 P.2d 829 (1997) (per curiam).

2. 345 S.C. 378, 548 S.E.2d 207 (2001).

3. Mattison v. Johnston, 152 Ariz. 109, 730 P.2d 286 (Ariz.App.1986).

4. 11 Ariz.App. 145, 462 P.2d 838 (1969).

5. 861 P.2d 531 (Wyo.1993).

term without any specifics and without any separate consideration, but it became binding when it was later reduced to writing and supported by a raise.

§ 8.9 Reasonableness of Duration, Activity, and Geographic Limitation

A covenant not to compete must be reasonable in duration, activity, and geographic limits in order to be enforceable. Whether a court will reform an unreasonable covenant depends upon the jurisdiction's rule on overbreadth.

The extreme examples are the easiest. For example, a covenant cannot operate in an area where the employer no longer engages in the activity the covenant was designed to protect. Nor can an employer prevent a former employee from soliciting customers of the firm with whom the employee had no significant contact during employment.

The typical case involves a covenant that overly restricts the time, activity, and area in which the former employee may not compete. In *The Phone Connection, Inc. v. Harbst,*[1] the employer sought to enforce a five-year restriction that prohibited the former employee from competing in a two-state area. The opinion begins by reaffirming the jurisdiction's three-pronged test for the reasonableness of covenants not to compete: "(1) Is the restriction reasonably necessary for the protection of the employer's business; (2) is it unreasonably restrictive of the employee's rights; and (3) is it prejudicial to the public interest?"[2] The court found the durational and geographic restrictions overbroad and entered the injunction for a two-year period limited to the counties in which the employer had established a trade area.

Other jurisdictions have similar approaches, although the test is articulated slightly differently in each state. In Connecticut, for example, the factors to assess the reasonableness of a restraint are "(1) the length of time the restriction is in effect; (2) the geographical scope of the restriction; (3) the fairness of the protection afforded the employer; (4) the extent of the restraint on the employee's ability to pursue his occupations; and (5) the extent of any interference with the public interest."[3] In the case of an electrical engineer in a firm that used ultrasonics, the former employee was reasonably restrained for a period of one year from working in any aspect of this highly technical business in any location. The court reasoned that the sophisticated and international nature of this business justified the restraint.

Covenants are premised on agreement of the parties at the time of contracting, so an ambiguous term in the restriction may void the

§ 8.9
1. 494 N.W.2d 445 (Iowa App.1992).
2. Id. at 449.

3. Branson Ultrasonics Corp. v. Stratman, 921 F.Supp. 909, 913 (D.Conn.1996).

agreement. In one case,[4] the Arkansas Supreme Court found unenforceable a restrictive covenant that defined the geographic location as ten miles from one known location "or such others as established" by the employer. The problem that the court discerned with this ambiguous provision was that the employer could control the area of future restriction without the consent of the employee.

Relevant to the inquiry of reasonableness is the hardship to the former employer as well as to the public that wishes to use the services of the particular individual. These factors were weighed in the case of a veterinarian who was enjoined for one year from practicing within five miles of the city where the former employer was located.[5] The restraint was reasonable because it was sufficiently limited in that it allowed the veterinarian to be able to continue to earn a living and it permitted the public to seek her continued services with only some inconvenience. The public was not deprived of similar services within the city itself, where other providers offered small-animal medicine.

The interest of the public in the services provided by the person sought to be enjoined is also relevant to the court's decision whether to enforce the noncompetition agreement. For example, a physician will not be enjoined from practicing in a particular area if the effect would be to deprive the public of that specialty. In *Dick v. Geist*,[6] the Idaho court refused to enforce covenants against two practitioners of pediatrics and neonatology because it found that these restrictions would have had a drastic impact on the provision of care to critically ill newborns in Twin Falls, Idaho. Similarly, a North Carolina court refused to grant an injunction because the public interest required there to be more than one physician in that specialty in the vicinity.[7] In contrast, in a case involving less specialized medical care, a court ruled that the public health needs could be just as easily served by having the physician practice in another community.[8]

§ 8.10 Nonsolicitation Agreements

Restrictions on the post-employment solicitation of a former employer's customers are related to noncompetition restrictions, but distinct from them. A former employee may be restricted from approaching a former employer's customer even under circumstances when a more general restriction on competition may be unenforceable. The customer restriction is more narrowly tailored to the employer's interest and is therefore given more deference by the courts. Some jurisdictions have characterized the difference as a restraint on an activity compared with a prohibition on competition and therefore a less stringent test of reasonableness is appropriate.

---

4. HRR Arkansas v. River City Contractors, 350 Ark. 420, 87 S.W.3d 232 (2002).

5. Hopper v. All Pet Animal Clinic, 861 P.2d 531 (Wyo.1993).

6. 107 Idaho 931, 693 P.2d 1133 (1985).

7. Iredell Digestive Disease Clinic v. Petrozza, 92 N.C.App. 21, 373 S.E.2d 449 (1988), affirmed, 324 N.C. 327, 377 S.E.2d 750 (1989).

8. See Bauer v. Sawyer, 8 Ill.2d 351, 134 N.E.2d 329 (1956).

The Restatement of Contracts takes the position that a restrictive covenant is easier to justify if it is limited to the taking of the former employer's customers rather than a restriction on competition in general.[1] This distinction has prompted some courts to find that state statutes restricting noncompetition agreements do not apply to nonsolicitation agreements unless they are expressly included in the act. The Oregon Supreme Court endorsed analysis that separates form from substance in such cases, however. In *Dymock v. Norwest Safety Protective Equipment,*[2] the state court of appeals rejected the argument that a nonsolicitation agreement fell outside the scope of the state statute governing noncompetition agreements because the restriction covered not only customers with whom the employer had done business in the past but also future "targets" of business. Such a covenant extended beyond nonsolicitation and functionally prevented future competition. The Supreme Court endorsed the lower court's reasoning on this point.

Applying this justification principle, courts are most likely to uphold customer restraints that are as narrowly drawn as possible. In *General Commercial Packaging, Inc. v. TPS Package Engineering, Inc.,*[3] for example, the Ninth Circuit applied California law and upheld a restriction on taking a major customer despite the state's statutory provision against restraints in trade. That provision restricts covenants not to compete when they prevent people from engaging in their profession, but it was not an impediment to enforcing a provision in a contract that specifically prohibited performing work for a long-time major customer. The court was influenced by the specificity of the restraint and its centrality to the former employee's contract to serve the employer with respect to this particular customer. The case involved a subcontractor who was hired specifically to work for that major client, such that the defendant's direct dealing with the customer had the effect of "cutting out" the plaintiff employer. Upholding the former employee's contractual promise not to do so was a reasonable restriction on the defendant's right to do business and an enforcement of the plaintiff's legitimate business interest.

The narrow restriction in *General Commercial Packaging,* naming a specific major customer, contrasts with provisions that prohibit former employees from dealing with any former customer of the employer. Provisions are usually considered overbroad if the former employee had not personally served those customers before and if the individual had never represented the firm's good will to those customers.

The employer's legitimate interest in its clientele becomes a question of fact. The question is whether the relationship is a longstanding one with a major client, as in *General Commercial Packaging*, or an insignificant one unworthy of protection. A long list of customers is more

§ 8.10

1. Restatement (Second) of Contracts § 188, comment g (1981)

2. 172 Or.App. ,399, 19 P.3d 934, rev'd on other grounds, 334 Or. 55, 45 P.3d 114 (2002).

3. 126 F.3d 1131 (9th Cir.1997).

likely to be insignificant than a short one. In *Corroon & Black of Illinois, Inc. v. Magner,*[4] an Illinois court considered seven factors to assess the strength of the relationship between the employer and its customers in customer list cases. These factors are: (1) number of years needed to develop a clientele; (2) amount of money invested in developing the clientele; (3) degree of difficulty in developing the clientele; (4) amount of personal contact by the employee; (5) extent of the employer's knowledge of its clientele; (6) length of time customers have been associated with the employer; and (7) continuity of the relationship between the employer and its customers. When these factors favor the employer, the relationship is "nearly permanent" and protectable. The *Corroon & Black* opinion concludes that an employer has a legitimate interest enforceable through a covenant not to compete where the relationship with the customer is "nearly permanent" and the former employee would not have had contact with the customers in question but for the association with the former employer.

A legitimate employer interest in carefully cultivated customers is protectable, whereas a list of customers that could be divined from other sources is not. An insurance company, for example, has a legitimate interest in preventing former employees from "exploiting the customer relationships developed at its expense and in its name,"[5] but not in prohibiting contact with customers whose names were obtained from a public list.

The employer must show not only that the customer list was confidential information but also that the former employee had access to it. The Restatement takes the position that the employer does not have a protectable interest unless the employee has access to the confidential information and misappropriates it.[6] Thus, the Arkansas Supreme Court in *Rector–Phillips–Morse, Inc. v. Vroman*[7] refused to enforce a noncompetition covenant where there was no evidence that the former employee attempted to use confidential information from the employer. In contrast, the Massachusetts Supreme Judicial Court in *Blackwell v. E.M. Helides, Jr., Inc.*[8] upheld an agreement not to compete where the former employee had access to files with lists of customers and properties not available to the public.

Sources that refer customers are protectable in the same manner as the customers themselves. In *Norlund v. Faust,*[9] for example, an ophthalmologist named Faust had employed an optometrist named Norland to perform optometric services and to build referral relationships with other optometrists for the ophthalmologist's business. The employment agreement contained a post-employment noncompetition agreement in which Norland promised not to contact any optometrist from whom

4. 145 Ill.App.3d 151, 98 Ill.Dec. 663, 494 N.E.2d 785 (1986).

5. National Interstate Ins. Co. v. Perro, 934 F.Supp. 883 (N.D.Ohio 1996).

6. Restatement (Second) of Contracts § 188, illustration 7.

7. 253 Ark. 750, 489 S.W.2d 1 (1973).

8. 368 Mass. 225, 331 N.E.2d 54 (1975).

9. 675 N.E.2d 1142 (Ind.App.1997).

Faust had received a referral. Norland quit and violated his agreement by directly contacting the optometrists from whom Faust had received referrals. The court found the restriction enforceable even though there was no geographic restriction. The limitation was specific to optometrists who had previously referred patients to this doctor and thus it was a reasonable one.

§ 8.11   Injunctions Against the Use of Trade Secrets

The common law duty not to divulge trade secrets arises by virtue of a confidential position in employment and does not require any separate agreement. In *Webcraft Technologies v. McCaw*,[1] for example, a former employee deliberately breached her fiduciary duty by stealing trade secrets. The court found the breaches sufficiently clear and serious to justify injunctive relief even in the absence of a covenant not to compete. The court noted that the duty not to convert an employer's trade secrets to one's own use arises from the employment relationship and need not be set forth in contract.

Although the duty not to divulge trade secrets arises from the common law, it also derives from statute in those jurisdictions that have adopted the Uniform Trade Secrets Act (UTSA).

The UTSA defines a trade secret as

information, including a formula, pattern, compilation, program, device, method, technique, or process, that:

> (1) Derives independent economic value, actual or potential, from not being generally known to the public or to other persons who can obtain economic value from its disclosure or use; and

> (2) Is the subject of efforts that are reasonable under the circumstances to maintain its secrecy.[2]

The hallmark of a trade secret under this definition is its secrecy rather than its novelty. The key to its value is its relative secrecy, and protection is premised on reasonable efforts to protect its secrecy.

The necessary secrecy for a "trade secret" requires only efforts to protect the secrecy rather than success in doing so. The Minnesota Supreme Court explained in *Electro–Craft Corp. v. Controlled Motion, Inc.*[3] that the "mere intention" to maintain secrecy is insufficient to confer trade secret status. The degree of effort to maintain secrecy must be sufficient to put employees on notice of the confidentiality. Moreover, the degree of effort may vary with the circumstances. Matters that are obviously secret, such as formulas, require little additional protection. Other matters that are less obviously secret, such as motor dimensions, require substantially more effort for protection. In *Electro-Craft* the

§ 8.11
1. 674 F.Supp. 1039 (S.D.N.Y.1987).
2. Uniform Trade Secret Act § 3426.1(d) (1984).

3. 332 N.W.2d 890 (Minn.1983). See also Fireworks Spectacular, Inc. v. Premier Pyrotechnics, Inc., 86 F.Supp.2d 1102 (D.Kan.2000) (customer list trade secret).

employer failed to establish that electric motor drawings were a trade secret, however, only because there had been too little effort to protect their secrecy.

Customer lists can qualify as trade secrets under both the UTSA and common law. Their qualification for this status depends first upon the same factors that create a legitimate employer interest in the lists for the purpose of nonsolicitation agreements. Specifically, the list must be the product of special effort and not widely known or easily accessible. Second, as with all trade secrets, the employer must have made an effort to maintain its secrecy. There was insufficient effort in *Allied Supply Co. v. Brown,*[4] for example, to keep a customer list secret because the employer had made multiple copies and had permitted employees to take the list home.

The question of whether a particular customer list is "readily acquired information" is often the subject of litigation. Although a list that could be obtained from a phone book is not a trade secret, information about which customers have interests in particular products can be a trade secret, especially if compiled over years of experience. The Washington Supreme Court has observed that "a trade secret plaintiff need not prove that every element of an information compilation is unavailable elsewhere. Such a burden would be insurmountable since trade secrets frequently contain elements that by themselves may be in the public domain but together qualify as a trade secret."[5]

Details concerning customers may suffice to make a list a trade secret. In *Kovarik v. American Family Insurance Group,*[6] for example, an insurance agent began to work for a competitor and solicited former clients. The court upheld the validity of his noncompetition agreement that he not solicit customers for one year, but the further question was whether he could be enjoined from all use of the customer lists beyond this period. Applying the state's UTSA, the court held that even though the customers' names may be from readily available sources, the list could still be a trade secret if the specific attributes of such customers are important to the seller and are not obvious. Such specific attributes can include the amounts and types of insurance purchased, the due dates and amounts of premiums, the character, description, and location of insured property, and characteristics of the insured including age, physical condition, dependents, financial condition, and credit history. These special attributes were sufficient to establish a trade secret in this case.

The distinction between types of customer information that are protected and unprotected as trade secrets is well illustrated by a case applying New Hampshire law, *Carriage Hill Health Care v. Hayden.*[7] The employer in this case was a dental supply company. The list in question contained the names, addresses, and telephone numbers of its

4. 585 So.2d 33 (Ala.1991).

5. Boeing Co. v. Sierracin Corp., 108 Wash.2d 38, 738 P.2d 665, 675 (Wash. 1987).

6. 108 F.3d 962 (8th Cir.1997).

7. 1997 WL 833131 (D.N.H.1997).

dentist customers, which included virtually every dentist practicing in Maine. Because this list could be compiled by anyone with a telephone directory, it was not a trade secret. The company failed to prove any creativity in the compilation of the list nor any significant expenditure of resources. Thus, the use of this list by the former employee for a letter to announce his change of employment to a competitor was not actionable. Any further use he might have made of information about pricing and the purchase history of individual customers, however, could amount to a trade secret.

The issue of federal preemption has arisen with respect to the UTSA in a few cases. The issue is whether federal copyright law[8] preempts any state statute relating to trade secrets. The leading opinions have held that state UTSA enactments are not preempted by federal copyright law because the state acts require the additional element of breach of a trust or a confidential relationship that is beyond the requirement of the federal law.[9]

Most trade secret cases have involved injunctions against the use of the secret, but the Indiana Supreme Court relied upon a state statute that broadly protects trade secrets to find that an employee who threatened to misappropriate trade secrets could be enjoined from working for a competitor altogether. In *Ackerman v. Kimball International*,[10] a former employee was enjoined from accepting employment with a competitor under the Indiana trade secrets statute that permits injunction of "actual or threatened misappropriation" of trade secrets. The court reasoned that such an injunction is appropriate in circumstances where a genuine threat of misappropriation existed in light of the employee's wrongful acquisition of customer and supplier lists before termination and where enjoining the former employee from working for competitors was arguably necessary to remedy the threat of disclosure. The court thus found it unnecessary to consider the enforceability of a covenant not to compete in the employment contract and issued an injunction broader than that covenant would have permitted.

Some jurisdictions have adopted the "inevitable disclosure" doctrine to support an injunction against employment for a competitor even in the absence of actual or threatened misappropriation of trade secrets. The leading case is *PepsiCo, Inc. v. Redmond*,[11] which held that unless the employee has "an uncanny ability to compartmentalize information" the employee will necessarily rely—consciously or subconsciously—upon knowledge of the former employer's trade secrets in performing his or her new job duties. In that case, PepsiCo sought to enjoin a former employee from working for the Quaker Oats Company, with whom the employer was in fierce competition in the sports drinks market. The

8. 17 U.S.C.A. §§ 101–914. The Copyright Act expressly provides for federal preemption in section 301.

9. See Avtec Sys. v. Peiffer, 21 F.3d 568 (4th Cir.1994); Trandes Corp. v. Guy F. Atkinson Co., 996 F.2d 655 (4th Cir.), cert.

denied, 510 U.S. 965, 114 S.Ct. 443, 126 L.Ed.2d 377 (1993).

10. 652 N.E.2d 507 (Ind.1995).

11. 54 F.3d 1262 (7th Cir.1995).

former employee held a high position at PepsiCo that gave him access to trade secrets regarding its products and marketing. He had signed a confidentiality agreement which PepsiCo sought to enforce to prevent him from assuming duties at Quaker Oats. There was no proof of actual or threatened disclosure, but the Seventh Circuit found that disclosure was "inevitable" because of the high degree of similarity between the positions, the degree of competition between the employers, and the former employee's "lack of forthrightness" before accepting the new job.

A California case with similar facts declined to adopt the inevitable disclosure doctrine. In *Whyte v. Schlage Lock Co.*,[12] the former employee knew trade secrets, signed a confidentiality agreement, and was not forthright about his departure to work for another employer in a fiercely competitive industry. Finding nothing in California law to support the doctrine, the court rejected it as incorrectly balancing the competing public policies of employee mobility and protection of trade secrets. It reasoned that because the inevitable disclosure doctrine permits an injunction without proof of actual or threatened use of trade secrets, the "result is not merely an injunction against the use of trade secrets, but an injunction restricting employment."[13] Relying on the logic of a law review article[14] the court concluded that to hold otherwise would give the employer a virtual noncompetition agreement without payment, while binding the employee with a court-imposed restriction with no opportunity to negotiate terms.

Damages for misappropriation of trade secrets can be measured by several means: (1) the actual loss to the holder of the trade secret, (2) the unjust enrichment of the misappropriator of the trade secret, or (3) a reasonable royalty for use of the trade secret. For example, a California court used the unjust enrichment method and calculated the earnings attributable to misappropriated names from a customer list. In that case,[15] a roof repair company's customer list was found to be a trade secret which former employees misappropriated to start a rival company. The court calculated that approximately one-third of their business was derived from the list, so the damages awarded were one-third of their earnings.

§ 8.12 Duty of Loyalty

Employees in positions of trust owe a common law fiduciary duty of loyalty to their employers during the time of their employment. Section 387 of the Restatement (Second) of Agency provides: "Unless otherwise agreed, an agent is subject to a duty to his principal to act solely for the benefit of the principal in all matters connected with his agency."[1]

---

12. 101 Cal.App.4th 1443, 125 Cal. Rptr.2d 277 (2002).

13. 125 Cal.Rptr.2d at 292.

14. John H. Matheson, *Employee Beware: The Irreparable Damage of the Inevitable Disclosure Doctrine*, 10 Loyola Consumer L.Rev. 145 (1998).

15. Morlife, Inc. v. Perry, 56 Cal. App.4th 1514, 66 Cal.Rptr.2d 731 (1997).

§ 8.12

1. Restatement (Second) of Agency § 387 (1957).

Courts have interpreted this principle to mean that an employee in a position of trust is bound to act at all times solely for the benefit of the employer, has a duty to use best efforts on behalf of the employer, and may not act in a manner inconsistent with the agency during employment.

The fiduciary obligation of an employee in a position of trust prevents that employee from competing with the employer during the period of agency. The Restatement defines the duty as one "not to compete with the principal concerning the subject matter of his agency."[2] Thus, such an employee cannot compete with the employer's business prior to the termination of the employment relationship if the competition relates to the specific aspect of the business with which the agent is involved. Some courts have said that "mere preparation" for a competing business during the time of employment is not a breach of the trust, however.

The question often becomes one of defining the line between "mere preparation" for future competition with the employer and failure to act in good faith for the employer's interests while making those preparations. Soliciting co-workers to join the future competing business may cross that line. In *Jet Courier Service v. Mulei,*[3] for example, the Colorado Supreme Court held that an employee may have breached his duty of loyalty to his employer if, before he left employment, he solicited his employer's customers for his future competing business. The trial court erred in holding that such a breach cannot occur unless the competing business is already in existence. The employee in this case was a regional manager of an air courier service who allegedly solicited customers as well as the employer's pilots for his planned competing business. The court noted that though his conduct did not rise to the level of tortious interference with contract, the agent's duty of loyalty is broader than the tort standard.

When an agent plans a competing business, any discussion with future customers must not amount to solicitation of the employer's customers. As one court has explained, even "if prospective customers undertake the opening of negotiations which the employee could not initiate, he must decline to participate in them."[4]

The duty of loyalty may also be breached by soliciting co-workers as well as customers. In *Feddeman & Co. v. Langan Associates, P.C.,*[5] the president met with some directors and other employees to formulate a plan for buying out the company and, if unsuccessful, resigning in a manner that would injure their then employer. This group distributed model resignation letters to other employees and told them that they could join the group in resigning and working for the new competing firm. This conduct fell below the state's required standard of good faith

---

2. Restatement (Second) of Agency § 393 (1957).

3. 771 P.2d 486 (Colo.1989).

4. Community Counselling Serv., Inc. v. Reilly, 317 F.2d 239 (4th Cir.1963).

5. 260 Va. 35, 530 S.E.2d 668 (2000).

and loyalty and was a breach of fiduciary duty because it amounted to more than mere preparation for departure from the company.

The duty of loyalty during the time of employment is distinguishable from any duty not to compete after termination of employment. Even if the employee has no duty after termination, any competing conduct during the time of employment is a violation of the duty of loyalty. In *Knott's Wholesale Foods v. Azbell,*[6] for example, a food distributorship sales representative told customers along his assigned route that he would be going into business for himself and that he could supply the same products at the same prices as the distributorship. The court found that these statements went beyond merely notifying customers of his intentions and constituted active solicitation in violation of his common law duty of loyalty. It was irrelevant to this claim that there was no agreement between the parties for the sales representative to refrain from competition after employment.

A critical fact in such cases is whether the employee is actively soliciting business while still employed by the plaintiff. In contrast to *Azbell*, the employee in *Nilan's Alley, Inc. v. Ginsburg*[7] asked his employer's customers if they would consider doing business with him if he were to leave and form his own business. These conversations were not a breach of fiduciary duty because they were "brief, non-specific, and strictly hypothetical."[8]

The employee's duty of loyalty during employment can be breached by conduct other than soliciting customers for a competing business. A dramatic illustration of different conduct is provided in *Food Lion v. Capital Cities.*[9] The employer in that case unknowingly hired two ABC television reporters with falsified resumes to work as a deli clerk and meat wrapper. The goal of the reporters was to investigate allegations that the employer engaged in unsanitary meat-handling practices. They wore microphones and made secret videotapes during their employment for the purpose of injuring their second employer, the grocery store, for the benefit of their primary employer, a television station. The unflattering results of the investigation were aired on the station's show Prime Time Live. The grocery sued on several grounds and ultimately prevailed only on a claim of breach of the duty of loyalty and a trespass claim premised on the breach of the duty of loyalty.

Although the two employers were not in competition, the conduct of the employees was a breach of their duty of loyalty to the grocery store because their intent was to injure it. Despite their lack of competition, the two employers had interests that were "diametrically opposed" because the station wished to expose the practices of the grocery in a harmful way. The court distinguished situations where an employee has two jobs and performs the second less well because of fatigue; the fundamental difference in interests of the employers was controlling.

---

6. 1996 WL 697943 (Tenn.App.1996).

7. 208 Ga.App. 145, 430 S.E.2d 368 (1993).

8. 430 S.E.2d at 370.

9. 194 F.3d 505 (4th Cir.1999).

Although the employees performed their grocery jobs well, their intent was to injure that employer and thus they breached their duty of loyalty. The employer received nominal damages.

The monetary recovery in a breach of loyalty claim is different from claims for breach of noncompetition agreements. The former employer does not need to show losses caused by the disloyalty but may instead seek to disgorge in restitution any profit by the former employee that is traceable to the disloyalty. In *Gomez v. Bicknell*,[10] the employee had covertly pursued a prospective client for his own gain in breach of his duty of loyalty to his employer's business of providing merger and acquisition services. The former employer sued under two theories: breach of the noncompetition agreement and breach of the duty of loyalty. Although the former employer was entitled to nominal damages for the violation of the restrictive covenant, further recovery in damages required proof of actual loss. The former employer offered no proof that the loss of the client was attributable to the breach of the covenant as opposed to other causes. For the claim for breach of the duty of loyalty, however, it was not necessary to prove that the former employer suffered any loss. The question of recovery for that claim is in restitution, to disgorge unjust enrichment from the disloyal former employee. The proof of his gross profits from the client satisfied the former employer's burden and the former employee could reduce recovery to net profits with proper proof of expenses.

10. 302 A.D.2d 107, 756 N.Y.S.2d 209 (App.Div.2002).

Chapter 9

DISCHARGE

Table of Sections

§ 9.1 Introduction

The employment at will doctrine, formulated in 1877 by American treatise writer Horace G. Wood, provided that an employee without a contract for a fixed term could be fired for any reason or no reason at all.[1] This rule was soon widely followed in the United States, and by the

§ 9.1

1. Horace G. Wood, A Treatise on the Law of Master and Servant (1877).

end of the nineteenth century the presumption of terminability at will had become the unquestioned and central rule of employment law. For the first half of the twentieth century the employment at will rule went virtually unchallenged, although two developments undoubtedly influenced the later course of employment law. First, the National Labor Relations Act, passed in 1935, gave employees federally protected rights to organize, join unions, and bargain collectively. Eventually, most collective bargaining agreements contained protection from discharge except for "just cause," with arbitration to resolve grievances. Second, the emergence of civil service protection for state and local government employees further increased the number of workers who could not be discharged arbitrarily.

The first major judicial crack in the employment at will rule came in 1959. In *Petermann v. Teamsters Local 396*,[2] a union business agent was fired after he refused his employer's order to commit perjury in testimony before a state legislative committee. In recognizing a cause of action for wrongful discharge, the court held that the right to discharge an at-will employee could be limited by statute or public policy.

Major civil rights legislation enacted in the 1960s gave further support to the concept that unchallenged employer prerogative in hiring and firing decisions had to give way to other social interests. During the next two decades a series of state court decisions, as well as influential commentary, increased the pace of reform of the at-will doctrine. Employees challenged unfair discharges with a variety of legal theories, and gradually three major "exceptions" to the at-will doctrine emerged. They are (1) breach of an express or implied promise, including representations made in employee handbooks; (2) discharge in violation of public policy; and (3) breach of the implied covenant of good faith and fair dealing. Almost every state accepts at least one of these causes of action. In the public sector, protections also came from the United States Supreme Court's decision that employees who have a property interest in their job may not have that interest taken from them without due process.

As these exceptions to the employment at will doctrine came to be recognized, courts also began to permit other claims arising from the employment relationship to be pursued. These included interference with economic advantage or contractual relations, fraud and misrepresentation, invasion of privacy, defamation, and intentional infliction of emotional distress. Although these torts had long existed, courts rarely allowed their use in employment settings prior to the sea change in the employment at will rule. These topics are discussed in this chapter as well as in preceding chapters.

§ 9.2 Written Contracts

Relatively few workers have individual written contracts of employment. Those most likely to have them include executives and other

---

2. 174 Cal.App.2d 184, 344 P.2d 25 (1959).

highly paid employees, employees with special knowledge and skill, and sales personnel who work on commission. Aside from detailing the terms and conditions of employment, often including limitations on the employer's ability to fire the employee, these contracts may also contain covenants not to disclose the employer's trade secrets and other proprietary information and not to compete with the employer following termination of the employment.

In all cases where a breach of a written contract is alleged, a threshold issue is whether a legally enforceable contract exists. Generally, the burden of proof rests with the party asserting the existence of a contract. The next issue is whether any terms of the contract have been breached. At common law, an individual employed under a contract for a definite term may not be fired before the expiration of the term except for cause (or material breach), unless the contract provides otherwise. The term may be stated as a specific period of time or as a project to be completed. A failure to renew at the end of a stated term is simply that, and not the equivalent of a firing. On the other hand, a written contract with no stated duration and no stated task to be completed is generally terminable at will by either party. These contracts of indefinite duration serve only to regulate the terms of employment, such as commissions, when the contract is in effect.

The jurisdictions are divided over the specificity with which the term of the contract must be expressed in order to take it out of the at-will rule. In some states, written statements (in either the contract itself or a confirmation letter) setting forth a monthly or annual salary indicate a contract for a term of one year, while in others, the manner in which the salary is expressed does not affect the characterization of the contract as one for a term or one at will. Although employer promises of "permanent" or "lifetime" employment occur more often as part of oral representations and inducements to employees than in written contracts, they are occasionally found in written contracts. In *Shoen v. Amerco, Inc.,*[1] the Nevada Supreme Court held that a written contract stating it was "the intent of the parties to provide the employee with employment for a lifetime," was enforceable because it was supported by the plaintiff's promise to make himself available as a lifetime consultant and not to provide any services to competing companies. The court also indicated that a contract for permanent or lifetime employment might be upheld without the requirement of additional consideration where the parties' intent was clear.

Employment contracts with no specific termination date, but with a notice provision for termination, are generally considered continually in force until notice is given. Once notice is given, the contract assumes a definite term, until the last day of the notice period. During this period, the employer must have cause to fire the employee. In *Shivers v. John H. Harland Co., Inc.,*[2] an employee working under a contract with a

§ 9.2

1. 111 Nev. 735, 896 P.2d 469 (1995).
2. 310 S.C. 217, 423 S.E.2d 105 (1992).

fifteen-day notice period was fired without notice and without cause. On a certified question from the Fourth Circuit, the South Carolina Supreme Court held that the employee's damages were fifteen days of lost wages and benefits. The court reasoned that the proper measure of damages was the amount necessary to put the employee in the position he would have enjoyed if there had been no employer breach. Because the contract would have been fulfilled if the employer had simply given fifteen days' notice instead of firing him summarily, the damages accrued only for the notice period.

§ 9.3   Employment Handbooks, Manuals, and Personnel Policies

The practice of providing employees with employment handbooks, manuals, or written personnel policies developed as employing firms grew larger and more sophisticated. Employment handbooks give employers the opportunity to provide large numbers of employees with standardized instruction about company policy in a more efficient and cost-effective manner than individual training. Employment handbooks can range from vague statements of the firm's policies to detailed descriptions of discharge, discipline, grievance, promotion, vacation, compensation, and benefit policies. Issuing employment manuals allows employers to regularize employment practices and to create an environment of fair treatment and settled expectations for their employees. In addition, employers may reap the benefit of a more committed and loyal work force. Sometimes employers issue employment manuals containing job security language in order to defeat or preempt a union organization campaign.

Before the 1980s, courts generally held that promises and statements made by employers in employment handbooks and manuals did not give rise to any contractual obligations. Some courts reasoned that the promises in the manuals were unenforceable because they lacked consideration. The employee's labor was seen as the consideration supporting the employer's promise to pay wages, and additional consideration, beyond the employee's continued labor, was required to support any other promises the employer made. Although most employees could not satisfy this requirement, cases did arise in which the requisite additional consideration to support promises of job security existed. For instance, quitting an existing job, especially one with protection from arbitrary discharge, or moving to another city to take an offered job was sometimes found sufficient to support employer promises of job security. Another aspect of this view of consideration prevented the enforcement of any employer promises made after the employee began work, because the employee would have nothing left to give as consideration. A second reason cited by many courts for their refusal to enforce promises in employment manuals was the absence of mutuality of obligation. Enforcing employer promises of job security would create an inequality, the courts reasoned, because employees could always terminate the employment relationship at will, while the employer would be bound by its promise of job security.

During the 1980s, most state supreme courts reconsidered the effect of employment handbooks and concluded that under the right circumstances they may create an implied employment contract. Today most states hold that promises contained in an employment manual may bind an employer. A minority either continue to reject this theory or have not yet definitively resolved the matter.

This so-called "handbook exception" to the employment-at-will rule has been articulated in two basic ways. The manner in which a state's courts have justified recognition of this cause of action is not always crucial, but occasionally the particular theory adopted by a court affects later handbook issues, such as the validity of employer attempts at modification.

Most of the states that recognize the handbook exception have adopted a unilateral contract analysis. In unilateral contract terms, the offeror-employer makes a promise limiting its prerogatives, such as the right to fire at will, by communicating the promise to employees in a handbook, manual, or other document, and the offeree-employee accepts the offer by commencing or continuing to work. The performance by the employee is consideration for the employer's promise; further consideration is not required. Moreover, a unilateral contract, by definition, does not require mutuality of obligation.

A typical statement of the elements of the cause of action under this analysis comes from *Duldulao v. Saint Mary of Nazareth Hospital Center,*[1] in which the Illinois Supreme Court held that the employee must prove three things to prevail.

First, the language of the policy statement must contain a promise clear enough that an employee would reasonably believe that an offer was made. Second, the statement must be disseminated to the employee in such a manner that the employee is aware of its contents and reasonably believes it to be an offer. Third, the employee must accept the offer by commencing or continuing to work after learning of the policy statement. When these conditions are present, then the employee's continued work constitutes consideration for the promises contained in the statement, and under traditional principles a valid contract is formed.

A second, less widely accepted theory of handbook enforcement comes from the decision of the Michigan Supreme Court in *Toussaint v. Blue Cross & Blue Shield.*[2] This theory treats handbooks as an obligation independent of traditional contract analysis. Rather, promises in employee manuals are seen as binding the employer because of the benefit the employer obtains by issuing the handbook in the first place.

§ 9.3

1. 115 Ill.2d 482, 106 Ill.Dec. 8, 505 N.E.2d 314 (1987).

2. 408 Mich. 579, 292 N.W.2d 880 (1980).

The employer secures an orderly, cooperative and loyal work force, and the employee the peace of mind associated with job security and the conviction that he will be treated fairly * * *. It is enough that the employer chooses, presumably in its own interest, to create an environment in which the employee believes that, whatever the personnel policies and practices, they are established and official at any given time, purport to be fair, and are applied consistently and uniformly to each employee. The employer has then created a situation "instinct with obligation."

Under either theory, litigation over the enforceability of handbook language raises a number of issues: the specificity of the language relied on by the employee, the relationship between that language and other employer representations, the adequacy of notice to employees of the existence of the handbook, and the effect of handbook modifications on incumbent employees. Additionally, although most employment handbook litigation involves the issue of both substantive and procedural job security—if, when, and under what circumstances an employer may fire an employee—language in employment manuals may also be a source of legal rights and obligations in other areas, such as layoffs, wages, severance pay, disciplinary penalties short of discharge, and arbitration requirements.

Specificity of Handbook Language

Regardless of the theory adopted to enforce handbooks, the language on which one or both parties rely must be sufficiently specific. This determination is an objective one, based on the parties' reasonable expectations and outward manifestations, not on either the employer or the employee's subjective beliefs. Many of these "definiteness of language" cases reach their conclusion by looking at a number of different provisions in the handbook to determine whether a reasonable reading of the entire document supports the employee's contention that the right to fire at will has been restricted.

All courts recognizing the handbook exception would find that, absent a disclaimer, language explicitly providing that discharge can occur only for cause binds the employer, but courts have also found for cause limitations in other, less direct, language. For instance, a detailed list of exclusive grounds for discipline and discharge, coupled with pretermination procedures, such as progressive discipline or investigation requirements, are normally construed as a contract not to discharge employees for offenses not on the list or without following the prescribed procedures. Cases involving "laundry lists" of dischargeable offenses often turn on the specific language describing the list. Language of exclusivity ("the types of separation are: * * *") generally binds the employer to its list, whereas when the dischargeable offenses "include, but are not limited to" those listed in the handbook, the employer will normally be allowed to fire for other reasons. Similarly, terms that preserve employer discretion to avoid its normal discharge reasons and procedures generally have that effect.

Some courts hold that descriptions of the standards of behavior and performance expected of employees are the equivalent of a cause standard. For instance, in *Cummings v. South Portland Housing Authority,*[3] the employee manual provided that "[t]he employment of personnel and all actions effecting [sic] employees shall be based solely on merit, ability (performance) and justice," and "[a]n employee who provides unsatisfactory service or who is guilty of substantial violation of regulations shall be subject to dismissal without prior notice." Noting that the Maine Supreme Court has described "for cause" to mean "conduct affecting the ability and fitness of the employee to perform his duties," the First Circuit held that the manual created a for cause restriction on the employer's ability to fire.

On the other hand, in *Robertson v. Utah Fuel Co.,*[4] an employee handbook contained a policy on substance abuse stating that employees who voluntarily requested treatment before testing positive on a workplace drug test would be offered rehabilitation assistance, which would be partially covered by the employer's medical plan. The plaintiff voluntarily sought treatment, but was then fired after he refused to accept a demotion following his treatment. The court held that the substance abuse policy could not reasonably be read to contain a guarantee that employees would not be disciplined or treated adversely because they had sought treatment.

Hunter v. Board of Trustees of Broadlawns Medical Center[5] illustrates the exclusive-list theory in an unusual set of facts. The employee manual described seven types of separation from employment (voluntary resignation, voluntary quit, retirement, three-day quit, expired leave, discharge for cause, and staff reduction). The employer eliminated the plaintiff's position and laid him off under the procedures for staff reduction, but several months later it created a new position and filled it with someone else. In a suit challenging the layoff, the Iowa Supreme Court held that the manual language constituted a contractual commitment that employment could be terminated only for one of the seven reasons. It also held that the meaning of the term "staff reduction" and whether a staff reduction had actually taken place were matters of contract interpretation for the trier of fact.

Disclaimers

The first courts that permitted employees to enforce promises in employment handbooks, under either unilateral contract theory or under the *Toussaint* theory, stated that employers were always free to include statements that employment remained at will. In *Woolley v. Hoffman–La Roche, Inc.,* for instance, the New Jersey Supreme Court remarked:

All that need be done is the inclusion in a very prominent position of an appropriate statement that there is no promise of any kind by the employer contained in the manual; that regardless of what the

3. 985 F.2d 1 (1st Cir.1993).

4. 889 P.2d 1382 (Utah App.1995), cert. denied, 899 P.2d 1231 (Utah 1995).

5. 481 N.W.2d 510 (Iowa 1992).

manual says or provides, the employer promises nothing and remains free to change wages and all other working conditions without having to consult anyone and without anyone's agreement; and that the employer continues to have the absolute power to fire anyone with or without good cause.[6]

Generally, courts require a disclaimer to be clear and unequivocal, conspicuously placed, and communicated to or acknowledged by the employee. Employers that require employees to sign an acknowledgement of the disclaimer usually have success defending against claims based on their handbooks, assuming the disclaimer language is clear and they do not make representations inconsistent with at-will status. Some of the most effective disclaimers have been contained in the employment application form, which applicants must sign, and not in an employee handbook. Similarly, courts generally accept disclaimers printed in large type or placed at the beginning of the handbook.

In *Butler v. Walker Power, Inc.,*[7] the employer issued a handbook containing a three-step discipline process and required employees to sign an acknowledgement providing, "I understand that this Handbook is not an expressed or implied contract of employment, but rather an overview of working rules and benefits, which can be changed at the discretion of the Company." The court distinguished between the durational status of employment and the incidents of employment and held that the disclaimer could be read to apply only to the former. Thus, employees were entitled to the progressive discipline process, although ultimately they remained at will. The court speculated that an employee might be able to prove damages resulting from the employer's failure to follow the discipline procedure, but no such evidence was presented in the case.

A number of cases turn on the placement and visibility of the disclaimer. In *McDonald v. Mobil Coal Producing, Inc.,*[8] both the application form and the employee handbook contained disclaimers, but the Wyoming Supreme Court held as a matter of law that they were not sufficiently conspicuous to bind the employee. The court noted that neither disclaimer was in larger print, capitalized, or set off by a border, and the handbook disclaimer was contained in a general welcoming section. The court also criticized the disclaimer as failing to give "persons untutored in contract law" a clear explanation of its effect on the employment relationship. Similarly, in *Jones v. Central Peninsula General Hospital,*[9] the Alaska Supreme Court held that a disclaimer consisting of one sentence in an eighty-five page detailed policy manual did not unambiguously and conspicuously inform employees that the manual was not part of their employment contract. On the other hand, in *Anderson v. Douglas & Lomason Co.,*[10] the Iowa Supreme Court surveyed the case law from states that require a disclaimer in an employee handbook to be conspicuous and found that this requirement created too

6. 99 N.J. 284, 491 A.2d 1257, modified, 101 N.J. 10, 499 A.2d 515 (1985).

7. 137 N.H. 432, 629 A.2d 91 (1993).

8. 820 P.2d 986 (Wyo.1991).

9. 779 P.2d 783 (Alaska 1989).

10. 540 N.W.2d 277 (Iowa 1995).

much uncertainty. Therefore, it rejected any special requirements for disclaimers and held that the rules applying to interpretation of other handbook language should be applied equally to disclaimers. Similarly, the South Carolina Supreme Court has said that a disclaimer is only one factor to consider in determining the effect of handbook language and that a handbook with both promissory language and a disclaimer is inherently ambiguous.[11]

Regardless of the prominence of the disclaimer and the clarity of its language, its effect can sometimes be overcome by other, inconsistent, employer behavior. In *Leahy v. Starflo Corp.*,[12] a conspicuous disclaimer appeared at the front of the employer's policy manual, but at some point the personnel director circulated to supervisors a letter stating, "If you are not aware of it we have had a disclaimer in our Employee Handbooks since about 1981 * * *. A disclaimer in the Employee Handbook is one thing but what does the Company Policy say? Read Policy #120–01 or Procedure #A04–003." Leahy was a manager and received this letter. The court agreed with his contention that the personnel director's letter was ambiguous and could be interpreted as a waiver of the disclaimer. In *Brown v. United Methodist Homes for the Aged*,[13] the employment manual contained a disclaimer, and the employer later distributed a memo explaining the concept of at-will employment. At trial, however, one of the employer's supervisors testified, "You don't just terminate a person because you want to terminate them. You have got to have some kind of cause." The Kansas Supreme Court held that this evidence was enough to create an issue of fact about the effect of the disclaimer.

In *Swanson v. Liquid Air Corp.*,[14] the employee, a truck driver, received a 200–page employment manual that included a disclaimer, although the accompanying cover letter did not refer to it. A few years later, in response to unrest among the drivers, the employer issued a Memorandum of Working Conditions, with a "Work Rights" section providing that employees who had not completed ninety days of employment could be terminated at will, and that otherwise, "Dishonesty, drinking or use of drugs on duty, recklessness resulting in an accident, or the carrying of unauthorized passengers shall be deemed sufficient and proper cause for discharge without prior notice. In all other instances of misconduct, at least one warning shall be given." This Memorandum did not refer to the disclaimer in the earlier manual. The Washington Supreme Court held that whether the parties intended the Memorandum to modify the contract created by the earlier-issued manual was a question of fact.

Communication to Employees

Under unilateral contract analysis, an employer policy cannot be considered an offer unless it is communicated to employees. Obviously,

11. Fleming v. Borden, 316 S.C. 452, 450 S.E.2d 589 (1994).

12. 314 S.C. 546, 431 S.E.2d 567 (1993).

13. 249 Kan. 124, 815 P.2d 72 (1991).

14. 118 Wash.2d 512, 826 P.2d 664 (1992).

an employee handbook or personnel manual that the employer distributes to all employees has been adequately communicated, whereas a policy that is never distributed or otherwise made known to employees has not. Generally, rank-and-file workers may not base breach of handbook claims on the terms of policies circulated only to supervisors and not otherwise made known to them, although the supervisors who receive the policies may have more success. For instance, in *Feges v. Perkins Restaurants, Inc.,*[15] the employer distributed to its managers a policy manual describing a system of progressive discipline. The managers used the manual in discussing company policies with new hires, but the manual itself was not generally distributed to all employees. When a store manager was fired in violation of the progressive discipline system, the Minnesota Supreme Court held that the issue was not whether the policy had been disseminated to all employees, but whether it had been communicated to the employee seeking to invoke it in a way that objectively manifested an offer for a contract applicable to that individual.

Although communication of the handbook is necessary for a valid offer under unilateral contract theory, many courts, especially those using the *Toussaint* rationale, do not require that an employee have actually relied on the terms of the handbook or continued to work intending an exchange for the promises in the handbook. In *Woolley v. Hoffmann–La Roche, Inc.,*[16] the New Jersey Supreme Court expressed the concern that requiring reliance would result in protection only for those employees who actually read the handbook, and not for the others, and therefore it presumed reliance. In *Kinoshita v. Canadian Pacific Airlines, Ltd.,*[17] the Supreme Court of Hawaii went one step further and permitted two employees to sue for breach of rules in a generally distributed set of employee policies even though they may not in fact have received all of the communications addressed to employees. Citing *Toussaint,* the court said the employer could not avoid liability for breach of the policies just because a particular employee was unaware of the rules.

Modification

The application of unilateral contract theory to employment manuals means that employees may enforce manuals issued after their initial hire, because continuing to work after the issuance constitutes consideration for the promises in the manuals. Many early cases were brought by employees hired at-will who were seeking to enforce after-hire promises of job security, but more recent litigation has involved employer policy changes running in the opposite direction. Often an employer with an existing policy manual promising just cause for dismissal amends the manual to revoke or diminish those promises and/or to insert an at-will disclaimer. The amendments will be part of the handbook "offer"

---

15. 483 N.W.2d 701 (Minn.1992).

16. 99 N.J. 284, 491 A.2d 1257, modified, 101 N.J. 10, 499 A.2d 515 (1985).

17. 68 Hawaii 594, 724 P.2d 110 (1986).

communicated to new employees, but can they modify the rights of incumbent workers? Although language in some early handbook cases might be read to support the position that once an employee has "accepted" an employer promise of job security by continuing to work after its promulgation, the employer may not unilaterally revoke or reduce that promise, other courts cited the employer's ability to change handbook language as a mark of the fundamental fairness of the handbook exception.

In *In re Certified Question (Bankey v. Storer Broadcasting Co.)*,[18] the Michigan Supreme Court held that although employers must comply with unrevoked promises of job security contained in an employee handbook, they are free unilaterally to change those promises at any time, even if the original handbook did not expressly reserve the right to do so. The court required only that the employer give affected employees reasonable notice of the policy change and that the change not be made in bad faith. A later Michigan case has held that *Bankey* does not require actual notice to each employee, as long as the method used to distribute the amendments was uniform and reasonable,[19] and the Sixth Circuit, applying Michigan law, has found that electronic posting of an updated handbook constituted reasonable notice.[20]

Michigan does not base its treatment of handbooks on a unilateral contract theory, but a few states that do have reached similar results. In *Gaglidari v. Denny's Restaurants, Inc.*,[21] the Washington Supreme Court also adopted a reasonable notice, uniformly given rule for modifications. Plaintiff received an employee handbook when she was hired. Although the employer amended the handbook a number of times over the years, including the addition of a disclaimer, it gave these new editions only to new employees, not to incumbent workers. The employer argued that new employees may have left copies of the subsequent handbook editions in the employee lounge where the plaintiff would have had a chance to read them, but the court rejected that argument. Reasonable notice of the changes requires more than conjecture or fortuity. Although the plaintiff was not bound by the terms of these later-issued handbooks, she had in fact received an alcoholic beverage manual containing rules similar to those in the newer handbook editions. Accordingly, the beverage manual did operate to modify her employment contract. Once she received it, she accepted the offer of new terms of employment it contained and provided consideration by remaining on the job. A later case from the Washington Court of Appeals read *Gaglidari* to mean that an employee's refusal to agree to the employer's reasonable new terms of

18. 432 Mich. 438, 443 N.W.2d 112 (1989), answer to certified question conformed to, 882 F.2d 208 (6th Cir.1989).

19. Grow v. General Prods., Inc., 184 Mich.App. 379, 457 N.W.2d 167 (1990), appeal denied, 439 Mich. 871, 478 N.W.2d 92 (1991).

20. Highstone v. Westin Engineering, 187 F.3d 548 (6th Cir.1999).

21. 117 Wash.2d 426, 815 P.2d 1362 (1991).

employment constituted a constructive resignation that justified her termination.[22]

In *Asmus v. Pacific Bell*,[23] the California Supreme Court held that an employer may unilaterally modify a policy that contains a specified condition of indefinite duration, if the employer makes the change after reasonable notice and without interfering with employees' vested benefits.

On the other hand, the Wyoming Supreme Court, on questions certified from the Tenth Circuit, held that the principle of additional consideration applies when an employer attempts to modify an implied job security provision to restore at-will status and that an employee's continued employment is not sufficient consideration for this modification.[24] The Supreme Court of Connecticut held that when an employer issues a handbook that "substantially interferes with an employee's legitimate expectations about the terms of employment," the mere fact that the employee continues to work following notice of the new terms is not conclusive evidence of consent; rather, the question is one of fact.[25] Similarly, the Seventh Circuit, applying Illinois law, held that an employer's unilateral issuance of an amended manual containing a disclaimer did not modify the provisions of the original handbook without acceptance and consideration, which could not be inferred from the fact that the employee continued to work with knowledge of the amendments.[26]

Similarly, in *Demasse v. ITT Corp.*,[27] in which the employer attempted to eliminate provisions of its handbook specifying that layoffs would be in reverse order of seniority, the Arizona Supreme Court held that an employer cannot unilaterally modify the terms of an employee handbook by publishing a later handbook that permits unilateral modification or rescission. The new handbook was merely an offer to modify the existing handbook, and continued employment alone did not constitute consideration for the modification. "The burden is on the employer to show that the employee assented with knowledge of the attempted modification and understanding of its impact on the underlying contract." In *Ex parte Amoco Fabrics & Fibers Co.*,[28] the Alabama Supreme Court held that an employer's issuance of a disclaimer did not unilaterally change the terms of its policy and procedures manual without evidence that the employees assented to the terms of the disclaimer.

Assuming the employer has properly amended its handbook, there can still remain an issue of the effect of the amendment's language. In

22. See Govier v. North Sound Bank, 91 Wash.App. 493, 957 P.2d 811 (1998).

23. 23 Cal.4th 1, 96 Cal.Rptr.2d 179, 999 P.2d 71 (2000).

24. Brodie v. General Chem. Corp., 934 P.2d 1263 (Wyo.1997).

25. Torosyan v. Boehringer Ingelheim Pharm., Inc., 234 Conn. 1, 18, 662 A.2d 89, 99 (1995).

26. Robinson v. Ada S. McKinley Community Servs., Inc., 19 F.3d 359 (7th Cir. 1994) (applying Ill. law).

27. 194 Ariz. 500, 984 P.2d 1138 (1999).

28. 729 So.2d 336 (Ala.1998).

Preston v. Claridge Hotel & Casino, Ltd.,[29] the original handbook contained a progressive discipline system and representations of "maximum job security." A few years later the employer issued a revised handbook with a disclaimer stating that it was "not intended to create, nor should be construed to constitute, a contract of employment between the Company and any one or all of its personnel." The court said that this language failed to explain the impact of the disclaimer on the previous representations of job security and therefore was not effective in creating at-will status.

Courts do state that the employer may not unilaterally modify or revoke employee rights that are already vested, accrued, or earned, such as vacation pay, but generally they do not place job security in this category.[30] Employees are entitled to rely on unrevoked promises of job security, and employers probably would not be permitted to manipulate the timing of handbook amendments in order to retaliate against a particular employee. Nevertheless, courts normally do not regard job security as an employment right that accrues with the passage of time. *Zuelsdorf v. University of Alaska*[31] presents a set of facts, unique to academic institutions, in which the plaintiffs enjoyed some measure of vested job security. The plaintiffs were untenured faculty members, and under the university's policies they were entitled to fifteen months' notice of nonretention. On May 19, 1986, the university amended its policies to provide for only twelve months' notice and promptly gave notice to the plaintiffs. The Alaska Supreme Court held that the plaintiffs' right to fifteen months' notice had vested on March 31, 1986, the beginning of the applicable fifteen-month period for that academic year, and the university could not later unilaterally eliminate that right. Presumably, however, the plaintiffs' right did not remain vested forever, and the university could apply its new twelve-month rule during the next academic year.

Arbitration Provisions and Other "Forum Selection" Clauses

During the mid 1990s issues involving the enforceability and effect of handbook provisions requiring the use of internal appeals procedures or arbitration of some sort began to be raised as defenses to suits alleging breach of handbook terms. In its 1988 decision in *Cannon v. National By–Products, Inc.,*[32] the Iowa Supreme Court held that the plaintiff's failure to pursue administrative remedies contained in the employer's handbook did not bar his suit for breach of the handbook's provisions. The court concluded that the "only prejudice which might arise on defendant's behalf as a result of plaintiff's failure to seek in-house review is the loss of an opportunity to avoid litigation."

29. 231 N.J.Super. 81, 555 A.2d 12 (1989).

30. See, e.g., In re the Wage Claim of Langager v. Crazy Creek Prods., Inc., 287 Mont. 445, 954 P.2d 1169 (1998).

31. 794 P.2d 932 (Alaska 1990).

32. 422 N.W.2d 638 (Iowa 1988).

To the extent that a trend can be perceived in more recent cases, however, it appears to be in favor of enforcing dispute resolution provisions. In *O'Brien v. New England Telephone & Telegraph Co.*,[33] the Supreme Judicial Court of Massachusetts held that a breach of contract claim based on representations in an employee handbook fails as a matter of law if the plaintiff did not pursue grievance procedures contained in the handbook. In *Ex parte McNaughton*,[34] the Alabama Supreme Court dealt with a handbook containing a clear at-will statement and an agreement to arbitrate disputes arising out of the employment, plus a signed acknowledgment incorporating the arbitration provision. The court rejected the employee's arguments of unconscionability and lack of mutuality of remedy, finding that the agreement did not bar ultimate redress by the employee, but only the means by which that redress may be sought. Although the parties may not have been bound by any other terms of the handbook, said the court, they had agreed to be bound by the arbitration provision. In *City of Odessa v. Barton*,[35] the Texas Supreme Court held that a city employee had no independent claim for breach of the just-cause promise in the city's personnel manual, because the manual also limited him to administrative review as the exclusive remedy for challenging the adverse employment decision.

In *Cheek v. United Healthcare of the Mid–Atlantic, Inc.*,[36] however, the Maryland Court of Appeals held that a former employee did not have to arbitrate his claims of breach of contract, negligent misrepresentation, and failure to pay earned compensation, because the arbitration agreement was unenforceable for lack of consideration. Although the employee had promised to arbitrate his claims, the employer's promise to arbitrate was illusory; the company reserved the right to alter, amend, modify, or revoke the arbitration agreement at any time and without notice.

Finally, a decision by the Alaska Supreme Court illustrates the other side of arbitration provisions. In *Ross v. City of Sand Point*,[37]an employee had pursued the employer's grievance policy and prevailed. The employer refused to follow the decision of the grievance committee and fired the employee. The court held that the grievance policy created an implied contract that the employee would not be fired if he won through that process.

§ 9.4   Oral Contracts

Even in the heyday of the employment at will doctrine, courts were willing to enforce express oral promises of job security, assuming the employee could meet a number of exacting requirements, including specificity of the promise, independent consideration, and the statute of frauds. Although the erosion of the at-will doctrine has meant the

33. 422 Mass. 686, 664 N.E.2d 843 (1996).

34. 728 So.2d 592 (Ala.1998), cert. denied, 528 U.S. 818, 120 S.Ct. 59, 145 L.Ed.2d 52 (1999).

35. 967 S.W.2d 834 (Tex.1998).

36. 378 Md. 139, 835 A.2d 656 (2003).

37. 952 P.2d 274 (Alaska 1998).

relaxation or elimination of these requirements with respect to promises contained in employment handbooks, courts continue to scrutinize oral contracts rigorously. Unlike generally-distributed employee handbooks containing company-wide policies, oral representations of job security or other employment conditions are usually unique promises made specifically to one employee, often in the context of preemployment interviews or negotiations. As a result, although the enormous variety of factual settings makes it difficult to find precise rules common to these cases, in many situations the employee will be able to prove reliance on the employer's promise. Indeed, if there is one theme in the modern oral contract cases, it is that courts attempt to find a way to enforce employer promises of job security where the employee has reasonably relied to his or her detriment on those promises.

Specificity of Language

A threshold issue in all cases involving oral promises is whether the employer's language was sufficiently clear and definite to be enforced. Promises of "permanent" or "lifetime" employment have proved particularly problematic. Some courts regard such promises as offering only steady employment for an indefinite period of time, which is the equivalent of employment at will. Others see them as a commitment to employment as long as the employer remains in operation, as subject to termination for just cause, or as employment until the employee retires or dies.

In all cases, courts search for objective evidence of the parties' intent. Oral representations for permanent employment must be more than mere expressions of optimistic hopes for a long relationship; they must be clear and unequivocal enough to overcome the presumption that employment is at will. For instance, although North Dakota adheres to the general rule that a promise of "permanent employment," "life employment," or "as long as the employee chooses" does not overcome the at-will presumption, in *Aaland v. Lake Region Grain Cooperative*,[1] the board of directors voted to allow the plaintiff to remain in his job "until a replacement has been found and he finds another position." The court held that a grant of summary judgment for the employer was improper because the employer's promise was for a duration that could be determined by an ascertainable event, and a jury could find that the parties intended the plaintiff to be employed for a reasonable time to allow him to look for another job. Similarly, in *Rooney v. Tyson*,[2] the New York Court of Appeals answered a certified question from the Second Circuit involving the definiteness of an oral promise between a fight trainer and a boxer that was to last "for as long as the boxer fights professionally." The court held that this promise stated a duration that was understandable and determinable enough to take the relationship out of employment at will. "Though the times are not precisely predicta-

§ 9.4
1. 511 N.W.2d 244 (N.D.1994).

2. 91 N.Y.2d 685, 674 N.Y.S.2d 616, 697 N.E.2d 571 (1998).

ble and calculable to dates certain, they are legally and experientially limited and ascertainable by objective benchmarks.''

The context in which the statements were made often helps courts distinguish between enforceable and unenforceable promises. In *Rowe v. Montgomery Ward & Co., Inc.,*[3] the Michigan Supreme Court held that a manager's statement to an employee hired to fill one of several identical appliance sales positions that she "would have a job as long as [she] sold" did not alter the at-will nature of the employment. It distinguished cases in which the employer negotiated specifically about job security with an employee hired for a singular executive position. In the latter cases, the court said, it is much more reasonable to find that the terms of the employment contract were negotiable and that the parties intended to restrict the employer's ability to fire at will.

In *Kurtzman v. Applied Analytical Industries, Inc.,*[4] the plaintiff had a secure position with another employer, was actively recruited by the defendant, and ultimately accepted the defendant's job offer and moved from New England to North Carolina. Before he took the job, the plaintiff engaged in extensive negotiations with the defendant and received many oral assurances of job security. Eight days after he began work at the new job, he was asked to complete an employment application containing at-will language. This was the first time the plaintiff had seen the application, and he testified that he considered the signing a mere formality and that, in light of his lengthy discussions with the defendant's managers, the at-will language did not apply to him. Approximately seven months later, the plaintiff was fired. The North Carolina Supreme Court held that neither the employer's oral assurances nor the employee's relocation to accept employment altered the employee's employment at will status.

Consideration

Although most courts have abandoned the requirement that employees give consideration in addition to their continued labor in exchange for promises contained in employment handbooks, the doctrine of additional consideration remains relatively intact in cases involving oral promises, especially if the promise is for permanent employment. Provision of independent consideration helps clarify the parties' intent; if the employee suffers a substantial detriment in exchange for the promise of job security, it is more likely that the employer and employee viewed the promise as serious. In *Shebar v. Sanyo Business Systems Corp.,*[5] the plaintiff, who had worked for Sanyo for several years as an at-will employee, received a job offer from Sony. In response to his letter of resignation, Sanyo's president told the plaintiff that if he stayed with Sanyo he would have a job for the rest of his life. The New Jersey Supreme Court construed this as a promise to discharge plaintiff only for cause and held that a jury could find it was supported by the relinquish-

---

3. 437 Mich. 627, 473 N.W.2d 268 (1991).

4. 347 N.C. 329, 493 S.E.2d 420 (1997).

5. 111 N.J. 276, 544 A.2d 377 (1988).

ment of the job opportunity at Sony. The court cautioned, however, that "not every relinquishment of a prior job or job offer constitutes additional consideration to support the modification of an at-will employment into employment with termination for cause only." What makes the decision in *Shebar* notable is that New Jersey does not require additional consideration to support promises of discharge only for cause contained in employment handbooks. Not all states have addressed this doctrine after their recognition of the handbook exception, but a number of states continue to require additional consideration to support oral promises of job security.

Statute of Frauds

Almost all of the states have enacted laws modeled on the English Statute of Frauds of 1677, and these statutes used to be a major obstacle to the enforcement of oral promises of employment. Statutes of frauds provide that agreements, promises, or undertakings are void if the terms of the agreement are not to be performed within one year from the time of making, unless the agreement is in writing and signed by the party to be sued. The purpose of the statute of frauds is said to be the prevention of fraud when parties attempt to prove legal transactions that are thought particularly susceptible to deception, mistake, and perjury. The general effect of the statute of frauds is to render void oral contracts for longer than one year.

Most modern courts, however, construe the statute narrowly so that it rarely bars enforcement of oral promises of job security. They do this by holding that the statute applies only to those contracts that, at the time of making, could not possibly or conceivably be completed within a year. Thus, promises of "permanent" or "lifetime" employment are capable of full performance within a year, because the employee could die or the employer could go out of business within that time. Similarly, a promise that the employer will fire the employee only for cause is capable of performance within a year. On the other hand, a promise of employment until the worker is sixty-five, made when he or she is younger than sixty-four, falls within the statute. The New York Court of Appeals has held that an oral agreement to pay a bonus consisting of a percentage of the company's annual pre-tax profits did not fall within the statute. That the employee's compensation could not be calculated until after the passage of year did not, standing alone, render the agreement void.[6]

A few states distinguish between performance of a contract within one year, which takes a contract out of the statute of frauds, and termination of the contract within one year, which does not. For instance, in *Graham v. Central Fidelity Bank*,[7] the plaintiff alleged an oral contract for employment terminable only for cause. The Virginia Supreme Court held that a discharge for cause is not a performance of the

6. Cron v. Hargro Fabrics, Inc., 91 N.Y.2d 362, 670 N.Y.S.2d 973, 694 N.E.2d 56 (1998).

7. 245 Va. 395, 428 S.E.2d 916 (1993).

contract within the meaning of the statute of frauds, but a termination of the contract because of its breach. The possibility of termination within the first year of performance did not remove the contract from Virginia's statute of frauds, and therefore the promise plaintiff alleged was not enforceable. The Washington Supreme Court ruled that the fact that an oral employment contract of a fixed duration longer than a year could be terminated by either party with six months' notice did not take the agreement out of the statute.[8]

Modification

In *Bullock v. Automobile Club of Michigan*,[9] decided the same day as *In re Certified Question (Bankey v. Storer Broadcasting Co.)*,[10] which permitted unilateral amendments of employee handbooks, the Michigan Supreme Court held that an employer may not unilaterally modify an express oral promise of job security. Bullock alleged he had received oral assurances at the time of hiring that he would have a lifetime job as long as he did not steal. Sometime after Bullock was hired, the employer issued an employee handbook with an at-will disclaimer. The court held that at most the handbook constituted an offer to modify the discharge-for-cause provision of Bullock's express oral contract. On the other hand, the court found an effective modification in *Scholz v. Montgomery Ward & Co.*[11] When she was hired, Scholz had been promised she would not have to work on Sunday. A few years later the employer issued a handbook with a "sign off" sheet providing that employees could be fired with or without cause. Scholz signed the sheet; sometime later, she was fired for refusing to work on Sundays. The court held that by signing the sign off sheet, Scholz agreed to a modification of all previous oral promises made to her, including the promise of no Sunday work.

Promissory Estoppel

Courts sometimes invoke the doctrine of promissory estoppel to enforce oral representations of job security on which an employee has detrimentally relied. Under the doctrine of promissory estoppel, courts need not find all of the elements of contract formation—offer, acceptance, and consideration. Rather, "[a] promise which the promisor should reasonably expect to induce action or forbearance on the part of the promisee or a third person and which does induce such action or forbearance is binding if injustice can be avoided only by enforcement of the promise."[12] Promissory estoppel may provide a remedy in situations where traditional contract analysis would not. For instance, in *Grouse v. Group Health Plan, Inc.*,[13] the defendant promised plaintiff a job, and in

---

8. French v. Sabey Corp., 134 Wash.2d 547, 951 P.2d 260 (1998).

9. 432 Mich. 472, 444 N.W.2d 114 (1989), cert. denied, 493 U.S. 1072, 110 S.Ct. 1118, 107 L.Ed.2d 1024 (1990).

10. 432 Mich. 438, 443 N.W.2d 112 (1989), answer to certified question conformed to 882 F.2d 208 (6th Cir.1989).

11. 437 Mich. 83, 468 N.W.2d 845 (1991).

12. Restatement (Second) of Contracts § 90 (1979).

13. 306 N.W.2d 114 (Minn.1981).

reliance on that promise, the plaintiff quit his existing job and gave up an offer of yet a third job. The defendant then reneged on its offer. The Minnesota Supreme Court held that the plaintiff could invoke the doctrine of promissory estoppel to recover his reliance damages from the defendant, even though the promised job would have been at will and plaintiff could have been fired at any time.

To establish promissory estoppel, the plaintiff must show a clear and unambiguous promise; as with oral contracts generally, vague statements of future employment will not support a cause of action for promissory estoppel. Moreover, reasonable reliance by the employee is required; employees who can not show some acts of a substantial nature will not prevail on a claim of promissory estoppel.

§ 9.5 Contracts Implied From Conduct

Many courts hold that terms of an employment contract, especially those dealing with job security, may be implied from the overall conduct and relationship of the parties. These implied-in-fact contracts may arise from oral representations, terms in employment handbooks, the nature of the employment, the past practices of the particular employer, the course of dealing between the employer and the employee, the custom in the trade or industry, and other circumstances that show the existence of contractual terms. This theory can be helpful to employees who may reasonably believe they have been promised job security, but who cannot allege any explicit words to that effect. Even when employees can point to express oral promises or handbook provisions, their claims may well be bolstered by proof of other employer conduct consistent with these representations.

In Kansas, all employment contract litigation not involving individual written contracts is channeled into this course of conduct theory. In *Morriss v. Coleman Co., Inc.,*[1] male and female coworkers who were not married to each other were fired after their supervisor learned they had taken an overnight trip together. They sued for breach of an implied contract of discharge for cause only and based their claim on the employer's personnel manual, the employer's established method of dealing with employees, and other verbal and nonverbal conduct indicating that the employer would treat its employees fairly. The Kansas Supreme Court held that the plaintiffs had raised legitimate factual issues concerning the existence of an implied contract not to fire employees without just cause.

In *Kestenbaum v. Pennzoil Co.,*[2] the New Mexico Supreme Court held that oral statements made by an employer may be sufficient to create an implied just cause contract. Kestenbaum presented a variety of evidence to establish that his employment contract was for an indefinite period of time and allowed involuntary removal only for a good reason.

---

1. 241 Kan. 501, 738 P.2d 841 (1987).

2. 108 N.M. 20, 766 P.2d 280 (1988), cert. denied, 490 U.S. 1109, 109 S.Ct. 3163, 104 L.Ed.2d 1026 (1989).

First, evidence was presented that during the initial employment negotiations, plaintiff's immediate supervisor stated that the employment would be long term and permanent as long as the plaintiff did his job. Second, a former operations manager and other company officials testified that the company discharged permanent employees only for "a good reason, a just cause." Third, both the insurance benefits manual and the policy manual contained provisions describing conversion privileges after termination of employment, but neither manual made mention of termination without cause. The court rejected the defendant's approach of considering each piece of evidence individually.

Although most cases involve allegations of implied contracts to discharge only for cause, the parties' conduct may give rise to other obligations as well. In *Metcalf v. Intermountain Gas Co.*,[3] the Idaho Supreme Court found that although there was no basis to support a general change in the plaintiff's at-will status, a promise not to fire employees for using their accumulated sick leave could be implied from the existence of the policy allowing the accrual of that leave.

Longevity of service, combined with other factors, can help establish a course of conduct. A series of California cases seemed to focus almost exclusively on the employee's years of service. In *Cleary v. American Airlines, Inc.*,[4] the California Court of Appeals relied on the employee's eighteen years of service and the employer's grievance and discharge policies to find an implied contract to discharge only for cause. In *Pugh v. See's Candies, Inc.*,[5] the plaintiff had thirty-two years of employment. In *Foley v. Interactive Data Corp.*,[6] the California Supreme Court found that employment for six years and nine months was long enough for conduct to occur on which an implied just-cause contract could be based. In *Guz v. Bechtel National, Inc.*,[7] however, the court took a step back from those decisions and held that "an employee's mere passage of time in the employer's service, even where marked with tangible indicia that the employer approves the employee's work, cannot alone form an implied-in-fact contract that the employee is no longer at will * * *. A rule granting such contract rights on the basis of successful longevity alone would discourage the retention and promotion of employees."

§ 9.6   Implied Covenant of Good Faith and Fair Dealing

A little more than one-fifth of the states permit the use of the implied-in-law covenant of good faith and fair dealing to challenge discharges or other employer actions in certain limited situations. That an implied covenant of good faith and fair dealing attaches to all contracts has been widely recognized in general contract law, but most courts have rejected the application of the doctrine to employment

---

3. 116 Idaho 622, 778 P.2d 744 (1989).

4. 111 Cal.App.3d 443, 168 Cal.Rptr. 722 (1980).

5. 116 Cal.App.3d 311, 171 Cal.Rptr. 917 (1981).

6. 47 Cal.3d 654, 254 Cal.Rptr. 211, 765 P.2d 373 (1988).

7. 24 Cal.4th 317, 100 Cal.Rptr.2d 352, 8 P.3d 1089 (2000).

contracts because of concerns that the doctrine is amorphous, too broad, and destructive of employer prerogatives. Most courts view the invocation of the implied covenant as the plaintiff's attempt to impose a just cause requirement on an employment relationship as a matter of law, where, as a matter of fact, the relationship is at will, and they decline to adopt it for that reason.

A careful look at the cases in which courts have applied the implied covenant, however, reveals that for the most part they do not involve the artificial creation of job security. Rather, the covenant is used to prevent employers from depriving employees of benefits the employees have already earned. (Consistent with this limitation, virtually all of the states that recognize the implied covenant hold that its violation leads to remedies in contract, not in tort.) For instance, in *Fortune v. National Cash Register Co.*,[1] the employer fired a twenty-five year at-will employee on the next business day after he obtained a $5,000,000 order from a customer in his sales territory. The court held that the firing, motivated by a desire to avoid paying a commission to the employee, breached the implied covenant of good faith and fair dealing.

Similarly, in *Metcalf v. Intermountain Gas Co.*[2] the employer reduced a full-time at-will employee to part-time status (eventually to only two hours per day) because she was using sick leave she had accrued under the employer's leave policies. The Idaho Supreme Court permitted her to sue for breach of the implied covenant, which it concluded is violated by "any action by either party which violates, nullifies or significantly impairs any benefit of the employment contract."

In *Hall v. Farmers Insurance Exchange*,[3] the Oklahoma Supreme Court permitted an insurance agent to recover for a breach of the implied covenant when the insurance group with which he contracted terminated his agency in retaliation for his protests on behalf of another agent who had also been terminated. The court, however, was careful in its characterization of the proof as to the group's intent; the evidence supported a finding that the group intended to deprive the agent of his income from renewal premiums on policies he had already sold and to parcel that income among its other, less obstreperous agents. Three years later, in *Burk v. K–Mart Corp.*,[4] the court distinguished *Hall* and held that there is no implied covenant of good faith and fair dealing governing an employer's decision to fire in an at-will situation. The Connecticut Supreme Court has reached a similar conclusion, that employment contracts contain an implied-in-law covenant of good faith designed to fulfill the reasonable expectations of the parties, but that the covenant does not impose a good cause provision on an at-will relationship.[5]

§ 9.6

1. 373 Mass. 96, 364 N.E.2d 1251 (1977).

2. 116 Idaho 622, 778 P.2d 744 (1989).

3. 713 P.2d 1027 (Okl.1985).

4. 770 P.2d 24 (Okl.1989).

5. Carbone v. Atlantic Richfield Co., 204 Conn. 460, 528 A.2d 1137 (1987).

In *K Mart Corp. v. Ponsock,*[6] Nevada's implied covenant case, an employee was fired a few months before he would have become 100 percent vested in the employer's pension plan. The court noted that if the employer had merely fired Ponsock arbitrarily and without warning, he would have had a contractual remedy under the employee handbook; it was the improper motive of defeating his contractual benefits that converted the action into a bad faith discharge. Then, in *Shoen v. Amerco, Inc.,*[7] the Nevada Supreme Court explained that *Ponsock* was based on the presence of "the type of employer-employee relationship which presents the elements of reliance, trust, and dependency." In *Shoen* the plaintiff founded the U–Haul Rental System and managed the business for over forty-one years. He made gifts of stock to his children and eventually turned over the running of the business to his oldest sons. He alleged that his sons terminated his employment in retaliation for his testimony at a federal tax trial against one of them, and that another son assaulted and harassed him. The court said that "[a] betrayal of the kind of relationship Shoen has with Amerco could be found to go well beyond the bounds of ordinary liability for breach of contract," and therefore summary judgment should not have been granted on his good faith and fair dealing claim.

In *Hoffman–La Roche, Inc. v. Campbell,*[8] the Alabama Supreme Court permitted use of the implied covenant where the employee claimed, among other things, that he was fired so that the employer would not have to pay him sick leave benefits under its employee handbook. Later cases in Alabama have restricted *Campbell* to situations where a contract of some sort, either an express contract or a handbook, exists.[9]

There are a few cases not involving the deprivation of benefits earned through employment in which courts have applied the covenant to bar extreme overreaching by employers where no other cause of action seemed to exist. A few of these are early cases that today would be handled through other doctrines. For instance, in *Monge v. Beebe Rubber Co.,*[10] an employee was fired after she refused her foreman's sexual advances. Today, her claim would be for sexual harassment under Title VII and perhaps for the tort of outrage or intentional infliction of emotional distress. The New Hampshire Supreme Court has since limited *Monge* to cases in which the discharge implicates public policy.[11]

In *Gates v. Life of Montana Insurance Co.,*[12] the Montana Supreme Court held that an employee handbook setting forth procedures to be followed before an employee could be fired did not apply to the plaintiff because she started work before the employer issued the handbook. The

---

6. 103 Nev. 39, 732 P.2d 1364 (1987).

7. 111 Nev. 735, 896 P.2d 469 (1995).

8. 512 So.2d 725 (Ala.1987).

9. See, e.g., Hanson v. New Technology, Inc., 594 So.2d 96 (Ala.1992).

10. 114 N.H. 130, 316 A.2d 549 (1974).

11. See, e.g., Cilley v. New Hampshire Ball Bearings, Inc., 128 N.H. 401, 514 A.2d 818 (1986).

12. 196 Mont. 178, 638 P.2d 1063 (1982).

court went on, however, to permit her to sue for breach of the implied covenant of good faith and fair dealing because the handbook created reasonable expectations that she would be treated fairly. Had this case arisen initially today, the court would undoubtedly have found the handbook contractually binding, because virtually all states have abandoned the notions of independent consideration that led to the rejection of the contract-in-fact theory in *Gates.* Montana went on to apply the implied covenant theory broadly and to impose for-cause requirements on at-will relationships, but most of these claims are now preempted by the state's Wrongful Discharge from Employment Act.

Merrill v. Crothall–American, Inc.[13] is an example of a decision applying the covenant to facts that did not fit into any other cause of action. The employer, which provided facilities management services for institutions such as schools and hospitals, had a contractual obligation to supply a Director of Plant Operations for a health care facility by October 14, 1986. On that date it offered the job to Merrill, even though he expressed concern about his qualifications. A few months later, Merrill was fired. He alleged that the employer hired him because it needed a "warm body" to fill the position and never intended to employ him on a long-term basis. Indeed, he contended that the employer was interviewing the person who replaced him only two days after he (Merrill) began work. He claimed that the employer induced him to take the job under the belief that the job, while at-will, would be of indefinite duration, all the while concealing its intention to employ him only temporarily. The Delaware Supreme Court reversed a grant of summary judgment for the employer and held that Merrill had adequately pled a cause of action for breach of the implied covenant of good faith and fair dealing. The court said that to breach the implied covenant, the employer's conduct

> must constitute an aspect of fraud, deceit, or misrepresentation * * *. The lodestar here is candor. An employer acts in bad faith when it induces another to enter into an employment contract through actions, words, or the withholding of information, which is intentionally deceptive in some way material to the contract.

The court did note, however, that it was not imposing a just cause standard or even considering what, if any, reasons for firing an at-will employee might breach the covenant. Here, it was the deceptive inducement that constituted the breach, and the firing was only the logical extension of that wrong.

Then there are two states, Alaska and Wyoming, that imply a covenant of good faith and fair dealing in all employment contracts. Alaska channels all of its wrongful discharge litigation through the implied covenant doctrine. It clearly recognizes the implied covenant in situations where the employer has impaired the employee's right to receive the benefits of employment,[14] but it also applies it to require that

13. 606 A.2d 96 (Del.1992).

14. See Jones v. Central Peninsula Gen. Hosp., 779 P.2d 783 (Alaska 1989).

the parties act in a manner that a reasonable person would regard as fair. In practice, this appears to mean that an employer must treat like employees alike, that an employer may not fire or suspend employees for reasons that violate public policy, and that a public employer may not fire an employee for an unconstitutional reason, but it does not mean that all employment relationships have a just cause requirement imposed on them.

In *Wilder v. Cody Country Chamber of Commerce*,[15] the Wyoming Supreme Court ended a decade of litigation in the state over recognition of the implied covenant and held that every employment contract contains an implied covenant of good faith and fair dealing. The claim gives rise to damages in tort, but only in the presence of "a special relationship of trust and reliance" between the employee and employer. According to the court, "[t]rust and reliance may be found by the existence of separate consideration, common law, statutory rights, or rights accruing with longevity of service." The court found as a matter of law that there was no breach of the implied covenant in *Wilder*, where the plaintiff had worked for the employer for only three years, and there was no evidence that the plaintiff was fired to avoid payment of benefits already earned under his employment contract.

Finally, the New Mexico Supreme Court has held that a covenant of good faith and fair dealing is to be implied in all employment contracts that are not at-will, and that the claim sounds in contract, not tort.[16] Nebraska implies a covenant of good faith and fair dealing as to termination of employment contracts providing that an employee may not be fired without good cause.[17]

Thus, with the exception of these four, jurisdictions that accept the implied covenant do so in situations where the employer has acted with the purpose of denying the employee benefits accrued through his or her employment. The confusion about the reach of the covenant comes primarily from decisions in a few states. The California courts had permitted the covenant to be used to create job security for long-term employees. In *Cleary v. American Airlines, Inc.*,[18] an employee claimed his discharge violated both company policy and the covenant of good faith and fair dealing. The California Court of Appeals said:

> [t]ermination of employment without legal cause after such a period of time offends the implied-in-law covenant of good faith and fair dealing contained in all contracts * * *. As a result of this covenant, a duty arose on the part of the employer * * * to do nothing which would deprive plaintiff * * * of the benefits of the employment bargain—benefits described in the complaint as having accrued during plaintiff's 18 years of employment.

15. 868 P.2d 211 (Wyo.1994).

16. Bourgeous v. Horizon Healthcare Corp., 117 N.M. 434, 872 P.2d 852 (1994).

17. Jeffers v. Bishop Clarkson Mem. Hosp., 222 Neb. 829, 387 N.W.2d 692 (1986)

18. 111 Cal.App.3d 443, 168 Cal.Rptr. 722 (1980).

Cases like *Cleary* led to a great deal of litigation in California over the nature of the covenant and the amount of time on the job necessary to invoke its protections. Although the implied covenant theory is still available, the California Supreme Court diminished its attractiveness with its decision in *Foley v. Interactive Data Corp.*,[19] limiting damages available for a breach of the covenant to contractual remedies. Further, although not required for its holding, the court in *Foley* engaged in a lengthy discussion of the problem of distinguishing between breaches of contract and breaches of the implied covenant, and said that, unless limited, the implied covenant could provide the basis for challenging "virtually any firing (indeed any breach of a contract term in any context)." In *Guz v. Bechtel National, Inc.*,[20] the court called a claim for breach of the covenant "superfluous" where breach of an actual contract term is involved, and "invalid" where it alleges "a breach of obligations beyond the agreement's actual term."

§ 9.7 Constructive Discharge

Ordinarily, an employee who quits his or her job does not have a claim for discharge in breach of contract or retaliatory discharge. If, however, the conditions that caused the employee to quit constitute a "constructive discharge," courts will treat the employee as if he or she had been fired. Most constructive discharges fall into one of two basic fact patterns. First, the employer can cause a constructive discharge by materially breaching the employee's contract of employment in some manner short of termination. Second, the employer can make working conditions so intolerable that the employee feels compelled to quit. It is important to remember that constructive discharge itself does not constitute a cause of action; proof that a quit was really a constructive discharge merely satisfies the discharge element in a claim for breach of contract or retaliatory discharge. The employee must still prove that the underlying circumstances that led him or her to quit were somehow wrongful.

Employer Breach of Contract

Not surprisingly, most cases involving constructive discharge caused by the employer's breach of contract arise with respect to employees who have express contracts of employment. If an employee was hired for a particular position, a material change in duties, a significant reduction of rank and responsibility, or a reassignment to another position, if not contemplated by the parties' agreement, will normally entitle the employee to quit and sue for damages. As one court put it, "[w]hile a material breach of an employment contract need not completely frustrate the entire purpose of the contract, it must be so important that it makes continued performance by the plaintiff virtually pointless."[1] In

19. 47 Cal.3d 654, 254 Cal.Rptr. 211, 765 P.2d 373 (1988).

20. 24 Cal.4th 317, 100 Cal.Rptr.2d 352, 8 P.3d 1089 (2000).

§ 9.7

1. Gibson v. City of Cranston, 37 F.3d 731, 737 (1st Cir.1994) (applying R.I. law).

Van Steenhouse v. Jacor Broadcasting of Colorado, Inc.,[2] a radio station took a talk show host off the air for the remainder of the term of her contract, but it continued to pay her. Her employment contract contained a noncompete clause, which made her unable to quit and immediately go to work for a competitor. The Colorado Supreme Court found that the station had materially breached the contract, recognizing that certain kinds of employees can be damaged by not being able to work, even while receiving full pay.

Another ground for a finding of constructive discharge is the employer's refusal to pay agreed-upon wages. In *Brock v. Mutual Reports, Inc.,*[3] the employer removed the plaintiff from his position as vice-president in charge of news operations and reassigned him to a reporter's job. The court agreed that the plaintiff had suffered a significant demotion constituting a constructive discharge, but it found the "discharge" was justified because the plaintiff had failed to perform his managerial duties competently. The employer, therefore, had cause to demote, and thus the constructive discharge was not a breach of contract.

Intolerable Working Conditions

A constructive discharge can also occur if the employee quits because of intolerable working conditions. A great deal of case law fleshing out the contours of this branch of constructive discharge doctrine exists under Title VII, where the intolerable working conditions are likely to be the result of racial, ethnic, or sexual harassment, but the theory can apply equally to claims of retaliatory discharge or discharge in breach of contract. Under the majority rule, the employer must have created or maintained working conditions so intolerable that any reasonable employee would have felt compelled to quit rather than endure them. A minority view requires the employee to prove that the employer created the intolerable conditions with the specific intent of forcing the employee to quit.

Relatively minor abuse of an employee is not sufficient for a constructive discharge. Unfavorable evaluations, criticisms of poor performance, transfers, and demotions, without more, do not justify an employee's resignation. Rather, the adverse working conditions must generally be ongoing, repetitive, pervasive, and severe. Indeed, in many cases, the intolerable working conditions that permit a finding of constructive discharge may also state a claim for intentional infliction of emotional distress and other torts of outrage. Occasionally, however, one very serious incident, standing alone, can be enough to warrant a finding of constructive discharge. In *Hammond v. United of Oakland, Inc.,*[4] the employee claimed his supervisor coerced him into signing a letter of resignation by brandishing a knife. The court held that a jury could find

2.   958 P.2d 464 (Colo.1998).
3.   397 A.2d 149 (D.C.App.1979).

4.   193 Mich.App. 146, 483 N.W.2d 652 (1992).

this incident made his working conditions so intolerable he felt compelled to quit.

As with the first branch of constructive discharge doctrine, an employee cannot prevail merely by proving the intolerable nature of the working conditions; the working conditions must be related to the facts giving rise to the employee's claim of retaliatory discharge or breach of contract. In *Kestell v. Heritage Health Care Corp.,*[5] a case arising under Montana's Wrongful Discharge from Employment Act, the Montana Supreme Court found the plaintiff, a highly qualified and experienced supervisor, was justified in quitting after the employer abruptly removed him from his office, isolated him in a remote area of the facility, and deprived him of any meaningful activity. The court then went on to address the statutory defense of good cause, because the "discharge" might have been justified by legitimate business reasons.

§ 9.8 Cause

Issues of "just cause," or "good cause," or simply "cause" can arise in three settings. First, by operation of law, an employment contract for a definite term may not be terminated without cause before the expiration of the term, unless the contract provides otherwise. Second, written contracts, whether for a term or for an indefinite period, may contain explicit just cause protection. Third, courts may find that oral agreements, employee handbooks, or courses of conduct have created just cause protection.

As a general matter, cause may be divided into two categories: (1) business or economic reasons unrelated to the employee, and (2) employee misconduct or inadequate performance. The first category, economic reasons, is the easiest. If the employment agreement is for an indefinite term, a bona fide reduction in force or a plant closing or reorganization will establish cause. On the other hand, a cessation of business due to poor economic conditions may not establish cause for a discharge under a contract for a definite term, unless the contract can be read to support discharge for that reason.

The second category, employee-based reasons, includes inadequate performance as well as offenses against the employer or its business, such as resume fraud, sexual harassment, fighting, drinking, assaulting a customer, and insubordination. Not all employee misconduct will meet the standard for cause, however. The misconduct must be *substantial.* Thus, a minor neglect of duty, an excusable absence, a minor misrepresentation, rudeness, and even filing a defamation action against the employer have been held not to establish cause. Moreover, in some situations misconduct, such as the failure to follow unreasonable orders, may be justified. Courts are reluctant to find cause based on employee activity off the job unless there is a direct, adverse effect on the employer's business.

5. 259 Mont. 518, 858 P.2d 3 (1993).

Although not yet specifically addressed by many courts, a threshold issue in cause cases involving alleged employee misconduct is whether the employee must actually have committed the acts of which he or she is accused. There is a split of authority on the matter, but several recent decisions may well prove influential. In *Cotran v. Rollins Hudig Hall International, Inc.*,[1] the California Supreme Court held that when an employee working under an implied good cause agreement is fired for misconduct, the question for the jury is whether "the factual basis on which the employer concluded a dischargeable act had been committed [was] reached honestly, after an appropriate investigation and for reasons that are not arbitrary or pretextual." The California court relied in part on *Baldwin v. Sisters of Providence in Washington, Inc.*,[2] an employee handbook case, in which the Washington Supreme Court said that without language indicating a contrary intent, the employer did not contract away its fact-finding prerogative when it imposed a cause standard on itself. Thus, a discharge for cause "is one which is not for any arbitrary, capricious, or illegal reason and which is * * * based on facts (1) supported by substantial evidence and (2) reasonably believed by the employer to be true." Similar decisions have been reached by the Supreme Courts of Alaska, Nevada, New Mexico, North Dakota, Oregon, and Wyoming.

On the other hand, in *Toussaint v. Blue Cross & Blue Shield of Michigan*,[3] the Michigan Supreme Court's handbook case, the court concluded that it should be the trier of fact, not the employer, who decides whether the misconduct leading to the employee's firing actually occurred. Otherwise, said the court, "[a] promise to terminate employment for cause only would be illusory if the employer were permitted to be the sole judge and final arbiter of the propriety of the discharge. There must be some review of the employer's decision if the cause contract is to be distinguished from the satisfaction contract." Under this view, the employer's good faith belief in the employee's wrongdoing is not enough; the employee must actually be guilty of the conduct with which he or she is charged.

The *Cotran* court did not have to reach the separate question whether the reasons given by the employer for the firing are legally sufficient to constitute cause, but it did provide some parameters on the meaning of the term. In implied employment contracts, cause is "fair and honest reasons, regulated by good faith on the part of the employer, that are not trivial, arbitrary, or capricious, unrelated to business needs or goals, or pretextual." Putting its entire holding together, cause is "[a] reasoned conclusion * * * supported by substantial evidence gathered through an adequate investigation that includes notice of the claimed misconduct and a chance for the employee to respond." *Cotran* thus provides a measure of "due process" in the private sector workplace.

§ 9.8

1. 17 Cal.4th 93, 69 Cal.Rptr.2d 900, 948 P.2d 412 (1998).

2. 112 Wash.2d 127, 769 P.2d 298 (1989).

3. 408 Mich. 579, 292 N.W.2d 880 (1980).

Instead of providing for discharge only for cause, some employment contracts permit discharge if an employee's performance is not "acceptable" or "satisfactory" to the employer. Courts generally agree that this satisfaction standard is inherently subjective and permits discharges as long as the employer is actually and in good faith dissatisfied with the employee. Employees fired under a satisfaction contract may prevail only by showing that the employer was not in fact dissatisfied with them, or that the employer fired them for reasons other than dissatisfaction.

§ 9.9   Public Policy Exception—Generally

Every state except Alabama, Florida, Georgia, Louisiana, Maine, New York, and Rhode Island, recognizes the public policy exception to the employment at will rule in at least one form. Arizona and Montana have statutes regulating employment termination.

The public policy exception does not displace the employment-at-will rule; rather, it provides a means for identifying certain grounds for firing that will support a cause of action for wrongful discharge. Although the courts of each state must decide whether and how to apply the public policy exception, most cases involving the exception can be grouped into one or more of four broad categories. These categories are (1) refusing to perform unlawful acts, (2) exercising legal rights, (3) reporting illegal activity (whistleblowing), and (4) performing public duties. Some cases may fall into more than one category, and some may not fit neatly into any, but these four groups are a helpful way to think about state law on wrongful discharge.

Scope of the Exception

Although the public policy exception is particularly important for private sector at-will employees, in most states it also covers government workers, some of whom may enjoy the protection of civil service laws, tenure laws, and constitutional due process rights. Many states have not yet reached the question whether workers covered by collective bargaining agreements or individual contracts with just cause protection may take advantage of the public policy exception as well.

Whether the exception encompasses adverse employment actions short of discharge has not yet arisen often, probably because of the lower potential for damages and the possibility of retaliation for filing suit against a current employer. The Kansas Supreme Court has recognized a cause of action for demotion in retaliation for filing a workers' compensation claim, as "a necessary and logical extension of the cause of action for retaliatory discharge."[1]

The "Public" Quality of the Policy

In an important decision, *Foley v. Interactive Data Corp.*,[2] the Supreme Court of California stated that the policy on which a claim for

§ 9.9
1. Brigham v. Dillon Cos., Inc., 262 Kan. 12, 20 935 P.2d 1054, 1059–1060 (1997).

2. 47 Cal.3d 654, 254 Cal.Rptr. 211, 765 P.2d 373 (1988).

discharge in violation of public policy is based must be "fundamental," "substantial," and "well established" at the time of the discharge, and it must involve a matter that affects society at large rather than a purely personal or proprietary interest of the employee or the employer. In *Foley*, the plaintiff was fired because he had given his employer information about criminal investigations of his supervisor for activity the supervisor allegedly engaged in while working for a different firm. Under California law, an employee is an agent of the employer and is required to disclose to the principal all information relevant to the subject matter of the agency. Foley contended that this statement of law imposed a duty on him to report relevant business information to management, and that he should be protected for having done so. The court, however, found that some statutes, including the one on which Foley relied, simply regulate conduct between private individuals or impose requirements whose fulfillment does not implicate public policy concerns.

Although this distinction may be hard to draw in some cases, many other courts have also limited the policy to those that benefit the public. As the Supreme Court of Virginia reasoned, public policy is "the policy underlying existing laws designed to protect the property rights, personal freedoms, health, safety, or welfare of the people in general," as distinguished from those "private rights established by the employer's internal regulations, [the violation of which] would have no impact upon any public policy established by existing laws for the protection of the public generally."[3]

Constitutional Provisions as Sources of Public Policy

The United States Constitution is a problematic source for the public policy to support a claim of wrongful discharge, because most federal constitutional provisions protect only against abuses of government power. With some exceptions, the same is true for state constitutional protections. Accordingly, attempts to assert against private sector employers federal and state constitutional provisions that require government action generally fail. For instance, in *Prysak v. R.L. Polk Co.*,[4] the Michigan Court of Appeals held that a private employer was not bound by provisions in the United States and Michigan Constitutions guaranteeing freedom of speech, neither of which extends to private conduct. Similarly, in *Barr v. Kelso–Burnett Co.*,[5] the Illinois Supreme Court rejected a public policy claim against a private sector employer based on the First Amendment and the Equal Protection and Due Process Clauses of the Fourteenth Amendment to the United States Constitution and the right to privacy under the Illinois Constitution, which also applies only to government action. A notable exception to the refusal of most courts to find a source of public policy for suits against private employers in constitutional provisions applicable only to the

---

3. Miller v. SEVAMP, Inc., 234 Va. 462, 362 S.E.2d 915, 919 (1987).

4. 193 Mich.App. 1, 483 N.W.2d 629 (1992).

5. 106 Ill.2d 520, 88 Ill.Dec. 628, 478 N.E.2d 1354 (1985).

government is *Novosel v. Nationwide Insurance Co.*[6] In *Novosel,* a district manager was discharged for refusal to participate in a lobbying effort in support of a bill before the state legislature. The court permitted him to sue based on the policy of the First Amendment to the U.S. Constitution, as well similar provisions of the Pennsylvania Constitution.

Statutes and Regulations as Sources of Public Policy

Obviously, state courts recognizing the public policy exception find that policy in appropriate state statutes and regulations, but most also permit suits based on the public policy embodied in federal laws or regulations. An Ohio court has held that a public policy must apply uniformly across the state; therefore, a plaintiff who alleged a violation of a municipal ordinance failed to state a claim for discharge in violation of public policy.[7] The chief question about the use of statutes as the source of public policy may well be whether a public policy claim may be maintained if the statute in question has its own enforcement scheme. This issue is addressed later in this chapter.

Nonlegislative Sources of Public Policy

Early cases dealing with the public policy exception often contained broad statements of the possible sources of public policy, but the more recent trend has been to restrict public policy to legislative sources. Courts sometimes voice the concern that employers have notice they are violating public policy at the time of the firing. According to the Maryland Court of Appeals, "recognition of an otherwise undeclared public policy as a basis for a judicial decision involves the application of a very nebulous concept to the facts of a given case, and * * * declaration of public policy is normally the function of the legislative branch."[8] Where nonlegislative sources have been permitted, they have most commonly been case law and codes of professional ethics.

Despite the acknowledgment by many courts that the plaintiff must find a source of public policy in law, once in a while a case presents a compelling fact pattern a court cannot deny. In *Gardner v. Loomis Armored, Inc.,*[9] on a question certified from the United States District Court for the Eastern District of Washington, the Washington Supreme Court engaged in "a delicate balancing of interests" in a case that did not fit neatly into any of the established categories of public policy discharges. The plaintiff, a guard and driver of an armored truck, left the truck unattended to go to the aid of a bank manager who was being chased by a man with a knife. The plaintiff was fired for violating an express company rule against leaving trucks unattended. After analyzing a number of statutes plaintiff claimed embodied the public policy involved in his case, the court decided that the most appropriate policy was that "of saving persons from life threatening situations." The court

6.   721 F.2d 894 (3d Cir.1983).

7.   Greenwood v. Taft, Stettinius & Hollister, 105 Ohio App.3d 295, 663 N.E.2d 1030 (1995).

8.   Adler v. American Standard Corp., 291 Md. 31, 432 A.2d 464, 472 (1981).

9.   128 Wash.2d 931, 913 P.2d 377 (1996).

agreed that defendant's rule was legitimate and work-related, but it held that on balance, the rule was outweighed by the narrow public policy it had identified.

§ 9.10 Public Policy Exception—Refusal to Perform Unlawful Act

Virtually all states that recognize the public policy exception apply it to the situation in which an employee is fired for refusing to commit a criminal act. In the earliest wrongful discharge case, *Petermann v. International Brotherhood of Teamsters, Local 396,*[1] the employer ordered an at-will employee to testify falsely at a legislative hearing and then fired the employee when he refused to do so. The court held that the employer's conduct violated the state's public policy of encouraging truthful testimony and therefore was an abuse of the employer's right to fire at will. The facts in *Petermann,* coercing an employee to commit the crime of perjury, are so compelling that in hindsight the outcome cannot be questioned. Not all "illegal act" cases may be as easy to resolve as *Petermann,* however. There are many factual permutations that can alter the basic analysis of *Petermann*; as with the rest of the public policy exception, most courts have not yet addressed them.

Some of the possible variations can be illustrated by litigation in Texas, which has perhaps the narrowest view of this exception. In *Sabine Pilot Service, Inc. v. Hauck,*[2] the Texas Supreme Court recognized a public policy exception for an at-will employee fired "for the *sole reason* that the employee refused to perform an illegal act" involving criminal penalties. Texas courts have refused to extend the exception to situations in which the employee was fired for refusing to commit an illegal act that would have resulted only in civil penalties, or for refusing to perform a legal act the legality of which the employee in good faith questioned.

Although Indiana apparently requires that the employee have been fired for refusing to commit an illegal act for which he or she would have been personally liable, its court of appeals extended that rule to a situation where no monetary sanction would have been imposed. In *Remington Freight Lines, Inc. v. Larkey,*[3] a truck driver was fired when he refused to drive an overloaded truck through Illinois. The employer argued that Illinois law imposed no monetary fine on a truck that is less than 2,000 pounds overweight; thus, although there would have been a technical violation, the driver would not have been personally liable. The court remarked that the evidence did support a finding that the truck was more than 2,000 pounds over the statutory limit, but it also rejected the employer's argument that there must be an actual penalty attached to the violation before a wrongful discharge cause of action would be recognized.

§ 9.10

1. 174 Cal.App.2d 184, 344 P.2d 25 (1959).

2. 687 S.W.2d 733 (Tex.1985).

3. 644 N.E.2d 931 (Ind.App.1994).

In *Fitzgerald v. Salsbury Chemical, Inc.*,[4] the Iowa Supreme Court held that an employee who alleged he was fired because the employer feared he intended to testify truthfully on behalf of another employee in a potential lawsuit stated a claim for discharge in breach of public policy. The court refused to require that the employer have ordered the employee to commit perjury before finding the public policy against perjury to be implicated.

Another variation on the illegal act cases involves violations of statutes or regulations that may not embody a policy against employment-related retaliation. For instance, in *Tatge v. Chambers & Owen, Inc.*,[5] the plaintiff was fired because he refused to sign a nondisclosure/noncompete agreement. He argued that the agreement was unlawful under a Wisconsin statute prohibiting unreasonable restraint of trade, and therefore his refusal to sign was protected under the public policy exception. The Wisconsin Supreme Court disagreed, saying that the statute's expression of policy was to render the agreement void and unenforceable, not to protect employees against retaliatory discharge. The employee was not put at any risk by signing the agreement, which could not be enforced against him. Similarly, in *Reilly v. Waukesha County*,[6] a child-care worker at a county children's center was fired when she refused to violate a state regulation by supervising juveniles in both a secure and a non-secure unit during a shift when she was the only female staff member available. Although administrative regulations can be the basis for public policy in Wisconsin, the court found no violation of public policy in Reilly's discharge. The safety of juveniles in residential facilities was the policy underlying the regulation, but the mechanics of the regulation did not "reif[y] a discrete fundamental and well-defined public policy." Rather, Reilly's supervisor could reasonably have believed that her refusal jeopardized the safety of the juveniles by removing supervision from one of the two groups.

There is also the question whether the exception should extend to individuals who participated in the unlawful activity, rather than refusing and being fired. In *Wheless v. Willard Grain & Feed, Inc.*,[7] a pollution control supervisor was fired after he admitted that his employer's environmental regulatory reports, required by state law, contained data he believed to be false. The Oklahoma Supreme Court refused to find a cause of action because he had been a party to the false statements, even though he argued that he went along with the misreporting because he was afraid of being fired if he refused.

Some courts have permitted suit where the employee was fired for refusing to commit a tortious act, although these cases are few. For instance, in *Delaney v. Taco Time International, Inc.*,[8] the plaintiff was

---

4. 613 N.W.2d 275 (Iowa 2000).

5. 219 Wis.2d 99, 579 N.W.2d 217 (1998).

6. 193 Wis.2d 527, 535 N.W.2d 51 (Ct. App.1995).

7. 964 P.2d 204 (Okla.1998).

8. 297 Or. 10, 681 P.2d 114 (1984).

fired for refusing to sign a false and potentially defamatory statement about another employee. Similarly, in *Kessler v. Equity Management, Inc.,*[9] the plaintiff, an apartment rental agent, was fired for refusing to enter tenants' apartments and search through their papers to find income information. The court characterized the discharge as based on the refusal to commit an unlawful or tortious act and said that the combination of the two wrongs, the tort of invasion of privacy and the trespass, permitted the public policy suit.

§ 9.11 Public Policy Exception—Exercise of a Right

The second category of public policy exceptions encompasses employees who are fired because they have exercised a right afforded them by state law. Courts generally require that this right relate to employment; employees must enjoy the right because of their status as employees, and not because of some other status they may have, such as citizen or taxpayer. A rare example of an exception to this rule is *Bowman v. State Bank of Keysville,*[1] in which two employees who also owned stock in the employer corporation were fired because they refused to vote their stock as the company wished. The Virginia Supreme Court found a public policy in the state securities and corporation laws, which contemplate freedom from coercion in exercising shareholders' rights.

Many of the early public policy cases involved firings in retaliation for an employee's filing of a workers' compensation claim. Almost all states now protect employees in this situation. In many states the workers' compensation laws expressly permit employees to sue if they are fired in retaliation for filing claims. In almost all of the remaining states, courts permit suit under the public policy exception. Although employees covered by statutory remedies do not need to rely on the public policy exception to vindicate their rights, they may nevertheless attempt to avoid the statute and bring a common law claim if they view the statutory remedies as less favorable.

It is important to note that in virtually all jurisdictions it is not unlawful to fire an employee for absenteeism, including absenteeism caused by recuperation from a work-related injury or illness, as long as the employer applies a uniform and neutral absenteeism rule. Under the Family and Medical Leave Act,[2] however, employees of employers with fifty or more employees have a right to twelve weeks of unpaid leave to recover from an injury or illness, and they may not be fired for absenteeism during that time. A number of states have similar medical leave laws. In addition, if the worker's injury has created a disability within the meaning of the Americans with Disabilities Act, employers have duties of accommodation that may include providing extra leave.

---

9. 82 Md.App. 577, 572 A.2d 1144 (1990).

2. 29 U.S.C.A. §§ 2611–2653.

§ 9.11

1. 229 Va. 534, 331 S.E.2d 797 (1985).

Among the jurisdictions that have addressed the issue, there is a split as to whether allegations that an employee was fired in anticipation that he or she would file a workers' compensation claim are adequate to state a cause of action. A split also exists on whether an employee who was fired by one employer because the employee had filed a workers' compensation claim against a previous employer has a public policy cause of action.

In *Zimmerman v. Buchheit of Sparta, Inc.,*[3] a sharply divided Illinois Supreme Court held that an employee who alleged she was demoted and discriminated against for filing a workers' compensation claim did not state a cause of action. Three justices would have limited the public policy cause of action to discharge, two would no longer permit it at all, even based on retaliatory discharge, and two would have permitted it to include demotions that involve a loss of income and benefits. The Kansas Supreme Court has, however, recognized a cause of action for demotion in retaliation for having filed a workers' compensation claim.[4]

Oklahoma has permitted a public policy tort claim to be brought by employees who were fired because they sued one of their employer's customers for on-the-job injuries they suffered while helping the customer.[5] The court reasoned that the discharge impermissibly interfered with the recovery regime contemplated by the state's workers' compensation law, which regulates the procedure for third-party tort claims. At least two courts have disagreed about whether a claim exists for an employee who was fired because he or she had filed a workers' compensation claim against a previous employer.[6]

Other state laws may provide work-related rights protected by the public policy exception. In *D'Angelo v. Gardner,*[7] an employee who had an unclosed surgical wound was fired when he refused to perform work requiring contact with cyanide. The Nevada Supreme Court used the state occupational safety and health act as its source of public policy and held that firing an employee for refusing to work in unreasonably dangerous conditions violates that policy.

> It requires little analysis to perceive that the legislative purpose underlying these provisions would be substantially undermined if employers were permitted to discharge employees simply for protesting working conditions which they reasonably believe constitute a hazard to their own health or safety, or the health or safety of others * * *. The public policy thus implicated extends beyond the question of fairness to the particular employee; it concerns protection of employees against retaliatory dismissal for conduct which, in

3. 164 Ill.2d 29, 206 Ill.Dec. 625, 645 N.E.2d 877 (1994).

4. Brigham v. Dillon Cos., 262 Kan. 12, 935 P.2d 1054 (1997).

5. Groce v. Foster, 880 P.2d 902 (Okla. 1994).

6. Compare Nelson Steel Corp. v. McDaniel, 898 S.W.2d 66 (Ky.1995) (no cause of action), with Jensen v. Hercules, Inc., 524 N.W.2d 748 (Minn.App.1994) (employees alleging they were not hired by a successor employer because they had filed workers' compensation claims against the predecessor employer may sue both companies).

7. 107 Nev. 704, 819 P.2d 206 (1991).

light of the statutes, deserves to be encouraged, rather than inhibited.

Similarly, in *Wilcox v. Niagara of Wisconsin Paper Corp.,*[8] Wilcox, the company's director of computer operations, was fired after he failed to come to work on a weekend. The year before, Wilcox had undergone heart bypass surgery. During the week he was fired, he had worked sixty-one hours, including thirty-five hours on Thursday and Friday alone. He went home at 9:30 p.m. on Friday after suffering angina pains and was hospitalized later that evening. He was released from the hospital on Saturday with instructions to take it easy. The court held Wilcox was entitled to a trial on whether a Wisconsin statute prohibiting employment that is "dangerous or prejudicial to the person's life, health, safety or welfare" established a public policy violated by the employer.

In *Amos v. Oakdale Knitting Co.,*[9] the North Carolina Supreme Court held that the employer violated public policy by firing employees for refusing to work for less than the statutory minimum wage under state law. The plaintiffs' other remedies did not preempt the public policy exception.

Courts have protected employees who have been fired for refusing to take a polygraph test when a state statute forbade such a requirement. The Iowa Supreme Court permitted a retaliatory discharge claim to be brought by an employee who was fired because she filed a claim for partial unemployment benefits.[10] Courts also have protected employees who were fired in violation of state statutes prohibiting various forms of economic exploitation of workers.

§ 9.12 Public Policy Exception—Reporting Illegal Activity

The third category of public policy exceptions to the employment at will rule is discharge for reporting illegal or harmful activity. Three-quarters of the states have statutes protecting employee "whistleblowers" in some situations, and the majority of the litigation in this area falls under one of these laws. A number of states with no applicable statutory protection for whistleblowers nevertheless permit employees to bring retaliatory discharge actions under the public policy exception. Issues that can arise in these common law cases include whether the exception covers those who report wrongdoing only within the company, or whether the employee must report externally; whether the employee must be free of any personal wrongdoing; and whether the employee must be correct about the nature of the reported activity. As always with the public policy exceptions, the overarching consideration is the public or private nature of the harm.

If a court is willing to recognize the whistleblower exception, it will, of course, recognize it where the employee has reported to appropriate

8. 965 F.2d 355 (7th Cir.1992).

9. 331 N.C. 348, 416 S.E.2d 166 (1992).

10. Lara v. Thomas, 512 N.W.2d 777 (Iowa 1994).

law enforcement officials a violation of the criminal law or a law protecting health and safety, committed by the employer or co-workers. A few state courts, however, specifically describe the cause of action as requiring reports of violations of laws relating to the public health, safety, or welfare. For instance, in *Mistishen v. Falcone Piano Co.*,[1] a piano marketing technician who was fired for complaining to her supervisor about defects in pianos was found not to state a claim because the alleged violations of state unfair and deceptive trade practices law of which she complained did not threaten public health or safety.

Whether to permit suits by workers who have complained only to supervisors or other members of management, and not to outside authorities, can be more troublesome. These internal whistleblowing cases can present difficulties because it may appear that the employee's complaints rest on dubious information or simply constitute a difference of opinion about the wisdom of company policy. *House v. Carter–Wallace, Inc.*,[2] reflects this concern. The court distinguished internal from external reporting of wrongdoing, concluding that going outside the company to report violations to some public authority was a necessary predicate for public policy protection. A mere difference of professional opinion between an employee and those with decisionmaking power in a corporation is not a sufficient basis to establish a wrongful discharge. The court noted that the plaintiff did not take or threaten to take "effective action" to prevent the corporate actions of which he complained.

Wright v. Shriners Hospital for Crippled Children[3] highlights the tension over protecting whistleblowers whose complaints fall in the gray area between allegations of illegalities and disagreements with employer policy, albeit in a situation of external reporting. In *Wright* the Massachusetts Supreme Judicial Court found no violation of public policy in the firing of a nurse in reprisal for her critical remarks to a survey team. The majority was unwilling to find the firing violated the public policy represented by state laws requiring reports of patient abuse, because the nurse did not complain about abuse, neglect, or mistreatment of patients. Rather, she reported her concerns about a lack of consistent procedures and standards for patient care, and a breakdown in communications between the nursing staff and the physicians. This report, said the majority, was about "an internal matter, and 'internal matters,' * * * could not be the basis of a public policy exception to the at-will rule." The dissent argued that, "[g]iven the public interest in good patient care, it must be the public policy of the Commonwealth to protect, if not encourage, hospital employees who perceive and report detriments to patient care. Only when problems are identified can they be adequately addressed; an employee's failure to report perceived detriments to patient care may allow the problems to persist. A hospital

§ 9.12

1. 36 Mass.App.Ct. 243, 630 N.E.2d 294 (1994), review denied, 418 Mass. 1102, 636 N.E.2d 278 (1994).

2. 232 N.J.Super. 42, 556 A.2d 353, certification denied, 117 N.J. 154, 564 A.2d 874 (1989).

3. 412 Mass. 469, 589 N.E.2d 1241 (1992).

employer therefore violates public policy when it fires an employee for trying to improve the quality of patient care."

On the other hand, some states have extended protection to internal whistleblowers. The Seventh Circuit, applying Illinois law, held that a department store employee who alleged he was fired in retaliation for reporting to management suspicious behavior on the part of his supervisor had a cause of action for retaliatory discharge.[4] Even though the employee did not report the matter to the police, Illinois public policy was held to protect vigilant employees who alert their employers to suspected criminal activity in the workplace. The court reasoned that "[a] report to an employer does not transform a violation of the Illinois Criminal Code from a matter of public concern into a private dispute. The employee who chooses to approach his employer should not be denied a remedy simply because a direct report to law enforcement agencies might effectuate the exposure of crime more quickly. This would be a nonsensical distinction."

Occasionally, the employer will defend a whistleblower's suit by arguing that the plaintiff was involved in the wrongdoing that he or she eventually reported and that, having "unclean hands," the employee may not seek redress. Few reported common law cases have raised this issue. One is *Paolella v. Browning–Ferris, Inc.,*[5] in which the Third Circuit held that a salesman who claimed he was fired for protesting an illegal billing scheme in which he participated could maintain a whistleblower cause of action under Delaware law, because it could find nothing in the law of that state requiring nonparticipation by the plaintiff. Similarly, in *Dahl v. Combined Insurance Co.,*[6] the South Dakota Supreme Court, in permitting a wrongful discharge claim brought by a district manager for an insurance company who alleged he was fired because he reported to the state Division of Insurance that premiums collected by certain agents were not being submitted to the company, stated that the whistleblowing cause of action cannot be invoked by employees who report wrongdoing out of concern for their own proprietary interests, as revenge against an employer, or for personal gain.

Most of the litigation raising the issue whether the employee must be correct about the unlawfulness of the activities he or she reports arise under specific whistleblower statutes, but some states with common law causes of action have dealt with the matter. For instance, in *Allum v. Valley Bank of Nevada,*[7] the Nevada Supreme Court held that an employee bringing a whistleblowing claim does not have to prove that his or her employer actually engaged in the illegal conduct; the employee must only show that he or she reasonably suspected, in good faith, that the employer's conduct was illegal.

4. Belline v. K–Mart Corp., 940 F.2d 184 (7th Cir.1991).

5. 158 F.3d 183 (3d Cir.1998).

6. 2001 S.D. 12, 621 N.W.2d 163 (2001).

7. 114 Nev. 1313, 970 P.2d 1062 (1998).

§ 9.13 Public Policy Exception—Performance of a Duty

Some courts have found that employees are entitled to public policy protection when they are fired for performing a public duty. The definition of a public duty sufficient to be protected from firing, however, generally proves difficult, beyond a few well-recognized categories. Many states now protect by statute service in an emergency as a volunteer firefighter, Red Cross volunteer, or other similar endeavors, although most of these laws apply only to the public sector. Most common law public duty cases involve obligations that are compelled by law. This category includes serving on a jury, obeying a subpoena, testifying in a legal proceeding, and, more recently, reporting abuse of children, the elderly, patients, and institutionalized individuals.

Almost every state has a statute prohibiting the firing of an employee because of jury service. In some states, the statute expressly permits fired employees to sue; in the others, the courts may allow fired employees to bring an action under the public policy exception.

Courts have protected employees who were fired for obeying a subpoena and for testifying truthfully, although these cases are sometimes difficult to distinguish from discharges for refusal to commit perjury.[1] In *Hummer v. Evans*,[2] an AIDS education consultant was fired after writing a letter to a judge saying that a convicted HIV-positive rapist awaiting sentencing could help in providing HIV prevention messages to children. The Idaho Supreme Court permitted his public policy suit, finding that since the letter was written in response to a subpoena, it should be protected to the same extent as live testimony. In *Carl v. Children's Hospital*,[3] a nurse alleged she was fired because she testified before the District of Columbia Council in opposition to legislation that would have limited recovery of damages in medical malpractice cases. The court held that she stated a claim for discharge in breach of public policy, reasoning that employees should have the right to speak out publicly on issues affecting the public without fear of retaliation by their employers.

Testifying at grievance hearings has not always been accorded the same type of public policy recognition, however. In *Miller v. SEVAMP, Inc.*,[4] an employee was held to have no cause of action in tort for her discharge, allegedly in retaliation for her appearance as a witness at a fellow employee's grievance hearing. The Virginia Supreme Court acknowledged that the right to testify was protected by the employer's personnel manual but held that violation of the manual would not impact upon public policy. "[S]uch a retaliatory act would impinge only upon private rights established by the employer's internal regulations." In a similar setting, however, the California Supreme Court held that an employee who testified truthfully concerning another employee's claim of

§ 9.13

1. See, e.g., Fitzgerald v. Salsbury Chem., Inc., 613 N.W.2d 275 (Iowa 2000).

2. 129 Idaho 274, 923 P.2d 981 (1996).

3. 702 A.2d 159 (D.C.1997) (en banc).

4. 234 Va. 462, 362 S.E.2d 915 (1987).

sexual harassment at an administrative investigation was protected against retaliatory discharge because, in part, the court viewed sexual harassment as sufficiently a matter of public policy.[5]

Reporting suspected abuse of children or hospital patients might be classified as the performance of a public duty, especially in states that require teachers and health care providers to make such reports. In *Hausman v. St. Croix Care Center,*[6] nurses who were fired after they reported suspected abuse of patients to a state ombudsman, pursuant to an affirmative obligation imposed by state law, were permitted to sue under this exception. The court specifically rejected reliance on the refusal to violate the law and whistleblowing categories of the public policy exception. Similarly, a Missouri court permitted suit by a nursing home employee who claimed she was fired for reporting abuse of patients; the court characterized its result as implying a private cause of action under a state statute that required the reporting of abuse and neglect and prohibited retaliation against employees who made reports.[7]

An Oregon court held that the firing of a bank employee for refusing to disclose confidential financial information about customers to the corporation that owned the bank fell within the public obligation branch of the exceptions to the employment at will doctrine.[8]

§ 9.14 Employer Fraud

An employer that misrepresents facts about the employment in order to induce an applicant to accept a job or an incumbent employee to turn down an offer from another employer may be found liable for fraud or, much less commonly, negligent misrepresentation. This claim sounds in tort, not in contract. The plaintiff sues not for wrongful discharge, but for fraud in the inducement, and promises that do not give rise to a claim for breach of contract may well support a claim for fraud.

The elements of fraud are generally stated as: (1) a misrepresentation of a material fact; (2) made knowingly; (3) with the intent to mislead, which induces; (4) reasonable reliance by the misled party; and (5) resulting damage to the misled party. Actionable misrepresentations can include the defendant's omission of facts when it has stated other facts it knows will create a false impression unless it also discloses the omitted facts, as well as the failure to correct a material representation once the defendant learns it is false. Mere nondisclosure, however, is not sufficient to establish fraud, unless circumstances exist that establish a legal duty to make a disclosure.

The traditional formulation of fraud requires proof that the defendant misrepresented present or existing facts. For instance, in *Stewart v.*

---

5. Gantt v. Sentry Ins., 1 Cal.4th 1083, 4 Cal.Rptr.2d 874, 824 P.2d 680 (1992).

6. 214 Wis.2d 655, 571 N.W.2d 393 (1997).

7. Clark v. Beverly Enter.–Mo., Inc., 872 S.W.2d 522 (Mo.App.1994).

8. Banaitis v. Mitsubishi Bank, Ltd., 129 Or.App. 371, 879 P.2d 1288 (1994), review dismissed, 321 Or. 511, 900 P.2d 508 (1995).

Jackson & Nash,[1] an attorney alleged that she resigned her position with one law firm and joined the defendant law firm because the defendant told her it had secured a large environmental law client and was in the process of establishing an environmental law practice. After two years, the defendant had still not established an environmental law section, and the plaintiff learned that there never was an environmental law client. The Second Circuit characterized these promises by the defendant as misrepresentations of present fact.

The corollary of the present or existing fact rule is that an action for fraud may not be based on unfulfilled promises or statements about future events. The courts have, however, created a few exceptions to the general rule, two of which can be helpful in many employment cases. First, a fraud claim may be based on promises made with a present intent not to perform them. Another promise made to the plaintiff in *Stewart v. Jackson & Nash* was that she would head the firm's new environmental law section as soon as it was established. This promise did not relate to existing fact, because the environmental law section did not exist at the time, but the court said the facts could support a claim that the promise was made with a preconceived intention of not performing it.

Similarly, in *Shebar v. Sanyo Business Systems Corp.,*[2] plaintiff, who worked for Sanyo, used an executive search firm to secure a job offer from Sony. When he submitted his resignation to his superiors at Sanyo, they told him they would not permit him to resign and assured him he would have a job at Sanyo for life. Based on this conversation, plaintiff rescinded his acceptance of the Sony offer. When he told his contact at the search firm what he had done, the contact expressed surprise at Sanyo's behavior, claiming he had knowledge that Sanyo was trying to find a replacement for the plaintiff. Plaintiff immediately confronted his superiors, who denied the whole thing and claimed that the search firm was just trying to get him to take the Sony job so that it could receive its placement fee. Four months later, Sanyo fired the plaintiff. The court reversed a grant of summary judgment for Sanyo, finding that plaintiff stated a claim for fraud on the theory that at the time the Sanyo executives were denying any efforts to replace him, they intended to fire him shortly.

The second exception to the present facts rule involves promises containing implied representations of fact that the promisor knows to be false. For instance, the plaintiff in *Varnum v. Nu–Car Carriers, Inc.*[3] invested $60,000 of his own money in equipment in order to become a truck driver for the defendant. During the discussions that led to the hiring, the defendant's representative told him that the company's dispatch system was run on a first-in, first-out basis that gave all drivers

---

1. 976 F.2d 86 (2d Cir.1992) (applying N.Y. law).

2. 218 N.J.Super. 111, 526 A.2d 1144 (1987), affirmed, 111 N.J. 276, 544 A.2d 377 (1988).

3. 804 F.2d 638 (11th Cir.1986) (applying Fla. law), cert. denied, 481 U.S. 1049, 107 S.Ct. 2181, 95 L.Ed.2d 838 (1987).

equal access to trips and that the recent average gross income for drivers had been $7000 per month. What the representative failed to tell the plaintiff was that the company was in the middle of negotiations with the union to change to a seniority-based dispatch system, which would effectively give all trips to more senior drivers and completely cut out newly-hired drivers. There was evidence that the company favored the change and that the individual with whom the plaintiff was dealing knew all of this. The Eleventh Circuit, applying Florida law, held that the defendant's representation about what the plaintiff could expect to earn, without any disclosure about the impending change in the seniority system, would support a cause of action for fraud.

The other elements of a claim for fraud have not received as much attention from the courts. The plaintiff must show reasonable reliance on the defendant's misrepresentations. This element was found lacking in *Shelby v. Zayre Corp.*,[4] where the employee signed an at-will disclaimer in the employment application and admitted she had read and understood it. The hiring representative, in response to her questions, then told her she would have permanent employment and would not be laid off immediately after the store's grand opening. She quit her current job, took the job with the defendant, and was fired a week later. The Alabama Supreme Court held that she could not reasonably have relied on the employer's misrepresentations in light of the clear disclaimer she had just signed.

The fraud plaintiff must also show that he or she was damaged by the defendant's fraud. *Stromberger v. 3M Co.*[5] contains an interesting discussion of this point. In an effort to induce sales representatives to take an early retirement incentive offer, the employer announced that it was raising its sales quotas significantly. This announcement prompted the plaintiff, who thought the new quotas were too high, to retire. Thereafter, however, the employer did not enforce its new quotas consistently, and plaintiff sued for fraud. The court found no evidence of any deliberate falsehoods in the announcement of the new sales quota; mere negligence will not support a claim for fraud. It also opined that the plaintiff had not been defrauded of anything. The plaintiff's theory was that the employer lied to get rid of him, but he was an at-will employee and could have been fired at any time. He did not allege any contractual right of which he had been deprived by being persuaded to take early retirement. In fact, said the court, the only consequence of the alleged fraud was to enrich plaintiff by the $39,000 in severance benefits he received from the retirement incentive program.

In *Hunter v. Up–Right, Inc.*,[6] the California Supreme Court held that misrepresentation of facts as part of a wrongful termination does not constitute fraud. The plaintiff resigned after the employer told him (falsely) his job was being eliminated. The court said that this misrepre-

4. 474 So.2d 1069 (Ala.1985).

5. 990 F.2d 974 (7th Cir.1993) (applying Ill. law).

6. 6 Cal.4th 1174, 26 Cal.Rptr.2d 8, 864 P.2d 88 (1993).

sentation merely acted to convert a voluntary resignation into a constructive discharge, but that the employee's only claim was for the breach of contract caused by the discharge itself. The court cited *Foley v. Interactive Data Corp.*[7] as limiting the scope of damages for breach of employment contract suits, and it said it would be difficult to have a wrongful termination case in which an employer misrepresentation was a separately actionable fraud.

Hunter did suggest in dicta that a claim for fraud might still lie if the employer's misrepresentation was intended not to induce the employee to quit, but to change his or her position in some other way. That situation presented itself in *Lazar v. Superior Court of Los Angeles.*[8] The plaintiff alleged that he worked for a family-owned company, earned $120,000 a year, and lived in New York with his family. A company in California began recruiting him; when he expressed concern about job security and relocation, the employer led him to believe that it was financially stable and that he could stay in his job as long as his work was good. Plaintiff then accepted the offer and moved with his family to California. In fact, the employer's representations were knowingly false, and it was planning a merger that would eliminate plaintiff's job. Two years after his move, plaintiff was fired. The California Supreme Court held that plaintiff had stated the elements of the tort of fraud and distinguished *Hunter* on the ground that Lazar had relied to his detriment on the misrepresentations, whereas Hunter's reliance was not to his detriment.

As opposed to the tort of fraud, the tort of negligent misrepresentation requires that a duty of care exist between the parties to the communication. The elements of the tort of negligent misrepresentation are generally set forth as (1) justifiable reliance by a party (2) to his or her detriment (3) on false or misleading information prepared without reasonable care (4) by one who owed the relying party a duty of care. To find a duty of care, there must be some close nexus between the parties, such as contractual privity or its equivalent. An employer may have an obligation to exercise reasonable care in making representations to a prospective employee during pre-employment negotiations. On the other hand, the president of a company may not owe a duty to individual employees when making statements about the company's profitability and long-term prospects.[9]

§ 9.15   Abusive Discharge

In its heyday, the employment at will doctrine permitted employers to fire an employee not only for any reason, but in any manner. For example, in one case,[1] a railroad ticket agent was fired because there

---

7. 47 Cal.3d 654, 254 Cal.Rptr. 211, 765 P.2d 373 (1988).

8. 12 Cal.4th 631, 49 Cal.Rptr.2d 377, 909 P.2d 981 (1996).

9. See, e.g., Jordan v. The Earthgrains Cos., Inc., 155 N.C.App. 762, 576 S.E.2d 336 (2003).

§ 9.15

1. Henry v. Pittsburg & L.E.R. Co., 139 Pa. 289, 21 A. 157 (1891).

were financial irregularities in his department, even though there was no evidence that the agent was personally responsible. The railroad then told the local newspaper that the agent had been fired for dishonesty. The Pennsylvania Supreme Court held that the agent had no claim against the railroad.

Today, just as certain reasons for discharge are actionable, so too are discharges effected in an abusive manner—regardless of the merits of the discharge decision itself. These are often referred to as abusive discharges, although some courts use "abusive" discharge as synonymous with "wrongful" discharge. For clarity, as used here, abusive discharge is a description of the circumstances surrounding a discharge rather than a distinct cause of action. Abusive discharge cases can involve claims for an intentional tort (assault, battery, false imprisonment), intentional infliction of emotional distress, defamation, invasion of privacy, the tort of outrage, and other theories.

The legal theories underlying each of these causes of action are discussed at greater length in other sections of this book. This section will focus on five stages in which abusive discharge actions may arise: (1) the employer's method of investigating alleged employee misconduct; (2) the employer's method of disciplining individual employees short of discharge; (3) the employer's method of deciding which employee to discharge for a particular offense; (4) the employer's method of informing the individual of the discharge; and (5) the employer's conduct after the employee's termination.

Investigations

Overzealous surveillance, interviews, and interrogation are a frequent source of litigation. Interrogating an employee for three hours without a break and then summarily firing him,[2] and threatening an employee for hours while using loud, obscene language and gestures[3] have been held to constitute intentional infliction of emotional distress. Coercive interrogation may be more likely to be actionable when the employer knows that the employee is in poor health.[4]

Unreasonable interrogation also may give rise to an action for false imprisonment. For example, detaining an employee to secure a confession has been held to be actionable.[5] On the other hand, if the employee is free to leave, even if leaving would result in discharge, the employee cannot sustain an action for false imprisonment.

Other actionable conduct has included intentionally placing company-endorsed checks in an employee's possession to make it appear that she was stealing from the company and conspiring with a security firm so that an employee would fail a polygraph examination.

2. Crump v. P & C Food Markets, Inc., 154 Vt. 284, 576 A.2d 441 (1990).

3. Kaminski v. United Parcel Serv., 120 A.D.2d 409, 501 N.Y.S.2d 871 (1986).

4. Dean v. Ford Motor Credit Co., 885 F.2d 300 (5th Cir.1989) (applying Tex. law).

5. Parrott v. Bank of Am. Nat. Trust & Sav. Ass'n, 97 Cal.App.2d 14, 217 P.2d 89 (1950).

Outrageous Treatment

An employer's overall pattern of dealing with an employee may be so outrageous that it constitutes intentional infliction of emotional distress. Employees who quit rather than endure the treatment may also have a claim for wrongful discharge on the theory that their quitting was a constructive discharge. For example, in *Wilson v. Monarch Paper Co.,*[6] the plaintiff was a sixty-year-old vice-president of a corporation. When a new president took over, the plaintiff was given three options: (1) he could take a sales job at half his former pay; (2) he could be terminated with three months severance pay; or (3) he could accept a job as warehouse supervisor with the same pay but a reduction in benefits. He chose the third option, but the warehouse position turned out to be a janitorial job, in which he had the responsibility for sweeping the floors and cleaning the employee cafeteria. He quit after four months because of a severe case of clinical depression and respiratory problems caused by dust. The Fifth Circuit affirmed an award of $3.4 million for age discrimination and intentional infliction of emotional distress. The Fifth Circuit noted two "ironies" in the case: first, that there would have been no liability for intentional infliction of emotional distress if Monarch had simply fired Wilson; and second, that the decision may have the effect of "civilizing" discrimination, or requiring employers "to behave like ladies and gentlemen when discriminating."

Shoen v. Amerco,[7] in which the court found a binding contract for lifetime employment, involved a dispute between the man who founded the U–Haul Rental System and his sons, to whom he had turned over the business. The father alleged that following his testimony, under subpoena, at an IRS tax trial against one of the sons, one son verbally threatened him and attempted to assault him, his sons discontinued his compensation to cause him financial hardship and emotional distress, and one of the sons knew the distress these actions would cause because the two had been in counseling together. The court held that these allegations supported a claim for intentional infliction of emotional distress.

Racial, ethnic, and sexual harassment on the job can violate Title VII, and courts may find the same conduct to be tortious under state law as well. In *Ford v. Revlon, Inc.,*[8] the plaintiff complained repeatedly about the sexual harassment of her supervisor, yet the company did not respond, even though it had a policy against sexual harassment that required investigation of complaints. This failure to investigate supported a claim for intentional infliction of emotional distress.

Discharge Decision

The basis for discharge is distinct from the method of discharge. Because an employer owes no duty to an at-will employee to refrain from negligence in making a discharge decision, it cannot be liable for negli-

---

6. 939 F.2d 1138 (5th Cir.1991).   **8.** 153 Ariz. 38, 734 P.2d 580 (1987).

7. 111 Nev. 735, 896 P.2d 469 (1995).

gent investigation of alleged wrongdoing. Employer negligence may, however, be relevant if cause is required for discharge.

In instances of suspected employee wrongdoing, more than one employee may be under suspicion. The manner in which the employer determines responsibility can be tortious. In *Agis v. Howard Johnson Co.*,[9] the manager of a restaurant notified all of the waitresses that someone was stealing from the cash register and that, until the person or persons were discovered, he would begin firing the waitresses in alphabetical order. The plaintiff, Debra Agis, was the first to be fired, and she sued for intentional infliction of emotional distress. The Massachusetts Supreme Judicial Court held that the plaintiff had pled facts sufficient to establish extreme and outrageous conduct.

Method of Discharge

A wide range of employer actions at the time of discharge have given rise to abusive discharge claims. In general, the courts have been reluctant to recognize causes of action unless the employer has engaged in truly outrageous conduct. For example, escorting an employee off the premises generally does not constitute intentional infliction of emotional distress. In *Bolton v. Department of Human Services*,[10] a social worker was fired following a disagreement about a guardianship petition for a resident of a center for developmentally disabled individuals. His supervisor accompanied him to his office, stayed while he packed his belongings, and, in full view of other employees, accompanied him to the main entrance of the facility. The lower court found that this conduct constituted defamation by action; it conveyed a statement that the employee was dishonest and could not be trusted to leave the building by himself. The Minnesota Supreme Court reversed and held there is no defamation "where there is no word spoken or conduct other than a simple escorting of the plaintiff to the exit door upon his termination * * *." A supervisor's yelling at an employee on the sales floor that he did not trust the employee did not constitute extreme and outrageous conduct,[11] but the use of abusive racial epithets in the course of discharge did.[12] In another case,[13] the Oregon Court of Appeals held that employees failed to state a claim for intentional infliction of emotional distress where the employer, in firing them, directed them to hold hands, demanded that they surrender their keys, accused them of being liars and saboteurs, and ordered them off the premises without an opportunity to collect their personal items.

On the other hand, in *Archer v. Farmer Brothers Co.*,[14] five days after the plaintiff suffered a heart attack, two supervisors went to the

---

9. 371 Mass. 140, 355 N.E.2d 315 (1976).

10. 540 N.W.2d 523 (Minn.1995).

11. Newberry v. Allied Stores, Inc., 108 N.M. 424, 773 P.2d 1231 (1989).

12. Alcorn v. Anbro Eng'g, Inc., 2 Cal.3d 493, 86 Cal.Rptr. 88, 468 P.2d 216 (1970).

13. Watte v. Maeyens, 112 Or.App. 234, 828 P.2d 479, review denied, 314 Or. 176, 836 P.2d 1345 (1992).

14. 70 P.3d 495 (Colo. App.2002), affirmed, 90 P.3d 228 (Colo. 2004).

home of the plaintiff's mother-in-law, where the plaintiff was recuperat-
ing, entered uninvited, and, finding the plaintiff in bed, announced they
had termination papers for him to initial. Although the plaintiff was
under investigation for alleged misconduct, he was a twenty-two-year
employee with a good reputation who was near retirement, and he had
no reason to believe he would be fired. The court upheld a verdict for
intentional infliction of emotional distress, noting that the supervisors'
actions could have triggered another heart attack and that the plaintiff
attempted suicide that evening.

Post–Discharge Acts

The most common basis for liability after a discharge is through
defamatory communications to third parties, such as prospective employers. Nevertheless, other actions are possible. For example, in *Diamond
Shamrock Refining & Marketing Co. v. Mendez,*[15] the plaintiff worked for
ten years as one of four chief operators at a refinery. At the end of one
night shift he was ordered to clean up some debris, including loose nails,
that had been left by carpenters working in the area. He threw the nails
in a small box and placed the box in his lunch bag. He forgot about the
nails and took the bag home. He was later fired for theft, and word of his
discharge for stealing was widely disseminated around the plant. The
lower court held that the excessive publication of the incident placed the
plaintiff in a false light, which was actionable as an invasion of privacy.
The Texas Supreme Court, however, reversed and remanded the case for
further evidence of whether the employer acted with actual malice.

In *Taiwo v. Vu,*[16] the plaintiff was a certified school teacher who was
hired by the defendant to bring a day care center into compliance with
state law. The plaintiff soon resigned when the defendant would not
agree to follow state laws. When the plaintiff attempted to obtain her
paycheck for prior service, the defendant assaulted, battered, and falsely
imprisoned her; she filed false police reports against the plaintiff and her
husband; and she induced another employee to lie to the police about the
plaintiff. The Supreme Court of Kansas held that the defendant's post-
termination conduct was so extreme and outrageous as to permit recovery for intentional infliction of emotional distress.

In *Kroger Co. v. Willgruber,*[17] the defendant appealed from a jury
verdict in favor of the plaintiff on a claim for intentional infliction of
emotional distress caused by the events that followed his discharge. The
plaintiff had worked for the company for thirty-two years; he was fired
at a Christmas lunch in 1990. He was then told that to qualify for a
severance package, he had to sign a complete release. To induce him to
sign, the company falsely told him that he would be eligible for a job as
assistant sales manager at a facility in South Carolina. Although the
plaintiff told the company that he was "mighty upset, mighty sick"
about the situation, the company sent him to South Carolina to interview for the nonexistent job. When the plaintiff returned home, he had a

15. 844 S.W.2d 198 (Tex.1992).   **17.** 920 S.W.2d 61 (Ky.1996).
16. 249 Kan. 585, 822 P.2d 1024 (1991).

complete breakdown. His wife telephoned the company and was told that she should get medical help for her husband and that he should sign the release. The plaintiff applied for disability benefits, and the company tried to persuade the plaintiff's insurance carrier to deny the claim by alleging that he was faking, that he was working for another company and taking money under the table, and by "items of a personal nature so derogatory to Willgruber and his family that they are unworthy of repetition in a published opinion." When the carrier finally started paying benefits, the employer demanded that it engage in surveillance of the plaintiff. The court held that these facts satisfied the elements of the tort of intentional infliction of emotional distress and supported the jury's verdict.

§ 9.16 Interference With the Employment Relationship

Third parties who improperly cause an employee to be fired or who otherwise interfere with the employee's economic expectations in his or her job may be liable to the employee for tortious interference with contract. The third party may be a former employer, someone who does business with the employee's employer, or even the employee's supervisor or other coworker. For instance, if a firm threatens an employer with loss of business or makes other similar threats to compel the employer to fire an employee, the firm may be liable to the employee for interference if its efforts succeed. A supervisor who makes or recommends a decision to fire an employee may be liable for tortious interference with the employee's employment if the supervisor acted for his or her personal interests. Although an employer normally cannot interfere with its own contract, an employee's current employer may be liable for interference with a prospective employment relationship if it improperly induces the employee to revoke or reject an offer of new employment.

According to the *Restatement (Second) of Torts*, a person who "intentionally and improperly interferes with the performance of a contract * * * between another and a third person by inducing or otherwise causing the third person not to perform the contract" is liable to the other for the loss resulting from the failure to perform.[1] Relying on the Restatement definition, most courts recite four elements for the tort of interference with contract: (1) a valid contract subject to interference; (2) knowledge of the contractual relationship by the interferor; (3) intentional and improper interference inducing or causing a breach or termination of the contractual relationship; and (4) resulting damages. A closely related claim is the tort of interference with prospective contractual relation, which involves situations in which the injured party had not yet entered into a contract.[2] Its elements are (1) a relationship between the plaintiff and a third party with the probability of future economic benefit; (2) knowledge of this relationship by the defendant; (3)

§ 9.16

1. Restatement (Second) of Torts § 766 (1979).

2. Restatement (Second) of Torts § 766B (1979).

intentional and improper interference by the defendant to prevent the relationship from maturing; and (4) resulting damage.

Employment contracts for a definite term and other for-cause employment relationships are clearly protected against tortious interference; virtually all states, even some that are generally hostile to wrongful discharge claims, protect at-will employment contracts as well. For instance, the Alabama Supreme Court, which has yet to recognize a common law cause of action against an employer for discharge of an at-will employee, has described at-will employment as a "property right" worthy of protection in the context of a tortious interference claim against a third party.[3] Indeed, in *Haddle v. Garrison*,[4] in which the question was whether 42 U.S.C.A. § 1985(2) contains a requirement of a constitutionally protected property interest, the Supreme Court remarked that the harm alleged, "essentially third-party interference with at-will employment relationships," has long been a compensable injury under state tort law, under the claims of intentional interference with contractual relations and intentional interference with prospective contractual relations.

The crucial element of most intentional interference claims is the requirement that the interference be improper, or, stated another way, that the defendant have acted without justification. Some courts hold that justification is an affirmative defense as to which the defendant bears the burden of persuasion. Factors relevant to determining whether the defendant's actions were justified include the nature of the defendant's conduct, the interests it was advancing, its motives, the relationship between the defendant and the employee, and the balance between the societal interests in protecting the defendant's freedom of action and the employee's contractual interests.

Some courts say that a third party is privileged or justified in interfering with another's contractual rights if the third party acts in a bona fide exercise of its own rights or if it has a right in the subject matter that is equal or superior to the rights of the other. If the interferor goes beyond what is necessary to protect its legitimate interests or uses improper means to achieve its ends, it will lose the defense of justification. While actual malice, in the sense of ill will, spite, or hostility, generally need not be proven, as a practical matter its presence often affects the justification calculus. For instance, the employee in *Hatten v. Union Oil Co. of California, Inc.*[5] worked as a crane operator for one of Union Oil's independent contractors until he was replaced at the demand of the Union superintendent. There was evidence that Union was concerned about Hatten's safety record, but there was also evidence supporting Hatten's contention that the superintendent had a

3. Hall v. Integon Life Ins. Co., 454 So.2d 1338 (Ala.1984).

4. 525 U.S. 121, 119 S.Ct. 489, 142 L.Ed.2d 502 (1998).

5. 778 P.2d 1150 (Alaska 1989).

personal grudge against him. This support for a finding of ill will was sufficient to create a jury question on Union's justification defense.

Most courts broaden the scope of the justification defense when the defendant and the plaintiff are fellow employees. Because corporate employers can act only through their agents, the decision or recommendation to fire an employee has to come from another employee, generally a supervisor or manager. Some courts simply hold that, as agents of the employer, supervisors are legally indistinguishable from the employer and therefore cannot be liable for intentional interference with another employee's contract of employment. Most, however, cast their decisions in terms of the justification defense and hold that corporate officers or agents are privileged to cause another employee's discharge if their actions are within the scope of their employment or related to a legitimate corporate interest and not for their own personal interests or motivated by actual malice.

For instance, in *Hunter v. Board of Trustees of Broadlawns Medical Center,*[6] the Iowa Supreme Court held that the evidence supported a jury's verdict against Meyer, the executive director of a hospital, who fired the plaintiff within two weeks of assuming his position. Meyer and Hunter had been competitors for the executive director position. Testimony revealed that Meyer disliked Hunter and openly snubbed him in public. He decided to fire Hunter without considering Hunter's job evaluations and without giving him any reason for the decision. The court held that this evidence was enough to show that Meyer exceeded his privilege to make discharge decisions.

§ 9.17 Statutory Protection—Federal Law

Most federal statutes regulating occupational safety and health, public health, and the environment contain provisions protecting public and private employees against retaliation for reporting violations or otherwise asserting rights under these laws. In addition, all federal employment statutes seek to protect employees who exercise their rights under them by prohibiting employer retaliation.

The whistleblower protections in two specific federal statutes have particular significance to employers. The first is the whistleblower provision contained in the Sarbanes–Oxley Act of 2002.[1] It prohibits any publicly traded company, its officers, employees, contractors, or agents, from retaliating against an employee for engaging in either of two broadly defined sorts of protected activity. The first protected activity is providing information, causing information to be provided, or otherwise assisting in the investigation of conduct that "the employee reasonably believes constitutes" wire fraud, bank fraud, securities fraud, or violation of "any rule or regulation of the Securities and Exchange

6. 481 N.W.2d 510 (Iowa 1992).   fied at 18 U.S.C.A. § 1514A.

§ 9.17

1. The whistleblower provision is codi-

Commission, or any provision of Federal law relating to fraud against shareholders." The information or assistance must be provided to or the investigation conducted by a federal regulatory or law enforcement agency, any member or committee of Congress, or a person with supervisory authority over the employee, or any other person working for the employer who has the authority to investigate, discover, or end misconduct. The second protected activity is filing, causing to be filed, testifying, participating in or otherwise assisting in a proceeding that has been filed or is about to be filed, with the employer's knowledge, relating to a violation of any of the provisions listed in the first category. Thus, formal and informal, and internal and external whistleblowing are protected, and the employee must meet only a standard of reasonable belief in the wrongdoing, not correctness.

Complaints of retaliation must be filed with the Department of Labor within ninety days of the alleged retaliatory act. The Department must investigate the complaint and make a determination within sixty days of receipt of the complaint. If the Department finds reasonable cause to believe a violation has occurred, the employer may request a hearing before an administrative law judge. Either party may appeal the ALJ's order to the United States Court of Appeals. If, however, the Department does not issue a final decision within 180 days after the complaint was filed, and the delay was not caused by bad faith conduct by the complainant, the employee may bring a civil action in federal district court. In either case the employee is entitled to make whole relief, including reinstatement, back pay with interest, and "compensation for any special damages sustained as a result of the discrimination, including litigation costs, expert witness fees, and reasonable attorney fees."

Sarbanes–Oxley also contains a criminal sanction for retaliation against whistleblowers.[2] Under this provision, anyone who "knowingly, with the intent to retaliate, takes any action harmful to any person" for giving truthful information to a law enforcement officer about the commission or possible commission of "any Federal offense" is subject to a fine or imprisonment of not more than ten years.

The second important federal statute sometimes used by whistleblowers is the False Claims Act.[3] This act was originally passed to prevent profiteering during the Civil War and authorizes private citizens to sue on behalf of the United States for fraud and misuse of federal funds. Amendments in 1986 require an award to the citizen or *qui tam* plaintiff of from ten to thirty percent of the amount recovered or received in settlement. The Act also contains an antiretaliation provision, prohibiting discharge or other adverse actions against an employee "because of lawful acts done by the employee on behalf of the employee or others in furtherance of an action" under the Act. Although *qui tam* defendants may not bring counterclaims for contribution or indemnifica-

2. 18 U.S.C.A. § 1513(e).   **3.** 31 U.S.C.A. §§ 3729–3730; 18 U.S.C.A. § 287.

tion, apparently they may assert counterclaims for "independent damages," including claims for such wrongs as breach of the duty of loyalty, breach of fiduciary duty, breach of the implied covenant of good faith and fair dealing, libel, and interference with economic relations.

Until the year 2000, some whistleblowers tried to use the Racketeer Influenced and Corrupt Organizations Act (RICO)[4] as a source of protection from employment-related retaliation. Section 1964(c) of RICO authorizes a private cause of action with treble damages for anyone injured in his or her business or property by reason of a RICO violation.[5] The RICO violations, three substantive offenses and a conspiracy offense, are specified in section 1962: (a) investment of proceeds of a pattern of racketeering activity in an enterprise; (b) acquisition or maintenance of control of an enterprise through a pattern of racketeering activity; (c) conducting the affairs of an enterprise through a pattern of racketeering activity; and (d) conspiracy to violate (a), (b), or (c). Section 1961(1) contains a list of federal crimes and other violations of federal law that constitute "racketeering activity;" a "pattern of racketeering activity" requires at least two of these so-called predicate acts.[6] In *Beck v. Prupis*,[7] the Supreme Court held that a person injured by an overt act done in furtherance of a RICO conspiracy does not have a cause of action under section 1964(c) if the overt act is not an act of racketeering. Therefore the former president, CEO, director, and shareholder of an insurance holding company who was fired after he allegedly discovered that other officers and directors were engaging in unlawful acts of racketeering could not maintain his action under the civil conspiracy provisions of RICO, as his firing was not itself an act of racketeering or otherwise unlawful under the statute.

Finally, two federal statutes, the Civil Service Reform Act[8] and the Whistleblower Protection Act,[9] protect federal employees from retaliation for whistleblowing.

§ 9.18   Statutory Protection—State Law

State Whistleblower and Antiretaliation Laws

All but a few states have whistleblower protection laws. About two-thirds of these protect only public sector employees and sometimes employees of state contractors; the rest protect both public and private sector employees. In addition, Arizona's Employment Protection Act and Montana's Wrongful Discharge from Employment Act, discussed later in this section, prohibit public and private sector employers from firing workers in retaliation for reporting violations of public policy.

The scope of protection under these laws varies from state to state. Some state laws require employees to report their concerns internally

---

4. 18 U.S.C.A. §§ 1961–1968.

5. Id. § 1964(c).

6. Id. § 1961(1), (5).

7. 529 U.S. 494, 120 S.Ct. 1608, 146 L.Ed.2d 561 (2000).

8. 5 U.S.C.A. § 2301(b)(9).

9. Id.

first and to give employers a reasonable time to correct alleged improprieties. For example, Ohio requires that the employee first notify the employer of a violation orally and then submit a written report to the employer describing in detail the alleged violation. If the employer fails to remedy the violation within twenty-four hours, the employee may then file a complaint with the appropriate government agency. (If the offense alleged is a violation of the air pollution control, solid and hazardous wastes, safe drinking water, or water pollution control laws, the employee may report directly, either orally or in writing, to any appropriate official or agency with regulatory authority.)

Twelve other states have employer notification requirements similar to Ohio's,[1] although Colorado requires only a good faith attempt at notification, and in Florida, internal reporting is unnecessary if it would be futile and there is an imminent danger to public health and safety. Four other states specifically reject any requirement that the employee report the alleged violation to the employer.[2]

In states specifying a statutory reporting scheme, it is essential that employees follow these procedures. The failure to do so may result in loss of statutory protection. For instance, in one case involving Ohio's whistleblower law, the employee complained orally to several company officials, including the company's president, that minor employees were consuming alcohol on company premises, but she did not follow up with a written report as required by the statute. (There was some evidence that she had drafted a memorandum to the president, but she was fired before she gave it to him.) The court held that her failure to comply with the statutory requirements precluded her suit.[3]

The kinds of allegations protected by statute vary significantly among the states and between public and private employees. In general, whistleblowing statutes covering public employees protect from retaliation for reporting violations of laws or regulations, mismanagement, gross waste of money, abuse of authority, neglect of duty, or endangerment of public health and safety. In *City of Houston v. Leach*,[4] the court held that reports of improper expenditures of public funds, extortion of money and favors by city employees, and misbehavior by public officials involved matters of public interest protected by the Texas whistleblower act.

In contrast, statutes covering private sector employees are often more limited in their scope. As a general matter, these workers are protected from retaliation for disclosing or threatening to disclose violations of laws, rules, or regulations to any appropriate government agency. Statutes in seven states protect employees who have objected to or refused to participate in a violation of a law, rule, or regulation.[5] Some

---

1. Cal., Colo., Fla., Me., Mass., Mich., Mont., N.H., N.J., Nev., N.Y., and Wis.

2. Kan., Ky., Mo., and Or.

3. Bear v. Geetronics, Inc., 83 Ohio App.3d 163, 614 N.E.2d 803 (1992).

4. 819 S.W.2d 185 (Tex.App.1991).

5. Florida, Illinois, Massachusetts, Minnesota, New Hampshire, North Carolina, and Utah.

state statutes, however, are much narrower. Louisiana's whistleblower law covers only reports of violations of environmental laws, rules, and regulations. New York also has a very strict law that protects an employee who discloses or threatens to disclose a violation that "creates and presents a substantial and specific danger to the public health and safety." New York courts have held that refusal to participate in fiscal improprieties, reporting of fraudulent billing of the City of New York, and reporting the neglect of a mental patient are all unprotected under this law.

Whistleblower laws generally do not protect reporting of alleged violations of company policy, waste, or mismanagement by private sector employers. For example, an employee who reported alleged breaches of his employer's contract with the U.S. Navy was not protected by Maine's Whistleblower Protection Act. That Act requires that the employee have reasonable cause to believe the employer is violating a law, but the employee was claiming only a breach of contract.[6] Similarly, except in Wisconsin, state laws do not protect reports of unethical conduct.

Generally, employee complaints will be protected if they are made in good faith and with reasonable belief in their truth, even if the factual assertions are later found to be incorrect. Three states require that employees take steps to verify the accuracy of any allegations.[7] California requires a sworn statement as to the truth or believed truth of the matters reported.

Most state laws are silent on the question whether an employee's own wrongdoing will negate the protection of the law. Four states specifically remove the statutory protection from an employee who has participated in the unlawful activity he or she reported.[8] In Louisiana, an employee who has participated in the wrongdoing remains protected only if the employer requested his or her involvement in the challenged activity.

In addition to state whistleblower protection, most state labor laws contain provisions protecting employees who file complaints, assist investigations, testify in proceedings, or otherwise assert their rights under the particular law. In contrast with the whistleblower laws, these provisions apply only to the assertion of rights under the specific law of which they are a part. For example, state fair employment practice laws commonly prohibit retaliation against employees who file complaints alleging discrimination. State occupational safety and health laws generally prohibit retaliation against employees who file complaints or assert their rights to a safe workplace. Many state workers' compensation laws prohibit retaliation because workers have filed claims for compensation. Not all of these provisions specifically authorize employees to sue for retaliation, but states that recognize the public policy exception to the

6. Bard v. Bath Iron Works Corp., 590 A.2d 152 (Me.1991).

7. Ind., N.C., and Ohio.

8. Alaska, Fla., Mo., and Or.

employment at will rule often use these provisions as the basis for a wrongful discharge suit.

Employment Termination Statutes

Montana was the first state to prohibit wrongful discharge by statute. The 1987 Montana Wrongful Discharge From Employment Act, preempts the state's common law of wrongful discharge.[9] It provides only three grounds for wrongful discharge actions: (1) if the discharge was in retaliation for the employee's refusal to violate public policy or for reporting a violation of public policy; (2) if the discharge was not for good cause and the employee had completed the employer's probationary period of employment; and (3) if the employer violated the express provisions of its own written personnel policy. The Act does not apply to employees covered by a written collective bargaining agreement or a written contract of employment for a specific term.

The Act defines "good cause" as "reasonable job-related grounds for dismissal based on a failure to satisfactorily perform job duties, disruption of the employer's operation, or other legitimate business reason." "Public policy" is defined as "a policy in effect at the time of the discharge concerning the public health, safety, or welfare established by constitutional provision, statute, or administrative rule."

The most noteworthy parts of the Montana Act may be its recovery limits and its exhaustion of remedies requirement. If the employer is found to have committed a wrongful discharge, the employee may be awarded "lost wages and fringe benefits for a period not to exceed 4 years from the date of discharge, together with interest thereon." The statute imposes a duty to mitigate on the employee. Although the Act does not permit recovery of compensatory damages for pain and suffering or emotional distress, punitive damages are available "if it is established by clear and convincing evidence that the employer engaged in actual fraud or actual malice in the discharge of the employee" in violation of the statutory prohibition against discharge for refusal to violate public policy or for reporting a violation of public policy.

If the employer has written internal procedures under which an employee may appeal a discharge within its organizational structure, it must notify the employee of their existence and supply a copy of the procedures within seven days of the date of the discharge. The employee must exhaust those procedures before he or she may file suit under the Act, unless the procedures have not been completed within ninety days from the date of initiation. The Act also permits arbitration by a neutral party. The incentive to arbitrate is created by awarding reasonable attorney's fees to a party willing to arbitrate that prevails over a party unwilling to arbitrate. A valid offer to arbitrate that has been made and accepted becomes the exclusive remedy for the wrongful discharge dispute and the arbitrator's award is final and binding, subject to review under the provisions of the Uniform Arbitration Act.

9.   Mont.Code Ann. § 39–2–913.

In 1996, Arizona enacted its own Employment Termination Act,[10] in a somewhat delayed reaction to the 1985 decision of *Wagenseller v. Scottsdale Memorial Hospital*,[11] in which the Arizona Supreme Court held that an employer that allegedly fired an employee for refusing to expose herself during a staff performance of the song "Moon River" could be liable for discharge in violation of public policy. The Legislature declared that while the result in the case was correct, the court had no authority to create a cause of action.

The Arizona statute sets forth four exclusive grounds for a claim for termination of employment: (1) discharge in breach of an employment contract; (2) discharge in violation of an Arizona statute; (3) discharge for nine enumerated public policy reasons, including refusal to commit an act or omission that would violate the state constitution or statutes, and internal and external whistleblowing; and (4) in the case of a public employee, if the employee has a right to continued employment under the constitution.

Finally, in 1991 the Commissioners on Uniform State Laws proposed the Model Employment Termination Act, which would displace all common law rights and claims of a terminated employee against the employer, its officers, directors, and other employees based on the termination. To date, no state has adopted this Act.

§ 9.19   Federal Preemption

Among the reasons offered for the willingness of state courts to create common law exceptions to the employment at will rule is that Congress and the state legislatures had already enacted many statutory exceptions to the rule in the form of civil rights laws, antiretaliation provisions in various remedial labor laws, and whistleblower protection laws. As judicial recognition of the various wrongful discharge theories grew, however, so did the potential for overlap or conflict with, and preemption or preclusion by, the statutory schemes. For instance, if a statute contains an antiretaliation provision, with administrative adjudication of claims and limited remedies, may a claimant choose instead to seek relief under state tort law, with its right to jury trial and the availability of compensatory and punitive damages? The resolution of this question depends, first, on whether the conflict is between a federal statute and state law, or between a state statute and a state common law claim. Some federal statutes preempt state law simply by substituting a body of federal substantive law for state rules of decision, while others oust state court subject matter jurisdiction entirely and force the claim into another forum. If a state statute precludes a common law claim, the result usually is that the claim must be brought in an administrative forum prescribed by the statute, rather than in court. This section discusses the doctrine of federal preemption as it applies to state discharge claims, while the next section will deal with whether the

10.   Ariz. Rev. Stat. Ann. § 23–1501.   **11.**   147 Ariz. 370, 710 P.2d 1025 (1985).

existence of a state statute precludes the bringing of a suit under the common law.

Preemption by Federal Statute—Generally

Under the Supremacy Clause of Article VI of the United States Constitution, Congress has the power to preempt state law. The existence and scope of federal preemption are matters of congressional intent, and the Supreme Court often remarks that the general presumption is against preemption of state law, especially when the state is exercising its traditional police powers. Federal preemption doctrines apply to both state statutes and state common law.

Preemption may be express or implied. Express preemption is precisely that: the federal statute contains explicit language preempting state law. The best example in the area of employment law is the Employee Retirement Income Security Act, which contains an extremely broad preemption provision.[1] On the opposite end of the spectrum, many federal labor laws contain saving clauses expressly permitting the enforcement of state laws that provide rights equal to or greater than those in the federal statute. These include Title VII of the Civil Rights Act of 1964,[2] the Americans with Disabilities Act,[3] the Fair Labor Standards Act,[4] and the Family and Medical Leave Act.[5] Cases involving either express preemption or saving provisions generally raise questions about the meaning and scope of the federal provision and whether the state law falls within it. The Supreme Court has held that when a statute contains express preemption language, courts should restrict their analysis to that provision and should not apply any of the rules governing implied preemption.[6]

If Congress is silent on the issue of preemption, the courts turn to whether the federal law nevertheless impliedly preempts state law. There are two or three fairly fluid categories of implied preemption, which the Supreme Court describes in language that has become almost boilerplate. First, a state law is impliedly preempted if Congress has legislated so comprehensively in an area that it has occupied the entire field of regulation. Under field preemption, any state law within that field is preempted, even if it complements or duplicates the federal law. Second, state law is impliedly preempted if compliance with both the federal law and the state law is impossible. Third, state law is impliedly preempted if it stands as an obstacle to the accomplishment of Congress' objectives in enacting the federal law. (The Supreme Court sometimes describes this third category as a subset of the second category, conflict preemption.) Aside from the National Labor Relations Act (NLRA), the Labor Management Relations Act (LMRA), and the Railway Labor Act,

---

§ 9.19

1. ERISA § 514, 29 U.S.C.A. § 1144.

2. Title VII § 708, 42 U.S.C.A. § 2000e–7. See also 42 U.S.C.A. § 2000h–4.

3. ADA § 501(b), 42 U.S.C.A. § 12201(b).

4. FLSA § 18, 29 U.S.C.A. § 218.

5. FMLA § 401(b), 29 U.S.C.A. § 2651(b).

6. Cipollone v. Liggett Group, Inc., 505 U.S. 504, 112 S.Ct. 2608, 120 L.Ed.2d 407 (1992).

which are discussed below, few federal laws can be said to occupy the field of employment law. Similarly, very few instances of actual-conflict, impossibility-of-compliance preemption exist. Thus, most preemption issues involving federal statutes without express preemption or saving provisions fall in the last category, interference with Congressional objectives.

English v. General Electric Co.[7] illustrates the Supreme Court's approach to these implied preemption issues in a retaliatory discharge case. *English* involved whether section 210 of the Energy Reorganization Act of 1974,[8] a whistleblower provision, preempted a nuclear whistle-blower's state law claim for intentional infliction of emotional distress. As with most preemption situations in which the plaintiff wishes to pursue a state common law claim, the remedy provided by section 210 has some significant drawbacks, including a thirty-day limitation period for filing complaints, prosecution by the Secretary of Labor through an administrative hearing process, unavailability of punitive damages (although the statute does permit the Secretary to award compensatory damages), and judicial review only in the courts of appeals. In addition, the statute has an "unclean hands" provision; its remedies are not available to an employee who "deliberately causes a violation of" the Act. English had actually attempted to pursue her federal remedy, but her complaint had been dismissed for failure to file within thirty days of the violation.

The Court marched through the standard federal preemption analysis. The Energy Reorganization Act does not contain an express preemption provision. Although nuclear safety is an area of field preemption, the Court has defined the field narrowly. To come within the preempted zone, a state law "must have some direct and substantial effect on the decisions made by those who build or operate nuclear facilities concerning radiological safety levels." While the costs of paying whistleblowers' claims for intentional infliction of emotional distress might eventually cause nuclear industry employers to alter their safety policies, any such effect, said the Court, was not direct or substantial enough to fall within the preempted field. Turning to obstacle preemption, the Court rejected the notion that the mere existence of a detailed federal regulatory or enforcement scheme preempts state law. It then specifically rejected each of the "special features" the employer claimed warranted preemption— the unclean hands provision, the lack of authorization for awards of punitive damages, and the short filing period.

Before *English,* some courts sidestepped the question of preemption through means such as narrowly construing the scope of the federal statute or holding that the wrongful discharge cause of action is supported only by public policies found in state law. Avoiding the issue should no longer be necessary, however. Short statutes of limitations, administrative resolution of complaints, and limits on recovery are

7. 496 U.S. 72, 110 S.Ct. 2270, 110 L.Ed.2d 65 (1990).

8. 42 U.S.C.A. § 5851.

common features of many antiretaliation and protective provisions in federal labor laws. Absent significant features distinguishing other federal laws from section 210, *English* would seem to compel findings that these statutes do not preempt state wrongful discharge claims. Indeed, *English* has been the basis for holdings of non-preemption of state law discharge claims by OSHA's antiretaliation provision, the whistleblower provision of the Surface Transportation Assistance Act, the Farm Credit Act, the Bankruptcy Code's protection of workers who file for bankruptcy, and the Immigration Reform and Control Act.

In addition to these three implied preemption categories, several lines of cases delineate the extent to which the National Labor Relations Act, the Labor Management Relations Act, and the Railway Labor Act preempt state law. These cases rarely, if ever, recite or rely on precedent from the implied preemption cases, and the boilerplate descriptions of doctrine in the implied preemption cases rarely cite them. They exist in doctrinal worlds of their own.

National Labor Relations Act Preemption

Under the rule in *San Diego Building Trades Council v. Garmon,*[9] an employee's state law claim is preempted by the NLRA, and the National Labor Relations Board (Board) has primary jurisdiction over the matter, if the claim involves conduct that is arguably protected activity under section 7 or arguably prohibited as an unfair labor practice under section 8 of the NLRA. For instance, a worker who alleges he or she was fired in retaliation for union organizing or other pro-union activities (or, for that matter, for anti-union activities) is limited to filing an unfair labor practice charge with the Board; any state claim based on the discharge is preempted by the NLRA. The Supreme Court has permitted exceptions to *Garmon*'s preemption rule when the conduct involves "interests * * * deeply rooted in local feeling and responsibility," and the controversy presented to the state court is not identical to the one that could have been presented to the Board. This exception is generally limited to state court actions involving violence, defamation, and intentional infliction of emotional distress.

A common misperception among those not familiar with the NLRA is that unfair labor practices always involve union activity. Although most do, an important category of unfair labor practices can occur in the complete absence of a union. Employee activity can be protected under section 7 of the NLRA if it is "concerted" and undertaken for "mutual aid or protection." Many disputes that might be brought under one of the state common law theories discussed in this chapter, such as protests over uncomfortable or dangerous working conditions, unlawful employer conduct, or workplace harassment, involve activity "for mutual aid or protection." If the employer fires workers in retaliation for protected activity, it has committed an unfair labor practice, and any state claims the workers attempt to pursue should be preempted by the NLRA.

9. 359 U.S. 236, 79 S.Ct. 773, 3 L.Ed.2d 775 (1959).

The potential impact of this rule is blunted by its limitation to activity that is "concerted." The requirement of concert is satisfied in a nonunion workplace if two or more employees act together, or if one employee acts "with or on the authority of" coworkers or seeks "to initiate or to induce or to prepare for group action." A nonunion employee acting totally alone is not engaged in concerted activity, and the employer does not commit an unfair labor practice by retaliating against him or her.

Invocation of a right under a collective bargaining agreement is, however, concerted activity even if the worker acts alone, because the agreement is an integral part and extension of the admittedly concerted collective bargaining process. Therefore, an employer that fires a worker for asserting a contractual right commits an unfair labor practice, and any state law claim the worker might wish to bring is preempted by the NLRA. Few reported decisions actually deal with this situation under doctrines of NLRA preemption. By definition, these workers also have rights under the collective bargaining agreement, and courts are much more likely to dispose of attempts to bring state claims under the rules governing preemption by section 301 of the Labor Management Relations Act.

A second branch of NLRA preemption, often called *Machinists* preemption,[10] preempts state regulation of conduct neither arguably protected nor arguably prohibited by the NLRA, but which Congress nevertheless intended to be left unregulated. *Machinists* preemption cases usually involve state interference in the collective bargaining process or in the use of economic weapons during a strike, but under certain circumstances worker discharge claims can trigger this branch of preemption. A few federal courts have preempted claims asserting just cause protection by unionized employees who were fired after the collective bargaining agreement expired, but before the employer and the union reached a bargaining impasse on a new contract. These courts reasoned that permitting suit in this situation would limit the parties' bargaining options by imposing contractual terms.

The most significant rejection of *Machinists* preemption in a worker discharge suit is *Belknap, Inc. v. Hale*.[11] In that case, the Supreme Court permitted state claims for misrepresentation and breach of contract brought by strike replacement workers who claimed the employer promised them "permanent" jobs but later fired them to make room for returning strikers. The Court agreed with the employer that the ability to hire striker replacements is an economic weapon that should be unregulated, but it did not agree that this weapon included the right to break promises to the replacements with impunity.

---

10. See International Ass'n of Machinists & Aerospace Workers, Lodge 76 v. Wisconsin Employment Relations Comm'n, 427 U.S. 132, 96 S.Ct. 2548, 49 L.Ed.2d 396 (1976).

11. 463 U.S. 491, 103 S.Ct. 3172, 77 L.Ed.2d 798 (1983).

Section 301 Preemption

Section 301 of the LMRA,[12] which creates federal court jurisdiction over suits to enforce collective bargaining agreements, preempts state law governing those disputes. The Supreme Court has held that section 301 authorizes the creation of a body of federal common law, and it has used that power to fashion powerful presumptions in favor of specific enforcement of arbitration clauses contained in collective bargaining agreements and to impose finality on arbitrators' decisions. For employees seeking to enforce rights under a collective bargaining agreement containing grievance and arbitration provisions, the contractual remedies are, for all practical purposes, exclusive. Employees may not bring their claim in court, even if the union refuses to take their grievance to arbitration, unless they can prove that the union breached its duty of fair representation to them. A decision that an employee's suit is preempted by section 301 often means that he or she has no remedy left, because either the time for filing a grievance under the contract or the six-month statute of limitations for section 301 actions will have long since passed. Like ERISA, section 301 is an area of "complete federal preemption," and state court complaints that do not explicitly rely on federal law must be recharacterized as federal question cases arising under section 301 if they involve interpretation of a collective bargaining agreement.

In *Allis–Chalmers Corp. v. Lueck,*[13] the Supreme Court said that an employee's state law claim is preempted by section 301 if its "resolution * * * is substantially dependent upon analysis of the terms of an agreement made between the parties in a labor contract." The Court also distinguished between actions that are based on "nonnegotiable state-law rights" and those that are "inextricably intertwined" with the collective agreement. Applying this analysis to the facts of the case, the Court found that an employee's claim for bad faith failure to pay disability benefits under the terms of a collective bargaining agreement was preempted by section 301. That the claim was a tort under state law was irrelevant, for the tort duties allegedly breached derived from the contract.

The Court broadened the scope of section 301 preemption a few years later in *Lingle v. Norge Division of Magic Chef, Inc.,*[14] in which an employee sued her employer under Illinois tort law, claiming she had been fired in retaliation for filing a workers' compensation claim. The lower courts had held her claim preempted because the facts needed to prove her retaliatory discharge claim were identical to those that would have proved lack of just cause under the collective bargaining agreement. The Supreme Court disagreed with this standard and said that "as long as the state-law claim can be resolved without interpreting the agreement itself, the claim is 'independent' of the agreement for § 301 pre-

12. 29 U.S.C.A. § 185.

13. 471 U.S. 202, 105 S.Ct. 1904, 85 L.Ed.2d 206 (1985).

14. 486 U.S. 399, 108 S.Ct. 1877, 100 L.Ed.2d 410 (1988).

emption purposes." Section 301 preempts a worker's state law claim "if the resolution of [the claim] depends upon the meaning of a collective-bargaining agreement." Because Lingle's retaliation claim could be resolved without resort to the collective bargaining agreement, it was not preempted. The *Lingle* test, however, throws a wider preemption net than does the *Allis–Chalmers* formulation, which requires that the state law claim substantially depend on the labor contract. The *Lingle* test seemingly includes cases in which the contract interpretation issue is not an element of the worker's claim, but is only injected into the case as a defense.

Finally, in *Livadas v. Bradshaw*,[15] the Court summarized the state of section 301 preemption. In that case it held that the National Labor Relations Act prevents state officials from refusing to enforce the state wage payment law in cases involving unionized workers. In dealing with the state's defense that its actions were compelled by *Lingle*, the Court said that section 301 preemption turns on the legal character of the claim as independent of rights under the collective bargaining agreement. "[W]hen the meaning of contract terms is not the subject of dispute, the bare fact that a collective-bargaining agreement will be consulted in the course of state-law litigation plainly does not require the claim to be extinguished." The Court held that because the plaintiff's claim required the court only to look at the collective bargaining agreement to determine her rate of pay, there was not even a "colorable argument" for preemption. Her claim was "entirely independent of any understanding embodied in the collective-bargaining agreement between the union and the employer."

In spite of the Court's attempt at clarification, the lower courts have struggled with the "thicket" of "thorny jurisdictional questions" involved in section 301 preemption. A few categories of easy cases have emerged. First, state law claims similar to Lingle's, alleging wrongful discharge in retaliation for filing a workers' compensation claim, are not preempted by section 301, nor are claims of discrimination under a state fair employment practices law, even where the collective bargaining agreement contains a nondiscrimination clause. Second, section 301 does not preempt state claims involving promises made to employees before they became a member of the bargaining unit and covered by the collective agreement. Third, section 301 does preempt state law claims founded in contract law, such as breach of contract, promissory estoppel, breach of the covenant of good faith and fair dealing, and other claims based directly on a violation of the collective agreement.

In *Cramer v. Consolidated Freightways, Inc.*,[16] employees sued their employer for invasion of privacy and intentional infliction of emotional distress when they discovered the employer had installed video and audio recording devices behind two-way mirrors in the restroom facilities of its

---

15. 512 U.S. 107, 114 S.Ct. 2068, 129 L.Ed.2d 93 (1994).

16. 255 F.3d 683 (9th Cir.2001) (en banc), cert. denied, 534 U.S. 1078, 122 S.Ct. 806, 151 L.Ed.2d 692 (2002).

truck terminal. The employer's asserted purpose was to detect drug use by its drivers, even though the California penal code prohibited the installation or maintenance of a two-way mirror in a restroom. The employer argued the plaintiffs' claims were preempted by section 301 and pointed to provisions in the collective bargaining agreement that addressed camera surveillance to prove theft and dishonesty and another that prohibited alcohol and drug use on the job and authorized drug testing. The court rejected this contention, stating that more than a "hypothetical connection" or "creative linkage" between the plaintiffs' claim and the collective bargaining agreement had to be found. Similarly, other post-*Lividas* courts have found no preemption where only reference to, not interpretation of, the collective bargaining agreement is necessary.[17]

Railway Labor Act Preemption

Preemption issues similar to those involving section 301 also arise under the Railway Labor Act (RLA), which provides for compulsory and binding arbitration of "minor disputes," those "growing out of grievances, or out of the interpretation or application of agreements concerning rates of pay, rules, or working conditions."[18] A minor dispute is one that "may be conclusively resolved by interpreting the existing [collective bargaining] agreement." Although the arbitration mandate under the RLA is statutory, while arbitration under section 301 requires a contract containing an arbitration provision, preemption under either statute depends on the relationship of the employee's state law cause of action to the collective bargaining agreement. In *Hawaiian Airlines, Inc. v. Norris*,[19] the Supreme Court held that the Railway Labor Act (RLA) does not preempt state law wrongful discharge claims brought by a mechanic who alleged he was fired for refusing to sign a maintenance record for a plane he considered unsafe and for reporting his concerns to the Federal Aviation Administration. The Court adopted the *Lingle* test developed under section 301 of the Labor Management Relations Act. To the extent they were not already doing so, since *Norris* the lower courts have used section 301 precedent in deciding RLA preemption cases.[20]

§ 9.20 Preemption and Preclusion by State Statute

The existence of state statutory remedies also raises preemption issues, particularly because state statutes are the most fruitful source of public policy to support a tort claim for wrongful discharge. In recognizing the first wrongful discharge claims, many state courts found the public policy in statutes that did not explicitly provide protection against retaliation, or that provided some remedy other than a private cause of action, such as a criminal sanction or civil penalty. If, however, a state

---

17. See, e.g., Gregory v. SCIE, 317 F.3d 1050 (9th Cir.2003).

18. 45 U.S.C.A. §§ 153 First (I), 184.

19. 512 U.S. 246, 114 S.Ct. 2239, 129 L.Ed.2d 203 (1994).

20. See, e.g., Hirras v. National R.R. Passenger Corp., 44 F.3d 278 (5th Cir. 1995).

statute does provide a remedy against retaliatory discharge, sooner or later the courts will have to decide whether common law wrongful discharge actions based on the public policy found in the statute are preempted or superseded by the statutory remedial scheme. Unlike preemption by federal statute, no single or uniform method has developed to analyze conflicts between state statutes and the common law. Indeed, the courts rarely use the term "preemption" in discussing these problems. Whether a plaintiff can maintain a common law claim where a state statutory remedy also exists depends on the approach taken by the courts of that state and the particular statute and claims at issue.

Some state courts simply declare that they created the public policy exception to the employment at will doctrine in the first place precisely to provide a remedy that would not otherwise exist. These courts therefore limit public policy wrongful discharge claims to discharges for which there is no statutory remedy. For instance, a plaintiff who alleged she was fired because of her gender would have to bring her claim under the state employment discrimination statute, not as a tort for violation of the state's public policy against gender discrimination. While this view bars a public policy tort claim based on the statute, it should not bar claims for other injuries that are outside the scope of the statute. Thus, if the facts support them, workers should still be able to maintain claims for other torts, such as intentional infliction of emotional distress, or for breach of contract.

This view has historical appeal, and it protects the integrity of the administrative scheme established to enforce the discrimination statute. It also creates the possibility for some interesting dilemmas. If the company does not employ enough workers to be covered by the state discrimination statute, or if it is otherwise exempt from statutory coverage, may the discharged employee pursue a state tort claim, or would the maintenance of the claim conflict with the legislature's decision to exempt businesses like this employer? Permitting the worker to maintain the tort claim brings about the odd result that employees whose employers are covered by the state discrimination law are restricted to their administrative remedies, whereas employees of small firms can recover potentially larger awards of compensatory and punitive damages in a civil action. (In recent years, most decisions have permitted employees of an employer too small to be covered by a state statute to bring common law claims, although not all of these jurisdictions would prohibit the employee of a covered employer from bringing the same suit).

Additionally, permitting the maintenance of an independent common law cause of action for discharge in violation of a public policy manifested in a statute with its own remedial provisions seems the necessary consequence of requiring, as most courts do, a clearly mandated legislative public policy. After all, the legislative public policy is most clearly mandated where the legislature also has provided a remedial structure. If the remedial structure within the legislative directive is found exclusive just because it exists, the public policy exception becomes limited to more tangential rights, those not protected by a statutory remedy.

A variation on this approach, illustrated by a question certified to the Kansas Supreme Court by the Tenth Circuit, is to preclude the common law claim only if the statute asserted by the employer provides an adequate alternative remedy. In *Flenker v. Willamette Industries, Inc.,*[1] the court concluded that a common law cause of action for whistleblowing is not precluded by the whistleblower provisions of OSHA, finding the OSHA remedy inadequate because the decision to pursue the claim is made by an administrative agency, not by the claimant.

A second approach to the preemption question, taken by some states, is the "new right-exclusive remedy," or "antecedent existence" doctrine, which says that a statutory action is the exclusive remedy if the common law action does not predate the enactment of the statute. This doctrine necessarily involves an historical inquiry into the state of the common law at the time the statute was enacted and a decision as to how broadly or narrowly plaintiff's common law claim should be defined. It also shares the same infirmity as the first approach, in that it unnecessarily limits the common law powers of the courts to define the scope of judicially created rules. In addition, it has a counter-intuitive aspect: common law claims created after statutory enactment are preempted, even though presumably the legislature could not have known of them or expressed its wishes about them at the time it considered the statute.

A third approach is to determine whether the legislature intended the statute at issue to be the exclusive remedy for the wrong with which it deals. This method has the advantage of requiring actual analysis of the language of the statute and the legislative history to determine whether the legislature intended to preclude common law claims. Unlike the first approach discussed above, under this view statutes with their own remedial schemes also support an independent common law claim unless the legislature indicated its preemptive intent. Unlike the second approach, later-created common law causes of action are not preempted without an expression of legislative intent.

As with the rules governing federal preemption, statutory language indicating exclusivity ("the procedures contained in this section * * * are the exclusive remedy under state law") generally preempts common law claims, while a saving provision bars preemption. Absent express language of either kind, some courts engage in a lengthy examination of legislative history and intent. Courts may point to permissive ("any employee aggrieved * * * may" file a complaint with the state agency) or mandatory ("a person claiming to be aggrieved * * * must" file a complaint) language, or they may cite the state workers' compensation law for the proposition that the legislature knew how to make a statutory remedy exclusive when it wanted to do so. This last analogy

§ 9.20
1. 266 Kan. 198, 967 P.2d 295 (1998).

works well for statutes enacted after recognition of common law exceptions to the employment at will rule, but it presumes too much for earlier-enacted statutes. Exclusivity of remedies was part of the grand compromise that led to the creation of the workers' compensation schemes, and employee personal injury suits against employers were well-known at the time. The same is not true for wrongful discharge claims, which are of fairly recent origin. A better view of the exclusivity question would simply be to adopt a presumption against exclusivity where the statute is silent. The legislature can, after all, always amend the statute if it disagrees.

A final form of preemption may occur not because a statutory remedy governs the employer's conduct, but because a statutory scheme covers the employee's injury. In some states worker claims for emotional distress caused by conditions of employment or by discharge are preempted by the exclusivity provisions of the state workers' compensation statute. In these states, some workers could have no remedy at all, because many states do not provide compensation payments for emotional disabilities. On the other hand, some states find claims for intentional infliction of emotional distress outside the exclusivity provisions either because the injuries result from intentional acts or because the injuries are not physical. Most courts faced with the question appear to hold that claims for defamation are not preempted by workers' compensation because damage to reputation is not covered by the statutory scheme. In California, discharges in violation of fundamental public policy are not part of the "compensation bargain," and therefore are not barred by workers' compensation.[2]

§ 9.21   Preclusion by Prior Proceedings

Questions of res judicata and collateral estoppel, or claim preclusion and issue preclusion, arise when a litigant has been involved in earlier litigation involving the incident at issue in the current proceeding. With discharge litigation, the most common source of preclusion arguments is an unemployment compensation proceeding.

A defense to an employee's claim for unemployment compensation is that the employee was fired for cause attributable to the employee or quit without good cause. Both employers and employees have attempted to use a prior adjudication in a state unemployment compensation case to preclude litigation of issues in subsequent wrongful discharge cases. If the employee was disqualified from receiving unemployment benefits because he or she was fired for misconduct, the employer will often attempt to preclude the employee from relitigating the issue of the reason for the discharge, or whether there was just cause for the discharge, in a later common law suit. Conversely, an employee who receives a favorable ruling on the reason for discharge or the justification for a quit may attempt to preclude the employer on that issue in a subsequent wrongful discharge action.

2. Gantt v. Sentry Ins., 1 Cal.4th 1083, 4 Cal.Rptr.2d 874, 824 P.2d 680 (1992).

The preclusion doctrine normally raised in these situations is collateral estoppel, or issue preclusion. Claim preclusion, or merger and bar, or "true res judicata," prevents a second action on a claim or any part of it, even as to issues the parties failed to raise in the first proceeding.[1] Claim preclusion will not apply, however, if limits on the jurisdiction or authority of the first tribunal prevented the parties from relying on certain theories or seeking certain relief.[2] Because unemployment compensation proceedings take place in administrative agencies with limited and specific statutory powers, the res judicata effects of agency determinations are rarely at issue.

Collateral estoppel, or issue preclusion, however, can apply to the factual determinations of adjudicative bodies with limited jurisdiction. According to the *Restatement (Second) of Judgments*, "[w]hen an issue of fact or law is actually litigated and determined by a valid and final judgment, and the determination is essential to the judgment, the determination is conclusive in a subsequent action between the parties, whether on the same or a different claim."[3] Although courts may arrange them in various manners, the elements of collateral estoppel generally are:

(1) the issue at stake must be identical to one actually litigated and necessarily adjudicated in the prior litigation;

(2) the party against whom estoppel is sought must have been a party to or in privity with a party to the prior proceeding;

(3) the first proceeding must have ended with a final judgment on the merits; and

(4) the party against whom the earlier decision is asserted must have had a full and fair opportunity to litigate the issue in the earlier proceeding.

The decisions of administrative agencies can be accorded preclusive effect if they satisfy certain requirements of procedural and substantive due process. Although not all states have adopted this rule, most jurisdictions apply preclusion doctrines to administrative determinations if the administrative procedures are adjudicatory in nature, if there is a method of appeal, and if it is clear that the legislature intended to make the administrative determination final in the absence of an appeal.

This last element, legislative intent, plus important policy considerations, cause some courts to deny collateral estoppel effect to unemployment compensation proceedings. If the evidence of a prior determination that an employer lacked just cause to discharge an employee were admissible in a subsequent wrongful discharge case, employers would routinely oppose the award of unemployment compensation benefits as a way of protecting against future liability for wrongful discharge. This

§ 9.21

1. Restatement (Second) of Judgments §§ 17–19 (1982).

2. Restatement (Second) of Judgments § 26 (1982).

3. Id. at § 27.

imposes additional costs on employers. Employees also would have the additional cost of hiring a lawyer to litigate issues surrounding the discharge, regardless of whether a subsequent wrongful discharge action were contemplated. The public interest also is not furthered by applying collateral estoppel because additional, contested unemployment compensation hearings are expensive. Moreover, if a result of increasingly adversarial unemployment compensation litigation is that more unemployment compensation claims are denied, the public welfare system may be forced to absorb additional costs to replace lost income attributable to unemployment.

In addition to these general policy reasons, courts often base their denial of preclusive effect on the absence of one or more of the elements of collateral estoppel. The factor most commonly recited is the lack of a full and fair opportunity to litigate the issue in the first proceedings. Courts point to the relatively small amount at stake and the informal, nontechnical nature of unemployment proceedings in finding that, as a practical matter, the parties had no reason for extensive litigation of the issue of the reason for termination.

Preclusion may also be denied on the ground that the issue decided in the unemployment proceedings is not identical to the issue on which preclusion is sought in the later wrongful discharge suit. For instance, a finding that an employee was not fired for misconduct (and thus is eligible to receive unemployment benefits) is not the equivalent of a finding that the discharge lacked just cause. Misconduct for unemployment compensation purposes requires a degree of fault or wanton disregard for the employer's interests, whereas the mere violation of a company rule may constitute just cause for dismissal under an employment contract. Conversely, a finding in the unemployment proceeding that the employee was fired for misconduct is not necessarily decisive of whether the employer had retaliatory or discriminatory motives for the firing. Even courts that estop the employee from relitigating the factual finding of misconduct generally permit the employee to proceed on allegations of unlawful motive.

Nevertheless, a minority view gives collateral estoppel effect in subsequent wrongful discharge suits to determinations in an unemployment compensation hearing, often without much analysis of the precise issues involved or the nature of unemployment compensation proceedings. For instance, in *Martinez v. Admiral Maintenance Service*,[4] the employee was denied unemployment benefits on the ground of misconduct and later sued for wrongful discharge in retaliation for filing a workers' compensation claim. Without any discussion of the motive issue, the Illinois Court of Appeals held that the reason for the employee's discharge had already been determined and precluded the later suit. *Martinez* has been superseded by statute in Illinois,[5] and several other states have also enacted statutes prohibiting the introduction of evidence

---

4. 157 Ill.App.3d 682, 110 Ill.Dec. 91, 510 N.E.2d 1122 (1987).

5. Ill.Rev.Stat. ch. 820, § 405/1900.

from an unemployment compensation hearing into a separate or subsequent action.

Occasionally, preclusion issues arise in contexts other than unemployment compensation hearings. For instance, in *Yapp v. Excel Corp.*,[6] the employee had settled a suit for unpaid overtime compensation under the Fair Labor Standards Act. The Tenth Circuit held that his later action for wrongful discharge in breach of public policy, breach of contract, promissory estoppel, negligent misrepresentation, and other torts was barred by claim preclusion. The court reasoned that both suits were based on the same transaction, the employee's employment relationship.

§ 9.22   Release and Waiver

Many employers ask workers whose employment has been terminated to sign a release or waiver of claims. In exchange for the receipt of various benefits, the employee agrees not to bring common law or statutory causes of action arising from his or her employment, including actions for wrongful discharge. Although some employment statutes, including the Fair Labor Standards Act and the Age Discrimination in Employment Act, restrict an employee's ability to waive his or her rights, generally courts uphold releases of other employment rights as long as the releases are knowing and voluntary, are supported by consideration, and do not purport to waive future claims. That the choice to settle and sign a release may have been difficult does not mean the decision was not voluntary.

A release may be invalidated if the employer induced the employee to sign it through misrepresentation, fraud, or duress. In most states, however, an employee wishing to avoid the effects of a release must tender back the consideration received within a reasonable time after he or she learns the facts supporting an argument of invalidity. If the employee continues to accept benefits under the release and acts in accordance with its terms after learning of any misrepresentation or other grounds for voiding the release, he or she will be deemed to have ratified the release. For instance, in a case involving Missouri law, the Eighth Circuit found ratification where the employee accepted and cashed his severance pay check, represented to potential future employers that he had resigned voluntarily, and received favorable references from his former employer.[1]

The Michigan Supreme Court has held that tender must occur no later than the commencement of any suit raising claims covered by the release. Thus, an amended pleading in which the employee offered to repay the benefits received under a release came too late, and her suit

---

6.   186 F.3d 1222 (10th Cir.1999).   Co., 771 F.2d 417 (8th Cir.1985).

§ 9.22

1.   Anselmo v. Manufacturers Life Ins.

was dismissed as barred by the release.[2] The Alaska Supreme Court, however, held that a trial court erred in dismissing a suit for failure to tender; the employee should have been given a reasonable time to tender the consideration, plus interest.[3] The tender must be unconditional, however. An employee's offer to give the former employer a second mortgage on his home instead of tendering back the consideration received in a termination agreement did not constitute a sufficient tender.

Although release or waiver is normally an affirmative defense, once a party establishes that the opponent signed a release that addresses the claim at issue, received adequate consideration, and breached the release, the opponent, in an employment case usually the former employee, has the burden of proving the release's invalidity. The employee must prove all of the elements necessary to invalidate the release. Thus, if the employee claims a termination agreement was procured by fraud, he or she must prove all the elements of fraud.

In *Kohn v. Jaymar–Ruby, Inc.,*[4] the court enforced an oral agreement in settlement of a wrongful discharge action, even though the confidentiality provisions of the agreement prevented it from being fully performed within one year. The agreement was reached at a court-mandated settlement conference, and the court found that the purpose of the writing requirement of the Statute of Frauds was not implicated in such a setting.

In *Picton v. Anderson Union High School District,*[5] a high school teacher who had resigned after being accused of engaging in unprofessional conduct with female students and raping one student sued the school district for breaching the nondisclosure provision in his resignation agreement by informing state teaching authorities of the facts surrounding his resignation. The California Court of Appeals held that the nondisclosure provision was void as against public policy because the school district had a statutory duty to notify the state of the facts.

§ 9.23 Remedies

The measure of damages for wrongful discharge depends on the theory of liability upon which the employee prevails. Traditional contract remedies are generally awarded when the firing violated an express employment contract or a contract implied from the terms of an employee handbook or the parties' course of conduct. Except in a few states, tort remedies are awarded when the firing violated public policy. Of those states that recognize the implied covenant of good faith and fair dealing, most permit only contract damages, either through a clear holding to that effect, or by implication.

2. Stefanac v. Cranbrook Educ. Community, 435 Mich. 155, 458 N.W.2d 56 (1990).

3. Thorstenson v. ARCO Alaska, Inc., 780 P.2d 371 (Alaska 1989).

4. 23 Cal.App.4th 1530, 28 Cal.Rptr.2d 780 (1994).

5. 50 Cal.App.4th 726, 57 Cal.Rptr.2d 829 (1996).

A major difference between contract and tort is that damages for emotional distress and punitive damages are generally not available under a breach of contract theory, but under the proper circumstances they can be elements of a recovery in tort. Beyond that relatively bright line, it is safe to say that many of the rules concerning damages in common law discharge cases are still evolving. Until the early 1980s, the dominance of the at-will rule restricted discharge claims almost entirely to those in which the employer breached a contract for a term by firing the employee without cause before the expiration of the term. In those cases, damages were generally calculated as the compensation for the remaining term of the contract. During the 1980s state courts recognized other theories of wrongful discharge, but these cases often reached the appellate courts on motions to dismiss or for summary judgment, and therefore no detailed discussion of damages was necessary. In the next phase of discharge litigation, which is occurring now, the parties have had full trials on the merits, and the appeals in these cases can be expected to generate clearer rules on damage formulations.

Back Pay

A general principle of both contract and tort law is that the plaintiff should be placed in the same economic position he or she would have enjoyed if the defendant's wrongful action had not taken place. Thus, a major element of damages in any discharge action is the compensation (wages, salary, commissions, or other payments, plus fringe benefits) the employee lost by reason of the discharge. As a general matter, the employee should recover back pay damages, less any mitigation amounts, from the date of the discharge until the date of trial, unless his or her employment would have ended earlier for a lawful reason. If, for instance, if the employee's position would have been abolished for a lawful reason before the date of trial, the employer's liability for back pay stops accruing as of that date.

If the employee worked under a contract for a term, the employee's back pay damages consist of the salary or other compensation for the remainder of the term, less amounts earned in mitigation. (This assumes that, as is likely, the trial takes place after the date on which the contract would have expired.) In cases where the only claim is breach of an employment contract containing a notice of termination requirement, courts have limited damages to the compensation for the period of the notice, less mitigation. Thus, if the employment contract requires fifteen days' notice of intent to terminate, but the employer fires the employee without notice, the employee may recover only fifteen days of wages and benefits. In *Wyatt v. BellSouth, Inc.,*[1] plaintiff, an at-will employee, sued his former employer for promissory estoppel. He alleged that when he agreed to take over management of a district with serious problems, the employer told him it "would conduct a full and fair investigation of any complaints of employees about him, would hear both sides of any controversy concerning his management of the district, and would view

§ 9.23

1.   757 So.2d 403 (Ala.2000).

any complaints about his management 'skeptically.' " The employer, however, fired him after holding secret meetings with the employees he supervised and without giving him a chance to rebut any allegations against him. On a question certified from the U.S. District Court for the Middle District of Alabama, the Alabama Supreme Court held that the measure of plaintiff's damages would be the wages and benefits he would have received during the time it would reasonably have taken the employer to conduct the investigation it promised

In *Phillips v. Butterball Farms Co.,*[2] the Michigan Supreme Court reversed a lower court decision holding that in a retaliatory discharge action damages for lost wages must be nominal because an at-will employee cannot show a reasonable expectation of continued employment. Rather, the court held that an at-will tort plaintiff may recover lost wages, as well as damages for mental and emotional distress. The parties failed to brief the question of front pay, so the court did not address it. In *Ford v. Trendwest Resorts,*[3] the Washington Supreme Court held that lost earnings are not an appropriate measure of damages when an employer breaches a contract to hire an at-will employee. Plaintiff Ford was fired from his at-will position after he came to work smelling of alcohol for a second time. The employer agreed to rehire him as an at-will employee in "a position equal to that which [he] held" after he had completed an alcohol counseling program. The employer, however, offered Ford a job that paid less than his previous job and fired him when he turned it down. Noting that contract damages are generally based on the injured party's expectation interest, the court said that Ford's expectations under an employment-at-will contract are no different from the employment itself, and that Ford could not reasonably have expected future earnings from an at-will job.

Front Pay/Future Damages

In addition to compensation lost in the past, plaintiffs often seek future damages, or front pay, for some period of time beyond the date of the trial. The duty to mitigate means that, if the court permits awards of front pay, they can go only to those plaintiffs who have not been able to find other comparable employment after their discharge; in many future damages cases, however, the employee has another job that pays less than the former employment and argues that the defendant should have to compensate him or her for the lifetime earnings differential.

The clearest cases warranting an award of future damages, or front pay, are those involving a contract for a term that has not expired by the time of trial. Most courts permit the employee to recover future damages for the contractual compensation for the remainder of the term, discounted to present value. Given the often lengthy delays inherent in litigation and the relatively short duration of most contracts for a definite term, there are not many modern era cases on this point.

2. 448 Mich. 239, 531 N.W.2d 144 (1995).   **3.** 146 Wn.2d 146, 43 P.3d 1223 (2002).

If the contract of employment is for an indefinite term, but the employer has created a just cause relationship through an employee handbook or other enforceable promises, many courts will permit the award of future damages beyond the date of the trial, on the theory that the just cause protection gave the plaintiff a reasonable expectation of continued employment. Permitting awards of front pay in this situation carries with it a much greater danger of speculation than in the contract for a term cases, where the front pay ends in any event on the date specified in the contract. To the extent that courts have addressed this issue, they deal with it by requiring plaintiffs to present evidence on their prospects for future employment, the amounts they would have earned from the defendant had they not been fired, and the anticipated length of their working lives, by leaving rebuttal of these matters to the employer, and by treating the amount of the front pay award as a jury question. This approach has the potential for large awards, covering long periods of time.

For instance, in *Beales v. Hillhaven, Inc.,*[4] the Nevada Supreme Court affirmed a jury verdict of $208,476 in front pay in favor of a plaintiff who was sixty-two at the time of trial. She had presented expert testimony that her front pay damages ranged from $49,152 to $315,791, based on the assumptions that she had little chance of finding comparable employment in the area and that she would have worked until either age sixty-five or age seventy. The court held that the jury was entitled to weigh the testimony and award an amount within the ranges suggested by her evidence. In *Diggs v. Pepsi–Cola Metropolitan Bottling Co., Inc.,*[5] the Sixth Circuit upheld an award of front pay for twenty-six and one-half years, based on the difference between the plaintiff's current salary and the salary he would have earned at Pepsi, and in *Stark v. Circle K Corp.,*[6] the Montana Supreme Court upheld a verdict for twenty-eight years of front pay based on the employer's failure to rebut expert testimony by the plaintiff's expert witness.

In *Worrell v. Multipress, Inc.,*[7] the Ohio Supreme Court engaged in one of the few lengthy discussions of the future damages issue in a modern common law discharge case. The court expressed concern for the interests of both plaintiff and defendant in front pay cases. Front pay is intended to assist in making injured plaintiffs whole by compensating them for the period in which they are seeking comparable employment; therefore, plaintiffs with employable and productive years ahead of them have an obligation to obtain other employment and should not receive awards of future damages representing the entire period until retirement. The court held that whether future damages are appropriate in a given case is a question of law for the court, to be determined by applying four factors: (1) the age of the employee and his or her reasonable prospects of obtaining comparable employment elsewhere; (2)

---

4. 108 Nev. 96, 825 P.2d 212 (1992).

5. 861 F.2d 914 (6th Cir.1988) (applying Mich. law).

6. 230 Mont. 468, 751 P.2d 162 (1988).

7. 45 Ohio St.3d 241, 543 N.E.2d 1277 (1989).

salary and other tangible benefits such as bonuses and vacation pay; (3) expenses associated with finding new employment; and (4) the replacement value of fringe benefits, such as automobile and insurance, for a reasonable time until the employee obtains another job.

If the rationale for awards of front pay where the employee had for-cause protection in the former employment is the reasonable expectation of continued employment that protection provided, at-will employees should normally not be eligible for future damages. There are a few decisions upholding future damage awards to at-will employees, although most contain little or no discussion of the theoretical basis for the award. It appears that the issue has not received much attention. By definition, these employees do not have breach of contract claims, so the challenge to their discharges will be under the public policy exception to the at-will rule, where compensatory damages for mental anguish and punitive damages are available. The parties undoubtedly focus more of their attention on these aspects of the case than on the front pay issue.

Reliance Damages

If they can find a theory of liability, at-will employees may be able to recover their reliance damages, even if no future damages are permitted. For instance, in *Pearson v. Simmonds Precision Products, Inc.,*[8] the plaintiff was hired as a senior test engineer on a design project for the B–2 bomber. During his preemployment interviews, he expressed concern about job security, given the unpredictable nature of defense contracting. The employer replied that much of its business was in nondefense areas, and that, even if the B–2 project failed, there would be work for him. The plaintiff accepted the job, moved to Vermont, and took out a loan to buy a house; within a few months, cutbacks in the B–2 project led to his discharge. Although he had signed a contract clearly indicating his at-will status, he prevailed against the employer on the theories of negligent failure to disclose and negligent misrepresentation. The employer knew at the time it was negotiating with him that the project was facing serious cutbacks and that there was a good chance his job would be eliminated, and therefore it had a duty to disclose that information to him. He was permitted to recover the damages he incurred in reliance on the employer's misrepresentations.

Damages for Emotional Distress

A major difference between contract and tort is that damages for emotional distress are generally not recoverable in an action for breach of contract. Most jurisdictions do permit the recovery of damages for emotional distress in common law retaliatory discharge cases. As the Washington Supreme Court reasoned, discharge in violation of public policy is an intentional tort, for which emotional distress damages are routinely available.[9]

8. 160 Vt. 168, 624 A.2d 1134 (1993).

9. Cagle v. Burns & Roe, Inc., 106 Wash.2d 911, 726 P.2d 434 (1986).

Punitive Damages

As with compensatory damages for emotional distress, recovery of punitive damages is normally restricted to actions that sound in tort. The purpose of punitive damages is said to be to punish the wrongdoer and to deter others from acting in a similar manner. States use various formulations for the degree of culpability that justifies an award of punitive damages. Under Arizona law, for example, the employee must show, by clear and convincing evidence, that the employer acted with "an evil mind;" factors considered include the reprehensibility of the conduct and the severity of harm likely to result, as well as the harm that in fact occurred, the duration of the misconduct, the defendant's awareness of harm or risk of harm, and any attempts to conceal it.[10] New Mexico requires a showing that the employer acted in bad faith, with a "culpable mental state."[11] Similarly, other states may use adjectives such as wanton, willful, malicious, oppressive, or fraudulent.

Some courts have refused to permit awards of punitive damages where the employer could not reasonably have known that its actions could result in liability. In *Springer v. Weeks & Leo Co.*,[12] for instance, the Iowa Supreme Court denied a claim for punitive damages on behalf of an employee who was fired in retaliation for filing a claim for workers' compensation benefits, on the ground that the discharge occurred before a tort action for retaliatory discharge had been recognized in Iowa. As time passes, of course, this defense to punitive damages will become increasingly less available to employers.

Most states do not permit awards of punitive damages in actions for breach of contract, unless the defendant's conduct is also an independent tort. This distinction explains the significance of the California Supreme Court's decision in *Foley v. Interactive Data Corp.*[13] that an action for breach of the covenant of good faith and fair dealing sounds in contract, not tort.

Duty to Mitigate

An employee seeking damages in a wrongful discharge action, whether brought in tort or in contract, has a duty to mitigate those damages by searching for and obtaining other, comparable employment. Any damages to which an employee may be entitled will be reduced by the amount of compensation he or she actually earned after the termination, and by amounts the employee failed to earn but could have earned if he or she had exercised reasonable diligence. Although mitigation is often referred to as a "duty" of the fired employee, failure to mitigate is in fact an affirmative defense. Thus, the employer has the burden of persuasion to show that the employee earned money in the interim or that comparable employment was available and the employee

---

10. Thompson v. Better–Bilt Alum. Prods. Co., 171 Ariz. 550, 832 P.2d 203 (1992).

11. McGinnis v. Honeywell, 110 N.M. 1, 791 P.2d 452 (1990).

12. 475 N.W.2d 630 (Iowa 1991).

13. 47 Cal.3d 654, 254 Cal.Rptr. 211, 765 P.2d 373 (1988).

failed to use reasonable efforts to obtain it. A few courts have held that an employee who was wrongfully fired out of malice, that is a willful and deliberate violation of the employee's rights, is entitled to back pay with no mitigation deduction.

As might be expected, most of the litigation surrounding the mitigation issue involves whether an employee who has not mitigated could have done so. The employee's obligation is to seek and obtain employment comparable to the position from which he or she was fired. Therefore, as a general matter, the employee does not have to change fields, take an inferior position, or relocate to find employment. If, however, the employee does take an inferior job, the amount earned is treated as mitigation and thereby reduces the award in the employee's wrongful discharge action. On the other hand, the employee may recover from the defendant any reasonable expenses incurred while seeking alternative employment.

Frye v. Memphis State University,[14] while perhaps a case with extreme facts, illustrates the effect of the placement of the burden of persuasion on the issue of mitigation. Frye, a tenured professor of psychology, was fired in 1979 because of alleged misuse of university computer facilities and privileges. The University reported Frye's discharge to the ethics committee of the American Psychological Association, Frye's professional association, and issued a press release essentially stating that Frye was dismissed because of fraud and theft. Not surprisingly, the firing received widespread media coverage in Memphis and became a matter of common knowledge within Frye's academic field nationally.

Frye eventually won reinstatement in 1988, but in the interim he did not look for another job because he believed his efforts would be futile. Frye argued, and experts testified, that the damage to his reputation caused by the firing, the University's press release, the media coverage, and the ethics investigation made it impossible for him to find a similar faculty position at another college or university. The Tennessee Supreme Court agreed that the University had failed to meet its burden of proving the availability of suitable and comparable substitute employment, that is, a position with "virtually identical promotional opportunities, compensation, job responsibilities, working conditions, and status." In deciding whether an employee has exercised reasonable diligence, the "individual characteristics of the employee and of the job market must be considered." The court added that the duty of mitigation did not require Frye to undertake a nationwide job search, especially because moving to another area would have adversely affected his consulting business in Memphis.

The best way for an employer to show a failure to mitigate is to introduce evidence that the employee rejected an offer of the identical job from which he or she was fired—that is, to show that it offered to reinstate the employee. To operate in this fashion, the offer of reinstate-

14. 806 S.W.2d 170 (Tenn.1991).

ment must be bona fide and made in good faith. It must not be conditioned on dismissal or compromise of the employee's claim, nor may it require a demotion, lower pay, or less responsibility. Even if the offer is to reinstate the employee to his or her old job with identical salary and benefits, the employee may still refuse if reasonable grounds exist for the refusal, as where further association between the parties would be offensive or degrading.

Most courts do not permit amounts an employee receives from collateral sources, such as unemployment compensation benefits, to be set off against a damages award, although the Michigan Supreme Court upheld a trial court's action in deducting from the damages in a breach of implied contract case the $6200 in unemployment compensation benefits received by the plaintiff.[15] The court refused to extend the collateral source rule, which would have prevented consideration of the amount of unemployment benefits, from tort actions to those based on breach of contract. Such a decision would conflict with the fundamental rule that the remedy for breach of contract is to make the nonbreaching party whole.

Reinstatement

Although most remedial labor statutes specifically authorize courts to order reinstatement of employees fired in violation of the statute, reinstatement is not normally ordered in common law cases. Historically, the rationale derives from the rule in equity that personal service contracts may not be specifically enforced. This rule was based on the doctrine of mutuality; an employee cannot be ordered to work for an employer, and therefore an employer should not be ordered to employ someone against its wishes. As a practical matter, reinstatement carries with it the potential for unhappiness and retaliation down the line. For all of these reasons, few employees seek reinstatement in common law actions.

After-Acquired Evidence

In *McKennon v. Nashville Banner Publishing Co.*,[16] a suit under the Age Discrimination in Employment Act, the United States Supreme Court held that evidence discovered by the employer after it fired the employee (in *McKennon*, allegedly because of her age) that the employee had engaged in job-related misconduct that would have caused a discharge had the employer known about it at the time affects only the available remedies but does not bar all recovery. The Court concluded that the objectives of both the ADEA and Title VII, deterring discrimination and compensating for injuries caused by unlawful discrimination, would not be served by barring recovery entirely. It recognized, however, the employer's legitimate interests in considering the employee's wrongdoing by stating that as a general matter reinstatement and front pay should not be permitted in a case involving after-acquired evidence, and

15. Corl v. Huron Castings, Inc., 450 Mich. 620, 544 N.W.2d 278 (1996).

16. 513 U.S. 352, 115 S.Ct. 879, 130 L.Ed.2d 852 (1995).

that back pay should be calculated from the date of the firing to the date the evidence was discovered.

McKennon has had some influence in state public policy cases. While some courts allow after-acquired evidence of misconduct to bar the claim entirely,[17] others follow *McKennon* and its rationale and hold that it limits remedies only.[18] In state law breach of contract claims, however, most courts that have addressed the issue have held that if an employer can prove it would have fired the employee if it had known of prior misconduct, the employee's claim is barred entirely.[19] Some of these courts point specifically to the *Restatement (Second) of Contracts*, under which a party is excused from performance upon the uncured material breach of the other. In fact, illustration 8 to section 237 is directly on point to the after-acquired evidence issue. It states:

> A and B make an employment contract. After the service has begun, A, the employee, commits a material breach of his duty to give efficient service that would justify B in discharging him. B is not aware of this but discharges A for an inadequate reason. A has no claim against B for discharging him.[20]

§ 9.24   Procedural Due Process and Public Employment

The Fourteenth Amendment provides that no one acting under color of state law shall "deprive any person of life, liberty, or property, without due process of law."[1] A public employee with a legally recognized interest in continued employment has a property right within the meaning of the Fourteenth Amendment that the state cannot take away without providing procedural due process.[2] All public employees, even those who do not have property rights in their jobs, have a protected liberty interest in the pursuit of their occupations under the Fourteenth Amendment, and employees who are fired in a manner that stigmatizes them have been deprived of that interest, unless the employer provides them procedural due process.[3]

Property Rights

Although federal law determines whether due process requirements have been met, state law determines whether a public employee has a property right in his or her job. This constitutionally protected property right can be shown through proof that a public employee has a legitimate

---

17. See, e.g., DePluzer v. Village of Winnetka, 265 Ill.App.3d 1061, 203 Ill.Dec. 31, 638 N.E.2d 1157 (1994), cert. denied, 514 U.S. 1127, 115 S.Ct. 1999, 131 L.Ed.2d 1001 (1995).

18. See, e.g., Baber v. Greenville County, 327 S.C. 31, 488 S.E.2d 314 (1997).

19. See, e.g., O'Day v, McDonnell Douglas Helicopter Co., 191 Ariz. 535, 959 P.2d 792 (1998).

20. Restatement (Second) of Contracts § 237, illustration 8 (1981).

§ 9.24

1. U.S. Const. amend. 14.

2. Cleveland Bd. of Educ. v. Loudermill, 470 U.S. 532, 105 S.Ct. 1487, 84 L.Ed.2d 494 (1985).

3. Bishop v. Wood, 426 U.S. 341, 96 S.Ct. 2074, 48 L.Ed.2d 684 (1976); Board of Regents v. Roth, 408 U.S. 564, 92 S.Ct. 2701, 33 L.Ed.2d 548 (1972).

claim of entitlement to continuing employment under state law, through a statute or regulation creating a term of office or establishing specific causes for which a public employee may be discharged, or through an express or implied contract providing protection from arbitrary dismissal. For instance, a tenured faculty member at a public school, college, or university has a constitutionally protected property right because tenure is a promise of continued employment. On the other hand, if an employee's status is provisional, probationary, or untenured, or if the employee cannot point to some other source of job security, he or she does not have a property right in the employment. Mere employment under consecutive annual contracts, without a statutory or contractual right to renewal, is not enough to establish a claim of entitlement; neither is employment under an employee handbook that does not create contractual rights under state law.

If a public employee has a protected property right in employment, the state cannot deprive him or her of that property without due process. In most situations, due process requires that before an employee may be fired, the employee must have notice of the charges and a meaningful opportunity to be heard. If there will be a posttermination hearing as well, then the pretermination stage may be limited to "some opportunity to be heard." At the posttermination stage, a full hearing is required. In *Gilbert v. Homar*,[4] the Supreme Court held that a hearing before the property deprivation is not always required. In that case, a state university police officer was suspended without pay because he had been arrested on a felony charge during a drug raid. In some situations, remarked the Court, where a state must act quickly or it would be impractical to provide predeprivation process, postdeprivation process satisfies the requirements of the Due Process Clause.

Due process notice requirements are satisfied by either oral or written notice of the charges against the employee, although states may require, as a matter of their own law, that the notice be in writing. To be sufficient, a notice must describe the general nature of the charges against the employee, the general substance of the evidence against him or her, the employer's intention to fire the employee on a specified date, and the employee's obligation to respond. The notice, however, need not be drafted with the particularity required in a criminal indictment. One purpose of the notice is to give the employee a chance to prepare a defense; another is to limit the employee's pretermination hearing to the charges delineated in the notice. Therefore, the notice must set forth specific rules alleged to be violated and specific conduct causing the violations. For example, a letter stating that the reason for an employee's discharge was a pattern of sexual harassment and including specific instances of the conduct was sufficient notice even though the letter did not include the names of the women allegedly harassed.[5]

4. 520 U.S. 924, 117 S.Ct. 1807, 138 L.Ed.2d 120 (1997).

5. Roberts v. Greiner, 182 W.Va. 137, 386 S.E.2d 504 (1989).

An employee must have an opportunity to be heard, either in writing or orally, at a pretermination hearing. The pretermination hearing need not be elaborate, especially if a more detailed posttermination procedure exists. The pretermination hearing need not be a full evidentiary hearing, the employee does not have a right to present witnesses in his or her defense or to confront and cross-examine adverse witnesses, and the employee is not entitled to a record of the proceedings. A pretermination hearing does not have to "definitively resolve the propriety of the discharge;" rather, "[i]t should be an initial check against mistaken decisions." Thus, a pretermination hearing should merely resolve "whether there are reasonable grounds to believe that the charges against the employee are true and support the proposed action." Pretermination warnings and an opportunity for a face-to-face meeting with supervisors has been held constitutionally sufficient. The decisionmaker at a pretermination hearing does not have to be an impartial outsider or an impartial insider. The individual proposing the discharge may also preside over the hearing. Moreover, the same party may order an investigation into the employee's conduct, issue a notice of proposed discharge, and sign the final discharge letter without violating an employee's due process rights at the pretermination stage.

At the posttermination stage, however, there must be a fair and impartial tribunal. Decisionmakers must not have a direct personal, substantial, and pecuniary interest in the outcome of the case, they must not have been the target of personal abuse or criticism from the employee, and they must not have had any investigative role in the dispute.

Liberty Interest

A public employee has a protected liberty interest in his or her "good name, reputation, honor, or integrity."[6] An injury to an employee's reputation alone, however, is not a deprivation of a liberty interest; rather, some alteration of a right or status recognized by state law must accompany the damage to reputation. Thus, a deprivation of a liberty interest occurs if a public employer fires or refuses to rehire an employee and at the same time makes false charges so stigmatizing that, as a practical matter, he or she is precluded from finding other government employment. Examples of stigmatizing charges are accusations of illegality, dishonesty, immorality, or even professional incompetence, while accusations of poor job performance have been held not to stigmatize in a way that infringes constitutionally protected liberty interests. Further, the charges made against the employee must be false, they must be made public, and the employee must have been denied a meaningful opportunity to clear his or her name. Unpublicized accusations or criticisms do not harm an employee's good name, reputation, honor, or integrity, nor do the inferences that may be drawn from a firing alone. Assertions surrounding a dismissal are considered "unpublicized" for due process

6. Bishop v. Wood, 426 U.S. 341, 348, 96 S.Ct. 2074, 48 L.Ed.2d 684 (1976); Board of Regents v. Roth, 408 U.S. 564, 92 S.Ct. 2701, 33 L.Ed.2d 548 (1972).

purposes if they are communicated only in a judicial proceeding after the discharge. Similarly, an employer's communications to a state unemployment office in response to a fired employee's claim for benefits have been held not to be "publicized."

An employee whose liberty interests have been violated is entitled to a hearing to clear his or her name. This hearing is for this limited purpose only; the employer is not required to rehire the employee if he or she can prove the inaccuracy of the stigmatizing statements.

Chapter 10

BANKRUPTCY, PLANT CLOSINGS, AND UNEMPLOYMENT COMPENSATION

Table of Sections

§ 10.1 Introduction

Every year millions of employees are adversely affected by economic exigencies experienced by their employers. Some are forced to accept compensation reductions, while others suffer temporary or permanent job losses. Even temporary unemployment can have devastating effects far beyond the critical disruption of income. Individuals whose personal identities are defined, at least partially, by their occupations suffer a loss of self-esteem during periods of forced idleness. Many experience increased medical problems caused by the frustration generated by their inability to locate other gainful employment.

This chapter will initially explore the ability of financially troubled companies to obtain relief through bankruptcy procedures and the rights of employees affected by employer bankruptcies. It will then consider state and federal plant closing laws that require employers to provide employees with advance notice of impending closures in certain circumstances. The chapter will finally examine the federally mandated unemployment compensation insurance system. It will discuss eligibility requirements and the situations that may result in worker disqualification.

§ 10.2 Bankruptcy—Generally

Companies experiencing financial difficulties often try to reduce operating expenses by decreasing labor costs. They may decide to lower wage rates and to diminish or discontinue costly fringe benefit programs. With respect to the eighty-five percent of workers who are not covered by collective bargaining agreements and who have no individual employment contracts, employers are generally free to modify their wages and their non-vested fringe benefits without even discussing the proposed changes with the affected employees. These companies need not file any bankruptcy petitions. Companies that wish to reduce the labor costs of employees covered by collective bargaining contracts, however, must either obtain the consent of the representative labor organizations or request bankruptcy court approval of the proposed modifications.

Modifying and Rejecting Bargaining Agreement Provisions

Chapter 11 of the Bankruptcy Code,[1] provides detailed procedures that must be followed by corporate debtors that wish to avoid liquidation through reorganization of their economically troubled businesses. Section 365(a) provides that a debtor or bankruptcy trustee "may assume or reject any executory contract * * * of the debtor."[2] In *NLRB v. Bildisco & Bildisco*,[3] the Supreme Court unanimously held that a collective bargaining agreement constitutes an "executory contract" that may be modified or rejected in bankruptcy proceedings if the agreement "burdens the estate and * * * the equities balance in favor of rejecting the labor contract." The *Bildisco* Court further held, by a five-to-four margin, that where its two-part rejection standard was satisfied, a debtor could reject its collective bargaining obligations as soon as it filed its bankruptcy petition. It was not required to wait until it received bankruptcy court approval. Nor did the debtor have to comply with the requirement of National Labor Relations Act (NLRA) section 8(d) that it obtain union consent before modifying the terms of an existing collective contract. The *Bildisco* majority concluded that the rights of a debtor under the Bankruptcy Code took precedence over the rights of a labor organization under the NLRA.

Following the *Bildisco* decision, organized labor lobbied successfully for a new Bankruptcy Code provision that prescribes stricter standards to be satisfied before an employer can modify or reject terms contained in an existing collective bargaining agreement. Congress acknowledged that employees differ substantially from ordinary commercial creditors. Employees derive most, if not all, of their income from their employment. When the wage and benefit provisions set forth in collective

§ 10.2
1. 11 U.S.C.A. §§ 1101–1174.
2. Id. § 365(a).

3. 465 U.S. 513, 104 S.Ct. 1188, 79 L.Ed.2d 482 (1984).

bargaining agreements are unilaterally decreased by their employers, the adversely affected employees must absorb the entire loss. Nonetheless, Congress also recognized the need to provide financially troubled employers with the flexibility required to enable them to achieve successful Chapter 11 reorganizations. If the standards regulating the rejection of bargaining agreement obligations were too restrictive, additional companies would fail, causing the unnecessary displacement of thousands of workers.

Section 1113 of the Bankruptcy Code specifies the prerequisites that must be satisfied if an economically depressed company wants to reject or modify bargaining agreement terms.[4] The company must "make a proposal to the authorized representative * * * based on the most complete and reliable information available at the time of such proposal, which provides for those necessary modifications in the employees benefits and protections that are necessary to permit the reorganization of the debtor." Such a proposal must assure "that creditors, the debtor and all of the affected parties are treated fairly and equitably." The employer must supply the representative labor organization with all relevant information and consult with that union in good faith. If the labor organization rejects the proposed changes "without good cause" and the company convinces the bankruptcy court that "the balance of the equities clearly favors rejection," it will be permitted to make the proposed modifications. The changes usually may not be effectuated until bankruptcy court approval has been obtained.

An employer seeking to modify the terms of an existing bargaining agreement must be careful to propose those changes that are reasonably necessary to successful reorganization. If the bankruptcy court finds that the proposed modifications go beyond what is realistically required, it will refuse to approve the requested concessions. For example, in *Wheeling–Pittsburgh Steel Corp. v. United Steelworkers of America*,[5] the court recognized that

> [t]he "necessary" standard cannot be satisfied by a mere showing that it would be desirable for the trustee to reject a prevailing labor contract so that the debtor can lower its costs. Such an indulgent standard would inadequately differentiate between labor contracts, which Congress sought to protect, and other commercial contracts, which trustees can disavow at will. * * * [section 1113] requires that "necessary" be construed strictly to signify only modifications that the trustee is constrained to accept because they are directly related to the Company's financial conditions and its reorganization.

On the other hand, courts have acknowledged that section 1113(b)(1)(A) does not oblige a petitioning employer to demonstrate that its proposed modifications include the absolutely minimal changes needed for a successful reorganization. It need only show that the proposed alterations are reasonably necessary.

---

4. 11 U.S.C.A. § 1113.   **5.** 791 F.2d 1074 (3d Cir.1986).

Proposed contractual alterations must ensure that "all of the affected parties are treated fairly and equitably." This language is designed to guarantee that the burden of economic hardship during the reorganization process does not disadvantage unionized employees to a disproportionate degree. Bankruptcy courts endeavor to satisfy this statutory mandate by conditioning approval of proposed collective bargaining agreement modifications upon a concomitant company promise to reduce other managerial costs in a commensurate manner.

Once a financially moribund company proposes changes in an existing bargaining agreement and provides the representative labor organization with the information it needs to evaluate the propriety of the suggested modifications, section 1113(b)(2) obliges the firm and the union "to confer in good faith in attempting to reach mutually satisfactory modifications." It is important to recognize that Congress chose the identical "confer in good faith" language used in section 8(d) of the NLRA to define the duty of labor-management parties to bargain in good faith. Nonetheless, because of the obvious exigencies involved in a reorganization effort, something less than extended and comprehensive collective bargaining should usually be sufficient to satisfy the Bankruptcy Code requirement. Management officials must offer labor leaders the opportunity to discuss proposed bargaining agreement changes and to consider less drastic alternatives that might equally address employer financial concerns. Where a company fails to provide the representative labor organization with a meaningful opportunity to explore the proposed contractual modifications, a request for bankruptcy court approval of the corporate reorganization plan is likely to be rejected. When a bankrupt firm proposes bargaining agreement modifications that are primarily designed to preserve firm equity and to avoid liability for early withdrawal from participation in a union pension fund and not to limit the negative impact of the bankruptcy on affected workers, the court is likely to find that the petitioning company has failed to confer with the representative labor organization in good faith.

Under section 1113(c)(2), a bankruptcy court may approve proposed bargaining agreement modifications only where "the authorized representative of the employees has refused to accept [the employer's] proposal without good cause." Neither the statute nor its legislative history delineates the applicable "good cause" standard. If a labor union can demonstrate that a company's suggested contractual changes are not really "necessary to permit the reorganization of the debtor" or do not assure that "all of the affected parties are [being] treated fairly and equitably," as mandated by section 1113(b)(1)(A), this will probably indicate that its refusal to assent to the proposed changes was for "good cause." On the other hand, if a labor organization simply rejected the employer's proposed contractual changes due to the possible effect on other bargaining agreements or because it did not wish to give up valuable fringe benefits, a court would likely conclude that it did not act with "good cause."

Even when all of the other statutory prerequisites are satisfied, a bankruptcy court cannot approve an employer's request for bargaining agreement modifications unless it finally determines, pursuant to section 1113(c)(3), that "the balance of the equities clearly favors rejection." A bankruptcy court must carefully weigh such factors as: (1) the likelihood of a successful reorganization if the requested contractual relief is approved; (2) the probable impact upon the interested parties if the business entity were forced into liquidation under Chapter 7; (3) the possibility of a devastating work stoppage if all of the proposed reductions are implemented; (4) the capacity of the affected workers to withstand the suggested compensation decreases; and (5) the number of jobs that would be preserved through a favorable reorganization. If a petitioning employer fails to demonstrate that the equities clearly favor relief, its suggested contract alterations will be denied.

United Food and Commercial Workers Union Local 211 v. Family Snacks, Inc.,[6] concerned the right of a company to reject bargaining agreement obligations *after* it had sold its firm assets to another business enterprise. The court acknowledged that once the assets have been sold, the selling firm is no longer in a position to reorganize. Although section 1113(b)(1)(A) speaks in terms of bargaining agreement changes that are "necessary to permit the reorganization of the debtor," the court indicated that this language should not be construed literally to preclude bargaining obligation modifications requested by companies that have sold their assets to other firms and thus do not technically require changes for successful "reorganizations." The court decided to interpret this language to permit collective contract changes by such selling companies whenever they can demonstrate that the requested modifications are "necessary to accommodate confirmation of a Chapter 11 plan." So long as the other statutory prerequisites are satisfied, firms selling their assets may still avail themselves of the contract modification rights set forth in section 1113 if such action is a necessary part of their proposed bankruptcy schemes.

In re United States Truck Company Holdings[7] concerned the right of a company going through a complete liquidation to use section 1113 to reject bargaining agreement obligations. Although the requirements of that section specifically refer to changes necessary to permit the successful "reorganization" of moribund firms, the court held that bargaining agreement modifications should also be allowed when necessary to assist liquidating companies. The petitioning entities must demonstrate that they have satisfied the statutory prerequisites to bargaining agreement changes. In liquidation settings, petitioning companies need not show that the requested changes are necessary to permit successful reorganizations, but rather to allow the prompt and efficient administration of the failing estates. Since U.S. Trucking Company Holdings failed to confer with the representative labor organization in good faith because it sought changes primarily designed to preserve firm equity and to avoid liability for early withdrawal from participation in the union pension fund and not to limit the negative impact on affected employees, the court rejected the firm's proposed bargaining agreement modifications.

Although an employer may normally not alter existing bargaining agreement provisions without satisfying the specific prerequisites set forth in section 1113, a company may be able to obtain interim relief in extraordinary cases. Section 1113(e) authorizes bankruptcy court approval of such interim modifications when the business firm can demonstrate at a special expedited hearing that immediate contractual changes are "essential to the continuation of the debtor's business" or are required in order to "avoid irreparable damage to the estate." When exigent circumstances warrant interim relief from collective bargaining agreement obligations, a court may approve the requested short-term changes even if those modifications do not constitute the actual "rejection" of contractual terms. If an employer is unable to convince the court that such exigent circumstances exist, interim relief will be denied.

Under section 365(k) of the Bankruptcy Code, the assignment of a contract by the trustee to an external entity relieves the trustee and the estate of liability for any contractual breach occurring after the assignment. In *American Flint Glass Workers Union v. Anchor Resolution*,[8] the court held that this provision operates independently from section 1113 and covers the assignment of existing collective bargaining agreements, but only where the third party assumes the collective contract *cum onere*—i.e., subject to all of the burdens and obligations under that agreement. If the contract assignment fails to oblige the assuming party to accept unconditional responsibility for the outstanding contractual obligations, the trustee and estate remain liable for the on-going contractual burdens. If the trustee wishes to modify the existing contractual obligations prior to the assignment, the trustee must do so pursuant to the requirements set forth in section 1113.

§ 10.3   Bankruptcy—Priority for Unpaid Compensation and Benefits

When a company seeks bankruptcy protection, it usually has outstanding wage and fringe benefit obligations. If it decides to reorganize under Chapter 11, it will incur additional wage and benefit liabilities during the reorganization. The Bankruptcy Code carefully distinguishes between pre-petition and post-petition wage and benefit obligations.

Although employees are not secured creditors, they are provided with certain wage and fringe benefit priorities under section 507 of the Bankruptcy Code. After outstanding liabilities are satisfied under the first and second priorities, pertaining to administrative expenses and to unsecured claims of parties furnishing goods, services, or credit to the petitioning firm after the filing of the petition and before appointment of

---

8.   197 F.3d 76 (3d Cir.1999).

the trustee, the remaining employer assets are used to reimburse employees for wages, salaries, and commissions earned within ninety days before the filing of the bankruptcy petition or the cessation of the debtor's business. The third priority also covers vacation, severance, and sick leave pay "earned" during the ninety day pre-petition/business cessation period.

Courts generally treat such benefits as if they accrue continuously as work is performed and limit third priority status to the amount of vacation, severance, and sick leave pay attributable to the ninety-day pre-petition/business cessation period. Employee claims for vacation, severance, and sick leave pay earned more than ninety days prior to the petition filing or business cessation are usually treated as unsecured, general claims not entitled to statutory priority. If a court finds, however, that a severance pay obligation constitutes "compensation for termination," it may conclude that the entire amount of such payments became due at the time of discharge. The total payment would then be entitled to third priority status, if the termination occurred during the ninety-day pre-petition/business cessation period.

When an employee has an individual employment contract for two or three years duration and the employer prematurely terminates that contractual relationship, the discharged employee may seek judicial redress. If the employer files a bankruptcy petition, section 502(b)(7) limits the period for which back pay may be awarded. That section provides that a bankruptcy court shall allow such a claim "except to the extent that—(7) if such claim is the claim of an employee for damages resulting from the termination of an employment contract, such claim exceeds—(A) the compensation provided by such contract, without acceleration, for one year following the earlier of—(1) the date of the filing of the petition: or (2) the date on which the employer directed the employee to terminate* * *." In *Anthony v. Interform Corp.,*[1] the Third Circuit held that the bankruptcy court had properly reduced a wrongfully terminated employee's back pay claim under a two-year employment contract to the one-year period set forth in section 502(b)(7).

It is important to recognize that the third priority applies only to "wages, salaries, or commissions." Although this priority has been liberally construed in favor of coverage, courts have refused to apply it to clearly non-compensation items such as moving expenses. Courts also have noted that the third priority was designed to protect individuals who reasonably need statutory protection. "Priority of payment was intended for the benefit only of those who are dependent upon their wages, and who, having lost their employment by the bankruptcy, would be in need of such protection." This consideration induced one court to deny the priority claim of an independent contractor who sought unpaid commissions on mobile homes he had sold for the bankrupt firm.

Fourth priority status is accorded to claims for unpaid employer contributions to employee benefit plans, such as pension, health insur-

§ 10.3
1. 96 F.3d 692 (3d Cir.1996).

ance, and life insurance programs, that pertain to services performed by employees within 180 days before the petition filing or business cessation. If the outstanding amount was earned over a period of more than 180 days, courts only grant priority status to the portion that accrued during the 180–day pre-petition/business cessation period. Sums earned more than 180 days before the filing of the bankruptcy petition or the business cessation are treated as unsecured claims not entitled to any statutory priority. The maximum amount of money subject to section 507(a)(4)(B) priority is equal to $2,000 times the number of employees covered by each plan, minus the aggregate amount paid to the employees under the third priority for wages, salaries, and commissions, *plus* the aggregate amount paid on behalf of the employees to any other benefit plan. The maximum aggregate amount payable to benefit plans under the fourth priority is thus $2,000 per employee. If the claims filed by different benefit plan administrators for unpaid employer contributions exceed $2,000 per covered worker, the various plans must divide the available funds on a pro rata basis.

Wages and benefits earned by employees *after* a bankruptcy petition has been filed and during the reorganization of their employer are accorded greater protection than pre-petition earnings. Section 507(a)(1) grants first priority to "administrative expenses allowed under section 503(b)." Section 503(b)(1)(A) indicates that "administrative expenses" include "the actual, necessary costs and expenses of preserving the estate, including wages, salaries, or commissions for services rendered after the commencement of the case." During a reorganization, the trustee will frequently continue to employ the personnel needed to continue basic operations. The compensation earned by these employees constitutes "administrative expenses" entitled to first priority status.

Questions occasionally arise with respect to the priority status of pension fund payments that become due during the post-petition period. To be eligible for section 507(a)(1) "administrative expense" priority, the amounts due must have actually been *earned* during the post-petition time frame. As a result, when pension fund contributions become due during the post-petition period, bankruptcy courts must differentiate between the portion of the pension obligation earned pre-petition and the portion earned post-petition, with only the part earned during the post-petition period being accorded section 507(a)(1) "administrative expense" priority.

The priority status of vacation pay, severance pay, and employer contributions to insurance programs and pension plans is directly related to the time frame during which those forms of deferred compensation accrued.

> Congress granted priority to administrative expenses in order to facilitate the efforts of the trustee or debtor in possession to rehabilitate the business for the benefit of all the estate's creditors. * * * Accordingly, an expense is administrative only if it arises out of a transaction between the creditor and the bankrupt's trustee or

debtor in possession * * * and "only to the extent that the consideration supporting the claimant's right to payment was both supplied to and beneficial to the debtor-in-possession in the operation of the business."[2]

Vacation pay, insurance obligations, and pension fund premiums earned by employees during the post-petition period are entitled to first priority status as administrative expenses. Vacation pay earned during the ninety-day period before the date the bankruptcy petition was filed is accorded third priority under section 507(a)(3), while insurance premiums and pension fund contributions earned during the 180 day pre-petition period are granted fourth priority status under section 507(a)(4).

Courts have had a more difficult time determining the priority status to be assigned to "severance pay." Courts that regard severance pay as a benefit that accrues on a week-to-week basis usually accord first priority status only to that portion of the severance pay earned during the post-petition period. These courts believe that the section 507(a)(1) priority was only intended to cover expenses incurred by the debtor-in-possession to maintain, preserve, or rehabilitate the bankrupt estate. Other courts, however, treat severance pay as "compensation for termination," and provide first priority for the entire amount due to workers who are discharged after the filing of the bankruptcy petition.

§ 10.4   Plant Closings and Mass Layoffs—State Laws

Fourteen states have laws regulating plant closings and/or work relocations. Some impose affirmative obligations upon employers, while others merely suggest voluntary conduct.

California[1] requires commercial and industrial firms that employ 75 or more employees to provide sixty-days advance notice of plant closings, relocations of all or substantially all operations to facilities 100 miles or more away from existing plants, or "mass layoffs" involving the "layoff during any 30-day period of 50 or more employees at a covered establishment." Advance notice must be given to the adversely affected employees, the Employment Development Department, the local workforce investment board, and the chief elected official of each city and county within which the termination, relocation, or mass layoff occurs. Failure to provide advance notice is excused when an employer is seeking capital or business that would enable it to avoid or postpone a relocation or termination and the employer reasonably and in good faith believes that giving the sixty-days notice would prevent it from obtaining the requisite capital or business. A covered firm that fails to provide the required advance notice is liable to the adversely affected workers for the days of notice not provided and to a civil penalty of up to $500 for each day of the employer's violation.

2. Trustees of Amalgamated Ins. Fund v. McFarlin's, Inc., 789 F.2d 98, 101 (2d Cir.1986), quoting In re Mammoth Mart, Inc., 536 F.2d 950, 954 (1st Cir.1976).

§ 10.4

1. Cal. Lab. Code pt. 4, div. 2 §§ 1400–1408.

Connecticut[2] requires companies with 100 or more employees to pay for the continuation of existing group health insurance for employees displaced by plant closings or relocations involving the removal of all or substantially all of the industrial or commercial operations in a covered establishment to a location outside Connecticut. The insurance must be provided for 120 days following the date of closing or relocation or until the displaced employees become eligible for other group health coverage.

Hawaii[3] requires companies with fifty or more employees to provide forty-five days advance notice of plant closures, partial plant closures, and relocations involving the removal of all or substantially all of the industrial or commercial operations in a covered establishment to a location outside Hawaii to affected employees and to the State Director of Labor Relations. In addition, section 394B–10 requires companies to pay displaced employees eligible for unemployment compensation the difference between their average weekly wages prior to a covered closure or relocation and their weekly unemployment compensation benefits during the four weeks following their displacement. Business firms that violate the duties imposed under this section may be required to pay each affected employee an amount equal to the total value of the wages, benefits, and other compensation earned by each during the three months preceding the closure or relocation. Employees may also obtain injunctive relief and reasonable attorney fees.

Illinois[4] requires private firms that must provide advance notice of plant closings or mass layoffs under the Worker Adjustment and Re-training Notification Act (WARN) and that have received state or local economic development incentives for doing business or continuing to conduct business in Illinois to provide copies of the WARN notice to the Governor, the Speaker and Minority Leader of the House, the President and Minority Leader of the Senate, and Mayor of each municipality in which the firm is located within the state. Companies failing to provide the required notices may have all or some of their incentive payments terminated and the due date of all or part of any indebtedness to the state or local government may be accelerated by notice given to the defaulting firm.

Maine[5] requires companies with 100 or more employees that terminate operations or remove all or substantially all industrial or commercial operations to a new location, within or outside Maine, 100 or more miles from the original location, to provide severance pay equal to one week's pay for each year of employment to all employees with at least three years of service, unless the closure or relocation is necessitated by a physical calamity. Business firms must also provide the Director of the State Bureau of Labor with sixty days advance written notice of proposed plant closures or relocations. Companies planning to relocate a covered plant outside Maine must provide the affected employees and

2. Conn.Stat.Ann. §§ 31–51o(a)–(c).

3. Haw.Rev.Stat. § 394B–1 to–8.

4. 30 Ill.Stat.Ann. § 760/15.

5. Me.Rev.Stat.Ann.tit. 26, § 625–B(1)–(7).

the local municipality with 60 days advance notice. Civil fines of up to $500 may be imposed upon violators, unless the failure to provide the required advance notice is due to a physical calamity or unforeseen circumstances.

Maryland[6] covers companies with at least fifty employees that have been in business for at least one year planning to relocate operations or to reduce the number of employees at a workplace by twenty-five percent or fifteen employees, whichever is greater, over any three-month period. The law suggests that covered employers voluntarily provide at least ninety days advance notice to affected employees. It also directs the State Secretary of Employment and Training to develop voluntary guidelines for companies to follow with respect to advance notice and the continuation of health and pension coverage.

Massachusetts[7] requests that companies with fifty or more employees voluntarily provide affected personnel and the State Director of the Division of Employment Security with advance notice of proposed plant closings that will result in the dislocation of at least ninety percent of workers. State law requires firms with twelve or more employees to provide the Director with advance notice of planned relocations within Massachusetts. Parties that knowingly violate this section may be fined up to $100.

Michigan[8] encourages employee-owned businesses with twenty-five or more employees to provide affected workers and the State Department of Labor with advance notice of plant closings or production relocations.

Minnesota[9] instructs the Commissioner of Jobs and Services to encourage business establishments contemplating plant closures, operational relocations, or substantial layoffs to provide advance notice to representative unions, affected employees, and the local government unit involved.

Montana[10] requires each state agency to notify affected employees, their representative labor organization, affected local governments, and a local newspaper of mass layoffs of at least 250 people that will be effectuated over a two-year period. The law does not cover private employers.

Oregon[11] requires employers covered by the Federal Worker Adjustment and Retraining Notification Act to provide advance notice of plant closures and mass layoffs to the Economic Development Department and directs that Department to apprise affected employers of programs and forms of assistance the Department and other state agencies can provide

6. Md. Code Ann. art. 83A, §§ 3–301 to 3–304.

7. Mass. Laws Ann. ch. 149, § 179B, ch. 151A, §§ 71A–G.

8. Mich.Comp. Laws § 450.731 to .737.

9. Minn.Stat. § 268.975 to .979.

10. Mont. Code Ann. §§ 39–2–1001 to 1004.

11. Or.Rev.Stat. § 285.453 to 285.463.

to communities, companies, and workers affected by plant closures and mass layoffs.

South Carolina[12] regulates only employers that require their employees to provide advance notice before they quit. The law requires covered firms to post written notices regarding proposed temporary or permanent plant closures not less than two weeks in advance or the same length of time required of employees before they resign. Violators are subject to fines of up to $5000 and are liable to employees for damages suffered because of their failure to provide them with adequate notice, except where the lack of advance notice is due to an unforeseen accident to machinery or an act of God.

Tennessee[13] requires companies with at least fifty but not more than ninety-nine full-time employees to provide advance notice to affected employees and the State Department of Labor of proposed plant closures, relocations more than fifty miles from the existing site, or reductions that will displace fifty or more employees within a three-month period. The statute does not specify the exact amount of advance notice that must be given.

Wisconsin[14] requires companies with at least fifty employees to provide affected employees, the Department of Industry, Labor, and Human Resources, and the highest official of the local municipality with sixty days advance notice of any planned plant closing that will displace twenty-five or more employees or any mass layoff affecting twenty-five employees or twenty-five percent of the company's workforce, whichever is greater, or 500 or more employees. Failure to provide such notice will be excused if: (1) the operations are relocated to another area within a reasonable commuting distance from the closed facility and the employer offers to transfer substantially all of the affected employees to the new location within six months; (2) the reductions are due to unforeseeable business circumstances or a natural or human-generated disaster beyond the control of the company; or (3) the firm was actively seeking capital or business to enable it to avoid or postpone indefinitely the closing or layoffs and the employer reasonably believed that giving the required notice would have prevented the company from obtaining the necessary capital or business. Companies that improperly fail to provide timely notice are liable to affected employees for the wages and benefits they would have earned during the period of omitted notice. They are also subject to penalties of up to $500 for each day they failed to provide timely notice to local municipality officials.

§ 10.5 Plant Closings and Mass Layoffs—Worker Adjustment and Retraining Notification Act (WARN)

In 1988, Congress enacted the Worker Adjustment and Retraining

12. S.C. Code § 41–1–40.

13. Tenn. Code §§ 50–1–601 to 50–1–604.

14. Wis.Stat.Ann. § 109.07.

Notification Act (WARN).[1] WARN covers companies that employ 100 full-time workers or 100 or more full-and part-time employees who work an aggregate of at least 4,000 hours per week, exclusive of overtime. "Part-time employees" include not only workers who average fewer than twenty hours per week, but also those persons who have been employed for fewer than six of the twelve preceding months.

A Department of Labor regulation extends WARN Act coverage to "public and quasi-public entities which engage in business * * * and which are separately organized from the regular government, which have their own governing bodies and which ave independent authority to manage their personnel and assets." In *Castro v. Chicago Housing Authority*,[2] the court found that both the WARN Act and its legislative history are silent with respect to whether municipal corporations are covered within the statutory definition of "business entities." Nonetheless, it concluded that the DOL regulation extending coverage to municipal corporations and quasi-public bodies constitutes a permissible construction of the statute.

Section 2102(a) requires covered employers to provide sixty days advance notice of planned "plant closings" and "mass layoffs" to affected employees or their representative labor organizations, if any, and to appropriate state and local government units. A "plant closing" involves "the permanent or temporary shutdown of a single site of employment, or one or more facilities or operating units within a single site of employment, if the shutdown results in an employment loss at the single site of employment during any thirty-day period for fifty or more employees excluding any part-time employees." The term "mass layoff" includes single site employment losses within a thirty-day period of at least thirty-three percent of the full-time employees and at least fifty full-time personnel, or the displacement of at least 500 full-time workers. "Employment losses" include terminations, other than discharges for cause or voluntary separations, layoffs exceeding six months in duration, and reductions in hours of work of more than fifty percent during each month of any six-month period. The Second Circuit has ruled, however, that "employment losses" do not include individuals displaced from a closed department who are immediately transferred to new positions at nearby facilities.

Graphic Communications International Union v. Quebecor Printing (USA) Corp.[3] concerned a company that notified employees on September 18 of a planned December layoff expected to last longer than six months. The layoff began on December 11, but on December 16, the firm decided to close the plant permanently, and it immediately notified the representative labor organization of this decision. The company argued that the September 18 notice of the planned December 11 layoff should also apply to the December 16 plant closure. The court rejected this

§ 10.5

1. 29 U.S.C.A. §§ 2101–2109.

2. 360 F.3d 721 (7th Cir.2004).

3. 252 F.3d 296 (4th Cir.2001).

claim, holding that different forms of employment losses require separate notices under WARN.

In *Viator v. Delchamps, Inc.*,[4] the court articulated the factors to be used to determine whether separate facilities should be considered a "single site of employment" for WARN Act purposes: (1) geographic proximity; (2) sameness of purpose; and (3) sharing of staff and equipment. Since the *Viator* court found that three separate grocery stores that were part of a chain and were located within twelve miles of each other did not share staff or equipment, they did not constitute a single employment site when they closed.

The WARN notice requirements do not apply to a plant closing or mass layoff caused by "any form of natural disaster," such as a flood, earthquake, or drought. Advance notice is not required for a relocation or consolidation of part or all of an employer's business, if, prior to the resulting plant closing or mass layoff, the company offers to transfer the employee being displaced to a different employment site within a reasonable commuting distance with no more than a six-month break in employment, or the employer offers to transfer the affected employee to another employment site, regardless of the distance from the prior facility, with no more than a six-month break in employment, and the employee accepts the transfer within thirty days of the offer or of the plant closing or mass layoff, whichever is later.

No advance notice is required when the closing involves a temporary facility or the closing or mass layoff is the result of the completion of a particular project, so long as the affected employees were hired with the understanding that their employment was limited to the duration of the facility or the particular project. The advance notice rules are similarly inapplicable to employment losses created by a strike or lockout that is not intended to evade the WARN notice obligations, and no advance notice need be given to economic strikers who are permanently replaced.

In certain situations, employers may be allowed to provide less than sixty-days advance notice of plant closings or mass layoffs, but they must clearly demonstrate that their circumstances fall within one of the statutory exceptions. A company "may order the shutdown of a single site of employment before the conclusion of the sixty-day period, if as of the time that notice would have been required, the employer was actively seeking capital or business which, if obtained, would have enabled the employer to avoid or postpone the shutdown and the employer reasonably and in good faith believed that giving the notice required would have precluded the employer from obtaining the needed capital or business."

A firm also may order a plant closing or mass layoff before the conclusion of the sixty-day notice period if the closing or layoff "is caused by business circumstances that were not reasonably foreseeable

---

4. 109 F.3d 1124 (5th Cir.), cert. denied,   109 (1997).
522 U.S. 862, 118 S.Ct. 165, 139 L.Ed.2d

as of the time that notice would have been required." Such circumstances may involve firms that have unexpectedly lost major customers, that have experienced unanticipated work stoppages, or have inexplicably lost anticipated business deals. If the exigent business circumstances are not truly "unforeseeable," courts are unlikely to find this exception applicable.

Companies relying upon either the actively seeking capital or business or the unforeseeable business circumstances exception must provide as much advance notice of the impending employee displacements as is practicable, and it must give a brief statement of the circumstances warranting a reduction in the notification period.

There are occasions when a mass layoff is not initially expected to exceed six months in duration. If such a layoff continues for more than six months, the failure to provide affected employees with sixty-days advance notice will constitute a violation, unless "(1) the extension beyond 6 months is caused by business circumstances (including unforeseeable changes in price or cost) not reasonably foreseeable at the time of the initial layoff; and (2) notice is given at the time it becomes reasonably foreseeable, that the extension beyond 6 months will be required."

There are times when the cumulative employment losses from two or more separate reductions at a single site of employment, each affecting an insufficient number of employees to trigger the WARN notice obligation, may be added together to create an advance notice duty. When such employment losses occur within a ninety-day period and the aggregate number of employees being displaced exceeds the statutory minimum, advance notice will be required, "unless the employer demonstrates that the employment losses are the result of separate and distinct actions and causes and are not an attempt by the employer to evade the requirements" of the Act.

Aggrieved employees, including personnel who suffer a reduction in their hours of work of more than fifty percent during each month during any six-month period, who are not provided with timely advance notice of plant closings or mass layoffs may maintain civil actions in federal district courts against the offending employers. Each employee is entitled to back pay for each day of violation at a rate of compensation not less than the higher of: (1) the average regular rate received by the employee during the last three years of that person's employment or (2) the final regular rate received by that employee. Although an early Third Circuit decision held that WARN Act back pay liability should be calculated on a *work day* basis, with aggrieved individuals being entitled to compensation for up to sixty *work days*, more recent decisions have concluded that Congress intended back pay to be determined on a *calendar day* basis with affected personnel being entitled to back pay for the number of work days falling during the sixty-*calendar-day* notice period. The offending employer is also liable to aggrieved personnel for the cost of their fringe benefit coverage during the period of violation, even if those employees did not suffer any compensable loss during that time frame. A company's liability is limited to a maximum of sixty days, but cannot exceed one-half of the total number of days the person was employed by the offending employer. The court may award the prevailing party reasonable attorney fees.

Williams v. Phillips Petroleum Co.[5] involved employees who were laid off during work force reductions. In exchange for additional severance benefits, they signed releases waiving all claims against their employer relating to their employment and their layoffs. When they subsequently filed WARN Act claims, the court found that their releases had validly waived their WARN Act rights, even though they did not expressly mention the WARN Act. The waiver language unambiguously covered their layoffs, and the releases advised them to seek legal advice and provided them with sufficient time to do so.

Section 2102(a) requires employers to give advance notice of plant closures and mass layoffs to labor organizations that represent the affected employees. When a company fails to provide a representative union with the requisite notice, may that union sue on behalf of the adversely affected bargaining unit members? In *UFCW Local 751 v. Brown Group, Inc.*,[6] a unanimous Supreme Court indicated that under modern associational standing concepts, an organization may sue to redress member injuries when: (1) its members would otherwise have standing to sue in their own right; (2) the interests it seeks to protect are germane to the organization's purpose; and (3) neither the claim asserted nor the relief requested requires the participation of individual members in the lawsuit. The Court noted that representative unions are expressly authorized to receive notice on behalf of affected personnel. It then found that since all three associational standing prerequisites were satisfied, labor organizations have standing to sue on behalf of adversely affected bargaining unit members.

WARN does not specify any statute of limitations for actions brought by aggrieved employees or their representative labor unions. In *North Star Steel Co. v. Thomas*,[7] the Supreme Court determined that courts presented with WARN Act cases should borrow the limitations period from the most analogous state statute. Several circuit courts have decided that state contract action limitation periods are most appropriate for WARN Act suits.

An employer that does not provide advance notice to the appropriate local government unit is subject to a civil penalty of not more than $500 for each day of the violation, up to a maximum of sixty days.

A firm's liability to an aggrieved employee shall be reduced by "(A) any wages paid by the employer to the employee for the period of the

5. 23 F.3d 930 (5th Cir.), cert. denied, 513 U.S. 1019, 115 S.Ct. 582, 130 L.Ed.2d 497 (1994).

6. 517 U.S. 544, 116 S.Ct. 1529, 134 L.Ed.2d 758 (1996).

7. 515 U.S. 29, 115 S.Ct. 1927, 132 L.Ed.2d 27 (1995).

violation; (B) any voluntary and unconditional payment by the employer to the employee that is not required by any legal obligation; and (C) any payment made by the employer to a third party or trustee (such as premiums for health benefits or payments to a defined contribution pension plan) on behalf of and attributable to the employee for the period of the violation." The company's liability is similarly reduced with respect to service credits granted to an employee under a defined benefit pension plan for the period of the violation. If an offending employer can demonstrate "that the act or omission that violated this chapter was in good faith and that the employer had reasonable grounds for believing that the act or omission was not a violation * * * the court may, in its discretion, reduce the amount of the liability or penalty provided * * *."

In *Frymire v. Ampex Corp.*,[8] the court held that severance benefits given "in lieu of notice" could not be used to offset WARN Act payments owed to employees who had not been given sufficient advance notice of layoffs, because contractually-required severance payments are not covered by section 2104(a)(2). The *Frymire* court indicated, however, that such a severance pay policy could be relevant under section 2104(a)(4) with respect to an employer's claim for a "good faith" reduction in WARN Act liability.

The specific remedies set forth in WARN are the exclusive remedies available for violations of that statute. Federal courts are expressly denied the authority to enjoin impending plant closings or mass layoffs. A court may, however, issue an injunction to prevent the dissipation of company assets needed to satisfy potential WARN liability. Punitive damages may not be awarded to aggrieved employees under WARN. Nonetheless, the rights and remedies provided to aggrieved employees under WARN are in addition to, and not in lieu of, any other contractual or statutory rights and remedies that may be available to displaced personnel.

§ 10.6   Unemployment Compensation—History and Financing

The original unemployment compensation insurance provisions were set forth in Titles III and IX of the Social Security Act. A federal payroll tax of 3.0% was imposed on covered employers. A credit of up to 90%, or 2.7%, was provided for amounts paid by employers into qualified state unemployment compensation funds. This offset feature was designed to induce state legislatures to adopt their own unemployment compensation laws to enable the employers in their respective states to benefit from the 2.7% tax credit. The remaining 0.3% portion of the federal payroll tax was to cover the cost of administering the federal/state unemployment compensation system. Within two years after the enactment of the

---

8.   61 F.3d 757 (10th Cir.1995), cert. dismissed, 517 U.S. 1182, 116 S.Ct. 1588, 134   L.Ed.2d 685 (1996).

Social Security Act, every state and the District of Columbia had established unemployment compensation programs.

Covered employers that did not pay the full 2.7% tax into a state unemployment fund were still allowed the 2.7% federal tax offset if they were assessed a state unemployment tax of less than 2.7% under experience-rating regulations that satisfied federal requirements. This rule enabled employers that did not lay off workers on a regular basis to contribute less than 2.7% to the state unemployment compensation fund while still receiving the entire 2.7% offset with respect to the 3.0% federal payroll tax.

As part of the Federal Unemployment Tax Act (FUTA), the federal payroll tax scheme is now codified in 26 U.S.C.A. §§ 3301–3311. These sections regulate the federal tax, the tax credits available to state unemployment compensation programs, and the minimal requirements state plans must satisfy to qualify for federal tax credit.

The FUTA currently imposes a 6.2% payroll tax on the first $7,000 paid annually by covered employers to each employee. Of this 6.2%, 6.0% constitutes the basic tax rate. The extra 0.2% represents a "temporary" surtax that partially finances extended unemployment benefits that are available during recessionary periods. This "temporary" surtax began in 1976 and has been repeatedly extended by Congress. Employers in states with federally approved unemployment compensation programs that do not have outstanding federal loans are given a tax credit of up to 90% of the basic 6.0% federal rate (i.e., 5.4%) toward assessed state unemployment taxes.

The full 5.4% credit is available to employers covered by a 5.4% state unemployment tax rate that do not actually contribute 5.4% to the state fund pursuant to an experience rating system that reduces their effective tax rate. The FUTA requires state experience-based tax reductions to be based on not less than three years of "experience with respect to unemployment or other factors bearing a direct relation to unemployment risk." All fifty states and the District of Columbia have established experience-rating systems.

§ 10.7 Unemployment Compensation—Included and Excluded Employers and Employees

The FUTA specifies the employers that state unemployment compensation programs must cover to enable states to qualify for the 5.4% federal tax credit. All states are required to cover:

(1) Employers that paid wages of $1,500 or more during any calendar quarter during the current or the preceding calendar year or that employed at least one worker on at least one day of each of twenty weeks during the current or the preceding calendar year.

(2) Employers that paid cash wages of $20,000 or more for agricultural labor during any calendar quarter during the current or the preceding calendar year or that employed at least ten agricultur-

al workers on at least one day of each of twenty weeks during the current or the preceding calendar year.

(3) Domestic service employers that paid cash wages of $1,000 or more during any calendar quarter during the current or the preceding calendar year for domestic service in a private home, local college club, or local chapter or a college fraternity or sorority.

(4) Nonprofit organizations that employed four or more employees for one day during each of twenty different weeks during the current or the preceding calendar year and state and local governments.

States are permitted to establish their own coverage standards, but they must satisfy the minimum federal requirements if their employers are to be entitled to the federal tax credit. Thirty-two states have adopted the basic federal definition of employer—i.e., a quarterly payroll of $1,500 during the current or the preceding calendar year or the employment of at least one worker in each of twenty weeks during the current or the preceding calendar year. Nine states and the District of Columbia include all employers that have any employees during the current year. The other nine states have requirements that are less restrictive than the federal standards.

§ 10.8 Unemployment Compensation—Employment Relationship

The FUTA and state unemployment compensation statutes only cover parties in an employer-employee relationship. In the federal enactment, the term "employee" is generally defined to include "any individual who, under the usual common law rules applicable in determining the employer-employee relationship, has the status of an employee." Fifteen states and the District of Columbia have used similar language in their statutes to cover all individuals in a "master-servant" or "contract-of-employment" relationship. Because these statutory definitions require application of common law doctrines, courts have frequently used the ten standards set forth in section 220 of the Restatement (Second) of Agency to determine whether a "master-servant" employment relationship exists:

(1) A servant is a person employed to perform services in the affairs of another and who with respect to the physical conduct in the performance of the services is subject to the other's control or right to control;

(2) In determining whether one acting for another is a servant or an independent contractor, the following matters of fact, among others, are considered:

(a) the extent of control which, by the agreement, the master may exercise over the details of the work;

(b) whether or not the one employed is engaged in a distinct occupation or business;

(c) the kind of occupation, with reference to whether, in the locality, the work is usually done under the direction of the employer or by a specialist without supervision;

(d) the skill required in the particular occupation;

(e) whether the employer or the workman supplies the instrumentalities, tools, and the place of work for the person doing the work;

(f) the length of time for which the person is employed;

(g) the method of payment, whether by the time or by the job;

(h) whether or not the work is a part of the regular business of the employer;

(i) whether or not the parties believe they are creating the relation of master and servant; and

(j) whether the principal is or is not in business.

In some cases, courts emphasize the so-called "control test" enunciated in both Paragraph 1 and part (a) of Paragraph 2 to resolve questions regarding the existence or nonexistence of an employment relationship. When the evidence demonstrates that the principal can exercise meaningful control over the individual's performance, courts usually find an employment relationship. In situations where the principal clearly lacks such control, independent contractor relationships are normally determined.

When the right-to-control factor does not unequivocally support an employment or an independent contractor relationship, courts generally evaluate the other Restatement factors. This occasionally occurs where the special skills possessed by the workers in question render close supervision impractical. The criteria supporting a covered master-servant relationship include: (1) the worker is not engaged in a distinct occupation or business; (2) the work is usually performed in the geographical area under the direction of an employer; (3) the work does not require the services of a highly skilled individual; (4) the principal supplies the tools and place of work; (5) the employment is for a considerable period of time and involves regular hours; (6) the individual is to work exclusively for one party; (7) the worker is to be paid by the hour, week, or month, and has not assumed the risk of loss if the work does not generate profits; (8) the work being performed is part of the regular business of the principal; (9) the parties thought that they were creating an employer-employee relationship; and (10) the principal party is engaged in a business activity.

Courts do not apply the Restatement factors on a strictly numerical basis. "The result in a particular case is governed by a weighing of all the factors in the light of the facts, and is almost completely 'a matter of judgment'." Even when the number of factors supporting an employment relationship is equal to or fewer than the number of factors indicating the presence of an independent contractor arrangement, an employer-employee relationship will generally be found if the employment relationship factors are more significant than the independent contractor factors. Courts often find an employment relationship in close cases, because they recognize that unemployment statutes are designed to protect individuals who are out of work. They thus interpret unemployment laws liberally to favor coverage.

Thirty-five states have adopted language providing unemployment compensation coverage that is usually considered more inclusive than the common law master-servant relationship. Their statutes cover all "service for remuneration," except where two or three exclusionary criteria are satisfied. Twenty-five states employ the so-called "ABC Test" that was incorporated in the Wisconsin unemployment compensation law in 1935. They include all individuals who perform remunerative services, unless an employer can demonstrate that:

(A) such individual has been and will continue to be free from control or direction over the performance of such service, both under his contract of service and in fact; and

(B) such service is either outside the usual course of the business for which such service is performed or that such service is performed outside of all the places of business of the enterprise for which such service is performed; and

(C) such individual is customarily engaged in an independently established trade, occupation, profession, or business.

Eight states include all persons who perform compensated services, unless a company can show that factors (A) and (C) are met, while Kansas includes all remunerated workers except where criteria (A) and (B) are satisfied.

Courts in several of the states that have incorporated the ABC Test apply their statutes as if their legislatures had codified the common law master-servant doctrine. They thus find covered employment relationships only in situations in which such relationships would be determined through application of the Restatement section 220 criteria. Courts in most ABC Test states, however, have assumed that the legislature envisioned broader coverage, and they frequently find covered employment relationships in circumstances that would probably not qualify for inclusion under the master-servant approach.

Under the ABC Test applied by the vast majority of courts operating in states with such statutory language, a company may normally escape unemployment compensation coverage only for workers who are truly free from employer control, who perform services outside the usual course of that company's business or who perform their work in their separate shops, *and* are engaged in an independent trade, occupation, profession, or business. If a company can merely establish the existence of one or two of these standards, most of the twenty-seven states that have incorporated all three exclusionary criteria will usually find a covered employment relationship.

The major controversies under the ABC Test concern individuals with attenuated work arrangements. These cases most often involve truck drivers, taxi drivers, commission salespeople, and home workers. When the principal retains the right to control the actual job performance of such persons, courts are likely to find covered employment relationships. For example, where truck drivers lease their vehicles from a freight company, drive exclusively or primarily for that carrier, and are expected to follow the instructions of that firm's dispatchers, employment relationships will normally be found. On the other hand, if the drivers own their own trucks, are able to work for various carriers, may hire their own assistants, and are permitted to determine whether they will carry particular loads, independent contractor arrangements will probably result. Similar standards are applied to taxi drivers. If they work primarily for one company, lease their vehicles from that firm, and are subject to meaningful company control with respect to their daily job performance, employment relationships are generally found. Where, however, the drivers own their taxis and basically decide when and how they will work, independent contractor status will normally be determined.

Salespeople who work for a specific firm, are compensated on a weekly or monthly basis, and are subject to the control of company managers are clearly covered employees. Even when such individuals are paid on a commission basis and work away from any company office, they will usually be considered covered employees if the other employment indicia are present. If, however, they are compensated on a commission basis, work primarily away from the principal's place of business, and are able to determine their own hours and the manner in which they will perform their work, courts applying the ABC Test will usually find independent contractor arrangements.

In a high-technology society, individuals will increasingly have the opportunity to work at home. They will be able to use computers and modems to conduct research, design products, and produce documents. When such home workers serve particular firms, are compensated on a weekly, monthly, or annual basis, and are subject to electronic or personal supervision over their job performance, they will be considered covered employees. Employment relationships will also be found when they are paid on a piece-work basis, so long as the principal retains the authority to control their job functions. Nonetheless, if such piece-work persons may work for different firms and they control their own hours and job performance, they will usually be considered uncovered independent contractors.

§ 10.9 Unemployment Compensation—Eligibility for Benefits

The mere fact that individuals are out of work does not necessarily indicate that they are entitled to unemployment compensation. They must first establish a requisite connection to covered employment. In all fifty states and the District of Columbia, people are only eligible for benefits if they earned at least a minimum amount of wages during the base period. Most states also require claimants to have been employed for at least a minimum amount of time during the base period. These eligibility rules are designed to limit the payment of unemployment benefits to those persons who are genuinely attached to the covered labor force. They also affect the amount of weekly benefits and the total weeks of benefits to be paid to each eligible claimant.

In forty-seven states and the District of Columbia, the "base period" is defined to include the first four calendar quarters of the last five completed calendar quarters preceding the filing of the claim for unemployment benefits. All fifty states and the District of Columbia restrict the receipt of unemployment benefits to those individuals who had specified minimum earnings during the base period. These statutory minima range from a low of $130 in Hawaii to a high of $3,400 in Florida. Most fall between $1,000 and $3,000. Every jurisdiction, except California, Colorado, Delaware, Massachusetts, Vermont, and Washington, also requires those applying for benefits to have been employed during at least two of the calendar quarters during the base period. Individuals who satisfy these requirements are eligible to apply for unemployment benefits when they are without work.

§ 10.10 Unemployment Compensation—Able to and Available for Work

Unemployment compensation is designed to provide financial assistance to individuals who are out of work and who wish to locate gainful employment. As a result, claimants are ineligible for benefits in all fifty states and the District of Columbia if they are not "able to work." This eligibility requirement generally relates to a person's physical and mental capacity to perform remunerative work. Claimants who are truly unable to engage in gainful employment must apply for workers' compensation if their conditions arose during and out of their employment or nonoccupational disability benefits if they did not.

The mere fact that claimants have a physical or mental problem does not automatically render them ineligible for unemployment benefits. So long as they are able to perform work suitable for persons with their training and experience, they will be found eligible for benefits. Even when they are not presently able to pursue their regular occupation, they will not lose their right to benefits if they are still able to engage in other remunerative employment. Doubts regarding this factor tend to be resolved in favor of eligibility.

The unemployment statutes in all fifty states and the District of Columbia contain eligibility provisions requiring benefit applicants to be available for work. Claimants must be able to demonstrate that they are ready and willing to work. State laws direct claimants to register at the appropriate public employment office, and this provides some evidence of availability. State unemployment offices usually require some additional indication that claimants are attempting to locate gainful employment.

The unemployment statutes in forty states and the District of Columbia require claimants to actively seek work if they wish to receive benefits. In these states, individuals are usually obliged to make reasonably diligent efforts each week to locate suitable employment. If unemployed persons normally obtain their jobs through union hiring halls, it may be sufficient for them to register for work with those entities. In other cases, they may be expected to file applications with firms that might have a need for workers with their skills and experience. Claimants who are unable to establish that they have made an active search for employment in these jurisdictions are likely to lose their benefit eligibility.

A temporary hiatus from the workforce does not necessarily result in a loss of claimant availability. For example, unemployed persons may take short vacations or enroll in training courses. So long as these individuals continue to look for employment and are willing to accept suitable jobs that may be found, they continue to be eligible for benefits. It is only when claimants effectively withdraw from the active labor force that they forfeit their right to receive unemployment compensation. Such ineligibility may result with respect to claimants who are forced to stay home to take care of young children or seriously ill family members and who are unable to remain available for work.

Claimants who relocate to different geographical areas while they are unemployed may encounter eligibility problems. This issue frequently arises when workers move to other regions to get married, to follow transferred spouses, or to find less expensive housing. Individuals who move to regions with as much potential for employment as the areas they left are generally considered "available for work," even when they move to different states. Difficulties may arise, however, when they relocate to areas that offer fewer job opportunities.

Numerous court decisions have liberally interpreted "availability" requirements to permit the payment of unemployment benefits to claimants who have relocated to areas with fewer job opportunities.

> The mere fact that a claimant has moved from one locality to another does not create a basis for holding him unavailable for work. If he registers for work in the new locality, and labor conditions there afford reasonable opportunities for work, he is available for work. Even if it appears that he might more readily have been employed had he remained in his former locality, he is nevertheless available for work if he is willing to take work for which opportunities exist in the new locality * * *. [T]he availability rule does not necessarily require that a claimant be available for his most recent work or his customary work. It is sufficient if he is able to do some type of work, and there is reasonable opportunity for securing such

work in the vicinity in which he lives.[1]

So long as there is a reasonable market in the new locale for the services the claimants are willing to perform, courts usually find them available for work. Nonetheless, when individuals relocate from one area to another and there are significantly diminished job opportunities in the new location, courts are likely to find the claimants unavailable for work.

Similar availability issues are raised by claimants who place restrictions upon the types of employment they will accept. People who are unable to withstand extreme job stress might refuse to consider employment opportunities that would involve unusual pressure. If they do not impose severe restrictions on the kinds of work they will perform and they remain willing to accept less stressful employment that is available, they will usually be found eligible for benefits. On the other hand, if claimants place undue limitations on the types of work they will accept, they will probably render themselves unavailable.

There are occasions when family or personal reasons cause claimants to indicate that they are unwilling to work the night shift or the day shift. For example, single parents with small children may refuse to consider anything but day work. If courts find that such limitations significantly reduce their availability for suitable employment, they will be found ineligible for benefits. This will be particularly likely where they impose restrictions that make it difficult for them to accept any full-time employment. A similar loss of eligibility may occur if claimants refuse to perform weekend work due to family obligations and this greatly diminishes their ability to locate work. Nonetheless, when such limitations do not significantly diminish employment opportunities, the claimants will usually be found available for work. For example, individuals who limit themselves to day or evening employment will still be found available for work, so long as suitable jobs are available during those hours. Unemployed individuals occasionally indicate that they are unwilling to accept employment that would require them to work on Saturdays or Sundays because of sincerely held religious convictions. States may not deny unemployment benefits to such persons based on their limited availability, because such action would contravene the free exercise clause of the First Amendment.

Some unemployed persons may impose other employment restrictions that may raise availability issues. These limitations may involve the physical environment, the location of work, the duration of employment, dress or grooming obligations, or compensation levels. The critical question in these cases involves the degree to which claimants have diminished the likelihood they will locate suitable employment. If their requirements significantly reduce their ability to find work, they will normally be found ineligible for benefits.

§ 10.10   A.2d 898 (1946).

1. Bliley Elec. Co. v. Unemployment Comp. Bd. of Review, 158 Pa.Super. 548, 45

Claimants occasionally indicate that they will only work in certain locations. If geographical restrictions meaningfully decrease job opportunities, they are likely to be found ineligible for benefits. Persons who previously performed home work may refuse to consider jobs that would require them to work elsewhere. Unless there continues to be a meaningful market for suitable home work, persons imposing such a restriction are likely to be found unavailable for work. A similar loss of eligibility will usually result for individuals who refuse to consider positions involving outdoor work.

People who are temporarily laid off from their regular jobs may inform prospective employers that they plan to return to their former positions as soon as they are available. Such representations are likely to induce firms to hire other applicants who can be expected to remain with them for prolonged periods. Courts often find that claimants who have limited their interim search to companies willing to hire short-term personnel have effectively rendered themselves unavailable for work.

Claimants are not usually obliged to seek employment that would involve remuneration substantially below that generally paid to individuals with their skill and experience. They are thus not rendered ineligible by virtue of their unwillingness to look for work involving truly substandard compensation. Nonetheless, as the period of their unemployment increases, they may be expected to "lower their sights." If they fail to do so, they may ultimately be found ineligible due to their unavailability.

§ 10.11 Unemployment   Compensation—Discharge   for Misconduct Connected With Employment

The unemployment statutes in all fifty states and the District of Columbia have provisions that disqualify claimants who have been recently terminated because of employment-related misconduct. In five states and the District of Columbia, the misconduct disqualification covers a specified number of weeks. In seven states, the disqualification is for a variable number of weeks, depending upon the severity of the misconduct involved. In the remaining thirty-eight states, the disqualification applies to the duration of the resulting period of unemployment. In these states, disqualified individuals may only regain their benefit eligibility through employment for a minimum number of weeks, post-termination earnings equal to a specified multiple of their weekly benefit amount, or a combination of these two factors. The most common provision requires post-termination earnings of from four to ten times their weekly benefit amount.

Twenty-two state unemployment statutes have additional disqualification provisions covering people terminated because of "gross misconduct." These special sections generally concern discharges based upon: admitted or convicted criminal theft connected with employment (Florida, Illinois, Indiana, Nevada, New York, Oregon, Utah, and Washington); work-related felony or misdemeanor convictions (Maine and Utah); employment-related dishonest or criminal act (Alabama); gross or aggravated misconduct at work (Maryland, Missouri and South Carolina); willful or flagrant employment-related misconduct (Maryland and Nebraska); or other similar acts of egregious misbehavior.

In fifteen states and the District of Columbia, the disqualification for gross misconduct is for the duration of the resulting unemployment. In the other seven states, the gross-misconduct disqualification is for six months, one year, or for a variable period of time.

The unemployment compensation system was created for the purpose of providing financial assistance to employees who become unemployed through no fault of their own. Courts are thus inclined to interpret eligibility rules liberally in favor of coverage. They also tend to interpret disqualification provisions narrowly to avoid benefit forfeitures in close cases. Nonetheless, when employers can demonstrate that claimants have engaged in disqualifying conduct, benefits will be withheld.

Courts have appropriately recognized that the general "misconduct" disqualification was designed to affect workers who have engaged in acts of wanton or willful misbehavior—deliberate violations of company rules or gross departures from accepted standards of conduct. Mere inadvertence or inattention will normally be insufficient to disqualify unemployment claimants. There must be evidence of intentional misconduct.

Misstatements on Job Applications

Individuals occasionally jeopardize their future right to unemployment benefits when they fill out their initial applications for employment. They may misrepresent their qualifications, their medical status, their criminal records, or other relevant factors. When applicants deliberately distort their job qualifications and their misstatements concern information that is material to their ability to perform the requisite work, they may lose their right to benefits if their misrepresentations are discovered and lead to their discharge. On the other hand, if they successfully perform their job tasks for several years before their previous misstatements are discovered, courts may find no disqualification, based upon the theory that their application falsifications were not truly material.

Job applicants do not always answer health questions completely. They may erroneously assume that inquiries regarding back problems, prior seizures, or chest pains are designed to elicit information regarding their current status. If they had such conditions several years ago but have had no recent incidents, they may decide not to mention those circumstances. When courts conclude that health omissions were due more to errors of judgment than to deliberate deceit, they usually refuse to disqualify the affected claimants. It is only when courts decide that job applicants willfully misrepresented medical information they realized was material with respect to the work they would perform that disqualification is likely to result. In close cases, doubts tend to be resolved in favor of the persons seeking unemployment benefits, because those alleging a disqualification must demonstrate claimant ineligibility.

Numerous cases involve claims that discharged workers are ineligible for unemployment benefits because of false job application statements they made with respect to questions about their criminal records. Even when it appears that applicants have deliberately concealed prior convictions, they will not be disqualified unless their omissions concerned material information. If their convictions did not involve violent acts or serious dishonesty and they were applying for positions that would not entail exposure to valuable property, their willful failure to provide the requested information may not prevent them from receiving benefits after they are terminated. If, however, the omitted convictions concerned violent behavior that would be relevant with respect to the way in which they might interact with fellow employees or the general public, they would probably be disqualified. A similar loss of eligibility would be likely where applicants failed to disclose conduct evidencing a lack of personal integrity and they were seeking employment in positions of trust. Even when their jobs do not involve positions of trust, they may still be disqualified if they are exposed to valuables owned by customers and they willfully fail to disclose previous convictions involving dishonesty.

Insubordination

Employees discharged because of insubordination may find themselves disqualified for benefits depending upon the seriousness of the surrounding circumstances. Workers who can demonstrate that they refused to obey supervisory directives because of mitigating circumstances, such as confusion regarding the exact orders to be carried out or a concern about the safety of the assigned tasks, will usually retain their eligibility. Nonetheless, employees who deliberately refuse to follow appropriate work directives will probably be disqualified. Such a result is particularly likely with respect to claimants who are discharged for repeated instances of insubordination.

Workers who are dissatisfied with supervisory instructions occasionally question those orders. If their inquiries are not made in an offensive manner, the employees will probably not lose their right to unemployment benefits. On the other hand, when objecting individuals use abusive or profane language to challenge work directives, they will frequently disqualify themselves. Such a loss of eligibility is especially likely when the abusive language is overheard by other employees. Workers who resort to threats of physical violence toward supervisory personnel will generally render themselves ineligible, except when the employees can show that the supervisors own improper conduct provoked their offensive responses.

Profanity and Violence

The behavior of employees toward fellow workers or third persons may render them ineligible for benefits. While the use of mere "shop talk" or isolated cursing incidents in private offices would normally not disqualify the terminated speakers, the use of excessive or abusive profanity would be likely to cause the disqualification of the offending individuals. When vulgar remarks are directed toward customers, disqualification is particularly likely.

Employees who are terminated because they threatened physical violence against other workers are normally found ineligible for benefits. Individuals who are discharged in response to unprovoked assaults committed against other workers or third persons tend to suffer a similar loss of eligibility. Only when claimants discharged for physical violence can show that they were simply defending themselves against the aggression of others or that their actions were isolated and not serious are they likely to avoid disqualification.

Poor Work Performance

One of the more difficult issues raised under misconduct disqualification provisions concerns the eligibility of individuals who have been discharged because of inefficient or negligent work performance. Although occasional performance lapses should not constitute "misconduct," isolated acts of gross negligence or repeated acts of mere negligence may result in disqualification.

> [T]he intended meaning of the term "misconduct" * * * is limited to conduct evincing such wilful or wanton disregard of an employer's interests as is found in deliberate violations or disregard of standards of behavior which the employer has the right to expect of his employee, or in carelessness or negligence of such degree or recurrence as to manifest equal culpability, wrongful intent or evil design, or to show an intentional and substantial disregard of the employer's interests or of the employee's duties and obligations to his employer. On the other hand, mere inefficiency, unsatisfactory conduct, failure in good performance as the result of inability or incapacity, inadvertencies or ordinary negligence in isolated instances, or good faith errors in judgment or discretion are not to be deemed "misconduct" within the meaning of the statute.[1]

Courts frequently experience difficulty when attempting to differentiate between nondisqualifying inadvertence and disqualifying "misconduct."

Occasional errors due to inattention will not normally be considered disqualifying misconduct. Nonetheless, if numerous mistakes are made, misconduct will often be found, particularly when the inattentive acts cause significant harm. Workers who engage in conduct evidencing a gross disregard for employer interests are also likely to be found ineligible for benefits. This factor explains the tendency of courts to disqualify workers who deliberately choose to sleep on the job. Even though employment-related accidents resulting from mere negligence do not result in a loss of benefit eligibility, mishaps caused by substantial departures from ordinary care (i.e., grossly negligent or reckless behavior) regularly lead to disqualification. The fundamental issue in these

§ 10.11

1. Fitzgerald v. Globe–Union, Inc., 35 Wis.2d 332, 338, 151 N.W.2d 136, 139–40 (1967), quoting Boynton Cab Co. v. Neubeck, 237 Wis. 249, 296 N.W. 636 (1941).

cases involves the degree of personal culpability exhibited by the terminated employees. Courts generally consider the degree of inattention, the number of occurrences, and the risk to important employer interests. While a single act of grossly negligent or reckless behavior may result in a loss of eligibility, most disqualification cases are based upon repeated acts of less blameworthy conduct. On the other hand, when employers are able to demonstrate that employees lack the ability to perform their basic job functions, courts may find disqualifying "just cause," based upon the belief that the workers' unsuitability for the positions in question constitutes sufficient "fault" to warrant a loss of benefit eligibility.

Absenteeism and Tardiness

Employers frequently terminate workers because of absenteeism or tardiness. When absenteeism or tardiness is found to constitute "misconduct," the affected individuals are disqualified from receiving benefits. Courts generally base their determinations on several factors: (1) the frequency of absence or lateness; (2) whether the absent individuals have notified their employer of expected non-attendance; and (3) the reasons for the claimants' behavior. Courts recognize that employers have the right to expect relatively prompt and regular attendance. When particular employees establish patterns of frequent absence or tardiness and are terminated because of that conduct, the discharged persons are often found to have engaged in disqualifying misconduct. A loss of eligibility is particularly likely when employees fail to provide valid reasons for their repeatedly absences.

In unusual circumstances, even a single absence may be found to constitute misconduct. When supervisors specifically deny employee requests for time away from work for personal reasons and the workers deliberately choose to ignore supervisory warnings of negative consequences if they fail to report for work, the offending persons may well lose their eligibility. If individuals critical to the production process are absent and they fail to notify their employer of their anticipated absence, they may forfeit their right to unemployment benefits. Nonetheless, when workers are not absent from work an excessive amount of time and they have valid reasons for their non-attendance, they will usually continue to be eligible for benefits, particularly if they attempt to provide their employer with advance notice.

Employees who fail to comply with company rules requiring advance notice of anticipated absences are occasionally found guilty of disqualifying misconduct, even when they are not away from work for prolonged periods. Nonetheless, when such persons have a valid reason for their failure to provide the requisite notice, they are unlikely to lose their right to benefits. They will similarly remain eligible if they seek in good faith to satisfy company rules that only require notice if the workers expect to be absent for more than a specific number of days.

Disqualification frequently results when employees are discharged because they have left work during their shift without permission, particularly when they have been previously warned about such improper conduct. Courts generally find that workers who are fired when they refuse to heed supervisory warnings regarding the adverse consequences that would result from continued poor attendance are guilty of disqualifying misconduct. On the other hand, when companies fail to warn employees with attendance problems that continued non-attendance will result in discipline, courts are less likely to disqualify people terminated for continued absenteeism.

Employees who are discharged because of absenteeism often claim that their non-attendance was caused by personal illness. If such claimants failed to notify their employer of anticipated absences and the reasons therefor, courts often find them disqualified. Even when workers with attendance difficulties have provided their employer with explanations for their conduct, if they have been repeatedly absent and have failed to supply independent evidence to support their health claims, they may be found ineligible for benefits. Although the overall records in such cases might not demonstrate an "intentional disregard" of employer interests, a determination that there is disqualifying misconduct is generally made if courts decide that the behavior of the claimants evidenced a "conscious," "wanton," or "reckless" indifference to employer needs. The failure of employees to notify their employer of anticipated absences or to provide credible evidence to substantiate health claims is often cited to show a conscious or reckless disregard for company interests.

Employees are occasionally absent from work due to personal reasons not related to their own health. For example, employees may remain at home to care for sick family members. If the workers are absent for prolonged periods of time and it is likely their non-attendance will continue, courts will regularly find that their resulting terminations were for disqualifying misconduct. If, however, the absences are not excessive and the employees notify their employer of the reasons for their non-attendance, they will normally remain eligible for benefits.

Individuals who are regularly late for work may lose their jobs and be found guilty of disqualifying misconduct. If they are repeatedly tardy and have no reasonable excuse for their behavior, a loss of eligibility will probably result. Their behavior will be found to evidence a deliberate or a reckless disregard for employer interests and result in a finding of disqualifying misconduct. On the other hand, occasional tardiness will almost never provide a basis for disqualification.

Use of Drugs or Alcohol

Employees who abuse drugs or alcohol often lose their jobs. If they are terminated because they reported for work in an unfit condition or they used alcohol or illicit drugs while at work, they will generally be found guilty of disqualifying misconduct. Individuals who are discharged because of their possession of illicit drugs on company premises will generally be found disqualified. A similar result is probable with respect to persons who contravene company rules against alcohol use while "on call." Employees violating rules prohibiting off-duty drinking or illegal drug use are often found disqualified if the employer can demonstrate that the rule is reasonably related to valid employment interests. On the other hand, when rules relating to off-duty drinking or illicit drug use have no demonstrable connection to appropriate company interests, people fired for violating those rules are unlikely to be found to have engaged in disqualifying misconduct.

Individuals terminated for work-related drinking or drug use occasionally argue that they are alcoholics or drug addicts whose compulsion to drink or use illegal drugs should preclude disqualification, because their "involuntary" consumption of alcohol or drugs should not be considered "willful" misconduct. Most courts have refused to accept this argument. Nonetheless, when workers with drinking problems have made good faith efforts to obtain treatment for their "chemical dependencies," some courts have sustained their right to receive unemployment benefits. A few of these courts might reach a similar conclusion with respect to drug addicts who have successfully completed drug rehabilitation programs.

Employers concerned about drug abuse are increasingly requiring employees to submit to drug tests. In *Southwood Door Company v. Burton*,[2] the Mississippi Supreme Court held that employers seeking to disqualify employees who have failed random drug tests must demonstrate by clear and convincing evidence that the testing procedures used comported with federal drug testing regulations–not less demanding state drug testing procedures that are preempted by federal regulations with respect to employee eligibility for unemployment benefits. Employers must thus show that they used split urine specimens and notified employees who tested positive of their right to request within seventy-two hours retests of the other half of their split urine specimens.

If individuals are terminated for refusing to submit to drug tests, should they be denied unemployment benefits? When company drug testing policies are reasonably applied, particularly when test requests are based on circumstances objectively suggesting drug abuse, employee refusals to comply may be found to constitute disqualifying misconduct. When, however, companies are unable to demonstrate a credible basis for suspecting drug use or a drug testing program is found to be unreasonable, an employee who tests positive or who refuses to cooperate will not be found disqualified. The mere fact that a worker has been involved in an on-the-job accident does not ipso facto establish a basis for suspecting drug use. More particularized information is normally required.

Refusal To Take a Polygraph

Although the Employee Polygraph Protection Act of 1988 severely restricts the right of employers to demand or request employee submission to lie detector tests, there are unusual situations in which polygraph

2. 847 So.2d 833 (Miss.2003).

tests may be directed. If the request is legitimate and a worker is terminated for refusing to submit, courts might well find the uncooperative worker disqualified for misconduct. Nonetheless, if a company request contravened the Employee Polygraph Protection Act or had no reasonable fact basis, persons fired for refusing to submit would most likely retain their benefit eligibility.

Religious Objections to Work

Employees are sometimes discharged when they refuse to work on Saturdays or Sundays or on the production of armaments due to sincerely held religious beliefs. Their former employer may challenge their right to unemployment benefits on the ground they were terminated because of misconduct. If states were to deny benefits to such individuals, they would impermissibly infringe upon the free exercise of religion guaranteed by the First Amendment.

Off–Duty Behavior

Courts often have to decide whether employees discharged because of behavior committed during off-duty hours are eligible for unemployment benefits. If individuals misuse or misappropriate company property during their off-duty hours, they will normally be found to have engaged in disqualifying misconduct. On the other hand, if employees commit relatively minor off-duty thefts that do not suggest that they can no longer be trusted at work, disqualification is unlikely. A loss of eligibility usually results with respect to workers who engage in off-duty acts of unprovoked violence against fellow employees, particularly if the altercations occur on company premises. Where, however, the workers in question merely respond to the aggression of other employees, disqualification will usually not result. Individuals involved in a labor dispute who are terminated for engaging in strike-related violence will generally be found guilty of disqualifying misconduct.

Employees involved in improper conduct during their off-duty hours away from company premises may find themselves disqualified from benefits, if their employer can demonstrate that their actions would be likely to have a negative impact on their employment relationship. For example, if workers develop off-duty ties with company customers that might endanger employer interests, they may be found guilty of misconduct connected with their employment. Employees who commit off-duty crimes may also forfeit their right to unemployment benefits, if their employer can show a reasonable relationship between their convictions and bona fide company interests. For example, individuals who engage in notorious criminal acts that would reflect negatively on the reputation of their employer will often lose their right to benefits. Disqualification is especially likely with respect to people who commit off-duty drug offenses. A loss of benefit eligibility will similarly result if the off-duty misconduct undermines the ability of the guilty persons to perform their usual job tasks—as where truck drivers lose their licenses. On the other hand, when off-duty criminal conduct has no demonstrable employment connection, disqualification is unlikely. This may even be true where the claimant has been arrested and forced to remain in jail pending trial because of an inability to afford bail.

Workers who experience financial problems may have their wages garnished. If they are terminated due to repeated garnishments caused by irresponsible personal behavior, they may be found guilty of disqualifying misconduct. Nonetheless, when the number of garnishments is not excessive and the affected employees can provide rational explanations for their economic difficulties, disqualification is unlikely.

§ 10.12   Unemployment Compensation—Voluntary Termination of Employment

Because unemployment compensation is designed to provide financial assistance to individuals who are out of work through no fault of their own, it might seem inappropriate to award benefits to employees who voluntarily sever their employment relationships. State legislatures have recognized, however, that workers occasionally resign because of bona fide reasons that should not cause them to forfeit their unemployment eligibility. As a result, the unemployment compensation statutes in all fifty states and the District of Columbia have sought to balance the competing interests by expressly disqualifying only employees who voluntarily terminate their employment without good cause. In most states and the District of Columbia, the disqualification continues for the entire period of their resulting unemployment. Eligibility in these states can only be restored through subsequent employment in which the disqualified persons earn specified minimum amounts.

In thirteen states, individuals who leave work voluntarily are not disqualified if they can show that they did so for "good cause." In the other thirty-seven states and the District of Columbia, the exception to disqualification is limited to good cause that is attributable to the employer or connected with the work. Employees who terminate their employment for purely personal reasons may only attempt to retain their benefit eligibility in states with disqualification provisions that except decisions based on "good cause." In states that require good cause attributable to the employer or connected with the work, wholly personal considerations are generally insufficient to prevent disqualification.

The rules pertaining to the voluntary termination disqualification vary substantially from state to state. In states with the general "good cause" exception, personal considerations may be accepted in some states that would be rejected in others. Even among the numerous states requiring good cause attributable to the employer or connected with work, different results are frequently achieved in cases involving similar circumstances. It is thus impossible to provide a set of universally applicable principles. The specific statutory language and pertinent judicial decisions must be examined in each state to ascertain the exact manner in which the voluntary termination disqualification is applied. Nonetheless, many common themes may be discerned.

When the right of claimants to receive benefits is challenged under voluntary termination disqualification provisions, three basic questions must usually be addressed: (1) did the individuals completely sever their employment relationships; (2) was their leaving "voluntary;" and (3) was their action based on "good cause" or "good cause attributable to their employer." Only when it is established that employees have voluntarily terminated their employment and have done so without appropriate cause will they be found disqualified.

Employment relationships are clearly severed when employees formally resign or retire. Persons who otherwise evidence an intention to abandon their employment will also be considered to have quit their jobs. For example, employees who fail to report to work for several months, or even several weeks, without contacting their employer will frequently be found to have relinquished their employment. When employees attempt to notify their employer of anticipated non-attendance or reasonably believe that it is obvious why they are not reporting (e.g., bad weather for outside work or temporary illness), courts are likely to find no cessation of employment.

Once courts decide that claimants severed their employment relationships, they must determine whether the workers did so "voluntarily." Because the answer to this question will relate directly to company claims that benefit applicants are statutorily disqualified, one might reasonably assume that the objecting employers would be obliged to establish that the applicants actually terminated their employment "voluntarily," and many courts have accepted this burden of proof allocation. Numerous courts have similarly placed the burden of persuasion on unemployment agencies when they, rather than companies, challenge the right of persons who have severed their employment relationships to receive benefits. Other courts, however, have decided that the burden of demonstrating that employment departures were not "voluntary" should be placed on the individuals seeking the compensation.

The mere fact that employees have not been discharged does not mean that they have terminated their employment "voluntarily." The surrounding circumstances must be evaluated in each contested case to determine whether the departures of the challenged claimants were in fact volitional. Even when employees have tendered their resignations, their ultimate loss of employment may not be found to be voluntary. If they sought to withdraw their resignations before they became effective but were told by their employer that they could not change their minds, courts frequently find that their separations were really "involuntary." Other courts, however, would probably reach the opposite conclusion.

Dillard Department Stores, Inc. v. Polinsky[1] involved unusual circumstances. An employee notified her employer that she planned to terminate her employment at the conclusion of the notice period. Instead of waiting for that date to arrive, the firm decided to discharge the worker immediately. Although the employer argued that the individual

§ 10.12

1. 247 Neb. 821, 530 N.W.2d 637 (1995).

should be ineligible for unemployment benefits because of her decision to relinquish her employment voluntarily without good cause, the court rejected this contention. It concluded that she had been effectively discharged by her employer and thus remained eligible for benefits even after the date on which she had originally intended to quit her job. While other jurisdictions have used the same rationale to allow continuing benefits to individuals terminated by their employers during the notice period, other courts have determined that compensation should only be available from the time of the discharge of such persons until the date on which they originally indicated they would voluntarily quit their jobs.

Employees occasionally resign because they fear they will be discharged if they do not act first. A number of courts have rejected employer assertions that these claimants should be treated as individuals who voluntarily terminated their employment. They have instead decided to treat these people as if they were involuntarily discharged. Businesses that wish to prevent claimants from receiving benefits must thus demonstrate that they would have been fired because of disqualifying misconduct. Other courts, however, have chosen to treat these actions as voluntary resignations, despite the impending discharge threats, rendering most of these persons ineligible for benefits. Workers who are found to have voluntarily terminated their employment will only be eligible for benefits if they can show that they left because of "good cause" or "good cause attributable to their employer." The different treatment is especially important in those cases in which the anticipated discharges that precipitated the preemptive resignations would not have been based on misconduct that would otherwise have rendered the employees disqualified.

Individuals are sometimes forced to sever employment relationships due to health problems. Courts have properly acknowledged that "where * * * an employee is impelled because of sickness and disease to terminate employment because continuance thereof would endanger his health and personal welfare, such termination is an involuntary rather than a voluntary act on the part of the employee * * *." When, however, the evidence suggests that workers were not really compelled to resign because of stated health reasons or they refused to consider other positions that would have accommodated their health difficulties, their decisions to leave will usually be considered voluntary. Nonetheless, if they can show that their decisions to depart were based on "good cause" or "good cause attributable to their employer," they may still avoid disqualification.

Retirement

Similar issues are raised with respect to workers who retire. Although retirement usually involves the complete cessation of employment, it does not necessarily entail voluntary action. When employees were compelled to end their employment pursuant to the terms of lawful mandatory retirement programs established by their employers, many courts appropriately treated such actions as involuntary. Some courts, however, refused to permit benefits in such cases, based upon the theory that employees who willingly accepted employment with firms they knew had compulsory retirement policies "voluntarily" agreed to terminate their employment when they reach the specified age.

In some cases it is not clear whether employment relationships have been terminated by employees or their employer. For example, after workers indicate that they plan to retire sometime in the future, their employer may advise them to leave immediately. If the workers did not intend to terminate their jobs at that time, their departures would usually be regarded as involuntary. On the other hand, an employer may notify workers that they are going to be discharged, but take no action to end their employment. If the affected individuals thereafter elected to leave, they would probably be considered to have departed voluntarily.

Good Cause Attributable to the Employer

Even when it is clear that claimants terminated their employment voluntarily, they can still avoid disqualification if they can demonstrate that they did so with either "good cause attributable to their employer" or simply "good cause." The majority of states require people who voluntarily sever their employment relationships to show that they acted with "good cause attributable to their employer" or "good cause connected with their employment."

In states that require claimants to establish good cause associated with their employer, it is obvious that wholly personal reasons will not suffice. The applicants must convince unemployment compensation administrators that they had a bona fide reason for ending their employment and that the proffered explanation is related to their previous employment. For example, employees may decide to resign when they are informed that their compensation is being reduced. If the size of the reduction is "substantial"—twenty to twenty-five percent or more—most courts will find that the claimants terminated their employment because of good cause associated with their employer. If, however, courts decide that the compensation decrease was not that significant—ten to fifteen percent or less—they will probably conclude that the claimants are disqualified.

Suppose compensation reductions are accompanied by corresponding work reductions, as where companies diminish the amount of overtime work or decrease the number of regular work hours? If the remuneration decrease is "substantial," courts will often find that the dissatisfied persons had "good cause attributable to their employer" for leaving to look for more rewarding employment. Individuals may similarly retain their benefit eligibility when they resign because of significantly increased workloads that are not accompanied by corresponding salary enhancements. When part-time employees who are ordered to work full-time terminate their employment, courts do not always agree whether they had "good cause" for their action.

Employees occasionally decide to quit not because of reduced compensation, but because of a lack of meaningful work. They are simply bored with the limited job tasks assigned to them. If they resign their positions, they will generally be found to have terminated their employment without good cause. If, however, they are induced to terminate their employment because of an inhospitable work environment, they may be able to avoid disqualification. For example, if employees are demoted without justification, they may have a valid reason for quitting, but not if their own conduct warranted the demotions.

When claimants allege that they have ended their employment because of mistreatment or harassment, courts generally apply a "reasonable person" standard. They ask whether the adverse circumstances in question would have induced reasonable employees to leave their jobs. Many court decisions have indicated that individuals encountering employment problems must initially notify management officials of the difficulties and provide their employer with the opportunity to correct the situation.

The mere fact that supervisors subject their subordinates to abusive language will normally be insufficient to provide good cause for resigning, even if the offending managers use raised voices. Nonetheless, if the verbal abuse becomes extreme or is accompanied by other forms of harassment, good cause will usually be found. When supervisors select their targets in a discriminatory fashion, the victims of their demeaning tactics will probably have good cause to quit. For example, if a manager arbitrarily refuses to give a particular employee the same pay increase given to other workers, grossly underpays an individual because of her gender, gives especially onerous job assignments to a disfavored worker, or makes clearly unwelcome sexual advances toward a particular employee, the victim would most likely have good cause to resign.

In some cases, unwelcome harassment comes from coworkers instead of supervisory personnel. If the tactics used are particularly abusive or are of a racial or sexual nature, good cause attributable to the employer will almost always be found. Only where the victims fail to ask their employer to rectify the situation, personally contributed to the abusive atmosphere and their employer reasonably sought to rectify the situation, or the harassment is not found to be sufficiently offensive to induce reasonable workers to resign will disqualification be likely to result.

Employees occasionally develop allergic reactions to substances in their work environments. When their conditions become sufficiently serious, they may be forced to terminate their employment. If the claimants can present competent testimony regarding their job-related health problems and demonstrate that they notified their employer of their difficulties but were unable to obtain reassignment to more healthful positions, they will usually be found to have terminated their employment because of good cause attributable to their employer. They may even be able to obtain benefits where they have departed because of their inability to tolerate the cigarette smoke generated by other workers. Nonetheless, if they are unable to establish the existence of an employment-related health problem or they made no real effort to relocate to a more suitable work environment, they will probably be found disqualified.

Courts similarly refuse to disqualify claimants who terminate their employment because of mental disorders caused or exacerbated by work-related circumstances. If claimants can show that job stress has meaningfully contributed to their mental difficulties, they will probably be found eligible for benefits. When, however, claimants who resign their positions are unable to establish a direct causal connection between their employment and their mental problems, they will normally be found disqualified.

Employees sometimes decide to resign when their employer moves their place of work to another community. Should they be disqualified from benefits due to the fact they have voluntarily terminated their employment? If they can show that the distance to the new location is excessive or that adequate public transportation is unavailable, they will probably be able to avoid disqualification. On the other hand, if the new facility is not too far from their former place of work, they will likely be found ineligible, especially if public transportation is available.

Individuals who decide to accept non-mandatory retirement will normally be considered disqualified. They are voluntarily terminating their employment without good cause attributable to their employer. Only when claimants can demonstrate that they are electing retirement because of circumstances providing good cause connected with their employment will they be found eligible for benefits. For example, if they were to accept retirement instead of a twenty-five to fifty percent reduction in their work hours, they would probably not be found disqualified.

Other Good Cause

The unemployment statutes in twenty-one states that disqualify employees who voluntarily terminate their employment without good cause attributable to their employer and in Ohio, a "good cause" state, provide an exception for workers who leave one firm to accept employment with another company. In Alabama, Florida, Missouri, Montana, South Dakota, and West Virginia, this exception is limited to situations in which persons on layoff from their regular employer give up interim positions to return to their usual jobs. In the other fifteen states that apply this exception, disqualification may be avoided when the individuals in question resign current positions to accept recall to their former employers or to obtain more advantageous permanent employment with other firms.

The unemployment statutes in thirteen states allow employees who voluntarily terminate their employment to avoid disqualification if they can demonstrate that they left their jobs because of "good cause." These individuals need not establish cause associated with their employment. If unemployment officials find their proffered personal reasons sufficiently compelling to justify their decisions to resign, they will continue to be eligible for benefits. Courts evaluating these cases generally ask whether the circumstances cited would have been likely to impel similar action by reasonable workers faced with the same situation. Due to the inherently subjective nature of this test, the decisions vary widely from state to state.

Many of the cases arising under "good cause" provisions involve family-related considerations. For example, employees may terminate their current employment and relocate to other areas to become married, to follow their spouses, or to care for ill family members. They may also move to different geographic areas for health reasons or because of economic factors. Although such individuals would generally be disqualified under statutes that only exempt workers who resign for good cause attributable to their employer, they may be able to retain their eligibility under enactments that merely require "good cause."

Some states have elected to deal with these issues through specific statutory provisions. These sections usually provide that employees who voluntarily terminate their employment to marry, to follow spouses to new locations, or to satisfy other marital, filial, or domestic obligations shall be ineligible for benefits. If these provisions apply equally to male and female claimants who resign to follow their spouses or to satisfy other familial duties, they generally survive constitutional challenges. They are only occasionally invalidated on the ground they impermissibly create irrebuttable presumptions that individuals who resign for marital or family reasons, as opposed to other considerations, have withdrawn from the labor market. Several of the statutory disqualification laws pertaining to people who resign because of marital or familial obligations exempt claimants who are the primary financial supporters of their families. Even though the enactments containing this exception tend to disqualify more women than men, they frequently survive constitutional claims. Nonetheless, courts sometimes invalidate such provisions under the equal protection clause of the Fourteenth Amendment.

Employees who terminate their employment to relocate with spouses are normally disqualified under statutes that expressly preclude the awarding of benefits to persons who voluntarily resign for such reasons. A similar loss of eligibility generally results with respect to people who terminate their employment because of family obligations in states with laws specifically disqualifying workers who resign for such reasons. Claimants who seek unemployment benefits in states with such explicit disqualification provisions are only likely to prevail when they can demonstrate that their family concerns were so substantial that their resignations should not be considered "volitional" acts.

A few states have enacted special provisions that treat individuals who resign due to family obligations quite differently. These laws expressly preserve the benefit eligibility of these claimants, so long as they can establish their availability for employment in their new circumstances. Under these enactments, employees who terminate their employment to follow spouses or to satisfy other familial duties retain their eligibility if they continue to actively seek suitable work.

In "good cause" states that do not have separate statutory sections defining the eligibility of individuals who voluntarily resign because of marital or familial obligations, it is not clear whether people who quit for such reasons will be entitled to benefits. Many courts avoid disqualification by finding that significant family concerns constitute "good cause." Other courts refuse to do so, however, unless the claimants can demonstrate truly compelling circumstances. Individuals who terminate their employment not to follow a current spouse, but to get married and reside with their new spouse, are less likely to be found eligible for benefits. If employees relocate to follow nonmarital "loved ones" with whom they are merely cohabiting, disqualification is especially likely.

When individuals become divorced or widowed they frequently experience financial difficulties. Similar economic problems may arise when one of two gainfully employed spouses is laid off. If people affected by such circumstances decide to give up their current employment to relocate to less expensive geographical areas, should they forfeit their right to unemployment benefits? If they can convince courts that their economic plight was urgent, good cause to resign may be found. In the absence of dire circumstances, however, disqualification is likely to result.

Employees may have to decide what to do when they or members of their immediate families develop serious medical conditions. Physicians may recommend relocation to more healthful environments, and they may accept that advice and terminate their employment. If courts conclude that their decisions to relocate were based on dire circumstances that would probably have induced other similarly situated workers to take the same action, "good cause" for their resignations may be determined. In most cases, however, courts find that good cause did not exist, because the claimants were not really forced to relocate.

The employment of female workers is frequently affected by pregnancy. Employer pressure[2] or personal considerations may induce individuals to terminate their employment during portions of their pregnancy. Should employees who resign or accept unpaid maternity leaves be disqualified from unemployment benefits? If state unemployment statutes unreasonably restricted the right of pregnant workers to obtain benefits, those limitations would probably contravene the equal protection clause of the Fourteenth Amendment. Furthermore, in 1976, Congress amended section 3304(a)(12) of the Federal Unemployment Tax Act to prohibit the disbursement of federal unemployment funds to states that deny compensation to claimants "solely on the basis of

---

2. Discrimination against employees because of pregnancy constitutes gender discrimination under Title VII of the Civil Rights Act of 1964. Section 701(k) of that enactment, 42 U.S.C.A. § 2000e(k), requires employers to treat women affected by pregnancy and related medical conditions "the same for all employment-related purposes * * * as other persons not so affected but similar in their ability or inability to work * * *." See § 2.2.

pregnancy." If state statutes or administrative decisions were to render applicants ineligible for benefits merely because of their pregnant status, the responsible states would forfeit their right to federal unemployment funds.

The Supreme Court has recognized that section 3304(a)(12) does not prevent states from disqualifying claimants who voluntarily terminate their employment for reasons unrelated to their employer. Although this federal provision forbids states from singling out pregnancy for disadvantageous treatment, it does not compel states to treat pregnancy in a preferential manner. States may thus apply to pregnant employees statutory provisions that disqualify workers who voluntarily terminate their employment without good cause attributable to their employer. Under such disqualification laws, claimants can avoid a loss of eligibility only if they can demonstrate that job-related circumstances adversely affected their pregnant condition and forced them to resign. If it is not clear that the employment environment caused the resignations, disqualification generally results.

When company personnel policies cause pregnant workers to terminate their employment, the affected individuals normally retain their eligibility for benefits either because they did not sever their employment "voluntarily" or they had good cause attributable to their employer for leaving. Under "good cause" disqualification provisions, pregnant employees who voluntarily quit their jobs may only preserve their eligibility if they can show a necessitous basis for terminating their employment that would have caused other similarly situated workers to take the same action. Benefit applicants must, of course, demonstrate that they remain able to and available for work. Doubts regarding their continued capacity to engage in gainful employment are frequently resolved against eligibility. Nonetheless, if a state enactment contained a conclusive presumption that pregnant women could not work for a specified period before and after delivery, that provision would be struck down under the due process clause of the Fourteenth Amendment.

§ 10.13 Unemployment Compensation—Refusal to Accept Suitable Employment

The unemployment compensation laws in all fifty states and the District of Columbia disqualify otherwise eligible individuals who refuse, without good cause, to accept "suitable" employment during the period of their unemployment. In thirty-eight states and the District of Columbia, claimants who reject suitable employment are disqualified for the duration of their unemployment. They can only regain eligibility through subsequent gainful employment for a minimum of time ranging from four weeks in Delaware, Illinois, and Minnesota to twelve weeks in Idaho and seventeen weeks in Florida. In six states, the disqualification period is fixed, running from three to seven weeks in every state but Colorado, which provides a twenty week period of ineligibility. The statutes in the remaining six states provide variable periods of disqualification that are dependent upon the particular circumstances involved.

Before a claimant can be disqualified under this kind of provision, there must be evidence that the person refused without good cause to accept employment that was "suitable" to the individual involved. Mere knowledge of job openings is not usually sufficient to establish disqualification. An offer must have been communicated to the claimant with sufficient detail to make the recipient realize that employment was available. If the claimant declined the offer without a valid reason and the unemployment agency found that the rejected work was "suitable" to the benefit recipient's skill, experience, and background, disqualification would normally result.

The test used to determine whether claimants have impermissibly refused to accept "suitable" employment is similar to the test applied to decide whether benefit applicants have made themselves "available" for appropriate work. Under both provisions, they must seek and be willing to accept employment that is commensurate with their skills, experience, and background. Many state unemployment statutes contain provisions listing factors that should be considered when suitability is being determined. The language contained in the North Carolina law is typical.

> In determining whether or not any work is suitable for an individual, the Commission shall consider the degree of risk involved to his health, safety, and morals, his physical fitness and prior training, his experience and prior earnings, his length of unemployment and prospects for securing local work in his customary occupation, and the distance of the available work from his residence.[1]

State statutes also codify the requirement set forth in section 3304(a)(5) of the Federal Unemployment Tax Act (FUTA)[2] which provides that

> compensation shall not be denied * * * to any otherwise eligible individual for refusing to accept new work * * *: (A) if the position offered is vacant due directly to a strike, lockout, or other labor dispute; (B) if the wages, hours, or other conditions of the work offered are substantially less favorable to the individual than those prevailing for similar work in the locality; [or] (C) if as a condition of being employed the individual would be required to join a company union or to resign from or refrain from joining any bona fide labor organization.

Cret v. Employment Department[3] concerned the right of Bakers' Union members to obtain unemployment benefits. While they were laid off due to a strike by other labor organizations, they refused to cross another union's picket line to perform non-bakery work at their employer's warehouse. Although the proffered warehouse positions were found to constitute "new work" with respect to the laid off bakery workers, the

§ 10.13
1. N.C.Gen.Stat. § 96–14 (3).
2. 26 U.S.C.A. § 3304(a)(5).
3. 146 Or.App. 139, 932 P.2d 560 (1997).

court found that their refusal to accept these jobs was due to the fact the positions involved "struck work." Their benefit eligibility was thus preserved by the section 3304(a)(5)(A) language precluding disqualification when the positions rejected were vacant as a result of a strike or other labor dispute.

It is also clear that First Amendment free exercise clause considerations prevent states from disqualifying persons who reject available employment that would require Saturday or Sunday work or participation in the production of armaments, where such job activities would conflict with sincerely held religious beliefs. Claimants who reject suitable job opportunities may still avoid disqualification if they can establish that they had "good cause" for their refusal to accept the offered positions. They must demonstrate that reasonable persons in their situations would have rejected the positions in question.

Unemployed persons who refuse to accept available work may claim that the positions were not "suitable," because they involved less demanding skills than their previous jobs, entailed difficult commutes, or required hours of work that would have interfered with family obligations. If the skills associated with the offered positions are wholly inconsistent with the training and experience of the claimants, the work is likely to be found unsuitable. The inability of individuals to find reasonable transportation to jobs may also excuse their failure to accept proffered employment, particularly where public transportation is unavailable. The fact that offered work would involve shifts that would conflict with the familial duties of claimants may similarly render that work unsuitable.

Unemployed persons may refuse to accept employment with terms and conditions not as beneficial as those associated with their previous work. If their rejection of the proffered jobs is based upon their unwillingness to work with older equipment or to tolerate less commodious environments, they would probably be disqualified, unless they could demonstrate that the circumstances were truly extreme. Claimants also may be reluctant to accept work outside their usual occupation. Such a restriction may be appropriate during the early period of their unemployment, but they may be required to expand their horizons as it becomes clear that no work is available in their preferred line of work. If they continue to reject employment for which they are qualified, they may forfeit their right to receive benefits.

A frequently litigated issue concerns the right of unemployed individuals to reject job offers that involve compensation significantly below that received in their prior positions. When the jobs in dispute entail remuneration levels "substantially" below what the claimants previously earned, courts regularly find the positions "unsuitable." Courts do not always agree on how substantial a wage decrease must be to render a position "unsuitable." Although a sixteen to twenty percent reduction is likely to result in an "unsuitable" finding, courts may occasionally reach the opposite conclusion. Conversely, while a six to ten percent wage decrease would usually be insufficient to render a job unsuitable, there may be occasions when it does.

After claimants have had a reasonable period of time to locate work paying wages commensurate with those associated with their previous employment, they are normally expected to "lower their sights" and accept lower paying jobs. Even when these positions involve significantly reduced compensation, their failure to accept them will probably result in their disqualification. The length of time claimants have to find well-paying positions will usually vary, depending upon the general economic circumstances in their geographical area and the likely availability of work for people possessing their particular skills. No definitive standard may be articulated. In some cases, benefit recipients may be required to lower their sights after only five to ten weeks of unemployment and accept positions paying ten, twenty, or even forty percent less than their prior jobs, while in other situations, claimants may be given more than seven months to seek well-paying work.

Even when claimants have been out of work for prolonged periods, section 3304(a)(5) of FUTA prevents them from being disqualified if they reject job offers that involve wages that are "substantially less favorable to the individual than those prevailing for similar work in the locality." The controlling factor is not whether the compensation offered is substantially below that previously earned by the people in question. The applicability of section 3304(a)(5) is instead determined by a comparison of the proffered wage with the levels of remuneration for similar jobs in the local geographical area.

When bona fide health considerations induce them to refuse otherwise suitable work, claimants generally retain their benefit eligibility. Claimants may similarly escape disqualification if they refuse to accept work in environments that would aggravate their allergy to cigarette smoke. They would, however, still be obliged to show that they remain able to and available for other suitable work despite their health limitations or they would lose their eligibility on that basis.

§ 10.14   Unemployment Compensation—Unemployed Due to a Labor Dispute

When labor disputes exist between companies and labor organizations, work stoppages may occur. Should employees be eligible for unemployment benefits while they are on strike or locked out by their employer or if they refuse to cross a picket line established by other workers? What if individuals are temporarily laid off because of a strike being conducted by other workers at the same facility or at another company plant? If permanent replacements are hired for striking employees, should the replaced strikers be able to obtain benefits?

The unemployment statutes in all fifty states and the District of Columbia have disqualification provisions that affect employees who are out of work because of labor-management controversies. Most contain language similar to the original Social Security Board draft bill provision, which was based upon the British labor dispute disqualification approach. Twenty-two states follow the draft bill approach and disqualify individuals whose unemployment is caused by a "stoppage of work due to a labor dispute." Eleven states and the District of Columbia use slightly different language that causes people to lose their benefit eligibility if they are out of work due to a "labor dispute in active progress." In ten states, employees are rendered ineligible during unemployment caused by the existence of a labor dispute. The remaining seven states use somewhat different formulations to disqualify claimants who are unemployed because of labor-management controversies.

Work Stoppages

Employees who engage in a work stoppage are usually considered voluntarily unemployed, and this partially explains the reason states have historically excluded strikers from unemployment benefits. Nevertheless, the Supreme Court has held that whether strikers should be disqualified is a matter of state law, and it has upheld both disqualification and payment of benefits.

The "voluntariness" factor is not applicable when workers are locked out by their employer. Nonetheless, many states apply the labor dispute disqualification to both strikers and locked out personnel. This is due to the fact that state legislatures have sought to maintain a neutral position during labor-management conflicts. They do not want to provide governmental assistance to individuals involved in labor disputes. State legislators also think it is unfair to compel businesses to subsidize employees who are exerting economic pressure against their employer.

In most states the period of disqualification only ends when the "stoppage of work due to a labor dispute" ends or the unemployment is no longer caused by a "labor dispute in active progress." Nevertheless, if disqualified claimants find truly permanent employment with different firms, they can regain their benefit eligibility. In most states they cannot eliminate their labor dispute disqualification through the acceptance of mere interim work. There must be evidence that they have completely severed the relationship with their previous employer and intend their new employment to be permanent. In several states, however, disqualified individuals can regain their eligibility by working several weeks in other employment during the continuing labor-management controversy, even if the interim work does not appear to be permanent. Courts in these states simply find when they are laid off from their new jobs that their unemployment is no longer due to a labor dispute at their place of "last employment." In New York, the disqualification continues for a maximum of seven consecutive weeks. New York claimants who are unemployed more than seven weeks are thereafter entitled to benefits.

Under the disqualification provisions contained in most state statutes, individuals are only rendered ineligible for benefits when the evidence indicates that they are totally or partially unemployed due to either a "stoppage of work" caused by a labor dispute or a "labor dispute in active progress." Application of these alternative formulations frequently results in identical eligibility determinations. Nonetheless, there are occasions when persons who would be disqualified under one would remain eligible under the other, and vice versa.

States that use "stoppage of work" language must initially determine what constitutes a "stoppage of work." It is generally agreed that this phrase concerns a reduction or cessation of employer operations, rather than a diminution with respect to the efforts of individual workers. As a result, a slight decrease in production caused by a walkout by a few employees is usually not considered a "stoppage of work." The concerted job action must generate a "substantial curtailment" of business operations. This was recognized in an early landmark case[1] that involved bakery workers who went on strike. Within fifteen minutes, their employer hired replacement employees and resumed normal operations. The Michigan Supreme Court logically recognized that because the circumstances of this case did not involve a significant production decline, there was no disqualifying "work stoppage." Other courts applying "stoppage of work" provisions similarly refuse to disqualify strikers who have been replaced by other people who are maintaining regular operations. Although courts have found it difficult to provide a precise definition of "substantial curtailment," they have generally agreed that a twenty-five to thirty percent reduction is sufficient. The requisite curtailment is most frequently measured in terms of decreased production, revenue, employees, and worker-hours.

Statutes that disqualify individuals who are unemployed due to a "labor dispute in active progress" are not concerned about the ability of struck firms to continue operations with replacement workers. They simply ask whether the persons seeking unemployment benefits are currently out of work because of an "active" labor dispute. Once it is established that the claimants are unemployed as a result of a present labor controversy, they are found ineligible for benefits—despite the fact their employer has remained open through the employment of permanent replacement workers.

Layoffs and Work Curtailments

There are times when an employer is induced by concern for property and machinery or a lack of orders due to customer stockpiling to reduce production in anticipation of an impending strike. If such pre-strike production curtailments are "substantial," they will generally be considered part of the disqualifying "stoppage of work." An analogous result may be reached when a company transfers a substantial amount of production from one plant to another to permit it to continue usual production during a strike at the first facility. After a labor dispute has been resolved, it may take several days or weeks for a business to resume normal operations. Most courts continue to disqualify striking individuals who have not yet been recalled, until "normal operations" have been

---

§ 10.14

1. Lawrence Baking Co. v. Unemployment Comp. Comm'n, 308 Mich. 198, 13 N.W.2d 260, cert. denied, 323 U.S. 738, 65 S.Ct. 43, 89 L.Ed. 591 (1944).

reestablished. A few, however, terminate the ineligibility of unrecalled strikers as soon as the "substantial curtailment" of operations has ended, even if full production has not yet been achieved. Because a disqualifying "stoppage of work" is only thought to commence once there has been a "substantial curtailment" of operations, it would seem reasonable to find a conclusion of that stoppage when the "substantial curtailment" has ended, instead of requiring a resumption of "normal operations."

A mere "stoppage of work," no matter how substantial the curtailment of normal operations, does not disqualify the affected employees, unless it is *caused by* a "labor dispute." Most unemployment statutes do not define the term "labor dispute." Nonetheless, it is generally recognized that the phrase includes any meaningful controversy concerning wages, hours, or conditions of employment or the organizational or representational rights of employees. When it is established that claimants are unemployed as a direct result of a work stoppage precipitated by a "labor dispute," they will be found disqualified. If, however, their stoppage of work is not attributable to a labor controversy, the out-of-work persons will retain their benefit eligibility. For example, if an employer decided during a strike to terminate certain operations, the strikers who formerly worked in the closed department would regain their eligibility, because their continued lack of employment would no longer be the result of the labor dispute.

Different results may occur in similar circumstances under statutes that disqualify employees who are unemployed due to a "labor dispute in active progress" rather than a "stoppage of work." The active progress provisions do not require any significant production curtailment, but rather a loss of employment by benefit applicants caused by an existing labor dispute. In states that use the active labor dispute formulation, it is generally recognized that a shut-down in anticipation of a future strike does not disqualify the laid off personnel, because their unemployment is not yet attributable to a "labor dispute in active progress." After a collective bargaining controversy has been resolved, the strikers who remain out of work until regular production is resumed are normally eligible for benefits during the hiatus between the dispute settlement and the date of their recall. Although they may still be out of work because of a "stoppage of work," their continued unemployment would no longer be due to an active labor dispute. On the other hand, if a labor union simply decides to terminate a work stoppage before the bargaining controversy has been resolved, those employees who are not able to regain their jobs immediately will remain ineligible for benefits in "active progress" states. Although there is no longer a "stoppage of work," these individuals are still unemployed because of a "labor dispute in active progress."

Employees are occasionally laid off by their employer because of a work stoppage by persons at another company facility or at a plant owned by an independent supplier or customer. It is important to remember that the disqualification provisions in most states only apply if claimants are unemployed because of a labor dispute at the "factory, establishment or other premises at which [they are or were] last employed." If their lack of work is caused by a labor-management controversy involving another company, including one closely related to their own employer, they will usually be found employed by a different "establishment" and retain their benefit eligibility. Even when the bargaining dispute concerns people employed at another facility of the same firm, the laid off personnel will not necessarily be disqualified.

Courts generally focus upon the geographical proximity of the plants in question and the functional integration of the production tasks being performed by the workers at each to determine whether they should be treated as a single "establishment" for disqualification purposes. Where the operations being performed at the different facilities are not functionally interrelated or the plants are not located close to each other, they are likely to be regarded as separate "establishments." Nonetheless, courts occasionally find a single "establishment" with respect to geographically dispersed factories that are functionally integrated, and these decisions significantly undermine the "establishment" limitation set forth in unemployment statutes. At the other extreme are decisions finding separate "establishments" for distinct departments at the same facility operated by a single employer, because of their lack of functional integration.

Lockouts

One of the more debated issues under labor dispute disqualification provisions concerns the treatment of employees locked out by their employer. Lockouts involve individuals who are willing to remain at work but who are laid off by their employer until an existing collective bargaining controversy can be resolved. If one believes that striking workers should be ineligible for benefits because their temporary lack of employment is attributable to their own voluntary decision to stop work, no disqualification should result when people are involuntarily locked out by their employer. Nonetheless, many courts have held that locked out individuals are not eligible for benefits because they are unemployed due to a "stoppage of work" or a "labor dispute in active progress." These courts have generally based their conclusion on both the literal language of the statutory provisions, which are not restricted to strikes, and the fact that many legislators voted for the labor dispute disqualification to preserve governmental neutrality during labor-management controversies.

Other state legislatures and judiciaries have focused upon the involuntary aspect of unemployment created by lockouts and have determined that employees adversely affected by such employer conduct should not necessarily forfeit their right to benefits. Twenty-eight states and the District of Columbia have, by judicial construction or legislative action, rendered the labor dispute disqualification inapplicable to most employer-initiated lockouts. Where, however, the lockout is precipitated by a whipsaw strike conducted by the employees' own labor union, many of these states apply the disqualification provision to the locked out personnel. For example, if a union struck one member of a multi-employer bargaining unit to exert economic pressure against both the struck firm and the other association members and the non-struck companies decided to lock out their union-represented employees to preserve the integrity of the multi-employer group, both the strikers and the locked out claimants would probably be denied benefits.

Brauneis v. State, Labor & Industry Review Commission[2] involved the unemployment benefit eligibility of employees who were locked out by one member of a multi-employer association after the labor organization representing association employees struck another association member. The court limited the "whipsaw strike" exception in the state unemployment compensation statute to work stoppages by unions against the employer that subsequently locks out its other workers. Since the strike in this case was directed at a different association member, and not at the locking out employer, the locked out workers were found entitled to benefits.

States that distinguish between disqualifying "strikes" and non-disqualifying "lockouts" must occasionally recognize that it is not always easy to determine which form of job action is occurring. An employer may make unreasonable bargaining demands in order to precipitate a non-compensable "strike," while a union may assert similarly outrageous positions and make strike threats to generate a compensable "lockout." Careful courts do not merely focus on the party that overtly began the work stoppage, but instead examine the underlying causative factors. If they determine that the company effectively caused the stoppage, a compensable "lockout" is likely to be found, while a non-compensable "strike" will probably be discerned where union warnings of an imminent walkout induce the firm to shut down.

Assisting Strikers

When the Social Security Board prepared the draft bill labor disqualification provision, the drafters recognized that individuals affected by, but not immediately involved in, a strike might provide important assistance to the strikers or derive personal benefits from the results of the work stoppage. This group included people unemployed during a labor dispute who honored picket lines, carried picket signs, or gave financial assistance to striking workers. It also comprised those whose wages, benefits, or employment conditions would be enhanced through resort to so-called "key worker" stoppages. Labor organizations used this device to exert maximum economic pressure on employers with a minimum of striker involvement. Unions would formally call out a few crucial employees. Without the assistance of these individuals, employers were forced to cease production and to lay off the remaining workers who would usually be the direct beneficiaries of any bargaining agreement achieved.

2.   236 Wis.2d 27, 612 N.W.2d 635, 2000 WI 69 (2000).

The drafters believed that people who were partially or totally unemployed due to a collective bargaining controversy who meaningfully assisted striking personnel or who were laid off as a result of "key worker" strikes should be disqualified with the actual strikers. The draft bill provision thus disqualified not only striking employees, but also those individuals who were laid off because of the labor-management dispute and who were "participating in or financing or directly interested in the labor dispute which caused the stoppage of work [or who belonged] to a grade or class or workers of which, immediately before commencement of the stoppage, there were members employed at the premises at which the stoppage occurs, any of whom [we]re participating in or financing or directly interested in the dispute."

Disqualification provisions incorporating the draft bill language or similar wording have been adopted by forty-one states and the District of Columbia. All of these provisions deny eligibility to employees who participate in work stoppages or who are directly interested in the outcome of the underlying labor disputes. Thirty of these states also disqualify individuals who are unemployed because of a labor-management controversy and who finance workers engaged in the concerted stoppage. Most of these states additionally disqualify people who are within a grade or class of workers employed at the premises affected by the labor dispute, some of whose members are participating in, financing, or directly interested in the controversy.

Courts must initially determine what constitutes "participating in" a labor dispute. Employees who voluntarily walk out to join a strike are obviously "participating in" the stoppage. Individuals who willingly refuse to cross a picket line established by striking employees are also likely to be found to be "participating in" the concerted job action. If the picket line is located at their place of employment, such sympathy strikers would be ineligible for benefits because they would be unemployed due to a labor dispute at the establishment at which they are or were last employed. They will only be able to obtain benefits if they can show that there was no work available for them and that it would have been futile for them to have tried to cross the established picket line. On the other hand, if truck drivers or delivery people are not employed by the business directly involved in the labor-management controversy and they simply honor a picket line at that other company's premises, they will probably not forfeit their benefit eligibility. They would not be out of work because of a labor dispute at *their* place of employment.

Other Work Stoppages

Employees of a struck enterprise do not automatically lose their benefit eligibility when they refuse to cross a picket line established by fellow employees. If they can demonstrate that they did not honor the picket line voluntarily but remained away from work because of a reasonable fear of bodily harm, they should be able to avoid disqualification. Courts generally require such claimants to show that they honestly and reasonably feared that meaningful physical harm would probably have resulted if they had attempted to pass through the picket line. While threats of immediate physical injury may be enough to excuse failures to report for work, mere verbal abuse or statements regarding possible future recriminations will normally not be sufficient to enable fearful individuals to avoid disqualification when they refuse to cross a picket line. The fact that sympathy strikers are motivated by a commitment to union solidarity will similarly not excuse their failure to report to work during a concerted stoppage being conducted by other company employees.

Individuals whose employment is temporarily interrupted by a work stoppage being conducted by other employees at their factory or establishment may also forfeit their right to benefits if they provide financial assistance to the strike participants. It is now generally recognized that the mere payment of regular dues to the labor organization involved in the concerted job action does not constitute "financing" under labor dispute disqualification provisions, even though some of the dues money may be used to support the striking workers. If, however, the normal dues rate were specially increased for the purpose of enhancing the strike fund, the persons paying the higher rate would most likely be considered financial supporters of the strikers. People who pay specific strike fund assessments or who make other direct financial contributions to employees involved in a work stoppage will usually lose their benefit eligibility.

Workers who are not immediately involved in a labor dispute at their place of employment may still lose their benefit eligibility if they are laid off because of that dispute and they are "directly interested in" the outcome of the underlying negotiations. If the wages, hours, or employment conditions of these employees are likely to be favorably or unfavorably affected by the terms of any strike settlement agreement, they would normally be considered "directly interested in" that controversy. If the benefit claimants are members of the labor organization involved in the bargaining dispute, there is a greater likelihood that they would be found "directly interested in" the results of that altercation. This statutory interpretation reflects the judicial belief that state legislatures intended to restrict the use of "key worker" strikes designed to benefit non-striking members of the same union.

Even if claimants are out of work due to a labor dispute involving other workers at their place of employment and they are not participating in, financing, or directly interested in that controversy, they may still be found ineligible for benefits. Most states deny them benefits if they are members of the same "grade or class" as persons employed at the same establishment who are participating in, financing, or directly interested in the existing labor-management conflict. To determine whether claimants are disqualified under the "grade or class" rule, it is necessary to decide what is meant by the term "grade or class." A few courts have inexplicably interpreted this provision so expansively that they have effectively placed all of the persons employed at the plant or establishment affected by the labor dispute within the same "grade or class." Most courts, however, have appropriately recognized that state legislators could not have intended such a pervasive disqualification.

Judges generally acknowledge that this specific statutory language was primarily designed to prevent the use of "key worker" strikes. They thus apply the "grade or class" exclusion to employees in the same job classifications or the same integrated production groups as the striking personnel. They often consider the types of work involved and the similarity of skills between the claimants and strike participants and supporters. If the persons seeking unemployment benefits are employed in the same bargaining unit as the labor dispute participants and supporters, they will almost always be found in the same "grade or class." Judges frequently cite the fact that claimants are members of the same labor organization as the workers involved in the labor dispute to support their determination that the benefit applicants are in the same "grade or class." Nonetheless, when claimants can establish that they are not employed in the same department, they are employed in distinct job classifications, and they perform different job functions, they are likely to be found outside the "grade or class" of the labor dispute participants.

§ 10.15 Unemployment Compensation—Procedure

State unemployment compensation laws are generally administered by commissions or boards consisting of from three to seven members (most often three) appointed by their respective governors. States that wish to receive administrative expenses from federal funds must satisfy certain criteria set forth in Title III of the Social Security Act. The state procedures must include:

> (1) Such methods of administration * * * as are found by the Secretary of Labor to be reasonably calculated to insure full payment of unemployment compensation when due; and

> (2) Payment of unemployment compensation solely through public employment offices or such other agencies as the Secretary of Labor may approve; and

> (3) Opportunity for a fair hearing, before an impartial tribunal, for all individuals whose claims for unemployment compensation are denied; * * *.[1]

Claims for unemployment benefits are generally initiated in public employment offices. Individuals who are voluntarily or involuntarily out of work register for work with the local public employment service. If no suitable employment is available, they usually file claims for unemployment compensation. They must supply information regarding their recent past employment and the reason for their current unemployment. Their immediate past employer will either have filed a form indicating the reasons for their loss of employment or that firm will be sent a form requesting such information. An employment agency deputy or claims

§ 10.15

1. 42 U.S.C.A. § 503(a).

examiner will review the file to determine whether the claimant: (1) has established sufficient credit in covered employment to be eligible for benefits and, if so, for what amount and duration of benefits; (2) is ready, willing, and able to work; and (3) is disqualified from receiving benefits under one of the statutory disqualification provisions. Individuals who file unemployment claims containing misrepresentations indicating that they had not worked during the benefit periods when they had actually done so, may be disqualified.

In the vast majority of cases, it is clear that claimants are eligible for benefits and are not disqualified. The deputy or examiner calculates the amount and duration of their benefits. After any prescribed waiting period has elapsed, they begin to receive their compensation. In a few cases, questions are raised about claimant eligibility or disqualification. In most instances involving controverted claims, the deputy or examiner reviews the files and decides whether the claimants are entitled to receive benefits. If the claimants are denied benefits, they may request internal agency review. If benefit eligibility is determined, the employers whose unemployment accounts are being charged may usually ask for agency review. In some states, deputies and examiners do not actually resolve controverted eligibility and disqualification questions. They merely complete the files and transmit them to the agency review board for the initial determinations. In most states, the initial appeal is considered by a single referee or commissioner, or by a three-member tripartite board consisting of one management representative, one worker representative, and one neutral person.

Parties dissatisfied by decisions reached by referees, commissioners, or review boards may normally appeal those determinations to final administrative appeals bodies. After final administrative determinations have been reached, dissatisfied parties may seek judicial review. Judicial review is expressly provided in most state unemployment compensation statutes. Even where the statute is silent with respect to this issue, judicial consideration would still be available, because "it is the duty of [the] court, when * * * a question of law is properly presented, to state the true meaning of the statute finally and conclusively." If judicial review were not available, substantial due process questions would be raised.

Under the traditional American rule, if applicable statutes do not expressly authorize attorney fee awards to prevailing parties, litigants have to accept responsibility for their own attorney fees. Only where courts find bad faith, vexatious, wanton, or oppressive behavior by parties will they approve attorney fee awards.

In a few states, court jurisdiction over unemployment claims extends to both factual and legal issues, and de novo hearings are conducted. In most states, however, only limited judicial review is available. Agency fact findings supported by substantial evidence are accorded judicial deference. Because agencies do not follow technical evidentiary rules, even credible hearsay evidence may be sufficient to support factual conclusions. Nevertheless, courts may occasionally refuse to sustain awards that are not supported by sufficient *admissible* evidence—refusing to rely on inadmissible hearsay. Legal interpretations are subject to closer judicial scrutiny, but deference is usually given to statutory constructions made by the expert administrative agency that was legislatively established to interpret and apply the state unemployment compensation law. Once final judicial decisions are rendered, they may be appealed to the state supreme court if the dissatisfied parties can demonstrate that significant legal issues are involved. Appeals to the United States Supreme Court are only available where substantial federal questions are raised.

Interstate Claims

There are occasions when unemployed individuals are unable to find suitable employment within their home states and they relocate to other states where they believe their job prospects will be better. If they were eligible for unemployment benefits in their former state, they may file for benefits in their new location. Under the Interstate Benefit Payment Plan that is universally followed, they may file for benefits in the state where they currently reside. That state acts as the agent for the state in which they previously earned their covered wages (the "liable state"). The local unemployment deputies or examiners obtain the relevant information from the claimants and transfer the information to the liable state which elicits additional information from their prior employers.

The rights of interstate claimants are determined by the unemployment agency of the liable state, in accordance with the legal doctrines applicable in the liable jurisdiction. The liable state agency decides whether the applicants are eligible for benefits and whether they are disqualified for any reason. If they are found eligible, the liable state calculates the amount and duration of their benefits and decides the employer account to be charged with their unemployment. The state where the claimants presently reside provides them with the appropriate benefit amounts and charges the liable state for the compensation paid out.

A similar interstate problem concerns individuals who have recently worked in several states for different covered employers. The Employment Security Amendments of 1970 specifically addresses this issue.

(9)(A)compensation shall not be denied or reduced to an individual solely because he files a claim in another state * * * or because he resides in another state * * * at the time he files a claim for unemployment compensation;

(B) the state shall participate in any arrangements for the payment of compensation on the basis of combining an individual's wages and employment covered under the State law with his wages and employment covered under the unemployment compensation law of other States which are approved by the Secretary of Labor * * * as reasonably calculated to assure the prompt and full payment of compensation in such situations. Any such arrangement shall include provisions for (1) applying the base period of a single State law to a claim involving the combining of an individual's wages and employment covered under two or more State laws, and (2) avoiding duplicate use of wages and employment by reason of such combining.[2]

The Employment Security Amendments caused states to participate in the Wage–Combining Arrangement. This Arrangement provides for the payment of benefits by the state in which multi-state claimants file (the "paying state"), even if those persons have earned no wage credits in the paying state. The paying state asks each state unemployment agency that has recorded covered earnings for the claimants during the relevant time period to furnish pertinent wage reports. In each case, the paying state then combines the different claimant earnings and determines claimant eligibility and the benefit amount and duration available under the paying state's unemployment compensation statute. The paying state sends quarterly reports to the other participating states. Those states are responsible for the same proportion of the benefits paid as the covered wages earned in that state bear to the total covered wages used to calculate the aggregate benefit amount.

§ 10.16 Unemployment Compensation—Benefit Levels and Duration

When covered employees become totally unemployed, they may immediately apply for benefits. If they are found eligible for benefits and they are not disqualified, they may receive compensation without any waiting period in twelve states. The other thirty-eight states and the District of Columbia normally require a one-week period of unemployment before claimants may begin to obtain benefits.

Once individuals who are totally or partially unemployed apply for benefits, state unemployment workers must determine the weekly benefit amounts and the duration of benefits available to them. Most states compute weekly benefits as a percentage of the earnings received during the calendar quarter of the base period in which claimants had their greatest earnings. This practice is designed to reflect the full-time earning capacity of workers. States usually set weekly benefit amounts as 1/23, 1/24, 1/25, or 1/26 of the earnings obtained by applicants during the relevant calendar quarters, resulting in benefit amounts ranging from fifty to fifty-six percent of average weekly earnings. States also specify minimum and maximum weekly benefit amounts available to unemployed individuals. The minimums range from $5.00 in Hawaii and $10.00 in Louisiana to $94.00 in Washington and $88.00 in Oregon. The maximum amounts range from $190.00 in Alabama and Mississippi, to $496.00 in Rhode Island and $715.00 in Massachusetts. Twelve states provide weekly benefit supplements based upon the number of dependent children and spouses being cared for by claimants. Several of these states also consider dependent siblings and/or parents.

---

2.   26 U.S.C.A § 3304(a)(9)(A), (B).

Totally unemployed claimants are entitled to the weekly benefit amounts available to persons with their earnings during the relevant portion of the base period. If their covered earnings were unusually low, they will be awarded the specified minimum level of benefits. If they earned substantial sums during the base period, they will be subject to the prescribed maximum benefit amount. Applicants who are partially unemployed during a claim week usually receive the appropriate weekly benefit amounts reduced by the wages they actually earned during that week.

Fully covered claimants are generally entitled to a maximum of twenty-six weeks of benefits. During recessionary periods, however, the federal government occasionally provides special funds to enable states to offer additional weeks of compensation to individuals out of work for prolonged periods. In most cases, claimants are provided with an extra thirteen weeks of benefits. Congress frequently limits the availability of extended benefits to states with unemployment rates above the national average.

Under the Tax Reform Act of 1986, Congress decided to treat all unemployment benefits as taxable income.[1] These legislative changes have compounded the fact that benefit levels have failed to keep pace with inflation over the past two decades.

§ 10.17 Unemployment Compensation—Benefit Reductions and Repayment

State unemployment agencies must occasionally decide whether claimant benefit eligibility should be affected by their receipt of other forms of compensation, such as severance pay, supplemental unemployment benefits, workers' compensation, disability benefits, or retirement payments. The resolution of this issue depends upon the specific language contained in the applicable unemployment statute. When statutory provisions expressly cover different forms of collateral income, they either require a commensurate reduction in weekly benefit amounts or cause recipients to lose their benefit eligibility. These benefit reductions or disqualifications only cover weeks during which the external compensation is being received.

Many unemployment statutes provide that claimants will be considered eligible for benefits only for weeks "with respect to which no remuneration is paid or payable." When unemployed persons receive severance pay based upon their prior company service, courts often find no disqualification for the weeks covered by such payments, because they do not consider such deferred payments to constitute compensation pertaining to the weeks in which they are received. On the other hand, when the payments are in lieu of advance termination notice or are dismissal payments, courts are more likely to treat them as remuneration pertaining to the post-termination weeks covered by those payments. Because supplemental unemployment benefits provided by pri-

§ 10.16
1. See 26 U.S.C.A. § 85.

vate or public employers are generally viewed as deferred compensation based upon previous service, states usually decline to deduct such payments from statutorily prescribed unemployment benefits.

Courts frequently reach opposite conclusions concerning the eligibility of claimants during weeks in which they receive vacation pay or holiday pay. When vacation pay is given to employees being permanently terminated, it is often treated as non-disqualifying severance pay relating to previous service. Other courts, however, treat vacation pay as wages earned during the weeks in which they are received, causing a reduction in or loss of unemployment benefits for those weeks. Judges also disagree with respect to the impact of vacation pay received during periods of temporary unemployment. Analogous judicial disagreements often result with respect to claimants who receive holiday pay during weeks of unemployment. Some courts reduce or deny unemployment compensation during the weeks such "wages" are received, while others reach the opposite conclusion, treating holiday pay as deferred compensation relating to services performed prior to the current period of unemployment.

Some state unemployment statutes expressly provide that pension benefits received by otherwise eligible claimants must be deducted from their unemployment compensation. In these states, weekly benefit amounts are reduced for claimants receiving company-financed retirement income. Courts may even apply such benefit reduction mandates to Social Security benefits received by unemployed individuals. Other courts, however, limit such statutory reduction provisions to money obtained from employer-sponsored retirement programs, and they do not apply such legislative terms to social security payments received by unemployment claimants. In states that do not have specific provisions covering the receipt of pension money, courts usually refuse to permit the receipt of such deferred compensation to diminish the right of claimants to obtain full unemployment benefits.

There are occasions when unemployment benefits are awarded to claimants who are not entitled to such compensation. Recipients may obtain sums that exceed their appropriate weekly benefit amounts or they may obtain payments when they do not satisfy statutorily prescribed eligibility requirements. Although some of these erroneous payments may be due to inadvertent mistakes, others are due to deliberate misrepresentations. When benefits are improperly paid because of mistakes or misrepresentations made by claimants, state unemployment agencies may normally obtain court-ordered repayment of the sums involved. Repayment may also be directed when benefit recipients subsequently obtain backpay from their former employers covering the period of their unemployment. Individuals who make deliberate misrepresentations to unemployment agency personnel may also subject themselves to criminal liability. Judges will usually require restitution of benefits given to claimants due to mistakes made by unemployment agency personnel. Courts are less willing, however, to order the repayment of excess benefits generated by errors contained in unemployment reports prepared by employers.

Chapter 11

RETIREMENT

Table of Sections

§ 11.1 Introduction

During the second half of the twentieth century Americans depended on Social Security, private pensions, and individual savings to provide their retirement income. As inflation and economic circumstances diminished the ability of individuals to rely on their own resources or those of their families to support them in their old age, retirement security came to occupy an increasingly important place in public policy. After defense expenditures, Social Security represents the largest part of the national budget, and, as every politician knows, it is a troubling problem. As to private pensions, the federal government's largest tax loss is the exclusion accorded to pension contributions and their accumulated earnings. In 1989, private pension assets totalled almost $1.7 trillion and accounted for eighteen percent of the economy's total financial assets.

All this attention is a fairly recent phenomenon. Although a few companies established pension programs for their workers as early as the 1870s, and as many as 300 firms may have had pension programs by the early 1930s, most of these schemes did not have strong financial bases and failed during the Depression. At the same time, millions of Americans lost their jobs and their life savings, and the country was willing to support the notion that self-reliance might not be sufficient to provide for old age. The Social Security Act of 1935[1] evidenced an

§ 11.1
1. 49 Stat. 620, 42 U.S.C.A. §§ 301–433.

awareness of the need for a government program that would provide at least a subsistence level of retirement income for all.

The Social Security Act, however, represented a "minimalist compromise" that did not by itself provide an adequate retirement income, and therefore labor unions began to look to the negotiation of private pensions as a source of retirement security for their members. During World War II, when civilian labor was in short supply and wage control policies limited the ability of many companies to compete for workers by increasing wages, the War Labor Board encouraged the establishment of pension plans and other forms of fringe benefits as a means of attracting and keeping workers. Immediately after the war, workers and their unions concentrated primarily on increases in cash wages, but within a few years pensions and other employee benefits became important aspects of collective bargaining.

This trend was aided by three developments. Since 1921, the tax laws have given favorable treatment to pension plans, first by permitting employers to deduct contributions to the plans, and later by deferring the taxation of employees with respect to those contributions and by exempting the earnings of pension trusts from taxation. In 1942, these tax advantages were linked to a requirement that plans not discriminate in favor of highly compensated employees. Thus, companies that wanted to provide pension plans for their executives had to broaden coverage in order to qualify for favorable tax treatment. These features remain a part of the Internal Revenue Code, but until the passage of the Employee Retirement Income Security Act (ERISA) in 1974 the Code did very little to assure adequate funding of pension plans or to protect employees' interests in future benefit payments.

Second, in 1947 the Labor Management Relations Act (LMRA), also known as the Taft–Hartley Act,[2] was enacted. Among the perceived problems that prompted the passage of the LMRA was the possibility for abuse and corruption in union-sponsored pension plans. Accordingly, section 302 of the LMRA makes it a crime for an employer to pay anything of value to an employee representative, with a number of exceptions. One of the exceptions is section 302(c)(5), which permits employer payments to a trust administered by an equal number of management-and union-appointed trustees and "established for the sole and exclusive benefit of the employees of such employer" to provide pension and various health and welfare benefits.[3] Although section 302(c)(5) consists of only a few lines, the federal courts used it to assert jurisdiction over covered plans and began to develop a body of common law governing the behavior of Taft–Hartley fiduciaries. Section 302(c)(5) applies, however, only to collectively-bargained trusts with union-appointed trustees, and not to plans controlled entirely by employers, which continued after 1947 to be governed solely by state law. Moreover,

2. Pub. L. No. 80–101, 61 Stat. 136 (1947), codified at 29 U.S.C.A. §§ 141–187.

3. 29 U.S.C.A. § 186(c)(5).

as with the Internal Revenue Code, section 302(c)(5) did not provide protection against the failure of underfunded plans.

Third, in its 1948 decision in *Inland Steel Co.*,[4] the National Labor Relations Board held that pension benefits are a mandatory subject of bargaining. By requiring collective bargaining about pensions, this decision contributed significantly to a dramatic increase in pension plan coverage, as heavily unionized industries adopted or expanded plans. In 1940, seventeen percent of full-time workers were covered by pension plans; by 1970, that figure had leaped to fifty-two percent. *Inland Steel* also helped complete the transition from a view of pensions as merely a gratuity and thus not a binding obligation that employees could enforce against their employer (at least not until they actually started to receive payments upon retirement), to the view of pensions as a form of deferred compensation earned by employees throughout their working lives and therefore an enforceable right.

Without any systematic regulation of the structure, funding, and activities of pension plans, problems and abuses eventually surfaced as the first wave of workers under plans established during and after World War II began to retire and found that they had few, if any, rights to pension benefits. For instance, many plans did not permit employees to participate until they had reached a certain age and worked continuously for the company for a specified number of years. Breaks in employment because of events such as layoffs and disability often prevented workers from meeting the service requirement of their employer's plan. Similarly, many plans required a long period of continuous service, often as much as twenty or more years, before a worker's benefits would vest. In the early 1970s a Treasury Department study found that only one out of three workers participating in employer-sponsored plans had a fifty percent or greater vested right to his or her accrued benefits, and fifty-four percent of covered employees sixty years of age and older did not have vested rights to half of their accrued benefits.

In addition, although the concepts of using actuarial principles to predict future pension claims for defined benefit plans and funding those plans in advance were well-established, there was no requirement that plans be adequately funded. The most infamous plan failure involved the December 1963 closing of the Studebaker plant in South Bend, Indiana, and the termination of its pension plan with insufficient assets to pay all its liabilities. Over four thousand workers with vested rights in the plan lost all or part of their pension benefits.

Congress had previously made a half-hearted attempt to deal with some of these inadequacies by enacting the Welfare and Pension Plans Disclosure Act of 1958 (WPPDA).[5] The WPPDA did not impose substantive requirements or even give the government enforcement authority;

4. 77 N.L.R.B. 1 (1948), enforced, 170 F.2d 247 (7th Cir.1948), cert. denied, 336 U.S. 960, 69 S.Ct. 887, 93 L.Ed. 1112 (1949).

5. Pub. L. No. 85–836, 72 Stat. 997 (1958), codified at 29 U.S.C.A. §§ 301–309, repealed by ERISA, Pub. L. No. 93–406, 88 Stat. 851 (1974).

rather, it merely required administrators of most private sector plans to file plan descriptions and annual reports with the Secretary of Labor and furnish this same information to participants. The theory was that providing information to participants would enable them to police the operations of their own pension plans.

Interest in pension reform continued, spurred on by the termination of underfunded plans, attention in the popular press, and by a public perception that pension plans were not delivering on their promises. Conflicting interest groups and political wrangling prevented the passage of any pension reform legislation until 1974, when the enactment of ERISA ended the period when private pension plans were "the only large private accumulation of funds which have escaped the imprimatur of effective federal regulations."[6] As this chapter will detail, ERISA mandated minimum participation, vesting, accrual, and funding standards, established standards of conduct for plan fiduciaries, regulated plan termination, and set up a system of termination insurance. Pension reform has continued to the present, with a number of significant amendments to ERISA, many aimed at increasing eligibility for pension benefits, tightening the minimum standards imposed on plans, deterring plan terminations, and ensuring the solvency of the Pension Benefit Guaranty Corporation, which administers the termination insurance program.

The passage of ERISA coincided with and probably contributed to the beginning of a second stage of pension plan development. Since the early 1970s, private pension plan coverage has remained stable at between fifty-one and fifty-three percent of full-time workers. At the same time, coverage under defined contribution plans has increased, while coverage under defined benefit plans has decreased. Observers have attributed these trends to a number of factors, including shifts in employment from large, heavily unionized, high-wage companies to smaller, nonunion, low-wage firms and the increasing costs and administrative burdens imposed by ERISA and its subsequent amendments.

§ 11.2 ERISA—Coverage of Pension Plans

As discussed in Chapter 4, the Employee Retirement Income Security Act of 1974 (ERISA)[1] imposes minimum standards on employee benefit plans. All covered benefit plans, both pension plans and welfare plans, are subject to statutory structural requirements, reporting and disclosure obligations, fiduciary standards, preemption of state law, federal court enforcement, and civil and criminal remedies for violations. Pension plans, but not welfare plans, are also subject to participation, vesting, accrual, funding, and survivor's benefits requirements. In addition, Title IV of ERISA regulates the termination of pension plans, provides for plan termination insurance, and imposes liability on employ-

---

6. S. Rep. No. 127, 93d Cong., 1st Sess. 4 (1973), reprinted in 1974 U.S.C.C.A.N. 4834.

§ 11.2

1. 29 U.S.C.A. §§ 1001–1461.

ers who withdraw from multiemployer plans under certain circumstances.

Under ERISA a pension benefit plan is "any plan, fund, or program" established or maintained by an employer, a union, or both, that "(i) provides retirement income to employees, or (ii) results in a deferral of income by employees for periods extending to the termination of covered employment or beyond," regardless of the method of calculating contributions or benefits or of distributing benefits.[2] As authorized by the statute, the Secretary of Labor has exempted from coverage as pension plans certain severance pay and supplemental retirement income plans, although they remain covered by ERISA as welfare plans. Unlike the question of coverage as a welfare plan, the threshold issue of coverage under the statutory definition of pension plan has generated little litigation.

ERISA distinguishes between two types of pension plans: individual account, or defined contribution plans, and defined benefit plans. A defined contribution plan is a plan in which a separate account is established for each participant, and retirement benefits are based on the amount in that account. The employer makes annual contributions to each account in an amount established by the plan, generally expressed as a percentage of the employee's compensation. The employer fulfills its funding obligation completely by making its annual contribution. The plan's trustees then have the duty to manage the plan and invest its assets. Each account shares proportionately in the plan's investment gains or losses, and at retirement the employee's pension benefit depends solely on the amount in his or her account. Thus, the investment risk falls on the employee, not on the plan sponsor; if the plan performs poorly, the employee has less in his or her account and therefore a lower pension benefit. Of course, if the plan performs well, the employee benefits accordingly.

Defined contribution plans include money purchase plans, profit sharing plans, and stock bonus plans. Under a money purchase plan the employer's annual contribution is fixed by the terms of the plan and is not discretionary. Contributions under profit sharing plans no longer depend on the employer's having a profit: the major difference between money purchase and profit sharing plans is that employer contributions to a profit sharing plan may be discretionary. Profit-sharing plans may include "Section 401(k) features" permitting participants to elect to reduce their taxable earnings in exchange for contributions to the plan. Stock bonus plans are similar to profit sharing plans, except that employer contributions take the form of employer stock, and distributions may be in employer stock. Employee stock ownership plans (ESOPs) are a form of stock bonus plan.

A defined benefit plan, on the other hand, is a plan in which a certain retirement benefit is promised. Most defined benefit plans provide for a benefit in the form of a life annuity, payable at the plan's

2. ERISA § 3(2)(A), 29 U.S.C.A. § 1002(2)(A).

normal retirement age (generally sixty-five). The amount of the annuity is determined according to a formula, usually based on variables such as an employee's years of service and his or her average compensation for an entire career or a specified number of years before retirement. The employer must fund the plan so that the benefits fixed by the formula will be available to employees when they retire years in the future. Basically, ERISA requires plan sponsors to contribute the present value of the future benefit obligations for each year of service. These contributions are determined actuarially, taking into account the age and mortality of employees and their spouses, employee turnover, projected wage increases, and economic assumptions about interest rates and rates of return on plan investments. In a defined benefit plan, unlike a defined contribution plan, the investment risk falls on the plan sponsor. If the plan's investments perform poorly and are not sufficient to fund promised benefit payments, the sponsor of a defined benefit plan must make up the difference through increased contributions. Conversely, if investments produce higher-than-expected returns, the employer's funding obligation is reduced. Although defined benefit plans once predominated in the pension world, in the past quarter century there has been a marked shift to defined contribution plans.

ERISA also differentiates between single employer plans and multiemployer plans. A single employer plan is a plan sponsored by one employer, whether collectively bargained or not. Multiemployer plans, which are common in industries such as trucking, building and construction, and entertainment, that have patterns of multiemployer collective bargaining, are plans to which more than one employer contributes pursuant to one or more collective bargaining agreements. A major difference between the two kinds of plans is that multiemployer plans are also governed by section 302(c)(5) of the Taft–Hartley Act,[3] which requires jointly administered employee benefit plans to have an equal number of union-appointed and management-appointed trustees. Generally, collective bargaining agreements between the employers and the union establish the amounts of required employer contributions to the plan, but the plan's trustees set the benefit levels and eligibility criteria. In contrast, in single employer collectively bargained plans, the employer and union bargain over the benefit levels, but the employer usually administers the plan itself. Multiemployer plans share aspects of both defined benefit and defined contribution plans. From the employee's point of view, a multiemployer plan looks like a defined benefit plan, because benefits are determined according to a formula, whereas to the employer it is more like a defined contribution plan, because it requires fixed contributions.

The Internal Revenue Code also regulates pension plans extensively. The favorable tax treatment received by plans meeting its requirements, or "qualified" plans, accounts in large part for the widespread growth of pension plans since World War II. Subject to certain limits, employer

---

3. 29 U.S.C.A. § 186(c)(5).

contributions to qualified plans are deductible when made, the employee is not taxed on contributions or earnings until benefits are paid, and the trust itself is tax-exempt.

Although ERISA covers pension plans without regard to their tax-qualified status, most ERISA plans are also qualified plans. Many of ERISA's minimum standards for pension plans, including most of its participation, vesting, and funding requirements, are mirrored in the Code, but some significant plan standards are found only in the Code. The Code contains a number of provisions designed to prevent qualified plans from discriminating in coverage, contributions, or benefits in favor of highly compensated employees, and it limits the maximum amount of benefits that a qualified plan can pay.

As originally enacted, ERISA placed the authority to administer Title I with the Department of Labor. In 1978, the Labor Department transferred to the Treasury Department responsibility for most of ERISA's participation, vesting, and funding requirements, and Treasury transferred responsibility for most of the fiduciary standards and prohibited transaction provisions to Labor.

An important difference between enforcement under ERISA and under the Code is the nature of the remedies. Generally, if a plan violates any of the Code's provisions, the penalty is disqualification of the plan for the period of the violation. This means the employer loses the deduction for contributions to the plan, and vested employees realize taxable income, even if the benefits are not yet distributable. Individual participants and beneficiaries do not have a private cause of action to enforce the Code's provisions; generally only the IRS may bring enforcement actions. Under ERISA, on the other hand, participants and beneficiaries, as well as the Department of Labor, may bring civil enforcement actions. The remedy for a violation of ERISA's statutory standards is an order requiring the plan to comply retroactively and prospectively.

§ 11.3   ERISA—Requirements for Pension Plans

One of ERISA's main purposes is protecting employees' expectations that pension benefits promised by their employers will be available when they retire. To prevent harsh qualification and forfeiture rules and plan amendments limiting previously promised pension obligations, ERISA imposes minimum participation, vesting, and accrual requirements on most covered pension plans. To prevent employers from failing to set aside enough money to pay their future pension obligations, ERISA also imposes funding standards on defined benefit plans and money purchase plans. Welfare benefit plans, which typically do not involve the same kind of commitments extending over many years, are not subject to any of these requirements.

Years of Service

ERISA contains complicated rules for calculating years of service, the basic measurement for participation, vesting, and accrual. A year of service is 1,000 hours of service during a twelve-month period. Generally, plans must count all of an employee's years of service with the sponsoring employer in determining periods of service for participation, vesting, and accrual. An employee's participation, vesting percentage, or accrued benefits may, however, be affected by any "breaks in service." An employee incurs a one-year break in service if he or she does not have 500 hours of service during the twelve-month period designated by the plan. The Retirement Equity Act of 1984 softened the consequences of breaks in service by establishing the "rule of parity." Under this rule, which applies only to nonvested participants, a participant's prebreak years of service must be credited unless the participant has five consecutive one-year breaks in service, or, if longer, a number of consecutive years equal to his or her prebreak service. In other words, if a nonvested participant has a break in service but returns to work within five years, or before the duration of the layoff exceeds the prebreak service, all of his or her prebreak service must be counted for participation and vesting. The Retirement Equity Act of 1984 also created a special rule for maternity, paternity, or adoption leave. For purposes of the break-in-service rules, employees absent on a leave for these purposes must be treated as having completed the number of hours of service which would normally be credited, up to 501 hours. This credit is just enough to prevent the employee from incurring a one-year break in service. Under this provision, an employee could take a maternity leave and then take four more years off for child care without losing credit for her prebreak service. Of course, these reforms benefit only employees who actually return to their prebreak jobs; most workers do not retain recall rights after such a long absence. The Uniformed Services Employment and Reemployment Rights Act of 1994 (USERRA)[1] requires that employees who return to work after discharge from the armed services within the period of time specified in the Act must be credited with service for purposes of participation and vesting for the period of his or her military service.

Participation

Section 202 contains minimum standards for participation.[2] Pension plans must permit participation when an employee reaches the age of twenty-one or completes one year of service, whichever is later. A plan may delay participation until an employee has completed two years of service if it provides for 100 percent vesting after two years. Plans may not exclude employees from participation because they have reached a specified age.

Vesting

The concept of vesting and the requirement that vesting occur before retirement are key aspects of ERISA's reform of pension plan administration. An employee's right to participate in a pension plan matters only if at some point the employee vests in the plan. An accrued

1. 38   U.S.C.A.   §§ 4301–4333.   See § 4.32.

2.   29 U.S.C.A. § 1052.

benefit is "vested" or "nonforfeitable," terms ERISA uses interchangeably, when the participant's claim to the benefit, either immediately or on a deferred basis, is unconditional and legally enforceable against the plan. A benefit becomes vested when "the employee's right to the benefit would survive a termination of his employment."[3]

Section 203[4] establishes minimum standards for vesting of accrued benefits. First, all pension plans must provide that employees' rights to their normal retirement benefits become nonforfeitable upon the attainment of normal retirement age. This rule applies even if the employee does not have enough years of service to vest under one of the preretirement vesting schedules discussed below. ERISA permits plans to define "normal retirement age" as the later of age sixty-five or the tenth anniversary of the commencement of an employee's participation in the plan. Although plans may not exclude employees from participation because of their age at the time of hire, defined benefit plans may redefine the normal retirement age for those workers who begin their participation within five years before the plan's normal retirement age as the fifth anniversary of the commencement of their participation.

Second, pension plans must provide that accrued benefits derived from employees' own contributions, if the plan requires or permits employee contributions, are nonforfeitable at all times. Third, for accrued benefits derived from the employer's contributions, plans must provide one of two preretirement vesting schedules, which were amended by the Tax Reform Act of 1986 to require faster vesting than under the original statute. (Amendments in 1996 eliminated, with respect to plan years beginning no later than January 1, 1999, a third option of ten-year cliff vesting for multiemployer plans.) Employees who satisfy the plan's preretirement vesting schedule have a nonforfeitable claim to their accrued benefits at retirement even if they leave their jobs before reaching the plan's normal retirement age.

The first preretirement vesting option is five-year "cliff" vesting; an employee who has completed five years of service must have a nonforfeitable right to 100 percent of the accrued benefit derived from employer contributions. Under this method, no vesting at all is required until the end of five years. The second option permits graduated vesting. It is met if employees are twenty percent vested in the employer-derived benefit after three years of service, with an additional twenty percent vesting in each successive year; the benefit must be 100 percent vested after seven years of service. Finally, the Internal Revenue Code requires all qualified plans to provide that accrued benefits vest, to the extent funded, when a plan is terminated or partially terminated, regardless of the vesting schedule chosen by the plan.[5]

---

3. Nachman Corp. v. Pension Benefit Guaranty Corp., 446 U.S. 359, 363–64, 100 S.Ct. 1723, 1727, 64 L.Ed.2d 354 (1980).

4. 29 U.S.C.A. § 1053.

5. 26 U.S.C.A. § 411(d)(3).

Plans may amend their vesting schedules, but any amendment may not reduce a participant's nonforfeitable accrued benefit. In addition, plans must give all participants with three years' service, even if not fully vested, the choice of having their nonforfeitable percentage computed under the preamendment schedule.

ERISA's preretirement vesting provisions were also intended to prevent enforcement of "bad boy" clauses, under which employees lose their otherwise vested pension benefits if they are fired for various forms of misconduct, such as dishonesty or theft, or if they compete with the employer after leaving their jobs. Because plan documents may not supersede the statutory vesting and nonforfeitability requirements, these provisions are void as they apply to vested accrued benefits. Plans may, however, apply forfeiture provisions to benefits that are not required to accrue, such as early retirement benefits or welfare benefits, and to benefits vested under a more liberal schedule than the statute requires. For instance, in *Clark v. Lauren Young Tire Center Profit Sharing Trust*,[6] the plan provided for 100 percent cliff vesting after six years at a time when ERISA's cliff vesting standard was ten years. The plan also called for forfeiture if an employee went to work for a competitor before he or she had completed ten years of service. The plaintiff was laid off after nine years and eight months' employment; two months later he took a job with a competitor. The court upheld the forfeiture on the ground that ERISA's prohibition on forfeitures does not apply to accrued benefits that have vested under the plan's schedule but would not be vested under one of the statutory minimum schedules.

ERISA does contain some exceptions to the basic rule of nonforfeiture of vested accrued benefits. Otherwise nonforfeitable accrued benefits may be lost because of (1) the death of the participant, unless a survivor's benefit must be paid; (2) suspension of benefits if the participant is reemployed under certain circumstances; (3) the adoption of certain plan amendments as approved by the Secretary of the Treasury; (4) the participant's withdrawal of mandatory employee contributions; (5) withdrawal of an employer from a multiemployer plan, as to precontribution service credits; and (6) amendment of a multiemployer plan under the provisions of the Multiemployer Pension Plan Amendments Act of 1980.

Many plans provide for the reduction of benefit payments by the amount of some other benefit the retiree is receiving. In *Alessi v. Raybestos–Manhattan, Inc.*,[7] the Supreme Court rejected arguments that an offset for workers' compensation awards constituted an impermissible forfeiture of vested pension rights. Pointing to the statutory definition of "nonforfeitable," the Court said that forfeiture connotes a total loss of a benefit, rather than a limit on the amount of the benefit. ERISA requires that the claim to a benefit become enforceable upon vesting, but it does not regulate the amount of the vested benefit, which is instead deter-

---

6. 816 F.2d 480 (9th Cir.1987).

7. 451 U.S. 504, 101 S.Ct. 1895, 68 L.Ed.2d 402 (1981).

mined by reference to the plan. The Court supported its decision with pre-ERISA Internal Revenue Service regulations permitting such offsets and by Congress' failure to prohibit the practice of integration, under which benefit levels are determined by including retirees' other sources of income.

Accrual

Alessi illustrates that vesting does not guarantee any particular amount or method of calculating a benefit; it merely allows the participant to enforce his or her claim to a particular percentage of the benefit provided for by the plan. When a participant becomes 100 percent vested, he or she has an enforceable right to the benefits accrued to date under the plan and to any additional benefits accrued in the future. Accrual rules help to determine the amount of the benefit to which a vested participant is entitled. As the Supreme Court remarked in *Nachman Corp. v. Pension Benefit Guaranty Corp.*, "the statutory definition of 'nonforfeitable' * * * describ[es] the quality of the participant's right to a pension rather than a limit on the amount he may collect."[8] Before the enactment of ERISA, a common plan practice was to "backload" benefits by providing for minimal accrual in the early years of employment, with accelerated accrual only as the employee neared retirement age. An employee who did not continue in employment until the plan's normal retirement age might be 100 percent vested, but have virtually no accrued benefits. Another of ERISA's reforms was to prevent an employer from avoiding the impact of the statutory preretirement vesting requirements through delayed accrual of this kind.

Section 204[9] establishes minimum standards for the accrual of benefits. Benefits must begin to accrue when an employee becomes a participant in the plan. The rules for defined contribution plans are simple. Contributions to the plan must be made annually as required by the plan and allocated to individual accounts for each participant. Gains or losses on the contributions are also allocated to the individual accounts. A participant's accrued benefit in a defined contribution plan is the balance in his or her account.

Defined benefit plans must accrue a portion of the normal retirement benefit for each year of participation. Section 204(b)(1) provides three accrual methods. First, the three percent method requires that the benefits accrued for each year of participation, up to 33 1/3 years, must be at least three percent of the normal retirement benefit. The normal retirement benefit for this purpose is the benefit to which the employee would be entitled if he or she had commenced participation at the earliest possible age and remained a participant continuously until the earlier of age sixty-five or the plan's normal retirement age. Second, the 133 1/3 percent method requires that the benefit accrued for any year be not more than 133 1/3 percent of the benefit accrued in earlier years. Third, the fractional method permits the accrued benefit to be deter-

8. 446 U.S. 359, 373, 100 S.Ct. 1723,   **9.** 29 U.S.C.A. § 1054.
1732, 64 L.Ed.2d 354 (1980).

mined by multiplying the normal retirement benefit by the fraction of the participant's years of participation over the total number of years the participant would have if he or she worked to normal retirement age. Defined benefit plans may not reduce accrued benefits because of the participant's age or years of service, and all plans, both defined benefit and defined contribution, must credit years of service after normal retirement age.

Commencement of Benefits

Unless the participant chooses to wait, payments of vested benefits must begin within sixty days after the end of the plan year in which the participant (1) reaches normal retirement age; (2) has participated in the plan for ten years; or (3) terminates service with the employer, whichever is latest. As discussed above, plans must continue benefit accruals on behalf of participants who continue working past normal retirement age. ERISA does not contain rules on how long an eligible participant may defer receipt of benefits, but the Internal Revenue Code requires the commencement of benefits no later than April 1 following the calendar year in which the participant reaches age 70 1/2.

ERISA does not require a plan to offer early retirement benefits. If a plan does offer early retirement benefits conditioned on the satisfaction of age and service requirements, ERISA requires the payment of actuarially reduced benefits to a participant who has satisfied the service requirement but left employment before reaching the required age when that individual does reach the plan's early retirement age.

Funding

ERISA's minimum funding standards apply to defined benefit plans and money purchase defined contribution plans, but not to profit sharing plans, stock bonus plans, and certain insurance plans. Each plan covered by the funding requirements must satisfy the minimum funding standard each year and maintain a funding standard account for each year. The minimum funding standard for a year is satisfied if the plan does not have an accumulated funding deficiency, an excess of total charges to the funding standard account over the total credits to that account.

For a money purchase plan, the minimum funding standard is satisfied for a year if the employer makes the contributions required under the terms of the plan. Determining whether a defined benefit plan has satisfied the minimum funding standard for a year requires complicated actuarial computations. The plan's funding standard account is charged with the plan's normal costs of that year's accrued benefits, plus amortization of unfunded past service liabilities, net experience losses, net losses from changes in actuarial assumptions, and any funding deficiencies previously waived, and certain other costs. The funding standard account is credited with contributions, amortization of net experience gains and net gains from changes in actuarial assumptions, and certain other amounts.

§ 11.4   ERISA—Survivor's Benefits

ERISA allows plans to stop payments of vested pension benefits when the participant dies, unless the plan is required to pay a survivor's annuity. As originally enacted, ERISA required a plan that offered pension benefits in the form of an annuity to offer as one option a "qualified joint and survivor annuity" (QJSA) payable during the lives of both the participant and his or her spouse. The participant could elect a single life annuity for his or her life only (instead of a QJSA) without the consent or, for that matter, the knowledge of the spouse; when the participant died, the spouse would be left with no pension income. In addition, in many situations ERISA did not require plans to provide rights for the nonemployee spouse if the participant died before retirement.

The Retirement Equity Act of 1984 (REA) amended section 205 of ERISA and the Internal Revenue Code to create significant new rights in a participant's pension for surviving spouses.[1] The concept of the QJSA was retained, with two important changes. Plans are now required to make payment of a QJSA upon the participant's retirement automatic unless specifically and correctly waived, and the nonemployee spouse, not the participant, has the waiver right. Additionally, the REA created a new survivor's right, the "qualified preretirement survivor annuity" (QPSA), which requires plans to provide an annuity for the life of the surviving spouse of a vested participant who dies before retirement. As with the QJSA, the QPSA is automatic, unless waived by the nonparticipant spouse.

With two exceptions, plans may require as a condition of payment of survivor's benefits that the participant and spouse have been married throughout the one-year period ending on the earlier of the date of retirement or the participant's death. Under the first exception, if the couple was married within the one-year period before the annuity starting date and remains married for at least one year before the date of death, the plan must pay survivor's benefits. Under the second, a "qualified domestic relations order" may provide that a former spouse be treated as the surviving spouse for purposes of the survivor's annuity, and in that case the one-year marriage rule is satisfied by one year of marriage at any time.

The QJSA is an annuity for the life of the participant, with a survivor annuity for the life of the participant's spouse. The survivor annuity must be not less than fifty nor more than 100 percent of the annuity payable during the joint lives of the couple. The total amount payable under the QJSA must be the actuarial equivalent of a single annuity for the life of the participant.

The QPSA must be at least the amount, or its actuarial equivalent, that would have been paid as a survivor annuity under the plan's QJSA. If the participant dies after reaching the earliest retirement age under

1.   29 U.S.C.A. § 1055.

the plan, the amount of the survivor's annuity is calculated as if the participant had retired with an immediate QJSA on the day before his or her death. If the participant dies before reaching the earliest retirement age under the plan, the amount is calculated as if the participant had (1) separated from service on the date of death, (2) survived to the earliest retirement age, (3) retired with an immediate QJSA at the earliest retirement age, and (4) died the day after he or she would have reached the earliest retirement age. If the participant separated from service before his or her death, the QPSA calculations are made using the date of separation, not the date of death. For defined contribution plans to which the QPSA applies, the QPSA must be an annuity for the life of the surviving spouse that is actuarially equivalent to at least fifty percent of the participant's vested account balance. All covered plans must begin QPSA benefit payments no later than the first month in which the participant could have taken early retirement.

Although the statute still speaks of the participant's right to elect to waive the survivor annuities, the nonparticipant spouse must consent to the participant's waiver before that waiver will be effective. The election to waive survivor annuities must designate a beneficiary or form of benefits, which may not be changed without spousal consent. The survivor annuities may be waived or any previous election revoked only during the "applicable election period." For the QJSA the election period is the ninety-day period ending on the annuity starting date. For the QPSA the period begins on the first day of the plan year in which the participant attains age thirty-five and ends on the earlier of the date of the participant's death or the annuity starting date. A waiver at any time other than the applicable election period is not effective. Plans do not have to permit waivers of survivor's rights if the plan fully subsidizes the costs of the benefits, so that joint and survivor's benefits are not lower than benefits in single life or some other form.

To enable participants to understand their rights and options with respect to the survivor annuities, plans must provide each participant a written explanation of the terms and conditions of the QJSA and the QPSA, the participant's right to elect to waive these annuities and the financial and other effects of that waiver, the right of the participant's spouse to consent or to withhold consent to the waiver, and the right to revoke a waiver and its effect. With respect to the QJSA, the statute requires this explanation to be provided "within a reasonable period of time before the annuity starting date," which Treasury Department regulations define as the nine-month period before the participant reaches the earliest retirement age under the plan.

Plans must provide information concerning the QPSA before the latest of (1) the period beginning with the first day of the plan year in which the participant turns thirty-two and ending with the close of the plan year preceding the plan year in which the participant reaches thirty-five, (2) a reasonable period after the person becomes a participant, or (3) a reasonable period after the survivor benefit requirements become applicable to the participant. If a participant separates from service before reaching age thirty-five, the QPSA notice must be provided within a reasonable period after separation. The statute requires notice only to the participant, however. As long as proper notice was given to the participant, claims by nonparticipant survivors that they did not receive or did not understand the notice, and therefore acted to their detriment, are rejected.

The spouse's consent to an election to waive the right to a survivor annuity must be in writing and either notarized or witnessed by a plan representative. A consent by one spouse affects only that spouse and does not waive the rights of any subsequent spouse of the same participant. Spousal consent to a waiver is not necessary if the participant establishes to the satisfaction of the plan that he or she is not married, or that the spouse can not be located. Prenuptial agreements purporting to waive survivor rights in a spouse's pension do not satisfy the statutory consent requirements because, among other reasons, ERISA requires that the spouse be married to the participant at the time of the waiver.

The plan is protected from liability for benefits paid if the fiduciary acts in accordance with ERISA's fiduciary standards in relying on a spouse's consent or in determining that the spouse's consent can not be obtained, but later learns that someone other than the spouse signed the consent or that the spouse could in fact have been located and consent obtained. In the absence of actual knowledge of fraud or coercion in the inducement of a spousal consent or actual knowledge of the invalidity of a consent, a plan fiduciary may rely on a waiver that on its face conforms to statutory requirements. ERISA's fiduciary standards may, however, require a plan to do more than merely accept a participant's assertions that a spouse cannot be located or does not exist. The difference between a signed, notarized document in which the spouse waives his or her rights and the participant's attempt to waive the spouse's rights by declaring that he or she cannot be found may require the fiduciary to conduct an independent investigation of the participant's representations as part of its duty of prudence.[2]

In *Boggs v. Boggs*,[3] the Supreme Court held that ERISA's qualified joint and survivor annuity provisions preempted Louisiana's community property laws, which would have given the plan participant's sons from his first marriage a portion of his second wife's survivor's annuity without her consent. The Court also held that ERISA's anti-alienation provisions preempted the state's community property laws that would have allowed the first wife to make a testamentary transfer of her interest in the participant's retirement benefits.

§ 11.5 ERISA—Alienation of Benefits

Complementing ERISA's provisions on vesting and nonforfeitability

2. See Lester v. Reagan Equip. Co. Profit Sharing Plan, 1992 WL 193499 (E.D.La. 1992).

3. 520 U.S. 833, 117 S.Ct. 1754, 138 L.Ed.2d 45 (1997).

of pension benefits is its antialienation provision, section 206(d)(1),[1] which protects participants from losing their benefits as a result of their dealings with third parties. Section 206(d)(1) accomplishes this goal by requiring that "[e]ach pension plan shall provide that benefits provided under the plan may not be assigned or alienated." Although the terms "assigned" and "alienated" often refer only to voluntary transfers, section 206(d)(1) applies to involuntary transfers as well, including attachment, garnishment, levy, execution, and constructive trust. Thus, a participant's creditors may not reach his or her pension benefits to satisfy their liens, even if the participant has a right to withdraw funds immediately or is awaiting a lump sum distribution. The antialienation rule does not apply, however, to funds that have already been distributed.[2] By its terms, section 206(d)(1) applies only to pension benefits, and in *Mackey v. Lanier Collection Agency & Service, Inc.,*[3] the Supreme Court held that ERISA does not preclude the garnishment of benefits from welfare plans.

A plan may permit a participant to assign the right to future benefit payments if the assignment is voluntary and revocable and does not exceed ten percent of any benefit payment.[4] A participant may also use nonforfeitable benefits as security for a loan from the plan under certain conditions.

Misconduct

In *Guidry v. Sheet Metal Workers National Pension Fund,*[5] the Supreme Court rejected an invitation to create an implied exception to section 206(a)(1) for criminal activity against the employer or union that sponsors the plan. After Guidry, a union officer and a trustee of a union pension fund, was convicted of embezzling funds from the union, the lower courts imposed a constructive trust on his pension benefits in favor of the union. The Court found that section 206(d)(1) reflects a considered choice by Congress to protect a participant's stream of retirement income and refused to approve any generalized equitable exceptions for employee malfeasance. Because Guidry had not been found to have breached any fiduciary duty to the plan, the Court expressly reserved the question whether section 409(a),[6] which creates personal liability for faithless plan fiduciaries and authorizes courts to impose appropriate equitable or remedial relief for fiduciary breaches, might override the command of section 206(d)(1).

In 1997 Congress amended section 206(d) to add new subsections (4) and (5) which deal with this issue. Section 206(d)(4) provides an exception to the antialienation rule for an order or requirement to pay arising under a judgment or conviction for a crime involving the plan, under a

§ 11.5
1. 29 U.S.C.A. § 1056(d)(1).
2. See, e.g., Wright v. Riveland, 219 F.3d 905 (9th Cir.2000).
3. 486 U.S. 825, 108 S.Ct. 2182, 100 L.Ed.2d 836 (1988).
4. ERISA § 206(d)(2), 29 U.S.C.A. § 1056(d)(2).
5. 493 U.S. 365, 110 S.Ct. 680, 107 L.Ed.2d 782 (1990).
6. 29 U.S.C.A. § 1109(a).

civil judgment in an action brought in connection with a violation or alleged violation of ERISA's fiduciary requirements, or pursuant to a settlement agreement between the Secretary and the participant or a settlement agreement between the PBGC and the participant in connection with a violation or alleged violation of the fiduciary requirements. The judgment, order, or settlement agreement must expressly provide for the offset of all or part of the amount ordered or required to be paid to the plan against the participant's benefits provided under the plan. If the benefits are subject to ERISA's rules on survivor's benefits, and if the participant is married at the time the offset is to be made, (1) either the spouse must consent to the offset by a notarized written statement or an election to waive the spouse's right to a QJSA or a QPSA must be in effect; (2) the spouse must have been required by the judgment, order, or settlement to pay an amount to the plan in connection with a violation of ERISA's fiduciary requirements; or (3) the judgment, order, or settlement must retain the spouse's right to receive his or her survivor's annuity. Section 206(d)(5) provides that for the purposes of section 206(d)(4), the survivor annuity is to be determine as if (1) the participant terminated his or her employment on the date of the offset, (2) there was no offset, (3) the plan permitted commencement of benefits only on or after normal retirement age, (4) the plan provided only the minimum-required QJSA, and (5) the amount of QJSA is equal to the amount of the survivor annuity payable under the minimum required QJSA. The "minimum-required" QJSA means the QJSA that is the actuarial equivalent of the participant's accrued benefit and under which the survivor annuity is fifty percent of the amount of the annuity payable during the joint lives of the participant and his or her spouse.

Qualified Domestic Relations Orders

As part of its reasoning for refusing to create an implied exception to ERISA's antialienation provision for employee malfeasance or criminal activity, the Court in *Guidry* cited the 1984 amendment to ERISA providing an express exception for qualified domestic relations orders. Under section 206(d)(3), the antialienation provisions do not apply to a "qualified domestic relations order" (QDRO).[7] Section 514 was also amended to exempt QDROs from ERISA preemption.[8] To be a QDRO, a judgment, decree, or order (including approval of a property settlement agreement) must be made pursuant to a state domestic relations law and must relate to child support, alimony, or marital property rights of a participant's spouse, former spouse, child, or other dependent (called "alternate payees" by the statute). The order must clearly specify the name and last known mailing address of the participant and each alternate payee, the amount or percent of the participant's benefits to be paid to each alternate payee, the number of payments or the period of time covered by the order, and each plan to which the order applies. The

---

7. 29 U.S.C.A. § 1056(d)(3).

8. ERISA § 514(b)(7), 29 U.S.C.A. § 1144(b)(7).

plan is protected from multiple QDROs that exceed the amount of the participant's benefits.

A QDRO may not require a plan to provide any type or form of benefit or option not otherwise provided under the plan, nor may it require a plan to increase benefits beyond those provided in the plan. An exception to this rule, however, is that a QDRO may require the plan to begin payments to the alternate payee when the participant reaches the age for early retirement under the plan, even if the participant does not actually retire at that time. Second, the QDRO may provide that the participant's former spouse is to be considered the surviving spouse for purposes of ERISA's survivor benefits provisions. Thus, a plan can be required to pay an ex-spouse the survivor benefits that would otherwise go to the participant's current spouse, or, if the participant did not remarry, would otherwise not have to be paid at all.

Orders that do not meet the QDRO standards are unenforceable as violations of section 206(d)(1) and are preempted by section 514. If a dispute exists about whether a state court order is a QDRO, the plan administrator may suspend payments to the alternate payee for up to eighteen months. ERISA's fiduciary duties apply to the payment of benefits, and a plan that has notice of a divorce or other decree that may satisfy the requirements of a QDRO may not simply ignore it in favor of other documents. An alternate payee under a QDRO is deemed a beneficiary under the plan "for purposes of any provision of this Act." Therefore, the alternate payee has standing to sue under ERISA's enforcement provisions.

Bankruptcy

In *Patterson v. Shumate*,[9] the Supreme Court resolved the tension between section 206(d)(1) and section 541(c)(2) of the Bankruptcy Code, which excludes from the debtor's estate property subject to a restriction on transfer that is enforceable under "applicable nonbankruptcy law."[10] Relying on a plain language reading of the Bankruptcy Code, the Court rejected the argument that "applicable nonbankruptcy law" refers only to state laws defining spendthrift trusts. Further, the Court noted that the requirement of section 206(d)(1) that pension plans include restrictions on alienation is enforceable under section 502(a) of ERISA. Therefore, a pension plan's antialienation provision is enforceable under nonbankruptcy law, namely ERISA, and funds in an ERISA-covered pension plan qualify for the exclusion in section 541(c)(2) of the Bankruptcy Code. These funds, which could be substantial, are thus excluded from the property of the bankruptcy estate and may not be used to pay the estate's debts.

Section 522(d)(10)(E) of the Bankruptcy Code permits a debtor who elects the federal exemptions in section 522(d) to exempt from the bankruptcy estate his or her right to receive "a payment under a stock

---

9. 504 U.S. 753, 112 S.Ct. 2242, 119 L.Ed.2d 519 (1992).

10. 11 U.S.C.A. § 541(c)(2).

bonus, pension, profitsharing, annuity, or similar plan or contract * * *, to the extent reasonably necessary for the support of the debtor and any dependent of the debtor.''[11] Although the petitioner in *Patterson* argued that this express exemption for pension benefits rendered superfluous a construction of section 541(c)(2) excluding a debtor's entire interest in a pension plan covered by ERISA, the Court noted that section 522(d)(10)(E) exempts a broader category of property than section 541(c)(2) excludes. Pension plans that are not covered by ERISA, such as governmental and church plans, are not subject to ERISA's antialienation requirement; neither are certain covered plans, such as IRAs, which are specifically excepted from section 206(d)(1). Some pre-*Patterson* appellate decisions had dealt with the superfluity argument by stating that section 522(d)(10)(E) exempts only pension benefits in pay status, whereas section 541(c)(2) excludes the entire undistributed corpus of a pension trust.

The *Patterson* Court declined to decide the scope of the section 541(c)(2) exclusion. Regardless of the resolution of this issue, use of the section 541(c)(2) exclusion can benefit some debtors much more than the section 522(d)(10)(E) exemption, which is pegged to a reasonable support standard. A young debtor with a potentially good future earning ability might not be able to protect his or her pension benefits under the exemption, whereas all of the benefits are shielded by the exclusion.

Taxes

Treasury Department regulations specify that section 206(d)(1) does not apply to federal tax levies, to the collection of a judgment for unpaid federal taxes, or to withholding for federal, state, or local taxes.[12] State tax levies, however, are prohibited.

§ 11.6 ERISA—Fiduciary Duties

The fiduciary provisions of ERISA, contained in Part 4 of Title I,[1] apply to virtually all employee benefit plans covered by ERISA. Thus, the fiduciary requirements apply to pension plans and to both funded and unfunded welfare plans. While most suits for breach of ERISA's fiduciary duties involve challenges to the management and disposition of pension fund assets, the actions of the fiduciaries of even unfunded welfare plans can also violate the statutory requirements. In addition to the fiduciary standards, Part 4 of Title I contains the requirements that all plans be established and maintained pursuant to a written instrument and, with certain exceptions, that their assets be held in trust by one or more trustees who are named in the plan documents or appointed by a named fiduciary.

11. Id. § 522(d)(10)(E).

12. 26 C.F.R. §§ 1.401(a)–13(b)(2),– 13(c)(2).

§ 11.6

1. ERISA §§ 401–414, 29 U.S.C.A. §§ 1101–1114.

Fiduciary Status

ERISA requires each plan to have one or more "named fiduciaries who * * * shall have authority to control and manage the operation and administration of the plan." ERISA defines "fiduciary" in functional terms. Under section 3(21)(A), a person is a fiduciary with respect to a plan to the extent he or she (1) exercises any discretionary authority or discretionary control concerning management of the plan or exercises any authority or control with respect to management or disposition of plan assets, (2) renders investment advice for a fee or other compensation with respect to plan assets or has the authority or responsibility to do so, or (3) has any discretionary authority or discretionary responsibility in the administration of the plan.[2]

In keeping with ERISA's remedial nature, courts have interpreted the term fiduciary broadly to include not only the fiduciary named in the plan documents, but also anyone who possesses or performs any of the three basic fiduciary functions, plan administration, asset management, or investment advice for a fee, even if that person has no formal relationship with the plan. Thus, while individuals who hold certain plan positions, such as a trustee, clearly have fiduciary status, a person who has no position with a plan may nevertheless be a fiduciary if he or she actually performs or controls the performance of a fiduciary function. For instance, in *Blatt v. Marshall & Lassman*,[3] an accounting firm ignored the request of a former partner to submit a notice of claim form on his behalf to the insurer of the firm's retirement plan, and as a result distribution of his vested benefits in the plan was delayed. Disposition of plan assets is a fiduciary function, and the return of contributions to plan participants is one method of disposition. The court found that by choosing to delay filing the notice of claim form, the firm exercised control over the disposition of plan assets and therefore became an ERISA fiduciary.

On the other hand, a person who performs only ministerial functions within a pre-established framework of policies and procedures and who has no power to make any independent decisions about the management of the plan or the disposition of plan assets does not satisfy the statutory definition. Thus, a person whose sole function is to apply a formula contained in the plan documents to calculate the amount of benefits to which a plan participant is entitled is not a fiduciary. Even a plan administrator may not qualify for fiduciary status if it merely processes claims and keeps records and does not exercise any discretion with respect to the plan or its assets.

Further, an individual is a fiduciary only to the extent that he or she performs fiduciary functions. An entity that limits its activities to one fiduciary function is not subject to ERISA's fiduciary standards as to its other activities relating to the plan. For instance, appointment and removal of plan fiduciaries are themselves fiduciary functions. If a

2. 29 U.S.C.A. § 1002(21)(A). **3.** 812 F.2d 810 (2d Cir.1987).

sponsoring employer appoints a plan administrator and delegates control over the plan and the disposition of claims to that administrator, the employer is an ERISA fiduciary with respect to the selection and retention of the administrator, but not with respect to the actual day-to-day administration of the plan.

A related concept is that some decisions that seriously affect the structure of the plan and the expectations of participants are simply not fiduciary in nature. By specifically permitting employer representatives to serve as fiduciaries,[4] ERISA contemplates that employers will often wear two hats with respect to benefit plans. Accordingly, the courts have distinguished between decisions that are employer or "settlor" functions, to which the fiduciary standards do not apply, and those that are fiduciary functions. Day-to-day corporate business decisions involving the workforce or the direction of the company, such as whether to keep employees on the payroll following the sale of a plant or whether the early retirement of a particular employee would be in the company's interest, are not subject to ERISA's fiduciary standards.

Settlor functions generally are the "design" decisions, such as whether to establish a plan, what level and type of benefits to offer, whether to amend the plan to reduce or eliminate nonvested benefits, and whether to terminate the plan. In *Lockheed Corp. v. Spink*,[5] the Supreme Court confirmed this point when it held that plan sponsors who alter the terms of a plan are not acting as fiduciaries when they do so. Then in *Hughes Aircraft Co. v. Jacobson*,[6] the Court once again held that an employer's decision to amend an ERISA plan (here a pension plan) does not implicate the statute's fiduciary duties. It rejected the lower court's distinction between the Lockheed plan, which was funded solely by employer contributions, and Hughes' plan, which involved employee contributions. Its holding "did not turn * * * on the type of plan being amended for the simple reason that the plain language of the statute defining fiduciary makes no distinction." Because many of the settlor decisions are motivated by the employer's desire to save money, they rarely satisfy ERISA's fiduciary requirement that they be "solely in the interest of the participants and beneficiaries." The courts reason that if ERISA's fiduciary provisions applied to the decision to reduce or eliminate a current benefit, few, if any, reductions would be allowed, and a decision to offer a benefit, once made, could never be revoked. ERISA's vesting and accrual requirements prevent the reduction or elimination of vested benefits and nonvested accrued benefits, but courts have found that the statutory fiduciary standards do not control employers' decisions to reduce or eliminate welfare benefits, to which the vesting and accrual requirements do not apply. As the litigation over retiree health benefits indicates, promises in the plan documents, in collective bargaining agreements, or in other statements may obligate an employer to

4. ERISA § 408(c)(3), 29 U.S.C.A. § 1108(c)(3).

5. 517 U.S. 882, 116 S.Ct. 1783, 135 L.Ed.2d 153 (1996).

6. 525 U.S. 432, 119 S.Ct. 755, 142 L.Ed.2d 881 (1999).

continue to provide a welfare benefit, but ERISA's fiduciary standards do not.

Finally, firms or individuals who render professional advice to plans are generally not fiduciaries, as long as they do not cross the line between advising plan fiduciaries and actually exercising control over the plan. Thus, attorneys, accountants, and actuaries who advise plans in their professional capacities may be pursued, if at all, for malpractice under state law, not for breach of ERISA's fiduciary standards. In *Pegram v. Herdrich,*[7] the Court held, unanimously, that a health mainte-nance organization and its physicians do not act as ERISA fiduciaries when they make what the Court called "mixed eligibility decisions," decisions about the diagnosis and treatment of a beneficiary's condition. In a footnote, however, the Court remarked that "fiduciary duty to disclose is not necessarily coextensive with fiduciary responsibility for the subject matter of the disclosure * * *."

Fiduciary Duties

ERISA codifies strict principles of fiduciary duty developed by the common law of trusts. Section 404(a)(1) imposes four basic interrelated statutory standards embodying the trust requirements of loyalty and care.[8] The first is the exclusive benefit rule. Fiduciaries must discharge their duties "solely in the interest of the participants and beneficiaries" of the plan and "for the exclusive purpose" of providing benefits and defraying reasonable administrative expenses. Complementing the exclu-sive benefit rule are the noninurement rule of section 403(c)(1),[9] which provides that, with certain exceptions, plan assets may not inure to the benefit of the employer, and the prohibited transactions provisions, sections 406, 407, and 408, discussed below. The second fiduciary stan-dard is the "prudence" standard of care for administration and invest-ment decisions. The third requires diversification of plan investments, and the fourth commands fiduciaries to act in accordance with plan documents to the extent they are consistent with the terms of the statute.

Under the exclusive benefit rule fiduciaries must act with "complete and undivided loyalty to the beneficiaries of the trust,"[10] and "with an eye single"[11] to the interests of participants and beneficiaries. They may not act in their own personal interests or in the interest of some third party. As discussed above, however, ERISA does permit employees of the employer that sponsors the plan to serve as plan fiduciaries,[12] and it also allows fiduciaries to invest as much as ten percent of the trust's assets in the stock of the employer that sponsors the plan.[13] In the leading case of

---

7. 530 U.S. 211, 120 S.Ct. 2143, 147 L.Ed.2d 164 (2000).

8. 29 U.S.C.A. § 1104(a)(1).

9. 29 U.S.C.A. § 1103(c)(1).

10. Freund v. Marshall & Ilsley Bank, 485 F.Supp. 629, 639 (W.D.Wis.1979).

11. Donovan v. Bierwirth, 680 F.2d 263, 271 (2d Cir.), cert. denied, 459 U.S. 1069, 103 S.Ct. 488, 74 L.Ed.2d 631 (1982).

12. ERISA § 408(c)(3), 29 U.S.C.A. § 1108(c)(3).

13. ERISA § 407(a)(3), 29 U.S.C.A. § 1107(a)(3).

Donovan v. Bierwirth,[14] the Second Circuit noted these aspects of the statute and said that fiduciaries do not violate their statutory duties merely because an action that benefits the plan also benefits the plan sponsor or even themselves. The fiduciaries must be extremely careful, however, to concentrate on the interests of the participants and beneficiaries. *Bierwirth* involved the actions of the trustees of the Grumman Corporation's pension fund, who were also officers of Grumman, in causing the fund to purchase large quantities of Grumman stock during the 1981 Grumman–LTV takeover battle. In finding a breach of ERISA's exclusive benefit rule, the court said that the trustees were obligated to engage in an intensive and scrupulous independent investigation of their options and "to take every feasible precaution to see that they had carefully considered the other side." In *Leigh v. Engle*,[15] the Seventh Circuit added that the extent and duration of the fiduciaries' actions favoring the interests of corporate officers must also be considered in determining a breach of the exclusive benefit rule.

The prudence standard of section 404(a)(1)(B) requires fiduciaries to act "with the care, skill, prudence, and diligence under the circumstances then prevailing that a prudent man acting in a like capacity and familiar with such matters would use in the conduct of an enterprise of a like character and with like aims." Although most of the ERISA prudence cases involve investment decisions, courts have applied the standard to other fiduciary actions. For instance, in *Central States, Southeast & Southwest Areas Pension Fund v. Central Transport, Inc.*,[16] the Court found a fiduciary duty to collect employer contributions derived from the common law duties of a trustee to preserve and maintain trust assets. In an influential early case, *Freund v. Marshall & Ilsley Bank*,[17] a district court found that a fiduciary's duty of prudence extends to his or her resignation, so that resignation without making adequate provision for the continued prudent management of the plan is a breach of fiduciary duty. The duty of prudence may require a fiduciary to investigate a participant's claim in connection with a waiver of survivor's benefits that he cannot locate his estranged wife.[18]

In *Varity Corp. v. Howe*,[19] the Supreme Court, citing the district court's findings of fact, upheld its conclusion that Varity was "wearing its 'fiduciary' * * * hat" when it made misrepresentations to its employees about benefits in order to induce the employees to become employees of a newly-created subsidiary. The subsidiary ultimately ended up in receivership, with workers losing nonpension benefits. The factual context in which the misleading statements were made, by individuals who had plan-related authority to make them, along with their plan-related nature, supported the conclusion that Varity was acting as a fiduciary,

---

14. 680 F.2d 263 (2d Cir.), cert. denied, 459 U.S. 1069, 103 S.Ct. 488, 74 L.Ed.2d 631 (1982).

15. 727 F.2d 113 (7th Cir.1984).

16. 472 U.S. 559, 105 S.Ct. 2833, 86 L.Ed.2d 447 (1985).

17. 485 F.Supp. 629 (W.D.Wis.1979).

18. Lester v. Reagan Equip. Co. Profit Sharing Plan, 1992 WL 193499 (E.D.La. 1992).

19. 516 U.S. 489, 116 S.Ct. 1065, 134 L.Ed.2d 130 (1996).

not merely as an employer. Varity argued that it had the authority to amend or terminate the plan at any time without triggering fiduciary responsibilities, but the Court responded that "it does not follow that making statements about the likely future of the plan is also beyond the scope of plan administration." The Court declined to reach the question whether ERISA fiduciaries have a duty to disclose truthful information on their own initiative or in response to employee questions, since *Varity* involved knowing deception.

In the wake of *Varity* there has been a great deal of litigation over this fiduciary duty of disclosure. Most of the lower courts have held that when "serious consideration" is being given to a plan amendment, a fiduciary duty arises not to make material misrepresentations, either negligently or intentionally, to participants.[20] The leading definition of serious consideration of a change in plan terms is that it does not occur until (1) a specific proposal (2) is being discussed for purposes of implementation (3) by senior management with the authority to implement the change.[21] A number of courts have also held that the fiduciary may have a duty to provide information beyond the specific scope of a participant's request.[22] There is disagreement, however, whether the duty not to make misleading statements can arise in the absence of the participant's inquiry.[23]

In *Krohn v. Huron Memorial Hospital*,[24] the Sixth Circuit held that a fiduciary has an affirmative duty to inform participants and beneficiaries of the existing provisions of a plan. In *Krohn* an employee was seriously injured, and her husband asked the employer about disability benefits. Although the employee was eligible for both short-and long-term disability benefits, the employer provided information only about short-term benefits. This failure was found to be a breach of the employer's fiduciary duty. The employer's defense that the information was readily available in its SPD was rejected; "[p]roviding a summary plan description several years before the request for information does not excuse the [employer] from its duty to respond fully and accurately to later inquiries about benefits."

In *Watson v. Deaconess Waltham Hospital*,[25] the First Circuit found no breach of fiduciary duties in the failure of a hospital to give an employee information about its long-term disability plan when the employee switched from part-time to full-time employment and became eligible for benefits under the plan. The court described "two related strands of ERISA cases: those involving plaintiffs seeking substantive

20. See, e.g., Mushalla v. Teamsters Local No. 863 Pension Fund, 300 F.3d 391 (3d Cir. 2002).

21. Fischer v. Philadelphia Elec. Co., 96 F.3d 1533 (3d Cir.1996), cert. denied, 520 U.S. 1116, 117 S.Ct. 1247, 137 L.Ed.2d 329 (1997).

22. See, e.g., Bixler v. Central Pennsylvania Teamsters Health & Welfare Fund, 12 F.3d 1292 (3d Cir. 1993).

23. Compare Martinez v. Schlumberger, Ltd., 338 F.3d 407 (5th Cir. 2003) (inquiry required), with Bowerman v. Wal–Mart Stores, Inc., 226 F.3d 574 (7th Cir. 2000) (no inquiry necessary).

24. 173 F.3d 542 (6th Cir.1999).

25. 298 F.3d 102 (1st Cir. 2002).

remedies, such as reinstatement or retroactive benefits, based on a fiduciary's failure to comply with ERISA's technical notice and disclosure requirements; and those involving a fiduciary's failure to communicate information relevant to the beneficiary's employment decisions." The court said that a technical violation of ERISA's notice requirements, without more, cannot be a fiduciary breach. While a fiduciary may have an obligation to convey accurate information to a beneficiary, including material information that the beneficiary did not specifically request, "fiduciaries need not generally provide individualized unsolicited advice." Any affirmative duty to provide material information about a plan arises only if there is some reason the fiduciary should have known that failure to give the information would be harmful to the beneficiary.

The fourth fiduciary duty is the duty to act in accordance with plan documents to the extent they are consistent with Titles I and IV of ERISA. In *Varity Corp. v. Howe*,[26] the Court rejected the argument that extending the duty of loyalty beyond plan management to individual beneficiaries would cause plan administrators to interpret the plan as requiring payments to individuals instead of preserving plan assets. Citing *Firestone Tire & Rubber Co. v. Bruch*,[27] the Court remarked that "characterizing a denial of benefits as a breach of fiduciary duty does not necessarily change the standard a court would apply when reviewing the administrator's decision to deny benefits." Moreover, the Court opined that an award of "appropriate" equitable relief under § 502(a)(3) should not be necessary where another section of ERISA provided "adequate relief for a beneficiary's injury."

Prohibited Transactions

ERISA's prohibited transactions provisions forbid fiduciary self-dealing and other transactions with the potential for misuse of fund assets. These transactions are defined by the relationship between the plan and the other parties to the arrangement. Subject to certain exceptions, section 406(a)[28] prohibits fiduciaries from engaging in various transactions with a "party in interest," which includes fiduciaries, counsel, or employees of the plan, persons providing services to the plan, employers whose employees are covered by the plan, unions whose members are covered by the plan, and other related individuals or entities. Prohibited are the sale, exchange, or lease of property, loans and extensions of credit, furnishing of goods or services, transfer of assets, or the acquisition of employer securities or property beyond limits permitted by section 407(a).

The Secretary of Labor is authorized to establish exemptions from this section for some transactions. Other transactions, such as certain loans to parties in interest who are also plan participants or beneficiaries, and the payment of reasonable compensation for services to the

26. 516 U.S. 489, 116 S.Ct. 1065, 134 L.Ed.2d 130 (1996).

27. 489 U.S. 101, 109 S.Ct. 948, 103 L.Ed.2d 80 (1989).

28. 29 U.S.C.A. § 1106(a).

plan, are specifically exempted. Section 406(b)(1) prohibits fiduciaries from dealing with plan assets for their own accounts.[29] Section 406(b)(2) prohibits fiduciaries from acting in a transaction involving the plan on behalf of a party whose interests are adverse to those of the plan, its participants, or beneficiaries.[30] Section 406(b)(3) prohibits kickbacks to fiduciaries.[31]

Fiduciary Liability

Section 409(a)[32] imposes personal liability on a fiduciary to make good any losses to the plan resulting from a breach of statutory duties and to restore to the plan any profits the fiduciary made through the misuse of plan assets, even if the plan did not suffer any loss. The fiduciary is also subject to "such other equitable or remedial relief as the court may deem appropriate." Unlike suits for denials of benefit claims, where relief runs from the plan to the participant or beneficiary, relief in section 409(a) suits runs from the fiduciary personally to the plan. In *Massachusetts Mutual Life Insurance Co. v. Russell*,[33] the Supreme Court held that section 409(a) does not authorize an award of compensatory or punitive damages to a participant for a fiduciary's breach, and most of the courts of appeals have relied on *Russell* to deny compensatory or punitive damages in suits based on any of ERISA's other causes of action.

Section 405(a) imposes liability on a fiduciary for the breach of a co-fiduciary in three situations: (1) if the fiduciary knowingly participates in or tries to conceal a breach by a co-fiduciary; (2) if, by failing to comply with his or her own fiduciary duties, a fiduciary enables a co-fiduciary to commit a breach; and (3) if a fiduciary knows that a breach has taken place and fails to make reasonable efforts to remedy it.[34] Actual knowledge of the breach is required for co-fiduciary liability in the first and third situations, but not in the second. Similarly, although a fiduciary is not liable for breaches committed before he or she became a fiduciary, new fiduciaries have a duty to review prior investment decisions and to take reasonable actions to correct any breaches discovered in that review. A fiduciary found liable for the breach of a co-fiduciary probably does not have a right to contribution from the co-fiduciary. ERISA does not expressly provide such a right, and most courts have refused to recognize one, relying on *Russell*'s admonition against the creation of remedies not expressly provided for in ERISA and on Supreme Court decisions denying a right to contribution under other federal statutes.

Although ERISA expressly establishes co-fiduciary liability, there is no provision imposing liability on nonfiduciaries in connection with a fiduciary's breach. In *Mertens v. Hewitt Associates*,[35] the Supreme Court

29. 29 U.S.C.A. § 1106(b)(1).

30. 29 U.S.C.A. § 1106(b)(2).

31. 29 U.S.C.A. § 1106(b)(3).

32. 29 U.S.C.A. § 1109(a).

33. 473 U.S. 134, 105 S.Ct. 3085, 87 L.Ed.2d 96 (1985).

34. ERISA § 405(a), 29 U.S.C.A. § 1105(a).

35. 508 U.S. 248, 113 S.Ct. 2063, 124 L.Ed.2d 161 (1993).

held, five to four, that ERISA does not permit suit for money damages against nonfiduciaries who knowingly participate in a fiduciary's breach. It rejected arguments that section 502(*l*), added to ERISA by the Omnibus Budget Reconciliation Act of 1989,[36] demonstrates congressional intent to permit suits against nonfiduciaries for knowing participation in a fiduciary breach. Section 502(*l*) gives the Secretary of Labor authority to assess a civil penalty against fiduciaries or other persons for "any knowing participation" in a breach of fiduciary duty. The Court said that "other persons" referred to in section 502(*l*) could be beneficiaries, who are expressly liable in certain circumstances.

The Court distinguished *Mertens* in *Harris Trust & Savings Bank v. Salomon Smith Barney, Inc.*[37] The case arose out of a transaction alleged to have been prohibited by section 406, which imposes duties on plan fiduciaries but not specifically on the nonfiduciary party in interest. The Court held, unanimously, that the nonfiduciary party in interest may be sued under section 502(a)(3). In support of its conclusion, the Court pointed to section 502(*1*), which it found authorizes the Secretary to sue an "other person" under section 502(a)(5). If the Secretary can sue under section 502(a)(5), then "it follows" that participants, beneficiaries, or fiduciaries can sue the "other person" under the similarly worded section 502(a)(3). The dicta in *Mertens* about the scope of section 502(*1*) was dismissed as just that.

Section 410(a) declares that agreements or provisions purporting to relieve fiduciaries from responsibility or liability for their statutory obligations are void as against public policy. A plan may, however, purchase insurance for itself or its fiduciaries, as long as the insurer has recourse against the breaching fiduciaries. An employer, a union, or fiduciaries themselves may also purchase insurance protecting fiduciaries from liability for breach of fiduciary duties. There is no statutory recourse requirement for this second group of insurance policies. Citing the policy favoring settlement of disputes, the Eighth Circuit held that section 410(a) does not bar private unsupervised releases of statutory claims.[38]

§ 11.7 ERISA—Plan Insurance and Single Employer Plan Terminations

One of the major themes of ERISA's legislative history was the plight of workers and retirees who lost the pension benefits they had earned over many years when their employer terminated its pension plan without having fully funded it. Congress dealt with this problem in Title IV of ERISA, which established the Pension Benefit Guaranty Corporation (PBGC), an independent corporation within the Department of Labor, to administer rules for pension plan terminations and a

36. ERISA § 502(*1*), 29 U.S.C.A. § 1132(*1*), as amended by Pub. L. No. 101–239, 103 Stat. 2123.

37. 530 U.S. 238, 120 S.Ct. 2180, 147 L.Ed.2d 187 (2000).

38. Leavitt v. Northwestern Bell Tel. Co., 921 F.2d 160 (8th Cir.1990).

program of pension insurance. Title IV applies to most tax-qualified defined benefit pension plans. Defined contribution plans are not covered by the PBGC insurance program because by definition they are always fully funded as long as the contributing employer makes the promised annual contributions.

Significant amendments in 1980 effectively created two different insurance programs administered by the PBGC, the single employer program and the multiemployer program. The single employer program guarantees certain benefits provided for under a terminated single employer plan, and the PBGC has a statutory claim against the sponsoring employer for any amounts it pays to satisfy the guarantees. The multiemployer program provides loans and grants to insolvent multiemployer plans. PBGC insurance is funded through premiums and employer obligations to the PBGC on the termination of a plan.

PBGC Guarantees

To be guaranteed by the PBGC, a benefit under a single employer defined benefit plan must satisfy three requirements: it must be nonforfeitable; it must be a pension benefit; and the participant or beneficiary must be entitled to the benefit. As to the first requirement, a benefit is nonforfeitable if it is vested under the terms of the plan or ERISA's requirements. Section 411(d)(3) of the Internal Revenue Code requires qualified plans to provide that all benefits become nonforfeitable, to the extent funded, upon the termination of the plan. Benefits that become nonforfeitable solely as a result of plan termination, however, are treated as forfeitable for purposes of PBGC guarantees. Thus, a participant who was not vested under the plan or under ERISA's minimum standards before the termination of the plan is not entitled to a PBGC-guaranteed benefit, even though he or she became vested by operation of law on the termination date. Second, to qualify as a pension benefit, a benefit must be payable as an annuity. Third, a participant or beneficiary is entitled to a benefit if the benefit was in pay status when the plan was terminated; if the participant had elected an optional form of benefit payable at normal retirement age before the plan terminated; if the participant had satisfied the plan conditions necessary to receive the benefit, other than application for the benefit, satisfaction of a waiting period, or retirement; or if, absent an election by the participant, the benefit would be payable on retirement.

In addition to these requirements, ERISA contains two significant limits on the amount of insured benefits under a single employer plan. First, a benefit is fully insured only if it has been in effect for five years before the plan's termination. Benefit increases made within the five-year period are insured on a graduated basis, at a rate of the greater of twenty dollars per month or twenty percent of the benefit or increase in benefit for each year the amendment was in effect before the termination of the plan. The five-year phase-in rule applies only if the plan was terminated for a reasonable business purpose and not just to obtain PBGC payments.

The second limit on PBGC guarantees is a cap on the amount of the guarantee. The maximum guaranteed benefits payable to a participant cannot exceed the actuarial value of a benefit in the form of a life annuity payable in monthly installments beginning at age sixty-five equal to the *lower* of (1) a dollar amount adjusted each year to take into account increases in the Social Security base, or (2) the participant's average monthly wages over his or her five highest paid years of employment.

Single Employer Plan Terminations

As originally enacted, ERISA did not place any conditions on the voluntary termination of a single employer plan. Although the sponsoring employer was liable to the PBGC for any unfunded guaranteed benefits, this liability was capped at thirty percent of the employer's net worth. In addition, the employer was responsible only for benefits covered by PBGC insurance. Because the PBGC does not insure all of a plan's benefits, employers could terminate their plans and walk away from many unfunded benefits. The Single Employer Pension Plan Amendments Act of 1986 (SEPPAA)[1] restricted the conditions under which single employer plans may be terminated, and the Pension Protection Act of 1987 (PPA)[2] increased the sponsoring employer's responsibility to pay unfunded benefit obligations.

SEPPAA established two, and only two, kinds of voluntary single employer plan terminations: standard terminations and distress terminations.[3] A plan amendment converting a defined benefit plan to a defined contribution plan constitutes a plan termination and must satisfy the requirements for either a standard or a distress termination. SEPPAA also added a provision explicitly recognizing that neither a standard nor a distress termination may take place in violation of the terms of an existing collective bargaining agreement.

A standard termination may take place only if the plan has enough assets to pay all "benefit liabilities." A distress termination may take place only if the sponsoring employer meets one of three tests: (1) it has filed, or has had filed against it, a petition seeking liquidation under the Bankruptcy Code or similar state laws; (2) it has filed, or has had filed against it, a petition seeking reorganization under the Bankruptcy Code or similar state laws, and the bankruptcy court has determined that plan termination is necessary for a successful reorganization; or (3) it demonstrates to the PBGC that it will be unable to pay its debts when due and stay in business or that the costs of providing pension coverage have become unreasonably burdensome solely because of a decline in its work force.

§ 11.7

1. Title XI, Pub.L. No. 99–272, 100 Stat. 237 (1986).

2. Title IX, Omnibus Budget Reconciliation Act of 1987, Pub. L. No. 100–203, 101 Stat. 1330 (1987).

3. ERISA § 4041(a)(1), 29 U.S.C.A. § 1341(a)(1).

If the plan seeking a distress termination does not have enough assets to satisfy all PBGC-guaranteed benefits, the PBGC must begin an involuntary termination.[4] In addition, the PBGC may unilaterally begin an involuntary termination if the plan (1) has not met minimum funding requirements; (2) will be unable to pay benefits when due; (3) has made a large distribution to a substantial owner at a time when other nonforfeitable benefits are unfunded; or (4) may reasonably be expected to cause increasing long-run loses for the PBGC if the plan is not terminated.[5]

Allocation of Plan Assets

ERISA establishes a set of six priority categories for the payment of benefits from a plan's assets. They are: (1) benefits attributable to voluntary employee contributions; (2) benefits attributable to mandatory employee contributions; (3) annuity benefits in pay status or eligible to be in pay status for three years before the plan's termination date, but limited to the lowest benefit level payable under the plan in the five years before termination; (4) benefits guaranteed by the PBGC and benefits that would have been guaranteed but for the limits on guarantees for substantial owners; (5) all other nonforfeitable benefits; and (6) all other benefits.

All benefits within a category must be satisfied before any assets may be distributed to the next lower category. If assets are insufficient to pay all of the benefits in a category, they are prorated among the benefits in that category, with one exception for category five. Category five includes benefits that the PBGC does not insure because of the five-year phase-in rule and the guaranteed benefit ceiling. If a plan's assets will be exhausted before all benefits in category five are paid, the assets are allocated first to benefits under provisions of the plan that have been in effect for five years before the termination. After this first allocation, any remaining assets are allocated to benefits in category five under the next earliest plan amendment. Allocation within category five continues in this method until no assets are left.

A trustee of a terminated plan may recover for the benefit of the plan "the recoverable amount" of all payments to a participant within the three-year period preceding the termination date. The recoverable amount is generally any payments exceeding $10,000 for a twelve-month period. Payments for death or total disability may not be recovered, and the PBGC may waive recovery if it would cause the participant substantial economic hardship.

Employer Liability

A standard termination cannot take place unless all of a plan's benefit liabilities are paid, but a distress or an involuntary termination can occur without payment of all benefit liabilities. Because the PBGC does not insure all benefits, participants can lose benefits that are not

---

4. ERISA § 4041(c)(3)(B)(iii), 29 U.S.C.A. § 1341(c)(3)(B)(iii).

5. ERISA § 4042(a), 29 U.S.C.A. § 1342(a).

insured by the PBGC and not paid by the statutory allocation of the plan's assets. The sponsoring employer and all members of any controlled group of which it is a member remain liable, however, for all of the plan's benefit liabilities, both insured and uninsured. The PBGC is authorized to collect this amount and pay part of the participants' unpaid benefit liabilities above PBGC-guaranteed levels.

ERISA creates a statutory lien in favor of the PBGC for thirty percent of the net worth of all entities owing termination liability. This provision was part of the statute as originally enacted, when employers in good financial shape could voluntarily terminate an insufficient plan and walk away from most of the liability for unfunded benefits. The restrictions on terminations enacted by SEPPAA and PPA make termination of insufficient plans unlikely unless those liable are already in bankruptcy or very close to it. If the statutory lien has been perfected before the filing of a bankruptcy petition, it will be given the same priority in bankruptcy as a tax lien. The lien does not arise until the date of the plan termination, however. If, as is likely, bankruptcy proceedings have begun before termination, the Bankruptcy Code's prohibition on the creation or perfection of a lien against a bankrupt debtor will bar the PBGC lien, and claims for unfunded benefits are treated as unsecured claims of general creditors.

Restoration of Plans

The PBGC has broad discretionary authority to stop a plan termination in process or restore a terminated plan to its pretermination status. Although the PBGC has occasionally used this authority to grant requests of plan administrators to withdraw a notice of termination or restore a terminated plan, it has invoked it against the wishes of the plan sponsor or administrator only in the case of "follow-on" plans. The PBGC defines a follow-on plan as a new benefit plan adopted following the termination of an insufficient plan and designed to provide substantially the same benefits as if no termination had taken place. The PBGC views these plans as an attempt to abuse the insurance system by obtaining an indirect corporate subsidy of an underfunded plan.

The PBGC's first effort to force restoration of a plan involved three of the LTV Corporation's pension plans, which were involuntarily terminated in 1987 for failure to meet minimum funding standards. Later that same year LTV agreed with its union to establish new pension arrangements that would pay the difference between PBGC-guaranteed benefits and the benefits promised under the terminated plans. The PBGC objected to these new plans and filed suit to force restoration of the terminated plans. In *PBGC v. LTV Corp.*,[6] the Supreme Court agreed with the PBGC that the anti-follow-on policy was a permissible construction of its statutory authority and rejected LTV's arguments that the PBGC should have considered the labor and bankruptcy laws before making its decision.

---

6. 496 U.S. 633, 110 S.Ct. 2668, 110 L.Ed.2d 579 (1990).

Asset Reversions

Changes in conditions underlying a defined benefit plan's actuarial assumptions may cause the plan to become overfunded as well as underfunded. In the case of an overfunded plan, ERISA's minimum funding standards permit the sponsoring employer to reduce its contributions, but the statute's exclusive benefit and noninurement rules do not permit it simply to withdraw excess assets from an ongoing plan. Both of these rules, however, contain express exceptions for the recapture of assets upon plan termination. Under section 4044(d), excess assets in a terminated pension plan can revert to the sponsoring employer under certain conditions.

First, all liabilities of the plan, both vested and nonvested, must be satisfied. This includes all benefits in the six categories discussed above plus any other benefit liabilities. If some of the plan's assets are attributable to mandatory employee contributions, the excess assets must be apportioned between those attributable to the employees' contributions and those attributable to the employer's contributions. Second, the distribution of excess assets must not contravene any other law. Third, the plan must specifically provide for the reversion of excess assets to the employer upon plan termination. Any amendment permitting reversion must have been in effect for at least five years before the termination.

§ 11.8 ERISA—Multiemployer Plan Termination

As originally enacted, ERISA's insurance program for multiemployer plans and its provisions for termination of multiemployer plans were similar to those for single employer plans. Multiemployer plans could be voluntarily terminated, and the PBGC guaranteed benefits at the same level as for single employer plans. As with the original rules governing single-employer plans, if a terminated multiemployer plan had insufficient assets to pay guaranteed benefits, a contributing employer's liability was capped at thirty percent of its net worth. Unlike single employer plans, liability for insufficient multiemployer plans was imposed only on employers that remained with the plan until it terminated or that withdrew from the plan within five years before termination. In any event, when ERISA was enacted, concerns about the effect of the termination insurance program on multiemployer plans caused Congress to delay automatic coverage of terminations of multiemployer plans. In the meantime, Congress gave the PBGC discretion to cover multiemployer plans on an individual basis while the PBGC gathered information about the potential financial impact of full insurance coverage.

The ability of a multiemployer plan to meet its benefit commitments depends on a stable or growing contribution base. Multiemployer plans commonly have a self-insurance feature that permits employees to retain benefit credits earned through service with a contributing employer, even though that employer later stops contributing to the plan. Employers that remain in the plan and any newly entering employers have the burden of funding the unfunded benefit obligations for the employees of the withdrawn employer. As long as a withdrawing employer is replaced by new entrants or employment with the remaining contributing employers expands, the plan can remain financially sound. Many multiemployer plans, however, cover workers in declining industries with a decreasing number of employers and an increasing proportion of retirees to current workers. If employers that contribute to a multiemployer plan go out of business and are not replaced by new contributors, the few remaining members of the plan could be saddled with all of its unfunded liabilities.

A congressionally-mandated PBGC study concluded that ERISA's original insurance program might actually exacerbate this situation by giving employers an incentive to withdraw from multiemployer plans, thereby preventing financially troubled plans from working out their problems and encouraging plan terminations. Employers that suspected a plan was in trouble and guessed correctly by withdrawing before the last five years of a plan could avoid all liability for unfunded benefits. As employer withdrawals caused the contribution base to dwindle, the remaining employers might find termination of the plan, with the statutory cap on their liability, a much more attractive option than continuing to fund benefit liabilities attributable to the withdrawn employers. Because PBGC insurance would pay all of the plan's guaranteed benefits, and future benefits for active workers could be provided at a lower cost under a new plan than current contributions under the troubled plan, active employees and their union might well agree to a termination.

In response to this study, Congress completely rewrote the multiemployer insurance program in the Multiemployer Pension Plan Amendments Act of 1980 (MPPAA).[1] The MPPAA contains several major reforms intended to strengthen multiemployer plans and discourage plan termination. First, the MPPAA imposes a continuing funding obligation on employers that withdraw from a multiemployer plan. Second, it creates the status of reorganization, under which multiemployer plans in financial difficulty can attempt to prevent insolvency by requiring increased employer contributions and reducing benefit payments. Third, it makes plan insolvency, not plan termination, the event that triggers PBGC financial assistance. Fourth, it reduces the level of guaranteed benefits for participants in multiemployer plans. Fifth, it requires continued funding of terminated multiemployer plans.

Withdrawal Liability

If the amount of litigation generated is any indication, the most controversial of the MPPAA's reforms is undoubtedly its requirement that a withdrawing employer continue to fund part of the plan's unfunded obligations. The MPPAA imposes withdrawal liability on all employers that withdraw from a multiemployer plan, without regard to whether the plan terminates within five years of an employer's withdrawal. The

§ 11.8

1. Pub. L. No. 96–364, 94 Stat. 1208.

Act also repealed the cap on the amount of an employer's liability. The withdrawal liability provisions are intended to protect the funding base of multiemployer plans and to eliminate an employer's incentives to withdraw.

When an employer withdraws from a multiemployer plan, the plan's trustees must determine the amount of its withdrawal liability, notify the withdrawing employer of the amount, and collect it. An employer's withdrawal liability is basically its proportionate share of the plan's "unfunded vested benefits" (UVBs), the difference between the value of nonforfeitable benefits under the plan and the value of the plan's assets. Withdrawal liability is a one-time obligation (although an employer may satisfy its liability with periodic installment payments), and the employer's obligation to the plan ceases upon payment in full. Calculation of the precise amount of withdrawal liability requires a number of complex actuarial assumptions and methods. Disputes over the trustees' calculations are subject to mandatory arbitration, with federal court review of the arbitrator's award. The MPPAA provides a presumption of correctness for the plan sponsor's determinations, for the actuarial assumptions and methods used to determine the plan's UVBs, and for the arbitrator's findings of fact.

In *Connolly v. PBGC*,[2] the Court considered and rejected arguments that the MPPAA's withdrawal liability provisions constitute a taking in violation of the Fifth Amendment. In a concurrence, however, Justices Powell and O'Connor suggested that in some circumstances imposition of withdrawal liability might be so arbitrary and irrational as to violate the due process clause of the Fifth Amendment and that as applied in particular cases the MPPAA may violate the taking clause. In *Concrete Pipe & Products of California, Inc. v. Construction Laborers Pension Trust*,[3] however, the Court rejected a variety of due process challenges to the MPPAA's scheme of presumptions. First, the Court held that the employer is not denied an impartial adjudicator, even though the statute places determination of withdrawal liability in the trustees, subject to section 4221's presumptions. The trustees act in an enforcement capacity, not an adjudicative one. The first adjudication under the MPPAA is before the arbitrator. The Court construed the presumption of correctness for the sponsor's factual determinations (a statutory scheme the Court called "incoherent") as placing the burden of persuasion on the employer to disprove the determinations by a preponderance of the evidence. The presumption of correctness for the actuarial assumptions and methods also raised no due process problem, because, unlike the trustees, the actuary is not vulnerable to bias in his or her determinations. Finally, the Court rejected claims that, as applied, the MPPAA violates substantive due process and constitutes a taking without just compensation.

2. 475 U.S. 211, 106 S.Ct. 1018, 89 L.Ed.2d 166 (1986).

3. 508 U.S. 602, 113 S.Ct. 2264, 124 L.Ed.2d 539 (1993).

Reorganization

The MPPAA created the status of reorganization to help underfunded plans prevent or at least delay insolvency. A plan is in reorganization for a plan year if its "reorganization index" for that year is greater than zero. Plans in reorganization must increase their minimum funding standards and pay benefits only in annuity form. In addition, a plan in reorganization may retroactively reduce or eliminate benefits increased or added by an amendment that has been in effect less than five years. Participants and beneficiaries must receive at least six months' advance notice of any reduction in benefits, and reductions of retirees' benefits must be proportional to reductions in the benefits of active employees. Any change in eligibility requirements or in the form of benefits may not apply to retirees or to employees within five years of the plan's normal retirement age.

At the end of the plan year in which a plan enters reorganization and every third year thereafter, the plan must determine whether it may become insolvent within the next three years. If it determines that it may become insolvent, it must give notice to the Secretary of the Treasury, the PBGC, the contributing employers, the union, and the participants and beneficiaries.

Insolvency as the Insured Event

Another major reform in the MPPAA was to change the insured event for multiemployer plans from plan termination to insolvency. PBGC assistance is available only in the event of "unavoidable plan insolvency," and it takes the form of loans which the plan is obligated to repay. Plan termination, either through a mass withdrawal of all employers or through a plan amendment that stops the crediting of service, does not trigger PBGC payments. Employers that were members of a terminated multiemployer plan must continue contributing to the plan until all benefit liabilities are fully funded, or they must pay withdrawal liability if they have withdrawn from the plan.

A plan is insolvent when its "available resources," its cash, marketable assets, contribution obligations, and withdrawal liability payments, are not sufficient to pay benefits when due during the year.[4] When a plan becomes insolvent, it must reduce benefit payments to the "resource benefit level," a level at which the plan's assets will be sufficient to pay the benefits that year. If the plan does not have enough assets to pay benefits at the level guaranteed by the PBGC, the PBGC will provide financial assistance in the amount necessary to pay guaranteed benefits. The plan administrator must give notice of the plan's insolvency to the Secretary of the Treasury, the PBGC, contributing employers, the union, and participants and beneficiaries. The plan must also give notice of the amount of benefits it will be able to pay during the plan year.

4. ERISA § 4245(b)(1), 29 U.S.C.A. § 1426(b)(1).

PBGC Guarantees

As with guarantees for single employer plans, a benefit under a multiemployer plan must be a nonforfeitable pension benefit to which the participant or beneficiary is entitled. As amended by the MPPAA, the PBGC guarantees for benefits under a multiemployer plan are less than the guarantees for single employer plans. Whereas benefit increases within five years before plan termination are insured on a gradual basis for single employer plans, the PBGC does not provide any insurance for benefit increases made by amendment to a multiemployer plan unless they have been in effect for at least five years from the earlier of plan insolvency, plan termination by mass withdrawal, or the first plan year in which benefits are reduced in plan reorganization.[5] In addition, the ceiling on guaranteed benefits under multiemployer plans is significantly lower than under single employer plans. Under amendments made by the Consolidated Appropriations Act of 2001,[6] the maximum amount the PBGC will guarantee is 100 percent of the first eleven dollars of the monthly benefit accrual rate and seventy-five percent of the next thirty-three dollars for each year of service.

As with the other parts of the MPPAA, the stated rationale for a guarantee of such "modest" proportions was to eliminate the incentives to permit plan insolvency and mass withdrawal, but another reason certainly was to protect the PBGC from massive liability for guaranteed benefits. The relatively high guarantees under the original law did not discourage plan termination, and contributing employers to a multiemployer plan could often dump large unfunded liabilities on the PBGC. Concerns about an impending financial crisis for the PBGC led Congress to guarantee only very low levels of benefits, with the hope that even very troubled plans could remain operational.

Voluntary Terminations

Multiemployer plans may be terminated voluntarily in two ways, through plan amendment and through mass withdrawal. A plan amendment providing that participants will receive no credit for service with any employer after a specified date terminates the plan. The date of termination is the later of the date of the amendment's adoption or its effective date. Although benefit accruals cease as of the termination date, the trustees must continue to administer the plan until it is closed out or until a trustee is appointed. Contributing employers must continue to fund the plan's unfunded benefit liabilities through the payment of contributions or withdrawal liability until the plan is fully funded. If the plan has sufficient assets to satisfy all obligations for nonforfeitable benefits, the trustees may distribute the assets and close out the plan. If the plan enters reorganization or becomes insolvent following termination, the rules discussed above governing reorganization or insolvency apply.

5. ERISA § 4022A(b)(1), 29 U.S.C.A. § 1322a(b)(1).

6. Pub.L. 106–554, § 1(a)(6), 114 Stat. 2763.

A plan termination by mass withdrawal occurs when every employer has withdrawn from a multiemployer plan or when the obligation of all employers to contribute to the plan stops. The date of termination in this situation is the earlier of the date on which the last employer withdraws or the first day of the first plan year for which no employer has a contribution obligation to the plan. At that point, the only assets that will ever be available to the plan are its assets at termination and its claims for withdrawal liability. Therefore, the plan sponsor must determine the value of the plan's assets, including withdrawal liability claims, and the value of its nonforfeitable benefits and reduce benefits "not eligible" for PBGC guarantees to the extent necessary to ensure that the plan will be able to pay benefits when due. For purposes of this reduction, the only benefits not eligible for PBGC guarantees are non-pension benefits and benefits in effect for less than five years. The dollar amount cap on guaranteed benefits in the event of plan insolvency does not apply to this determination. If the terminated plan ultimately becomes insolvent, however, the MPPAA's insolvency provisions, with the cap on guaranteed benefits, does apply. Following termination by mass withdrawal, the trustees must pay benefits only in annuity form.

Involuntary Terminations

The PBGC may involuntarily terminate a multiemployer plan under section 4042, the same provision that allows involuntary terminations of single employer plans.[7] As with single employer plans, the PBGC may begin termination proceedings if the plan (1) has not met ERISA's minimum funding standards; (2) will be unable to pay benefits when due; (3) has made a large distribution to a substantial owner at a time when other nonforfeitable benefits are unfunded; or (4) may reasonably be expected to cause increasing long-run losses for the PBGC if the plan is not terminated.

Additionally, under certain circumstances the PBGC may order the partition of a multiemployer plan, either on its own initiative or on petition of the plan sponsor. The PBGC must find that a contributing employer's Chapter 11 bankruptcy has caused or will cause a substantial reduction in contributions to the plan, the plan is likely to become insolvent, contributions will have to be increased significantly in reorganization, and partition will significantly reduce the likelihood of insolvency. The PBGC must give notice to the plan sponsor and affected participants and beneficiaries. Under a plan partition, liabilities for nonforfeitable benefits "directly attributable" to service with the bankrupt employer and an "equitable share" of the multiemployer plan's assets are transferred to a new plan. This new plan is treated as if it had been terminated by mass withdrawal, so that benefits must be reduced to the level guaranteed by the PBGC, as described above. Although the partitioned plan has only one sponsor, the bankrupt employer, if it is or becomes insolvent, it is dealt with under the multiemployer plan rules.

---

7. 29 U.S.C.A. § 1342.

§ 11.9 Age Discrimination in Pensions and Other Employee Benefits

The Age Discrimination in Employment Act (ADEA)[1] prohibits discrimination in employment on the basis of age against individuals aged forty and over. As originally enacted, the ADEA protected individuals between the ages of forty and sixty-five. A 1978 amendment increased the upper age limit to seventy, and in 1986 the upper limit was eliminated entirely for most workers. Section 4(f)(2) of the ADEA, however, permitted an employer to observe the terms of a "bona fide employee benefit plan" as long as the plan was not "a subterfuge to evade the purposes of [the] Act."[2] In a 1977 decision, *United Air Lines, Inc. v. McMann*,[3] the Supreme Court interpreted the term subterfuge to mean "a scheme, plan, stratagem, or artifice of evasion" and held that a pension plan requiring retirement at age sixty that had been adopted before the enactment of the ADEA could not possibly be characterized as a subterfuge. The 1978 amendments, which increased the upper age limit to seventy, also overruled the result in *McMann* by adding to section 4(f)(2) the clause, "except that no such employee benefit plan shall require or permit the involuntary retirement of any individual * * * because of the age of such individual."

Thus, while pension plans could no longer require an employee to retire because of his or her age, section 4(f)(2) continued to permit benefit plans to provide different benefits to workers on the basis of their age. In 1979, the Department of Labor, which was then charged with enforcing the ADEA, took an "equal cost or equal benefit" view of section 4(f)(2); plans had to provide equal benefits to all workers regardless of age, or spend approximately the same amount on all workers. Any age-based distinction in an employee benefit plan that could not be justified by the higher cost of providing the benefit to older workers was a "subterfuge." The EEOC, which assumed ADEA enforcement later that year, adopted Labor's position. The lower courts generally reached the same conclusion as the agencies.

In *Public Employees Retirement System v. Betts*,[4] the Supreme Court rejected this cost-justification requirement. *Betts* involved a plan that provided disability retirement benefits, computed with reference to the employee's last salary, to employees under sixty. Workers who became disabled after age sixty received only their regular pension, based on age and years of service. June Betts took disability retirement at sixty-one. Her monthly age-and-service pension benefit was $158.50, but she would have received $355 per month if she had been permitted to take disability retirement instead. Because the state did not claim that this discrimination against older workers was justified by age-related cost considerations, the Sixth Circuit found the plan violated section 4(f)(2).

§ 11.9

1. 29 U.S.C.A. §§ 621–634. See also Ch. 2.

2. 29 U.S.C.A. § 623(f)(2).

3. 434 U.S. 192, 98 S.Ct. 444, 54 L.Ed.2d 402 (1977).

4. 492 U.S. 158, 109 S.Ct. 2854, 106 L.Ed.2d 134 (1989).

The Supreme Court reversed. It reaffirmed its *McMann* holding that "subterfuge" requires a showing of subjective intent, not just a lack of cost justification, and it found in the legislative history congressional intent to exempt bona fide employee benefit plans from the ADEA completely. Therefore, the general prohibitions of section 4(a)(1) do not apply to employee benefit plans, and section 4(f)(2) is not an affirmative defense, but rather a definition of prohibited employer conduct. A benefit plan that distinguishes on the basis of age cannot be a subterfuge to evade the purposes of the Act, said the Court, "unless it discriminates in a manner forbidden by the Act's substantive provisions." Section 4(f)(2) protects a benefit plan as long as it "is not a method of discriminating in other, nonfringe-benefit aspects of the employment relationship."

Congressional reaction to *Betts* was swift. In 1990, Congress enacted the Older Workers Benefit Protection Act (OWBPA).[5] A new section 11(*l*) was added to overrule the holding in *Betts* that the ADEA's substantive prohibitions do not apply to employee benefit plans. It provides that "[t]he term 'compensation, terms, conditions, or privileges of employment' encompasses all employee benefits, including such benefits provided pursuant to a bona fide employee benefit plan."[6] Section 4(f)(2) was completely rewritten to codify the EEOC's equal benefit or equal cost regulation, which is cited in the amended section, and to place the burden of persuasion on the defendant. The word "subterfuge" was eliminated from the section, to make it clear that, with certain exceptions also enacted by the OWBPA, "the *only* justification for age discrimination in an employee benefit is the increased cost in providing the particular benefit to older individuals."[7] A new section 4(k) provides that the Act applies to seniority systems and employee benefit plans regardless of the date they were adopted.[8]

In *Erie County Retirees Association v. County of Erie*,[9] the employer placed Medicare-eligible retirees into an HMO that allegedly provided benefits inferior to those provided to younger retirees. The court held that this age-based distinction could possibly be saved by section 4(f)(2)(B)(i), the safe harbor provision added to the ADEA by OWBPA, which permits an equal benefit-equal cost defense. The court went on to state that in determining whether the employer was providing an equal benefit, the lower court should take into account both the Medicare-provided and the employer-provided benefits received by the older retirees. In looking to the equal cost prong of the analysis, however, the district court must consider only the cost incurred by the employer, not the costs Medicare incurs on behalf of the older retirees. On remand, the district court held against the employer.[10] The employer conceded it had

5. Pub. L. No. 101–433, 104 Stat. 978 (1990).

6. 29 U.S.C.A. § 630(*l*).

7. S. Rep. No. 101–263, 101st Cong., 2d Sess., at 18, reprinted in 1990 U.S.C.C.A.N. 1509, 1523 (emphasis in original).

8. 29 U.S.C.A. § 623(k).

9. 220 F.3d 193 (3d Cir. 2000), cert. denied, 532 U.S. 913, 121 S.Ct. 1247, 149 L.Ed.2d 153 (2001).

10. Erie County Retirees Association v. County of Erie, 140 F.Supp.2d 466 (W.D.Pa. 2001).

not satisfied the equal cost test, and the court found the benefits provided to the older retirees were in fact inferior to those provided younger retirees.

In August 2001 the EEOC revoked its policy on retiree health benefits and announced a review of the issue. On July 14, 2003, it issued a proposed rule that would exempt from the ADEA reductions in benefits or elimination of employer-sponsored health coverage when retirees become eligible for Medicare or state-sponsored health plans.[11]

Exceptions for Certain Pension Plan Practices

The OWBPA excepts certain practices of defined benefit plans that arguably do not comply with the equal benefit or equal cost rule of section 4(f)(2)(B). Section 4(*l*)(1)(A) permits employee benefit pension plans to establish a minimum age as a condition of eligibility for normal or early retirement benefits.[12] Section 4(*l*)(1)(B) permits defined benefit plans to provide for payments that constitute the subsidized portion of early retirement benefits and for Social Security bridge payments intended to substitute for Social Security benefits that will become available at age sixty-two or sixty-five.[13]

Coordination of Severance Benefits

Before *Betts* the lower courts had held that section 4(f)(2) prohibited employers from coordinating pension benefits and severance pay, and the legislative history of the OWBPA confirms that severance pay and pension benefits are not fungible. The OWBPA does, however, authorize coordination of severance benefits in certain narrowly defined circumstances. Under section 4(*l*)(2), if a contingent event unrelated to age, such as a plant closing or layoff, entitles employees to severance pay, employers may deduct from the severance pay the value of any retiree health benefits received by an individual eligible for an immediate pension. If the pension is actuarially reduced, the severance pay deduction must be reduced by the same percentage as the reduction in pension benefits. For instance, if an employee receives a pension benefit that is actuarially reduced by ten percent, the value of any retiree health benefits the employee receives must also be reduced by ten percent before the employer may set them off against the severance pay.

Employers may also deduct from severance pay the value of any additional pension benefits provided to the worker solely because of the contingent event, but only if the worker is eligible for not less than an immediate and unreduced pension. The retiree health plan must provide certain levels of benefits if the employer wishes to set them off against severance pay, and the statute specifies the values that employers may assign to retiree health benefits. If an employer deducts the value of retiree health benefits from an employee's severance pay and then does not provide those benefits, the employee may sue under the ADEA for specific performance.

11. 68 Fed. Reg. 41542 (July 14, 2003), proposing new 29 C.F.R. § 1625.32.

12. 29 U.S.C.A. § 623(*l*)(1)(A).

13. Id. § 623(*l*)(1)(B)(i), (ii).

Section 4(*l*)(3) permits employers to reduce long-term disability benefits by any pension benefits that the individual voluntarily elects to receive or by any pension benefits for which an individual who has reached the later of age sixty-two or normal retirement age is eligible.

Early Retirement Incentives

During the restructuring and downsizing of American industries in the 1980s, many employers adopted programs intended to encourage workers to retire before the pension plan's normal retirement age. Although these programs were linked to an employee's age, the courts held that the mere offer of an early retirement incentive does not raise an inference of age discrimination. Rather, early retirement programs were characterized as favoring older workers by offering them extra benefits, with the dispositive issue whether acceptance of an early retirement offer was truly voluntary. The OWBPA affirms this case law by adding section 4(f)(2)(B)(ii), which permits employers to maintain voluntary early retirement incentive plans "consistent with the relevant purpose or purposes of this Act."[14] The legislative history indicates that a voluntary early retirement incentive plan must give employees enough time to consider their choices, particularly if the employer has not previously offered retirement counseling, and provide complete and accurate information about the benefits available under the plan. In addition, the background must be free from threats, intimidation, and coercion. Many of Congress' concerns about the voluntariness of a decision to retire early are also reflected in the new requirements for waivers of age discrimination claims, discussed below.

The legislative history also states that early retirement programs may offer incentives, such as payment of a flat dollar amount, service-based benefits, a percentage of salary, flat dollar or percentage increases in pension benefits, and imputation of years of service and/or age. Early retirement plans that deny or reduce benefits to workers above a certain age while providing them to younger workers may conflict with the purposes of the ADEA, as may plans that exclude older workers based on age-related stereotypes.

Waivers

Employers often condition payment of benefits under an early retirement incentive program, as well as payments under individually tailored separation agreements, on the execution of a release of claims against the company. Although the courts have developed a "knowing and voluntary" standard to measure the validity of releases under Title VII, there was a question whether that body of law could be incorporated into the ADEA. The ADEA uses many of the enforcement provisions of the Fair Labor Standards Act, which does not permit unsupervised waivers, and therefore, the argument went, a release of age discrimination claims would not be valid unless approved by the EEOC. Most courts rejected this contention and applied some form of a knowing and

---

14.   29 U.S.C.A. § 623(f)(2)(B)(ii).

voluntary test to ADEA releases, but the issue remained controversial. The EEOC promulgated regulations permitting employees to release ADEA claims under certain circumstances, but Congress prohibited the agency from implementing them.

The OWBPA resolves the issue of waivers of ADEA claims by adding a new section 7(f),[15] which adopts the general rule that a waiver will not be valid unless it is knowing and voluntary. The statute goes beyond the case law, however, by establishing seven minimum standards that any waiver must meet. First, the waiver must be part of an agreement between the employee and the employer that is written in a manner that the employee or the average eligible individual can understand. Second, the waiver must specifically refer to rights or claims arising under the ADEA. Third, the waiver must not include rights or claims arising after the date it is executed. Fourth, the employee must receive consideration in addition to anything of value to which he or she is already entitled. Fifth, the employee must be advised in writing to consult with an attorney before signing the agreement. Sixth, the employee must be given at least twenty-one days in which to consider the agreement. Seventh, the agreement must provide for at least a seven-day grace period after its execution, within which the employee may revoke it. The agreement may not become effective or enforceable until after the revocation period has expired.

If the waiver is sought as part of an exit incentive or other termination program offered to a group or class of employees, the waiting period is extended from twenty-one to forty-five days. In addition, at the beginning of the forty-five day period, the employer must inform the employee in writing of the group of employees covered by the program, any eligibility factors and time limits for the program, the job titles and ages of all employees who are eligible or selected for the program, and the ages of all employees in the same job classification or unit who are not eligible or selected for the program.

Waivers given in settlement of an EEOC charge or a lawsuit satisfy the knowing and voluntary requirement if they meet the first five tests described above and if the employee has a reasonable period of time within which to consider the settlement agreement. No waiver agreement may affect the EEOC's right to enforce the ADEA, or interfere with an employee's right to file a charge or participate in an EEOC investigation or proceeding. The party asserting the validity of a waiver has the burden of proving satisfaction of the statute's requirements.

In *Oubre v. Entergy Operations, Inc.*,[16] the Supreme Court refused to apply the common law doctrines of ratification and tender back to waivers that are invalid under the OWBPA. The Court concluded that the OWBPA governs the effect under federal law of waivers or releases on ADEA claims, and it does not require tender back of consideration received before an employee may challenge an allegedly defective waiver.

---

15. 29 U.S.C.A. § 626(f).   **16.** 522 U.S. 422, 118 S.Ct. 838, 139 L.Ed.2d 849 (1998).

Benefit Accruals after Normal Retirement Age

ERISA permits pension plans to specify a normal retirement age, usually sixty-five,[17] and it defines the concept of accrued benefits under a defined benefit plan in terms of the plan's normal retirement age.[18] The ADEA, however, prohibits employers from requiring most employees to retire because of their age or from discriminating against them in any other manner because of their age.

Under 1986 amendments to ADEA, ERISA, and the Internal Revenue Code, plans may not exclude employees from participation on the basis of age, and neither benefit accruals under a defined benefit plan nor allocations to an employee's account under a defined contribution plan may be stopped or reduced because the employee has reached the plan's normal retirement age.[19]

Relationship Between ERISA Section 510 and the ADEA

Section 510 of ERISA prohibits employers from discriminating against employees in order to interfere with their rights under covered plans. Thus, an employer violates section 510 if it fires an employee to prevent him or her from becoming vested in the employer's pension plan. Although some lower courts had found that evidence that an employer's action was timed in relation to the availability of pension benefits supports a claim of age discrimination, in *Hazen Paper Co. v. Biggins*,[20] the Supreme Court held that pension status may not be deemed a proxy for age in most situations, and that "an employer does not violate the ADEA just by interfering with an older employee's pension benefits that would have vested by virtue of the employee's years of service."

§ 11.10 Sex Discrimination in Pensions

Because women as a group live longer than men as a group, from an actuarial standpoint employee benefits tied to life expectancy, such as life annuities, cost more for women than for men. In *City of Los Angeles Department of Water & Power v. Manhart*,[1] the employer maintained an unusual kind of pension plan, a defined benefit plan that required unequal employee contributions. The plan used sex-based mortality assumptions, and it required higher contributions from female employees so that both men and women would receive the same monthly benefit payments upon retirement. The Supreme Court held that this plan discriminated against women workers in violation of Title VII of the Civil Rights Act of 1964. Title VII requires that employees be treated as

17. ERISA § 3(24), 29 U.S.C.A. § 1002(24).

18. ERISA § 3(23)(A), 29 U.S.C.A. § 1002(23)(A).

19. ADEA § 4(i), 29 U.S.C.A. § 623(i); ERISA §§ 202(a)(2), 204(b)(1)(H), 204(b)(2), 29 U.S.C.A. §§ 1052(a)(2), 1054(b)(1)(H), 1054(b)(2); 26 U.S.C.A. §§ 411(a)(8), 411(b)(1)(H), 411(b)(2), as amended by Pub. L. No. 99–509, §§ 9201, 9202.

20. 507 U.S. 604, 113 S.Ct. 1701, 123 L.Ed.2d 338 (1993).

§ 11.10

1. 435 U.S. 702, 98 S.Ct. 1370, 55 L.Ed.2d 657 (1978).

individuals, not as members of groups, and the use of actuarial tables based on group characteristics violates that principle. The Court remarked that it did not intend its holding to "revolutionize the insurance and pension industries," and it suggested that employers were free to give equal sums to male and female workers for the purchase of pension benefits in the open insurance market.

In many ways *Manhart* was an easy case, because the present discrimination was readily apparent; women workers had larger payroll deductions than men and consequently took home smaller checks each payday. The lower courts disagreed on *Manhart's* application to pension plans that required equal contributions on behalf of men and women workers but paid smaller pension benefits to women. In *Arizona Governing Committee v. Norris*,[2] a five-to-four Supreme Court majority found those plans in violation of Title VII as well. The State of Arizona maintained a defined contribution plan under which the state used the employee's contribution to buy an annuity contract from an insurance company chosen by the employee from an approved list. When the employee retired, he or she could choose among different payment options. For one of these options, a life annuity, all of the companies used sex-based mortality assumptions. Thus, in converting her individual account to a life annuity, Norris would receive a smaller monthly payment than would a man with an identical employment history. The Court found that discriminatory benefit payments were just as unlawful as discriminatory contributions. "[T]he classification of employees on the basis of sex is no more permissible at the pay-out stage of a retirement plan than at the pay-in stage." The Court rejected the state's arguments that its conduct was lawful because it offered other, nondiscriminatory payment options from which employees could choose or because it was merely offering the equivalent of what workers could buy on the open insurance market.

A different five-to-four majority in *Norris* declined to impose a retroactive remedy, however, reasoning that the Court's decision could not have been anticipated, despite *Manhart* and a number of intervening lower court decisions. According to this majority, the State of Arizona had taken a reasonable approach to *Manhart's* suggestion of an open-market exception. Moreover, the Court reasoned that retroactive relief could jeopardize the financial integrity of many pension plans, especially public-sector plans such as the one at issue in *Norris*. Instead, the Court required defined contribution plans to use unisex mortality assumptions only for contributions made after August 1, 1983, the date of the judgment in *Norris*.

After *Norris* the lower courts struggled with the issue of retroactivity in other contexts, until the Court finally resolved the question in *Florida v. Long*.[3] After *Norris* the State of Florida began using sex-neutral mortality tables to compute benefits under its defined benefit

---

2. 463 U.S. 1073, 103 S.Ct. 3492, 77 L.Ed.2d 1236 (1983).

3. 487 U.S. 223, 108 S.Ct. 2354, 101 L.Ed.2d 206 (1988).

plan for employees retiring in the future. A group of men who retired before *Norris* claimed that their joint and survivor annuities, computed with sex-based mortality tables, violated Title VII. The Court pronounced that *Norris*, not *Manhart*, had first resolved the legality of pension discrimination at the pay-out stage. It then concluded that retroactive relief for pre-*Norris* retirees would not be equitable because of the effect on the plans' reserves, the complexities of pension funding in an industry that had once used sex-based tables exclusively, the lack of authoritative guidance from the courts, the potential for harm to other retirees, and the willingness of the pension industry to comply after *Norris*. By retroactive relief, the Court meant two things. Any order affecting payments already made is retroactive in nature, but so too are orders affecting future payments to the extent those payments are based on pre-*Norris* contributions. Thus, the pre-*Norris* retirees, for whom by definition no post-*Norris* contributions had been made, were not entitled to any adjustment of their benefits.

In 1989, the EEOC issued a policy guidance on *Long* in which it concluded that post-*Norris* retirees under defined benefit plans have a right to benefits computed using unisex mortality assumptions only to the extent that payments are derived from post-*Norris* contributions.[4] The EEOC takes the position that *Long* does permit retroactive relief for participants in defined contribution plans that do not promise any particular level of benefit. Participants in those plans are entitled to have unisex assumptions applied to all post-*Norris* benefits, regardless of whether they were derived from pre-or post-*Norris* contributions. Some defined contribution plans, however, do guarantee a minimum benefit level, and the EEOC recognized that to that extent unisex assumptions do not have to be used for pre-*Norris* contributions.

Although the plaintiffs in *Manhart* and *Norris* were women, *Long* illustrates that abandoning the use of sex-based mortality assumptions often benefits men as a class. For instance, *Long* involved the reduction required to convert a single life annuity to a joint and survivor annuity. Following *Norris*, a plan may not reduce a male participant's annuity more to take into account his wife's assumed longer life expectancy than it does for a female participant who elects a survivor's benefit for her husband.

---

4. Policy Guidance on Retroactive Relief for Discriminatory Retirement Plans, re- printed in BNA Fair Emp. Prac. Manual 405:4001.

*

Appendix

RESEARCHING EMPLOYMENT LAW

Analysis

Section 1. Introduction

Employment Law provides a strong base for analyzing even the most complex problem involving issues related to employment law. Whether

931

your research requires examination of case law, statutes, administrative decisions, expert commentary, or other materials, West books and Westlaw are excellent sources of information.

To keep you informed of current developments, Westlaw provides frequently updated databases. With Westlaw, you have unparalleled legal research resources at your fingertips.

Additional Resources

If you have not previously used Westlaw or if you have questions not covered in this appendix, call the West Reference Attorneys at 1–800–REF–ATTY (1–800–733–2889). The West Reference Attorneys are trained, licensed attorneys, available 24 hours a day to assist you with your Westlaw search questions. To subscribe to Westlaw, call 1–800–344–5008 or visit westlaw.com at **www.westlaw.com**.

Section 2. Westlaw Databases

Each database on Westlaw is assigned an abbreviation called an *identifier*, which you can use to access the database. You can find identifiers for Westlaw databases in the online Westlaw Directory and in the printed *Westlaw Database Directory*. When you need to know more detailed information about a database, use Scope. Scope contains coverage information, lists of related databases, and valuable search tips.

The following chart lists selected Westlaw databases that contain information pertaining to employment law. For a complete list of employment law databases, see the online Westlaw Directory or the printed *Westlaw Database Directory*. Because new information is continually being added to Westlaw, you should also check the tabbed Westlaw page and the online Westlaw Directory for new database information.

Selected Employment Law Databases on Westlaw

Database	Identifier	Coverage
Combined Federal Materials		
Federal Labor and Employment—Combined Labor Materials	FLB—ALL	Varies by source
PersonNet® EEOC Multibase	PNET–EEOC	Varies by source
PersonNet FLRA Multibase	PNET–FLRA	Varies by source
Federal Case Law		
Equal Employment Opportunity Commission Federal Sector—Court Cases	EEOC–CS	Begins with 1982

Database	Identifier	Coverage
Federal Civil Rights—Cases	FCIV–CS	Begins with 1789
Federal Civil Rights—Supreme Court Cases	FCIV–SCT	Begins with 1790
Federal Civil Rights—Courts of Appeals Cases	FCIV–CTA	Begins with 1891
Federal Civil Rights—District Courts Cases	FCIV–DCT	Begins with 1789
Federal Labor and Employment—Cases	FLB–CS	Begins with 1789
Federal Labor and Employment—Supreme Court Cases	FLB–SCT	Begins with 1790
Federal Labor and Employment—Courts of Appeals Cases	FLB–CTA	Begins with 1891
Federal Labor and Employment—District Courts Cases	FLB–DCT	Begins with 1789
Federal Labor Relations Authority—Court Cases	FLRA–CS	Begins with 1980
Wage and Hour Cases	WH–CS	Begins with 1945

State Case Law		
Multistate Civil Rights Cases	MCIV–CS	Varies by state
Individual State Civil Rights Cases	XXCIV–CS (where XX is a state's two-letter postal abbreviation	Varies by state
Multistate Labor and Employment Cases	MLB–CS	Varies by state
Individual State Labor and Employment Cases	XXLB–CS (where XX is a state's two-letter postal abbreviation)	Varies by state
Multistate Workers' Compensation Cases	MWC–CS	Varies by state
Individual State Workers' Compensation Cases	XXWC–CS (where XX is a state's two-letter postal abbreviation	Varies by state
Public Employee Reporters—Combined	PER	Varies by state
Individual State Public Employee Reporter	XX–PER (where XX is a state's two-letter postal abbreviation)	Varies by state

Database	Identifier	Coverage
Briefs, Pleadings, and Other Court Documents		
Andrews Disability Litigation Reporter Court Documents	ANDISLR–DOC	Begins with 2000
Andrews Employment Litigation Reporter Court Documents	ANEMPLR–DOC	Begins with 2000
Andrews Sexual Harassment Litigation Reporter Court Documents	ANSEXHLR–DOC	Begins with 2000
Federal Labor and Employment Briefs	FLB–BRIEF	Begins with 1885
White–Collar Crime Reporter Court Documents	ANWCCR–DOC	Begins with 2000
Federal Statutes, Rules, and Regulations		
Federal Civil Rights— U.S. Code Annotated	FCIV–USCA	Current data
Federal Civil Rights— Code of Federal Regulations	FCIV–CFR	Current data
Federal Civil Rights— Federal Register	FCIV–FR	Begins with July 1980
Federal Labor and Employment—Code and Regulations	FLB–CODREG	Varies by source
Federal Labor and Employment—U.S. Code Annotated	FLB–USCA	Current data
Federal Labor and Employment—Code of Federal Regulations	FLB–CFR	Current data
Federal Labor and Employment—Federal Register	FLB–FR	Begins with July 1980
Federal Labor and Employment—Final, Temporary, and Proposed Regulations	FLB–REG	Varies by source
Wage and Hour Statutes	WH–ST	Current data
Americans with Disabilities Code of Federal Regulations	AWD–CFR	Current data
Americans with Disabilities Federal Register	AWD–FR	Begins with July 1980

Database	Identifier	Coverage
Arnold & Porter Legislative History: Americans with Disabilities Act of 1990	ADA–LH	Full history
Arnold & Porter Legislative History: Employee Retirement Income Security Act of 1974	ERISA–LH	Full history
Arnold & Porter Legislative History: Family and Medical Leave Act	FAMLV–LH	Full history

State Statutes, Rules, and Regulations

State Statutes—Annotated	ST–ANN–ALL	Varies by jurisdiction
Individual State Statutes—Annotated	XX–ST–ANN (where XX is a state's two-letter postal abbreviation)	Varies by jurisdiction
State Administrative Code Multibase	ADC–ALL	Current data
Individual State Administrative Code	XX–ADC (where XX is a state's two-letter postal abbreviation)	Current data
Wage and Hour Regulations	WH–REG	Current data
Wage and Hour Statutes	WH–ST	Current data

Federal Administrative Materials

Americans with Disabilities Act Technical Assistance Manuals	ADA–TAM	Informational booklets: 1991 Manuals: 1992
Federal Labor and Employment—Department of Labor Wage and Hour Opinion Letters	FLB–WHO	Fair Labor Standards Act opinion letters: begins with January 1970 Family and Medical Leave Act opinion letters: begins with June 1993
Federal Labor and Employment—Equal Employment Opportunity Commission (EEOC) Multibase	FLB–EEOC–ALL	Varies by source
Federal Labor and Employment—Federal Mine Safety and Health Review Commission	FLB–FMSHRC	Begins with 1979

Database	Identifier	Coverage
Federal Labor and Employment—Occupational Safety and Health Review Commission	FLB–OSRC	Begins with 1971
National Disability Law Reporter	NDLRPTR	Begins with 1990
Wage and Hour Administrative Decisions	WH–ADMIN	Begins with 1935
State Administrative Materials		
California Fair Employment and Housing Commission Decisions	CA–FEHC	Begins with 1978
California Fair Political Practices Commission	CA–ETH	Opinions: begins with 1975 Advice letters: begins with 1985
California Occupational Safety and Health Appeals Board Decisions	CA–OSHA	Begins with 1974
California State Personnel Board Decisions	CASPB	Begins with 1992
City of New York Conflicts of Interest Board	NYC–ETH	Advisory opinions: begins with 1990 Decisions: begins with 1992 Rules: current through August 1995
ENFLEX®State Environmental, Health, and Safety Regulations	ENFLEX–STATE	Current data
Individual State Environmental, Health, and Safety Regulations	ENFLEX–XX (where XX is a jurisdiction's two-letter postal abbreviation)	Current data
Hawaii Department of Labor and Industrial Relations, Occupational Safety and Health Decisions	HI–OSHA	Begins with 1994
Illinois Human Rights Commission Decisions	ILCIV–ADMIN	Begins with 1991
Massachusetts Commission Against Discrimination Decisions	MACIV–ADMIN	Begins with 1999

Database	Identifier	Coverage
Washington Commission of Employment Security Precedential Decisions	WAPREC–DEC	Begins with April 1954
Washington Public Employment Relations Commission Decisions	WALB–ADMIN	Begins with 1976
West Virginia Education and State Employees Grievance Board Decisions	WVLB–ADMIN	Begins with 1994
Multistate Workers' Compensation—Administrative Decisions	MWC–ADMIN	Varies by state
Individual State Workers' Compensation Administrative Decisions	XXWC–ADMIN (where XX is a state's two-letter postal abbreviation)	Varies by state

Legal Texts, Periodicals, and Practice Materials

Americans with Disabilities Texts and Periodicals	AWD–TP	Varies by source
Civil Rights—Law Reviews, Texts, and Bar Journals	CIV–TP	Varies by publication
Labor and Employment—Law Reviews, Texts, and Bar Journals	LB–TP	Varies by publication
Avoiding and Defending Wrongful Discharge Claims	ADWDC	Current data
Berkeley Journal of Employment and Labor Law	BERKJELL	Selected coverage begins with 1984 (vol. 6); full coverage begins with 1994 (vol. 15)
BNA's Wage and Hour Manual	BNA–WHM	Current data
Comparative Labor Law and Policy Journal	CLLPJ	Selected coverage begins with 1988 (vol. 9); full coverage begins with 1993 (vol. 15)
Corporate Compliance Series: Combined Employment Titles	CORPC–EMP	Current data
Defense of Equal Employment Claims	DEFEECL	Second edition

Database	Identifier	Coverage
Disability Discrimination in Employment	DISDE	Current data
Dispute Resolution Journal	DRJ	Selected coverage begins with 1993 (vol. 48)
Employee Dismissal Law and Practice	JW–EMPDIS	Third edition
Employee Rights and Employment Policy Journal	EREPJ	Full coverage begins with 1997 (vol. 1)
Employment Coordinator	EMPC	Current data
Employment Law Checklists and Forms	EMPL–CF	Current data
Federal and State Guide to Employee Medical Leave, Benefits, and Disabilities Laws	FSGEML	Current edition
Hofstra Labor and Employment Law Journal	HOFLELJ	Selected coverage begins with 1984 (vol. 2); full coverage begins with 1993 (vol. 10, no. 2)
HR Series Fair Employment Practices	HRS–FEP	Current data
Into the Jury Box: A Disability Accommodation Guide for State Courts	ABA–DISJURY	1994 edition
Industrial and Labor Relations Review	INDLRR	Selected coverage begins with 1991 (vol. 44); full coverage begins with 1994 (vol. 47, no. 2)
Labor Lawyer	LABLAW	Selected coverage begins with 1987 (vol. 3)
Litigating Age Discrimination Cases	LITADCS	Current data
Litigating Wrongful Discharge Claims	LITWDCS	Current data
Manual on Employment Discrimination and Civil Rights Actions in the Federal Courts	MEDCRA	Current edition
Occupational Safety and Health Law	OSHL	Current data

Database	Identifier	Coverage
Pattern Discovery: Employment Discrimination	PDED	Second edition
Practical Guide to the Occupational Safety and Health Act	GUIDEOSHA	Current data
Sex-Based Employment Discrimination	SBEDIS	Current data
Statistics of Discrimination	STATDIS	Current data
University of Pennsylvania Journal of Labor and Employment Law	UPAJLEL	Full coverage begins with 1998 (vol. 1)
Wage and Hour Law: Compliance and Practice	WHLCP	Current data
West's® Legal Forms—Employment	WESTLF–EMPL	Current data

News and Information

Andrews Disability Litigation Reporter	ANDISLR	Begins with November 2003
Andrews Employment Litigation Reporter	ANEMPLR	Begins with November 1996
Andrews Sexual Harassment Litigation Reporter	ANSEXHLR	Begins with November 1996
ARBIT Private Database	ARBIT	Begins with 1963
Cal—OSHA Reporter	CA–COR	Begins with August 1974
Discrimination Law Update	DISCRIMLU	Begins with January 1997
EEOC Compliance Newsletter	EEOCCOMPL	Begins with March 2002
Employment Alert	EMPALERT	Begins with July 1999
Employment Law Report	OAKELR	Begins with October 2001
Employment Law Strategist	EMPLST	Begins with March 1995
Employment Law Update	EMLUP	Begins with 1996
Federal Labor and Employment—News Releases	FLB–NR	Varies by agency

Database	Identifier	Coverage
Individual State Employment Law Letter	SMXXEMPLL (where XX is a state's two-letter postal abbreviation)	Varies by state
Labor News	LBNEWS	Varies by source
Termination of Employment Bulletin	TERMEMPB	Begins with February 2001
Westlaw Topical Highlights—Labor and Employment	WTH–LB	Current data
White-Collar Crime Reporter	ANWCCR	Begins with November 1996
Directories		
West Legal Directory%2 F–Civil Rights	WLD–CIV	Current data
West Legal Directory—Employment Law/Employee	WLD–EMPLE	Current data
West Legal Directory—Employment Law/Employer	WLD–EMPLR	Current data
West Legal Directory—Labor Law	WLD–LAB	Current data

Section 3. Retrieving a Document with a Citation: Find and Hypertext Links

3.1   Find

Find is a Westlaw service that allows you to retrieve a document by entering its citation. Find allows you to retrieve documents from any page in westlaw.com without accessing or changing databases. Find is available for many documents, including case law (state and federal), the *United States Code Annotated*® (USCA®), state statutes, administrative materials, and texts and periodicals.

To use Find, simply type the citation in the *Find this document by citation* text box at the tabbed Westlaw page and click **GO**. The following list provides some examples:

To find this document:	Access Find and type:
Raytheon Co. v. Hernandez 124 S.Ct. 513 (2003)	**124 sct 513**
American Broadcasting Cos. v. Wolf 52 N.Y.2d 394 (1981)	**52 ny2d 394**
29 U.S.C.A. § 203	**29 usca 203**
29 C.F.R. § 1604.8	**29 cfr 1604.8**

To find this document:	Access Find and type:
Cal. Gov't Code § 12940	**cal govt code s 12940**
Fla. Stat. Ann. § 435.09	**fl st s 435.09**

For a complete list of publications that can be retrieved with Find and their abbreviations, click **Find** on the toolbar and then click **Publications List**.

3.2 Hypertext Links

Use hypertext links to move from one location to another on Westlaw. For example, use hypertext links to go directly from the statute, case, or law review article you are viewing to a cited statute, case, or article; from a headnote to the corresponding text in the opinion; or from an entry in a statutes index database to the full text of the statute.

Section 4. Searching with Natural Language

Overview: With Natural Language, you can retrieve documents by simply describing your issue in plain English. If you are a relatively new Westlaw user, Natural Language searching can make it easier for you to retrieve cases that are on point. If you are an experienced Westlaw user, Natural Language gives you a valuable alternative search method to the Terms and Connectors search method described in Section 5.

When you enter a Natural Language description, Westlaw automatically identifies legal phrases, removes common words, and generates variations of terms in your description. Westlaw then searches for the concepts in your description. Concepts may include significant terms, phrases, legal citations, or topic and key numbers. Westlaw retrieves the documents that most closely match the concepts in your description, beginning with the document most likely to match.

4.1 Natural Language Search

Access a database, such as the Federal Labor and Employment—Cases database (FLB–CS). Click **Natural Language** and type the following description in the text box:

age discrimination in employment

4.2 Browsing Search Results

Best Mode: To display the best portion (the portion that most closely matches your description) of each document in a Natural Language search result, click the **Best** arrows at the bottom of the right frame.

Term Mode: **Click the** Term **arrows at the bottom of the right frame to display portions of the document that contain your search terms.**

Previous/Next Document: Click the left or right **Doc** arrow at the bottom of the right frame to view the previous or the next document in the search result.

Section 5. Searching with Terms and Connectors

Overview: With Terms and Connectors searching, you enter a query consisting of key terms from your issue and connectors specifying the relationship between these terms.

Terms and Connectors searching is useful when you want to retrieve a document for which you know specific details, such as the title or the fact situation. Terms and Connectors searching is also useful when you want to retrieve all documents containing specific terms.

5.1   Terms

Plurals and Possessives: Plurals are automatically retrieved when you enter the singular form of a term. This is true for both regular and irregular plurals (e.g., **child** retrieves *children*). If you enter the plural form of a term, you will not retrieve the singular form.

If you enter the nonpossessive form of a term, Westlaw automatically retrieves the possessive form as well. However, if you enter the possessive form, only the possessive form is retrieved.

Compound Words and Abbreviations: When a compound word is one of your search terms, use a hyphen to retrieve all forms of the word. For example, the term **non-discrimination** retrieves *non-discrimination*, *nondiscrimination*, and *non discrimination*.

When using an abbreviation as a search term, place a period after each of the letters to retrieve any of its forms. For example, the term **e.e.o.c.** retrieves *EEOC, E.E.O.C., E E O C* and *E. E. O. C.* Note: The abbreviation does not retrieve the phrase *Equal Employment Opportunity Commission*, so remember to add additional alternative terms such as **"equal employment opportunity commission"** to your query.

The Root Expander and the Universal Character: When you use the Terms and Connectors search method, placing the root expander (!) at the end of a root term generates all other terms with that root. For example, adding the ! to the root *discriminat* in the query

age /s discriminat!

instructs Westlaw to retrieve such terms as *discriminate*, *discriminated*, *discriminating*, and *discrimination*.

The universal character (*) stands for one character and can be inserted in the middle or at the end of a term. For example, the term

withdr*w

will retrieve *withdraw* and *withdrew*. Adding three asterisks to the root *elect*

elect* * *

instructs Westlaw to retrieve all forms of the root with up to three additional characters. Terms such as *elected* or *election* are retrieved by this query. However, terms with more than three letters following the root, such as *electronic,* are not retrieved. Plurals are always retrieved, even if the plural form of the term has more than three letters following the root.

Phrase Searching: To search for an exact phrase, place it within quotation marks. For example, to search for references to *disparate impact*, type **"disparate impact"**. When you are using the Terms and Connectors search method, you should use phrase searching only if you are certain that the terms in the phrase will not appear in any other order.

5.2 Alternative Terms

After selecting the terms for your query, consider which alternative terms are necessary. For example, if you are searching for the term *constitutional*, you might also want to search for the term *unconstitutional*. You should consider both synonyms and antonyms as alternative terms. You can also use the Westlaw thesaurus to add alternative terms to your query.

5.3 Connectors

After selecting terms and alternative terms for your query, use connectors to specify the relationship that must exist between search terms in your retrieved documents. The connectors are described below:

Type:	To retrieve documents with:	Example:
& (and)	both terms	**age & discriminat!**
a space (or)	either term or both terms	**sex! gender**
/p	search terms in the same paragraph	**hostile /p environment**
/s	search terms in the same sentence	**disparate /s impact**
+s	the first search term preceding the second within the same sentence	**burden +s prov! proof**
/n	search terms within *n* terms of each other (where *n* is a number from 1 to 255)	**vicarious! /3 liab!**
+n	the first search term preceding the second by *n* terms (where *n* is a number from 1 to 255)	**wrongful! +3 terminat!**
" "	search terms appearing in the same order as in the quotation marks	**"bona fide occupational qualification"**

Type:	To exclude documents with:	Example:
% (but not)	search terms following the % symbol	**age % gender**

5.4 Field Restrictions

Overview: Documents in each Westlaw database consist of several segments, or *fields*. One field may contain the citation, another the title, another the synopsis, and so forth. Not all databases contain the same fields. Also depending on the database, fields with the same name may contain different types of information.

To view a list of fields and their contents for a specific database, see Scope for that database. Note that in some databases not every field is available for every document.

To retrieve only those documents containing your search terms in a specific field, restrict your search to that field. To restrict your search to a specific field, type the field name or abbreviation followed by your search terms enclosed in parentheses. For example, to retrieve a U.S. Supreme Court case titled *Raytheon v. Hernandez*, access the Federal Labor and Employment—Supreme Court Cases database (FLB–SCT) and search for your terms in the title field (ti):

ti(raytheon & hernandez)

The fields discussed below are available in Westlaw case law databases you might use for researching issues related to employment law.

Digest and Synopsis Fields: The digest (di) and synopsis (sy) fields summarize the main points of a case. The synopsis field contains a brief description of a case. The digest field contains the topic and headnote fields and includes the complete hierarchy of concepts used by West's editors to classify the headnotes to specific West digest topic and key numbers. Restricting your search to the synopsis and digest fields limits your result to cases in which your terms are related to a major issue in the case.

Consider restricting your search to one or both of these fields if

• you are searching for common terms or terms with more than one meaning, and you need to narrow your search; or

• you cannot narrow your search by using a smaller database.

For example, to retrieve U.S. Supreme Court cases that discuss age as a bona fide occupational qualification (BFOQ), access the FLB–SCT database and type the following query:

sy,di(age /p "bona fide occupational qualification" b.f.o.q.)

Headnote Field: The headnote field (he) is part of the digest field but does not contain the topic names or numbers, hierarchical classification information, or key numbers. The headnote field contains a one-sentence summary for each point of law in a case and any supporting citations given by the author of the opinion. A headnote field restriction is useful when you are searching for specific statutory sections or rule numbers. For example, to retrieve headnotes from federal courts of appeals cases that cite 29 U.S.C.A. § 203, access the Federal Labor and Employment—Courts of Appeals Cases database (FLB–CTA) and type the following query:

he(29 +s 203)

Topic Field: The topic field (to) is also part of the digest field. It contains the hierarchical classification information, including the West digest topic names and numbers and the key numbers. You should restrict search terms to the topic field in a case law database if

- a digest field search retrieves too many documents; or

- you want to retrieve cases with digest paragraphs classified under more than one topic.

For example, the topic Labor and Employment has the topic number 231H. To retrieve federal district court cases that discuss layoffs due to plant closings, access the Federal Labor and Employment—District Courts Cases database (FLB–DCT) and type a query like the following:

to(231h) /p plant factory /s clos! /p lay-off

To retrieve cases classified under more than one topic and key number, search for your terms in the topic field. For example, to retrieve recent state cases discussing covenants not to compete, which may be classified to such topics as Contracts (95), Injunctions (212), and Labor and Employment (231H), access the Multistate Labor and Employment Cases database (MLB–CS) and type a query like the following:

to(non-compet! "not to compete") & da(aft 2002)

For a complete list of West digest topics and their corresponding topic numbers, access the Custom Digest by choosing **Key Numbers and Digest** from the *More* drop-down list on the toolbar.

> *Note*: Slip opinions and cases from topical services do not contain the West digest, headnote, and topic fields.

Prelim and Caption Fields: When searching in a database containing statutes, rules, or regulations, restrict your search to the prelim (pr) and caption (ca) fields to retrieve documents in which your terms are important enough to appear in a section name or heading. For example, to retrieve federal statutes regarding unlawful employment practices, access the Federal Labor and Employment—U.S. Code Annotated database (FLB–USCA) and type the following query:

pr,ca(unlawful /s employment /s practice)

5.5 Date Restrictions

You can use Westlaw to retrieve documents *decided* or *issued* before, after, or on a specified date, as well as within a range of dates. The following sample queries contain date restrictions:

da(2003) & disparate /s impact

da(aft 1998) & disparate /s impact

da(5/20/1988) & disparate /s impact

You can also search for documents *added to a database* on or after a specified date, as well as within a range of dates, which is useful for updating your research. The following sample queries contain added-date restrictions:

ad(aft 2002) & disparate /s impact

ad(aft 11/9/2001 & bef 6/23/2002) & disparate /s impact

Section 6. Searching with Topic and Key Numbers

To retrieve cases that address a specific point of law, use topic and key numbers as your search terms. If you have an on-point case, run a search using the topic and key number from the relevant headnote in an appropriate database to find other cases containing headnotes classified to that topic and key number. For example, to search for federal cases containing headnotes classified under topic 78 (Civil Rights) and key number 1123 (Constructive Discharge), access the Federal Civil Rights— Cases database (FCIV–CS) and type the following query:

78k1123

For a complete list of West digest topics and their corresponding topic numbers, access the Custom Digest by choosing **Key Numbers and Digest** from the *More* drop-down list on the toolbar.

Note: Slip opinions and cases from topical services do not contain West topic and key numbers.

6.1   Custom Digest

The Custom Digest contains the complete topic and key number outline used by West attorney-editors to classify headnotes. You can use the Custom Digest to obtain a single document containing all case law headnotes from a specific jurisdiction that are classified under a particular topic and key number.

Access the Custom Digest by choosing **Key Numbers and Digest** from the *More* drop-down list on the toolbar. Select up to 10 topics and key numbers from the easy-to-browse outline and click **Search selected**. Then follow the displayed instructions.

For example, to research issues involving employment, scroll down the Custom Digest page until topic 231H, *Labor and Employment*, is displayed. Click the plus symbols (+) to display key number information. Select the check box next to each key number you want to include in your search, then click **Search selected**. Select the jurisdiction from which you want to retrieve headnotes and, if desired, type additional search terms and select a date restriction. Click **Search**.

6.2 KeySearch

KeySearch is a research tool that helps you find cases and secondary sources in a specific area of the law. KeySearch guides you through the selection of terms from a classification system based on the West Key Number System® and then uses the key numbers and their underlying concepts to provide a query for you.

To access KeySearch, click **KeySearch** on the toolbar. Then browse the list of topics and subtopics and select a topic or subtopic to search by clicking the hypertext links. For example, to search for cases that discuss violations of the Occupational Safety and Health Act (OSHA), click **Employment Law** at the first KeySearch page. Then click **Occupational Safety and OSHA** and **Violations and Penalties** at the next two pages. Select the source from which you want to retrieve documents and, if desired, type additional search terms. Click **Search**.

Section 7. Verifying Your Research with Citation Research Services

Overview: A citation research service, such as KeyCite, is a tool that helps you ensure that your cases, statutes, regulations, and administrative decisions are good law; retrieve cases, legislation, articles, or other documents that cite them; and verify the spelling and format of your citations.

7.1 KeyCite for Cases

KeyCite for cases covers case law on Westlaw, including unpublished opinions. KeyCite for cases provides the following:

- direct appellate history of a case, including related references, which are opinions involving the same parties and facts but resolving different issues

- negative indirect history of a case, which consists of cases outside the direct appellate line that may have a negative impact on its precedential value

- the title, parallel citations, court of decision, docket number, and filing date of a case

- citations to cases, administrative decisions, secondary sources, and briefs on Westlaw that have cited a case

- complete integration with the West Key Number System so you can track legal issues discussed in a case

7.2 KeyCite for Statutes and Regulations

KeyCite for statutes and regulations covers the USCA, the *Code of Federal Regulations* (CFR), statutes from all 50 states, and regulations from selected states. KeyCite for statutes and regulations provides

- links to session laws or rules amending or repealing a statute or regulation

- statutory credits and historical notes
- citations to pending legislation affecting a statute
- citations to cases, administrative decisions, secondary sources, and briefs that have cited a statute or regulation

7.3   KeyCite for Administrative Materials

KeyCite for administrative materials includes the following:

- National Labor Relations Board decisions beginning with 1935
- Board of Contract Appeals decisions (varies by agency)
- Board of Immigration Appeals decisions beginning with 1940
- Comptroller General decisions beginning with 1921
- Environmental Protection Agency decisions beginning with 1974
- Federal Communications Commission decisions beginning with 1960
- Federal Energy Regulatory Commission (Federal Power Commission) decisions beginning with 1931
- Internal Revenue Service revenue rulings beginning with 1954
- Internal Revenue Service revenue procedures beginning with 1954
- Internal Revenue Service private letter rulings beginning with 1954
- Internal Revenue Service technical advice memoranda beginning with 1954
- *Public Utilities Reports* beginning with 1974
- U.S. Merit Systems Protection Board decisions beginning with 1979
- U.S. Patent and Trademark Office decisions beginning with 1984
- U.S. Tax Court (Board of Tax Appeals) decisions beginning with 1924
- U.S. patents beginning with 1976

7.4   KeyCite Alert

KeyCite Alert monitors the status of your cases, statutes, regulations, and administrative decisions and automatically sends you updates at the frequency you specify when their KeyCite information changes.

Section 8. Researching with Westlaw: Examples

8.1   Retrieving Law Review Articles

Recent law review articles are often a good place to begin researching a legal issue because law review articles serve as an excellent introduction to a new topic or review for an old one, providing terminology to help you formulate a query; as a finding tool for pertinent primary authority, such as cases, statutes, and rules; and in some instances, as persuasive secondary authority.

Suppose you need to gain background information on whether an employer can enforce English-only language restrictions in the workplace.

Solution

- To retrieve law review articles relevant to your issue, access the Labor and Employment—Law Reviews, Texts, and Bar Journals database (LB–TP). Using the Natural Language search method, type a description like the following:

  english only language restrictions in the work-place

- If you have a citation to an article in a specific publication, use Find to retrieve it. For more information on Find, see Section 3.1 of this appendix. For example, to retrieve the article found at 73 Tex. L. Rev. 871, access Find and type

  73 tex l rev 871

- If you know the title of an article but not the journal in which it was published, access the LB–TP database and search for key terms in the title field. For example, to retrieve the article "English–Only Rules and the Role of Perspective in Title VII Claims," type the following Terms and Connectors query:

  ti(english-only & perspective)

8.2 Retrieving Case Law

Suppose you need to retrieve federal cases discussing failure to pay employees for hours worked "off the clock" in violation of the Fair Labor Standards Act (FLSA).

Solution

- Access the FLB–CS database. Type a Terms and Connectors query such as the following:

  off-the-clock /p "fair labor standards act" f.l.s.a.

- When you know the citation for a specific case, use Find to retrieve it. For example, to retrieve *Tum v. Barber Foods, Inc.,* 331 F.3d 1 (1st Cir. 2003), access Find and type

  331 f3d 1

- If you find a topic and key number that is on point, run a search using that topic and key number to retrieve additional cases discussing that point of law. For example, to retrieve federal cases containing headnotes classified under topic 231H (Labor and Employment) and key number 2318 (Meal or Break Periods), access the FLB–CS database and type the following query:

  231hk2318

- To retrieve cases written by a particular judge, add a judge field (ju) restriction to your query. For example, to retrieve federal courts of appeals cases written by Judge Reinhardt that contain headnotes classified under topic 231H (Labor and Employment), access the FLB–CTA database and type the following query:

  ju(reinhardt) & to(231h)

- You can also use KeySearch and the Custom Digest to retrieve cases and headnotes that discuss the issue you are researching.

8.3 Retrieving Statutes and Regulations

Suppose you need to retrieve federal statutes and regulations dealing with mine safety.

Solution

- Access the Federal Labor and Employment—Code and Regulations database (FLB–CODREG). Search for your terms in the prelim and caption fields using the Terms and Connectors search method:

pr,ca(mine /s safety)

- When you know the citation for a specific statute or regulation, use Find to retrieve it. For example, to retrieve 30 U.S.C.A. § 820, access Find and type

30 usca 820

- To look at surrounding sections, use the Table of Contents service. Click **Table of Contents** on the Links tab in the left frame. To display a section listed in the Table of Contents, click its hypertext link. You can also use Documents in Sequence to retrieve the sections following 30 U.S.C.A. § 820 even if the subsequent sections were not retrieved with your search or Find request. Choose **Documents in Sequence** from the Tools menu at the bottom of the right frame.

8.4 Retrieving Administrative Decisions

Suppose you need to retrieve state workers' compensation decisions discussing the personal comfort doctrine.

Solution

- Access the Multistate Workers' Compensation—Administrative Decisions database (MWC–ADMIN) and type the following query:

personal /5 comfort /p doctrine

8.5 Using KeyCite

Suppose one of the cases you retrieve in your case law research is *Pittston Coal Group v. Sebben*, 109 S.Ct. 414 (1988).

Solution

- Use KeyCite to retrieve direct and negative indirect history for *Pittston*. Access KeyCite and type **109 sct 414**.

- Use KeyCite to display citing references for *Pittston*. Click **Citing References** on the Links tab in the left frame.

8.6 Following Recent Developments

If you are researching issues related to employment law, it is important to keep up with recent developments. How can you do this efficiently?

Solution

One of the easiest ways to follow recent developments in employment law is to access the Westlaw Topical Highlights—Labor and Employment database (WTH–LB). The WTH–LB database contains summaries of recent legal developments, including court decisions, legislation, and materials released by administrative agencies. When you access the WTH–LB database, you automatically retrieve a list of documents added to the database in the last two weeks.

You can also use the WestClip® clipping service to stay informed of recent developments of interest to you. WestClip will run your Terms and Connectors queries on a regular basis and deliver the results to you automatically. You can run WestClip queries in legal and news and information databases.

*

Table of Cases

E

G

H

N

Q

R

T

Table of Statutes

UNITED STATES CODE ANNOTATED
11 U.S.C.A.—Bankruptcy

Sec.	This Work Sec.	Note
1113(e)	10.2	
1114	4.26	7
1501	1.11	3
15101—151326	1.11	3

15 U.S.C.A.—Commerce and Trade

Sec.	This Work Sec.	Note
1011—1015	4.30	27
1671—1677	4.12	1
1681—1681t	1.11	1

17 U.S.C.A.—Copyrights

Sec.	This Work Sec.	Note
101—914	8.11	8

18 U.S.C.A.—Crimes and Criminal Procedure

Sec.	This Work Sec.	Note
287	9.17	3
874	4.11	7
1513(e)	9.17	2
1514A	9.17	1
1961—1968	9.17	4
1961(1)	9.17	6
1961(5)	9.17	6
1964(c)	9.17	5
2510—2521	5.5	1

26 U.S.C.A.—Internal Revenue Code

Sec.	This Work Sec.	Note
85	10.16	1
411(a)(8)	11.9	19
411(b)(1)(H)	11.9	19
411(b)(2)	11.9	19
411(d)(3)	11.3	5
411(d)(3)	11.7	
3304(a)(5)	10.13	2
3304(a)(9)(A)	10.15	2
3304(a)(9)(B)	10.15	2

28 U.S.C.A.—Judiciary and Judicial Procedure

Sec.	This Work Sec.	Note
1875	4.34	1
2412(d)(1)(A)	4.28	13

29 U.S.C.A.—Labor

Sec.	This Work Sec.	Note
50—50b	1.4	7

UNITED STATES CODE ANNOTATED
29 U.S.C.A.—Labor

Sec.	This Work Sec.	Note
101—115	Intr.	5
141—187	11.1	2
141—197	Intr.	13
151—169	1.13	1
151—169	Intr.	8
158(a)(3)	1.4	2
158(b)(2)	1.4	1
185	1.4	4
185	4.13	2
185	9.19	12
186(c)	4.29	1
186(c)(5)	11.1	3
186(c)(5)	11.2	3
201—219	Intr.	11
203(d)	4.2	10
203(e)(1)	4.2	11
203(e)(4)	4.8	10
203(g)	4.2	12
203(g)	4.5	1
203(l)	4.7	1
203(l)	4.7	3
203(m)	4.3	2
203(m)	4.3	15
203(o)	4.5	10
203(r)	4.15	1
203(r)(1)	4.2	2
203(r)(2)	4.2	4
203(s)(1)(A)(i)	4.2	6
203(s)(1)(A)(ii)	4.2	7
203(s)(1)(B)	4.2	8
203(s)(1)(C)	4.2	8
203(s)(2)	4.2	9
203(t)	4.3	15
203(y)	4.8	16
206(a)	4.2	1
206(a)(1)	4.3	1
206(d)	4.14	1
206(g)	4.6	24
207(a)	4.2	1
207(e)	4.4	1
207(f)	4.4	6
207(i)	4.6	26
207(k)	4.8	14
207(o)	4.8	7
207(p)(1)	4.8	15
211(c)	4.10	5
212(a)	4.7	7
212(c)	4.7	6
213(a)(1)	4.6	1
213(a)(3)	4.15	1
213(a)(17)	4.6	23
213(b)	4.6	25
213(b)(20)	4.8	13
213(c)	4.7	3
213(c)(1)	4.7	5
213(c)(2)	4.7	5
213(c)(7)	4.7	4
213(d)	4.7	3
215(a)(1)	4.10	3
215(a)(3)	4.9	1

ENERGY REORGANIZATION ACT

	This Work	
Sec.	**Sec.**	**Note**
210	9.19	

ETHICS IN GOVERNMENT ACT

	This Work	
Sec.	**Sec.**	**Note**
501(b)	5.11	

FAIR LABOR STANDARDS ACT

	This Work	
Sec.	**Sec.**	**Note**
3(d)	4.2	10
3(e)(1)	4.2	11
3(e)(4)	4.8	10
3(g)	4.2	12
3(g)	4.5	1
3(l)	4.7	1
3(l)	4.7	3
3(m)	4.3	
3(o)	4.5	
3(r)(1)	4.2	2
3(r)(2)	4.2	4
3(s)(1)(A)(i)	4.2	6
3(s)(1)(A)(ii)	4.2	7
3(s)(1)(B)	4.2	8
3(s)(1)(C)	4.2	8
3(s)(2)	4.2	9
3(y)	4.8	
6	4.3	
6(a)	4.2	1
6(g)	4.6	24
7	4.3	
7	4.6	
7	4.8	
7(a)	4.2	1
7(a)	4.4	
7(e)	4.4	
7(h)	4.4	
7(i)	4.6	
7(k)	4.8	
7(o)	4.8	
7(o)(2)(A)(i)	4.8	
7(p)	4.8	
7(p)(1)	4.8	
11(c)	4.10	
12(a)	4.7	
12(c)	4.7	
13	4.6	
13(a)(1)	4.6	
13(a)(1)	4.8	
13(a)(17)	4.6	
13(a)(17)	4.6	23
13(b)	4.6	
13(b)(20)	4.8	
13(c)	4.7	3
13(c)(1)	4.7	5
13(c)(2)	4.7	5
13(c)(7)	4.7	4
13(d)	4.7	3
15(a)(1)	4.10	

FAIR LABOR STANDARDS ACT

	This Work	
Sec.	**Sec.**	**Note**
15(a)(3)	4.9	
15(a)(3)	4.10	
16(a)	4.10	
16(b)	4.9	
16(b)	4.10	
16(c)	4.10	
16(e)	4.10	
17	4.9	
17	4.10	
18	9.19	4

FAMILY AND MEDICAL LEAVE ACT

	This Work	
Sec.	**Sec.**	**Note**
401(b)	9.19	5

FEDERAL MINE SAFETY AND HEALTH ACT

	This Work	
Sec.	**Sec.**	**Note**
103	6.33	
104(b)	6.33	
818	6.33	
820	6.33	
820(d)	6.33	

FEDERAL UNEMPLOYMENT TAX ACT

	This Work	
Sec.	**Sec.**	**Note**
3304(a)(5)	10.13	
3304(a)(12)	10.12	

GOVERNMENT IN SUNSHINE ACT

	This Work	
Sec.	**Sec.**	**Note**
321	2.5	

LABOR MANAGEMENT RELATIONS ACT

	This Work	
Sec.	**Sec.**	**Note**
301	1.4	
301	4.13	
301	4.26	
301	9.19	
302	11.1	
302(c)	4.19	
302(c)	4.29	
302(c)(5)	11.1	

NATIONAL INDUSTRIAL RECOVERY ACT

	This Work	
Sec.	**Sec.**	**Note**
7(a)	Intr.	

OCCUPATIONAL SAFETY AND HEALTH ACT

Sec.	This Work Sec.	Note
18(c)	6.3	
20	6.5	
20(b)	6.5	
21	6.16	
22	6.5	
24	6.14	

OMNIBUS CRIME CONTROL AND SAFE STREETS ACT

Sec.	This Work Sec.	Note
Tit. III	5.5	
Tit. III	5.5	1

PORTAL–TO–PORTAL ACT

Sec.	This Work Sec.	Note
4	4.5	
4(a)	4.5	7
10	4.10	
11	4.10	

RACKETEER–INFLUENCED AND CORRUPT ORGANIZATIONS ACT

Sec.	This Work Sec.	Note
1961(1)	9.17	
1962	9.17	
1964(c)	9.17	

REHABILITATION ACT

Sec.	This Work Sec.	Note
501	1.25	
501	3.2	
501	3.3	
503	1.25	
503	3.2	
504	1.25	
504	1.26	
504	3.2	
504	3.2	2
504	3.4	

SOCIAL SECURITY ACT

Sec.	This Work Sec.	Note
Tit. II	4.23	
Tit. III	10.6	
Tit. III	10.15	
Tit. IX	10.6	
Tit. XVI	4.23	

TAFT–HARTLEY ACT

Sec.	This Work Sec.	Note
302(c)(5)	11.2	

WORKER ADJUSTMENT AND RETRAINING NOTIFICATION ACT

Sec.	This Work Sec.	Note
2102(a)	10.5	

STATE STATUTES

ARIZONA REVISED STATUTES

Sec.	This Work Sec.	Note
23–1501	9.18	10

WEST'S ANNOTATED CALIFORNIA CONSTITUTION

Art.	This Work Sec.	Note
XI, Ch. 10, Subd.(b)	1.15	4

WEST'S ANNOTATED CALIFORNIA GOVERNMENT CODE

Sec.	This Work Sec.	Note
12926.1	3.15	2
12940	1.25	5

WEST'S ANNOTATED CALIFORNIA LABOR CODE

Sec.	This Work Sec.	Note
1400—1408	10.4	1
3602(a)	7.36	2

WEST'S COLORADO REVISED STATUTES ANNOTATED

Sec.	This Work Sec.	Note
8–2–113(3)	8.6	6
13–25–125.5	1.8	8

CONNECTICUT GENERAL STATUTES ANNOTATED

Sec.	This Work Sec.	Note
31–48B	5.5	7
31–51o(a)—(c)	10.4	2

DELAWARE CODE

Tit.	This Work Sec.	Note
2707	8.6	5

WEST'S FLORIDA STATUTES ANNOTATED

Sec.	This Work Sec.	Note
542.335(j)	8.5	14

GEORGIA CONSTITUTION

Art.	This Work Sec.	Note
III, § VI, para.V(c)	8.6	3

GEORGIA CODE

Sec.	This Work Sec.	Note
13–8–2.1(g)(1)	8.6	2

HAWAII REVISED STATUTES

Sec.	This Work Sec.	Note
394B–1 to 394B–8	10.4	3
394B–10	10.4	

ILLINOIS SMITH–HURD ANNOTATED

Ch.	This Work Sec.	Note
30, § 760/15	10.4	4

ILLINOIS REVISED STATUTES

Ch.	This Work Sec.	Note
820, § 405/1900	9.21	5

LOUISIANA REVISED STATUTES— CRIMINAL EVIDENCE

Art.	This Work Sec.	Note
23:921(F)	8.6	7

MAINE REVISED STATUTES ANNOTATED

Tit.	This Work Sec.	Note
26, § 625–B(1)—(7)	10.4	5

MARYLAND ANNOTATED CODE

Art.	This Work Sec.	Note
83A, §§ 3–301 to 3–304	10.4	6

MASSACHUSETTS GENERAL LAWS ANNOTATED

Ch.	This Work Sec.	Note
149, § 19(B)(1)	1.18	3

MASSACHUSETTS GENERAL LAWS ANNOTATED

Ch.	This Work Sec.	Note
149, § 179B	10.4	7
151A, §§ 71A—71G	10.4	7

MICHIGAN COMPILED LAWS ANNOTATED

Sec.	This Work Sec.	Note
445.774a	8.6	1
450.731 to 450.737	10.4	8

MINNESOTA STATUTES ANNOTATED

Sec.	This Work Sec.	Note
181.933	1.8	7
268.975 to 268.979	10.4	9
363.01 to 363.20	1.25	6
363A.20	3.15	1

MONTANA CODE ANNOTATED

Sec.	This Work Sec.	Note
39–2–913	9.18	9
39–2–1001 to 39–2–1004	10.4	10

NEW JERSEY STATUTES ANNOTATED

Sec.	This Work Sec.	Note
10:5–12	1.25	1

NEW YORK, MCKINNEY'S CIVIL RIGHTS LAW

Sec.	This Work Sec.	Note
48	1.25	3
48a	1.25	3

NORTH CAROLINA GENERAL STATUTES

Sec.	This Work Sec.	Note
96–14(3)	10.13	1

OREGON REVISED STATUTES

Sec.	This Work Sec.	Note
285.453 to 285.463	10.4	11
656.850(1)	1.30	2
659.227	1.25	2

RHODE ISLAND GENERAL LAWS

Sec.	This Work Sec.	Note
28–6.1–1 to 28–6.1–4	1.18	4

SOUTH CAROLINA CODE

Sec.	This Work Sec.	Note
40–68–70(A)	1.30	1
41–1–40	10.4	12

TENNESSEE CODE ANNOTATED

Sec.	This Work Sec.	Note
50–1–601 to 50–1–604	10.4	13

UTAH CODE ANNOTATED

Sec.	This Work Sec.	Note
34–38–1 to 34–38–15	1.26	27
58–59–102(3)	1.30	3

WISCONSIN STATUTES ANNOTATED

Sec.	This Work Sec.	Note
109.07	10.4	14
111.372	1.25	4

FEDERAL RULES OF CIVIL PROCEDURE

Rule	This Work Sec.	Note
4(a)	6.32	
8(a)(2)	2.8	
12(b)(6)	6.27	
15(a)	6.27	
15(b)	6.29	
23(b)(3)	4.10	
26(b)(1)	6.28	
30	6.28	
32	6.28	
37	6.28	
53	6.28	
56	6.28	
60(b)	6.21	

FEDERAL RULES OF EVIDENCE

Rule	This Work Sec.	Note
614(b)	6.29	
615	6.29	

FEDERAL RULES OF APPELLATE PROCEDURE

Rule	This Work Sec.	Note
15	6.32	

COMMISSION RULES OF PROCEDURE

Rule	This Work Sec.	Note
6	6.27	

COMMISSION RULES OF PROCEDURE

Rule	This Work Sec.	Note
7	6.22	
11(f)	6.28	
22	6.29	
22(a)	6.29	
34	6.27	
34(a)	6.27	
34(b)	6.27	
35	6.27	
38(a)	6.22	
38(b)	6.22	
38(c)	6.22	
41	6.27	
41(b)	6.30	
52(c)	6.28	
52(d)	6.28	
52(e)	6.30	
53(a)(2)	6.28	
54	6.28	
55	6.28	
64(b)	6.30	
67(h)	6.29	
67(j)	6.29	
69	6.29	
71	6.29	
73	6.29	
73(b)	6.29	
74	6.30	
90	6.30	
90(b)(2)	6.30	
91(a)	6.31	
92(b)	6.31	
92(c)	6.31	
100	6.27	
103	6.22	

EXECUTIVE ORDERS

No.	This Work Sec.	Note
11246	2.15	
11246	2.19	
12196	6.2	6
12564	1.26	

CODE OF FEDERAL REGULATIONS

Tit.	This Work Sec.	Note
3, § 1964	2.19	3
20, § 718.202(a)(4)	7.26	2
20, § 725.493(a)(1)	7.26	6
20, § 725.493(b)	7.26	7
26, § 1.401(a)–13(b)(2)	11.5	12
26, § 1.401(a)–13(c)(2)	11.5	12
29, Pt. 70	6.28	1
29, §§ 531.30—531.32	4.3	3
29, Pt. 541	4.6	2
29, § 541.1	4.6	17
29, § 541.3	4.6	20
29, § 541.5	4.6	21
29, § 541.5d	4.8	11

Index

†

0-314-15028-5